FINE ART
IDENTIFICATION AND PRICE GUIDE

second edition

S U S A N   T H E R A N

The CONFIDENT COLLECTOR™

AVON BOOKS ◆ NEW YORK

THE CONFIDENT COLLECTOR: FINE ART IDENTIFICATION AND PRICE GUIDE (2nd edition) is an original publication of Avon Books. This edition has never before appeared in book form.

AVON BOOKS
A division of
The Hearst Corporation
1350 Avenue of the Americas
New York, New York 10019

Second Edition copyright © 1992 by Auction Index, Inc.
Cover Photograph: The reproduction on the front cover is entitled *The Flower Carrier* by Diego Rivera, courtesy of San Francisco Museum of Modern Art
The Confident Collector and its logo are trademarked properties of Avon Books.
Published by arrangement with the author
ISBN: 0-380-76924-7

Library of Congress Cataloging in Publication Data:

Theran, Susan.
  Fine art : identification and price guide / Susan Theran. — 2nd ed.
    p. cm. — (The Confident Collector)
  Rev. ed. of: The official price guide to fine art. 1st ed. 1987.
  1. Art—Prices.   I. Theran, Susan. Official price guide to fine art.   II. Title.   III. Series.
N8675. T48   1992   92-24926
707'.5—dc20   CIP

First Avon Books Trade Printing: September 1992

AVON TRADEMARK REG. U.S. PAT. OFF. AND IN OTHER COUNTRIES, MARCA REGISTRADA, HECHO EN U.S.A.

Printed in the U.S.A.

ARC   10   9   8   7   6   5   4   3   2   1

This book is dedicated to my father, Max Fargotstein,
who gave me a wonderful gift:
the gift of feeling I could accomplish whatever I wanted.

Acknowledgments

There are due many thanks to the people who have helped this book come into being . . .

A thank you to Dorothy Harris, editorial director of The Confident Collector (Avon Books), whose genuine professionalism and support has, as always, made the creation of this book a pleasure.

A special thank you to Susan Ebert who took my words and turned them into prose.

and, thank you:

• to the art experts who were so generous with their time: Jeffrey Brown, Cathy Corbin, Leonard L. Davis, III, Tom Denzel, Dean Failey, and Alice Levi Duncan.

• to the many libraries and museums throughout the country who provided their services and information, and most especially to the librarians at the Boston Public Library's Fine Arts Department for their ongoing help and support.

• to Victor Smith of Datatech, without whose programs and expertise this book would not have been possible.

• to my staff, who worked so tirelessly compiling the database and research-ing artists: Kathy Acerbo, Joyce Ananian, Kristin Dalton, Andrea Des Jardins, Cindy McCabe, Anne Rouillard, Ruth Schmidt, Faye Stark, Michelle Tarlow, Sally Theran, Tessa Virr, and Trudy Weinstein.

• to my business experts, whose counsel and good humor throughout the year made my life a little easier–Joel Blattstein, Sheldon Fogelman, and Eliot Schein.

• and most of all, to my daughters, Sally and Rachel, whose everpresent love and ephemeral patience make it all worthwhile.

Auction House Acknowledgments

Special appreciation and thanks to the many auction houses who provide catalogs and prices in a timely manner for the Auction Index database. All of these are listed in Appendix C.

And a special thank-you to the auction houses who so generously provided the photographs and some of the stories behind the captions. They are James R. Bakkar Galleries, Barridoff Galleries, Blackwood/March Auctioneers, Frank H. Boos Gallery, Richard A. Bourne Co., Butterfield & Butterfield, Christie's New York, William Doyle Galleries, DuMouchelle Art Galleries, Robert C. Eldred Co., Robert L. Foster Auctioneers, Freeman/Fine Arts, Morton M. Goldberg Galleries, Grogan & Company, Leslie Hindman Auctioneers, Arthur James Galleries, John Moran Auctioneers, Mystic Fine Arts, Nadeau's Auction Gallery, Neal Auction Company, Oliver's Auction Gallery, Osona Auctioneers, Sanders & Mock Associ-ates, Selkirk's, Skinner's Inc., C. G. Sloan & Company, Inc., Sotheby's Inc., Adam A. Weschler & Son, Gustave J. S. White Auctioneers, Wolf's Auctioneers, and Young Fine Arts Gallery.

Table of Contents

Introduction ────────────────────

When Japanese industrialists spend millions on Impressionist paintings, it makes news and draws worldwide attention.* The media hype that accompanies mega-sales in the art auction world obscures one vitally important fact—for every million dollar painting, there are thousands of works by recognized artists that sell for considerably less than $10,000. In fact, in the last ten years 40% of all the art sold at auction in the United States went for less than $1,000, and 30% sold in the $1,000–$5,000 range. While prices have increased in the last five years since the predecessor volume of this *Price Guide* appeared, much more work is being sold, and it is still possible to buy at affordable prices.

Finding, buying, and collecting art—whether paintings, sculpture, or photographs—has become a compelling interest for thousands of people, and for good reason. They have been caught up in an extraordinary adventure, filled with excitement, learning, the thrill of the chase, possible disappointment, and, very often, success!

Collecting art encompasses everything from an occasional visit to a flea market to a concerted, focused, meticulously prepared search. How you collect depends on you. There are no rules but your own.

The passionate impulse to collect that led to the first volume of this book, covering the prices of art at auction in America from 1980–1985, remains. An important section has been added on "How To Sell."

This volume includes prices published in *Leonard's ANNUAL Price Index* from September 1986–August 1990. Sixty percent of the listed artists were not included in the first volume because their work was not sold at auction during that time. Conversely, sixty percent of the artists whose sales records appeared in the first volume have not sold in the last five years, and are not included here. For complete coverage, you would be wise to peruse both.

The art market keeps changing. It has become more sophisticated and competitive at every level. Now, more than ever, the well-informed buyer has the edge. Good luck as you use this book to find and buy the works you are seeking.

Look Before You Leap ────────────────────

You've probably already taken many of the first steps that culminate in collecting. Most of us begin to develop an interest in fine art by visiting

───────────

*Van Gogh's *Portrait Du Dr. Gachet* sold for $82,500,000 at Christie's on May 15, 1990, and two days later, Renoir's *Au Moulin de la Galette* sold for $78,100,000 at Sotheby's. Both works were bought by the same Japanese industrialist.

museums. There is no better place to start–the phrase "museum quality" denotes the highest standard of workmanship. Museums with extensive collections provide exposure to an encyclopedic variety of styles and artistic media. Smaller museums, especially those with specialized collections, provide an opportunity to study a particular aspect of art in depth.

In every case, museum going will help you develop your own eye for quality. Examine the individual works carefully. Analyze their composition. How does the artist lead you into the work? Are you made to focus on the foreground and then drawn further back? Are you led immediately to a particular point on the canvas? What are the primary lines of composition? How are light and shadow achieved? What did the artist set out to accomplish? Does the painting tell a story? If it is a portrait, does it convey personality? It is the ability of paintings to spark these questions that contributes to their quality. Your ability to respond to them is an indication of your growing understanding of what quality means in art.

At the same time, you will be sharpening your taste and defining your preferences. Is your eye drawn to particular subjects? Do you like still lifes? Landscapes? Animals? Domestic interiors? Abstract shapes? Do you prefer specific color ranges? Do you like looking at pictures of activities you enjoy? What kinds of artistic media attract you? Do you like chalk, pencil, watercolor? Do you like finished paintings, or do you prefer oil sketches? A few leisurely afternoons in a museum will help you make such determinations.

Galleries offer a way of learning about the works of individual artists. Owners are generally knowledgeable and most have chosen to sell art because they love it. Keep in mind, however, that galleries are governed by the realities of the marketplace. Many, but by no means all, are willing to take the time to help educate potential customers and share their often specialized and unique information. Most collectors agree that the very best galleries are the ones which will take the time to educate, confident that their investment in time will ultimately show a return in sales.

Classes, courses, lectures, and workshops offered by museums and historical societies afford additional opportunities to learn. Frequently, individual lectures are planned to coincide with annual or semi-annual exhibits and shows. Since smaller institutions often cannot afford to advertise, you will have to call for information or watch local newspaper "calendars" for announcements.

Above all, you must read–art books, magazines, exhibition catalogs, and auction catalogs. When, after conscientious museum going and gallery visits, you determine you are seriously interested in, for example, the Connecticut Impressionists, and want to begin collecting this late 19th- to early 20th-century group, your next stop is the library. Who were the Connecticut Impressionists? In what part of the state did they paint? Who was associated with the movement? By doing your own research, you'll pull together the bits of information gleaned from museum labels and dealers, and begin to assemble a composite body of data. You don't need to be an expert before you begin to buy art–the learning process is continuous. If you're like most collectors, once you've been drawn into a subject, you'll want to learn more and more.

Thorough knowledge and study lay the groundwork for serious collecting. Anyone who builds a valuable collection has worked hard, studying and learning.

Developing Your Taste

The best way to begin is by buying.

Buy what you can afford. Buy in little shops. Buy in junk shops. Buy in antique shops, flea markets, and at low-priced auctions. But buy!

Nothing else shapes your eye so quickly. Nothing sharpens your taste like making a purchase. In making a financial commitment, you make a statement of your likes and dislikes. It is a process subject to constant refinement.

What catches your eye?

Will the first item in your collection be a scene that you recognize, something that evokes a feeling or memory which you want to preserve? For many people, collecting starts with something very specific that is tied to a strong personal interest and then extends and develops. Many real or armchair sailors collect maritime scenes. Gardeners often are drawn to pictures of flowers. Mountain scenes are popular with many collectors.

Discovering what you really like is akin to stripping paint from a piece of old furniture. As you work through to the essence of your taste, you will reveal successive layers of appreciation for different types of work. In the process, you will refine your taste–and you may end up selling some of your early acquisitions.

But, begin by buying. Don't be afraid to make mistakes.

In the course of building a collection you will develop a consistent eye. That is, over time you will find everything you buy fits together. Buying will enable you to develop a sureness of taste, and the confidence of your own judgments.

Where to Buy Art

Buying art is somewhat less straightforward than buying a washing machine, but it's more absorbing and more fun. The sheer variety of places in which you can look, and the process of looking are at once an education and an activity in themselves.

Yard Sales, Garage Sales, and Flea Markets

Yard sales, garage sales, and flea markets are a boon to weekend collectors. Someone we know who has a phenomenal memory for artists' names has been very successful (and very lucky) at turning up pictures that others have cleaned out of their attics. If your personal database is less complete this book is a reliable substitute.

The first rule for getting to any of these sales is *be early*. Most flea markets advertise in the classified section of local newspapers and list their hours. (Some open at dawn.) Often dealers will sell right out of their cars to early arrivals–even before they've had a chance to set up their displays. One word of caution–"early birds" aren't always welcome, particularly at garage sales. But it may be worth the risk of a chilly reception on the chance that you'll catch the proverbial worm.

At a flea market you'll find most old paintings and drawings in the antiques section. Check a map of the field when you arrive, since some markets divide dealers' merchandise into old and new, and you can waste a great deal of time trudging past racks of bubble gum and shoelaces before you find the right area. But don't overlook the "junk" area. Some of the best buys may be in the section reserved for sellers who have just cleaned out their attics or garages and don't know what they have.

Some flea markets are held regularly, even weekly. Others are occasional—sponsored by service groups, churches, or fraternal organizations.

The queen of the flea markets is held three times a year (May, July, and September) in Brimfield, Massachusetts. Thousands of dealers set up their displays on acres of fields for this event that attracts purchasers not only from the Northeast but the entire nation and abroad. Some European dealers buy a year's stock of American antiques and paintings at Brimfield.

One veteran Brimfield connoisseur recommends arriving before dawn. The show opens at 5:00 A.M. and the line begins to form two hours earlier. "Carry a flashlight," she advises, so you can see what's displayed on the tables, and spot the dealers walking around carrying signs that read, "I buy penknives," or "I buy old cameras." Take the time to savor the unique character of this enormous show, which includes the spectacle of pairs of collectors or dealers who race from one display to the next, using walkie-talkies to announce finds to their partners.

Brimfield runs for a week—you may find the very best buys if you're there before first light, but good quality material is on sale all day long. Brimfield is a joy for collectors, and a good place for dealers as well. Many of them save unique pieces to bring to this market, which attracts thousands of sophisticated purchasers.

Other noteworthy flea markets around the nation include the annual indoor event at the Atlantic City Convention Center conducted each March by the Brimfield Association.

Remingers #1 Antique Market is a Pennsylvania institution. Held every Sunday year round in Adamstown, this indoor/outdoor spectacular welcomes over 500 dealers each week in its indoor space. In good weather, hundreds more open their stands outdoors. Antiques and collectibles are the mainstay here.

Unbeknownst to most sports fans, the Pasadena Rose Bowl hosts a different sort of competition on the second Sunday of every month. At the Rose Bowl Flea Market and Swap Meet nearly anything is sold and bought by thousands of sellers and shoppers.

Flea markets and garage and yard sales are fun to go to, and great places to buy. They are good sources for watercolors, drawings . . . and fakes. Chances are strong that the painting you find signed "Picasso" wasn't the work of Pablo. Even a name-plaque on the frame does not assure that a piece is actually the work of the designated artist. (You might, however, find an original of a more obscure artist.) Some prints, especially chromolithographs, closely resemble paintings. Also, some prints were painted over, closely following the original lines. They are often very difficult to detect. They turn up at places like Brimfield, but they occasionally also turn up at auction, and are sold as "painted by the artist who did the original work for the print."

When you decide to buy at a flea market, yard, or garage sale, examine the condition of the work carefully. Flea market merchandise is sold "as is."

Usually it's helpful to ask where the work came from–that is, attic, base-ment, or Aunt Gertrude. Most sellers know something about what they're selling, and though there won't be a provenance (history) supplied for a picture at a yard sale, there may well be an interesting story attached to it. Some material could be "hot." Last year a painting stolen from a New England historical society surfaced at a church flea market where it was purchased for under $100. The work was recognized when it was brought in for appraisal.

The rule of purchase at yard sales and flea markets is–make an offer. There is usually little science, knowledge, or reason for the price written on the tag. Be ready to negotiate.

One final note.

Don't go to any of these sales expecting to find a lost masterwork. When you buy, buy because you are drawn to the work, because it appeals to you, because it is consistent with the things you like and own, and because you can afford it.

Second Hand, Junk, and Consignment Stores, and Antique Shops

One step up from garage sales and flea markets (and sometimes a very short step indeed) is browser's paradise–second hand, junk, and consignment shops. With growing numbers of people in the art market, there's more competitive shopping in these stores than before but there are still finds. Often the owners of these emporia will pick up stray pictures or drawings in the process of acquiring an estate or cleaning out a garage or attic. Art may be almost hidden in many of these stores. Ask if there are any pictures. Look under tables and behind furniture.

Antique stores are another good source. It's hard to be knowledgeable about everything. Store owners may be expert about furniture but unaware of the value of a picture they have bought. They may have purchased a picture in order to acquire an entire estate and be willing to sell at minimal profit to move it, because they specialize in another field.

Wherever you are, look for frames. Good period frames are hard to find. In fact, there are now auctions just for frames! Even if you don't like the picture, the frame may be just what you need for your picture at home.

Dealing with Dealers

A first trip to a big-city gallery can be intimidating. The imposing front entrance and glacial sales staff can combine to keep beginning collectors at a distance. Yet the same people won't hesitate for a second to get out of the car at a country antiques store and ask if there are any pictures in the back room. It's a mistake to assume that a country dealer in a flannel shirt is any less knowledgeable about value and quality than his Madison Avenue or Newbury Street counterpart, or that his prices will be lower. The overhead will be higher in the city, and that will affect prices, but a higher turnover may enable a city gallery to work on a lower profit margin.

Some collectors who are just starting out may hesitate to visit dealers, for they're convinced this is the most expensive way to purchase, or concerned that they'll be pushed into something they really don't want. Others wouldn't begin to look for a work of art without the guidance of a professional.

If, in fact, you end up developing a very serious interest in collecting, you'll become an expert in the area that interests you. When you walk into a tiny up-country store and spot a small dirty canvas that looks promising, you'll have the knowledge you need to examine it carefully and decide if you want to add it to your collection.

Should that happen when you're just starting out, and it's a small purchase, go ahead and buy it. As long as the work really appeals to you, there's no such thing as a $150 error. But imagine a different scenario in which the price tag is substantially higher, and you really don't know whether the work is fairly priced, or even authentic. (Of course, you'll have this book in hand, and that will give you confidence and credibility if you decide to negotiate the price.) That's a compelling reason for making major purchases from dealers. Until, and even when, you develop your own store of knowledge, they are the professionals.

A good dealer knows an artist's work and style, can authenticate it, and can recognize whether it has been altered. Experienced dealers know a lot about the process of making art, and the scholarly and technical aspects of art history.

There were, for example, artists who painted the major elements of pictures, and then turned to apprentices to fill in the rest. Works completed during certain periods of an artist's life are worth more than others. There are nuances to a painting which will change its value. If there's a glass in a still life by an artist who didn't usually paint glass, the work is more valuable. If the artist worked in a realistic style during much of his career, but later became more impressionistic, the pictures from different periods will have differing values. If, in a particular picture, an artist introduced an element which later became characteristic of his work, the picture will have special or added value. Some artists chose not to sign their canvases, or signed them on the back so that they didn't disturb the aesthetic balance of the work. This is the type of specialized information for which you will turn to a dealer.

In addition to being a storehouse of knowledge, a dealer can be extremely helpful in locating the kind of work you find most appealing, particularly if your taste is very specialized. Once you've developed a relationship with a dealer, he or she will buy with you in mind and be able to sell to you with a lower markup because there will be a quicker turnover. An ongoing relationship with a reputable dealer is a good way to assure access to quality work. Every serious collector has a good working relationship with at least a few dealers. It's true that you may pay more when you buy from a dealer than you might at an auction, but you're paying for knowledge and time.

Note, too, that most dealers will generally not sell a painting unless it has been cleaned and, if needed, restored by a competent professional restorer. This can save both time and money for a collector.

The key question is, how do you find a dealer with whom you'll be comfortable? There are literally hundreds of galleries, shops, and dealers in most areas. Consult the *Art in America Gallery Guide*, available on newsstands in August and in many libraries. In larger cities you can begin by looking through the yellow pages, the gallery listings in newspapers and magazines, weekly calendar supplements, and even guidebooks. In smaller areas where galleries are dispersed, dealers often form regional associations and publish a listing of members and a map showing their locations. These are available in the stores, or at local, state-sponsored tourist information centers.

Galleries may specialize. Visit as many as you can until you find those dealers whose taste is very much like your own, and begin to cultivate a working relationship. Put your name on the mailing list so that you will be invited to previews and kept informed about publications.

Networking and talking with other collectors is essential. Talk to people at auctions. You may get to discover dealers you'd never meet otherwise because they don't generally sell to the public.

Terms

The term *dealer* covers such a broad range of operations that it will be useful to distinguish among the various types who operate at all different levels of the art market. On the very first rung of the ladder are *pickers*, people with good eyes, developed taste, and eternal optimism. They scour flea markets, yard sales, and country auctions, always on the lookout for the underpriced, unrecognized "find." Pickers have established relationships with lawyers representing estates, dealers, galleries, and individual collectors. They buy and sell to their contacts.

Then there are *door knockers*. The name says it all. Door knockers are a variety of picker who go door to door in search of old paintings, rugs, and furniture to resell to dealers or through auction houses.

Runners are the matchmakers, the link between dealers, or dealers and collectors. A very few who work the upper end of the market are essentially private dealers who make a handsome commission on costly works of art. Most live a far less glamorous existence, moving individual pieces from one dealer to the next, hoping to make a quick sale and a small profit. *Brokers* are a more elite version of runners, often relying on a large circle of acquaintances to keep up to date about what's for sale and who might be looking. Brokers never actually own any work (although they may take a piece on consignment). They direct their energies instead to bringing buyer and seller together.

Wholesalers don't maintain a retail space, but work directly with galleries rather than individual collectors.

Collector dealers start as collectors, but become so involved with their interest that they sell parts of their collections in order to "feed their habits" and upgrade or diversify their holdings.

Strategies

The term *dealer*, as it is usually used, means an individual who owns and runs a shop or gallery. But the word is so inclusive that it covers everything from an exquisitely decorated world famous gallery which commands instant name recognition, to the tiniest, most crowded, backstreet junkstore.

The range of dealers really runs the gamut from part-time entrepreneurs who do business out of the trunks of their cars, on up. Some limit their activities and only participate in shows. Some will see clients only by appointment.

With this variety, it is clear that no single strategy of dealing with dealers will work in all situations. What follows is the composite of advice from a number of dealers, collectors, and personal experience.

On your first visits to a dealer or gallery, you should make your interests and intentions clear. Establish yourself. Let the owner or salesperson know why you've come in. Are you there to learn or to buy? Do you know what you like? (This can be a particularly important question if you're in a major gallery. Some have enormous inventories, literally hundreds of paintings. It's no time to start trying to define your taste.)

Are you buying for visual and aesthetic pleasure? Are you buying for decoration–a blue painting to hang over the sofa? Or, are you buying for investment?

Know what your price range is, and state it, but don't be afraid to look at things you can't afford. Consider it another step in honing your eye and developing your own standards of taste by correlating quality and price.

Authenticity

Ask the dealer to show you the painting in a darkened room under a black light, an uncomplicated ultraviolet light which, when it shines on the canvas, will reveal inpainting and overpainting. The former is the precise repainting of a damaged area, the latter, the addition of too much new paint which alters the appearance of the work. Particularly in an older work, a certain amount of restoration is acceptable, and perhaps even desirable. A hundred year old painting can show some signs of wear around the edges. A skilled restorer can repair it, filling in the missing spots, enhancing the painting's appearance, and increasing its value. Inpainting is an absolute necessity when a torn or punctured canvas is repaired.

It's when the restorer's skill is abused and a painting is significantly changed from its original form that inpainting becomes a problem. Among the long list of items that can be added to a painting to make it seem more attractive are: parasols, balloons, American flags, baby carriages, little dogs, long white dresses, flowers, pretty women tending gardens or interiors, butterflies, and last, but by no means least, signatures and dates. It is to discover these abuses that a black light is used.

Under a black light, it's easy to detect changes that would otherwise be impossible to see. Paint that is only a few months or years old looks different from paint applied a century ago. Inpainting will fluoresce under a black light. However, some 20th-century pigments will always fluoresce. Surface cracks and other irregularities, changes in composition and color also become dramatically apparent. Some new techniques, however, do not show up under a black light. If you are buying at auction, some auction houses may give you a "condition" report before the sale.

Thus, if you've found a painting you like, ask to see it under a black light. In fact, a reputable dealer will be eager to show a canvas under a black light and quick to point out any alterations in the surface. If, however, he or she is reluctant to have the painting subjected to such scrutiny, you ought to look for another painting . . . and another dealer. (If you would like to buy your own black light, you can probably find one in a novelty store for less than an art supply store will charge. They're popular with young people because they make fluorescent posters glow.)

If you're looking at paintings in a less formal setting, it may be helpful to carry a magnifying glass so that you can closely examine the surface of the work. With the aid of a lens you can pick out an inscription or signature that would otherwise be difficult to see. You may also be able to tell if a signature or anything else has been added over the varnish that covers the original work.

A final step before making a purchase is to ask to have the picture removed from the frame. If the work is old and hasn't been restored, the canvas shouldn't be taut. The surface of the painting may show some craquelure, a web of tiny fine lines caused by the drying out of the canvas. When the canvas is out of the frame, you'll be able to see if the picture has been remounted–if the canvas has been tautened as a result of relining it with another canvas or a board. Ask the dealer why the work was relined. It may not affect the value of the painting, but it's something you should know. At the same time, you can see if the painting has been cropped, or even cut out of a larger work.

Provenance

Depending on the level at which you are buying, a painting may have a written provenance, a life history from the time it left the artist's easel to its arrival at the gallery, which includes the names of previous owners and the dates on which it changed hands. Obviously, the better known and more costly the painting the likelier and more necessary the provenance. Not surprisingly, a provenance adds to the value of a painting.

You might begin by asking about the painting's history. If the dealer has the estate, he may have the artist's notebook, preliminary sketches for the work (very collectible), or other information. Has the work been in a catalog? Was it included in an exhibit? This may or may not be pertinent to a given work. Quite a number of very fine works have never been shown publicly, and thus, their formal record is short. Because dealers' connections in the art world may give them access to works before any private buyers get to see them, the picture you're looking at may have remained in the hands of a single owner or family and be new to the market. It may, for example, have been the gift of the artist to the grandfather of the present owner, or have some similar history.

A less expensive work may have no written history at all, just the statement of the dealer to the effect that "I bought it from the Smith estate up in Westfield." If you're looking at the work of a relative unknown, this is an acceptable response. The dealer may be able to fill you in on the family that owned the painting, the general nature of the estate, and the artist as well.

Negotiating a Price

While the price that a dealer quotes to you is not necessarily the one you'll end up paying, the issue of price negotiations raises questions, eyebrows, and sometimes, tempers.

To negotiate or not to negotiate? Most dealers will insist that they won't. Many buyers will tell you they've tried and sometimes succeeded. If you're embarrassed, don't, but as a general rule of thumb, it's worth a try. Remember that if you can walk away from a potential purchase, there's a far greater chance of getting it at the price you're willing to pay than if you're caught up in the process and dead set on acquiring it.

The possibilities for negotiation depend very much upon the dealer, the gallery, the painting, and the realities of the marketplace. Galleries at prestigious addresses in major cities carry enormous overheads which are necessarily reflected in the prices of the paintings they sell. There is generally a close relationship between the location and prestige of the gallery, the desirability of the painting, and the readiness of the customer to make an offer and the dealer to accept it. This is complicated by the length of time the picture has been in the dealer's possession, and last, but by no means least, by the percentage which it has been marked up.

In other words, if you want to buy a picture which has been in a gallery for only a week, the dealer is not likely to negotiate. If the picture is still on the wall when you come back six months later, it's much more likely that you'll find some flexibility in the price.

Of course, the whole question of negotiation depends upon who you are talking to and where. We know one very genteel lady who successfully bargains at Cartier. While small informal stores which carry a mix of paintings and other things seem to invite bargaining more than others, serious collectors will negotiate anywhere.

Remember, too, that when you question a price, you are at least in part asking why it has been set at a certain level. If it seems especially high, there may be a good reason for it–the work may have some unique quality. Keep in mind as well that some dealers will overprice, expecting to be negotiated down.

Dealers maintain that it is not in their own interest to overprice paintings, since most guarantee that they will take a work back in trade for at least the original price. Most dealers will add that they will not try to outbid an individual collector at auction, since they will later have to resell the painting.

Bear in mind, too, that prices in this *Guide* were achieved at auction, a market that is frequently considered wholesale. It is perfectly reasonable for the dealer who has spent time and money acquiring, and possibly restoring, the work to make a profit on it. Your readiness to make an offer, and the dealer's willingness to be somewhat flexible about pricing, will constitute the negotiation.

Bills of Sale

For major purchases, for purposes of insurance and recordkeeping, it is important to secure a bill of sale. You can be assured of the authenticity of a work of art if the dealer will write out and sign the sales slip to read:

"One oil, title, *by* Robert Smith, size, location of signature, and any other significant details."

If the slip reads: "One oil, *signed* Robert Smith" or "One oil *inscribed* Robert Smith," or "One oil *attributed* to Robert Smith," then the dealer is not liable should the painting turn out to be a forgery. You can be forceful, or you can be innocent and say that your sister the attorney insisted that you ask for that specific wording, but don't leave the gallery without the dealer's written assurance that the work is "one [work] *by* [the artist]," as noted above.

Methods of Payment

You may find a greater degree of flexibility in price if you can pay cash; however, most people find it more convenient to make major purchases by check.

If you do pay cash, be sure to save your sales slip, since it is the only proof you will have to present to an insurance company in the event of loss.

Some dealers will permit you to pay for a painting in installments, but unless you are a well-established customer, you should not expect to be able to take the work home until it is completely paid for. (However, if you offer to let the dealer keep the painting until you finish paying for it, he may let you take it home.)

Auctions

You don't need a course in assertiveness training to bid at an auction. Neither do you need to sit absolutely still while bidding goes on around you, lest an auctioneer mistake some motion as a hidden signal. Auctions are entertaining to attend, and a good way to purchase art.

Terms

As in all specialized fields, there are specific terms used in auctions which you must understand before you begin. The most important, listed alphabetically, are:

Auction. A sale in which the auctioneer, acting as the agent for sellers (called *consignors*), offers a series of objects to prospective buyers who bid incrementally. The highest bidder buys the object. The auctioneer always encourages bidding to try to get the highest price, since his payment is generally a percentage of the sale.

Bought-in (sometimes called passed or unsold). If a lot does not achieve its reserve (see page 13) it is said to be bought-in by the auction house and will be returned to the consignor or be reoffered at a later sale. However, bear in mind that if, on its own momentum, bidding does not reach the reserve, the auction house will bid on behalf of the consignor against bids from the floor. Only if the work still does not reach its reserve is it bought-in. It's not always clear whether there's a reserve on an individual lot. A 1987 New York City law requires the house to announce the disposition of an unsold lot as passed, returned to owner, withdrawn, or bought-in. New York also requires that all lots with a reserve be marked with a black square or dot in the auction catalog.

Buyer premium. At most auctions, a premium amounting to 10% of the hammer price is added to the cost of each item. Sales tax is calculated on the total. An auctioneer who adds a buyer premium will usually indicate this in advertisements or catalogs.

Catalog sale. An auction for which a printed listing of lots is prepared and distributed in advance. Catalogs can be mimeographed lists with brief descriptions or beautifully illustrated, carefully researched, book-length publications.

Consignor. The individual who has asked the auction house to sell a particular piece or pieces.

Estimate. The price range within which an auction house expects to sell a particular lot. The estimate is included in the printed catalog. Reserve is usually two-thirds of the low estimate. For more expensive lots, reserve is often close to the low estimate. At best, an estimate is the auctioneer's best judgment based on the artist's sales history, and the condition and desirability of the particular piece.

Hammer price (knockdown). The price at which a lot is sold.

Inspection. See "preview."

Left bid (including mail bids). A bid submitted by a prospective buyer who can't attend the auction. These are executed by the auctioneer or a member of his staff during the sale.

Lot. An individual work or group of works offered for sale at one time.

Paddle. A numbered card which may be anything from an imprinted plastic paddle to a paper plate. It is given to bidders when they register and must be held aloft in order to bid.

Passed. If there is no interest from the floor and no bidding on the lot, it is passed over, and the auctioneer goes on to the next.

Preview (exhibition). The period before a sale reserved for the inspection or viewing of items to be auctioned. In larger auction houses, the preview period may be as long as a week. At smaller sales, the preview may be only the day of the sale. Generally, lots cannot be viewed after the sale starts. However, if it is really impossible to schedule a pre-sale inspection, call the auction house in advance and arrange to see the item when you arrive.

Prices realized. A listing of lots sold and the prices achieved. Some auction houses publish these prices and some do not. They may be published with or without the buyer premium.

Reserve. The lowest price which a consignor will accept for a lot. It is ordinarily used only for high-priced works. The reserve is often two-thirds of the low estimate. At the major houses, the reserve for more expensive paintings is frequently close to the low estimate. If reserve is not reached and the lot is bought-in, the piece may be offered again at a later sale. Reserves are rarely set at country sales, so that sparse attendance, or limited interest, may make it possible to pick up a good buy.

The ring (the pool). An informal agreement among dealers that they will not bid against each other for a specific lot. After the sale they adjourn to the parking lot for a "knockout" in which the lot is sold to one of the dealers in the pool. Each writes down the figure that he or she is ready to pay. The highest bidder ends up with the merchandise, while the others split the difference between the actual purchase price at the auction and the price reached in the post-auction action. Most merchandise sold in this manner leaves the parking lot at the price it should have fetched at the sale. The losers, clearly, are the auction house and the consignor. These activities amount to restraint of trade and are illegal in most states. Curiously, some members of the ring never actually deal in merchandise but manage to make a small living simply by participating. While the ring can be a potent force in controlling prices at an auction, an independent purchaser can beat it. Just set your price and stick to it.

Shill. An individual planted in the crowd by the house or by an individual consignor to bid up the price of a lot. Contracts at most houses forbid the consignor or his agent to bid on the lot he has consigned.

Telephone bid. A bid from someone not attending the auction, who makes advance arrangements with the house to bid actively during the auction. Telephone bidding is generally limited to higher priced works, and at important auctions, there may be a bank of telephones in place for long distance participation. (Not all telephone bidding is long distance. Sometimes, bidders use a pay phone in the auction house so they can bid without being identified.)

Underbidder. The losing bidder.

Withdrawn. A lot removed before the sale begins.

Types

Auctions vary widely in the selection, type, and quality of artwork they offer. At country auctions mixed offerings are the rule, and they will include furniture, paintings and drawings, rugs, bric-a-brac, and assorted collectibles. A painting sold at a country auction may have been hanging on the same wall for the past 100 years, or it might be the ten-year-old work of a summer painter. That stained work on paper may be an original watercolor, or it may have been clipped from a magazine and hung in a five and dime store frame.

Some auctioneers assemble a collection for a sale by combining lots from many different households or sources. Be aware that some dealers will consign "hard to sell" merchandise at these sales. Such sales are frequently held in halls and lodges, veterans' posts, or fraternal organizations and may include some paintings and watercolors.

Some paintings are usually put on the block at estate auctions, where the entire contents of a house are sold on site, often on a weekday. Estate auctions bring fresh, new, and thus particularly desirable material to the market.

Catalogs

One advantage of buying a work of art at a large auction house is that a great deal of your work has already been done for you. By the time something appears in an auction house catalog, it has already filtered through the first levels of professional assessment.

An auction house catalog, a listing of lots to be sold at a particular auction, can be anything from a mimeographed list to a splendidly printed and illustrated volume that looks a great deal like an expensive art book. A catalog can be a source of valuable information, but it should be read in the context in which it is created. An auction house catalog is a sales tool. It can be glamorous and packed with information, but it is compiled to help the house successfully market a product.

Catalogs, while useful art reference tools, are not definitive sources of information. The fact that a work is listed in a catalog does not legitimize it.

Catalogs are not always scholarly works. They may or may not be written by knowledgeable people. They are not infallible and may contain errors in attribution or authentication.

In reading an art auction catalog, it is important to remember that at the major houses, works are generally arranged chronologically, rather than in order of importance. Color illustrations often draw the reader's attention. Whether a lot is illustrated or not, or in black and white or in color, does not indicate importance. Remember that most auction houses charge consignors for illustrations, and charge more for color than black and white.

Auction houses list the title of the painting, if known. Otherwise they give a descriptive title.

A typical catalog description will include the artist's name; the title (in quotation marks or capital letters); whether and where the work is signed; the medium (oil on canvas, oil on board, pencil on paper, etc.); size and condition; and the price estimate. It may also provide information about the provenance of the work, or literature about the artist. (If you buy a picture at an auction, save the catalog, for it becomes part of the provenance.)

The auction house may indicate its confidence in the authenticity of a particular piece in the way it prints the artist's name. For example, if it catalogs a piece by Sir Jacob Epstein, you can be confident that it's by the great 20th-century English sculptor. A little less certainty will shorten the listing to Jacob Epstein. If there's more question, the name may appear as J. Epstein. Dropping a title or abbreviating a first name to an initial usually implies doubt. If the catalog description says "bears signature" or "apocryphal signature," the signature is false. If the catalog says "signature is inscribed," it was written by someone other than the artist. When you read the description, be aware that state laws vary, as does the buy back policy or guarantee. Terminology also varies from house to house. Christie's uses the term "cast from a model by" as its guarantee for bronzes. This term has been picked up by auction houses outside of New York state, but does not necessarily mean the same thing.

The same cautions apply to the use of such terms as "school," "school of," "studio of," and "circle of," whether in catalogs or anywhere else. "School of," as in "School of Raphael," is generally applied to the work of students or apprentices who studied with a renowned artist. An individual work by a member of the "school" may actually have been touched in one or two places by the master's brush. "Circle of" covers a broader area–the connection is more tenuous, but the work of art may still be very valuable. "After" means a copy of the work of an artist–perhaps by an art student sitting in a museum–at least a hundred years after the original was completed. "Attributed to" indicates that a work is *most probably* by a particular artist even though it is not signed.

Auction catalogs are compiled and published by the major houses six weeks to a few days before the actual sale. In the United States the art auction market is dominated by two huge New York houses, Sotheby's and Christie's. Together they account for 90% of all catalog lots sold annually and dominate the market. Their specialized sales are scheduled in the same seasons each year: major American paintings sales are traditionally early in December and the last week in May, Latin American sales at the end of May, etc. Both offer catalogs by subscription which assure that you are on the auction house mailing list and will receive their newsletter and notices of forthcoming sales. Most houses also send catalog subscribers lists of the prices realized at sales. Appendix C is a list of the major auction houses. All of them offer some art and sell by catalog or flyer.

Read carefully the "Conditions of Sale" at the front of each catalog, which provides important information on absentee bidding, establishing credit, shipping, insurance, and storage.

Strategy

One basic ground rule covers all purchasing at all auctions:

NEVER BID ON SOMETHING YOU HAVEN'T LOOKED AT FIRST.

Take advantage of the auction preview. Carefully examine the piece you are interested in. Re-examine it just before the sale begins. Sometimes a piece is damaged during the preview.

Inspect carefully. If you've done your reading and research, you'll be aware of the characteristic styles and signatures of the artists you're interested in. Don't be put off by small signs of wear or damage. Don't be afraid to bid on a dirty painting–at least a dirty painting hasn't been damaged by an amateur restorer. Most paintings can be cleaned. Holes can be repaired. torn canvas can usually be mended. Stains and acid can be removed from paper. Skilled restorers can perform near-miracles.

If you've received a catalog in which a piece is described, but not illustrated, ask the auction house to send a color photograph or transparency for you to examine. After you've looked at the illustration, know that you're interested enough to buy, but can't possibly attend the preview or the sale and don't want to risk a telephone bid on unseen merchandise, there's still hope. You can arrange with a dealer to bid for you. This method provides a built-in advantage–experience. A firsthand examination by a knowledgeable dealer can help a prospective purchaser decide whether or not to bid. The dealer will preview the painting, check its authenticity, examine its condition, assess its value, and look at the frame. The dealer will then call you from the auction house and discuss overall values, and you will be able to decide whether and how much to bid.

Dealers' commissions will vary for this service. Some charge 5% of the purchase price if they bid successfully for you. Some won't charge if they don't get the painting, but other will ask for a flat fee for time and effort. Fees vary and should be negotiated in advance.

Bidding

To bid in an auction you must secure a number by registering and presenting a valid form of identification, usually a driver's license and major credit card, which will enable the auctioneer to accept your check at the end. If you can't establish a line of credit, you will need to leave your merchandise until your check clears.

Bidding strategy is individual. There are as many different strategies as there are bidders. Some people like to be identified as bidders and other do not. Some prefer to get in early and join the action from the opening bid. Others will follow for a while before jumping in. There's no rule that bidding must begin at the auctioneer's opening figure. However, bidding will occasionally start at that level if the work is very desirable, or if an individual bidder has decided to try to bring action on that particular item to a quick close by getting a psychological jump on others who wanted to start much lower.

Before bidding starts on the lot you are interested in, make sure you know what you think the piece is worth. Keep this *Guide* at hand and remember that there are a number of factors that influence prices. Don't be discouraged by high estimates, for they may be wishful thinking. Write your top price for the lot on your catalog or on a pad of paper. Add 10% to give yourself some flexibility and then add another 10% for the buyer's premium. If there's a state sales tax, calculate that as well. Be sure that your opening bid is below what you're finally willing to pay. Be alert for symptoms of "auction fever," a potentially dangerous disease in which a purchaser decides to pay whatever is necessary to own a particular work.

Be prepared to exceed your own limit, but only a little. If you've decided that you'll spend $1,250 on a painting, and your last bid of $1,200 was followed by someone else's reluctant $1,300, go ahead to $1,350–you may get what you're after.

If you've left a bid with the auctioneer, make it an odd figure, such as $625, and consider giving instructions that will enable him to up to the next level on your behalf. In this way you have an advantage, since the bidding goes up in round increments.

Don't be reluctant to bid against dealers. Unless a dealer is bidding on behalf of a client, he will have to resell the painting to make a profit, so he must begin by buying at a price he can mark up.

If you were hesitant, pulled out of the bidding, and the item you wanted was bought-in because it didn't reach its reserve, you may still be able to purchase it after the auction. Most auction house contracts empower the auction house to sell the consigned lot at its reserve price for up to sixty days after the sale. After consulting the consignor, the auction house may sell the lot below the reserve price.

How to Sell

Art collectors share certain fantasies. One of the most common follows this scenario: the much loved early 20th-century oil painting of a horse that hangs above the mantle, but was inherited from a favorite uncle who lived in a gracious, antique-filled home, turns out to be a very valuable British sporting painting.

That's the fantasy.

The reality is that every age has produced greater and lesser artists, and that our affection for a work does not enhance its value. Art has no absolute financial value. Value is created in the marketplace. Price is influenced by a variety of factors which include the artist's prestige, whether he is currently in vogue or out of fashion, the rarity of his work, the quality of the individual piece, previous auction records, condition, size, and subject matter.

Unpredictable elements may also come into play. If, for example, the auction prices achieved by an individual artist have been inflated by competition between two collectors, and one suddenly withdraws from the market, prices will drop.

While there are many variables that affect art prices, there are still some fundamental guidelines to follow if you want to sell a work of art.

Begin by ascertaining what you're selling. Do you have a provenance (history of ownership) for the work? Where was it bought and when? Is it the work of a listed artist? Is there a sales history? Check Bénézit (see p. 27), Falk (see p. 29), and *Leonard's ANNUAL Price Index*, and, of course, the first volume of *The Official Price Guide to Fine Art*.

Review your decision. Are you sure you want to sell? Do you want to keep the work a little longer, or keep it forever to leave to your family?

If you've decided to sell you should consider the next set of options; you can place the piece at auction, sell it directly to a dealer, or consign it on a commission basis.

Selling at Auction

Selling at auction assures maximum exposure to the largest possible audience. An experienced auction house will publicize a sale effectively, hoping to draw a large crowd of bidders on sale day. This is the most likely way to achieve fair market value for a piece, and the sales price becomes a matter of public record.

Most auction houses will be happy to help sell an estate, though the largest may sell only the best pieces themselves, and contract out the remainder. Sotheby's and Christie's will conduct an on-site sale only if the proceeds are expected to exceed $2–$3 million.

If you are selling only one or two pieces, take a *careful* photograph (of both the front *and* back if there are marks or labels there). Make an appointment with a local auction house, and bring it to the in-house art specialist. Or you can send a photograph to one of the New York houses. (Before mailing any material, it's a good idea to call ahead and secure the name of the appropriate department head so that you can direct the materials to the right individual. It also provides a name for follow-up.)

The photograph should include the artist's name, signature, the size of the work without the frame, support (canvas, board, paper, etc.), media, and the best provenance you can supply. Working from a photograph, even the instant variety, an expert can usually determine the value of a painting. If you think that you own an especially valuable work, a color transparency made by a professional will cost about $100, and may prove a good investment.

Another approach is to bring the work(s) to an appraisal day which all auction houses hold, either on their premises or as benefits for museums or historical societies. On these occasions, experts assess the value of work brought in and provide a verbal appraisal for a minimal fee.

In any event, try to get at least three appraisals to help ascertain the value of a work. This will help you safeguard against any unscrupulous appraiser who might set an artificially low value on a work and offer to buy it, only to resell it at its real worth.

One cautionary note–avoid having any restoration done on a work you are consigning to auction. Most paintings sell better before they are restored. If you think restoration is essential, consult the auction house, and ask for a recommendation. One classic restoration horror story concerns a work by Wifredo Lam which was ruined when the restorer removed all the impasto (paint applied in heavy layers or strokes). The end product looked like a poster.

If you decide to consign to auction, you will be asked to sign a contract with the auction house. There are a number of standard provisions with which you should be familiar.

Auction houses charge the consignor for insurance, shipping, photographs (for catalogs), handling, and the seller's commission. There is a charge, a percentage of the reserve, if the work is bought-in. There is also a withdrawal fee if you change your mind.

Standard commission rates prevail: 20% for lots under $2,000, 15% for lots between $2,000 and $7,500, and 10% for lots above $7,500.

If the fees sound high, remember they must offset the considerable expenses the house carries–rent, staff, storage, catalog, publicity, overhead, and viewing.

A dealer or appraiser who refers a seller to an auction house may be paid a finder's fee, which is paid by the house out of its commission. The need to pay the fee may limit the house's ability to adjust its commission rates.

But, because flexibility and variability are the rule in the auction world, there is often room to negotiate many of these provisions. If, for example, you agree to the reserve the house suggests, the house in turn may agree to waive the buyback commission. The best rule to remember is to ask every question about costs and procedures that comes to mind. Afterall, the auction house is there to serve you.

Working with a Dealer

Working with a dealer or a gallery presents two additional options–selling the work directly, or placing it on consignment. The fee in the latter option can range up to 25% of the sale price, or it may be a set commission plus the dealer's costs.

There are good reasons to take a work to a dealer, rather than to auction. Going "private" permits exclusivity. The right dealer may know just the right buyer. The right dealer can show only the work you've sold or consigned, and it won't have to compete with other pieces by the same artist. A good dealer is knowledgeable and can act discreetly. The dealer should be willing to agree that the work be shown only to select clients while consigned for an agreed period of time.

If you want to sell a work directly to a dealer, follow the same steps you would take if you wanted to buy. Call your local museum and ask for a reference. Call the Art Dealers Association Headquarters in New York (212-940-8590) and request a list of members; call the Private Art Dealers Association (PADA), a new organization based in New York, at 212-315-4820.

Pick a dealer who specializes in the kind of work you want to sell, and check how long the dealer has been in business. Take the time to check the credentials of any source you use. Try to protect yourself from untrained or self-appointed appraisers.

Trust is essential in this relationship. Some prospective sellers are hesitant about contracting for a commission sale, since it can be difficult to ascertain a final price. If you do choose to work with a dealer, be certain that the conditions of the sale are made explicit in writing at the time that you consign. Ask for a status report within two weeks.

Selling a painting poses some of the same questions as buying–establishing value, creating a working relationship with a sales agent, whether an auction house or dealer, and investigating the various mechanisms that are needed to achieve a sale. By proceeding thoughtfully and cautiously, you are more likely to achieve the result you hope for.

The Impossible Dream

It happens every year–at least once. The lost work reappears; a locked storage closet is opened in a warehouse; a dusty old canvas is brought out of an attic; a masterwork surfaces at a garage sale. It is the stuff that dreams are made of.

The odds against making a major find are overwhelming. However, there is always the possibility of turning up something undervalued or unrecognized. And if you succeed, what then?

The first step is to do your basic research. If the picture is signed, perhaps another work by the same artist is listed in this book, or some other art price guide. However, the name alone is not enough to authenticate the work, for the signature may have been added. Or, the painting may have the wrong attribution inscribed on a plaque on the frame, or on the back of the canvas. Don't believe something just because it's written down.

Next, have the work appraised. Take the picture to an established dealer or auction house. Most auction houses will give a free verbal appraisal. Get a second opinion.

Some museums hold appraisal days. Call for information. On a typical appraisal day, a museum will assemble outside experts, art specialists from auction houses and galleries, who will tell you who, what, and when, but will not set a dollar value. Charges vary from $5-$12 for a verbal opinion. Some charitable organizations or schools occasionally sponsor appraisal days.

Auction houses offer free verbal estimates, by appointment, at their main galleries. They will supplement the information provided by the museum by appraising the work for its "auction" value. Sotheby's and Christie's maintain offices around the country, and there are numerous smaller houses listed in Appendix C. If you can't bring the work in, mail a photograph to the appropriate department of your favorite auction house and ask for an unofficial appraisal. Auction houses are responsive to these inquiries, and will follow up immediately if they think you've made a find.

Get a second opinion, for appraisal is a highly subjective process and linked to the constant vagaries of the art market.

For everyone who cherishes the dream of making a find, hope is fed by stories like the one about the Martin Johnson Heade canvas that was sold at Bourne's in 1990.

Restoration

Great art is undaunted by time, but it can certainly be damaged. Even if it remains unblemished, a canvas which has hung for a century will darken with age. Or, it may have been harmed by too much attention. In most cases, a skilled restorer can make the painting look as it did when it was new.

You should bring exactly the same criteria to deciding whether to purchase a slightly damaged work of art as to one in pristine condition. If the painting moves you, and you can afford it, buy. Overlook *small* physical flaws, because they can be repaired. Restorers can accomplish near miracles with canvases that have holes or tears, or even water damage. Stains, mold,

Find Over the Fireplace

In the spring of 1990, the Richard Bourne Galleries on Cape Cod was asked to do a house appraisal by an owner who wanted to sell his silver and some of his furniture. When the appraiser walked in, he saw a painting of an orchid by Martin Johnson Heade hanging over the fireplace. The owner was completely unaware of the value of the work. The painting was sent to Theodore Stebbins, the Heade expert, for authentication. In August 1990 the painting, which had been framed under glass and was in pristine condition, sold for $550,000.

Martin Johnson Heade (1819–1904) was best known for his paintings of tropical birds and flowers and his eastern salt marsh landscapes. Born in Lumberville, Pennsylvania, he received his first training from Edward Hicks. His early paintings are signed M.J. Heed, his family name. When he was twenty, he changed his name to Heade and left for Europe, the first of many trips in search of subject matter. His wanderings took him to the Caribbean, South America, and all along the Eastern Seaboard of the United States.

Heade studied for a time with Hudson River School artists Frederic Church and John Kensett. His later landscapes are infused with light. Those 19th-century artists, painting from 1870 to 1890, who were concerned with the depiction of light and atmospheric effects, are called Luminists, a word coined in the 1960s. Heade was the archetypal Luminist painter. In his travels, Heade made three trips to Brazil and executed a variety of paintings of hummingbirds and orchids. After his marriage in 1884, at age 64, Heade settled in St. Augustine, Florida. During this period he painted Florida landscapes and still lifes. The orchid painting that was found over the fireplace was signed on the front, and on the back it was inscribed "M.J. Heade/Studio 7," the number of Heade's studio in St. Augustine in the late 1880s. From 1861 to 1944, Heade's works received little recognition. It was not until 1944, when one of his landscapes was hung in the Museum of Modern Art, that at long last his works began to be studied and appreciated. (Martin Johnson Heade, *Heliodore's Woodstar with a Pink Orchid*, oil on canvas, 15 x 20 in., Bourne, August 21, 1990, $550,000) and foxing (chemical impurities) can be removed from paper; fractured sculpture can be mended. Fire-damaged canvases present a particular problem. In some cases, fire may have damaged only the varnish covering the surface paint. This can be removed and fresh varnish applied. Sometimes fire affects the paint and turns it to a brownish hue which is neither reversible nor restorable. If you choose to buy a damaged work and have it restored, you may be getting a bargain and you'll actually come out ahead. Remember, however, that restoration can affect value, and the line between minor and major restoration may be fine where sensitive areas of the painting are concerned. Get the advice of a restorer or knowledgeable dealer before you purchase a work in poor condition.

A word of caution–restoration is a profession, not a hobby. Cleaning a canvas is not a do-it-yourself job. If you buy a dirty painting and can't afford a professional cleaning, leave it alone until you can have a restorer do the work. Don't touch the surface with anything more than a feather duster, and then only occasionally. Treat all paintings carefully. Don't expose a painting to extremes of humidity or temperature, don't hang a painting over a radiator or air conditioner and particularly not over a fireplace or wood stove.

Restoration, or conservation as it is also called, is a delicate procedure. A restorer has an arsenal of materials and techniques, but the same solvents and materials are available to both highly skilled and inept practitioners. The aim of restoration is to put a painting into good condition. Poor restoration can do more damage than the ravages of time.

Cleaning a canvas can be as simple as removing old varnish, lightly cleaning the surface, and applying a synthetic varnish that won't discolor.* The art and science of restoration combine in the decision of which materials to use, in what quantity, and, of the greatest importance, when to stop. Some artists signed their paintings after applying a preliminary coat of varnish. If a restorer fails to detect this, he may remove the signature. Other artists applied alternating layers of paint and varnish to build up a feeling of depth on the canvas. A restorer who doesn't recognize this technique will cause terrible damage.

Relining may be called for if the painting has lost its tautness. Relining is required to restore a punctured or torn canvas. In this process, the work is removed from its stretcher and adhered to another support (board, canvas, fiberglass, etc.). It is important to photograph or preserve in some manner any inscriptions or labels which are on the back prior to mounting. A modern rule of thumb is that restoration should be reversible so that, if a better technique is developed, it can be employed.

Sometimes all that is required to restore a work is a bit of inpainting, perhaps to touch up the edges where paint has chipped off at the stretcher line. Flaking or cracking paint requires more concerted attention. A variety of techniques can be used, and most often a painting will require a combination to complete the restoration.

Modern art, on the other hand, presents a different challenge to museums and collectors alike. Young artists often don't have the money to buy quality

---

* Restoration can dramatically change the way in which an artist's work is perceived. Subsequent to the cleaning of the Sistine Chapel, art historians have been forced to re-evaluate Michelangelo, long thought to have painted in muted colors. The cleaned ceiling of the chapel revealed amazingly vibrant colors.

This still life by John Joseph LaValley (1858–1930) was bought at auction in "as found" condition, badly in need of cleaning and with a large hole. Restorer Leonard Davis painstakingly removed the grime and varnish and stabilized the paint. He then mounted the canvas on linen to repair the hole, inpainted where needed, and applied a fresh coat of varnish, literally bringing the work back to its original condition. (Leonard L. Davis III, Newton, Massachusetts)

---

materials and costly pigments. Sometimes they don't prime their canvases. When they do start to sell, they may be tempted to invest in sports cars instead of art supplies. The results are awful–cheap paint on bad canvas can require attention in as little as five years.

Proper restoration is time consuming and expensive, but worth it. It is better to leave a canvas in the condition in which you bought it, than to have the job done poorly.

It must be noted that there is a significant body of opinion that holds that restoration can destroy the value of a work. For clumsy restoration, or restoration that changes the character of the original, that is undoubtedly true. Choosing the right restorer thus becomes vitally important.

Assume that you have purchased an "ancestor portrait" that seems lovely beneath the accumulated dirt, but has a small tear on the left side. How do you go about finding a restorer who will do the job well, but not charge an exorbitant price?

The cost of restoration varies widely, as does the quality. Probably the best source of referrals is a gallery owner, who will share your interest in paying a fair price for quality work. Major museums maintain their own restoration departments, but they will know of outside restorers, who, perhaps, once worked for the museum.

The price of restoration varies depending on the size of the work and its condition. In 1992, a highly skilled Boston restorer would have charged from $350-$500 to clean, reline, and do minor repairs on a 25 x 30 inch ancestor portrait. More elaborate procedures to deal with flaking, fly spots, fire, or water damage would increase the price two or three times or more.

In requesting an estimate for restoration, you may be asking for the impossible. A complex problem may involve x-raying, testing with a variety of solvents, or other preliminary steps to determine what the best approach will be. Once the preliminary work has been done, a conservator will discuss any unforeseen problems before proceeding. For example, a painting may appear to have a firm surface, but when tested, the paint may show a tendency to lift, indicating that it should be relined. Most conservators will give you a verbal listing of the work they will do, but will charge for a written one.

Art As Investment

Should you buy art as an investment?

"No!" is the resounding answer of dealers, gallery owners, auction house executives, and investment counselors.

Buy art because it moves you, because it is beautiful, because it appeals to you. Buy quality.

If these are your guidelines, it is quite possible that in ten or twenty years your purchases will be worth substantially more than what you first paid for them. Don't ever buy because you think that a currently underpriced field will come back into demand, or because you've read a glowing review of a popular young painter and you've heard that art is a gilt-edged investment.

Collecting art is an investment in the largest sense. It is an investment in time, in aesthetic pleasure, in developing your own eye and your expertise. If, along the way, your collection appreciates, the increase in value is an added benefit. It should never be a starting point.

Beware of a dealer who suggests a particular painting as a good investment. There's a sale pitch in marketing art, sometimes even a hard sell, and the hope that today's modest purchase will both enhance the living room and help send the children to college can be hard to resist.

"But what about those clever connoisseurs who bought the Impressionists in the 1950s?" you ask. "Haven't they sat smiling while prices for Impressionist works increased forty times and more?"

Indeed they have, but those same people who are fortunate enough to own paintings that now sell for millions made a significant investment when they first purchased, paying prices in the $40,000 range thirty or more years ago. (Note that the same $40,000 invested in an account paying 10% interest would have increased to over $1,120,000 in the same time period.)

Remember, too, that while public opinion of the Impressionists has done a complete about-face within a century, time has been less kind to other artists. During the '50s, '60s, and '70s, the paintings of 19th-century academicians William Adolphe Bouguereau and Sir Lawrence Alma-Tadema could be bought very inexpensively. Only recently have works by these artists commanded prices similar to what they sold for in the 19th century.

Similarly, 19th-century American painter Thomas Moran was immensely popular during his lifetime, and his works commanded high prices. He was later eclipsed by other artists, and only recently have his works again begun to sell for close to their original prices.

If, despite all these cautions, you are still intent on assembling your collection as an investment tool, you should bear a number of points in mind.

There is usually a strong correlation between cost and investment. Barring the occasional flukes and finds, investment quality work is expensive. Most works included in museum collections are important examples of an artist's style. A piece in a private collection does not need to be equally representative. In general but not always, a work is more valuable if it is a typical rather than an atypical example. A work that is both decorative and attractive is a safer bet than one that is not. The real trick is to find the museum quality paintings of the future today.

Studies and drawings done in preparation for major works are more valuable than those done for works that were never completed. Also, any documentation of a painting, especially if the artist has written about it in letters or in a diary, makes the work more valuable. A solid provenance enhances the value of an individual picture. A work that has been part of a major collection has accrued value; similarly, a work that has changed hands frequently, or been hawked around from dealer to dealer, may lose value. A work from a "good" period in the artist's career is more valuable than one produced in a less fertile time.

Where a work is sold can greatly affect its value, for art can be geographically chauvinistic. Scenes of the White Mountains of New Hampshire are popular in New England. Cowboy art is popular in the west. And some subjects do better than others–scenes of dead game are generally not sought after in the United States but are popular in Europe.

In general, pleasant subjects are more sought after than troubling ones: country scenes are more appealing than sickbeds; baskets of fresh flowers more attractive than those that are withered; bright and colorful pictures are more salable than gloomy and drab ones.

The size and shape of the work are of great importance. Some modern artists have produced canvases of heroic proportion, measuring ten by twenty feet. Few homes can accommodate such massive works, rendering them difficult to sell. Some dealers consider horizontal pictures easier to sell than vertical ones. The ratio 2 x 3 is thought to be the "ideal" proportion for a painting.

Assembling a collection of older art is a challenge, but the highest risks for the investor/collector are in contemporary art, for it hasn't stood the test of time. Chroniclers of the art market note that only about 5% of the artists who have their first one-person shows in major cities in any given year *ever* have another show. Another concern is that in the curious intersection of art and publicity, some young artists may be heavily promoted by a gallery with a healthy public relations budget and good press contacts. The difference between hype and a consistent display of talent may be difficult to ascertain.

There is, of course, another side to all this caution. Some of today's young artists will be tomorrow's masters, and a collector discerning and lucky enough to find this work will be able to combine aesthetic satisfaction with the pleasure of watching it appreciate.

A collector of contemporary work must be carefully attuned to every turn of the market, attend shows and gallery talks, visit artists' studios, and read the art press. While even the experts make mistakes, if you can buy the artists whom the curators, collectors, gallery owners, and artists themselves are buying, you're closer to the right track, but there are no guarantees. At best, buying contemporary work is a long-term investment, which may take ten years or more to appreciate, if it ever does. Some collectors think that the best time to buy is 30–40 years after an artist dies, when the sales price for his work hits a low.

One of the few characteristics that art and the traditional financial markets have in common is the tendency to run in cycles, with well-publicized periods of solid growth creating a bandwagon effect on purchases, only to be followed by a sharp decline in prices.

Double-digit inflation fuels speculation in the art market, but there are those who believe that art prices have been rising so much and so long that there could not be much more room for increase for a long time to come.

In short, you're more likely to find success as an investor by staying with more conventional financial instruments. Your investment in art belongs in a personal portfolio under "A" for aesthetic and "L" for love.

A Brief Guide to Art Research

This chapter will not make you a skilled art researcher. It will, however, provide you with basic approaches to art research, the names of the standard sources, and an overall method of developing your knowledge about a school or a movement in painting, or about an individual artist. A selective bibliography appears at the end of this chapter.*

The Library

General Art Reference Works and Encyclopedias

Where and how you begin to do art research depends very much on what you want to learn. If, fresh from a foray to a museum, you decide to explore a budding interest in flower painting, start at the main branch of your local library.

Inquire at the reference desk for general art sources. The three prime general reference books on the visual arts are *Encyclopedia of World Art*, *McGraw-Hill Dictionary of Art*, and *Praeger Encyclopedia of Art*. Each is well illustrated and geared to the general reader and beginning student. Each contains many articles on artists, periods, styles, terms, museums, and countries. Articles vary in length, from very short ones that define terms to more

---

* The approach assumes that you will begin your research in a library. However, it is also advisable to begin to build your own library of art reference books. An inexpensive, pocket-sized handbook, Ralph Mayer's *Dictionary of Art Terms and Techniques*, explains schools, techniques, styles, and art terms. Information is easy to retrieve.

Another very useful book is Lois Swan Jones' *Art Research Methods and Resources: A Guide to Finding Art Information*. This comprehensive guide, geared for more advanced researchers, surveys the basic sources, deals with research methods, and provides practical advice on how to obtain reference material. Of particular value is the inclusion of facsimiles of pages from major reference works and directions for their use. Jones also provides a dictionary of French, German, and Italian art terms.

substantial pieces on individual artists that include bibliographies. The five-volume McGraw-Hill work is especially accessible and readable.

Taking this first step and consulting a general reference book may give you all the information that you need or want to know. Should you require more data, there are various additional sources.

The Card Catalog

The card catalog lists every book in a library's collection. Holdings are indexed by author, subject, and title. If you are checking to see if the library owns a specific work, the author and title listings are the place to turn. If, however, you are pursuing a broader area, track it down in the subject catalog, starting with an inclusive topic, such as "painting," and then working through the subheadings to the one that will lead you to the pertinent titles. Research an artist by looking under his name. (See Appendix D for a detailed explanation of how artists' names are listed.) Types of books listed in a card catalog include:

Monographs. Books about individual artists that provide historical or biographical material and information about his or her more famous works.

Oeuvre catalogues. Systematic lists of each work of art in an artist's entire creative output, or the works in a specific medium.

Catalogues raisonnés. Similar to *oeuvre catalogues,* but provide a more complete citation for each work. (An auction catalog may try to give a particular lot added cachet by noting that it has been or will be listed in the *catalogue raisonné.*)

Exhibition catalogs. Document the exhibition of an artist's work at a museum or gallery.

Most public libraries will have some, but not all, of these resources. One time-tested way to find additional titles is to review the bibliography of related books and magazines that is usually found at the end of reference works. Librarians will be able to help you locate the more scholarly materials at an art library or in an adjacent larger city.

General Artist Dictionaries

There are no general dictionaries of artists in English, but there are two outstanding foreign language works that are the basic resources in the field. Many researchers turn first to Emmanuel Bénézit's *Dictionnaire Critique et Documentaire des Peintres, Sculpteurs, Dessinateurs et Graveurs.* Usually called "Bénézit," the ten-volume set, written in French, is an alphabetical listing of names with life dates and other basic information about international artists. It may include the names of cities where they studied and worked, and note any honors or awards given to them. Bénézit also provides facsimiles of some artists' signatures and some sales information. Last revised in 1976, the work retains certain idiosyncrasies. The names of some American and English artists, for example, are altered to the French versions–a Henry may be called a Henri; a Mary, Marie. You may occasionally hear an auctioneer say that an artist is listed in Bénézit–it's nice to know, but it doesn't really confer any value.

Another general reference, in German, is the highly regarded biographical dictionary compiled by Ulrich Thieme and Felix Becker, *Allgemeines Lexikon der bildenden Künstler von der Antike bis zur Gegenwart*, which runs to thirty-seven volumes. Generally preferred by scholars, it is a specialized, alphabetical index that contains material similar to that in Bénézit. At the end of each entry on an individual artist, there is a bibliography from which the data was drawn, with titles in the original language. Thieme-Becker, as it is usually called, was published from 1907 through 1950. Hans Vollmer's *Allegemeines Lexikon der bildenden Künstler des XX Jahrhunderts*, which covers artists born after 1870, is a supplement to Thieme-Becker.

Artist Indexes and General Indexes

An index can best be used as a jumping-off point for further research. Brief entries, listed alphabetically by the artist's last name, provide the complete name, nationality, life dates, and abbreviated notations of books or articles from which the information was compiled. The abbreviations used in a particular index are explained in the introduction to the individual work. These short listings direct you to longer articles and books about the artist in whom you are interested.

Patricia Havlice's two-volume *Index to Artistic Biography*, published in 1973, is a survey of sixty-four different biographical dictionaries exclusive of Thieme-Becker and Bénézit, and thus a valuable source of additional information. A supplement including material in seventy additional sources was published in 1981. Daniel Mallett's *Index of Artists*, first published in 1935, and its supplement which appeared in 1940, are other valuable biographical reference tools.

It is especially difficult to find information on little-known 20th-century artists, or on regional or very contemporary artists. The *Biography and Genealogy Master Index* is a guide to more than 725,000 listings in over fifty current editions of *Who's Who*. It includes the names of many individuals who are not listed anywhere else. *The New York Times Index* and *The New York Times Obituaries Index* are excellent sources of information about 20th-century artists. The latter, particularly, includes information about regional artists that may not be found elsewhere.

Major artists, movements, and periods are the subjects of books; less prominent names may become the special subjects of devoted researchers who publish articles in popular or scholarly periodicals. An index of periodical literature provides easy reference to recent articles on both major and minor artists. There are a number of specialized art indexes. Most libraries subscribe to *Art Index*, a quarterly which covers 230 journals and began publishing in 1929. (A selective list of art periodicals, tabloids, and newsletters appears in Appendix B.) As comprehensively as they survey periodical literature, none of the indexes include the highly respected tabloid *The Maine Antique Digest*, to which many avid collectors subscribe–a serious omission.

Specialized Artist Dictionaries and Directories

If you already know the basic facts about an artist's nationality and life dates, you may go directly to a specialized dictionary. Mantle Fielding's *Dictionary of American Painters, Sculptors and Engravers*, first published in 1925 and revised in 1974, is one of the better known dictionaries, though it is sometimes at variance with other sources and thus less reliable. Peter Falk's *Who Was Who in American Art*, compiled from the original thirty volumes of *American Art Annual, 1898-1933*, and from four volumes of *Who's Who in Art, 1935-1947*, includes biographical data and information about exhibitions, prizes, and membership in artist societies. Chris Pettey's *Dictionary of Women Artists* is international in scope and an excellent source on women artists born before 1900.

Other sources to check are George C. Groce and David H. Wallace's *New York Historical Society's Dictionary of Artists in America, 1565-1860*; William Young's *A Dictionary of American Artists, Sculptors and Engravers*; Peggy and Harold Samuels' *Artists of the American West*; and Eden Hughes' *Artists in California, 1786-1940*.

For information about contemporary American artists, consult *Who's Who in American Art*; the *Art in America Annual Guide to Galleries, Museums and Artists*; Samuels' *Contemporary Western Artists*; Paul Cummings' *A Dictionary of Contemporary American Artists*; and Les Krantz's *American Artists*.

If you are looking for information about a European artist, you will be able to turn to a number of standard texts. The basic biographical references for Italian art are Giulio Bolaffi's *Dizionario Enciclopedico Bolaffi dei Pittori e Degli Incisori Italiani: Dall' XI al XX Sècolo*, published in 1972, and A.M. Comanducci's *Dizionario Illustrato dei Pittori, Disegnatori e Incisori Italiani Moderni e Contemporanei*, last revised in 1962, which covers the 19th and 20th centuries.

Standard biographical references to British art include Christopher Woods' *Dictionary of Victorian Painters*, published in 1971; Grant Waters' *Dictionary of British Artists Working 1900-1950*, 1975; H.L. Mallalieu's *The Dictionary of British Watercolor Artists up to 1920*, 1976; and J. Johnson and A. Greutzner's *Dictionary of British Artists, 1880-1940*, 1976.

Additional Resources

Additional resources are available to a researcher intent on discovering information about a particular artist. Many are accessible by telephone, greatly easing the research process.

Archives of American Art

The Archives of American Art is a bureau of the Smithsonian Institution which documents the history of the visual arts in America by collecting and preserving original documents, diaries, letters, photographs, oral histories, and other materials.

The main offices of the Archives are in Washington, D.C., and regional offices are located in New York City, Boston, Detroit, San Francisco, and San Marino, California. Records in the Archives include artists' personal papers, letters, diaries, sketches, photographs, exhibition material, financial information, writings, and lectures. The Archives also contains the records of arts organizations and institutions, and the papers of critics, dealers, collectors, and scholars. In addition, the Archives publishes a newsletter which is available by subscription.

The Archives responds to telephone inquiries. If you are interested in a particular artist, call and ask if there is any information on file, and then make an appointment to see the material.

The National Museum of American Art

The Inventory of American Painting Executed Before 1914 was begun as a project to celebrate America's bicentennial in 1976. It is a little-known but invaluable source which now has information on over 22,000 artists and 262,000 paintings, indexed by artist, title, owner/location, and subject matter. While the information is maintained on computer, and the database is constantly updated, it is not absolutely accurate and may contain errors of date or spelling. However, up to twenty pages of information will be photocopied free of charge, and nominal charges apply to additional pages.

The Inventory of American Sculpture, another National Museum of American Art project, was begun in 1985. This is a new research database on the location, physical characteristics, and subject matter of outdoor monuments as well as sculpture in over 800 public and private collections. Information on each sculpture includes artist, title, medium, foundry identification, cast number, subject matter, location, and other data. Information on both sources is available by calling 202-357-2941.

Vertical Files

Many libraries maintain files of special material which is not listed in the card catalog, not shelved with books, and which may not be otherwise publicized. Generally filed under specific artists' names, these files preserve "casual" information that is quickly lost and almost impossible to replicate, and may include press releases, exhibition reviews, newspaper and magazine clippings, and obituaries. Librarians generally concentrate on artists working in the region. Historical societies also maintain excellent vertical files. If you can locate an artist's home town, call the library or museum there and inquire if they have such information and if they will duplicate these materials. Most will comply and charge only a small fee for the service. These ephemera or vertical files are gold mines of information unavailable anywhere else.

Associations

Many dictionaries will refer to the local or regional associations to which an artist belonged. Many of these groups maintained private archives, another resource of valuable information about individual artists. The *American Art Dictionary* and the *Encyclopedia of Associations* provide the addresses of associations, museums, and art clubs across the nation. The Society of Illustrators may have information on illustrators not found elsewhere. The Guild of Boston Artists, the National Academy of Design in New York, and the National Watercolor Society in Lakewood, California, may all preserve unique resources. Pursue your artist–it's a grown-up treasure hunt.

Price Guides

An artist's sales history is an invaluable record of information. Auction records are frequently the only source of public information about art prices, since those achieved from gallery sales and purchases from estates or personal collections may remain private. More detailed information about the price histories of artists at auction over the past five years is available in the parent publication of this volume, *Leonard's ANNUAL Price Index of Art Auctions,* published annually since 1981 by Auction Index, Inc., Newton, Massachusetts (617-964-2876). *Leonard's Index,* listed alphabetically by artist, includes every original work of art (exclusive of multiples) sold at auction at every major auction house in the United States. Updated annually, it provides the most current information, and can be found in many libraries. (Some surprising and prominent names turn up in *Leonard's Index.* The paintings of Zero Mostel, e. e. cummings, and Winston Churchill–all better known for other endeavors–have all sold at auction.)

Additional price information is available in Richard Hislop's *The Annual Art Sales Index,* which is published in England and covers international sales, but excludes all lots under $500 and any artists not listed in Bénézit.

Another index is Enrique Mayer's *International Auction Records,* translated from the French, which is published annually and includes prints in its price listings.

A Selective Bibliography

General Art Reference Works and Encyclopedias

Arts in America: A Bibliography. 4 vols. Edited by Bernard Karpel. Washington, D.C., Smithsonian Institution Press, 1979.

Encyclopedia of American Art. Edited by Milton Rugoff. New York, E.P. Dutton, 1981.

Encyclopedia of World Art. 15 vols. New York, McGraw-Hill Book Co., 1958.

Jones, Lois Swan. *Art Research Methods and Resources.* 2nd ed. Dubuque, Iowa, Kendall/Hunt Publishing Co., 1984.

Mayer, Ralph. *A Dictionary of Art Terms and Techniques*. New York, Harper and Row Publishers, 1981.

McGraw-Hill Dictionary of Art. 5 vols. Edited by Bernard S. and Shirley D. Meyers. New York, McGraw-Hill Book Co., 1969.

Phaidon Dictionary of Twentieth-Century Art. New York, Phaidon Publishers, 1973.

Praeger Encyclopedia of Art. 5 vols. New York, Praeger Publishers, Inc., 1971

General Artist Dictionaries

Bénézit, Emmanuel. *Dictionnaire Critique et Documentaire des Peintres, Sculpteurs, Dessinateurs et Graveurs*. 10 vols. 3rd ed. Paris, Grund, 1976.

Thieme, Ulrich, and Becker, Felix. *Allgemeines Lexikon der bildenden Künstler von der Antike bis zur Gegenwart; unter Mitwirkung von 300 Fachgelehrten des In-und Auslandes*. 37 vols. Leipzig, E.A. Seemann, 1907-50; reprint, 37 vols. Leipzig, F. Allmann, 1964.

Vollmer, Hans. *Allgemeines Lexikon der bildenden Künstler des XX. Jahrhunderts*. 6 vols. Leipzig, E.A. Seemann, 1953-62.

Artist Indexes and General Indexes

Art Index. 1 vol. Edited by Bertrum Deli. New York, H.W. Wilson Co., 1929+.

Biographical Dictionaries Master Index. Detroit, Michigan, Gale Research Co., 1975+.

Havlice, Patricia Pate. *Index to Artistic Biography*. 2 vols. Metuchen, New Jersey, The Scarecrow Press, Inc., 1973. Suppl. 1981.

Mallett, Daniel Trowbridge. *Mallett's Index of Artists*. New York, R.R. Bowker Co., 1935. Suppl. 1940; reprint, 1948.

New York Times Index. Vol. 1-1913. New York, New York Times Co., 1913+.

New York Times Obituaries Index, 1858-1968. New York, New York Times Co., 1970. Suppl. 1969-1978, 1980.

Specialized Artist Dictionaries and Directories

Art in America Annual Guide to Galleries, Museums, Artists. Edited by Walter Robinson. New York, Brant Art Publications, 1992.

Baigell, Matthew. *Dictionary of American Art*. New York, Harper and Row Publishers, 1979.

Catley, Bryan. *Art Deco and Other Figures*. Woodbridge, England. Antique Collectors Club, 1978.

Comanducci, Agostino Mario. *Dizionario Illustrato dei Pittori, Disegnatori e Incisori Italiani Moderni e Conemporanei*. Milano, Italy, Luigi Patuzzi Editore, 1970.

Dictionary of Contemporary American Artists. 4th ed. Edited by Paul Cummings. New York, St. Martin's Press, 1982.

Dizionario Enciclopedico Bolaffi dei Pittori e Degli Incisori Italiani: Dall'XI al XX Sècolo. 11 vols. Turin, Italy, Giulio Bolaffi Editore, 1972-76.

Encyclopedia of New Orleans Artists 1718-1918. New Orleans, The Historic New Orleans Collection, 1987.

Falk, Peter Hastings. *Who Was Who in American Art.* Madison, Connecticut, Sound View Press, 1985.

Fielding, Mantle. *Dictionary of American Painters, Sculptors and Engravers.* Poughkeepsie, New York, Apollo Book, 1983.

Groce, George C., and Wallace, David H. *The New York Historical Society's Dictionary of Artists in America, 1564-1860.* New Haven and London, Yale University Press, 1957.

Harper, J. Russell. *Early Painters and Engravers in Canada.* Toronto, Canada, University of Toronto Press, 1970.

Houfe, Simon. *The Dictionary of British Book Illustrators and Caricaturists.* Baron Publishing, Woodbridge, England, Antique Collectors Club, 1978.

Hughes, Edan Milton. *Artists in California, 1786-1940.* 2nd ed. San Francisco, Hughes Publishing Co., 1989.

Johnson, J., and Greutzner, A. *Dictionary of British Artists, 1880-1940:* An Antique Collector's Club Research Project Listing 41,000 Artists. Baron Publishing, Woodbridge, England, Antique Collectors Club, 1976.

Krantz, Les. *American Artists.* New York, Facts on File Publications, 1985.

Krantz, Les. *American Art Galleries.* New York, Facts on File Publications, 1985.

MacDonald, Colin S. *A Dictionary of Canadian Artists.* Ottawa, Canada, Canadian Paperbacks, 1972.

Mallalieu, H.L. *The Dictionary of British Watercolour Artists up to 1920.* Woodbridge, England, Antique Collectors Club, 1976.

Meyer, George H., Ed. *Folk Artists Biographical Index,* Detroit, Gale Research Co., 1987.

Naylor, Colin, and Genesis, P-Orridge. *Contemporary Artists.* New York, St. Martin's Press, 1977; 2nd ed., 1983.

Pettey, Chris. *Dictionary of Women Artists:* An International Dictionary of Women Artists Born Before 1900. Boston, Massachusetts, G.K. Hall Co., 1985.

Samuels, Peggy, and Samuels, Harold. *The Illustrated Biographical Encyclopedia of Artists of the American West.* Garden City, New York, Doubleday, 1976.

Samuels, Peggy, and Samuels, Harold. *Contemporary Western Artists.* New York, Crown Publishing, 1985.

Waters, Grant M. *Dictionary of British Artists Working 1900-1950.* Eastbourne Fine Art, Eastbourne, England, 1975.

Westphal, Ruth. *Plein Air Painters of California—The North.* Irvine, California, Westphal Publishing, 1986.

Westphal, Ruth. *Plein Air Painters of California—The Southland.* Irvine, California, Westphal Publishing, 1982, 1988.

Wood, Christopher. *The Dictionary of Victorian Painters.* 2nd ed. Antique Collectors Club, Woodbridge, England, 1978, 1981.

A Dictionary of American Artists, Sculptors and Engravers; From the Beginning Through the Turn of the Twentieth Century. Edited by William Young. Cambridge, Massachusetts, William Young and Co., 1968.

Association Directories

American Art Directory. 50th ed. New York, R.R. Bowker Co., 1986.

Encyclopedia of Associations. 21st ed. Detroit, Gale Research Co., 1987.

The Official Museum Directory: United States and Canada. 1st issue. Washington, D.C., American Association of Museums, 1971+.

Price Guides

The Annual Art Sales Index. 1st ed. Edited by Richard Hislop. Weybridge, Surrey, England, Art Sales Index, Ltd., 1969-70+.

Leonard's ANNUAL Price Index of Art Auctions. 1 vol. Edited by Susan Theran. Newton, Massachusetts, Auction Index, Inc., 1980+.

Mayer, Enrique. *International Auction Records: Engravings, Drawings, Watercolors, Paintings, Sculpture.* 1st English ed. Paris, Editions Enrique Mayer, 1967+.

Theran, Susan. *The Official Price Guide To Fine Art.* New York, House of Collectibles, 1987.

How to Use This Book

Fine Art: Identification and Price Guide is a compilation of prices of fine art sold at auction throughout the United States from September 1985 through August 1990. Prices of fine art are established in the marketplace–at galleries, private sales, and auctions. Only those established at auction are public record (in most cases governed by state regulations). These are the prices listed in this *Guide*.

The database for this volume consists of 37,388 names. Size limitations have forced us to refine it to 21,765 names, eliminating all artists whose top price was less than $600 at auction during this five-year period. You will find that there are famous artists, especially Old Masters such as Hieronymus Bosch and Vermeer, whose works are extremely rare and are not listed because their works have not been offered for sale during this period.

By providing data about the *actual prices* realized at auction for the work of thousands of artists, the *Fine Art: Identification and Price Guide* presents a baseline of information about the art market. Auction prices are sometimes considered to be wholesale and sometimes retail, depending on location and date of sale. This *Guide* will help you assess comparative price data for individual artists and will help you determine whether a particular work is fairly priced, overvalued or a bargain. The final consideration, however, must be the artistic quality of the painting, condition and other factors being equal.

The names of artists are listed exactly as they appear in the auction catalogs. Asterisks beside a name indicate that the expert cataloging the work found these letters indecipherable. In the case of some families of painters—the Breanskis, for example—not only did the artists choose similar subject matter, they also signed their names in a similar fashion. Attributions of such works are frequently confused. Our listings, therefore, reflect the manner in which these artists' works have been catalogued by the various auction houses. In other cases of similar names, prices have not been merged because of the uncertainty as to whether they were the same person.

The price range reflects the low and high prices for a category of work. Identical prices in "low" and "high" reflect that more than one work by the artist has sold but at the same price. If only one work by an artist was sold, the price will appear in the high column.

Price ranges are just that. Prices for an artist's work vary for a tremendous variety of reasons, including the importance and quality of the work, its size, and differences in medium. Other factors are the desire of competing bidders, condition, subject matter, framing, provenance, attendance, weather, etc. The price ranges in this book reflect these variables.

For the purpose of this *Guide*, fine art is categorized as paintings, drawings, and sculpture. Prints and etchings, while certainly within the category of fine art, are not included, because they are works that exist in multiples. Paintings include oil, tempera, acrylic, casein, and fresco. Drawings include watercolor, pastel, gouache, crayon, pencil, charcoal, pen and ink, and mixed media. Included in the sculpture category are bronzes, marble statuary, bas reliefs, constructions, mobiles, and assemblages. Appendix E provides a complete listing by category.

Indexing in this *Guide* conforms to the *Anglo-American Cataloging Rules* for names, revised in 1979. For reasons of size, we have not cross-indexed artists' names. Appendix D provides a brief summary of the cataloging rules. If there is any doubt, check all the possibilities.

Nationality and life dates are included for all artists where available. When conflicts have arisen as to their validity, we have been diligent in our research and have made informed decisions.

There is sometimes confusion about the authorship of a particular work. John Herring Sr. and his son, John Jr., are frequently confused. We've done our best to sort through all these problems and present accurate prices.

Prices reflect the popularity of a particular artist or style in a certain region, fads, and fashion in art. Above all they reflect the overall strength of the economy. The years between 1979 and 1990 were a highly speculative period for the entire art market. Prices for Western art rose during the oil crisis of 1981, fell sharply, and began to rise again for the quality pieces in 1990. Beginning with the Skull Collection in 1986, the first major collection of contemporary art to sell at auction, contemporary art prices rose very sharply. As we close the decade, record prices are still being set. The softening of prices is for those pieces which might have been bought for speculative or investment purposes only. Many feel that this is just a "rightening of the market."

Price is not the only index of value of an individual painting. Price will not tell you if a work is authentic. Neither will it tell you the unique characteristics or rarity of a painting. Note, too, that the price an artist sells for at auction is not necessarily what you will receive if you want to sell.

Finally, don't be discouraged by high prices. If you desire a work by a famous artist, it may be possible to buy a minor example for a reasonable sum. Slight sketches and smaller, less typical examples sell well below the prices of major canvases. The works of lesser known, undiscovered, or undervalued artists provide many good buying opportunities.

For more specific information on the works of a particular artist, refer to *Leonard's ANNUAL Price Index of Art Auctions,* the parent volume of this *Guide,* which provides more detailed information on titles of works sold, size, auction house, and date of sale.

Artists' Price Ranges

Artists' Price Ranges

A'BECKET, Maria
American d. 1904
paintings: (L) $358; (H) $1,100
sculpture: (H) $1,100

AACHEN, Johann von, or Hans von
German 1552-1616
paintings: (H) $6,050
drawings: (L) $2,750; (H) $6,050

AALTEN, Jacques van
American b. 1907
drawings: (H) $16,500

AARONS, George
American 1896-1980
paintings: (H) $5,500
sculpture: (H) $5,500

AARONSON, David
American b. 1923
paintings: (H) $825
drawings: (H) $275
sculpture: (H) $1,100

ABADES, Juan Martinez
Spanish b. 1862
paintings: (L) $9,350; (H) $14,300

ABAKANOWICZ, Magdalena
Polish b. 1930
sculpture: (H) $7,975

ABBATE, Niccolo dell'
Italian 1512-1571
paintings: (H) $297,000

ABBEMA, Louise
French 1858-1927
paintings: (L) $990; (H) $1,860

ABBETT, Robert
American b. 1926
paintings: (H) $8,360

ABBEY, Edwin Austin
American 1852-1911
drawings: (L) $154; (H) $13,200

ABBOTT, John White
paintings: (H) $4,675

ABBOTT, Lemuel Francis
English 1760-1803
paintings: (L) $1,870; (H) $5,500

ABBOTT, Lena H.
American early 20th cent.
paintings: (H) $1,650

ABBOTT, Yarnall
American 1870-1938
paintings: (L) $137; (H) $1,650

ABDELL, Doug
American b. 1947
sculpture: (L) $1,000; (H) $3,850

ABDY, Rowena Meeks
American 1887-c. 1945
paintings: (L) $6,050; (H) $13,200
drawings: (L) $138; (H) $825

ABEL, Frank
American 19th/20th cent.
paintings: (H) $990

ABEL-BOULINEAU, N.
French 20th cent.
paintings: (H) $10,450

ABEL-TRUCHET
French 1857-1918
paintings: (L) $3,190; (H) $9,350
drawings: (L) $880; (H) $2,640

ABELA, Eduardo
Cuban 1892-1966
paintings: (L) $4,425; (H) $7,700
drawings: (L) $2,200; (H) $2,750

ABERG, Charley
paintings: (H) $1,100
drawings: (H) $44

ABEYTA, Narcisco Platero, Ha So Deh
Navajo b. 1918
paintings: (H) $1,320
drawings: (H) $770

ABIETA, James
American 20th cent.
paintings: (H) $2,640

ABOUT, J.F.M.
paintings: (H) $1,760

ABRACHEFF, Nicolai
American b. 1897
paintings: (H) $1,980

ABRAHAM, Tancrede
French 1836-1895
paintings: (H) $2,750

ABRAHAMS, Helen
American
paintings: (H) $1,100

ABRAM
Continental 19th cent.
paintings: (H) $1,870

ABRAMS, Lucien
American 1870-1941
paintings: (L) $660; (H) $2,750

ABREU, Mario
Venezuelan b. 1918
paintings: (L) $1,650; (H) $7,150

ABRIL, Ben
American b. 1923
paintings: (L) $303; (H) $990

ABRY, Leon Eugene Auguste
Belgian 1857-1905
paintings: (H) $6,600

ABSOLON, John
English 1815-1895
drawings: (L) $198; (H) $1,650

ACCONCI, Vito
American b. 1940
drawings: (L) $6,600; (H) $15,400

ACEVES, Gustavo
Mexican b. 1957
paintings: (L) $2,750; (H) $3,080

ACHEFF, William
American b. 1947
paintings: (L) $1,320; (H) $16,500

ACHENBACH, Andreas
German 1815-1910
paintings: (L) $1,430; (H) $46,200
drawings: (L) $125; (H) $935

ACHENBACH, Gabrielle
paintings: (H) $3,300

ACHENBACH, Oswald
German 1827-1905
paintings: (L) $715; (H) $88,000
drawings: (H) $1,650

ACHESON, Alice Stanley
paintings: (H) $825
drawings: (H) $104

ACHILLE, Julie
French 1815-1881
paintings: (H) $660

ACHTSCHELLINCK, Lucas
Flemish 1626-1699
paintings: (H) $24,200

ACOSTA, A.
paintings: (H) $660

ACQUA, Cesare dell
Austrian 1821-1904
paintings: (H) $4,125

ADAM, Albrecht
German 1786-1862
paintings: (L) $26,400; (H) $29,700

ADAM, Denovan
paintings: (H) $1,760

ADAM, Edouard
French 1847-1922
paintings: (L) $1,320; (H) $3,300

ADAM, Edouard
French 1847-1929
paintings: (L) $1,100; (H) $3,850

ADAM, Emil
German 1843-1924
paintings: (L) $3,850; (H) $24,200
drawings: (H) $2,860

ADAM, Franz
German 1815-1886
paintings: (H) $44,000

ADAM, Gerhard
Continental 19th/20th cent.
paintings: (L) $1,100; (H) $1,320

ADAM, J.D.
paintings: (H) $2,200

ADAM, Joseph, Sr.
British 1842-1896
paintings: (L) $825; (H) $1,210

ADAM, Julius
German 1826-1874
paintings: (L) $16,500; (H) $42,350

ADAM, Julius
German 1852-1913
paintings: (L) $11,000; (H) $41,800

ADAM, Richard Benno
German 1873-1936
paintings: (L) $440; (H) $5,500
drawings: (H) $550

ADAM, William
American 1846-1931
paintings: (L) $412; (H) $990
drawings: (L) $330; (H) $385

ADAMS, Charles J.
British 1857-1931
paintings: (H) $1,760

ADAMS, Charles Partridge
American 1858-1942
paintings: (L) $440; (H) $8,800
drawings: (L) $275; (H) $1,045

ADAMS, Chauncey M.
American b. 1895
paintings: (H) $770

ADAMS, Ed
paintings: (H) $1,540

ADAMS, Edouard and Son
Anglo/French 1880-1910
paintings: (H) $2,640

ADAMS, Harry William
British 1868-1947
paintings: (H) $2,475

ADAMS, Herbert
American
sculpture: (L) $2,640; (H) $4,180

ADAMS, J.H.
paintings: (H) $1,650

ADAMS, Jeff
contemporary
paintings: (H) $1,760

ADAMS, John Clayton
British 1840-1906
paintings: (L) $220; (H) $13,200

ADAMS, John Otis
American 1851-1927
paintings: (L) $8,690; (H) $17,600

ADAMS, John Quincy
Austrian 1874-1933
paintings: (H) $38,500

ADAMS, Lilian
American b. 1899
paintings: (H) $770

ADAMS, Philip
American b. 1881
paintings: (L) $100; (H) $660

ADAMS, Robert
sculpture: (H) $770

ADAMS, Wayman
American 1883-1959
paintings: (L) $2,860; (H) $4,125

ADAMS, Willis Seaver
American 1844-1921
paintings: (L) $210; (H) $1,650
drawings: (H) $165

ADAMS, Woodhull
paintings: (H) $770

ADAMS, Wyman
paintings: (H) $770

ADAMSON, John
British 19th cent.
paintings: (H) $5,500

ADDAMS, Charles
drawings: (L) $440; (H) $825

ADDISON, Byron Kent
American b. 1937
sculpture: (H) $3,850

ADEMA, Gerhardus Jan
Dutch b. 1898
paintings: (H) $660

ADERENTE, Vincent
Italian/American 1880-1941
paintings: (H) $1,760

ADICKES, David
American
paintings: (L) $110; (H) $660

ADLER, Edmund
German 1871-1957
paintings: (L) $4,400; (H) $10,175

ADLER, Jankel
Polish 1895-1949
paintings: (L) $5,500; (H) $27,000
drawings: (L) $880; (H) $4,400

ADLER, Jules
French 1865-1952
paintings: (H) $5,500
drawings: (H) $660

ADLER, Oscar F.
American 19th/20th cent.
paintings: (L) $302; (H) $1,760

ADLER, Yankel
paintings: (H) $4,180

ADNET, Francoise
French b. 1924
paintings: (L) $308; (H) $1,100

ADNET, Jean and Jacques
French early 20th cent.
sculpture: (H) $2,420

ADOLPH, A.
German (?) 19th cent.
paintings: (H) $660

ADOLPHE, Albert Jean
American 1865-1940
paintings: (L) $121; (H) $1,760
drawings: (H) $1,210

ADRIAENSSEN, Alexander
Flemish 1557-1661
paintings: (L) $2,640; (H) $7,700

ADRIAN, Gilbert
American 1903-1959
paintings: (H) $700
drawings: (L) $275; (H) $11,000

ADRIAN, M.
German 19th cent.
paintings: (H) $6,050

ADRIANI, Camille
American 19th/20th cent.
paintings: (L) $137; (H) $2,310

ADRION, Lucien
French 1889-1953
paintings: (L) $385; (H) $9,900
drawings: (L) $660; (H) $1,320

ADZAK, Roy
sculpture: (H) $2,640

AELST, Evert van
Dutch 1602-1657
paintings: (H) $2,750

AELST, Pieter Coecke van, studio of
1502-1550
paintings: (H) $26,400

AELST, Willem van
Dutch 1625/26-c. 1683
paintings: (H) $13,200

AENVANCK, Theodor van
Flemish 1633-1690
paintings: (H) $44,000

AERNI, Franz Theodor
paintings: (H) $2,750

AERTSEN, Pieter
Dutch 1507/1508-1575
paintings: (L) $6,600; (H) $88,000
drawings: (H) $20,900

AFFLECK, Rafe
contemporary
sculpture: (H) $1,650

AFFLECK, William
British b. 1869
drawings: (L) $1,760; (H) $18,700

AFFORTUNATI, Aldo
Italian b. 1906
paintings: (H) $1,100

AFRICANO, Nicholas
American b. 1948
paintings: (L) $2,970; (H) $63,250
drawings: (L) $1,430; (H) $3,190
sculpture: (L) $6,050; (H) $44,000

AFRO, Afro BASALDELLA
Italian 1912-1976
paintings: (L) $5,775; (H) $253,000
drawings: (L) $1,760; (H) $35,750

AFSARY, Cyrus
American b. 1940
paintings: (L) $1,100; (H) $11,000

AGAM, Yaacov
Israeli b. 1928
paintings: (L) $9,900; (H) $44,000
drawings: (L) $1,760; (H) $11,000
sculpture: (L) $495; (H) $19,800

AGARD, Charles Jean
French b. 1866
paintings: (L) $4,400; (H) $8,250

AGASSE, Jacques Laurent
Swiss 1767-1849
paintings: (H) $385,000

AGGERUP, Agnes
Danish 19th cent.
paintings: (H) $15,400

AGNDE (?), E.
paintings: (H) $1,045

AGNEW, Clark
American 19th/20th cent.
paintings: (H) $5,500

AGOSTINELLI
French 20th cent.
paintings: (H) $880

AGOSTINI, Guido
Italian 19th cent.
paintings: (L) $3,300; (H) $7,150
drawings: (H) $352

AGOSTINI, Peter
contemporary
drawings: (L) $121; (H) $990

AGOSTINI, Tony
Italian b. 1816
paintings: (L) $495: (H) $1,320

AGRASOT Y JUAN, Joaquin
Spanish b. 1836
paintings: (L) $6,050; (H) $88,000
drawings: (L) $247; (H) $286

AGRESTI
paintings: (H) $935

AGRICOLA, Christoph Ludwig
German 1667-1719
drawings: (H) $3,575

AGUILA, A. del
Spanish 19th cent.
paintings: (L) $1,650; (H) $1,650

AGUILAR, Homero
paintings: (H) $4,180

AGULAR
Continental
sculpture: (H) $660

AHEARN, John
American b. 1951
sculpture: (L) $2,750; (H) $8,800

AHL, Henry Curtis
b. 1905
paintings: (H) $2,475

AHL, Henry Hammond
American 1869-1953
paintings: (L) $61; (H) $11,000
drawings: (L) $33; (H) $220

AHLBORN, August Wilhelm Julius
German 1796-1857
paintings: (H) $6,050

AHRBACH, C.
paintings: (H) $2,475

AHRENS, Carl
Canadian 1863/67-1936
paintings: (L) $77; (H) $770

AID, George Charles
American b. 1872
paintings: (H) $1,980

AIKEN, Charles Avery
American 1872-1965
paintings: (L) $165; (H) $750
drawings: (H) $165

AINSLEY, Dennis
French 1880-1952
paintings: (L) $38; (H) $1,100

AIRY, Anna
English 1882-1964
paintings: (H) $17,050

AITKEN, John Ernest
British 1881-1957
drawings: (L) $413; (H) $715

AITKEN, Robert Ingersoll
American 1878-1949
sculpture: (L) $1,045; (H) $15,400

AIVAZOFFSKI, Ivan
Constantinowitsch
Russian 1817-1900
paintings: (L) $4,400; (H) $58,300

AIZELIN, Eugene Antoine
French 1821-1902
sculpture: (L) $1,045; (H) $4,180

AIZENBERG, Roberto
Argentinian 20th cent.
paintings: (H) $8,250

AIZPIRI, Paul
French b. 1919
paintings: (L) $1,870; (H) $115,500
drawings: (L) $2,420; (H) $10,450

AJDUKIEWICZ, Sigismund
paintings: (L) $1,210; (H) $3,300

AJDUKIEWICZ, Tadeusz
Polish 1852-1916
paintings: (L) $2,475; (H) $14,300

AKAWIE, Tom
contemporary
paintings: (H) $1,650

AKELEY, Carl Ethan
American 1864-1926
sculpture: (L) $1,100; (H) $18,700

AKERS, Vivian Milner
American b. 1886
paintings: (L) $440; (H) $5,500

AKIN, Louis
American 1868-1913
paintings: (L) $220; (H) $3,300

AKINOBU, Kano
Japanese 1773-1826
drawings: (H) $2,860

AKKERINGA, Johan
Dutch b. 1864
paintings: (L) $440; (H) $2,420

ALAJALOV, Constantin
Russian/American b. 1900
paintings: (L) $770; (H) $825
drawings: (H) $55

ALARS, B.
paintings: (H) $1,760

ALAUX, Guillaume
French ac. 1883-1907; d. 1913
paintings: (L) $1,430; (H) $4,125

ALAUX, Gustave
French 1887-1965
paintings: (H) $660

ALAUX, Jean Pierre
French b. 1925
paintings: (L) $165; (H) $1,045

ALBAN, Samuel
paintings: (H) $715

ALBANI, Francesco
1578-1660
drawings: (H) $8,250

ALBAREDE, A.
paintings: (H) $770

ALBERIA, A.
paintings: (H) $2,860

ALBEROLA, Jean Michel
contemporary
paintings: (L) $2,200; (H) $9,350

ALBERS, Anton
paintings: (H) $770

ALBERS, Josef
American 1888-1976
paintings: (L) $12,100; (H) $198,000
drawings: (H) $1,760

ALBERT, Arthur
American 1919-1987
paintings: (L) $44; (H) $2,860
drawings: (L) $440; (H) $2,090

ALBERT, E. Maxwell
American b. 1890
paintings: (L) $137; (H) $1,320

ALBERT, Ernest
American 1857-1946
paintings: (L) $2,640; (H) $16,500
drawings: (L) $770; (H) $6,600

ALBERT, Hermann
paintings: (H) $2,970

ALBERTI, Cherubino
1553-1615
drawings: (H) $11,000

ALBERTI, G.
Italian 20th cent.
paintings: (H) $797

ALBERTI, Giovanni or Cherubino
drawings: (H) $1,650

ALBERTS, W.J.
American 20th cent.
paintings: (H) $660

ALBINSON, Dewey Ernest
American b. 1898
paintings: (L) $303; (H) $3,300

ALBORI, V.
paintings: (H) $8,250

ALBRECHT, Carl
German b. 1862
paintings: (H) $770

ALBRECHT, Kurt
American 20th cent.
paintings: (H) $9,350

ALBRIGHT, Adam Emory
American 1862-1957
paintings: (L) $1,100; (H) $63,800

ALBRIGHT, E.F.
paintings: (H) $935

ALBRIGHT, Henry James
American 1887-1951
paintings: (L) $100; (H) $1,100

ALBRIGHT, Herman Oliver
American 1876-1944
drawings: (L) $66; (H) $825

ALBRIGHT, Ivan Le Lorraine
American 1897-1983
paintings: (H) $11,000
drawings: (L) $770; (H) $2,750

ALBRIGHT, John A.
American 20th cent.
paintings: (L) $330; (H) $935

ALBRO, Maxine
American 1903-1966
paintings: (L) $138; (H) $1,320

ALCALAY, Albert
French/American 20th cent.
drawings: (L) $275; (H) $880

ALCAZAR Y RUIZ, Manuel
Spanish 19th cent.
paintings: (H) $8,800

ALDEMOLLO, Carlo
Italian b. 1825
paintings: (H) $8,800

ALDERTON, Henry Arnold
American 1896-1961
paintings: (L) $412; (H) $715

ALDIN, Cecil
English 1870-1930
paintings: (H) $8,250
drawings: (L) $2,310; (H) $9,900

ALDINE, Marc
Italian b. 1917
paintings: (L) $385; (H) $8,250

ALDRICH, George Ames
American 1872-1941
paintings: (L) $165; (H) $4,840

ALDRIDGE, Frederick James
English 1850-1933
drawings: (L) $275; (H) $825

ALDRIDGE, William Joseph
American
drawings: (H) $2,200

ALDRIN, Anders Gustave
American 1889-1970
paintings: (L) $385; (H) $4,125

ALEBON, J.
American 19th cent.
paintings: (H) $2,090

ALECHINSKY, Pierre
Belgian b. 1927
paintings: (L) $6,325; (H) $330,000
drawings: (L) $4,950; (H) $66,000

ALENKOPF, J.
paintings: (H) $660

ALENZA Y NIETO, Leonardo
paintings: (H) $4,620
drawings: (H) $660

ALEX, Kosta
American b. 1925
drawings: (L) $220; (H) $605
sculpture: (H) $5,500

ALEXANDER, C.
British 19th cent.
paintings: (H) $1,320

ALEXANDER, Clifford Grear
American 1870-1954
paintings: (L) $770; (H) $4,950

ALEXANDER, Francesca
American 1837-1917
paintings: (L) $4,180; (H) $5,500
drawings: (H) $3,850

ALEXANDER, Francis
American 1800-1880/81
paintings: (H) $660

ALEXANDER, Henry
American 1860-1895
paintings: (H) $12,100

ALEXANDER, John
American b. 1945
paintings: (L) $1,320; (H) $25,300
drawings: (H) $5,720

ALEXANDER, John White
American 1856-1915
paintings: (L) $20,900; (H) $517,000
drawings: (L) $330; (H) $24,200

ALEXANDER, Peter
American b. 1939
paintings: (H) $242
drawings: (H) $5,500

ALEXANDER, William
British 1767-1816
drawings: (H) $26,400

ALEXANDROFF, J.A.
Russian b. 1837
paintings: (H) $2,090

ALEXEIEFF, Alexandre
Russian b. 1901
paintings: (L) $660; (H) $1,000

ALEXEIEFF, Alexandre-Ignatjewitsch
Russian b. 1842
paintings: (H) $4,400

ALFANI, Domenico
Italian 1479/1480-1553
paintings: (H) $49,500

ALFIERI, J.
French 19th/20th cent.
paintings: (L) $88; (H) $4,675

ALFIERI, V.
sculpture: (H) $1,650

ALFINITO
paintings: (H) $715

ALGARDI, Alessandro
Italian 1595-1654
sculpture: (L) $52,250; (H) $115,500

ALIANI
Italian 19th cent.
paintings: (H) $825

ALICHIN, Harry
20th cent.
paintings: (H) $935

ALIGNY, Claude
French 1798-1871
paintings: (H) $1,500

ALKEN, H.
drawings: (H) $660

ALKEN, Henry
English 19th cent.
drawings: (H) $4,950

ALKEN, Henry, Jr.
British 1810-1894
paintings: (L) $2,530; (H) $14,300

ALKEN, Henry Thomas
English 1785-1851
paintings: (L) $3,025; (H) $143,000
drawings: (L) $880; (H) $9,900

ALKEN, Samuel
English
paintings: (L) $6,050; (H) $15,400

ALKEN, Samuel, Jr.
English c. 1784-1825
paintings: (L) $6,875; (H) $16,500

ALKEN, Samuel Henry
British 1810-1894
paintings: (L) $3,520; (H) $29,700

ALKEN, Sefferin
English 19th cent.
drawings: (H) $1,100

ALKEN, T.
English 19th/20th cent.
paintings: (H) $742

ALLAN, Archibald Russell Watson
English 1878-1959
paintings: (L) $1,210; (H) $1,210

ALLAN, M.
English 19th cent.
paintings: (H) $1,155

ALLAN, Robert Weir
English 1852-1942
paintings: (L) $440; (H) $1,320
drawings: (H) $550

ALLAN, Sir William
British 1782-1850
paintings: (H) $6,875

ALLAN, V.
paintings: (H) $660

ALLBON, Charles Frederick
British 19th cent.
drawings: (H) $715

ALLCHIN, Harry
American 19th/20th cent.
paintings: (L) $495; (H) $825

ALLEAUME, Ludovic
French b. 1859
paintings: (H) $4,950

ALLEGRAIN, Christophe Gabriel
French 18th cent.
sculpture: (L) $660; (H) $71,500

ALLEMANDE, Jean Baptiste
French 18th cent.
drawings: (H) $3,300

ALLEN, C.H.
paintings: (L) $44; (H) $990

ALLEN, Charles Curtis
American 1886-1950
paintings: (L) $110; (H) $2,970
drawings: (H) $330

ALLEN, Courtney
American b. 1896
paintings: (H) $880

ALLEN, Douglas
20th cent.
paintings: (H) $770
drawings: (L) $495; (H) $550

ALLEN, Frederick Warren
American 1888-1961
sculpture: (H) $6,600

ALLEN, Greta
paintings: (H) $880

ALLEN, Jasper van
American 20th cent.
paintings: (H) $880

ALLEN, Junius
American 1898-1962
paintings: (L) $247; (H) $3,850

ALLEN, Luther
American
paintings: (H) $13,750

ALLEN, Marion Boyd
American 1862-1941
paintings: (L) $275; (H) $8,250

ALLEN, Robert
paintings: (H) $1,320

ALLEN, Thomas
American 1849-1924
paintings: (L) $385; (H) $7,150
drawings: (L) $308; (H) $7,700

ALLEN, V.
American 20th cent.
paintings: (L) $412; (H) $2,200

ALLIEVI, Fernando
Argentinian b. 1954
drawings: (L) $2,640; (H) $4,400

ALLIGRE, F.
French 19th cent.
paintings: (H) $2,530

ALLINGHAM, Helen
English 1848-1926
drawings: (L) $412; (H) $9,350

ALLIOT, Leon
sculpture: (L) $1,100; (H) $4,400

ALLIOT, Lucien
French ac. 1905-1940
sculpture: (L) $110; (H) $8,080

ALLIS, C. Harry
American c. 1880-1938
paintings: (L) $165; (H) $1,100
sculpture: (L) $138; (H) $138

ALLISON, Roy
paintings: (H) $1,155

ALLORI, Alessandro
Italian 1535-1607
paintings: (H) $110,000

ALLORI, Alessandro di Cristofano,
workshop of
1535-1607
paintings: (H) $52,800

ALLORI, Cristofano
1577-1621
paintings: (L) $1,100; (H) $2,200

ALLOUARD, Henri
French 1844-1929
sculpture: (L) $825; (H) $2,200

ALLTER, M.
French 19th/20th cent.
paintings: (H) $935

ALLUSTANTE Y PALLARES, Joaquin
paintings: (L) $2,200; (H) $4,400

ALLWORTHY
paintings: (H) $825

ALMA-TADEMA, Lady Laura Teresa
English 1852-1909
paintings: (H) $22,000

ALMA-TADEMA, Sir Lawrence
English 1836-1912
paintings: (L) $3,080; (H) $242,000
drawings: (L) $330; (H) $20,900

ALMOND, William Douglas
British 19th cent.
paintings: (L) $357; (H) $880

ALONSO, Carlos
Argentinian b. 1929
paintings: (H) $15,400

ALONSO-PERES, Carlos
Spanish 19th/20th cent.
paintings: (H) $6,050

ALONZO, Dominique
French 20th cent.
sculpture: (L) $302; (H) $2,860

ALORDA Y PEREZ, Ramon
Spanish 19th cent.
drawings: (H) $1,870

ALOTT, Robert
paintings: (L) $3,300; (H) $14,300

ALOTT, Rudolf
French 19th/20th cent.
paintings: (H) $6,600

Victorian Art

Sir Lawrence Alma-Tadema (1836-1912) was a well-known painter of classical Greek and Roman subjects. Born in Holland, he entered the Antwerp Academy when he was sixteen and studied archaeology. In 1860 he became a pupil and assistant to Baron Leys, a well-known Belgian painter of historical scenes. In 1863, Alma-Tadema visited Pompeii and created a substantial collection of photographs, sketches, and drawings. From 1865 to 1870, his Pompeii period, he painted scenes of Greek and Roman antiquity.

In 1870, Alma-Tadema settled in London, becoming a British citizen in 1873. He was so enamored of ancient Rome that his home in a London suburb was remodeled as a Pompeiian villa. He was a prolific artist and numbered all of his works with Roman numerals, from Opus I, painted when he was fifteen, to CCCCXIII, painted two months before his death. His works were popular in Victorian England.

Alma-Tadema became a member of the Royal Academy in 1879, was knighted in 1899, and received the Order of Merit in 1905. He also produced stage sets and received a gold medal for his promotion of architecture in painting. *A Roman Scribe Writing Dispatches,* in a custom frame designed by Alma-Tadema, is one of the earliest works from his Pompeiian period. The painting is in keeping with the Victorian style of anecdotal, narrative work. Some Victorian painters painted historical scenes, and others, as a reaction to the Industrial Revolution, painted tranquil scenes of domesticity that appealed to the prevailing tastes of middle-class patrons. Many Victorian painters fell out of style in the 20th century and their reputations have only recently been revived.

In 1990 the McCormick Collection of Victorian paintings was offered for sale at Sotheby's. The McCormicks had gathered a collection of works by Victorian artists who had been honored during their lifetimes. When the sale was over, twenty-nine lots had sold for over $2.1 million. (Sir Lawrence Alma-Tadema, *A Roman Scribe Writing Dispatches*, oil on cradled panel, 22 x 15½ in., Sotheby's, February 28, 1990, $110,000)

ALPERIZ, Nicolas
Spanish b. 1869
paintings: (H) $4,400

ALPHONSE, L.V.
American 19th cent.
paintings: (H) $1,045

ALPOINTE
sculpture: (H) $935

ALPUY, Julio
sculpture: (H) $1,650

ALSINA, J.
paintings: (L) $2,750; (H) $2,860

ALSINA, J.
French 19th/20th cent.
sculpture: (L) $1,540; (H) $2,200

ALSLOOT, Denis van
Flemish 1570-1628
paintings: (H) $110,000

ALSTON, Abbey
British b. 1864
paintings: (H) $11,000

ALSTON, Frank H., Jr.
American 20th cent.
paintings: (H) $660

ALT, Dr.
drawings: (L) $5,500; (H) $8,250

ALT, Franz
Austrian 1821-1914
drawings: (L) $2,090; (H) $9,350

ALT, Jacob
German 1789-1872
paintings: (L) $770; (H) $1,540
drawings: (H) $715

ALT, Rudolf von
Austrian 1812-1905
drawings: (L) $2,970; (H) $33,000

ALTAMIRANO, Arturo Pacheco
paintings: (L) $2,200; (H) $4,950

ALTEN, Mathias J.
German/American 1871-1938
paintings: (L) $247; (H) $8,525

ALTENKIRCH, Otto
paintings: (H) $2,750

ALTOON, John
American 1925-1969
drawings: (L) $358; (H) $4,675

ALTSON, Abbey
British 19th/20th cent.
paintings: (L) $660; (H) $22,000

ALVAREZ, Mabel
American 1891-1985
paintings: (L) $1,870; (H) $3,025

ALVARO DI PIERO, Il Portoghese
Portugese 15th cent.
paintings: (H) $85,000

ALY, Salvatti
Italian 19th cent.
paintings: (H) $660

AMADO Y BERNARDET, Ramon
Spanish 1844-1888
paintings: (H) $825

AMAHL
paintings: (H) $880

AMAN-JEAN, Edmond Francois
French 1860-1935/36
paintings: (L) $2,750; (H) $46,750
drawings: (L) $19,800; (H) $27,500

AMARAL, Antonio Henrique
Brazilian b. 1935
paintings: (L) $1,210; (H) $28,600

AMARAL, Tarsila
drawings: (H) $3,850

AMARATICO, Joseph
American 1931-1986
paintings: (H) $440
drawings: (H) $715

AMAT, Frederic
contemporary
drawings: (H) $4,400

AMAT, Jose
paintings: (H) $3,300

AMATEIS, Edmond
sculpture: (H) $3,080

AMATO, A.
paintings: (H) $660

AMBERG, Wilhelm
German 1822-1899
paintings: (L) $1,320; (H) $3,740

AMBRESATH
English 20th cent.
paintings: (H) $825

AMBROGIANI, Pierre
French b. 1907
paintings: (H) $2,860
drawings: (H) $880

AMBROIS, Jules Francois Achille
paintings: (H) $2,420

AMBROS, Raphael von
paintings: (L) $3,300; (H) $8,250

AMBROSSI, A.J.
paintings: (H) $1,045

AMEGLIO, Merlo
Italian d. 1970
paintings: (L) $1,045; (H) $8,800

AMELE, Burdin
French b. 1834
paintings: (H) $1,045

AMENOFF, Gregory
American b. 1948
paintings: (L) $1,870; (H) $17,600
drawings: (H) $3,850

AMES, Adelbert
American early 20th cent.
paintings: (L) $880; (H) $880

AMES, Blanche
American 19th/20th cent.
paintings: (H) $1,100

AMES, Ezra
American 1768-1836
paintings: (L) $1,870; (H) $4,125

AMES, May
American d. 1946
paintings: (L) $143; (H) $715

AMICK, Robert Wesley
American 1879-1969
paintings: (L) $165; (H) $1,760
drawings: (L) $247; (H) $2,420

AMIGOMI, Pietro
Italian 20th cent.
drawings: (H) $2,475

AMIGONI, Jacopo
Italian 1675-1752
paintings: (L) $9,900; (H) $52,250

AMMAN, Jost
German/Swiss 1539-1591
drawings: (H) $66,000

AMORGASTI
sculpture: (L) $462; (H) $990

AMOROSI, Antonio
Italian 1660-c. 1736
paintings: (L) $2,750; (H) $44,000

AMORSOLO, Fernando Cueto
Filipino 20th cent.
paintings: (L) $990; (H) $7,480

AMSDEN, William King
American 20th cent.
paintings: (H) $990

AMSEL, Pearl
sculpture: (H) $4,675

AMSEL, Richard
American 1947-1985
drawings: (L) $6,600; (H) $15,400

AMUNDSON, Hjalmar
American b. 1905
paintings: (L) $110; (H) $1,500

AMYOT, C.G.
French 19th cent.
paintings: (H) $2,750

ANCELIN, P.
paintings: (H) $715

ANCHER, Michael Peter
Danish 1849-1927
paintings: (H) $2,310

ANDERS, Ernst
German 1845-1911
paintings: (L) $1,705; (H) $12,100

ANDERS, Robert
paintings: (H) $715

ANDERSEN, Carl Christian
Danish 1849-1906
paintings: (H) $24,200

ANDERSEN-LUNDBY, Anders
paintings: (H) $5,500

ANDERSON
paintings: (H) $1,210

ANDERSON, A.
Danish 19th cent.
paintings: (H) $1,540

ANDERSON, Abraham Archibald
American 1846-1940
paintings: (L) $247; (H) $1,210

ANDERSON, C. Stephen
American b. 1896
paintings: (H) $2,200

ANDERSON, C.A.
drawings: (H) $825

ANDERSON, C.W.
American 20th cent.
paintings: (H) $1,650

ANDERSON, Charles Goldborough
paintings: (H) $4,950

ANDERSON, Charles Webster
paintings: (H) $852

ANDERSON, David
contemporary
sculpture: (H) $660

ANDERSON, Doug
contemporary
paintings: (L) $1,650; (H) $2,750
drawings: (H) $88

ANDERSON, Emma
American c. 1870
drawings: (H) $1,210

ANDERSON, Harold N.
American b. 1894
paintings: (L) $2,420; (H) $3,300

ANDERSON, Harry
American b. 1906
drawings: (H) $1,870

ANDERSON, Jeremy
sculpture: (H) $2,090

ANDERSON, Karl
American 1874-1956
paintings: (L) $440; (H) $5,500
drawings: (L) $80; (H) $770

ANDERSON, Laurie
contemporary
drawings: (H) $1,760

ANDERSON, Lennart
paintings: (L) $2,420; (H) $5,500

ANDERSON, Neil
drawings: (H) $770

ANDERSON, Oscar
American b. 1873
paintings: (L) $110; (H) $880

ANDERSON, Victor Coleman
American 1882-1937
paintings: (L) $550; (H) $5,500
drawings: (H) $165

ANDERSON, Walter
American 1903-1965
drawings: (L) $1,210; (H) $2,310

ANDERSON, William
British ac. 1856-1893
paintings: (H) $3,025

ANDRE, Albert
French 1869-1954
paintings: (L) $440; (H) $44,000
drawings: (L) $660; (H) $880

ANDRE, Carl
American b. 1935
drawings: (H) $7,150
sculpture: (L) $18,700; (H) $198,000

ANDRE, Rene
French 20th cent.
paintings: (H) $770

ANDREA, John de
American b. 1941
sculpture: (L) $12,100; (H) $49,500

ANDREA, Mariano
paintings: (H) $715

ANDREA DI BARTOLO
Italian ac. 1389-1428
paintings: (H) $74,250

ANDREAE, Tobias
paintings: (H) $5,280

ANDREAS RICO
Italian 16th cent.
paintings: (H) $15,400

ANDREE, Ch.
French School 19th cent.
paintings: (H) $1,155

ANDREINI, Ferdinando
Italian b. 1843
sculpture: (H) $16,500

ANDREIS, Alex de
British 20th cent.
paintings: (L) $385; (H) $10,450

ANDREJEVIC, Milet
Yugoslav/American b. 1925
paintings: (L) $2,090; (H) $8,800

ANDREONI, Orazio
Italian late 19th cent.
sculpture: (L) $770; (H) $3,300

ANDREOTTI, Federico
Italian 1847-1930
paintings: (L) $715; (H) $66,000

ANDREW, Richard
American b. 1869
paintings: (L) $247; (H) $3,520
drawings: (H) $440

ANDREW, Walter
English 19th/20th cent.
paintings: (H) $1,540

ANDREWS, Ambrose
American 1824-1859
paintings: (L) $660; (H) $990

ANDREWS, Benny
b. 1930
paintings: (L) $550; (H) $4,400
drawings: (L) $110; (H) $935

ANDREWS, Eliphalat F.
American 1833-1915
paintings: (L) $275; (H) $5,390

ANDREWS, George H.
British/American
paintings: (L) $880; (H) $935

ANDREWS, George Henry
English 1816-1898
paintings: (L) $825; (H) $10,450

ANDREWS, Henry
Dutch 1801-1868
paintings: (H) $1,210

ANDREWS, James
American
drawings: (L) $605; (H) $770

ANDREY, James
sculpture: (L) $605; (H) $1,210

ANDRIESSEN, Hendrick
Dutch before 1607-1655
paintings: (H) $253,000

ANDRIEU, Mathurin Arthur
American
paintings: (H) $1,650

ANDRIEUX, Clement Auguste
French b. 1829
drawings: (L) $440; (H) $3,850

ANDRION, Lucien
contemporary
paintings: (H) $1,320

ANDROMEDA
paintings: (H) $825

ANDUJAR, Plutarco
paintings: (H) $2,200

ANDZOUSOW, Vadime
French
sculpture: (H) $7,150

ANELLI (?), V.
American 20th cent.
paintings: (H) $770

ANESI, Paolo
Italian c. 1700-c. 1761
paintings: (L) $6,600; (H) $31,900

ANGEL, Felix
drawings: (H) $1,100

ANGELIS, Clotilde de
drawings: (H) $880

ANGELVY, G.A.
French late 19th cent.
paintings: (H) $715

ANGENOT, O.
French/American 19th/20th cent.
paintings: (H) $2,090

ANGLADA-CAMARASA, Hermen
Spanish 1873-1959
paintings: (L) $50,600; (H) $101,200

ANGLADE, Gaston
French 1854-1919
paintings: (L) $302; (H) $2,200

ANGLIA, Emilio
sculpture: (H) $715

ANGO, Jean Robert
French ac. 1759-1769
drawings: (L) $825; (H) $4,400

ANGRAND, Charles
French 1854-1926
paintings: (H) $11,000

ANGUIANO, Raul
Mexican b. 1915
paintings: (H) $4,125
drawings: (L) $247; (H) $1,430

ANGUIER, Michel Andre, workshop of
French 18th cent.
sculpture: (H) $13,200

ANIEV
sculpture: (H) $1,980

ANIVITTI, Filippo
Italian b. 1876
paintings: (L) $1,760; (H) $4,400
drawings: (L) $132; (H) $2,090

ANKARCRONA, Henrik August
Swedish b. 1831
paintings: (H) $2,090

ANKER, Albert
drawings: (H) $880

ANNA, Alessandro d'
drawings: (L) $2,970; (H) $3,410

ANNENKOV, Yuri, Georges
ANNENKOPF
Russian 1890/94-1974
drawings: (L) $495; (H) $4,400

ANNIGONI, Pietro
drawings: (H) $660

ANQUETIN, Louis
French 1861-1932
paintings: (H) $8,800

ANRROY, Anton van
Dutch 20th cent.
drawings: (H) $1,760

ANSDELL, Richard
English 1815-1885
paintings: (L) $1,045; (H) $198,000

ANSELMI, Michelangelo
paintings: (H) $17,600

ANSHUTZ, Thomas Pollock
American 1851-1912
paintings: (L) $1,100; (H) $1,540,000
drawings: (L) $110; (H) $60,500

ANTES, Horst
German b. 1936
paintings: (L) $44,000; (H) $71,500
drawings: (L) $605; (H) $15,400

ANTHONISEN, George R.
American
sculpture: (H) $1,045

ANTHONY, Carol
American b. 1943
paintings: (H) $3,300
drawings: (H) $2,200

ANTHONY, Jean B.
Belgian b. 1854
paintings: (H) $3,740

ANTOINE, Fr.
paintings: (H) $1,760

ANTOKOLSKY, Mark
sculpture: (H) $2,750

ANTOLINEZ, Francisco
paintings: (H) $9,350

ANTONIA, Aurilio
sculpture: (H) $1,870

ANTONIANI, Pietro
Italian d. 1805
paintings: (H) $52,800

ANTONIAZZO ROMANO, studio of
Italian ac. 1461-d. 1508/09
paintings: (H) $57,750

ANTONINI
drawings: (H) $4,950

ANTONIO, Cristobal di
Spanish 19th cent.
paintings: (H) $2,200

ANTONISSEN, Henri Joseph
paintings: (H) $4,400

ANTRAL, Louis Robert
French 1895-1940
paintings: (H) $2,750

ANTUNEZ, Nemesio
Chilean b. 1918
paintings: (L) $1,540; (H) $4,400

ANTY, Henri d'
French b. 1910
paintings: (L) $330; (H) $1,650
drawings: (H) $66

ANUSKIEWICZ, Richard
American b. 1930
paintings: (L) $357; (H) $13,200
sculpture: (H) $605

AOVATTI, S.
Italian 19th cent.
paintings: (H) $715

APARICI, Antonio
paintings: (H) $2,200

APOL, Armand Adrien Marie
paintings: (H) $2,640

APOL, Louis
Dutch b. 1850
paintings: (L) $2,200; (H) $2,640
drawings: (H) $1,760

APOLLODORO DI PORCIA,
Francesco
Italian 16th cent.
paintings: (H) $49,500

APPEL, Charles P.
American b. 1857
paintings: (L) $440; (H) $16,500

APPEL, Karel
Dutch/American b. 1921
paintings: (L) $1,980; (H) $115,500
drawings: (L) $2,420; (H) $19,800
sculpture: (L) $2,090; (H) $22,000

APPERLEY, George Owen Wynne
British 1884-1961
paintings: (H) $29,700
drawings: (L) $82; (H) $220

APPERT, George
paintings: (L) $1,210; (H) $2,860

APPIAN, Adolphe
French 1818-1898
paintings: (H) $1,650

APPIAN, Louis
drawings: (H) $2,420

APPLEBAUM, Leon
contemporary
sculpture: (H) $1,100

APPLETON, George Washington
American 1805-1831
paintings: (H) $1,100

APSHOVEN, Thomas van
Flemish 1622-1664
paintings: (L) $4,675; (H) $12,100

ARAKAWA, Shusaku
Japanese b. 1936
paintings: (L) $2,860; (H) $176,000
drawings: (L) $4,180; (H) $126,500
sculpture: (H) $7,700

ARALOV, Vladimir Nikolaevitch
paintings: (H) $3,575

ARAMN
drawings: (H) $5,775

ARANGO, Alejandro
Mexican b. 1950
paintings: (H) $1,430

ARANIS
French 20th cent.
paintings: (H) $715

ARAPOFF, Alexis
Russian/American 1904-1948
paintings: (L) $1,210; (H) $5,500
drawings: (L) $110; (H) $1,430

ARAUJO, Carlos
paintings: (H) $7,700

ARAUJO, Emanuel
Brazilian b. 1940
sculpture: (H) $13,200

ARBEIT, Eugene
French b. 1825
paintings: (H) $1,980

**ARCANGELO DI COLA DA
CAMERINO**
Italian ac. 1416-1425
paintings: (H) $1,100,000

ARCHER, J.H.
American 19th cent.
paintings: (H) $27,500

ARCHIPENKO, Alexander
Russian 1887-1964
drawings: (L) $3,850; (H) $24,200
sculpture: (L) $2,530; (H) $517,000

ARCHULETA, Tony
American
paintings: (H) $990

ARCIERI, Charles F.
American
paintings: (H) $11,000

ARCOS Y MEGALDE, Santiago
Chilean 1865-1912
paintings: (H) $2,200
drawings: (H) $1,540

ARCUCCIO, Angelillo
paintings: (H) $6,325

ARDISSONE, Yolande
French 19th/20th cent.
paintings: (L) $1,210; (H) $2,090

ARDON, Mordecai
Israeli b. 1896
paintings: (H) $47,300

ARELLANO, Juan de
Spanish 1614-1676
paintings: (L) $9,350; (H) $715,000

ARENTZ, Arent, called Cabel
Dutch 1586-1635
paintings: (H) $44,000

ARENTZ, Josef M.
American 1903-1969
paintings: (L) $44; (H) $1,100
drawings: (L) $11; (H) $660

ARERA
French 19th cent.
paintings: (H) $8,800

ARESTI, Carlos
Chilean b. 1944
paintings: (L) $6,050; (H) $9,900

AREVALO, Javier
paintings: (H) $1,540

ARGIENTO, Nicholas, Duster
contemporary
paintings: (L) $990; (H) $1,540

ARGYROS, Oumbertos
Greek 1877-1963
paintings: (L) $9,900; (H) $12,100

ARIAS, J.
paintings: (H) $1,870

ARIOLLA, Fortunato
American 1827-1872
paintings: (L) $8,800; (H) $27,500

ARISSE, G.
French early 20th cent.
sculpture: (H) $3,300

ARIZA, Gonzalo
Colombian b. 1912
paintings: (L) $5,500; (H) $25,300

ARIZMENDI, Jose Sanz
Spanish 1885-1929
paintings: (H) $2,475

ARKHIPOV, Abram Efimovitch
Russian 1862-1930
paintings: (L) $440; (H) $660

ARLES, Jean Henry d'
French 1734-1784
paintings: (H) $99,000

ARMAN, Armand FERNANDEZ
French b. 1928
sculpture: (L) $800; (H) $363,000

ARMAND-DUMARESQ, Edouard
French 1826-1895
paintings: (L) $1,760; (H) $3,080

ARMBRUSTER, Tom
contemporary
sculpture: (H) $1,650

ARMENISE, Raffaello
Italian 1852-1925
paintings: (H) $9,900

ARMENTIA, Gustavo Lopez
paintings: (L) $3,300; (H) $3,850

ARMENTO, Louis S.
sculpture: (L) $770; (H) $2,640

ARMER, Laura Adams
American 1874-1963
paintings: (L) $3,575; (H) $8,800

ARMER, Ruth
American 1896-1977
paintings: (L) $44; (H) $660
drawings: (H) $467

ARMET Y PORTANEL, Jose
Spanish 19th cent.
paintings: (H) $27,500

ARMFIELD, Edward
British 19th cent.
paintings: (L) $577; (H) $7,700

ARMFIELD, Edwin
paintings: (H) $3,520

ARMFIELD, George
British ac. 1840-1875/80
paintings: (L) $550; (H) $16,500

ARMFIELD, Maxwell Ashby
English 1882-1972
paintings: (L) $1,045; (H) $19,800

ARMIN, Emil
American 1895-1983
paintings: (H) $660
drawings: (L) $275; (H) $880

ARMIN, L.C.
Austrian ? 19th/20th cent.
paintings: (H) $1,650

ARMINGTON, Frank Milton
Canadian 1876-1940
paintings: (H) $3,740
drawings: (H) $1,100

ARMITAGE, H.A.
paintings: (H) $935

ARMITAGE, Kenneth
English b. 1916
sculpture: (L) $1,700; (H) $49,500

ARMITAGE, Thomas Liddall
British 19th/20th cent.
paintings: (L) $2,420; (H) $33,000

ARMLEDER, John
b.Switzerland 1948
paintings: (H) $27,500
sculpture: (L) $14,300; (H) $27,500

ARMOR, Charles
American b. 1844
paintings: (L) $302; (H) $2,420

ARMORSOLO, Fernando
Filipino 20th cent.
paintings: (H) $935

ARMOUR, Lieutenant-Colonel George
Denholm
drawings: (L) $1,980; (H) $12,100

ARMOUR, Samuel E.
Anglo/American b. 1890
paintings: (L) $220; (H) $660

ARMS, John Taylor
American 1887-1953
drawings: (L) $440; (H) $825

ARMSTRONG, David
American
drawings: (L) $3,520; (H) $4,180

ARMSTRONG, David Maitland
1836-1918
paintings: (H) $1,000

ARMSTRONG, Rolf
American 1881-1960
drawings: (H) $1,100

ARMSTRONG, Sam
American 20th cent.
drawings: (L) $600; (H) $8,800

ARMSTRONG, William M.
American 1862-1906
paintings: (L) $880; (H) $2,750

ARMSTRONG, William W.
Canadian 1822-1914
paintings: (L) $660; (H) $3,080

ARNALD, George
British 1763-1841
paintings: (L) $2,200; (H) $14,300

ARNAUTOFF, Victor Mikhail
American 1896-1979
paintings: (L) $880; (H) $1,100

ARNECLIO, Merio
contemporary
paintings: (H) $1,210

ARNEGGER, Alois
Austrian 1879-1967
paintings: (L) $242; (H) $4,950

ARNEGGER, Alwin
German 1883-1916
paintings: (L) $440; (H) $1,430

ARNEGGER, G.
Italian 20th cent.
paintings: (L) $275; (H) $990

ARNESEN, Vilhelm
Danish b. 1865
paintings: (H) $1,650

ARNESON, Robert
American b. 1930
sculpture: (L) $935; (H) $18,700

ARNETT, J.A.
Dutch 19th/20th cent.
paintings: (H) $1,100

ARNETT, J.R.
late 20th cent.
paintings: (H) $660

ARNETT, Joe Anna
American contemporary
paintings: (H) $12,000

ARNODIO, G.
paintings: (L) $550; (H) $660

ARNOLD
paintings: (L) $220; (H) $715

ARNOLD, E.
American 20th cent.
paintings: (H) $1,320

ARNOLD, Edward
b. Germany 1824 d. U.S. 1866
paintings: (L) $18,700; (H) $44,000

ARNOLD, Grant
American b. 1904
paintings: (H) $2,200

ARNOLD, Henry
sculpture: (L) $2,090; (H) $2,420

ARNOLD, James
American 20th cent.
paintings: (L) $330; (H) $1,100

ARNOLD, John
American 20th cent.
paintings: (L) $110; (H) $825

ARNOLD, John James Trumbull
American 1812-c. 1865
paintings: (H) $5,500

ARNOLD, Reginald Ernst
English 1853-1938
paintings: (L) $468; (H) $18,700

ARNOLD-KAISER, Bernita
American
paintings: (H) $6,600

ARNOLDI, Charles
American b. 1946
paintings: (L) $5,500; (H) $23,100
drawings: (L) $440; (H) $6,600
sculpture: (L) $4,400; (H) $22,000

ARNOT, J.
Dutch 19th cent.
paintings: (H) $1,100

ARNOUX, Michel
French 1833-1877
paintings: (L) $1,540; (H) $3,850

ARNTZ, Constant
paintings: (H) $4,620

ARNTZ, Michael
contemporary
sculpture: (H) $1,100

ARNTZENIUS, Floris
contemporary
paintings: (H) $2,750

ARNULL, George
British 19th cent.
paintings: (L) $5,500; (H) $15,400

ARNULL, George
French 19th cent.
paintings: (H) $660

ARON, Toni
Austrian 1859-1920
paintings: (H) $2,860

ARONSON, Boris
drawings: (H) $1,000

ARONSON, David
American b. 1923
drawings: (L) $38; (H) $1,320
sculpture: (L) $440; (H) $3,300

ARP, Jean, or Hans
French 1887-1966
paintings: (L) $28,600; (H) $85,250
drawings: (L) $2,420; (H) $17,600
sculpture: (L) $2,090; (H) $990,000

ARP, Jean and Sophie Tauber ARP
drawings: (H) $7,700

ARPA, Jose
Spanish/American b. 1862
paintings: (L) $4,400; (H) $5,225

ARPAD, Romek
Hungarian b. 1883
paintings: (L) $121; (H) $1,100

ARRANTS, Shirley
American
drawings: (L) $1,100; (H) $1,200

ARREGUI, Romana
French b. 1875
paintings: (H) $3,300

ARRENEGER, Alois
paintings: (H) $1,320

ARRIAGA, Juan Antt.
paintings: (H) $2,310

ARRIETA, Jose Agustin
Mexican 1802-1879
paintings: (L) $30,800; (H) $38,500

ARRIOLA, Fortunato
American 1827-1872
paintings: (H) $12,100

ARRIOLA, Fortunato
Mexican 1827-1872
paintings: (H) $3,025

ARROYA, R.
Spanish 19th cent.
paintings: (H) $27,500

ARSENIUS, Jorg Johann
paintings: (H) $4,950

ARSON, A.
sculpture: (H) $770

ARSON, Alphonse Alexandre
sculpture: (L) $308; (H) $3,850

ARTAL, Ramos Manuel
paintings: (H) $1,540

ARTAUD, L.
sculpture: (H) $825

ARTEAGA Y ALFARO, Matias
paintings: (H) $12,100

ARTER, Charles J.
American d. 1923
paintings: (L) $467; (H) $2,640

ARTHOIS, Jacques d' and David
TENIERS
Flemish 17th cent.
paintings: (H) $22,000

ARTHUR, Reginald
English 19th cent.
paintings: (L) $121; (H) $4,180

ARTHURS, Stanley Massey
American 1877-1950
paintings: (L) $176; (H) $6,600
drawings: (H) $385

ARTIGUE, Albert Emile
French ac. 1875-1901
paintings: (H) $8,800

ARTS, Dorus
paintings: (H) $715

ARTSCHWAGER, Richard
American b. 1924
paintings: (L) $7,700; (H) $990,000
drawings: (L) $1,870; (H) $14,300
sculpture: (L) $8,250; (H) $308,000

ARTZ, Constant
Dutch 1870-1951
paintings: (L) $1,100; (H) $3,520
drawings: (H) $4,400

ARTZ, David Adolf Constant
Dutch 1837-1890
paintings: (L) $1,100; (H) $16,500
drawings: (L) $467; (H) $1,760

ARUNDALE, Francis Vyvyan Jago
English 1807-1853
drawings: (H) $2,750

ARUS, Joseph Raoul
French 1848-1921
paintings: (H) $4,950

ARVILLAND
American 19th cent.
drawings: (H) $2,500

ARVILLAND
French ac. Bordeaux 1850-1878
drawings: (H) $3,000

ARYTON, Michael
sculpture: (H) $4,950

ARZYBASHEFF, Boris
1899-1965
drawings: (H) $700

ASCENZI, E.
Italian
paintings: (L) $330; (H) $2,860
drawings: (L) $242; (H) $1,650

ASCH, Pieter Jansz van
Dutch 1603-1678
paintings: (L) $2,200; (H) $11,000

ASCIONE, Aniello
Italian ac. 1680-1708
paintings: (H) $17,600

ASHBAUGH, Dennis
paintings: (H) $825

ASHBROOK, Paul
American b. 1867
paintings: (L) $935; (H) $1,320

ASHER, Julius Ludwig
paintings: (H) $825

ASHFUTEL, A.
drawings: (H) $1,760

ASHLEY, Anita
American 19th/20th cent.
drawings: (H) $1,100

ASHLEY, Clifford W.
American 1862-1941
paintings: (H) $2,200

ASHLEY, Clifford W.
American 1881-1947
paintings: (L) $4,000; (H) $9,000
drawings: (L) $250; (H) $1,600

ASHLEY, Frank N.
American b. 1920
paintings: (L) $275; (H) $1,155
drawings: (L) $990; (H) $3,960

ASHTON, Frederico
Italian b. 1836
paintings: (H) $825

ASHTON, Sir John William
English 1881-1963
paintings: (L) $550; (H) $660

ASHURST(?), W.H.
paintings: (H) $2,200

ASKENAZY, Maurice
American
paintings: (H) $8,800

ASKENAZY, Mischa
American 1888-1961
paintings: (H) $8,800

ASKEVOLD, Anders Monsen
Swedish 1834-1900
paintings: (L) $2,200; (H) $12,650

ASOMA, Tadashi
contemporary
paintings: (L) $1,760; (H) $2,640

ASPETTATI, Antonio Mario
paintings: (L) $605; (H) $990

ASPETTI, Tiziano
Italian 1565-1607
sculpture: (H) $1,650

ASPETTI, Tiziano, studio of
Italian 16th cent.
sculpture: (H) $24,970

ASPEVIG, Clyde
American
paintings: (H) $1,000

ASPLAND, Theophile Lindsay
paintings: (H) $990

ASPREY, M.
paintings: (H) $715

ASSELIN, Maurice
French 1882-1947
paintings: (H) $1,320

ASSELYN, Jan
Dutch 1610-1652/60
paintings: (L) $6,050; (H) $82,500

ASSERETO, Gioacchino
Italian 1600-1649
paintings: (L) $77,000; (H) $110,000

ASSETTO, Franco
Italian b. 1911
paintings: (L) $11; (H) $770

AST, Balthasar van der
Dutch c. 1590-c. 1656
paintings: (L) $55,000; (H) $935,000

ASTE, Jean Louis
French b. 1864
paintings: (H) $11,000

ASTE, Joseph d'
French early 20th cent.
sculpture: (H) $1,650

ASTI, Angelo
French 1847-1903
paintings: (L) $66; (H) $7,150

ASTUDILLO, Ever
Colombian b. 1948
drawings: (H) $1,100

ATALAYA, Enrique
Spanish 19th/20th cent.
paintings: (L) $1,320; (H) $13,200
drawings: (H) $495

ATAMIAN, Charles Garabed
Turkish 20th cent.
paintings: (L) $1,430; (H) $5,500

ATENCIO, Gilbert, Wah PEEN
American b. 1930
paintings: (L) $220; (H) $1,045
drawings: (H) $1,320

ATHERTON, John
American, d.Canada 1900-1952
paintings: (H) $1,045
drawings: (H) $400

ATKEN, ** van
English 19th cent.
paintings: (H) $715

ATKINS, Albert Henry
d. 1951
sculpture: (H) $3,300

ATKINS, Samuel
British ac. 1787-1808
drawings: (L) $192; (H) $4,840

ATKINS, W.H.
American b. 1926
paintings: (L) $330; (H) $6,000

ATKINSON, James, the elder
1775-1833
paintings: (H) $1,980

ATKINSON, John
English 19th cent.
paintings: (H) $990
drawings: (H) $770

ATL, Dr., Geraldo MURILLO
Mexican 1875-1964
paintings: (L) $22,000; (H) $72,600
drawings: (L) $11,000; (H) $11,000

ATLAN, Jean
French 1913-1960
paintings: (H) $58,850

ATLEE, J.W.
drawings: (H) $825

ATRIJGAJEFF, Nikolaj Alexejewitsch
Russian 1823-1892
paintings: (H) $2,750

ATTANASIO, Natale
Italian 1845/46-1923
paintings: (H) $17,600

ATTENDU, Antoine Ferdinand
French
paintings: (H) $2,750

ATWOOD, Robert
American b. 1892
paintings: (L) $357; (H) $3,410

ATWOOD, William Edwin
American 19th/20th cent.
paintings: (H) $2,200

AUBERT
sculpture: (H) $880

AUBERT, Jean Ernest
French 1824-1906
paintings: (L) $825; (H) $6,325

AUBERT, Rene Raymond Louis
French 20th cent.
paintings: (H) $2,200

AUBINIERE, Madame C.A. de l',
Georgina M.
French ac. 1876-1891
drawings: (H) $715

AUBLET, Albert
French 1851-1938
paintings: (L) $4,950; (H) $44,000

AUBRY, Charles
drawings: (H) $1,320

AUBRY, Emile
French 1880-1964
paintings: (L) $467; (H) $3,850

AUCK, R.E. (L)
paintings: (H) $935

AUDUBON, John James
American 1780/85-1851
drawings: (L) $82,500; (H) $253,000

AUDUBON, John Woodhouse
American 1812-1868
paintings: (L) $3,850; (H) $20,900

AUDY, Jonny
French ac. 1872-1876
drawings: (H) $8,250

AUERBACH, Frank
British b. 1931
paintings: (L) $66,000; (H) $660,000
drawings: (H) $4,400

AUERBACH-LEVY, William
Russian/American 1889-1964
paintings: (L) $1,100; (H) $3,520
drawings: (H) $220

AUFRAY, Joseph Athanase
French b. 1836
paintings: (L) $3,080; (H) $3,575

AUGE, Philippe
French 20th cent.
paintings: (L) $330; (H) $2,970

AUGUST, Carl E.
Belgian late 19th cent.
paintings: (H) $1,650

AUGUSTE, Robert Joseph
French 1725-1804
sculpture: (H) $20,900

AUGUSTI, Cesare
Italian 19th cent.
paintings: (H) $3,300

AUGUSTIN, Jean Baptiste Jacques
French 1759-1832
drawings: (H) $1,430

AUGUSTINE, L.
19th/20th cent.
paintings: (H) $770

AUGUSTINES, Eduardo
paintings: (H) $3,850

AULT, George C.
American 1891-1948
paintings: (L) $3,300; (H) $55,000
drawings: (L) $440; (H) $3,300

AURELI, Giuseppe
Italian 1858-1929
paintings: (L) $275; (H) $2,420
drawings: (L) $550; (H) $9,900

AUS, Carol
Norwegian b. 1868
paintings: (H) $770

AUSSANDON, Hippolyte
paintings: (H) $935

AUSSANDON, Joseph Nicolas
Hippolyte
French b. 1836
paintings: (H) $242,000

AUSTEN, Alexander
British 19th/20th cent.
paintings: (L) $880; (H) $1,320

AUSTEN, Winifred
British 19th/20th cent.
drawings: (H) $1,700

AUSTIN, Arthur Everett, Jr.
American
paintings: (H) $3,850

AUSTIN, Charles Percy
American 1883-1948
paintings: (L) $715; (H) $15,400
drawings: (H) $77

AUSTIN, Darrel
American b. 1907
paintings: (L) $220; (H) $990

AUSTIN, F.G.
American
paintings: (H) $2,200

AUSTIN, R.S.
British 19th cent.
paintings: (L) $440; (H) $2,090

AUSTRIAN, Ben
American 1870-1921
paintings: (L) $154; (H) $14,000
drawings: (L) $725; (H) $1,500

AUTIO, Rudy
American b. 1926
sculpture: (L) $5,280; (H) $35,200

AUVED, A.
Dutch School 19th cent.
paintings: (H) $1,540

AVED, Jacques Andre
French 1702-1766
paintings: (H) $11,000

AVEDISIAN, Edward
American b. 1935/36
paintings: (L) $110; (H) $1,320

AVERCAMP, Hendrick
Dutch 1585-1634/63
paintings: (H) $159,500

AVERKAMP, Barent
Dutch 1612-1679
paintings: (H) $33,000

AVERY, A.S.
American
paintings: (H) $1,430

AVERY, Kenneth Newell
American b. 1883
paintings: (L) $385; (H) $6,600

AVERY, Milton
American 1893-1965
paintings: (L) $302; (H) $198,000
drawings: (L) $605; (H) $68,750

AVERY, Sally
American 20th cent.
paintings: (L) $495; (H) $2,475

AVILLOND
American 19th cent.
drawings: (H) $2,200

AVISON, George
American b. 1885
paintings: (L) $467; (H) $1,210

AVONT, Pieter van
Flemish 1600-1632
paintings: (H) $4,620

AVONT, Pieter van and Isaac van
OOSTEN
Flemish early 17th cent.
paintings: (H) $24,200

AXEL, Captain A.
American late 19th/early 20th cent.
paintings: (L) $550; (H) $660

AXENTOWICZ, Theodor
Polish 1859-1938
paintings: (L) $1,320; (H) $38,500

AYARS, Margaret T.
American 19th/20th cent.
paintings: (H) $660

AYERS, C.L.
paintings: (H) $5,060

AYLING, Albert W.
English ac. 1853-1892, d. 1905
drawings: (H) $1,100

AYLWARD, J.W.
British 20th cent.
drawings: (H) $1,210

AYRTON, Michael
English 1921-1975
paintings: (H) $1,650
drawings: (L) $440; (H) $770
sculpture: (L) $880; (H) $3,960

AZACETA, Luis Cruz
Cuban b. 1942
drawings: (H) $3,575

AZEMA, Louis
French 1876-1963
paintings: (H) $3,300

AZUZ, David
contemporary
drawings: (H) $3,520

BAADSGAARD, Alfrida Vilhelmine
Ludovica
Danish 1839-1912
paintings: (L) $3,575; (H) $10,450

BABAYEV, Rasim
Russian b. 1927
paintings: (H) $5,280

BABB, John Staines
British ac. 1870-1900
drawings: (L) $24,750; (H) $33,000

BABCOCK, Herb
contemporary
sculpture: (L) $385; (H) $660

BABER, Alice
American b. 1928
paintings: (L) $440; (H) $550
drawings: (L) $660; (H) $770

BABUREN, Dirck van
Dutch 1570/90-1623/24
paintings: (L) $44,000; (H) $220,000

BACARDY, Don
drawings: (H) $16,500

BACCHI, Cesare
Italian 20th cent.
paintings: (L) $1,430; (H) $3,300

BACCI
Italian 19th/20th cent.
paintings: (H) $935

BACCI, Edmondo
paintings: (L) $143; (H) $2,860
drawings: (H) $1,650

BACCIGALUPO, Rose
paintings: (L) $550; (H) $825

BACH, Elvira
German b. 1951
paintings: (L) $6,600; (H) $8,800

BACH, Guido
paintings: (H) $2,860

BACH, Oscar B.
American
paintings: (H) $24,200

BACHARDY, Don
drawings: (H) $770

BACHARINI, A.
sculpture: (H) $1,100

BACHE, Otto
Danish 1839-1914
paintings: (L) $13,750; (H) $17,600

BACHELDER, J.M.
American 19th cent.
drawings: (H) $3,300

BACHELDER, Jonathan Badger
American 1825-1894
paintings: (H) $825
drawings: (H) $137

BACHELIER, Jean Jacques
French 1724-1806
paintings: (H) $121,000

BACHENIN, Valeri
Russian b. 1943
paintings: (H) $3,520

BACHMAN, Max
b. Germany 1862 d. N.Y.C. 1921
sculpture: (L) $6,600; (H) $12,100

BACHMAN, Otto
Swiss b. 1915
paintings: (L) $550; (H) $1,210

BACHMANN, Adolphe
Swiss 19th/20th cent.
paintings: (L) $467; (H) $2,090
drawings: (H) $110

BACHMANN, Alfred
German b. 1863
paintings: (L) $605; (H) $2,750

BACHMANN, Karl
Hungarian 1874-1924
paintings: (L) $715; (H) $880
drawings: (H) $495

BACHRACH-BARRE, Helmut
German b. 1898
paintings: (H) $1,650

BACKEN, O.P.
early 20th cent.
paintings: (H) $6,050

BACKER, Francois Joseph Thomas de
Flemish 1812-1872
paintings: (H) $6,600

BACKER, Jacob Adriaensz
paintings: (L) $6,600; (H) $9,900

BACKER, Jacob de
Flemish c. 1560-1590
drawings: (H) $36,300

BACKUS, A.E.
paintings: (H) $4,950

BACKUS, George J.
American 19th cent.
paintings: (H) $660

BACKVIS, Francois
French mid-19th cent.
paintings: (L) $3,575; (H) $18,700

BACON, Arch
American
sculpture: (H) $2,700

BACON, Charles Roswell
American 1868-1913
paintings: (L) $220; (H) $4,620

BACON, Francis
Irish 1909–1992
paintings: (L) $137,500; (H) $6,270,000

BACON, Henry
American 1839-1912
paintings: (L) $357; (H) $33,000
drawings: (L) $220; (H) $1,980

BACON, I. Lewis
American 1853-1910
paintings: (L) $440; (H) $1,045

BACON, Irving R.
American 1875-1962
paintings: (L) $440; (H) $770

BACON, Julia L.
paintings: (L) $660; (H) $935

BACON, Peggy
American 1895-1987
paintings: (H) $3,850
drawings: (L) $220; (H) $1,100

BACQUE, Daniel Joseph
French 1874-1947
sculpture: (L) $880; (H) $1,980

BADEN, Hans Jurriaensz van
Dutch c. 1604-1663
paintings: (H) $9,350

BADGER, James W.
American 19th cent.
paintings: (H) $1,320

BADGER, Joseph
American 1708-1765
paintings: (H) $1,870

BADGER, S.F.M.
American ac. 1890
paintings: (L) $3,300; (H) $16,500

BADIN, Jean Jules
French b. 1843
paintings: (H) $15,400

BADURA, Ben
paintings: (H) $725

BAECHLER, Donald
American b. 1956
paintings: (L) $4,400; (H) $33,000

BAEDER, John
American b. 1938
paintings: (L) $20,900; (H) $27,500
drawings: (L) $3,850; (H) $27,500

BAELLIEUR, Cornelis de
Flemish 17th cent.
paintings: (H) $6,875

BAER, Jo
American b. 1929
paintings: (L) $9,900; (H) $71,500

BAER, Lillian
sculpture: (H) $2,530

BAER, William Jacob
American 1860-1941
paintings: (L) $880; (H) $2,750

BAERT, H.
Belgian ac. 1840
paintings: (H) $715

BAES, Emile
Belgian b. 1879
paintings: (H) $6,050

BAES, Firmin
drawings: (L) $1,540; (H) $2,640

BAGG, Henry Howard
American 1852-1928
paintings: (L) $132; (H) $1,650

BAGLIONE, Giovanni
drawings: (H) $1,430

BAHAR, Bijan
contemporary
sculpture: (L) $1,045; (H) $2,750

BAHICA, A.
paintings: (H) $990

BAHIEU, Jules G.
Belgian 19th cent.
paintings: (L) $385; (H) $2,090

BAIL, Franck Antoine
French 1858-1924
paintings: (L) $5,500; (H) $24,200

BAIL, Joseph
French 1862-1921
paintings: (L) $1,100; (H) $33,000

BAILEY, Clayton
American 20th cent.
sculpture: (H) $2,090

BAILEY, Frederick Victor
British 20th cent.
paintings: (H) $16,500
sculpture: (H) $9,900

BAILEY, G.
paintings: (H) $2,420

BAILEY, George H.
American 19th cent.
paintings: (H) $3,850

BAILEY, La Force
drawings: (H) $990

BAILEY, T.
American 19th/20th cent.
paintings: (L) $49; (H) $990

BAILEY, Walter Alexander
American b. 1894
paintings: (L) $209; (H) $825

BAILEY, William
American b. 1930
paintings: (L) $132,000; (H) $253,000
drawings: (L) $247; (H) $30,800

BAILEY, William E.
paintings: (H) $4,675

BAILLE, Louis
drawings: (H) $990

BAILLOT
sculpture: (H) $770

BAILLY, A.
American School 19th cent.
sculpture: (H) $5,225

BAILY, Edward Hodges
ac. 1788-1867
sculpture: (H) $1,100

BAIN, Marcel Adolphe
French 1878-1937
paintings: (L) $220; (H) $8,800

BAINEY, J.
British 19th cent.
paintings: (H) $1,100

BAIRD, John
drawings: (H) $1,320

BAIRD, Nathaniel Hughes
British b. 1865
paintings: (L) $935; (H) $6,600
drawings: (H) $825

BAIRD, Sylvia E.
contemporary
paintings: (H) $4,100

BAIRD, William Baptiste
American b. 1847, ac. 1872-1899
paintings: (L) $330; (H) $8,250
drawings: (L) $385; (H) $1,320

BAISCH, Hermann
German 1846-1894
paintings: (L) $1,210; (H) $9,350

BAISHI, Qi
Chinese 1864-1957
drawings: (H) $14,850

BAIZE, Wayne
American b. 1943
drawings: (L) $800; (H) $1,650

BAIZERMAN, Saul
American
sculpture: (H) $5,500

BAJ, Enrico
Italian b. 1924
paintings: (L) $2,970; (H) $24,200
drawings: (L) $2,200; (H) $29,700

BAKALOWICZ, Ladislaus
Polish 1833-1904
paintings: (L) $550; (H) $3,300

BAKALOWICZ, Stephan
Wladislawowitsch
Russian b. 1857
paintings: (H) $5,775

BAKER, Bryant
American 1881-1970
sculpture: (H) $770

BAKER, E.
paintings: (L) $220; (H) $1,210

BAKER, Edith
19th cent.
paintings: (H) $1,320

BAKER, Elisha Taylor
American 19th cent.
paintings: (L) $990; (H) $13,200

BAKER, Ernest
American
paintings: (L) $825; (H) $2,530

BAKER, George
paintings: (H) $4,675

BAKER, George
Canadian 19th cent.
drawings: (L) $154; (H) $825

BAKER, George A.
American 1821-1880
paintings: (H) $2,860

BAKER, George Herbert
American 1878-1943
paintings: (L) $300; (H) $1,650

BAKER, George O.
American b. 1882
paintings: (H) $1,650

BAKER, Gladys
American 1821-1880
paintings: (L) $715; (H) $880

BAKER, Jack
contemporary
paintings: (H) $1,320

BAKER, Lucy
20th cent.
sculpture: (H) $1,320

BAKER, Lulu
British 19th cent.
paintings: (H) $825

BAKER, Ralph
American 1908-1976
drawings: (L) $605; (H) $770

BAKER, Samuel Colwell
American 1874-1964
paintings: (H) $1,100

BAKER, Thomas, called Baker of
Leamington
English 1809-1869
paintings: (L) $2,200; (H) $7,700

BAKER, W.R.
American
paintings: (H) $880

BAKER, William Bliss
American 1859-1887
drawings: (L) $605; (H) $4,180

BAKHUYZEN, Gerardina Jacoba van de Sande
Dutch 1826-1895
paintings: (L) $5,280; (H) $17,050
drawings: (H) $12,100

BAKHUYZEN, Hendrik van de Sande
Dutch 1795 1860
paintings: (L) $2,310; (H) $28,600

BAKHUYZEN, Julius Jacobus van de Sande
Dutch 1835-1925
paintings: (L) $1,650; (H) $8,800
drawings: (H) $1,000

BAKHUYZEN, Ludolf, or BACKHUYZEN
Dutch 1631-1708
paintings: (L) $2,640; (H) $44,000

BAKKER, Jacob
Dutch 1608-1651
paintings: (H) $1,100

BAKSHI, Ralph
drawings: (L) $286; (H) $660

BAKST, Leon
Russian 1866-1924
paintings: (H) $39,600
drawings: (L) $220; (H) $48,400

BALACA, Ricardo
paintings: (H) $3,300

BALASSI, Mario
Italian 1604-1667
paintings: (H) $11,000

BALCIAR, Gerald
American
sculpture: (H) $700

BALDERO, J.G.
Italian 19th cent.
paintings: (H) $3,850

BALDESSARI, John
American b. 1931
sculpture: (H) $52,800

BALDI, Lazzaro
Italian 1624-1703
drawings: (H) $1,650

BALDOCK, James Walsham
British ac. 1867-1887
paintings: (L) $990; (H) $16,600

BALDRIDGE, Cyros Le Roy
American
drawings: (H) $1,210

BALDUCCI, Giovanni, called Cosci
Italian c. 1560-1631
drawings: (L) $825; (H) $3,080

BALDWIN, B.
British 19th cent.
paintings: (H) $770

BALE, Charles Thomas
English ac. 1868-1875
paintings: (L) $385; (H) $5,500

BALE, Edwin
British 1838-1923
paintings: (H) $2,475

BALE, T.C.
British 19th cent.
paintings: (H) $3,300

BALEN, Hendrik van
Flemish
paintings: (H) $44,000

BALEN, Hendrik van, the elder
Flemish 1575-1632
paintings: (L) $16,500; (H) $24,750

BALEN, Jan van
Flemish 1611-1654
paintings: (H) $5,225

BALENCIAGA
drawings: (H) $1,430

BALESTRA, Antonio
Italian 1666-1740
paintings: (L) $20,900; (H) $46,200
drawings: (L) $495; (H) $4,950

BALESTRIERI, Lionello
Italian 1872-1958
paintings: (L) $16,500; (H) $18,700
drawings: (H) $715

BALFOUR, Helen Johnson
American 1857-1925
drawings: (H) $990

BALINK, Henry C.
Dutch/American 1882-1963
paintings: (L) $165; (H) $13,970

BALIS, C.
American ac. c. 1850
paintings: (H) $2,310

BALL, Adrien Joseph Verhoeven
Belgian 1824-1882
paintings: (H) $4,675

BALL, Joseph
French 1862-1921
paintings: (H) $8,800

BALL, L. Clarence
American 1858-1915
paintings: (L) $220; (H) $1,100
drawings: (L) $165; (H) $412

BALL, M.L.
American
drawings: (H) $2,200

BALL, Thomas
American 1819-1911
paintings: (H) $3,850
sculpture: (L) $412; (H) $55,000

BALLA, Giacomo
Italian 1871-1958
paintings: (L) $165,000; (H) $4,400,000
drawings: (L) $24,750; (H) $660,000
sculpture: (L) $2,200; (H) $2,200,000

BALLAINE, Jerrold
paintings: (L) $935; (H) $5,500
drawings: (H) $110

BALLANTYNE, John
British 1815-1897
paintings: (L) $825; (H) $11,000

BALLANTYNE, Keith
American
paintings: (H) $1,540

BALLARD, Richard
paintings: (H) $800

BALLARN, Frans van
paintings: (H) $990

BALLAVOINE, Jules Frederic
French ac. 1880-1900
paintings: (L) $1,430; (H) $60,500

BALLESIO
Italian 19th cent.
drawings: (H) $5,500

BALLESIO, Federico
Italian 19th cent.
paintings: (H) $16,500
drawings: (L) $192; (H) $10,450

BALLESIO, G.
Italian 19th cent.
paintings: (H) $2,750

BALLIN, Hugo
American b. 1879
paintings: (L) $308; (H) $660

BALLING, Peter Hansen
Norwegian 1823-1906
paintings: (L) $2,420; (H) $2,420

BALLINGER, Harry
American b. 1892
paintings: (L) $247; (H) $825

BALLIQUANT
French 19th cent.
paintings: (L) $605; (H) $2,310

BALLOVOINE, Jules Frederic
paintings: (H) $2,750

BALLOWS, Albert F.
American 1829-1883
paintings: (H) $880

BALLUE, Pierre
French 1855-1928
paintings: (L) $660; (H) $1,650

BALOGH, Komoczi
Hungarian 19th/20th cent.
paintings: (L) $1,760; (H) $2,200

BALSAMO, Salvatore
Italian 1894-1922
paintings: (L) $990; (H) $2,860

BALTEN, Pieter
Flemish c. 1525-c. 1598
paintings: (H) $38,500

BALTHUS, Count Balthazar
KLOSSOWSKI de Rola
Polish/French b. 1908
paintings: (L) $99,000; (H) $2,090,000
drawings: (L) $2,035; (H) $319,000

BAUDRY DE BALZAC, Therese
French 1774-1831
drawings: (H) $1,650

BAMA, James
American b. 1926
paintings: (L) $9,350; (H) $36,300

BAMBERGER, Fritz
German 1814-1873
paintings: (L) $6,600; (H) $7,150

BAMBI, S.
  paintings: (H) $715

BAMFYLDE, Coppelstone Warre
  British d. 1791
  paintings: (H) $1,320

BANCEL, Louis
  sculpture: (H) $1,320

BANCHIERI, Giuseppe
  Italian b. 1927
  paintings: (L) $110; (H) $3,080

BANCROFT, Milton
  American 1867-1947
  paintings: (L) $110; (H) $605
  drawings: (L) $33; (H) $1,100

BAND, Max
  Lithuanian/Amer. b. 1900
  paintings: (L) $110; (H) $1,650

BANDECK, Fritz Muller
  German 19th/20th cent.
  paintings: (H) $1,650

BANDINELLI, Baccio
  Italian 1493-1560
  drawings: (L) $1,100; (H) $44,000

BANDO, Toshio
  b. 1890
  paintings: (H) $2,200

BANG, Peter Marius
  Danish b. 1829
  paintings: (H) $27,500

BANK, J.O.
  paintings: (H) $6,050

BANKS, Robert
  drawings: (L) $1,100; (H) $5,280

BANKS, William
  paintings: (H) $3,300

BANNARD, Walter Darby
  American b. 1931
  paintings: (L) $220; (H) $2,860

BANNISTER, Edward Mitchell
  American 1833-1901
  paintings: (L) $1,650; (H) $5,500

BAPTISTE, E.JM.
  Haitian 20th cent.
  paintings: (H) $1,045

BAQUERO, Mariano
  Spanish 19th cent.
  drawings: (H) $41,250

BAR, Bonaventure de
  French 1700-1729
  paintings: (H) $4,400

BARABAN-CAHAGNET, Blanche
Marie
  French 20th cent.
  paintings: (H) $1,210

BARAIN, J.
  paintings: (H) $825

BARANYA, Gustov Lorincz von
  Hungarian 1886-1938
  paintings: (H) $7,700

BARATTA, Carlo Alberto
  drawings: (H) $990

BARATTI, Filippo
  Italian 19th/20th cent.
  paintings: (L) $3,410; (H) $4,070

BARAU, Emile
  French 1851-1930
  paintings: (H) $1,870

BARAUD, J.
  paintings: (H) $1,100

BARBAGELATA, Giovanni
  ac. by 1484-c. 1508
  paintings: (H) $22,000

BARBARINI, Emil
  Austrian 1855-1930
  paintings: (L) $2,530; (H) $3,850

BARBARINI, Franz
  Austrian 1804-1873
  paintings: (L) $1,540; (H) $5,500

BARBARINI, Gustav
  Austrian 1840-1909
  drawings: (H) $2,090

BARBARINO, Nicolo
  paintings: (H) $990

BARBASAN, Mariano
  Spanish 1864-1924
  paintings: (L) $11,000; (H) $38,500

BARBAUD, Auguste
  American early 19th cent.
  paintings: (H) $1,210

BARBE, Jules Edouard Desire
  French 19th cent.
  paintings: (H) $825

BARBEDIENNE, Blanc
  sculpture: (H) $1,760

BARBEDIENNE, Ferdinand
French 1810-1892
sculpture: (H) $1,650

BARBER, Alfred R.
British 19th cent.
paintings: (L) $8,250; (H) $18,700

BARBER, C.J.
paintings: (H) $2,200

BARBER, George
American b. 1910
paintings: (H) $1,760

BARBER, John
paintings: (H) $1,980

BARBER, Reginald
English ac. 1882-1908
paintings: (H) $1,430

BARBER, Sam
American 20th cent.
paintings: (L) $176; (H) $1,320

BARBIER, George
drawings: (L) $1,100; (H) $3,520

BARBIER, N.
paintings: (H) $1,980

BARBIER, Nicolas Francois
1768-1826
drawings: (H) $1,375

BARBIERS, Pieter Pietersz.
Dutch 1749-1842
drawings: (H) $2,200

BARBINI, Alfredo
contemporary
sculpture: (H) $3,300

BARBOT
Continental School 19th cent.
paintings: (H) $2,310

BARBUDO-SANCHEZ, Salvador
Spanish 1857-1917
paintings: (L) $3,080; (H) $68,200

BARCELO, Miguel
Spanish b. 1957
paintings: (L) $6,050; (H) $46,750
drawings: (L) $5,500; (H) $16,500

BARCHUS, Eliza R.
American 1857-1959
paintings: (L) $220; (H) $3,300

BARCLAY, J.
drawings: (H) $1,210

BARCLAY, J. Edward
drawings: (H) $1,100

BARCLAY, McClelland
American 1891-1943
paintings: (L) $440; (H) $6,000
sculpture: (H) $880

BARD, James
American 1815-1897
paintings: (L) $11,000; (H) $132,000
drawings: (H) $88,000

BARD, James and John
American 19th cent.
paintings: (L) $38,500; (H) $55,000

BARDONE, Guy
French b. 1927
paintings: (L) $440; (H) $3,520

BARDUT-DAVRAY, Luc
paintings: (H) $2,420

BARDWELL, Thomas
ac. 1735-c. 1780
paintings: (H) $6,050

BARE, E.
French 19th cent.
paintings: (H) $5,280

BARE, Ed W.
19th cent.
paintings: (H) $1,760

BAREAU, Georges
French b. 1866
sculpture: (L) $1,100; (H) $4,125

BARENGER, James
British 1745-1813
paintings: (L) $2,750; (H) $3,960

BARENGER, James
English 1780-1831
paintings: (H) $20,900

BARGUE, Charles
drawings: (L) $1,540; (H) $2,200

BARIL
sculpture: (H) $770

BARILARI, Enrique
Argentinian b. 1931
paintings: (L) $4,125; (H) $8,250

BARILE, Xavier J.
American b. 1891
paintings: (L) $110; (H) $3,520

BARILLOT, Eugene
French 19th cent.
sculpture: (H) $1,760

BARILLOT, Leon
French 1844-1929
paintings: (L) $385; (H) $4,950

BARISON, G.
paintings: (H) $770

BARK, Jared
contemporary
drawings: (H) $1,100

BARKER, George
American 1882-1965
paintings: (L) $330; (H) $3,025
drawings: (H) $302

BARKER, J.
paintings: (L) $660; (H) $825

BARKER, J.
British 1820-1865
paintings: (H) $3,520

BARKER, J.H.
British 19th cent.
paintings: (H) $1,210

BARKER, John
British 19th cent.
paintings: (L) $605; (H) $2,750

BARKER, Joseph, of Bath
English 19th cent.
paintings: (H) $4,400

BARKER, L.M.
American 19th cent.
drawings: (H) $1,430

BARKER, Thomas, of Bath
British 1769-1847
paintings: (L) $880; (H) $7,150
drawings: (H) $605

BARKER, Thomas Jones
British 1815-1882
paintings: (L) $2,200; (H) $14,300

BARKER, Wright
British d. 1941
paintings: (L) $1,650; (H) $13,200

BARKS, Carl
American contemporary
drawings: (L) $550; (H) $1,320

BARKTON, H.
paintings: (H) $715

BARLACH, Ernst
German 1870-1938
drawings: (L) $4,620; (H) $11,000
sculpture: (L) $2,200; (H) $77,000

BARLAND, A.
English 19th cent.
paintings: (H) $1,320

BARLAND, Adams
British ac. 1843-1863
paintings: (L) $715; (H) $5,500

BARLOW, Francis
c. 1626-1704
drawings: (H) $3,300

BARLOW, John Noble
American 1861-1924
paintings: (L) $165; (H) $2,200

BARLOW, Myron
American 1873-1938
paintings: (L) $2,750; (H) $38,500
drawings: (L) $330; (H) $2,200

BARNABE, Duilio
Italian 1914-1961
paintings: (L) $660; (H) $12,100

BARNARD, Edward Herbert
American 1855-1909
paintings: (L) $3,190; (H) $15,400

BARNARD, Frederick
English 1846-1896
paintings: (H) $5,280

BARNARD, George Grey
American 1863-1938
sculpture: (L) $2,200; (H) $3,960

BARNES, Abram
American 19th cent.
paintings: (H) $1,045

BARNES, E.C.
English ac. 1856-1882
paintings: (L) $715; (H) $1,980

BARNES, E.H.
paintings: (L) $121; (H) $715

BARNES, Edward Charles
British 19th cent.
paintings: (L) $2,200; (H) $4,620

BARNES, Ernest Harrison
American b. 1873
paintings: (L) $77; (H) $2,090

BARNES, Frank
New Zealander 19th/20th cent.
paintings: (H) $6,050

BARNES, George B.
paintings: (H) $935

BARNES, Gertrude Jameson
American b. 1865
paintings: (L) $1,650; (H) $3,850

BARNES, Matthew
American 1880-1951
paintings: (L) $440; (H) $935

BARNET, Will
American b. 1911
paintings: (L) $2,420; (H) $25,300
drawings: (H) $5,500

BARNETT, Herbert
American 1910-1972
paintings: (L) $176; (H) $825

BARNETT, Les
American
drawings: (L) $650; (H) $850

BARNEY, Alice Pike
American b. 1860
paintings: (H) $660
drawings: (H) $770

BARNEY, Frank A.
American b. 1862
paintings: (L) $100; (H) $825

BARNJUM, Frederick S.
Canadian(?) 19th cent.
paintings: (H) $1,650

BARNOIN, Henri Alphonse
French 1882-1935
paintings: (L) $3,080; (H) $14,300

BARNSLEY, James MacDonald
American/Canadian 1861-1929
paintings: (L) $1,375; (H) $1,430
drawings: (H) $825

BAROCCI, Federico, called Fiori da Urbino
Italian 1526/35-1612
drawings: (L) $7,150; (H) $121,000

BARON, Henri Charles Antoine
French 1816-1885
paintings: (L) $1,760; (H) $6,050
drawings: (L) $275; (H) $440

BARONE, Antonio
American b. 1889
paintings: (L) $192; (H) $22,000
drawings: (H) $440

BARQUE, Charles
paintings: (H) $2,420

BARR, G.R.
British
paintings: (H) $8,525

BARR, William
American 1867-1933
paintings: (L) $330; (H) $4,400

BARRABAND, Jacques
French 1767-1803
drawings: (H) $1,320

BARRAGAN, Luis
paintings: (H) $3,300

BARRAL(?), A***
sculpture: (H) $1,925

BARRANTI, P.
Italian 20th cent.
sculpture: (L) $1,650; (H) $5,720

BARRATT, Thomas, of Stockbridge
paintings: (H) $6,600

BARRAU, Laureano
Spanish b. 1864
paintings: (H) $55,000
drawings: (H) $2,310

BARRAUD, Francis
British 1856-1924
paintings: (H) $6,600

BARRAUD, Francois
paintings: (H) $3,025

BARRAUD, Henry
English 1811-1874
paintings: (L) $6,600; (H) $88,000

BARRAUD, William
English 1810-1850
paintings: (L) $2,750; (H) $51,700

BARRE, Jean Auguste
drawings: (H) $1,650

BARRE, Martin
French b. 1924
paintings: (H) $24,200

BARREAU, A.
French/American 19th cent.
paintings: (H) $1,650

BARREDA, Antonio
paintings: (H) $5,225

BARREDA, Ernesto
Latin American b. France 1927
paintings: (L) $2,860; (H) $8,250

BARREL, W.R.
drawings: (H) $1,210

BARRERA, Antonio
Colombian b. 1948
paintings: (L) $3,850; (H) $16,500

BARRET, George, Jr.
British 1767-1842
drawings: (H) $1,100

BARRET, George, Sr.
British 1732-1784
paintings: (L) $3,300; (H) $60,500

BARRETT, Elizabeth Hunt
American b. 1863, exhib. 1875-1879
paintings: (L) $220; (H) $2,200
drawings: (L) $110; (H) $110

BARRETT, George
paintings: (H) $2,310

BARRETT, John
British 19th cent.
paintings: (H) $2,200

BARRETT, William S.
American 1854-1927
paintings: (H) $660
drawings: (L) $55; (H) $550

BARRIAS, Louis Ernest
French 1841-1905
sculpture: (L) $825; (H) $24,750

BARRIE, Erwin S.
b. 1886
paintings: (L) $55; (H) $770

BARRIER, Gustave
French 20th cent.
paintings: (L) $605; (H) $880

BARRIES, G.T.
American 1842-1937
paintings: (H) $990

BARRIOS, Armando
South American b. 1920
paintings: (L) $8,250; (H) $17,600

BARRITT, Robert Carlyle
American b. 1898
paintings: (H) $660

BARRON, Hugh
English 1745-1791
paintings: (H) $2,420

BARROW, John Dobson
American
paintings: (L) $220; (H) $2,860

BARROW, Julian
American 20th cent.
paintings: (H) $770

BARRY, J.
paintings: (H) $1,980

BARRY, John
ac. 1784-1827
paintings: (H) $1,045

BARRYMORE, Lionel
American 1878-1954
paintings: (H) $2,475

BARSAU, George
sculpture: (H) $1,045

BARSCH, Wulf Erich
contemporary
paintings: (H) $1,650

BARSE, George Randolph, Jr.
American 1861-1938
paintings: (L) $3,190; (H) $8,250
drawings: (L) $880; (H) $3,850

BARSOTTI, Hercules
paintings: (H) $6,600

BARSTOW, G.M.
American 19th cent.
paintings: (H) $660

BARSTOW, J.
paintings: (H) $2,860

BARTAK, F.
Czechoslovakian
sculpture: (H) $660

BARTELL, Ira
contemporary
paintings: (H) $660

BARTHE, Richmond
American 1901-1989
sculpture: (H) $4,125

BARTHELEMY, L.
sculpture: (L) $330; (H) $1,870

BARTHOLDI, Frederic Auguste
French 1834-1904
drawings: (H) $12,100
sculpture: (L) $880; (H) $148,500

BARTHOLOMEW, Truman C.
paintings: (H) $2,640

BARTHOLOMEW, Valentine
English 1799-1879
drawings: (H) $1,650

BARTHOLOMEW, William Newton
American 1822-1898
paintings: (L) $450; (H) $1,300
drawings: (L) $44; (H) $220

BARTLETT, Charles William
British 1860-1940
drawings: (H) $1,210

BARTLETT, Dana
American 1878/82-1957
paintings: (L) $468; (H) $5,500
drawings: (L) $550; (H) $3,190

BARTLETT, Frederic Clay
American b. 1873
paintings: (H) $2,970

BARTLETT, Gray
American 1855-1951
paintings: (L) $715; (H) $2,750

BARTLETT, Jennifer
American b. 1941
paintings: (L) $8,800; (H) $99,000
drawings: (L) $2,530; (H) $44,000
sculpture: (L) $33,000; (H) $137,500

BARTLETT, L.
paintings: (H) $715

BARTLETT, Paul Wayland
American 1865-1925
sculpture: (L) $715; (H) $29,700

BARTOLI, Jacques
French b. 1920
paintings: (H) $2,090

BARTOLINI, Frederico
Italian 19th/20th cent.
paintings: (H) $49,500
drawings: (L) $3,025; (H) $8,800

BARTOLO DI FREDI
Italian c. 1330-1410
paintings: (H) $121,000

BARTOLOMIN, Ulma de
Italian 19th-20th cent.
paintings: (H) $715

BARTOLOMMEO, Fra, called Baccio
della Porta
Italian 1472-1517
drawings: (L) $12,650; (H) $440,000

BARTOLOMMEO, Giuliano
paintings: (H) $1,210

BARTOLOMMEO DI GIOVANNI
Italian ac. 1483-1511
paintings: (L) $90,200; (H) $247,500

BARTOLUZZI, M.H.
Italian 20th cent.
paintings: (H) $1,100

BARTON
paintings: (H) $715

BARTON, Donald Blagge
American b. 1903
paintings: (L) $605; (H) $1,870

BARTON, Harry
American 20th cent.
paintings: (L) $110; (H) $660

BARTON, Loren
American 1893-1975
drawings: (H) $770

BARTSCH, A.
paintings: (H) $748

BARTSCH, Ernst L.
American ac. 1898-1936
paintings: (H) $715

BARTSCH, Wilhelm
German 1871-1953
paintings: (L) $495; (H) $715

BARTTENBACH, Hans
German b. 1908
paintings: (L) $1,155; (H) $1,210

BARUCCI, Pietro
Italian 1845-1917
paintings: (L) $1,980; (H) $27,500

BARUZZI, Cincinnato
Italian d. 1878
sculpture: (H) $52,250

BARWICK, John
British ac. 1835-1876
paintings: (L) $1,980; (H) $10,450

BARWIG, Franz
Austrian b. 1868
sculpture: (L) $275; (H) $4,180

BARYE
sculpture: (L) $550; (H) $3,740

BARYE, Alfred
French 19th cent.
sculpture: (L) $385; (H) $11,000

BARYE, Antoine Louis
French 1795-1875
paintings: (L) $2,200; (H) $3,850
drawings: (L) $8,250; (H) $80,000
sculpture: (L) $154; (H) $93,500

BARZANTI, Licinio
Italian 1857-1944
paintings: (L) $121; (H) $880

BARZANTI, Peter
Italian 19th/20th cent.
sculpture: (L) $462; (H) $1,100

BAS, Edward le
British 1904-1966
paintings: (L) $440; (H) $6,875

BASCHENIS, Evaristo, studio of
Italian 17th cent.
paintings: (H) $99,000

BASCOM, Andrew J.
American 19th cent.
paintings: (L) $495; (H) $1,430

BASCOM, G.
American 19th/20th cent.
paintings: (H) $715

BASCOM, Ruth Henshaw
American 1772-1848
drawings: (L) $4,400; (H) $66,000

BASELITZ, Georg
German b. 1938
paintings: (L) $35,200; (H) $797,500
drawings: (L) $2,310; (H) $39,600

BASKERVILLE, Charles, Jr.
American b. 1896
paintings: (L) $220; (H) $660
drawings: (L) $33; (H) $825

BASKIN, Leonard
American b. 1922
drawings: (L) $165; (H) $4,400
sculpture: (L) $220; (H) $19,800

BASOLI, Antonio
1774-1848
drawings: (L) $3,850; (H) $4,950

BASQUIAT, Jean Michel
American 1960-1988
paintings: (L) $4,950; (H) $440,000
drawings: (L) $825; (H) $159,500
sculpture: (L) $35,200; (H) $319,000

BASSANI, P.
paintings: (H) $935

BASSANO, Francesco Giambattista da
Ponte, called Francesco Giambattista
the younger
Italian c. 1549-1592
paintings: (H) $77,000

BASSANO, Gerolamo, studio of
paintings: (H) $7,150

BASSANO, Gerolamo da Ponte, called
Gerolamo
Italian c. 1566-1621
paintings: (H) $5,500

BASSANO, Jacopo
Italian 1510/18-1592
paintings: (H) $440,000
drawings: (L) $5,500; (H) $23,100

BASSANO, Leandro
Italian 1557-1622
paintings: (L) $4,400; (H) $20,900

BASSEN, Bartholomeus van
Dutch 1590-1652
paintings: (H) $15,400

BASSEN, Bartolomeus van and Jan
PYNAS
Dutch 17th cent.
paintings: (H) $49,500

BASSEPORTE, Madeleine Francoise
French 1701-1780
drawings: (H) $16,500

BASSETT, Reveau
American b. 1897
paintings: (L) $2,200; (H) $6,600

BASSETTI, Marcantonio
Italian 1588-1630
paintings: (H) $66,000

BASSFORD, Franklyn
American 19th cent.
paintings: (H) $16,500

BASSFORD, Wallace
American
paintings: (L) $220; (H) $1,980
drawings: (H) $154

BASSIN, L.
French 20th cent.
sculpture: (H) $825

BASTANIER, Hans
paintings: (H) $1,100

BASTERT, Nicolas
Dutch 1854-1939
paintings: (L) $330; (H) $4,950

BASTIANI, **
sculpture: (H) $7,150

BASTIANI, Lazzaro di Jacopo
Italian c. 1423-1512
paintings: (H) $52,250

BASTIDE
paintings: (L) $412; (H) $4,400

BASTIDE, P.
late 19th cent.
sculpture: (H) $2,750

BASTIEN, Alfred Theodore Joseph
Belgian 1873-1955
sculpture: (H) $3,850

BASTIEN-LEPAGE, Jules
French 1848-1884
paintings: (L) $2,750; (H) $9,900
drawings: (L) $1,980; (H) $8,800

BASTON, Andre
French 19th cent.
paintings: (L) $1,540; (H) $1,540

BASYE, Joyce
American b. 1947
paintings: (H) $2,310

BATCHELLER, Frederick S.
American 1837-1889
paintings: (L) $715; (H) $6,600

BATE, Firmin
sculpture: (H) $1,320

BATEMAN, James
British 1815-1849
paintings: (H) $3,300

BATEMAN, Robert
British 19th cent.
paintings: (H) $6,050

BATES, A.
paintings: (H) $2,420

BATES, David
British 1840-1921
paintings: (L) $330; (H) $8,250
drawings: (L) $1,320; (H) $1,925

BATES, David and Sydney Richard
PERCY
paintings: (H) $2,750

BATES, Dewey
American 1851-1891
paintings: (L) $385; (H) $46,200

BATES, Frederick Davenport
English b. 1867
paintings: (L) $247; (H) $1,650

BATES, Gladys
American b. 1896
paintings: (H) $66
sculpture: (H) $1,980

BATES, Henry
British 19th cent.
paintings: (H) $825

BATES, Kenneth
American b. 1904
paintings: (L) $25; (H) $1,045

BATHIEU, J.
paintings: (H) $1,430

BATIGNE, Francois Victor
French 19th/20th cent.
paintings: (H) $4,180

BATON, Claude
French 20th cent.
paintings: (H) $2,090

BATONI, Pompeo
Italian 1708-1787
paintings: (L) $1,980; (H) $110,000
drawings: (L) $770; (H) $12,100

BATOWSKI-KACZOR, Stanislas
Polish b. 1866
paintings: (L) $2,200; (H) $3,520

BATTACHI, A.
Italian 19th cent.
sculpture: (H) $2,200

BATTAGLIA, Alessandro
Italian 1870-1940
paintings: (L) $9,350; (H) $49,500
drawings: (H) $1,540

BATTAGLIA, Clelia Bompiani
Italian 1848-1927
drawings: (L) $275; (H) $1,100

BATTAGLIA, E.
sculpture: (L) $275; (H) $880

BATTELLH (?), E.W.
paintings: (H) $1,760

BATTI, Leon
late 19th cent.
sculpture: (H) $2,750

BATTISTA, Giovanni
Italian 1858-1925
drawings: (L) $187; (H) $880

BATTISTA, M.
19th cent.
drawings: (H) $1,100

BAUCHANT, Andre
French 1873-1958
paintings: (L) $660; (H) $41,800
drawings: (H) $880

BAUCHE, Leon Charles
paintings: (H) $880

BAUDE, Francois Charles
French 1880-1953
paintings: (H) $3,300

BAUDERON, Louis
French b. 1809
paintings: (L) $660; (H) $2,420

BAUDESSON, Nicolas
French c. 1611-1680
paintings: (H) $7,700

BAUDIT, Amedee
French 1825-1890
paintings: (L) $1,980; (H) $2,530
drawings: (H) $357

BAUDOUIN, Eugene
French 1842-1893
paintings: (H) $1,650

BAUDOUIN, Paul Albert
French 1844-1931
paintings: (H) $660
drawings: (H) $385

BAUDOUIN, Pierre Antoine
French 1723-1769
drawings: (H) $1,100

BAUDRY, Paul
French 1828-1886
paintings: (L) $1,650; (H) $2,200
drawings: (L) $2,420; (H) $3,520

BAUDUIN, Roland
French 19th cent.
paintings: (H) $1,320

BAUER, A***
19th cent.
paintings: (H) $1,760

BAUER, Carl Ferdinand
Austrian 1879-1954
paintings: (H) $4,950

BAUER, F.
Austrian 19th cent.
paintings: (H) $798

BAUER, Marius Alexander Jacques
Dutch 1867-1932
paintings: (H) $1,100

BAUER, Rudolf
German/American 1889-1953
paintings: (L) $4,400; (H) $93,500
drawings: (L) $330; (H) $16,500

BAUER, W.
German 19th cent.
paintings: (H) $1,430

BAUER, W.C.
American
drawings: (H) $770

BAUER, Willi
German b. 1923
paintings: (L) $99; (H) $880

BAUER, William C.
drawings: (H) $770

BAUER-RADNAY, Elizabeth de
Hungarian/American 1897-1972
drawings: (H) $2,970

BAUERLE, Karl Wilhelm Friedrich
German 1831-1912
paintings: (H) $13,200

BAUERMEISTER, Mary
German b. 1934
sculpture: (L) $1,320; (H) $16,500

BAUERNFEIND, Gustave
Austrian 1848-1904
drawings: (H) $1,430

BAUFFE, Victor
Dutch ac. 19th cent.
paintings: (L) $495; (H) $1,210
drawings: (H) $605

BAUGIN, Lubin
French 1612/13-1663
paintings: (H) $71,500

BAUM, Carl
American
paintings: (L) $2,860; (H) $7,700

BAUM, Charles
American b. 1892
paintings: (L) $7,700; (H) $16,500

BAUM, Joseph
American 19th cent.
paintings: (H) $1,100

BAUM, Walter Emerson
American 1884-1956
paintings: (L) $132; (H) $19,800
drawings: (L) $100; (H) $3,250

BAUMAN, F.
European 19th cent.
paintings: (H) $880

BAUMANN, Ida
paintings: (H) $9,900

BAUMANN, Karl Herman
American 1911-1984
paintings: (L) $1,430; (H) $10,450
drawings: (L) $495; (H) $2,475

BAUMANN, L.
paintings: (H) $825

BAUMEISTER, Mary
drawings: (H) $5,060

BAUMEISTER, Willi
German 1889-1955
paintings: (H) $110,000

BAUMES, Amedee
French b. 1820
paintings: (H) $5,500

BAUMGARTNER, A.
paintings: (H) $935

BAUMGARTNER, H.
Swiss 19th cent.
paintings: (L) $1,760; (H) $13,200

BAUMGARTNER, Johann Wolfgang,
and Studio
1712-1761
paintings: (H) $6,600

BAUMGARTNER, John Jay
American 1865-1946
drawings: (L) $880; (H) $1,430

BAUMGARTNER, Peter
German 1834-1911
paintings: (L) $24,200; (H) $44,000

BAUMGARTNER, Warren W.
American 1894-1963
paintings: (L) $302; (H) $3,190
drawings: (L) $110; (H) $1,870

BAUMGRAS, Peter
American 1827-1904
paintings: (L) $220; (H) $1,100

BAUMHOFFER, Walter M.
American b. 1904
paintings: (L) $330; (H) $6,600

BAUR, Johann Wilhelm, or BAUER
French d. 1640
drawings: (L) $6,050; (H) $7,975

BAUTER, C.
paintings: (H) $2,310

BAXTER, Charles
English 1809-1879
paintings: (H) $1,925

BAXTER, Elijah, Jr.
American 1849-1939
paintings: (L) $132; (H) $1,540

BAXTER, Reginald
paintings: (H) $6,050

BAXTER, Robert
paintings: (H) $1,200

BAYER, Herbert
Austrian/American b. 1900
paintings: (L) $880; (H) $1,100

BAYER, J.
paintings: (H) $660

BAYERS, Fannie
paintings: (L) $440; (H) $1,430

BAYES, Alfred Walter
English 1832-1909
paintings: (L) $467; (H) $1,870

BAYES, Gilbert
English 1872-1953
sculpture: (H) $22,000

BAYEU Y SUBIAS, Ramon
Spanish 1746-1793
paintings: (H) $57,200

BAYHA, Edwin F.
American 19th/20th cent.
paintings: (H) $37,400

BAYLINSON, A.S.
American 1882-1950
paintings: (L) $440; (H) $6,820

BAYLISS, Sir Wyke
British 1835-1906
drawings: (H) $770

BAYNARD, Ed
American b. 1940
paintings: (L) $137; (H) $1,870

BAYNE, Walter McPherson
British 1795-1859
paintings: (H) $3,300

BAYNES, Frederick Thomas
drawings: (H) $935

BAZAINE, Jean
French b. 1904
paintings: (H) $60,500
drawings: (L) $330; (H) $15,400

BAZILE, Castera
Haitian 1923-1965
paintings: (L) $2,200; (H) $3,520

BAZIN, Francois
French
sculpture: (H) $660

BAZIN, Frederick
sculpture: (H) $3,300

BAZIN, L.E.
drawings: (H) $1,320

BAZIOTES, William
American 1912-1963
paintings: (L) $22,000; (H) $385,000
drawings: (L) $1,320; (H) $66,000

BAZZANI, Giuseppe
Italian 1690/1701-1769
paintings: (L) $20,900; (H) $63,250

BAZZANI, Luigi
Italian 1836-1926/27
paintings: (H) $6,600

BAZZANTI
Italian
sculpture: (L) $2,090; (H) $3,300

BAZZARO, Leonardo
Italian 1853-1937
paintings: (H) $5,500

BAZZICALUVA, Ercole
Italian 1600-1640
drawings: (L) $605; (H) $1,650

BAZZONI, A.
sculpture: (H) $6,325

BEACH, Chester
American 1881-1956
sculpture: (L) $440; (H) $14,850

BEACH, Thomas
English 1738-1806
paintings: (L) $1,100; (H) $74,250

BEADLE, James Prinsep
paintings: (H) $7,150

BEAL, Gifford
American 1879-1956
paintings: (L) $110; (H) $72,600
drawings: (L) $82; (H) $4,620

BEAL, Jack
American b. 1931
paintings: (L) $3,080; (H) $27,500

BEAL, Reynolds
American 1867-1951
paintings: (L) $935; (H) $40,700
drawings: (L) $121; (H) $6,875

BEALE, Mary
English 1632/33-1697/99
paintings: (L) $1,650; (H) $4,400

BEALL, Cecil Calvert
American 1892-1967
paintings: (L) $100; (H) $700
drawings: (H) $550

BEAMAN, Gamaliel W.
American 1852-1937
paintings: (L) $220; (H) $1,760

BEAN, Caroline van Hook
American 1879/80-1980
paintings: (L) $66; (H) $99
drawings: (L) $33; (H) $2,750

BEAQUESNE, Wilfrid Constant
paintings: (H) $1,980

BEARD, Adelia Belle
American d. 1920
paintings: (H) $660

BEARD, Daniel Carter
American 1850-1941
drawings: (H) $1,540

BEARD, James Henry
American 1812/14-1893
paintings: (L) $1,210; (H) $12,100

BEARD, William Holbrook
American 1825-1900
paintings: (L) $770; (H) $8,250

BEARDEN, Romare
American 1914-1988
paintings: (L) $5,280; (H) $16,500
drawings: (L) $1,320; (H) $66,000

BEARDSLEY, Aubrey
English 1872-1898
drawings: (L) $165; (H) $1,980

BEARE, George
English ac. 1744-1749
paintings: (L) $4,400; (H) $37,400

BEARS, Orlando Hand
American 1811-1851
paintings: (L) $11,000; (H) $77,000

BEATON, Sir Cecil
English 1904-1980
drawings: (L) $110; (H) $3,300

BEATTIE-BROWN, William
Scottish 1831-1909
paintings: (L) $687; (H) $715

BEATTY, E.V.
British 19th cent.
paintings: (H) $1,320

BEATTY, Frank T.
American b. 1899
paintings: (H) $825
drawings: (L) $55; (H) $770

BEATTY, John Wesley
American 1850-1924
paintings: (L) $220; (H) $1,320

BEAUBIEN, A.J.
American 20th cent.
paintings: (H) $770

BEAUCHAMP, John
paintings: (H) $660

BEAUCHAMP, Robert
American b. 1923
paintings: (L) $825; (H) $2,640
drawings: (H) $495

BEAUDESERL, C.
paintings: (H) $715

BEAUDIN, Andre
French 1895-1980
sculpture: (H) $5,500

BEAUDOUIN, Frank
American 20th cent.
paintings: (H) $990

BEAUDUIN, Jean
Belgian 1851-1916
paintings: (L) $440; (H) $9,350

BEAUFRERE, Adolphe
French 1876-1960
drawings: (H) $2,860

BEAUGUREAU, Francis
American b. 1920
paintings: (L) $825; (H) $3,300
drawings: (L) $330; (H) $1,500

BEAULEY, William
American
paintings: (H) $770

BEAUMONT, Arthur E.
American 1890-1978
paintings: (L) $605; (H) $1,540
drawings: (L) $1,100; (H) $1,760

BEAUMONT, Arthur J.
Anglo/American 1877/79-1956
paintings: (L) $82; (H) $1,870

BEAUMONT, Charles
American 19th cent.
paintings: (H) $825

BEAUMONT, Claudio Francesco
Italian 1694-1766
drawings: (L) $880; (H) $2,860

BEAUMONT, Lillian Adele
American 1880-1922
paintings: (H) $2,090

BEAUMONT, T.D.
British 19th cent.
paintings: (L) $253; (H) $1,320

BEAUMONT, W.
paintings: (L) $3,300; (H) $3,300

BEAUQUESNE, Wilfrid Constant
French
paintings: (L) $522; (H) $5,500

BEAUVAIS, Arnold
drawings: (H) $4,125

BEAUVAIS, F.
French
paintings: (H) $4,125

BEAUX, Cecilia
American 1863-1942
paintings: (L) $8,250; (H) $25,300
drawings: (H) $3,300

BEAVER, Fred
American (Creek) b. 1911
paintings: (L) $275; (H) $825

BEAVIS, Richard
English 1824-1896
paintings: (L) $600; (H) $6,600
drawings: (H) $220

BEBIE, Henry
American c. 1824-1888
paintings: (H) $4,400

BECCAFUMI, Domenico
Italian 1486-1551
drawings: (H) $7,425

BECHER, Arthur E.
German/American 1877-1941
paintings: (L) $264; (H) $4,125

BECHER, Bernd and Hilla
contemporary
drawings: (L) $7,700; (H) $35,200

BECHI, Luigi
Italian 1830-1919
paintings: (L) $1,760; (H) $35,200

BECHTLE, Robert
American b. 1932
paintings: (L) $19,800; (H) $60,500
drawings: (L) $6,600; (H) $8,800

BECK, A.R.
paintings: (H) $770

BECK, Claude
paintings: (H) $990

BECK, Clifford
American Indian b. 1946
drawings: (L) $220; (H) $880

BECK, E.
sculpture: (H) $2,530

BECK, George
paintings: (H) $990

BECK, I.F.
Scandinavian 19th cent.
paintings: (H) $11,000

BECK, Joel
paintings: (H) $1,100

BECK, Raphael
American d. 1947
paintings: (H) $900

BECK, Rosemary
American
paintings: (L) $330; (H) $660

BECKEN, Brian A.
American 20th cent.
paintings: (H) $5,500

BECKER, August
German 1822-1887
paintings: (H) $1,210

BECKER, Carl Ludwig Friedrich
German 1820-1900
paintings: (L) $2,090; (H) $4,950

BECKER, Frederick W.
American b. 1888
paintings: (L) $220; (H) $1,650
drawings: (L) $121; (H) $700

BECKER, Georges
French b. 1845
paintings: (H) $1,320

BECKER, Joseph
American 1841-1910
paintings: (H) $1,045

BECKER, Maurice
Russian/American 1889-1975
paintings: (L) $550; (H) $935

BECKER, Q.
paintings: (H) $825

BECKER, William G.
British 19th/20th cent.
paintings: (L) $1,045; (H) $1,100

BECKER-WEGELI, Friedy
paintings: (L) $198; (H) $880

BECKERS, Franz
Dutch 1898-1983
paintings: (H) $990

BECKETT, Ernest F.
British 19th/20th cent.
paintings: (H) $1,000

BECKLEY, Bill
American b. 1946
drawings: (H) $880

BECKMAN, Jessie Mary
American 1856-1929
paintings: (H) $770

BECKMAN, William
American 20th cent.
paintings: (H) $49,500
drawings: (L) $2,090; (H) $38,500

BECKMANN, Ludwig
German 1822-1902
paintings: (H) $3,520

BECKMANN, Max
American 1884-1950
paintings: (L) $44,000; (H) $1,540,000
drawings: (L) $605; (H) $110,000

BECKWITH, Arthur
American 1860-1930
paintings: (L) $358; (H) $2,475

BECKWITH, James Carroll
American 1852-1917
paintings: (L) $247; (H) $58,300
drawings: (L) $550; (H) $3,300

BECQUER, Joaquin
Spanish 1805-1841
paintings: (H) $2,200

BECQUEREL, Andre Vincent
French ac. early 20th cent.
sculpture: (L) $110; (H) $2,310

BEDA, Francesco
Italian 1840-1900
paintings: (L) $1,650; (H) $46,200

BEDA, Giulio
paintings: (H) $1,980

BEDINGFIELD
paintings: (L) $220; (H) $880

BEE, Lonie
b. 1902
paintings: (H) $1,900

BEECHER, Amariah Dwight
American b. 1839
paintings: (L) $143; (H) $1,650

BEECHEY, Admiral Richard Brydges
British 1808-1895
paintings: (L) $1,210; (H) $44,000

BEECHEY, Sir William
English 1753-1839
paintings: (L) $495; (H) $46,200

BEECQ, Jan Karel Donatus van
Dutch 1638-1722
paintings: (H) $39,600

BEEK, Bernardus Antonie van
Dutch b. 1875
paintings: (L) $550; (H) $715

BEEK, Theodor von der
German b. 1838
paintings: (L) $605; (H) $14,300

BEELER, Joe
American b. 1931
paintings: (L) $4,125; (H) $11,000
sculpture: (L) $1,650; (H) $5,500

BEELT, Cornelis
Dutch 1660-c. 1702
paintings: (H) $6,050

BEER, Cornelis de
paintings: (H) $5,500

BEER, Jan de
Belgian c. 1480/1490-c. 1536/1542
paintings: (H) $187,000

BEER, John
British ac. 1895-1915
paintings: (H) $2,475
drawings: (L) $660; (H) $770

BEERBOHM, Sir Max
drawings: (L) $275; (H) $660

BEERS, Jan van
Belgian 1852-1927
paintings: (L) $220; (H) $4,950

BEERSTRATEN, Anthonie
Dutch ac. 1639-1665
paintings: (H) $19,800

BEERSTRATEN, Jan Abrahamsz
Dutch 1622-1666
paintings: (L) $3,025; (H) $20,900

BEERT, Osias, I
Flemish c. 1570-1624
paintings: (L) $110,000; (H) $902,000

Native American

Harrison Begay (Haskay Yah Ne Yah, Warrior Who Walked Up to His Enemy) is one of the first well-known contemporary Navajo artists. Begay was born in 1917 and lived for a short while in White Cone, Arizona. He had little formal education and studied mainly at home. In 1934 he returned to high school in Santa Fe, New Mexico, and also studied art under Dorothy Dunn. In 1940-1941, Begay studied architecture at Black Mountain College in North Carolina. During World War II he served for three years in the U.S. Army Signal Corps in the South Pacific. The Japanese had broken all of the American codes except the Navajo language, and many Navajos played a vital role in communications.

Harrison Begay is a painter, illustrator, printmaker, and muralist. Begay began exhibiting in 1946, and his paintings have been reproduced in multiples as silk screens. He has received numerous awards, and his works have been exhibited at many museums including the Museum of Modern Art in New York. Navajos weaving, wild horses, antelopes, a Navajo dance, and a Navajo girl with sheep are recurrent themes in Begay's work. The works of many artists such as Begay are sold in specialized ethnographic sales mixed in with baskets and rugs. (Harrison Begay, *The Shepherdess*, tempera on white paper, 11 x 14 in., Skinner, June 29, 1990, $935)

BEEST, Albert van
Dutch 1820-1860
paintings: (L) $412; (H) $18,000

BEEST, Albertus van
paintings: (H) $3,850

BEET, Cornelius de
American 1779-1840
paintings: (L) $6,600; (H) $13,200

BEETZ-CHARPENTIER, Elisa
French 20th cent.
sculpture: (L) $660; (H) $2,200

BEFANI, Achille Formis
Italian 1832-1906
paintings: (H) $4,950

BEGA, Cornelis Pietersz
Dutch 1620-1664
paintings: (L) $825; (H) $60,500

BEGAS, R.
Continental 19th cent.
paintings: (H) $1,595

BEGAY, Harrison, Haskay Yah Ne Yah
American (Navajo) b. 1917
paintings: (L) $137; (H) $935
drawings: (L) $22; (H) $110

BEGAZZI, R.
sculpture: (H) $880

BEGEYN, Abraham
paintings: (H) $11,000

BEGUINE, Michael Leonard
French 1855-1929
sculpture: (L) $1,870; (H) $4,125

BEHM, Karl
German 1858-1905
paintings: (H) $3,740

BEHN, Fritz
sculpture: (H) $3,575

BEHNCKE, Nile Jurgen
American 1892-1954
paintings: (H) $110
drawings: (L) $16; (H) $770

BEHR, Carel Jacobus
Dutch 1812-1895
paintings: (H) $3,740

BEHR, Johann Philipp
German d. 1756
paintings: (H) $5,500

BEHRENS, Hermann
paintings: (H) $2,750

BEICH, Mary
paintings: (H) $715

BEICH-MUNSTEKOG
German 19th/20th cent.
paintings: (H) $715

BEIHONG, Xu
Chinese 1895-1953
drawings: (H) $31,900

BEIL, C.A.
American
sculpture: (H) $900

BEINASCHI, Giovanni Battista
Italian 1636-1688
drawings: (L) $990; (H) $9,625

BEINKE, Fritz
German 1842-1907
drawings: (H) $4,400

BEJARANO, Manuel Cabral
paintings: (H) $15,400

BEL-GEDDES, Norman
drawings: (L) $2,530; (H) $3,080

BELAY, Pierre de
French 1890-1947
paintings: (L) $385; (H) $4,620

BELENOK, Pyotr
Russian b. 1938
paintings: (L) $1,760; (H) $2,860

BELIMBAU, Adolfo
Italian b. 1845
paintings: (H) $1,320

BELINE, George
drawings: (H) $2,200

BELKIN, Arnold
Canadian/American b. 1930
paintings: (L) $660; (H) $5,775

BELKNAP, Zedekiah
American 1781-1858
paintings: (L) $880; (H) $82,500

BELL, A.D.
drawings: (L) $550; (H) $1,100

BELL, Arthur George
British 1848/49-1916
paintings: (H) $2,860
drawings: (H) $660

BELL, Cecil C.
American b. 1906
paintings: (L) $99; (H) $8,800
drawings: (L) $660; (H) $1,980

BELL, Charles
American ac. 1930
paintings: (H) $990

BELL, Charles
American b. 1935
paintings: (L) $26,400; (H) $187,000
drawings: (L) $4,400; (H) $14,300

BELL, Clara Louise
American b. 1886
paintings: (H) $2,970

BELL, D.C.
American 19th cent.
paintings: (H) $935

BELL, Edward
paintings: (H) $5,500

BELL, Edward August
American b. 1862
paintings: (L) $605; (H) $13,200

BELL, F.C.
English 19th cent.
paintings: (H) $853

BELL, George C.
American 19th cent.
drawings: (H) $1,430

BELL, John
British 1811-1895
paintings: (H) $1,650

BELL, John
British 19th cent.
paintings: (H) $4,000

BELL, John W.
American 19th cent.
paintings: (H) $1,760

BELL, Larry
American b. 1939
paintings: (H) $1,430
drawings: (L) $660; (H) $4,950
sculpture: (L) $7,700; (H) $22,000

BELL, Stuart H.
British 1823-1896
paintings: (L) $770; (H) $1,045

BELL, T.B.
paintings: (H) $2,200

BELLA, Stefano Della
Italian 1610-1664
drawings: (H) $1,870

BELLAMY, A.
English School late 19th/early 20th
cent.
paintings: (H) $1,045

BELLAN, Henri Ferdinand
paintings: (H) $880

BELLANGE, Jacques
drawings: (H) $3,080

BELLANGE, Joseph Louis Hippolyte
French 1800-1866
paintings: (L) $3,025; (H) $52,250
drawings: (L) $165; (H) $1,320

BELLANGER, Camille Felix
French 1853-1923
paintings: (L) $9,350; (H) $137,500

BELLANGER, Georges
French 1847-1918
paintings: (H) $6,600

BELLANGER-ADHEMAR, Paul
French b. 1868
paintings: (H) $1,540

BELLANO, A.
Italian 19th cent.
paintings: (H) $9,350

BELLAY, R.
French c. 1900
paintings: (H) $1,320

BELLE, Alexis Simon
French 1674-1734
paintings: (L) $10,450; (H) $35,200

BELLE, Marcel
paintings: (H) $3,300

BELLECOUR, Etienne Prosper Berne
French 1838-1910
paintings: (H) $9,900

BELLECOUR, Jean Berne
French b. 1874
paintings: (H) $5,500

BELLEI, Gaetano
Italian 1857-1922
paintings: (L) $935; (H) $37,400

BELLEMONT, Leon
paintings: (H) $3,300

BELLENGE, Michel Bruno
French 1726-1793
paintings: (H) $12,100

BELLENGER, Georges
French 1847-1918
paintings: (H) $660

BELLERMANN, Ferdinand
German 1814-1889
paintings: (L) $14,300; (H) $55,000

BELLET, Anna
paintings: (H) $990

BELLET, Auguste Emile
paintings: (L) $3,300; (H) $6,600

BELLEVOIS, Jacob
Dutch 1621-1675
paintings: (L) $1,430; (H) $36,300

BELLI, Giovacchino
Italian 1756-1822
drawings: (L) $770; (H) $4,950

BELLIAS, Richard
French 1921-1974
paintings: (L) $500; (H) $4,400

BELLIMBAU, Adolfo
Italian b. 1845
paintings: (H) $6,600

BELLINA (?), E.
American School
paintings: (H) $2,090

BELLINCIONI, E.
paintings: (H) $825

BELLINI, Filippo
drawings: (H) $2,750

BELLINI, Giovanni
Italian 1430-1516
paintings: (H) $352,000

BELLINI, Giovanni, circle of
Italian
paintings: (H) $19,800

BELLIS, Daisy Maude
American b. 1887
paintings: (L) $165; (H) $660

BELLIS, Hubert
Belgian 1831-1902
paintings: (L) $192; (H) $19,800

BELLMER, Hans
German/French b. 1902
paintings: (H) $10,450
drawings: (L) $715; (H) $7,150

BELLOLI, Andrei Franzovich
Russian d. 1881
paintings: (H) $17,050

BELLON, Jean
French b. 1944
paintings: (L) $825; (H) $1,980

BELLONI, Giorgio
Italian 1861-1944
paintings: (H) $3,080

BELLONI, Serge
Continental 20th cent.
paintings: (L) $605; (H) $990

BELLOTTI, Pietro
Italian 1627-1700
paintings: (H) $34,100

BELLOTTO, Bernardo
Italian 1720/24-1780
paintings: (H) $1,870,000

BELLOTTO, Bernardo, studio of
Italian 18th cent.
paintings: (L) $35,200; (H) $192,500

BELLOWS, Albert Fitch
American 1829-1883
paintings: (L) $1,430; (H) $39,600
drawings: (L) $880; (H) $19,800

BELLOWS, George
American 1882-1925
paintings: (L) $3,740; (H) $1,430,000
drawings: (L) $440; (H) $220,000

BELLOWS, J.F.
American
paintings: (H) $1,320

BELLUCCI, Antonio
Italian 1654-1726
paintings: (L) $10,450; (H) $60,500

BELOT, H.
paintings: (H) $1,650

BELTRAME, Alfredo
Italian 19th cent.
paintings: (H) $990

BELTRAN-MASSES, Federico
Spanish b. 1885
paintings: (L) $7,975; (H) $42,900

BELVEDERE, Andrea, called Abate
Andra
Italian 1642-1732
paintings: (L) $17,600; (H) $41,800

BEMAN, W.E.
paintings: (H) $2,035

BEMEL, Karl Sebastian von
German 1743-1796
drawings: (H) $2,760

BEMELMANS, Ludwig
Austrian/American 1898-1963
paintings: (L) $110; (H) $825
drawings: (L) $121; (H) $1,760

BEMIS, W.L.
American School 19th cent.
paintings: (H) $1,210

BEMMEL, Peter von
German 1685-1754
paintings: (L) $4,125; (H) $4,400

BEMTINCK, Ottoline
Dutch 19th cent.
paintings: (H) $3,960

BEN TRE, Howard
American b. 1949
sculpture: (L) $5,500; (H) $22,000

BEN-ZION
American 1897-1987
paintings: (L) $55; (H) $10,450
drawings: (L) $55; (H) $192

BENASCHI, Giovanni Battista
paintings: (L) $2,200; (H) $3,850

BENASSIT, E.
19th cent.
paintings: (H) $1,650

BENASSIT, Louis Emile
French 1833-1902
paintings: (L) $770; (H) $1,980

BENBRIDGE, Henry
American 1744-1812
paintings: (H) $6,050

BENDA, Wladyslaw T.
American 1873-1948
drawings: (L) $660; (H) $660

BENDER, Bill
American b. 1920
paintings: (L) $1,045; (H) $1,320

BENDER, Sarah E.
American d. 1915
paintings: (H) $2,090

BENDER, Stanislaus
paintings: (H) $35,750

BENDIXEN, Siegfried Detlev
German 1786-1864
drawings: (H) $1,980

BENEDETTI, Andries
Flemish 1620-after 1649
paintings: (L) $13,200; (H) $121,000

BENEDITO-VIVES, Manuel
Spanish 1875-1963
paintings: (H) $4,400

BENEKER, Gerrit A.
American 1882-1934
paintings: (L) $110; (H) $23,000
drawings: (L) $330; (H) $550

BENERAIS, G. de
paintings: (H) $2,090

BENET, Eugene Paul
sculpture: (H) $2,310

BENGLIS, Lynda
American b. 1941
sculpture: (L) $1,100; (H) $22,000

BENGSTON, Billy Al
American b. 1934
paintings: (L) $550; (H) $13,200
drawings: (L) $1,100; (H) $4,400

BENHOLD
paintings: (H) $2,860

BENKER, A.
German 19th cent.
paintings: (L) $550; (H) $1,980

BENLLIURE Y GIL, Jose
Spanish 1855-1914
paintings: (L) $12,100; (H) $165,000

BENLURE
paintings: (H) $660

BENN, Ben
American 1884-1983
paintings: (L) $220; (H) $4,180
drawings: (L) $330; (H) $2,090

BENNEKER, Louis F.
American 1876-1937
paintings: (L) $110; (H) $1,320

BENNER, Emmanuel Michel, called
MANY
French 1873-1965
paintings: (L) $1,760; (H) $29,700

BENNER, J.
French 19th cent.
paintings: (H) $715

BENNES, J.
sculpture: (H) $2,640

BENNETT, A.
paintings: (H) $660

BENNETT, A.H.
English late 19th cent.
paintings: (H) $1,320

BENNETT, Frank Moss
English 1874-1953
paintings: (L) $1,320; (H) $9,350

BENNETT, Joseph
American b. 1899
paintings: (L) $330; (H) $715

BENNETT-BROWN, Mae
American 20th cent.
paintings: (H) $700

BENOIS, Alexander Nikolaievitch
Russian 1870-1960
paintings: (H) $1,100
drawings: (L) $275; (H) $12,100

BENOIS, Nicolai
drawings: (L) $110; (H) $1,100

BENOIT, Rigaud
Haitian 20th cent.
paintings: (H) $13,750

BENOLDI, Walter
paintings: (L) $110; (H) $660

BENSA, C.
Italian 19th cent.
drawings: (H) $935

BENSA, Joseph
paintings: (H) $1,100

BENSELL, Edmond
American 19th cent.
paintings: (H) $2,420

BENSELL, George Frederick
American 1837-1879
paintings: (L) $715; (H) $2,475

BENSO, Giulio
Italian 1601-1668
drawings: (L) $1,320; (H) $5,500

BENSON, Ambrosius
Flemish 1495-1550
paintings: (L) $9,900; (H) $46,200

BENSON, Eugene
American 1839-1908
paintings: (L) $1,100; (H) $20,900

BENSON, Frank W.
American 1862-1951
paintings: (L) $605; (H) $583,000
drawings: (L) $1,760; (H) $24,000

BENSON, J.
paintings: (H) $1,100

BENSON, John P.
American 1865-1947
paintings: (L) $1,100; (H) $4,125

BENSON, Tressa Emerson
American b. 1896
paintings: (L) $528; (H) $3,025
drawings: (L) $110; (H) $1,100

BENSOU, O.
paintings: (H) $1,100

BENTHAM-DINSDALE, John
paintings: (H) $6,600

BENTHELSEN, Johann
paintings: (H) $935

BENTIER, Francisgne Edouard
paintings: (H) $2,640

BENTLEY, Alfred
British d. 1923
paintings: (H) $1,100

BENTLEY, Claude
American b. 1915
paintings: (H) $825
drawings: (H) $33

BENTLEY, John William
American b. 1880
paintings: (L) $357; (H) $14,300

BENTLEY, Lester W.
American b. 1908
paintings: (L) $165; (H) $1,320

BENTON, Dwight
American b. 1834
paintings: (L) $330; (H) $1,650

BENTON, Fletcher
American b. 1931
paintings: (H) $825
sculpture: (L) $1,650; (H) $4,400

BENTON, L.D.
American 19th cent.
paintings: (H) $5,600

BENTON, Thomas Hart
American 1889-1975
paintings: (L) $1,650; (H) $1,540,000
drawings: (L) $82; (H) $176,000
sculpture: (L) $6,600; (H) $9,680

BENTURE
paintings: (H) $660

BENVENUTO DI GIOVANNI
Italian 1436-1518
paintings: (H) $13,750

BENWELL, Joseph Austin
English 19th cent.
drawings: (H) $6,050

BENZONI
Italian 19th cent.
paintings: (H) $1,980

Regionalist School

Born in Missouri, Thomas Hart Benton (1889-1975) was raised in Washington, D.C., the son of a congressman. He studied at Western Military Academy and drew sketches and cartoons for a local newspaper. In 1907 he enrolled in classes at the Chicago Art Institute but left in 1908 for Paris, where he remained for three years, and studied at the Academie Julian. During this period he developed a close friendship with Stanton Macdonald-Wright, one of the first American abstract artists.

Influenced by Cubism, Synchromism, and the aesthetics of abstraction, Benton became a Modernist painter. He returned to the United States in 1916 and settled in New York. In 1918 he was employed as a draftsman at the Norfolk, Virginia, Naval Base, and his attention turned to more realistic themes reflecting his Missouri background. He abandoned Modernism in the 1920s and became a "born again" realist.

Benton was the most vocal of the Regionalist painters, voicing their desire to establish a genuinely American art by utilizing American subject matter and repudiating innovative artistic styles. Other important realists were John Steuart Curry and Grant Wood. During the 1920s and 1930s the Regionialists' stance against formalism and the glorification of agrarian life was shared by the Social Realists of the Soviet Union and the Mexican muralists. Benton also painted murals of contemporary American life, most notably at the New School for Social Research in New York (1930-1931) and the Whitney Museum of American Art (1932).

During the 1930s, Benton taught at the Art Students League; his most famous pupil was Jackson Pollock, whose paintings later evolved into the Modernism Benton so detested. (Thomas Hart Benton, *Spring Storm*, tempera on board, 18¾ x 26¾ in., Wolf's, April 23, 1988, $187,000)

BENZONI, C.B.
Italian 19th cent.
sculpture: (H) $22,000

BENZONI, Giovanni Maria
Italian 1809-1873
sculpture: (L) $5,500; (H) $330,000

BEQUEREL
sculpture: (H) $3,080

BERAIN, Jean
French 1640-1711
drawings: (H) $20,900

BERAN, Bruno
Czechoslovakian early 20th cent.
paintings: (L) $1,155; (H) $1,155

BERANGER, Charles
French 1816-1853
paintings: (L) $4,400; (H) $6,600

BERANGER, L.
paintings: (H) $2,475
drawings: (H) $1,650

BERARD, Christian
French 1902-1949
paintings: (H) $15,400
drawings: (L) $825; (H) $8,800

BERAUD, Jean
French 1849-1936
paintings: (L) $5,500; (H) $2,860,000
drawings: (L) $1,980; (H) $17,600

BERCHEM, Claesz Pietersz
paintings: (H) $9,900

BERCHEM, Nicolaes
Dutch 1620-1683
paintings: (L) $2,750; (H) $16,500
drawings: (H) $5,225

BERCHERE, Narcisse
French 1819-1891
paintings: (L) $1,210; (H) $3,410
drawings: (L) $550; (H) $660

BERCHMANS, Emile
drawings: (H) $2,420

BERCKHEYDE, Gerrit Adrianensz
Dutch 1638-1698
paintings: (L) $19,800; (H) $148,500

BERDANIER, Paul F., Sr.
American b. 1879
paintings: (L) $132; (H) $6,050

BEREA, Dimitri
Rumanian 1908-1975
paintings: (L) $440; (H) $2,750

BERG, Ann
paintings: (H) $1,980

BERG, George Louis
American 1868/70-1941
paintings: (L) $138; (H) $2,530

BERG, J. van
paintings: (H) $907

BERG, Ralph Tuffy
American
sculpture: (L) $3,500; (H) $6,800

BERG, Ro
contemporary
sculpture: (H) $6,050

BERG, Simon van den and Wouter VERSCHUUR
paintings: (H) $19,800

BERGAMINI, Francesco
Italian 19th cent.
paintings: (L) $1,540; (H) $11,000

BERGE, Bernardus Gerardusten
Dutch 1825-1875
paintings: (H) $1,320

BERGE, Edward
American 1876-1924
sculpture: (L) $825; (H) $15,400

BERGE, Henri
drawings: (L) $550; (H) $660

BERGE, James Franklin
American 20th cent.
paintings: (H) $1,100

BERGEN, C.
German 19th cent.
paintings: (H) $7,700

BERGEN, Dirck van
paintings: (H) $8,250
drawings: (H) $550

BERGEN, John van
drawings: (H) $1,650

BERGER, Ernst
Austrian 1857-1919
paintings: (H) $11,000

BERGER, Jason
American b. 1923
paintings: (L) $2,200; (H) $2,475

BERGERE, F.M.
paintings: (H) $1,650

BERGERON, Eugene
French 19th cent.
paintings: (H) $2,090

BERGEVIN, Edouard de
French 19th/20th cent.
paintings: (H) $1,650

BERGFELD, A.
paintings: (H) $1,650

BERGHE, Charles Auguste van den
Belgian 1798-1853
paintings: (H) $27,500

BERGHE, Christoffel van den
Dutch 1590?-1642
paintings: (H) $60,500

BERGHE, Herman van den
Belgian 19th/20th cent.
paintings: (H) $2,750

BERGI, G.
Italian
sculpture: (H) $660

BERGLER, Joseph, the Younger
Austrian 1753-1829
paintings: (L) $605; (H) $5,500

BERGMAN
Austrian
sculpture: (H) $1,100

BERGMAN, Anna Eva
contemporary
paintings: (H) $2,640

BERGMAN, C.
European School
paintings: (H) $660

BERGMAN, Franz
Austrian 19th/20th cent.
sculpture: (L) $66; (H) $4,950

BERGMAN, Herman
Finnish (?)
sculpture: (H) $3,410

BERGMAN, N.
paintings: (H) $1,540

BERGMAN, Oskar
Swedish 1879-1963
drawings: (H) $990

BERGMANN
paintings: (H) $1,650

BERGMANN, Julius Hugo
German 1861-1940
paintings: (H) $6,600

BERGNER, Yossl
Israeli contemporary
paintings: (L) $1,265; (H) $2,200

BERGSLIEN, Knud Larsen
Norwegian 1827-1908
paintings: (H) $24,200

BERGSOE, Johann Fredrik
Danish 1841-1897
paintings: (H) $2,860

BERGSTROM, Charles J.
American 20th cent.
paintings: (H) $660

BERGUE, Tony Francis de
French b. 1820
paintings: (L) $1,045; (H) $1,760

BERINGUIER, Eugene
French 1874-1949
paintings: (H) $11,000

BERJON, Antoine
drawings: (H) $5,390

BERK, Henrietta
paintings: (H) $3,300

BERKBURGH, *G***
paintings: (H) $3,025

BERKE, Ernest
American b. 1921
paintings: (H) $4,125
sculpture: (L) $2,640; (H) $3,300

BERKELEY, Stanley
British 1855-1909
paintings: (H) $82,500

BERKES, Antal
Hungarian 1874-1938
paintings: (L) $193; (H) $3,850

BERKOWITZ, Leon
American 20th cent.
paintings: (H) $3,575

BERLAND, Henel
American
paintings: (H) $935

BERLANT, Tony
American b. 1941
sculpture: (L) $990; (H) $17,600

BERLIN, S.
Continental 19th cent.
paintings: (H) $715

BERMAN, Eugene
Russian/American 1899-1972
paintings: (L) $1,100; (H) $10,450
drawings: (L) $385; (H) $7,700

BERMAN, Leonid
Russian 1896/98-1976
paintings: (L) $77; (H)$6,600
drawings: (H) $77

BERMAN, Saul
Russian/American b. 1899
paintings: (L) $770; (H) $7,150
drawings: (L) $50; (H) $1,760

BERMAN, W.E.
American 19th cent.
paintings: (H) $2,090

BERMAN, Wallace
contemporary
drawings: (L) $1,650; (H) $6,600

BERMUDEZ, Cundo
Cuban b. 1914
paintings: (L) $1,650; (H) $31,900
drawings: (L) $2,200; (H) $6,050

BERNADOTTE, Prins Eugen, of
Sweden
Swedish 1865-1947
paintings: (H) $33,000

BERNARD, Auguste Henri
French 20th cent.
paintings: (H) $825

BERNARD, Emile
French 1868-1941
paintings: (L) $528; (H) $286,000
drawings: (L) $209; (H) $1,870

BERNARD, Francois
French b. 1814
paintings: (L) $715; (H) $4,675

BERNARD, J. van
Dutch 19th cent.
paintings: (H) $4,950

BERNARD, Jean Joseph, called
Bernard De Paris
French b. 1740
drawings: (L) $660; (H) $2,200

BERNARD, Joseph
French
sculpture: (H) $16,500

BERNARD, Joseph
French 1864-1933
paintings: (H) $6,820

BERNARD, Joseph Antoine
French 1866-1931
sculpture: (H) $2,750

BERNARD, Jules Francois
French 20th cent.
paintings: (H) $4,950

BERNARO, L.
paintings: (H) $660

BERNATH, Aurel
paintings: (H) $935

BERNATH, Sandor
American b. 1892
drawings: (L) $165; (H) $1,870

BERNDORF
sculpture: (H) $1,320

BERNE-BELLECOUR, Etienne Prosper
French 1838-1910
paintings: (L) $880; (H) $66,000
drawings: (L) $495; (H) $550

BERNEDE, Pierre Emile
French b. 1820
paintings: (H) $3,575

BERNEKER, Louis Frederick
American 1872-1937
paintings: (L) $275; (H) $24,200
drawings: (H) $110

BERNEKER, Maud
American b. 1882
paintings: (H) $1,045

BERNI, Antonio
Argentinian 1905-1981
paintings: (L) $1,540; (H) $33,000
drawings: (H) $3,300

BERNIER, George
Belgian 1862-1918
paintings: (L) $880; (H) $990

BERNINGER, Edmund
German b. 1843
paintings: (L) $1,870; (H) $13,200

BERNINGHAUS, Charles
American b. 1905
paintings: (L) $324; (H) $715

BERNINGHAUS, Oscar Edmund
American 1874-1952
paintings: (L) $1,210; (H) $57,750
drawings: (L) $1,320; (H) $20,900

BERNSTEIN, Rick
contemporary
sculpture: (H) $715

BERNSTEIN, Theresa
American b. 1895
paintings: (L) $330; (H) $16,500
drawings: (H) $2,200

BERNT, Rudolf
Austrian 1844-1914
drawings: (L) $550; (H) $2,200

BERONNEAU, Andre
French 20th cent.
paintings: (L) $550; (H) $2,640

BEROUD, Louis
French b. 1852
paintings: (L) $1,870; (H) $187,000

BEROUJON, Regis
French 19th cent.
paintings: (H) $715

BERRETTARI, P.G.
sculpture: (H) $3,850

BERRETTINI, Pietro, called Pietro da
Cortona
1596-1669
drawings: (H) $16,500

BERROCAL
sculpture: (L) $176; (H) $2,200

BERROCAL, Miguel
Spanish b. 1933
sculpture: (L) $132; (H) $12,100

BERRY, Carroll Thayer
American 1886-1978
paintings: (L) $165; (H) $880

BERRY, Nathaniel L.
American b. 1859
paintings: (L) $192; (H) $1,210

BERRY, Patrick Vincent
American 1852-1922
paintings: (L) $357; (H) $4,950

BERSHAD, Helen
paintings: (H) $1,870

BERSTEIN, Richard
drawings: (H) $2,200

BERTALAN, Albert
Hungarian 20th cent.
paintings: (L) $1,210; (H) $1,375

BERTAULD
paintings: (H) $1,980

BERTAUX, Jacques
French c. 1745-1818
paintings: (H) $49,500

BERTE
paintings: (H) $715

BERTELLI, Guiseppe
sculpture: (H) $27,500

BERTELS, George
American 20th cent.
paintings: (H) $990

BERTHELEMY, Jean Simon
French 1743-1811
paintings: (H) $181,500

BERTHELON, Eugene
French 1829-after 1914
paintings: (L) $1,320; (H) $3,520

BERTHELSEN, Johann
Danish/American b. 1883
paintings: (L) $220; (H) $8,140
drawings: (L) $248; (H) $990

BERTHELYER, Latham
American 20th cent.
paintings: (H) $770

BERTHOLD, Joachim
sculpture: (H) $1,980

BERTHOT, Jake
American b. 1939
paintings: (L) $550; (H) $11,000
drawings: (L) $290; (H) $660

BERTHOU, Paul F.
sculpture: (H) $1,540

BERTHOUD, A.
ac. 19th cent.
paintings: (H) $1,650

BERTHOUD, Auguste Henri
Swiss 1829-1887
paintings: (H) $13,200

BERTIER, Francisque Edouard
French 19th cent.
paintings: (H) $1,760

BERTIN, Alexandre
French 19th/20th cent.
paintings: (L) $935; (H) $3,850

BERTIN, Jean Victor
French 1775-1842
paintings: (H) $17,600
drawings: (H) $825

BERTIN, Roger
French b. 1915
paintings: (H) $4,950

BERTLING, Carl
German b. 1835
paintings: (H) $770

BERTOIA, Harry
Italian/American 1915-1978
paintings: (L) $550; (H) $30,800
drawings: (H) $418

BERTOLANI, Gaetano
1758/59-1856
drawings: (H) $1,650

BERTOLINGRANDE, E.
Italian 19th/20th cent.
paintings: (H) $825

BERTON, A.
British 19th/20th cent.
paintings: (H) $1,650

BERTON, Louis
French 19th cent.
paintings: (L) $1,100; (H) $18,700

BERTON, Paul Emile
paintings: (H) $880

BERTONI, Mae
American b. 1929
drawings: (H) $1,100

BERTOS, Francesco
Italian 17th/18th cent.
sculpture: (L) $13,200; (H) $19,800

BERTRAM, Abel
French 1871-1954
paintings: (L) $550; (H) $8,800

BERTRAND, Elise
paintings: (H) $2,310

BERTRAND, Gaston
paintings: (H) $935

BERTRAND, James
English 1823-1887
paintings: (H) $7,150

BERTRAND, Jeanne
sculpture: (H) $660

BERTRAND, Paulin Andre
French 1852-1940
paintings: (L) $7,150; (H) $11,000

BERTRAND-PERRONY, A.
French d. 1903
paintings: (H) $4,125

BERTZIK
Northern European late 19th cent.
paintings: (H) $5,500

BERY, C.
American
paintings: (H) $715

BERZEVIZY, Julius
Hungarian/American b. 1875
paintings: (L) $121; (H) $660

BERZONI, G.M.
sculpture: (H) $3,025

BESAREL, B.
sculpture: (H) $4,950

BESCHEY, Balthasar
Flemish 1708-1776
paintings: (L) $2,200; (H) $22,000

BESNARD, Paul Albert
French 1849-1934
paintings: (H) $19,800
drawings: (L) $770; (H) $8,800

BESS
paintings: (H) $825

BESS, Forrest
contemporary
paintings: (L) $2,860; (H) $7,150

BESSA, Pancrace
French 1772-1835
paintings: (H) $8,800

BESSE, Raymond
French 1899-1969
paintings: (L) $413; (H) $880

BESSER, Arne
paintings: (H) $1,980

BESSIN, L.
sculpture: (H) $825

BESSIRE, Dale
American b. 1892
paintings: (H) $1,210

BESSON
paintings: (H) $2,200

BESSON, Charles A., Jr.
French 19th cent.
paintings: (H) $2,200

BESSON, Melanie
French 19th cent.
paintings: (H) $2,200

BESSONOF, Boris
Russian 20th cent.
paintings: (L) $6,600; (H) $7,700

BEST, Arthur William
American 1865-1935
paintings: (L) $110; (H) $2,200

BEST, David
American contemporary
paintings: (H) $605
sculpture: (L) $248; (H) $880

BEST, Hans
German 19th/20th cent.
paintings: (H) $4,400

BEST, Harry Cassie
American 1863-1936
paintings: (L) $248; (H) $1,540

BEST, Mary Ellen
British 1809-1891
drawings: (L) $1,045; (H) $17,600

BESTI, Prof. G., or BESJI or BESFI
19th/20th cent.
sculpture: (L) $660; (H) $6,050

BETBEDER, Faustin
French 19th/20th cent.
paintings: (H) $6,600

BETHKE, Hermann
German 1825-1895
paintings: (L) $6,050; (H) $12,100

BETTANNIER, A.
20th cent.
paintings: (H) $660

BETTERA, Bartolomeo
Italian 1639-1700
paintings: (H) $35,200

BETTINGER, Hoyland B.
American 1890-1950
paintings: (L) $330; (H) $3,245
drawings: (H) $935

BETTINGER, Paul
American 20th cent.
paintings: (L) $352; (H) $880

BETTRIDGE, and JENNENS
American 19th cent.
paintings: (H) $1,100

BETTS, Anna Whelan
American 19th/20th cent.
paintings: (L) $990; (H) $5,500

BETTS, E.F.
American 20th cent.
paintings: (H) $6,050

BETTS, Harold Harrington
American b. 1881
paintings: (L) $55; (H) $2,200

BETTS, Louis
American 1873-1961
paintings: (L) $165; (H) $27,500

BETZ, Andre
paintings: (H) $770

BETZEVIZY, J.
American 20th cent.
paintings: (H) $770

BEUGHDT, L.
paintings: (H) $880

BEUGHOLT, L.
paintings: (H) $4,180

BEUL, Franz de
Dutch 1849-1919
paintings: (L) $220; (H) $3,300

BEUL, Henri de
Belgian 1845-1900
paintings: (L) $1,045; (H) $5,500

BEUL, Laurent de
Belgian 1821-1872
paintings: (L) $550; (H) $5,000

BEUYS, Joseph
German 1921-1986
paintings: (L) $12,100; (H) $66,000
drawings: (L) $3,300; (H) $121,000
sculpture: (L) $1,925; (H) $242,000

BEVORT, Jean
Dutch 20th cent.
paintings: (L) $413; (H) $660

BEVRO (?), J.B.V.
paintings: (H) $1,760

BEWLEY, Murray P.
American b. 1884
paintings: (L) $3,080; (H) $3,575

BEYER, Ed
1820-1865
paintings: (H) $880

BEYEREN, Abraham van
Dutch 1620/21-c. 1675/90
paintings: (H) $264,000

BEYET, H.
American 20th cent.
paintings: (H) $2,145

BEYLE, Pierre Marie
French 1838-1902
paintings: (H) $5,500

BEYLINSON, A.S.
American 20th cent.
drawings: (H) $660

BEYRER, Eduard Maximilian
sculpture: (H) $2,090

BEYSCHLAG, Robert
German 1838-1903
paintings: (L) $6,600; (H) $9,900

BEZOMBES, Roger
French b. 1913
paintings: (L) $330; (H) $5,775

BEZZI, R.
paintings: (H) $1,045

BIALA, Janice
Polish/American b. 1903
paintings: (L) $176; (H) $715

BIALKOWSKI, N.
paintings: (H) $660

BIANCHI, A.
Italian 20th cent.
paintings: (H) $4,620

BIANCHI, A.M.
sculpture: (H) $1,100

BIANCHI, Isidoro
Italian 1602-1690
paintings: (H) $99,000

BIANCHI, Mose
Italian 1836-1893
paintings: (H) $44,000

BIANCHI, Pietro
paintings: (L) $4,675; (H) $11,000

BIANCHIAI, C.
paintings: (H) $3,850

BIANCHINI, A.
American School 19th cent.
sculpture: (H) $715

BIANCHINI, C.
Italian 19th cent.
paintings: (H) $1,540

BIANCHINI, E.
Italian School 19th/20th cent.
paintings: (L) $440; (H) $1,100

BIANCHINI, V.
Italian 19th/20th cent.
paintings: (L) $82; (H) $2,420

BIANCO, Baccio del
drawings: (H) $3,520

BIANCO, G.
Italian 19th cent.
paintings: (H) $1,430

BIANCO, Pamela
drawings: (H) $3,025

BIARD, Francois Auguste
French 1798-1882
paintings: (L) $13,200; (H) $165,000

BIARD, William Baptiste
American b. 1847
paintings: (H) $1,320

BIBER, A. van
paintings: (H) $2,750

BIBIENA, Carlo Galli
drawings: (H) $2,310

BIBIENA, Ferdinando Galli
Italian 1657-1743
drawings: (L) $1,980; (H) $3,080

BIBIENA, Giuseppe Galli
Italian 1696-1756
drawings: (L) $1,650; (H) $18,700

BICCI, Neri di
Italian 1419-1491
paintings: (H) $17,600

BICHARD, A.
French
drawings: (H) $16,500

BICKERSTAFF, George
American 1893-1954
paintings: (L) $165; (H) $1,870

BICKFORD, Nelson Norris
American 1846-1943
paintings: (H) $5,060
sculpture: (H) $440

BICKFORD, Sid
American 1862-1947
paintings: (L) $495; (H) $4,510

BICKNELL, Albion Harris
American 1837-1915
paintings: (L) $220; (H) $5,500

BICKNELL, Evelyn M.
American 1857-1936
paintings: (L) $275; (H) $825
drawings: (L) $110; (H) $660

BICKNELL, Frank Alfred
American 1866-1943
paintings: (L) $440; (H) $24,200
drawings: (L) $467; (H) $1,430

BIDA, Alexandre
French 1823-1895
drawings: (L) $352; (H) $1,870

BIDAULD, Jean Joseph Xavier
French 1758-1846
paintings: (L) $8,800; (H) $11,000

BIDAULT
drawings: (H) $1,760

BIDDLE, George
American c. 1885-1973
paintings: (L) $880; (H) $7,700
drawings: (H) $192

BIDDLE, Laurence
English b. 1888
paintings: (H) $990

BIDLO, Mike
American b. 1935
paintings: (L) $2,420; (H) $19,800

BIDO, Candido
paintings: (H) $6,600

BIDWELL, Mary W.
19th cent.
paintings: (H) $2,530

BIE, Cornelis de
Dutch 1621-1654/64
paintings: (H) $2,860

BIE, Erasmus de
Flemish 1629-1675
paintings: (H) $12,650

BIEDERMAN, Charles
American b. 1906
paintings: (H) $4,950
sculpture: (H) $8,800

BIEDERMAN, James
American b. 1947
drawings: (H) $4,400
sculpture: (H) $7,920

BIEDERMANN, Edward
American
drawings: (H) $6,600

BIEDERMANN-ARENDTS, Hermine
German b. 1855
paintings: (L) $1,430; (H) $3,300

BIEGAS, Boleslas
Polish 1877-1954
sculpture: (L) $4,400; (H) $13,200

BIEGEL, Peter
British b. 1913
paintings: (H) $7,700

BIEHLE, August
American b. 1885
paintings: (L) $2,970; (H) $5,500
drawings: (L) $110; (H) $1,650

BIENAIME, Luigi
Italian early 19th cent.
sculpture: (L) $4,400; (H) $8,800

BIENNER, Carle J.
American 1864-1952
paintings: (H) $5,500

BIENNOURRY, Victor Francois Eloi
drawings: (H) $660

BIENVETU, Gustave
French 19th/20th cent.
paintings: (L) $1,760; (H) $11,000

BIERHALS, Otto
American b. 1879
paintings: (L) $137; (H) $8,250
drawings: (H) $352

BIERSTADT, Albert
German/American 1830-1902
paintings: (L) $330; (H) $2,640,000
drawings: (L) $660; (H) $20,900

BIESBROECK, J. van
sculpture: (H) $1,430

BIESEL, Fred
American b. 1893
paintings: (H) $880

BIEVRE, Marie de
Belgian b. 1865
paintings: (L) $3,850; (H) $52,250

BIGARI, Vittorio
Italian 1692-1776
paintings: (L) $3,300; (H) $33,000
drawings: (L) $1,540; (H) $7,700

BIGATTI, Tommaso
ac. c. 1800
drawings: (L) $6,600; (H) $19,800

BIGAUD, Wilson
Haitian b. 1931
paintings: (L) $385; (H) $4,675

BIGELOW, Daniel Folger
American 1823-1910
paintings: (L) $110; (H) $1,705

BIGELOW, Folger Allen
American
paintings: (H) $880

BIGGS, Walter
American 1886-1968
paintings: (L) $220; (H) $11,000
drawings: (L) $1,500; (H) $2,310

BIGGS, William Redmore
British 1755-1828
paintings: (H) $3,300

BIGOT, Alphonse
American 1828-1873
paintings: (H) $5,500

BIGOT, Georges
Japanese ac. late 19th cent.
paintings: (H) $7,700

BIHAN, D.L.
British ac. 1850's
paintings: (H) $6,050

BIHARI
paintings: (H) $660

BILBAO, Gonzalo
Spanish b. 1860
paintings: (H) $35,200

BILCOQ, Marie Marc Antoine
French 1755-1838
paintings: (H) $12,100

BILINSKY, Boris
drawings: (H) $1,100

BILIVERT, Giovanni
1576-1644
drawings: (H) $15,400

BILL, Max
Swiss b. 1908
paintings: (L) $23,100; (H) $88,000
sculpture: (L) $825; (H) $46,750

BILLE, Carl Ludwig
Danish 1815-1898
paintings: (L) $1,760; (H) $17,600

BILLE, Vilhelm
paintings: (H) $715

BILLET, Etienne
French 1821-1888
paintings: (L) $286; (H) $9,350

BILLET, Leon
French 19th cent.
paintings: (H) $1,100

BILLET, Pierre
French 1837-1922
paintings: (L) $1,430; (H) $38,500

BILLINGS, Hammat and William
RIMMER
sculpture: (H) $3,520

BILLINGS, Henry J.
American b. 1894
paintings: (L) $192; (H) $1,320

BILLINGS, Moses
American 1809-1884
paintings: (L) $2,420; (H) $3,850

BILLMAN, S.H.
American
drawings: (L) $4,070; (H) $6,600

BILLOTTE, Leon Joseph
French b. 1815
paintings: (L) $1,650; (H) $2,860

BILS, Claude
French 1884-1968
paintings: (H) $3,300

BILT, Cornelis van der, called
Cornelius BILTIUS
Dutch ac. c. 1670
paintings: (L) $14,300; (H) $68,750

BILTIUS, Jacobus
Dutch 1640?-1679?
paintings: (L) $15,400; (H) $38,500

BIMMERMANN, Caesar
German 19th cent.
paintings: (L) $4,950; (H) $14,300

BINCK, Georges
European 19th cent.
paintings: (H) $880

BINDER, Alois
German b. 1857
paintings: (L) $220; (H) $1,980

BINDER, Erwin
sculpture: (H) $1,210

BINDER, Tony
paintings: (H) $1,045

BINET, Georges
paintings: (L) $990; (H) $7,480

BINET, Victor Jean Baptiste Barthelemy
French 1849-1924
paintings: (L) $4,125; (H) $6,050

BINFORD, Julian
American
paintings: (H) $3,300

BINGHAM, George Caleb
American 1811-1879
paintings: (L) $7,150; (H) $11,000

BINGHAM, George Caleb, studio of
American 1811-1879
paintings: (H) $33,000

BINGHAM, James R.
20th cent.
paintings: (H) $715

BINGO, G.
paintings: (H) $2,750

BINICH, A.
paintings: (H) $1,760

BINKS, Reuben Ward
English exhib. 1934
paintings: (L) $5,500; (H) $24,200
drawings: (L) $550, (11) $3,080

BINOIT, Peter
German 1590/93-1632
paintings: (H) $60,500

BINTKOWSKI, W.
Russian 19th/20th cent.
paintings: (H) $2,750

BIONDO, Giovanni del
Italian 1356-1392
paintings: (L) $110,000; (H) $181,500

BIORN, Emil
Norwegian/American b. 1864
paintings: (L) $385; (H) $1,540

BIPSHAM, Henry Collins
American
paintings: (H) $880

BIRCH, Samuel John Lamorna
English 1869-1955
paintings: (H) $13,200

BIRCH, T.
American
paintings: (H) $1,100

BIRCH, Thomas
American 1779-1851
paintings: (L) $1,155; (H) $55,000

BIRCH, W.
paintings: (H) $7,700

BIRCHALL, William Minshall
American/English b. 1884
drawings: (L) $137; (H) $1,760

BIRCHFIELD, Charles
drawings: (H) $660

BIRCHOFF, Lina
paintings: (H) $715

BIRD, Edward
English 1762 or 1772-1819
paintings: (H) $1,980

BIRD, G.T.
English 20th cent.
paintings: (H) $715

BIRD, John Alexander Harrington
English 1846-1936
paintings: (H) $15,400
drawings: (L) $660; (H) $9,900

BIRDSALL, Amos
American 1865-1938
paintings: (L) $220; (H) $1,100

BIRDSALL, Bryon
American 20th cent.
drawings: (L) $660; (H) $3,300

BIRK, C.
American 19th cent.
paintings: (L) $522; (H) $2,090

BIRKS, E.
British 19th cent.
paintings: (H) $770

BIRLEY, Sir Oswald
New Zealander 1880-1979
paintings: (H) $5,500

BIRNEY, A.
American 19th cent.
paintings: (H) $4,950

BIRNEY, William Verplanck
American 1858-1909
paintings: (L) $550; (H) $27,500
drawings: (L) $22; (H) $495

BIRNIE, A.D.
paintings: (H) $1,100

BIRO, Geza
Hungarian b. 1919
paintings: (H) $4,950

BIROLLI, Renato
Italian 1906-1959
paintings: (L) $1,045; (H) $34,100

BIRREN, Joseph
American 1864-1933
paintings: (L) $522; (H) $6,600

BIRTLES, Harry
English 19th cent.
paintings: (H) $880

BISBING, Henry
1849-1919
paintings: (H) $770

BISCAINO, Bartolommeo
Italian 1632-1657
paintings: (H) $60,500
drawings: (H) $6,600

BISCHOFF, Elmer
contemporary
paintings: (H) $5,500

BISCHOFF, Franz A.
Austrian/American 1864-1929
paintings: (L) $495; (H) $38,500
drawings: (L) $303; (H) $3,025

BISHOP, A.F.
American 19th cent.
paintings: (H) $825

BISHOP, Brooke
American 20th cent.
paintings: (H) $935

BISHOP, Emily C.
American
sculpture: (H) $660

BISHOP, Isabel
American b. 1902
paintings: (H) $3,300
drawings: (L) $715; (H) $3,850

BISHOP, Richard Evett
American 1887-1975
paintings: (L) $330; (H) $7,150

BISON, Giuseppe Bernardino
Italian 1762-1844
drawings: (L) $467; (H) $7,700

BISPHAM, H.C.
paintings: (H) $1,320

BISPHAM, Henry
paintings: (H) $1,650

BISPHAM, Henry Collins
American 1841-1882
paintings: (L) $880; (H) $16,500

BISSCHOP, Abraham
Dutch 1670-1731
paintings: (H) $126,500

BISSCHOP, Jan de, Johannes
EPISCOPIUS
Dutch c. 1628-1671
drawings: (L) $3,300; (H) $5,500

BISSELL, George Edwin
American 1839-1920
sculpture: (L) $1,430; (H) $4,950

BISSELL, Kate E.
American
paintings: (H) $3,850

BISSIER, Julius
German/Swiss 1893-1965
paintings: (L) $8,800; (H) $33,000
drawings: (L) $4,125; (H) $26,400

BISSIERE, Roger
French 1886/88-1964
paintings: (H) $6,050

BISSON
paintings: (H) $1,100

BISSON, Edouard
French b. 1856
paintings: (L) $1,980; (H) $6,600

BISSON, Lucienne
French 1884-1964
paintings: (L) $880; (H) $3,300

BISSON, Pierre
paintings: (H) $880

BISTTRAM, Emil J.
Hungarian/American b. 1895
paintings: (L) $2,750; (H) $52,800
drawings: (L) $715; (H) $8,800

BITNEY, Bye
American
paintings: (H) $6,250

BITRAN, Albert
French b. 1929
drawings: (H) $3,300

BITTAR, Pierre
paintings: (L) $7,150; (H) $7,700

BITTER, Ary
French 1883-1960
sculpture: (L) $110; (H) $2,640

BITTINGER, Charles
American 1879-1970
paintings: (L) $375; (H) $4,400

BIVA, Henri
French 1848-1928
paintings: (L) $2,475; (H) $22,000

BIVA, Paul
French 1851-1900
paintings: (H) $2,750

BIVEL, Fernand Achille Lucien
French 1888-1950
paintings: (H) $2,750

BIXBEE
paintings: (H) $665

BIXBEE, William Johnson
American 1850-1921
paintings: (L) $55; (H) $1,000
drawings: (L) $247; (H) $2,250

BIZARD, S.
sculpture: (H) $825

BIZZELLI, Giovanni
Italian 1556-1612
paintings: (H) $8,800
drawings: (H) $4,400

BJARNORAHTS
paintings: (H) $825

BJELSKI, Nikolai Bogdanoff
paintings: (H) $5,500

BJORGUM, N.
Swedish 20th cent.
paintings: (H) $687

BJORIK, O.
paintings: (H) $770

BLAAS, Carl von
Austrian 1815-1894
paintings: (L) $11,000; (H) $13,750

BLAAS, Eugen von
Austrian 1843-1931
paintings: (L) $1,760; (H) $286,000
drawings: (H) $4,620

BLAAS, Eugene de
Austrian 1843-1931
paintings: (L) $18,700; (H) $286,000

BLAAS, Julius von
Austrian 1845-1922
paintings: (L) $770; (H) $16,500

BLACHE, Christian
paintings: (H) $1,100

BLACK, Andrew
English 1850-1916
paintings: (H) $1,760

BLACK, Edwin
English ac. 1880-1894
paintings: (H) $797

BLACK, Francois
sculpture: (H) $1,540

BLACK, La Verne Nelson
American 1887-1938/39
paintings: (L) $3,850; (H) $16,500
drawings: (L) $935; (H) $1,320

BLACK, Mary C.
American d. 1943
paintings: (H) $1,100

BLACK, Olive Parker
American 1868-1948
paintings: (L) $66; (H) $11,000

BLACKBURN, Joseph
American ac. 1750-1774
paintings: (H) $3,025

BLACKBURN, Morris
American 1902-1979
paintings: (L) $250; (H) $1,018
drawings: (L) $165; (H) $935

BLACKLOCK, Thomas Bromley
British 1863-1903
paintings: (H) $1,100

BLACKLOCK, William Kay
English b.1872, exhib.1897-1922
paintings: (H) $5,500

BLACKMAN, Walter
American 1847-1928
paintings: (L) $110; (H) $5,280

BLACKMORE, Arthur Edward
Anglo/American 1854-1921
paintings: (L) $150; (H) $3,300

BLACKTON, James Stuart
American 1875-1941
paintings: (L) $468; (H) $6,325

BLACZ
sculpture: (L) $1,210; (H) $3,740

BLADIER, Emile
French 19th cent.
sculpture: (H) $1,155

BLAGDEN, Allen
American b. 1938
paintings: (H) $1,320
drawings: (L) $715; (H) $2,200

BLAI, Boris
American b. 1893
sculpture: (H) $2,200

BLAIKLEY, Alexander
American
drawings: (H) $8,250

BLAINE, Nell
American b. 1922
paintings: (L) $550; (H) $2,860
drawings: (H) $660

BLAIR, Lee Everett
American b. 1911
drawings: (H) $2,475

BLAIR, Marc
French b. 1924
paintings: (L) $2,200; (H) $2,420

BLAIR, Mary
drawings: (H) $1,100

BLAIR, Robert
paintings: (H) $330
drawings: (L) $440; (H) $715

BLAIR, Streeter
American 1888-1966
paintings: (L) $193; (H) $770

BLAIR-BRUCE, William
Canadian 1859-1906
paintings: (H) $4,125

BLAIS, Jean Charles
French b. 1956
drawings: (H) $17,600

BLAKE, Benjamin
paintings: (H) $715

BLAKE, Buckeye
American
paintings: (H) $750

BLAKE, Leo B.
American 1887-1976
paintings: (L) $176; (H) $3,850

BLAKE, William
English 1757-1827
drawings: (L) $264; (H) $352,000

BLAKELOCK
paintings: (H) $1,650

BLAKELOCK, Ralph Albert
American 1847-1919
paintings: (L) $275; (H) $49,500
drawings: (H) $990

BLAKELY, Dudley Moore
American
paintings: (H) $880

BLAMPIED, Edmund
English 1886-1966
drawings: (L) $880; (H) $1,540

BLANC, Celestin Joseph
French 1818-1888
paintings: (H) $770

BLANCH, Arnold
American 1896-1968
paintings: (L) $242; (H) $2,420
drawings: (H) $440

BLANCH, Lucille
American b. 1895
paintings: (L) $440; (H) $5,500

BLANCHARD, A.
French 20th cent.
paintings: (H) $6,600

BLANCHARD, Antoine
paintings: (L) $110; (H) $10,450

BLANCHARD, Blanche
American 1866-1959
paintings: (H) $935
drawings: (L) $935; (H) $1,650

BLANCHARD, Jacques
French 1600-1638
paintings: (L) $4,400; (H) $7,700

BLANCHARD, Louis
French 19th cent.
paintings: (H) $1,760

BLANCHARD, Maria
Spanish/French 1881-1932
paintings: (L) $15,400; (H) $418,000

BLANCHARD, Maurice
contemporary
paintings: (L) $715; (H) $715

BLANCHARD, Remy
paintings: (H) $715

BLANCHE, Arnold
American
paintings: (H) $1,760

BLANCHE, Jacques Emile
French 1861-1942
paintings: (L) $1,705; (H) $77,000
drawings: (H) $15,400

BLANCHE, Lucille
paintings: (H) $1,430

BLANCHE, M.
paintings: (H) $1,045

BLANCO, Dionisio
Dominican Republic b. 1935
paintings: (L) $1,650; (H) $6,050

BLANEY, Dwight
American 1865-1944
paintings: (H) $1,650
drawings: (L) $22; (H) $1,210

BLANKIMAN
paintings: (H) $1,540

BLANQUETTE, La
French
sculpture: (H) $715

BLARENBERGE, Henri Joseph van
French 1741-1826
drawings: (H) $9,900

BLARENBERGHE, Henri Desire van
French 1734-1812
drawings: (H) $19,800

BLAS, G.
paintings: (H) $1,210

BLAS, O.
Italian 19th cent.
drawings: (H) $880

BLASHFIELD, Edwin Howland
American 1848-1936
paintings: (L) $550; (H) $18,700
drawings: (L) $165; (H) $3,575

BLASS, Charlotte
American b. 1908
paintings: (L) $82; (H) $2,200
drawings: (L) $60; (H) $120

BLASS, Julius von
Austrian b. 1845
paintings: (H) $4,400

BLASSET, E.
French 19th cent.
paintings: (H) $13,200

BLATAS, Arbit
Lithuanian b. 1908
paintings: (L) $110; (H) $4,950
drawings: (L) $110; (H) $715

BLATTER, B.
paintings: (H) $1,210

BLAU, Tina
Austrian 1845-1916
paintings: (H) $4,675

BLAUVELT, Charles F.
American 1824-1900
paintings: (L) $1,870; (H) $3,410

BLAVVETT, Charles
drawings: (H) $1,760

BLAZEBY, J.
English 19th cent.
paintings: (H) $3,300

BLECKNER, Ross
American b. 1949
paintings: (L) $3,300; (H) $187,000
drawings: (L) $5,500; (H) $14,300

BLEEKER, Uwe
Dutch 20th cent.
paintings: (H) $770

BLEIMANN, Michel
French 1825-1892
paintings: (H) $13,200

BLEKER, Dirck
Dutch 1622-1672
paintings: (H) $34,100

BLENNER, Carle John
American 1864-1952
paintings: (L) $110; (H) $16,500

BLENT, C.
American 19th cent.
paintings: (L) $4,675; (H) $13,200

BLES, Hendrik Met de, called
CIVETTA in Italy
Flemish c. 1480/1500-after 1550
paintings: (L) $49,500; (H) $308,000

BLES, Joseph
Dutch 1792-1883
paintings: (L) $2,750; (H) $2,750

BLEULER, Johann Heinrich
drawings: (H) $4,950

BLEULER, Louis
Swiss 1792-1850
drawings: (L) $1,870; (H) $7,150

BLEUMNER, Oscar F.
American 1867-1938
drawings: (L) $357; (H) $1,100

BLEZER, De
sculpture: (H) $4,950

BLIECK, Daniel de
Dutch d. 1673
paintings: (H) $8,800

BLIGNY, Albert
French 1849-1908
paintings: (H) $1,650
drawings: (H) $302

BLINKS, Thomas
English 1860-1912
paintings: (L) $3,520; (H) $60,500

BLISH, Carolyn
American 20th cent.
paintings: (H) $1,430

BLISS, Robert
American b. 1925
paintings: (L) $165; (H) $660

BLOCH, Albert
American 1882-1961
paintings: (L) $26,400; (H) $27,500

BLOCH, Alexandre
French 19th/20th cent.
paintings: (H) $880

BLOCH, Julius Thiengen
German/American 1888-1966
paintings: (L) $275; (H) $1,320
drawings: (L) $66; (H) $330

BLOCH, Martin
German/English 1883-1954
paintings: (L) $1,980; (H) $2,860

BLOCK, Adolph
American b. 1906
sculpture: (H) $1,210

BLOCK, Joseph
German b. 1863
paintings: (L) $660; (H) $990

BLOCK, Louis
English 1846-1909
drawings: (H) $990

BLOCKI, Eugene W.
Italian 19th cent.
paintings: (H) $660

BLOCKSMA, Dewey
Canadian contemporary
sculpture: (H) $1,650

BLODGETT, Walton
American b. 1908
drawings: (L) $55; (H) $935

BLOEMAERT, Abraham
Dutch c. 1564-1651
paintings: (L) $18,700; (H) $25,300
drawings: (L) $2,420; (H) $18,700

BLOEMAERT, Adrien
1609-1666
paintings: (H) $7,150
drawings: (L) $1,870; (H) $4,180

BLOEMAERT, Hendrick
Dutch 1601-1672
paintings: (H) $2,640

BLOEMAERT, Pseudo-Hendrick
17th cent.
paintings: (H) $44,000

BLOEMEN, Jan Frans van, called
ORIZZONTE
Flemish 1662-1749
paintings: (L) $3,520; (H) $44,000

BLOEMEN, Pieter van, called
STANDARD
Flemish 1657-1720
paintings: (L) $4,950; (H) $49,500

BLOEMERS, Arnoldus
Dutch 1786/92-1844
paintings: (L) $23,100; (H) $35,750

BLOIS, Francois B. de
Canadian c. 1829-1913
paintings: (L) $715; (H) $1,650

BLOM, Gustav Vilhelm
Danish b. 1853
paintings: (H) $3,960

BLONAY, Margarite de
Swiss b. 1895
drawings: (H) $55
sculpture: (L) $192; (H) $770

BLONDAT, Max
French 1879-1926
sculpture: (L) $2,750; (H) $5,500

BLONDEL, Emile
French 1893-1970
paintings: (L) $550; (H) $3,300

BLONDEL, George Francois
French 1730-1791
drawings: (H) $3,960

BLONDEL, J.D.
paintings: (H) $1,017

BLONDEL, Merry Joseph
French 1781-1853
paintings: (L) $1,980; (H) $39,600
drawings: (H) $880

BLOODGOOD, M.S.
paintings: (H) $3,410

BLOOM, Hyman
American b. 1913
paintings: (L) $1,320; (H) $12,100
drawings: (L) $220; (H) $1,760

BLOOMER, Hiram Reynolds
American 1845-1910/11
paintings: (L) $138; (H) $4,675
drawings: (H) $248

BLOOMERS, Bernardus Johannes
Dutch 1845-1914
paintings: (L) $1,100; (H) $28,600
drawings: (L) $770; (H) $8,525

BLOOMFIELD, Harry
paintings: (H) $2,420

BLOOT, Pieter de
Dutch c. 1602-1658
paintings: (L) $1,870; (H) $9,900

BLOSER, Florence Parker
American 1889-1935
paintings: (L) $715; (H) $880

BLOSER, Paul B.
American 20th cent.
paintings: (H) $742

BLOUNT, G.
American 19th/20th cent.
paintings: (H) $4,400

BLOWER, David H.
American b. 1901
drawings: (L) $275; (H) $1,210

BLUEMNER, Oscar F.
German/American 1867-1938
paintings: (L) $22,000; (H) $396,000
drawings: (L) $55; (H) $52,800

BLUHM
paintings: (H) $5,775

BLUHM, Norman
American b. 1920
paintings: (L) $1,540; (H) $46,200
drawings: (L) $550; (H) $660

BLUM, Charles
sculpture: (H) $880

BLUM, Edith C.
American ac. 1930's
paintings: (L) $110; (H) $3,300

BLUM, Helen
American ac. 1915-1920
paintings: (H) $715

BLUM, Jerome
American
paintings: (L) $715; (H) $1,210

BLUM, Keith
paintings: (H) $770

BLUM, Ludwig
Israeli 20th cent.
paintings: (L) $137; (H) $7,425

BLUM, Marselle
European 19th cent.
paintings: (H) $660

BLUM, Maurice
French b. 1832
paintings: (L) $495; (H) $3,960

BLUM, Robert Frederick
American 1857-1903
paintings: (L) $26,400; (H) $220,000
drawings: (L) $605; (H) $55,000

BLUM-SIEBERT, Ludwig
German b. 1853
paintings: (H) $6,875

BLUMBERG, Ron
American School 20th cent.
paintings: (H) $2,750

BLUME, Edmund
German b. 1844
paintings: (L) $165; (H) $3,575

BLUME, Peter
American b. 1906
paintings: (H) $24,200
drawings: (L) $330; (H) $3,080

BLUMENSCHEIN, Ernest Leonard
American 1874-1960
paintings: (L) $9,900; (H) $79,750
drawings: (L) $440; (H) $2,640

BLUNT, John S.
American 1798-1835
paintings: (L) $1,045; (H) $15,400

BLY, Frank
American 20th cent.
paintings: (H) $660

BLYTH, R. Henderson
English b. 1919
paintings: (H) $1,650

BLYTHE, David Gilmour
American 1815-1865
paintings: (L) $3,630; (H) $60,500

BOARDMAN, Rosina Cox
American 20th cent.
paintings: (H) $880

BOARDMAN, William
American
paintings: (H) $5,500

BOBBETT, C.A.
19th cent.
drawings: (H) $1,870

BOBERMAN, Voldemar
Russian b. 1897
paintings: (H) $660

BOCCACCINO, Giovanni di Agostino
Italian ac. late 15th cent.
drawings: (H) $93,500

BOCCACCINO, Camillo
Italian 1501-1546
drawings: (H) $11,550

BOCCIONI, Umberto
Italian 1882-1916
paintings: (L) $60,500; (H) $605,000

BOCH, Anton
paintings: (H) $1,870

BOCHERO, Peter Charlie
American c. 1895-1962
paintings: (H) $4,125

BOCHMANN, Gregor von
paintings: (H) $4,180
drawings: (H) $220

BOCHNER, Mel
American b. 1940
paintings: (L) $19,800; (H) $31,900
drawings: (L) $3,300; (H) $8,250

BOCK, Frederick William
American b. 1876
paintings: (L) $1,100; (H) $2,420

BOCK, Richard Walter
American
sculpture: (H) $7,150

BOCK, Theophile Emile Achille de
Dutch 1851-1904
paintings: (L) $770; (H) $20,900
drawings: (H) $825

BOCKLIN, Arnold
Swiss 1827-1901
paintings: (L) $1,650; (H) $6,325

BOCKSDORFER, Christoph
Swiss d. 1522
drawings: (H) $71,500

BOCTOR, Istwan
paintings: (H) $990

BODDIEN, Georg von
German b. 1850
paintings: (H) $5,500

BODDINGTON, Edwin Henry
English 1836-c. 1905
paintings: (L) $385; (H) $2,200

BODDINGTON, Henry John
English 1811-1865
paintings: (L) $990; (H) $9,350

BODDINGTON, Thomas F.
British 19th cent.
paintings: (H) $880

BODELSON, Dan
American b. 1949
paintings: (H) $7,500

BODEMANN, Willem
Dutch 1806-1880
paintings: (H) $4,400

BODENDIECK
sculpture: (H) $880

BODENMULLER, Alphons
German 1847-1886
paintings: (L) $1,980; (H) $4,840

BODIN, A.
19th cent.
paintings: (H) $1,870

BODIS
20th cent.
paintings: (H) $770

BODLEY, Josselin Reginald Courtenay
British 20th cent.
paintings: (L) $121; (H) $1,430

BODMER, Karl
Swiss 1809-1893
paintings: (H) $4,125

BODOY, Ernest Alexandre
French ac. 1874
paintings: (L) $1,210; (H) $20,900

BOECKHORST, Jan van
paintings: (H) $4,400

BOEH, H.
English 19th cent.
paintings: (H) $935

BOEHM, Edward
German b. 1830
paintings: (H) $715

BOEHME, Karl Theodor
German b. 1866
paintings: (H) $2,200

BOEHNER, Alexander
European early 20th cent.
paintings: (H) $825

BOEL, A.P.
Scottish 19th/20th cent.
paintings: (H) $825

BOEL, J.H.
19th cent.
paintings: (L) $165; (H) $935

BOEMM, Ritta
Hungarian 19th cent.
paintings: (L) $330; (H) $660
drawings: (H) $412

BOERI, A.
paintings: (H) $907

BOERI, Jacques
paintings: (H) $1,540

BOERO, Jacques
Italian 19th/20th cent.
sculpture: (H) $1,980

BOERO, Nilda
Italian 19th cent.
sculpture: (H) $3,300

BOERS, Marianne
American b. 1945
drawings: (L) $715; (H) $2,750

BOESE, Henry
American b. 1824, ac. 1844-1860
paintings: (L) $550; (H) $15,400

BOESEN, Johannes
Danish 1847-1916
paintings: (L) $880; (H) $7,700

BOETTCHER, Christian Edward
German 1818-1889
paintings: (H) $4,400

BOETTI, Alighiero
Italian contemporary
drawings: (L) $3,520; (H) $8,800

BOEVER, Jean Francois de
Belgian 1872-1949
paintings: (H) $3,575

BOFILL, Antoine
Spanish ac. c. 1921
sculpture: (L) $209; (H) $3,190

BOGART, George Hirst
American 1864-1923
paintings: (H) $907

BOGDANOFF-BJELSKI, Nikolai
Petrowitsch
Russian 1868-1935
paintings: (L) $8,800; (H) $14,300

BOGDANY, Jakob
Hungarian 1660-1724
paintings: (L) $11,000; (H) $104,500

BOGER
sculpture: (H) $880

BOGERT, George Hirst
American 1864-1944
paintings: (L) $275; (H) $2,750

BOGERT, John Hirst
American
paintings: (H) $990

BOGGIANI, Guido
Italian 1861-1902
paintings: (L) $660; (H) $6,050

BOGGS, Frank Myers
American/French 1855-1926
paintings: (L) $1,650; (H) $49,500
drawings: (L) $90; (H) $2,475

BOGH, Carl Henrik
Danish 1827-1893
paintings: (L) $3,850; (H) $13,200
drawings: (H) $3,300

BOGHOSIAN, Varujan
American b. 1926
sculpture: (L) $1,980; (H) $16,500

BOGMAN, Hermanus Charles
Christian
Dutch 1861-1921
paintings: (L) $605; (H) $770

BOHDE, George W.
paintings: (H) $1,100

BOHLAND, Gustav
Austrian/American 1897-1959
sculpture: (H) $1,320

BOHLER, Joseph
American
drawings: (L) $247; (H) $1,800

BOHM, C. Curry
American b. 1894
paintings: (L) $77; (H) $2,420

BOHM, Max
American 1868-1923
paintings: (L) $330; (H) $44,000
drawings: (L) $121; (H) $220

BOHM, Pal
Hungarian 1839-1905
paintings: (L) $605; (H) $2,860

BOHROD
American b. 1907
paintings: (H) $1,100

BOHROD, Aaron
American b. 1907
paintings: (L) $192; (H) $7,700
drawings: (L) $200; (H) $6,600

BOICHARD, Joseph Alexandre
early 19th cent.
paintings: (H) $935

BOILAUGES, Fernand
paintings: (L) $660; (H) $935

BOILLEAU, Philip
American 1864-1917
paintings: (L) $1,375; (H) $2,750
drawings: (H) $275

BOILLY, Eugene
French ac. 1850's-1860's
paintings: (H) $1,320

BOILLY, Julien Leopold, Jules
French 1796-1874
drawings: (L) $880; (H) $11,000

BOILLY, Louis Leopold
French 1761-1845
paintings: (L) $3,740; (H) $90,750
drawings: (H) $7,150

BOISROND, Francois
French b. 1959
paintings: (L) $1,100; (H) $2,860

BOISSEAU, Alfred
American 1823-1903
paintings: (L) $495; (H) $1,100

BOISSEAU, Emile Andre
French 1842-1923
sculpture: (L) $1,870; (H) $4,950

BOISSIER, Gaston Maurice Emile
French 19th/20th cent.
paintings: (H) $35,200

BOIT, Edward Darley
American 1840-1915/16
paintings: (L) $1,650; (H) $6,000
drawings: (L) $440; (H) $2,200

BOIT, M.C.
Continental 19th cent.
paintings: (H) $5,500

BOITARD, Francois
Dutch c. 1671-1715
drawings: (L) $286; (H) $2,090

BOIVIN, Emile
French b. 1846
paintings: (H) $880

BOIZARD, C.V.
paintings: (L) $115; (H) $1,980

BOKER, Carl
paintings: (L) $12,100; (H) $16,500

BOKS, Evert Jan
Dutch 1838-1914
paintings: (L) $3,850; (H) $9,350

BOL, Ferdinand
Dutch 1616-1680
paintings: (L) $2,090; (H) $99,000
drawings: (L) $11,000; (H) $60,000

BOL, Hans
Dutch 1534-1593
paintings: (L) $4,400; (H) $55,000
drawings: (H) $20,900

BOLAND, Charles
Continental 19th cent.
paintings: (H) $18,700

BOLDINI, Giovanni
Italian 1842-1931
paintings: (L) $5,500; (H) $1,650,000
drawings: (L) $6,050; (H) $451,000

BOLE, Jeanne
French ac. 1870-1883
paintings: (H) $17,600

BOLIN, Alex
paintings: (H) $2,310

BOLINGER, Franz Joseph
American 20th cent.
paintings: (L) $302; (H) $2,420

BOLINGER, Truman
American b. 1944
sculpture: (L) $385; (H) $1,650

BOLLENDONK, W.
paintings: (L) $330; (H) $1,100

BOLLES, Reginald Fairfax
paintings: (H) $1,045

BOLLI
Italian 19th cent.
paintings: (H) $825

BOLLING, Leslie Garland
American b. 1898
sculpture: (H) $4,675

BOLLONGIER, Hans
Dutch 1600-after 1644
paintings: (H) $24,200

BOLMER, M. DeForest
American 1854-1910
paintings: (L) $220; (H) $800

BOLOGNA, Giovanni da
sculpture: (H) $1,540

BOLOMEY, Benjamin Samuel
drawings: (H) $2,475

BOLOTOWSKY, Ilya
Russian/American 1907-1981
paintings: (L) $1,650; (H) $19,800

BOLTANSKI, Christian
French b. 1944
sculpture: (H) $22,000

BOLTON-JONES, Hugh
American 1848-1927
paintings: (H) $1,980

BOLTRAFFIO, Giovanni Antonio
Italian 1467-1516
paintings: (L) $46,200; (H) $121,000

BOMBELLI, Sebastiano
paintings: (H) $990

BOMBLED, Louis Charles
French 1862-1927
paintings: (L) $385; (H) $4,950
drawings: (H) $1,430

BOMBOIS, Camille
French 1883-1970?
paintings: (L) $3,250; (H) $121,000

BOMMEL, Elias Pieter van
Dutch 1819-1890
paintings: (L) $3,575; (H) $44,000

BOMPARD, Maurice
French 1857-1936
paintings: (L) $330; (H) $3,300

BOMPIANI, Augusto
Italian 1852-1930
drawings: (L) $605; (H) $2,420

BOMPIANI, Roberto
Italian 1821-1908
paintings: (H) $1,100

BOMPIANI-BATTAGLIA, Clelia
Italian 1846/47-1927
drawings: (L) $825; (H) $4,675

BON, Max
paintings: (H) $1,980

BON DE BOULLOGNE
French 1649-1717
paintings: (H) $19,800

BONALUMI, Agostino
Italian b. 1935
paintings: (L) $1,650; (H) $1,650

BONAMARTE, Leo
American 20th cent.
drawings: (H) $900

BONAMY, Philippe
French 20th cent.
paintings: (H) $990

BONAR, James King
American b. 1864
paintings: (H) $3,850

BONAVIA, Carlo
Italian ac. 1740-1756
paintings: (L) $11,000; (H) $176,000

BOND, Charles V.
paintings: (H) $990

BOND, James
British 19th/20th cent.
paintings: (H) $825

BOND, Joseph
English 1868-1912
paintings: (H) $660

BOND, R. Sebastian
paintings: (H) $880

BOND, William Joseph J.C.
English 1833-1926/28
paintings: (H) $1,430

BONDELL, Charles
Continental 19th cent.
paintings: (H) $660

BONDOUX, Jules Georges
French(?) d. 1920
paintings: (H) $8,800

BONDUEL, Leon
sculpture: (H) $4,675

BONE, Muirhead
Scottish 1876-1953
drawings: (L) $60; (H) $935

BONECCHI, Matteo
c. 1672-after 1754
paintings: (L) $2,750; (H) $6,600

BONELLI, G.
Italian 19th cent.
paintings: (H) $660

BONEVARDI, Marcelo
Argentinian b. 1929
paintings: (L) $1,100; (H) $23,100
drawings: (L) $1,210; (H) $19,800
sculpture: (L) $9,350; (H) $24,200

BONFIELD, George Robert
American 1802-1898
paintings: (L) $605; (H) $2,860

BONFIELD, William van de velde
American 19th cent.
paintings: (L) $495; (H) $1,650

BONFILS, Gaston
French 19th cent.
paintings: (L) $605; (H) $2,750

BONFIT, S.
paintings: (H) $770

BONFORT, Vernet
French 20th cent.
paintings: (L) $330; (H) $2,420

BONGART, Sergei
Russian/American b. 1918
paintings: (H) $1,100

BONGHI
Italian
paintings: (L) $605; (H) $1,210

BONHAM, Horace
American 1835-1892
paintings: (H) $28,600

BONHEUR
19th cent.
paintings: (H) $825

BONHEUR, Ferdinand
French 19th cent.
paintings: (H) $770

BONHEUR, Isidore Jules
French 1827-1901
sculpture: (L) $412; (H) $38,500

BONHEUR, Juliette Peyrol
French 1830-1891
paintings: (L) $2,000; (H) $6,600

BONHEUR, Rosa
French 1822-1899
paintings: (L) $358; (H) $63,250
drawings: (L) $220; (H) $231,000
sculpture: (L) $192; (H) $2,750

BONHOMME, Leon
French 1870-1924
drawings: (L) $440; (H) $1,870

BONIFAZI, A.
paintings: (H) $880

BONINGTON, Richard Parkes
English 1801-1828
paintings: (H) $220,000
drawings: (L) $467; (H) $5,500

BONIROTE, Pierre
French 1811-1891
paintings: (H) $6,000

BONITO, Giuseppe
Italian 1705-1789
paintings: (L) $48,400; (H) $352,000

BONNAFFONS
19th cent.
paintings: (H) $4,180

BONNAR, James
American 1885-1961
paintings: (L) $300; (H) $3,520

BONNARD, Pierre
French 1867-1947
paintings: (L) $3,300; (H) $7,480,000
drawings: (L) $550; (H) $44,000
sculpture: (L) $4,620; (H) $11,000

BONNAT, Leon Joseph Florentin
French 1833-1922
paintings: (L) $880; (H) $17,600

BONNEFOY, Henry Arthur
French 1839-1917
paintings: (L) $660; (H) $7,975

BONNEMAISON, Jules de
French b. 1809
paintings: (L) $660; (H) $8,250

BONNER, L.K.
American 20th cent.
paintings: (H) $660

BONNET, Franz de
paintings: (H) $770

BONNY, G.
British 19th cent.
paintings: (H) $990

BONNY, J.
British 19th/20th cent.
paintings: (L) $330; (H) $1,540

BONO, Primitif
Italian ac. 1920-1940
paintings: (L) $605; (H) $1,320

BONOME, Santiago Rodriguez
sculpture: (L) $4,125; (H) $5,225

BONOMICI, Lionel
Italian 20th cent.
paintings: (H) $935

BONONE, Carlo
paintings: (H) $10,450

BONTE, Paula
German 1840-1902
paintings: (H) $1,760

BONTECOU, Lee
American b. 1931
drawings: (L) $1,650; (H) $3,025
sculpture: (L) $950; (H) $22,000

BONVIN, Francois
French 1817-1887
paintings: (H) $8,750
drawings: (L) $660; (H) $8,250

BONVIN, Leon
French 1834-1866
drawings: (H) $17,600

BOODLE, Walter
paintings: (H) $1,045

BOOG, Carle Michel
American b. 1877
paintings: (L) $220; (H) $9,350
drawings: (H) $6,600

BOOG, Frank Myers
American
paintings: (H) $4,620

BOOGAARD, Willem Jacobus
Dutch 1842-1887
paintings: (L) $1,430; (H) $15,400

BOOK, Harry M.
paintings: (H) $1,200

BOOM, Charles
Dutch b. 1858
paintings: (H) $825

BOOM, Karel
Dutch b. 1858
paintings: (H) $1,980

BOON, Constantin
Dutch 19th cent.
paintings: (L) $660; (H) $2,200

BOONEN, Arnold
Dutch 1669-1729
paintings: (H) $10,450

BOOTH, Cameron
American b. 1892
paintings: (H) $2,250

BOOTH, Franklin
American 1874-1943/48
paintings: (L) $132; (H) $330
drawings: (L) $220; (H) $7,500

BOOTH, Herb
American
drawings: (L) $3,600; (H) $4,500

BOOTH, T.
American 19th cent.
paintings: (H) $1,760

BOQUET, P.J.
paintings: (H) $3,300

BORATIN, A.
c. 1900
sculpture: (H) $1,375

BORCHERS, Dean
American
sculpture: (H) $850

BORDEN LIMNER
paintings: (L) $5,500; (H) $18,700

BORDENAVE, Pierre
French
paintings: (H) $2,090

BORDIGNON, Noe
Italian 1841-1920
paintings: (L) $16,500; (H) $19,800

BORDUAS, Paul Emile
Canadian 1905-1960
paintings: (L) $15,400; (H) $176,000

BOREIN, John Edward
American 1872-1943
drawings: (L) $220; (H) $41,800

BOREN, James
American 1921-1990
paintings: (H) $4,950
drawings: (L) $1,320; (H) $15,000

BOREN, Rick
American contemporary
paintings: (H) $1,870

BORES, Francisco
Spanish 1898-1972
paintings: (L) $220; (H) $132,000
drawings: (L) $935; (H) $1,760

BORG, Carl Oscar
American 1879-1947
paintings: (L) $325; (H) $41,250
drawings: (L) $55; (H) $13,200

BORGES, Jacobo
Venezuelan b. 1931
paintings: (L) $8,250; (H) $66,000
drawings: (H) $2,420

BORGLUM, Elizabeth Collins
American 1848-1922
paintings: (L) $660; (H) $715

BORGLUM, John Gutzon
American 1867-1941
paintings: (L) $550; (H) $3,300
drawings: (H) $121
sculpture: (L) $2,200; (H) $38,500

BORGLUM, Solon
American 1868-1922
sculpture: (L) $8,800; (H) $110,000

BORGMANN, Paul
German 1851-1893
paintings: (H) $16,500

BORGONI, Mario
paintings: (H) $660

BORIE, Adolphe
American 1877-1934
paintings: (L) $1,100; (H) $7,700

BORIEN, Edward
American 1872-1945
paintings: (H) $7,150

BORIONE, Bernard Louis
French 19th/20th cent.
paintings: (L) $302; (H) $3,575
drawings: (L) $605; (H) $1,650

BORISSOVA, Aimme Liouba
French 19th/20th cent.
paintings: (H) $1,100

BORKOBE, H.
paintings: (H) $2,860

BORMAN, Johannes
Dutch ac. 1653-1659
paintings: (H) $40,700

BORMEL, Eugen
German b. 1858
sculpture: (L) $264; (H) $2,310

BOROFSKY, Jonathan
American b. 1942
paintings: (L) $4,950; (H) $46,750
drawings: (L) $2,420; (H) $24,200
sculpture: (L) $1,980; (H) $18,700

BORONDA, Lester D.
American 1886-1953
paintings: (L) $137; (H) $1,650

BOROVIKOVSKY, Vladimir Lukitsch
Russian 1757-1825
paintings: (H) $6,600

BORRANI, Odoardo
Italian 1834-1905
paintings: (L) $52,800; (H) $154,000

BORRAS Y ABELLA, Vicente
Spanish 19th cent.
paintings: (H) $1,320

BORRELL, Julio
paintings: (H) $4,400

BORREMANS, Guglielmo
Flemish 17th/18th cent.
paintings: (H) $1,650

BORROMINI, Francesco
Italian 1599-1667
drawings: (H) $88,000

BORSDORF
Continental
sculpture: (H) $1,870

BORSE
sculpture: (H) $5,500

BORSELEN, Jan Willem van
Dutch 1825-1892
paintings: (L) $666; (H) $12,100

BORSOS, Josef
Hungarian 1821-1883
paintings: (H) $1,100

BORSSOM, Anthonie van
paintings: (H) $7,700

BORSTEIN, Elena
American b. 1922
paintings: (H) $8,250

BORSTEL, R.A.
British ac. 1914-1918
paintings: (L) $1,540; (H) $2,200

BORTIGNONI, Giuseppe
Italian 19th cent.
paintings: (H) $5,500

BORTNYIK, Sandor
drawings: (L) $495; (H) $17,600

BORTOLUZZI, Camillo
Italian 1868-1933
paintings: (L) $1,320; (H) $2,750

BORTSOME(?), Filippo
drawings: (H) $770

BOS, Georges van den
Belgian 1835-1911
paintings: (L) $2,475; (H) $4,950

BOS, Henk
Dutch b. 1901
paintings: (L) $1,265; (H) $4,180
drawings: (L) $176; (H) $264

BOS, J.
Dutch 1825-1898
paintings: (H) $880

BOSA, Louis
Italian/American 1905-1981
paintings: (L) $27; (H) $2,310
drawings: (L) $220; (H) $495

BOSBOOM, Johannes
Dutch 1817-1891
paintings: (H) $990
drawings: (L) $770; (H) $4,125

BOSCH, Edouard van den
Belgian 1828-1878
paintings: (H) $1,870

BOSCH, Ernst
German 1834-1917
paintings: (H) $2,640

BOSCH, Pieter van den
Dutch 1613-1663
paintings: (L) $4,400; (H) $22,000

BOSCH, T. du
paintings: (H) $660

BOSCHETTI, B.
sculpture: (L) $1,650; (H) $1,980

BOSCHETTO, Giuseppe
Italian b. 1841
paintings: (H) $880

BOSCO, Pierre
French b. 1909
paintings: (H) $990

BOSCOLI, Andrea
Italian c. 1550/60-1606
drawings: (L) $990; (H) $16,500

BOSE
Continental
sculpture: (H) $5,500

BOSELLI, Felice
Italian 1650-1732
paintings: (H) $24,200

BOSKERCK, Robert Ward van
American 1855-1932
paintings: (L) $330; (H) $6,050

BOSLEY, Frederick A.
American 1881-1941
paintings: (L) $522; (H) $37,400

BOSMAN, Richard
American b. 1944
paintings: (L) $2,750; (H) $16,500

BOSS, Henry Wolcott
American 1820-1916
paintings: (H) $5,225

BOSSARD, Hans Heinrich
Swiss b. 1874
paintings: (L) $495; (H) $1,100

BOSSCHAERT, Ambrosius, I
Flemish 1573-1621
paintings: (H) $550,000

BOSSCHAERT, Jean Baptiste
Flemish 1667-1746
paintings: (L) $8,800; (H) $42,900

BOSSCHAERT, Johannes
Dutch 17th cent.
paintings: (H) $198,000

BOSSCHE, Balthasar van den
Flemish 1681-1715
paintings: (L) $11,550; (H) $15,400

BOSSCHE, Dominique van den
Belgian b. 1906
sculpture: (H) $1,045

BOSSE, Abraham
French 1602-1676
drawings: (H) $1,650

BOSSI DA ESTE, Francesco
ac. c. 1800
paintings: (H) $37,400

BOSSOLI, Carlo
Italian 1815-1874
drawings: (H) $110,000

BOSSUET, Francois Antoine
Belgian 1800-1889
paintings: (L) $8,250; (H) $23,100

BOSTIK, T.
American
paintings: (H) $660

BOSTON, Frederick James
American 1855-1932
paintings: (L) $303; (H) $4,000
drawings: (H) $110

BOSTON, Frederick J. and Joseph H.
19th/20th cent.
paintings: (H) $1,200

BOSTON, Joseph H.
American 1860-1954
paintings: (L) $143; (H) $41,000

Unknown Painter

Nadeau's Auction Gallery is a country-style auction house in Colchester, Connecticut, that issues no formal catalogs and holds sales in an old barn. An estate consigned a painting by Joseph H. Boston in the fall of 1988. The previous high for the artist was $1,485; the gallery estimated the painting at $2,500-$4,000. The oil was in a period frame and badly in need of a cleaning but very appealing, showing women in fancy dress and parasols, with the painted slant providing the feel of the ferry boat.

After the painting sold for $41,000, many followers of the art market tried to research the artist but were frustrated. Little is known about Joseph H. Boston. A resource especially useful in providing information on lesser-known artists is Peter Falk's *Who Was Who in American Art*. The book is a compilation of 30 volumes of the American Art Annual, the predecessor of *Who's Who in American Art* and also includes four volumes of *Who's Who from 1934 to 1947*. The original information was solicited directly from artists and is reliable and sometimes unique.

Joseph H. Boston (1860-1954) was born in Bridgeport, Connecticut, and worked in New York City. He belonged to the Society of American Art, Salmagundi Club, Brooklyn Art Club, and National Arts Club and was an associate member of The National Academy of Design. His works are in the Brooklyn Art Institute. The Archives of American Art also has a listing of the location of some of his paintings. (Joseph H. Boston, *Ferry Boat Interior*, oil on canvas, 27 x 35 in., Nadeau, January 8, 1989, $41,000)

BOSWORTH, Elizabeth N.
paintings: (H) $2,200

BOTELLO, Angel
Spanish 1913-1986
paintings: (L) $1,760; (H) $31,900
sculpture: (H) $1,320

BOTERO, Fernando
Colombian b. 1932
paintings: (L) $6,600; (H) $715,000
drawings: (L) $4,675; (H) $121,000
sculpture: (L) $3,520; (H) $385,000

BOTH, Andries Dirksz
Dutch 1612-1650
drawings: (L) $1,870; (H) $14,300

BOTH, Jan
Dutch c. 1615-1652
paintings: (L) $990; (H) $88,000

BOTKE, Cornelius J.
American 1887-1954
paintings: (L) $468; (H) $5,225

BOTKE, Jessie Arms
American 1883-1971
paintings: (L) $440; (H) $27,500
drawings: (L) $66; (H) $1,100

BOTKIN, Henry Albert
American b. 1896
paintings: (L) $220; (H) $2,200

BOTT, E.F.
19th cent.
paintings: (H) $1,210

BOTT, R.C.
paintings: (H) $24,200

BOTT, R.T.
British ac. 1847-1862
paintings: (H) $4,070

BOTTANI, Giuseppe
paintings: (H) $6,325
drawings: (H) $1,045

BOTTI, Rinaldo
drawings: (H) $880

BOTTICELLI, Sandro, Alessandro di
Mariano FILIPEPI
Italian 1444/45-1510
paintings: (H) $539,000
drawings: (H) $88,000

BOTTICINI, Francesco
1446-1497
paintings: (H) $35,750

BOTTINELLI, Antonio
Italian 1827-1898
sculpture: (L) $2,200; (H) $16,500

BOTTINGER, G.F.
paintings: (H) $850

BOTTINI, David
contemporary
sculpture: (L) $2,200; (H) $2,475

BOTTINI, Georges
French 1873-1906
drawings: (L) $2,530; (H) $4,620

BOTTON, Jean de
French/American 1909-1978
paintings: (L) $248; (H) $2,310

BOUANGER
paintings: (H) $770

BOUAT, H.
paintings: (H) $11,000

BOUCART, Gaston Hippolyte
French b. 1878
paintings: (L) $550; (H) $1,045

BOUCHARD, Adolphe
drawings: (H) $990

BOUCHARD, Henri
French 1870-1960
sculpture: (H) $1,540

BOUCHARD, Paul Louis
paintings: (H) $6,600

BOUCHARD, Pierre Francois
French 1831-1889
paintings: (H) $9,625

BOUCHAUD, Etienne
paintings: (H) $715

BOUCHE, Louis Alexandre
French 1838-1911
paintings: (L) $165; (H) $3,300

BOUCHE, Rene
paintings: (L) $11; (H) $2,310

BOUCHENE, Dimitri
paintings: (L) $220; (H) $3,080
drawings: (L) $77; (H) $880

BOUCHER, Alfred
French 1850-1934
sculpture: (L) $2,090; (H) $13,200

BOUCHER, Auguste
paintings: (L) $550; (H) $1,100

BOUCHER, Ferdinand Jean Edouard
French b. 1888
drawings: (H) $1,430

BOUCHER, Francois
French 1703-1770
paintings: (L) $77,000; (H) $1,925,000
drawings: (L) $2,090; (H) $159,500

BOUCHER, Francois, and Assistants
French 1703-1770
paintings: (H) $550,000

BOUCHER, Francois, and studio
French 18th cent.
paintings: (L) $45,100; (H) $159,000

BOUCHER, Francois, studio of
1703-1770
paintings: (H) $22,000

BOUCHER, Jean
French 1870-1939
sculpture: (H) $2,200

BOUCHERVILLE, Adrien de
paintings: (H) $6,050

BOUCHOR, Joseph Felix
French 1853-1935
paintings: (L) $2,090; (H) $10,450

BOUCHOT, Francois
French 1800-1842
paintings: (H) $4,675

BOUCKHORST, Jan van
Dutch 1588-1631
drawings: (H) $16,500

BOUCLE, Pierre
c. 1610-1673
paintings: (H) $60,500

BOUDET, Pierre
paintings: (H) $1,210

BOUDEWYNS, Adriaen Frans
paintings: (L) $9,350; (H) $10,450

BOUDEWYNS, Adriaen Frans and
Mathys SCHOEVAERDTS
paintings: (H) $14,300

BOUDIER, Raoul
paintings: (H) $5,500

BOUDIN, Eugene
French 1824-1898
paintings: (L) $8,800; (H) $1,540,000
drawings: (L) $770; (H) $60,500

BOUDOT, Leon
paintings: (H) $14,300

BOUDRY, Alois
paintings: (H) $2,860

BOUGH, Samuel
Scottish 1822-1878
paintings: (L) $605; (H) $4,400
drawings: (H) $440

BOUGHTON, George Henry
Anglo/American 1833-1905
paintings: (L) $302; (H) $33,000
drawings: (L) $55; (H) $4,620

BOUGHTON, T.
British 19th cent.
paintings: (H) $770

BOUGUEREAU, Elizabeth Jane
Gardner
American 1851-1922
paintings: (L) $4,950; (H) $81,400

BOUGUEREAU, William Adolphe
French 1825-1905
paintings: (L) $2,000; (H) $253,000
drawings: (L) $3,575; (H) $14,300

BOUILLON, Michel
Flemish mid 17th cent.
paintings: (L) $8,800; (H) $41,800

BOULANGER, Gustave Clarence
Rodolphe
French 1824-1888
paintings: (L) $4,730; (H) $33,000
drawings: (H) $440

BOULAY, Paul Auguste
French 20th cent.
paintings: (H) $880

BOULAYS, P. la
Belgian 19th/20th cent.
paintings: (H) $3,300

BOULET, Cyprien Eugene
French 1877-1927
paintings: (H) $6,050

French Landscape Painter

Eugene Boudin (1824-1898) was the son of a French sailor. While working in a stationery and picture-framing shop in the port city of Le Havre, he became friendly with Constant Troyon and Jean Francois Millet, both members of the French Barbizon School of landscape painting. Encouraged by the two artists, he began to paint and ultimately studied in Paris. After traveling to Belgium and Holland, he returned to Normandy, where he remained for the rest of his life.

Boudin's early landscapes were pastel studies of the sky and sea. In 1858 at Le Havre, Boudin met Claude Monet, who was then only eighteen, and persuaded him to take up landscape painting. In 1862, Monet introduced Boudin to Johan Barthold Jongkind, the Dutch master of *plein-air* (open-air) painting. Jongkind moved Boudin away from the Barbizon convention of landscape painting–creating a romanticized ideal of countryside–and encouraged him to rely solely on his own observations. Jongkind's marine scenes and views of ports were studies of the effects of light and atmosphere and greatly influenced both Boudin and Monet. Boudin began to paint beach scenes peopled with crowds of fashionably dressed men and women. His paintings are regarded as a link between the painters of the Barbizon School and the Impressionists, and he showed in the first Impressionist exhibition of 1874. Unlike the others, he did not continue to experiment but stayed with the style he had developed in the 1860s. *Le Havre,* a vibrant painting of the French seaport, was painted in 1877. Consigned from the estate of San Francisco socialite Whitney Warren, the oil sold for $231,000. (Eugene Boudin, *Le Havre,* oil on canvas, 9¾ x 14¼ in., Butterfield, April 25, 1989, $231,000)

BOULIER, Lucien
French 1882-1963
paintings: (L) $440; (H) $2,420
drawings: (L) $825; (H) $1,045

BOULINEAU, Aristide
paintings: (H) $2,310

BOULLONGNE, Bon de
French 1649-1717
paintings: (L) $1,320; (H) $1,650

BOULOGNE, Louis de
French 1654-1733
paintings: (H) $6,050
drawings: (L) $1,870; (H) $33,000

BOULT, A.S.
British ac. 1815-1853
paintings: (H) $6,600

BOULT, Francis Cecil
British ac. 1877-1895
paintings: (L) $4,180; (H) $6,875

BOULTBEE, John
English ac. 1775-1788
paintings: (L) $3,300; (H) $4,950

BOUMAN, Johannes
Dutch b. c. 1602
paintings: (H) $99,000

BOUN, V.
American 19th cent.
paintings: (H) $770

BOUNDEY, Burton Shepard
American 1879-1962
paintings: (L) $550; (H) $7,700

BOUNIER, M.
paintings: (H) $770

BOUQUET
paintings: (H) $660

BOUQUET, Andre
French b. 1897
paintings: (L) $605; (H) $935

BOUQUET, Michel
French 1807-1890
paintings: (H) $1,430
drawings: (H) $880

BOUQUIER, Gabriel
drawings: (H) $2,090

BOURAINE, A.
French 20th cent.
sculpture: (L) $550; (H) $3,850

BOURAINE, Marcel
French ac. 1918-1935
sculpture: (L) $990; (H) $6,050

BOURDELLE, Emile Antoine
French 1861-1929
drawings: (L) $990; (H) $1,320
sculpture: (L) $660; (H) $1,760,000

BOURET, Eutrope
French 1833-1906
sculpture: (L) $126; (H) $3,080

BOURGAIN, Gustave
French d. 1921
paintings: (L) $1,540; (H) $99,000

BOURGEOIS, Douglas
American 20th cent.
paintings: (H) $2,200

BOURGEOIS, Eugene
French 1855-1909
paintings: (L) $825; (H) $4,620

BOURGEOIS, Louise
American b. Paris 1911
paintings: (L) $1,320; (H) $26,400

BOURGEOIS-BORGEX, Louis
French b. 1873
paintings: (H) $2,640

BOURGES, Pauline Elise Leonide
French 1838-1910
paintings: (L) $800; (H) $1,925

BOURGOIN, Francois Jules
French ac. 1796-1812
paintings: (H) $26,400

BOURGUIGNON, Hubert Francois,
called Gravelot
1699-1773
drawings: (H) $825

BOURLARD, Antoine Joseph
Flemish 1826-1899
paintings: (H) $5,500

BOURNE, Gertrude Beals
American 1897-1962
drawings: (L) $72; (H) $1,870

BOURNE, Jean Baptiste Clement
French ac. 1844-1866
paintings: (L) $935; (H) $3,300

BOUSSUET, Francois Antoine
Belgian 1800-1889
paintings: (L) $13,750; (H) $30,800

BOUT, Pieter
paintings: (L) $2,530; (H) $7,150

BOUT, Pieter and Adriaen Franz
BOUDEWYNS
17th/18th cent.
paintings: (L) $11,000; (H) $17,600

BOUTELLE, De Witt Clinton
American 1817/20-1884
paintings: (L) $248; (H) $30,800

BOUTER, Cornelis
Dutch 1888-1966
paintings: (L) $1,210; (H) $7,150

BOUTER, Pieter
Dutch 1887-1968
paintings: (H) $935

BOUTERWEK, Friedrich
German 1806-1867
paintings: (H) $20,900

BOUTET DE MONVEL, Bernard
French 1884-1949
paintings: (L) $1,870; (H) $9,350

BOUTET DE MONVEL, Louis
Maurice
French 1851-1913
drawings: (H) $2,860

BOUTKJEWICH(?), J.
Polish School late 19th cent.
paintings: (H) $3,575

BOUTON, C.
European 20th cent.
paintings: (H) $3,300

BOUTON, H. A. Bedyl von
Continental 19th cent.
paintings: (H) $990

BOUTS, Albrecht
paintings: (H) $8,800

BOUTS, Pieter
paintings: (H) $3,850

BOUTTATS, Frederik, the elder
Flemish d. 1661
paintings: (H) $19,800

BOUVAL, Maurice
French d.c. 1920
sculpture: (L) $467; (H) $825

BOUVARD
paintings: (H) $2,200

BOUVARD, Antoine
French d. 1956
paintings: (L) $1,100; (H) $12,100

BOUVARD, Hugues de
Austrian 19th cent.
paintings: (L) $3,300; (H) $4,400

BOUVARD, Noel A.
French 1912-1975
paintings: (H) $2,475

BOUVE, Rosamond Smith
American early 2oth cent.
paintings: (H) $14,300

BOUVIER, Auguste
paintings: (H) $330
drawings: (L) $1,320; (H) $2,860

BOUVIER, Joseph
19th cent.
paintings: (L) $660; (H) $990

BOUVIER, Jules
drawings: (H) $1,210

BOUVIER, Pietro
paintings: (H) $3,300

BOUVRAL, Maurice
sculpture: (H) $1,650

BOUYSSOU, Jacques
French b. 1926
paintings: (L) $1,980; (H) $3,080

BOUZGOUIN, E.
Continental
sculpture: (H) $1,650

BOVERIE, L.
Belgian b. 1888
drawings: (H) $1,320

BOWDEN, J.
paintings: (H) $1,100

BOWDEN, W.
paintings: (H) $3,520

BOWDISH, Nelson S.
1831-1916
paintings: (H) $660

BOWDOIN, Harriette
American d. 1947/48
paintings: (L) $990; (H) $1,045
drawings: (L) $110; (H) $247

BOWEN, Benjamin James
American 1859-1930
paintings: (L) $523; (H) $3,190

BOWEN, John
paintings: (H) $880

BOWEN, P.T.
American circa 1836
paintings: (H) $935

BOWEN, Paul
paintings: (H) $1,870

BOWER, Alexander
American 1875-1952
paintings: (L) $165; (H) $2,420
drawings: (L) $220; (H) $467

BOWER, J.S.
American ac. 1850
paintings: (L) $330; (H) $495
drawings: (L) $220; (H) $10,450

BOWER, Maurice
American 1889-1980
drawings: (L) $220; (H) $825

BOWERS, Cheryl
paintings: (H) $4,125

BOWERS, George Newall
American 1849-1909
paintings: (L) $330; (H) $2,860

BOWIE, Frank Louville
American 1857-1936
paintings: (L) $137; (H) $2,310

BOWKETT, Nora
English late 19th cent.
paintings: (H) $715

BOWLER, Joseph
b. 1928
paintings: (H) $1,500

BOWMAN, M.E.
American 19th/20th cent.
paintings: (L) $770; (H) $990

BOWSER, David Bustill
American 1820-1900
paintings: (H) $20,900

BOXER, Stanley
paintings: (L) $550; (H) $3,520

BOYCE, George Price
British 1826-1897
drawings: (H) $13,200

BOYCE, William Thomas Nicholas
British 1858-1911
drawings: (H) $660

BOYD, of Harrisburg
American early 19th cent.
paintings: (H) $10,450

BOYD, Clarence
paintings: (H) $1,980

BOYD, Elizabeth Frances
Scottish ac. 1896-1935
paintings: (L) $55; (H) $2,970

BOYD, Rutherford
American 1884-1951
paintings: (L) $550; (H) $6,600
drawings: (H) $1,045

BOYD, Theodore Penleigh
Australian 1890-1923
paintings: (H) $5,170

BOYDEN, Dwight Frederick
American 1860-1933
paintings: (L) $200; (H) $1,045

BOYE, Abel Dominque
French 1864-1934
paintings: (H) $3,300

BOYER
paintings: (H) $770

BOYER, Emile
French 1877-1948
paintings: (L) $770; (H) $4,400
sculpture: (L) $330; (H) $770

BOYER, V. and Pierre LENORDEZ
French 19th cent.
sculpture: (H) $3,025

BOYLE, Charles Wellington
American 1861-1925
paintings: (H) $4,400

BOYLE, F.
American 1820-1906
paintings: (L) $330; (H) $660

BOYLE, John J.
American 1852-1917
sculpture: (H) $19,800

BOYLE, Mark
Scottish b. 1934
sculpture: (H) $2,310

BOYLE, Neil
American
paintings: (H) $2,500

BOYLES, N.
American 20th cent.
sculpture: (H) $1,210

BOZE, Honore
British 1830-1908
paintings: (L) $7,150; (H) $16,500

BOZZALLA, Giuseppe
Italian 1874-1958
paintings: (H) $2,750

BRABAZON, Hercules
English 1821-1906
drawings: (L) $192; (H) $9,625

BRACHT, Eugen
Swiss 1842-1921
paintings: (L) $3,520; (H) $7,700

BRACK, Emil
drawings: (H) $2,860

BRACKEN, Clio Hinton Huneker
American 1870-1925
sculpture: (L) $2,750; (H) $8,800

BRACKETT, Sidney Lawrence
American 1852-1910
paintings: (L) $358; (H) $3,190
drawings: (H) $330

BRACKETT, Walter M.
American 1823-1919
paintings: (L) $385; (H) $7,700

BRACKMAN, David
British 19th cent.
drawings: (H) $6,600

BRACKMAN, Robert
American 1898-1980
paintings: (L) $770; (H) $18,150
drawings: (L) $880; (H) $3,410

BRACONY, Leopold
Italian/American 19th/20th cent.
sculpture: (L) $264; (H) $8,800

BRACQUE, Georges
sculpture: (H) $3,300

BRACQUEMOND, Felix
French 1833-1914
drawings: (L) $990; (H) $4,400

BRACQUEMOND, Pierre
French 20th cent.
paintings: (H) $880

BRACY, Arthur E.
paintings: (L) $715; (H) $1,210

BRACY, C.E.
American 20th cent.
paintings: (H) $825

BRAD, J.
American 19th cent.
paintings: (H) $825

BRADBURY, Bennett
American 20th cent.
paintings: (L) $275; (H) $1,320

BRADBURY, Gideon Elden
American 1833-1904
paintings: (L) $715; (H) $3,850

BRADDON, Charles E.
b. 1906
paintings: (H) $1,760

BRADE, J.
paintings: (L) $412; (H) $1,540

BRADER, F.A.
American 19th cent.
drawings: (L) $4,675; (H) $8,250

BRADFORD, Dean
American 20th cent.
paintings: (H) $990

BRADFORD, William
American 1823/30-1892
paintings: (L) $99; (H) $90,200
drawings: (L) $400; (H) $4,950

BRADISH, Alvah
American 1806-1901
paintings: (L) $2,420; (H) $2,640

BRADLEY, Basil
English 1842-1904
drawings: (H) $1,760

BRADLEY, Cuthbert
drawings: (H) $1,980

BRADLEY, J.
paintings: (H) $29,700

BRADLEY, John
American 19th cent.
paintings: (L) $1,980; (H) $2,750

BRADLEY, Martin
British 20th cent.
paintings: (L) $550; (H) $880

BRADY, Robert
contemporary
sculpture: (H) $4,950

BRAEKELEER, Adrien Ferdinand de
Belgian 1818-1904
paintings: (L) $13,200; (H) $23,100

BRAEKELEER, Ferdinand de
Dutch 1792-1883
paintings: (H) $9,900
drawings: (H) $1,980

BRAGG, Charles
American 20th cent.
paintings: (H) $523
drawings: (H) $990

BRAIL, Achille Jean Theodore
French 19th cent.
paintings: (H) $38,500

BRAITH, Anton
German 1826-1895
paintings: (H) $27,500

BRAITH, Anton
German 1836-1905
paintings: (L) $1,155; (H) $33,000
drawings: (H) $110

BRAKENBURG, Richard
Dutch 1650-1702
paintings: (L) $1,540; (H) $18,700

BRALEY, Clarence E.
American 19th cent.
paintings: (L) $192; (H) $990
drawings: (L) $110; (H) $2,200

BRAMER, Leonard
Dutch 1596-1674
paintings: (L) $1,650; (H) $33,000
drawings: (H) $1,320

BRAMHALL, W.T.
paintings: (H) $1,100

BRAMLEY, Robert
paintings: (L) $990; (H) $1,650

BRAMSON, Phyllis
contemporary
drawings: (H) $2,090

BRANCACCIO, Carlo
Italian b. 1861
paintings: (L) $2,200; (H) $115,500

BRANCACCIO, Giovanni
paintings: (H) $1,100

BRANCHARD, Emile
paintings: (H) $770
drawings: (H) $88

BRANCHO Y MURILLO, Jose Maria
Spanish 19th cent.
paintings: (H) $33,000

BRANCUSI, Constantin
Rumanian 1876-1957
paintings: (L) $38,500; (H) $385,000
drawings: (L) $19,800; (H) $121,000
sculpture: (L) $264,000; (H) $8,800,000

BRANCUSI, Constantin and Edward
STEICHEN
drawings: (H) $143,000

BRAND, Christian Hulfgott
b. 1695/d. after 1756
paintings: (H) $7,700

BRAND, Myra
American 19th cent.
paintings: (H) $660

BRANDAO-GIONO, Wilson
paintings: (L) $2,420; (H) $5,280

BRANDEGEE, Rob B.
American 1848-1922
paintings: (L) $176; (H) $750

BRANDEIS, Antonietta
Czechoslovakian b. 1849
paintings: (L) $528; (H) $16,500

BRANDEIS, Johann
Austrian 1818-1872
paintings: (H) $1,100

BRANDI, Domenico
Italian 1683-1736
paintings: (L) $990; (H) $8,250

BRANDI, Giacinto
Italian 1623-1691
paintings: (L) $3,080; (H) $20,900

BRANDIEN, Carl W.
American 20th cent.
paintings: (L) $308; (H) $1,320

BRANDIS, August von
German b. 1862
paintings: (L) $1,210; (H) $2,475

BRANDNER, Karl C.
American b. 1898
paintings: (L) $66; (H)$1,980
drawings: (H) $99

BRANDOIN, Michel Vincent
Swiss 1733-1807
drawings: (H) $3,740

BRANDON, Jacques Emile Edouard
French School 1831-1897
paintings: (H) $2,310
drawings: (H) $39,600

BRANDRETH, Courtenay
paintings: (L) $385; (H) $2,090

BRANDRETT, Anthony
American 20th cent.
paintings: (H) $1,210

BRANDRIFF, George Kennedy
American 1890-1936
paintings: (L) $220; (H) $14,300

BRANDT, Carl Ludwig
American 1831-1905
paintings: (L) $275; (H) $3,080

BRANDT, Edgar
sculpture: (L) $4,950; (H) $88,000

BRANDT, Henry
American b. 1862
paintings: (L) $467; (H) $1,100

BRANDT, Josef von
Polish 1841-1915/28
paintings: (L) $8,800; (H) $27,500

BRANDT, Karl C.
Swedish d. 1930
paintings: (H) $5,500

BRANDT, Otto
German 1828-1892
paintings: (L) $357; (H) $3,575

BRANDT, Paul
drawings: (H) $880

BRANDT, Rexford Elson
American b. 1914
paintings: (L) $192; (H) $275
drawings: (L) $2,090; (H) $3,300

BRANDT, S. Kielland
Danish 19th/20th cent.
paintings: (H) $1,402

BRANDT, Van
Dutch 20th cent.
paintings: (H) $1,045

BRANDT, Warren
American b. 1918
paintings: (H) $1,210

BRANGWYN, Sir Frank
British 1867-1956
paintings: (L) $495; (H) $41,800
drawings: (L) $242; (H) $5,280

BRANK, Rockwell
American 20th cent.
paintings: (L) $220; (H) $660

BRANNAN, Sophie M.
American 1878-1962
paintings: (L) $121; (H)$880
sculpture: (H) $1,540

BRANSOM, John Paul
American 1885-1979
paintings: (H) $550
drawings: (L) $88; (H) $950

BRANWHITE, Charles
English 1817-1883
paintings: (L) $825; (H) $1,100
drawings: (H) $1,210

BRAQUAVAL, Louis
French 1854-1919
paintings: (L) $3,300; (H) $4,400

BRAQUE, Georges
French 1882-1963
paintings: (L) $3,300; (H) $4,675,000
drawings: (L) $17,600; (H) $660,000
sculpture: (L) $19,800; (H) $132,000

BRASCH, Magnus
drawings: (H) $1,320

BRASHER, Rex
American 20th cent.
drawings: (L) $220; (H) $715

BRASILIER, Andre
French b. 1929
paintings: (L) $275; (H) $225,500

BRATBY, John
British b. 1928
paintings: (L) $165; (H) $2,860

Cubism

Cubism, the result of a 1907 collaboration between Georges Braque and Pablo Picasso, was the most radical revolution in art since the Renaissance. Inspired by Cezanne, who advocated viewing nature as a series of geometric planes, the two began a movement that was later broadened by Juan Gris and Fernand Leger and greatly influenced twentieth-century art. Analytical Cubism, the first stage in the movement's development, depicted subject matter as overlapping geometric planes that were made transparent to indicate depth. Sometimes the subject was simultaneously rendered from several different points of view. Color use was largely limited to browns and grays. In Synthetic Cubism, the second phase, artists included actual objects (newspapers, printed letters, numerals, cloths, pieces of wood, etc.) in the picture, employing them as colored and textured shapes combined with forms abstracted from objects in nature.

Georges Braque (1882-1963) was born in Argenteuil, France. He followed his father's trade and became a house painter, but by 1900 he had begun to study at the Ecole des Beaux-Arts in Paris. His first paintings were brightly colored in the Fauvist manner, but after seeing the Cezanne Retrospective in 1907, Braque began to paint in a geometric, analytical manner. That same year he was introduced to Picasso, and the two soon began to work in close association, visiting each other's studio almost every day. Braque painted still lifes (often with musical instruments) and sometimes landscapes; Picasso was drawn to the human figure.

Braque was seriously wounded in World War I, and after his recovery his style changed and became less angular. He concentrated on still lifes and during the 1920s, produced some of his most outstanding works. In a long productive life, Braque painted, created an important body of sculpture, drew book illustrations, designed decor and costumes for theater and ballet, executed decorative designs for the ceiling of the Louvre, and designed stained-glass windows and jewelry. In 1961, when he was seventy-nine, he became the first living artist to have his work exhibited in the Louvre.

Le Tampon Buvard was painted in 1911, the period in which Braque began to introduce stenciled letters into his paintings, a prelude to the introduction of collages. (Georges Braque, *Le Tampon Buvard*, oil on canvas, 12 ⅛ x 10 ⅛ in., Christie's, May 15, 1990, $1,320,000)

BRAUN, Larry
sculpture: (H) $1,980

BRAUN, Maurice
American 1877-1941
paintings: (L) $440; (H) $35,750
drawings: (H) $440

BRAUN, P.
19th cent.
paintings: (H) $990

BRAUNER, Olaf
American 1869-1947
paintings: (H) $935

BRAUNER, Victor
Rumanian 1903-1966
paintings: (L) $4,950; (H) $148,000
drawings: (L) $25,300; (H) $27,500

BRAUNS, P.
German School 19th cent.
paintings: (H) $1,100

BRAUNTUCH, Troy
American b. 1954
drawings: (L) $715; (H) $17,600

BRAVO, Claudio
Chilean b. 1936
paintings: (L) $3,850; (H) $148,500
drawings: (L) $1,430; (H) $63,250
sculpture: (H) $15,400

BRAY, Arnold
American ac. 1920-1940
paintings: (L) $303; (H) $990

BRAY, Jan de
Dutch c. 1626/27-1697
paintings: (H) $7,150

BRAY, Salomon de
1597-1664
paintings: (H) $19,800

BRAYER, Yves
French b. 1907
paintings: (L) $1,100; (H) $28,600
drawings: (H) $467

BREA, Lodovico
paintings: (H) $4,400

BREACH, E.R.
British ac. 1868-1886
paintings: (H) $4,125

BREAKSPEARE, William A.
English 1855/56-1914
paintings: (L) $385; (H) $3,300

BREANSKI, Alfred Fontville de
British 19th cent.
paintings: (L) $1,760; (H) $1,760

BREANSKI, Alfred de
paintings: (L) $418; (H) $13,200
drawings: (H) $2,860

BREANSKI, Alfred de
British 1869-1893
paintings: (H) $1,430

BREANSKI, Alfred de
British ac. 1880-1919
paintings: (L) $1,100; (H) $9,075

BREANSKI, Alfred de
British 1852-1928
paintings: (L) $715; (H) $29,700

BREANSKI, Alfred de
British 19th cent.
paintings: (L) $1,650; (H) $39,600

BREANSKI, Alfred de
British d. c. 1945
paintings: (L) $440; (H) $3,520

BREANSKI, Alfred de, Jr.
British c. 1904
paintings: (L) $440; (H) $8,250

BREANSKI, Alfred de, Jr.
British 1877-1957
paintings: (L) $825; (H) $2,475

BREANSKI, Alfred de, Sr.
paintings: (L) $660; (H) $15,400

BREANSKI, Gustave de
British c. 1856-1898
paintings: (L) $275; (H) $1,650

BREBIETTE, Pierre
paintings: (H) $3,080

BRECHER, Samuel
Austrian/American 1897-1982
paintings: (L) $880; (H) $9,020

BRECHERET, Victor
Brazilian 1894-1955
sculpture: (H) $88,000

BRECKENRIDGE, Hugh Henry
American 1870-1937
paintings: (L) $522; (H) $825
drawings: (L) $385; (H) $3,850

BREDA, Carl Fredrik van
paintings: (H) $4,400

BREDAEL, Alexander van
Flemish 1663-1720
paintings: (H) $16,500

BREDAEL, Josef van
Flemish 1688-1739
paintings: (H) $12,100

BREDAEL, Pieter van
paintings: (H) $1,760

BREDAL, Neils Anders
paintings: (H) $6,600

BREDIN, Rae Sloan
American 1881-1933
paintings: (L) $6,250; (H) $35,200
drawings: (H) $165

BREDOW, Gustav Adolf
German b. 1875
paintings: (H) $10,450

BREDSDORFF, Axel
paintings: (H) $1,210

BREDT, Ferdinand Max
German 1860-1921
paintings: (H) $1,760

BREE, Anthony de
English 19th/20th cent.
paintings: (L) $6,050; (H) $9,900

BREE, Joseph van
Dutch 19th/20th cent.
paintings: (H) $2,860

BREE, Philippe Jacques van
Belgian 1786-1871
paintings: (H) $11,000

BREEDE, Alex
American 19th cent.
paintings: (H) $1,430

BREEN, J.T.
American 20th cent.
paintings: (L) $192; (H) $1,045

BREEVORT, James Renwick
American 1832-1918
paintings: (L) $1,100; (H) $1,760
drawings: (H) $330

BREHM, George
American b. 1878
paintings: (H) $900
drawings: (H) $385

BREHMER, Emil
paintings: (H) $990

BREIDWIESER, T.H.
Hungarian
paintings: (H) $1,650

BREITKOPF, Franz
American
paintings: (H) $3,300

BREITNER, George Hendrik
Dutch 1857-1923
drawings: (H) $28,600

BREJCHA, Vernon
American b. 1942
sculpture: (H) $770

BREKELENKAM, Quiringh Gerritsz
van
Dutch 1620-1668
paintings: (L) $12,100; (H) $28,600

BRELING, Heinrich
German b. 1849
paintings: (L) $1,540; (H) $5,500

BRELL, J. Peru
Spanish 19th cent.
paintings: (H) $8,800

BRELY, Auguste de la
French 1838-1906
paintings: (H) $1,650

BREMER, R.
Continental School 19th cent.
paintings: (H) $1,650

BREN, Claire Trevor
paintings: (L) $605; (H) $3,080

BRENA, Jose Kuri
sculpture: (H) $5,225

BRENDEKILDE, Hans Andersen
Danish 1857-1920
paintings: (L) $7,150; (H) $23,100

BRENNEISEN, Heinrich
American early 20th cent.
paintings: (H) $715

BRENNER, Adam
Austrian 1800-1891
paintings: (H) $2,860

BRENNER, Carl C.
American 1838-1888
paintings: (L) $715; (H) $7,150

BRENNER, Victor David
Russian/American 1871-1924
sculpture: (L) $110; (H) $3,740

BRENNIR, Carl
British 19th cent.
paintings: (L) $825; (H) $2,200

BRENOT, Pierre Laurent
French b. 1913
paintings: (H) $1,045

BRERETON, James Joseph
British b. 1954
paintings: (H) $700

BRESDIN, Rodolphe
French 1822-1885
drawings: (H) $71,500

BRESLAU, Robert
sculpture: (H) $4,125

BRESSIN, A.
French 19th/20th cent.
paintings: (H) $15,400

BRESSLER, Emile
Swiss b. 1886
paintings: (L) $1,100; (H) $2,310
drawings: (H) $187

BREST, Germain Fabius
French 1823-1900
paintings: (H) $24,200

BRESTER, Anna Richards
paintings: (H) $770

BRET, Paul Marie Leonce
French b. 1902
paintings: (H) $3,740

BRETLAND, Thomas
English 1802-1874
paintings: (L) $2,860; (H) $7,700

BRETON, Andre
French 1896-1966
drawings: (L) $6,050; (H) $7,150

BRETON, Charles Eugene
sculpture: (H) $715

BRETON, Emile
paintings: (H) $5,500

BRETON, Jacqueline
drawings: (H) $4,180

BRETON, Jules Adolphe
French 1827-1906
paintings: (L) $1,430; (H) $1,650,000

BRETON, Paul Eugene
sculpture: (H) $1,760

BRETT, Dorothy Eugenie
Anglo/American 1883-1977
paintings: (L) $1,210; (H) $11,000

BRETT, Harold M.
American 1880-1955
paintings: (L) $450; (H) $4,400
drawings: (L) $121; (H) $715

BREU, Jorg, the elder
German 1475/80-1537
drawings: (H) $77,000

BREU, Marie
paintings: (H) $2,475

BREUER, Henry Joseph
American 1860-1932
paintings: (L) $275; (H) $3,025
drawings: (L) $220; (H) $467

BREUER, T.
sculpture: (L) $770; (H) $1,540

BREUL, Hugo
German/American 1854-1910
paintings: (L) $220; (H) $715

BREVOORT, James Renwick
American 1832-1918
paintings: (L) $1,100; (H) $9,350
drawings: (H) $715

BREWER, Adrian Louis
American 1891-1956
paintings: (H) $1,650
sculpture: (H) $660

BREWER, H.J.
paintings: (H) $1,650

BREWER, John
British 18th/19th cent.
drawings: (H) $770

BREWER, Nicholas Richard
American 1857-1949
paintings: (L) $150; (H) $4,400

BREWERTON, George Douglas
American 1820-1901
paintings: (L) $440; (H) $770
drawings: (L) $138; (H) $3,025

BREWSTER, A.R.
paintings: (L) $110; (H) $3,300
drawings: (L) $165; (H) $935

BREWSTER, Anna Richards
American 1870-1952
paintings: (L) $140; (H) $1,760

BREWSTER, G. Douglas
American
drawings: (H) $1,540

BREWSTER, John, Jr.
American 1766-1854
paintings: (L) $4,950; (H) $852,500
drawings: (H) $2,860

BREWSTER, Marvin M.
American
sculpture: (H) $1,100

**BREYDAEL, Karel, called Cavalier
d'Anvers**
Flemish 1678-1733
paintings: (L) $4,675; (H) $4,950

BRIANCHON, Maurice
French b. 1899
paintings: (L) $5,775; (H) $110,000
drawings: (L) $2,530; (H) $4,180

BRIANTE, Ezelino
Italian 1901-1970
paintings: (L) $1,100; (H) $1,210

BRIARD
paintings: (H) $12,100

BRICE, William
American 20th cent.
paintings: (H) $1,210

BRICHER, Alfred Thompson
American 1837-1908
paintings: (L) $550; (H) $176,000
drawings: (L) $77; (H) $52,800

BRICKDALE, Eleanor Fortescue
English 1871-1945
drawings: (L) $660; (H) $13,200

BRIDAHAM, Lester Burbank
paintings: (H) $1,320

BRIDGE, Helen
American 20th cent.
paintings: (H) $880

BRIDGE, W.B.
paintings: (H) $440
drawings: (L) $935; (H) $1,210

BRIDGEHOUSE, Robert
paintings: (H) $29,700

BRIDGES, Fidelia
American 1834-1923
paintings: (L) $2,860; (H) $13,200
drawings: (L) $275; (H) $9,900

BRIDGMAN, Frederick Arthur
American 1847-1928
paintings: (L) $1,870; (H) $418,000

BRIDGMAN, George B.
American b. 1864
paintings: (L) $605; (H) $1,320

BRIE, Anthonie de
paintings: (H) $2,750

BRIGANTE, Nicholas P.
American b. 1895
paintings: (L) $137; (H) $2,200
drawings: (L) $165; (H) $660

BRIGANTI, T.
Italian 19th/20th cent.
paintings: (H) $4,675

BRIGATTI, N.
paintings: (H) $715

BRIGAUD, Frederick
sculpture: (H) $2,475

BRIGDEN, B.
paintings: (H) $715

BRIGDORF, Ferdinand
paintings: (H) $990

BRIGGS, Austin
American 1909-1973
paintings: (L) $400; (H) $2,200

BRIGGS, Lucius A.
American 1852-1937
drawings: (L) $330; (H) $1,980

BRIGGS, Lamar
American 20th cent.
drawings: (H) $1,100

BRIGHAM, R. Jordan
American 19th cent.
paintings: (H) $660

BRIGHAM, W.H.
paintings: (H) $660

BRIGHT, Harry
British ac. 1867-1892
drawings: (L) $440; (H) $3,025

BRIGHT, Henry
English 1814-1873
paintings: (L) $880; (H) $1,980
drawings: (H) $550

BRIGHTWELL, Walter
American b. 1914
paintings: (H) $1,650

BRIGL, Wilhelm
paintings: (H) $715

BRIGNONI, Sergio
paintings: (H) $26,400

BRIL, Paul
Flemish 1554-1626
paintings: (L) $1,650; (H) $88,000

BRILLOUIN, Louis Georges
French 1817-1893
paintings: (L) $2,090; (H) $3,300

BRINDEAU, Louis Edouard
French d. 1943
drawings: (H) $1,045

BRINDISI, Remo
paintings: (H) $3,410

BRINDLE, Melbourne
paintings: (H) $12,100

BRINK, Guido
American contemporary
sculpture: (H) $825

BRINKMAN, Tracy Beeler
American b. 1958
sculpture: (H) $5,000

BRION, Gustave
French 1824-1877
paintings: (L) $1,320; (H) $10,450
drawings: (H) $550

BRIOSCHI, Carlo
Austrian School
paintings: (H) $1,595

BRISCOE, F.W.
English 19th cent.
paintings: (H) $687

BRISCOE, Franklin D.
American 1844-1903
paintings: (L) $308; (H) $8,250
drawings: (H) $440

BRISSAUD, Pierre
French b. 1885
drawings: (H) $660

BRISSET, Emile
French 19th cent.
paintings: (L) $1,650; (H) $1,760

BRISSON
paintings: (L) $330; (H) $880

BRISSOT, Franck
paintings: (H) $770

BRISSOT DE WARVILLE, Felix
Saturnin
French 1818-1892
paintings: (L) $308; (H) $10,450
drawings: (L) $220; (H) $220

BRISTOL, John Bunyan
American 1826-1909
paintings: (L) $440; (H) $11,000
drawings: (H) $990

BRISTOW, Edmund
English 1787-1876
paintings: (L) $357; (H) $19,800

BRITTON, C.W.
American 19th cent.
paintings: (H) $770

BRIZZI, Francesco
1574-1623
paintings: (H) $2,200

BROCAS, Eugene Mary
French b. 1813
paintings: (H) $4,290

BROCAS, S.F.
Irish 19th cent.
drawings: (H) $1,210

BROCH, A.
paintings: (H) $2,420

BROCHART, Constant Joseph
French 1816-1899
drawings: (L) $495; (H) $4,400

BROCHERT, Bernard Christian
Russian b. 1863
paintings: (H) $1,760

BROCK, Sir Thomas
English 1847-1922
sculpture: (H) $1,210

BROCKHURST, Gerald Leslie
English b. 1890
paintings: (L) $374; (H) $1,870

BROCZIK, Wencelas
paintings: (H) $1,650

BRODEL
paintings: (H) $1,320

BRODERS
paintings: (L) $522; (H) $852

BRODERSON, Morris
American b. 1928
paintings: (L) $1,650; (H) $3,800
drawings: (L) $303; (H) $3,575

BRODIE, William
English
sculpture: (H) $5,940

BRODOWSKI, Thaddaeus
Polish 1821-1848
paintings: (H) $3,300

BROE, Vern
American 20th cent.
paintings: (L) $385; (H) $2,250

BROECK, Clemence van den
paintings: (L) $1,320; (H) $1,650

BROECK, Elias van den
Dutch 1650-1708
paintings: (L) $21,450; (H) $110,000

BROEMEL, Carl
American b. 1891
paintings: (H) $165
drawings: (L) $5; (H) $990

BROKAW, D.
19th cent.
paintings: (H) $1,650

BROMLEY, Frank C.
American 1860-1890
paintings: (L) $605; (H) $2,200

BROMLEY, John W.
English 19th cent.
paintings: (H) $2,310

BROMLEY, Valentine Walker
British 1848-1877
paintings: (H) $1,650

BROMLEY, William
British ac. 1835-1888
paintings: (H) $9,350

BROMLEY, William, III
paintings: (L) $3,410; (H) $35,750

BRON, Aghille
French 19th/20th cent.
paintings: (H) $1,320

BRON, Louis
Dutch 20th cent.
paintings: (H) $880

BRONCKHORST, Johannes
Dutch 1618-1727
drawings: (H) $2,420

BRONKHORST, Johannes
drawings: (H) $1,320

BRONSON, Clark
American b. 1939
sculpture: (L) $2,500; (H) $2,750

BROODTHAERS, Marcel
Belgian 1924-1976
drawings: (H) $20,900
sculpture: (H) $77,000

BROOK, Alexander
American 1898-1980
paintings: (L) $192; (H) $6,380
drawings: (L) $275; (H) $467

BROOK, H.J.
19th cent.
paintings: (H) $4,200

BROOKE, Joseph
British 18th cent.
paintings: (H) $3,575

BROOKE, Richard Norris
American 1847-1920
paintings: (L) $495; (H) $12,100

BROOKER, Harry
English ac. 1876-1902
paintings: (L) $880; (H) $18,700

BROOKES, Samuel Marsden
American 1816-1892
paintings: (L) $3,850; (H) $17,600

BROOKING, Charles
English 1723-1759
paintings: (H) $8,800

BROOKS, Alden Finney
American 1840-c. 1938
paintings: (L) $165; (H) $3,300
drawings: (L) $192; (H) $303

BROOKS, Allan
Canadian 1869-1946
drawings: (L) $2,420; (H) $3,410

BROOKS, Cora S.
American 20th cent.
paintings: (L) $1,265; (H) $1,760

BROOKS, Henry Howard
American b. 1898, ac. 1934
paintings: (L) $44; (H) $3,520

BROOKS, J.B.
paintings: (H) $2,750

BROOKS, Jacob
paintings: (H) $1,100

BROOKS, James
American b. 1906
paintings: (L) $3,300; (H) $41,250
drawings: (L) $1,870; (H) $2,310

BROOKS, Maria
British ac. 1869-1890
paintings: (L) $8,800; (H) $110,000

BROOKS, Newton
American 19th cent.
paintings: (H) $44,000

BROOKS, Nicholas Alden
American ac. 1880-1904
paintings: (L) $935; (H) $26,400

BROOKS, Richard Edwin
American
sculpture: (L) $770; (H) $880

BROOKS, S.
paintings: (H) $1,045

BROOKS, Thomas
English 1818-1891
paintings: (H) $71,500

BROOME, William
paintings: (H) $2,420

BROOS, Jean Jacques Z.
Flemish 19th cent.
paintings: (H) $1,320

BROQUET
paintings: (H) $825

BROSCO, C.
sculpture: (H) $715

BROSE, Carl
sculpture: (L) $880; (H) $3,300

BROSE, Morris
sculpture: (H) $907

BROSHARD
French 20th cent.
paintings: (H) $825

BROU, Adele de
Belgian 19th cent.
paintings: (H) $2,860

BROUGIER, Adolphe
German b. 1870
paintings: (H) $2,475

BROUILLET, Pierre Andre
French 1857-1914
paintings: (H) $104,500

BROULOWSKY, L. and N.
paintings: (H) $2,310

BROUWER, Adriaen
Flemish 1605/06-1638
paintings: (L) $1,650; (H) $55,000

BROUWER, Gien
Dutch 20th cent.
paintings: (L) $715; (H) $825

BROWEN, Byron
drawings: (H) $990

BROWER, T.D.
paintings: (H) $1,045

BROWERE, Albertis del Orient
American 1814-1887
paintings: (L) $1,000; (H) $2,640

BROWN, A.E.D.G. Stirling
British late 19th/20th cent.
paintings: (H) $9,350

BROWN, A.K.
British 1849-1922
paintings: (L) $1,210; (H) $2,860
drawings: (H) $385

BROWN, Anna Wood
American 19th/20th cent.
paintings: (L) $192; (H) $660

BROWN, Arthur William
Canadian/American 1881-1966
paintings: (L) $176; (H) $225
drawings: (L) $66; (H) $770

BROWN, Benjamin Chambers
American 1865-1942
paintings: (L) $550; (H) $26,400
drawings: (L) $825; (H) $1,100

BROWN, Byron
American 1907-1961
paintings: (L) $880; (H) $1,320
drawings: (L) $605; (H) $660

BROWN, C.P.
American 20th cent.
paintings: (L) $55; (H) $1,045

BROWN, Carlyle
American 1919/20-1964
paintings: (L) $176; (H) $1,100
drawings: (L) $385; (H) $1,980

BROWN, Carroll
19th/20th cent.
paintings: (L) $55; (H) $880
drawings: (H) $3,500

BROWN, Cecil, Major
British 1868-1926
paintings: (H) $2,860

BROWN, Christopher
American contemporary
paintings: (H) $4,125
drawings: (H) $2,200

BROWN, D. Crosby
paintings: (H) $2,200

BROWN, David Lee
contemporary
drawings: (H) $38
sculpture: (H) $1,760

BROWN, E.
paintings: (H) $3,520

BROWN, E.
British 19th cent.
paintings: (H) $2,420

BROWN, Edmund
American 19th cent.
sculpture: (H) $88,000

BROWN, Florinne
American 19th cent.
paintings: (H) $1,100

BROWN, Francis F.
American b. 1891
paintings: (L) $110; (H) $990

BROWN, Frank
paintings: (H) $880

BROWN, Frank A.
American b. 1876
paintings: (L) $330; (H) $660
drawings: (H) $440

BROWN, Frank W.
paintings: (H) $660

BROWN, Fred C.
American
paintings: (H) $8,800

BROWN, G.
American 19th/20th cent.
paintings: (H) $1,100

BROWN, George Appleton
American
drawings: (H) $4,180

BROWN, George Elmer
American 1871-1946
paintings: (H) $2,750

BROWN, George Henry Alan
English b. 1862
paintings: (H) $1,540
drawings: (H) $350

BROWN, George Loring
American 1814-1889
paintings: (L) $110; (H) $13,200
drawings: (L) $358; (H) $2,090

BROWN, H.E.
American 19th cent.
paintings: (L) $385; (H) $825
drawings: (H) $825

BROWN, Harley
American contemporary
drawings: (L) $715; (H) $2,970

BROWN, Harrison B.
American 1831-1915
paintings: (L) $220; (H) $11,000

BROWN, Horace
American b. 1876
paintings: (L) $143; (H) $660

BROWN, J.
paintings: (L) $137; (H) $935
drawings: (H) $176

BROWN, J.
American ac. c. 1803-1808
paintings: (H) $13,200

BROWN, James
American b. 1818
paintings: (L) $3,300; (H) $159,000
drawings: (L) $1,870; (H) $19,800
sculpture: (L) $7,150; (H) $14,300

BROWN, James Francis
American 1862-1935
paintings: (L) $247; (H) $4,675

BROWN, Joan
American b. 1938
paintings: (L) $468; (H) $16,500
drawings: (L) $935; (H) $2,750

BROWN, Joe
sculpture: (L) $302; (H) $5,775

BROWN, John Appleton
American 1844-1902
paintings: (L) $467; (H) $8,800
drawings: (L) $165; (H) $16,500

BROWN, John George
Anglo/American 1831-1913
paintings: (L) $275; (H) $192,500
drawings: (L) $880; (H) $6,050

BROWN, John Lewis
French 1829-1890
paintings: (L) $440; (H) $27,500
drawings: (L) $302; (H) $330

BROWN, Joseph Randolph
American b. 1861
paintings: (L) $83; (H) $4,950
drawings: (L) $55; (H) $798

BROWN, L.M.
American 20th cent.
paintings: (L) $175; (H) $800
drawings: (H) $75

BROWN, Louis
French 19th cent.
paintings: (H) $1,210

BROWN, M.E.D.
American ac. 19th cent.
paintings: (L) $9,350; (H) $11,000

BROWN, Marnell
American
paintings: (H) $1,450

BROWN, Mather
American, b. London 1761/62-1831
paintings: (L) $495; (H) $4,675

BROWN, Paul
American 1893-1958
paintings: (H) $126
drawings: (L) $220; (H) $4,125

BROWN, Paul F.
American 1871-1944
drawings: (H) $1,100

BROWN, Peter
British ac. 1758-99
drawings: (H) $1,540

BROWN, R. Woodley
English 19th cent.
paintings: (L) $192; (H) $1,320

BROWN, R.G.
British ac. 1844-1859
paintings: (L) $550; (H) $3,300

BROWN, Robert
paintings: (L) $880; (H) $990

BROWN, Robert A.
American b. 1895
paintings: (H) $1,980

BROWN, Roger
American b. 1941
paintings: (L) $4,620; (H) $28,600
sculpture: (L) $1,100; (H) $20,900

BROWN, Roy H.
American 1879-1956
paintings: (L) $44; (H) $1,650

BROWN, T**
British 19th cent.
paintings: (H) $2,310

BROWN, W.
paintings: (L) $495; (H) $880

BROWN, W. Warren
Canadian late 19th cent.
paintings: (L) $110; (H) $770

BROWN, W.F.
paintings: (H) $770

BROWN, Walter Emerson
paintings: (H) $1,100

BROWN, Walter Francis
American 1853-1929
paintings: (L) $715; (H) $2,860
drawings: (L) $225; (H) $440

BROWN, William Beattie
English 1831-1909
paintings: (H) $2,750

BROWN, William E.
American
drawings: (H) $3,190

BROWN, William H.
paintings: (H) $3,300

BROWN, William J.
American 20th cent.
paintings: (H) $935

BROWN, William Mason
American 1828-1898
paintings: (L) $330; (H) $50,600

BROWNE, Byron
American 1907-1961
paintings: (L) $715; (H) $22,000
drawings: (L) $110; (H) $4,675

BROWNE, Charles Francis
American 1859-1920
paintings: (L) $99; (H) $7,150

BROWNE, Edward
paintings: (H) $3,080

BROWNE, George
American
paintings: (H) $1,650

BROWNE, George Elmer
American 1871-1946
paintings: (L) $55; (H) $12,100
drawings: (L) $110; (H) $1,045

BROWNE, Hablot Knight, Phiz
English 1815-1882
paintings: (L) $3,740; (H) $12,100
drawings: (L) $176; (H) $2,750

BROWNE, Henriette
French 1829-1901
paintings: (H) $15,400

BROWNE, Margaret Fitzhugh
American 1884-1972
paintings: (L) $77; (H)$3,300
drawings: (H) $82

BROWNE, Matilda
American 1869-1953
paintings: (L) $605; (H) $770
drawings: (L) $303; (H) $1,650

BROWNE, Nassau Blair
British 19th/20th cent.
paintings: (H) $990

BROWNE, Tom
English 1872-1910
paintings: (H) $1,650

BROWNE, W.H.
American
paintings: (H) $38,500

BROWNE, William Garf.
American 19th cent.
paintings: (H) $770

BROWNELL, Charles de Wolf
American 1822-1909
paintings: (L) $5,060; (H) $20,900

BROWNELL, Franklin P.
American 1857-1946
paintings: (H) $412
drawings: (L) $110; (H) $825

BROWNLOW, George Washington
English exhib. 1858-1875
paintings: (H) $3,575

BROWNSCOMBE, Jennie Augusta
American 1850-1936
paintings: (L) $165; (H) $9,350
drawings: (L) $137; (H) $6,050

BROZIK, Wenceslas de
Bohemian 1851-1900/01
paintings: (L) $1,320; (H) $39,600

BRUCE, Edward
American 1879-1943
paintings: (L) $165; (H) $10,450

BRUCE, James Christie
American (?) 19th/20th cent.
paintings: (H) $1,100

BRUCE, Joseph A.
American 1838-1908
paintings: (H) $990

BRUCE, William
paintings: (H) $2,200

BRUCE, William
American 19th/20th cent.
paintings: (H) $6,600

BRUCE, William Blair
Canadian 1857/59-1906
paintings: (L) $1,100; (H) $10,725

BRUCH, K.
Continental 19th cent.
paintings: (H) $1,320

BRUCK, Lajos
Hungarian 1846-1910
paintings: (H) $1,760

BRUCKER, Edmund
American b. 1912
paintings: (H) $2,420

BRUCKMAN, Lodewijk
Dutch/American b. 1903
paintings: (L) $440; (H) $3,080

BRUCKYER, T.
paintings: (H) $3,960

BRUEGHEL, Jan, called Velvet
BRUEGHEL the elder
Flemish 1568-1625
paintings: (L) $99,000; (H) $2,035,000

BRUEGHEL, Jan, studio of the younger
Flemish 17th cent.
paintings: (L) $16,500; (H) $71,500

BRUEGHEL, Jan, the younger
Flemish 1601-1678
paintings: (L) $16,500; (H) $550,000

BRUEGHEL, Jan (the younger) and
Pieter van AVONT
17th cent.
paintings: (H) $27,500

BRUEGHEL, Jan and Hendrick van
BALEN, the younger
Flemish 17th cent.
paintings: (H) $66,000

BRUEGHEL, Pieter, III
Flemish b. 1589
paintings: (H) $33,000

BRUEGHEL, Pieter, the elder
Flemish 1525-1569
paintings: (L) $275,000; (H) $495,000

BRUEGHEL, Pieter, the younger
Flemish c. 1564-1637/8
paintings: (L) $55,000; (H) $2,970,000

BRUEL, H.
drawings: (L) $220; (H) $1,430

BRUESTLE, Bertram G.
American b. 1902
paintings: (L) $220; (H) $3,300

BRUESTLE, George M.
American 1871/72-1939
paintings: (L) $495; (H) $6,600

BRUFF, Joseph Goldsborough
American 1804-1889
drawings: (H) $715

BRUGAIROLLES, Victor
French 1869-1936
paintings: (L) $1,760; (H) $3,025

BRUGGHEN, Girard van der
Dutch 1811-1891
paintings: (H) $2,200

BRUGO, Giuseppe
Italian 19th/20th cent.
paintings: (H) $1,000
drawings: (H) $495

BRUKMAN, Lodewyk
b. 1903
paintings: (H) $990

BRUMIDI, Constantino
American 1805-1880
paintings: (H) $3,190

BRUMMOND, Marie
contemporary
drawings: (H) $715

BRUN, Gaston
French b. 1873
paintings: (H) $660

BRUNDAGE, Frances I.
American b. 1854
drawings: (L) $500; (H) $800

BRUNDKROZIR
19th cent.
sculpture: (H) $660

BRUNEAU, Adrien
French 19th/20th cent.
drawings: (H) $715

BRUNEL DE NEUVILLE, Alfred
Arthur
French 19th cent.
paintings: (L) $880; (H) $24,200

BRUNER, P.
Continental 19th cent.
paintings: (H) $935

BRUNERY, Francois
Italian b. 1845, ac. 1898-1909
paintings: (L) $660; (H) $23,100

BRUNERY, Marcel
French 20th cent.
paintings: (H) $10,450

BRUNIN, Leon
Belgian 1861-1949
paintings: (L) $187; (H) $7,150

BRUNINI, C.
sculpture: (H) $3,300

BRUNNER, A.F.
paintings: (L) $2,090; (H) $2,090

BRUNNER, F. Sands
American b. 1886
paintings: (H) $2,100

BRUNNER, Ferdinand
Austrian b. 1870
paintings: (H) $7,700

BRUNNER, Hattie K.
drawings: (L) $500; (H) $2,090

BRUNNER (?), Art
paintings: (H) $3,300

BRUNNER-LACOSTE, Emile Henri
French 1838-1881
paintings: (L) $2,100; (H) $6,600

BRUNTON, Richard
d. 1832
drawings: (H) $4,070

BRUSH, George De Forest
American 1855-1941
paintings: (L) $550; (H) $46,200
drawings: (L) $880; (H) $3,300

BRUSKIN, Grisha
Russian b. 1945
paintings: (H) $39,600

BRUSSEL, Anneke Van
contemporary
drawings: (H) $7,700

BRUSSET, Jean Paul
French b. 1914
paintings: (H) $1,650

BRUTON, Margaret
American 1894-1983
paintings: (H) $715

BRUTT, Ferdinand
paintings: (L) $209; (H) $1,045

BRUYERE, Elise
c. 1776-1842
paintings: (H) $16,500

BRUYN, Abraham de
paintings: (H) $22,000

BRUYN, Barthel, the elder
1493-1555
paintings: (H) $18,700

BRUYN, Barthel, the elder
German c. 1493-1553/57
paintings: (L) $33,000; (H) $170,500

BRUYN, Cornelis Johannes de
Dutch ac. c. 1763 to c. 1828
paintings: (L) $5,500; (H) $22,000

BRUYN, Jan Cornelis de
paintings: (H) $3,080

BRUYNEEL, V.
sculpture: (H) $6,600

BRUYNESTEYN
paintings: (L) $412; (H) $715

BRUZZI, Stefano
Italian 1835-1911
paintings: (L) $13,200; (H) $66,000

BRYANT, A.M.
Australian 19th/20th cent.
paintings: (H) $935

BRYANT, Everett Lloyd
American 1864-1945
paintings: (L) $220; (H) $12,100
drawings: (H) $4,675

BRYANT, Harold Edward
paintings: (H) $1,100

BRYANT, Henry C.
American 1812-1881
paintings: (H) $1,870

BRYANT, Jack
sculpture: (H) $3,300

BRYANT, Nanna Mathews
American
sculpture: (L) $385; (H) $1,650

BRYCE, Gilbert
British 19th cent.
paintings: (H) $2,200

BRYER, C*** de
17th cent.
paintings: (H) $38,500

BRYERS, Duane
American b. 1911
paintings: (L) $2,530; (H) $9,900
drawings: (H) $83

BRYSON, Hope Mercereau
American 20th cent.
drawings: (H) $4,125

BUBARNIK, A. Gyula
Hungarian 20th cent.
paintings: (H) $2,090

BUCCI, Ermocrate
Italian 19th cent.
paintings: (L) $1,540; (H) $3,190

BUCHANAN, T.
British 19th cent.
paintings: (H) $19,800

BUCHANON, J.
British 19th cent.
paintings: (H) $1,540

BUCHBINDER, Simeon
German 19th cent.
paintings: (H) $7,150

BUCHEL, Charles
American 20th cent.
paintings: (H) $715

BUCHEL, Charles A.
British 19th/20th cent.
paintings: (H) $1,100

BUCHET, Gustave
paintings: (H) $5,750

BUCHHOLTZ, T.T.
Russian b. 1857
paintings: (H) $5,225

BUCHHOLZ, Erich
German b. 1891
paintings: (H) $60,500
drawings: (H) $1,650

BUCHTA, Anthony
American b. 1890
paintings: (L) $275; (H) $825
drawings: (H) $55

BUCK, A.
paintings: (H) $880

BUCK, Carl
American
paintings: (H) $2,420

BUCK, Claude
American b. 1890
paintings: (L) $330; (H) $1,100

BUCK, William H.
Norwegian/American 1840-1888
paintings: (L) $1,100; (H) $33,000

BUCKER
paintings: (H) $1,210

BUCKLER, Charles E.
American b. 1869
paintings: (L) $275; (H) $1,375

BUCKLEY, Charles F.
English 1841-1869
drawings: (L) $154; (H) $2,200

BUCKLEY, John Michael
American 1891-1958
paintings: (L) $605; (H) $1,760

BUCKLEY, Stephen
British b. 1944
sculpture: (H) $6,325

BUCKLIN, Arnold
late 20th cent.
paintings: (H) $880

BUCKLIN, William Savery
American 1851-1928
paintings: (L) $1,210; (H) $1,870
drawings: (L) $110; (H) $1,430

BUCKMASTER, Ernest
Australian 1897-1968
paintings: (H) $3,025

BUCKNER, Richard
paintings: (H) $2,860

BUCKSTONE, Frederick
British 19th cent.
paintings: (H) $1,650

BUDELOT, Philippe
French ac. 1793-1841
paintings: (L) $2,200; (H) $4,950

BUECKL, Heinrich
paintings: (H) $2,200

BUEHR, Karl Albert
German/American b. 1866
paintings: (L) $110; (H) $3,300

BUEL, Franz de
paintings: (H) $1,100

BUEL, Henri de
paintings: (H) $1,650

BUEL, Laurent de
paintings: (H) $1,650

BUELL, Marge Henderson
paintings: (H) $770

BUENGIORNO, D.
paintings: (H) $825

BUENO, Antonio
paintings: (H) $5,500

BUERGERNISS, Carl
American
paintings: (H) $770

BUFANO, Beniamino Benevenuto
American 1898-1970
sculpture: (L) $935; (H) $1,980

BUFF, Conrad
Swiss/American 1886-1975
paintings: (L) $660; (H) $11,000
drawings: (L) $357; (H) $1,100

BUFFET, Amedee
French 1869-1934
paintings: (H) $2,090

BUFFET, Bernard
French b. 1928
paintings: (L) $550; (H) $797,500
drawings: (L) $198; (H) $71,500
sculpture: (H) $1,760

BUFFIN, Carlos
French 19th/20th cent.
paintings: (H) $22,000

BUGATTI, Carlo
drawings: (L) $154; (H) $660

BUGATTI, Rembrandt
Italian 1883/85-1916
sculpture: (L) $8,800; (H) $137,500

BUGGE, Frieda
Danish
paintings: (H) $715

BUGGIANI, Paolo
contemporary
paintings: (L) $110; (H) $1,870

BUGIARDINI, Giulio
Italian 1475-1554
paintings: (H) $99,000

BUGZESTER, Max
contemporary
paintings: (L) $1,045; (H) $1,210

BUHLER, Augustus W.
American 1853-1920
paintings: (L) $1,100; (H) $2,090
drawings: (H) $357

BUHLER, Fritz Zuber
Swiss 1822-1896
paintings: (H) $715

BUHLMANN, Johann Rudolf
Swiss 1802-1890
paintings: (H) $2,750

BUHLMAYER, Conrad
Austrian 1835-1883
paintings: (H) $2,860

BUHLMAYER, F.
German 19th cent.
paintings: (H) $1,100

BUHOT, Louis Charles Hippolyte
mid-19th cent.
paintings: (H) $1,870

BUICIO
contemporary
sculpture: (H) $1,100

BUILD, Augustus Donfred H.
sculpture: (H) $16,500

BUISSERET, Louis
Belgian 20th cent.
paintings: (L) $550; (H) $770

BUKILL, G.
sculpture: (H) $1,210

BULAND, Jean Eugene
French 1852-1927
paintings: (H) $82,500

BULENS, Rene
French late 19th/20th cent.
sculpture: (H) $880

BULL, Charles Livingston
American 1874-1932
paintings: (H) $880
drawings: (L) $275; (H) $2,310

BULLE, Reverend David
American 19th cent.
paintings: (H) $715

BULLEID, George Lawrence
English 1858-1911
drawings: (H) $7,150

BULLER, Audrey
paintings: (H) $935

BULLOCK, Edith
English d. 1911
paintings: (H) $1,045

BUNBURY, H.W.
British 1750-1811
paintings: (H) $4,400

BUNCE, Kate Elizabeth
British 1858-1927
paintings: (H) $23,100

BUNCE, Louis
drawings: (H) $2,090

BUNCE, William Gedney
American 1840-1916
paintings: (L) $358; (H) $1,650
drawings: (H) $330

BUNCH, C.V.
Scandinavian 20th cent.
paintings: (H) $715

BUNDY, E.W.
British 19th cent.
paintings: (H) $1,900

BUNDY, Edgar
English 1862-1922
paintings: (H) $4,400

BUNDY, Horace
American 1814-1883
paintings: (L) $330; (H) $45,100

BUNDY, John Elwood
American 1853-1933
paintings: (L) $1,045; (H) $2,420
drawings: (L) $220; (H) $660

BUNN, George
American 19th/20th cent.
paintings: (L) $418; (H) $6,000

BUNNER, Andrew Fisher
American 1841-1897
paintings: (L) $1,100; (H) $4,950
drawings: (L) $302; (H) $1,210

BUNNETT
Continental School 19th cent.
paintings: (H) $3,410

BUNNEY, John
drawings: (H) $2,090

BUNNIK, Jan van
paintings: (H) $5,500

BUNNY, Rupert Charles Wulsten
Australian 1864-1947
paintings: (L) $10,450; (H) $242,000

BUONACCORSI, Jim
sculpture: (H) $990

BUONACCORSI, Piero, called Perino
del Vaga
Italian 1500/1-1547
drawings: (L) $18,700; (H) $374,000

BUONAMICO, Agostino, called Tassi
Italian 1566-1644
paintings: (H) $4,400

BUONGIORNO, Donatus
Italian/American b. 1865
paintings: (L) $330; (H) $1,210

BUONO, Leon Giuseppe
Italian b. 1888
paintings: (L) $77; (H) $1,650

BUONOROTTE
paintings: (H) $1,540

BURBANK, Addison Buswell
American b. 1895
paintings: (H) $1,045

BURBANK, Elbridge Ayer
American 1858-1949
paintings: (L) $110; (H) $6,600
drawings: (L) $385; (H) $880

BURBIER
American
paintings: (H) $770

BURCH, ***van der
paintings: (H) $9,625

BURCH, Alice
American 1909-1975
paintings: (L) $44; (H) $715

BURCHARD, Pablo
Chilean b. 1876
paintings: (H) $7,150

BURCHFIELD, Charles E.
American 1893-1967
drawings: (L) $137; (H) $143,000

BURCHMAN, Jerrold
contemporary
drawings: (H) $715

BURDICK, Horace Robbins
American 1844-1942
paintings: (L) $39; (H) $1,045
drawings: (L) $33; (H) $1,155

BUREAU, Leon
sculpture: (L) $495; (H) $2,750

BUREAUD, J.
sculpture: (H) $715

BUREN, Daniel
French b. 1938
paintings: (H) $4,400

BURFIELD, James M.
British ac. 1865-1883
paintings: (L) $880; (H) $990

BURGDORFF, Ferdinand
American 1883-1975
paintings: (L) $187; (H) $3,300
drawings: (L) $275; (H) $3,300

BURGER, Anton
German 1824-1905
paintings: (H) $7,700

BURGER, Franz
Tyrolean b. 1857
paintings: (H) $3,850

BURGER, Fritz
German b. 1867
paintings: (H) $660

BURGER, Leopold
Austrian 1861-1903
paintings: (H) $1,980

BURGERS, Hendricus Jacobus
Dutch 1834-1899
paintings: (L) $1,045; (H) $18,700

BURGESS, Adelaide
British ac. 1857-1886
paintings: (H) $880

BURGESS, John Bagnold
English 1830-1897
paintings: (L) $220; (H) $27,500

BURGESS, Ruth Payne
American d. 1934
paintings: (L) $522; (H) $1,430

BURGH, Cornelis Jacobsz. van der
Dutch b. 1640
paintings: (H) $14,300

BURGH, Hendrik van den
Dutch
paintings: (H) $198,000

BURGHARDT
European 19th cent.
paintings: (H) $2,090

BURGHART, C.
American 19th/20th cent.
paintings: (H) $1,320

BURGUM, John
American ac. 1875-1885
paintings: (H) $1,870

BURKE, Patrick
contemporary
paintings: (H) $1,320

BURKEL, Heinrich
German 1802-1869
paintings: (L) $22,000; (H) $49,500

BURKER, W.H.
paintings: (H) $875

BURKHARD, Henri
American b. 1892
paintings: (L) $220; (H) $1,650

BURKHARDT
Russian 19th cent.
paintings: (H) $1,210

BURKHARDT, Emerson C.
American 1905-1969
paintings: (L) $350; (H) $2,200
drawings: (H) $55

BURKHARDT, Hans
American b. 1904
paintings: (L) $1,100; (H) $2,750
drawings: (L) $275; (H) $1,100

BURKHAVEN (?), Van der
European late 19th cent.
paintings: (H) $880

BURLE-MARX, Roberto
Brazilian b. 1909
paintings: (H) $5,500

BURLEIGH, Charles H. H.
British 1875-1956
paintings: (H) $24,200
drawings: (H) $77

BURLEIGH, Sydney R.
American 1853-1931
drawings: (L) $55; (H) $1,650

BURLIK, David
American 20th cent.
paintings: (H) $660

BURLIN, Paul
American 1886-1969
paintings: (L) $935; (H) $1,980
drawings: (H) $495

BURLINGAME, Charles Albert
American 1860-1930
paintings: (L) $55; (H) $2,200

BURLINGAME, Dennis Meighan
paintings: (H) $1,100

BURLINGAME, Sheila Hale
American 1893-1969
sculpture: (L) $275; (H) $26,400

BURLINGAME, Will
American
paintings: (L) $1,500; (H) $2,300

BURLIUK, David
Russian/American 1882-1967
paintings: (L) $55; (H) $275,000
drawings: (L) $110; (H) $1,760

BURMEISTER, Paul
German b. 1847
paintings: (L) $1,320; (H) $3,960

BURN, E.
American 19th/20th cent.
paintings: (H) $2,860

BURNAND, Eugene
paintings: (H) $4,400

BURNE, H.
paintings: (H) $715

BURNE-JONES, Sir Edward Coley
English 1833-1898
drawings: (L) $3,025; (H) $82,500

BURNETT, J. Stuart
sculpture: (H) $4,675

BURNETT, Thomas Stuart
Scottish 1853-1888
sculpture: (H) $2,750

BURNETTE, M. (Mabel?)
American ac. 1920s
paintings: (L) $935; (H) $1,100

BURNHAM, Anita
American b. 1880
paintings: (H) $2,860

BURNHAM, T.M.
British 19th cent.
paintings: (H) $950

BURNHAM, Thomas Mickell
American 1818-1866
paintings: (L) $950; (H) $27,500

BURNITZ, Karl Peter
German 1824-1886
paintings: (H) $4,950

BURNS
American 19th cent.
paintings: (H) $3,575

BURNS, J.
American 19th cent.
paintings: (H) $4,400

BURNS, Mark
American b. 1950
sculpture: (H) $1,650

BURNS, Maurice K.
American 20th cent.
paintings: (L) $302; (H) $2,640

BURNS, Milton Jewett
American 1853-1933
paintings: (L) $990; (H) $5,280

BURNS(?), J.
American
paintings: (H) $880

BURNS-WILSON, Robert
American 1851-1916
drawings: (H) $990

BURNSIDE, Cameron
American 1887-1952
paintings: (H) $550
drawings: (H) $770

BURPEE, William Partridge
American b. 1846
paintings: (L) $2,750; (H) $23,100
drawings: (L) $220; (H) $990

BURR, Alexander Hohenlohe
British 1837-1899
paintings: (L) $825; (H) $4,950

BURR, George Brainerd
American 1876-1950
paintings: (L) $385; (H) $5,500

BURR, George Elbert
American 1859-1939
paintings: (H) $6,050
drawings: (L) $330; (H)$935

BURR, John
Scottish/English 1831/36-1893/94
paintings: (L) $550; (H) $2,750

BURRAGE, Mildred
American 1890-1983
paintings: (H) $1,018

BURRAS, Thomas, Of Leeds
British 19th cent.
paintings: (H) $13,200

BURREDGE, Betsey
American School 19th cent.
drawings: (H) $1,430

BURRELL, James
paintings: (H) $4,180

BURRI, Alberto
Italian b. 1915
drawings: (H) $24,200
sculpture: (L) $55,000; (H) $473,000

BURRIDGE, Walter Wilcox
American
paintings: (H) $1,100

BURRILL, Edward
American b. 1835
paintings: (L) $55; (H) $1,760

BURRINGTON, Arthur Alfred
British 1856-1925
paintings: (H) $7,700

BURRINI, Giovanni Antonio
drawings: (L) $3,300; (H) $6,875

BURRISS, Riley Hal
b. 1892
drawings: (L) $605; (H) $880

BURROUGHS, A. Leicester
British 19th cent.
paintings: (H) $2,860

BURROUGHS, Bryson
American 1869-1934
paintings: (L) $198; (H) $2,090

BURT, C.S.
American
paintings: (H) $4,180

BURT, Charles Thomas
English 1823-1902
paintings: (L) $1,210; (H) $2,090

BURT, James
American ac. 1835-1849
paintings: (L) $2,860; (H) $4,950

BURTON, Arthur Gibbes
American b. 1883
paintings: (L) $308; (H) $2,090

BURTON, Arthur P.
paintings: (H) $1,210

BURTON, Charles
American ac. 1820-1832
drawings: (H) $35,200

BURTON, Scott
American b. 1939
sculpture: (L) $13,200; (H) $19,800

BURTON, Sir Frederick
British 1816-1900
paintings: (H) $1,100

BURY, Louis de
paintings: (H) $935

BURY, Pol
Belgian b. 1922
sculpture: (L) $770; (H) $29,700

BUSACK, Charles G.
American 19th/20th cent.
paintings: (H) $1,100

BUSCH, Clarence F.
American b. 1887
paintings: (L) $352; (H) $2,090

BUSCH, Hans
American 20th cent.
drawings: (H) $4,290

BUSCH, L.C.
German 20th cent.
sculpture: (H) $1,045

BUSCH, S. van den
Belgian 19th/20th cent.
drawings: (H) $1,650

BUSCHER, Franz
American 19th cent.
paintings: (H) $3,300

BUSCIOLANO, Vincenzo
Italian b. 1851
paintings: (H) $880

BUSH, Harry
English 1883-1957
paintings: (L) $440; (H) $7,425

BUSH, Jack
Canadian 1903/09-1977
paintings: (L) $15,400; (H) $66,000

BUSH, Norton
American 1834-1894
paintings: (L) $1,100; (H) $18,700

BUSH-BROWN, Margaret Lesley
American
paintings: (H) $770

BUSIRI, Giovanni Battista
Italian c. 1698-1757
drawings: (H) $825

BUSON, D.
European 19th cent.
paintings: (H) $1,100

BUSON, Peter Nikolaus
German 1783-1830
paintings: (H) $1,430

BUSQUETS, Jean
French 20th cent.
paintings: (L) $467; (H) $935

BUSSE, Jacque
French b. 1922
paintings: (H) $880

BUSSEY, Reuben
British 1818-1893
paintings: (H) $770

BUSSIERE, Ernest
sculpture: (H) $2,640

BUSSIERE, Gaston
French 1862-1929
paintings: (H) $8,800

BUSSON
paintings: (H) $1,650

BUSSON, Charles
French 1822-1908
paintings: (H) $4,400

BUSSON, Georges Louis Charles
French 1859-1933
paintings: (L) $1,870; (H) $5,775
drawings: (L) $2,750; (H) $3,575

BUSSON DU MAURIER, Georges
Louis Palmella
French 1834-1896
drawings: (H) $880

BUTHAUD, Rene
French b. 1886
paintings: (L) $4,400; (H) $22,000
drawings: (L) $4,400; (H) $10,450

BUTIN, Ulysee Louis Auguste
French 1837-1883
paintings: (L) $440; (H) $1,760

BUTLER
19th cent.
paintings: (H) $1,320

BUTLER, A. La Verne
19th cent.
paintings: (H) $1,320

BUTLER, Charles E.
British 1864-1918
paintings: (L) $220; (H) $4,950

BUTLER, Courtland
b. 1871
paintings: (H) $1,210

BUTLER, Fray Guillermo
Argentinian 1880-1961
paintings: (H) $3,025

BUTLER, Georges
Swiss 19th/20th cent.
paintings: (H) $1,430

BUTLER, Herbert E.
British 19th cent.
paintings: (H) $1,100

BUTLER, Howard Russell
American 1856-1934
paintings: (L) $110; (H) $7,150
drawings: (L) $357; (H) $550

BUTLER, James
American b. 1925
paintings: (L) $495; (H) $1,210

BUTLER, Lady Elizabeth Southerden
English 19th cent.
paintings: (H) $1,100

BUTLER, Mary
American 1865-1946
paintings: (L) $55; (H) $1,540
drawings: (L) $28; (H) $165

BUTLER, Reg
English b. 1913
paintings: (L) $4,400; (H) $115,500
drawings: (H) $352
sculpture: (H) $11,550

BUTLER, Rozel Oertle
American 20th cent.
paintings: (L) $2,200; (H) $6,600

BUTLER, Theodore Earl
American 1876-1937
paintings: (L) $4,950; (H) $60,500
drawings: (L) $357; (H) $2,420

BUTLER, Thomas
British ac. 1750-1759
paintings: (L) $5,280; (H) $143,000

BUTMAN, Frederick A.
American 1820-1871
paintings: (L) $385; (H) $5,500

BUTNER, Hans
German 19th cent.
paintings: (H) $3,850

BUTTER, Tom
American b. 1952
sculpture: (L) $3,300; (H) $8,250

BUTTERFIELD, Charles
paintings: (H) $825

BUTTERFIELD, Deborah
American b. 1949
sculpture: (L) $8,250; (H) $50,600

BUTTERI, Giovanni Maria
Florentine c. 1540-1606
paintings: (H) $20,900
drawings: (H) $15,400

BUTTERSWORTH, James E.
American 1817-1894
paintings: (L) $5,500; (H) $242,000

BUTTERSWORTH, Thomas
English ac. 1797-1830
paintings: (L) $1,320; (H) $48,400
drawings: (H) $412

BUTTI, E.
sculpture: (H) $715

BUTTNER, Hans
German b. c. 1850
paintings: (L) $660; (H) $12,100

BUTTON, Albert Prentice
American b. 1872
paintings: (L) $88; (H) $1,870
drawings: (L) $99; (H) $605

BUTTON, John
American b. 1929
paintings: (H) $660
drawings: (L) $330; (H) $825

BUTZKE, B.
sculpture: (L) $1,100; (H) $1,100

BUXTON, Robert Hugh
English b. 1871
drawings: (H) $3,740

BUYKO, Anton
drawings: (L) $440; (H) $880

BUZIO, Lidya
contemporary
sculpture: (H) $3,740

BUZZELLI, Joseph Anthony
American b. 1907
sculpture: (H) $660

BUZZI, A.
Italian 20th cent.
drawings: (H) $1,155

BUZZI, Federigo
paintings: (H) $1,870

BYARS, James Lee
sculpture: (H) $9,350

BYKLE
American 20th cent.
paintings: (H) $880

BYLANDT, Alfred van
Belgian 1829-1890
paintings: (L) $1,100; (H) $1,980

BYLANT, A. de
British ac. 1853-1874
paintings: (L) $2,420; (H) $3,575

BYLERT, Jan van
Dutch 1603-1671
paintings: (L) $3,080; (H) $11,000

BYLERT, Jan van and Bernardus
ZWAERDERCROON
Dutch 17th cent.
paintings: (H) $17,600

BYLES, William Hounson
English b. 1872
paintings: (L) $880; (H) $2,200

BYMAN, T.
paintings: (H) $1,700

BYNG, Robert
paintings: (H) $1,980

BYRD, Henry
ac. 1866-1884
paintings: (H) $2,090

BYRNE, Francis Barry and Walter
Burley GRIFFIN
drawings: (H) $1,650

CABAILLOT, Louis Simon, called
LASALLE
French b. 1810
paintings: (L) $2,750; (H) $7,700

CABAILLOT-LASSALLE, Camille
French b. 1839
paintings: (H) $3,300

CABALLERO, Luis
Columbian b. 1943
paintings: (H) $2,200
drawings: (L) $2,090; (H) $13,200

CABALLERO, Maximo
Spanish 19th/20th cent.
paintings: (L) $8,250; (H) $30,800

CABANEL, Alexandre
French 1823-1889
paintings: (L) $7,150; (H) $38,500
drawings: (H) $2,200

CABANYES, Alejandro de
Spanish b. 1877
paintings: (H) $2,750

CABEL, Adriaen van der
1631-1705
paintings: (H) $18,700

CABELLERO, Luis
drawings: (H) $4,400

CABIE, Louis Alexandre
French 1853-1939
paintings: (L) $1,760; (H) $5,500

CABOT, Edward Clarke
American 1818-1901
drawings: (L) $165; (H) $990

CABRAL, R.
American 20th cent.
paintings: (H) $850

CABRERA, Miguel
Mexican 1695-1768
paintings: (H) $8,800

CABRERA, Ricardo Lopez
Spanish 1864-1950
paintings: (H) $9,900

CABUZEL, Auguste Hector
paintings: (H) $9,350

CACCIA, Guglielmo, Il Moncalvo
Italian 1568-1625
paintings: (H) $2,200
drawings: (L) $1,980; (H) $7,150

CACCIAPOUTI, G.
sculpture: (H) $880

CACCIARELLI, Victor
drawings: (L) $770; (H) $1,320

CACCIARELLI, Victor
Italian 19th cent.
paintings: (H) $2,420
drawings: (L) $660; (H) $825

CACCIERELLI, Umberto
Italian 19th cent.
paintings: (H) $3,080

CACHOIS, Eugene Henri
paintings: (H) $1,870

CACHOUD, Felix
paintings: (H) $990

CACHOUD, François Charles
French 1866-1943
paintings: (L) $660; (H) $13,200
drawings: (L) $412; (H) $550

CADENASSO, Giuseppe
Italian/American 1858-1918
paintings: (L) $715; (H) $18,700
drawings: (L) $330; (H) $2,090

CADES, Giuseppe
Italian 1750-1799
drawings: (H) $2,530

CADMUS, Paul
American b. 1904
paintings: (L) $7,700; (H) $154,000
drawings: (L) $550; (H) $9,900

CADORET, Michel
drawings: (H) $1,430

CADORIN, Guido
Italian b. 1892
paintings: (H) $5,775

CADY, Harrison
American 1877-1970
paintings: (L) $660; (H) $6,325
drawings: (L) $137; (H) $3,740

CADY, Henry
American b. 1849
paintings: (L) $385; (H) $4,620
drawings: (L) $247; (H) $605

CAESAR, Doris
American 1892-1971
sculpture: (L) $247; (H) $3,300

CAETANI, Lelia
paintings: (H) $1,100

CAFE, Thomas Watt
English 1856-1925
paintings: (H) $1,430

CAFFE, Nino
Italian 1909-after 1967
paintings: (L) $715; (H) $12,100

CAFFERTY, James H.
American 1819-1869
paintings: (H) $4,400
drawings: (H) $385

CAFFI, L.
Italian 19th cent.
paintings: (H) $715

CAFFI, Margherita
Italian ac. 1660-1700
paintings: (H) $24,200

CAFFIERI, Hector
British 1847-1932
paintings: (H) $6,600
drawings: (L) $770; (H) $12,100

CAFFYN, Walter Wallor
English ac. 1876-1898; d. 1898
paintings: (L) $522; (H) $4,950

CAGHLIN, J.
paintings: (H) $1,870

CAGLI, Corrado
Italian b. 1910
paintings: (L) $1,760; (H) $3,850

CAGLIANI, Luigi
Italian 20th cent.
paintings: (L) $93; (H) $495
drawings: (L) $176; (H) $770

CAGNACCI, Guido
Italian 1601-1681
paintings: (L) $55,000; (H) $236,500

CAGNIART, Emile
French 1851-1911
paintings: (H) $7,700

CAGNIERE, Julien
paintings: (H) $825

CAHARI, Carlo
paintings: (H) $715

CAHEN-MICHEL, Lucien
French b. 1888
paintings: (H) $115
drawings: (H) $880

CAHLN, R.H.
American 19th cent.
paintings: (H) $1,320

CAHOON, Charles D.
American 1861-1951
paintings: (L) $522; (H) $30,800

CAHOON, Martha
American b. 1905
paintings: (L) $300; (H) $4,500
drawings: (L) $220; (H) $650

CAHOON, Ralph
American 1910-1982
paintings: (L) $1,925; (H) $18,250

CAHOON, Ralph, and Barbara
SPARRE
American
paintings: (H) $19,000

CAILLAUX, Rodolphe
paintings: (H) $1,210

CAILLE, Leon
French 1836-1907
paintings: (L) $357; (H) $4,950

CAILLEBOTTE, Gustave
French 1848-1894
paintings: (L) $41,250; (H) $715,000
drawings: (H) $577,500

CAIN, Auguste Nicolas
French 1822-1894
sculpture: (L) $302; (H) $7,700

CAIN, Georges Jules Auguste
French 1856-1919
paintings: (L) $1,320; (H) $4,950

CAIRA, D**
French 19th cent.
paintings: (H) $2,090

CAIRE, E. Barbot
Continental School 19th cent.
paintings: (H) $1,650

CAIRO, Francesco del, called Il
Cavaliere del CAIRO
Italian 1598-1674
paintings: (H) $19,800

CAISNE, Henri de
Flemish 1799-1852
paintings: (H) $4,400

CALABRIA, Ennio
paintings: (H) $1,320

CALAME, Alexandre
Swiss 1810-1864
paintings: (H) $4,950

CALBET, Antoine
French 1860-1944
paintings: (H) $550
drawings: (H) $715

CALCAGNO, Lawrence
American b. 1916
paintings: (L) $412; (H) $550
drawings: (H) $1,870

CALCAR, Jan Stephan von
paintings: (H) $6,050

CALDECOTT, Randolph
English 1846-1886
drawings: (H) $137,500

CALDER, Alexander
American 1898-1976
paintings: (L) $1,980; (H) $55,000
drawings: (L) $550; (H) $55,000
sculpture: (L) $880; (H) $2,090,000

CALDER, Alexander Stirling
American 1870-1945
sculpture: (L) $825; (H) $8,800

CALDERON, Charles Clement
French 19th/20th cent.
paintings: (L) $990; (H) $4,840

CALDERON, Philip Hermogenes
French 1833-1898
paintings: (L) $495; (H) $11,000

CALDWELL, Atha Haydock
American 19th/20th cent.
paintings: (H) $1,210

CALFYN, W. W.
British 19th cent.
paintings: (H) $3,025

CALGI, Corrado
drawings: (H) $880

CALIARI, Carletto
Italian 1570-1596
drawings: (H) $3,410

CALIARI, Gabrielli
paintings: (H) $4,400

CALIFANO, John
Italian/American 1864-1924
paintings: (L) $77; (H) $36,300

CALIGA, Isaac Henry
American b. 1857
paintings: (L) $1,100; (H) $1,760
drawings: (H) $220

CALISCH, Moritz
Dutch 1819-1870
paintings: (H) $715

CALISSENDORF, A.
German 19th cent.
paintings: (H) $1,430

CALLCOTT, Sir Augustus Wall
English 1779-1844
paintings: (L) $352; (H) $4,620
drawings: (H) $275

CALLE, Paul
American b. 1928
paintings: (L) $23,100; (H) $55,000
drawings: (H) $4,510

CALLET, Antoine Francois
French 1741-1823
paintings: (H) $16,500

CALLON, John K.
American 19th cent.
paintings: (H) $2,800

CALLOT, Jacques
French 1592-1635
drawings: (L) $20,900; (H) $341,000

CALLOW, George D.
English exhib. 1858-1873
paintings: (L) $660; (H) $880

CALLOW, John
English 1822-1878
paintings: (L) $935; (H) $2,100

CALLOW, William
English 1812-1908
paintings: (L) $825; (H) $3,520
drawings: (H) $3,520

CALMETTES, Pierre
French b. 1874
paintings: (H) $1,100

CALOGERO, Jean
Italian b. 1922
paintings: (L) $176; (H) $880

CALOGIRO
Continental 20th cent.
paintings: (H) $935

CALOSCI, Arturo
Italian 1854/55-1926
paintings: (L) $1,430; (H) $1,650

CALRAET, Abraham van
1642-1722
paintings: (L) $11,000; (H) $22,000

CALS, Adolphe Felix
French 1810-1880
paintings: (H) $1,800

CALVAERT, Dionys
1540-1619
drawings: (H) $10,450

CALVERLEY, Charles
American
sculpture: (L) $770; (H) $1,320

CALVERT, Elizabeth
American 20th cent.
paintings: (H) $880

CALVERT, Frederick
English 19th cent.
paintings: (L) $715; (H) $2,090

CALVERT, Henry
English ac. 1826-1854
paintings: (L) $1,100; (H) $38,500

CALVERT, Louis
paintings: (H) $990

CALVERT, Sam
English ac. 1882-1885
paintings: (L) $440; (H) $825

CALVES, Leon Georges
French b. 1848
paintings: (L) $1,320; (H) $1,760

CALVET, Henri Bernard
paintings: (L) $1,320; (H) $1,650

CALVI, Ercole
Italian 1824-1900
paintings: (H) $7,150

CALVI, Jacopo Alessandro
1740-1815
drawings: (H) $770

CALYO, Nicolino
Italian/American 1799-1884
paintings: (H) $3,520
drawings: (H) $225

CALZADA, Humberto
Cuban b. 1944
paintings: (L) $3,300; (H) $6,600

CALZADA MASTER
paintings: (H) $14,300

CAMACHO, Jorge
b. Cuba 1934
paintings: (L) $2,475; (H) $6,050

CAMACHO Y ARROYO, Augustin
paintings: (H) $2,420

CAMARASA, Herman Anglada
contemporary
paintings: (H) $19,800

CAMARGO, Sergio de
Brazilian b. 1930
paintings: (H) $6,600

CAMARRECO, J.L.
Continental 19th/20th cent.
paintings: (H) $1,320

CAMBIASO, Luca
Italian 1527-1585
paintings: (H) $18,700
drawings: (L) $880; (H) $12,100

CAMBIER, Guy
French 20th cent.
paintings: (L) $77; (H) $2,860

CAMBOS, Jean Jules
French 1828-1917
sculpture: (L) $880; (H) $3,575

CAMERON, David Young
British 1865-1945
paintings: (H) $825

CAMERON, Edgar Spier
American 1862-1944
paintings: (L) $385; (H) $3,300

CAMERON, G.L.
South American
paintings: (H) $2,035

CAMERON, Hugh
British 1835-1918
paintings: (L) $1,210; (H) $16,500

CAMERON, Marie Gelon
French 19th cent.
paintings: (H) $990

CAMERON, Sir David Young
Scottish 1865-1945
paintings: (H) $1,430

CAMERON, William Ross
American 1893-1971
paintings: (H) $990

CAMILLE, Carl
paintings: (H) $715

CAMILLIERI, Nicolas
Malta 19th cent.
drawings: (H) $1,155

CAMMANARO, M.
paintings: (H) $825

CAMMILLIERI, Nicolas S.
drawings: (H) $2,640

CAMOIN, Charles
French 1879-1965
paintings: (L) $550; (H) $71,500
drawings: (H) $5,500

CAMP, Jeffery
American 20th cent.
paintings: (H) $825

CAMPAGNE
sculpture: (H) $2,860

CAMPAGNOLA, Domenico
drawings: (H) $660

CAMPAIOLA
Italian late 19th/early 20th cent
sculpture: (H) $990

CAMPBELL
American 19th cent.
paintings: (H) $6,050

CAMPBELL, Blendon
American b. 1872
paintings: (L) $99; (H) $1,100

CAMPBELL, Byram C.
American ac. 1930's
paintings: (H) $2,090

CAMPBELL, C.
paintings: (H) $900

CAMPBELL, Charles
American b. 1905
paintings: (L) $220; (H) $660

CAMPBELL, David
drawings: (H) $1,100

CAMPBELL, Francis Soule and Amos
SEWELL
American
drawings: (H) $1,320

CAMPBELL, George F.
paintings: (H) $1,100

CAMPBELL, Isabella F.
American 1874-1968
paintings: (H) $1,100

CAMPBELL, Laurence A.
American 20th cent.
paintings: (L) $1,375; (H) $1,705

CAMPBELL, Lydia Douglas
drawings: (H) $770

CAMPBELL, R.
American 20th cent.
paintings: (H) $1,100

CAMPBELL, Steven
British b. 1946
paintings: (L) $9,350; (H) $22,000
drawings: (H) $3,850

CAMPBELL-PHILLIPS, John
American b. 1873
paintings: (H) $6,325

CAMPENDONK, Heinrich
German 1889-1957
drawings: (L) $1,980; (H) $82,500

CAMPES, Charles
French 19th cent.
paintings: (H) $2,420

CAMPHUYSEN, Govert Dircksz
Dutch 1623-1672
paintings: (L) $880; (H) $1,650

CAMPHUYSEN, Joachim
paintings: (H) $1,100

CAMPHUYSEN, Raphael Govertsz
Dutch 1597/98-1657
paintings: (H) $8,250

CAMPIGLI, Massimo
Italian 1895-1971
paintings: (L) $11,000; (H) $253,000
drawings: (L) $1,980; (H) $19,800

CAMPO, Federico del
Peruvian ac. 1880
paintings: (L) $34,100; (H) $198,000
drawings: (H) $2,420

CAMPOLIMI, S.
Italian 19th c.
paintings: (H) $28,600

CAMPOS, F. Molinas
Argentinian b. 1937
paintings: (L) $2,310; (H) $10,450
drawings: (L) $715; (H) $1,760

CAMPOTOSTO, Henry
Belgian d. 1910
paintings: (L) $1,650; (H) $6,050

CAMPOTOSTO, Octavio
paintings: (L) $1,045; (H) $1,210

CAMPRIANI, Alceste
Italian 1848-1933
paintings: (H) $20,900
drawings: (H) $2,420

CAMPUZANO Y AGUIRRE, Tomas
Spanish b. 1857
paintings: (H) $3,850

CAMRADT, Johannes Ludvig
Danish 1779-1849
paintings: (H) $23,100

CAMUS, Blanche Augustine
French 19th/20th cent.
paintings: (L) $1,430; (H) $16,500

CAMUS, Jean Marie
sculpture: (H) $825

CANAL, Gilbert von
Austrian b. 1849
paintings: (H) $1,650

CANALETTO, Antonio Canal
Italian 1697-1768
paintings: (L) $26,400; (H) $11,000,000
drawings: (L) $16,500; (H) $715,000

CANALETTO, Giovanni Antonio
Canale, studio of
Italian 1697-1768
paintings: (H) $55,000

CANAS, Benjamin
Brazilian b. 1933
paintings: (H) $8,800

CANAVERAL Y PEREZ, Enrique
Spanish 19th cent.
paintings: (H) $7,700

CANCIO, Carlos
Puerto Rican b. 1961
paintings: (H) $6,600

CANDIA, Domingo
paintings: (L) $9,900; (H) $10,450

CANDIDO, Sal
Italian 19th cent.
paintings: (H) $46,750

CANEDALLE, R.
American
paintings: (H) $1,100

CANELLA, Antonio
Italian 19th cent.
drawings: (L) $137; (H) $770

CANELLA, Giuseppe
Italian 1788-1847
paintings: (L) $143; (H) $14,850

CANEVARI, Carlo
Italian 20th cent.
paintings: (L) $137; (H) $1,650

CANFIELD
paintings: (H) $1,210

CANIFF, Milton
American b. 1907
paintings: (H) $110
drawings: (L) $275; (H) $2,750

CANINI, Giovanni Angelo
Italian 1617-1666
drawings: (H) $6,050

CANJURA, Noe
contemporary
paintings: (L) $385; (H) $1,650

CANLI (?), Rot A.
sculpture: (H) $2,750

CANNELLA, Pizzi
contemporary
paintings: (L) $5,500; (H) $19,800

CANNICCI, Nicolo
Italian 1846-1906
paintings: (H) $45,100

CANOVA, Antonio
sculpture: (L) $1,100; (H) $2,475

CANOW, Carl
German 1814-1880
paintings: (L) $99; (H) $715

CANT, J.Y.
British 19th cent.
paintings: (H) $1,540

CANTARINI, Simone, called Simone
da Pesaro IL PESARESE
Italian 1612-1648
paintings: (H) $17,600
drawings: (L) $880; (H) $4,950

CANTATORE, Domenico
paintings: (L) $1,200; (H) $2,250

CANTU, Federico
Mexican b. 1908
paintings: (H) $2,420
drawings: (L) $330; (H) $528

CANU, Yvonne
French b. 1921
paintings: (L) $825; (H) $11,000

CANUTI, Domenico Maria
Italian 1620-1684
drawings: (H) $2,200

CAPALTI, Alessandro
paintings: (H) $2,640

CAPARN, Rhys
sculpture: (H) $1,210

CAPEINICK, Jean
Belgian 1838-1890
paintings: (H) $9,900

CAPELLE, Jan van de
Dutch c. 1624-1679
paintings: (H) $990,000

CAPEN, Nathaniel
American 1841
paintings: (H) $6,325

CAPOBIANCHI, Vittorio
Italian ac. 1870-1880
paintings: (H) $4,675

CAPOGROSSI, Giuseppe
Italian b. 1900
paintings: (H) $19,250

CAPON, George Emile
contemporary
paintings: (H) $4,180

CAPONE, Gaetano
Italian 1845-1920/24
paintings: (L) $82; (H) $13,200

CAPPELLI, Pietro
Italian d. 1724
paintings: (H) $4,400

CAPPIELLO, Leonetto
French 1875-1942
paintings: (H) $2,750

CAPPIELLO, Suzanne
French 20th cent.
paintings: (L) $2,475; (H) $2,860

CAPPONI, Raffaelo, called Raffaelo del
Garbo
Italian 1466/76-1524
paintings: (H) $17,600

CAPRILE, Vincenzo
Italian 1856-1936
paintings: (H) $3,850
drawings: (H) $330

CAPRINOZZI, Marco
drawings: (H) $2,200

CAPRITE, V.
paintings: (H) $660

CAPRON, Jean Pierre
French b. 1921
paintings: (L) $357; (H) $1,650

CAPULETTI
Italian 20th cent.
paintings: (H) $2,750

CAPUTO, Ulisse
Italian 1872-1948
paintings: (L) $1,100; (H) $22,000

CARA, Henry
Australian/English 19th cent.
paintings: (H) $770

CARABAIN, Jacques Francois
Belgian 1834-1892
paintings: (L) $1,540; (H) $30,800

CARABAIN, Victor
Belgian 19th/20th cent.
paintings: (H) $2,200

CARABIN, Rupert
sculpture: (H) $9,900

CARACCI, Annibale
paintings: (H) $935

CARACCIOLO, Giovanni Battista,
called Battistello
Italian c. 1570-1637
paintings: (L) $5,775; (H) $121,000

CARADOSSI, Vittorio
Italian ac. 1910
sculpture: (H) $61,600

CARANGA, Achille E. Conrad de
French 1829-1889 ·
paintings: (H) $5,940

CARAUD, Joseph
French 1821-1905
paintings: (L) $4,510; (H) $17,600
drawings: (H) $880

CARBEE, Scott Clifton
American 1860-1946
paintings: (L) $412; (H) $10,450

CARBINO, Jon
paintings: (H) $825

CARBONELL, Rafael
paintings: (H) $2,200

CARBOULD, Alfred
paintings: (H) $1,500

CARDENAS, Agustin
Cuban b. 1927
sculpture: (L) $5,500; (H) $44,000

CARDENAS, Juan
paintings: (H) $18,700

CARDENAS, M.T.
paintings: (H) $3,850

CARDENAS, Santiago
Colombian b. 1937
paintings: (L) $5,170; (H) $10,450
drawings: (H) $1,100

CARDI, Lorenzo
paintings: (H) $4,950

CARDI, Ludovico, called Il CIGOLI
Italian 1559-1613
paintings: (L) $28,600; (H) $132,000

CARDON, Claude
English 19th cent.
drawings: (H) $1,100

CARDONA, Juan
Spanish 19th/20th cent.
paintings: (H) $19,800

CARDOSSI, Vittorio
Italian late 19th/20th cent.
sculpture: (H) $99,000

CARDUCCI, Adolfo
Italian b. 1901
paintings: (L) $1,100; (H) $1,540

CARDUCHO, Vincente
Italian 1576/78-1638
paintings: (H) $20,900

CARDWELL, Holme
sculpture: (H) $5,500

CARELLI, Consalve
Italian 1818-1900
paintings: (L) $1,100; (H) $93,500
drawings: (L) $523; (H) $605

CARELLI, Gabriel
Italian/English 1821-1900
drawings: (L) $220; (H) $1,650

CARELLI, Giuseppe
Italian 1858-1921
paintings: (L) $308; (H) $6,600

CARENA, Felice
Italian b. 1879/80
paintings: (H) $6,050

CARESME, Philippe
drawings: (H) $3,300

CAREY, Ted
paintings: (H) $2,420

CARGNEL, Vittore Antonio
Italian 1872-1931
paintings: (H) $770

CARIANI, Giovanni de Busi
1485/90-after 1547
paintings: (H) $154,000

CARILLO, Lilia
Mexican b. 1930
paintings: (L) $3,850; (H) $5,225

CARINI
American
paintings: (H) $4,950

CARL, Ewan B.
American 19th cent.
paintings: (H) $660

CARLANDI, Onorato
Italian 1848-1939
drawings: (L) $110; (H) $2,420

CARLEBUR, Francois
paintings: (H) $4,620

CARLES, Arthur B.
American 1880/82-1952
paintings: (L) $1,980; (H) $44,000
drawings: (L) $110; (H) $1,980

CARLES, Jean Antonin
French 1851-1919
sculpture: (L) $462; (H) $3,575

CARLETON, Anne
American 1878-1968
paintings: (L) $825; (H) $1,650

CARLETTI, Alicia
Argentinian b. 1946
drawings: (H) $2,200

CARLEVARIS, Luca
Italian 1665-1731
paintings: (L) $93,500; (H) $143,000

CARLIER, Emile Joseph
French 1849-1927
sculpture: (L) $242; (H) $1,870

CARLIER, Modeste
Belgian 1820-1878
paintings: (L) $2,640; (H) $19,800

CARLIN, Andrew B.
American 1816-after 1871
paintings: (H) $8,800

CARLIN, James
paintings: (H) $660
drawings: (H) $825

CARLIN, James
American
drawings: (H) $770

CARLIN, John
American 1813-1891
paintings: (L) $495; (H) $4,950

CARLINE, George F.
English 1855-1920
paintings: (L) $330; (H) $2,750

CARLONE, Carlo
Italian 1686-1775/76
paintings: (H) $18,700
drawings: (H) $4,180

CARLONE, Giovanni Battista
drawings: (H) $1,100

CARLROSA, Mario Cornilleau Raoul
French 1855-1913
paintings: (H) $3,410

CARLSEN, Carl
Danish 1853-1917
paintings: (H) $9,900

CARLSEN, Dines
American 1901-1966
paintings: (L) $385; (H) $18,700

CARLSEN, R.
paintings: (H) $1,870

CARLSEN, Soren Emil
Danish/American 1853-1932
paintings: (L) $770; (H) $66,000
drawings: (L) $715; (H) $4,675

CARLSON, F.
American 20th cent.
paintings: (L) $440; (H) $990

CARLSON, John Fabian
Swedish/American 1875-1945
paintings: (L) $357; (H) $41,800
drawings: (L) $1,045; (H) $7,150

CARLSON, John Frederick
American
paintings: (H) $1,650

CARLSON, John P.
paintings: (H) $1,320

CARLSON, Ken
American b. 1907
paintings: (L) $4,500; (H) $5,000
drawings: (L) $412; (H) $770

CARLSON, William
American b. 1950
sculpture: (L) $3,080; (H) $4,400

CARLTON, Fred
English 19th cent.
paintings: (L) $660; (H) $880

CARLTON, Helen
drawings: (H) $4,125

CARMICHAEL, Franklin
Canadian 1890-1945
paintings: (H) $30,800

CARMICHAEL, James Wilson
British 1800-1868
paintings: (L) $522; (H) $14,850

CARMIENCKE, Johann Hermann
German/American 1810-1867
paintings: (L) $357; (H) $14,300

CARMIGNANI, Guido
Italian 1838-1909
paintings: (H) $4,950

CARNEO, Antonio
paintings: (L) $9,900; (H) $16,500

CARNEVALI, Nino
Italian b. 1849
paintings: (H) $660

CARNEVARI, Carlo
paintings: (H) $1,650

CARNICERO, Antonio
Spanish 1748-1814
paintings: (H) $57,750

CARNIER, H.
French 19th/20th cent.
paintings: (L) $176; (H) $990

CARO, Anthony
English b. 1924
sculpture: (L) $4,400; (H) $85,250

CARO, Lorenzo de
paintings: (H) $5,500

CARO-DELVAILLE, Henry
French 1876-1926
paintings: (L) $110; (H) $13,200

CAROLSFELD, Julius Schnorr von
German 1794-1872
drawings: (L) $715; (H) $825

CAROLUS, Jean
Belgian 19th cent.
paintings: (L) $1,430; (H) $18,700

CAROLUS-DURAN, Emile Auguste
French 1837-1917
paintings: (L) $990; (H) $407,000

CARON, Antoine
French 1520/21-1599
paintings: (H) $60,500

CARON, Paul Archibald
paintings: (H) $6,600

CAROSELLI, Angelo
Italian 1585-1653
paintings: (H) $39,600

CAROSELLI, Cesare
Italian b. 1847
paintings: (H) $2,640

CAROT, Jules Etienne
paintings: (H) $4,400

CAROT, L.
Belgian late 19th/early 20th cent
paintings: (H) $1,540

CAROTO, Giovanni Francesco
Italian c. 1480-1555
paintings: (H) $61,600
drawings: (H) $88,000

CARPACCIO, Vittore
Italian c. 1465-1525
drawings: (H) $187,000

CARPEAUX, Jean Baptiste
French 1827-1875
sculpture: (L) $132; (H) $24,200

CARPENTER, A.R.
British exhib. 1868-1890
paintings: (H) $660

CARPENTER, Fred Green
American b. 1882
paintings: (L) $407; (H) $2,970
drawings: (H) $66

CARPENTER, Louise M.
American 1867-1963
paintings: (L) $275; (H) $1,540

CARPENTER, Margaret Sarah
English 1793-1872
paintings: (L) $3,850; (H) $4,950
drawings: (H) $825

CARPENTERO, Henri Joseph
Gommarus
Belgian 1820-1874
paintings: (L) $770; (H) $5,500

CARPENTIER, Evariste
Belgian 1845-1922
paintings: (L) $4,400; (H) $22,000

CARPENTIER, Madeleine
French b. 1865
paintings: (L) $1,980; (H) $5,170

CARPENTIERS, Adriaen
ac. by 1739-1778
paintings: (H) $3,575

CARPI, Girolamo da
1501-1556
drawings: (L) $1,320; (H) $2,200

CARPIONE, Giulio, the elder
Italian 1611-1674
paintings: (H) $28,600

CARPIONI, Giulio
paintings: (H) $9,900

CARR, Lyell
American 1857-1912
paintings: (L) $880; (H) $5,225

CARR, M. Emily
Canadian 1871-1945
paintings: (L) $59,400; (H) $90,750

CARR, Samuel S.
American 1837-1908
paintings: (L) $165; (H) $82,500

CARRA, Carlo
Italian 1881-1966
paintings: (L) $24,200; (H) $385,000

CARRACCI, Agostino
Italian 1557-1602
drawings: (H) $363,000

CARRACCI, Annibale
Italian c. 1560-1609
paintings: (H) $605
drawings: (H) $19,800

CARRACCI, Antonio
Italian 1583-1618
paintings: (H) $13,200

CARRACCI, Lodovico
Italian 1555-1619
paintings: (H) $27,500
drawings: (H) $28,600

CARREE, Michiel
Dutch 1657-1747
paintings: (L) $660; (H) $7,150
drawings: (H) $3,520

CARRENO, Mario
Cuban/American b. 1913
paintings: (L) $1,760; (H) $286,000
drawings: (L) $385; (H) $13,200

CARRENO, Ramon
Colombian b. 1951
sculpture: (H) $8,525

CARRERE, F. Ouiclon
French early 20th cent.
sculpture: (H) $1,320

CARRICK, John Mulcaster
English ac. 1854-1878
paintings: (H) $44,000

CARRICK, Robert
British c. 1829-1904
drawings: (L) $770; (H) $1,210

CARRIER, A.
sculpture: (L) $550; (H) $715

CARRIER-BELLEUSE, Albert Ernest
French 1824-1887
sculpture: (L) $550; (H) $7,700

CARRIER-BELLEUSE, Louis Robert
French 1848-1913
paintings: (L) $7,700; (H) $10,450
sculpture: (H) $3,025

CARRIER-BELLEUSE, Pierre
French 1851-1932/33
paintings: (L) $1,320; (H) $13,200
drawings: (L) $4,125; (H) $44,000

CARRIERE, Eugene
French 1849-1906
paintings: (L) $3,300; (H) $20,900
drawings: (H) $275

CARRILLO, Lilia
paintings: (L) $3,850; (H) $5,280
drawings: (H) $440

CARRINGTON, James Yates
British 1857-1892
paintings: (L) $1,540; (H) $1,900

CARRINGTON, Leonora
English b. 1917
paintings: (L) $9,350; (H) $132,000
drawings: (L) $770; (H) $13,200
sculpture: (L) $4,950; (H) $8,250

CARROGIS, Louis, called Carmontelle
drawings: (L) $1,870; (H) $5,775

CARROLL, John
American 1892-1959
paintings: (L) $275; (H) $2,420
drawings: (H) $121

CARROLL, L.
paintings: (H) $770

CARROLL, Lawrence
contemporary
sculpture: (H) $16,500

CARRUTHERS, Roy
paintings: (L) $715; (H) $1,045

CARSMAN, Jon
contemporary
paintings: (L) $176; (H) $1,430

CARSON, Frank
American b. 1881
paintings: (L) $77; (H) $7,975
drawings: (L) $66; (H) $330

CARSON, W.A.
American 19th/20th cent.
paintings: (L) $21; (H) $1,100

CARSTENS, Julius Victor
paintings: (H) $1,870

CARTER, Clarence Holbrook
American b. 1904
paintings: (L) $3,850; (H) $38,500
drawings: (L) $522; (H) $4,180

CARTER, Clifford
paintings: (H) $1,320

CARTER, Dennis Malone
American 1827-1881
paintings: (L) $220; (H) $4,620

CARTER, E.S.
British 19th cent.
drawings: (H) $715

CARTER, Gary
American b. 1939
paintings: (L) $3,000; (H) $6,600
drawings: (L) $650; (H) $1,200
sculpture: (H) $4,200

CARTER, Hugh
English 1837-1903
drawings: (H) $1,265

CARTER, M.W.P.
paintings: (H) $1,045

CARTER, P.
European 19th cent.
paintings: (H) $1,100

CARTER, Pruett
American 1891-1955
paintings: (L) $385; (H) $2,475

CARTER, R.H.
Continental 20th cent.
drawings: (H) $1,540

CARTER, Raymond
d. 1939
paintings: (H) $1,210

CARTER, Samuel
paintings: (H) $55,000

CARTER, Sydney
British ac. 1894-1936
paintings: (H) $4,000
drawings: (L) $138; (H) $687

CARTER, William Sylvester
American b. 1909
paintings: (H) $1,210
drawings: (L) $440; (H) $825

CARTIER
sculpture: (H) $1,760

CARTIER, Jacques
French 20th cent.
paintings: (L) $247; (H) $4,400

CARTIER, Thomas Francois
French b. 1879
sculpture: (L) $523; (H) $3,300

CARTWRIGHT, Isabel Bronson
American b. 1885
paintings: (L) $352; (H) $8,250

CARTWRIGHT, William P.
British 1855-1915
paintings: (L) $220; (H) $1,100

CARUSO, Bruno
Italian b. 1927
paintings: (L) $143; (H) $1,540

CARUSO, Enrico
Italian 1873-1921
drawings: (H) $247
sculpture: (L) $605; (H) $660

CARVILL, V.F.
French 19th/20th cent.
drawings: (H) $880

CARVILLANI, Renato
sculpture: (H) $2,310

CARVIN, Louis Albert
French
sculpture: (L) $242; (H) $3,080

CARY, William de la Montagne
American 1840-1922
paintings: (L) $3,080; (H) $5,500

CARYBE, Hector Julio Bernabo
drawings: (H) $880

CARZOU
paintings: (H) $2,860

CASANODAY, Arcadio
Spanish 19th cent.
paintings: (H) $7,700

CASANOVA, A.
paintings: (L) $352; (H) $990

CASANOVA, Domingo A.
Continental 19th cent.
paintings: (H) $3,190
drawings: (H) $550

CASANOVA, Francesco
paintings: (L) $4,400; (H) $12,100

CASANOVA Y ESTORACH, Antonio
Spanish d. 1896
paintings: (L) $1,980; (H) $17,600
drawings: (H) $495

CASAS, Ernest
paintings: (H) $1,320

CASAS, G.
paintings: (H) $1,320

CASAS, Ramon
drawings: (L) $660; (H) $1,980

CASCELLA, Michele
Italian b. 1892
paintings: (L) $1,760; (H) $14,300
drawings: (L) $715; (H) $7,700

CASCELLA, Tommaso
Italian 1890-1968
paintings: (H) $4,400

CASCIARO, Giuseppe
Italian 1863-1945
paintings: (L) $1,980; (H) $11,000

CASE, Edmund E.
American 1840-1919
paintings: (L) $300; (H) $2,600

CASE, Richard
paintings: (H) $3,600

CASEMBROT, Abraham
Dutch 17th cent.
paintings: (H) $22,000

CASER, Ettore
Italian/American 1880-1944
paintings: (L) $330; (H) $1,980

CASEY, John Joseph
American 1878-1930
paintings: (H) $3,740

CASEY, Tim
contemporary
paintings: (H) $1,650

CASHWAN, Samuel Adolph
American b. Russia 1900
sculpture: (L) $550; (H) $17,600

CASILE, Alfred
French 1847-1909
paintings: (L) $550; (H) $6,050

CASILEAR, John W.
American 1811-1893
paintings: (L) $550; (H) $39,600
drawings: (H) $5,500

CASNELLI, Victor
American 1865-1961
drawings: (L) $192; (H) $3,300

CASOLANI, Andrea
drawings: (H) $2,860

CASQUE, Le
paintings: (H) $1,870

CASS, George Nelson
American d. 1882
paintings: (L) $242; (H) $2,970

CASSATT, Mary
American 1844-1926
paintings: (L) $18,700; (H) $3,080,000
drawings: (L) $176; (H) $4,510,000

CASSEL, Jno.
American early 20th cent.
paintings: (L) $330; (H) $880

CASSELL, Frank
paintings: (L) $660; (H) $825

CASSELLI, Henry
b. 1946
drawings: (H) $11,000

CASSIDY, Ira Diamond Gerald
American 1879-1934
paintings: (L) $5,500; (H) $19,800
drawings: (L) $1,100; (H) $40,000

CASSIERS, Hendrick
Belgian 1858-1944
paintings: (H) $2,750
drawings: (L) $50; (H) $1,045

CASSIGNEUL, Jean Pierre
French b. 1935
paintings: (H) $770
drawings: (H) $60,500

CASSON, A.J.
Canadian b. 1898
paintings: (L) $5,060; (H) $11,550

CASTADDO
paintings: (H) $880

CASTAGNARY, Marie Amelie
French 19th cent.
paintings: (H) $2,860

CASTAGNOLA, Gabriele
Italian 1828-1883
paintings: (L) $247; (H) $4,400

CASTAIGNE, J. Andre
French 1860-1930
paintings: (L) $770; (H) $24,200

CASTALDO, Amaylia
American b. 1906
paintings: (L) $33; (H) $990

CASTAN, Pierre Jean Edmond
French b. 1817
paintings: (L) $3,080; (H) $19,800

CASTANEDA, Alfredo
Mexican b. 1932
paintings: (L) $3,300; (H) $44,000
drawings: (L) $2,200; (H) $4,400

CASTANEDA, Felipe
Mexican b. 1938
sculpture: (L) $3,300; (H) $15,400

CASTANO, G.
Mexican 20th cent.
paintings: (H) $660

CASTANO, John
1896-1978
paintings: (H) $1,200

CASTEELS, Pieter
Flemish 1684-1749
paintings: (L) $34,100; (H) $85,250

CASTEGNARO, Felice
Italian b. 1872
paintings: (L) $770; (H) $770

CASTEL, Moshe
Israeli b. 1909
paintings: (L) $3,300; (H) $11,000

CASTELLAN, Federico
American b. 1914
paintings: (H) $10,175

CASTELLANI, Enrico
Italian b. 1930
paintings: (H) $19,800

CASTELLANOS, Julio
Mexican 1905-1947
paintings: (H) $3,080
drawings: (H) $2,530

CASTELLI, Bartolomeo, called
SPADINO, JR.
18th cent.
paintings: (H) $55,000

CASTELLI, Giovanni Paolo, called LO
SPADINO
Italian ac. 1687
paintings: (H) $29,700

CASTELLI, Luciano
Italian/Swiss b. 1951
paintings: (L) $1,320; (H) $28,600
drawings: (L) $5,280; (H) $7,700

CASTELLI, Luciano and SALOME
20th cent.
paintings: (H) $17,600

CASTELLO, Bernardo
Italian 1557-1629
drawings: (H) $2,860

CASTELLO, Francesco da
paintings: (H) $8,800

CASTELLO, Giovanni Battista
Italian
drawings: (H) $8,800

CASTELLO, Valerio
Italian 1624-1659
paintings: (L) $159,500; (H) $1,100,000

CASTELLON, Federico
Spanish/American 1914-1971
paintings: (L) $55; (H) $1,430
drawings: (L) $275; (H) $4,620

CASTER, James
American 20th cent.
paintings: (H) $770

CASTEX-DEGRANGE, Adolphe Louis
paintings: (H) $8,800

CASTIGLIONE, Giovanni Benedetto
Italian 1609-1665
paintings: (L) $4,675; (H) $71,500
drawings: (H) $104,500

CASTIGLIONE, Giuseppe
Italian 1829-1908
paintings: (L) $550; (H) $31,900

CASTILLO, Jorge
Spanish b. 1933
paintings: (L) $6,380; (H) $14,300
drawings: (H) $3,300

CASTILLO, Sergio
sculpture: (H) $825

CASTLE, Wendell
American b. 1932
sculpture: (H) $132,000

CASTLE-KEITH, W.
American early 20th cent.
paintings: (L) $550; (H) $935

CASTOLDI, Guglielmo
Italian b. 1852
paintings: (L) $550; (H) $4,400

CASTON, E.J.
19th cent.
paintings: (H) $3,080

CASTRES, E.
paintings: (H) $770

CASTRES, Edouard
Swiss 1838-1902
paintings: (L) $1,320; (H) $22,000

CASTRO, Gabriel Henriquez de
Dutch 1808-1953
drawings: (H) $2,970

CASWELL, H.
American
drawings: (H) $880

CATALA, Luis Alvarez
Spanish 1836-1901
paintings: (L) $1,650; (H) $41,250

CATALAN, Ramos
Chilean 20th cent.
paintings: (L) $120; (H) $660

CATALDI, Amieto
sculpture: (H) $1,980

CATEIGNON, Ernest
French ac. 1887-1910
paintings: (H) $2,200

CATHELIN, Bernard
French b. 1920
paintings: (L) $880; (H) $34,100

CATHERWOOD, Frederick
English 1799-1854
drawings: (H) $2,420

CATLIN, George
American 1796-1872
paintings: (H) $539,000
drawings: (L) $16,500; (H) $71,500

CATOIRE, X.
20th cent.
paintings: (H) $4,125

CATS, Jacob
1741-1799
drawings: (L) $880; (H) $6,050

CATTLE, T.
paintings: (H) $2,860

CATTRANI, Baldassare
paintings: (L) $2,200; (H) $3,300
drawings: (L) $1,045; (H) $1,045

CAUCANNIER, Jean Denis Antoine
French late 19th cent.
paintings: (H) $4,180

CAUCHOIS, Eugene Henri
French 1850-1911
paintings: (L) $440; (H) $20,900

CAUDRELIER, Gerard
paintings: (H) $4,180

CAUHOIS, H.
Dutch 20th cent.
paintings: (H) $1,430

CAULAERT, J.D. van
20th cent.
paintings: (L) $2,090; (H) $4,250

CAULLERY, Louis de
Flemish 16th/17th cent.
paintings: (L) $3,300; (H) $55,000

CAUSEY, J.
sculpture: (H) $1,760

CAUSSE, Julien
French 19th cent.
sculpture: (L) $440; (H) $13,200

CAUSSIN, Marc L.
sculpture: (H) $1,100

CAUVET, Gilles Paul
drawings: (H) $1,100

CAVAILLES, Jean Jules Louis
French 1901-1977
paintings: (L) $550; (H) $6,050

CAVALCANTE, Lito
Brazilian b. 1926
paintings: (H) $2,750

CAVALERI, Lodovico
Italian 1867-1942
paintings: (L) $1,980; (H) $5,775

CAVALIERE, Alik
contemporary
sculpture: (H) $2,860

CAVALLINO, Bernardo
Italian 1616-1656/58
paintings: (H) $1,925,000

CAVALLON, Giorgio
American b. 1904
paintings: (L) $7,150; (H) $99,000

CAVANAUGH, Robert
American
sculpture: (H) $1,150

CAVE, Jules Cyrille
French b. 1859
paintings: (H) $4,400

CAVEDONE, Giacomo
Italian 1577-1660
drawings: (H) $6,600

CAVET(?)
paintings: (H) $2,420

CAVIEDES, Hipolito Hidalgo de
Spanish b. 1902
paintings: (H) $7,150

CAWSE, John
British c. 1779-1862
paintings: (H) $1,650

CAWTHORNE, Neil
British b. 1936
paintings: (L) $330; (H) $18,700

CAYRON, Jules
French 1868-1940
paintings: (L) $3,575; (H) $5,500

CAZAUBON, A.
French 19th/20th cent.
paintings: (H) $2,530

CAZIN, Jean Charles
French 1841-1901
paintings: (L) $357; (H) $33,000
drawings: (H) $165

CEAN
drawings: (H) $1,320

CECCARELLI, Naddo
first half of 14th cent.
paintings: (H) $407,000

CECCHI, Adriano
Italian b. 1850
paintings: (L) $2,200; (H) $15,400

CECCOBELLI, Bruno
Italian b. 1952
paintings: (L) $3,300; (H) $12,100

CECCONI, Lorenzo
Italian 19th/20th cent.
paintings: (H) $4,400

CECIONI, Adriano
Italian 1838-1886
sculpture: (H) $3,300

CECO DEL CARAVAGGIO
Italian ac. 1619
paintings: (H) $71,500

CEDERSTROM, Thurne Nikolaus von
Swedish 1843-1924
paintings: (H) $8,250

CEELY, Lincoln
paintings: (H) $6,160

CEJUDO, J. Rio
paintings: (H) $1,650

CELESTI, Andrea
Italian 1637-1700
paintings: (H) $30,800

CELIS, Perez
Argentinian b. 1939
paintings: (L) $4,180; (H) $13,200

CELMINS, Vija
b. 1939
drawings: (L) $19,800; (H) $23,100

CELOMMI, Pasquale
Italian 1851-1928
paintings: (L) $2,970; (H) $11,000

CELOS, Julien
Belgian 1884-1953
paintings: (H) $1,100

CELOSTIN
paintings: (H) $770

CEMIN, SAINT CLAIR
American b. 1951
sculpture: (L) $2,200; (H) $57,750

CEMIR
19th cent.
sculpture: (H) $990

CENTURION, Emilio
Argentinian 1894-1970
paintings: (H) $2,475

CEPEDA, Ender
Venezuelan b. 1945
paintings: (H) $4,400

CERAMANO, Charles Ferdinand
Belgian 1829-1909
paintings: (L) $550; (H) $5,500

CERARD, T.
paintings: (H) $3,080

CERCONE, Ettore
Italian 1850-1896
paintings: (H) $13,200

CERES
18th cent.
paintings: (H) $2,640

CEREZO
paintings: (H) $1,045

CEREZO, Mateo, the younger
Spanish 1635-1685
paintings: (H) $1,430

CERIA, Edmond
French 1884-1955
paintings: (H) $1,100

CERIEZ, Theodore
paintings: (H) $1,980

CERMANO, Charles Ferdinand
Belgian 1829-1909
paintings: (H) $6,325

CERNY, Charles
20th cent.
paintings: (L) $358; (H) $660

CERQUOZZI, Michelangelo and
Viviano CODOZZI
17th cent.
paintings: (H) $42,900

CERRINI, Giovanni Domenico
Italian 1609-1681
paintings: (H) $44,000

CERUTI, Giacomo
Italian 1698-1767
paintings: (H) $20,900

CERVI, Giulio
Italian 19th cent.
paintings: (L) $1,650; (H) $22,000

CESAR, Cesar BALDACCINI
French b. 1921
drawings: (H) $3,300
sculpture: (L) $594; (H) $82,500

CESARI, Giuseppe, Cavalier d'Arpino
Italian 1560/68-1640
drawings: (L) $4,950; (H) $44,000

CESTARO, Jacopo
Italian 18th cent.
paintings: (H) $13,200

CEULEN, Cornelis Janssens van
Dutch 1593-1664
paintings: (L) $3,300; (H) $143,000

CEZANNE, Paul
French 1839-1906
paintings: (L) $41,800; (H) $11,550,000
drawings: (L) $6,875; (H) $858,000

CHAB, Victor
b. Argentina 1930
paintings: (L) $2,090; (H) $17,600

CHABANIAN, Arsene
Armenian 1864-1899
paintings: (H) $275
drawings: (L) $357; (H) $935

CHABAS, Maurice
French 1862-1947
paintings: (L) $2,750; (H) $14,300

CHABAS, Paul Emile
French 1869-1934/37
paintings: (L) $467; (H) $13,200

CHABAUD, Auguste Elisee
French 1882-1955
paintings: (L) $2,090; (H) $3,300
drawings: (II) $100

CHABELLARD, J. Charles
French 19th/20th cent.
paintings: (H) $8,800

CHABLIS
paintings: (H) $660

CHABRILLAC, Charles Raymond
French b. 1804
paintings: (H) $770

CHABRY, Leonce
French 1832-1883
paintings: (H) $990

CHADEAYNE, Robert O.
American b. 1897
paintings: (L) $250; (H) $990

CHADWICK, Lynn
English b. 1914
drawings: (L) $770; (H) $4,400
sculpture: (L) $3,850; (H) $60,500

CHADWICK, William
American 1879-1962
paintings: (L) $467; (H) $27,500

CHAESE, Emilie
American b. 1868
paintings: (L) $1,540; (H) $6,050

CHAFFEE, Oliver
American 1881-1944
paintings: (L) $55; (H) $1,650
drawings: (L) $132; (H) $523

CHAFFEE, Samuel R.
American 19th/20th cent.
paintings: (H) $495
drawings: (L) $55; (H) $1,045

CHAGALL, Marc
Russian/French 1887-1985
paintings: (L) $99,000; (H) $14,850,000
drawings: (L) $385; (H) $935,000
sculpture: (H) $60,500

CHAIGNEAU, Jean Ferdinand
French 1830-1906
paintings: (L) $1,100; (H) $4,180

CHAILLOUX, Robert
French b. 1913
paintings: (L) $302; (H) $742

CHAILLY, Victor
French 19th cent.
paintings: (H) $1,100

CHALEYE, Jean
French 1878-1960
paintings: (H) $770

CHALEYE, Joannes
French 1878-1960
paintings: (H) $6,050

CHALFANT, Jefferson David
American 1856-1931
paintings: (H) $24,200

CHALLA?, F.
English 19th cent.
paintings: (H) $660

CHALIAPIN, Boris
Russian/American 1904/07-1979
drawings: (H) $660

CHALLE, Charles Michel Ange
French 1718-1778
drawings: (L) $1,430; (H) $1,430

CHALLET
paintings: (H) $770

CHALLICE, Annie J.
English 19th cent.
paintings: (H) $1,430

CHALLIE, Jean
contemporary
paintings: (H) $1,540

CHALLIE, Jean Laurent
French 1880-1943
paintings: (H) $3,520

CHALMERS, Hector
paintings: (H) $1,430

CHALMERS, Lady Elizabeth
British 1894-1939
paintings: (H) $1,100

CHALON, Alfred Edward
Swiss 1780-1860
paintings: (L) $2,475; (H) $4,400

CHALON, Henry Bernard
English 1770-1849
paintings: (L) $3,025; (H) $41,250

CHALON, J.J.
paintings: (H) $1,760

CHALON, John James
British 1778-1854
paintings: (H) $44,000
drawings: (H) $165

CHALON, Kingsley S.
English 19th/20th cent.
paintings: (L) $770; (H) $825

CHALON, Louis
French b. 1866
drawings: (H) $4,400
sculpture: (L) $660; (H) $28,600

CHALONER, Holman Waldron
American 1851-1930
paintings: (H) $6,050

CHAMAILLARD, Ernest Henri
Ponthier de
French 1862-1930
paintings: (H) $6,600

CHAMBELLAN, Rene Paul
American 1893-1955
sculpture: (H) $49,500

CHAMBERLAIN, ***
British 19th cent.
paintings: (H) $1,980

CHAMBERLAIN, Elwynn
American b. 1928
paintings: (H) $12,100

CHAMBERLAIN, Esther
American early 19th cent.
drawings: (H) $715

CHAMBERLAIN, John
American b. 1927
sculpture: (L) $1,430; (H) $253,000

CHAMBERLAIN, Norman Stiles
American 1887-1961
paintings: (L) $550; (H) $6,600

CHAMBERLAIN, Wynn
American b. 1929
paintings: (L) $1,100; (H) $8,250

CHAMBERLIN, Frank Tolles
American 1873-1961
paintings: (L) $1,100; (H) $2,090
drawings: (H) $550

CHAMBERLIN, Mason
paintings: (H) $1,100

CHAMBERS, C. Bosseron
American b. 1883
paintings: (L) $825; (H) $1,430

CHAMBERS, Charles Edward
American 1883-1941
paintings: (L) $660; (H) $3,025

CHAMBERS, George, Jr.
English ac. 1848-1862
paintings: (L) $1,100; (H) $29,700

CHAMBERS, George, Sr.
English 1803-1840
paintings: (L) $2,200; (H) $7,700

CHAMBERS, George W.
American 19th cent.
paintings: (L) $264; (H) $30,800

CHAMBERS, J.K.
American d. 1916
paintings: (L) $302; (H) $750

CHAMBERS, Richard Edward Elliot
Irish/American 1863-1944
drawings: (L) $55; (H) $1,210

CHAMBERS, Thomas
American 1808-1866
paintings: (L) $525; (H) $88,000

CHAMBERS, Thomas
British 1724-1789
paintings: (H) $3,410

CHAMPAIGNE, Jean Baptiste de
French 1631-1681
paintings: (H) $14,850

CHAMPHEY, Benjamin
paintings: (H) $770

CHAMPLIN, Ada Belle
American
paintings: (L) $1,045; (H) $2,200

CHAMPNEY, Benjamin
American 1817-1907
paintings: (L) $193; (H) $14,300
drawings: (L) $302; (H) $1,980

CHAMPNEY, James Wells
American 1843-1903
paintings: (L) $247; (H) $9,900
drawings: (L) $138; (H) $8,250

CHAN, Eddie
drawings: (H) $950

White Mountain Painter

Since the beginning of the 19th century, the extraordinary scenery of the White Mountains in New Hampshire has made them a mecca for artists. Benjamin Champney (1817-1907) is known as the father of the White Mountain School. Champney trained as a lithographer in Boston, and then followed the fashion and went to Paris to study. There he met another student, John Frederick Kensett, who was also to become a noted landscape painter. The two traveled throughout Europe before returning to the United States.

In 1851, Champney and Kensett made a walking and sketching tour of the White Mountains and were impressed by the beauty of New Hampshire, comparing it favorably to Switzerland. Kensett returned to New York, Champney to Boston, and both spread the word of the beauty of the White Mountains. Soon, North Conway, New Hampshire was a summer artists' colony. Samuel Lancaster Gerry, Harrison Bird Brown, George Loring Brown, Alfred T. Ordway, Horace Robbins Burdick, John Joseph Enneking, Frank Shapleigh, Willard Metcalf, and Edward Hill were some of the artists who, along with Champney and Kensett, summered in the White Mountains. Champney built a summer home and studio in North Conway and lived there till his death at age ninety. Champney is best known for landscapes of the White Mountains but toward the end of his life, when he was confined to a wheelchair, he painted numerous florals of his wife's garden. (Benjamin Champney, *White Mountain Landscape*, oil on canvas, 10 x 15 ½ in., Sanders & Mock, June 2, 1989, $7,150)

CHANCRIN, Rene
French 20th cent.
paintings: (H) $1,100

CHANDLER, John Green
American 1815-1879
paintings: (L) $750; (H) $5,225

CHANDLER, Joseph Goodhue
American 1813-1880
paintings: (H) $40,700

CHANDLER, Winthrop
American
paintings: (H) $11,000

CHANEY, Lester Joseph
American b. 1907
paintings: (L) $44; (H) $1,870

CHANNING, Norwood
English 19th cent.
paintings: (H) $4,400

CHAPAUD, Marc
French 20th cent.
paintings: (L) $110; (H) $715

CHAPELAIN-MIDY, Roger
contemporary
paintings: (L) $935; (H) $6,325

CHAPERON, Eugene
drawings: (H) $825

CHAPIN, Bryant
American 1859-1927
paintings: (L) $302; (H) $13,200
drawings: (H) $330

CHAPIN, C.H.
American c. 1830-after 1874
paintings: (L) $192; (H) $1,980
drawings: (H) $275

CHAPIN, Charles C.
American
paintings: (H) $6,600

CHAPIN, Charles E.
American
paintings: (H) $1,760
drawings: (H) $770

CHAPIN, Francis
American 1899-1965
paintings: (L) $385; (H) $1,320
drawings: (L) $55; (H) $660

CHAPIN, Lucy Grosvenor
American d. 1939
paintings: (L) $110; (H) $1,320
drawings: (H) $110

CHAPLEAU, Eugene Jean Alexandre
French b. 1882
paintings: (L) $550; (H) $715

CHAPLET, Roger
20th cent.
paintings: (L) $715; (H) $990

CHAPLIN, Charles
French 1825-1891
paintings: (L) $715; (H) $49,500
drawings: (H) $3,850

CHAPLIN, Charlie
drawings: (L) $880; (H) $1,155

CHAPMAN, Carlton T.
American 1860-1925/26
paintings: (L) $137; (H) $7,700
drawings: (L) $66; (H) $500

CHAPMAN, Charles
paintings: (L) $286; (H) $660

CHAPMAN, Charles S.
American 1879-1962
paintings: (L) $55; (H) $4,950
drawings: (L) $187; (H) $357

CHAPMAN, Conrad Wise
Italian/American 1842-1910
paintings: (L) $770; (H) $27,500
drawings: (H) $7,700

CHAPMAN, John Gadsby
American 1808-1889/90
paintings: (L) $286; (H) $3,575

CHAPMAN, John Gadsby and Robert
Swain GIFFORD
American
drawings: (H) $990

CHAPMAN, John Linton
American 1839-1905
paintings: (L) $55; (H) $6,600

CHAPMAN, John Watkins
British ac. 1880-1903
paintings: (H) $22,000

CHAPMAN, Mary Louise
American 19th cent.
paintings: (H) $1,980

CHAPMAN, Minerva
American b. 1858
paintings: (H) $1,650

CHAPOTON, Gregoire
French 1845-1916
paintings: (H) $9,900

CHAPOVAL, Youla
paintings: (H) $2,420
drawings: (H) $1,650

CHAPPEL, Alonzo
American 1828-1887
paintings: (H) $4,400
drawings: (L) $220; (H) $2,860

CHAPPEL, S.
paintings: (H) $715

CHAPPELL, R.
paintings: (H) $825

CHAPPELL, Reuben
English 1870-1940
paintings: (L) $2,200; (H) $3,520
drawings: (H) $532

CHAPU, Henri Michel Antoine
French 1833-1891
sculpture: (L) $198; (H) $3,740

CHAPY, R.
European 19th cent.
sculpture: (H) $935

CHARBONNET, Marie Natalie
American ac. 1845-1924
paintings: (H) $1,650

CHARCHOUNE, Serge
Russian 1888-1975
paintings: (L) $2,310; (H) $77,000

CHARDIN, Jean Baptiste Simeon
French 1699-1779
paintings: (L) $184,999; (H) $2,530,000

CHARLAMOFF, Alexei Alexeiewitsch
Russian b. 1842/49
paintings: (L) $3,850; (H) $66,000

CHARLEMONT, Eduard
Austrian 1848-1906
paintings: (L) $6,500; (H) $17,600
drawings: (H) $605

CHARLEMONT, Hugo
Austrian b. 1850
drawings: (H) $660

CHARLES, Jacques
drawings: (H) $1,210

CHARLES, James
British 1851-1906
paintings: (H) $27,500

CHARLES, James
British 19th cent.
paintings: (H) $688

CHARLESON, Malcolm Daniel
Canadian b. 1888
paintings: (H) $660

CHARLET, Emile
Belgian b. 1851
paintings: (H) $1,320

CHARLET, Frantz
Belgian 1862-1928
paintings: (L) $3,300; (H) $28,600

CHARLET, Nicolas Toussaint
French 1792-1845
paintings: (L) $660; (H) $5,500

CHARLOT, Jean
French 1898-1979
paintings: (L) $440; (H) $28,600
drawings: (L) $137; (H) $3,850

CHARLOT, Louis
paintings: (L) $550; (H) $1,300

CHARMAN, Frederick Montague
American 1894-1986
paintings: (H) $400
drawings: (L) $27; (H) $800

CHARMAN, Jessie Bone
American 1895-1986
drawings: (L) $200; (H) $1,200

CHARMAN, Rodney
20th cent.
paintings: (H) $1,320

CHARMY, Emile
paintings: (H) $4,180

CHARNAY, Armand
French 1844-1916
paintings: (L) $2,530; (H) $14,300

CHAROL, D.
sculpture: (L) $308; (H) $2,750

CHARON, Guy
paintings: (L) $2,860; (H) $3,410

CHARPENTIER, Alexandre Louis
Marie
  French
  sculpture: (H) $770

CHARPENTIER, Constance Marie
  French 1767-1849
  paintings: (H) $8,800

CHARPENTIER, Felix Maurice
  French 1858-1924
  sculpture: (L) $198; (H) $5,225

CHARPENTIER, Jean Baptiste
  French 1728-1806
  paintings: (L) $3,575; (H) $22,000

CHARPENTIER, Michel
  French 20th cent.
  paintings: (H) $1,210

CHARPIN, Albert
  French 1842-1924
  paintings: (H) $660

CHARPIN, C.D.
  paintings: (L) $1,100; (H) $1,760

CHARPIN, F.
  paintings: (H) $990

CHARRETON, Victor
  French 1864-1936
  paintings: (L) $5,225; (H) $77,000

CHARRON, Amadee
  French 1837-?
  sculpture: (H) $3,850

CHARTON, Ernest
  French 1813-1905
  paintings: (H) $49,500

CHARTRAN, Theobold
  French 1849-1907
  paintings: (H) $2,640

CHARTRAND, Esteban
  Latin American 1825-1889
  paintings: (L) $3,520; (H) $10,450

CHARTRAND, Philipe
  Latin American
  paintings: (H) $2,750

CHASE, Adelaid Cole
  American 1869-1944
  paintings: (H) $990

CHASE, Elsie Rowland
  American 1863-1937
  paintings: (H) $3,850

CHASE, Frank Swift
  American 1886-1958
  paintings: (L) $357; (H) $8,250

CHASE, Henry, called Harry
  American 1853-1889
  paintings: (L) $1,210; (H) $5,610
  drawings: (H) $550

CHASE, Jessie Kalmbach
  American 1879-1970
  paintings: (H) $1,650

CHASE, Louisa
  American b. Panama 1951
  paintings: (L) $1,870; (H) $17,600

CHASE, Richard
  American b. 1891
  paintings: (L) $500; (H) $675

CHASE, Richard A.
  American 1892-1985
  paintings: (L) $495; (H) $990

CHASE, Sidney M.
  American 1877-1957
  paintings: (L) $220; (H) $7,700

CHASE, William Merritt
  American 1849-1916
  paintings: (L) $4,400; (H) $1,100,000
  drawings: (L) $1,760; (H) $2,200,000

CHASHNIK, Ilya Grigorevich
  Russian 1902-1929
  drawings: (L) $23,100; (H) $38,500

CHASSELAT, Pierre
  French 1753-1814
  drawings: (H) $9,900

CHASSERIAU, Theodore
  French 1819-1856
  paintings: (H) $286,000
  drawings: (L) $13,200; (H) $46,200

CHASSON, Pierre
  French 20th cent.
  paintings: (H) $1,430

CHATAUD, Marc Alfred
  French b. 1833
  paintings: (H) $2,750

CHATEIGNON, Ernest
  French ac. 19th cent.
  paintings: (L) $1,650; (H) $2,750

CHATELET, Claude Louis
French 1753-1794/95
paintings: (H) $82,500
drawings: (H) $12,100

CHATOV, C.
paintings: (L) $605; (H) $935

CHATTAWAY, William
sculpture: (H) $3,300

DU CHATTEL, Fredericus Jacobus van
Rossum du
Dutch 1856-1917
paintings: (L) $440; (H) $1,980
drawings: (H) $880

CHATTERTON, Clarence K.
American 1880-1973
paintings: (L) $55; (H) $16,500
drawings: (H) $440

CHAUDET, Antoine Denis
French 1763-1810
sculpture: (L) $550; (H) $3,025

CHAUVIN, August
paintings: (H) $1,650

CHAVALLIAUD, Leon Joseph
French 1858-1921
sculpture: (H) $1,650

CHAVANNES, Alfred
Swiss 1836-1894
paintings: (H) $1,100

CHAVET, Victor Joseph
French 1822-1906
paintings: (L) $1,540; (H) $1,650

CHAVEZ, Gerardo
paintings: (H) $13,200
drawings: (H) $3,080

CHAVEZ, Jose de
Spanish 19th cent.
paintings: (H) $10,450

CHEADLE, Henry
English b. 1852
paintings: (L) $385; (H) $715

CHECA Y SANZ, Ulpiano
Spanish 1860-1916
paintings: (H) $49,500

CHEDANNE, Marcel
drawings: (H) $1,210

CHEE, Robert
American (Navajo) 1938-1971
paintings: (L) $137; (H) $660
drawings: (H) $55

CHELINS
sculpture: (H) $990

CHELMINSKI, Jan van
Polish 1851-1925
paintings: (L) $242; (H) $4,400

CHELMONSKI, Josef
Polish 1850-1914
paintings: (H) $8,800

CHEMELLIER, George Petit de
French d. 1908
sculpture: (H) $1,650

CHEMIAKIN, Mikhail
Russian 20th cent.
drawings: (L) $1,320; (H) $13,200

CHEMIAKINE, Michel
Russian b. 1940
paintings: (H) $22,000
drawings: (L) $3,740; (H) $15,400

CHEMIELINSKI, W.T.
paintings: (L) $605; (H) $1,210

CHEMIN, Joseph Victor
French 1825-1901
sculpture: (L) $275; (H) $2,475

CHEN, Hilo
Chinese b. 1942
paintings: (L) $2,750; (H) $9,350
drawings: (L) $495; (H) $1,650

CHENEWERCK, Henry
Continental 19th cent.
paintings: (H) $1,650

CHENEY, Harold W.
American
paintings: (L) $330; (H) $2,750

CHENEY, Russell
American 1881-1945
paintings: (L) $125; (H) $1,540

CHERC
sculpture: (L) $605; (H) $2,750

CHERET, Gustave Joseph
French 1838-1894
sculpture: (L) $880; (H) $4,400

CHERET, Joseph
sculpture: (L) $1,320; (H) $2,090

CHERET, Jules
French 1836-1932
paintings: (L) $3,850; (H) $14,300
drawings: (L) $550; (H) $16,500

CHERNOW, Ann
paintings: (H) $1,100

CHERON, Louis
French 1660-1725
drawings: (L) $1,100; (H) $2,200

CHERRY, Kathryn
American 1880-1931
paintings: (L) $357; (H) $2,310

CHERSELL, John
British 18th cent.
paintings: (H) $1,100

CHERUBINI, Andrea
Italian 19th cent.
paintings: (L) $77; (H) $5,500

CHERUBINI, Carlo
Italian b. 1897
paintings: (L) $880; (H) $1,210

CHERUBINO, or Giovanni ALBERTI
Italian 1553-1615 or 1558-1601
drawings: (H) $13,200

CHERY, Jacques Richard
Haitian b. 1929
paintings: (H) $1,870

CHESNEY, Lee
contemporary
paintings: (H) $660

CHESTER, E.
English 19th cent.
paintings: (L) $121; (H) $1,540

CHESTNUT, Billy Dohlman
American 20th cent.
drawings: (H) $1,760

CHEURET, Albert
French ac. 19th/20th cent.
sculpture: (L) $825; (H) $41,800

CHEVALIER, Charles
paintings: (H) $1,320

CHEVALIER, Helene
paintings: (H) $1,760

CHEVALIER, Nicholas
paintings: (H) $13,200

CHEVALIER, Peter
contemporary
paintings: (L) $1,650; (H) $9,350
drawings: (L) $550; (H) $880

CHEVALIER, Robert Magnus
British ac. 1876-1908
paintings: (H) $6,600
drawings: (H) $440

CHEVILLIARD, Vincent Jean Baptiste
French 1841-1904
paintings: (L) $4,950; (H) $6,000
drawings: (H) $550

CHEVIOT, Lillian
British 19th/20th cent.
paintings: (L) $2,640; (H) $9,900

CHEVOLLEAU, Jean
French b. 1924
paintings: (H) $3,850

CHEYSSIAL, Georges Robert
French b. 1907
paintings: (H) $3,190

CHI, Chen
Chinese/American b. 1912
drawings: (L) $875; (H) $1,870

CHIA, Sandro
Italian b. 1946
paintings: (L) $5,500; (H) $126,500
drawings: (L) $1,045; (H) $51,700
sculpture: (L) $9,900; (H) $110,000

CHIA, Sandro and Rainer FETTING
drawings: (H) $1,320

CHIALIVA, Luigi
Swiss/Italian 1842-1914
paintings: (L) $4,950; (H) $16,500
drawings: (L) $1,100; (H) $3,850

CHIANELLI, Mervine
contemporary
sculpture: (H) $1,760

CHIAPARELLI, P.O.
sculpture: (L) $1,540; (H) $2,090

CHICAGO, Judy
American b. 1939
drawings: (L) $770; (H) $2,640

CHICHESTER, Cecil
American b. 1891
paintings: (L) $75; (H) $935

CHIDLEY, A.
British 20th cent.
drawings: (H) $1,250

CHIERICI, Gaetano
Italian 1838-1920
paintings: (L) $8,800; (H) $297,000

CHIFFLART, Nicolas Francois
drawings: (H) $3,080

CHIGONNET, P.
sculpture: (H) $2,090

CHIGOT, Eugene
paintings: (H) $2,750

CHIHULY, Dale
American b. 1941
sculpture: (L) $1,320; (H) $12,100

CHILD, Edwin Burrage
American 1868-1937
paintings: (L) $66; (H) $2,310
drawings: (H) $110

CHILD, J.T.
paintings: (H) $1,650

CHILDS, Elias
British 19th cent.
paintings: (H) $2,310

CHILLIDA, Eduardo
Spanish b. 1924
drawings: (H) $1,430

CHIMENTI, Jacopo, called Jacopo da
Empoli
Italian 1554-1640
paintings: (H) $2,750
drawings: (H) $3,630

CHINNERY, George
British 1748-1847
drawings: (L) $88; (H) $3,520

CHINTREUIL, Antoine
French 1814/16-1873
paintings: (L) $6,600; (H) $10,450
drawings: (H) $330

CHIPARUS, Demetre
Rumanian ac. 1914-1933
sculpture: (L) $880; (H) $176,000

CHIRIACKA, Ernest
American b. 1920
paintings: (L) $330; (H) $11,000

CHIRICO, Giorgio de
Italian 1888-1978
paintings: (L) $16,500; (H) $5,280,000
drawings: (L) $2,090; (H) $269,500
sculpture: (L) $6,050; (H) $41,800

CHITTENDEN, Alice Brown
American 1860-1934
paintings: (L) $303; (H) $27,500
drawings: (L) $44; (H) $770

CHMELKOFF, Peter Mikhailovitch
Russian 1819-1890
paintings: (H) $5,775

CHMIELINSKI, W.T.
Polish 19th/20th cent.
paintings: (L) $275; (H) $880
drawings: (H) $88

CHO, Chang Young
paintings: (L) $660; (H) $1,320

CHOATE, Nathaniel
American 1899-1965
sculpture: (H) $5,500

CHOCARNE-MOREAU, Paul Charles
French 1855-1931
paintings: (L) $2,750; (H) $16,500

CHONG, Manuel Neto
Panamanian b. 1927
paintings: (H) $2,750

CHOPARD, G.
drawings: (H) $1,100

CHOPIN, F.
sculpture: (H) $990

CHOPPARD-MAZEAU, Caroline
Leonie Jeanne
French 19th/20th cent.
paintings: (H) $5,500

CHOPPIN, Paul
sculpture: (H) $1,980

CHOQUET, Rene
Continental 19th cent.
paintings: (L) $248; (H) $935

CHOQUET, Rene
French 19th/20th cent.
paintings: (H) $6,600

CHOTKA
sculpture: (L) $308; (H) $3,080

CHOULET
sculpture: (H) $770

Packaging Art

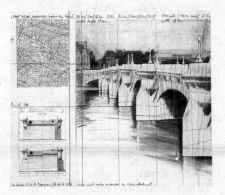

Bulgarian-born Christo (Christo Javacheff, b. 1935) emigrated in 1956—first to Vienna, Switzerland, and Paris and then to New York in 1964. He first gained recognition with his assemblages of oil casks in Cologne in 1961 and in Paris in 1962. His work is conceptual art, in which the underlying concept is more important than the physical structure. He is known as the originator of "packaging" art (*empaquetages*), in which familiar objects are wrapped in canvas or transparent packaging. The first of these packages were small in scale, but they gradually increased in size. In 1969 he wrapped a million square feet of Australian coastline in white polypropylene, his first colossal environmental project. Christo's packaging is a commentary on a consumer society and focuses attention on the beauty of the environment.

In 1969 he swathed the Chicago Museum of Contemporary Art in tarpaulins, and in 1974 he draped the walkways of Kansas City's Loose Park in saffron nylon. In 1976, after four years of planning, Christo created "Running Fence," an eighteen-foot-high, twenty-four-mile-long ribbon of white nylon cutting across California's Marin and Sonoma counties. The fence stood for only two weeks, at a cost in excess of $3 million. Money for the project was raised in part by selling drawings and scale models of the project. He also has wrapped Miami's Key Biscayne Bay and the Pont Neuf in Paris.

(Christo, *The Pont Neuf, Wrapped, Project for Paris*, 28 x 33 in., left panel: street map, bridge diagram, and colored crayons on paper mounted on board; right panel: collage on board, Christie's, February 23, 1990, $88,000)

CHOULTSE, Ivan
Russian 1877-after 1932
paintings: (L) $220; (H) $10,450

CHOVA, V.
sculpture: (H) $1,980

CHRETIEN, Eugene Ernest
sculpture: (H) $3,520

CHRIST, J.
Continental 19th cent.
paintings: (H) $2,750

CHRISTENSEN, Anthonore
Danish 1849-1926
paintings: (L) $1,650; (H) $4,400

CHRISTENSEN, Dan
American b. 1942
paintings: (L) $440; (H) $4,950
drawings: (H) $715

CHRISTENY
Continental 20th cent.
paintings: (H) $880

CHRISTIAN, G.
Scandinavian 19th cent.
paintings: (H) $1,210

CHRISTIANSEN, Nils H.
Swedish 1876-1903
paintings: (L) $330; (H) $1,320

CHRISTINA, Anna
drawings: (H) $7,150

CHRISTO, Christo JAVACHEFF
Bulgarian/American b. 1935
paintings: (L) $13,200; (H) $214,500
drawings: (L) $2,750; (H) $143,000
sculpture: (H) $165,000

CHRISTY, Howard Chandler
American 1873-1952
paintings: (L) $522; (H) $115,500
drawings: (L) $110; (H) $18,700

CHRUSCLCKI, Eugene
paintings: (H) $1,320

CHRUVINI, A.
Italian 19th cent.
paintings: (H) $8,250

CHRYSSA
Greek/American b. 1933
sculpture: (L) $2,750; (H) $33,000

CHUANG CHE
paintings: (H) $1,650

CHUIKOV, Ivan
Russian b. 1935
paintings: (L) $15,400; (H) $90,200

CHUMLEY, John
American
drawings: (H) $660

CHURCH, E.F.
American 19th cent.
paintings: (H) $880

CHURCH, Frederic Edwin
American 1826-1900
paintings: (L) $5,170; (H) $8,250,000
drawings: (H) $550

CHURCH, Frederick Stuart
American 1842-1924
paintings: (L) $330; (H) $44,000
drawings: (L) $83; (H) $3,300

CHURCH, Henry
American 1836-1908
paintings: (H) $33,000

CHURCHILL, Alfred Vances
American b. 1864
paintings: (L) $110; (H) $935

CHURCHILL, Sir Winston
English 1874-1965
paintings: (H) $44,000

CHURCHILL, William
paintings: (H) $880

CHURCHILL, William Worcester
American 1858-1926
paintings: (L) $880; (H) $9,075

CHWALA, Adolf
Czechoslovakian 1836-1900
paintings: (H) $880

CIALLI, G.
paintings: (H) $16,500

CIAN, Fernand
Italian ac. 1911-1928
sculpture: (L) $550; (H) $2,750

CIANI, Cesare
Italian 1854-1925
paintings: (H) $990

CIAPPA, Carlo
Italian 19th/20th cent.
paintings: (H) $2,000

CIARAI, Olga
Italian 20th cent.
paintings: (H) $4,070

CIARDI, Beppe
Italian 1875-1932
paintings: (L) $9,020; (H) $11,550

CIARDI, Emma
Italian 1879-1933
paintings: (L) $2,200; (H) $5,060

CIARDIELLO, Michel
Italian b. 1839
paintings: (L) $11,000; (H) $11,000

CICCORELLI, A.
sculpture: (H) $825

CICERI, Eugene
French 1813-1890
paintings: (H) $660
drawings: (L) $165; (H) $1,760

CICERO, Carmen
American b. 1926
paintings: (L) $770; (H) $1,210

CICKOWSKY, N.
paintings: (H) $715

CIDONCHA, Rafael
Spanish b. 1952
paintings: (H) $3,300

CIGNAROLI, Gianbettino
paintings: (H) $2,640

CIGNAROLI, Scipione
drawings: (H) $1,430

Reversal of Fortune

Frederic Edwin Church (1826-1900) was the leading landscape painter of the mid-19th century. Born in Hartford, Connecticut, the son of a wealthy insurance executive, he began a two-year study with Thomas Cole, founder of the Hudson River School of landscape painting, when he was eighteen. Church gained artistic recognition early and became a member of the National Academy when he was only twenty-three. Like his teacher, Church painted scenes of the Catskill Mountains; but while Cole's paintings became increasingly Romantic and allegorical in style, Church painted in a realistic manner.

In 1853, Church began to travel widely and painted heroic scenes of Niagara Falls, the Andes, volcanos, jungles, icebergs, the Alps, Jamaica, and the Aegean. As was popular in his day, some of these paintings were panoramas of great size. Church's paintings were spectacular and filled with specific depictions of vegetation, atmosphere, and fauna. They appealed to the public's relish for the exotic and its growing preoccupation with science. In 1877, when he was only fifty-one, arthritis crippled Church's right hand. Although he managed to paint with his left hand, his paintings lacked their previous vigor. By 1883 different schools of painting began to supplant realistic depictions and Church's paintings fell out of favor. At the time of his death in 1900, Church had been virtually forgotten as an artist. A memorial exhibition of his paintings was held at the Metropolitan Museum of Art in 1900, but it was not until the 1980s that his work was once again appreciated.

Home by the Lake was painted in 1852; it was inspired by two Catskill scenes that Thomas Cole painted while Church was his student. The composition is basically the same: a log cabin with puffing chimney in a clearing near the shore of a reflecting lake. Each painting depicts cows and a small boat and cumulus clouds over the rocky hills. Although the paintings contain similar elements, they are different, indicating Church's interest in the realistic depiction of landscapes. *Home by the Lake* was deaccessioned by the Walker Art Center and sold at Sotheby's in May 1989. The painting has been widely exhibited and was scheduled for inclusion in the Church exhibition at the National Gallery in the winter of 1989 to 1990. The landscape, which sold for $8,250,000, is now in the collection of JoAnn and Julian Ganz, Jr. (Frederic E. Church, *Home by the Lake*, oil on canvas, 32 x 48¼ in., Sotheby's, May 24, 1989, $8,250,000)

CIKOVSKY, Nicolai
Russian/American b. 1894
paintings: (L) $275; (H) $3,850
drawings: (L) $55; (H) $990

CILFONE, Gianni
American b. 1908
paintings: (L) $330; (H) $990

CIMA, Luigi
Italian 1860-1938
paintings: (L) $385; (H) $10,450

CIMA DA CONEGLIANO, studio of
paintings: (H) $30,800

CIMAROLI, Gianbattista
Italian ac. c. 1700-1753
paintings: (L) $3,300; (H) $44,000

CIMIOTTI, Gustave
American 1875-after 1929
paintings: (L) $248; (H) $1,430
drawings: (L) $55; (H) $140

CINALLI, Ricardo
Argentinian b. 1948
drawings: (H) $4,400

CINISELLI, G.
Italian 19th cent.
sculpture: (H) $2,420

CINQUEGRANA, Livia
American b. 1894
paintings: (L) $200; (H) $880

CINTHOIN, Jules
French 19th cent.
paintings: (H) $2,200

CIPOLLA, Fabio
Italian b. 1854
paintings: (H) $1,540

CIPPER, Giacomo Francesco, called IL
TODESCHINI
Italian c. 1670-1738
paintings: (L) $5,500; (H) $35,200

CIPRIANI, A.
sculpture: (L) $528; (H) $3,190

CIPRIANI, Giovanni Battista
Italian 1727-1785/1790
drawings: (L) $110; (H) $1,760

CIPRIANI, J.A.
sculpture: (H) $1,100

CIPRIANI, Nazzareno
Italian 1843-1925
paintings: (L) $2,420; (H) $4,400
drawings: (H) $192

CIPRICO, Marguerite F.
American 1891-1973
paintings: (H) $1,100

CIPUANI, A.
sculpture: (H) $1,650

CIRCIGNANI, Niccolo, called Il
Pomarancio
ac. 1564-1598
drawings: (H) $16,500

CIRINO, Antonio
American 1889-1982/83
paintings: (L) $466; (H) $11,000

CIRY, Michel
French b. 1919
paintings: (L) $3,410; (H) $4,400

CISSARD, Geo Ma
sculpture: (H) $660

CITTADINI, Pier Francesco
paintings: (L) $3,850; (H) $17,600

CIVITA, Vincenzo
Italian c. 19th cent.
drawings: (L) $3,520; (H) $4,180

CLAESSINS, Pieter, II
Flemish d. 1623
paintings: (H) $22,000

CLAESZ, Aert, called Aertgen van
Leyden
Dutch 1498-1564
paintings: (H) $170,500

CLAESZ, Pieter
Dutch 1597-1661
paintings: (L) $44,000; (H) $88,000

CLAESZ, Anthony, I
Dutch 1592-1635
paintings: (H) $28,600
drawings: (H) $3,850

CLAGHORN, Joseph C.
American 1869-1947
paintings: (L) $264; (H) $2,200
drawings: (L) $440; (H) $1,430

CLAGUE, Richard
American 1816-1878
paintings: (H) $11,550
drawings: (H) $2,200

CLAIR, Charles
French 19th/20th cent.
paintings: (L) $935; (H) $5,500

CLAIRE, Auguste Jean
French 19th/20th cent.
paintings: (H) $3,850

CLAIRE, Vincent
Continental 1855-1925
paintings: (H) $2,750

CLAIRIN, Georges Jules Victor
French 1843-1919
paintings: (L) $1,210; (H) $52,250
drawings: (L) $302; (H) $1,430

CLAIRIN, Pierre Eugene
French 1897-1980
paintings: (L) $187; (H) $4,180

CLAITON, J.
Continental School 19th cent.
paintings: (L) $660; (H) $770

CLAPHAM, Mark
contemporary
paintings: (L) $5,000; (H) $6,500

CLAPP, Clinton W.
American mid-19th cent.
paintings: (L) $220; (H) $1,320

CLAPP, William Henry
American 1879-1954
paintings: (L) $55; (H) $12,100
drawings: (L) $275; (H) $577

CLARA, Jose
Spanish b. 1878
drawings: (L) $1,100; (H) $2,200

CLARA, Juan
Spanish 1875/78-1958
sculpture: (L) $247; (H) $825

CLARE, George
English ac. c. 1860-1900
paintings: (L) $990; (H) $4,620
drawings: (L) $550; (H) $2,420

CLARE, J.
English 19th/20th cent.
paintings: (H) $715

CLARE, Oliver
British c. 1853-1927
paintings: (L) $330; (H) $4,400

CLARE, Oliver and George
paintings: (H) $2,090

CLARE, Vincent
British c. 1855-1925/30
paintings: (L) $440; (H) $8,800

CLARK, A.
paintings: (H) $2,200

CLARK, Albert
English 19th cent.
paintings: (L) $1,980; (H) $3,300

CLARK, Albert James
British ac. 1890-1943
paintings: (H) $13,200

CLARK, Allan
American 1896/98-1950
sculpture: (L) $550; (H) $4,400

CLARK, Alson Skinner
American 1876-1949
paintings: (L) $308; (H) $14,300

CLARK, Benton H.
American 1895-1964
paintings: (L) $110; (H) $9,075

CLARK, C. Myron
American 1858-1923
paintings: (L) $110; (H) $2,475
drawings: (L) $44; (H) $1,045

CLARK, Claude C.
British 19th cent.
paintings: (H) $1,760

CLARK, E.H.
American 19th/20th cent.
paintings: (H) $715

CLARK, Eliot Candee
American 1883-1980
paintings: (L) $70; (H) $7,700
drawings: (L) $45; (H) $450

CLARK, F. Myron
paintings: (H) $880

CLARK, Frederick Albert
paintings: (L) $440; (H) $3,080

CLARK, Frederick H.
American
paintings: (H) $1,980

CLARK, George Herritt
American d. 1904
paintings: (L) $165; (H) $990

CLARK, James
British 1858-1943
paintings: (L) $4,400; (H) $15,400

CLARK, James, Sr.
paintings: (H) $2,420

CLARK, James Lippitt
American 1883-1957
sculpture: (L) $1,100; (H) $7,700

CLARK, Joseph
paintings: (H) $1,100

CLARK, Lemuel
paintings: (H) $2,035

CLARK, Octavius T.
British 1850-1921
paintings: (L) $302; (H) $715

CLARK, P.
American 19th cent.
drawings: (H) $990

CLARK, Richard
contemporary
drawings: (H) $660

CLARK, Roland
American 1874-1957
paintings: (L) $577; (H) $5,830

CLARK, S.
paintings: (L) $302; (H) $3,850

CLARK, S. Joseph
British 19th cent.
paintings: (H) $1,760

CLARK, S.J.
British 19th cent.
paintings: (L) $825; (H) $6,600

CLARK, W.
paintings: (H) $1,210

CLARK, W.A.
paintings: (L) $385; (H) $1,870

CLARK, W.W.
British 20th cent.
paintings: (H) $935

CLARK, Walter
American 1848-1917
paintings: (L) $302; (H) $5,500

CLARK, William
British 19th cent.
paintings: (L) $357; (H) $2,100

CLARK, William
British ac. 1827-1841
paintings: (L) $600; (H) $900

CLARKE, Emery
paintings: (H) $1,700

CLARKE, F.
paintings: (H) $1,540

CLARKE, Frederick
paintings: (H) $770

CLARKE, James L.
American 1883-1969?
sculpture: (H) $17,600

CLARKE, James W.
drawings: (H) $1,650

CLARKE, John Clem
American b. 1937
paintings: (L) $495; (H) $12,100

CLARKE, Samuel
paintings: (H) $1,210

CLARKSON, Ralph Elmer
American c. 1890
paintings: (H) $1,870

CLARY-BAROUX, Adolphe
French d. 1933
paintings: (H) $2,750

CLARYS, Alexander
Belgian 1857-1930
paintings: (H) $3,850

CLASCO, Joseph
drawings: (H) $770

CLAUDE, Eugene
French 1841-1922
paintings: (L) $4,400; (H) $5,720

CLAUDE, Jean Maxime
French 1823-1904
paintings: (H) $770
drawings: (H) $770

CLAUDEL, Camille
French 1864-1943
sculpture: (L) $33,000; (H) $110,000

CLAUS, Emile
Belgian 1849-1924
paintings: (H) $26,400

CLAUS, William A.J.
American b. 1862
paintings: (L) $82; (H) $1,100

CLAUSADES, P.T. de
paintings: (H) $2,420

CLAUSADES, Pierre de
French 19th cent.
paintings: (L) $1,100; (H) $2,200

CLAUSELL, Joaquin
Mexican 1866-1935
paintings: (L) $4,400; (H) $34,100

CLAUSEN, C.
Danish 19th cent.
drawings: (H) $6,600

CLAUSEN, Franciska
Danish b. 1899
drawings: (L) $12,100; (H) $15,400

CLAUSEN, Sir George
English 1852-1944
paintings: (L) $495; (H) $143,000
drawings: (H) $660

CLAVE, Antoni
French b. Spain 1913
paintings: (L) $1,540; (H) $220,000
drawings: (L) $770; (H) $77,000
sculpture: (H) $5,720

CLAVER, Francois
French b. 1918
paintings: (L) $550; (H) $1,210

CLAVIERE, Bernard de
French 20th cent.
paintings: (H) $4,400

CLAXTON
American 20th cent.
paintings: (H) $3,300

CLAY, Elizabeth Fisher
American
paintings: (H) $1,100

CLAY, Jordan
American
paintings: (L) $1,500; (H) $2,000

CLAYES, Berthe Des
American
drawings: (H) $825

CLAYS, Paul Jean
Belgian 1819-1900
paintings: (L) $82; (H) $17,600
drawings: (H) $880

CLAYTON, J. Hughes
English 19th/20th cent.
drawings: (L) $220; (H) $1,100

CLEARY, Joseph
American 19th cent.
paintings: (H) $2,750

CLEAVES, W.P.
American 19th cent.
paintings: (H) $990

CLEENEWERCK, Henry
Belgian 19th cent.
paintings: (L) $770; (H) $20,900

CLEGG and GUTTMAN
contemporary
drawings: (H) $12,650

CLEMENCIN, Francois Andre
French b. 1878
sculpture: (L) $990; (H) $6,050

CLEMENS, Paul
contemporary
paintings: (L) $165; (H) $8,800

CLEMENT, Marie Louise
French 20th cent.
paintings: (H) $6,600

CLEMENT-RENE, Paul Henri
French 20th cent.
paintings: (H) $935

CLEMENT-SERVEAU
French 1886-1972
paintings: (L) $2,200; (H) $24,200

CLEMENTE, Francesco
Italian b. 1952
paintings: (L) $7,975; (H) $286,000
drawings: (L) $1,000; (H) $66,000

CLEMENTE, S.
paintings: (H) $770

CLEMENTS, Alexander H.
American 1818-1896
paintings: (H) $6,600

CLEMENTS, George H.
American 1854-1935
paintings: (L) $605; (H) $1,100
drawings: (L) $303; (H) $440

CLEMINSON, Robert
English ac. 1865-1868
paintings: (L) $880; (H) $3,850

CLERE, Jacques Francois Camille
French b. 1825
paintings: (H) $1,210

CLERGET, Alexandre
sculpture: (H) $715

CLERGET, Hubert
drawings: (H) $880

CLERICI, Fabrizio
Italian b. 1913
drawings: (L) $55; (H) $2,090

CLERICI, Leone
sculpture: (L) $2,090; (H) $3,080

CLERISSEAU, Charles Louis
French 1721-1820
paintings: (L) $15,400; (H) $24,200
drawings: (L) $600; (H) $11,000

CLERMONT-GALLERANDE,
Adhemar Louis Vicomte de
French d. 1895
paintings: (H) $55,000

CLERSON, Jules
paintings: (H) $2,420

CLESINGER, Jean Baptiste
French 1814-1883
sculpture: (L) $522; (H) $17,600

CLESSE, Louis
Belgian 1889-1961
paintings: (H) $1,760

CLEVE, Cornelis van
French 1520-d. after 1567
paintings: (L) $3,300; (H) $35,200

CLEVE, Hendrik van, III
paintings: (H) $28,600

CLEVE, Joos van
paintings: (H) $38,500

CLEVELY, John
British 1747-1786
drawings: (H) $1,540

CLIFFORD, Edward
Amer. or British 19th cent.
drawings: (H) $3,410

CLIME, Winfield Scott
American 1881-1958
paintings: (L) $247; (H) $5,775
drawings: (L) $165; (H) $550

CLINGER, Robert
American 20th cent.
paintings: (L) $220; (H) $935

CLIVALA, A.
paintings: (H) $990

CLOAR, Carroll
American b. 1913
paintings: (L) $308; (H) $11,000

CLODION, Claude MICHEL
French 1738-1814
sculpture: (L) $330; (H) $352,000

CLORISET
paintings: (L) $825; (H) $3,575

CLOSE, Chuck
American b. 1940
drawings: (L) $10,450; (H) $88,000

CLOSKY
contemporary
paintings: (H) $1,210

CLOSSON, William Baxter Palmer
American 1848-1926
paintings: (L) $900; (H) $4,400
drawings: (H) $440

CLOTTU, Jean
French (?) 19th cent.
paintings: (H) $1,760

CLOUGH, Charles
contemporary
drawings: (H) $1,650

CLOUGH, George C.
paintings: (H) $2,860

CLOUGH, George L.
American 1824-1901
paintings: (L) $242; (H) $7,700

CLOUGH, Jane B.
American b. 1881
sculpture: (H) $2,420

CLOUGH, Prunella
English b. 1919
paintings: (H) $2,970

Maquette

John H. and Ernestine A. Payne Fund. Courtesy of Museum of Fine Arts, Boston.

A maquette (or bozzetto) is a small clay or wax model that serves as a three-dimensional "sketch" for a sculptor. In November 1989, the Boston Museum of Fine Arts purchased at auction at Christie's a terra-cotta maquette by Clodion. The maquette is a preliminary study for an important late work, *The Deluge*, a terra-cotta dating from about 1800 and in the museum's collection since 1981.

Clodion (1738-1814) was a French sculptor whose real name was Claude Michel. Clodion's works from the 1760s until the time of the French Revolution were lighthearted, classical subjects in the Rococo style, which were very popular with French nobility. After the Revolution he changed his style to accommodate the sterner Neoclassical taste of the Napoleonic period. The study and the finished work are of particular interest because they demonstrate the transformation in Clodion's style. The study is the only surviving free-standing model by the artist. The maquette is smaller and rougher than the final version and is unsigned. The two can be viewed side by side at the Boston Museum of Fine Arts. (Clodion, *Study for the Deluge*, terra-cotta, $10^{3/8}$ in. high, Christie's, November 1, 1989, $143,000)

CLOUSTON, Thomas
British 18th cent.
drawings: (L) $495; (H) $1,200

CLOVER, Joseph
paintings: (H) $3,575

CLOVIO, Giulio
c. 1500-1578
drawings: (H) $19,800

CLOWES, Daniel
English ac. 1790-1835
paintings: (L) $2,200; (H) $22,000

CLOWES, David
paintings: (H) $3,960

CLURE, W.M.
American 19th/20th cent.
paintings: (H) $1,320

CLUSMANN, William
American 1859-1927
paintings: (L) $3,960; (H) $11,000
drawings: (L) $440; (H) $1,980

CLUTZ, William
contemporary
paintings: (H) $935

CLUZEL, Brodman
sculpture: (H) $715

CLYME, John
European 20th cent.
paintings: (H) $2,475

CLYMER, John F.
American 1907-1989
paintings: (L) $302; (H) $51,700
drawings: (H) $55

COALE, Griffith Baily
American b. 1890
paintings: (L) $2,090; (H) $26,400

COATES, Edmund C.
American 1816-1871
paintings: (L) $770; (H) $12,100

COATES, Randolph
American b. 1891
paintings: (L) $1,100; (H) $3,080

COBB, Darius
American 1834-1919
paintings: (L) $165; (H) $1,760

COBB, Dawis
paintings: (H) $3,520

COBB, Henry Ives
American 1859-1931
paintings: (L) $88; (H) $1,760
drawings: (L) $330; (H) $550

COBB, Mildred
paintings: (H) $660

COBBETT, Edward John
English 1815-1899
paintings: (L) $1,100; (H) $3,080

COBELLE, Charles
French b. 1902
paintings: (L) $5; (H) $2,420
drawings: (L) $935; (H) $1,760

COBO, Chema
contemporary
drawings: (H) $11,000

COBURN, Frank
American 1866-1931
paintings: (L) $165; (H) $3,520

COBURN, Frederick Simpson
Canadian b. 1871
paintings: (H) $30,800

COCCAPANI, Sigismondo
paintings: (H) $27,500

COCCORANTE, Leonardo
Italian 1700-1750
paintings: (L) $7,150; (H) $15,400

COCHIN, Charles Nicolas
French 1715-1790
drawings: (L) $880; (H) $4,400

COCHRAN, Allen D.
American 1888-1971
paintings: (L) $82; (H) $8,250
drawings: (H) $125

COCK, Cesar de
Flemish 1823-1904
paintings: (L) $1,100; (H) $1,870

COCK, Jan de, the putative
first half 16th cent.
paintings: (H) $71,500

COCK, Xavier de
Belgian 1818-1896
paintings: (H) $9,000

COCK, de
European 19th cent.
paintings: (H) $2,750

COCKBURN, James Pattison
British 1778-1847
drawings: (H) $825

COCKCROFT
paintings: (H) $715

COCKERELL, Christabel A., Lady
Frampton
British 19th cent.
paintings: (H) $2,750

COCKS, John H.
American 1850-1938
drawings: (L) $825; (H) $990

COCTEAU, Jean
French 1889-1963
drawings: (L) $220; (H) $12,100
sculpture: (L) $2,200; (H) $7,700

CODAZZI, Niccolo
Italian c. 1648-1693
paintings: (H) $9,900

CODAZZI, Viviano
Italian 1603-1672
paintings: (L) $14,300; (H) $31,900

CODAZZI, Viviano and Domenico
GARGIULIO, called Micco SPADARO
17th cent.
paintings: (H) $60,500

CODDE, Pieter
Dutch 1599-1678
paintings: (H) $110,000

CODINO Y LANGLIN, Victoriano
Spanish 1844-1911
paintings: (H) $16,500

CODMAN, Charles
American 1800-1842
paintings: (L) $660; (H) $8,800

CODMAN, E.E.
American
sculpture: (L) $935; (H) $3,300

CODMAN, John Amory
American 1824-1886
paintings: (L) $578; (H) $7,700

CODRON, Jef
French 19th cent.
paintings: (H) $7,150

COECKE VAN AELST, Pieter, I
Flemish 1502-1550
paintings: (L) $10,450; (H) $104,500

COELLO, Alonzo Sanchez, studio of
1531/32-1588
paintings: (H) $52,250

COENE, Constantinus Fidelio
Flemish 1780-1841
paintings: (L) $1,870; (H) $7,700

COENE, Jean Baptiste and Louis Marie
Dominique ROBBE
Belgian
paintings: (H) $13,200

COENE, Jean Henri
Flemish b. 1805
paintings: (H) $8,800

COESSIN, Charles
paintings: (H) $935

COESSIN DE LA FOSSE, Charles
Alexandre
French b. 1829
paintings: (H) $5,500

COFFERMANS, Marcellus
Flemish 1535?-after 1575
paintings: (L) $14,300; (H) $82,500

COFFIN, Elizabeth Rebecca
American 1851-1930
paintings: (L) $357; (H) $3,080

COFFIN, George Albert
American
drawings: (H) $660

COFFIN, W. Haskell
American 1878-1941
paintings: (L) $688; (H) $3,080
drawings: (L) $440; (H) $2,420

COFFIN, William Anderson
American 1855-1925
paintings: (L) $715; (H) $6,820

COGNEE, Philippe
contemporary
paintings: (H) $3,080

COGNIET, L.
paintings: (H) $1,100

COGNIET, Leon
French 1794-1880
paintings: (H) $30,250
drawings: (H) $825

COGSWELL, William
American 1819-1903
paintings: (L) $247; (H) $2,420

COHEN
paintings: (H) $770

COHEN, Frederick E.
paintings: (H) $660

COHEN, Lewis
American 1857-1915
paintings: (L) $440; (H) $1,540

COHEN, M. August
paintings: (H) $1,100

COHN, Michael
contemporary
sculpture: (H) $1,980

COIGNARD, James
French b. 1925
paintings: (L) $605; (H) $3,960

COIGNARD, Louis
French 1810-1883
paintings: (L) $1,210; (H) $1,650

COKER, W.
paintings: (H) $1,430

COL, David and Eugene R. MAES
paintings: (H) $11,000

COL, Jan David
Belgian 1822-1900
paintings: (L) $3,300; (H) $28,600

COLACICCO, Salvatore
Italian 20th cent.
paintings: (L) $715; (H) $935

COLBURN, Eleanor Ruth
American 1866-1939
paintings: (L) $440; (H) $3,300
drawings: (H) $330

COLBURN, Gertrude
sculpture: (H) $1,980

COLBY, Victor
sculpture: (H) $660

COLE, Alphaeus P.
American b. 1876
paintings: (L) $132; (H) $5,500

COLE, Charles Octavius
American b. 1814
paintings: (L) $500; (H) $12,100
drawings: (H) $1,430

COLE, E.
paintings: (L) $88; (H) $715

COLE, E.
English 19th/20th cent.
paintings: (L) $55; (H) $825

COLE, Elias V.
paintings: (H) $1,320

COLE, G.
English(?) 19th cent.
paintings: (L) $330; (H) $3,080

COLE, George
British 1810-1883
paintings: (L) $1,017; (H) $19,800

COLE, George Vicat
English 1833-1893
paintings: (L) $550; (H) $4,400

COLE, H.
English 19th cent.
paintings: (L) $825; (H) $825

COLE, J.
paintings: (L) $357; (H) $660

COLE, James
paintings: (H) $1,650

COLE, Joseph Foxcroft
Anglo/American 1837-1892
paintings: (L) $330; (H) $6,050

COLE, Lyman E.
paintings: (H) $1,650

COLE, Philip Tennyson
British ac. 1878-1889
paintings: (H) $1,540

COLE, Thomas
American 1801-1848
paintings: (L) $1,017; (H) $1,045,000
drawings: (L) $385; (H) $16,500

COLE, Thomas C.
American 1888-1976
paintings: (L) $60; (H) $3,080

COLEMAN, Anne Gordon
American 19th cent.
paintings: (H) $2,750

COLEMAN, C.
Italian 19th cent.
paintings: (H) $1,320

COLEMAN, Charles Caryl
American 1840-1928
paintings: (L) $660; (H) $93,500
drawings: (L) $880; (H) $6,600

COLEMAN, Enrico
Italian 1846-1911
paintings: (L) $385; (H) $10,450
drawings: (L) $5,500; (H) $8,250

COLEMAN, F.
Italian b. 1851
paintings: (H) $1,870

COLEMAN, F.D.
19th cent.
paintings: (H) $880

COLEMAN, Francesco
Italian b. 1851
paintings: (H) $5,500
drawings: (H) $1,980

COLEMAN, G.
American
drawings: (H) $770

COLEMAN, Glenn O.
American 1887-1932
paintings: (L) $5,775; (H) $8,000

COLEMAN, Harvey
American 1884-1959
paintings: (L) $275; (H) $880

COLEMAN, J.
British 19th cent.
paintings: (H) $660

COLEMAN, Loring W.
American 20th cent.
paintings: (L) $400; (H) $660

COLEMAN, M.
Continental 20th cent.
paintings: (H) $2,090

COLEMAN, Mary Darter
American b. 1894
paintings: (L) $275; (H) $1,760

COLEMAN, Michael
American b. 1941
paintings: (H) $11,550
drawings: (L) $2,750; (H) $7,000

COLEMAN, Michael
American b. 1946
paintings: (L) $110; (H) $16,500
drawings: (L) $2,750; (H) $13,750

COLEMAN, S.T.
sculpture: (H) $1,100

COLEMAN, Samuel
American 1832-1920
paintings: (H) $1,650
drawings: (L) $121; (H) $715

COLEMAN, William Stephen
English 1829/30-1904
paintings: (L) $1,980; (H) $10,450
drawings: (L) $220; (H) $275

COLESCOTT, Robert
contemporary
drawings: (H) $2,475

COLFER, John Thomas
20th cent.
paintings: (L) $413; (H) $1,870

COLHE, A.E.
English 19th cent.
paintings: (L) $385; (H) $660

COLI, Giovanni and Filippo
GHERARDI
1636-1681; 1643-1704
paintings: (L) $2,200; (H) $68,200

COLIN, G.
sculpture: (H) $1,705

COLIN, George
drawings: (H) $990

COLIN, Georges
sculpture: (L) $2,310; (H) $3,850

COLIN, Gustave
French 1828-1910
paintings: (L) $1,320; (H) $2,750

COLIN, M.
French 19th cent.
paintings: (H) $5,500

COLIN, Paul
paintings: (H) $3,850

COLINET, Claire Jeanne Roberte
French ac. 1929
sculpture: (L) $550; (H) $35,200

COLLAS, A.
French mid-19th cent.
sculpture: (H) $1,540

COLLE, Leopold
Austrian b. 1869
paintings: (H) $2,200

COLLE, Michel Auguste
French 1872-1949
paintings: (H) $6,600

COLLIER, Alan Caswell
paintings: (H) $2,640

COLLIER, Evert
Dutch ac. 1662, d. 1702/03
paintings: (L) $1,760; (H) $35,200

COLLIER, Imogen
British 19th/20th cent.
paintings: (H) $1,980

COLLIER, John, The Hon.
British 1850-1934
paintings: (L) $3,520; (H) $29,700

COLLIER, Thomas
drawings: (H) $825

COLLIN, Benjamin
Danish/American 1896-1979
paintings: (H) $770

COLLIN, Bernard
Swiss 1896-1979
drawings: (H) $770

COLLIN, Louis Joseph Raphael
French 1850-1916
paintings: (L) $3,000; (H) $37,400

COLLIN, R.
paintings: (H) $1,100

COLLIN, Raphael
French 1850-1916
paintings: (H) $5,280

COLLINI, P.
paintings: (H) $1,650

COLLINS, Ben
American 20th cent.
paintings: (H) $2,310

COLLINS, Charles
British d. 1921
paintings: (H) $1,650

COLLINS, Earl
American 20th cent.
paintings: (L) $550; (H) $3,740

COLLINS, F.
American 19th cent.
paintings: (H) $3,300

COLLINS, J.R.
English 19th cent.
paintings: (H) $770

COLLINS, Reginald F.
Canadian d. 1974
paintings: (H) $1,100

COLLINS, Thomas
English ac. 1857-1893
paintings: (H) $1,760

COLLINS, William
English 1788-1847
paintings: (L) $1,980; (H) $7,150

COLLINSON, J.
Continental School 19th cent.
paintings: (H) $6,600

COLLINSON, James
British 1825-1881
paintings: (H) $60,500

COLLINSON, Robert
British b. 1832
paintings: (H) $8,800

COLLO, E.
20th cent.
paintings: (H) $1,100

COLLS, E.
English late 19th cent.
paintings: (H) $742

COLLUM, W.F.
American early 20th cent.
paintings: (H) $850

COLMAN, James
paintings: (H) $825

COLMAN, R. Clarkson
American b. 1884
paintings: (L) $99; (H) $2,750

COLMAN, Samuel
American 1832-1920
paintings: (L) $1,485; (H) $35,200
drawings: (L) $192; (H) $3,520

COLOMANUS, M.
English 19th cent.
paintings: (H) $1,375

COLOMBEL, Nicolas
French 1644-1717
paintings: (L) $2,640; (H) $4,400

COLOMBIER, Amelie
sculpture: (H) $1,540

COLOMBO, Ambrogio
Italian 1821-1890
sculpture: (H) $1,430

COLOMBO, Gian Battista Innocenzo
Swiss 1717-1793
paintings: (H) $14,300

COLOMBO, Grange
sculpture: (H) $1,760

COLOMBO, J.
Italian 19th cent.
sculpture: (H) $3,025

COLOMBO, R.
European 19th cent.
sculpture: (L) $385; (H) $1,100

COLOMBO, Virgilio
Italian 19th cent.
drawings: (L) $605; (H) $3,575

COLONELLI-SCIARRA, Salvatore
Italian ac. 1729
paintings: (H) $115,500

COLSON, Guillaume Francois
French 1785-1850
paintings: (H) $8,800

COLSON, Jean Francois Gille
paintings: (H) $1,760

COLSOULLE, G.
paintings: (H) $1,100

COLT, Morgan
American 20th cent.
paintings: (H) $4,620
drawings: (H) $660

COLTMAN, Ora
American b. 1860
paintings: (L) $110; (H) $742
drawings: (L) $77; (H) $82

COLUCCI, Gio
Italian b. 1892
paintings: (L) $550; (H) $1,210
sculpture: (H) $495

COLUNGA, Alejandro
Mexican b. 1948
paintings: (L) $5,500; (H) $23,100
drawings: (L) $1,870; (H) $22,550
sculpture: (L) $1,980; (H) $5,500

COLVIN
paintings: (H) $1,320

COLVIN, J.M.
paintings: (H) $1,210

COLVIN, Marta
sculpture: (H) $2,200

COLWAY, James
drawings: (L) $1,320; (H) $1,760

COMAN, Charlotte Buell
American 1833-1924
paintings: (L) $550; (H) $2,640
drawings: (H) $125

COMBAS, Robert
French b. 1957
paintings: (L) $4,400; (H) $14,300
drawings: (H) $3,080

COMERRE, Leon Francois
French 1850-1916
paintings: (L) $4,675; (H) $30,250
drawings: (H) $880

COMERRE-PATON, Jaqueline
French b. 1859
paintings: (H) $13,200

COMFORT, Charles Fraser
paintings: (H) $6,050

COMINOTTO, Thommaso
drawings: (H) $5,225

COMMARIEUX, Raymond
drawings: (H) $6,820

COMMUNAL, Joseph Victor
French 1876-1962
paintings: (L) $385; (H) $5,500

COMOLERA, Paul
sculpture: (L) $440; (H) $1,760

COMPARD, Emile
French 1900-1977
paintings: (H) $880
drawings: (H) $110

COMPRIS, Maurice
American 1885-1939
paintings: (L) $412; (H) $1,650

COMPTE-CALIX, Francois Claudius
French 1813-1880
paintings: (L) $2,420; (H) $11,000

COMPTON, Edward Harrison
British b. 1881
drawings: (L) $935; (H) $1,210

COMPTON, Edward Theodore
English 1849-1921
paintings: (L) $11,000; (H) $13,200

COMPTON, F.C.
English 19th cent.
paintings: (H) $1,210

COMTE, N.M.
paintings: (H) $660

COMTE, Pierre Charles
French 1823-1895
paintings: (L) $1,100; (H) $30,800

COMTOIS, Henry le
paintings: (H) $1,980

CONANT, E.A.
American 19th cent.
paintings: (H) $715

CONANT, Lucy Scarborough
American 1867-1921
paintings: (H) $467
drawings: (L) $110; (H) $660

CONAWAY, J.
paintings: (H) $1,100

CONCA, Sebastiano
Italian c. 1676/80-1764
paintings: (H) $11,000

CONDAMY, Charles Ferdinand de
French 19th cent.
paintings: (H) $3,190
drawings: (L) $495; (H) $990

CONDO, George
American b. 1967
paintings: (L) $2,750; (H) $93,500
drawings: (L) $2,200; (H) $7,700

CONDORA
French 19th cent.
sculpture: (H) $1,430

CONDY, Nicholas Matthew
English 1816-1851
paintings: (L) $1,650; (H) $3,600

CONE, Marvin D.
American 1891-1964
paintings: (L) $880; (H) $33,000

CONELY, William B.
American 1830-1911
paintings: (H) $2,200

CONFORTINI, Jacopo
drawings: (H) $1,320

CONGDON, Anne Ramsdell
American 1873-1958
paintings: (L) $1,100; (H) $6,600
drawings: (L) $550; (H) $935

CONGEPIED, C.
sculpture: (H) $1,540

CONKEY, Samuel
American 1830-1904
paintings: (H) $938

CONKLIN, Mabel
American b. 1871
sculpture: (L) $825; (H) $1,650

CONLEY, Stephen
contemporary
paintings: (L) $660; (H) $880

CONNARD, C.E.
paintings: (H) $880

CONNARD, Philip
British 1875-1958
paintings: (H) $14,300

CONNAWAY, Jay Hall
American 1893-1970
paintings: (L) $302; (H) $5,170

CONNELL, Edwin D.
American b. 1859
paintings: (L) $77; (H) $3,575

CONNELLY, Chuck
American b. 1956?
paintings: (L) $550; (H) $14,300

CONNELLY, Pierce Francis
American 1841-1902
sculpture: (L) $550; (H) $2,750

CONNELLY, S.
paintings: (H) $880

CONNER, Bruce
American b. 1933
drawings: (L) $4,950; (H) $15,400
sculpture: (H) $12,100

CONNER, John Anthony
American 20th cent.
paintings: (L) $220; (H) $2,200

CONNER, John Ramsey
American 1869-1952
paintings: (L) $55; (H) $12,100

CONNER, McCauley
b. 1913
drawings: (H) $950

CONNER, Paul
American 1881-1968
paintings: (L) $302; (H) $1,320

CONNOR, Charles
American b. 1857
paintings: (H) $4,125

CONNRAD, Phillip
British 1876-1958
paintings: (L) $880; (H) $1,320

CONOLLY, Thurloe
paintings: (H) $1,980

CONRAD, Albert
paintings: (H) $4,400

CONRAD, J.T.
American 19th cent.
paintings: (H) $5,500

CONRADE, Alfred Charles
British 1863-1955
drawings: (L) $330; (H) $770

CONRADER, George
paintings: (H) $7,700

CONRADI, H.
paintings: (H) $2,640

CONROY, George T.
20th cent.
paintings: (L) $330; (H) $687

CONROY, R.
British 19th cent.
paintings: (H) $1,210

CONSAGRA, Pietro
Italian b. 1920
sculpture: (L) $605; (H) $33,000

CONSTABLE, John
English 1776-1837
sculpture: (L) $1,017; (H) $39,600

CONSTABLE, William
American 1783-1861
drawings: (L) $137; (H) $1,045

CONSTANT, Benjamin
French 1845-1902
paintings: (L) $1,100; (H) $38,500
drawings: (H) $990

CONSTANT, C.
paintings: (H) $715

CONSTANT, David Adolf
paintings: (H) $5,500

CONSTANT, George
paintings: (L) $440; (H) $825
drawings: (L) $220; (H) $495

CONSTANT, Maurice
sculpture: (L) $247; (H) $1,430

CONSTANT-ROUX
sculpture: (H) $1,650

CONSTANTIN, S.
French or Belgian 19th cent.
paintings: (H) $2,200

CONSTANTINE, George Hamilton
drawings: (H) $1,980

CONSTANTINI, Giuseppe
Italian 19th/20th cent.
paintings: (L) $6,050; (H) $8,250
drawings: (L) $880; (H) $2,420

CONSUELO-FOULD
French 1862-1927
paintings: (H) $1,100

CONTE, Pierre Charles
French 1823-1895
paintings: (H) $2,310

CONTEL, Jean Charles
French 1895-1928
paintings: (H) $660

CONTENCIN, Charles Henry
French 20th cent.
paintings: (H) $990

CONTENOT, D.H.
French
sculpture: (H) $770

CONTENT, Daniel
American b. 1902
paintings: (L) $2,200; (H) $4,180

CONTI, Antonio
drawings: (H) $3,025

CONTI, Bernardino dei
Italian 1450-1525
paintings: (H) $6,600

CONTI, Gino Emilio
Italian/American b. 1900
paintings: (L) $385; (H) $2,750

CONTI, P.
c. 1900
sculpture: (H) $715

CONTI, Primo
paintings: (L) $2,750; (H) $4,400

CONTI, Tito
Italian 1842-1924
paintings: (L) $440; (H) $4,400

CONTOIT, Louis
American 19th/20th cent.
paintings: (L) $1,210; (H) $1,320

CONTWAY, Jay
American
sculpture: (L) $900; (H) $2,200

CONVENTI, Francesco
sculpture: (H) $1,210

CONWAY, Douglas
paintings: (H) $1,100

CONWAY, Fred
American 1900-1972
paintings: (H) $935
drawings: (L) $220; (H) $330

CONWAY, John S.
American 1852-1925
paintings: (L) $3,520; (H) $6,050

COOK, Charles A.
English b. 1878
paintings: (H) $715

COOK, Ebenezer Wake
English b. 1843
drawings: (H) $6,050

COOK, G.
paintings: (H) $1,045

COOK, Gordon
paintings: (L) $3,025; (H) $5,225

COOK, Howard Norton
American b. 1901
drawings: (L) $330; (H) $18,700

COOK, John A.
American 1870-1936
drawings: (L) $88; (H) $825

COOK, Nelson
American 1817-1892
paintings: (L) $247; (H) $1,045

COOK, Otis
American b. 1900
paintings: (L) $302; (H) $1,320

COOK, Robert
American b. 1921
sculpture: (L) $220; (H) $2,860

COOK, William Edward
drawings: (H) $715

COOKE, Edward William
English 1811-1880
paintings: (L) $605; (H) $7,150
drawings: (H) $1,540

COOKE, G.
English 19th cent.
paintings: (H) $770

COOKE, George
American 1793-1849
paintings: (L) $1,870; (H) $4,950

COOKE, John
British ac. 1887-1903
paintings: (H) $8,250

COOKESLEY, Margaret Murray
English 19th cent.
paintings: (L) $3,520; (H) $12,100

COOL, Delphine de
French b. 1830
paintings: (H) $13,200

COOLE, Brian
British 19th cent.
paintings: (L) $412; (H) $1,540

COOLEY, C.C.
English 19th cent.
paintings: (H) $1,815

COOLIDGE, Cassius Marcellus
American 1844-1934
paintings: (L) $1,430; (H) $13,200

COOMANS, Auguste
Belgian ac. c. 1850
paintings: (L) $770; (H) $1,320

COOMANS, Diana
Belgian 19th cent.
paintings: (L) $660; (H) $9,350

COOMANS, Heva
Belgian 19th cent.
paintings: (H) $6,160

COOMANS, Joseph
paintings: (H) $11,000

COOMANS, Pierre Olivier Joseph
Belgian 1816-1889
paintings: (L) $935; (H) $8,250

COOMBS, Delbert Dana
American 1850-1938
paintings: (H) $3,520
drawings: (L) $55; (H) $2,200

COOPER, Abraham
English 1787-1868
paintings: (L) $2,200; (H) $57,750

COOPER, Alice
sculpture: (H) $2,200

COOPER, Astley David Montague
American 1865-1924
paintings: (L) $44; (H) $6,490

COOPER, Colin Campbell
American 1856-1937
paintings: (L) $220; (H) $77,000
drawings: (L) $220; (H) $14,300

COOPER, Edwin
English 1785-1833
paintings: (L) $3,300; (H) $6,600
drawings: (L) $880; (H) $6,050

COOPER, Emma Lampert
American 1860-1920
paintings: (L) $110; (H) $6,050
drawings: (H) $462

COOPER, G.H.
drawings: (H) $880

COOPER, George
American 1796-1849
paintings: (H) $1,430

COOPER, Helen A.
paintings: (L) $330; (H) $990

COOPER, Henry
English 19th cent.
paintings: (L) $605; (H) $1,100

COOPER, John
American
paintings: (H) $12,100

COOPER, Lillian
American 19th/20th cent.
paintings: (H) $1,320

COOPER, M.
American 19th/20th cent.
paintings: (H) $880

COOPER, Rita
Dutch 20th cent.
paintings: (L) $825; (H) $1,210

COOPER, Robert
English 19th cent.
paintings: (H) $3,300

COOPER, Thomas George
British ac. 1857-1896
paintings: (H) $1,540

COOPER, Thomas Sidney
English 1803-1902
paintings: (L) $605; (H) $55,000
drawings: (L) $132; (H) $1,870

COOPER, W.B.
drawings: (H) $2,420

COOPER, W.H.
paintings: (L) $220; (H) $1,540

COOPER, William H.
paintings: (H) $1,980

COOPER, William Sidney
English ac. 1871-1908
paintings: (L) $880; (H) $3,740
drawings: (H) $715

COOPSE, Pieter
ac. mid-17th cent.
paintings: (H) $35,750

COORMAN, C.E.
paintings: (H) $3,080

COOSEMANS, Alexander
Flemish baptized 1627, d. 1689
paintings: (H) $25,300

COOSEMANS, Joseph
Belgian 1828-1904
paintings: (H) $1,760

COPE, Charles West
English 1811-1890
drawings: (L) $385; (H) $825

COPE, George
American 1855-1929
paintings: (L) $935; (H) $16,500

COPE, Gordon Nicholson
American b. 1906
paintings: (L) $550; (H) $3,850

COPELAND, Alfred Bryant
American 1840-1909
paintings: (L) $88; (H) $9,625

COPELAND, Charles
American 1858-1945
paintings: (H) $12,100
drawings: (H) $357

COPLAND, J.
American
paintings: (H) $990

COPLEY, John Singleton
American 1737-1815
paintings: (L) $18,700; (H) $330,000
drawings: (H) $19,800

COPLEY, Robert
contemporary
paintings: (H) $6,600

COPLEY, William
American b. 1919
paintings: (L) $880; (H) $19,800
drawings: (L) $330; (H) $400

COPP, William
American b. 1891
paintings: (L) $99; (H) $770

COPPEDGE, Fern Isabel
American 1883/88-1951
paintings: (L) $412; (H) $12,100

COPPENOLLE, Jacques van
French d. 1915
paintings: (L) $1,650; (H) $7,425

COPPER, J.
American 18th cent.
paintings: (H) $4,950

COPPIN, John
Canadian/American b. 1904
paintings: (L) $38; (H) $660

COPPINI, Pompeo
American 1870-1957
sculpture: (H) $45,100

COPPOLA, Carlo
paintings: (H) $5,500

COPPOLA, Giovanni Andrea
paintings: (H) $1,100

COQUE, Emile de le
paintings: (H) $770

COQUIER, L.
paintings: (H) $3,300

CORBE
paintings: (H) $1,650

CORBELLINI, Luigi
Italian 1901-1968
paintings: (L) $176; (H) $3,190
drawings: (H) $138

CORBET
paintings: (H) $825

CORBETT, Edward
American 1919-1971
paintings: (L) $550; (H) $1,430
drawings: (H) $770

CORBETT, Josephine Gilmer
American
paintings: (H) $1,650

CORBINO, Jon
Italian/American 1905-1964
paintings: (L) $248; (H) $4,125
drawings: (L) $352; (H) $2,420

CORBOULD, Alfred
paintings: (H) $2,050

CORBOULD, Aster R.C.
British 19th cent.
paintings: (H) $1,650

CORCHON Y DIAQUE, Federico
Spanish 19th cent.
paintings: (H) $6,600

CORCK, Albert
American early 20th cent.
paintings: (H) $770

CORCOS, Lucille
American 1908-1973
paintings: (L) $2,200; (H) $4,400

CORCOS, Vittorio Matteo
Italian 1859-1933
paintings: (L) $13,200; (H) $66,000

CORDERO, Francisco
Mexican 19th cent.
paintings: (L) $1,760; (H) $6,050

CORDEY, P.
paintings: (H) $935

CORDIER
French 19th cent.
sculpture: (H) $1,540

CORDIER, H.
French 19th cent.
paintings: (H) $880

CORDREY, John
British 18th/19th cent.
paintings: (H) $4,950

CORELLI, Augusto
Italian b. 1853
paintings: (H) $1,980
drawings: (L) $1,100; (H) $1,430

CORELLI, G.
drawings: (H) $1,210

CORENENBERG, A.J.
Continental School 19th cent.
paintings: (H) $6,600

CORENZIO, Belisario
c. 1560-1643
drawings: (H) $8,800

CORINI, Professor
19th/20th cent.
sculpture: (H) $7,480

CORINTH, Lovis
German 1858-1925
paintings: (H) $990
drawings: (L) $110; (H) $880

CORLEY, H.
paintings: (H) $2,090

CORMIER, Joseph J. Emmanuel,
Joseph J. Emmanuel DESCOMPS
French 1869-1952
sculpture: (L) $880; (H) $8,800

CORMON, Fernand Anne Piestre
French 1845-1924
paintings: (L) $1,320; (H) $27,500

CORNARO, V.
paintings: (H) $1,650

CORNE, Michel
American b. Italy 1752-1832
paintings: (H) $12,100

CORNEAU, Eugene
paintings: (H) $990

CORNEILLE, Cornelius Guillaume van
BEVERLOO
Dutch b. 1922
paintings: (L) $6,600; (H) $170,500
drawings: (L) $4,620; (H) $18,700

CORNEILLE, Michel
1642-1708
drawings: (H) $17,600

CORNEILLE DE LYON
Flemish/French 1500?-1574/75
paintings: (H) $35,200

CORNEILLE DE LYON, and Studio
Flemish/French 16th cent.
paintings: (H) $99,000

CORNEJO, Francisco
American d. 1963
paintings: (H) $660
drawings: (H) $660

CORNELISZ, Cornelis, called Cornelis
van Haarlem
Dutch 1562-1638
paintings: (L) $7,150; (H) $41,800

CORNELISZ, Jacob van Oostsanen,
called Jacob D'Amsterdam
Dutch c. 1477-1533
paintings: (L) $4,620; (H) $5,775

CORNELIUS
Continental 19th cent.
paintings: (H) $2,200

CORNELL, Joseph
American 1903-1972
drawings: (L) $1,980; (H) $60,500
sculpture: (L) $3,080; (H) $495,000

CORNER, Thomas C.
American 1865-1938
paintings: (L) $495; (H) $3,520

CORNET, Alphonse
French 19th cent.
paintings: (L) $1,210; (H) $1,320

CORNIELLE
drawings: (H) $10,450

CORNIL, Gaston
French b. 1883
paintings: (H) $23,100

CORNOYER, Paul
American 1864-1923
paintings: (L) $660; (H) $35,200
drawings: (L) $522; (H) $1,100

CORNU, Pierre
French b. 1895
paintings: (H) $6,050
drawings: (H) $660

CORNU, Vital
French 1851-?
sculpture: (H) $990

CORNWALL, W. H.
British 19th cent.
paintings: (H) $6,875

CORNWELL, Dean
American 1892-1960
paintings: (L) $302; (H) $7,150
drawings: (L) $88; (H) $1,980

CORONEL, Pedro
Mexican b. 1923
paintings: (L) $8,250; (H) $88,000
drawings: (H) $6,050
sculpture: (L) $3,300; (H) $4,675

CORONEL, Rafael
Mexican b. 1932
paintings: (L) $1,760; (H) $143,000
drawings: (L) $1,540; (H) $2,475

COROT, Jean Baptiste Camille
French 1796-1875
paintings: (L) $8,250; (H) $1,375,000
drawings: (L) $687; (H) $11,000

CORPORA, Antonio
paintings: (L) $7,500; (H) $8,000

CORRADI, Konrad
Swiss 1813-1878
drawings: (L) $1,980; (H) $4,620

CORRADINI, C.
Italian 19th cent.
paintings: (L) $2,200; (H) $2,530

CORRADO, Cagli
paintings: (H) $4,180

CORREA, Benito Rebolledo
Chilean 1880-1964
paintings: (L) $3,520; (H) $22,000

CORREA, Juan
paintings: (H) $22,000

CORREA, Raphael
South American 19th/20th cent.
paintings: (H) $3,300

CORREA DE VIVAR, Juan
paintings: (H) $2,860

CORREGGIO
drawings: (H) $29,700

CORREGGIO, J.
American School 19th cent.
paintings: (H) $1,600

CORRELLI
Italian 19th cent.
drawings: (H) $880

CORRODI, Arnold
Italian
paintings: (H) $12,100

CORRODI, Hermann David Salomon
Italian 1844-1905
paintings: (L) $2,420; (H) $33,000

CORRODI, Salomon
Swiss 1810-1892
drawings: (L) $1,650; (H) $8,800

CORSI, Nicholas de
Italian b. 1882
paintings: (L) $935; (H) $1,430

CORSI, S.
Italian 19th cent.
paintings: (L) $2,750; (H) $11,000

CORSICA, Felix Calvelli
20th cent.
paintings: (H) $660

CORSINI, Raffael
Italian 19th cent.
drawings: (L) $7,150; (H) $15,000

CORT, Hendrik Frans de
Dutch 1742-1810
paintings: (L) $9,900; (H) $11,000

CORT?, A.
American School 19th/20th cent.
paintings: (H) $715

CORTAN, J.
paintings: (H) $1,870

CORTAZZ
American 20th cent.
drawings: (H) $770

CORTE, H. de
Belgian 20th cent.
paintings: (H) $715

CORTES, Edouard
French b. 1882
paintings: (L) $247; (H) $68,750
drawings: (L) $1,980; (H) $15,400

CORVOS, V.
paintings: (H) $1,650

CORWIN, Charles Abel
American 1857-1938
paintings: (L) $143; (H) $16,500
drawings: (H) $3,300

CORZAS, Francisco
Mexican b. 1936
paintings: (L) $3,575; (H) $71,500
drawings: (L) $1,650; (H) $3,300

COSENZA, Giuseppe
Italian b. 1847
paintings: (H) $3,850

COSSIERS, Jan
Flemish 1600-1671
paintings: (L) $5,500; (H) $17,600

COSSON, Marcel
French 1878-1956
paintings: (L) $1,760; (H) $22,000

COSTA
paintings: (H) $924

COSTA, Decava
paintings: (H) $3,300

COSTA, E.
paintings: (L) $1,650; (H) $2,640

COSTA, Emmanuele
Italian b. 1875
paintings: (L) $440; (H) $4,950
drawings: (H) $110

COSTA, Giovanni
Italian 1826/1833-1903
paintings: (L) $1,100; (H) $14,300

COSTA, Giovanni Battista
Italian 1858-1938
paintings: (L) $2,090; (H) $14,300

COSTA, Giuseppe
Italian 1852-1912
paintings: (H) $3,850

COSTA, Joachim
sculpture: (H) $1,650

MENDES DA COSTA, Joseph
Dutch 1806-1893
drawings: (L) $1,980; (H) $3,740

COSTA, O.
Italian 19th cent.
paintings: (H) $1,980

COSTA, Olga
Mexican b. 1913
paintings: (L) $1,980; (H) $33,000
drawings: (L) $1,320; (H) $11,000

COSTA, Oreste
Italian b. 1851
paintings: (L) $550; (H) $26,400

COSTANTINI, Giuseppe
Italian 1844-1894
paintings: (L) $660; (H) $4,400

COSTANZI, Placido
Italian c. 1690-1759
paintings: (L) $23,100; (H) $30,800

COSTE, Jean Baptiste
French 18th/19th cent.
drawings: (H) $1,900

COSTER, Adam de
paintings: (H) $18,700

COSTER, Jules de
Belgian 1883-1972
paintings: (H) $8,250

COSTIGAN, John Edward
American 1888-1972
paintings: (L) $715; (H) $6,050
drawings: (L) $495; (H) $2,970

COSWAY
British 18th/19th cent.
paintings: (H) $2,750

COSWAY, Richard
British 1742-1821
paintings: (L) $990; (H) $7,700

COT, Pierre Auguste
French 1837-1883
paintings: (L) $35,750; (H) $99,000

COTAN, Juan Sanchez
paintings: (H) $6,050

COTES, Francis
English 1725/26-1770
paintings: (L) $1,900; (H) $17,600
drawings: (H) $4,950

COTMAN, John Sell
English 1782-1842
drawings: (L) $605; (H) $37,400

COTTET, Charles
French 1863-1925
paintings: (L) $660; (H) $4,400

COTTINGHAM, Robert
American b. 1935
paintings: (L) $20,900; (H) $198,000
drawings: (L) $1,650; (H) $16,500

COTTON, John W.
American 1868-1931
paintings: (L) $1,430; (H) $2,475
drawings: (L) $330; (H) $550

COTTON, Marietta Leslie
American ac. 1889-1931
paintings: (L) $880; (H) $1,760

COTTON, William
American 1880-1958
paintings: (L) $1,100; (H) $6,600
drawings: (L) $660; (H) $1,100

COUDER, Alexandre
French 1808-1879
paintings: (H) $1,210

COUDER, Gustave Emile
French d. 1903
paintings: (L) $2,200; (H) $44,000

COUDJOIS, Henri
Belgian 19th cent.
paintings: (H) $2,475

COUDRAY, Georges Charles
French ac. 1883-1903
sculpture: (L) $550; (H) $1,430

COUDRAY, Marie Antoinette Lucien
French b. 1864
sculpture: (L) $2,420; (H) $4,675

COULDERY, Horatio H.
British 1832-1893
paintings: (L) $3,850; (H) $9,350

COULON, B.
paintings: (H) $1,760

COULON, G.
French b. 1914
paintings: (L) $550; (H) $880

COULON, George D.
American 1823-1904
paintings: (L) $715; (H) $2,200
drawings: (L) $605; (H) $3,520

COULON, Georges
French 1914-1988
paintings: (L) $880; (H) $1,210

COULON, Noel
sculpture: (H) $12,100

COULTER, William Alexander
American 1849-1936
paintings: (L) $418; (H) $15,400
drawings: (H) $880

COULTOU
sculpture: (H) $1,980

COUMONT, Charles
Flemish ac. 1842
paintings: (L) $2,200; (H) $25,300

COUNET, Cl. J.M.
sculpture: (H) $2,530

COUPER, William
American
sculpture: (L) $1,650; (H) $4,950

COUPIN DE LA COUPERIE, Marie
Philippe
French 1773-1851
paintings: (H) $4,950

COURBET, Gustave
French 1819-1877
paintings: (L) $1,100; (H) $715,000
drawings: (H) $1,430

COURBET, Gustave, and assistant
French 19th cent.
paintings: (H) $17,600

COURBET, Gustave and Cherubin
PATA
19th cent.
paintings: (H) $22,000

COURBET, Gustave and Marcel
ORDINAIRE
French 1819-1877
paintings: (H) $44,000

COURTAT, Louis
French d. 1909
paintings: (L) $8,250; (H) $13,750

Photorealism

Photorealism is a movement dating from the late 1960s in which subjects were depicted with a minute and impersonal precision of detail. The motifs are simple: urban landscapes, shop fronts, cars, horses, and faces. The paintings are monumental, and their cold mechanical finish recalls Surrealism. Photorealists focused on technical problems, treating all parts of the image impartially, capturing reflections and highlights. The work is closer to formal abstraction than to realism. Artists associated with the movement are Robert Cottingham, Chuck Close, Richard Estes, and Michael Gorman.

Robert Cottingham (b. 1935) was born in Brooklyn, New York, and studied at Pratt Institute. He gained recognition during the late 1960s and 1970s with paintings that were close-ups of the shiny surfaces of signs on building facades. Like many of the Photorealists, he begins by photographing signs and facades to be used as models. Letters and forms of word play figure prominently in his work. His fascination with letters and his use of brilliant colors and oblique angles are a product of his earlier career in advertising and illustration. His works are in the Whitney, Guggenheim, Smithsonian, Hirshhorn, and many other museums. (Robert Cottingham, *Ajax*, acrylic on paper, 24½ x 39½ in., Christie's, May 4, 1989, $26,400)

COURTENS, Franz
paintings: (H) $1,320

COURTET, Augustin
French 1821-1891
sculpture: (H) $1,430

COURTOIS, Guillaume, Guglielmo
CORTESE
French 1628-1679
paintings: (H) $4,950
drawings: (L) $1,925; (H) $7,700

COURTOIS, Gustave Claude Etienne
French 1853-1923
paintings: (L) $275; (H) $33,000

COURTOIS, Jacques, called LE
BOURGUIGNON
French 1621-1676
paintings: (L) $4,675; (H) $19,800

COURVOISIER, Jules
Swiss b. 1884
drawings: (H) $880

COUSE, Eanger Irving
American 1866-1936
paintings: (L) $1,100; (H) $71,500
drawings: (L) $1,320; (H) $6,600

COUSIN, Charles
French 19th cent.
paintings: (L) $209; (H) $4,400

COUSTEAU, Guillaume
French 1716-1777
sculpture: (L) $324; (H) $1,705

COUSTOU
French 18th cent.
sculpture: (H) $1,210

COUTAUD, Lucien
French 1904-1977
drawings: (L) $880; (H) $3,520

COUTOURIER, Rene
French 20th cent.
paintings: (H) $715

COUTRE, Thomas
paintings: (H) $2,200

COUTTS, Alice
American
paintings: (L) $1,650; (H) $4,400

COUTTS, Gordon
American 1868/80-1937
paintings: (L) $193; (H) $4,180

COUTURE, Thomas
French 1815-1879
paintings: (L) $33,000; (H) $82,500
drawings: (L) $1,540; (H) $8,250

COUTURIE, Ninette
American 19th/20th cent.
paintings: (L) $990; (H) $1,100

COUTURIER
paintings: (H) $770

COUTURIER, Philibert Leon
French 1823-1901
paintings: (L) $500; (H) $16,500

COUVER, J. van
Dutch 1836-1909
paintings: (H) $1,980

COUVERT, G.
paintings: (H) $3,850

COUWENBERG, Christian van
Dutch 1604-1667
paintings: (L) $14,300; (H) $60,500

COVARRUBIAS, Miguel
Mexican 1904-1957
paintings: (L) $8,800; (H) $25,300
drawings: (L) $187; (H) $16,500

COVENTRY, Robert M.S.
paintings: (H) $3,300

COWAN, John
Scottish ac. 1773-1777
drawings: (H) $8,000

COWAN, John P.
American b. 1920
drawings: (L) $2,500; (H) $8,525

COWARD, Sir Noel
British 19th/20th cent.
paintings: (L) $1,540; (H) $3,300

COWDERY, Eva D.
American exhib. 1897-98, 1905
paintings: (L) $215; (H) $4,950

COWDERY, Jennie Van Fleet
American 20th cent.
paintings: (H) $770

COWELL, William Wilson
American b. 1856
paintings: (H) $1,155

COWIE, A.B.
British 19th cent.
paintings: (H) $1,200

COWIESON, Agnes M.
English ac. 1899-1912
paintings: (H) $825

COWLAND, Alice C.
American 20th cent.
drawings: (H) $770

COWLES, Russell
American 1887-1979
paintings: (L) $600; (H) $1,430

COWPER, Frank Cadogan
British 1877-1958
paintings: (H) $46,750

COX, Albert Scott
American 1863-1920
paintings: (L) $275; (H) $2,750

COX, Allyn
American 1896-1982
paintings: (L) $77; (H) $1,430
drawings: (L) $33; (H) $247

COX, David
paintings: (L) $550; (H) $6,050
drawings: (L) $300; (H) $2,200

COX, David, Sr.
British 1783-1859
paintings: (L) $550; (H) $6,050
drawings: (L) $357; (H) $5,775

COX, David, Jr.
British 1809-1885
drawings: (L) $412; (H) $935

COX, David
British 19th cent.
paintings: (L) $605; (H) $2,750

COX, Everard M.
paintings: (H) $742

COX, Frank
ac. 1890-1899
paintings: (H) $935

COX, Garstin
British b. 1892
paintings: (L) $440; (H) $2,750

COX, George J.
American 1884-1946
paintings: (H) $825

COX, Jimmy
American contemporary
paintings: (H) $3,500
sculpture: (H) $6,500

COX, Kenyon
American 1856-1917/19
paintings: (H) $550
drawings: (H) $1,045

COX, Louise
American 1865-1945
paintings: (H) $3,410

COX, Palmer
Canadian/American 1840-1924
drawings: (L) $110; (H) $5,225

COX, Timmy
American 20th cent.
paintings: (H) $1,430

COXE, Reginald Cleveland
American b. 1855
paintings: (H) $2,750

COY, I.H.
drawings: (H) $4,675

COYPEL, Charles Antoine
French 1694-1752
paintings: (L) $9,900; (H) $77,000
drawings: (L) $1,100; (H) $5,225

COYPEL, Noel, studio of
paintings: (L) $5,500; (H) $23,100

COYPEL, Noel Nicolas
French 1690-1734
drawings: (H) $6,600

COZENS, Alexander
English c. 1717-1786
drawings: (H) $2,090

COZENS, William
paintings: (H) $2,200

COZZA, Francesco
Italian 1605-1682
paintings: (L) $2,420; (H) $74,250

COZZENS, Frederick Schiller
American 1846-1928
drawings: (L) $110; (H) $8,250

CRABEELS, Florent Nicolas
Belgian 1829-1896
paintings: (L) $11,000; (H) $11,550

CRADDOCK, Marmaduke
British c. 1660-1717
paintings: (L) $3,300; (H) $15,400

CRAESBEECK, Joos van
Flemish c. 1606-1654/61
paintings: (L) $660; (H) $29,700

CRAFTY, Victor Gerusez
French c. 1840-1906
drawings: (H) $8,800

CRAGG, Tony
English b. 1949
sculpture: (L) $20,900; (H) $55,000

CRAIG
paintings: (H) $1,100

CRAIG, Charles
American 1846-1931
paintings: (L) $440; (H) $8,250
drawings: (H) $605

CRAIG, Frank
British 1874-1918
paintings: (H) $2,310
drawings: (H) $1,400

CRAIG, Henry Robertson
British 1916-1984
paintings: (L) $330; (H) $6,050

CRAIG, R.H.
American
paintings: (H) $715

CRAIG, Thomas Bigelow
American 1849-1924
paintings: (L) $250; (H) $4,950
drawings: (L) $165; (H) $1,320

CRAIG, William
American 1829-1875
drawings: (L) $770; (H) $2,750

CRALI, Tullio
paintings: (H) $3,080

CRAM, Allen Gilbert
American 1886-1947
paintings: (L) $825; (H) $5,280

CRAMER, Helene
German b. 1844
paintings: (H) $6,875

CRAMER, Konrad
German/American 1888-1965
paintings: (L) $3,300; (H) $24,200
drawings: (H) $165

CRAMER, Molly
German b. 1862
paintings: (L) $137; (H) $1,430

CRAMPTON, W.J.
British 19th cent.
paintings: (L) $88; (H) $880

CRANACH, Lucas, the elder, studio of
German 14th/15th cent.
paintings: (H) $14,300

CRANACH, Lucas, the elder
German 1472-1553
paintings: (L) $88,000; (H) $748,000

CRANACH, Lucas, the younger
German 1515-1586
paintings: (H) $22,000

CRANACH, Lucas, the younger, and studio
paintings: (H) $15,400

CRANCH, Christopher Pearse
American 1813-1892
paintings: (L) $880; (H) $3,740

CRANDALL, Bradshaw
American 1896-1966
paintings: (H) $330
drawings: (L) $192; (H) $2,420

CRANE, Fred E.
paintings: (L) $467; (H) $990

CRANE, Robert Bruce, or Bruce
American 1857-1937
paintings: (L) $605; (H) $42,900

CRANE, Walter
English 1845-1915
paintings: (L) $22,000; (H) $385,000
drawings: (L) $220; (H) $20,900

CRANE, Wilbur
American
paintings: (L) $220; (H) $1,870

CRANFORD, Kenneth
American 19th cent.
paintings: (H) $1,980

CRANK, James
American 20th cent.
paintings: (H) $1,320

CRAPELET, Louis Amable
French 1822/23-1867
drawings: (H) $1,980

CRARARA, A. Piazza
sculpture: (H) $1,650

CRASKE, Leonard
American
sculpture: (H) $27,500

CRATZ, Benjamin
American b. 1888
paintings: (H) $880

CRAVEN, E.
American 19th/20th cent.
paintings: (H) $1,760

CRAWFORD, Brenetta Herman
American 1876-1956
paintings: (L) $330; (H) $770

CRAWFORD, Esther Mabel
American b. 1872
paintings: (H) $1,320

CRAWFORD, J.
American 19th cent.
paintings: (H) $6,820

CRAWFORD, Ralston
American 1906-1977
paintings: (L) $22,000; (H) $82,500
drawings: (L) $770; (H) $15,400

CRAWFORD, Robert C.
British 19th cent.
paintings: (H) $880

CRAWFORD, Thomas
American 1813-1857
sculpture: (H) $44,000

CRAWFORD, Thomas, studio of
American
sculpture: (H) $7,700

CRAWSHAW, J.I.
English 19th cent.
paintings: (H) $990

CRAYER, Gaspar de
Flemish 1584-1669
paintings: (L) $6,050; (H) $27,500

CREALOCK, John
British 1871-1959
paintings: (L) $825; (H) $9,900

CREDELOS, Richard
American 20th cent.
paintings: (H) $715

CREE, James
American 1867-1951
drawings: (H) $1,540

CREEFT, Jose de
Spanish b. 1884
drawings: (H) $440
sculpture: (L) $220; (H) $16,500

CREIGHTON, Bessy
American b. 1884
paintings: (H) $1,540

CREMONINI, Leonardo
Italian b. 1925
paintings: (L) $4,620; (H) $19,800

CRENTANOVE, G.
Italian 19th/20th cent.
sculpture: (H) $1,760

CREO, Leonard
American b. 1923
paintings: (L) $88; (H) $660

CREPIN, Louis Phillipe
paintings: (H) $4,125

CRESPI, Daniele
Italian 1598-1630
paintings: (L) $3,850; (H) $8,800

CRESPI, Giovanni Battista, Il Cerano
Italian 1575-1633
paintings: (L) $17,600; (H) $20,900

CRESPI, Giuseppe Maria
Italian 1665-1747
paintings: (H) $11,000
drawings: (H) $52,250

CRESPI, Giuseppe Maria, studio of
Italian 18th cent.
paintings: (H) $23,100

CRESPI, Luigi
Italian c. 1709/10-1779
paintings: (H) $77,000

CRESPI, Luigi, and studio
paintings: (H) $22,000

CRESSINGHAM, A.E.
American 19th cent.
paintings: (H) $1,375

CRESSWELL, William N.
American
drawings: (H) $1,760

CRESWICK, Thomas
English 1811-1869
paintings: (L) $175; (H) $4,950

CRETEN-GEORGE
drawings: (H) $660

CRETI, Donato
Italian 1671-1749
paintings: (H) $770
drawings: (L) $1,650; (H) $18,700

CREVEL, Rene
paintings: (H) $3,300

CRICHELOW, Ernie
American School 20th cent.
paintings: (H) $2,310

CRIEFELDS, Richard
1853-1939
paintings: (H) $880

CRILEY, Theodore Morrow
American 1880-1930
paintings: (H) $1,760

CRILLEY
American 20th cent.
paintings: (H) $2,970

CRIMEAN, Robert
sculpture: (H) $4,950

CRIPPI, Roberto
drawings: (H) $5,750

CRISP, Arthur
American b. 1881
paintings: (L) $990; (H) $1,320

CRISP, G.
British 20th cent.
paintings: (H) $770

CRISPE, E.N.
British 20th cent.
paintings: (H) $825

CRISS, Francis
Anglo/American 1901-1973
paintings: (L) $1,155; (H) $18,700

CRISTADORO, Charles
American
sculpture: (H) $19,800

CRITE, Allan Rohan
American b. 1910
paintings: (L) $495; (H) $825
drawings: (H) $330

CRITZ, John de, studio of
paintings: (H) $25,300

CRIVELLI, Angelo Maria, called
Crivellone
Italian d. 1730/60
paintings: (L) $2,200; (H) $8,800

CRIVELLI, Vittorio
Italian ac. 1480-1501
paintings: (H) $36,300

CROCHEPIERRE, Andre
French b. 1860
paintings: (H) $2,530

CROCHET, Jules Emile
paintings: (H) $8,800

CROCIFISSI, Simone dei
Italian 1330-1399
paintings: (H) $484,000

CROCKER, Charles Matthew
American 1877-1950
paintings: (L) $467; (H) $3,300
drawings: (H) $413

CROCKER, John Denison
French/American b. 1823
paintings: (L) $330; (H) $2,970

CROCKETT, S.D.
British 1806-1865
paintings: (L) $1,980; (H) $2,090

CROCKFORD, Duncan
Canadian 20th cent.
paintings: (H) $1,210

CROCKWELL, Spencer Douglass
American 1904-1968
paintings: (L) $660; (H) $3,300

CROEGAERT, Georges
Dutch b. 1848
paintings: (L) $1,100; (H) $88,000

CROFT, Arthur
British b. 1828
drawings: (H) $715

CROISY, Aristide
sculpture: (H) $1,760

CROMARTY, A.
paintings: (H) $825

CROME, John
English 18th/19th cent.
paintings: (L) $1,320; (H) $1,320

CROME, John, called Old Crome
English 1768-1821
paintings: (L) $1,210; (H) $1,320

CROME, John Berney
English 1793/94-1842
paintings: (L) $3,300; (H) $3,850

CROME, William Henry
paintings: (H) $3,300

CROMWELL, Joane
American d. 1966
paintings: (L) $110; (H) $1,100

CROOK, Don
American
paintings: (H) $4,000

CROOKS, Ron
American b. 1925
paintings: (L) $935; (H) $1,925

CROOS, Anthony Jansz van der
Dutch c. 1606-after 1662
paintings: (L) $13,200; (H) $88,000

CROOS, Pieter van der
Dutch b. c. 1610
paintings: (L) $3,520; (H) $20,900

CROPSEY, Jasper Francis
American 1823-1900
paintings: (L) $605; (H) $209,000
drawings: (L) $1,320; (H) $17,600

CROSATO, Giovanni Battista
paintings: (H) $2,640

CROSBIE, A.R.
British early 20th cent.
paintings: (H) $660

CROSBY, O.R.
American 19th cent.
paintings: (H) $825

CROSBY, Ray
American 20th cent.
paintings: (H) $1,210

CROSBY, William
English ac. 1859-1873
paintings: (L) $2,310; (H) $5,500

CROSIO, Luigi
Italian 1835-1915
paintings: (L) $6,050; (H) $7,150

CROSMAN, John H.
American 20th cent.
paintings: (L) $303; (H) $2,250

CROSS, Anson Kent
American 1862-1944
paintings: (L) $330; (H) $1,980

CROSS, H.H.
paintings: (L) $715; (H) $935

CROSS, Henri Edmond
French 1856-1910
paintings: (L) $2,310; (H) $770,000
drawings: (L) $385; (H) $30,800

CROSS, Henry H.
American 1837-1918
paintings: (L) $385; (H) $77,000

CROSS, Penni Anne
American b. 1939
drawings: (L) $3,575; (H) $6,500

CROSS, Sally
1874-1950
paintings: (H) $1,100

CROSS, Watson, Jr.
American b. 1918
drawings: (L) $121; (H) $2,200

CROSSLAND, James Henry
paintings: (H) $1,650

CROTTI, Jean
French 1878-1958
paintings: (H) $2,640

CROUCH, A.
English 19th cent.
paintings: (H) $825

CROVELLO, William G.
American 20th cent.
sculpture: (L) $1,650; (H) $6,325

CROWE, Eyre
English 1824-1910
paintings: (L) $1,540; (H) $2,200

CROWE, Phillip
American contemporary
paintings: (H) $7,800

CROWELL, A.E.
paintings: (L) $770; (H) $1,210

CROWELL, Lucius
American 1911-1988
paintings: (H) $1,072

CROWLEY, Herbert
American 20th cent.
paintings: (H) $800

CROWLEY, J.M.
American c. 1835
drawings: (H) $2,750

CROWNINSHIELD, Frederick
American 1845-1918
paintings: (L) $1,100; (H) $6,270

CROZIER, William
contemporary
sculpture: (L) $550; (H) $8,800

CRUICKSHANK, William
English ac. 1866-1877
paintings: (L) $770; (H) $1,760
drawings: (L) $1,045; (H) $4,620

CRUIKSHANK, George
English 1792-1878
paintings: (H) $110
drawings: (L) $88; (H) $935

CRUIKSHANK, Robert Isaac
English 1789-1856
drawings: (L) $412; (H) $770

CRUIKSHANK, William, or
CRUICKSHANK
Scottish/Canadian 1844/49-1922
paintings: (L) $110; (H) $1,760
drawings: (L) $770; (H) $4,620

CRUISE, Aluyk Boyd
American 1909-1988
drawings: (L) $9,350; (H) $9,900

CRUM, R.
drawings: (H) $23,100

CRUYL, Lieven
1640-1720
drawings: (H) $8,250

CRUYS, Cornelis
Dutch d. 1660
paintings: (H) $49,500

CRUZ, Olger Villegas
sculpture: (H) $6,600

CRUZ-DIEZ, Carlos
Venezuelan b. 1923
paintings: (H) $23,100
drawings: (H) $9,900
sculpture: (H) $4,950

CSADEK (?), J.
sculpture: (H) $1,045

CSAKY
sculpture: (H) $8,250

CSAKY, Joseph
Hungarian/French 1888-1971
paintings: (L) $22,000; (H) $22,000
drawings: (H) $6,600

CSOT
Hungarian b. 1930
paintings: (L) $121; (H) $715

CSUK, Jeno
Hungarian 19th cent.
paintings: (H) $770

CUARTAS, Gregorio
Colombian b. 1938
paintings: (L) $1,100; (H) $6,050
drawings: (L) $770; (H) $935

CUATRI, Frederico
Mexican 20th cent.
paintings: (H) $770

CUBLEY, Henry Hadfield
English ac. 1882-1904
paintings: (L) $330; (H) $1,320

CUCCHI, Enzo
Italian b. 1950
paintings: (L) $14,300; (H) $121,000
drawings: (L) $2,200; (H) $60,500
sculpture: (H) $79,750

CUCUEL, Edward
American 1875/79-1951
paintings: (L) $100; (H) $41,800
drawings: (H) $990

CUENOV, Daniele E.
French 20th cent.
paintings: (H) $880

CUEVAS, Jose Luis
Mexican b. 1933/34
drawings: (L) $247; (H) $8,250

CUGAT, Xavier
Argentinian 20th cent.
paintings: (H) $935

CUITT, George, Sr.
paintings: (H) $2,310

CULBERTSON, Josephine
American 1852-1939
paintings: (L) $385; (H) $1,320

CULLIN, Isaac J.
British ac. 1881-1920
paintings: (L) $24,750; (H) $44,000

CULLOCH, H.M.
paintings: (H) $715

CULLUM, John
British ac. 1833-1849
paintings: (H) $1,100

CULMER, Henry Lavender Adolphus
American 1854-1914
paintings: (H) $2,475

CULOSILA, B.
paintings: (H) $990

CULVER, Charles
American b. 1908
drawings: (L) $88; (H) $1,870

CULVERHOUSE, Johann Mongels
Dutch b. 1820, ac. 1859-1891
paintings: (L) $550; (H) $25,300

CUMBERWORTH, Charles
French 1811-1852
sculpture: (L) $770; (H) $7,700

CUMING, Beatrice
American 1903-1975
paintings: (L) $209; (H) $1,210

CUMMING, Arthur
American 19th cent.
paintings: (L) $275; (H) $1,540
drawings: (L) $165; (H) $500

CUMMING, Charles Atherton
American 1858-c. 1932
paintings: (L) $660; (H) $2,860

CUMMINGS, e.e.
American 1894-1962
paintings: (H) $528
drawings: (H) $1,045

CUNAEUS, Conradyn
Dutch 1828-1895
drawings: (H) $1,100

CUNEO, Cyrus C.
American 1878/79-1916
paintings: (H) $2,750

CUNEO, Rinaldo
American 1877-1939
paintings: (L) $550; (H) $2,750

CUNLIFFE, David
paintings: (H) $14,300

CUNNINGHAM, Earl
American 1893-1978
paintings: (L) $575; (H) $7,700

CUNNINGHAM, John Wilton
American d. 1903
paintings: (L) $660; (H) $1,760

CUNY, E.R.
paintings: (H) $1,320

CUPRIEN, Frank W.
American 1871-1948
paintings: (L) $467; (H) $8,800

CURADZE, H.
Continental 19th cent.
sculpture: (H) $770

CURFI, S.
French 19th/20th cent.
paintings: (H) $825

CURIOS, John
paintings: (H) $660

CURIOT, Gustave C.G.
paintings: (H) $990

CURNOCK, James
British b. 1839
drawings: (H) $2,475

CURRADI, Francesco
Italian 1570-1661
paintings: (H) $2,200
drawings: (L) $1,430; (H) $7,150

CURRAN, Charles Courtney
American 1861-1942
paintings: (L) $578; (H) $99,000
drawings: (L) $286; (H) $1,980

CURRIER, Edward Wilson
American 1857-1918
paintings: (L) $110; (H) $2,750

CURRIER, Joseph Frank
American 1843-1909
drawings: (L) $1,430; (H) $1,650

CURRIER, Mary Ann
contemporary
paintings: (H) $41,250
drawings: (H) $22,000

CURRIER, Walter Barron
American 1879-1934
paintings: (L) $165; (H) $3,300

CURRY, John Steuart
American 1897-1946
paintings: (L) $8,250; (H) $82,500
drawings: (L) $302; (H) $18,700

CURRY, Robert F.
American b. 1872
paintings: (L) $330; (H) $990

CURTIN, Thomas R.
American 19th/20th cent.
paintings: (L) $50; (H) $770

CURTIS, Alice Marion
American 1847-1911
paintings: (L) $715; (H) $1,600
drawings: (H) $66

CURTIS, Charles
American circa 1820
paintings: (H) $990

CURTIS, Ellen Hunt
American 20th cent.
paintings: (H) $2,200

CURTIS, G.V.
American 19th/20th cent.
paintings: (H) $880

CURTIS, George
American 1826-1881
paintings: (L) $1,540; (H) $9,460

CURTIS, George Vaughan
British 1859-1943
paintings: (H) $4,180

CURTIS, Hughes
American 20th cent.
sculpture: (H) $660

CURTIS, Ida Maynard
American 1860-1959
paintings: (L) $55; (H) $1,540

CURTIS, Leland
American b. 1897
paintings: (L) $220; (H) $1,430
drawings: (L) $275; (H) $440

CURTIS, Philip C.
American 20th cent.
paintings: (L) $3,850; (H) $9,350

CURTIS, Ralph W.
American
paintings: (L) $330; (H) $770

CURTIS, Robert J., attrib.
German/American c. 1816-after 1850
paintings: (H) $110,000

CURTIS, Sidney W.
paintings: (H) $770

CURTIS, William Fuller
American b. 1873
paintings: (L) $1,100; (H) $5,500
sculpture: (L) $9,900; (H) $11,000

CURTS, T.
sculpture: (L) $462; (H) $1,100

CURZON, Paul Alfred de
French 1820-1895
paintings: (L) $3,700; (H) $16,500

CUSACHS Y CUSACHS, Jose
Spanish 1851-1908
paintings: (L) $770; (H) $137,500

CUSHING, Howard Gardiner
American 1869-1915
paintings: (L) $275; (H) $20,900

CUSHING, Val
contemporary
sculpture: (L) $770; (H) $2,530

CUSHMAN, Warren
American b. 1845
paintings: (H) $750

CUSTER, Edward L.
American 1837-1880
paintings: (L) $1,210; (H) $4,400

CUSTIS, Eleanor Parke
American 1897-1983
paintings: (H) $6,325
drawings: (L) $220; (H) $5,500

CUTHBERT, Virginia
American b. 1908
paintings: (H) $2,750

CUTTING, Francis Harvey
American 1872-1964
paintings: (L) $330; (H) $825

CUVENES, Johan
paintings: (H) $79,750

CUYLENBORCH, Abraham van
Dutch before 1620-1658
paintings: (H) $6,050

CUYNERS?, F.
Belgian 19th cent.
paintings: (H) $1,650

CUYP, Aelbert
Dutch 1620-1691
paintings: (L) $18,700; (H) $198,000

Indian Chief

Osceola was chief of the Seminoles during their second war with the United States. He was captured in 1837 and imprisoned at Fort Moultrie, South Carolina, and died a year later. After his death, the 3,000 surviving Seminoles were sent to live on a reservation in Oklahoma.

Robert J. Curtis (c. 1816-after 1850) was born in Germany, emigrated to the United States as a boy, and settled in Charleston, South Carolina. In January 1838, a month before Osceola died, Curtis was commissioned by his patron, Dr. Robert Baker, to travel to Fort Moultrie to paint a portrait of the chief. The painting was so well received that Curtis advertised that he would produce copies for all interested buyers. The original, which now hangs in the Charleston Museum, was in the Charleston Exposition of 1901-1902, and was bought by the museum in 1927. A painting of Osceola, identical to the original by Curtis in every detail, and with an impeccable provenance, was attributed to Curtis and offered at auction on Nantucket Island in the summer of 1990. Estimated at $80,000-$100,000, the painting sold for $110,000; it is now in the William Reese Company (Robert J. Curtis (attrib.), *Osceola, War Chief of the Seminoles (1803-1838)*, oil canvas, 30 x 25 in., Osona, August 4, 1990, $110,000)

CUYP, Benjamin Gerritsz
Dutch 1612-1652
paintings: (L) $1,540; (H) $35,200

CUYP, Jacob Gerritsz
Dutch 1594-c. 1651
paintings: (L) $4,950; (H) $165,000

CUZZINI
sculpture: (H) $935

CYBOULLE, Aman
French ac. 1868-80
drawings: (H) $2,310

CYGAN, Z.
Polish 20th cent.
paintings: (H) $715

CYKOWSKI, Jan
early 20th cent.
sculpture: (H) $770

CYRSKY, Frank
American contemporary
paintings: (H) $1,980

CZACHORSKI, Ladislas de
Polish 1850-1911
paintings: (H) $8,800

CZACHORSKI, Wiadyslaw
paintings: (H) $11,000

CZENCZ, Janos
paintings: (H) $1,870

CZERNOTZKY, Ernst
Austrian b. 1869
paintings: (L) $1,430; (H) $1,540

CZERNUS, Tibor
paintings: (L) $4,950; (H) $14,850

CZOBEL, Bela Adalbert
Hungarian b. 1883
paintings: (H) $2,530

D'ACOSTA, Hy. Walker
Spanish 19th cent.
paintings: (H) $7,150

D'AGOTY, Pierre Edouard Gautier
1775-1871
paintings: (H) $3,850

D'AIRE, Paul
French ac. 1890-1910
sculpture: (L) $330; (H) $1,540

D'ALESSARDI, Michele
American
sculpture: (H) $1,320

D'ANGELO, R.A.
sculpture: (L) $121; (H) $880

D'ANGERS, Pierre Jean David
sculpture: (H) $935

D'AOUST, Enrique
Mexican 20th cent.
paintings: (H) $3,850

D'ARCANGELO, Allan
American b. 1930
paintings: (L) $55; (H) $18,150
drawings: (L) $330; (H) $1,540
sculpture: (H) $2,090

D'ARGELE
French 19th cent.
paintings: (H) $687

D'ASCENZO, Nicola
Italian/American b. 1869/71
paintings: (L) $55; (H) $1,540
drawings: (L) $165; (H) $440

D'ASTE, Joseph
sculpture: (L) $220; (H) $1,100

D'AVENNES, Emile Prisse
drawings: (L) $1,100; (H) $2,200

D'AZEGLIO, Massimo
1798-1866
paintings: (L) $110; (H) $1,100

D'ENTRAYGUES, Charles Bertrand
French b. 1851
paintings: (L) $7,700; (H) $77,000

D'EPINAY, Prosper
sculpture: (H) $3,520

D'ESPAGNAT, George
French 1870-1950
drawings: (H) $1,320

D'ESPOSITO, Vincent
drawings: (H) $770

D'LEON, Omar
paintings: (L) $3,080; (H) $3,300

D'ORSAY, Count Alfred Guillaume
Gabriel
French 1801-1852
paintings: (H) $11,550

D'ORSI, A.
sculpture: (H) $880

D'OTEMAR, Marie Adolph Edouard
Modert
French 19th cent.
paintings: (H) $825

DA, Popovi
American Indian
paintings: (H) $990

DA CHIRICO, V. Colombo
drawings: (H) $3,080

DABO, Leon
American 1868-1960
paintings: (L) $110; (H) $39,600

DACHENHAUS, E. von
paintings: (H) $2,420

DACOSTA, Milton
Brazilian b. 1915
paintings: (H) $15,400

DADAIX
sculpture: (H) $1,650

DADD, Frank
drawings: (H) $2,640

DADDI, Bernardo
Italian 1290-1330/55
paintings: (H) $159,500

DADELBEEK, G***
Dutch 18th cent.
paintings: (H) $4,400

DADO
paintings: (L) $9,900; (H) $22,000

DAEL, Jan Frans van
Flemish 1764-1840
drawings: (H) $825

DAELE, Casimir van den
Belgian 1818-1880
paintings: (H) $2,860

DAEN, Lindsay
Austrian/American b. 1923
sculpture: (L) $440; (H) $1,430

DAGGY, Richard
paintings: (L) $2,090; (H) $3,245
drawings: (H) $220

DAGNAN-BOUVERET, Pascal
Adolphe Jean
French 1852-1929
paintings: (L) $4,400; (H) $20,900

DAGNAUX, Albert Marie Adolphe
French 1861-1933
paintings: (H) $550,000
drawings: (H) $143

DAGNON-BOUVERET, J.A.P.
paintings: (H) $8,250

DAGUERRE, Louis Jacques Mande
French 1787-1851
drawings: (H) $6,600

DAHL, Hans
Norwegian 1849-1937
paintings: (L) $275; (H) $28,600
drawings: (L) $605; (H) $5,500

DAHL, J.
Danish 19th cent.
paintings: (H) $6,050

DAHL, Michael
Swedish
paintings: (H) $3,850

DAHL, Siegwald
German 1827-1902
paintings: (L) $2,420; (H) $25,300

DAHLAGER, Jules
American 20th cent.
paintings: (L) $770; (H) $1,320

DAHLGREEN, Charles W.
American 1864-1955
paintings: (L) $140; (H) $2,090

DAHLGREN, Carl
Danish/American 1841-1920?
paintings: (L) $275; (H) $4,400
drawings: (L) $330; (H) $440

DAHLGREN, Marius
American 1844-1920
paintings: (H) $2,200

DAHN, Walter
contemporary
paintings: (L) $3,850; (H) $15,400

DAHRES-DAUBIGNY
paintings: (H) $1,430

DAILEY, Dan
American b. 1947
sculpture: (L) $1,650; (H) $5,500

DAINGERFIELD, Elliott
American 1859-1932
paintings: (L) $412; (H) $7,700
drawings: (L) $165; (H) $330

DAINI, Augusto
Italian 19th cent.
drawings: (L) $880; (H) $2,860

DAIO, David
contemporary
paintings: (H) $1,320

DAIWAILLE, Alexander Joseph and
Eugene VERBOECKHOVEN
paintings: (H) $11,000

DAKIN, J.
British 19th/20th cent.
paintings: (H) $1,045

DAKIN, Sidney Tilden
American 1876-1935
paintings: (L) $165; (H) $1,430

DALBREUSE, J.
sculpture: (H) $1,320

DALBY, David, called DALBY of York
English 18th/19th cent.
paintings: (L) $3,300; (H) $44,000

DALBY, John
British 1826-1853
paintings: (L) $4,070; (H) $27,500

DALBY, Joshua
British ac. 1838-1893
paintings: (H) $30,250

DALE, F.W.
paintings: (H) $770

DALEE, J.
American ac. c. 1826-1848
drawings: (H) $3,740

DALENS, Dirk, the elder
paintings: (H) $5,500

DALEY, William and Catherine
contemporary
sculpture: (H) $3,850

DALI, Louis
French 20th cent.
paintings: (L) $193; (H) $1,210

DALI, Salvador
Spanish 1904-1989
paintings: (L) $35,200; (H) $4,070,000
drawings: (L) $825; (H) $440,000
sculpture: (L) $880; (H) $148,500

DALLAIRE, Jean Phillipe
Canadian
paintings: (L) $17,600; (H) $30,800

DALLIN, Cyrus Edwin
American 1861-1944
sculpture: (L) $275; (H) $41,800

DALMAU, Emilio Poy
Spanish b. 1876
paintings: (H) $1,760

DALOU, Aime Jules
French 1838-1902
sculpture: (L) $495; (H) $25,300

DALVIT, Oskar
Swiss b. 1911
paintings: (H) $880

DALY, Matt A.
paintings: (H) $770

DALZIEL, James
British 19th cent.
paintings: (H) $2,310

DAM, Vu Cao
French/Indonesian b. 1908
paintings: (L) $1,430; (H) $3,080

DAMAIGE, H.
sculpture: (L) $1,210; (H) $1,320

DAMERON, Emile Charles
French 1848-1908
paintings: (H) $6,050

DAMEZ, Sophie
French b. 1943
paintings: (L) $247; (H) $770

DAMIAN, Horia
Romanian b. 1922
paintings: (L) $2,200; (H) $2,420

DAMM, Johan Frederik
Danish 1820-1894
paintings: (H) $13,200

DAMME, Frans van
Flemish b. 1860
paintings: (H) $1,870

DAMME-SYLVA, Emile van
Belgian 1853-1935
paintings: (L) $550; (H) $1,540

DAMOYE, Pierre Emmanuel
French 1847-1916
paintings: (L) $1,320; (H) $35,200

DAMPIER, William
American 1910-1985
paintings: (L) $275; (H) $770

DAMROW, Charles
American b. 1916
paintings: (L) $55; (H) $715

DAMSCHROEDER, Jan Jacobus
Matthijs
German 1825-1905
paintings: (L) $935; (H) $7,700

DANA, C.G.
American 19th/20th cent.
paintings: (L) $522; (H) $1,100

DANA, William Parsons Winchester
American 1833-1927
paintings: (L) $495; (H) $1,540

DANBY
paintings: (H) $1,430

DANBY, E.R., Mrs.
English 19th cent.
paintings: (H) $825

DANBY, James Francis
British 1816-1875
paintings: (L) $220; (H) $4,400

DANBY, Thomas
English 1818-1886
paintings: (H) $1,100

DANCIG, F.
European 19th cent.
paintings: (H) $1,430

DANCKERTS DE RY, Peter
Dutch 1605-1659/61
paintings: (H) $1,980

DANDINI, Cesare
Italian 1595-1658
paintings: (L) $2,640; (H) $85,250

DANDINI, Pietro
Italian 1646-1712
paintings: (H) $35,200
drawings: (L) $605; (H) $715

DANDINI, Vincenzo
paintings: (L) $16,500; (H) $17,600
drawings: (H) $187

DANDRE-BARDON, Michel Francois
French 1700-1778/83
drawings: (H) $1,320

DANDRIDGE, Bartholomew
English 1691-1751
paintings: (H) $15,400

DANERI, Eugenio
Argentinian 1891-1970
paintings: (H) $6,600

DANHAUSER, Josef
Austrian 1805-1845
paintings: (H) $5,775

DANIELL, William
British 1769-1837
drawings: (L) $1,650; (H) $3,300

DANIELL, William Swift
American 1865-1933
paintings: (H) $440
drawings: (L) $523; (H) $990

DANIELLI, Giovanni
Italian 1824-1890
paintings: (H) $990

DANIELS, George Fisher
American b. 1821
paintings: (L) $2,250; (H) $24,200

DANKWORTH, August
paintings: (H) $1,430

DANLOUX, Henri Pierre
French 1753-1809
paintings: (L) $4,400; (H) $170,500

DANN, Frode N.
American b. 1892
drawings: (H) $5,225

DANNAT, William Turner
American 1853-1929
paintings: (L) $1,320; (H) $1,870

DANNEL, F.
19th cent.
paintings: (H) $880

DANNENBERG, Alice
Russian/French b. 1861
paintings: (H) $1,320

DANNER, Sara Kolb
American 1894-1969
paintings: (L) $303; (H) $5,225

DANSAERT, Leon
Belgian 1830-1909
paintings: (L) $2,640; (H) $7,150

DANTON, D.
American 19th cent.
paintings: (H) $660

DANTON, F., Jr.
American 19th cent.
paintings: (H) $7,700

DANTU, George Victor Laurent
French b. 1876
paintings: (L) $605; (H) $4,290

DANTZIG, Meyer M.
American 20th cent.
paintings: (L) $330; (H) $825

DANZ, Robert
German b. 1841
paintings: (H) $35,200

DANZIGER, Joan
sculpture: (H) $1,430

DANZNIANY, H.G.
sculpture: (H) $825

DAOUR, Jeanne
French b. 1914
paintings: (L) $385; (H) $660

DAPHNIS, Nassos
American b. 1914
paintings: (L) $1,430; (H) $4,620

DAQIAN, Zhang
Chinese 1899-1983
drawings: (L) $5,500; (H) $6,050

DARBEFEUILLE, Victor Sacha
French 19th/20th cent.
paintings: (L) $5,500; (H) $12,100

DARBES, Joseph Friedrich August
German 1747-1810
paintings: (H) $1,760

DARBOUR, Marguerite Mary
French 19th/20th cent.
paintings: (L) $2,420; (H) $3,850

DARBOVEN, Hanne
b. Germany 1941
drawings: (H) $7,150

DARBY, Henry F.
American b. c. 1831
paintings: (L) $1,045; (H) $3,630

DARGELAS, Andre Henri
French 1828-1906
paintings: (H) $11,000

DARIANS, H.
paintings: (H) $1,100

DARIEN, Andre
paintings: (H) $990

DARIEN, Henri Gaston
French 1864-1926
paintings: (L) $3,190; (H) $41,250

DARLEY, Felix Octavius Carr
American 1822-1888
paintings: (L) $1,320; (H) $36,300
drawings: (L) $44; (H) $2,090

DARLEY, Felix Octavius Carr and
Randolph John ROGERS
American 19th cent.
drawings: (H) $990

DARLING, Jay Norwood, "Ding"
American b. 1876
paintings: (L) $2,090; (H) $2,400

DARLING, Wilder M.
American 1856-1933
paintings: (L) $495; (H) $1,210
drawings: (H) $275

DARLING, William S.
American 1882-1963
paintings: (L) $660; (H) $3,025

DARMANIN, Jose Miralles
Spanish b. 1851
paintings: (H) $5,775

DARNAUT, Hugo
Austrian 1851-1937
paintings: (H) $1,320

DARONDEAU, Stanislas Henri Benoit
French 1807-1841
paintings: (H) $1,210

DARRIE, Louis
19th cent.
paintings: (H) $880

DARRIEUX, Charles Rene
French b. 1879
paintings: (L) $825; (H) $6,600

DARRU, Louis
French 19th cent.
paintings: (L) $6,050; (H) $11,000

DART, Richard Pousette
American b. 1916
paintings: (H) $22,000

DASBURG, Andrew Michael
American 1887-1979
paintings: (L) $1,650; (H) $121,000
drawings: (L) $3,850; (H) $18,700

DASH, Robert
American b. 1932
paintings: (L) $550; (H) $1,870

DASHENG, Huang
late 19th cent.
paintings: (H) $880

DASSON, Henri
sculpture: (H) $11,000

DASTUGUE, Maxime
French 19th cent.
paintings: (L) $1,100; (H) $6,600

DAUBIGNY
paintings: (L) $330; (H) $3,850

DAUBIGNY, Charles Francois
French 1817-1878
paintings: (L) $990; (H) $126,500
drawings: (L) $990; (H) $7,700

DAUBIGNY, Karl Pierre
French 1846-1886
paintings: (L) $825; (H) $20,900

DAUCHOT, Gabriel
French b. 1927
paintings: (L) $523; (H) $2,200

DAUDIN, Henry Charles
French b. 1861
paintings: (H) $4,400

DAUGHTERY, James Henry
American 1889-1974
paintings: (L) $660; (H) $26,400
drawings: (L) $200; (H) $11,000

DAUMIER, Honore
French 1808-1879
paintings: (L) $38,000; (H) $1,100,000
drawings: (L) $1,650; (H) $253,000
sculpture: (L) $1,870; (H) $57,750

DAUMIER, Jean
French b. 1919
paintings: (L) $880; (H) $6,875

DAUVERGNE, R.J.
sculpture: (H) $3,025

DAUX, Charles Edmond
French 19th cent.
paintings: (L) $605; (H) $19,800

DAVEAU, Flavian
French 19th cent.
paintings: (L) $165; (H) $1,320

DAVELOOSE, Jean Baptiste
Belgian 1807-1886
paintings: (L) $1,045; (H) $2,420

DAVENPORT, Rebecca
American b. 1943
paintings: (L) $770; (H) $4,950

DAVEY, Randall
American 1887-1964
paintings: (L) $440; (H) $16,500
drawings: (L) $250; (H) $3,080
sculpture: (H) $715

DAVID, Fernand
sculpture: (L) $242; (H) $1,980

DAVID, Gerard
Flemish 1460-1523
paintings: (H) $33,000

DAVID, Hermine
French 1886-1971
paintings: (L) $990; (H) $3,850
drawings: (L) $77; (H) $220

DAVID, Jacques Louis
French 1748-1825
paintings: (H) $4,070,000
drawings: (L) $7,700; (H) $18,700

DAVID, Jules
French
drawings: (H) $1,430

DAVID, Michael
contemporary
paintings: (H) $5,500

DAVID, Pierre Jean, called David
D'Angers
sculpture: (H) $1,320

DAVID, Stanley S.
American
paintings: (L) $8,800; (H) $15,400

DAVIDSON, Allan
British 1873-1932
paintings: (H) $1,430

DAVIDSON, Clara D.
American b. 1874
paintings: (H) $3,520

DAVIDSON, Daniel Pender
Scottish 20th cent.
paintings: (H) $660

DAVIDSON, Herbert
paintings: (L) $275; (H) $1,100

DAVIDSON, Jo
American 1883-1952
drawings: (L) $154; (H) $220
sculpture: (L) $93; (H) $12,100

DAVIDSON, Julian O.
American 1853-1894
paintings: (L) $330; (H) $2,860
drawings: (L) $330; (H) $4,400

DAVIDSON, Karen
drawings: (H) $660

DAVIDSON, Morris
American 1898-1979
paintings: (H) $770

DAVIDSON, Thomas
British ac. 1863-1893
paintings: (L) $605; (H) $8,250

DAVIE, Alan
English b. 1920
paintings: (L) $1,320; (H) $93,500
drawings: (L) $1,540; (H) $4,950

DAVIES
paintings: (H) $1,100

DAVIES, A.
paintings: (L) $770; (H) $1,430

DAVIES, Albert Webster
American 1889-1967
paintings: (L) $132; (H) $1,320

DAVIES, Arthur Bowen
American 1862-1928
paintings: (L) $165; (H) $35,200
drawings: (L) $165; (H) $6,050

DAVIES, Harold Christopher
American 1891-1976
paintings: (H) $1,650
drawings: (L) $137; (H) $990

DAVIES, J.
British 19th cent.
paintings: (H) $1,045

DAVIES, James Hey
English b. 1848
paintings: (H) $1,540

DAVIES, Ken
American b. 1925
paintings: (L) $1,870; (H) $3,850

DAVIES, Norman Prescott
English 1862-1915
paintings: (H) $2,750

DAVIES, Warren
paintings: (H) $880

DAVIES, William Steeple
American
drawings: (H) $1,430

DAVIHOT
French 20th cent.
paintings: (H) $825

DAVILA, Jose Antonio
b. New York 1935
paintings: (L) $3,300; (H) $22,000

DAVILLA, Fernando
paintings: (H) $3,300

DAVIS
British 19th cent.
paintings: (H) $825

DAVIS, Alexander Jackson
American 1803-1892
paintings: (H) $462
drawings: (H) $880

DAVIS, Arthur Alfred
English ac. 1877-1884
paintings: (L) $3,740; (H) $6,050

DAVIS, Brad
American b. 1942
paintings: (L) $6,050; (H) $7,700

DAVIS, Charles F.
British 19th/20th cent.
paintings: (H) $1,430

DAVIS, Charles Harold
American 1856-1933
paintings: (L) $770; (H) $13,500
drawings: (L) $80; (H) $550

DAVIS, Debby
contemporary
paintings: (H) $330
sculpture: (L) $330; (H) $1,320

DAVIS, Edward
paintings: (H) $2,860

DAVIS, Gene
American b. 1920
paintings: (L) $1,870; (H) $28,600
drawings: (L) $308; (H) $825

DAVIS, Gladys Rockmore
American 1901-1967
paintings: (L) $165; (H) $6,600
drawings: (H) $440

DAVIS, H.A.
American 19th cent.
paintings: (H) $1,210

DAVIS, Henry William Banks
English 1833-1914
paintings: (L) $3,520; (H) $25,300

DAVIS, J.A.
American b. 1824, ac. c. 1838-1854
drawings: (L) $660; (H) $8,800

DAVIS, John Scarlett
English 1804-1841/45
paintings: (H) $6,600

DAVIS, Joseph H.
Canadian/American d. 1837
drawings: (L) $2,750; (H) $28,600

DAVIS, Leonard M.
American 1864-1938
paintings: (L) $55; (H) $1,980

DAVIS, Marsha
American
paintings: (H) $1,250

DAVIS, Miles
paintings: (H) $1,100

DAVIS, O.E.
American 19th cent.
drawings: (H) $990

DAVIS, Paul
paintings: (H) $1,100

DAVIS, Richard Barrett
English 1782-1854
paintings: (L) $1,650; (H) $66,000

DAVIS, Ron
American b. 1937
paintings: (L) $605; (H) $44,000
drawings: (H) $4,950
sculpture: (L) $4,180; (H) $16,500

DAVIS, Stan
American b. 1942
paintings: (L) $6,050; (H) $9,625

DAVIS, Stark
paintings: (H) $990

DAVIS, Stark
American b. 1885
paintings: (L) $220; (H) $2,860

DAVIS, Stuart
American 1894-1964
paintings: (L) $1,980; (H) $880,000
drawings: (L) $770; (H) $99,000

DAVIS, Theodore Russell
American 1840-1894
drawings: (L) $275; (H) $2,750

DAVIS, Vestie
American 1903-1978
paintings: (H) $4,290

DAVIS, W.
paintings: (H) $1,980

DAVIS, W.H.
English d. 1865
paintings: (L) $880; (H) $7,700

DAVIS, W.M.
drawings: (H) $935

DAVIS, Warren B.
American 1865-1928
paintings: (L) $192; (H) $17,600

DAVIS, William B.
paintings: (H) $4,620

DAVIS, William Henry
English ac. 1803-1849
paintings: (L) $1,430; (H) $4,400

DAVIS, William M.
American 1829-1920
paintings: (L) $242; (H) $22,000
drawings: (H) $9,350

DAVIS, William R.
American 20th cent.
paintings: (L) $1,100; (H) $5,775

DAVIS, Willis E.
American 1855-1910
paintings: (H) $1,760

DAVIS (?), Mary DeForest
American 2nd half 19th cent.
paintings: (H) $1,760

DAVISON, Wilfred P.
American 19th/20th cent.
paintings: (H) $1,100
drawings: (H) $495

DAVOL, Joseph
American 1864-1923
paintings: (L) $440; (H) $1,100

DAWE, George
British 1781-1829
paintings: (H) $1,760

DAWES, Edwin M.
American 1872-1934/45
paintings: (L) $247; (H) $715
drawings: (H) $440

DAWSON, Alfred
British 1860-1894
paintings: (H) $1,870

DAWSON, Henry Thomas
British ac. 1860-1878
paintings: (L) $357; (H) $15,400

DAWSON, Manierre
American 1887-1969
paintings: (H) $57,750

DAWSON, Montague
English 1895-1973
paintings: (L) $1,540; (H) $176,000
drawings: (L) $2,640; (H) $17,600

DAWSON, S.
paintings: (H) $660

DAWSON-WATSON, Dawson
Anglo/American 1864-1939
paintings: (L) $467; (H) $14,300

DAWYDOFF, Iwan Grigorievich
Russian 1826/31-1856
paintings: (H) $6,050

DAY, Francis
American 1863-1942
paintings: (L) $467; (H) $14,000

DAY, G.F.
British 19th cent.
paintings: (H) $7,150

DAY, Larry
American b. 1921
paintings: (L) $192; (H) $1,650
drawings: (H) $165

DAYES, Edward
English 1761/63-1804
paintings: (H) $15,400

DAYEZ, Georges
contemporary
paintings: (L) $110; (H) $5,500

DAYON, Michael
American b. 1939
sculpture: (H) $660

DE BEUL, Franz
Belgian 1849-1919
paintings: (L) $412; (H) $935

DE BUT
sculpture: (H) $935

DE CAMP, Joseph Rodefer
American 1858-1923
paintings: (L) $715; (H) $55,000

DE CAMP, Ralph Earll
American 1858-1936
paintings: (H) $770

DE CRAMO, A.B.C.
paintings: (H) $154
drawings: (H) $2,310

DE CREEFT, Jose
Spanish/American 1884-1982
sculpture: (H) $4,950

DE DIEGO, Julia
American
paintings: (H) $3,080

DE ERDELY, Francis
American 1904-1959
paintings: (L) $770; (H) $14,300

DE FOREST, Henry J.
Canadian 1860-1924
paintings: (H) $2,475

DE FOREST, Lockwood
American 1850-1932
paintings: (L) $110; (H) $1,760

DE FORREST, Grace Bauker
American b. 1897
paintings: (H) $4,290

DE FRANCISCI, Anthony
Italian/American 1887-1964
sculpture: (H) $9,900

DE HAAFT, Cornelia
American 20th cent.
paintings: (H) $935

DE HAAS, Mauritz Frederik Hendrik
Dutch/American 1832-1895
paintings: (L) $660; (H) $35,200

DE HAVEN, Franklin
American 1856-1934
paintings: (L) $110; (H) $6,050
drawings: (H) $55

DE KOONING, Elaine
American b. 1920
paintings: (L) $1,540; (H) $9,900
drawings: (L) $550; (H) $990

DE KOONING, Willem
American b. 1904
paintings: (L) $11,000; (H) $20,680,000
drawings: (L) $1,760; (H) $1,870,000

FUENTE, Manuel de la
sculpture: (H) $20,900

DE LONGPRE, Paul
French/American 1855-1911
paintings: (L) $522; (H) $4,950
drawings: (L) $770; (H) $11,550

DE LONGPRE, Raoul
French/American 1855-1911
paintings: (L) $2,860; (H) $35,750
drawings: (L) $495; (H) $8,800

DE LUCE, Percival
American 1874-1914
paintings: (L) $165; (H) $5,500
drawings: (H) $1,760

DE MARIA, Nicola
contemporary
paintings: (H) $22,000
drawings: (L) $8,800; (H) $28,600

DE MARIA, Walter
American b. 1935
drawings: (L) $1,540; (H) $14,300
sculpture: (L) $8,800; (H) $110,000

DE MONI, Louis
paintings: (H) $4,950

DE MORGAN, Evelyn Pickering
English 1855-1919
paintings: (L) $9,900; (H) $22,000
drawings: (L) $1,870; (H) $23,100

DE NAGY, Ernest
American 1906-1944
paintings: (L) $220; (H) $1,045

DE NATHAN, Raoul
paintings: (H) $825

DE NIRO, Robert
American b. 1922
drawings: (H) $660

DE NITTIS
paintings: (H) $825

DE PINELLI, A.
paintings: (H) $1,650

DE RIBCOWSKI, Dey
American 1880-1936
paintings: (L) $302; (H) $3,410

DE SAINT MEMIN, Charles Balthazer Feuret
American 1770-1852
drawings: (H) $4,400

DE SIMONE
American
drawings: (H) $1,760

DE SIMONE
Italian 19th/20th cent.
drawings: (L) $605; (H) $3,520

DE VALDENUIT, Thomas Bluget
American 1763-1846
drawings: (H) $1,155

DE VOLL, F. Usher
American 1873-1941
paintings: (H) $30,800

DE WINT, Peter
English 1784-1849
drawings: (L) $33; (H) $1,980

DE WITT, Jerome Pennington
late 19th cent.
paintings: (H) $660

DE WOLFE, Sarah E. Bender
American 1852-1935
paintings: (H) $770

DE YONG, Joe
American 1894-1975
paintings: (L) $110; (H) $1,045
drawings: (H) $193

DE'ROSSI, Francesco, called Salviati
Italian 1510-1563
drawings: (H) $49,500

DE'VECCHI, Giovanni
c. 1537-1615
drawings: (H) $3,300

DEAKIN, Edward
paintings: (H) $880

DEAKIN, Edwin
American 1838-1923
paintings: (L) $413; (H) $8,800
drawings: (L) $187; (H) $715

DEALER
paintings: (H) $3,300

DEAN, Laura E.
paintings: (H) $1,210

DEAN, Mabel
American 19th/20th cent.
paintings: (H) $742

DEAN, Peter
American contemporary
paintings: (L) $605; (H) $1,320

DEAN, Walter Lofthouse
American 1854-1912
paintings: (L) $165; (H) $3,575

DEARLE, John H.
British ac. 1853-1891
drawings: (L) $825; (H) $1,650

DEARN, W.
English 19th cent.
paintings: (H) $1,100

DEARTH, Henry D.
American
paintings: (H) $1,760

DEARTH, Henry Golden
American 1864-1918
paintings: (L) $330; (H) $5,280

DEAS, Charles
American 1818-1867
paintings: (L) $38,500; (H) $165,000

DEBAT, E.
paintings: (L) $715; (H) $1,320

DEBAT-PONSON, Edouard Bernard
French 1847-1913
paintings: (L) $4,950; (H) $25,300

DEBAY, J.
sculpture: (H) $715

DEBEUL, Armand
Belgium 1874-?
paintings: (H) $1,100

DEBEUL, H.
Belgian 19th cent.
paintings: (H) $4,675

DEBLAS, E.
European 19th cent.
paintings: (H) $660

DEBLOCK, Eugenius Frans
American
paintings: (H) $770

DEBLOIS, B.
paintings: (H) $1,210

DEBLOIS, Francois B.
Canadian c. 1829-1913
paintings: (L) $770; (H) $2,090

DEBOCK, Theophile Emile Archille
Dutch 1851-1904
paintings: (H) $1,650

DEBRAS, Louis
French 1820-1899
paintings: (L) $880; (H) $1,375

DEBRAUX, Rene Charles Louis
French 19th/20th cent.
paintings: (H) $1,320

DEBRE, Olivier
French b. 1920
paintings: (L) $660; (H) $50,600

DEBREANSKI, Gustave
English 19th cent.
paintings: (H) $1,760

DEBROCK, Eugene
Dutch 19th cent.
paintings: (H) $1,540

DEBRUS, A.
French 19th cent.
paintings: (H) $2,750

DEBRUS, Alexandre
French 19th cent.
paintings: (H) $8,800

DEBUT, Jean Didier
French 1824-1893
sculpture: (L) $935; (H) $6,820

DEBUT, Marcel
French b. 1865
sculpture: (L) $154; (H) $5,500

DECAMPS, Alexandre Gabriel
French 1803-1860
paintings: (L) $2,530; (H) $10,450
drawings: (L) $550; (H) $4,400

DECANDDER, S.
Belgian 19th cent.
paintings: (H) $5,500

DECHAR, Peter
American b. 1942
paintings: (L) $715; (H) $2,860

DECKER, Joseph
German/American 1853-1924
paintings: (L) $5,500; (H) $759,000
drawings: (H) $500

DECKER, Robert M.
American b. 1847
paintings: (L) $88; (H) $4,400

DECKLEMANN, Andreas
German 1820-1882
paintings: (H) $2,970

DECLOCHE, Paul Joseph
paintings: (H) $715

DECOENE, Henri
Belgian 1798-1866
paintings: (H) $8,250

DECONTI
paintings: (H) $880

DECOTE, George
French b. 1870
paintings: (H) $1,760

DECOUR
sculpture: (H) $1,320

DEDECKER, Tom
American b. 1951
paintings: (L) $1,980; (H) $4,000

DEDREUX, Alfred
French 1810-1860
drawings: (L) $1,430; (H) $22,000

DEERDELY, Francis
drawings: (H) $1,430

DEFAUX, Alexandre
French 1826-1900
paintings: (L) $440; (H) $7,700

DEFEURE, Georges
drawings: (L) $1,100; (H) $1,210

DEFFNER, Ludwig
German 19th/20th cent.
paintings: (L) $880; (H) $3,080

DEFILLO, Pena
Dominican b. 1928
paintings: (H) $2,750

DEFIZE, Alfred
Belgian 19th/20th cent.
paintings: (H) $1,430

DEFONTE, Edmond Alphonse
French b. 1862
paintings: (L) $462; (H) $20,900

DEFOREST, Roy
American b. 1930
paintings: (L) $330; (H) $27,500
drawings: (L) $1,320; (H) $6,050

DEFRANCE, James
contemporary
paintings: (H) $1,100

DEFREES, T.
American
paintings: (H) $825

DEFREGGER, Franz von
German 1835-1921
paintings: (L) $495; (H) $137,500

DEGAS, Edgar
French 1834-1917
paintings: (L) $37,400; (H) $3,850,000
drawings: (L) $1,760; (H) $7,975,000
sculpture: (L) $34,100; (H) $10,175,000

DEGOTTEX, Jean
contemporary
paintings: (H) $9,900

DEGRAILLY, Victor
American 1804-1889
paintings: (H) $7,700

DEGRANGE, Adolphe Louis, called
CASTEX-DEGRANGE
French b. 1840
paintings: (H) $2,200

DEHAAS, Johannes H.L.
Flemish 1832-1908
paintings: (H) $2,420

DEHASPE, Francois
Belgian b. 1874
paintings: (H) $935

DEHAVEN, T.
American 19th cent.
paintings: (H) $1,100

DEHN, Adolf Arthur
American 1895-1968
paintings: (L) $66; (H) $10,450
drawings: (L) $440; (H) $4,950

DEHODENCQ, Alfred
French 1822-1882
paintings: (L) $550; (H) $10,450
drawings: (H) $110

DEHODENCQ, Edme
French 1822-1882
drawings: (H) $2,090

DEIBL, Anton
German 1833-1883
paintings: (L) $1,760; (H) $3,300

DEIKE, Clara
American 20th cent.
paintings: (L) $110; (H) $1,650

DEIKER, Johannes Christian
German b. 1822
paintings: (H) $4,675

DEILMAN, Frederick
paintings: (H) $1,980

DEISGINSKYISSI, G.
sculpture: (H) $19,800

DEITERS, Heinrich
German 1840-1916
paintings: (H) $3,410
drawings: (H) $2,200

DEJOINER, Oscar D.
American 1860-1924
paintings: (H) $1,100

DEJONKER, C.
drawings: (H) $715

DEJUINNE, Francois Louis
French 1786-1844
paintings: (H) $33,000

DEL CAMPO, Federico
Peruvian 19th cent.
drawings: (H) $8,250

DEL MUE, Maurice Auguste
Franco/American 1875-1955
paintings: (L) $330; (H) $1,320

DEL SARTO, Andrea
Italian 1486/88-1530/31
drawings: (H) $165,000

DEL TORRE, Giulio
Italian 1856-1932
paintings: (H) $6,600

DELABASSEE, Jean Theodore
French early 20th cent.
sculpture: (H) $1,760

DELABRIERE, E.
sculpture: (H) $1,100

DELABRIERRE, Paul Edouard
French 1829-1912
sculpture: (L) $357; (H) $3,960

DELACHAUX, Leon
Swiss 1850-1918
paintings: (H) $1,980

DELACROIX, Eugene
French 1798-1863
paintings: (L) $16,500; (H) $5,500,000
drawings: (L) $440; (H) $550,000

DELACROIX, Henri Eugene
French 1845-1930
paintings: (L) $2,310; (H) $5,225

DELAGE, Pierre
European 19th cent.
paintings: (L) $770; (H) $3,300

DELAGRANGE, Leon Noel
French 1872-1910
sculpture: (L) $990; (H) $14,300

DELAHAYE, Louis
French 19th cent.
paintings: (H) $6,050

DELAHOGUE, Alexis Auguste
French 1867-1930
paintings: (L) $1,210; (H) $3,300

DELANCE, Paul Louis
French 1848-1924
paintings: (L) $357; (H) $5,500

DELANDRE, Robert Paul
French 1879-1961
sculpture: (H) $4,400

DELANEY, Joseph
American b. 1904
paintings: (L) $55; (H) $1,540

DELANNOY, Maurice
French b. 1885
sculpture: (H) $990

DELANNOY, P.
Continental School early 20th cent.
sculpture: (H) $1,045

DELANO, Gerard Curtis
American 1890-1972
paintings: (L) $550; (H) $17,600
drawings: (H) $1,760

DELANOY, Hippolyte Pierre
French 1849-1899
paintings: (L) $1,430; (H) $3,850

DELANOY, Jacques
French 1820-1890
paintings: (H) $6,050

DELAPORTE, Eugene
French b. 1914
paintings: (L) $550; (H) $2,640
drawings: (L) $2,310; (H) $2,420

DELAROCHE, Paul, Hippolyte
DELAROCHE
French 1797-1856
paintings: (H) $1,760
drawings: (L) $2,310; (H) $2,420

DELARUE, Charles
French b. 1927
paintings: (H) $1,210

DELARUE, Lucien
French b. 1925
paintings: (L) $412; (H) $825

DELASALLE, Angele
French 19th cent.
paintings: (H) $990

DELASALLE, Edouard Henri
sculpture: (H) $1,210

DELATTRE, Henri
French 1801-1876
paintings: (H) $8,800

DELAUNAY, Jules Elie
French 1828-1891
paintings: (H) $4,400
drawings: (H) $3,520

DELAUNAY, Paul
American b. Paris, 1883
sculpture: (H) $990

DELAUNAY, Robert
French 1885-1941
paintings: (L) $93,500; (H) $550,000
drawings: (L) $9,075; (H) $44,000

DELAUNAY, Sonia
Russian/French 1885/86-1979
paintings: (L) $6,600; (H) $341,000
drawings: (L) $440; (H) $36,300

DELAUNAY, T.
paintings: (H) $990

DELBOS, Julius
American b. 1879
paintings: (L) $33; (H) $2,200
drawings: (L) $11; (H) $605

DELBY, F.
20th cent.
drawings: (H) $750

DELECLUSE, Etienne Jean
French 1781-1863
paintings: (H) $15,950

DELEN, Dirk van
Dutch 1605-1671
paintings: (L) $5,225; (H) $79,750

DELESSARD, Auguste Joseph
French 1827-1890
paintings: (H) $2,860

DELFF, Cornelis Jacobsz
Dutch 1571-1643
paintings: (H) $30,800

DELFGAAUW, Gerard Johannes
Dutch 1882-1947
paintings: (H) $1,650

DELFIN, Victor
Peruvian b. 1927
sculpture: (L) $170; (H) $18,700

DELFOSSE, Georges Marie Joseph
paintings: (H) $8,800

DELGADO, Maria Elena
Mexican
sculpture: (H) $1,760

DELHOMME, Leon Alexandre
French late 19th cent.
sculpture: (L) $220; (H) $3,300

DELHOMMEAU, Charles
sculpture: (H) $3,850

DELL'ACQUA, Cesare Felix Georges
Austrian/Italian 1821-1904
paintings: (L) $1,870; (H) $4,250

DELLENBAUGH, Frederick S.
American 1853-1935
paintings: (L) $13,200; (H) $20,900

DELOBBE, Francois Alfred
French 1835-1920
paintings: (L) $990; (H) $11,000

DELOCK, Xavier
French 19th cent.
paintings: (H) $880

DELORME, Raphael
French 20th century
paintings: (L) $5,500; (H) $19,800

DELORT, Charles Edouard
French 1841-1895
paintings: (L) $3,025; (H) $16,500
drawings: (H) $1,650

DELORT, Charles Edward and
Maurice LELOIR
19th cent.
paintings: (H) $1,430

DELPY, Henri Jacques
French 1877-1957
paintings: (L) $935; (H) $1,540

DELPY, Hippolyte Camille
French 1842-1910
paintings: (L) $1,200; (H) $55,000
drawings: (H) $165

DELPY, Lucien Victor Felix
French b. 1898
paintings: (L) $330; (H) $825

DELSAUX, G.W.
Belgian 1862-1945
paintings: (H) $1,100

DELSAUX, Jeremie
Belgian 1852-1927
paintings: (H) $1,870

DELUC, Gabriel
French 1850-1916
paintings: (H) $5,500

DELUCA, A.
sculpture: (L) $3,850; (H) $8,250

DELUCE, Percival
American 1847-1914
paintings: (H) $1,210

DELUCO
sculpture: (H) $990

DELUERMOZ, Henri
French 1876-1943
paintings: (H) $5,500

DELVAUX, Paul
Belgian b. 1897
paintings: (L) $220,000; (H) $770,000
drawings: (L) $7,150; (H) $104,500

DELVILLE, Jean
Belgian 1867-1953
paintings: (L) $7,700; (H) $49,500
drawings: (H) $440,000

DEMACHY, Pierre Antoine
French 1723-1807
paintings: (L) $8,250; (H) $55,000
drawings: (H) $44,000

DEMAINE, Harry
American 1880-1952
drawings: (L) $192; (H) $770

DEMANET, Victor
French 19th/20th cent.
sculpture: (H) $1,100

DEMAREST, Suzanne
French contemporary
paintings: (L) $88; (H) $1,870

DEMARNE, Jean Louis
French 1744/54-1829
paintings: (L) $2,640; (H) $22,000

DEMESTER
paintings: (H) $935

DEMETROPOULOS, Charles P.
American 1912-1976
paintings: (H) $132
drawings: (L) $300; (H) $2,090

DEMING, Edwin Willard
American 1860-1942
paintings: (L) $110; (H) $9,900
drawings: (L) $110; (H) $880
sculpture: (H) $5,500

DEMMY, Tho
English
drawings: (H) $1,100

DEMONT, Adrien
French 1851-1928
paintings: (H) $1,320

DEMONT-BRETON, Virginie
French 1859-1935
paintings: (H) $4,400

DEMONTE, Bruno
drawings: (L) $1,430; (H) $3,080

DEMONTE, Rosalia
Brazilian 20th cent.
drawings: (L) $605; (H) $1,650

DEMONTE, Yvonne
drawings: (H) $1,650

DEMUTH, Charles
American 1883-1935
paintings: (H) $39,600
drawings: (L) $550; (H) $308,000

DEMYANOV, Mikhail Alexandrovich
Russian 1873-1913
paintings: (H) $7,975

DEN BOS, G. van
Dutch 19th cent.
paintings: (H) $5,060

DENARIE, Paul
French 1859-1942
paintings: (H) $1,210

DENATO
sculpture: (H) $2,420

DENDEVILLE, Raymond Auguste
contemporary
paintings: (H) $1,210

DENENS, Jan
before 1671
paintings: (H) $9,900

DENES, Agnes
contemporary
drawings: (L) $2,860; (H) $3,850

DENIERE AND CARRIER-BELLEUSE
sculpture: (H) $660

DENIRO, Robert
American b. 1922
paintings: (H) $1,100

DENIS, Luizo
Belgian 19th cent.
paintings: (H) $13,200

DENIS, Maurice
French 1870-1943
paintings: (L) $10,450; (H) $49,500
drawings: (L) $550; (H) $20,900

DENIS, Simon Joseph Alexander
Clement
paintings: (H) $7,975

DENNER, Balthasar
German 1685-1749
paintings: (L) $935; (H) $7,700

DENNEULIN, Jules
French 1835-1904
paintings: (H) $8,250

DENNINGHOFF, H.
Continental 19th cent.
paintings: (H) $1,760

DENNIS
paintings: (H) $1,400

DENNIS, J. M.
American
paintings: (L) $165; (H) $1,400
drawings: (L) $137; (H) $330

DENNIS, Roger Wilson
American b. 1902
paintings: (L) $132; (H) $3,850

DENNIS, S.A.
American late 19th cent.
paintings: (H) $2,090

DENNY, Gideon Jacques
American 1830-1886
paintings: (L) $825; (H) $6,050

DENOLL, H. Usher
American 20th cent.
paintings: (H) $770

DENT, Rupert Arthur
paintings: (H) $4,125

DENTON, Troy
American 20th cent.
paintings: (H) $1,320

DENTZ, T.
American 20th cent.
paintings: (H) $1,540

PENNE, Charles Olivier de
French 1831-1897
paintings: (H) $3,575
drawings: (H) $2,750

DEPIVAY, C.
sculpture: (H) $880

DEPLECHIN, Valentin Eugene
sculpture: (H) $2,200

DEPZ, A.O.
sculpture: (H) $1,650

DER GARABEDIAN, G.
American 20th cent.
paintings: (H) $2,200

DERAIN, Andre
French 1880-1954
paintings: (L) $3,250; (H) $682,000
drawings: (L) $82; (H) $165,000
sculpture: (L) $4,180; (H) $8,250

DERBY, Sophie
sculpture: (H) $1,650

DERBY, William
English 19th cent.
paintings: (H) $1,375

DERCHEU, Jules Alexandre
French 1864-1912
sculpture: (H) $1,760

DERENDINGER, C.
Continental 19th cent.
paintings: (H) $1,320

DERENNE
French 20th cent.
sculpture: (L) $275; (H) $880

DERICKS, Louis
French 19th cent.
paintings: (H) $60,500

DEROME, Albert Thomas
American 1885-1959
paintings: (H) $1,320

DERRICK, William Rowell
American 1858-1941
paintings: (L) $302; (H) $2,310
drawings: (L) $175; (H) $467

DERRY, Patrick Vincent
American 1843-1913
paintings: (H) $990

DERUJINSKY, Gleb W.
Russian/American 1888-1975
sculpture: (L) $770; (H) $23,100

DERY, Kalman
Hungarian b. 1859
paintings: (L) $1,980; (H) $3,300

DERYKE, William
paintings: (H) $6,600

DESANGES, Louis William
British b. 1822
paintings: (H) $2,200

DESAR, Louis Paul
American 1867-1952
paintings: (H) $4,620

DESATNICK, Mike
American b. 1943
paintings: (L) $440; (H) $10,500

DESBOIS, Jules
French 1851-1935
sculpture: (H) $7,700

DESBORDES, Constant
paintings: (L) $770; (H) $11,550

DESBOUTIN, Marcelin Gilbert
French 1823-1902
paintings: (H) $11,000

DESBROSSES, Jean Alfred
French 1835-1906
paintings: (H) $1,900

DESCAMPS, Guillaume Desire Joseph
French 1779-1858
paintings: (H) $990

DESCHAMPS, Frederic
French b. 19th cent.
sculpture: (H) $3,025

DESCHAMPS, Joseph
French
sculpture: (H) $13,200

DESCHAMPS, Leon
French
sculpture: (H) $1,100

DESCHAMPS, Louis
French 1846-1902
paintings: (L) $1,100; (H) $3,520

DESCOMPS, Jean Bernard
sculpture: (L) $1,210; (H) $3,850

DESCUBES, A.
French or British 19th/20th cent.
drawings: (L) $1,045; (H) $9,350

DESERVI
paintings: (H) $1,430

DESFONTAINES, F.B.
paintings: (H) $1,760

DESFONTAINES, Jacques Francois
Jose Swebach
paintings: (H) $18,700

DESFRICHES, Aignan Thomas
1715-1800
drawings: (H) $8,250

DESGOFFE, Alexandre
French 1805-1882
paintings: (H) $8,800

DESGOFFE, Blaise
French 1830-1901
paintings: (L) $2,750; (H) $16,500

DESGRANGE, Jeanne, DESGRANGE-
SELMERSHEIMA
French 19th/20th cent.
paintings: (L) $4,400; (H) $38,500
drawings: (H) $880

DESHAYES, Charles Felix Edouard
French b. 1831
paintings: (L) $880; (H) $2,750

DESHAYS DE COLLEVILLE, Jean
Baptiste Henri
French 1729-1765
paintings: (L) $1,925; (H) $17,600

DESIR-LUCAS, Louis Marie
French 1869-1949
paintings: (H) $3,850

DESJARLAIT, Patrick Robert
American Indian
paintings: (L) $1,430; (H) $3,630

DESNOYER, Francois
drawings: (H) $2,200

DESORIA, Jean Baptiste Francois
paintings: (H) $8,800

DESPALLARGUES, Pedro
late 15th cent.
paintings: (H) $44,000

DESPIAU, Charles
French 1874-1946
drawings: (L) $193; (H) $1,870
sculpture: (L) $8,800; (H) $19,800

DESPORTES, Alexandre Francois
French 1661-1743
paintings: (L) $1,320; (H) $341,000

DESPUJOLS, Jean
French b. 1883
paintings: (H) $16,500

DESRAIS, Claude Louis
French 1746-1816
drawings: (L) $1,870; (H) $3,850

DESSAR, Louis Paul
American 1867-1952
paintings: (L) $412; (H) $2,860
drawings: (L) $110; (H) $165

DESTOUCHES, Johanna von
German 1869-1956
paintings: (H) $7,150
drawings: (H) $220

DESTREE, Johannes Joseph
Belgian 1827-1888
paintings: (L) $253; (H) $1,320

DESVARREAUX, Raymond
paintings: (H) $4,400

DESVARREUX-LARPENTEUR, James
American b. 1847
paintings: (L) $440; (H) $3,300

DETAILLE, Jean Baptiste Edouard
French 1848-1912
paintings: (L) $52,800; (H) $55,000
drawings: (L) $550; (H) $11,000

DETMOLD, Edward Julius
English 1883-1957
drawings: (H) $880

DETREVILLE, Richard
American 1864-1929
paintings: (L) $220; (H) $1,210

DETRIER, Pierre Louis
French 1822-1897
sculpture: (L) $2,035; (H) $4,950

DETROY, Leon
French 1857-1955
paintings: (L) $1,100; (H) $1,760

DETTI, Cesare Auguste
Italian 1847-1914
paintings: (L) $770; (H) $39,600
drawings: (L) $462; (H) $1,800

DETTMANN, Walter
German 20th cent.
paintings: (L) $467; (H) $1,100

DETWILLER, Frederick Knecht
American 1882-1953
paintings: (L) $110; (H) $1,760

DEULLY, Eugene Auguste Francois
French b. 1860
paintings: (H) $29,700

DEUMANCY, K.
paintings: (H) $1,760

DEUTMANN, F.
paintings: (H) $1,000

DEUTSCH, Boris
Russian/American b. 1895
paintings: (H) $7,150

DEUTSCH, David
American b. 1943
paintings: (L) $11,000; (H) $22,000
drawings: (H) $3,520

DEUTSCH, Ludwig
Austrian b. 1855
paintings: (L) $2,750; (H) $66,000

DEVAGNE
German 19th cent.
paintings: (H) $1,100

DEVAMBEZ, Andre
French 1867-1943
paintings: (L) $880; (H) $4,950

DEVAUX, Jules Ernest
French b. 1837
paintings: (L) $2,640; (H) $5,775

DEVE, Eugene
French 1826-1887
paintings: (H) $880

DEVEDEUX, Louis
French 1820-1874
paintings: (H) $17,600

DEVELOUR, J. van
paintings: (H) $1,100

DEVENTER, Jan Frederik van
Dutch 1822-1886
paintings: (H) $9,350

DEVENTER, Willem Antonie van
Dutch 1824-1893
paintings: (L) $935; (H) $3,850

DEVERIA, Eugene Francois Marie
Joseph
French 1808-1865
drawings: (H) $1,540

DEVICH, John
American
paintings: (H) $1,650

DEVILLE, Vickers
British 19th/20th cent.
paintings: (H) $1,210

DEVILLERS, P.
French 19th cent.
paintings: (H) $770

DEVILLIERS, Louis Pierre Dufourny
French 18th cent.
sculpture: (H) $6,820

DEVIS, Arthur William
English 1763-1822
paintings: (L) $3,740; (H) $7,700

DEVIS, Thomas Anthony
paintings: (H) $1,650

DEVOIS, Arie
Dutch 1631-1680
paintings: (H) $2,750

DEVOLL, F. Usher
American 1873-1941
paintings: (L) $550; (H) $2,420
drawings: (H) $83

DEVORE, Richard
contemporary
sculpture: (L) $2,420; (H) $4,180

DEVOS, Vincent
paintings: (H) $660

DEVRIENT, W.
Continental 19th cent.
drawings: (H) $990

DEVRIEZ, P.
French early 20th cent.
sculpture: (H) $10,450

DEVRIEZ, Philippe
Polish ac. 1918-1935
sculpture: (H) $2,860

DEWEHRT, Friedrich
German b. 1808
paintings: (H) $2,200

DEWEY, Charles Melville
American 1849-1937
paintings: (L) $357; (H) $3,520
drawings: (L) $1,100; (H) $7,150

DEWHURST, Wynford
British b. 1864
paintings: (L) $2,200; (H) $3,300

DEWING, Thomas Wilmer
American 1851-1938
paintings: (L) $440; (H) $594,000
drawings: (L) $165; (H) $46,200

DEWITT, R.
American 19th/20th cent.
paintings: (H) $2,200

DEXTER, William
contemporary
sculpture: (H) $1,430

DEYGAS, Regis Jean Francois
paintings: (H) $9,900

DEYI, Wu
Chinese d. 1920
drawings: (H) $1,760

DEYROLLE, Theophile Louis
French d. 1923
paintings: (H) $5,500

DEZA, Oscar Mario
paintings: (H) $1,430

DI CAVALCANTI, Emiliano
Brazilian b. 1897
paintings: (L) $8,800; (H) $66,000
drawings: (L) $1,210; (H) $9,900

DI ROSA, Herve
contemporary
paintings: (H) $2,420

DI SUVERO, Mark
American b. 1933
drawings: (L) $1,045; (H) $5,225
sculpture: (L) $1,870; (H) $319,000

DIAGUE, R.C.
paintings: (H) $1,870

DIAM, Peter
American 20th cent.
paintings: (H) $990

DIAMOND, Martha
paintings: (L) $1,320; (H) $6,600

DIAQUE, Ricardo
French 19th cent.
paintings: (L) $2,090; (H) $2,640

DIART, Jules Edouard
French 19th cent.
paintings: (L) $440; (H) $1,650

DIAS PENNADES, J.
paintings: (H) $2,860

DIAZ, N.
Spanish 19th cent.
paintings: (H) $2,310

DIAZ DE LA PENA, Narcisse Virgile
French 1807-1876
paintings: (L) $462; (H) $55,000

DIAZ DE LEON, Francisco
drawings: (H) $22,000

DIBBETS, Jan
Dutch/American b. 1941
drawings: (L) $12,100; (H) $33,000

DIBDIN, Thomas Colman
English 1810-1893
drawings: (L) $143; (H) $1,870

DICK, Dorothy
American 20th cent.
sculpture: (H) $990

DICK, James L.
American 1834-1868
paintings: (L) $1,430; (H) $5,060

DICK, Sir William Reid
English 1879-1961
sculpture: (H) $1,540

DICKERMAN, Albert
American 19th/20th cent.
paintings: (H) $4,400

DICKINSON, Edwin W.
American 1891-1979
paintings: (L) $12,100; (H) $26,400
drawings: (L) $550; (H) $3,300

DICKINSON, Preston
American 1891-1930
paintings: (L) $3,575; (H) $374,000
drawings: (L) $7,150; (H) $26,400

DICKINSON, Sidney Edward
American b. 1890
paintings: (L) $495; (H) $1,430

DICKMAN, Charles John
American 1863-1943
paintings: (L) $660; (H) $1,320

DICKSEE, Herbert Thomas
English 1862-1942
drawings: (L) $660; (H) $7,700

DICKSEE, John
paintings: (H) $2,200

DICKSEE, Sir Frank
British 1853-1929
paintings: (H) $4,180
drawings: (L) $88; (H) $264,000

DICKSEE, Thomas Francis
paintings: (H) $4,950

DICKSON, Jane
contemporary
drawings: (H) $11,000

DIDDAERT, Henri
Belgian 19th cent.
paintings: (H) $1,540

DIDIER, Clovis Francois Auguste
French b. 1858
paintings: (H) $5,500

DIDIER, Jules
French 1831-1892
paintings: (L) $2,200; (H) $8,250
drawings: (H) $495

DIDIER-POUGET, William
French 1864-1959
paintings: (L) $330; (H) $4,675

DIEBENKORN, Richard
American b. 1922
paintings: (L) $30,800; (H) $1,760,000
drawings: (L) $2,420; (H) $198,000

DIEBOLT, A.A.
American 19th cent.
paintings: (H) $1,650

DIEFENBACH, Karl Wilhelm
German 1851-1931
paintings: (H) $1,100

DIEFFENBACHER, August Wilhelm
paintings: (H) $4,400

DIEGHEM, G.H. van
paintings: (L) $418; (H) $1,210

DIEHL, Arthur Vidal
American 1870-1929
paintings: (L) $110; (H) $4,000
drawings: (H) $385

DIELMAN, Frederick
German/American 1847/48-1935
paintings: (H) $1,210
drawings: (L) $28; (H) $6,600

DIELMAN, Pierre Emmanuel
Belgian 1800-1858
paintings: (H) $3,080

DIELMANN, F.
paintings: (H) $4,950

DIEPENBECK, Abraham van
Flemish 1599-1675
paintings: (H) $77,000

DIEPOLD, Maximilian Klein von
German b. 1873
paintings: (L) $800; (H) $1,320

DIEPRAAN, A.
Dutch 1622-1670
paintings: (H) $1,265

DIERCKX, Pierre Jacques
paintings: (H) $1,430

DIERICKX, Joseph
Belgian 1865-1959
paintings: (H) $12,100

DIES, Albert Christophe
Austrian 1755-1822
drawings: (H) $1,045

DIEST, Willem van
paintings: (H) $4,400

DIETERICH, Wilhelm Hunt
drawings: (H) $770

DIETERLE, Georges Pierre
French b. 1844
paintings: (H) $2,640

DIETERLE, Marie
French 1856-1935
paintings: (L) $1,430; (H) $17,600
drawings: (H) $1,100

DIETRICH, Adelheid
German b. 1827
paintings: (L) $11,000; (H) $79,750

DIETRICH, Christian Wilhelm Ernst
German 1712-1774
paintings: (L) $660; (H) $35,200

DIETTERLIN, Bartholomaeus
German/French c. 1590-after 1630
drawings: (L) $4,950; (H) $27,500

DIETZ, H. R.
American b. 1860
paintings: (L) $2,750; (H) $4,125

DIETZSCH, Barbara Regina
German 1706-1783
drawings: (L) $3,300; (H) $16,500

DIETZSCH, Margareta Barbara
drawings: (H) $4,950

DIEU, Antoine
drawings: (H) $2,860

DIEVENBACH, Henricus Anthonius
paintings: (L) $880; (H) $1,430

DIGHTON, Joshua
British 19th/20th cent.
paintings: (H) $2,860

DIGNAN, Mary E.
American
paintings: (H) $880

DIGNIMONT, Andre
French 1891-1965
drawings: (L) $220; (H) $1,320

DIJCKMANNS, J.
Continental 19th cent.
paintings: (H) $4,180

DIJCKMANS, J.L.
Dutch 20th cent.
paintings: (L) $3,300; (H) $4,180

DIJK, Wim. L. van
Brazilian 20th cent.
paintings: (H) $962

DIKE, Phil
American b. 1906
drawings: (H) $1,100

DILDINE, Emaline
American early 19th cent.
drawings: (H) $3,300

DILIGEON, Charles Alfred
French 1825-1897
paintings: (H) $1,980

DILL, Laddie John
American b. 1943
paintings: (L) $2,090; (H) $10,450
drawings: (L) $770; (H) $4,950
sculpture: (L) $1,320; (H) $4,125

DILL, Ludwig
German 1848-1940
paintings: (L) $880; (H) $2,750

DILL, Otto
German 1884-1957
paintings: (L) $5,225; (H) $18,700

DILLENS, Adolf Alexander
Flemish 1821-1877
paintings: (L) $825; (H) $16,500

DILLENS, Adolf and Albright
DILLENS
19th cent.
paintings: (H) $2,640

DILLENS, Julien
Belgian 1849-1904
sculpture: (H) $5,500

DILLER, Burgoyne
American 1906-1965
paintings: (H) $35,200
drawings: (L) $7,150; (H) $19,800
sculpture: (H) $99,000

DILLER, F.
Continental 19th/20th cent.
sculpture: (L) $65; (H) $1,100

DILLION, Julia McEntee
American
paintings: (H) $9,020

DILLON, Frank
British 1823-1909
paintings: (L) $660; (H) $7,700

DILLON, Julia McEntee
American 1834-1919
paintings: (L) $605; (H) $9,020

DINCKEL, George W.
American b. 1890
paintings: (L) $55; (H) $770
drawings: (L) $193; (H) $253

DINE, Jim
American b. 1935
paintings: (L) $3,300; (H) $660,000
drawings: (L) $1,650; (H) $385,000
sculpture: (L) $16,500; (H) $132,000

DINEA, Francesco
Italian 1845-1902
paintings: (H) $990

DINET, Etienne
French 1861-1929
paintings: (L) $1,045; (H) $38,500
drawings: (H) $303

DING, Henri Marius
French 1844-1898
sculpture: (H) $2,860

DINGLE, Andrian
paintings: (H) $935

DINGLE, Thomas
British 19th cent.
paintings: (H) $1,430

DINTEREN, Kees van
Dutch 20th cent.
paintings: (H) $797

DIRANIAN, Serkis
Turkish 19th cent.
paintings: (L) $2,090; (H) $6,875

DIRCKS, Auguste
paintings: (H) $4,950

DIRK, Nathaniel
American b. 1895
paintings: (H) $275
drawings: (L) $330; (H) $1,650

DIRKS, Andreas
German 1866-1922
paintings: (H) $825

DIRKS, Rudolph
American 1877-1968
paintings: (L) $121; (H) $1,980

DISCART, Jean
French 19th cent.
paintings: (H) $18,700

DISLER, Martin
contemporary
paintings: (L) $1,760; (H) $6,325
drawings: (L) $1,100; (H) $2,860

DISNEY, Walt
American 1901-1966
drawings: (H) $110,000

DITRIEG
Dutch ? 19th cent.
paintings: (H) $1,430

DITSCHEINER, Adolf Gustav
German 1846-1904
paintings: (H) $19,800

DITT-ZEIGLER, Lee Woodward
American 1868-1934
paintings: (H) $1,210

DITTMAN, Edmund
German 19th cent.
paintings: (L) $2,200; (H) $3,300

DITZLER, Anton
German 1811-1845
paintings: (H) $1,100

DIVITA, Frank
American
sculpture: (L) $850; (H) $1,600

DIX, Charles T.
American 1838-1873
paintings: (L) $220; (H) $990
drawings: (L) $16; (H) $220

DIX, Otto
German 1891-1969
paintings: (H) $16,500
drawings: (L) $330; (H) $85,800

DIXON, Charles
British 1872-1934
paintings: (L) $1,760; (H) $3,520
drawings: (L) $770; (H) $3,500

DIXON, Francis Stilwell
American 1879-1967
paintings: (L) $165; (H) $4,070

DIXON, G.
American 19th/20th cent.
paintings: (L) $660; (H) $660

DIXON, M.R.
American 19th/20th cent.
paintings: (L) $2,200; (H) $2,750

DIXON, Maynard
American 1875-1946
paintings: (L) $1,540; (H) $192,500
drawings: (L) $138; (H) $8,800

DIZIANI, Antonio
Italian 18th cent.
paintings: (L) $7,700; (H) $19,800

DIZIANI, Gaspare
Italian 1689-1767
paintings: (L) $24,200; (H) $33,000
drawings: (L) $990; (H) $10,450

DJORDJEVIC, Petar
Yugoslavian b. 1935
paintings: (H) $1,760

DO, Giovanni
Italian d. 1656
paintings: (H) $35,200

DOAN, Edmund
paintings: (H) $2,475

DOAN, Effie
paintings: (L) $440; (H) $660

DOBROWSKY, Josef
Australian 1889-1962
paintings: (H) $4,400

DOBSON, Henry John
British b. 1858
paintings: (L) $358; (H) $660

DOBSON, William Charles Thomas
German/English 1817-1898
drawings: (H) $4,400

DOBUJINSKY, Mstislav
Russian/American 20th cent.
drawings: (L) $660; (H) $1,100

DOCH, F. van den
Continental 19th/20th cent.
paintings: (H) $1,100

DOCHARTY, A. Brownlie
Scottish ac. 1842-1892
paintings: (H) $935

DOCHARTY, James
British 1829-1878
paintings: (H) $2,420

DODD, Arthur Charles
British ac. 1878-1890
paintings: (H) $4,400

DODD, Charles Tattershall
British 1815-1878
paintings: (H) $1,320

DODD, Louis
American
paintings: (L) $2,750; (H) $7,700

DODD, Mark Dixon
American b. 1888
paintings: (L) $505; (H) $12,100

DODD, Robert
English 1748-1816
paintings: (H) $8,800

DODGE, Frances Farrand
American b. 1878
paintings: (H) $770

DODGE, William de Leftwich
American 1867-1935
paintings: (L) $550; (H) $9,350
drawings: (L) $440; (H) $4,180

DODSON, Sarah Paxton Ball
American 1847-1906
paintings: (H) $6,050

DOES, Simon van der
Dutch 1653-c. 1717
paintings: (H) $11,000

DOESBURG, Theo van
Dutch 1883-1931
paintings: (L) $88,000; (H) $165,000

DOESJAN, Adriaan
Dutch 1740-1817
drawings: (H) $4,400

DOHANOS, Stevan
American b. 1907
paintings: (L) $2,090; (H) $6,600
drawings: (L) $330; (H) $8,800
sculpture: (H) $1,760

DOIGNEAU, Edouard Edmond
French b. 1865
paintings: (H) $2,200

DOKE, Sallie George
American 19th/20th cent.
paintings: (H) $880

DOKOUPIL, Georg Jiri
Czechoslovakian b. 1954
paintings: (L) $2,690; (H) $7,700

DOLCI, Carlo
Italian 1616-1686
paintings: (L) $2,420; (H) $1,760,000

DOLE, William
contemporary
drawings: (L) $935; (H) $2,750

DOLEY, Peter
American b. 1907
paintings: (L) $605; (H) $990

DOLICE, Leon
American 20th cent.
paintings: (L) $143; (H) $1,210
drawings: (L) $83; (H) $825

DOLIVET, E.
sculpture: (H) $715

DOLL, Anton
German 1826-1887
paintings: (L) $825; (H) $17,600
drawings: (H) $990

DOLL, C.***
paintings: (H) $715

DOLLAND, W. Ansley
British 19th cent.
drawings: (L) $660; (H) $1,155

DOLLMAN, John Charles
English 1851-1934
paintings: (L) $14,300; (H) $40,700
drawings: (H) $467

DOLLY, A.
paintings: (H) $715

DOLPH, John Henry
American 1835-1903
paintings: (L) $660; (H) $11,000

DOMBA, R.
paintings: (H) $1,320

DOMBA, R.
Italian School 19th cent.
paintings: (H) $715

DOME, Ken
Australian 20th cent.
drawings: (H) $1,210

DOMELA, Cesar
Dutch b. 1900
drawings: (L) $1,870; (H) $7,700
sculpture: (L) $3,300; (H) $13,200

DOMENCH, Pla
Spanish b. 1917
paintings: (H) $1,375

DOMENICH and PFEFTER
French
sculpture: (H) $1,870

DOMENICHINO, Domenico
ZAMPIERI
Italian 1581-1641
paintings: (H) $1,540,000
drawings: (H) $8,250

DOMERGUE, Jean Gabriel
French 1889-1962
paintings: (L) $880; (H) $52,250
drawings: (H) $1,760

DOMINGO Y FALLOLA, Roberto
Spanish 1867-1956
drawings: (L) $176; (H) $7,700

DOMINGO Y MARQUES, Francisco
Spanish 1842-1920
paintings: (L) $6,600; (H) $8,800

DOMINGO Y MUNOZ, Jose
Spanish 19th cent.
paintings: (H) $770

DOMINGUEZ, Oscar
Spanish 1906-1958
paintings: (L) $22,000; (H) $176,000

DOMINICIS, Achille du
Italian 19th cent.
paintings: (H) $6,600
drawings: (L) $495; (H) $605

DOMINIQUE, John Augustus
American b. 1893
paintings: (L) $247; (H) $880

DOMMERSEN, Cornelis Christian
Dutch 1842-1928
paintings: (L) $1,870; (H) $8,800

DOMMERSEN, Pieter Christian
Dutch 1834-1903
paintings: (L) $2,200; (H) $4,400

DOMMERSEN, William
Dutch d. 1927
paintings: (L) $687; (H) $3,300

DOMOTO, Hisao
Japanese b. 1928
paintings: (L) $121; (H) $22,000

DONA, Lydia
contemporary
paintings: (L) $550; (H) $7,700

DONADONI, Stefano
Italian 1844-1911
paintings: (H) $770
drawings: (L) $165; (H) $990

DONAGHY, John
American 1838-1931
paintings: (L) $1,100; (H) $2,970

DONAHUE, Vic
American 20th cent.
paintings: (L) $330; (H) $935

DONAHUE, William Howard
American b. 1881
paintings: (H) $1,100

DONALD, John Milne
English 1819-1858
paintings: (L) $330; (H) $6,600

DONALDSON, Alice Willits
drawings: (L) $715; (H) $770

DONALDSON, Andrew Benjamin
British 1840-1919
paintings: (H) $5,500
drawings: (H) $220

DONAT, F.R.
French 19th cent.
paintings: (L) $1,870; (H) $2,420

DONAT, M.
paintings: (L) $407; (H) $880

DONATI, Enrico
Italian/American b. 1909
paintings: (L) $522; (H) $17,600
drawings: (L) $1,540; (H) $8,800

DONATI, Lavaro
Italian 20th cent.
paintings: (L) $132; (H) $715

DONATI, Lazzaro
Italian b. 1926
paintings: (L) $88; (H) $1,430
drawings: (L) $22; (H) $440

DONCKER, Herman Mijnerts
Dutch before 1620-c. 1656
paintings: (L) $7,700; (H) $19,800

DONDUCCI, Giovanni Andrea, called
IL MASTELLETTA
1575-1655
paintings: (H) $5,500

DONEAUD, Jean Eugene
paintings: (H) $7,700

DONGEN, Dionys van
paintings: (H) $4,400

DONGEN, Kees van
Dutch/French 1877-1968
paintings: (L) $9,350; (H) $1,760,000
drawings: (L) $55; (H) $93,500

DONLE, J.
drawings: (H) $1,320

DONNATO, H.
paintings: (H) $4,400

DONNELLY, Thomas
American
paintings: (H) $1,430

DONNITHORNE, Peter
paintings: (H) $3,850

DONOHO, Gaines Ruger
American 1857-1916
paintings: (L) $302; (H) $15,400
drawings: (L) $33; (H) $935

DONOUY, Alexandre Hyacinthe
1757-1841
paintings: (H) $20,900

DONOVAN, C.V.
American 19th/20th cent.
paintings: (H) $660

DONZIO, Lettou
paintings: (H) $660

DOORN, Jan van
Dutch b. 1916
paintings: (L) $440; (H) $1,980

DOOYEWAARD, Willem
Dutch b. 1892
paintings: (L) $440; (H) $935

DORAZIO, Piero
Italian b. 1927
paintings: (L) $5,720; (H) $23,100
drawings: (L) $880; (H) $880

DORE, Gustave
French 1832-1883
paintings: (L) $13,200; (H) $605,000
drawings: (L) $440; (H) $11,000
sculpture: (H) $26,400

DOREN, Emile van
paintings: (H) $935

DORET, R.
paintings: (H) $2,200

DORIAN, C.S.
19th/20th cent.
paintings: (L) $55; (H) $1,045

DORIES, E.
paintings: (H) $1,540

DORIGNY, Michel
drawings: (H) $715

DORIOT, Theodore
French 19th cent.
sculpture: (L) $770; (H) $907

DORNER, Max
paintings: (H) $1,210

DORPH, Anton Laurids Johannes
Danish 1831-1914
paintings: (H) $7,700

DORSCH, Ferdinand
paintings: (H) $1,650
drawings: (H) $220

DORSEY, William
American 20th cent.
paintings: (H) $2,475

DOSSENA, Alceo
Italian ac. 1880
sculpture: (H) $13,200

DOSSO DOSSI, Giovanni de LUTERO
Italian c. 1490-1542
paintings: (H) $4,070,000

DOU, Gerrit
Dutch 1613-1675
paintings: (L) $26,400; (H) $330,000

DOUAY, M.
sculpture: (H) $3,960

DOUCET, Henri Lucien
French 1856-1895
paintings: (H) $3,520

DOUGHERTY, Paul
American 1877-1947
paintings: (L) $357; (H) $16,500
drawings: (L) $220; (H) $550

DOUGHERTY, Rush
contemporary
sculpture: (H) $1,430

DOUGHTY, Thomas
American 1793-1856
paintings: (L) $2,200; (H) $132,000

DOUGLAS, Earl Graham
American 1879-1954
paintings: (H) $880

DOUGLAS, Edward Algernon Stuart
English 19th cent.
paintings: (L) $1,430; (H) $22,000

DOUGLAS, Edwin
British 1848-1914
paintings: (L) $11,550; (H) $27,500

DOUGLAS, James
Scottish ac. late 19th cent.
drawings: (H) $1,320

DOUGLAS, Sir William Fetes
Scottish 1822-1891
paintings: (L) $1,980; (H) $8,250

DOUGLAS, Walter
American b. 1868
paintings: (L) $137; (H) $1,540
drawings: (H) $192

DOUMET, Zacharie Felix
French 1761-1818
drawings: (H) $7,150

DOUST, Jan van
Continental School 19th/20th cent.
paintings: (L) $605; (H) $14,300

DOUW, Simon Jansz. van
Flemish 1630-1677
paintings: (H) $6,600

DOUZETTE, Louis
German 1834-1924
paintings: (L) $550; (H) $3,575
drawings: (L) $198; (H) $440

DOVE, Arthur
American 1880-1946
paintings: (L) $34,100; (H) $484,000
drawings: (L) $193; (H) $22,000

DOW, Arthur Wesley
American 1857-1922
paintings: (L) $1,100; (H) $46,200

DOWALSKOFF, J.A.
Russian 19th cent.
drawings: (H) $11,000

DOWLING, Robert
English 1827-1886
paintings: (H) $1,100

Ferrarese School

Giovanni de Lutero (called Dosso Dossi, c. 1490-1542) was an Italian painter of the Ferrarese School who spent most of his life in Ferrara executing religious paintings, stage sets, and designs for majolica and tapestries for the royal court. Few of his religious works have survived; his secular works, following in the tradition of Giorgione and Titian, are very sensual. He painted allegorical and mythological scenes using opulent colors and lyrical landscapes. In January 1989, a long-lost painting by Dosso Dossi was offered at Christie's. A rarity, the allegorical scene realized $4.07 million. (Dosso Dossi, *An Allegory with a Male and Female Figure*, oil on canvas, 70½ x 85½ in., Christie's, January 11, 1989, $4,070,000)

DOWNES, P.S.
American 1893
drawings: (L) $2,750; (H) $5,775

DOWNES, Rackstraw
English b. 1939
paintings: (H) $25,300
drawings: (H) $4,180

DOWNIE, John P.
English 1871-1945
paintings: (H) $4,730

DOWNING, Joe
American b. 1925
paintings: (L) $286; (H) $1,540
drawings: (H) $77

DOWNING, Thomas
American b. 1928
paintings: (L) $440; (H) $3,025

DOWNMAN, John
British 1750-1824
paintings: (L) $2,750; (H) $3,850
drawings: (L) $462; (H) $3,080

DOWNS, Albert E.
American School 19th cent.
paintings: (H) $825

DOWNS, Robert
paintings: (H) $660

DOYEN, Gustave
French b. 1837
paintings: (H) $3,300

DOYER, Jacobus Schoenmaker
Dutch 1792-1867
paintings: (H) $5,775

DOYLE, Joe
American 20th cent.
paintings: (L) $110; (H) $715

DOYLE, John
drawings: (H) $715

DOYLE, John
British 1797-1868
paintings: (H) $4,400

DOYLE, Margaret Byron
American early 19th cent.
drawings: (H) $2,420

DOYLE, Sam
American 1906-1987
paintings: (L) $1,540; (H) $3,850

DRAEGER, Ella M.
paintings: (H) $1,430

DRAKE, Peter
contemporary
paintings: (H) $3,300

DRAKE, William A.
American b. 1891
paintings: (L) $440; (H) $2,090

DRAKE, William Henry
American 1856-1926
paintings: (H) $330
drawings: (L) $200; (H) $1,650

DRAPELL, Joseph
contemporary
paintings: (L) $220; (H) $1,760

DRASSER
paintings: (H) $2,860

DRATZ-BARAT, Charles
French early 20th cent.
paintings: (H) $1,760

DRAVER, Orin
paintings: (L) $495; (H) $825

DRAYTON, Grace
American 1877-1936
drawings: (L) $27; (H) $1,700

DRAZAN, M.
drawings: (H) $5,280

DRECHSLER, Johann Baptist
Austrian 1756-1811
paintings: (H) $71,500

DREHER, N.
paintings: (H) $5,500

DREIBHOLZ, Christiaan Lodewyk
Willem
Dutch 1799-1874
paintings: (H) $6,050

DREIER, Katherine S.
American 1877-1952
paintings: (L) $3,850; (H) $14,300

DRENNAN, Vincent Joseph
American b. 1902
paintings: (L) $55; (H) $660

DRESSLER, Adolph
sculpture: (H) $990

DREUX, Alfred de
French 1810-1860
paintings: (L) $16,500; (H) $55,000

DREW, Clement
American 1806/08-1889
paintings: (L) $192; (H) $7,600

DREW, George W.
American b. 1875
paintings: (L) $154; (H) $3,025

DREWES, Werner
German/American b. 1899
paintings: (L) $1,760; (H) $27,500
drawings: (H) $1,210

DREYFUS, Bernard
paintings: (H) $2,640

DREYFUSS-STEER, J.
paintings: (H) $660

DRIAN
Continental 20th cent.
drawings: (L) $2,200; (H) $2,475

DRIBEN, Peter
paintings: (H) $2,000

DRIELST, Egbert van
Dutch 1746-1818
paintings: (L) $40,700; (H) $44,000
drawings: (L) $2,860; (H) $3,300

DRIFT, Johannes Adrianus van der
paintings: (L) $770; (H) $2,640
drawings: (H) $1,100

DRINKARD, David
b. 1948
paintings: (H) $2,200

DRISCOLE, H.A.
19th cent.
paintings: (L) $275; (H) $990

DRIVIER, Leon Ernest
French 1878-1951
sculpture: (H) $2,090

DROLLING, Martin
French 1752-1817
paintings: (L) $6,325; (H) $46,750
drawings: (H) $3,300

DROLLING, Michel Martin
French 1786-1851
paintings: (H) $2,860

DROOGSLOOT, Joost Cornelisz
Dutch 1586-1666
paintings: (L) $2,200; (H) $47,300

DROPSEY, Henry
sculpture: (L) $165; (H) $8,250

DROST, Willem
d. 1678
paintings: (H) $38,500

DROUAIS, Francois Hubert
French 1727-1775
paintings: (L) $11,000; (H) $31,900

DROUAIS, Jean Germain
1763-1788
drawings: (H) $3,300

DROUET, Jan van
paintings: (H) $715

DROUIN, J. and E. PETIT
paintings: (H) $2,640

DROUOT, Edouard
French 1859-1945
sculpture: (L) $605; (H) $2,860

DROWN, William Staples
American d. 1915
paintings: (L) $165; (H) $2,750
drawings: (L) $203; (H) $330

DRUMMOND, Arthur
British 1871-1951
paintings: (H) $6,600

DRUMMOND, Arthur
Canadian b. 1891
paintings: (H) $1,980

DRUMMOND, J.
paintings: (H) $660

DRUMMOND, J.
Scottish 19th cent.
paintings: (H) $3,575

DRUMMOND, Samuel
British 1765-1844
paintings: (L) $770; (H) $1,045

DRUOT, E. and Moris
sculpture: (L) $3,300; (H) $4,180

DRURY, Edward Alfred
sculpture: (H) $1,320

DRYDEN, Helen
American b. 1887
paintings: (H) $1,045

DRYSDALE, Alexander John
American 1870-1934
paintings: (L) $247; (H) $4,620
drawings: (L) $286; (H) $3,630

DU BOIS, Gaston
Continental 19th/20th cent.
paintings: (H) $8,250

DU BOIS, Guy Pene
American 1884-1958
paintings: (L) $357; (H) $137,500
drawings: (L) $550; (H) $6,050

DU BOIS, Yvonne Pene
American b. 1913
paintings: (L) $165; (H) $2,870
drawings: (H) $110

DU PASSAGE, Arthur Marie Gabriel
Comte
   French 1838-1900
   sculpture: (L) $2,420; (H) $26,400

DU PASSAGE, Charles Marie, Vicomte
   sculpture: (H) $2,860

DU VAL, Charles Allen
   British 1808-1872
   paintings: (H) $1,430

DUBAUT, Pierre Olivier
   French 1886-1968
   drawings: (H) $1,210

DUBBELS, Hendrik Jacobsz
   Dutch 1620/1621-1676
   paintings: (L) $11,000; (H) $16,500

DUBE, Matti
   French b. 1861
   paintings: (H) $2,750

DUBOIS, Arsene
   French 19th cent.
   paintings: (H) $6,600

DUBOIS, Charles
   paintings: (H) $1,210

DUBOIS, Emile Fernand
   French early 20th cent.
   sculpture: (H) $825

DUBOIS, Ernest Henri
   French 1863-1931
   sculpture: (H) $7,700

DUBOIS, Ferdinand
   sculpture: (H) $1,210

DUBOIS, Francois
   French 1790-1871
   paintings: (H) $8,800

DUBOIS, Guy
   drawings: (H) $660

DUBOIS, Henri Pierre Hippolyte
   French 1837-1909
   paintings: (H) $8,800

DUBOIS, Jules
   French 19th cent.
   paintings: (H) $770

DUBOIS, Maurice Pierre
   French 20th cent.
   paintings: (H) $4,400

DUBOIS, Paul
   French 1829-1905
   sculpture: (L) $495; (H) $3,080

DUBOIS, Simon
   Flemish 1632-1708
   drawings: (H) $935

DUBOIS, Willem
   Dutch d. 1680
   paintings: (H) $3,575

DUBOURG, Louis Alexandre
   French 1825-1891
   paintings: (H) $3,300

DUBOURG, Louis Fabricius
   drawings: (H) $1,320

DUBOY, Paul
   sculpture: (H) $1,980

DUBRAY-BESNARD, Charlotte
Gabrielle
   French b. 1855
   sculpture: (H) $60,500

DUBREUIL, V.
   paintings: (H) $990

DUBREUIL, Victor
   American late 19th cent.
   paintings: (L) $1,155; (H) $13,200

DUBUCAND, Alfred
   French 1828-1894
   sculpture: (L) $176; (H) $7,700

DUBUFE, Edouard Louis
   French 1820-1883
   paintings: (L) $6,050; (H) $6,600

DUBUFE, Edouard Marie Guillaume
   French 1853-1909
   paintings: (H) $2,750
   drawings: (L) $660; (H) $1,540

DUBUFFET, Jean
   French b. 1901
   paintings: (L) $22,000; (H) $5,170,000
   drawings: (L) $1,980; (H) $220,000
   sculpture: (L) $49,500; (H) $687,500

DUC, Arthur Jacques le
   French 1848-1912
   sculpture: (H) $3,300

DUC, E. Champion
   paintings: (H) $880

DUCHAMP, Marcel
French 1887-1968
drawings: (L) $6,600; (H) $26,400
sculpture: (L) $1,100; (H) $88,000

DUCHAMP, Suzanne
paintings: (L) $2,420; (H) $3,300

DUCHAMP-VILLON, Raymond
French 1876-1918
sculpture: (L) $12,100; (H) $1,100,000

DUCHATEAU, Marie Therese
French 1870-1953
paintings: (H) $29,700

DUCHEMIN, Victoire
French ac. 1864-1879
paintings: (H) $1,870

DUCHOISEUIL
French 19th cent.
sculpture: (L) $605; (H) $15,400

DUCK, Jacob
Dutch c. 1600-after 1660
paintings: (L) $15,400; (H) $220,000

DUCKWORTH, Ruth
British b. Germany 1919
sculpture: (L) $660; (H) $8,800

DUCLERC, Ch.
paintings: (H) $1,430

DUCOIN, A.
Continental 19th/20th cent.
paintings: (H) $2,200

DUCREUX, Joseph
French 1735-1802
paintings: (H) $1,650

DUCROS, Abraham Louis Rodolphe
Swiss 1748-1810
paintings: (H) $770

DUDAN, C.
paintings: (H) $1,320

DUDFIELD, Gloria
paintings: (H) $1,100

DUDGEON, James
English 19th cent.
paintings: (H) $935

DUDITS, A.
Continental 19th cent.
paintings: (H) $1,320

DUDLEY, Frank V.
American 1868-1957
paintings: (L) $165; (H) $4,180

DUESBERRY, Joellyn
contemporary
drawings: (H) $4,125

DUESBURY, Horace
American 1851-1904
paintings: (H) $825

DUESSEL, Henry A.
American 19th/20th cent.
paintings: (L) $220; (H) $770

DUEZ, Ernest Ange
French 1843-1896
paintings: (L) $26,400; (H) $29,700
drawings: (H) $715

DUFAUG, G.A.
French 19th cent.
paintings: (H) $20,900

DUFAUX, Frederic
paintings: (L) $935; (H) $1,650

DUFF, John
sculpture: (H) $5,500

DUFF, John T.
American
paintings: (H) $1,320

DUFFAUT, Prefete
Haitian b. 1923
paintings: (L) $154; (H) $6,600

DUFFIELD, William
paintings: (H) $5,500

DUFFY, Richard H.
American b. 1881
sculpture: (H) $1,320

DUFNER, Edward
American 1871/72-1957
paintings: (L) $2,860; (H) $220,000
drawings: (L) $1,320; (H) $3,025

DUFOUR, Bernard
contemporary
paintings: (H) $4,950

DUFOUR, P.
paintings: (H) $1,650

DUFRENOY, E.G.
paintings: (H) $12,100

DUFRESNE, Charles
French 1876-1938
paintings: (L) $2,420; (H) $17,600
drawings: (L) $2,750; (H) $2,860

DUFY, Jean
French 1888-1964
paintings: (L) $1,430; (H) $52,250
drawings: (L) $302; (H) $25,300

DUFY, Raoul
French 1877-1953
paintings: (L) $19,800; (H) $1,815,000
drawings: (L) $275; (H) $231,000

DUGEN, A. van
Dutch 1878-1946
paintings: (H) $1,320

DUGHET, Gaspard, called Gaspard
Poussin
French 1615-1675
paintings: (L) $4,125; (H) $9,350

DUHEN, Jacques Joseph
French 1748-1840
paintings: (H) $6,600

DUISBERG, C.
paintings: (H) $660

DUJARDIN, Karel
Dutch c. 1622-1678
paintings: (L) $4,400; (H) $209,000

DUKE, Alfred
British 1847-1904
paintings: (L) $467; (H) $5,500

DUKE, Theo
paintings: (H) $1,320

DUKES, Charles
paintings: (H) $1,650

DULAC, Edmund
French/English 1882-1953
drawings: (L) $3,080; (H) $39,600

DULUAR, Joardy
paintings: (L) $44; (H) $660

DULUARD, Hippolyte Francois Leon
French b. 1871
paintings: (L) $880; (H) $1,650

DUMAIGE, Etienne-Henri
French 1830-1888
sculpture: (L) $330; (H) $6,600

DUMAREST, Alph.
Continental 19th cent.
paintings: (H) $9,900

DUMAY, C.
American 19th cent.
paintings: (H) $990

DUMBAR, Harold C.
paintings: (H) $880

DUMIEN, Henri
French b. 1909
paintings: (H) $880

DUMITRESCO, Natalia
contemporary
paintings: (L) $1,430; (H) $1,650

DUMMER, H. Boylston
American 1878-1945
paintings: (L) $247; (H) $990

DUMOND, Frank Vincent
American 1865-1951
paintings: (L) $550; (H) $6,600
drawings: (L) $110; (H) $8,250

DUMONT, Edme
sculpture: (H) $2,750

DUMONT, Francois
Belgian 19th cent.
paintings: (H) $1,210

DUMONT, Frank
paintings: (H) $1,540

DUMONT, Jean, called LE ROMAIN
drawings: (H) $1,320

DUMONT, Paul
American ac. c. 1915-1930
paintings: (H) $660

DUMONT, Pierre
contemporary
paintings: (L) $9,350; (H) $14,300

DUMONT, Pierre
French 1660-1737
paintings: (L) $2,090; (H) $4,620

DUMONT, Pierre
French 1884-1936
paintings: (L) $2,640; (H) $6,875

DUMONT, R.
French 19th cent.
paintings: (H) $715

DUMONT, Rene
French School 19th cent.
paintings: (L) $880; (H) $1,540

DUMORTIER, Prosper
Flemish 1805-1879
paintings: (H) $715

DUMOULIN
Belgian 19th cent.
paintings: (H) $825

DUNAND, Jean
Swiss 1877-1942
paintings: (L) $49,500; (H) $143,000
drawings: (H) $3,850

DUNAND, Pierre
sculpture: (H) $5,500

DUNBAERT, Leon
Belgian 1830-1909
paintings: (H) $1,540

DUNBAR, Harold
American 1882-1953
paintings: (L) $77; (H) $1,650
drawings: (L) $27; (H) $350

DUNCAN, Edmund
English 19th cent.
drawings: (H) $1,210

DUNCAN, Edward
English 1803-1882
drawings: (L) $715; (H) $3,520

DUNCAN, Geraldine Birch
American 1883-1972
paintings: (H) $1,100

DUNCAN, Walter
British 19th cent.
drawings: (H) $715

DUNCANSON, Robert S.
American 1817/22-1872
paintings: (L) $200; (H) $11,000

DUNCKHAM, H.
British 19th cent.
paintings: (H) $700

DUNEI, L.
paintings: (H) $990

DUNHAM, Carroll
American b. 1949
paintings: (L) $38,500; (H) $66,000
drawings: (L) $4,400; (H) $60,500

DUNHAM, Horace C.
American b. 1893
drawings: (H) $715

DUNINGTON, A.
English exhib. 1885
paintings: (H) $770

DUNKELBERGER, R.
American School 20th cent.
paintings: (L) $1,155; (H) $1,155

DUNLAP, Eugene
American ac. 1930s-1940s
paintings: (L) $275; (H) $1,870

DUNLAP, Helena
American 1876-1955
paintings: (H) $17,600

DUNLAY, Thomas R.
American 20th cent.
paintings: (L) $193; (H) $6,050

DUNLOP, E.
paintings: (H) $1,760

DUNLOP, Roland
British 20th cent.
paintings: (H) $1,650

DUNN, Harvey Hopkins
American b. 1879
paintings: (H) $6,600

DUNN, Harvey T.
American 1884-1952
paintings: (L) $2,640; (H) $52,250

DUNNING, Robert Spear
American 1829-1905
paintings: (L) $880; (H) $286,000

DUNNINGTON, A.
paintings: (H) $660

DUNNINGTON, Albert
English 19th cent.
paintings: (L) $1,100; (H) $1,600

DUNOYER DE SEGONZAC, Andre
French 1884-1974
paintings: (L) $5,500; (H) $74,250
drawings: (L) $192; (H) $60,500

DUNSMORE, John Ward
American 1856-1945
paintings: (L) $99; (H) $2,530
drawings: (L) $220; (H) $330

DUNSTAN, Bernard
English b. 1920
paintings: (H) $3,300

DUNTON, W. Herbert "Buck"
American 1878-1936
paintings: (L) $2,090; (H) $30,800
drawings: (H) $577

DUNTRE, J.
paintings: (H) $715

DUNTZE, Johannes Bertholomaus
German 1823-1895
paintings: (L) $6,325; (H) $13,200

DUPAIN, Edmond Louis
French b. 1847
paintings: (H) $6,600

DUPAS, Jean
French 1882-1964
paintings: (L) $2,420; (H) $143,000
drawings: (L) $825; (H) $82,500

DUPERREX, W.
paintings: (L) $1,210; (H) $1,870

DUPLESSIS, Michel
paintings: (H) $1,210

DUPONT, Gainsborough
English c. 1754-1797
paintings: (L) $880; (H) $3,575

DUPONT, Louise
French 19th cent.
paintings: (H) $1,650

DUPONT-ZIPCY, Emile
French 1822-1885
paintings: (H) $4,950

DUPRAT, Albert Ferdinand
Italian b. 1882
paintings: (L) $605; (H) $1,540

DUPRAY, Henry Louis
French 1841-1909
paintings: (L) $825; (H) $2,420

DUPRE, Henri
French contemporary
paintings: (L) $330; (H) $825

DUPRE, Jules
French 1811-1889
paintings: (L) $550; (H) $29,700

DUPRE, Julien
French 1851-1910
paintings: (L) $1,650; (H) $170,500
drawings: (H) $1,100

DUPRE, Leon Victor
French 1816-1879
paintings: (L) $935; (H) $26,400

DUPREE, L.
French 19th cent.
paintings: (H) $2,310

DUPUIS, Pierre
French 1610-1682
paintings: (L) $1,500; (H) $93,500

DUPUY, L.
French 19th cent.
paintings: (H) $950

DUPUY, Paul Michel
French 1869-1949
paintings: (L) $3,740; (H) $66,000

DURA, G.
Italian 19th cent.
drawings: (L) $110; (H) $935

DURA, Gaetano
Italian 19th cent.
drawings: (H) $1,870

DURAN, Carolus
paintings: (H) $880

DURAND, Asher B.
American 1796-1886
paintings: (L) $2,200; (H) $297,000
drawings: (H) $3,850

DURAND, Carolus
paintings: (H) $1,760

DURAND, Elias W.
American 19th cent.
paintings: (L) $275; (H) $3,080

DURAND, F.G.
paintings: (H) $880

DURAND, Francisque
French 19th cent.
paintings: (H) $1,870

DURAND, Gustave
French 19th/20th cent.
paintings: (H) $2,750

DURAND, J.
American 19th cent.
paintings: (H) $1,760

DURAND, J.C.
British 19th cent.
paintings: (L) $302; (H) $2,750

DURAND, John
d. c. 1820
paintings: (H) $1,400

DURAND, John
American ac. 1766-1782
paintings: (H) $28,600

DURAND-BRAGER, A.
paintings: (H) $2,750

DURAND-BRAGER, Jean Baptiste
Henri
French 1814-1879
paintings: (L) $2,310; (H) $4,620

DURANT, Albert
French 1886-1941
paintings: (H) $4,400

DURANT, Andre
French 20th cent.
paintings: (H) $2,860

DURANT, D.
20th cent
paintings: (H) $660

DURCK, Frederich
German 1809-1884
paintings: (H) $6,600

DUREAU, George
contemporary
drawings: (L) $247; (H) $990

DUREN, Terence Romaine
American 1907-1968
paintings: (L) $132; (H) $5,500
drawings: (L) $110; (H) $1,100

DURENCEAU, Andre
paintings: (L) $650; (H) $1,100

DURENNE, Eugen Antoine
French 1860-1944
paintings: (H) $17,600

DURER, Albrecht
German 1471-1528
drawings: (L) $11,000; (H) $440,000

DURET, Francisque Joseph
French 1804-1865
sculpture: (L) $577; (H) $6,325

DUREVIL, Michel
French 20th cent.
paintings: (L) $440; (H) $4,675

DUREY, Rene
French 1890-1959
paintings: (H) $3,850

DURGIN, Lyle
American 19th/20th cent.
paintings: (H) $1,650

DURIEUX, Caroline
American 1896-1989
drawings: (H) $2,640

DURRIE, George Henry
American 1820-1863
paintings: (L) $220; (H) $385,000

DURRIE, John
American b. 1818
paintings: (H) $19,800

DURST, J.
paintings: (H) $1,320

DURU, Jean Baptiste
French School 18th cent.
paintings: (H) $49,500

DUSART, Cornelis
1660-1704
paintings: (L) $18,700; (H) $19,800

DUSSEK, Edward Adrian
paintings: (H) $1,430

DUTERTRE, Andre
drawings: (H) $1,210

DUTEURTRE, Pierre Eugene
French b. 1911
paintings: (L) $440; (H) $1,045

DUTILLIEU, J.
Belgian 1876-1960
paintings: (L) $907; (H) $3,960

DUTTON, Thomas G.
paintings: (H) $1,650
drawings: (L) $2,860; (H) $3,080

DUVAL
Continental 19th cent.
paintings: (H) $1,540

DUVAL, Charles
paintings: (H) $1,100

DUVAL, Constant Leon
French b. 1877
paintings: (H) $2,200

DUVAL, Etienne
Swiss 1824-1914
paintings: (H) $1,100

DUVAL, Eugene Emmanuel Pineau,
called Amaury Duval
drawings: (H) $1,760

DUVAL, P.
paintings: (H) $660

DUVAL, R.
French School 19th/20th cent.
paintings: (H) $2,750

DUVAL, T.
paintings: (H) $770

DUVENECK, Frank
American 1848-1919
paintings: (L) $550; (H) $8,800
drawings: (L) $3,300; (H) $4,400

DUVENT, Charles Jules
French 1867-1940
paintings: (L) $495; (H) $49,500

DUVERGER, Theophile Emmanuel
French b. 1821
paintings: (L) $1,650; (H) $23,100

DUVERNET
sculpture: (H) $1,210

DUVIEUX, Henri
French 19th cent.
paintings: (L) $175; (H) $9,350

DUVIVIER
drawings: (L) $1,540; (H) $1,760

DUYK, F.
paintings: (L) $935; (H) $990

DUYK, Frans
Belgian 19th cent.
paintings: (H) $1,100

DUYNEN, Isaac van
paintings: (H) $2,860

DUYOT
paintings: (H) $880

DUYVEN, Steven van
paintings: (H) $2,860

DUZER, Van
paintings: (L) $2,200; (H) $3,850

DVORAK, Franz
Bohemian/Czech b. 1862
paintings: (L) $550; (H) $22,000

DWIGHT, Mabel
American b. 1876
paintings: (L) $715; (H) $1,540

DYCK, Anthony van
paintings: (H) $1,100
drawings: (H) $412

DYCK, Philip van
1680-1753
paintings: (H) $8,250

DYCK, Sir Anthony van
Flemish 1599-1641
paintings: (L) $231,000; (H) $374,000
drawings: (H) $143,000

DYCK, Sir Anthony van, and assistant
Flemish 1599-1641
paintings: (H) $38,500

DYCK, Sir Anthony van, and studio
Flemish 17th cent.
paintings: (H) $242,000

DYCZKOWSKI, Eugene Matthew
American 1899-1987
paintings: (L) $2,200; (H) $7,700

DYE, Charlie
American 1906-1972/73
paintings: (L) $13,200; (H) $46,200

DYE, Clarkson
American 1869-1955
paintings: (L) $440; (H) $3,300

DYER, H. Anthony
American 1872-1943
paintings: (L) $275; (H) $1,100
drawings: (L) $165; (H) $1,320

DYER, Hezekiah Anthony
American 1872-1943
paintings: (H) $935
drawings: (L) $165; (H) $1,540

DYF, Marcel
French b. 1899
paintings: (L) $330; (H) $16,500

DYK, Anton van
Dutch 20th cent.
paintings: (H) $1,210

DYKE, Pieter van
English 18th cent.
paintings: (H) $660

DYKE, Samuel P.
American ac. 1855-1870
paintings: (L) $192; (H) $1,100

DZIGURSKI, Alex
Yugoslav/American b. 1911
paintings: (L) $220; (H) $2,750

DZUBAS, Friedel
German/American b. 1915
paintings: (L) $1,100; (H) $33,000

EAKINS, Murray Thomas
sculpture: (H) $1,100

EAKINS, Susan MacDowell
American 1851-1938
paintings: (L) $88; (H) $4,180

EAKINS, Thomas
American 1844-1916
paintings: (L) $1,430; (H) $2,420,000
drawings: (L) $1,375; (H) $3,520,000

EARHART, John Franklin
American b. 1853
paintings: (L) $165; (H) $1,320

EARL, George
British op. 1856-1883
paintings: (L) $1,320; (H) $71,500

EARL, Jack
American b. 1934
sculpture: (H) $2,090

EARL, Maud
English ac. 1884-1934; d. 1943
paintings: (L) $825; (H) $17,600

EARL, Percy
British ac. 1909-1930
paintings: (L) $4,400; (H) $17,600

EARL, Ralph
American 1751-1801
paintings: (L) $2,310; (H) $7,700

EARL, Ralph E.W.
American c.1785-1838
paintings: (H) $44,000

EARL, Thomas
paintings: (H) $3,300

EARLE
paintings: (H) $1,980

EARLE, Charles
English 1832-1893
drawings: (H) $3,520

EARLE, Lawrence Carmichael
American 1845-1921
paintings: (L) $440; (H) $2,475
drawings: (L) $220; (H) $1,760

EARNIST, Florence Reinhold
American 20th cent.
paintings: (H) $660

EAST, H.
English 19th cent.
paintings: (H) $1,540

EAST, Sir Alfred
English 1849-1913
paintings: (L) $495; (H) $12,100

EASTLAKE, Charles
English 19th/20th cent.
paintings: (L) $660; (H) $825

EASTLAKE, Sir Charles Lock
English 1793-1865
drawings: (H) $1,650

EASTMAN, Emily
American b. 1804; ac. 1820-1830
drawings: (L) $330; (H) $3,190

EASTMAN, William J.
American 1888-1950
paintings: (L) $55; (H) $880
drawings: (L) $44; (H) $330

EASTWOOD, Raymond J.
American b. 1898
paintings: (L) $475; (H) $1,100

EATON, Charles Harry
American 1850-1901
paintings: (L) $121; (H) $4,400

EATON, Charles Warren
American 1857-1937
paintings: (L) $385; (H) $14,300
drawings: (L) $220; (H) $4,125

EATON, Dorothy
American b. 1893
paintings: (L) $660; (H) $1,540

EATON, Hugh M.
drawings: (H) $880

EATON, J.G.
paintings: (H) $935

EATON, Joseph Oriel
American 1829-1975
paintings: (L) $2,310; (H) $2,750

EATON, Wyatt
Canadian/American 1849-1896
paintings: (H) $7,150

EAUBONNE, Louis Lucien d'
French 1834-1894
paintings: (H) $3,410

EBERHARD, Heinrich
paintings: (L) $2,200; (H) $2,530

EBERLE
paintings: (H) $3,300

EBERLE, Abastenia St. Leger
American 1878-1942
sculpture: (L) $2,310; (H) $30,800

EBERLE, Adolf
German 1843-1914
paintings: (L) $4,400; (H) $17,600

EBERLEIN, Gustav Heinrich
German 1847-1926
sculpture: (H) $8,800

EBERT, Anton
Czechoslovakian 1845-1896
paintings: (H) $7,700

EBERT, Carl
German 1821-1885
paintings: (L) $6,600; (H) $7,500

EBERT, Charles H.
American 1873-1959
paintings: (L) $55; (H) $24,200

EBERT, L.
paintings: (H) $825

EBNER, Lajos Deak
Hungarian 1850-1934
paintings: (H) $1,980

EBNER, Ludwig
paintings: (H) $8,250

EBURT, Emanuel (?)
drawings: (H) $1,650

ECHEVERRIA, Enrique
paintings: (L) $770; (H) $3,080

ECHTLER, Adolf
German 1843-1914
paintings: (L) $3,850; (H) $15,400

ECK, Ernst
paintings: (H) $1,100

ECKART, Charles
contemporary
paintings: (H) $935

ECKEN, Charles Vanden
Belgian 19th cent.
paintings: (H) $1,650

ECKENBRECHER, Karl P.Themistocles
von
German 1842-1921
paintings: (L) $880; (H) $3,300

ECKENFELDER, Friedrich
German b. 1861
paintings: (H) $13,200

ECKERMANS, Alice
Continental 19th/20th cent.
paintings: (H) $1,980

ECKERT, Henri Ambrose
German 1807-1840
paintings: (H) $4,125

ECKHARDT, Edris
American b. 1907
sculpture: (L) $82; (H) $770

EDAM, M.
paintings: (H) $1,870

EDDY, Don
American b. 1944
paintings: (L) $6,050; (H) $60,500

EDDY, Henry Stephens
American 1878-1944
paintings: (L) $165; (H) $1,320

EDE, Frederic
American 1865-after 1909
paintings: (L) $715; (H) $3,850

EDELFELT, Albert
Finnish 1854-1905
paintings: (L) $22,000; (H) $418,000

EDELMANN, Hanno
German 20th cent.
paintings: (H) $770

EDGAR, W.
Australian 19th cent.
paintings: (H) $2,310

EDGAR, William
Australian 1870-1903
paintings: (H) $1,650

EDGERLY, Beatrice E., Mrs. J. Harvard
Macpherson
American
paintings: (H) $3,850

EDIE, Stuart Carson
American b. 1908
paintings: (L) $110; (H) $825

EDISS, Theodore N.
American 20th cent.
paintings: (H) $1,100

EDLICH, Stephen
American b. 1944
paintings: (L) $935; (H) $4,400
drawings: (L) $880; (H) $5,500

EDMONDS, Francis William
American 1806-1863
paintings: (L) $16,500; (H) $17,600

EDMONDSON, Edward, Jr.
American 1830-1884
paintings: (L) $385; (H) $3,410

EDMONDSON, Leonard
drawings: (H) $1,760

EDMONDSON, William John
American 1868-1951/1966
paintings: (L) $192; (H) $9,900

EDOUART, August
French 1789-1861
drawings: (L) $1,870; (H) $2,420

EDRIDGE, Henry
British 1769-1821
drawings: (L) $264; (H) $2,420

EDSON, Allan
paintings: (H) $2,860

EDT, F.
American 19th cent.
paintings: (H) $1,000

EDUARDO, Jorge
contemporary
paintings: (L) $5,500; (H) $11,000

EDWARD
paintings: (L) $605; (H) $1,760

EDWARD, Alfred S.
British 1852-1915
paintings: (H) $1,760

EDWARDS, George Wharton
American 1869-1950
paintings: (L) $1,540; (H) $28,600
drawings: (L) $330; (H) $9,900

EDWARDS, Harry C.
American 1868-1922
paintings: (L) $77; (H) $1,430
drawings: (L) $176; (H) $1,430

EDWARDS, James
English 19th cent.
paintings: (H) $660

EDWARDS, John
paintings: (H) $1,650

EDWARDS, Lionel
English 1877/78-1966
paintings: (L) $303; (H) $19,800
drawings: (L) $4,950; (H) $11,000

EDWARDS, M.E.
paintings: (H) $2,750

EDWARDS, Stephen Dale
American b. 1948
sculpture: (H) $825

EDWARDS, Sydenham Teast
English c. 1768-1819
paintings: (H) $9,075

EDY-LEGRAND, Edouard Leon Louis
French 1892-1970
drawings: (L) $2,090; (H) $2,310

EDZARD, Dietz
German 1893-1963
paintings: (L) $385; (H) $18,700

EDZGERADZE, Giya
Russian b. 1953
paintings: (H) $13,200

EECKHOUT, Gerbrand van den
Dutch 1621-1674
paintings: (H) $88,000

EECKHOUT, Jakob Joseph
Belgian 1793-1861
paintings: (H) $3,740

EECKHOUT, Victor
Flemish 1821-1879
paintings: (H) $3,740

EERELMAN, Otto
Dutch b. 1839
drawings: (H) $20,900

EERTVELT, Andries van, or Artvelt
Flemish 1590-1652
paintings: (L) $7,700; (H) $44,000

EGBERGON, A. Javan
paintings: (H) $660

EGERTON, Daniel Thomas
British ac. 1824, d. 1842
paintings: (L) $660; (H) $26,400

EGGELING, Viking
contemporary
drawings: (H) $1,320

EGGEMEYER, Maude Kaufman
American b. 1877
paintings: (L) $165; (H) $935

EGGENHOFER, Nick
American b. 1897
paintings: (L) $2,000; (H) $20,900
drawings: (L) $99; (H) $55,000

EGGER, Ernest
paintings: (H) $1,155

EGGERT, Sigmund
German 1839-1896
paintings: (L) $715; (H) $6,325

EGGLESTON, Anna C.
American late 19th cent.
paintings: (H) $1,210

EGGLESTON, Benjamin
American 1867-1937
paintings: (L) $82; (H) $7,700

EGGS, G.
paintings: (H) $1,100

EGLAN, Max
German/American b. 1825
paintings: (L) $385; (H) $1,980

EGUSQUIZA, Rogelio de
Spanish 1845-1913
paintings: (L) $9,900; (H) $104,500

EHLINGER, M.
paintings: (H) $1,100

EHRENBERG, Wilhelm van
Dutch 1630-c. 1676
paintings: (H) $9,900

EHRET, Georg Dyonis
German/British 1710-1770
drawings: (L) $3,300; (H) $6,600

EHRIG, William C.
American 20th cent.
paintings: (L) $220; (H) $1,155

EICHENS, Edward
drawings: (H) $660

EICHHOLTZ, Jacob
American 1776-1842
paintings: (L) $1,650; (H) $8,800

EICHHOLTZ, Rebecca
American 19th/20th cent.
paintings: (H) $935

EICHINGER, E. Erwin
Austrian 19th/20th cent.
paintings: (L) $330; (H) $11,000

EICHINGER, O.
paintings: (L) $550; (H) $3,575

EICHINGER, Oswald
German b. 1915
paintings: (L) $880; (H) $990

EICHINGER, Otto
Austrian 20th cent.
paintings: (L) $385; (H) $4,400

EICHSTAEDT, Rudolf
German b. 1857
paintings: (L) $3,300; (H) $4,125

EICKELBERG, Willem Hendrik
Dutch 1845-1920
paintings: (L) $1,650; (H) $2,250

EILSHEMIUS, Louis Michel
American 1864-1942
paintings: (L) $55; (H) $6,050
drawings: (L) $44; (H) $2,200

EINSLE, Anton
Austrian 1801-1871
paintings: (H) $1,980

EISELE, Charles Christian Carl
American 20th cent.
paintings: (L) $550; (H) $1,870

EISEN, Charles Dominique Joseph
French 1720-1778
drawings: (H) $3,960

EISEN, Francois
Flemish c. 1695-after 1778
paintings: (H) $13,200

EISENBERG, J.
sculpture: (H) $2,200

EISENBERGER, L.
German c. 1895-1920
sculpture: (L) $715; (H) $770

EISENDIECK, Suzanne
German b. 1908
paintings: (L) $330; (H) $11,550
drawings: (H) $3,080

EISENHUT, Ferencz
Hungarian 1857-1903
paintings: (H) $33,000

EISENLOHR, Edward G.
American 1872/73-1961
paintings: (H) $1,870

EISENSCHITZ, Willy
French 1889-1974
paintings: (L) $1,045; (H) $1,760

EISLER, Georg
paintings: (L) $935; (H) $1,870

EISMANN, Johann Anton
1604-1698
paintings: (H) $14,300

EITEL, Jacques
French b. 1926
paintings: (L) $522; (H) $1,540

EJSMOND, Franz von
Polish b. 1859
paintings: (H) $4,400

EKENAES, Jahn
Norwegian b. 1847
paintings: (L) $4,950; (H) $22,000

EKVALL, Knut
Swedish 1843-1912
paintings: (L) $8,800; (H) $44,000

ELAND, John Shenton
paintings: (L) $550; (H) $1,980

ELASIS, Ed
sculpture: (H) $660

ELDRED, Lemuel D.
American 1848-1921
paintings: (L) $468; (H) $11,000
drawings: (L) $300; (H) $825

ELDRIDGE, Cyrus
American
paintings: (H) $1,980

ELDRIDGE, Marion
American 20th cent.
paintings: (H) $1,210

ELGOOD, George Samuel
English 1851-1943
paintings: (L) $495; (H) $907
drawings: (H) $137

ELIAERTS, Jean Francois
Belgian 1761-1848
paintings: (H) $57,750

ELIAS, Nicolaes, called Pickenoy
Dutch 1591-1655
paintings: (L) $13,200; (H) $28,600

ELIASOPH, Paula
American 1895-1983
paintings: (H) $3,850

ELIM, F.
French 20th cent.
paintings: (L) $302; (H) $3,025

ELK, Ger van
Dutch b. 1944
drawings: (H) $22,000

ELKAN, Benno
American b. 1877
sculpture: (H) $2,750

ELKINS, H.J.
paintings: (L) $1,210; (H) $2,090

ELKINS, Henry Arthur
American 1847-1884
paintings: (L) $550; (H) $5,500

ELLENSHAW, Peter
English b. 1931
paintings: (L) $385; (H) $4,950

ELLERMAN, F.C.
British 1853-1908
paintings: (H) $1,870

ELLIGER, Ottmar, I
Swedish 1633-1679
paintings: (H) $27,500

ELLINGER, David
American 1940-1980
paintings: (L) $467; (H) $1,485

ELLIOT, Daniel Giraud
drawings: (H) $2,200

ELLIOT, J.
paintings: (H) $1,980

ELLIOTT, Charles Loring
American 1812-1868
paintings: (L) $660; (H) $1,320

ELLIOTT, James
British ac. 1882-1897
paintings: (H) $825

ELLIOTT, Ruth Cass
American b. 1891
paintings: (H) $1,320

ELLIS, Edwin
English 1841-1895
paintings: (H) $770
drawings: (L) $110; (H) $440

ELLIS, F. M.
American
paintings: (H) $742

ELLIS, Fremont F.
American b. 1897
paintings: (L) $1,760; (H) $11,000

ELLIS, Joseph F.
British 1783-1848
paintings: (H) $6,325

ELLIS, Paul H.
Continental 19th/20th cent.
drawings: (H) $1,320

ELLIS, Richard
American 20th cent.
paintings: (L) $2,750; (H) $4,125

ELLIS, W.E.
English 19th cent.
paintings: (H) $1,045

ELLIVAL, Charles
paintings: (H) $2,090

ELLSWORTH, Clarence Arthur
American 1885-1961
paintings: (L) $55; (H) $1,430
drawings: (H) $192

ELLSWORTH, James Sanford
American c. 1802-1874
drawings: (L) $2,860; (H) $6,050

ELLWOOD, Evelyn
contemporary
paintings: (H) $2,200

ELMER, E.
American
paintings: (H) $2,420

ELMER, Edwin Romanzo
American 1850-1923
paintings: (H) $7,700

ELMER, Stephen
English c. 1714-1796
paintings: (L) $8,800; (H) $24,200

ELMORE, Alfred W.
British 1815-1881
paintings: (H) $5,225
drawings: (H) $121

ELMORE, Richard
English 19th cent.
paintings: (H) $715

ELSHEIMER, Adam
German 1574/78-1610/20
paintings: (H) $450,000

ELSLEY, Arthur John
English b. 1861; ac. 1903
paintings: (L) $16,500; (H) $104,500

ELSNER, Fritz Richter
sculpture: (H) $2,970

ELTEN, Hendrick Dirk
Dutch/American 1829-1904
paintings: (H) $4,840

ELTON, K.
paintings: (H) $1,870

ELVGREN, Gil
American
paintings: (L) $770; (H) $3,080

ELWELL, D. Jerome
American 1847/57-1912
paintings: (L) $110; (H) $2,200
drawings: (L) $225; (H) $250

ELWELL, Frank Edwin
American b. 1858
sculpture: (H) $1,540

ELWELL, Frederick William
drawings: (H) $770

ELWELL, R. Farrington
American 1874-1962
paintings: (L) $55; (H) $1,100
drawings: (L) $66; (H) $303
sculpture: (L) $1,540; (H) $5,500

ELY, Harriet Gardner
19th cent.
paintings: (H) $1,430

ELZINGRE, Edouard
Swiss 20th cent.
drawings: (H) $1,045

EMBRY, Norris
American 1921-1981
paintings: (L) $770; (H) $1,980

EMELE, Wilhelm
German 1830-1905
paintings: (H) $4,950

EMERSON, Edith
American b. 1888
paintings: (L) $192; (H) $900

EMERSON, Louise
American b. 1901
paintings: (L) $275; (H) $742

EMERSON, William C.
American 19th/20th cent.
paintings: (L) $495; (H) $1,210

EMMANUEL
French late 19th/20th cent.
sculpture: (H) $3,740

EMMERIK, Govert van
Dutch 1808-1882
paintings: (H) $1,540

EMMET, Lydia Field
American 1866-1952
paintings: (L) $18,150; (H) $50,600
drawings: (L) $3,850; (H) $5,500

EMMONS, Chansonetta S.
paintings: (H) $880

EMMONS, Dorothy Stanley
American b. 1891
paintings: (L) $110; (H) $4,180

EMMONS, T.F.
American 20th cent.
paintings: (L) $715; (H) $880

EMMS, John
English 1843-1912
paintings: (L) $715; (H) $77,000

EMPAIN, Joseph
paintings: (H) $2,200

EMSLIE, Alfred Edward
English 1848-1917
paintings: (H) $3,740

ENCKE, Fedor
German 1851-1926
paintings: (L) $302; (H) $10,450

ENDARA CROW, Gonzalo
Ecuadorean b. 1936
paintings: (L) $4,950; (H) $18,700

ENDER, Axel Hjalmar
Norwegian 1853-1920
paintings: (L) $4,400; (H) $24,200

ENDER, Edouard
Austrian 1822-1883
paintings: (L) $1,430; (H) $2,860

ENDER, Johann Nepomuk
drawings: (H) $1,100

ENDER, Thomas
Austrian 1793-1875
paintings: (L) $2,420; (H) $15,400

ENDERS, Frank
American 19th/20th cent.
paintings: (L) $357; (H) $770
drawings: (L) $88; (H) $715

ENFIELD, H.
paintings: (L) $462; (H) $825

ENFIELD, Henry
British b. 1849
paintings: (H) $880

ENGEL, Johann Friedrich
German 1844-1921
paintings: (L) $2,310; (H) $3,080

ENGEL, Jules
drawings: (H) $880

ENGELEN, Louis van
Belgian b. 1856
paintings: (H) $4,840

ENGELEN, Piet van
Belgian 1863-1921
paintings: (H) $8,800

ENGELHARDT, Edna Palmer
American 20th cent.
paintings: (L) $770; (H) $990

ENGELHARDT, Georg
German 1823-1883
paintings: (H) $11,000

ENGELHARDT, Walter Albert
American 1893-1956
paintings: (L) $176; (H) $880

ENGELHART, Joseph
American b. 1859
paintings: (L) $220; (H) $1,210

ENGELS, Robert
German b. 1866
paintings: (H) $715

ENGLE, Harry
American 1891-1970
paintings: (H) $2,420

ENGLE, Harry Leon
American b. 1870
paintings: (L) $88; (H) $1,430

ENGLEHARDT, George
German 1823-1883
paintings: (H) $1,650

ENGLEHART, John J.
American 19th/20th cent.
paintings: (L) $248; (H) $715

ENGLES, Leo
Belgian 1882-1952
paintings: (H) $1,375

ENGLISH, Frank F.
American 1854-1922
paintings: (L) $3,080; (H) $6,930
drawings: (L) $95; (H) $3,300

ENGLISH, John A.
American 20th cent.
paintings: (H) $1,760

ENGLISH, Mabel Bacon
American b. 1861
paintings: (H) $770

ENGLISH, P.
20th cent.
paintings: (L) $440; (H) $660

ENJOLRAS, Delphin
French b. 1857
paintings: (L) $6,600; (H) $11,000
drawings: (L) $2,860; (H) $8,250

ENNEKING, John Joseph
American 1841-1916
paintings: (L) $220; (H) $61,000
drawings: (H) $770

ENNEKING, Joseph Eliot
American d. 1916
paintings: (L) $400; (H) $6,490

ENNIS
Belgian 19th/20th cent.
paintings: (H) $1,760

ENNIS, George Pearse
American 1884-1936
paintings: (L) $880; (H) $7,150
drawings: (L) $330; (H) $660

ENNISKERRY, and C.E. KANE
drawings: (H) $1,100

ENRIGHT, Maginel Wright, Barney
American 1881-1966
paintings: (H) $1,100

ENRIQUEZ, Carlos
b. Cuba, 1900-1957
paintings: (L) $4,400; (H) $6,050
drawings: (H) $1,980

ENSOR, James
Belgian 1860-1949
paintings: (L) $11,000; (H) $528,000
drawings: (L) $2,860; (H) $34,100

ENTRAYGUES, Charles Bertrand d'
French b. 1851
paintings: (H) $6,600

ENWRIGHT, J.J.
American 19th/20th cent.
paintings: (L) $165; (H) $770

ENZINGER, H.
paintings: (H) $2,090

EPHRATA CLOISTER
American
drawings: (H) $1,650

EPINAY, Prosper d'
French 1836-1914
sculpture: (L) $3,520; (H) $6,050

EPP, Rudolf
German 1834-1910
paintings: (L) $3,575; (H) $30,800

EPPENSTEINER, John Joseph
American b. 1893
paintings: (H) $1,540

EPPINK, Norman
American b. 1906
paintings: (H) $6,600

EPPLE, Emil
German
sculpture: (H) $2,200

EPREUVE, Ire
sculpture: (H) $880

EPSTEIN, Henri
Polish 1892-1944
paintings: (L) $550; (H) $5,720

EPSTEIN, Jehudo
Polish 1870-1946
paintings: (L) $825; (H) $3,300
drawings: (H) $1,650

EPSTEIN, Sir Jacob
English 1880-1959
drawings: (L) $715; (H) $2,970
sculpture: (L) $825; (H) $17,600

EQUSQUIZA, Roland
paintings: (H) $10,450

ERDMANN, Otto
German 1834-1905
paintings: (L) $3,000; (H) $41,250

ERDOSSY, Bela
Hungarian b. 1871
paintings: (L) $495; (H) $770

ERDTELT, Alois
German 1851-1911
paintings: (H) $2,640

ERELMAN, Otto
German 19th/20th cent.
paintings: (H) $770

ERIC
drawings: (L) $2,200; (H) $2,310

ERICSON, David
Swedish/American 1870/73-1946
paintings: (L) $385; (H) $3,575

ERICSON, Johan
Swedish 1849-1925
paintings: (H) $2,860

ERIKSEN, Edvard
Danish early 20th cent.
sculpture: (H) $1,430

ERISTOFF-KASAK, Princess Marie
Russian 19th cent.
paintings: (H) $15,400

ERMELS, Johann Franciscus
paintings: (H) $9,900

ERNI, Hans
Swiss b. 1909
paintings: (L) $10,450; (H) $16,500
drawings: (L) $1,100; (H) $12,650

ERNST, Jimmy
German/American b. 1920
paintings: (L) $880; (H) $24,200
drawings: (L) $550; (H) $2,200

ERNST, Max
French 1891-1976
paintings: (L) $19,800; (H) $687,500
drawings: (L) $7,700; (H) $31,900
sculpture: (L) $1,650; (H) $181,500

ERNST, Rudolph
Austrian b. 1854
paintings: (L) $1,980; (H) $132,000
drawings: (H) $4,950

ERRO
paintings: (H) $1,320

ERTE, Romain de TIRTOFF
Russian 1892-1990
paintings: (L) $3,740; (H) $17,600
drawings: (L) $715; (H) $23,100
sculpture: (L) $2,310; (H) $20,900

ERTZ, Bruno
American b. 1873
paintings: (H) $220
drawings: (L) $137; (H) $770

ERTZ, E.
British/American 19th cent.
paintings: (H) $990

ERTZ, Edward Frederick
American b. 1862
paintings: (L) $412; (H) $6,050

ERUBELLIN, J.
French 19th cent.
paintings: (H) $14,300

ERXLEBEN, August
German 19th cent.
paintings: (H) $1,540

ES, Jacob Fopsen van
Flemish c. 1596-1666
paintings: (L) $16,500; (H) $77,000

ESCALIERI
paintings: (H) $660

ESCHBACH, Louis
French 19th cent.
paintings: (H) $935

ESCHBACH, Paul Andre Jean
American 1881-1961
paintings: (L) $935; (H) $1,100

ESCHKE, Herman
German b. 1859
paintings: (H) $990

ESCHKE, Wilhelm Benjamin Hermann
paintings: (H) $2,640

ESCOBAR, Daniel
paintings: (H) $22,000

ESCOLA, Salvador
Spanish 19th cent.
paintings: (H) $5,500

ESCOSURA, Ignacio Leon
Spanish 19th cent.
paintings: (H) $2,750

ESCUEL, Pablo
paintings: (L) $385; (H) $715

ESCURIAZ, Diego Lopez de
ac. c. 1587-1589
drawings: (H) $5,225

ESMERALDO, Servulo
sculpture: (H) $1,650

ESPAGNAT, Charles d'
paintings: (H) $30,800

ESPAGNAT, Georges d'
French 1870-1950
paintings: (L) $3,850; (H) $198,000
drawings: (L) $440; (H) $2,970

ESPINO, Richard
American 1888-1954
paintings: (H) $770

ESPINOSA, Professor
Spanish 19th/20th cent.
paintings: (H) $1,980

ESPINOSA, Jeronimo Jacinto
Spanish 1600-1680
paintings: (L) $13,200; (H) $20,900

ESPOSITO, Gaetano
Italian 1858-1911
paintings: (H) $28,600
drawings: (H) $715

ESPOSITO, V.
Italian 19th/20th cent.
drawings: (L) $440; (H) $825

ESPOY, Angel
American 1869-1962
paintings: (L) $138; (H) $6,050

ESSEN, Cornelis van
paintings: (H) $2,310

ESSEN, Jan van
paintings: (H) $2,420
drawings: (H) $1,430

ESSEN, Johannes Cornelis van
Dutch 1854-1936
paintings: (H) $2,200
drawings: (H) $1,045

ESSIG, George Emerick
American b. 1838
paintings: (L) $319; (H) $1,980
drawings: (L) $192; (H) $1,760

ESTE, Gaudi
Venezuelan b. 1947
sculpture: (L) $4,620; (H) $13,200

ESTES, Florence
paintings: (H) $660

ESTES, Richard
American b. 1936
paintings: (L) $29,700; (H) $550,000
drawings: (L) $1,000; (H) $16,500

ESTEVE, Augustin
Spanish 1753-1809
paintings: (L) $15,400; (H) $44,000

ESTEVE, Maurice
French b. 1904
paintings: (L) $28,600; (H) $104,500

ESTEVE Y MARQUES, Agustin
Spanish 1753-c. 1809
paintings: (H) $77,000

ESTEVE Y MARQUES, Agustin,
studio of
paintings: (H) $10,450

ETCHEVERRY, Hubert Denis
French 1867-1950
paintings: (L) $1,650; (H) $30,800

ETIENNE, A.
paintings: (H) $770

ETIENNE, Francois Theophile
paintings: (H) $1,100

ETIENNE, H.
French 19th cent.
paintings: (H) $1,320

ETIENNE-MARTIN
sculpture: (H) $17,600

ETNIER, Stephen Morgan
American b. 1903
paintings: (L) $220; (H) $4,675

ETROG, Sorel
American b. 1933
sculpture: (L) $1,100; (H) $35,750

ETTING, Emlen P.
American b. 1905
paintings: (L) $44; (H) $2,640

ETTINGER, Churchill
American 20th cent.
drawings: (H) $715

ETTY, William
English 1787-1849
paintings: (L) $550; (H) $38,500

EUBANKS, Tony
American b. 1939
paintings: (L) $2,420; (H) $15,400

EUGENE, H.N.
French 19th cent.
paintings: (L) $935; (H) $935

EULER, Carl
German b. 1815
paintings: (H) $1,320

EURICH, Richard
English b. 1903
paintings: (L) $3,520; (H) $7,150
drawings: (H) $110

EURICK, Richard
paintings: (H) $2,200

EUSEBI, Luis
paintings: (H) $880

EUSTON, Jacob Howard
American b. 1892
paintings: (L) $110; (H) $715
drawings: (L) $110; (H) $467

EUWER, Anthony Henderson
American b. 1877
drawings: (L) $82; (H) $1,045

EVANS, Bruce
American b. 1939
paintings: (L) $660; (H) $2,750

EVANS, De Scott
American 1847-1898
paintings: (L) $2,310; (H) $23,100

EVANS, Donald
American 1946-1977
drawings: (L) $3,300; (H) $12,100

EVANS, E.L.
American ac. 1892
drawings: (H) $825

EVANS, F.
English 20th cent.
paintings: (H) $522
drawings: (H) $935

EVANS, Grace L.
American b. 1877
paintings: (H) $660

EVANS, J.
19th cent.
drawings: (H) $3,300

EVANS, J.
American ac. c. 1827-1855
drawings: (L) $5,500; (H) $6,600

EVANS, J.R.
paintings: (H) $1,210

EVANS, Jessie Benton
American 1866-1954
paintings: (L) $220; (H) $715

EVANS, Joe
1857-1898
paintings: (H) $4,620

EVE, Jean
French 1900-1968
paintings: (L) $1,045; (H) $4,950

EVELIER
paintings: (H) $660

EVENERL(?), K.
paintings: (H) $880

EVERDINGEN, Allart van
Dutch baptized 1621,buried 1675
paintings: (L) $15,400; (H) $22,000
drawings: (L) $440; (H) $9,350

EVERDINGEN, Caesar Boetius van
Dutch c. 1617-1678
paintings: (H) $286,000

EVERDINGEN, Cesar van
paintings: (H) $8,800

EVEREN, Jay van
American
drawings: (H) $2,090

EVERGOOD, Philip
American 1901-1973
paintings: (L) $385; (H) $38,500
drawings: (L) $88; (H) $16,500

EVERS, J.
American 1797-1884
paintings: (H) $1,760

EVERSEN, Adrianus
Dutch 1818-1897
paintings: (L) $935; (H) $28,600

EVRARD, Paula
Belgian 1876-1927
paintings: (H) $6,600

EWBANK, P.
paintings: (H) $8,250

EWING, Harris
paintings: (L) $770; (H) $990

EXTER, Alexandra
Russian 1884-1949
paintings: (L) $2,530; (H) $3,300
drawings: (L) $660; (H) $6,050

EYBERGEN, Johanna G. van
Dutch 1865-1950
paintings: (H) $3,080

EYCK, Caspar van
1613-1673
paintings: (L) $2,200; (H) $7,150

EYCKEN, Charles van den
paintings: (L) $3,300; (H) $18,700

EYCKEN, Charles van den
Belgian 1859-1923
paintings: (L) $4,400; (H) $52,800

EYCKEN, Charles van den
Belgian b. 1809
paintings: (L) $2,970; (H) $11,000

EYCKEN, Felix van der
Belgian 19th cent.
paintings: (H) $1,045

EYCKEN, Jean Baptiste van
Belgian 1809-1853
paintings: (L) $2,420; (H) $3,300

EYDEN, William Arnold
American b. 1893
paintings: (L) $275; (H) $1,155

EYER, Johann Adam
American
drawings: (H) $19,800

EYLES, D. C.
American d. 1975
paintings: (H) $990

EYMER, Arnoldus Johannes
Dutch 1803-1863
paintings: (H) $7,425

EYTEL, Carl A.
American 1862-1925
paintings: (H) $1,430

EZEKIEL, Moses Jacob
American 1844-1917
sculpture: (L) $3,080; (H) $26,400

FABBI, Alberto
Italian 1858-1906
paintings: (H) $4,400

FABBI, Fabio
Italian 1861-1946
paintings: (L) $1,430; (H) $41,250
drawings: (L) $550; (H) $2,860

FABER, E.
paintings: (H) $770

FABER DE CREUZNACH, Conrad
German d. 1553
paintings: (H) $82,500

FABER DU FAUR, Otto von
German 1828-1901
paintings: (L) $3,520; (H) $13,200

FABIEN, Henri
American
paintings: (H) $990

FABIEN, Louis
French b. 1924
paintings: (L) $220; (H) $2,200

FABRE, Francois Xavier
1766-1837
paintings: (H) $2,860

FABRES Y COSTA, Antonio Maria
Spanish b. 1854
paintings: (L) $5,500; (H) $74,250
drawings: (H) $2,200

FABRI-CANTI, Jose
French 20th cent.
paintings: (L) $1,045; (H) $12,650

FABRIS, Pietro
Italian 18th cent.
paintings: (H) $77,000
drawings: (L) $23,100; (H) $31,900

FABRITIS, *C***
paintings: (H) $8,800

FABRITIUS, Barent
Dutch ac. 1624-1673
paintings: (H) $7,700

FABRITIUS DE TENGNAGEL,
Frederik Michael Ernst
Danish 1781-1849
paintings: (H) $8,800

FACCINI, Pietro
Italian 1560-1602
paintings: (H) $71,500
drawings: (L) $5,940; (H) $29,700

FACCIOLI, Silvio
Italian 19th cent.
paintings: (H) $770

FACHINATTI, C.
paintings: (H) $1,650

FAED, James, Jr.
British 1857-1920
paintings: (H) $770

FAED, James, Sr.
British 1821-1911
paintings: (L) $3,300; (H) $3,300

FAED, John
British 1820-1902
paintings: (L) $3,850; (H) $4,400

FAED, Thomas
Scottish 1826-1900
paintings: (L) $990; (H) $13,200

FAED, William C.
paintings: (H) $660

FAEHNLEIN, Louis
French ac. 1895-1930
paintings: (H) $15,400

FAEHODRICH, E.
paintings: (H) $660

FAES, Peter
Flemish 1750-1814
paintings: (L) $9,900; (H) $22,000

FAGANI, Joseph
paintings: (H) $1,540

FAGERER, Fr.
paintings: (H) $935

FAGG, Arthur J.
British 19th cent.
paintings: (H) $2,310

FAGGIONI
sculpture: (H) $1,650

FAGOTTO, H.
sculpture: (H) $2,090

FAHEY, James
British 1804-1885
drawings: (H) $1,760

FAHNESTOCK, Wallace Weir
American b. 1877
paintings: (L) $440; (H) $825

FAHRINGER, Karl
Austrian 1874-1952
drawings: (L) $385; (H) $990

FAHRWASSEN, Paul Lehmann
paintings: (H) $715

FAIRCHILD, Elizabeth Nelson
English c. 19th cent.
paintings: (L) $132; (H) $990

FAIRFIELD, Hannah
American ac. 1836-1839
paintings: (L) $8,800; (H) $46,750
drawings: (H) $4,950

FAIRLIE, Henry
drawings: (H) $3,080

FAIRMAN, Frances C.
British 1836-1923
paintings: (L) $935; (H) $8,525

FAIRMAN, James
Scottish/American 1826-1904
paintings: (L) $522; (H) $18,700

FAIRNETTI, C.
Italian 19th/20th cent.
paintings: (H) $1,540

FAISTENBERGER, Anton
paintings: (H) $2,310

FAIVRE, Antoine Jean Etienne
French 1830-1905
paintings: (L) $6,600; (H) $49,500

FAIVRE, Jules Abel
French 1867-1945
paintings: (H) $2,420

FAIVRE, Justin
American b. 1902
paintings: (H) $275
drawings: (H) $990

FALANGE, Enrico
17th cent.
paintings: (H) $1,650

FALBE, Joachim Martin
German 1709-1782
paintings: (H) $1,430

FALCHETTI, Giuseppe
Italian b. 1843
paintings: (L) $1,760; (H) $2,640

FALCHETTI, Giuseppe
Italian b. 1940
paintings: (H) $1,980

FALCIATORE, Filippo
Italian ac. 1728-1768
paintings: (H) $121,000

FALCONER, John M.
American 1820-1903
paintings: (H) $880
drawings: (H) $1,045

FALCONET, Etienne Maurice
French 1716-1791
sculpture: (L) $770; (H) $2,750

FALCONET, Pierre Etienne
French 1741-1791
drawings: (H) $24,200

FALERO, Luis Riccardo
Spanish 1851-1896
paintings: (L) $6,050; (H) $20,900

FALGUIERE, A.
French 1831-1900
sculpture: (H) $2,750

FALGUIERE, Jean Alexandre Joseph
French 1831-1900
sculpture: (L) $412; (H) $6,050

FALIANY, E.
Italian 19th cent.
paintings: (H) $742

FALK, Max
paintings: (H) $1,100

FALKE, G.
paintings: (H) $1,100

FALKENSTEIN, Claire
sculpture: (L) $3,850; (H) $4,400

FALKLAND, H.
British 19th cent.
paintings: (H) $990

FALLINI
paintings: (H) $770

FALTER, John
American 1910-1982
paintings: (L) $200; (H) $8,800
drawings: (H) $650

FAN, James
paintings: (L) $330; (H) $990

FANCESCHI, M. de
Italian 19th/20th cent.
paintings: (H) $687

FANCOLINI, C.
paintings: (H) $880

FANELLI, Francesco, workshop of
mid-17th cent.
sculpture: (H) $6,050

FANFANI, Enrico
Italian 19th cent.
paintings: (L) $770; (H) $11,000

FANGE, F.
Continental 19th cent.
paintings: (H) $6,050

FANGEL, Maud Tousey
drawings: (H) $850

FANROSE
sculpture: (H) $1,540

FANTACCHIOTTI, Odoardo
sculpture: (H) $7,700

FANTIN-LATOUR, Henri
French 1836-1904
paintings: (L) $7,700; (H) $3,080,000
drawings: (L) $1,045; (H) $8,800

FANTIN-LATOUR, Victoria Dubourg
French 1840-1926
paintings: (L) $12,100; (H) $49,500

FANVOL, G.
French 19th cent.
paintings: (H) $7,150

FARAI, Gennaro
Italian 1879-1958
paintings: (H) $715

FARASYN, Edgar
Belgian 1858-1938
paintings: (L) $1,760; (H) $23,100

FARBER, Manny
American 20th cent.
paintings: (L) $165; (H) $660

FARETO, Pietro
paintings: (H) $3,300

FARINA, Isidoro
Italian 19th cent.
paintings: (H) $17,600

FARINATI, Paolo
Italian 1524-1606
drawings: (L) $715; (H) $10,450

FARINGTON, Joseph
paintings: (H) $2,640

FARLEY, Rachel V.
American
paintings: (H) $1,540

FARLEY, Richard Blossom
American 1875-1951?
paintings: (L) $440; (H) $3,300

FARLOW, Harry
American b. 1882
paintings: (L) $110; (H) $825

FARM, Gerald
American b. 1935
paintings: (H) $3,575

FARMER, J.
paintings: (H) $3,300

FARMER, John
Australian 19th cent.
paintings: (H) $2,200

FARNDON, Walter
American 1876-1964
paintings: (L) $605; (H) $4,950

FARNHAM, H. Cyrus
American
paintings: (H) $1,210

FARNHAM, Sally James
American 1876-1943
sculpture: (L) $1,210; (H) $49,500

FARNSWORTH, Alfred V.
American 1858-1908
paintings: (H) $523
drawings: (L) $990; (H) $2,475

FARNSWORTH, Jerry
American b. 1895
paintings: (L) $220; (H) $1,760

FARNUM, Herbert Cyrus
American b. 1866
paintings: (L) $220; (H) $4,950

FARNY, Henry F.
American 1847-1916
paintings: (L) $4,950; (H) $5,060
drawings: (L) $935; (H) $203,500
sculpture: (L) $770; (H) $825

FARQUHARSON, David
British 1829/40-1907
paintings: (L) $1,870; (H) $2,475

FARQUHARSON, Joseph
Scottish 1846-1935
paintings: (L) $1,650; (H) $2,200

FARR, Charles Griffin
paintings: (L) $935; (H) $4,675

FARR, Ellen B.
American 1840-1907
paintings: (L) $93; (H) $1,430

FARR, Helen
American ac. 1934
paintings: (H) $880

FARRE, Henri
French/American 1871-1934
paintings: (L) $220; (H) $11,000

FARRER, Henry
American 1843-1903
drawings: (L) $605; (H) $18,700

FARRIER, Edgar G.
British 1827-1902
paintings: (H) $3,000

FARRIER, Robert
paintings: (H) $990

FARRINGTON, E.
English late 19th cent.
paintings: (H) $687

FARSKY, Oldrich
paintings: (L) $198; (H) $715

FARSKY, Otto
American 19th/20th cent.
paintings: (L) $330; (H) $2,200

FASCE, F.
Italian 19th cent.
drawings: (L) $467; (H) $26,400

FASSETT, Truman E.
American b. 1885
paintings: (L) $3,850; (H) $14,300

FASSIN, Nicolas Henri Joseph de
Belgian 1728-1811
paintings: (H) $13,200

FATENA, P.
Italian 19th cent.
drawings: (H) $880

FATH, Rene Maurice
French 1850-1922
paintings: (H) $1,980

FATORI
sculpture: (L) $1,485; (H) $1,650

FATTORI, Giovanni
Italian 1825-1908
paintings: (L) $1,650; (H) $1,870

FAUGERON, Adolphe
French b. 1806
paintings: (L) $475; (H) $9,900

FAULEY, Albert
American 1858-1919
paintings: (H) $880

FAULKER, J.
paintings: (H) $770

FAULKNER, Charles
British 19th/20th cent.
paintings: (L) $990; (H) $8,250

FAULKNER, Frank
American b. 1946
paintings: (L) $154; (H) $7,700

FAULKNER, Herbert W.
paintings: (H) $770

FAULKNER, John
British 1830-1888
paintings: (L) $1,650; (H) $4,125
drawings: (L) $385; (H) $2,530

FAULKNER, John and J.F.
WAINWRIGHT
drawings: (H) $1,650

FAURE, J.
French 19th cent.
paintings: (H) $2,200

FAURE, Marie
paintings: (L) $302; (H) $1,320

FAURE DE BROUSSE, Vincent Desire
French b. 19th cent.
sculpture: (L) $550; (H) $1,980

FAURET, Jean Joseph Leon
paintings: (H) $1,650

FAURNIER, Alex
French 19th/20th cent.
paintings: (H) $1,700

FAUSER-ISERLOHN
20th cent.
sculpture: (H) $990

FAUSETT, William Dean
American b. 1913
paintings: (L) $110; (H) $776
drawings: (L) $22; (H) $550

FAUSKY, O.
Continental 19th cent.
paintings: (H) $770

FAUST, Jean
French 19th cent.
paintings: (H) $16,500

FAUSTO, Biggi
sculpture: (H) $880

FAUTRIER, Jean
French 1898-1964
paintings: (L) $9,350; (H) $30,800
drawings: (L) $990; (H) $3,410

FAVAI, Gennaro
Italian 1879-1958
paintings: (H) $1,182
drawings: (L) $165; (H) $715

FAVE, Paul
French 19th/20th cent.
paintings: (H) $2,200

FAVIER, P.
paintings: (H) $1,100

FAVORY, Andre
paintings: (H) $4,180
drawings: (H) $242

FAVRAY, Antoine de
paintings: (H) $4,125

FAVRE, M.C.
sculpture: (H) $1,650

FAVRE, Maurice
sculpture: (H) $1,100

FAVRETTO, Giacomo
Italian 1849-1887
paintings: (L) $4,400; (H) $22,550

FAWCETT, Ada M.
British 19th cent.
paintings: (H) $770

FAWCETT, Dean
paintings: (H) $880

FAWCETT, John
contemporary
drawings: (H) $935

FAWCETT, Robert
Anglo/American 1903-1967
drawings: (L) $100; (H) $1,650

FAWKES, H.C.
English 20th cent.
paintings: (L) $412; (H) $770

FAY, Arlene Hooker
American
drawings: (L) $2,800; (H) $4,000

FAY, Clark
American 20th cent.
paintings: (H) $770

FAY, Ludwig Benno
German 1859-1906
paintings: (H) $2,860

FAY, Redmond
American 19th cent.
paintings: (L) $495; (H) $1,430

FAYRAL
sculpture: (L) $330; (H) $1,540

FAZZINI, Pericle
Italian b. 1913
paintings: (L) $1,650; (H) $3,520
drawings: (L) $550; (H) $550

FEARINGTON, Jennifer
contemporary
paintings: (H) $770

FEARNLEY, Thomas
Norwegian 1802-1842
paintings: (H) $67,100

FEBRARI, R.
sculpture: (L) $2,200; (H) $2,310

FEBVRE, Edouard
French 20th cent.
paintings: (L) $660; (H) $1,980

FEBVRE (?)
French 19th cent.
paintings: (H) $990

FECHIN, Nicolai
Russian/American 1881-1955
paintings: (L) $9,350; (H) $176,000
drawings: (L) $495; (H) $6,000

FEDAER, Otto
paintings: (H) $1,650

FEDDERSEN, Hans Peter, Jr.
German b. 1848
paintings: (H) $2,530

FEDELER, Carl Justus Harmen
paintings: (H) $2,090

FEDER, Maurice Adolphe
French b. 1886
paintings: (L) $2,200; (H) $2,860
drawings: (L) $220; (H) $660

FEDERICO, Cavalier Michelle
Italian b. 1884
paintings: (L) $220; (H) $4,400

FEDERICO, Miche.
paintings: (H) $770

FEDERLE, Helmut
contemporary
drawings: (H) $1,320

FEDOROFF, Ivan Kousmitch
Russian b. 1853
paintings: (H) $9,350

FEELEY, Paul
American 1910-1966
paintings: (L) $33; (H) $8,800

FEHDMER, Eugene
Dutch late 19th cent.
paintings: (H) $1,980

FEHER, Joseph
American b. 1908
paintings: (L) $385; (H) $1,700

FEHNRICH
sculpture: (H) $660

FEID, Josef
paintings: (H) $12,650

FEIERTAG, Karl
Austrian 1874-1944
paintings: (H) $5,775
drawings: (L) $660; (H) $990

FEINIF, K.
paintings: (H) $715

FEININGER, Lyonel
German/American 1871-1956
paintings: (L) $35,200; (H) $495,000
drawings: (L) $660; (H) $60,500
sculpture: (L) $2,200; (H) $16,500

FEININGER, Theodore Lux
American b. 1910
paintings: (H) $880

FEINSTEIN, Sam
contemporary
paintings: (H) $825

FEITELSON, Lorser
American 1898-1978
paintings: (L) $3,300; (H) $7,700

FEKETE, D.
paintings: (H) $880

FELBER, Carl
Swiss 1880-1932
paintings: (H) $990

FELDBAUER, Max
German b. 1869
paintings: (L) $660; (H) $990
drawings: (L) $110; (H) $220

FELDHUTTER, Ferdinand
German 1842-1898
paintings: (L) $825; (H) $5,280

FELDMANN, Wilhelm
German b. 1859
paintings: (L) $770; (H) $990

FELGENTREFF, Paul
German 1854-1933
paintings: (H) $11,000

FELGUEREZ, Manuel
Latin American contemporary
paintings: (L) $2,640; (H) $9,350
drawings: (H) $1,210

FELICE, Giordano
paintings: (L) $110; (H) $1,980

FELICIAN, H.
Italian 19th cent.
paintings: (H) $2,860

FELIX, Karl Eugene
Austrian 1837-1906
paintings: (L) $330; (H) $1,210

FELIX, Lafortune
Haitian b. 1935
paintings: (L) $660; (H) $660

FELIXMULLER, Conrad
German b. 1897
paintings: (H) $74,800

FELLING, J.
sculpture: (H) $880

FELLING, Schmidt
sculpture: (H) $880

FELLOWS, Fred
American b. 1934
paintings: (L) $3,500; (H) $6,500
drawings: (H) $2,200

FELS, Jacob
Dutch b. 1816
paintings: (H) $990

FELTUS, Alan Evan
paintings: (H) $660

FELUSIO (?), T.
paintings: (H) $1,650

FENETTI, F.M.
American 19th cent.
paintings: (H) $1,400

FENEULLE, Luigi Augusto
drawings: (H) $1,870

FENIMORE, J.
American ac. 1850
paintings: (H) $935

FENN, Harry
American 1845-1911
drawings: (L) $220; (H) $6,050

FENNELL, Nora H.
American 19th/20th cent.
paintings: (H) $1,100

FENSON, Robin
English 19th/20th cent.
paintings: (L) $50; (H) $715

FENSON, Roger
paintings: (H) $935

FENTON, Beatrice
American
sculpture: (H) $1,760

FENTON, John
paintings: (H) $880

FENTON, Walter Scott
American
paintings: (H) $1,100

FENYES, Adolf
Hungarian 1867-1945
paintings: (L) $3,520; (H) $4,400

FEO, Charles de
paintings: (H) $1,045
drawings: (H) $300

FER, Edouard
French 20th cent.
paintings: (L) $264; (H) $4,620

FERAT, Serge
French 1881-1958
paintings: (H) $990
drawings: (L) $1,100; (H) $2,860

FERBER, Herbert
American b. 1906
paintings: (H) $495
drawings: (H) $550
sculpture: (L) $550; (H) $7,700

FERDINANDI, Francesco, called
Imperiali
Italian ac. c. 1730
paintings: (L) $9,350; (H) $9,900

FERENZ, Anton Johan
Hungarian d. 1874
paintings: (H) $2,200

FERENZONA, Raoul Dal Molin
Italian 20th cent.
paintings: (H) $1,100

FERG, Franz de Paula
Austrian 1689-1740
paintings: (L) $4,950; (H) $36,000

FERGUSON, Elizabeth
American 1884-1925
paintings: (H) $715

FERGUSON, F.
paintings: (H) $660

FERGUSON, Henry A.
American 1842-1911
paintings: (L) $412; (H) $4,200

FERMATI, T.
Italian 19th cent.
paintings: (H) $1,870

FERNANDEZ, Agustin
Cuban b. c. 1928
paintings: (L) $412; (H) $17,600
drawings: (L) $44; (H) $3,300

FERNANDEZ, Eduardo Pelayo
Spanish b. 1850
paintings: (H) $14,300

FERNANDEZ, Jesse
drawings: (H) $1,210

FERNANDEZ, Rafa
b. Costa Rica
paintings: (H) $3,850

FERNELEY, Claude Lorraine
English 1822-1891/92
paintings: (L) $1,760; (H) $4,675

FERNELEY, John
paintings: (H) $3,300

FERNELEY, John, Jr.
English c. 1815-1862
paintings: (L) $6,600; (H) $44,000

FERNELEY, John E., Sr.
English 1781/82-1860
paintings: (L) $1,430; (H) $319,000

FERNLUND, Peter Petrovitch
Russian 19th cent.
paintings: (H) $990

FERRAND
sculpture: (L) $440; (H) $1,320

FERRAND, C.
paintings: (H) $687

FERRAND, Marcel Plaza
Chilean 20th cent.
paintings: (H) $2,750

FERRANTI, Carlo
Italian 19th cent.
paintings: (H) $2,750
drawings: (L) $825; (H) $1,870

FERRARA, Jackie
American b. 1929
sculpture: (L) $7,150; (H) $16,500

FERRARA, Joe
American
paintings: (L) $1,400; (H) $3,400

FERRARI, A.
Italian 20th cent.
paintings: (H) $2,200

FERRARI, Arturo
Italian b. 1861
paintings: (H) $990

FERRARI, Carlo
Italian 1813-1871
paintings: (L) $11,000; (H) $66,000

FERRARI, G.
French 19th/20th cent.
sculpture: (H) $2,420

FERRARI, Giovanni B.
Italian 1829-1906
paintings: (L) $1,760; (H) $2,530

FERRARI, Gregorio de
Italian 1644-1726
drawings: (H) $990

FERRARI, Lorenzo de
Italian 1680-1744
paintings: (H) $30,800
drawings: (L) $1,650; (H) $3,080

FERRARI, Virginio
Italian/American contemporary
sculpture: (H) $1,045

FERREN, John
American 1905-1970
paintings: (L) $935; (H) $15,400
drawings: (L) $605; (H) $1,980

FERRER, Joaquin
paintings: (H) $1,870

FERRER-COMAS, Edouard
Spanish 19th cent.
paintings: (H) $16,500

FERRI, Ciro
Italian 1634-1689
drawings: (L) $2,750; (H) $4,950

FERRIER, Gabriel
French 1847-1914
paintings: (L) $4,400; (H) $4,840

FERRIER, James
English 19th cent.
drawings: (H) $1,650

FERRIERES, Martin
contemporary
paintings: (L) $990; (H) $1,760

FERRIS, G.
paintings: (H) $880

FERRIS, Jean Leon Jerome
American b. 1863
paintings: (L) $13,750; (H) $16,500
drawings: (L) $110; (H) $1,980

FERRIS, R.D.
American
paintings: (H) $2,640

FERRISS, Hugh
American 1889-1962
drawings: (L) $13,200; (H) $20,900

FERROND
sculpture: (H) $1,100

FERRONI, Egisto
Italian 1835-1912
paintings: (L) $385; (H) $825

FERRY, Georges
paintings: (H) $1,760

FERRY, J.
paintings: (H) $990

FERSTEL, L.
paintings: (H) $770

FERVILLE-SUAN, Charles Georges
French 19th cent.
sculpture: (H) $2,750

FERY, John
Hungarian/American 1865-1934
paintings: (L) $77; (H) $7,425
drawings: (L) $275; (H) $440

FESENMAIER, Helene
drawings: (H) $715

FESSER, E.
American 1881
drawings: (H) $2,750

FETTI, Domenico
paintings: (H) $1,980

FETTING, Rainer
German/American b. 1949
paintings: (L) $7,150; (H) $34,100
drawings: (H) $6,050

FEUCHERE, Jean Jacques
French 1807-1852
sculpture: (L) $715; (H) $3,850

FEUDEL, Arthur
American b. 1857
paintings: (H) $715
drawings: (L) $110; (H) $275

FEUDEL, Constantin
paintings: (H) $1,100

FEUERBACH, Anselme
German 1829-1880
paintings: (H) $2,200

FEUERMAN, Carole Jeane
American b. 1945
paintings: (L) $23,100; (H) $35,750

FEUILLE, J.F.
paintings: (H) $715

FEURE, Georges de
French 1868-1943
drawings: (L) $3,080; (H) $165,000

FEUVRE, Louis Albert le
French ac. c. 1875-1905
sculpture: (H) $2,200

FEYEN, Jacques Eugene
French 1815-1908
paintings: (H) $1,210

FEYEN-PERRIN, Francois Nicolas
Augustin
French 1826-1888
paintings: (L) $770; (H) $9,900

FIASCHI, A.
Italian 19th/20th cent.
sculpture: (H) $880

FIASCHI, P.C.E.
Italian 19th/20th cent.
sculpture: (L) $1,045; (H) $3,300

FICHEL, Benjamin Eugene
French 1826-1895
paintings: (L) $1,320; (H) $22,000
drawings: (H) $248

FICHI, F.
sculpture: (H) $1,210

FIDLER, Anton
Austrian ac. 1825-1855
paintings: (H) $11,000

FIDLER, Harry
British 20th cent.
paintings: (H) $4,675

FIDRIT, Charles Andre
French 1881-1927
paintings: (H) $24,200

FIEDLER, J.
paintings: (H) $1,320

FIELD, Edward Loyal
American 1856-1914
paintings: (L) $302; (H) $2,640
drawings: (L) $55; (H) $250

FIELD, Erastus Salisbury
American 1805/1807-1900
paintings: (L) $4,180; (H) $66,000
drawings: (H) $385

FIELD, Freke
British ac. 1890-1894
paintings: (L) $4,400; (H) $57,750

FIELDING, Anthony Vandyke Copley
English 1787-1855
paintings: (H) $3,520
drawings: (L) $385; (H) $6,050

FIELDING, Ernest
British 19th cent.
paintings: (H) $2,750

FIELDING, G.
19th cent.
paintings: (L) $770; (H) $990

FIELDS, George
British 19th cent.
paintings: (L) $550; (H) $715

FIENE, Ernest
American 1894-1965
paintings: (L) $138; (H) $28,600
drawings: (L) $385; (H) $1,760

FIERAVINO, Francesco, Il Maltese
paintings: (H) $1,320

FIERRO, Pancho
drawings: (H) $3,850

FIGARI, Pedro
Uruguayan 1861-1938
paintings: (L) $4,400; (H) $88,000

FIGINO, Ambrogio
Italian 1548-1608
drawings: (H) $1,650

FILATOV, Nikolai
Russian b. 1951
paintings: (H) $16,500

FILDES, Sir Luke Samuel
English 1844-1927
paintings: (L) $550; (H) $2,200

FILIPPELLI, Cafiero
b. 1889
paintings: (L) $605; (H) $880

FILLATREAU, Benoist
French b. 1843
paintings: (H) $3,850

FILLERUP, Peter M.
American b. 1953
sculpture: (L) $302; (H) $2,750

FILLON, Andre
contemporary
paintings: (L) $4,950; (H) $6,600

FILLON, Arthur
French 1900-1974
paintings: (L) $1,760; (H) $2,860

FILMUS, Tully
American b. 1903
paintings: (L) $660; (H) $1,045

FILOSA, Giovanni B.
Italian 1850-1935
drawings: (L) $550; (H) $8,800

FINALY, C.
paintings: (H) $770

FINCH, E.E.
American ac. c. 1833-1850
paintings: (L) $2,420; (H) $6,600

FINCHER, W.
paintings: (H) $1,300

FINCK, Hazel
American b. 1894
paintings: (H) $8,800

FINCK, Ludwig
German b. 1857
paintings: (H) $1,540

FINELLI, Edoardo
drawings: (H) $880

FINES, E.
paintings: (H) $1,650

FINES, Eugene Francois
French b. 1826
paintings: (L) $1,800; (H) $8,250

FINI, Leonor
Italian b. 1908
paintings: (L) $8,800; (H) $154,000
drawings: (L) $242; (H) $6,600

FINK, Aaron
American b. 1955
paintings: (L) $935; (H) $2,420

FINK, August
German 1846-1916
paintings: (H) $13,200

FINK, Frederick
American 1817-1849
paintings: (H) $1,650

FINKELGREEN, David
American 1888-1931
paintings: (H) $1,430

FINKERNAGEL, E.
paintings: (H) $4,180

FINNEY, Harry
Continental 19th cent.
paintings: (H) $6,600

FINOGLIA, Paolo Domenico
Italian ac. 1640-1656
paintings: (H) $49,500

FINSTER, Reverend Howard
American b. 1916
paintings: (L) $1,430; (H) $4,400

FIORENTINO, Pseudo Pier Francesco
15th cent.
paintings: (H) $165,000

FIORENZO DI LORENZO
Italian c. 1445-c. 1525
paintings: (H) $12,100

FIORETTI
paintings: (H) $660

FIOT, Maximilien
sculpture: (H) $2,420

FIRLE, Walter
German 1859-1929
paintings: (H) $44,275

FIRMIN, Claude
French 1864-1944
paintings: (H) $2,200

FIRMIN-GIRARD, Marie Francois
French 1838-1921
paintings: (L) $4,400; (H) $137,500

FISCHBACH, Johann
paintings: (H) $3,740

FISCHER, A.O.
paintings: (H) $3,300

FISCHER, Adolf, called Fischer Gurig
German b. 1860
paintings: (H) $770

FISCHER, Anton Otto
American 1882-1962
paintings: (L) $550; (H) $8,525

FISCHER, B.
American 19th cent.
paintings: (L) $550; (H) $880

FISCHER, C.
American
paintings: (H) $17,600

Outsider Art

"Outsiders" was a term first used by British art historian Rodger Cardinal in 1972 to explain the paintings of Jean Dubuffet to the English-speaking public. The term has been adapted in the United States and an outsider is commonly defined as "a colorful, uneducated, 'down-home' eccentric (frequently from the rural South) who turns to art late in life, often to exorcise private demons or convey a visionary message."*

Outsider art, the work of self-taught artists who once worked in isolation and went unrecognized, now fetches high prices. The most visible of the outsiders is the Reverend Howard Finster (b. 1916), who has been profiled in *The Wall Street Journal* and *Rolling Stone,* has painted the cover art for a Talking Heads album, and has been a guest on "The Tonight Show." Born in the Sand Mountains of Alabama, his formal education ended with the sixth grade. He became a fundamentalist preacher while trying his hand at twenty-two trades. In 1976, while patching some bicycles with white tractor enamel, he had a "vision" and began to create works of art. He has produced thousands in the past fifteen years. Finster draws upon his religious beliefs and vivid imagination to create whimsical, fantastic, and unconventional art in a variety of media. One hundred of his works were included in a recent retrospective exhibition organized by the Museum of American Folk Art, and in 1990-1991 the Smithsonian sponsored a traveling exhibition of his paintings, sculptures, and cutouts–"The Road to Heaven Is Paved by Good Works: The Art of Reverend Howard Finster." (Reverend Howard Finster, *Cheetah,* oil on wood, 35 x 26 in., Sotheby's, January 24, 1990, $4,400)

*Eleanor E. Gaver, "Inside the Outsiders," *Art & Antiques Magazine,* VII, no. vi, (Summer 1990) pp. 72-86, 159, 161, 163.

FISCHER, Carl
Danish 19th/20th cent.
paintings: (H) $1,650

FISCHER, F.
paintings: (H) $880

FISCHER, Gottlob
paintings: (H) $2,970

FISCHER, Heinrich
paintings: (H) $4,620

FISCHER, Joel
contemporary
sculpture: (H) $15,400

FISCHER, L.
American 20th cent.
paintings: (L) $495; (H) $1,100

FISCHER, Ludwig
Austrian b. 1825
paintings: (L) $467; (H) $880

FISCHER, Ludwig Hans
German 1848-1915
paintings: (L) $522; (H) $25,300

FISCHER, Paul
Danish 1860-1934
paintings: (L) $1,100; (H) $55,000

FISCHER, Vilhelm Theodor
Danish 1857-1928
paintings: (H) $44,000

FISCHER-ELPONS, George
German b. 1866
paintings: (H) $935

FISCHL, Eric
American b. 1948
paintings: (L) $11,000; (H) $715,000
drawings: (L) $3,850; (H) $49,500

FISCHMAN, Charles
French b. 1928
paintings: (H) $825

FISCUS, Gordon W.
American b. 1902
paintings: (L) $605; (H) $880

FISEN, Engelbert
Flemish 1655-1733
paintings: (H) $28,600

FISH, Janet
American b. 1938
paintings: (L) $5,500; (H) $104,500
drawings: (L) $1,430; (H) $19,800

FISHER, Alvan
American 1792-1863
paintings: (L) $4,070; (H) $26,400
drawings: (H) $22,000

FISHER, Anna S.
American d. 1942
paintings: (H) $2,475
drawings: (H) $125

FISHER, C.G.
British 19th cent.
paintings: (H) $660

FISHER, Edgar H.
British 1870-1939
paintings: (H) $1,320

FISHER, Harrison
American 1875-1934
paintings: (H) $358
drawings: (L) $248; (H) $24,200

FISHER, Heinrich
German 19th cent.
paintings: (H) $715

FISHER, Horace
British d. 1893
paintings: (H) $6,600
drawings: (L) $110; (H) $220

FISHER, Hugh Antoine
American c. 1850/67-1916
paintings: (L) $192; (H) $3,410
drawings: (L) $110; (H) $1,760

FISHER, Hugo Melville
American 1876/78-1946
paintings: (L) $165; (H) $3,300
drawings: (L) $138; (H) $715

FISHER, Joshua
British b. 1859
drawings: (H) $935

FISHER, Mark
Anglo/American 1841-1923
paintings: (L) $1,760; (H) $9,900

FISHER, Paul
drawings: (H) $2,860

FISHER, Samuel Melton
British 1860-1939
paintings: (H) $15,400

FISHER, Vernon
American b. 1943
paintings: (L) $6,820; (H) $35,750

FISHER, Virginia
drawings: (L) $110; (H) $715

FISHER, William
paintings: (H) $880

FISHER, William
American b. 1890
paintings: (L) $385; (H) $825

FISHER, William Mark
Anglo/American 1841-1923
paintings: (L) $88; (H) $6,600

FISHER-CLAY, Elizabeth Campbell
American 1871-1959
paintings: (L) $440; (H) $3,300

FISKE, Charles Albert
American 1837-1915
paintings: (H) $770

FISKE, Gertrude
American 1879-1961
paintings: (L) $577; (H) $52,800

FITGER, Arthur Heinrich Wilhelm
German 1840-1909
paintings: (H) $8,800

FITLER, William Crothers
American 1857-1915
paintings: (L) $500; (H) $1,870
drawings: (L) $110; (H) $1,760

FITSCH, Eugene Camille
paintings: (L) $286; (H) $825

FITZGERALD, Edmond James
American b. 1912
paintings: (L) $605; (H) $1,980
drawings: (H) $358

FITZGERALD, Eugenia Toledano
American 19th/20th cent.
paintings: (H) $825

FITZGERALD, James
American 1899-1971
drawings: (H) $880

FIUSCHI, P.C.E.
sculpture: (L) $1,705; (H) $3,300

FIX-MASSEAU, Pierre Felix
French 1869-1925
sculpture: (H) $1,430

FJAESTAD, Gustav Edolf
Swedish 1868-1948
paintings: (H) $17,600

FLACH, G.A.
paintings: (H) $660

FLACK, Audrey
American b. 1931
paintings: (L) $33,000; (H) $104,500
drawings: (H) $5,500

FLAGG, Charles Noel
American 1848-1916
paintings: (L) $385; (H) $1,100

FLAGG, H. Peabody
American b. 1859
paintings: (L) $99; (H) $935
drawings: (L) $88; (H) $385

FLAGG, James Montgomery
American 1877-1960
paintings: (L) $550; (H) $2,860
drawings: (L) $110; (H) $2,860

FLAGG, Jared Bradley
American 1820-1899
paintings: (H) $3,080

FLAHERTY, Charles
American 19th cent.
paintings: (H) $1,100

FLAHERTY, James Thorpe
American 19th cent.
paintings: (L) $4,400; (H) $4,400

FLAMENG, Francois
French 1856-1923
paintings: (L) $1,210; (H) $49,500
drawings: (H) $137

FLAMENG, Marie Auguste
French 1843-1893
paintings: (L) $1,045; (H) $1,760

FLAMM, Albert
German 1823-1906
paintings: (L) $9,350; (H) $22,000

FLANAGAN, Barry
English b. 1941
sculpture: (H) $26,400

FLANAGAN, John B.
American
drawings: (H) $770

FLANDRIN, Jean Hippolyte
French 1809-1864
paintings: (H) $715
drawings: (H) $1,760

FLANDRIN, Jules
French 1871-1947
paintings: (L) $660; (H) $1,650

FLANDRIN, Paul Hippolyte
French 1856-1921
paintings: (H) $1,540

FLANDRIN, Paul Jean
French 1811-1902
drawings: (L) $2,640; (H) $7,480

FLANNAGAN, John
American 1897-1942
drawings: (H) $2,640
sculpture: (L) $1,980; (H) $35,200

FLANNERY, Vaughn
American 1898-1955
paintings: (L) $1,540; (H) $1,540

FLAVIN, Dan
American b. 1933
drawings: (L) $7,150; (H) $12,100
sculpture: (L) $15,400; (H) $231,000

FLAVIN, Dan and Sonja
contemporary
sculpture: (H) $11,000

FLECK, Joseph
American b. 1893
paintings: (L) $5,500; (H) $18,700

FLEGEL, Georg
German 1563-1638
paintings: (H) $1,980,000

FLEISCHBEIN, Frantz
American 1804-1862
paintings: (L) $660; (H) $7,975

FLEISCHER, Max
German b. 1861
drawings: (L) $462; (H) $990

FLEMING, A.
British 20th cent.
paintings: (L) $605; (H) $1,100

FLERS, Camille
French 1802-1868
paintings: (H) $1,650

FLETCHER, Aaron Dean
American 1817-1902
paintings: (L) $2,640; (H) $7,150

FLETCHER, E.
American 19th/20th cent.
paintings: (H) $825

FLETCHER, Edwin
British 19th cent.
paintings: (L) $440; (H) $2,860

FLEUR, Johan Willem
Dutch 1888-1967
paintings: (H) $1,430

FLEURENT, Robert
French 1904-1981
paintings: (L) $143; (H) $1,650

FLEURY, Albert
American b. 1848
paintings: (H) $1,650

FLEURY, Francois Antonine Leon
French 1804-1858
paintings: (L) $880; (H) $2,475

FLEURY, J.V. de
English ac.1847-68, exhib.1892/93
paintings: (L) $1,210; (H) $3,300

FLG, Fritz
Dutch 19th cent.
paintings: (H) $797

FLINCK, Govaert
Dutch 1615/16-1660
paintings: (L) $11,550; (H) $407,000
drawings: (H) $44,000

FLINT, Francis Murray Russell
British b. 1915
paintings: (L) $715; (H) $2,475

FLINT, Sir William Russell
British 1880-1969
paintings: (L) $4,180; (H) $19,800
drawings: (L) $165; (H) $99,000

FLOCH, Joseph
Austrian/American b. 1895
paintings: (L) $715; (H) $7,700

FLOCKENHAUS, Heinz
German 20th cent.
paintings: (L) $1,375; (H) $3,300

FLOOD, Daro
American 20th cent.
sculpture: (L) $385; (H) $13,200

FLORES, Pedro Victor
Spanish b. 1897
paintings: (L) $550; (H) $2,090

FLORES, Peter
paintings: (L) $440; (H) $1,045

FLORIS, Frans
Italian 1516-1570
paintings: (L) $3,850; (H) $71,500

FLORQUIN, Louis
paintings: (H) $715

FLORY, Arthur
American 20th cent.
paintings: (L) $440; (H) $1,017

FLUMBASOIU, H.
paintings: (H) $660

FLUMMER, C.L.
American 19th cent.
paintings: (H) $3,080

FOCARDI, Elisina
paintings: (H) $1,540

FOCARDI, Giovanni
Italian 1842-1903
sculpture: (H) $4,950

FOCARDI, Piero
Italian b. 1889
paintings: (H) $825

FOCHT, Frederic
French b. 1879
sculpture: (L) $495; (H) $1,100

FOERSTER, C.A.
American 19th cent.
paintings: (H) $6,600

FOGARTY, Thomas
American 1873-1938
paintings: (L) $385; (H) $2,420

FOLCK, Adalbert John
American
paintings: (H) $1,650

FOLDES
contemporary
drawings: (H) $1,980

FOLDES, Peter
English b. 1922
paintings: (H) $1,320

FOLGER, James W.
drawings: (H) $770

FOLGER, James Walter
drawings: (H) $4,500

FOLINSBEE, John Fulton
American 1892-1972
paintings: (L) $220; (H) $14,300

FOLK, Pauline
drawings: (H) $660

FOLLETT, Foster
American b. 1872
paintings: (H) $1,430

FOLTZ, Philipp
German 1825-1877
paintings: (H) $4,950

FONDA, Harry Stuart
American 1863-1942/43
paintings: (H) $825

FONECHE
French 19th cent.
paintings: (H) $715

FONECHE, A.
French 20th cent.
paintings: (H) $4,400

FONG, Lai
Chinese ac. 1860-1880
paintings: (L) $4,675; (H) $20,000

FONGUEUSE, Maurice
French 20th cent.
paintings: (H) $770

FONSECA, Gonzalo
Uruguay b. 1922
sculpture: (H) $47,300

FONSECA, Harry
American contemporary
paintings: (L) $137; (H) $825

FONSELL
American
paintings: (H) $660

FONSSAGRIVES-PENN, Lisa
contemporary
sculpture: (H) $8,250

FONT, Constantin
French b. 1890
paintings: (H) $6,050

FONTAINE, Charles la
French 20th cent.
paintings: (L) $220; (H) $4,950

FONTAINE, Emmanuel
sculpture: (H) $2,200

FONTAINE, Victor
Belgian 1837-1884
paintings: (H) $4,125

FONTAINES, Andre des
French b. 1869
paintings: (L) $2,420; (H) $2,860
drawings: (L) $220; (H) $6,600

FONTANA, Ernesto
Italian 19th cent.
paintings: (H) $3,850

FONTANA, Lavinia
Italian 1552-1614
paintings: (H) $12,100

FONTANA, Lucio
Italian 1899-1968
paintings: (H)$132,000
drawings: (L) $275; (H) $25,300
sculpture: (L) $7,700; (H) $36,300

FONTANA, Roberto
Italian 1844-1907
paintings: (L) $1,650; (H) $3,190

FONTANAROSA, Lucian
French 1912-1975
paintings: (L) $1,320; (H) $2,750

FONTANE, Roberto
paintings: (H) $1,320

FONTANO, R.
Italian 19th/20th cent.
paintings: (H) $935

FONTEBASSO, Francesco Salvator
Italian 1709-1769
paintings: (L) $7,700; (H) $286,000

FONTENAY, Andre
French b. 1913
paintings: (H) $4,950

FONTYN, Pieter
Dutch 1773-1839
paintings: (H) $1,210

FOOTE, Mary
American 1872-1968
paintings: (L) $193; (H) $1,760

FOOTE, Will Howe
American 1874-1965
paintings: (L) $220; (H) $9,900

FOPPIANI, Gustavo
paintings: (L) $220; (H) $935

FERRABOSCO, Girolamo
Italian d. 1675
paintings: (L) $6,600; (H) $22,000

FORAIN, Jean Louis
French 1852-1931
paintings: (L) $4,950; (H) $44,000
drawings: (L) $220; (H) $6,050

FORAIN, Jeanne
sculpture: (H) $1,100

FORBES, Charles Stuart
American b. 1860
paintings: (L) $82; (H) $880
drawings: (H) $100

FORBES, Edwin C.
American 1839-1895
paintings: (L) $3,300; (H) $7,700
drawings: (L) $3,300; (H) $12,100

FORBES, Elizabeth Adela Stanhope
British 1859-1912
paintings: (L) $1,650; (H) $22,000

FORBES, Helen K.
American 1891-1945
paintings: (L) $400; (H) $3,850
drawings: (H) $165

FORBES, Leyton
English 19th/20th cent.
drawings: (L) $137; (H) $2,420

FORBES, Stanhope Alexander
Irish 1857-1948
paintings: (L) $880; (H) $28,600

FORD, Dale
American
sculpture: (H) $3,750

FORD, Edward Onslow
English 1852-1901
sculpture: (L) $2,090; (H) $3,300

FORD, Gordon Onslow
contemporary
paintings: (L) $220; (H) $13,200

FORD, Henry Chapman
American 1828-1894
paintings: (L) $522; (H) $7,700
drawings: (L) $165; (H) $1,540

FORD, W.
English 19th cent.
drawings: (H) $660

FORD, William H.
American 1823-1917
paintings: (H) $2,090

FORD, William Onslow
19th/20th cent.
paintings: (H) $880

FORDHAM, Hubbard
American 1794-1872
paintings: (H) $7,975

FORDNEY, B.F.
American
paintings: (H) $3,850

FOREST, Pierre
French 1881-1971
paintings: (H) $4,125

FORESTER, Russell
paintings: (H) $4,950

FORESTIER, Amedee
French 19th cent.
paintings: (H) $5,500

FORETT, Pierre
French 20th cent.
paintings: (H) $1,100

FORG, Gunther
German b. 1952
paintings: (L) $16,500; (H) $41,800
drawings: (L) $46,200; (H) $74,800

FORGY, J.D.
American 19th cent.
paintings: (H) $797

FORNAIROS, E.
paintings: (H) $825

FORRESTER, Alfred Henry, known as
Alfred CROWQUILL
English 1804-1872
drawings: (H) $1,045

FORSTER, George
American ac. c. 1860-1880
paintings: (L) $880; (H) $13,200

FORSTER, Hal
paintings: (H) $715

FORSTER, J.
American 20th cent.
paintings: (L) $605; (H) $990

FORSTER, Joseph Wilson
British ac. 1889-1916
paintings: (H) $14,300

FORSYTH, William
American 1854-1935
drawings: (L) $440; (H) $2,860

FORSYTHE, J.E.
American 20th cent.
drawings: (H) $1,650

FORSYTHE, Victor Clyde
American 1885-1962
paintings: (L) $1,210; (H) $5,500

FORT, Evelyn Corlett
paintings: (H) $3,740

FORT, Theodore
French 19th cent.
drawings: (L) $550; (H) $935

FORTE, Luca
Italian 18th cent.
paintings: (H) $88,000

FORTE, Vicente
paintings: (L) $880; (H) $4,620

FORTESCUE, William Banks
British 19th cent.
paintings: (H) $3,300

FORTESCUE-BRICKDALE, Eleanor
English 1871-1945
drawings: (L) $4,950; (H) $6,600

FORTI, Eduardo
Italian 19th cent.
paintings: (H) $22,000

FORTI, Enrico
paintings: (H) $1,045

FORTI, Ettore
Italian ac. 1893-1897
paintings: (L) $4,950; (H) $49,500

FORTI, Max
sculpture: (H) $2,475

FORTIN, Marc Aurele
Canadian b. 1888
paintings: (H) $52,800

FORTIN(?), E.
paintings: (H) $660

FORTING, E.
sculpture: (H) $1,045

FORTINI, A.
Italian 20th cent.
paintings: (H) $770

FORTINY
sculpture: (H) $1,210

FORTUNA, Alfredo
paintings: (H) $1,100

FORTUNATI, ***de
Italian 19th cent.
paintings: (H) $2,200

FORTUNE, Euphemia Charleton
American 1885-1969
paintings: (L) $3,575; (H) $13,200
drawings: (L) $880; (H) $2,750

FORTUNY, Lucia
French 20th cent.
paintings: (L) $990; (H) $2,310

FORTUNY Y CARBO, Mariano
Spanish 1838-1874
paintings: (L) $1,760; (H) $220,000
drawings: (L) $495; (H) $14,300
sculpture: (H) $2,090

FORTUNY Y DE MADRAZO,
Mariano
Spanish 1871-1949
paintings: (H) $5,500

FORTUNY Y MARSAL, Mariano
drawings: (H) $1,980

FOSCHI, Francesco
Italian d. 1805
paintings: (L) $7,700; (H) $60,500

FOSCHI, Pier Francesco
Italian 1502-1567
paintings: (H) $5,500

FOSHKO, Josef
Russian/American ac. 20th cent.
paintings: (L) $176; (H) $1,100

FOSS, Olivier
American b. 1920
paintings: (L) $270; (H) $935

FOSSATI, Domenico
Italian 1743-1784
drawings: (H) $3,025

FOSSE, Charles Alexander Coessin de la
French b. 1829
paintings: (H) $8,250

FOSSE, Charles de la
Italian 1636-1713
paintings: (H) $715

FOSSEY, Felix
drawings: (H) $825

FOSTER, Ben
American 1852-1926
paintings: (L) $82; (H) $4,400
drawings: (L) $132; (H) $385

FOSTER, H.
paintings: (H) $880

FOSTER, Hal
American 1892-1982
drawings: (L) $154; (H) $4,950

FOSTER, J.
paintings: (L) $303; (H) $1,045

FOSTER, James
paintings: (H) $825

FOSTER, John B.
American 19th/20th cent.
drawings: (L) $110; (H) $660

FOSTER, Myles Birkett
English 1825-1899
drawings: (L) $308; (H) $2,750

FOSTER, W.P.H.
paintings: (H) $1,210

FOSTER, Walter
paintings: (H) $1,155

FOSTER, Will
American 1882-1953
paintings: (L) $468; (H) $5,225

FOSTER, William Frederick
American b. 1883
paintings: (H) $715

FOUBERT, Emile Louis
French 1840-1910
paintings: (L) $3,575; (H) $7,150

FOUCQUIER, Jacques
c. 1580/90-1659
paintings: (H) $4,400

FOUJITA, Tsuguharu
Japanese 1886-1968
paintings: (L) $33,000; (H) $6,050,000
drawings: (L) $440; (H) $385,000

FOULKES, Llyn
American b. 1934
paintings: (H) $2,200
drawings: (L) $990; (H) $1,980

FOULQUIER, Francois Joseph
drawings: (H) $1,650

FOUNTAIN, Grace R.
American 1857-1942
paintings: (H) $715

FOUQUERAY, Charles
French 1872-1956
drawings: (L) $3,080; (H) $15,400

FOURAU, Hughes
drawings: (H) $2,640

FOURIE, Albert Auguste
French b. 1854
paintings: (L) $1,650; (H) $8,800

FOURNIER, Alexis Jean
American 1865-1948
paintings: (L) $110; (H) $3,850
drawings: (L) $385; (H) $825

FOURNIER, Alexis Jean and John A.
COOK
American
drawings: (H) $825

FOURNIER, Alfred Victor
French 19th/20th cent.
paintings: (L) $523; (H) $1,045

FOURNIER, Louis Edouard Paul
French b. 1857
paintings: (H) $9,900
drawings: (H) $1,320

FOURNIER, Victor Edmond Charles
French 1872-1904
paintings: (H) $6,600

FOUS, Jean
French 1901-1971
paintings: (H) $660

FOWLER, Frank
American 1852-1910
paintings: (L) $303; (H) $2,860

FOWLER, O.R.
American
paintings: (H) $3,850

FOWLER, Robert
British 1853-1926
paintings: (L) $605; (H) $11,550

FOWLER, Trevor Thomas
American ac. 1830-1850's
paintings: (H) $3,025

FOWLER, Walter
British 19th cent.
paintings: (H) $1,650

FOWLER, William Henry
English 19th cent.
paintings: (L) $308; (H) $660

FOWLES, Arthur W.
British ac. 1840-60
paintings: (H) $4,400

FOX, Charles James
French 19th cent.
paintings: (L) $385; (H) $1,430

FOX, Ernest R.
British b. c. 1860
paintings: (L) $302; (H) $1,650

FOX, George
British 19th cent.
paintings: (L) $632; (H) $1,430

FOX, Henry Charles
English b. c. 1860
paintings: (H) $1,320
drawings: (L) $110; (H) $715

FOX, John
Canadian b. 1927
paintings: (H) $770

FOX, R. Atkinson
Canadian/American b. 1860
paintings: (L) $176; (H) $2,200
drawings: (H) $220

FOX, S.B.
paintings: (H) $770

FOY, Gray
paintings: (L) $715; (H) $1,540

FOYATIER, Denis
sculpture: (H) $1,100

FRABEL, Hans Godo
b. E. Germany 1941
sculpture: (H) $2,420

FRACANZANO, Francesco
Italian 1612-1656
paintings: (H) $25,300

FRACKMANN, H.W.
drawings: (H) $6,500

FRAGIACOMO, Pietro
Italian 1856-1922
paintings: (L) $220; (H) $10,450

FRAGONARD, Alexandre Evariste
French 1780-1850
paintings: (H) $33,000
drawings: (H) $2,860

FRAGONARD, Jean Honore
French 1732-1806
paintings: (L) $132,000; (H) $352,000
drawings: (L) $1,980; (H) $297,000

FRAILE, Alfonzo
Spanish b. 1930
paintings: (L) $110; (H) $1,100

FRAILLION, Paul
French 19th/20th cent.
paintings: (H) $1,430

FRAINT, E.
Continental 19th cent.
paintings: (H) $5,225

FRAIPONT, Georges
French 1873-1912
paintings: (H) $38,500

FRAKFURTER
paintings: (H) $825

FRAMPTON, Edward Reginald
English 1870/72-1923
paintings: (H) $12,100

FRANCAIS, F.L.
paintings: (H) $1,100

FRANCAIS, Louis
French 1814-1897
paintings: (H) $9,350

FRANCANZANO, Francesco
Italian after 1612-1656?
paintings: (H) $35,750

FRANCE, Ben
sculpture: (L) $137; (H) $660

FRANCE, Eurilda Loomis
American 1865-1931
paintings: (L) $330; (H) $8,800

FRANCES, Esteban
paintings: (H) $6,820

FRANCES, Fernanda
paintings: (H) $660

FRANCES Y PASCUAL, Placido
Spanish b. 1840
paintings: (H) $8,250

FRANCESCHI, Mariano de
Italian 1849-1896
paintings: (L) $550; (H) $6,600
drawings: (L) $352; (H) $1,760

FRANCESCHINI, Baldassare, called Il
Volterrano
Italian 1611-1689
drawings: (L) $1,320; (H) $26,300

FRANCESCHINI, J.**
sculpture: (H) $1,980

FRANCESCHINI, Marcantonio
Italian 1648-1729
paintings: (L) $385; (H) $8,800
drawings: (H) $6,600

FRANCESCO DE GIORGIO,
workshop of
Italian 1439-1501/02
paintings: (H) $41,800

FRANCESO, J.
paintings: (H) $770

FRANCHEVILLE, Clemence Andree
Lenique de
French b. 1875
paintings: (H) $2,420

FRANCHI, Franco
Italian
sculpture: (H) $4,950

FRANCHI, Pietro
Italian 19th cent.
sculpture: (H) $5,060

FRANCHINI, Antonio
French ac. 1847
sculpture: (H) $121,000

FRANCHINI, Antonio
Italian 19th cent.
paintings: (L) $1,600; (H) $1,760

FRANCHOYS, Peter
Flemish 1606-1681
paintings: (H) $6,600

FRANCIA, Francois Louis Thomas
French 1772-1839
drawings: (H) $880

FRANCIA, Giacomo
Italian 1486-1557
paintings: (L) $22,000; (H) $49,500

FRANCIS, John F.
American 1808-1886
paintings: (L) $2,200; (H) $264,000

FRANCIS, Sam
American b. 1923
paintings: (L) $3,850; (H) $1,870,000
drawings: (L) $990; (H) $550,000

FRANCIS, Thomas Edward
British fl. 1899-1912
paintings: (H) $1,650

FRANCISCI, Anthony de
American 1887-1964
sculpture: (L) $495; (H) $2,200

FRANCISCO, B.
paintings: (H) $715

FRANCISCO, John Bond
American 1863-1931
paintings: (L) $385; (H) $4,400
drawings: (H) $825

FRANCISI, Anthony de
American 1887-1934
sculpture: (H) $1,760

FRANCK, Albert Jacques
paintings: (H) $6,050

FRANCK, W.
English? 19th cent.
paintings: (H) $990

FRANCKEN, Frans, II
Flemish 1581-1642
paintings: (L) $4,400; (H) $38,500

FRANCKEN, Frans, III
Flemish 1607-1667
paintings: (L) $2,200; (H) $10,450

FRANCKEN, Frans, the elder
Flemish 1542-1616
paintings: (H) $17,600

FRANCKEN, Hieronymous, III
b. 1611
paintings: (H) $8,250

FRANCKENBERGER, Hans, the elder
German ac. 1530
drawings: (H) $37,400

FRANCO, Siron
paintings: (L) $5,280; (H) $8,250

FRANCOIS
French 19th cent.
paintings: (H) $4,675

FRANCOIS, Ange
Flemish b. 1800
paintings: (H) $5,500

FRANCOIS, Celestin
paintings: (H) $3,300

FRANCOIS, Pierre Joseph Celestin
Belgian 1759-1851
paintings: (L) $16,500; (H) $25,300

FRANCUCCI, Innocenzo, called
Innocenzo da Imola
1499/94-1547/50
paintings: (L) $18,700; (H) $19,800

FRANDZEN, Eugene M.
American 1893-1972
paintings: (L) $550; (H) $1,540
drawings: (L) $302; (H) $385

FRANETTA, C.
paintings: (H) $1,210

FRANGIAMORE, Salvatore
Italian 1853-1915
paintings: (L) $15,400; (H) $18,700

FRANK, C.
German or Swiss 19th cent.
paintings: (H) $660

FRANK, Charles H.
paintings: (L) $770; (H) $1,980

FRANK, Charles Lee
paintings: (H) $1,430

FRANK, Eugene C.
American 1845-1914
paintings: (L) $935; (H) $2,090

FRANK, Friedrich
drawings: (H) $1,870

FRANK, Gerald A.
American b. 1889
paintings: (L) $495; (H) $2,400

FRANK, Josef
Continental 19th cent.
paintings: (H) $1,100

FRANK, Mary
Anglo/American b. 1933
drawings: (H) $220
sculpture: (L) $220; (H) $9,900

FRANK, Sand
paintings: (H) $770

FRANK-WILL
French 1900-1951
paintings: (L) $3,740; (H) $24,200
drawings: (L) $1,210; (H) $7,700

FRANKE, Albert
German b. 1860
paintings: (L) $1,540; (H) $30,800

FRANKE, Albert Joseph
German 1893-1924
paintings: (H) $5,775

FRANKE, E.A.
European 19th cent.
paintings: (H) $1,430

FRANKEL, Ignaz, called Ingomar
Hungarian 1838-1924
paintings: (H) $13,200

FRANKEN, Paul von
German 1818-1884
paintings: (L) $1,650; (H) $4,180

FRANKEN, V.
paintings: (H) $1,100

FRANKENBERGER, Johann
German 1807-1874
paintings: (L) $330; (H) $1,320

FRANKENSTEIN, Godfrey Nicholas
American 1820-1873
paintings: (L) $468; (H) $16,500

FRANKENTHALER, Helen
American b. 1928
paintings: (L) $3,025; (H) $715,000
drawings: (H) $13,200
sculpture: (L) $3,300; (H) $5,500

FRANKFORT, Edward
Dutch 1864-1920
paintings: (H) $1,650

FRANKL, Walter
American 20th cent.
paintings: (L) $385; (H) $1,760

FRANKLIN
Continental 19th cent.
paintings: (H) $935

FRANKS, Gerald
American b. 1888
paintings: (H) $1,320

FRANQUELIN, Jean Augustin
French 1798-1839
paintings: (L) $2,750; (H) $93,500

FRANQUINET, Eugene P.
American 1875-1940
paintings: (H) $1,210

FRANSIOLI, Thomas Adrian
American b. 1906
paintings: (L) $88; (H) $4,950
drawings: (H) $1,045

FRANTZ, Marshall
paintings: (H) $715

FRANTZ, Marshall
American b. 1890
paintings: (H) $825

FRANZEN, August
American 1863-1938
paintings: (L) $440; (H) $6,600
drawings: (L) $33; (H) $2,200

FRAPPA, Jose
French 1854-1904
paintings: (L) $4,950; (H) $6,875

FRASER, Alex, Sr.
British 1786-1865
paintings: (H) $4,950

FRASER, Alexander
British 1828-1899
paintings: (H) $2,090

FRASER, Alexander
English 19th cent.
paintings: (L) $220; (H) $2,310

FRASER, Donald Hamilton
English b. c. 1930
paintings: (L) $176; (H) $1,100

FRASER, George Gordon
British 19th/20th cent.
paintings: (H) $6,600

FRASER, James Earle
American 1876-1953
sculpture: (L) $209; (H) $9,900

FRASER, John Arthur
Canadian/British 1839-1898
paintings: (H) $2,310

FRASER, Malcolm
American 1869-1949
paintings: (L) $110; (H) $880
drawings: (H) $220

FRASER, Thomas Douglass
American 1883-1955
paintings: (L) $1,100; (H) $2,475

FRASSATI, Gianni
paintings: (H) $1,320

FRATIN, Christophe
French c. 1800-1864
sculpture: (L) $660; (H) $7,150

FRATINO, Cesare
paintings: (H) $5,500

FRATTA, Domenico Maria
drawings: (L) $2,475; (H) $3,025

FRAUENFELDER, F.J.
Dutch 20th cent.
paintings: (H) $825
drawings: (L) $660; (H) $1,980

FRAZIER, C. James
American b. 1924
paintings: (L) $4,000; (H) $6,800

FRAZIER, Gertrude Busby
English early 20th cent.
paintings: (H) $1,265

FRAZIER, Kenneth
French/American 1867-1949
paintings: (L) $715; (H) $19,800
drawings: (L) $55; (H) $82

FREBORG, Jack
American b. 1931
drawings: (H) $990

FREDENTHAL, David
American 1914-1958
drawings: (L) $82; (H) $3,080

FREDERIC, Leon Henri Marie
Belgian 1856-1940
paintings: (H) $14,300

FREDERICKS, Ernest
American b. 1877
paintings: (L) $66; (H) $900

FREDERICKS, Marshall Maynard
sculpture: (H) $2,640

FREDOU, Jean Martial
French c. 1711-1795
drawings: (H) $4,500

FREEDLANDER, Arthur R.
American 1875-1940
paintings: (H) $660
drawings: (L) $192; (H) $440

FREEDMAN, Maurice
American 20th cent.
paintings: (L) $495; (H) $660

FREELAND, Anna C.
American 1837-1911
paintings: (H) $687
drawings: (H) $412

FREEMAN, Daniel W.
paintings: (H) $880

FREEMAN, Don
American 1908-1978
paintings: (L) $2,200; (H) $13,200
drawings: (H) $1,540

FREEMAN, J.
paintings: (L) $1,980; (H) $4,400

FREEMAN, Lloyd
American
paintings: (L) $110; (H) $1,210

FREEMAN, William
American 1927
sculpture: (H) $1,155

FREER, Frederick Warren
American 1849-1908
paintings: (L) $1,210; (H) $9,350
drawings: (L) $350; (H) $1,155

FREEZOR, George Augustus
British ac. 1861-1879
paintings: (H) $3,850

FREHS (?), O.
German 19th cent.
paintings: (H) $2,200

FREILICHER, Jane
American 20th cent.
drawings: (H) $1,045

FRELINGHUYSEN, Suzy
paintings: (H) $4,950

FREMIET, Emmanuel
French 1824-1910
sculpture: (L) $66; (H) $11,000

FREMINET, Martin
French 1567-1619
drawings: (H) $82,500

FRENCH, Daniel Chester
American 1850-1931
sculpture: (L) $550; (H) $4,400

FRENCH, Edwin Davis
American 1851-1906
paintings: (H) $825

FRENCH, Frank
1850-1933
paintings: (H) $1,760

FRENCH, G.B.
American
paintings: (H) $4,180

FRENCH, Jared
American b. 1905
paintings: (H) $60,500
drawings: (L) $2,750; (H) $4,620

FRENTZ, Rudolph
German 1831-1888
paintings: (H) $5,500

FRENZEL, Oscar
German b. 1855
paintings: (H) $2,750

FREQUENEZ, Paul Leon
French b. 1876
paintings: (L) $6,050; (H) $22,000

FRERE, Charles Edouard
French 1837-1894
paintings: (L) $990; (H) $3,575

FRERE, Charles Theodore
French 1814/15-1888
paintings: (L) $990; (H) $82,500
drawings: (L) $110; (H) $660

FRERE, Pierre Edouard
French 1819-1886
paintings: (L) $467; (H) $23,100
drawings: (H) $550

FRERICHS, William Charles Anthony
Belgian/American 1829-1905
paintings: (L) $880; (H) $22,000

FREUND, Harry Louis
American 1905-1979
paintings: (H) $990

FREVET(?)
sculpture: (H) $990

FREY, Eugene H.
Belgian b. 1864
paintings: (L) $715; (H) $1,760

FREY, Johann Georg
German School 18th cent.
paintings: (H) $797

FREY, Johann Wilheim
Austrian b. 1830
drawings: (H) $6,050

FREY, Joseph F.
American 1892-1977
paintings: (L) $330; (H) $1,210

FREY, Viola
American b. 1933
sculpture: (H) $24,200

FREY, Wilhelm
German 1826-1911
paintings: (H) $1,320

FREYBERG, Conrad
German b. 1842
paintings: (L) $1,760; (H) $12,100

FREYE, William
1812-1872
paintings: (H) $770

FRIANT, Emile
French 1863-1932
paintings: (H) $2,420
drawings: (H) $550

FRICK, Paul de
French 1864-1935
paintings: (L) $330; (H) $2,420

FRICKE, A.
German 19th cent.
paintings: (H) $2,860

FRICKER, Florence
American 20th cent.
paintings: (H) $1,650

FRIED, Lucien
paintings: (H) $660

FRIED, Pal
Hungarian 1893-1976
paintings: (L) $220; (H) $5,225
drawings: (L) $440; (H) $880

FRIEDEBERG, Pedro
sculpture: (H) $1,430

FRIEDENSON, Arthur
paintings: (H) $1,320

FRIEDENTHAL, David
American 1914-1958
paintings: (H) $1,210

FRIEDERICH, G.
German 19th cent.
paintings: (H) $1,100

FRIEDLANDER, Camilla
Austrian 1856-1928
paintings: (H) $4,400

FRIEDLANDER, Friedrich
Austrian 1825-1901
paintings: (L) $1,210; (H) $16,500

FRIEDLINGER, J.
European 19th cent.
paintings: (H) $1,650

FRIEDMAN, Arnold
American 1879-1946
paintings: (L) $2,310; (H) $4,180
drawings: (L) $165; (H) $495

FRIEDRICH, Johann Heinrich August
German 1789-1843
drawings: (H) $1,320

FRIEDRICH, M.G.
American 20th cent.
paintings: (L) $165; (H) $1,430

FRIEDRICH, Nikolaus
German b. 1865
sculpture: (L) $1,210; (H) $1,760

FRIEDRICH, Otto
Austrian 1862-1937
paintings: (H) $1,210

FRIEDRICHSEN, Ernestine
German 1824-1892
paintings: (H) $8,800

FRIELICHER, Jane
American b. 1924
paintings: (H) $28,600

FRIER, Harry
19th cent.
drawings: (H) $1,210

FRIES, Charles Arthur
American 1854-1940
paintings: (L) $385; (H) $4,675

FRIESE, Richard Bernhard Louis
German b. 1854
paintings: (H) $3,025

FRIESEKE, Frederick Carl
American 1874-1939
paintings: (L) $825; (H) $825,000
drawings: (L) $1,100; (H) $28,600

FRIESZ, Emile Othon
French 1879-1949
paintings: (L) $1,320; (H) $440,000
drawings: (L) $330; (H) $3,300

FRIGERIO, R.
Italian 19th/20th cent.
paintings: (L) $110; (H) $1,980

FRILLI, A.
Italian
sculpture: (L) $770; (H) $8,800

FRIMODT, Johanne Nicoline Louise
Danish b. 1861
paintings: (H) $29,700

FRIND, August
Austrian 1852-1924
paintings: (H) $24,200

FRINK, Dame Elizabeth
British b. 1930
sculpture: (L) $1,100; (H) $12,100

FRIPP, Charles Edwin
English 1854-1906
drawings: (L) $137; (H) $11,550

FRISCH
Continental 19th cent.
paintings: (L) $138; (H) $770

FRISCH, Johann Christoph
German 1738-1815
paintings: (L) $440; (H) $1,980

FRISHMUTH, Harriet Whitney
American 1880-1979
sculpture: (L) $825; (H) $231,000

FRISTRUP, Niels
Danish 1837-1909
paintings: (L) $13,750; (H) $20,900

FRITEL, Pierre
French b. 1853
paintings: (H) $17,600

FRITH, William Powell
English 1819-1909
paintings: (L) $605; (H) $121,000

FRITZ, Charles
American
paintings: (H) $1,700

FRITZ, Robert
contemporary
sculpture: (H) $2,420

FRITZEL, Wilhelm
German b. 1870
paintings: (H) $4,400

FRITZIUS, Harry
contemporary
paintings: (L) $1,650; (H) $2,090

FROHLICH, Bernhard
German 1823-1885
paintings: (L) $3,300; (H) $5,225

FROMANTIOU, Hendrik de
Dutch 1633-1694
paintings: (H) $22,000

FROMENTIN, Eugene
French 1820-1876
paintings: (L) $990; (H) $99,000
drawings: (L) $1,760; (H) $6,600

FROMET, E.
sculpture: (H) $1,760

FROMKES, Maurice
Russian/American 1872-1931
paintings: (L) $132; (H) $2,200

FROMUTH, Charles Henry
American 1861-1937
paintings: (L) $1,650; (H) $3,190
drawings: (L) $770; (H) $2,200

FROOT, Harry D.
English 19th/20th cent.
paintings: (L) $770; (H) $880

FROSCHL, Carl
b. 1848
paintings: (H) $2,860

FROST, Anna S.R.
American 1873-1955
paintings: (H) $1,870

FROST, Arthur Burdett
American 1851-1928
paintings: (L) $880; (H) $4,125
drawings: (L) $247; (H) $85,250

FROST, F.
American
paintings: (L) $770; (H) $935

FROST, F.S.
paintings: (L) $1,760; (H) $2,530

FROST, George Albert
American b. 1843
paintings: (L) $412; (H) $1,980

FROST, John, "Jack"
American 1890-1937
paintings: (L) $1,210; (H) $44,000
drawings: (L) $165; (H) $770

FROST, William Edward
English 1810-1877
paintings: (L) $1,100; (H) $6,600

FROTHINGHAM, James
American 1786-1864
paintings: (L) $286; (H) $3,300

FRY, William
English 19th/20th cent.
paintings: (H) $880

FRYER, G.
English 19th/20th cent.
paintings: (H) $715

FUCHS, Bernie
b. 1932
paintings: (H) $1,100

FUCHS, Emil
Austrian/American 1866-1929
paintings: (L) $880; (H) $1,100
drawings: (H) $110
sculpture: (L) $275; (H) $935

FUCHS, Ernst
Austrian b. 1930
paintings: (H) $6,325

FUCHS, Richard
German b. 1852
paintings: (L) $1,650; (H) $2,310

FUCHS, Therese
German 19th cent.
paintings: (L) $220; (H) $1,540

FUECHSEL, Hermann
German/American 1833-1915
paintings: (L) $137; (H) $40,700

FUEGER, Friedrich Heinrich
German 1775-1818
paintings: (H) $3,850

FUENTES, Giorgio
Italian 1756-1821
drawings: (L) $1,430; (H) $1,650

FUERTES, Louis Agassiz
American 1874-1927
paintings: (H) $14,300
drawings: (L) $400; (H) $18,700

FUES, Christian
German 1772-1836
paintings: (H) $2,200

FUGER, Friedrich Heinrich
German 1751-1818
paintings: (H) $22,000
drawings: (H) $1,210

FUHRKEN, Sophie
German 19th cent.
paintings: (H) $1,540

FUJINO
paintings: (H) $1,430

FUKUI, Ryonosuke
Japanese b. 1922
paintings: (L) $2,310; (H) $8,800

FUKUSHIMA, Tikashi
Japanese/Brazilian b. 1920
paintings: (H) $12,100

FULDE, Edward B.
American
paintings: (H) $1,650

FULLER, A.
American 19th cent.
paintings: (H) $6,050

FULLER, Alfred
American 1817-1893
paintings: (L) $110; (H) $1,320
drawings: (H) $385

FULLER, Arthur Davenport
American 1889-1966
paintings: (L) $880; (H) $1,210
drawings: (L) $385; (H) $990

FULLER, George
American 1822-1884
paintings: (L) $192; (H) $27,500

FULLER, Karl Hubert Maria
American
sculpture: (H) $3,850

FULLER, Richard Henry
American 1822-1871
paintings: (L) $357; (H) $7,700

FULLERTON, Robert
American 20th cent.
paintings: (H) $3,300

FULLEYLOVE, John
English 1845/47-1908
drawings: (L) $110; (H) $660

FULLONTON, Robert Dudley
American 1876-1933
paintings: (L) $302; (H) $825

FULLUN, D.
British ac. 1860
paintings: (H) $990

FULMARGE, George
American 20th cent.
paintings: (H) $2,530

FULOP, Karoly
American b. 1898
paintings: (H) $3,300
drawings: (H) $3,025
sculpture: (H) $4,125

FULTON, David
British b. 1850
paintings: (H) $3,025

FULTON, Fitch
American b. 1879
paintings: (L) $1,210; (H) $4,675

FULTON, R.
British late 18th cent.
drawings: (H) $1,210

FULTON, Samuel
English 1855-1941
paintings: (L) $220; (H) $1,760

FUNKE, Anton
Dutch 1869-1955
paintings: (H) $1,980

FUNKE, Helene
paintings: (L) $1,320; (H) $12,100

FUNNO, Michele
Italian 19th cent.
drawings: (H) $2,000

FURCY DE LAVAULT, Albert Tibule
French 19th cent.
paintings: (L) $2,200; (H) $15,400

FURINI, Francesco
Italian 1604-1646
paintings: (L) $9,625; (H) $33,000
drawings: (H) $18,700

FURLONG, Thomas
American 20th cent.
paintings: (H) $1,540

FURMAN, John
American
drawings: (H) $5,500

FURNEAUX, Charles
American 1835-1913
paintings: (L) $467; (H) $1,300

FURSE, Charles Wellington
paintings: (H) $660

FURSMAN, Frederick F.
American 1874-1943
paintings: (L) $302; (H) $3,300

FURST
paintings: (H) $3,850

FURST, August
Italian 19th/20th cent.
paintings: (L) $1,100; (H) $2,475

FURST, Emil
American
paintings: (H) $2,200

FUSELI, Henri, Johann Hans Heinrich
FUSSLI
Swiss 1741-1825
drawings: (H) $11,000

FUSSELL, Alexander
drawings: (H) $660

FUSSELL, Charles Lewis
American 1840-1909
paintings: (L) $2,200; (H) $3,520
drawings: (H) $11,000

FYFE, Samuel H.
British 19th cent.
paintings: (H) $6,600

FYFE, William Baater Collier
British 1836-1882
paintings: (H) $11,550

FYSON, John J.
American 19th/20th cent.
paintings: (H) $990

FYT, Jan
Flemish 1611-1661
paintings: (H) $132,000

GAAL, Ferenc
Hungarian b. 1891
paintings: (H) $770

GABANI, Giuseppe
Italian 1846-1899
drawings: (L) $1,100; (H) $6,050

GABINELLE, Rainer Zstranffy
Continental 19th/20th cent.
paintings: (L) $2,090; (H) $4,400

GABINI, P.
Italian 19th cent.
paintings: (H) $2,640

GABO, Naum
American 1890-1977
sculpture: (H) $473,000

GABRIEL, Francois
French 19th/20th cent.
paintings: (L) $1,540; (H) $3,850

GABRIEL, J.
Italian 19th cent.
paintings: (H) $880

GABRIEL, Paul Joseph Constantin
Dutch 1828-1903
paintings: (L) $1,760; (H) $1,980

GABRINI, Pietro
Italian 1856-1926
paintings: (L) $990; (H) $17,600
drawings: (L) $357; (H) $7,150

GADSBY, William Hippon
British 1844-1924
paintings: (H) $4,675

GAEDT
drawings: (H) $1,870

GAEL, Barent
Dutch 1635/45-1681
paintings: (L) $2,860; (H) $13,200

GAERTNER, Carl F.
American 1898-1952
paintings: (L) $88; (H) $1,650
drawings: (L) $55; (H) $990

GAETANO, Chierini
paintings: (H) $4,675

GAGE, George William
American b. 1887
paintings: (L) $770; (H) $1,650

GAGE, Harry Lawrence
American b. 1887
paintings: (L) $85; (H) $880

GAGE, Jane
American b. 1914
paintings: (L) $220; (H) $990

GAGEN, Robert Ford
British 1847-1926
drawings: (H) $2,200

GAGILIARDINI, Julien Gustave
French 1846-1927
paintings: (H) $4,500

GAGLIARDO, Gino
Italian 19th/20th cent.
paintings: (H) $2,310

GAGNEAU, Paul Leon
French d. 1910
paintings: (H) $715

GAGNI, P.
French 20th cent.
paintings: (L) $302; (H) $1,210

GAGNON, Clarence A.
Canadian 1882-1942
paintings: (L) $96,250; (H) $495,000

GAIGNEAU, Paul
paintings: (H) $1,100

GAINES, Charles
contemporary
drawings: (L) $2,640; (H) $3,850

GAINSBOROUGH, Thomas
English 1727-1788
paintings: (L) $1,320; (H) $176,000
drawings: (H) $126,500

GAISSER, Jakob Emmanuel
German 1825-1899
paintings: (L) $1,760; (H) $7,150

GAISSER, Max
German 1857-1922
paintings: (L) $1,870; (H) $8,800

GALAMUNICH, Yucca
sculpture: (H) $4,400

GALAN, Julio
Mexican b. 1958
paintings: (L) $3,300; (H) $8,250

GALBRUND
French 19th cent.
paintings: (H) $1,650

GALCOTA, L.R.
paintings: (L) $286; (H) $715

GALE, D.
American 19th cent.
paintings: (H) $1,540

GALE, George
American 1893-1951
drawings: (L) $100; (H) $2,700

GALEOTTI, Sebastiano
drawings: (H) $990

GALIANY, E.
paintings: (L) $660; (H) $2,420

GALIEN-LALOUE, Eugene
French 1854-1941
paintings: (L) $4,400; (H) $11,000
drawings: (L) $1,980; (H) $28,600

GALINDEZ, P.
Spanish 19th cent.
paintings: (H) $1,430

GALL, Francois
French 1912-1945
paintings: (L) $374; (H) $22,000
drawings: (L) $880; (H) $2,640

GALL, Joseph
French b. 1807
paintings: (H) $17,600

GALL, Theodore
sculpture: (H) $990

GALLAGHER, Michael
American b. 1898
paintings: (L) $2,200; (H) $12,100

GALLAGHER, Sears
American 1869-1955
paintings: (L) $770; (H) $1,430
drawings: (L) $110; (H) $2,750

GALLAIT, Louis
French 1810-1887
paintings: (L) $330; (H) $2,420

GALLARD, Michel de
French b. 1921
paintings: (L) $990; (H) $3,300

GALLARD-LEPINAY, Paul Char
Emmanuel
French 1842-1885
paintings: (H) $8,250

GALLATIN, Albert Eugene
American 1881/82-1952
paintings: (L) $3,575; (H) $20,900
drawings: (H) $15,400

GALLEGOS Y ARNOSA, Jose
Spanish 1859-1917
paintings: (L) $46,200; (H) $66,000
drawings: (L) $1,980; (H) $3,960

GALLI, Ferdinando
Italian b. 1814
paintings: (H) $1,540

GALLI, G.
Italian 19th cent.
paintings: (H) $8,800

GALLI, Giuseppe
Italian
paintings: (H) $11,000

GALLI, Riccardo
Italian 1869-1944
paintings: (H) $2,530

GALLI, Stanley Walter
American b. 1912
drawings: (H) $1,430

GALLIA, V.
paintings: (H) $660

GALLIARI, Bernardino
Italian 1707-1794
drawings: (H) $3,850

GALLIARI, Fabrizio
Italian 1707-1790
drawings: (H) $935

GALLIARI, G***
drawings: (L) $1,540; (H) $1,540

GALLISON, Henry Hammond
American 1850-1910
paintings: (L) $440; (H) $950
drawings: (H) $198

GALLITIN, Albert E.
1882-1952
paintings: (H) $800

GALLO, Frank
American b. 1933
sculpture: (L) $2,200; (H) $7,150

GALLO, Guiseppe
contemporary
paintings: (H) $6,325

GALLO, I.
sculpture: (L) $99; (H) $1,320

GALLO, Vincent
American contemporary
paintings: (L) $2,200; (H) $5,225
drawings: (L) $9,900; (H) $11,000

GALLON, Robert
English 1845-1925.
paintings: (L) $385; (H) $7,700

GALLOWAY, J.
British 19th cent.
paintings: (H) $880

GALOFRE Y GIMENEZ, Baldomero
Spanish 1848/49-1902
paintings: (L) $2,420; (H) $28,600
drawings: (L) $1,980; (H) $5,060

GALVAN, Jesus Guerrero
Mexican 1910-early 1970's
paintings: (L) $6,050; (H) $71,500
drawings: (L) $2,475; (H) $3,300

GAMARRA, Jose
b. 1934 Brazil
paintings: (L) $4,400; (H) $17,600

GAMBARD, Henri Augustin
French 1819-1882
paintings: (H) $27,500

GAMBARTES, Leonidas
Argentinian b. 1909
paintings: (H) $9,350

GAMBEY, Andre
French 19th cent.
paintings: (H) $880

GAMBEY, Leon
French 1883-1914
paintings: (H) $3,300

GAMBLE, John Marshall
American 1863-1957
paintings: (L) $220; (H) $19,800

GAMBLE, Roy C.
American 1887-1964
paintings: (L) $27; (H) $1,870
drawings: (L) $165; (H) $302

GAMBOGI, Emile
paintings: (H) $880

GAMBOGI, G.
late 19th cent.
sculpture: (L) $935; (H) $16,500

GAMMELL, Robert Hale Ives
American 1893-1981
paintings: (L) $412; (H) $11,000

GAMMERITH, F.L.
German 19th cent.
paintings: (H) $1,045

GAMMIER, J.
American 20th cent.
paintings: (H) $660

GAMPENRIEDER, Karl
German b. 1860
paintings: (H) $29,700

GANDOLFI, Gaetano
Italian 1734-1802
paintings: (L) $45,100; (H) $49,500
drawings: (L) $880; (H) $3,850

GANDOLFI, Mauro
Italian 1764-1834
drawings: (L) $4,620; (H) $9,350

GANDOLFI, Ubaldo
Italian 1728-1781
drawings: (L) $2,860; (H) $15,400

GANNAM, John
American
drawings: (H) $3,960

GANNE, Pierre Christian
French 20th cent.
paintings: (H) $1,210

GANNE, Yves
paintings: (L) $209; (H) $880

GANNI, Y.
Italian 19th cent.
drawings: (H) $715

GANS, E.D.
Dutch 1832-1874
paintings: (H) $1,870

GANSO, Emil
German/American 1895-1941
paintings: (L) $330; (H) $11,000
drawings: (L) $110; (H) $1,760

GANT, J.
paintings: (H) $1,430

GANTCKEFF
sculpture: (H) $825

GANTNER, Bernard
French b. 1928
paintings: (L) $209; (H) $2,530
drawings: (L) $300; (H) $880

GANZ, Edwin
Swiss b. 1871
paintings: (H) $4,400

GARABEDIAN, Charles
American b. 1924
paintings: (L) $11,000; (H) $14,300

GARABEDIAN, Giragos der
Armenian/American b. 1893
paintings: (L) $165; (H) $1,100

GARAT, Francis
French 19th cent.
paintings: (L) $3,300; (H) $15,400
drawings: (L) $1,100; (H) $1,100

GARAY, M. de
paintings: (H) $10,450
drawings: (H) $308

GARAY Y AREVALO, Manuel
Spanish 19th cent.
paintings: (L) $3,850; (H) $22,000

GARBER, Daniel
American 1880-1958
paintings: (L) $1,980; (H) $154,000
drawings: (L) $230; (H) $5,610

CAPPONI, Raffaelino de, called
Raffaelo del Garbo
Italian 1466-1524
paintings: (H) $47,300

GARCIA, David
French b. 1936
paintings: (L) $1,100; (H) $1,980

GARCIA, H.
Chilean 20th cent.
paintings: (H) $700

GARCIA, Joaquin Torres
Uruguayan 1874-1949
paintings: (L) $24,200; (H) $82,500
drawings: (L) $2,200; (H) $8,250

GARCIA, Juan
Spanish 19th cent.
paintings: (H) $9,350

GARCIA Y MENCIA, Antonio
Spanish 19th cent.
drawings: (H) $6,050

GARCIA Y RAMOS, Jose
Spanish b. 1852
paintings: (L) $2,090; (H) $28,600
drawings: (H) $550

GARCIA Y RODRIGUEZ, Manuel
Spanish b. 1863
paintings: (L) $1,430; (H) $33,000

GARDANNE, August
French 19th cent.
paintings: (L) $1,430; (H) $1,925

GARDENER, F.J.H.
British 20th cent.
drawings: (L) $660; (H) $880

GARDET, Georges
French b. 1863
sculpture: (L) $165; (H) $4,125

GARDEUR, Charles
French 19th cent.
paintings: (L) $330; (H) $1,210

GARDINER, Eliza D.
American 1871-1955
paintings: (H) $880
drawings: (H) $550

GARDINER, J.H.
American contemporary
drawings: (H) $770

GARDINIER, A.V.
Continental 19th cent.
paintings: (H) $660

GARDNER, Derek
paintings: (H) $3,300

GARDNER, Elizabeth
American/French 1851-1922
paintings: (H) $44,000

GARDNER, F.J.H.
British 20th cent.
drawings: (L) $1,000; (H) $3,000

GARDNER, G.
English ac. 1884-1886
drawings: (H) $1,650

GARDNER, Walter
English/American b. 1902
paintings: (H) $825

GARDNER, William Biscombe
English 1847/49-1917/19
drawings: (H) $1,210

GARET, Jedd
American b. 1955
paintings: (L) $66; (H) $19,800
drawings: (L) $33; (H) $3,850
sculpture: (H) $11,000

GARF, Carl C.
American
paintings: (H) $3,300

GARF, Salomon
Dutch 1879-1943
paintings: (H) $5,500

GARGIOLLO, A.
Italian 19th cent.
drawings: (L) $385; (H) $4,400

GARIBALDI, Joseph
French b. 1863
paintings: (L) $1,100; (H) $6,050

GARINE, M.
Italian 19th cent.
paintings: (H) $660

GARINEI, Giovanni
Italian 1846-1900
paintings: (H) $2,860

GARINEI, M.
paintings: (H) $1,045

GARINEI, Michele
paintings: (L) $165; (H) $990

GARINO, Angelo
Italian b. 1860
paintings: (L) $990; (H) $9,350

GARIOT, Paul Cesare
French b. 1811
paintings: (H) $990

GARLAND, Charles Trevor
British ac. 1874-1901
paintings: (H) $9,075

GARLAND, H.
sculpture: (H) $2,750

GARLAND, Henry
English ac. 1854-1892
paintings: (L) $550; (H) $3,750

GARLAND, Valentine T.
paintings: (H) $2,750

GARMAN, Ed
American
paintings: (L) $2,420; (H) $12,100

GARMAN, Michael
American 20th cent.
drawings: (L) $1,100; (H) $3,630
sculpture: (H) $275

GARNER, E.M.
European 20th cent.
paintings: (L) $880; (H) $1,210

GARNERAY, Ambrose Louis
French 1783-1857
paintings: (H) $7,700

GARNIER, Alfred
paintings: (H) $1,045

GARNIER, Jean
French ac. c. 1885-1910
sculpture: (L) $176; (H) $1,210

GARNIER, Jules Arsene
French 1847-1889
paintings: (L) $660; (H) $19,800

GARNIER, Michel
French ac. 1793-1814
paintings: (H) $66,000

GARNIER, Pierre
French b. 1847
paintings: (H) $5,500

GARRETT, Edmund Henry
American 1853-1929
paintings: (L) $165; (H) $2,090
drawings: (L) $302; (H) $1,400

GARRIDO, Eduardo Leon
Spanish 1856-1949
paintings: (L) $2,310; (H) $77,000

GARRIDO, Leandro Ramon
Spanish 1868-1909
paintings: (H) $1,870

GARRY, D.D.
paintings: (H) $1,650

GARSIDE, Thomas H.
Canadian b. 1906
drawings: (H) $1,320

GARTH, John
American 1894-1971
paintings: (L) $220; (H) $1,210

GARTHWAITE, William
British 1821-1889
paintings: (H) $1,320

GARTNER, L.
paintings: (H) $1,650

GARTNER, L.
European 19th cent.
paintings: (L) $1,980; (H) $4,180

GARZI, Luigi
Italian 1638-1721
paintings: (L) $4,180; (H) $11,000

GARZOLINI, Giuseppe
Italian 1850-1938
paintings: (H) $1,100

GASCARS, Henri
c. 1635-1701
paintings: (H) $5,500

GASKELL, George Arthur
English 19th cent.
paintings: (H) $825

GASPARD, Leon
Russian/American 1882-1964
paintings: (L) $1,100; (H) $275,000
drawings: (L) $825; (H) $2,420

GASPARI, Antonio
Italian 1670-c. 1730
paintings: (H) $29,700

GASPARINI, Luigi
Italian 19th/20th cent.
paintings: (H) $2,090

GASPARO, Oronzo
American b. 1903
paintings: (H) $715

GASQ, Paul Jean Baptiste
French 1860-1944
sculpture: (L) $1,760; (H) $3,080

GASSER, Henry Martin
American 1909-1981
paintings: (L) $330; (H) $7,150
drawings: (L) $88; (H) $4,950

GAST, John
American 19th cent.
drawings: (L) $330; (H) $1,320

GASTAN, Gustave
Swiss 1823-1892
paintings: (L) $577; (H) $742

GASTIN, A.J.
paintings: (H) $825

GASTIRE, L**
Continental 19th cent.
paintings: (H) $770

GATCH, Lee
American 1902/09-1968
paintings: (L) $880; (H) $6,600
drawings: (L) $1,980; (H) $6,050

GATEWOOD, Bill
contemporary
paintings: (H) $660

GATSKI, Gerald
paintings: (H) $2,200

Taos Artist

Leon Gaspard (1882-1964) was born in Russia, the son of a retired army officer who dealt in furs and rugs. As a boy he went on extended trading trips with his father. Gaspard studied art in Odessa and Moscow before going to Paris at age seventeen to enroll at the Academie Julian under the tutelage of Edouard Toudouze and William Adolphe Bouguereau. Success came while he was still a student—a New York collector bought thirty-five of his Parisian sketches. Flushed with success, he took his American bride on a two-year horseback honeymoon in Siberia. Gaspard served in the French Air Corps during the World War I. He was shot down and wounded but recovered and joined his wife in New York. They settled in Taos, New Mexico, in 1918. The terrain and Indian life reminded Gaspard of Siberia, and his bright, colorful paintings of New Mexico life brought him great success. Gaspard traveled extensively and painted productively until his death. (Leon Gaspard, *New Year's Day in Smolenski*, oil on artist board, 24 3/8 x 24 3/8 in., Boos, July 27, 1990, $126,500)

GATTI, Ceasare
Italian 19th cent.
paintings: (H) $1,045

GATTO, Victor Joseph
American 1893-1965
paintings: (L) $1,210; (H) $2,530

GAUBAULT, Alfred Emile
French d. 1895
paintings: (L) $1,650; (H) $4,950

GAUDEFROY, Alphonse
French 1845-1936
paintings: (L) $2,860; (H) $3,850

GAUDET, Gabriel
French late 19th/early 20th cent
sculpture: (H) $990

GAUDET, H.
sculpture: (H) $660

GAUDEZ, Adrien Etienne
French 1845-1902
sculpture: (L) $220; (H) $10,450

GAUDEZ-CHENNEVIERE, Cecile
Delphine
French b. 1851
drawings: (H) $1,980

GAUDFROY, F.D.
paintings: (H) $2,640

GAUDIER-BRZESKA, Henri
French 1891-1915
drawings: (H) $5,500

GAUERMANN, Friedrich
Austrian 1807-1862
paintings: (L) $14,300; (H) $308,000

GAUFFIER, Louis
French 1761-1801
paintings: (L) $825; (H) $52,250
drawings: (H) $275

GAUGENGIGL, Ignaz Marcel
German/American 1855/56-1932
paintings: (L) $2,970; (H) $77,000

GAUGUIN, Paul
French 1848-1903
paintings: (L) $99,000; (H) $24,200,000
drawings: (L) $1,100; (H) $77,000
sculpture: (L) $5,280; (H) $60,500

GAUL, Arrah Lee
American ac. 1915-1933
paintings: (L) $66; (H) $1,100

GAUL, August
German 1869-1921
sculpture: (H) $1,760

GAUL, Gilbert, or William Gilbert
American 1855-1919
paintings: (L) $522; (H) $22,000

GAUL, Gustave
Austrian 1836-1888
paintings: (L) $1,210; (H) $2,200

GAULD, David
British 1865-1936
paintings: (H) $2,750

GAULEY, Robert David
American 1875-1943
paintings: (L) $330; (H) $3,520
drawings: (L) $121; (H) $742

GAULLI, Giovanni Battista, Il Baciccio
paintings: (L) $8,800; (H) $17,600
drawings: (L) $5,775; (H) $13,750

GAULOIS, Jules
French ac. 1848-1853
paintings: (H) $8,800

GAUME, Henri Rene
French b. 1834
paintings: (H) $5,720

GAUSS, Eugen
American
sculpture: (L) $330; (H) $2,640

GAUSSEN, Adolphe Louis
French b. 1871
paintings: (L) $770; (H) $1,430

GAUSSON, Leo
contemporary
paintings: (L) $440; (H) $1,650

GAUTHERIN, Jean
French 1840-1890
sculpture: (L) $1,100; (H) $5,775

GAUTHERIN, Jules
late 19th cent.
sculpture: (L) $935; (H) $1,870

GAUTHIER, Jacques
sculpture: (H) $2,475

GAUTIER, Armand Desire
French 1825-1894
paintings: (L) $1,100; (H) $1,210

GAUTIER, C.
drawings: (H) $2,200

GAUTIER, Francois
French 19th cent.
paintings: (H) $2,750

GAUTIER, Jacques Louis
b. 1831
sculpture: (H) $2,090

GAUTIER D'AGOTY, Jacques Fabien
French 1710-1781
paintings: (H) $3,520

GAVAGNIN, Giuseppe
Italian 19th cent.
paintings: (H) $7,700

GAVARDIE, Jean de
French 1909-1961
paintings: (H) $1,320

GAVARNI, Paul
French 1804-1866
drawings: (L) $413; (H) $3,300

GAVARNI, Sulpice Guillaume
Chevalier
French 1804-1866
drawings: (H) $2,750

GAVENCKY, Frank J.
American b. 1888
paintings: (H) $6,050

GAW, William Alexander
American 1891-1973
paintings: (L) $220; (H) $2,200

GAY, August
American 1891-1949
paintings: (H) $4,400

GAY, Edward
Irish/American 1837-1928
paintings: (L) $385; (H) $18,700
drawings: (L) $275; (H) $880

GAY, Edward and Arthur Fitzwilliam
TAIT
American 19th/20th cent.
paintings: (H) $2,750

GAY, George Howell
American 1858-1931
paintings: (L) $137; (H) $2,420
drawings: (L) $66; (H) $2,750

GAY, Patricia
American 1876-1965
paintings: (H) $3,850

GAY, Walter
American 1856-1937
paintings: (L) $220; (H) $70,400
drawings: (L) $308; (H) $6,600

GAY, Winckworth Allan
American 1821-1910
paintings: (L) $825; (H) $3,740
drawings: (L) $55; (H) $165

GAYLOR, Samuel Wood
American b. 1883
paintings: (H) $5,500

GAYRARD, Paul Joseph Raymond
French 1807-1855
sculpture: (L) $2,420; (H) $5,280

GAZE, Harold
American 20th cent.
drawings: (L) $1,650; (H) $3,850

GAZUL, Xaviar
Hatian b. 1783
paintings: (H) $9,075

GAZZERI, Ernesto
Italian c. 1894
sculpture: (L) $990; (H) $23,100

GEBHARDT, Friedrich Wilhelm
German 1827-1893
paintings: (H) $1,100

GEBHARDT, Karl
German 1860-1917
paintings: (H) $4,400

GEBHARDT, Ludwig
Bavarian 1830-1908
paintings: (H) $1,430

GEBLER, Friedrich Otto
German 1838-1917
paintings: (L) $12,100; (H) $31,900

GECHTER, Jean Francois Theodore
French
sculpture: (L) $1,870; (H) $3,300

GECHTER, T.
sculpture: (H) $770

GECHTER, Thomas
sculpture: (H) $1,100

GECHTOFF, Leonid
American 20th cent.
paintings: (L) $165; (H) $2,200
drawings: (L) $176; (H) $231

GECHTOFF, Sonia
American b. 1926
paintings: (H) $825
drawings: (L) $935; (H) $2,750

GEDDES, Matthew
American b. 1899
paintings: (H) $1,100

GEDLEK, Ludwig
Polish/Austrian school b. 1847
paintings: (L) $1,210; (H) $7,150

GEEFS, Fanny Corr
Irish 1807/14-1883
paintings: (H) $2,200

GEERHAERDTS, Marcus, the younger
follower of
paintings: (H) $4,950

GEERTZ, Julius
German 1837-1902
paintings: (H) $935

GEEST, Juliaen Franciscus de
ac. by 1657-d. 1699
paintings: (H) $5,500

GEETERE, Georges de
French 19th/20th cent.
paintings: (L) $7,700; (H) $17,600

GEETS, Willem
Belgian 1838-1919
paintings: (L) $1,925; (H) $13,200

GEGERFELT, Wilhelm von
Swedish 1844-1920
paintings: (H) $3,850
drawings: (H) $825

GEGOUX, J.
paintings: (H) $880

GEH, A.A.
paintings: (H) $1,100

GEHRIG, Jacob
German 1846-1922
paintings: (H) $1,100

GEHRY, Frank
American b. Canada 1929
sculpture: (H) $53,900

GEIBEL, Casimir
Austrian 1839-1896
paintings: (L) $1,210; (H) $4,675

GEIBEL, K.
paintings: (H) $660

GEIGER, Peter Johann Nepomuk
Austrian 1805-1880
drawings: (H) $2,860

GEIGER, Richard
Austrian 1870-1945
paintings: (L) $165; (H) $3,300

GEIGER, Robert
German 1859-1903
paintings: (L) $1,210; (H) $4,950

GEIGER, Willi
1878-1971
paintings: (H) $660

GEIS, Joseph W.
paintings: (L) $60; (H) $1,320

GEISLER, B.
paintings: (L) $2,310; (H) $2,640

GELANZE, Giuseppe
Italian b. 1867
paintings: (L) $275; (H) $825

GELDER, Aert de
Dutch 1645-1727
paintings: (L) $6,600; (H) $28,600

GELDER, Eugene van
paintings: (L) $1,650; (H) $2,200

GELDER, Lucia Mathilde von
German 1865-1899
paintings: (H) $2,200

GELERDTS, Flore
Belgian 19th/20th cent.
paintings: (L) $7,700; (H) $9,900

GELHAAR, Emil
American 1862-1934
paintings: (H) $1,100

GELHAY, Edouard
French b. 1856
paintings: (L) $1,540; (H) $9,350

GELIBERT, Gaston
French 1850-after 1931
paintings: (H) $13,200

GELIBERT, Jules Bertrand
French 1834-1916
paintings: (L) $2,200; (H) $6,325
drawings: (L) $990; (H) $2,860
sculpture: (L) $550; (H) $715

GELIBERT, Jules and Gaston
French 19th cent.
drawings: (H) $2,420

GELLI, Edoardo
Italian 1852-1933
paintings: (H) $990

GELMUYDEN, R.E.
Dutch 19th/20th cent.
drawings: (H) $2,200

GEMITO, Vincenzo
Italian 1852-1929
sculpture: (L) $440; (H) $9,900

GEMOGNE
sculpture: (H) $825

GEMPT, Bernard de
Dutch 1826-1879
paintings: (H) $8,250

GEN PAUL
French 1895-1975
paintings: (L) $660; (H) $37,400
drawings: (L) $440; (H) $5,500

GENDROT, Felix Albert
American b. 1866
paintings: (L) $220; (H) $2,200

GENGE, C.
paintings: (H) $1,760

GENICHIRO, Inokuma
Japanese b. 1902
drawings: (H) $19,800

GENIN, John
American 1830-1895
paintings: (L) $66; (H) $3,520

GENIN, Lucien
French 1894-1958
paintings: (L) $5,500; (H) $6,050
drawings: (L) $275; (H) $6,050

GENIS, Rene
French b. 1922
paintings: (L) $247; (H) $4,125

GENISSON, Jules Victor
Belgian 1805-1860
paintings: (L) $3,850; (H) $6,050

GENNARELLI, Amedeo
French, b. Naples ac. 1913-1930
sculpture: (L) $1,430; (H) $5,720

GENNARI, Benedetto
drawings: (H) $1,650

GENNARI, Benedetto, the younger
Italian 1633-1715
paintings: (H) $3,300

GENNAY, A.
sculpture: (L) $385; (H) $935

GENOELS, Abraham, called
ARCHIMEDES
1640-1723
drawings: (H) $2,860

GENOVES, Juan
contemporary
paintings: (L) $3,080; (H) $6,600

GENTH, Lillian Matilda
American 1876-1953
paintings: (L) $99; (H) $9,350

GENTILINI, Franco
Italian b. 1909
paintings: (H) $2,860

GENZMER, Berthold
German 1858-1927
paintings: (L) $1,760; (H) $10,450

GEORGE, Juliette
paintings: (H) $1,650

GEORGE, Vesper Lincoln
American 1865-1934
paintings: (L) $302; (H) $7,150
drawings: (L) $193; (H) $550

GEORGES
Haitian 20th cent.
drawings: (H) $990

GEORGES, F.
French 19th/20th cent.
paintings: (H) $1,210

GEORGI, Edwin A.
American 1896-1964
paintings: (H) $1,210

GEORGI, Otto Friedrich
German 1819-1874
paintings: (L) $8,250; (H) $31,900

GEORGIUS, R.
paintings: (H) $770

GERARD, Francois Pascal Simon,
Baron
French 1770-1837
paintings: (H) $17,600

GERARD, Jasper, or GEERAERTS
paintings: (H) $36,300

GERARD, Pascal
French 20th cent.
paintings: (L) $3,080; (H) $3,190

GERARD, Paul
French 20th cent.
paintings: (L) $110; (H) $715

GERARD, Rolf
paintings: (H) $6,325

GERARD, Theodore
Belgian 1829-1895
paintings: (L) $3,850; (H) $41,250

GERBER, Henriette
German 19th cent.
paintings: (L) $440; (H) $4,950

GERDAGO
French 20th cent.
sculpture: (L) $330; (H) $7,150

GERE, Charles March
drawings: (H) $1,045

GERFORD, A.
German 19th cent.
paintings: (H) $990

GERGELY, Imre
Hungarian 1868-1915
paintings: (L) $440; (H) $4,400

GERHARDT, Eduard
German 1813-1888
paintings: (L) $2,860; (H) $5,720

GERICAULT, Theodore
French 1791-1824
paintings: (L) $82,500; (H) $2,420,000
drawings: (L) $3,080; (H) $88,000

GERIN, Michelle
sculpture: (H) $60,500

GERINI, Lorenzo di Niccolo
Italian 14th/15th cent.
paintings: (H) $93,500

GERINI, Niccolo di Pietro
Italian ac. 1368; d. 1415
paintings: (H) $82,500

GERIRET, A.
paintings: (H) $770

GERLACH, Albert
paintings: (H) $1,100

GERLASH, Anthony
American
paintings: (H) $2,420

GERMAIN, Jacques
French b. 1915
paintings: (L) $3,080; (H) $7,500

GERMAIN, Jean Baptiste
late 19th cent.
sculpture: (L) $165; (H) $4,840

GERMASCHEFF, Michail
Markianowits
Russian b. 1868
paintings: (H) $935

GERNEZ, Paul Elie
French 1888-1948
drawings: (H) $17,000

GEROME, Francois
French 20th cent.
paintings: (L) $110; (H) $2,310

GEROME, J.
paintings: (H) $1,100

GEROME, Jean Leon
French 1824-1904
paintings: (L) $7,150; (H) $2,200,000
drawings: (L) $275; (H) $7,700
sculpture: (L) $1,045; (H) $440,000

GEROME, Joannes D.
French 19th cent.
paintings: (H) $1,980

GERRY, Samuel Lancaster
American 1813-1891
paintings: (L) $440; (H) $9,350
drawings: (H) $660

GERTLER, Mark
English 1891/92-1939
paintings: (H) $29,700

GERVAIS, Paul Jean
French 1859-1936
paintings: (H) $26,400

GERVELLI
drawings: (H) $1,210

GERVEX, Henri
French 1852-1929
paintings: (L) $660; (H) $49,500
drawings: (L) $660; (H) $4,125

GERVEX, Madeleine
paintings: (H) $660

GERZSO, Gunther
Mexican b. 1916
paintings: (L) $522; (H) $56,100
drawings: (L) $550; (H) $5,500
sculpture: (L) $6,050; (H) $20,900

GESINUS, Bob
Belgian 20th cent.
paintings: (L) $660; (H) $1,320

GESNE, Jean Victor Albert de
French 1834-1903
paintings: (L) $3,300; (H) $14,300

GESSA Y ARIAS
Spanish 1840-1920
paintings: (L) $605; (H) $880

GESSINGER, E.
paintings: (H) $1,045

GESSNITZER, Joseph
Austrian 19th cent.
paintings: (H) $1,760

GESSNITZER, T.C.
German 19th cent.
paintings: (H) $2,860

GEST, Margaret Ralston
American
paintings: (H) $2,420

GEUDENS, Albert
Belgian b. 1869
paintings: (H) $1,265

GEYER, H.
paintings: (H) $660

GEYGER, Ernst Moritz
German b. 1861
sculpture: (L) $825; (H) $7,150

GEYLING, Carl
Austrian 1814-1880
paintings: (H) $1,045

GEYP, Adriaan Marinus
Dutch 1855-1926
paintings: (L) $385; (H) $3,080

GEZA, Peske
paintings: (H) $1,320

GHERADINI, Melchiore
paintings: (H) $7,700

GHERARDI, Giuseppe, studio of
paintings: (H) $4,400

GHERARDI, Giuseppe
Italian 19th cent.
paintings: (L) $715; (H) $1,210

GHERARDI, Luigi
drawings: (H) $1,045

GHERARDINI, Alessandro
Italian 1655-1723/28
paintings: (H) $5,500

GHEYN, Jacob de, II
Dutch 1565-1629
paintings: (H) $88,000

GHEYN, Jacob de, II, follower of
drawings: (H) $2,090

GHEZZI, Pier Leone
Italian 1674-1755
drawings: (L) $1,320; (H) $2,200

GHIGLION GREEN, Maurice
paintings: (H) $1,045

GHIKAS, Panos George
American b. 1922
paintings: (L) $935; (H) $2,860

GHIRARDINI, Stefano
paintings: (H) $3,850

GHIRLANDAJO, Ridolfi de Domenico
Italian 1483-1561
paintings: (L) $19,800; (H) $23,100

GHISLANDI, Vittorio, called Fra
Galgario
Italian 1655-1743
paintings: (L) $7,700; (H) $33,000

GHISOLFI, Giovanni
Italian 1632-1683
paintings: (H) $27,500

GHIZE, Eleanor de
American b. 1896
paintings: (H) $1,320

GIACHI, E.
paintings: (L) $220; (H) $880

GIACOMETTI, Alberto
Swiss 1901-1966
paintings: (L) $6,050; (H) $3,190,000
drawings: (L) $2,310; (H) $68,750
sculpture: (L) $4,400; (H) $4,950,000

GIACOMETTI, Alberto and Diego
Swiss 20th cent.
sculpture: (L) $4,950; (H) $66,000

GIACOMETTI, Diego
Swiss 1902-1985
sculpture: (L) $605; (H) $462,000

GIACOMOTTI, Felix Henri
drawings: (H) $880

GIALLI
paintings: (H) $1,540

GIALLINA, Angelos
Greek b. 1857
drawings: (L) $605; (H) $7,700

**GIAMBOLOGNA/SUSINI
WORKSHOP, EARLY 17TH
CENTURY**
sculpture: (L) $44,000; (H) $82,500

GIAMPETRINO
paintings: (L) $13,200; (H) $13,200

GIANI, E.
Italian 19th cent.
paintings: (H) $1,210

GIANI, Felice
Italian c. 1760-1823
drawings: (L) $2,750; (H) $3,300

GIANI, P.
paintings: (H) $660

GIANNETTI, Raffaele
Italian 1837-1915
paintings: (L) $3,960; (H) $8,800

GIANNI, Gian
Italian 19th cent.
paintings: (L) $330; (H) $11,000
drawings: (L) $138; (H) $467

GIANNI, H.
Italian 19th cent.
paintings: (H) $770
drawings: (L) $77; (H) $825

GIANNI, M.
Italian late 19th cent.
drawings: (L) $88; (H) $935

GIANNY, A.
Italian 19th/20th cent.
drawings: (H) $770

GIAQUINTO, Corrado
Italian c. 1690-1765
paintings: (L) $24,200; (H) $275,000

GIARDIELLO, Giovanni
Italian 19th/20th cent.
paintings: (H) $1,980

GIARDIELLO, Giuseppe
Italian 19th cent.
paintings: (L) $1,430; (H) $3,850

GIARDIELLO, J.
Italian 19th/20th cent.
paintings: (L) $2,640; (H) $7,150

GIARIZZO, Carmelo
paintings: (H) $4,400

GIBB, J.
19th cent.
paintings: (H) $1,430

GIBBISON, J.
paintings: (H) $990

GIBBONS, Arthur
American b. 1947
sculpture: (L) $3,025; (H) $6,600

GIBBS, George
American 1870-1942
drawings: (L) $220; (H) $3,575

GIBBS, J.
American 19th/20th cent.
paintings: (H) $1,320

GIBBS, Percy William
British ac. 1894-1925
paintings: (H) $5,500

GIBORY, A.
paintings: (H) $1,650

GIBRAN, Kahlil
American b. Lebanon 1883, d. 1931
drawings: (L) $220; (H) $4,950
sculpture: (L) $1,870; (H) $2,860

GIBSON, Charles Dana
American 1867-1944
paintings: (L) $715; (H) $2,310
drawings: (L) $110; (H) $8,000

GIBSON, George
American 20th cent.
drawings: (L) $385; (H) $1,760

GIBSON, John
British 1790-1866
sculpture: (H) $242,000

GIBSON, John Vincent
British ac. 1861-1888
paintings: (H) $1,760

GIBSON, Thomas
c. 1680-1751
paintings: (H) $11,000

GIBSON, William Alfred
English 19th cent.
paintings: (L) $220; (H) $4,400

GIDE, Francois Theophile Etienne
French 1822-1890
paintings: (H) $2,750

GIEBERICH, Oscar H.
American b. 1886
paintings: (L) $385; (H) $1,210

GIES, Joseph W.
American 1860-1935
paintings: (L) $99; (H) $2,420

GIFFINGER, R.
19th cent.
paintings: (L) $1,430; (H) $4,125

GIFFORD, Charles Henry
American 1839-1904
paintings: (L) $330; (H) $23,100
drawings: (L) $300; (H) $8,000

GIFFORD, H.
paintings: (H) $3,300

GIFFORD, James
English 19th cent.
paintings: (H) $6,050

GIFFORD, John
British 19th cent.
paintings: (L) $4,400; (H) $6,875

GIFFORD, John
British 20th cent.
paintings: (H) $5,500

GIFFORD, Robert Swain
American 1840-1905
paintings: (L) $440; (H) $6,050
drawings: (L) $220; (H) $990

GIFFORD, Sanford Robinson
American 1823-1880
paintings: (L) $495; (H) $363,000
drawings: (H) $550

GIFFORD, William B.
Continental 19th/20th cent.
paintings: (L) $715; (H) $990

GIGLI, R.
drawings: (L) $110; (H) $2,420

GIGNOUX, Regis Francois
French/American 1816-1882
paintings: (L) $660; (H) $34,100

GIHON, Albert D.
paintings: (H) $770

GIHON, Clarence Montfort
American 1871-1929
paintings: (L) $440; (H) $4,400

GIKOW, Ruth
American b. 1913
paintings: (L) $605; (H) $1,210
drawings: (H) $121

GILARDI, Pier Celesting
Italian 1837-1905
paintings: (H) $1,980

GILBERT, Alfred
English 1854-1934
drawings: (H) $2,200

GILBERT, Andre
sculpture: (H) $3,960

GILBERT, Arthur
paintings: (H) $10,450

GILBERT, Arthur
British 1819-1895
paintings: (L) $600; (H) $1,210

GILBERT, Arthur Hill
American 1893/94-1970?
paintings: (L) $247; (H) $18,700

GILBERT, C.
American early 19th cent.
drawings: (H) $3,300

GILBERT, C. Ivar
American 20th cent.
paintings: (L) $176; (H) $1,980
drawings: (L) $137; (H) $200

GILBERT, C.M.
American 20th cent.
paintings: (H) $990

GILBERT, I.
American ac. ca. 1833-40
paintings: (H) $20,900

GILBERT, Joseph Francis
English 1792-1855
paintings: (H) $23,100

GILBERT, Octave
French 19th/20th cent.
drawings: (H) $1,045

GILBERT, Sir Alfred
English 1854-1934
sculpture: (H) $7,150

GILBERT, Sir John
English 1817-1897
paintings: (H) $1,650
drawings: (L) $770; (H) $2,200

GILBERT, Terence J.
British 20th cent.
paintings: (H) $4,400

GILBERT, Victor Gabriel
French 1847-1933
paintings: (L) $495; (H) $66,000
drawings: (H) $3,300

GILBERT, W.J.
British 19th cent.
paintings: (L) $1,980; (H) $5,500

GILBERT & GEORGE
American contemporary
paintings: (L) $15,400; (H) $198,000

GILBERT-ROLFE, Jeremy
contemporary
drawings: (H) $1,760

GILCHRIST, Herbert
British 19th cent.
paintings: (H) $1,045

GILCHRIST, Philip Thomas
British 20th cent.
paintings: (L) $900; (H) $3,000

GILCHRIST, William Wallace, Jr.
American 1879-1926
paintings: (L) $248; (H) $35,200
drawings: (L) $44; (H) $990

GILE, Seldon Connor
American 1877-1947
paintings: (L) $605; (H) $46,750
drawings: (H) $550

GILES, Geoffrey Douglas, Major
British 1857-1941
paintings: (L) $715; (H) $18,700

GILES, Horace P.
American
paintings: (L) $110; (H) $1,375

GILES, Howard
American 1876-1955
paintings: (L) $165; (H) $715
drawings: (H) $110

GILES, J.
British 19th cent.
paintings: (H) $1,210

GILES, James William
British 1801-1870
paintings: (H) $1,980

GILES, M.
British 19th cent.
paintings: (H) $1,320

GILES, William
drawings: (H) $770

GILHOOLY, David
American b. 1943
sculpture: (L) $550; (H) $13,200

GILIO, Carlo
drawings: (H) $2,200

GILIOLI, Emile
French b. 1911
sculpture: (L) $1,500; (H) $11,000

GILKERSON, William
American 20th cent.
drawings: (L) $350; (H) $1,000

GILL, De Lancey W.
American 1859-1940
paintings: (H) $4,125
drawings: (L) $110; (H) $660

GILL, Edmund
English 1820-1894
paintings: (L) $231; (H) $2,750
drawings: (H) $330

GILL, Marquita
paintings: (L) $247; (H) $5,225

GILL, William
English 19th cent.
paintings: (H) $3,520

GILLEMANS, Jan Pauwel, II
Flemish 1651-1704
paintings: (L) $6,600; (H) $57,750

GILLEMANS, Jan Pauwel, the elder
1618-1675
paintings: (L) $16,500; (H) $28,600

GILLEOUX
paintings: (H) $880

GILLES, F.
Continental 19th cent.
drawings: (H) $770

GILLES, Werner
contemporary
drawings: (H) $1,045

GILLESPIE, Gregory
American b. 1936
paintings: (L) $3,520; (H) $8,800

GILLIAM, Ed
contemporary
paintings: (H) $770

GILLIAM, Sam
American b. 1933
paintings: (L) $1,320; (H) $2,640
drawings: (L) $770; (H) $1,980

GILLIG, Jacob
Dutch 1636-1701
paintings: (L) $1,650; (H) $12,100

GILLOL Y GRANELL, Antonio y
Spanish b. 1870
paintings: (H) $4,400

GILLOT, Claude
drawings: (L) $1,870; (H) $3,850

GILLOT, Gustave
sculpture: (L) $550; (H) $1,320

GILMAN, J.F.
American 19th cent.
paintings: (H) $990

GILOT, Francoise
French contemporary
paintings: (L) $825; (H) $1,540
drawings: (L) $440; (H) $605

GILPIN, Sawrey
British 1733-1807
paintings: (L) $8,800; (H) $46,200

GILSOUL, Victor Olivier
Belgian b. 1867
paintings: (H) $9,900

GIMENO, Andres
paintings: (H) $1,320

GIMENO, Francisco
paintings: (H) $660

GIMIGNANI, Giacinto
Italian 1611-1681
paintings: (H) $20,900

GIMIGNANI, Lodovico
Italian 1643-1697
paintings: (H) $12,100

GIMINEZ, F. Fernandez
drawings: (L) $165; (H) $858

GIMOUX
19th cent.
paintings: (L) $550; (H) $1,210

GINESTET, E.
paintings: (H) $1,650

GINNIVER, Charles
contemporary
sculpture: (L) $880; (H) $6,600

GINOUX, F.E.
American 19th cent.
paintings: (H) $1,210

GINSBERG, Varda
paintings: (L) $3,300; (H) $6,050

GINZBURG, Yankel
American
paintings: (L) $495; (H) $2,530

GIOBBI, Edward
American b. 1926
paintings: (L) $1,650; (H) $1,760
drawings: (H) $770

GIOFFREDO, Mario
drawings: (H) $770

GIOJA, Belisario
Italian 1829-1906
paintings: (H) $88,000
drawings: (L) $440; (H) $2,750

GIOJA, Edoardo
Italian 1862-1937
paintings: (H) $1,210
drawings: (L) $715; (H) $1,540

GIOLI, Francesco
Italian 1846-1922
paintings: (H) $6,050

GIONO, Wilson Brandao
paintings: (H) $3,300

GIORDANO, Felice
Italian 1880-1964
paintings: (L) $302; (H) $1,600
drawings: (H) $165

GIORDANO, Luca
Italian 1632-1705
paintings: (L) $5,500; (H) $88,000
drawings: (L) $528; (H) $4,000

GIORDANO, Luca, studio of
paintings: (H) $3,850

GIOVANI, G.
paintings: (H) $1,430

GIOVANI, P.
paintings: (H) $1,980

GIOVANNETTI, Vittoria
Italian 1900-1968
paintings: (H) $770

GIOVANNINI, Vincenzo
Italian 1816-1868
paintings: (L) $320; (H) $34,100

GIOVATTI
Continental 19th cent.
paintings: (H) $1,100

GIPS, Cornelis
paintings: (H) $1,045

GIRADET, Edouard Henri
Swiss 1819-1880
paintings: (H) $5,060

GIRARD, Noel Jules
French 1816-1886
sculpture: (H) $4,950

GIRARD-RABACHE, Helene
French 19th/20th cent.
paintings: (H) $4,400

GIRARDET, Edouard Henri
Swiss 1819-1880
paintings: (L) $825; (H) $6,600

GIRARDET, Eugene Alexis
French 1853-1907
paintings: (L) $5,500; (H) $77,000

GIRARDET, Karl
Swiss 1813-1871
paintings: (H) $33,000

GIRARDIN, Frank J.
American 1856-1945
paintings: (L) $165; (H) $935
drawings: (H) $44

GIRARDOT
French 19th/20th cent.
paintings: (H) $2,475

GIRARDOT, Ernest Gustave
English 19th/20th cent.
paintings: (L) $1,320; (H) $7,150

GIRAUD, Pierre Francois Eugene
French 1806-1881
paintings: (H) $7,150

GIRAUD-RIVIERE
sculpture: (H) $1,980

GIRAULT, T.
paintings: (H) $2,200

GIRIN, David Eugene
French 1848-1917
paintings: (L) $800; (H) $13,200

GIRODET-TRIOSON, Anne Louis
French 1767-1824
paintings: (H) $132,000

GIRODET-TRIOSON, Anne Louis,
studio of
paintings: (H) $23,100

GIROLAMO DI BENVENUTO DI
GIOVANNI DEL GUASTA
Italian 1470-1524
paintings: (H) $60,500

GIROLAMO DI TOMMASO DA
TREVISO, the younger
Italian 1497-1544
paintings: (H) $49,500

GIRONELLA, Alberto
Mexican b. 1929
paintings: (L) $3,300; (H) $33,000

GIROTTO, Napoleon
European 19th cent.
paintings: (H) $1,100
drawings: (L) $99; (H) $1,870

GIROUX, Charles
Franco/American b.c. 1828, ac. 1868-
1885
paintings: (H) $10,450

GIROUX, Ernest
French/Italian b. 1851; ac. 1883-1887
paintings: (L) $1,980; (H) $7,150

GIRTIN, Thomas
English 1775-1802
drawings: (L) $385; (H) $2,970

GISBERT, Antonio
Spanish b. 1835
paintings: (L) $8,800; (H) $52,800

GISCHIA, Leon
paintings: (H) $3,575

GISOT, H.
paintings: (H) $1,210

GISSON, Andre
paintings: (L) $357; (H) $7,425

GIULLIANI, G.
Italian 19th cent.
drawings: (H) $1,100

GIUSIANO, Eduardo
paintings: (H) $1,980

GIUSTI, Guglielo
Italian 19th/20th cent.
drawings: (L) $495; (H) $880

GIUSTO, Faust
Italian 19th cent.
paintings: (L) $6,050; (H) $10,450

GLACKENS, Louis M.
American 1866-1933
drawings: (L) $88; (H) $770

GLACKENS, William J.
American 1870-1938
paintings: (L) $2,000; (H) $715,000
drawings: (L) $121; (H) $22,000

GLADDING, C.
Continental 19th cent.
paintings: (H) $687

GLADDINGS, Timothy Allen
American 1818-1864
paintings: (H) $4,620

GLADENBECK, Ges
sculpture: (H) $1,485

GLAGDEN, Allen
American b. 1938
drawings: (H) $2,200

GLAIZE, Auguste Barthelemy
French 1807-1893
paintings: (H) $12,100

GLANCY, Michael
contemporary
sculpture: (L) $1,980; (H) $3,850

GLANKOFF, Sam
contemporary
drawings: (H) $12,650

GLANSDORFF, Hubert
Belgian 1877-1963
paintings: (L) $3,025; (H) $5,500

GLANTZMAN, Judy
American b. 1956
paintings: (H) $1,100

GLARNER, Fritz
American 1899-1972
paintings: (L) $154,000; (H) $330,000
drawings: (H) $7,700

GLASCO, Joseph
American b. 1925
paintings: (L) $154; (H) $1,320
drawings: (L) $44; (H) $550

GLASGOW, Bernard
American
paintings: (L) $440; (H) $1,320

GLASNER, Jakob
Polish b. 1879
paintings: (H) $1,320

GLATZ, Oscar
Hungarian 1872-1958
paintings: (L) $1,980; (H) $1,980
drawings: (H) $275

GLATZ, Theodor
paintings: (H) $1,430

GLAUBER, Jan
paintings: (H) $13,200

GLAUBER, Johannes
Dutch 1646-1726
paintings: (H) $15,400

GLEASON, Joe Duncan
American 1881-1959
paintings: (L) $412; (H) $3,850
drawings: (L) $660; (H) $715

GLEHN, Wilfrid Gabriel de
English b. 1870
paintings: (L) $17,600; (H) $33,000
drawings: (H) $1,760

GLEITSMAN, Louis A.
American 1883-1970
paintings: (L) $330; (H) $880

GLEITSMAN, Raphael
American b. 1910
paintings: (L) $2,200; (H) $33,000
drawings: (L) $220; (H) $1,210

GLEIZES, Albert
French 1881-1953
paintings: (L) $50,600; (H) $467,500
drawings: (L) $1,100; (H) $126,500

GLEN, Robert
American
sculpture: (H) $3,300

GLENDENING, Alfred Augustus, Jr.
English ac. 1861, d. 1907
paintings: (L) $1,100; (H) $28,600

GLENDENING, Alfred Augustus, Sr.
British 19th cent.
paintings: (L) $1,870; (H) $3,300

GLENNY, Alice R.
American b. 1858
paintings: (H) $1,760

GLERDINEN
paintings: (H) $1,400

GLERUP, S***
Danish 19th cent.
paintings: (H) $3,080

GLIMES, D.
paintings: (H) $715
GLIMES, P. de
paintings: (H) $2,640
GLINDONI, Henry Gillard
English 1852-1912/13
paintings: (L) $5,500; (H) $9,350
drawings: (H) $192
GLINTENKAMP, Hendrik
American 1887-1946
paintings: (L) $550; (H) $1,760
drawings: (L) $121; (H) $825
GLOAG, Isobel Lilian
British 1865-1917
paintings: (H) $19,800
GLOJA, B.
drawings: (H) $1,320
GLOVER, John
British 1767-1849
paintings: (L) $990; (H) $3,850
GLUCK, Louis Theodore Eugene
French 1820-1898
paintings: (H) $6,050
GLUCKMANN, Grigory
Russian b. 1898
paintings: (L) $220; (H) $14,000
GLUGING, Franzig
German 20th cent.
paintings: (L) $1,320; (H) $1,375
GLYNDON, F.
American 20th cent.
paintings: (H) $1,540
GOBBI, A.
paintings: (H) $1,650
GOBBIS, Giuseppe
Italian 18th cent.
paintings: (L) $30,800; (H) $66,000
GOBER, Robert
American b. 1954
sculpture: (H) $55,000
GOBERT, Pierre
French 1662-1744
paintings: (L) $2,310; (H) $16,500
GOBI, A.
Italian 19th cent.
paintings: (H) $3,575

GOBL, Wahl Camilla
German 1871-1965
paintings: (H) $935
GODARD, A.
sculpture: (L) $330; (H) $1,430
GODARD, Gabriel
b. 1933
paintings: (L) $150; (H) $1,540
GODCHAUX
French 19th cent.
paintings: (H) $9,900
GODCHAUX, ***
Continental 19th cent.
paintings: (H) $6,875
GODCHAUX, Roger
French b. 1878
paintings: (L) $7,700; (H) $14,300
sculpture: (L) $330; (H) $14,300
GODDARD, George Bouverie
British 1832-1886
sculpture: (H) $15,400
GODDARD, Margaret E.
American
paintings: (H) $1,540
GODDING, Emiel Hendrik Karel
Belgian 1841-1898
paintings: (H) $2,530
GODERIS, Hans
paintings: (H) $5,500
GODET, Henri
French b. 1863
sculpture: (L) $660; (H) $3,850
GODFREY, William
Australian late 19th/early 20th cent
paintings: (H) $2,200
GODINAU, Jacobus Ludovicus
Belgian 1811-1873
paintings: (H) $6,050
GODWARD, John William
British 1861-1922
paintings: (L) $825; (H) $46,750
GODWIN, Clara
American
paintings: (H) $715
GODWIN, Frances Bryant
American 1892-1975
sculpture: (L) $330; (H) $4,070

GOEBEL, Carl
Austrian 1824-1899
drawings: (H) $770

GOEBEL, Rod
paintings: (L) $495; (H) $2,860

GOEBL-WAHL, Camilla
Austrian 1871-1965
paintings: (II) $1,760

GOEGROIRE
19th cent.
sculpture: (H) $1,320

GOEMANS, G.
Flemish 19th cent.
paintings: (H) $2,640

GOENEUTTE, Norbert
French 1854-1894
paintings: (H) $14,300
drawings: (H) $14,300

GOERG, Edouard Joseph
French,b.Australia 1893-1968/69
paintings: (L) $6,600; (H) $22,000

GOETINCK
paintings: (H) $4,180

GOETSCH, Gustav
American b. 1877
paintings: (L) $66; (H) $467
drawings: (H) $1,100

GOETZ, Henri
American b. 1909
paintings: (L) $2,750; (H) $3,575

GOETZ, R.V.
American 20th cent.
paintings: (L) $1,210; (H) $1,375

GOETZEOMANN
paintings: (H) $1,980

GOGH, Vincent van
Dutch 1853-1890
paintings: (L) $231,000; (H) $82,500,000
drawings: (L) $60,500; (H) $429,000

GOHLER, Hermann
German b. 1874
paintings: (L) $302; (H) $880

GOINGS, Ralph
American b. 1928
paintings: (H) $77,000
drawings: (L) $9,350; (H) $15,400

GOITIA, Francisco
paintings: (H) $12,100

GOLA, Emilio
Italian 1852-1923
paintings: (H) $935

GOLD, Albert
American b. 1906
paintings: (L) $247; (H) $3,300

GOLDBECK
paintings: (L) $418; (H) $3,465

GOLDBECK, Walter Dean
American 1882-1925
paintings: (H) $1,072

GOLDBERG, Chaim
drawings: (H) $1,430

GOLDBERG, Glenn
American b. 1953
paintings: (L) $880; (H) $23,100

GOLDBERG, Michael
American b. 1924
paintings: (L) $650; (H) $27,500
drawings: (H) $1,320

GOLDBERG, Rube
American 1883-1970
drawings: (L) $88; (H) $220
sculpture: (H) $825

GOLDCAP, F.B.
drawings: (H) $1,925

GOLDEN, Roland
American 20th cent.
paintings: (L) $770; (H) $990
drawings: (L) $880; (H) $2,310

GOLDER, C.H.
American 19th cent.
paintings: (H) $93,500

GOLDIN, Leon
American b. 1923
paintings: (H) $2,200

GOLDING, Cecil
American 20th cent.
paintings: (H) $880

GOLDING, Tomas L.
Venezuelan b. 1909
paintings: (H) $770

GOLDMAN, I.
American 20th cent.
paintings: (H) $1,265

GOLDSCHEIDER
early 20th cent.
sculpture: (H) $1,210

GOLDSCHEIDER, A.
sculpture: (H) $1,870

GOLDSCHMIDT, Henrique
drawings: (H) $2,640

GOLDSMITH, Callander
English ac. 1880-1910
paintings: (L) $440; (H) $1,210

GOLDSMITH, Walter H.
British 19th cent.
paintings: (L) $110; (H) $2,640
drawings: (L) $22; (H) $302

GOLDSTEIN, Jack
Canadian b. 1945
paintings: (L) $1,540; (H) $35,200

GOLDTHWAIT, Harold
British 19th/20th cent.
paintings: (H) $1,100

GOLDTHWAITE, Anne
American 1875-1944
paintings: (L) $1,760; (H) $2,420
drawings: (L) $330; (H) $550

GOLDTHWAITE, Harold
paintings: (H) $935

GOLINKIN, Joseph Webster
American b. 1896
paintings: (H) $2,090

GOLL, A.
paintings: (H) $990

GOLLINGS, William Elling
American 1878-1932
paintings: (L) $1,100; (H) $8,250
drawings: (L) $660; (H) $3,300

GOLTZ, Walter
American 1875-1956
paintings: (L) $302; (H) $880

GOLUB, Leon
American b. 1922
paintings: (L) $4,180; (H) $24,200

GOMEZ, Gabriel
Spanish 19th cent.
paintings: (H) $4,125

GOMEZ Y GIL, Guillermo
Spanish 19th cent.
paintings: (H) $4,400

GOMEZ Y MIR, Eugenio
Spanish 19th cent.
paintings: (H) $35,200

GOMEZ Y PLASENT, Vicente
paintings: (H) $6,050

GOMSONN, J.
paintings: (H) $1,430

GONDI, Thomas
paintings: (H) $935

GONDOUIN, Emmanuel
French 1883-1934
paintings: (L) $660; (H) $9,350

GONGORA, Leonel
Columbian b. 1932
paintings: (L) $550; (H) $735
drawings: (L) $137; (H) $193

GONTARD, R.D.
French 19th/20th cent.
paintings: (H) $1,925

GONTCHAROVA, Natalia
Russian 1881-1962
paintings: (L) $3,190; (H) $209,000
drawings: (L) $605; (H) $14,300

GONTIER, Pierre Camille
French 19th cent.
paintings: (L) $3,190; (H) $68,200
drawings: (L) $605; (H) $10,175

GONZAGA, Pietro
drawings: (L) $880; (H) $1,650

GONZALES, Eva
French 1849-1883
paintings: (H) $154,000
drawings: (H) $187,000

GONZALES, Jeanne
paintings: (H) $4,400

GONZALES, Juan Amos
paintings: (H) $3,300

GONZALEZ, Arthur
American contemporary
sculpture: (H) $4,840

GONZALEZ, Beatriz
Columbian b. 1936
paintings: (H) $2,750

GONZALEZ, Isidoro y Romero
Spanish 19th cent.
paintings: (H) $3,300

GONZALEZ, Juan
Spanish 1854-1933?
paintings: (H) $2,640

GONZALEZ, Juan Antonio
Spanish b. 1842
paintings: (L) $3,300; (H) $19,800

GONZALEZ, Julio
Spanish 1876-1942
drawings: (L) $6,050; (H) $37,400
sculpture: (L) $9,625; (H) $1,320,000

GONZALEZ, Vincente Palmardli
Spanish 1834-1896
paintings: (H) $1,650

GOOD, John Willis
English exhib. 1870-1878
sculpture: (L) $385; (H) $3,080

GOOD, Thomas Sword
English 1789-1872
paintings: (H) $1,100

GOODALE
American 20th cent.
paintings: (H) $935

GOODALL, Edward Alfred
English 1819-1908
drawings: (H) $3,300

GOODALL, Frederick
English 1822-1904
paintings: (L) $440; (H) $264,000

GOODALL, G.W.
British 1830-1889
paintings: (L) $660; (H) $715

GOODALL, Peggy
American 20th cent.
paintings: (H) $4,180

GOODALL, W.
British 19th cent.
drawings: (L) $495; (H) $660

GOODALL, Walter
paintings: (H) $3,850

GOODE, Joe
American contemporary
drawings: (L) $1,320; (H) $3,575

GOODELL, Ira Chaffee
American 1800-c. 1875
paintings: (H) $24,200

GOODELL, J.C.
American ac. c. 1825-1832
paintings: (H) $3,960

GOODELMAN, Aaron J.
American
sculpture: (H) $2,860

GOODMAN, Bertram
American b. 1904
paintings: (L) $55; (H) $1,430

GOODMAN, H.K.
American ac. c. 1845-1850
paintings: (L) $14,300; (H) $30,800

GOODMAN, Job
American 20th cent.
drawings: (L) $33; (H) $935

GOODMAN, Maude
English 19th cent.
paintings: (L) $330; (H) $935

GOODMAN, Michael
American b. 1903
drawings: (H) $4,400

GOODNOUGH, Robert
American b. 1917
paintings: (L) $308; (H) $18,700
drawings: (L) $330; (H) $1,540

GOODWIN, Albert
English 1845-1932
drawings: (L) $6,050; (H) $14,300

GOODWIN, Arthur Clifton
American 1866-1929
paintings: (L) $385; (H) $29,700
drawings: (L) $165; (H) $19,800

GOODWIN, Harry
English 19th cent.
paintings: (H) $990
drawings: (H) $154

GOODWIN, Helen A.
19th/20th cent.
paintings: (H) $660

GOODWIN, Karl
American
paintings: (H) $1,430

GOODWIN, Philip Russell
American 1881/82-1935
paintings: (L) $220; (H) $20,900
drawings: (L) $440; (H) $1,100
sculpture: (H) $165

GOODWIN, Richard La Barre
American 1840-1910
paintings: (L) $605; (H) $29,700
drawings: (L) $138; (H) $220

GOOL, Jan van
paintings: (H) $7,700

GOOSEN, Frits J.
Dutch b. 1943
paintings: (L) $44; (H) $1,100

GOOSENS, Josse
German b. 1876
paintings: (H) $2,200

GORBATOFF, Constantin
Russian b. 1876
paintings: (L) $605; (H) $5,500
drawings: (L) $715; (H) $3,300

GORCHOV, Ron
American b. 1930
paintings: (L) $242; (H) $3,300

GORDER, Luther Emerson van
American b. 1861
paintings: (L) $385; (H) $4,400
drawings: (L) $247; (H) $275

GORDIGIANI, Michele
Italian 1830-1909
paintings: (H) $1,980

GORDINE, Dora
British b. 1906
sculpture: (H) $1,100

GORDON, Bern.
American 19th cent.
paintings: (H) $2,640

GORDON, Sir John Watson
English 1790-1864
paintings: (L) $770; (H) $23,100

GORDY, Robert
paintings: (H) $2,640

GORE, Ken
paintings: (L) $33; (H) $1,980

GORE, William Henry
British 20th cent.
paintings: (H) $11,000

GORGE, Emile
paintings: (H) $1,540

GORGON, Vinzenz
Austrian 1891-1961
paintings: (H) $1,320

GORGUET, Auguste Francois Marie
French 1862-1917
paintings: (H) $3,300

GORHAM, Sidney
American
paintings: (H) $660

GORI, A.
sculpture: (L) $1,320; (H) $4,675

GORKA, Paul
American 20th cent.
paintings: (L) $121; (H) $1,155

GORKY, Arshile
Armenian/American 1904-1948
paintings: (L) $10,450; (H) $880,000
drawings: (L) $1,100; (H) $264,000

GORLEY, Philip A.
Irish b. 1944
paintings: (L) $330; (H) $770

GORMAN, Carl Nelson
American Indian 1907-1966
paintings: (H) $1,100
drawings: (H) $550

GORMAN, R.C.
American b. 1933
paintings: (L) $1,100; (H) $4,180
drawings: (L) $605; (H) $4,620

GORMITT, Carl
paintings: (H) $8,525

GORMON, James O.
American 19th cent.
paintings: (H) $3,300

GORNIK, F.
sculpture: (H) $825

GORNIK, Friedrich
Austrian 19th cent.
sculpture: (L) $313; (H) $1,100

GORRA, Guilio
Italian 1832-1884
paintings: (H) $4,675

GORSLINE, Douglas
American 1913-1985
sculpture: (L) $330; (H) $1,870

GORSON, Aaron Henry
American 1872-1933
paintings: (L) $134; (H) $30,800
drawings: (L) $55; (H) $495

GORTER, Arnold Marc
Dutch 1866-1933
paintings: (L) $330; (H) $9,350

GORTZIUS, Geldorp
Flemish 1503-1618
paintings: (H) $30,800

GORY, A.
ac. 1895-1930
sculpture: (L) $1,100; (H) $24,200

GORY, J.
sculpture: (H) $4,950

GOSE, J.F.
paintings: (H) $1,155

GOSLING, William
British 1824-1883
paintings: (L) $1,045; (H) $1,980

GOSSELIN, Ferdinand Jules Albert
French b. 1862
paintings: (H) $5,500

GOTSCHKE, Walter
drawings: (H) $3,520

GOTT, J.
sculpture: (H) $1,650

GOTTLIEB, Adolph
American 1903-1974
paintings: (L) $1,650; (H) $352,000
drawings: (L) $2,860; (H) $88,000

GOTTLIEB, Harry
American b. 1895
paintings: (L) $418; (H) $2,640
drawings: (L) $72; (H) $522

GOTTLIEB, Moritz
Polish 1856-1879
drawings: (H) $7,150

GOTTWALD, Frederick
American 1860-1941
paintings: (L) $495; (H) $3,850

GOTZE, M.
sculpture: (H) $1,540

GOTZINGER, Hans
Austrian b. 1867
drawings: (H) $660

GOUBIE, Jean Richard
French 1842-1899
paintings: (L) $19,800; (H) $74,250

GOUDRAY, *****
sculpture: (H) $4,950

GOUDT, Hendrik
drawings: (H) $3,080

GOUGELET, J.
French 19th/20th cent.
drawings: (H) $1,650

GOUILLET, Jules
French b. 1826
paintings: (H) $4,400

GOULD, Alexander Carruthers
British 1870-1948
paintings: (H) $5,500

GOULD, Thomas Ridgeway
American 1818-1881
sculpture: (H) $770

GOULD, Walter
American 1829-1893
paintings: (L) $2,860; (H) $110,000
drawings: (H) $1,760

GOULET, Lorrie, Mrs. Jose de Creeft
American b. 1925
sculpture: (L) $110; (H) $3,520

GOUPIL, Jules Adolphe
French 1839-1883
paintings: (L) $770; (H) $16,500

GOUPIL, Leon Lucien
French 1834-1890
paintings: (L) $330; (H) $1,500

GOURDAULT, Pierre
French 1880-1915
paintings: (H) $2,200

GOURDON, Rene
French 19th cent.
paintings: (L) $275; (H) $825

GOURGUE, Jacques Enguerrand
Haitian b. 1930
paintings: (L) $550; (H) $3,080

GOURLET, W.M.
British
paintings: (H) $935

GOUROISIER, G.
paintings: (H) $990

GOURY, Juliette
Franco/American 20th cent.
drawings: (H) $990

GOUTTET, M.
paintings: (H) $2,200

GOUY, M.A.
American 19th cent.
paintings: (L) $1,210; (H) $3,740

GOVAERTS, Abraham
Flemish 1589-1626
paintings: (H) $15,400

GOW
paintings: (H) $1,870

GOW, Mary L.
British 1851-1929
paintings: (H) $104,500
drawings: (H) $3,300

GOWAN, George R.
paintings: (L) $605; (H) $825

GOYA Y LUCIENTES, Francisco
Jose de
Spanish 1746-1828
drawings: (L) $170,500; (H) $715,000

GOYEN, Jan Jansz van
paintings: (H) $935

GOYEN, Jan van
Dutch 1596-1656
paintings: (L) $2,200; (H) $880,000
drawings: (L) $2,200; (H) $28,600

GOYO, Hashiguchi
Japanese c. 1880/88-1921
drawings: (L) $11,000; (H) $28,600

GOZZARD
paintings: (H) $770

GOZZARD, J.W.
English 19th cent.
paintings: (L) $220; (H) $1,430
drawings: (H) $440

GOZZARD, William
Continental 19th cent.
paintings: (L) $660; (H) $2,200

GOZZOLI, Benozzo, studio of
drawings: (H) $12,100

GRAAT, Barend
1628-1709
paintings: (H) $8,800

GRAAT, Barent
paintings: (H) $3,575

GRABACH, John R.
American 1880/86-1981
paintings: (L) $825; (H) $28,600
drawings: (L) $880; (H) $4,400

GRABHEIN, Wilhelm
German b. 1859
paintings: (H) $1,700

GRABONE, Arnold
German 20th cent.
paintings: (L) $605; (H) $770

GRABWINKLER, Paul
Austrian b. 1880
paintings: (H) $770
drawings: (H) $8,250

GRACHOV
Russian late 19th/early 20th cent.
sculpture: (L) $770; (H) $1,870

GRACIANO, Clovis
drawings: (H) $1,100

GRAEB, Karl George Anton
German 1816-1884
paintings: (H) $14,000

GRAECEN, Edmund
American 1877-1949
paintings: (H) $4,950

GRAEF, Oscar
paintings: (H) $1,430

GRAEGER, Gregoria
sculpture: (H) $660

GRAEME, Colin
British 19th cent.
paintings: (L) $1,100; (H) $9,900

GRAF, Carl
American 1890-1947
paintings: (L) $33; (H) $4,400

GRAF, Ilma
paintings: (H) $1,430

GRAFILI, Gublielamo
sculpture: (H) $770

GRAFLY, Charles
paintings: (H) $66
sculpture: (H) $880

GRAFTON, Robert W.
American 1876-1936
paintings: (L) $935; (H) $9,625

GRAHAM, Charles
American 1852-1911
drawings: (H) $6,050

GRAHAM, Clancy
English 19th cent.
paintings: (H) $990

GRAHAM, Donald
American 20th cent.
paintings: (H) $6,050

GRAHAM, Florence
British 19th cent.
paintings: (H) $40,700

GRAHAM, George
British 19th cent.
paintings: (H) $6,270

GRAHAM, Gloria
American b. 1940
sculpture: (H) $990

GRAHAM, John
Russian/American 1881/90-1961
paintings: (L) $3,850; (H) $275,000
drawings: (L) $1,320; (H) $82,500

GRAHAM, Peter
English 1836-1921
paintings: (L) $605; (H) $7,150

GRAHAM, Robert A.
American 1873-1946
paintings: (L) $242; (H) $2,090

GRAHAM, Robert MacDonald
American b. 1919
paintings: (H) $33,000

GRAHAM, Robert McDowell
American b. 1938
sculpture: (L) $4,400; (H) $9,900

GRAHAM, Stanley
Scottish 19th/20th cent.
paintings: (H) $660

GRAHAM, Thomas Alexander
Ferguson
British 1840-1906
paintings: (H) $1,800

GRAILLY, Victor de
French 1804-1889
paintings: (L) $770; (H) $9,625
drawings: (H) $550

GRAIZE, Pierre Paul Leon
French 1842-1932
paintings: (H) $19,800

GRANACCI, Francesco
Italian 1477-1543
paintings: (H) $71,500

GRANDCHAMP, Louis Emile Pinel de
French d. 1894
paintings: (H) $6,930

GRANDCHAMPS, F.
paintings: (H) $1,540

GRANDEE, Joe
paintings: (H) $1,650

GRANDGERARD, Lucien Henri
French 1880-1965
paintings: (L) $550; (H) $660

GRANDIN, Elizabeth
American 20th cent.
paintings: (H) $1,760

GRANDIN, Eugene
French 19th cent.
drawings: (L) $357; (H) $3,300

GRANDJEAN, Edmund Georges
French 1844-1908
paintings: (H) $88,000

GRANDMAISON, Nickola de
drawings: (L) $4,125; (H) $4,950

GRANER, Ernst
Austrian b. 1865
drawings: (L) $935; (H) $2,420

GRANER Y ARUFFI, Luis
b. Spain 1867-1929
paintings: (L) $880; (H) $18,700

GRANET, Francois Marius
French School 1775-1849
drawings: (H) $2,860

GRANGER, Edward
English late 19th cent.
sculpture: (H) $2,640

GRANGER, Genevieve
French
sculpture: (L) $605; (H) $1,650

GRANGER, Henry Ward
American
paintings: (H) $6,600

GRANT
20th cent.
paintings: (H) $715

GRANT, Carleton
British ac. 1890's
paintings: (H) $660

GRANT, Carlton
drawings: (H) $2,200

GRANT, Charles Henry
American 1866-1938
paintings: (L) $715; (H) $1,100

GRANT, Clement Rollins
American 1849-1893
paintings: (L) $2,200; (H) $6,600
drawings: (H) $935

GRANT, Donald
American b. 1951
paintings: (L) $2,200; (H) $16,500

GRANT, Duncan
British 1885-1978
drawings: (L) $550; (H) $1,650

GRANT, Durnell
American
drawings: (L) $825; (H) $2,420

GRANT, Dwinell
American
drawings: (L) $1,100; (H) $1,870

GRANT, Edouard Rodolphe
French 19th cent.
paintings: (H) $1,100

GRANT, Frederic M.
American b. 1886
paintings: (L) $330; (H) $17,600

GRANT, Gordon Hope
American 1875-1962
paintings: (L) $247; (H) $13,200
drawings: (L) $137; (H) $3,300

GRANT, H.
paintings: (H) $1,430

GRANT, J. Jeffrey
American 1883-1960
paintings: (L) $275; (H) $715
drawings: (L) $110; (H) $605

GRANT, J.A.
paintings: (L) $121; (H) $3,850

GRANT, Marthe
paintings: (L) $935; (H) $1,760

GRANT, Mimi
American
drawings: (H) $1,000

GRANT, William James
British 1829-1866
paintings: (L) $5,500; (H) $17,600

GRANVILLE-SMITH, Walter
American 1870-1938
paintings: (L) $192; (H) $8,800
drawings: (L) $132; (H) $8,800

GRASDORP, Willem
Dutch 1678-1723
paintings: (H) $1,980,000

GRASHOF, Otto
paintings: (H) $8,800

GRASSET, Eugene
Swiss 1841-1917
drawings: (H) $1,100

GRASSI, Nicola
paintings: (H) $9,350

GRATCHEFF, Alexei Petrovitch
Russian c. 1780-after 1850
sculpture: (L) $550; (H) $3,300

GRATCHEFA, Georgi Ivanovich
1860-1893
sculpture: (L) $1,760; (H) $7,700

GRATZ, Meyer
paintings: (H) $1,100

GRATZ, Rudolf
paintings: (H) $3,300

GRAU, Enrique
Colombian b. 1920
paintings: (L) $12,100; (H) $38,500
drawings: (L) $1,760; (H) $8,800

GRAU-SALA, Emile
Spanish 1911-1975
paintings: (L) $715; (H) $85,250
drawings: (L) $137; (H) $24,200

GRAUBNER, Gotthart
drawings: (H) $1,210

GRAUER, William C.
American b. 1896
paintings: (L) $82; (H) $3,740
drawings: (L) $187; (H) $1,760

GRAVE, Charles de
ac. 1609
drawings: (H) $990

GRAVELOT, Hubert Francois
Bourguignon d'Anville
French 1699-1773
drawings: (L) $275; (H) $24,200

GRAVES, Abbott Fuller
American 1859-1936
paintings: (L) $357; (H) $57,750
drawings: (L) $302; (H) $4,290

GRAVES, C.A.
paintings: (H) $825

GRAVES, Captain
American ac. 1860-1890
paintings: (L) $935; (H) $1,650

GRAVES, Michael
American contemporary
drawings: (H) $852

GRAVES, Morris
American b. 1910
paintings: (L) $3,080; (H) $12,650
drawings: (L) $425; (H) $6,600

GRAVES, Nancy
American b. 1940
paintings: (L) $14,300; (H) $44,000
drawings: (L) $275; (H) $19,800
sculpture: (L) $14,300; (H) $132,000

GRAY, Jack L.
American 20th cent.
paintings: (H) $3,300

GRAY, Charles Alden
American 1858-1933
paintings: (L) $770; (H) $1,320

GRAY, Cleve
American b. 1918
paintings: (L) $220; (H) $13,200
drawings: (H) $66

GRAY, D.
German 1820-1915
paintings: (H) $1,320

GRAY, Eileen
American
drawings: (L) $4,125; (H) $25,300

GRAY, G.
paintings: (H) $1,760

GRAY, George
paintings: (H) $1,760

GRAY, Henry Percy
American 1869-1952
paintings: (L) $2,200; (H) $2,750
drawings: (L) $400; (H) $46,750

GRAY, Henry Peters
American 1819-1877
paintings: (L) $1,870; (H) $9,900

GRAY, Jack L.
American 1927-1981
paintings: (L) $385; (H) $22,000
drawings: (L) $110; (H) $1,200

GRAY, Jim
American
drawings: (H) $1,650

GRAY, Kate
English 19th century
paintings: (H) $825

GRAY, Mary Chilton
American
paintings: (L) $1,045; (H) $2,750

GRAY, Una
American ac. 1930
paintings: (H) $1,100

GRAY, Urban
American 19th cent.
paintings: (H) $1,045

GRAY, Walter
American
paintings: (H) $17,600

GRAY, William
English 19th cent.
paintings: (H) $1,540

GRAZZINI, Eufemio
Italian 1823-before 1907
paintings: (H) $935

GREACEN, Edmund W.
American 1877-1949
paintings: (L) $1,320; (H) $88,000

GREACEN, Nan
American b. 1909
paintings: (L) $165; (H) $7,150
drawings: (H) $14,300

GREASON, William
American b. 1884
paintings: (L) $66; (H) $2,090

GREATOREX, Eliza Pratt
American 1820-1897
paintings: (H) $3,575

GREATOREX, Katherine Honora
American
paintings: (H) $11,000

GREAVES, Walter
British 1846-1930
paintings: (H) $935
drawings: (H) $110

GREAVES, William A.
American 1847-1900
paintings: (L) $500; (H) $715

GREB, Nam
sculpture: (L) $247; (H) $2,860

GREBBER, Pieter Franz de
c. 1600-c. 1652/53
paintings: (L) $2,640; (H) $6,050

**GRECO, El, Domenikos
THEOTOKOPOULOS**
Spanish 1541?-1614
paintings: (H) $429,000

GRECO, El, studio of
c. 1541-1614
paintings: (H) $27,500

GRECO, Emilio
Italian b. 1913
drawings: (L) $605; (H) $3,300
sculpture: (L) $2,200; (H) $264,000

GREEN, Alfred H.
English 19th century
paintings: (H) $3,300

GREEN, Balcomb
contemporary
paintings: (H) $880

GREEN, Bernard I.
American 1887-1951
paintings: (H) $1,320

GREEN, Charles
English 1840-1898
drawings: (L) $550; (H) $8,250

GREEN, Charles Edwin Lewis
American b. 1844
paintings: (L) $770; (H) $7,150
drawings: (H) $880

GREEN, Elizabeth Shippen
American 1871-1954
paintings: (H) $2,310

GREEN, Frank Russell
American 1856/59-1940
paintings: (L) $138; (H) $8,525
drawings: (H) $88

GREEN, George
contemporary
paintings: (L) $2,475; (H) $16,500

GREEN, George Pycock Everett
English ac. 1841-1873
paintings: (H) $1,210

GREEN, Gertrude
American b. 1904
paintings: (H) $1,650

GREEN, J.G.
American 19th cent.
drawings: (H) $2,000

GREEN, Leroy
American 20th cent.
paintings: (H) $1,210

GREEN, Roland
English 1896-1971
drawings: (L) $1,650; (H) $2,090

GREEN, William Bradford
American 1871-1945
paintings: (L) $61; (H) $2,530
drawings: (H) $28

GREENAWAY, Kate
English 1846-1901
paintings: (H) $357
drawings: (L) $330; (H) $17,600
sculpture: (H) $165

GREENBAUM, Joseph
American 1864-1940
paintings: (L) $193; (H) $3,575

GREENBERG, Maurice
American b. 1893
paintings: (H) $660

GREENBLAT, Rodney Alan
American b. 1960
paintings: (L) $880; (H) $16,500
drawings: (L) $825; (H) $2,420
sculpture: (L) $330; (H) $11,000

GREENE, Albert van Nesse
American b. 1887
paintings: (L) $330; (H) $3,575
drawings: (L) $275; (H) $577

GREENE, Balcomb
American b. 1904
drawings: (H) $4,400

GREENE, Edward D.E.
1823-1879
paintings: (H) $900

GREENE, Gertrude
American 1911-1956
drawings: (L) $2,200; (H) $5,225

GREENE, J. Barry
American 1895-1966
paintings: (L) $110; (H) $1,540

GREENE, Saya
American 20th cent.
sculpture: (H) $1,045

GREENE, Stephen
American contemporary
paintings: (L) $880; (H) $2,860
drawings: (H) $385

GREENE, Walter L.
American 19th/20th cent.
paintings: (L) $440; (H) $1,375
drawings: (L) $220; (H) $440

GREENEVELD, G.
European 20th cent.
paintings: (H) $825

GREENLEAF, Jacob I.
American 1887-1968
paintings: (L) $165; (H) $2,200

GREENLEES, James
paintings: (H) $1,100

GREENOUGH, Richard Saltonstall
American 1819-1904
sculpture: (L) $1,980; (H) $8,800

GREENWOOD, Ethan Allen
American 1779-1856
paintings: (L) $495; (H) $3,575

GREENWOOD, George Parker
British 1850-1904
paintings: (L) $1,870; (H) $1,870

GREENWOOD, Joseph H.
American 1857-1927
paintings: (L) $330; (H) $9,350

GREER, A.D.
American b. 1904
paintings: (L) $275; (H) $5,500

GREEVES, Richard
sculpture: (H) $2,640

GREGOIRE, Jean Louis
French 1840-1890
sculpture: (L) $385; (H) $5,775

GREGOR, Harold
American b. 1929
paintings: (L) $1,100; (H) $13,200

GREGORY, Arthur V.
Australian 1862-1952
drawings: (H) $1,155

GREGORY, Charles
drawings: (H) $660

GREGORY, Charles
English 19th/20th cent.
paintings: (H) $8,250

GREGORY, George
English 1849-1938
paintings: (L) $1,210; (H) $2,640

GREGORY, John
English/American 1879-1958
sculpture: (L) $1,870; (H) $14,300

GREIFFENHAGEN, Maurice
British b. 1862
paintings: (L) $1,210; (H) $3,850

GREILSAMER, Alphonse
French 20th cent.
paintings: (H) $1,430

GREITZER, Jack
American b. 1910
paintings: (H) $275
drawings: (L) $2,640; (H) $7,975

GREIVE, Petrus Franciscus
Dutch 1811-1872
paintings: (H) $2,475

GRELL, Louis Frederick
American b. 1887
paintings: (L) $330; (H) $1,650

GRELLE, Martin
American b. 1954
paintings: (H) $10,000

GREMKE, Henry Dietrick
American 1869-1939
paintings: (L) $275; (H) $4,125
drawings: (L) $66; (H) $330

GRENET, Edward
French b. U.S. 1857
paintings: (L) $225; (H) $5,225

GRENIER, F.
paintings: (H) $880

GRENIER, Francois
paintings: (L) $825; (H) $1,540

GRENIER, Henry
French ac. 1922
paintings: (H) $770
drawings: (L) $550; (H) $715

GRENNESS, J.
contemporary
paintings: (H) $1,870

GRETHA
sculpture: (H) $1,210

GRETZNER, Harold
American 1902-1977
paintings: (H) $1,045
drawings: (L) $660; (H) $1,430

GREVENBROECK, Alessandro
Italian 17th/18th cent.
paintings: (L) $4,400; (H) $13,200

GREUZE, Jean Baptiste
French 1725-1805
paintings: (L) $2,750; (H) $517,000
drawings: (L) $30,800; (H) $57,750

GREVIN, Alfred
French 1827-1892
sculpture: (H) $770

GREY, Edith F.
drawings: (H) $1,045

GREY, Gregor
British 19th cent.
paintings: (H) $8,525

GREY, Henry Peters
American 1819-1877
paintings: (H) $660

GREYER, Emil
paintings: (H) $770

GREYER, Ernst
Austrian b. 1907
paintings: (H) $1,430

GREYTAK, Don
American
drawings: (L) $1,000; (H) $1,100

GRIBBLE, Bernard Finegan
British 1873-1962
paintings: (H) $880

GRIEVES, Bob V.
American 20th cent.
sculpture: (H) $1,430

GRIFANY, J.
paintings: (H) $7,700

GRIFFANY, J.
paintings: (L) $7,700; (H) $12,100

GRIFFIER, Jan, the elder
paintings: (L) $9,350; (H) $17,600

GRIFFIN, David
American b. 1952
paintings: (L) $3,800; (H) $4,400

GRIFFIN, James Martin
American 1850-1931
paintings: (L) $220; (H) $413
drawings: (H) $990

GRIFFIN, Thomas Bailey
American ac. 1860-1899
paintings: (L) $330; (H) $3,300

GRIFFIN, Thomas Bartholomew
American
paintings: (H) $3,300

GRIFFIN, W.G.
American 20th cent.
paintings: (H) $825

GRIFFIN, Walter
American 1861-1935
paintings: (L) $302; (H) $14,300
drawings: (L) $110; (H) $2,640

GRIFFIN, William
British 1838-1865
paintings: (H) $7,150

GRIFFITH
American 20th cent.
paintings: (H) $1,650

GRIFFITH, E.N.
American 19th cent.
paintings: (H) $15,400

GRIFFITH, Grace Allison
American 1885-1955
drawings: (L) $715; (H) $3,575

GRIFFITH, Louis Oscar
American 1875-1956
paintings: (L) $687; (H) $1,650

GRIFFITH, Marie Osthaus
German, lived in Ohio
paintings: (L) $660; (H) $12,100
drawings: (H) $440

GRIFFITH, William Alexander
American 1866-1940
paintings: (L) $302; (H) $1,980

GRIGGS, Samuel W.
American 1827-1898
paintings: (L) $192; (H) $9,900

GRIGNION, Charles
English 1754-1804
drawings: (H) $1,100

GRIGORESCU, Nicolae Jon
Rumanian 1838-1907
paintings: (L) $3,850; (H) $4,400

GRIGORIEV, Boris
Russian 1886-1939
paintings: (L) $1,320; (H) $11,000
drawings: (L) $55; (H) $2,090

GRILLO, John
American b. 1917
paintings: (L) $121; (H) $1,045
drawings: (L) $412; (H) $440

GRILO, Sarah
Argentinian b. 1921
paintings: (L) $2,200; (H) $8,800

GRIMALDI, Giovanni Francesco
Italian 1606-1680
paintings: (H) $9,350
drawings: (L) $2,200; (H) $3,850

GRIMBERGHE, Comte Edmond de
German 1865-1920
paintings: (H) $35,750

GRIMELUND, Johannes Martin
Norwegian 1842-1917
paintings: (L) $715; (H) $3,300

GRIMES, Frances
American
sculpture: (H) $6,600

GRIMM, Paul
American 1892-1974
paintings: (L) $137; (H) $2,750

GRIMMER, Abel
Flemish 1570/73-1619/40
paintings: (H) $66,000

GRIMMER, Jacob
drawings: (H) $1,100

GRIMOU, Alexis
French 1680-1733/40
paintings: (H) $55,000

GRIMSHAW, John Atkinson
English 1836-1893
paintings: (L) $6,050; (H) $35,000

GRIMSTONE, Edward
English ac. 1837-1879
paintings: (H) $1,210

GRINNELL, George Victor
American 1878-1946
paintings: (L) $330; (H) $1,870

GRINNELL, Roy
American b. 1934
paintings: (L) $1,650; (H) $3,300

GRIPS, Charles Joseph
Belgian 1852-1920
paintings: (H) $9,350

GRIS, Juan
Spanish 1887-1927
paintings: (L) $69,300; (H) $2,640,000
drawings: (L) $5,775; (H) $528,000

GRISARD, D.
sculpture: (L) $192; (H) $1,045

GRISET, Ernest
French 1844-1907
paintings: (H) $330
drawings: (L) $165; (H) $1,320

GRISET, Ernest Henry
drawings: (H) $8,250

GRISON, Francois Adolphe
French 1845-1914
paintings: (L) $1,430; (H) $22,000
drawings: (H) $1,870

GRISSOT, P.
paintings: (H) $990

GRISWOLD, Casimir Clayton
American 1834-1918
paintings: (L) $440; (H) $2,200
drawings: (L) $77; (H) $220

GRITCHENKO, Alexis
paintings: (L) $550; (H) $7,480
drawings: (L) $110; (H) $308

GRITTEN, Henry C.
paintings: (H) $3,300

GRIVAUX, Charles Georges
paintings: (H) $30,800

GRIVAZ, Eugene
French 1852-1915
drawings: (H) $3,575

GROB, Conrad
Swiss 1828-1904
paintings: (H) $16,500

GROBON, Francois Frederic
French 1815-1901
paintings: (L) $2,420; (H) $5,500

GROEBER, Hermann
paintings: (H) $3,080

GROENEVELDT, Thomas Tadema
Dutch 19th cent.
paintings: (L) $1,430; (H) $1,650

GROENEWEGEN, A.J.
Dutch 19th cent.
paintings: (H) $1,045
drawings: (H) $625

GROENEWEGEN, Adrianus Johannes
Dutch 1874-1963
drawings: (L) $220; (H) $1,210

GROESBECK, Dan Sayre
American 1878-1950
paintings: (H) $1,100

GROLL, Albert Lorey
American 1866-1952
paintings: (L) $275; (H) $7,920
drawings: (L) $600; (H) $2,200

GROLL, Ch.
German 19th cent.
paintings: (H) $1,100

GROLLERON, P.
paintings: (H) $1,900

GROLLERON, Paul Louis Narcisse
French 1848-1901
paintings: (L) $770; (H) $25,300

GROM-ROTTMAYER, Hermann
1877-1953
paintings: (H) $990

GROMAIRE, Marcel
French 1892-1971
paintings: (L) $8,800; (H) $88,000
drawings: (L) $770; (H) $17,600

GROMME, Owen
American b. 1896
paintings: (L) $22,000; (H) $27,500

GRONDARD, Philippe
French 19th/20th cent.
paintings: (L) $440; (H) $1,650

GRONLAND
paintings: (H) $880

GRONLAND, Nelius
French b. 1859
paintings: (H) $1,980

GRONLAND, Theude
German 1817-1876
paintings: (L) $13,200; (H) $22,000

GROOME, Esther M.
American b. 1929
paintings: (L) $137; (H) $3,850

GROOMS, Red
American b. 1937
paintings: (L) $13,200; (H) $51,700
drawings: (L) $2,420; (H) $66,000
sculpture: (L) $1,320; (H) $77,000

GROOT, Frans Arnold Breuhaus de
Dutch 1824-1872
paintings: (H) $25,300

GROOTH, George Christophe
Russian 1716-1749
paintings: (H) $8,800

GROOTVELT, Jan Hendrich van
paintings: (H) $3,080

GROPPER, William
American 1897-1977
paintings: (L) $880; (H) $46,200
drawings: (L) $132; (H) $2,640

GROS, Baron Jean Louis Baptiste de
French 1793-1870
paintings: (L) $25,300; (H) $52,250

GROS, Lucien Alphonse
French 1845-1913
paintings: (H) $4,950

GROSE, David C.
American ac. 1860-1880
paintings: (L) $165; (H) $5,500

GROSE, H.E.
American
paintings: (H) $2,090

GROSPERRIN, Claude
paintings: (H) $1,210

GROSS, Chaim
American b. 1904
paintings: (L) $275; (H) $495
drawings: (L) $99; (H) $3,025
sculpture: (L) $275; (H) $37,400

GROSS, Oskar
Austrian/American 1871-1963
paintings: (L) $82; (H) $5,500

GROSS, Peter Alfred
American 1849-1914
paintings: (L) $55; (H) $715

GROSSENHEIDER, Richard Philip
American 1911-1975
drawings: (H) $2,750

GROSSER, Maurice
American b. 1903
paintings: (L) $550; (H) $1,760

GROSSMAN, Joseph
American b. 1889
paintings: (L) $528; (H) $825

GROSSMAN, Nancy
American b. 1940
drawings: (L) $550; (H) $2,200
sculpture: (L) $4,400; (H) $12,100

GROSSMANN
German/American 20th cent.
paintings: (H) $770

GROSVENOR, Caroline
American 19th cent.
drawings: (H) $1,210

GROSVENOR, Robert
American b. 1937
paintings: (H) $3,080
sculpture: (H) $19,800

GROSZ, George
German/American 1893-1959
paintings: (L) $1,980; (H) $16,500
drawings: (L) $660; (H) $148,500

GROUARD, John E.
American 19th cent.
paintings: (H) $3,000

GROUX, Henry de
Belgian 1867-1930
drawings: (H) $1,650

GROVE, Maria
Danish 19th cent.
paintings: (H) $9,900

GROVER, Dorothy Reno
American 1908-1975
paintings: (L) $248; (H) $2,475

GROVER, Oliver Dennett
American 1861-1927
paintings: (L) $209; (H) $9,900

GROWEN, A.J.
European 19th cent.
paintings: (H) $1,100

GRUBACS, Carlo
German 19th cent.
paintings: (L) $2,750; (H) $18,700

GRUBER, Aaronel de Roy
American 20th cent.
sculpture: (H) $715

GRUBER, Carl
Austrian 1803-1845
drawings: (L) $1,100; (H) $1,100

GRUBER, Francis
French 1912-1948
paintings: (H) $71,500

GRUBGES, M.
paintings: (H) $770

GRUET, Robert
Continental 19th cent.
sculpture: (H) $2,200

GRUGER, Frederic Rodrigo
American 1871-1953
drawings: (L) $99; (H) $1,000

GRUGER, Frederic Rodrigo and Peter
NEWELL
American
paintings: (H) $770

GRUN, F.
French 19th cent.
paintings: (H) $2,420

GRUN, Jules Alexandre
French 1868-1934
paintings: (H) $17,600

GRUND, F.
German 19th cent.
paintings: (H) $2,090

GRUND, Johann
Austrian 1808-1887
paintings: (L) $3,575; (H) $8,800

GRUND, Norbert Joseph Carl
Czechoslovakian 1717-1767
paintings: (L) $3,300; (H) $11,000

GRUNENWALD, Jakob
German 1822-1896
paintings: (L) $6,600; (H) $46,200

GRUNEWALD, Gustavus
German 1805-1878
paintings: (L) $25,300; (H) $33,000

GRUNWALD, Isaac
Swedish 1889-1946
paintings: (H) $3,850

GRUPPE, Carl
American b. 1893
paintings: (II) $1,100

GRUPPE, Charles Paul
Canadian/American 1860-1940
paintings: (L) $137; (H) $13,200
drawings: (L) $50; (H) $2,200

GRUPPE, Emile Albert
American 1896-1978
paintings: (L) $61; (H) $28,600
drawings: (L) $632; (H) $715

GRUPPE, Karl Heinrich
sculpture: (H) $3,300

GRUPPE, Robert C.
American 20th cent.
paintings: (L) $50; (H) $962

GRUST, F.A.
paintings: (H) $935

GRUST, F.G.
Dutch 19th/20th cent.
paintings: (L) $825; (H) $3,575

GRUST, Theodor
German 19th cent.
paintings: (H) $3,025

GRUTZNER, Eduard von
German 1846-1925
paintings: (L) $1,430; (H) $55,000

GRUYTER, Jacob Willem de
paintings: (H) $880

GRYEF, Adriaen de
Flemish 1670-1715
paintings: (H) $2,200

GSCHOSMANN, L.
German b. 1901
paintings: (H) $880

GSELL, Laurent
French 1860-1944
paintings: (L) $1,650; (H) $8,800

GUACCIMANNI, Alessandro
Italian 1864-1927
paintings: (H) $24,200
drawings: (H) $110

GUACCIMANNI, Vittorio
Italian b. 1858
paintings: (H) $2,475

GUADAGNINI, Anacleto
Italian 1832-1919
paintings: (H) $2,420

GUALDI, Pietro
Italian b. 1716
paintings: (L) $23,100; (H) $38,500

GUARDABASSI, Guerrino
Italian b. 1841
paintings: (L) $825; (H) $6,600
drawings: (L) $55; (H) $1,650

GUARDI, Francesco
Italian 1712-1793
paintings: (L) $38,500; (H) $4,510,000
drawings: (L) $7,700; (H) $99,000

GUARDI, Francesco and Giacomo
18th/19th cent.
drawings: (H) $77,000

Rockport Art Association

Gloucester and Rockport are small towns on Cape Ann, Massachusetts, whose beaches and dunes have been depicted by many artists. During the 19th century, Fitz Hugh Lane, Frank Duveneck, Winslow Homer, Childe Hassam, and John Sloan painted the ocean landscape of Cape Ann. Many artists settled in Gloucester and Rockport, and the area became a thriving summer art colony. In 1921 a group of artists met under the leadership of artist Aldro Hibbard to form the Rockport Art Association. The association did not represent a particular style but was formed to promote the artists and to attract tourists to the area. Some of the many artists who have belonged to the Rockport Art Association are Aldo Hibbard, Anthony Thieme, Reynolds Beale, and Emile Gruppe.

Emile Albert Gruppe (1896–1978) was born in Rochester, New York, the son of landscape artist Charles P. Gruppe. He followed in his father's footsteps by becoming an artist and studied in New York at the National Academy of Design and the Art Students League; George Bridgeman, Charles Chapman, Richard Miller, and John F. Carlson were some of his teachers. After studying in New York and serving in the navy during World War I, Gruppe settled permanently in Gloucester, Massachusetts. In 1942 he founded the Gruppe Summer School for Art. Gruppe is best known for his Impressionist landscapes. In 1989, the heirs of the estate of a fellow Rockport artist who had painted with Gruppe in the 1920s and 30s consigned *March Snow*. The painting realized a strong price when it sold for $17,050. (Emile Albert Gruppe, *March Snow*, oil on canvas, 30 x 36 in., Blackwood/March, November 28, 1989, $17,050)

GUARDI, Giacomo
Italian 1764-1835
paintings: (L) $3,080; (H) $77,000
drawings: (L) $7,150; (H) $23,100

GUARDI, Giovanni Antonio
Italian 1698-1760
drawings: (L) $9,350; (H) $45,100

GUARINO, Salvatore Anthony
American b. 1882
paintings: (H) $7,150

GUARNIERI, F.
Italian 20th cent.
paintings: (L) $302; (H) $715

GUASTAVINO, Clement Pujol de
French ac. 1878-1889
paintings: (L) $6,325; (H) $17,600

GUAYASAMIN, Oswaldo
Ecuadorean b. 1919
paintings: (L) $4,950; (H) $35,200
drawings: (L) $1,980; (H) $3,300

GUBIN, Selma
American 1903-1974
paintings: (H) $1,100

GUDDEN, Rudolf
German b. 1863
paintings: (H) $660

GUDE, Hans Frederik
Norwegian 1825-1903
paintings: (H) $9,570

GUDIASHVILI, Lado
drawings: (H) $1,650

GUDIN, Henriette
French 19th cent.
paintings: (L) $2,750; (H) $5,500

GUDIN, Herminie
French 19th cent.
paintings: (H) $24,200

GUDIN, Jean Antoine Theodore
French 1802-1880
paintings: (L) $121; (H) $1,320

GUDMUNDSEN-HOLMGREN, Johan
Danish 1858-1912
paintings: (H) $3,850

GUE, David John
American 1836-1917
paintings: (L) $264; (H) $5,390

GUELDRY, Ferdinand Joseph
French b. 1858
paintings: (L) $4,620; (H) $19,800

GUERBE
sculpture: (L) $440; (H) $2,200

GUERCINO, Giovanni Francesco
BARBIERI
Italian 1591-1666
paintings: (L) $7,150; (H) $71,500
drawings: (L) $6,600; (H) $82,500

GUERIN, Armand Marie
French b. 1913
paintings: (L) $198; (H) $2,530

GUERIN, Charles
paintings: (H) $1,760

GUERIN, Jules
American 1866-1946
drawings: (L) $176; (H) $1,980

GUERIN, Pierre Narcisse
French 1774-1833
drawings: (L) $248; (H) $2,420

GUERMACHEFF, Michael
Russian b. 1867
paintings: (L) $385; (H) $2,420

GUERRA, Achille
Italian 1832-1903
paintings: (L) $1,320; (H) $16,500

GUERRA, Carlos Hernandez
paintings: (L) $4,070; (H) $6,050

GUERRERO, Jose
Spanish/American b. 1914
paintings: (L) $908; (H) $2,090

GUERRERO, Luis Garcia
Mexican b. 1921
paintings: (H) $13,200

GUERRERO, Rosario
Mexican b. 1944
paintings: (H) $990

GUERRESCHI, Giuseppe
1929-1985
paintings: (L) $110; (H) $1,870
drawings: (H) $44

GUERRIER, M.
contemporary
paintings: (H) $880

GUERRIER, Raymond
contemporary
paintings: (H) $2,200

GUERVAL
sculpture: (H) $1,870

GUERY, Arman
French 1850-1912
paintings: (H) $3,575

GUES, Alfred F.
French b. 1837
paintings: (L) $660; (H) $880

GUETON, Antonin
French 1886-1941
sculpture: (H) $3,575

GUEY, Fernand L.
paintings: (H) $770

GUEYTON, G.
French 19th cent.
sculpture: (L) $1,100; (H) $1,925

GUGEL, Karl Adolf
German 1820-1885
paintings: (H) $4,950

GUGLIELMI, Luigi
Italian b. 1804
paintings: (H) $1,925

GUGLIELMI, O. Louis
American 1906-1956
paintings: (L) $1,430; (H) $34,100

GUICHI, L.
sculpture: (H) $1,430

GUIDI, Giuseppe
Italian 1881/84-1931
paintings: (L) $2,035; (H) $5,720
drawings: (L) $1,760; (H) $6,050

GUIDI, Virgilio
Italian b. 1891/92
paintings: (L) $2,090; (H) $16,500

GUIDOBONO, Domenico
drawings: (H) $2,200

GUIGNARD, Alexandre Gaston
French 1848-1922
paintings: (H) $3,300

GUIGNARD, Gaston
French 1848-1922
paintings: (H) $30,800

GUIGOU, Paul
French 1834-1871
paintings: (L) $104,500; (H) $253,000

GUILBERT, E.
sculpture: (H) $880

GUILBERT, Octave
French 20th cent.
paintings: (H) $2,090

GUILD, James
American 1797-1841
drawings: (H) $1,320

GUILLAUME, Albert
French 1873-1942
paintings: (L) $6,600; (H) $19,800

GUILLAUMET, Gustave Achille
French 1840-1887
paintings: (L) $330; (H) $8,250
drawings: (L) $220; (H) $8,250

GUILLAUMIN, Armand
French 1841-1927
paintings: (L) $4,400; (H) $148,500
drawings: (L) $110; (H) $33,000

GUILLE, Louis Ernest
paintings: (H) $1,210

GUILLEMET, Jean Baptiste Antoine
French 1843-1918
paintings: (L) $495; (H) $4,400

GUILLEMIN, Barye
sculpture: (H) $2,475

GUILLEMIN, Emile
French 1841-1907
sculpture: (L) $275; (H) $23,100

GUILLEMINET, Claude
French b. 1821
paintings: (L) $660; (H) $5,170

GUILLERMO, Juan
mid-late 20th cent.
paintings: (H) $1,870

GUILLERMOT, C.T.
French 19th cent.
paintings: (L) $660; (H) $12,100

GUILLET-SAGUEZ, A.
French 19th cent.
paintings: (H) $4,950

GUILLON, Eugene Antoine
French b. 1834
paintings: (L) $2,640; (H) $6,600

GUILLONNET, Octave Denis Victor
French 1872-1967
paintings: (L) $605; (H) $27,500

GUILLOU, Alfred
French 1844-1926
paintings: (L) $825; (H) $52,800

GUINCOURT, E.
Italian 19th cent.
paintings: (H) $2,200

GUINEA, Anselmo de
Spanish 1855-1906
drawings: (H) $1,210

GUINO
sculpture: (H) $1,100

GUINZBURG, Frederic Victor
American
sculpture: (L) $330; (H) $7,700

GUIO, A.
sculpture: (H) $1,540

GUION, Molly
American b. 1910
paintings: (H) $1,650

GUIPON, Leon
American 1872-1910
paintings: (H) $1,650

GUIRAUD-RIVIERE, Maurice
French b. 1881
sculpture: (L) $880; (H) $57,200

GUIRMAND, Paul
French b. 1926
drawings: (H) $990

GUISSARD (?), Henri
paintings: (H) $715

GUISTO, Faust
19th cent.
paintings: (H) $5,280

GUITTON, Edward
paintings: (H) $660

GULLAGER, Christian
American 1762-1826
paintings: (H) $14,300

GULLEMINET, Claude
paintings: (H) $2,860

GULUCHE, J. le
sculpture: (H) $1,650

GUMERY, A.
American
paintings: (H) $1,045

GUMME
paintings: (L) $110; (H) $660

GUMPERTZ, Clara
Austrian b. 1863
paintings: (H) $1,320

GUNDLACH, Max
American 20th cent.
paintings: (H) $715

GUNN, Edwin H.
American 1876-1940
paintings: (H) $715
drawings: (L) $605; (H) $880

GUNOT
paintings: (H) $1,045

GUNTHER, Georg
German b. 1886
paintings: (H) $2,750

GUORD, A.
19th/20th cent.
paintings: (H) $660

GURR, Lena
American b. 1897
paintings: (H) $1,100

GURSCHNER, Gustav
Austrian b. 1873
sculpture: (L) $220; (H) $5,500

GURVICH, Jose
Lithuanian 1927-1974
paintings: (H) $12,100

GUSCHONIK, F.
Continental 20th cent.
paintings: (H) $4,400

GUSSOW, Bernard
Russian/American 1881-1957
paintings: (L) $110; (H) $6,600
drawings: (L) $88; (H) $880

GUSSOW, Carl
German 1843-1907
paintings: (H) $1,540

GUSTAVSON, Henry
American 1864-1912
paintings: (L) $440; (H) $880
drawings: (H) $192

GUSTEMER, G.
American ac. 1840-1850
paintings: (H) $35,750

GUSTIN, Paul Morgan
American b. 1886
paintings: (L) $358; (H) $825

GUSTON, Philip
Canadian/American 1913-1980
paintings: (L) $4,950; (H) $550,000
drawings: (L) $1,650; (H) $71,500

GUTE, Herbert J.
American 1908-1977
paintings: (L) $357; (H) $14,850
drawings: (L) $165; (H) $495

GUTGEMON, Gustave
German 19th cent.
paintings: (H) $1,430

GUTHERZ, Carl
American 1844-1907
paintings: (L) $1,650; (H) $6,600

GUTIERREZ, Ernesto
Spanish 19th/20th cent.
paintings: (L) $770; (H) $2,200

GUTIERREZ, F.A.
drawings: (L) $1,980; (H) $2,200

GUTTMAN, Bernhard
German 1869-1936
paintings: (L) $247; (H) $1,540
drawings: (L) $110; (H) $220

GUTTUSO, Renato
Italian b. 1912
paintings: (L) $3,520; (H) $35,200
drawings: (H) $660

GUTZON, Borglum
1867-1941
sculpture: (H) $742

GUY, Francis
Anglo/American 1760-1820
paintings: (L) $3,850; (H) $26,400

GUY, Seymour Joseph
Anglo/American 1824-1910
paintings: (L) $220; (H) $25,300

GUYOT, A.
paintings: (H) $5,280

GUYOT, E.
drawings: (H) $1,210

GUYOT, Georges-Lucien
drawings: (L) $138; (H) $154
sculpture: (L) $880; (H) $1,595

GUYS, Constantin
French 1802-1892
drawings: (L) $330; (H) $3,960

GWATHMEY, Robert
American b. 1903
paintings: (L) $2,530; (H) $24,200
drawings: (L) $825; (H) $7,150

GWYN, Woody
contemporary
paintings: (H) $4,620

GWYNN, William
British ac. 1795-1838
paintings: (H) $2,750

GYNGELL, Albert
English/S. African 1866-1949
paintings: (H) $1,045

GYORGY, Nemeth
paintings: (L) $286; (H) $825

GYOSAI
Japanese 1831-1889
drawings: (H) $3,300

GYSELAAR, M*** de
b. Brussels ac. 1813-1820
drawings: (L) $660; (H) $880

GYSELINCKX, Joseph
Belgian 19th cent.
paintings: (L) $990; (H) $3,850

GYSELS, Pieter
Flemish 1621-1690
paintings: (L) $8,250; (H) $57,750
drawings: (H) $412

HORTON, William Samuel
American 1865-1936
paintings: (H) $1,760

HAACKE, Hans
German/American b. 1936
sculpture: (H) $99,000

HAAG, Carl
German 1820-1915
paintings: (L) $27; (H) $880
drawings: (L) $990; (H) $13,200

HAAG, Hans Johann
Austrian b. 1841
paintings: (H) $1,650

HAAG, Hy.
American 20th cent.
paintings: (H) $2,200

HAAG, Jean Paul
French 19th cent.
paintings: (L) $935; (H) $3,575

HAAGEN, Joris van der
Dutch 1615-1669
paintings: (H) $20,900

HAAKMAN, Leon
paintings: (H) $660

HAANEN, Casparis
Dutch 1778-1849
paintings: (H) $25,300

HAANEN, Cecil van
Dutch 1844-1914
paintings: (L) $110; (H) $7,700

HAANEN, G. (?)
Continental 19th cent.
paintings: (H) $660

HAANEN, Georg Gillis van
Dutch 1807-1876
paintings: (L) $357; (H) $4,125

HAANEN, Remigius Adrianus van
Dutch 1812-1894
paintings: (L) $880; (H) $4,950

HAAPANEN, John Nichols
American b. 1891
paintings: (L) $77; (H) $1,650

HAARDT, J.
Dutch 20th cent.
paintings: (H) $1,540

HAARLEM, Cornelis Cornelisz. van
Dutch 1562-1638
paintings: (L) $9,350; (H) $44,000

HAAS, Johannes Hubertus
Leonardus de
Belgian 1832-1880/1908
paintings: (L) $990; (H) $6,875

HAAS, Mauritz Frederik Hendrick de
Dutch 1832-1895
paintings: (L) $1,760; (H) $6,600

HAAS, Richard John
American b. 1936
drawings: (H) $2,750

HAAS, William de
paintings: (L) $2,640; (H) $3,080

HAASE, Hermann
sculpture: (L) $302; (H) $660

HAAXMAN, Pieter Alardus
Dutch 1814-1887
paintings: (H) $3,850

HABERLE, John
American 1853/56-1933
paintings: (L) $20,900; (H) $517,000
drawings: (L) $99; (H) $3,850

HABERMANN, Franz von
drawings: (H) $935

HABICH, Ludwig
German
sculpture: (H) $1,210

HACCOU, Johann Cornelis
Dutch 1798-1893
paintings: (H) $1,320

HACHENBERGER, Henry
drawings: (H) $1,625

HACKAERT, Jacob Philip
German 1737-1807
paintings: (H) $85,250

HACKER
American 19th cent.
paintings: (H) $3,300

HACKER, Arthur
British 1858-1919
paintings: (L) $330; (H) $4,400

HACKER, Dieter
German b. 1942
paintings: (L) $5,500; (H) $16,500
drawings: (L) $1,540; (H) $4,400
sculpture: (H) $8,250

HACKER, Homer
American 20th cent.
drawings: (L) $715; (H) $770

HACKER, Horst
German 1842-1906
paintings: (L) $3,300; (H) $19,800

HACKERT, Jacob Phillipp
German 1737-1807
paintings: (L) $2,090; (H) $93,500
drawings: (L) $3,300; (H) $4,620

HACKETT, Malcolm
American 20th cent.
paintings: (H) $825

HADDON, Arthur Trevor
British 1864-1941
paintings: (L) $605; (H) $9,350
drawings: (H) $1,320

HADDON, David W.
English 19th cent.
paintings: (L) $247; (H) $880

HADER, Elmer Stanley
American 1889-1973
drawings: (H) $26,400

HADLEY, H.
English 19th cent.
paintings: (H) $1,430

HADLEY, Raymond
paintings: (H) $880

HADZI, Dimitri
American b. 1921
sculpture: (L) $1,045; (H) $1,540

HAELSZEL, Johann Baptist
German 1712-1777
paintings: (H) $11,000

HAEN, David de
paintings: (H) $6,600

HAENGER, M.
Continental 19th/20th cent.
paintings: (H) $1,760

HAENGER, Max
German 19th cent.
paintings: (H) $1,155

HAENGER, Merio
Continental 19th/20th cent.
paintings: (H) $1,540

HAENSBERGEN, Jan van
Dutch 1642-1705
paintings: (L) $2,860; (H) $13,200

HAFENRICHER, Hans
sculpture: (H) $1,100

HAFFNER, Feliz
French 1818-1875
paintings: (H) $1,760

HAFNER, Charles Andrew
American b. 1888
sculpture: (L) $990; (H) $30,800

HAGARTY, James
British ac. 1762-1783
paintings: (H) $6,600

HAGBORG, August Wilhelm Nikolaus
Swedish 1852-1925
paintings: (L) $2,090; (H) $121,000

HAGEDORN, Friedrich
Latin American
drawings: (H) $11,000

HAGEL, Frank
American
drawings: (L) $850; (H) $1,200

HAGEMAN, S.
Dutch 20th cent.
paintings: (H) $1,540

HAGEMANN, Godefroy de
French d. 1877
paintings: (H) $3,750

HAGEMANN, Oskar H.
German b. 1888
paintings: (L) $440; (H) $770

HAGEMEISTER, Karl
paintings: (H) $3,300

HAGEN, Eduard von
German 1834-1909
paintings: (L) $550; (H) $880

HAGEN, Thomas
paintings: (H) $1,870

HAGENDORN, Karl
contemporary
drawings: (H) $880

HAGER, Charles
Belgian early 20th cent.
sculpture: (H) $4,180

HAGERBAUMER, David
drawings: (L) $605; (H) $880

HAGERUP, Nels
American 1864-1922
paintings: (L) $143; (H) $2,475
drawings: (H) $193

HAGG, Jacob
Swedish 1839-1941
paintings: (H) $3,850

HAGGERTY, Isabel
American 20th cent.
paintings: (H) $2,750

HAGHE, Louis
Belgian b. 1806,d. London 1885
drawings: (L) $440; (H) $4,620

HAGUE, J. Edward Homerville
British b. 1885
paintings: (H) $1,870

HAGUE, Joshua Anderson
British 1850-1916
paintings: (H) $660

HAGUE, Michael
drawings: (L) $1,210; (H) $3,520

HAGUE, Raoul
American b. 1904
sculpture: (L) $4,620; (H) $60,500

HAHN, Georg
German 1841-1889
paintings: (L) $3,520; (H) $9,900

HAHN, Gustav Adolph
German 1811-1872
paintings: (L) $990; (H) $3,300

HAHN, W.
paintings: (H) $2,860

HAHN, William
American 1829-1887
paintings: (L) $4,675; (H) $9,130
drawings: (H) $935

HAHN, Wm.
paintings: (H) $4,950

HAIER, Joseph
Austrian 1816-1891
paintings: (H) $880

HAIGH, Alfred
British 1870-1963
paintings: (L) $1,430; (H) $4,950
drawings: (H) $1,100

HAINES, Lizzie
American 19th cent.
paintings: (L) $302; (H) $2,530

HAINS, Raymond
French b. 1926
drawings: (L) $6,600; (H) $7,150

HAINS, W.D.
American School 19th cent.
paintings: (H) $1,870

HAINSCOUGH (?), ****
sculpture: (H) $6,600

HAJDU, Etienne
French b. 1907
sculpture: (L) $2,250; (H) $17,600

HALAHMY, Oded
Iraqi contemporary
sculpture: (L) $825; (H) $1,430

HALAUSKA, Ludwig
German 1827-1882
paintings: (H) $8,800

HALBERG-KRAUSS, Fritz
German 1874-1951
paintings: (L) $2,200; (H) $5,280

HALBERT, Samuel
American 1884-1930
paintings: (H) $1,650

HALE, A.
American 19th/20th cent.
drawings: (H) $1,000

HALE, Ellen Day
American 1855-1940
paintings: (L) $165; (H) $27,500
drawings: (L) $220; (H) $1,980

HALE, James W.
paintings: (H) $4,950

HALE, Lilian Westcott
American 1881-1963
paintings: (L) $14,300; (H) $22,000
drawings: (L) $275; (H) $3,850

HALE, Philip Leslie
American 1865-1931
paintings: (L) $2,200; (H) $132,000
drawings: (L) $385; (H) $14,300

HALEM, Henry
contemporary
drawings: (H) $1,540

HALEY, Robert Duane
American 1892-1959
paintings: (H) $2,750

HALICKA, Alice
Polish 1895-1975
paintings: (L) $1,210; (H) $1,870
drawings: (H) $286

HALKETT, Francois Joseph Clement
Belgian ac. 1886
paintings: (L) $6,600; (H) $13,200

HALKO, Joe
American b. 1940
sculpture: (L) $500; (H) $1,000

HALL, Charles
paintings: (L) $1,210; (H) $1,375

HALL, Cyrneius
American
paintings: (H) $2,090

HALL, F.W.
paintings: (H) $770

HALL, Frederick
British 1860-1948
paintings: (L) $9,350; (H) $68,750

HALL, George Henry
American 1825-1913
paintings: (L) $357; (H) $46,750
drawings: (H) $209

HALL, George S.
paintings: (H) $2,750

HALL, Harry
English 1814-1882
paintings: (L) $4,950; (H) $220,000

HALL, Henry R.
British
paintings: (H) $990

HALL, J.
American 19th/20th cent.
paintings: (H) $1,650

HALL, Sadie van Patten
American 20th cent.
paintings: (H) $770

HALL, Susan
contemporary
paintings: (L) $1,100; (H) $1,100

HALLADY, John R.
American
paintings: (H) $1,210

HALLE, Charles
paintings: (H) $4,125

HALLE, Leo
paintings: (H) $990

HALLE, Noel
French 1711-1781
paintings: (L) $6,050; (H) $20,900

HALLE, Oscar
paintings: (H) $880

HALLELT, Frederick A.
paintings: (H) $715

HALLER, G.
English 19th cent.
paintings: (H) $990

HALLETT, Hendricks A.
American 1847-1921
paintings: (L) $99; (H) $7,700
drawings: (L) $82; (H) $385

HALLETT, W.
American 19th cent.
paintings: (L) $385; (H) $700

HALLEY, Peter
American b. 1953
paintings: (H) $143,000
drawings: (H) $3,300

HALLINAN, T.
European 20th cent.
paintings: (H) $990

HALLMARK, George
American b. 1949
paintings: (H) $5,000

HALLOWELL, George H.
American 1871-1926
paintings: (H) $4,950
drawings: (L) $220; (H) $6,050

HALLOWELL, Robert
American 1886-1939
drawings: (L) $770; (H) $2,200

HALLOWELL, William
drawings: (H) $1,210

HALOW, E.J.
American 19th/20th cent.
paintings: (L) $275; (H) $880

HALPERT, Samuel
American 1884-1930
paintings: (L) $550; (H) $2,860
drawings: (L) $187; (H) $1,650

HALS, Dirk
Dutch 1591-1656
paintings: (L) $15,400; (H) $71,500

HALS, Frans
Dutch c.1580-1666
paintings: (H) $572,000

HALS, Harmen Franz
1611-1669
paintings: (H) $28,600

HALSALL, William F.
American 1841-1919
paintings: (L) $400; (H) $5,200

HALVERSON, Jean
American
drawings: (L) $750; (H) $1,400

HAM, Gordon R.
American 20th cent.
paintings: (H) $825

HAMBIDGE, Jay
American 1867-1924
paintings: (H) $165
drawings: (L) $418; (H) $1,100

HAMBLIN, Sturtevant J.
American ac. c. 1837-1856
paintings: (L) $2,420; (H) $104,500

HAMBOURG, Andre
French b. 1909
paintings: (L) $880; (H) $33,000
drawings: (L) $440; (H) $748

HAMBRIDGE, Jay
American 1867-1924
drawings: (H) $660

HAMDY-BEY, Osman Edhem Pacha
Zadeh
Turkish 1842-1910
paintings: (H) $60,500

HAMELIN, E.C.
paintings: (H) $715

HAMEN Y LEON, Juan van der
Spanish 1596-1632
paintings: (H) $550,000

HAMEN Y LEON, Juan van der,
studio of
paintings: (H) $24,200

HAMILTON, Edward Wilbur Dean
American 1862/64-1943
paintings: (H) $8,250
drawings: (H) $330

HAMILTON, Gawen
English 1697-1773
paintings: (L) $16,500; (H) $38,500

HAMILTON, Hadassah
American 19th cent.
paintings: (H) $700

HAMILTON, Hamilton
Anglo/American 1847-1928
paintings: (L) $550; (H) $6,050
drawings: (L) $495; (H) $8,800

HAMILTON, Helen
American early 20th cent.
paintings: (L) $110; (H) $990

HAMILTON, Hugh Douglas
Irish 1736/39-1806/08
drawings: (H) $990

HAMILTON, James
British 1645?-1705?
paintings: (L) $1,430; (H) $3,850

HAMILTON, James
Irish/American 1819-1878
paintings: (L) $358; (H) $14,300

HAMILTON, James Whitelaw
Scottish 1860-1932
paintings: (L) $350; (H) $1,760

HAMILTON, Johann Georg de
paintings: (H) $6,600

HAMILTON, John McLure
American 1853-1936
paintings: (L) $825; (H) $44,000
drawings: (L) $440; (H) $1,760

HAMILTON, Karl Wilhelm
Flemish 1668-1754
paintings: (L) $8,800; (H) $9,350

HAMILTON, Thomas Alexander
American 19th cent.
paintings: (L) $143; (H) $715

HAMILTON, William R.
American 1810-1865
paintings: (L) $330; (H) $12,650

HAMLIN, A.
American
paintings: (H) $31,900

HAMLIN, Edith A.
American b. 1902
paintings: (H) $1,320

HAMLIN, Genevieve Karr
American b. 1896
sculpture: (L) $770; (H) $1,430

HAMMAN, Edouard Michel Ferdinand
French b. 1850
paintings: (L) $2,090; (H) $2,860

HAMME, Alexis van
Belgian 1818-1875
paintings: (L) $2,970; (H) $16,500

HAMMER, John Johann
German 1842-1906
paintings: (L) $3,520; (H) $4,400

HAMMERAS, Ralph
American 20th cent.
paintings: (L) $198; (H) $1,100

HAMMERSHOI, Wilhelm
Danish 1864-1916
paintings: (L) $4,620; (H) $90,750

HAMMOND, Arthur J.
American b. 1875
paintings: (L) $88; (H) $3,630
drawings: (H) $165

HAMMOND, John A.
Canadian 1843-1939
paintings: (L) $1,072; (H) $1,155

HAMMOND, Richard Henry
American b. 1854
paintings: (H) $660

HAMMOND, Robert John
British 20th cent.
paintings: (H) $1,430

HAMON, Jean Louis
French 1821-1874
paintings: (L) $110; (H) $68,750

HAMPE, Ernst Heinrich Wilhelm
German 1806-1862
paintings: (H) $1,320

HAMPTON, Herbert
sculpture: (H) $715

HAMPTON, John Wade
American b. 1918
paintings: (L) $3,850; (H) $6,050

HAMZA, Hans
Austrian 1879-1945
paintings: (H) $1,210

HAMZA, Johann
German b. 1850
paintings: (L) $3,850; (H) $13,200

HAMZA, Joseph
German 1850-1927
paintings: (H) $1,750

HAN, H.N.
paintings: (H) $6,050

HANAU, Jean
French b. 1899
paintings: (L) $440; (H) $1,100

HANBURY, Una
20th cent.
sculpture: (H) $1,210

HANCOCK, Charles
British 1795-1868
paintings: (L) $1,045; (H) $13,200

HANCOCK, Charles
English 1802-1877
paintings: (H) $4,675

HAND, I.
British 19th cent.
paintings: (H) $7,150

HAND, Orville
paintings: (H) $770

HAND, Thomas
English d. c. 1804
paintings: (L) $2,420; (H) $3,575

HANDMANN, Emmanuel
paintings: (L) $577; (H) $962

HANGER, Max
German b. 1874
paintings: (L) $990; (H) $2,200

HANICOTTE, Augustin
French 1870-1957
paintings: (H) $3,520

HANISCH, Alois
Austrian 1866-1937
paintings: (H) $2,200

HANJE
Dutch 20th cent.
paintings: (H) $660

HANKEY, Lucille
American
drawings: (H) $825

HANKEY, William Lee
English 1869-1952
paintings: (L) $3,300; (H) $16,500
drawings: (L) $121; (H) $3,850

HANKS, Jervis F.
American
paintings: (H) $1,430

HANNA, Thomas King
American 1872-1957
paintings: (L) $3,025; (H) $7,975
drawings: (L) $77; (H) $715

HANNAH, Duncan
American b. 1952
paintings: (L) $2,750; (H) $5,500

HANNAH, H.K.
American 19th/20th cent.
paintings: (H) $1,700

HANNAH, Robert
British 1812-1909
paintings: (H) $3,850

HANNAUX, Emmanuel
French b. 1855
sculpture: (L) $2,750; (H) $17,600

HANNEMAN, Adriaen
Dutch b. c. 1601-1671
paintings: (L) $1,870; (H) $27,500

HANNIS
American 19th cent.
paintings: (H) $1,540

HANNON, Theodore
Belgian 1851-1917
paintings: (H) $29,700

HANNOT, Jan
late 17th cent.
paintings: (H) $22,000

HANOCQ, Ferdinand
French 19th cent.
drawings: (H) $770

HANOTEAU, Hector
paintings: (H) $4,400

HANSCH, Anton
paintings: (H) $935

HANSCOM, Trude
American b. 1898
paintings: (L) $715; (H) $1,045

HANSEN, Armin Carl
American 1886-1957
paintings: (L) $1,100; (H) $27,500
drawings: (L) $468; (H) $3,025

HANSEN, B.H.
Danish 19th cent.
paintings: (H) $1,100

HANSEN, Ejnar
Danish/American 1884-1965
paintings: (L) $138; (H) $1,650
drawings: (H) $412

HANSEN, F.
Continental School 19th cent.
paintings: (L) $990; (H) $990

HANSEN, F.
European 19th/20th cent.
paintings: (H) $880

HANSEN, Frank
American
paintings: (H) $715

HANSEN, Hans
English 1853-1923
drawings: (H) $935

HANSEN, Heinrich
Danish 1821-1890
paintings: (H) $1,045

HANSEN, Herman Wendelborg
German/American 1854-1924
paintings: (L) $2,475; (H) $66,000
drawings: (L) $275; (H) $20,900

HANSEN, Josef Theodor
Danish 1848-1912
paintings: (L) $3,630; (H) $7,700

HANSEN, Lambertus Johannes
Dutch 1803-1859
paintings: (L) $880; (H) $1,760

HANSEN, Sigvard Marius
Danish b. 1859
paintings: (L) $220; (H) $1,760

HANSEN, Stephen
American contemporary
sculpture: (L) $2,640; (H) $2,860

HANSON, Duane
American b. 1925
sculpture: (L) $209,000; (H) $297,000

HANSON, Leon
Australian 20th cent.
paintings: (H) $1,650

HANSON, Peter
American 1821-1887
paintings: (L) $660; (H) $3,300

HANSSENGER, John
contemporary
paintings: (H) $990

HAPPENEN, John Nichols
American b. 1891
paintings: (H) $1,100

HAPSMANS, M.
American 20th cent.
drawings: (H) $660

HAQUETTE, Georges
French 1854-1906
paintings: (L) $577; (H) $3,080

HARBESON, Georgiana Brown
American b. 1894
drawings: (H) $797

HARCOURT, George
paintings: (H) $4,400

HARDER, Heinrich
German 1858-1914
paintings: (H) $3,850

HARDIME, Pieter
Flemish 1677/78-c. 1758
paintings: (L) $6,600; (H) $35,200

HARDIN, Helen, Tsa Sah Wee Eh
Native American 1946-1984
drawings: (L) $192; (H) $715

HARDING, Chester
American
paintings: (H) $8,800

HARDING, George
American 1882-1959
drawings: (L) $11; (H) $825

HARDING, J.L.
American ac. c. 1825
paintings: (L) $1,540; (H) $1,650

HARDING, James Duffield
English 1798-1863
drawings: (L) $495; (H) $1,320

HARDING, John L.
American ac. 1848-1882
paintings: (H) $1,980

HARDMAN, James
British ac. 1799-1846
paintings: (H) $4,400

HARDWICK, Melbourne H.
American 1857-1916
paintings: (L) $247; (H) $1,870
drawings: (L) $55; (H) $1,870

HARDY, Anna Eliza
American 1839-1934
paintings: (L) $880; (H) $2,640
drawings: (H) $220

HARDY, Dorofield
paintings: (H) $770

HARDY, Dudley
English c. 1866-1922
paintings: (H) $770

HARDY, Frederick Daniel
British 1826-1911
paintings: (L) $6,600; (H) $11,000

HARDY, George
British 1822-1909
paintings: (L) $1,650; (H) $1,650

HARDY, Heywood
English 1843-1932
paintings: (L) $6,050; (H) $73,700
drawings: (L) $495; (H) $2,090

HARDY, James, Jr.
English 1832-1889
paintings: (L) $660; (H) $1,430

HARDY, Jeremiah Pearson
American 1800-1888
drawings: (H) $1,870

HARDY, R.
English 19th cent.
paintings: (H) $1,430

HARDY, Thomas Bush
English 1842-1897
paintings: (L) $600; (H) $2,475
drawings: (L) $286; (H) $6,600

HARE, A.
paintings: (H) $660

HARE, C.K.
English 19th cent.
paintings: (H) $1,100

HARE, David
American b. 1917
sculpture: (H) $6,875

HARE, John C.
American
drawings: (L) $110; (H) $688

HARE, John Knowles
American 1884-1947
paintings: (L) $248; (H) $1,980
drawings: (L) $138; (H) $1,430

HARE, St. George
British b. 1857
paintings: (H) $14,300

HARE, William
American ac. c. 1842-1859
paintings: (H) $6,600

HAREL, E. Albert
French b. 1876
paintings: (H) $2,860

HARGENS, Charles
American b. 1893
paintings: (L) $137; (H) $3,575

HARGITT, Edward
English 1835-1895
paintings: (H) $2,090

HARGRAVE, Harry S.
American ac. 1930's
paintings: (H) $715

HARGREAVES, Edgar W.
American 20th cent.
drawings: (L) $275; (H) $935

HARGUAR, Hans
paintings: (H) $935

HARIA, Josef
European 20th cent.
drawings: (H) $1,210

HARING, Keith
American 1958-1990
paintings: (L) $1,210; (H) $148,500
drawings: (L) $687; (H) $41,800
sculpture: (L) $35,750; (H) $231,000

HARING, Keith and Eric ORR
contemporary
drawings: (H) $7,150

HARING, Keith and Kermit OSWALD
contemporary
paintings: (L) $10,450; (H) $11,000

HARING, Keith and L.A. 2
contemporary
sculpture: (L) $1,650; (H) $15,400

HARINGTON, Mary
American
paintings: (H) $1,430

HARITONOFF, Nicholas B.
American 1880-1944
paintings: (H) $8,525

HARLES, Victor Joseph
American b. 1894
paintings: (L) $137; (H) $3,520

HARLEY, George Willis
British 19th/20th cent.
paintings: (H) $880

HARLEY, Herbert E.
British 19th cent.
paintings: (H) $825

HARLOW, G.H.E.
English b. 1808
drawings: (H) $825

HARLOW, George Henry
English 1787-1819
paintings: (L) $5,500; (H) $10,450
drawings: (L) $605; (H) $1,430

HARLOW, Louis K.
American 1850-1930
drawings: (L) $38; (H) $660

HARMAN, Fred
American 1902-1983?
paintings: (L) $3,300; (H) $7,000

HARMER, Alexander F.
American 1856-1925
paintings: (L) $880; (H) $5,500
drawings: (H) $1,210

HARMON, Charles Henry
American 1859-1936
paintings: (L) $385; (H) $1,210
drawings: (H) $1,540

HARMON, James and Harry
ANDERSON
  contemporary
  sculpture: (L) $220; (H) $880

HARMS, Alfred
  American 19th/20th cent.
  paintings: (H) $825

HARNDEN, William
  American 1920-1983
  paintings: (L) $440; (H) $1,760

HARNE, G.
  American 19th cent.
  paintings: (H) $742

HARNETT, William Michael
  American 1848/51-1892
  paintings: (L) $38,500; (H) $264,000
  drawings: (H) $2,420
  sculpture: (H) $8,250

HARNEY, E.
  paintings: (H) $935

HARNEY, Paul E.
  American 1850-1915
  paintings: (L) $154; (H) $1,870
  drawings: (H) $495

HAROLD, E.
  paintings: (H) $660

HARPER
  18th/19th cent.
  paintings: (H) $1,210

HARPER, Edward S.
  American 20th cent.
  paintings: (H) $1,100

HARPER, W.A.
  paintings: (H) $990

HARPER, William St. John
  American 1851-1910
  paintings: (L) $16,500; (H) $52,800
  drawings: (H) $18,700

HARPIGNIES, Henri Joseph
  French 1819-1916
  paintings: (L) $1,210; (H) $33,000
  drawings: (L) $220; (H) $24,200

HARPSAU
  paintings: (H) $1,540

HARQUETTE, Georges
  French 19th cent.
  paintings: (H) $4,675

HARRIET, Fulchran Jean
  French 1778-1805
  paintings: (H) $15,400

HARRIS, Albert
  paintings: (L) $352; (H) $715

HARRIS, Charles Gordon
  American b. 1891
  paintings: (L) $275; (H) $1,870
  drawings: (L) $137; (H) $770

HARRIS, Charles X.
  American b. 1856
  paintings: (L) $605; (H) $4,675

HARRIS, Edwin
  British 19th cent.
  paintings: (L) $2,200; (H) $44,000
  drawings: (L) $55; (H) $4,400

HARRIS, G.
  paintings: (H) $880

HARRIS, George Edgerly
  paintings: (H) $2,200

HARRIS, H.
  British 19th/20th cent.
  paintings: (L) $248; (H) $825

HARRIS, H.H.
  paintings: (H) $1,870

HARRIS, Henry
  British 1805-1865
  paintings: (L) $880; (H) $1,760
  drawings: (H) $187

HARRIS, J.T.
  paintings: (H) $1,540

HARRIS, John, II
  British 1791-1873
  paintings: (H) $1,210

HARRIS, Lawren Stewart
  Canadian 1885-1970
  paintings: (L) $440; (H) $330,000

HARRIS, Mary Aubin
  American b. 1864
  paintings: (H) $660

HARRIS, R.
  English 18th cent.
  paintings: (L) $3,300; (H) $5,500

HARRIS, Sam Hyde
  American 1889-1977
  paintings: (L) $330; (H) $7,350

HARRIS, William E.
English 19th cent.
paintings: (L) $1,100; (H) $2,750

HARRISON, Alexander
American 1853-1930
paintings: (L) $660; (H) $20,900

HARRISON, Birge Lowell
American 1854-1929
paintings: (L) $825; (H) $37,400

HARRISON, C.P.
American 19th cent.
paintings: (H) $1,540

HARRISON, F.E.
English ac. 1862-1867
paintings: (H) $2,200

HARRISON, G.L.
British ac. 1870's-1880's
drawings: (H) $1,540

HARRISON, John Cyril
British 1898-1985
drawings: (L) $605; (H) $990

HARRISON, Lowell Birge
American 1854-1929
drawings: (H) $16,500

HARRISON, Mark Robert
American 1819-1894
paintings: (H) $1,320

HARRISON, Thomas Alexander
American 1853-1930
paintings: (L) $467; (H) $4,400

HARROWING, Walter
British ac. 1877-1904
paintings: (L) $1,760; (H) $2,750

HART, B.
American ac. 1810-1860
paintings: (H) $742

HART, George Overbury (Pop)
American 1868-1933
paintings: (H) $495
drawings: (L) $264; (H) $2,530

HART, J.
American 19th cent.
paintings: (H) $1,540

HART, James McDougal
American 1828-1901
paintings: (L) $880; (H) $30,800
drawings: (L) $522; (H) $1,540

HART, James McDougal and Arthur
Fitzwilliam TAIT
paintings: (H) $17,600

HART, James Turpin
paintings: (H) $1,210

HART, Joel Tanner
American 1810-1877
sculpture: (H) $9,900

HART, Letitia Bennet
American b. 1867
paintings: (L) $1,100; (H) $1,925

HART, Louis B.
paintings: (H) $3,080

HART, Mary Theresa
American b. 1872
paintings: (L) $330; (H) $2,750

HART, Solomon Alexander
British 1806-1881
paintings: (H) $1,540

HART, T.R.
British 19th cent.
paintings: (H) $4,125

HART, William
paintings: (L) $1,760; (H) $19,800

HART, William Howard
American 1863-1934
paintings: (H) $5,280

HART, William M.
American 1823-1894
paintings: (L) $605; (H) $39,600
drawings: (L) $275; (H) $1,100

HARTIG, Hans
German b. 1873
paintings: (H) $715

HARTIGAN, Grace
American b. 1922
paintings: (L) $1,760; (H) $6,050
drawings: (L) $550; (H) $7,150

HARTING, George W.
American b. 1877
paintings: (H) $880

HARTING, Lloyd
American 1901-1974
drawings: (L) $550; (H) $1,045

HARTING, Marinus
Dutch b. 1816
paintings: (L) $935; (H) $3,080

HARTINGER, Anton
Austrian 1806-1890
drawings: (H) $26,400

HARTLAND, Henry Albert
Irish 1840-1893
drawings: (L) $412; (H) $825

HARTLEY, Charles D.
paintings: (H) $990

HARTLEY, Jonathan Scott
American 1845-1912
sculpture: (L) $192; (H) $18,700

HARTLEY, Marsden
American 1877-1943
paintings: (L) $6,600; (H) $550,000
drawings: (L) $440; (H) $24,400

HARTLEY, Rachel
American b. 1884
paintings: (L) $165; (H) $8,250

HARTMAN, Bertram
American 1882-1960
paintings: (L) $165; (H) $4,950
drawings: (L) $110; (H) $3,300

HARTMAN, George
American 20th cent.
paintings: (L) $165; (H) $1,650

HARTMAN, Robert
contemporary
paintings: (H) $715

HARTMANN, Johann Jacob
paintings: (H) $4,950

HARTMANN, Johann Joseph
1753-1830
drawings: (H) $6,325

HARTMANN, Ludwig
German 1835-1902
paintings: (L) $34,100; (H) $55,000

HARTNELL, Nathaniel
British ac. 1829-1864
paintings: (H) $2,310

HARTRATH, Lucie
American 1868-1962
paintings: (L) $550; (H) $8,800

HARTSHORNE, Howard Morton
American 19th/20th cent.
paintings: (L) $138; (H) $5,225

HARTSON, Walter C.
German b. 1866
paintings: (L) $303; (H) $1,320
drawings: (L) $165; (H) $935

HARTUNG, Hans
German b. 1904
paintings: (L) $6,050; (H) $93,500
drawings: (L) $6,600; (H) $44,000

HARTUNG, Heinrich
German 1851-1919
paintings: (H) $1,320

HARTUNG, J.
paintings: (H) $1,045

HARTUNG, J.
American 19th cent.
paintings: (H) $660

HARTWELL, George, Prior-Hamblen
School
American
paintings: (L) $12,100; (H) $14,850

HARTWELL, Nina Rosabel
American 19th/20th cent.
paintings: (H) $19,800

HARTWICH, Herman
American 1853-1926
paintings: (L) $880; (H) $24,200

HARTWICK, George Gunther
American ac. 1847-1857
paintings: (L) $352; (H) $9,350

HARTWICK, Herman
American 1853-1926
paintings: (H) $11,000

HARTWIG, Heinie
American 20th cent.
paintings: (L) $110; (H) $1,265

HARTWIG, J.F.
paintings: (H) $660

HARVARD, James
American b. 1937
paintings: (L) $13,200; (H) $22,000

HARVEY, Andre
sculpture: (H) $4,125

HARVEY, Edward A.
1862-1917
paintings: (H) $770
drawings: (L) $44; (H) $55

HARVEY, Eli
American 1860-1957
sculpture: (L) $220; (H) $9,900

HARVEY, G., Gerald Harvey JONES
American b. 1933
paintings: (L) $3,740; (H) $35,000
sculpture: (H) $3,850

HARVEY, George
paintings: (L) $2,420; (H) $6,600
drawings: (H) $11

HARVEY, George
American ac.1837-1840
paintings: (H) $203,500

HARVEY, George W.
American 1835-1920
paintings: (L) $330; (H) $1,045
drawings: (L) $176; (H) $1,100

HARVEY, George W.
American b. 1855
paintings: (L) $330; (H) $605
drawings: (L) $143; (H) $1,100

HARVEY, Henry T.
American
paintings: (L) $165; (H) $935

HARVEY, Paul
American 1878-1948
paintings: (L) $330; (H) $1,045

HARVEY, W. Craig
American b. 1882
paintings: (L) $66; (H) $1,100

HARWEY, J.
paintings: (H) $1,210

HARWIG, B.
German 19th cent.
paintings: (H) $3,025

HARWOOD, James Taylor
American 1860-1940
paintings: (H) $2,200

HARZE, Leopold
sculpture: (H) $3,850

HASAEUS, *****
sculpture: (H) $4,950

HASBROUCK, Du Bois Fenelon
American 1860-1917
paintings: (L) $275; (H) $4,675
drawings: (L) $17; (H) $1,650

HASCH, Carl
Austrian 1834/35-1897
paintings: (L) $3,300; (H) $3,575

HASEGAWA, Kiyoshi
Japanese b. 1891
paintings: (H) $10,725

HASELTINE, Charles F.
American 1840-1915
paintings: (L) $275; (H) $1,210

HASELTINE, Herbert
American 1877-1962
sculpture: (L) $4,950; (H) $35,200

HASELTINE, James Henry
American d. 1907
sculpture: (L) $2,420; (H) $9,350

HASELTINE, William Stanley
American 1835-1900
paintings: (L) $495; (H) $71,500
drawings: (L) $1,760; (H) $6,600

HASILER, E.
European 19th cent.
paintings: (H) $1,540

HASKELL, Ernest
American 1876-1925
drawings: (H) $770

HASKELL, Joseph Allen
American 1808-1894
paintings: (L) $450; (H) $2,400

HASKELL, Sarah E.
American 19th cent.
paintings: (H) $2,090

HASKELL, William H.
paintings: (H) $1,430

HASKINS, John
English 20th cent.
paintings: (H) $1,430

HASLAM, Ron
20th cent.
paintings: (H) $687

HASLEHUST, E.W.
English School 20th cent.
drawings: (L) $176; (H) $935

HASSAM, Frederick Childe
American 1859-1935
paintings: (L) $18,700; (H) $3,190,000
drawings: (L) $990; (H) $990,000

HASSELL, Edward
British 19th cent.
paintings: (H) $1,650

HASTINGS, Howard L.
American 19th cent.
paintings: (L) $137; (H) $715

HASTINGS, Rafael
paintings: (H) $7,700

HATCH, Emily Nichols
American 1871-1959
paintings: (L) $82; (H) $990

HATFIELD, Joseph Henry
American 1863-1928
paintings: (L) $660; (H) $2,530

HATHAWAY, Bruce
British 20th cent.
paintings: (L) $1,100; (H) $1,320

HATHAWAY, Dr. Rufus
American 1770-1822
paintings: (H) $90,000

HATHAWAY, George M.
American c. 1852-1903
paintings: (L) $275; (H) $3,850
drawings: (L) $198; (H) $3,630

HATHAWAY, M.
paintings: (H) $1,210

HATTIN
paintings: (L) $440; (H) $880

HATTORI, Hiroshi
contemporary
paintings: (H) $715

HAU, Eva
Russian 19th cent.
drawings: (L) $12,100; (H) $15,400

HAUBER
sculpture: (H) $1,760

HAUBTMANN, Michael
Czech/German 1843-1921
paintings: (L) $880; (H) $1,870

HAUCHECORNE, Gaston
French
sculpture: (H) $770

HAUGHTON, M.
paintings: (H) $770

HAUNOLD, Charles
paintings: (H) $935

HAUNOLD, Karl Franz Emanuel
Austrian 1832-1911
paintings: (H) $6,325

HAUPT, Erik Guide
German/American b. 1891
paintings: (L) $198; (H) $1,320
drawings: (L) $247; (H) $412

HAUPTMANN, Karl
German 19th/20th cent.
paintings: (H) $770

HAUSCH, Alexander Fiodorovich
Russian b. 1873
paintings: (H) $6,050

HAUSCHILD, Maximilian
German 1810-1895
paintings: (H) $6,600

HAUSER, John
American 1858/59-1913/18
paintings: (L) $1,045; (H) $27,500
drawings: (L) $220; (H) $7,150

HAUSER, Karl Ludwig
German 1810-1873
paintings: (H) $880

HAUSHALTER, George M.
American b. 1862
paintings: (L) $440; (H) $990

HAUSHOFER, Maximilian
German 1811-1866
paintings: (H) $715

HAUSMANN, Raoul
paintings: (L) $660; (H) $1,650

HAUTOT, Rachel Lucy
sculpture: (H) $2,860

HAUZET (?), R.
German 19th cent.
paintings: (H) $1,045

HAVANNES, John
American
sculpture: (H) $1,375

HAVARD, James
American b. 1937
paintings: (L) $825; (H) $82,500
drawings: (L) $1,100; (H) $44,000

HAVELL, Alfred Charles
British 1855-1928
paintings: (H) $15,400

HAVELL, Charles Richards
British 19th cent.
paintings: (H) $4,180

HAVELL, Edmund, Jr.
English 1819-after 1895
paintings: (L) $13,200; (H) $15,400

HAVELL, Robert, Jr.
American 1793-1878
paintings: (L) $2,090; (H) $2,750

HAVELL, William
paintings: (L) $770; (H) $7,700

HAVENS, James D.
American 1900-1960
paintings: (H) $990

HAVERS, Alice
paintings: (H) $3,520

HAVET, C.
paintings: (H) $660

HAWKINS, Lewis Welden
English d. 1910
paintings: (H) $4,125

HAWKINS, Welden
American 19th cent.
paintings: (H) $660

HAWKINS, William
American b. 1895
paintings: (H) $18,700

HAWKSETT, Samuel
Irish 1776-1851
paintings: (H) $825

HAWLEY, Hughson
Anglo/American 1850-1936
drawings: (L) $550; (H) $880

HAWN, Jacques
sculpture: (H) $880

HAWTHORNE, Charles Webster
American 1872-1930
paintings: (L) $495; (H) $44,000
drawings: (L) $330; (H) $42,000

HAWTHORNE, E.D.
American 19th cent.
paintings: (H) $4,070

HAWTHORNE, Marion C.
American 1870-1945
drawings: (H) $1,100

HAY, Bernard
English b. 1864
paintings: (L) $440; (H) $9,350

HAYDEN, Charles H.
American 1856-1901
paintings: (L) $522; (H) $2,640

HAYDEN, Edward Parker
American b. 1922
paintings: (L) $192; (H) $2,750

HAYDEN, Henri
French 1883-1970
paintings: (L) $1,650; (H) $23,100
drawings: (L) $110; (H) $19,800

HAYE, H.
English 19th cent.
paintings: (H) $742

HAYEK, Hans Von
Austrian 1869-1940
paintings: (L) $550; (H) $1,980

HAYER, N.
sculpture: (H) $660

HAYES, Charles
English 19th cent.
paintings: (H) $2,090

HAYES, Claude
Irish 1852-1922
paintings: (L) $715; (H) $4,620

HAYES, David V.
American b. 1931
drawings: (H) $220
sculpture: (H) $825

HAYES, Edd
American
sculpture: (H) $4,400

HAYES, Edwin
Irish 1819/20-1904
paintings: (L) $660; (H) $12,100

HAYES, Frederick William
English 1848-1918
paintings: (L) $357; (H) $880

HAYES, George
English 19th cent.
paintings: (H) $3,300

HAYES, Lee
American b. 1854
paintings: (H) $660

HAYES, William Jacob
19th cent.
paintings: (H) $990

HAYEZ, Francesco
Italian 1791-1881
paintings: (L) $8,800; (H) $8,800

HAYLLAR, Edith
British 1860-1948
paintings: (H) $4,400

HAYLLAR, James
English 1829-1920
paintings: (L) $1,210; (H) $6,600

HAYLLAR, Jessica
British 1858-1940
paintings: (L) $660; (H) $27,500

HAYMAN, F.
paintings: (H) $715

HAYMSON, John
American 20th cent.
drawings: (L) $132; (H) $4,675

HAYNES, John William
British 1836-1908
paintings: (L) $303; (H) $2,310

HAYNES, Nancy
sculpture: (L) $3,520; (H) $3,850

HAYNES-WILLIAMS, John
British 19th cent.
paintings: (L) $220; (H) $2,200

HAYS, Barton S.
American 1826-1914
paintings: (L) $990; (H) $2,750

HAYS, Bret
British 1880-1940
paintings: (H) $1,650

HAYS, George A.
American b. 1854
paintings: (L) $165; (H) $4,000
drawings: (L) $220; (H) $468

HAYS, William Jacob, Sr.
American 1830-1875
paintings: (L) $330; (H) $4,180

HAYTER, John
English 1800-1895
paintings: (H) $1,320

HAYTER, Sir George
English 1792-1871
paintings: (H) $7,150

HAYTER, Stanley William
English 1901-1988
paintings: (L) $4,675; (H) $10,450
drawings: (L) $990; (H) $5,500

HAYWARD, Arthur
English b. 1889
paintings: (H) $2,420

HAYWARD, Frank
American
paintings: (L) $440; (H) $660

HAYWARD, Peter
American b. 1905
paintings: (L) $143; (H) $715

HAZAK, Eli
sculpture: (H) $1,980

HAZARD, Arthur Merton
American 1872-1930
paintings: (L) $110; (H) $2,530
drawings: (H) $385

HAZARD, Garnet
Canadian
paintings: (H) $990

HAZARD, S.
American
paintings: (H) $1,045

HAZEL, C. van der
Belgian 1876-1942
paintings: (H) $1,100

HAZELTON, Mary Brewster
American 19th/20th cent.
paintings: (L) $11; (H) $2,090
drawings: (H) $330

HAZELTON, W.B.
paintings: (H) $2,750

HEAD, Cecil
American b. 1906
paintings: (L) $2,860; (H) $2,970

HEAD, Edith
American 1899/1907-1981
paintings: (H) $23,100

HEADE, Martin Johnson
American 1819-1904
paintings: (L) $7,700; (H) $1,925,000
drawings: (L) $1,760; (H) $7,150

HEADLEY, S.T.
English 19th cent.
paintings: (H) $1,100

Provenance

A provenance is "the record of the ownership of a work of art. A complete provenance accounts for the whereabouts of a work from leaving the artist's studio to the present day."* The provenance of a work of art can greatly enhance its value.

Edith Head (1899/1907-1981) was a Hollywood costume designer whose career spanned fifty years. After receiving her M.A. at Stanford, she studied costume design. In 1923 she began work at Paramount Studios, and by 1938 she was named head designer. In the course of her long career she won eight Oscars, had over 1,000 screen credits to her name, and exerted substantial influence on American fashion. Head's sarong for Dorothy Lamour in *The Jungle Princess* (1936) was widely copied across the country; in 1991 the sarong is again back in fashion. At the auction of the Bette Davis estate at William Doyle Galleries, a framed crayon drawing by Edith Head, depicting Davis in *All About Eve*, and inscribed "Bette from Edith," was estimated at $1,200-$1,800; the lot sold for $23,100. (Edith Head, *All About Eve*, crayon on paper, Doyle, April 11, 1990, $23,100)

---

*Chilvers, Ian and Harold Osbourne, ed., *The Oxford Dictionary of Art*. (New York: Oxford University Press, 1988), p. 402.

HEALEY, G.R.
paintings: (H) $2,200

HEALY, George Peter Alexander
American 1808/13-1894
paintings: (L) $99; (H) $7,150
drawings: (H) $467

HEAPHY, J.
paintings: (H) $3,520

HEAPHY, Thomas Frank
paintings: (H) $7,150

HEARD, Joseph
English 1799-1859
paintings: (L) $4,400; (H) $13,200

HEARNE, Thomas
English 1744-1817
drawings: (L) $220; (H) $1,155

HEATH, Frank L.
American 1857-1921
paintings: (L) $935; (H) $4,400

HEATHCOTE, E**S**
British 19th/20th cent.
paintings: (H) $2,860

HEATON, Augustus G.
American 1844-1930
paintings: (L) $385; (H) $5,500

HEATON, Edward
American b. 1824
drawings: (H) $1,100

HEBALD, Milton Elting
American b. 1917
sculpture: (L) $1,100; (H) $1,650

HEBER, Carl Augustus
American 1857-1956
sculpture: (H) $770

HEBERER, Charles
American 19th cent.
paintings: (H) $3,850

HEBERT, Emile
sculpture: (L) $825; (H) $6,600

HEBERT, Ernest
French 1817-1908
drawings: (H) $1,540

HEBERT, Pierre Eugene Emile
French 1828-1893
sculpture: (L) $7,700; (H) $9,900

HECHT, Victor David
American b. 1873
paintings: (H) $3,190

HECK, R.
Northern School 19th cent.
paintings: (H) $2,090

HECKEL, Erich
German 1883-1970
paintings: (H) $148,500
drawings: (L) $550; (H) $23,100

HECKENDORF, Franz
German 1888-1962
paintings: (H) $2,750

HEDA, Gerrit Willemsz
Dutch b. before 1702
paintings: (L) $33,000; (H) $352,000

HEDA, Willem Claesz.
Dutch 1594-c. 1670
paintings: (L) $170,500; (H) $451,000

HEDRICK, Wally
paintings: (H) $1,650

HEEM, Cornelis de
Dutch 1631-1695
paintings: (L) $11,000; (H) $242,000

HEEM, David Davidsz. de
Dutch c. 1610-after 1669
paintings: (L) $22,000; (H) $55,000

HEEM, Jan Davidsz de
Dutch 1606-1684
paintings: (L) $35,200; (H) $6,600,000

HEEMSKERCK, Jacoba van
drawings: (L) $440; (H) $880

HEEMSKERCK, Maarten van
Dutch 1498-1574
paintings: (H) $74,250
drawings: (H) $50,600

HEEMSKERK, Egbert van, the elder
Dutch 1610-1680
paintings: (L) $770; (H) $5,500

HEEMSKERK VAN BEEST, Jacob
Eduard van
Dutch 1828-1894
paintings: (H) $6,600

HEER, Guillaume de
drawings: (H) $3,520

HEEREMANS, Thomas
Dutch c. 1640-1697
paintings: (L) $2,750; (H) $52,800

HEERSCHOP, Hendrik
Flemish c. 1620-1672
paintings: (H) $6,325

HEES, Gustav Adolf van
German b. 1862
paintings: (H) $1,980

HEESAKKER, Thomas
Dutch 20th cent.
paintings: (L) $550; (H) $1,430

HEFFER, Edward A.
British 19th cent.
paintings: (L) $770; (H) $880

HEFFNER, Karl
German 1849-1925
paintings: (L) $165; (H) $33,000

HEGG, Teresa
Swedish 19th/20th cent.
drawings: (H) $770

HEGI, Johann S.
drawings: (H) $4,950

HEGLER, John Jacob
American 1812-1856
paintings: (H) $3,630

HEHIANCHI, J.L.
paintings: (H) $6,050

HEICKE, Joseph
Austrian 1811-1861
paintings: (H) $2,420

HEIDE, Johannes Wilhelm van der
Dutch b. 1878
paintings: (H) $2,750

HEIDEN, John Peter
American
paintings: (H) $2,200

HEIDER, Frank
Scottish early 20th cent.
paintings: (H) $1,650

HEIKKA, Earle E.
American 1910-1941
sculpture: (L) $1,100; (H) $12,000

HEIL, Charles Emile
American 1870-1953
paintings: (L) $220; (H) $880
drawings: (L) $110; (H) $577

HEIL, Daniel van
paintings: (H) $2,860

HEIL, Daniel van
Flemish 1604-1662
paintings: (L) $2,860; (H) $4,400

HEILBUTH, Ferdinand
French 1826-1889
paintings: (L) $440; (H) $22,000
drawings: (L) $1,100; (H) $16,500

HEILMANN, Ernst
paintings: (H) $2,200

HEILMANN, Jean Gaspard
paintings: (H) $4,620

HEILMAYER, Karl
German 1829-1908
paintings: (L) $1,650; (H) $6,050

HEIM, Francois Joseph
drawings: (L) $825; (H) $1,100

HEIMBACH, Wolfgang
German 1613-c. 1678
paintings: (H) $121,000

HEIMERDINGER, Friedrich
paintings: (H) $1,540

HEIMERL, Josef
Austrian 19th/20th cent.
paintings: (L) $825; (H) $935

HEIMHIZER, Marcellus
American
drawings: (H) $2,200

HEIMIG, Walter
German b. 1881
paintings: (H) $2,750

HEIN, Hendrick Jan
Dutch 1822-1866
paintings: (H) $6,050

HEINBERG, A.
paintings: (H) $880

HEINE, A.
German 19th cent.
paintings: (H) $2,420

HEINEFETTER, Johann
German 1815-1902
paintings: (H) $2,750

HEINEMAN, Julie
American 19th/20th cent.
paintings: (H) $5,500

HEINEMANN, Fritz
sculpture: (L) $80; (H) $770

HEINER, Karl
Austrian 20th cent.
paintings: (H) $880

HEINISCH, Karl Adam
German 1847-1927
paintings: (H) $8,250

HEINRICH, Franz
Austrian 1802-1890
paintings: (H) $2,200

HEINS, D.
paintings: (H) $16,500

HEINSBERGEN, Anthony
American 20th cent.
paintings: (L) $165; (H) $990

HEINSIUS, Johann Ernst
German 1740-1812
paintings: (L) $2,420; (H) $3,850

HEINTZ, Joseph, the younger
Swiss c. 1600-c. 1678
paintings: (L) $30,800; (H) $49,500

HEINZ, F.
German(?) 19th cent.
paintings: (H) $1,100

HEINZE, Adolph
American b. 1887
paintings: (L) $286; (H) $770
drawings: (H) $495

HEISCHMANN, Harry G.
American 19th/20th cent.
paintings: (H) $715

HEISEN, Mat
sculpture: (H) $715

HEISKELL
paintings: (H) $3,080

HEISLER, W.O.
paintings: (H) $715

HEISS, Johann
German 1640-1704
paintings: (H) $5,225

HEITER, Michael M.
American b. 1883
paintings: (L) $770; (H) $935

HEITKAMP, Irving
American d. 1917
paintings: (H) $1,320

HEITLAND, Wilmot Emerton
American b. 1893
paintings: (H) $1,320
drawings: (L) $330; (H) $550

HEITMULLER, August
German 1873-1935
paintings: (H) $1,320

HEIZAN
late 19th cent.
paintings: (L) $60,500; (H) $60,500

HEIZER, Michael
American b. 1944
paintings: (L) $4,950; (H) $22,000
drawings: (L) $1,650; (H) $15,400
sculpture: (L) $3,300; (H) $33,000

HEKKING, Joseph Antonio
German/American ac. 1859-1885
paintings: (L) $440; (H) $19,800

HELA, D.
paintings: (H) $990

HELBERGER, Alfred Hermann
German b. 1871
paintings: (H) $3,300

HELBIG, A.
German 19th cent.
paintings: (H) $880

HELCK, Peter
American b. 1893/97
drawings: (L) $110; (H) $4,400

HELD, Al
American b. 1928
paintings: (L) $1,870; (H) $319,000
drawings: (L) $440; (H) $27,500

HELD, John, Jr.
American 1889-1958
drawings: (L) $66; (H) $1,700
sculpture: (H) $4,400

HELDNER, Colette Pope
American 20th cent.
paintings: (L) $247; (H) $2,090

HELDNER, Knute
American 1884/86-1952
paintings: (L) $220; (H) $6,050

HELFFERICH, Willem
Dutch 20th cent.
paintings: (L) $1,760; (H) $3,575

HELIKER, John
American b. 1909/10
paintings: (L) $110; (H) $6,325
drawings: (L) $330; (H) $1,100

HELION, Jean
French b. 1904
paintings: (H) $14,300
drawings: (L) $4,950; (H) $10,725

HELK, Peter
drawings: (L) $357; (H) $2,860

HELLBUSCH, H.
19th/20th cent.
paintings: (H) $2,200

HELLEMANS, Jean Pierre
Belgian 1787-1845
paintings: (H) $7,700

HELLER, Eugenie M.
American 20th cent.
paintings: (L) $990; (H) $4,400

HELLESEN, Thorvald
paintings: (H) $3,500

HELLEU, Paul Cesar
French 1859-1927
paintings: (L) $1,100; (H) $110,000
drawings: (L) $523; (H) $220,000

HELLHOF, Heinrich
German 1868-1914
paintings: (H) $1,760

HELMER, Philipp
German 1846-1912
paintings: (L) $770; (H) $770

HELMICK, Howard
American 1845-1907
paintings: (H) $1,100
drawings: (L) $880; (H) $2,420

HELMONT, Matheus van
Flemish 1623-1674/79
paintings: (L) $9,900; (H) $33,000

HELMONT, Zeger Jacob van
Flemish 1683-1726
paintings: (H) $7,700

HELPS, Francis
English ac. 1910-1940
paintings: (H) $1,320

HELSBY, Alfredo
Chilean ac. c. 1889-1931
paintings: (L) $352; (H) $2,860
drawings: (L) $165; (H) $247

HELST, Bartholomeus van der
Dutch 1613-1670
paintings: (H) $8,250

HELVERDINK, E.A.
Dutch 19th cent.
paintings: (H) $1,760

HELY, Laurent
French early 20th cent.
sculpture: (L) $2,200; (H) $16,500

HEM, Pieter van der
Dutch b. 1885
paintings: (H) $7,700

HEMESSEN, Jan Sanders van
Flemish c. 1504-c. 1566
paintings: (L) $3,025; (H) $29,700

HEMESSEN, Jan van, studio of
ac. 1519-d. after 1566
paintings: (H) $44,000

HEMESSEN, Katharina van
American 1527/28-1587
paintings: (L) $14,300; (H) $14,300

HEMMDIN, Elisabeth
American
drawings: (H) $3,960

HEMMRICH, Georg
paintings: (H) $1,320

HEMSLEY, William
English b. 1819; ac. 1848-1893
paintings: (L) $2,530; (H) $8,250

HEMY, Bernard Benedict
English ac. 1875-1910; d. 1913
paintings: (L) $1,650; (H) $1,925

HEMY, Charles Napier
British 1841-1917
paintings: (L) $2,475; (H) $26,400
drawings: (L) $1,430; (H) $4,400

HENCKE, Albert
American 1865-1936
paintings: (L) $275; (H) $990

HENDERSON, Charles Cooper
English 1803-1877
paintings: (L) $1,210; (H) $18,700
drawings: (L) $495; (H) $2,090

HENDERSON, David English
American 1832-1887
paintings: (H) $935
drawings: (H) $209

HENDERSON, Jack
paintings: (L) $660; (H) $715

HENDERSON, Jacob S.
American
drawings: (H) $1,760

HENDERSON, John
British 1754-1845
paintings: (L) $522; (H) $1,100

HENDERSON, John
British 1860-1924
paintings: (H) $2,090

HENDERSON, John
British late 19th/early 20th cent
paintings: (H) $880

HENDERSON, Joseph Morris
English 1863-1936
paintings: (L) $1,540; (H) $3,850

HENDERSON, W.S.P.
English exhib. 1836-1874
paintings: (L) $605; (H) $2,640

HENDERSON, William
British ac. 1874-1892
paintings: (H) $4,400

HENDERSON, William Penhallow
American 1877-1943
paintings: (H) $220
drawings: (L) $330; (H) $5,280

HENDON, Cham
paintings: (L) $880; (H) $2,200

HENDRICI, John
paintings: (H) $825

HENDRIKS, E.
Dutch 20th cent.
paintings: (H) $1,210

HENDRIKS, Gerardus
Dutch 19th cent.
paintings: (L) $1,210; (H) $11,000

HENDRIKS, W.
Dutch early 20th cent.
paintings: (H) $990

HENDRIKS, Willem
Dutch 1828-1891
paintings: (L) $770; (H) $2,860

HENDRIKS, Willem
Dutch 1863-1941
paintings: (H) $1,760

HENDRIX, Jimi
American 1942-1970
drawings: (L) $3,300; (H) $5,500

HENFELD, Ernie
American contemporary
sculpture: (L) $330; (H) $3,080

HENKE, Bernard
American 1888-1945
paintings: (L) $137; (H) $880

HENKEL, Charles
American
paintings: (H) $19,800

HENLEY, Lionel Charles
British b. 1843
paintings: (L) $2,475; (H) $6,600

HENNAH, Joseph Edward
English b. 1897
paintings: (L) $495; (H) $715

HENNER, Jean Jacques
French 1829-1905
paintings: (L) $330; (H) $28,600
drawings: (L) $880; (H) $990

HENNESSEY, Frank Charles
Canadian 1894-1941
drawings: (H) $1,650

HENNESSY, Patrick
paintings: (L) $900; (H) $1,210

HENNESSY, Richard
contemporary
paintings: (L) $55; (H) $2,750

HENNESSY, William John
Irish/American 1839/40-1917
paintings: (L) $440; (H) $3,850

HENNING, Albin
American c. 1943
paintings: (H) $770

HENNINGS, Ernest Martin
American 1886-1956
paintings: (L) $2,860; (H) $49,500
drawings: (L) $5,500; (H) $18,700

HENNINGSEN, Frants Peter Didrik
Danish 1850-1908
paintings: (H) $4,675
drawings: (H) $990

HENNINGSEN, Henning
Danish 19th/20th cent.
paintings: (H) $990

HENOCQUE, Narcisse
contemporary
paintings: (H) $2,530

HENRI, Andre
French 19th/20th cent.
paintings: (H) $7,700

HENRI, Florence
drawings: (H) $4,950

HENRI, Michel
French 20th cent.
paintings: (L) $192; (H) $1,210

HENRI, Robert
American 1865-1929
paintings: (L) $495; (H) $462,000
drawings: (L) $110; (H) $6,050

HENRICH, A.M.
20th cent.
paintings: (H) $2,420

HENRICI, John H.
American 19th/20th cent.
paintings: (L) $1,430; (H) $3,190

HENRILL, Hermann
American ac. c. 1845
drawings: (H) $4,400

HENRION, Armand
French b. 1875
paintings: (L) $770; (H) $1,210

HENRIOT, Camille
paintings: (H) $3,300

HENRY, Edward Lamson
American 1841-1919
paintings: (L) $550; (H) $192,500
drawings: (L) $110; (H) $4,510

HENRY, Edwin
American 20th cent.
paintings: (H) $900

HENRY, Harry Raymond
American 1882-1974
paintings: (H) $6,600

HENRY, J.
American
drawings: (H) $3,300

HENRY, James Levin
English 1855-c. 1904
drawings: (L) $110; (H) $660

HENRY, Michel
French 19th cent.
paintings: (L) $198; (H) $3,850

HENRY, Paul
Irish 1876-1958
paintings: (L) $3,300; (H) $9,900

HENSCHEL, Paul
Dutch b. 1889
paintings: (H) $1,650

HENSELER, Ernst
German b. 1852
paintings: (H) $19,800

HENSHALL, J.
British ac. 1848-1863
paintings: (H) $6,600

HENSHALL, John Henry
British b. 1856
drawings: (H) $7,700

HENSHAW, F.H.
paintings: (H) $2,475

HENSHAW, Frederick Henry
British 1807-1891
paintings: (L) $412; (H) $2,475
drawings: (H) $880

HENSHAW, Glenn Cooper
American 1881/85-1946
paintings: (L) $1,210; (H) $2,475
drawings: (L) $247; (H) $715

HENSTENBURGH, Herman
Dutch 1667-1726
drawings: (L) $3,300; (H) $39,600

HENTZE, Gudmund
drawings: (H) $1,210

HENWOOD, Thomas
British ac. 1842-1859
paintings: (H) $19,800

HENZELL, Issac
paintings: (H) $660
HEPPLE, Wilson
British 1854-1937
paintings: (H) $1,760
HEPWORTH, Barbara
English 1903-1975
drawings: (H) $44,000
sculpture: (L) $5,280; (H) $132,000
HERBERT, Emile
sculpture: (L) $495; (H) $1,650
HERBERT, Ernest
drawings: (H) $1,540
HERBERT, John Roger
paintings: (H) $1,980
HERBERT, Sidney
paintings: (L) $187; (H) $1,210
HERBERTE, Alfred
English d. 1861
drawings: (H) $880
HERBERTE, Edward Benjamin
English ac. 1860-1893
paintings: (L) $3,300; (H) $20,900
HERBIN, Auguste
French 1882-1960
paintings: (L) $4,950; (H) $319,000
drawings: (L) $2,750; (H) $24,300
HERBO, Fernand
contemporary
paintings: (H) $8,250
HERBO, Leon
Belgian 1850-1907
paintings: (L) $990; (H) $4,950
HERBST, Frank C.
American 20th cent.
paintings: (L) $55; (H) $1,320
drawings: (H) $1,320
HERDMAN, William Gawin
paintings: (H) $4,400
drawings: (H) $528
HERDT, Friedrich Wilhelm
German 1790-1840
paintings: (H) $1,540
HEREAU, Jules
French 1830/39-1879
paintings: (H) $5,060

HERERA, G.
Continental contemporary
paintings: (H) $1,210
HERGENRODER, Emilie
American d. 1925
paintings: (L) $165; (H) $660
HERGESHEIMER, Ella Sophronisba
American 1873-1943
paintings: (L) $770; (H) $1,210
HERIMULLER, Louis
American b. 1863
paintings: (H) $880
HERING, George Edwards
English 1805-1879
paintings: (H) $1,650
HERING, Harry
American 1887-1967
paintings: (L) $150; (H) $1,210
HERING, Henry
American 1874-1949
sculpture: (L) $770; (H) $4,675
HERKELMAN, Henk
Dutch 19th/20th cent.
paintings: (H) $1,210
HERKOMER, Sir Hubert von
German/English 1849-1914
paintings: (L) $248; (H) $418
drawings: (H) $2,420
HERLAND, Emma
French 1856-1947
paintings: (H) $8,800
HERLIN, M.
American 19th cent.
paintings: (H) $880
HERMAN, Roger
paintings: (L) $770; (H) $990
HERMANN, Charles
American
paintings: (H) $2,860
HERMANN, H.
Continental 19th cent.
paintings: (L) $1,760; (H) $2,750
HERMANN, Leo
French b. 1853
paintings: (L) $1,650; (H) $8,800

HERMANN, Ludwig
German 1812-1881
paintings: (L) $660; (H) $29,700

HERMANNS, Heinrich
German 1862-1942
paintings: (L) $550; (H) $3,575
drawings: (H) $1,045

HERMANNSTORFER, Joseph
German 1817-1901
paintings: (H) $2,640

HERMANS, T.(F.?) O.
North European 19th cent.
drawings: (H) $660

HERMANSEN, Olaf August
Danish 1849-1897
paintings: (L) $3,300; (H) $16,500

HERMANT, Beil
American late 19th cent.
sculpture: (H) $6,600

HERMANT, Leon
sculpture: (H) $1,980

HERMIDA, Juan de
paintings: (H) $2,860

HERMS, George
contemporary
sculpture: (L) $605; (H) $2,200

HERNANDEZ, Caesar
American 20th cent.
paintings: (H) $1,210
drawings: (H) $1,650

HERNANDEZ, Daniel
Peruvian 1856-1932
paintings: (L) $4,180; (H) $22,000
drawings: (H) $264

HERNANDEZ, J.
early 20th cent.
paintings: (H) $1,540

HERNANDEZ, Manuel
paintings: (L) $3,850; (H) $4,400

HERNDON, Charles
American contemporary
sculpture: (H) $1,100

HERNY, Bernard Benedict
paintings: (H) $660

HERON, Patrick
English b. 1920
drawings: (H) $660

HERP, Willem van, the elder
Flemish 1614-1677
paintings: (L) $4,400; (H) $24,200

HERPFER, Carl
German 1836-1897
paintings: (L) $3,300; (H) $17,600

HERPIN, Leon Pierre
French 1841-1880
paintings: (H) $3,850
drawings: (L) $275; (H) $1,320

HERR, Laetitia Neff
American b. 1881
paintings: (H) $715

HERREMANS, Lievin
Belgian 1858-1886
paintings: (H) $11,000

HERRENBURG, Johann Andreas
German 1824-1906
paintings: (H) $1,650

HERRERA, Francisco, the younger
Spanish 1622-1685
paintings: (H) $396,000

HERRERA, Velino Shije, Ma Pe We
American Indian b. 1902
paintings: (H) $770

HERRICK, C.K.
American 19th cent.
paintings: (H) $825

HERRICK, Henry W.
American 1824-1906
drawings: (L) $110; (H) $1,320

HERRIMAN, George
drawings: (H) $10,450

HERRING, Benjamin, Jr.
English 1830-1871
paintings: (L) $3,425; (H) $23,100

HERRING, Benjamin, Sr.
English 1806-1830
paintings: (H) $8,250

HERRING, J.F.
paintings: (L) $2,700; (H) $25,300

HERRING, John Frederick, Jr.
British 1815-1907
paintings: (L) $3,300; (H) $63,250
drawings: (H) $1,980

HERRING, John Frederick, Sr.
British 1795-1865
paintings: (L) $1,430; (H) $836,000

HERRING, SR., John Frederick and
James **POLLARD**
British 18th/19th cent.
paintings: (H) $632,500

HERRMANN, Carl Gustav
German b. 1857
paintings: (H) $1,980

HERRMANN, Frank Simon
American 1866-1942
paintings: (H) $935

HERRMANN, Hans
German 1813-1890
paintings: (H) $4,675

HERRMANN, Hans
German 1858-1942
paintings: (L) $1,870; (H) $15,400

HERRMANN, J.
German 19th cent.
paintings: (H) $7,150

HERRMANN, Leo
French 1853-1927
paintings: (H) $1,000

HERRMANN, Willi
Continental 19th cent.
paintings: (H) $1,650

HERRMANN-LEON, Charles
French 1838-1908
paintings: (L) $990; (H) $7,700

HERRMANNSTORFER, J.
German 1817-1901
paintings: (H) $2,475

HERSCH, Lee
American 1896-1953
paintings: (L) $77; (H) $1,980

HERSESHEIMER, Ella S.
American
paintings: (H) $2,200

HERSON, E.
French 19th cent.
paintings: (L) $522; (H) $1,650

HERTEL, Albert
German 1843-1912
paintings: (H) $1,980

HERTER, Adele
American 1869-1946
paintings: (L) $935; (H) $3,190

HERTER, Albert
American 1871-1950
paintings: (L) $935; (H) $99,000
drawings: (L) $1,650; (H) $6,600

HERTERICH
paintings: (H) $1,760

HERVE, Jules
French b. 1887
paintings: (L) $275; (H) $16,500

HERVE-MATHE, Jules Alfred
French b. 1868
drawings: (H) $3,630

HERVIER, A.
paintings: (H) $880

HERVIER, Adolphe
Dutch 1871-1891
drawings: (L) $990; (H) $1,045

HERVIER, Louis Adolphe
French 1818-1879
paintings: (L) $1,650; (H) $1,980

HERWEGEN-MANINI, Veronica
Maria
German b. 1851
paintings: (H) $880

HERZEL, Paul
American b. 1876
sculpture: (L) $99; (H) $20,900

HERZOG, Hermann
German/American 1832-1932
paintings: (L) $880; (H) $66,000
drawings: (L) $121; (H) $275

HESCHLER, David, workshop of
German 17th cent.
sculpture: (H) $44,000

HESKETH
American 20th cent.
sculpture: (H) $1,540

HESS, G.
German 19th cent.
paintings: (H) $1,320

HESS, J.N.
American 19th cent.
paintings: (H) $825

HESS, Sara
American b. 1880
paintings: (L) $38; (H) $1,650

HESSE, Eva
American 1936-1970
paintings: (H) $5,225
drawings: (L) $605; (H) $19,800
sculpture: (L) $5,500; (H) $110,000

HESSE, Hans Meyer von
paintings: (H) $2,310

HESSELIUS, John
American 1728-1778
paintings: (L) $4,400; (H) $44,000

HESTHAL, William Jurgen
American b. 1908
paintings: (H) $935
drawings: (L) $33; (H) $440

HETCHER, E.
English late 19th/early 20th cent
paintings: (H) $1,980

HETSCHER, C.
German 19th cent.
paintings: (H) $687

HETZ, Carl
paintings: (H) $1,980

HETZEL, George
French/American 1826-1906
paintings: (L) $660; (H) $14,300

HEULLANT, Felix Armand
French b. 1834
paintings: (H) $7,480

HEURELMANS
French
sculpture: (H) $1,430

HEURLIN, Magnus Rusty
American 19th/20th cent.
paintings: (H) $33,000

HEUSCH, Jacob de
Dutch 1657-1701
paintings: (L) $3,575; (H) $49,500

HEUSCH, Willem de
Dutch 1638-1692
paintings: (H) $4,675

HEUSER, Carl
German 19th cent.
paintings: (L) $1,650; (H) $3,025

HEUSTIS, Louise Lyons
American b. 1878
paintings: (H) $770

HEUSTON, Frank Zell
American 1880-1966
paintings: (L) $110; (H) $935

HEUTON, E.
paintings: (H) $660

HEUVEL, Theodore Bernard de
Flemish 1817-1906
paintings: (L) $2,640; (H) $6,050

HEVEL, R.
American 19th cent.
paintings: (H) $907

HEWEY, H.
paintings: (H) $880

HEWIT, Mabel A.
American 1903-1987
paintings: (L) $385; (H) $1,800
drawings: (H) $33

HEWITT, John Newton
American 1885-1958
paintings: (H) $1,100

HEY, Paul
French b. 1867
drawings: (H) $1,650

HEYDE, Charles Louis
American
paintings: (H) $3,500

HEYDEN, Jan van der
Dutch 1637-1712
paintings: (L) $16,500; (H) $77,000

HEYDENDAHL, Friedrich Joseph
Nicolai
German 1844-1906
paintings: (L) $1,700; (H) $2,750

HEYER, Arthur
German b. 1872
paintings: (L) $550; (H) $5,500

HEYERMANS, Jean Arnould
Belgian b. 1837
paintings: (L) $330; (H) $3,740

HEYLIGERS, Hendrik
Dutch 1877-1915
paintings: (H) $4,950

HEYM, C.
Continental 19th cent.
paintings: (H) $880

HEYN, August
German b. 1837
paintings: (H) $5,000

HIBBARD, Aldro Thompson
American 1886-1972
paintings: (L) $385; (H) $16,500
drawings: (L) $110; (H) $715

HIBBARD, Frederick Cleveland
American b. 1881
sculpture: (H) $1,540

HIBBARD, Marsh
American 20th cent.
paintings: (H) $2,475

HIBBARD, Mary
paintings: (H) $660

HIBEL, Edna
American b. 1917
paintings: (L) $110; (H) $7,700
drawings: (L) $220; (H) $467

HIBON, J.
paintings: (H) $1,100

HICK, Terrence
American b. 1950
paintings: (L) $2,500; (H) $4,000

HICKS, Edward
American 1780-1849
paintings: (H) $44,000

HICKS, George Edgar
British 1824-1914
paintings: (L) $10,450; (H) $33,000

HICKS, George H.
American 19th/20th cent.
paintings: (H) $1,265

HICKS, Thomas
American 1823-1890
paintings: (L) $990; (H) $297,000

HIDALGO DE CAVIEDES, Hipolito
Spain b. 1902
paintings: (H) $10,450

HIDDEMANN, Friedrich Peter
German 1829-1892
paintings: (L) $9,625; (H) $12,100

HIDER, F.
British 19th cent.
paintings: (L) $1,100; (H) $1,100

HIDER, Frank
19th/20th cent.
paintings: (L) $247; (H) $880

HIEBEL, Helaide
American
drawings: (H) $715

HIEBLOT, E.
paintings: (H) $825

HIER, A. van
Dutch 19th/20th cent.
paintings: (H) $1,650

HIERSCH-MINERBI, Joachim, Van
Hier
Austrian 1834-1903
paintings: (H) $3,520

HIGBY, Wayne
American b. 1943
sculpture: (L) $2,200; (H) $5,280

HIGGENSON, Stephen
drawings: (H) $800

HIGGINS, Eugene
American 1874-1958
paintings: (L) $33; (H) $6,600
drawings: (L) $33; (H) $1,210

HIGGINS, George F.
American ac. 1850-1884
paintings: (L) $44; (H) $3,080

HIGGINS, J.H.
paintings: (H) $1,210

HIGGINS, Victor Eugene
American 1884-1949
paintings: (L) $550; (H) $15,400
drawings: (L) $1,760; (H) $24,750

HIGHMORE, Joseph
English 1692-1780
paintings: (L) $6,600; (H) $10,450

HIGHSTEIN, Jene
contemporary
paintings: (H) $2,420
drawings: (H) $1,100

HIGUERO, Enrique Marin
drawings: (H) $1,100

HILAIRE, Camille
French b. 1916
paintings: (L) $2,530; (H) $20,900
drawings: (H) $1,650

HILAIRE, Hiler
paintings: (H) $1,430

HILAIRE, Jean Baptiste
drawings: (H) $3,960

HILBERT, Georges
French early 20th cent.
sculpture: (L) $1,100; (H) $12,100

HILDEBRANDT, Edouard
German 1818-1869
paintings: (L) $1,650; (H) $2,750
drawings: (L) $715; (H) $3,575

HILDEBRANDT, Fritz
paintings: (H) $6,050

HILDEBRANDT, Howard Logan
American 1872-1958
paintings: (L) $165; (H) $3,850
drawings: (L) $110; (H) $275

HILDITCH, George
paintings: (H) $2,420

HILER, Hilaire
American 1898-1966
paintings: (L) $3,080; (H) $4,180

HILET, T.
19th cent.
paintings: (H) $1,320

HILGART, V.
paintings: (H) $2,420

HILGERS, Carl
German 1818-1890
paintings: (L) $3,080; (H) $5,775

HILL, Albert D.
American ac. 1897-1898
paintings: (L) $1,210; (H) $4,675

HILL, Alice Stewart
American
paintings: (H) $1,210

HILL, Arthur
British 19th cent.
paintings: (H) $2,530

HILL, Arthur Turnbull
American 1868-1929
paintings: (L) $110; (H) $1,540

HILL, Edward
American 1843-1923
paintings: (L) $200; (H) $3,190

HILL, Edward Rufus
American 1851/52-1908
paintings: (L) $385; (H) $1,980

HILL, George Snow
American
paintings: (H) $825

HILL, Howard
American ac. 1860-1870
paintings: (L) $330; (H) $8,250

HILL, J. Henry
American 1839-1922
paintings: (H) $468
drawings: (H) $1,760

HILL, J. Henry
American b. 1870
drawings: (H) $1,870

HILL, J.W.
paintings: (H) $715

HILL, James John
British 1811-1882
paintings: (L) $1,210; (H) $15,400

HILL, John Henry
American 1839-1922
paintings: (L) $1,210; (H) $6,380
drawings: (L) $330; (H) $8,580

HILL, John William
Anglo/American 1812-1879
paintings: (L) $2,750; (H) $10,120
drawings: (L) $357; (H) $9,350

HILL, Mason M.
Continental 19th/20th cent.
paintings: (H) $1,980

HILL, S.H.
British 19th/20th cent.
paintings: (H) $875

HILL, Thomas
American b. England 1929, d. 1908
paintings: (L) $357; (H) $77,000

HILL, Thomas Virgil T.
American 1871-1922
paintings: (H) $2,200

HILLIARD, William Henry
American 1836-1905
paintings: (L) $165; (H) $2,090

HILLINGFORD, Robert Alexander
English 1825-1904
paintings: (L) $1,500; (H) $27,500

HILLINGS, John
American d. 1894
paintings: (H) $38,500

HILLS, Anna Althea
American 1882-1930
paintings: (L) $385; (H) $6,600
drawings: (L) $468; (H) $990

HILLS, Laura Coombs
American 1859-1952
paintings: (H) $9,350
drawings: (L) $55; (H) $45,100

HILLS, Robert
English 1769-1844
drawings: (L) $88; (H) $7,700

HILLSMITH, Fannie
American
paintings: (H) $4,400

HILLYER, David
British ac. 1850-1890
paintings: (H) $1,540

HILLYER, William
British 19th cent.
paintings: (H) $1,430

HILSTON, J.
English 19th cent.
paintings: (H) $1,815

HILT, H.
paintings: (H) $1,980

HILTON, John W.
American b. 1904
paintings: (L) $121; (H) $3,300
drawings: (H) $412

HILTON, William
1786-1839
paintings: (H) $7,700

HILVERDINK, Eduard Alexander
Dutch 1846-1891
paintings: (L) $412; (H) $3,960

HILVERDINK, Johannes
Dutch 1813-1902
paintings: (H) $1,210

HINCKLEY, Thomas H.
American 1813-1896
paintings: (L) $605; (H) $20,900

HINDS, Patrick Swazo, Grey Squirrel
American (Tesuque) b. 1929
paintings: (L) $467; (H) $1,650

HINE, Charles
American 1821-1871
paintings: (H) $1,760

HINES, Frederick
British ac. 1875-1897
paintings: (L) $192; (H) $715
drawings: (L) $165; (H) $1,100

HINES, Jack
drawings: (L) $302; (H) $880

HINES, Theodore
British ac. 1876-1889
paintings: (L) $440; (H) $2,420

HINEU, J.
sculpture: (H) $825

HINGER, Gaylord B.
British 20th cent.
paintings: (H) $1,100

HINGER, H.
American 19th cent.
paintings: (H) $770

HINKLE, Clarence
American 1880-1960
paintings: (L) $550; (H) $14,300
drawings: (L) $248; (H) $3,850

HINKLEY, Thomas Hewer
American 1813-1896
paintings: (H) $6,050

HINMAN, Charles
American b. 1932
paintings: (L) $550; (H) $10,450

HINOTTE
paintings: (H) $2,090

HINSDALE, Richard L.
American
paintings: (H) $15,400

HINTERMEISTER, Henry, "Hy"
American b. 1897
paintings: (L) $550; (H) $8,800
drawings: (H) $77

HINTERREITER, Hans
Swiss b. 1902
paintings: (L) $3,850; (H) $6,050

HINTON, Walter H.
American early 20th cent.
paintings: (H) $1,430
drawings: (H) $66

HINTZE, Johann Ferdinand Julius
German 1849-1877
paintings: (H) $4,400

HIOLIN, Louis Auguste
sculpture: (L) $660; (H) $6,600

HIPPOLYTE-LUCAS, Marie Felix
French 1854-1925
paintings: (L) $7,700; (H) $7,700

HIQUILY, Philippe
French b. 1925
sculpture: (H) $35,200

HIRD, Helen
drawings: (H) $770

HIREMY-HIRSCHL, Adolph
Austrian 1860-1933
paintings: (H) $9,900

HIRRSINGER, J.
German ac. 1906
paintings: (H) $935

HIRSCH, Alphonse
French 1843-1884
paintings: (H) $55,000

HIRSCH, H.E.
19th/20th cent.
sculpture: (H) $962

HIRSCH, Joseph
American 1910-1981
paintings: (L) $132; (H) $24,200
drawings: (L) $550; (H) $1,540

HIRSCH, Stefan
American 1899-1964
paintings: (L) $330; (H) $39,600

HIRSCHBERG, Carl
American 1854-1923
paintings: (L) $137; (H) $16,500

HIRSCHFELD, Al
American b. 1903
drawings: (L) $385; (H) $4,675

HIRSH, Alice
paintings: (L) $550; (H) $715

HIRSHFIELD, Morris
American 1872-1946
paintings: (H) $8,250

HIRST, Claude Raguet
American 1855-1942
paintings: (L) $1,100; (H) $44,000
drawings: (L) $2,090; (H) $14,300

HIRT, Heinrich
German 19th cent.
paintings: (L) $17,600; (H) $38,500

HIRTH DU FRENES, Rudolf
German 1846-1916
paintings: (L) $2,310; (H) $12,100

HISCHINGER
sculpture: (H) $715

HISPANUS, Johannes
ac. 15th/16th cent.
paintings: (H) $66,000

HITCH, Samuel
American 19th cent.
paintings: (H) $1,100

HITCHCOCK, David Howard
American 1861-1943
paintings: (L) $193; (H) $5,225

HITCHCOCK, George
American 1850-1913
paintings: (L) $825; (H) $66,000
drawings: (L) $605; (H) $660

HITCHCOCK, Lucius Wolcott
American 1868-1942
paintings: (L) $467; (H) $3,520
drawings: (H) $880

HITCHENS, Ivon
English b. 1893
paintings: (H) $14,300

HITCHINGS, Henry
American d. 1902
paintings: (H) $1,100
drawings: (L) $165; (H) $605

HITTELL, Charles J.
American 1861-1938
paintings: (H) $990

HITZ, Conrad
Swiss 1798-1866
paintings: (H) $3,300

HIVA, F.
Dutch School 19th cent.
paintings: (H) $1,045

HJORTH, G.R.
paintings: (H) $1,320

HLADIK, Farentisek
Czechoslovakian 1887-1944
paintings: (H) $2,090

HLAVACEK, Anton
Austrian 1842-1926
paintings: (H) $1,650

HLIDDEL, Freda Taylor
American 20th cent.
paintings: (H) $1,320

HOARE, William
paintings: (H) $4,950

HOBAN, Therese
American 19th cent.
paintings: (H) $825

HOBART, Clark
American 1880-1948
paintings: (L) $550; (H) $15,400
drawings: (H) $715

HOBART, Lewis P.
early 20th cent.
drawings: (H) $2,200

HOBBEMA, Meindert
Dutch 1638-1709
paintings: (L) $55,000; (H) $550,000

HOBBS, George Thompson
American b. 1846
paintings: (L) $110; (H) $5,280

HOBBS, Louise Allen
American
sculpture: (L) $770; (H) $1,430

HOBBS, Morris Henry
American b. 1892
drawings: (L) $264; (H) $990

HOBSON, H.E.
paintings: (H) $715

HOBSON-KRAUS, Katherine Thayer
sculpture: (H) $1,100

HOCH, Franz Xavier
German 1869-1916
paintings: (H) $1,430

HOCHMANN, Franz Gustav
German b. 1861
paintings: (L) $1,100; (H) $1,320

HOCHREIN, Lajos Karoly
Hungarian b. 1853
paintings: (H) $1,430

HOCKNEY, David
English b. 1937
paintings: (L) $25,300; (H) $2,200,000
drawings: (L) $3,190; (H) $357,500

HODE, Pierre
French 1889-1942
paintings: (H) $3,850

HODEBERT, Leon Auguste Cesar
French 1852-1914
paintings: (H) $660

HODGDON, Sylvester Phelps
American 1830-1906
paintings: (L) $220; (H) $2,200

HODGES, Frederick W.
paintings: (H) $770

HODGES, W.S.
English 1744-1797
paintings: (H) $4,950

HODGKIN, Eliot
British 20th cent.
drawings: (H) $660

HODGKIN, Howard
English b. 1932
paintings: (L) $60,500; (H) $506,000
drawings: (H) $15,400

HODGSON, John Evan
paintings: (L) $3,500; (H) $8,250

HODGSON, S.
paintings: (H) $770

HODGSON, Sylvester Phelps
American 1830-1906
paintings: (L) $550; (H) $770

HODICKE, Karl Horst
German 20th cent.
paintings: (L) $3,300; (H) $33,000
drawings: (L) $1,100; (H) $1,100

HOEBER, Arthur
American 1854-1915
paintings: (L) $412; (H) $7,425

HOECKER, Paul
German 1854-1910
paintings: (H) $1,650

HOEDRIENG
Continental 19th cent.
paintings: (H) $660

HOEF, Abraham van der, or HOEFF
Dutch ac. 1613-1649
paintings: (L) $4,950; (H) $8,525

HOEFFLER, Adolf
German 1826-1898
paintings: (L) $3,500; (H) $28,600

HOEN, Alfred Georges
French 1869-1954
paintings: (H) $825

HOENIGER, Paul
German 1865-1924
paintings: (L) $6,600; (H) $6,875

HOEPFNER, Franz
paintings: (L) $495; (H) $990

HOERMAN, Carl
paintings: (L) $275; (H) $2,530

HOERMANN, Theodor von
Austrian 1840-1895
paintings: (L) $41,800; (H) $63,250

HOERNER, M.E.
German 19th/20th cent.
paintings: (H) $660

HOERTZ, Frederick J.
American 20th cent.
paintings: (H) $1,045

HOESE, Jean de la
Belgian 1846-1917
paintings: (H) $1,980

HOET, G.
paintings: (H) $1,760

HOETGER, Bernhard
sculpture: (L) $495; (H) $3,000

HOEVENAAR, Jozef
paintings: (H) $5,500

HOEY, Joseph Ignace van
paintings: (H) $3,850

HOFBAUER, Ferdinand
Austrian 1801-1864
paintings: (H) $6,600

HOFEL, Johann Nepomuk
German 1786-1864
paintings: (H) $8,800

HOFER, A.
paintings: (H) $660

HOFER, Heinrich
German 1825-1878
paintings: (L) $4,400; (H) $10,450

HOFER, Karl
German 1878-1956
paintings: (L) $578; (H) $82,500
drawings: (H) $2,860

HOFF, Carl Heinrich
German
paintings: (H) $13,200

HOFF, Carl Hendrich, Sr.
German 1838-1890
paintings: (H) $2,200

HOFF, J.
paintings: (H) $1,100

HOFFBAUER, Charles C.J.
French/American 1875-1957
paintings: (L) $110; (H) $143,000
drawings: (L) $55; (H) $9,350

HOFFMAN, Arnold
American b. 1886
paintings: (L) $55; (H) $1,760

HOFFMAN, Frank B.
American 1888-1958
drawings: (H) $1,980

HOFFMAN, Gustave Adolph
German/American 1869-1945
paintings: (L) $248; (H) $3,500
drawings: (L) $121; (H) $407

HOFFMAN, Irwin D.
American b. 1901
paintings: (L) $522; (H) $660

HOFFMAN, K.
paintings: (H) $1,100

HOFFMAN, Malvina Cornell
American 1887-1966
sculpture: (L) $110; (H) $24,200

HOFFMAN, Murray
American
paintings: (H) $1,430

HOFFMANN, Harry Leslie
American 1874-1966
paintings: (L) $1,210; (H) $1,650
drawings: (H) $330

HOFFMANN, Josef
Austrian 1870-1956
drawings: (L) $1,760; (H) $2,200

HOFFMANN, O.
sculpture: (H) $3,190

HOFFMANN, P.
paintings: (H) $1,760

HOFFMANN, P.
German 19th cent.
paintings: (H) $2,750

Atypical Painting

Charles Hoffbauer (1875-1957) was a Parisian, the son of the leading authority on old Paris. His talent in drawing and painting was nurtured by his father; at age seventeen he began his formal art training at the École des Beaux-Arts. His first exhibition at the Paris Salon, when he was only twenty-three, won him an honorable mention.

By the time Charles Hoffbauer arrived in the United States in 1909, he had already earned an international reputation as one of France's leading academic painters. Hoffbauer spent the next several years traveling between Paris and New York. In 1913 he was commissioned to paint a large military mural for the Confederate Memorial Institute in Richmond, Virginia, but when World War I broke out in 1914, he returned to Paris to enlist as a private in the French infantry. He served as an official war artist.

After the war, Hoffbauer returned to finish the Confederate mural in Richmond and in 1921 was commissioned to paint a mural in the state capitol at Jefferson City, Missouri. Hoffbauer continued to paint murals and paintings, but in 1931, after seeing Walt Disney's *The Three Little Pigs*, he decided he wanted to become an animator. He became friendly with Walt Disney, and in 1939 Hoffbauer and his wife moved to Hollywood. Hoffbauer never became an animator; he continued to paint and also served as a technical advisor for military backgrounds for several movies. In 1953 the Hoffbauers moved to Boston and then settled permanently in Rockport, Massachusetts.

On the Beach was an atypical subject matter for Hoffbauer. It had been bought directly from him at his studio in Paris, and no one other than the consignor's family and friends had seen the painting for thirty years. When the original owner died, the heirs brought the painting to Skinner Galleries for an appraisal. The previous auction record for the artist was $10,000, but because this painting was well-executed, large, and of a desirable subject, it was estimated at $25,000-$35,000. The painting was on the cover of the auction catalog. When the heated bidding was over, *On the Beach* had sold for $143,000. (Charles C. J. Hoffbauer, *On the Beach*, oil on canvas, 25 ¼ x 32 in., Skinner, November 3, 1988, $143,000)

HOFLEHNER, Rudolf
American b. 1916
sculpture: (H) $33,000

HOFLER, Max
Cont. or British 20th cent.
paintings: (H) $1,320

HOFMAN, Pieter
Dutch 1755-1837
paintings: (H) $4,125

HOFMANN, A.
German 19th cent.
paintings: (L) $1,100; (H) $3,850

HOFMANN, Ansen
Scandinavian 19th cent.
paintings: (H) $1,650

HOFMANN, Charles C.
American 1821-1882
paintings: (L) $30,800; (H) $126,500

HOFMANN, E. Ansen
Austrian 19th/20th cent.
paintings: (L) $220; (H) $1,760

HOFMANN, Earl
American 20th cent.
paintings: (L) $880; (H) $2,090
drawings: (L) $110; (H) $220

HOFMANN, Hans
German/American 1880-1966
paintings: (L) $5,500; (H) $715,000
drawings: (L) $440; (H) $66,000

HOFMANN, Heinrich
German 19th cent.
paintings: (L) $770; (H) $1,540

HOFMANN, Ludwig von
drawings: (H) $880

HOFNER, Johann Baptist
German 1832-1913
paintings: (H) $4,400

HOGAN, Jean
paintings: (H) $1,100

HOGARTH, Michael
American 20th cent.
drawings: (H) $3,300

HOGER, R.A.
paintings: (H) $1,320

HOGERS, Jakob
paintings: (H) $3,300

HOGG, George C.
American
paintings: (H) $1,300

HOGGATT, William
paintings: (H) $1,650

HOGGETT, William
British 19th/20th cent.
paintings: (L) $495; (H) $2,750

HOGNER, Nils
American b. 1893
paintings: (H) $1,650

HOGNER, P.R.L.
American 20th cent.
paintings: (H) $2,640

HOGUET, Charles
French 1821-1870
paintings: (L) $4,125; (H) $6,050

HOHALB, Adolf
paintings: (H) $770

HOHANNESIAN, Garabed der
contemporary
paintings: (L) $660; (H) $880

HOHENREIN, L.S.
North European 19th cent.
paintings: (H) $1,980

HOHENSTEIN, Anton
American
paintings: (H) $1,540

HOHNE, W.
German 19th cent.
paintings: (H) $2,420

HOHNSTEDT, Peter L.
American 1872-1957
paintings: (L) $99; (H) $1,100

HOIN, Claude Jean Baptiste
French 1750-1817
paintings: (L) $3,850; (H) $14,300

HOINTEN(?), R.
paintings: (H) $1,100

HOIT, Albert Gallatin
American 1809-1856
paintings: (H) $11,000

HOIT, William B.
paintings: (H) $3,300

HOKUSAI, Katsushika
Japanese 1760-1849
drawings: (H) $55,000

Almshouse Painter

Almshouses, or poorhouses, were homes for the indigent during the nineteenth century. Charles Hofmann (1820-1882) was the first of three artists to specialize in painting views of Pennsylvania almshouses. The other two almshouse painters are John Rasmussen and Louis Mader. Hofmann was born in Germany, emigrated to New York in 1860, and settled in Reading, Pennsylvania. He first worked as a house and sign painter and after 1865 became an itinerant artist. His commissions included painting private farms, such as his view of *Henry Z. Van Reed's Farm and Paper Mill* (Abby Aldrich Rockefeller Art Center, Williamsburg, Virginia) and the *Benjamin Reber Farm* (National Gallery, Washington, D.C.).

From 1865 until his death, Hofmann lived as a vagrant, obtaining commissions when possible and periodically committing himself to the almshouse. His death entry in the pauper's register of the Berks County Almshouse, where Hofmann is buried in an unmarked grave, records the few facts known about his life: "Place of Settlement, none; Occupation, painter; Civil Condition, was never married; Habits, intemperate; and Cause of Pauperism, intemperance." Most of his works were of almshouses, most likely commissioned by the director of the almshouse who is often shown in a cartouche at the bottom center. Despite the appalling real-life conditions, the almshouses Hofmann depicted were bright and cheerful, rendered with minute anecdotal detail. Hofmann's paintings of the almshouses realize higher prices than do those of other scenes. (Charles C. Hofmann, *View of Benjamin Reber Farm, in Lower Heidelberg Township, Berks County, Pennsylvania,* oil on canvas, 25 x 34 ½ in., Sotheby's, January 28, 1988, $30,800)

Painter and Teacher

Hans Hofmann (1880-1966) was born in Germany. When he was sixteen, he invented the electromagnetic comptometer while serving as assistant to the director of public works for the state of Bavaria. At age nineteen, he entered art school and was sent to study in Paris by a wealthy patron. He remained there until 1914, developing friendships with Matisse, Picasso, Braque, and Delaunay, the proponents of Fauvism, Cubism, and Orphism.

In 1915 he opened his own school in Munich and was immediately successful. In the summer of 1930, he was invited to teach at the University of California, Berkeley. A trip the following summer persuaded him to remain, and he settled permanently in the United States. He taught at the Art Students League until he opened the Hans Hofmann School of Fine Art in New York (1933) and Provincetown (1934). From 1930 to 1935 he largely confined his work to drawing, but in the mid 1930s he returned to painting, creating works that were increasingly abstract.

His main focus remained his school; his teaching consisted of summarizing or reinterpreting the work of the great modern artists in the light of his own theory of tensions. He rejected the idea of preliminary preparations to art and insisted upon a spontaneous confrontation of the hand holding the brush with the canvas in front of it. Most of the young painters who were to become Abstract Expressionists were his students, notably Clifford Still and Jackson Pollock. In 1958 he closed his school to concentrate on his own work, but it was not until the 1960s that he realized recognition for his paintings.

Hofmann was a major influence on American painting for almost forty years. During the 1930s he was the champion of Modernism; in the 1940s he established principles that were intrinsic to Abstract Expressionism; and in the 1960s his interest in large areas of intensely saturated color were pivotal to the development of Color Field painting. Hofmann died in 1966, leaving seventy-five paintings to the University of California at Berkeley in gratitude for his first job in America. (Hans Hofmann, *Abstract*, ink drawing, 7 x 12 in., Mystic, February 22, 1990, $990)

HOLBECH, Niels Peter
Danish 1804-1889
paintings: (L) $385; (H) $4,070

HOLBERG, Richard A.
American 1889-1942
paintings: (L) $44; (H) $1,100

HOLBERG, Ruth Langland
American b. 1891
paintings: (L) $33; (H) $1,155
drawings: (L) $11; (H) $88

HOLBERTON, W.
paintings: (L) $1,600; (H) $2,860

HOLCOMB, Alice White
American 19th cent.
paintings: (H) $935

HOLCOMB, Vera
ac. c. 1885
paintings: (H) $1,265

HOLDEN, Albert William
British 1848-1932
paintings: (H) $715

HOLDEN, James Albert
American 19th/20th cent.
paintings: (H) $1,045
drawings: (H) $1,100

HOLDEN, Schuyler
American
paintings: (H) $2,750

HOLDER, Edward Henry
British d. 1917
paintings: (L) $1,045; (H) $2,860

HOLDREDGE, Ransom Gillet
American 1836-1899
paintings: (L) $187; (H) $5,500

HOLE, William Brassey
British 1846-1917
paintings: (H) $1,540

HOLFFERICH, Wilhelm
paintings: (L) $1,650; (H) $2,200

HOLGATE, Edwin Headley
Canadian 1892-1977
paintings: (H) $68,200

HOLIDAY, Gilbert
English 1879-1937
drawings: (L) $4,950; (H) $11,000

HOLIDAY, Henry
drawings: (H) $1,100

HOLINGS, Clark
American 20th cent.
paintings: (H) $6,050

HOLL, Francis Montague, "Frank"
English 1845-1888
paintings: (H) $104,500
drawings: (H) $110

HOLLAENDER, A.
Continental 19th/20th cent.
paintings: (H) $1,900

HOLLAMBY, C.
paintings: (H) $660

HOLLAMS, Florence Mabel
British 1877-1963
paintings: (L) $2,200; (H) $3,300

HOLLAND, Francis Raymond
American 1886-1934
paintings: (L) $440; (H) $11,000

HOLLAND, J.
English ac. 1755
paintings: (L) $770; (H) $770

HOLLAND, James, Jr.
British 1800-1870
paintings: (L) $935; (H) $11,000
drawings: (H) $715

HOLLAND, John
paintings: (H) $2,860

HOLLAND, John, Jr.
English 1830-1886
paintings: (H) $715

HOLLAND, Sir Nathaniel Dance
English 1734-1811
paintings: (L) $24,200; (H) $29,700

HOLLAND, Tom
American b. 1936
paintings: (L) $1,100; (H) $13,200
drawings: (L) $770; (H) $990
sculpture: (L) $880; (H) $3,575

HOLLANDER, Gino
contemporary
paintings: (L) $93; (H) $990

HOLLANDS, Una
paintings: (H) $935

HOLLEN, John E.
American act. 1850-1860
paintings: (L) $750; (H) $2,475

HOLLING, E.
American 19th/20th cent.
paintings: (H) $660

HOLLINGSWORTH, Ruth
British ac. 1906-34
paintings: (H) $1,650

HOLLINGSWORTH, Thomas
English ac. 1857-1885
paintings: (H) $2,750

HOLLIS, C.T.
paintings: (H) $990

HOLLISTER, Antoinette B.
American b. 1873
sculpture: (L) $605; (H) $1,760

HOLLOSY, Simon
paintings: (H) $3,520

HOLLOWAY, Charles
American 1859-1941
paintings: (H) $990
drawings: (L) $143; (H) $187

HOLLOWAY, F***
American 19th cent.
paintings: (H) $5,775

HOLLOWELL, Robert
American
paintings: (H) $660

HOLLYER, Eva
British ac. 1891-1898
paintings: (L) $880; (H) $10,725

HOLLYER, W.P.
American 19th cent.
paintings: (L) $2,750; (H) $3,850

HOLM, Carl Otto
American 1885-1918
paintings: (H) $1,430

HOLM, Just Jean Christian
paintings: (H) $6,600

HOLMBOE, Thorolf
Norwegian 1866-1935
paintings: (L) $660; (H) $1,870

HOLMES, A.C.
Scottish 19th cent.
drawings: (H) $1,320

HOLMES, Basil
English ac. 1844-1850
paintings: (H) $10,450

HOLMES, Ralph
American 1876-1963
paintings: (L) $138; (H) $2,750

HOLMES, Rhoda
British ac. 1881-1882
paintings: (H) $1,980

HOLMES, William Henry
American 1846-1933
drawings: (L) $121; (H) $1,100

HOLSLAG, Edward J.
American 1870-1925
paintings: (L) $495; (H) $935

HOLSOE, Carl Vilhelm
Danish 1863-1935
paintings: (L) $8,250; (H) $27,500

HOLSOE, Eilsa
Danish 19th cent.
paintings: (L) $6,600; (H) $6,875

HOLSOE, Niels
paintings: (H) $1,980

HOLST, Johannes
Continental 1880-1965
paintings: (L) $2,640; (H) $4,675

HOLST, Laurits Bernhard
Danish 1848-1934
paintings: (L) $715; (H) $1,925

HOLSTAYN, Josef
German 20th cent.
paintings: (L) $2,750; (H) $24,200

HOLSTEYN, Pieter, the younger
Dutch 1614-1687
drawings: (L) $7,150; (H) $12,100

HOLT, E.F.
English ac. 1850-1865
paintings: (L) $770; (H) $4,400

HOLT, Geoffrey
American 1882-1977
paintings: (L) $193; (H) $715

HOLTY, Carl Robert
American 1900-1973
paintings: (L) $605; (H) $7,700
drawings: (L) $110; (H) $4,125

HOLUB, Georg
Austrian 1861-1919
paintings: (L) $990; (H) $1,870

HOLYOAKE, Rowland
British 19th cent.
paintings: (H) $1,210

HOLYSTAYN, Josef
Austrian 19th/20th cent.
paintings: (L) $3,080; (H) $6,600

HOLZ, Johann Daniel
German b. 1867
paintings: (H) $880

HOLZER, Jenny
American b. 1950
paintings: (H) $19,800
sculpture: (L) $3,740; (H) $82,500

HOLZER, Joseph
Austrian 1824-1876
paintings: (H) $8,800

HOLZHAUER, Emil Eugen
American b. 1887
paintings: (H) $440
drawings: (H) $2,090

HOMBARY, W.
paintings: (L) $660; (H) $742

HOMER, Winslow
American 1836-1910
paintings: (L) $77,000; (H) $880,000
drawings: (L) $1,980; (H) $770,000

HOMEXT, H.M.
Dutch 19th cent.
drawings: (H) $1,210

HOMITZKY, Peter
paintings: (L) $1,000; (H) $1,100

HOMONNY, Linda de
paintings: (H) $1,200

HOND(?), T.
American 19th cent.
paintings: (H) $1,320

HONDECOETER, Gillis Claesz de
Dutch 1575-1638
paintings: (L) $22,000; (H) $93,500

HONDECOETER, Melchior de
Dutch 1636-1695
paintings: (L) $550; (H) $374,000

HONDIUS, Abraham Danielsz
Dutch c. 1625-1695
paintings: (L) $1,650; (H) $33,000

HONDIUS, Gerrit
Dutch/American 1891-1970
paintings: (L) $55; (H) $1,100
drawings: (L) $28; (H) $264

HONE, Nathaniel
paintings: (L) $3,850; (H) $9,900

HONEGGER, Gotfried
drawings: (H) $462
sculpture: (H) $880

HONIG, Mervin
paintings: (L) $77; (H) $1,320

HONTHORST, Gerrit van
Dutch 1590-1656
paintings: (L) $16,500; (H) $286,000
drawings: (H) $770

HONTHORST, Willem van
Dutch 1594-1666
paintings: (H) $4,620

HOOCH, David de
ac. 1650
paintings: (H) $33,000

HOOCH, Pieter de
Dutch 1629-1681
paintings: (L) $25,300; (H) $275,000

HOOG, Bernard de
Dutch 1867-1943
paintings: (L) $1,650; (H) $23,100
drawings: (L) $110; (H) $200

HOOGSTRATEN, Samuel van
Flemish 1627-1678
paintings: (L) $33,000; (H) $220,000

HOOM, K. van
paintings: (L) $440; (H) $1,045

HOOPER, J. and H. MELVILLE
paintings: (H) $1,430

HOOPER, John Horace
English ac. 1870-1899
paintings: (L) $440; (H) $4,125

HOOPER, William G.
British ac. 1870-1898
paintings: (H) $2,420

HOOPES, Florence Jane
American 1895-1984
paintings: (L) $110; (H) $1,155
drawings: (L) $55; (H) $825

HOORN, Eduard Jacobus van
Dutch 1863-1934
paintings: (L) $1,320; (H) $1,540

HOOVEN, Herbert Nelson
American b. 1897
paintings: (L) $908; (H) $935

Convent Painting

Samuel van Hoogstraten (1627-1678) was a Dutch painter, etcher, poet, director of the mint at Dordrecht, and art theorist. He received his first training as a painter from his father and then became a member of Rembrandt's atelier. As a writer he is best known for his handbook on painting, in which he reports his conversations with fellow students when they were Rembrandt's pupils. Hoogstraten's early paintings were modeled after Rembrandt, but as he matured, he developed his own style. He painted history, genre, portraits, and religious scenes, but he became known for his special interest in problems of perspective and illusionism.

In 1986 a Rhode Island convent was in need of funds to repair its roof and consigned Samuel van Hoogstraten's painting of a courtyard scene to Newport auctioneer Gustave White. The painting far exceeded expectations when it sold for $192,500. (Samuel van Hoogstraten, *Young Man in a Courtyard Reading a Book,* oil on canvas, 94 x 69 in., White, July 30, 1986, $192,500)

HOPE, C.A.W.
paintings: (H) $2,860

HOPE, C.H.
American
paintings: (H) $1,650

HOPE, James
American 1818/19-1892
paintings: (L) $1,320; (H) $9,900

HOPE, Robert
paintings: (H) $3,080

HOPE, Thomas H.
American, b.England d. 1926
paintings: (L) $137; (H) $1,650

HOPFGARTEN, A.
paintings: (L) $4,950; (H) $5,500

HOPKIN, Robert
Scottish/American 1832-1909
paintings: (L) $302; (H) $4,125
drawings: (L) $16; (H) $550

HOPKINS, Arthur
English 1848-1930
paintings: (H) $1,100
drawings: (H) $248

HOPKINS, Betty Lee
American 19th/20th cent.
paintings: (L) $935; (H) $1,045
drawings: (H) $165

HOPKINS, Budd
American b. 1931
paintings: (L) $605; (H) $2,750
drawings: (H) $1,210

HOPKINS, James R.
paintings: (H) $1,210

HOPKINS, Peter
American b. 1911
paintings: (L) $440; (H) $5,500

HOPKINS, Robert
American b. 1934
paintings: (L) $412; (H) $770
drawings: (H) $385

HOPKINS, William H.
English ac. 1853-1890, d. 1892
paintings: (H) $23,100

HOPKINS, William H. and Edmund
HAVELL
British 19th cent.
paintings: (H) $30,800

HOPKINSON, Charles S.
American 1869-1962
paintings: (L) $4,950; (H) $15,400
drawings: (L) $247; (H) $3,520

HOPKINSON, Glen S.
American
paintings: (H) $700

HOPKINSON, Harold
American
paintings: (H) $900

HOPLEY
drawings: (H) $850

HOPPE, Bernard
paintings: (H) $2,150

HOPPE, C.A.W.
German 19th cent.
paintings: (L) $1,320; (H) $2,475

HOPPENBROUWERS, Johannes F.
Dutch 1791-1866
paintings: (H) $880

HOPPER, Edward
American 1882-1967
paintings: (L) $88,000; (H) $2,310,000
drawings: (L) $825; (H) $137,500

HOPPIN, Thomas Frederick
American 1816-1872
paintings: (H) $1,870

HOPPNER, John
British 1758-1810
paintings: (L) $440; (H) $17,600

HORACIO
Mexican b. 1912
paintings: (L) $2,200; (H) $17,600

HORANE, Pierre
paintings: (H) $770

HOREMANS, Jan Josef
paintings: (L) $1,210; (H) $5,500

HOREMANS, Jan Josef, the elder
Flemish 1682-1759
paintings: (L) $4,180; (H) $23,100

HOREMANS, Jan Josef, the younger
Flemish 1714-c. 1790
paintings: (H) $16,500

HOREMANS, Pieter Jacob
Flemish 1700-1776
paintings: (L) $1,540; (H) $4,400

HORLOR, George William
British ac. 1849-1891
paintings: (L) $1,100; (H) $35,750

HORLOR, Joseph
British 19th cent.
paintings: (L) $660; (H) $2,420

HORN, M.
sculpture: (H) $3,630

HORNAK, Ian
American b. 1944
paintings: (H) $935

HORNBY, T.
British 19th cent.
paintings: (H) $3,200

HORNE, Else
American
sculpture: (H) $1,650

HORNEL, E.A.
British 1864-1933
paintings: (H) $4,125

HORNER, G. Christopher
paintings: (H) $13,200

HORNIBROOK, C.F.
paintings: (H) $1,430

HORSCHELT, Theodore
German 1829-1871
paintings: (H) $55,000

HORSEFALL, Robert Bruce
American 1869-1948
paintings: (L) $165; (H) $1,045

HORSFORD, A.J.
American d. 1877
paintings: (H) $880

HORSLEY, John Callcott
British 1817-1903
paintings: (L) $7,700; (H) $22,000

HORSSEN, Winand Bastien van
Dutch b. 1863
paintings: (H) $2,420

HORST, Gerrit Willemsz.
Dutch 1612-1652
paintings: (H) $88,000

HORSTMEIER, Albert
American
paintings: (H) $5,500

HORTER, Earle
American 1881-1940
paintings: (L) $550; (H) $66,000
drawings: (L) $132; (H) $11,000

HORTIG, Hans
paintings: (H) $1,650

HORTON, E.
British 19th cent.
paintings: (L) $77; (H) $1,100

HORTON, William Samuel
American 1865-1936
paintings: (L) $770; (H) $26,400
drawings: (L) $39; (H) $12,100

HORWARTER, Josef Eugen
Austrian 1854-1925
paintings: (L) $468; (H) $935

HORY, Elmyr de
French 20th cent.
paintings: (L) $1,320; (H) $2,200

HOSCHEDE-MONET, Blanche
French 1865-1947
paintings: (H) $12,100

HOSENFELDER, Christian Friedrich
German 1706-1780
paintings: (L) $11,000; (H) $15,400

HOSKINS, Gayle Porter
American 1887-1962
paintings: (L) $242; (H) $4,950
drawings: (L) $247; (H) $357

HOSMER, Harriet
American 1830-1908
sculpture: (H) $18,700

HOSMER, Lawrence F.
American b. 1895
paintings: (H) $1,100

HOTT, Henry
American
drawings: (H) $6,050

HOTTINGER, William A.
American b. 1890
paintings: (H) $880

HOTTOT, Louis
French 1834-1905
sculpture: (L) $550; (H) $1,430

HOUBEN, Henri
Belgian 20th cent.
paintings: (L) $1,650; (H) $1,760

HOUBRAKEN, Arnold
Dutch 17th cent.
paintings: (L) $770; (H) $1,650

HOUDON, F.
sculpture: (H) $2,750

HOUDON, Jean Antoine
French 1741-1828
sculpture: (L) $550; (H) $2,860,000

HOUGH, William
English 19th cent.
drawings: (L) $687; (H) $825

HOUGUE, Jean de la
French 1874-1959
paintings: (H) $1,870

HOUKE, Van der
Dutch
paintings: (L) $495; (H) $1,072

HOULDITCH, John
paintings: (H) $7,700

HOUQUET, Charles
French 19th cent.
paintings: (H) $990

HOURTAL, Henri
paintings: (H) $660

HOUSE, Howard Elmer
American b. 1877
paintings: (H) $935
drawings: (H) $220

HOUSE, Van
paintings: (H) $2,200

HOUSSOT, Louis
French 1824-1890
paintings: (H) $3,520

HOUSSY, F.W.
paintings: (H) $700

HOUSTON, John Adam
Scottish, b.France 1812/13-1884, d.
London
paintings: (L) $605; (H) $1,760

HOUSTON, Ken
English 20th cent.
paintings: (L) $302; (H) $770

HOUSTON, William
American 19th cent.
paintings: (H) $4,400

HOUT, P. In'T, Jr.
paintings: (H) $715

HOUTEN, Gerard van
drawings: (H) $880

HOUTMAN, M***
ac. early 19th cent.
drawings: (H) $9,350

HOUYOUX, Leon
paintings: (L) $440; (H) $1,210

HOVE, Bartholomeus Johannes van
Dutch 1790-1880
paintings: (L) $4,950; (H) $19,800
drawings: (H) $1,760

HOVE, Hubertus van
Dutch 1814-1865
paintings: (L) $132; (H) $2,420

HOVEN, Gottfried von
German 1868-1921
paintings: (H) $770

HOVEN, H. den
paintings: (H) $715

HOVENDEN, H.C.
American 19th cent.
drawings: (H) $1,485

HOVENDEN, Helen Corson
1846-1935
paintings: (H) $3,300

HOVENDEN, Thomas
Irish/American 1840-1895
paintings: (L) $1,500; (H) $17,600
drawings: (L) $1,045; (H) $5,500

HOVENER, Johannes, or Jan
Dutch 20th cent.
paintings: (L) $660; (H) $825

HOVER, Edward
paintings: (H) $4,180

HOVSEPIAN, Leon
American b. 1915
drawings: (L) $231; (H) $1,018

HOW, Kenneth G.
American b. 1883
paintings: (H) $3,520

HOWARD, B.K.
American b. 1872
paintings: (L) $192; (H) $3,410

HOWARD, Bessie J.
American 20th cent.
paintings: (L) $165; (H) $660

HOWARD, Edith Lucile
paintings: (H) $3,520

HOWARD, Hugh Huntington
American 1860-1927
paintings: (L) $38; (H) $1,650
drawings: (L) $55; (H) $275

HOWARD, John Langley
American b. 1902
drawings: (H) $990

HOWARD, Marion
American b. 1883
paintings: (L) $880; (H) $2,970
drawings: (H) $60

HOWARD, W.
paintings: (H) $3,300
drawings: (L) $75; (H) $660

HOWARD, Wil de Vray, Wilhelm
Rudolf Hermann
German b. 1879
paintings: (H) $935

HOWARD, William
paintings: (L) $770; (H) $880

HOWE
American late 19th cent.
paintings: (H) $935

HOWE, of Edinburgh
paintings: (H) $5,500

HOWE, Charles
American
drawings: (H) $3,850

HOWE, James
British 1780-1836
paintings: (H) $14,300

HOWE, Oscar, Mazuha Hokshina
American Indian b. 1915
drawings: (L) $3,080; (H) $4,510

HOWE, William H.
American 1846-1929
paintings: (L) $247; (H) $1,980
drawings: (H) $715

HOWELL
paintings: (L) $143; (H) $715
drawings: (H) $77

HOWELL, Felicie Waldo
American 1897-1968
paintings: (L) $770; (H) $27,500
drawings: (L) $2,310; (H) $17,600

HOWELL, Frank
American 20th cent.
drawings: (H) $770

HOWELL, Raymond
American 20th cent.
paintings: (H) $852

HOWELL, Samuel
paintings: (H) $880

HOWELLS, Alice
American d. 1939
paintings: (H) $1,540
drawings: (H) $110

HOWES, Samuel P.
American 1806-1881
paintings: (H) $2,090

HOWITT, John Newton
American 1885-1958
paintings: (L) $82; (H) $2,640

HOWITT, Samuel
British 1765-1822
drawings: (L) $286; (H) $1,760

HOWLAND, Alfred Cornelius
American 1838-1909
paintings: (L) $440; (H) $4,950

HOWLAND, J.D.
American b. 1843
paintings: (H) $6,050

HOWSE, George
English d. 1860
drawings: (H) $825

HOY, Charles de
paintings: (H) $1,100

HOYD, Thomas
British 19th cent.
drawings: (H) $990

HOYLAND, John
English b. 1934
paintings: (L) $44; (H) $9,900
drawings: (H) $242

HOYOLL, Phillip
German b. 1816
paintings: (L) $385; (H) $1,760

HOYOS, Ana Mercedes
Colombian b. 1942
paintings: (L) $7,700; (H) $27,500

HOYOS, Ricardo Martinez de
Mexican 20th cent.
paintings: (H) $6,050

HOYT, Edith
American b. 1894
paintings: (H) $2,750

HUBACEK, William
American 1866-1958
paintings: (L) $275; (H) $14,300

HUBBARD, C.A.M.
American 19th/20th cent.
paintings: (H) $1,100

HUBBARD, Charles
American 1801-1876
paintings: (L) $577; (H) $1,650

HUBBARD, Charles D.
American 1876-1951
paintings: (L) $220; (H) $660

HUBBARD, Lydia M.B.
American 1849-1911
paintings: (H) $1,980

HUBBARD, Richard William
American 1817-1888
paintings: (L) $550; (H) $4,675

HUBBARD, Whitney Myron
American b. 1875
paintings: (L) $357; (H) $4,180

HUBBELL, Charles H.
American 20th cent.
paintings: (H) $715

HUBBELL, Henry Salem
American 1870-1949
paintings: (L) $330; (H) $6,600

HUBER, E.
Dutch 19th cent.
paintings: (H) $1,430

HUBER, Josef Ignaz
b. 1759
paintings: (H) $1,320

HUBER, Leon
French 1858-1928
paintings: (L) $770; (H) $17,600

HUBERT, A.
Austrian 19th cent.
paintings: (H) $3,740

HUBERT, A.
Continental School 19th cent.
paintings: (H) $770

HUBERT, Laurent
French ac. 1749-died c. 1780
drawings: (H) $792

HUBERT, Leon
French b. 1887
paintings: (H) $1,650

HUBLIN, Emile August
French b. 1830
paintings: (L) $3,850; (H) $18,700

HUBNER, Carl
German 1797-1831
paintings: (H) $11,000

HUBNER, Carl Wilhelm
German 1814-1879
paintings: (L) $1,650; (H) $6,600

HUBNER, Ulrich
German b. 1872
paintings: (H) $2,475

HUCHON, S. (?)
sculpture: (H) $3,025

HUCHTENBURGH, Jan van
Dutch 1647-1733
paintings: (L) $9,900; (H) $17,600

HUCHTHAUSEN, David
American b. 1951
sculpture: (L) $660; (H) $5,720

HUDDLESTONE, Denis Lawler
paintings: (H) $990

HUDLESTON, C.E.
English School late 19th cent.
drawings: (H) $880

HUDSON, Charles Bradford
American 1865-1938/39
paintings: (L) $302; (H) $2,420
drawings: (H) $192

HUDSON, Charles William
American 1871-1943
paintings: (H) $1,650
drawings: (H) $385

HUDSON, Grace Carpenter
American 1865-1937
paintings: (L) $1,760; (H) $56,100
drawings: (L) $330; (H) $1,870

HUDSON, Henry John
British ac. 1910
paintings: (H) $4,950

HUDSON, John Bradley
American 1832-1903
paintings: (L) $165; (H) $467
drawings: (L) $165; (H) $825

HUDSON, R.
paintings: (H) $770

HUDSON, Robert
American b. 1938
paintings: (H) $440
sculpture: (L) $5,500; (H) $8,800

HUDSON, Samuel Adams
American 1813-1894
paintings: (H) $3,520

HUDSON, Thomas
English 1701-1779
paintings: (L) $2,300; (H) $198,000

HUDSON, Thomas Bradford
American 20th cent.
paintings: (H) $2,200

HUDSON, William, Jr.
American b. 1787
paintings: (H) $770

HUEBLER, Douglas
American b. 1924
drawings: (H) $5,500

HUEPPEL, L.
paintings: (H) $770

HUERTAS, Segundo
contemporary
paintings: (L) $412; (H) $687

HUET, Christophe
French d. 1759
paintings: (H) $77,000

HUET, Ernestine
American
paintings: (H) $880

HUET, Francois, called Villiers Huet
French 1772-1813
drawings: (H) $5,225

HUET, Jean Baptiste
French
paintings: (L) $11,000; (H) $19,800
drawings: (L) $660; (H) $23,100

HUET, Jean Baptiste, the elder
French 1745-1811
paintings: (L) $11,000; (H) $34,100
drawings: (L) $2,750; (H) $4,400

HUET, Paul
French 1803-1869
paintings: (H) $1,100
drawings: (H) $308

HUFFEL, Nicolaas Gerhard van
Dutch 1869-1936
paintings: (H) $3,300

HUFFINGTON, John C.
American 1864-1929
paintings: (L) $176; (H) $660
drawings: (H) $176

HUFNAGAL, A.S.
paintings: (H) $1,320

HUGE, J.F.
American 1809-1878
drawings: (L) $10,450; (H) $14,300

HUGENHOLTZ, Arina
Dutch 1848-1934
paintings: (H) $880

HUGENTOBLER, E.J.
American 20th cent.
paintings: (L) $440; (H) $770

HUGGINS, William
British 1820-1884
paintings: (L) $4,620; (H) $24,200

HUGGINS, William John
English 1781-1845
paintings: (L) $3,300; (H) $9,900

HUGGLER, Arnold
Swiss early 20th cent.
sculpture: (H) $2,200

HUGH, Charles Desire
French 19th cent.
paintings: (H) $1,200

HUGH, W.
British 19th cent.
paintings: (H) $3,000

HUGHES, Arthur
British 1832-1915
paintings: (L) $330; (H) $22,000

HUGHES, Daisy Marguerite
American 1883-1968
paintings: (L) $138; (H) $6,600

HUGHES, Edward
British 1832-1908
paintings: (H) $1,650

HUGHES, Edward Robert
English 1851-1914
drawings: (H) $7,150

HUGHES, Edwin
English 19th cent.
paintings: (L) $385; (H) $770

HUGHES, George E.
American b. 1907
paintings: (H) $4,950

HUGHES, George Frederick
British ac. 1873-1879
paintings: (H) $1,430

HUGHES, J.
possibly American 19th cent.
paintings: (H) $17,600

HUGHES, J.T.
Scottish 19th cent.
paintings: (L) $264; (H) $715

HUGHES, John Joseph
British 19th cent.
paintings: (L) $302; (H) $1,760

HUGHES, Lilly Jones
English 19th/20th cent.
paintings: (H) $770

HUGHES, Marilyn
American
drawings: (H) $900

HUGHES, Paul
paintings: (H) $1,045

HUGHES, Stanley C.
American
paintings: (H) $1,450
drawings: (H) $1,500

HUGHES, Talbot
English 1869-1942
paintings: (L) $1,650; (H) $18,700
drawings: (H) $1,870

HUGHES, William
English 1842-1901
paintings: (L) $3,025; (H) $5,280

HUGHTO, Darryl
contemporary
paintings: (H) $5,500

HUGNET, Georges
drawings: (H) $2,420

HUGO, Francois
sculpture: (L) $3,750; (H) $9,500

HUGO, Jean
French b. 1894
paintings: (L) $110; (H) $19,800
drawings: (L) $286; (H) $4,620

HUGO, Victor
French 1802-1885
drawings: (H) $68,200

HUGUET, Victor Pierre
French 1835-1902
paintings: (L) $2,200; (H) $9,900

HUILLIOT, Pierre Nicolas
paintings: (H) $7,700

HUISHAMP, John M.
paintings: (H) $825

HULBERT, Charles Allen
American d. 1939
paintings: (L) $60; (H) $1,870

HULDAH, Cherry Jeffe
American 20th cent.
paintings: (L) $330; (H) $7,150

HULETT, J.G.
American 19th cent.
paintings: (H) $1,300

HULETT, Ralph
American 1915-1974
drawings: (L) $198; (H) $1,210

HULINGS, Clark
American b. 1922
paintings: (L) $12,000; (H) $143,000
drawings: (H) $1,300

HULK, Abraham, Jr.
British ac. 1876-1898
paintings: (L) $385; (H) $3,300
drawings: (H) $44

HULK, Abraham, Sr.
Dutch/English 1813-1897
paintings: (L) $1,650; (H) $6,600

HULK, Hendrik
Dutch 1842-1937
paintings: (L) $825; (H) $3,190

HULK, Johannes Frederik
Dutch 1829-1911
paintings: (L) $2,090; (H) $5,500

HULK, John Frederik
Dutch 1855-1913
paintings: (L) $880; (H) $12,500

HULK, T.
paintings: (H) $660

HULK, William F.
English b. 1852; ac. 1875-1906
paintings: (L) $220; (H) $3,300

HULL, Gregory
paintings: (L) $1,760; (H) $3,300

HULL, John
paintings: (H) $1,100

HULL, Marie
American 1890-1980
paintings: (L) $330; (H) $1,540

HULLETT, J.G.
American 19th cent.
paintings: (H) $900

HULLINGS, Clark
American b. 1922
sculpture: (H) $36,300

HULME, Frederick William
English 1816-1884
paintings: (L) $1,650; (H) $18,700

HULSDONCK, Jacob van
Flemish 1582-1647
paintings: (L) $27,500; (H) $143,000

HULSEBOS, R.
paintings: (H) $825

HULSMANN, H.
American 19th/20th cent.
paintings: (L) $121; (H) $770

HULST, J. van der
Belgian 19th cent.
paintings: (H) $660

HULTBERG, John
American b. 1922
paintings: (L) $440; (H) $880
drawings: (L) $275; (H) $1,045

HUMANN, O. Victor
American
paintings: (L) $165; (H) $660

HUMBLOT, Robert
French 1907-1962
paintings: (L) $495; (H) $9,350

HUMBORG, Adolf
Austrian b. 1847
paintings: (L) $880; (H) $16,500

HUME, Edith
British 19th cent.
paintings: (H) $1,540

HUMES, Ralph Hamilton
sculpture: (H) $2,200

HUMPHREY, Ralph
American b. 1932
paintings: (L) $660; (H) $24,200
sculpture: (H) $7,700

HUMPHREY, Walter Beach
American b. 1892
paintings: (L) $385; (H) $2,530
drawings: (L) $110; (H) $264

HUMPHREYS, Malcolm
American b. 1894
paintings: (H) $1,100
drawings: (H) $25

HUMPHRISS, Charles H.
b. England 1867 d. N.Y.C. 1934/40
sculpture: (L) $605; (H) $28,600

HUMPLIK, Joseph
sculpture: (H) $1,320

HUNAEUS, Andreas Herman
Danish 19th cent.
paintings: (H) $1,100

HUNDERTWASSER, Fritz
STOWASSER
Austrian b. 1928
paintings: (H) $19,800
sculpture: (H) $1,540

HUNLEY, Katherine Jones
American 1883-1964
paintings: (H) $660

HUNT, Bryan
American b. 1947
drawings: (L) $4,950; (H) $14,300
sculpture: (L) $18,700; (H) $126,500

HUNT, C.
British 19th cent.
paintings: (L) $3,850; (H) $6,600

HUNT, Cecil Arthur
English 1873-1965
paintings: (L) $605; (H) $715
drawings: (H) $220

HUNT, Charles
paintings: (L) $550; (H) $11,000

HUNT, Charles
British 1803-1877
paintings: (L) $2,200; (H) $14,850
drawings: (L) $385; (H) $440

HUNT, Charles D.
American 1840-1914
paintings: (L) $413; (H) $2,200
drawings: (L) $110; (H) $495

HUNT, E. Hall
drawings: (H) $1,210

HUNT, Edgar
English 1876-1953
paintings: (L) $4,400; (H) $26,400

HUNT, Edward Aubrey
British 1855-1922
paintings: (L) $440; (H) $5,280
drawings: (L) $165; (H) $605

HUNT, Esther Anna
American 1875-1951
drawings: (L) $330; (H) $2,750

HUNT, Geoff
paintings: (H) $5,390

HUNT, George C.
paintings: (H) $715

HUNT, Lynn Bogue
American 1878-1960
paintings: (L) $220; (H) $9,500
drawings: (L) $1,155; (H) $10,500

HUNT, Maria
British 19th cent.
paintings: (H) $1,650

HUNT, Millson
19th cent.
paintings: (L) $77; (H) $1,430

HUNT, Richard
American b. 1938
drawings: (H) $110
sculpture: (L) $275; (H) $11,000

HUNT, Richard Morris and Daniel
Huntington
American
drawings: (H) $1,210

HUNT, Thomas L.
American 1882-1938
paintings: (L) $330; (H) $35,750

HUNT, W.
American 19th cent.
paintings: (L) $440; (H) $3,190

HUNT, Walter
British 1861-1941
paintings: (L) $14,300; (H) $33,000

HUNT, Wayne Henry, Wolf Robe
Native American b. 1905
paintings: (H) $770

HUNT, William
sculpture: (H) $1,650

HUNT, William
British 19th cent.
paintings: (H) $2,640

HUNT, William Henry
British 1790-1864
paintings: (L) $1,320; (H) $1,980
drawings: (L) $687; (H) $2,200

HUNT, William Holman
British 1827-1910
paintings: (H) $3,300
drawings: (L) $8,800; (H) $17,600

HUNT, William Morris
American 1824-1879
paintings: (L) $330; (H) $33,000
drawings: (L) $275; (H) $6,050

HUNTER, Clementine
American 1887-1988
paintings: (L) $220; (H) $3,850

HUNTER, Colin
Scottish, d. London 1841-1904
paintings: (L) $440; (H) $2,900

HUNTER, Edward
drawings: (H) $770

HUNTER, Frances Tipton
American 1896-1957
paintings: (H) $500
drawings: (L) $412; (H) $1,650

HUNTER, Fred Leo
American 1858-1943
paintings: (L) $303; (H) $1,540
drawings: (L) $121; (H) $247

HUNTER, George Sherwood
British ac. 1882, d. 1920
paintings: (L) $770; (H) $2,200

HUNTER, Harper R.
paintings: (H) $1,320

HUNTER, Isabel
American 1878-1941
paintings: (L) $1,760; (H) $4,400

HUNTER, John Young
British 1874-1955
paintings: (L) $715; (H) $82,500
drawings: (L) $632; (H) $1,100

HUNTER, Lizbeth Clifton
American b. 1868
drawings: (L) $55; (H) $715

HUNTER, Robert
Irish 18th cent.
paintings: (H) $4,400

HUNTER, Robert Douglas
American b. 1928
paintings: (L) $110; (H) $2,310

HUNTINGTON, Anna Vaughn Hyatt
American 1876-1973
sculpture: (L) $990; (H) $110,000

Naive Art

Naive Art is a term applied to painting produced in sophisticated societies but lacking conventional expertise in representational skills. Lacking formal training, naive painters can characteristically fail to render perspective, yet their work retains a vigor and freshness, as well as a powerful sense of creativity, which combine to make it very appealing. Colors are usually bright and the vision childlike or literal-minded. Naive folk art by contemporary artists has become increasingly collectible in recent years.

Clementine Hunter (1887-1988) was a black folk artist who worked most of her life as a field hand and kitchen maid on a cotton plantation in Louisiana. After finding a paintbrush that had been abandoned by a New Orleans artist, she began in 1946 to paint naively stylized scenes of life among black people in the rural south. (Clementine Hunter, *Washday at Melrose*, oil on board, 15 x 30 in., Goldberg, April 28, 1990, $1,320)

HUNTINGTON, Daniel
American 1816-1906
paintings: (L) $220; (H) $5,775
drawings: (H) $880

HUNTINGTON, Dwight W.
American
drawings: (L) $1,100; (H) $3,080

HUNTINGTON, Ellui B.
drawings: (H) $1,210

HUNTINGTON, Margaret Wendell
American 1867-1958
paintings: (H) $1,100

HUNTLEY, R.
British 19th cent.
paintings: (H) $1,870

HUPE, Martial
French 19th/20th cent.
paintings: (H) $6,875

HURD, L. Fred
American 19th cent.
drawings: (L) $110; (H) $1,210

HURD, Peter
American 1904-1984
paintings: (L) $385; (H) $28,600
drawings: (L) $550; (H) $30,250

HURLEY, Edward Timothy
American 1869-1950
paintings: (L) $1,210; (H) $4,510

HURLEY, Wilson
American b. 1924
paintings: (H) $4,125

HURSON, Michael
contemporary
drawings: (H) $2,200

HURT, Louis B.
British 1856-1929
paintings: (L) $1,870; (H) $35,750

HUS, Zultan
paintings: (H) $660

HUSE, Marion
American b. 1896
paintings: (L) $400; (H) $1,650

HUSENETT, A.V.
drawings: (H) $880

HUSER, A.C.
paintings: (H) $3,300

HUSON, Thomas
British 1844-1920
paintings: (H) $2,200

HUSSET, Henri Robert
sculpture: (H) $1,760

HUSTON, William
American 19th cent.
paintings: (H) $3,740
drawings: (L) $110; (H) $275

HUTCHENS, Frank Townsend
American 1869-1937
paintings: (L) $137; (H) $4,950
drawings: (L) $27; (H) $1,200

HUTCHINSON, D.C.
American 1869-1954
paintings: (H) $1,430

HUTCHINSON, Frederick W.
American 1871-1953
paintings: (L) $137; (H) $825

HUTCHINSON, James S.
American 19th cent.
drawings: (H) $1,540

HUTCHINSON, R.
paintings: (H) $2,530

HUTCHISON, Robert Gemmell
British 1855-1936
paintings: (L) $1,210; (H) $9,350

HUTSUM, Jan van
Dutch 1682-1749
paintings: (H) $2,475

HUTTER, Wolfgang
contemporary
drawings: (H) $990

HUTTERSHEIM, E.
paintings: (H) $880

HUTTY, Alfred Herber
American 1877/78-1954
paintings: (H) $770
drawings: (L) $330; (H) $1,430

HUUBRAL, C.A.
Continental School 19th cent.
paintings: (H) $8,800

HUVE, Jean Jacques
French 1742-1808
drawings: (H) $3,300

HUYGENS, Francois Joseph
Belgian 1820-1908
paintings: (L) $770; (H) $3,300

HUYGENS, Leon
paintings: (H) $880

HUYS, Pieter
paintings: (H) $4,620

HUYSMANS, Cornelis
Flemish 1648-1727
paintings: (L) $4,840; (H) $10,450

HUYSMANS, Jacob
Flemish c. 1633-after 1696
paintings: (L) $1,320; (H) $110,000

HUYSMANS, Jan Baptist
Belgian b. 1826
paintings: (H) $3,300

HUYSMANS, Jan Baptist
Flemish 1654-1716
paintings: (H) $3,300

HUYSUM, Jan van
Dutch 1682-1749
paintings: (L) $22,000; (H) $396,000
drawings: (L) $2,250; (H) $10,450

HUYSUM, Justus van, the elder
Dutch 1659-1716
paintings: (L) $2,090; (H) $66,000

HUYSUM, Justus van
Dutch
paintings: (L) $8,800; (H) $13,200

HUZEL
sculpture: (H) $770

HYDE, H.H.
American early 20th cent.
paintings: (H) $660

HYDMAN-VALLIEN, Ulrica
contemporary
sculpture: (H) $715

HYETT, Will J.
American b. 1876
paintings: (H) $990

HYLANDER
paintings: (H) $2,640

HYND, Frederick S.
American b. 1905
paintings: (L) $303; (H) $1,100
drawings: (L) $209; (H) $275

HYNEMAN, Herman N.
American 1859-1907
paintings: (L) $495; (H) $1,650

HYNER, Arend
paintings: (H) $715

HYON, George Louis
French b. 1855
paintings: (L) $1,100; (H) $3,850

HYPPOLITE, Hector
Haitian 1894-1948
paintings: (L) $11,550; (H) $38,500

IACOVLEFF, Alexandre
French 1887-1938
paintings: (L) $2,970; (H) $3,520
drawings: (L) $385; (H) $1,100

IANELLI, Arcangelo
Brazilian b. 1922
paintings: (L) $4,675; (H) $6,600

IANNELLI, Alfonso
American b. 1888
paintings: (L) $275; (H) $1,210
drawings: (L) $165; (H) $2,475

IBBETSON, Julius Caesar
English 1759-1817
paintings: (L) $1,760; (H) $13,200

IBELS, Henri Gabriel
drawings: (L) $605; (H) $3,520

ICART, Louis
French 1888-1950
paintings: (L) $1,100; (H) $99,000
drawings: (L) $275; (H) $9,350

ICAZA, Ernesto
paintings: (L) $3,850; (H) $7,700

IDIGORAS, Louis
American 20th cent.
paintings: (H) $1,320

IFFLAND, Franz
ac. 1885-1915
sculpture: (L) $176; (H) $935

IFOLD, Frederick
British 19th cent.
paintings: (H) $2,640

IGLER, Gustav
Hungarian b. 1842
paintings: (L) $5,720; (H) $28,600

IGNATIEV, Alex
Russian/American b. 1913
paintings: (L) $605; (H) $3,575
drawings: (H) $550

ILLAVA, Karl
American early 20th cent.
sculpture: (H) $1,760

ILLES, Aladar Edvi
paintings: (L) $907; (H) $2,750

ILLIERS, Gaston d'
French b. 1876
sculpture: (L) $242; (H) $2,420

ILSTED, Peter Vilhelm
Danish 1861-1933
paintings: (L) $24,200; (H) $63,250

ILYIN, Peter A.
Russian/American 1887-1958
paintings: (L) $77; (H) $1,045
drawings: (H) $660

IMBAULT, Leonce Edouard
French 1845-1882
paintings: (H) $4,180

IMERGLIA, Paul
paintings: (H) $2,420

IMHOF, Joseph A.
American 1871-1955
paintings: (H) $660
drawings: (L) $110; (H) $4,400

IMMENDORF, Jorg
German b. 1945
paintings: (L) $15,400; (H) $49,500

IMMERMAN, David
American
paintings: (H) $990

IMRE, Greguss
Hungarian d. 1910
paintings: (H) $3,520

INDIA, Bernardino
c. 1528-1590
drawings: (H) $7,150

INDIANA, Robert
American b. 1928
paintings: (L) $6,050; (H) $104,500
drawings: (L) $1,760; (H) $2,970
sculpture: (H) $35,200

INDONI, Filippo
Italian 19th cent.
paintings: (L) $550; (H) $4,950
drawings: (L) $550; (H) $12,100

INDUNO, Domenico
Italian 1815-1878
paintings: (H) $253,000
drawings: (H) $528

INDUNO, Girolamo
Italian 1827-1890
paintings: (L) $16,500; (H) $102,300

INFANTE-ARANA, Francesco
Russian b. 1943
paintings: (H) $35,200

INGANNI, Enrico
Italian 19th cent.
drawings: (H) $1,430

INGEN, Hendrikus Alexander van
Dutch 1846-1920
paintings: (L) $1,320; (H) $2,530

INGEN, Henry van
American 1833-1899
paintings: (H) $3,300

INGERLE, Rudolph F.
American b. 1879
paintings: (L) $275; (H) $2,640

INGERMANN, Keith
paintings: (L) $22; (H) $1,760
drawings: (L) $33; (H) $121

INGHAM, Charles Cromwell
Irish/American 1796-1863
paintings: (L) $577; (H) $1,430

INGLES, Kathleen Beverly Robinson
sculpture: (H) $1,540

INGLIS, John J.
Irish/American 1867-1946
paintings: (L) $330; (H) $1,760

INGMAN, Lucie
Danish 19th cent.
paintings: (H) $4,400

INGRAM, Walter Rowlands
sculpture: (H) $6,600

INGRAM, William Ayerst
English 1855-1913
paintings: (L) $990; (H) $1,265
drawings: (H) $165

INGRE, Maurice
paintings: (L) $2,530; (H) $8,800

INGRES, Jean Auguste Dominique
French 1780-1867
paintings: (H) $1,430,000
drawings: (L) $1,430; (H) $286,000

INJALBERT, Jean Antoine
sculpture: (L) $550; (H) $1,925

INMAN, Henry
American 1801-1846
paintings: (L) $523; (H) $2,860

INMAN, Jerry
American
drawings: (H) $1,000

INMAN, John O'Brien
American 1828-1896
paintings: (L) $330; (H) $11,000

INNERST, Mark
American b. 1957
paintings: (H) $35,750
drawings: (H) $10,450

INNESS, George
paintings: (H) $6,600

INNESS, George
American 1825-1894
paintings: (L) $605; (H) $935,000
drawings: (H) $1,320

INNESS, George, Jr.
American 1853-1926
paintings: (L) $440; (H) $12,100
drawings: (L) $1,320; (H) $1,870

INNOCENT, Frank
French 20th cent.
paintings: (H) $770

INNOCENTI
paintings: (L) $1,210; (H) $2,640

INNOCENTI, Camilio
Italian b. 1861
paintings: (L) $935; (H) $7,150
drawings: (H) $1,320

INNOCENTI, Gugliemo
Italian 19th cent.
paintings: (L) $192; (H) $7,700

INOKUMA, Genichiro
paintings: (H) $2,200

INSLEY, Albert
American 1842-1937
paintings: (L) $330; (H) $6,600
drawings: (L) $220; (H) $1,100

INSLEY, Will
contemporary
paintings: (L) $220; (H) $352
drawings: (L) $2,640; (H) $3,520

INUKAI, Kyohei
American b. 1913
paintings: (L) $495; (H) $18,700

IPCAR, Dahlov
American b. 1917
paintings: (H) $2,200
drawings: (H) $1,210

IPOUSTEGUY, Jean
French b. 1920
sculpture: (L) $4,400; (H) $31,900

IPSEN, Ernest L.
American 1869-1951
paintings: (L) $330; (H) $11,000
drawings: (L) $77; (H) $165

IPSEN, Kent
American b. 1933
sculpture: (H) $990

IRARRAZABAL, Mario
sculpture: (H) $4,400

IRELAND, Edouard A.
German 1830-1896
paintings: (H) $990

IRELAND, LeRoy
Italian 1889-1970
paintings: (L) $250; (H) $1,320

IRELAND, T. (or J.)
British ac. 1870s-1900
paintings: (L) $418; (H) $935
sculpture: (H) $935

IRELAND, Taylor
English 19th/20th cent.
drawings: (H) $1,045

IRIARTE
Colombian b. 1920
paintings: (H) $16,500

IROLLI, Vincenzo
Italian 1860-c. 1937/42
paintings: (L) $770; (H) $88,000
drawings: (L) $302; (H) $8,800

IRVINE, Sadie
ac. 20th cent.
paintings: (H) $1,760
drawings: (L) $302; (H) $660

IRVINE, Wilson Henry
American 1869-1936
paintings: (L) $880; (H) $52,800
drawings: (L) $275; (H) $2,200

IRVING, I.
paintings: (H) $715

IRVING, Jeanette Bowman
20th cent.
paintings: (H) $825

IRVING, John Beaufain
American 1826-1877
paintings: (L) $247; (H) $3,080

IRWIN, Robert
American b. 1928
paintings: (L) $14,300; (H) $198,000
sculpture: (L) $52,800; (H) $93,500

IRWIN, William Hyde
American b. 1903
paintings: (H) $1,210

ISAAKS, ***
paintings: (H) $5,500

ISABEY, Jean Baptiste
French 1767-1855
drawings: (L) $770; (H) $1,760

ISABEY, Louis Gabriel Eugene
French 1803-1886
paintings: (L) $1,000; (H) $27,500
drawings: (L) $770; (H) $1,980

ISAILOFF, Alexandre
French b. 1869
paintings: (H) $2,750

ISENBART, Marie Victor Emile
French 1846-1921
paintings: (L) $825; (H) $16,500

ISENBRANT, Adriaen
Flemish c. 1490-1551
paintings: (L) $99,000; (H) $170,500

ISENBURGER, Eric
American b. 1902
paintings: (L) $550; (H) $3,300

ISENDYCK, Anton van
Belgian 1801-1875
paintings: (L) $1,430; (H) $1,870

ISER(?)
paintings: (H) $880

ISHIKAWA, Kinichiro
drawings: (H) $797

ISOLA, Giancarlo
Brazilian b. 1924
paintings: (L) $330; (H) $4,620

ISOLA, Giancarlo
Italian b. 1927
paintings: (H) $825

ISRAEL, Daniel
Austrian 1859-1901
paintings: (L) $880; (H) $8,800

ISRAELS, Isaac
Dutch 1865-1934
paintings: (L) $1,980; (H) $104,500

ISRAELS, Joseph
Dutch 1824-1911
paintings: (L) $165; (H) $46,200
drawings: (L) $550; (H) $7,150

ISSELSTEYN, Adrianus van
d. 1684
paintings: (H) $9,900

ISSUPOFF, Alessio
Russian/Italian 1889-1957
paintings: (L) $1,100; (H) $4,400
drawings: (H) $385

ISTRATI, Alexander
contemporary
paintings: (L) $1,045; (H) $2,090

ISTVANFFY, Gabrielle Rainer
Hungarian b. 1857
paintings: (H) $770

ITAMI, Michi
paintings: (H) $4,400

ITAYA, Foussa
Japanese b. 1919
paintings: (L) $220; (H) $2,750

ITO, Miyoko
American b. 1918
drawings: (H) $1,045

IVANOFF, Alexander Andreievitch
Russian 1806-1858
paintings: (H) $7,150

IVANOFF, Nicolai
Russian b. 1853
paintings: (H) $1,870

IVANOVITCH, Paul
Austrian b. 1859
paintings: (H) $8,800

IVANOWSKI, Sigismund de
Russian/American 1875-1944
paintings: (L) $110; (H) $6,050
drawings: (H) $302

IVANYI-GRUNWALD, Bela
Hungarian 1867-1940
paintings: (L) $2,750; (H) $3,300
drawings: (L) $137; (H) $300

IVES, Chauncey Bradley
American 1810/12-1894
sculpture: (L) $4,400; (H) $88,000

IVES, Percy
American 1864-1928
paintings: (L) $55; (H) $1,870

IVESTER-LLOYD, Thomas
British 1873-1942
drawings: (H) $6,600

IVONYI-GRUNWALD, Beld
paintings: (H) $1,320

IZART, M.A.
paintings: (H) $3,300
IZQUIERDO, Maria
Mexican b. 1908
paintings: (L) $5,775; (H) $99,000
drawings: (L) $8,250; (H) $55,000
JAARIMA, H.A.
Dutch 20th cent.
paintings: (H) $1,210
JABONCAN, E.G.
paintings: (H) $2,640
JACK, Richard
paintings: (L) $440; (H) $3,300
JACKEL, M**
Austrian 19th cent.
paintings: (H) $1,760
JACKMAN, Oscar Theodore
American 1878-1940
paintings: (L) $825; (H) $1,650
JACKMAN, Reva
American 1892-1966
paintings: (L) $358; (H) $4,950
JACKMAN, Theodore
paintings: (H) $770
JACKSON, Alexander Young
Canadian b. 1882
paintings: (L) $3,300; (H) $363,000
JACKSON, Annie Hurlburt
American 1877-d. c. 1960
drawings: (L) $880; (H) $2,640
JACKSON, Billy Morrow
American 20th cent.
paintings: (H) $1,650
JACKSON, Diana
American b. 1944
paintings: (L) $450; (H) $775
JACKSON, Elbert McGran
American 1896-1962
paintings: (L) $2,300; (H) $4,400
JACKSON, George
paintings: (H) $4,950
JACKSON, Harry
American b. 1924
paintings: (H) $880
drawings: (H) $715
sculpture: (L) $1,980; (H) $154,000

JACKSON, J.
paintings: (H) $1,540
JACKSON, James R.
paintings: (H) $5,720
JACKSON, John
English 1778-1831
paintings: (H) $1,650
drawings: (H) $165
JACKSON, Lee
American b. 1909
paintings: (L) $330; (H) $3,520
JACKSON, Louise W.
American 19th/20th cent.
drawings: (L) $220; (H) $660
JACKSON, Martin
American 1871-1955
paintings: (L) $198; (H) $1,045
JACKSON, Suzanne
paintings: (H) $1,650
JACKSON, W.
paintings: (H) $880
JACOB, Alexandre
French b. 1876
paintings: (L) $110; (H) $990
JACOB, Betty
American contemporary
sculpture: (L) $1,100; (H) $1,650
JACOB, Max
French 1876-1944
paintings: (H) $8,250
drawings: (L) $330; (H) $2,530
JACOB, Ned
American b. 1938
paintings: (H) $7,500
drawings: (H) $3,080
JACOB, R.
American
paintings: (H) $850
JACOBI, J.C.
paintings: (H) $33,000
JACOBI, Marcus
paintings: (H) $1,320
JACOBI, Otto Reinhold
Canadian 1812-1901
paintings: (H) $29,700

JACOBI, Rudolph
American b. 1889
paintings: (H) $1,045
drawings: (L) $110; (H) $330

JACOBS, Adolphe
Belgian ac. 1887-1910
paintings: (H) $52,250

JACOBS, Emil
paintings: (H) $7,150

JACOBS, F.
paintings: (H) $4,400

JACOBS, Francois
French 19th/20th cent.
paintings: (L) $4,400; (H) $8,250

JACOBS, Franz
Dutch 19th cent.
paintings: (H) $1,650

JACOBS, Henry
sculpture: (H) $1,430

JACOBS, M.
American
paintings: (H) $1,650

JACOBS, Michel
American 1877-1958
paintings: (H) $2,200

JACOBS, N.S.
drawings: (H) $1,210

JACOBS, Paul Emil
German 1802-1866
paintings: (H) $5,775

JACOBS, R.
paintings: (H) $660

JACOBSEN, Albert
American 20th cent.
drawings: (H) $1,045

JACOBSEN, Antonio
American 1850-1921
paintings: (L) $1,100; (H) $49,500

JACOBSEN, Sophus
Norwegian 1833-1912
paintings: (L) $2,310; (H) $16,500

JACOBSON
drawings: (L) $66; (H) $825

JACOBUS, C.
paintings: (H) $6,875

JACOBUSZ
Continental 19th cent.
paintings: (H) $3,300

JACOMIN, Alfred Louis Vigny
French 1842-c. 1913
paintings: (L) $2,200; (H) $4,400

JACOPIN, Achille Emille
French 1874-?
sculpture: (H) $3,300

JACOPO DI CIONE
Italian 1308-1394
paintings: (H) $330,000

JACOULET, Paul
b. Japan, French 1902-1960
drawings: (L) $9,350; (H) $23,100

JACOVLEFF, Alexandre
French 1887-1938
paintings: (L) $495; (H) $1,320

JACQUAND, Claude
French 1804-1878
paintings: (H) $770

JACQUART, Lucie
contemporary
paintings: (H) $3,850

JACQUE, Charles Emile
French 1813-1894
paintings: (L) $550; (H) $68,200
drawings: (L) $330; (H) $4,400

JACQUE, Charles Emile and Louis
Remy MATIFAS
French 19th cent.
paintings: (H) $28,600

JACQUEMART, Andre
sculpture: (H) $2,420

JACQUEMART, Henri Alfred Marie
French 1824-1896
sculpture: (L) $385; (H) $5,225

JACQUEMART, Nelie Barbe
Hyacinthe, b. ANDRE
French 1841-1912
paintings: (H) $4,950

JACQUEMON, Pierre
contemporary
paintings: (H) $1,100
drawings: (H) $88

JACQUES, Emil
paintings: (L) $220; (H) $3,960

JACQUES, Maurice
paintings: (H) $880

JACQUET
French
sculpture: (H) $2,090

JACQUET, Alain
paintings: (H) $6,050

JACQUET, C.
French 19th cent.
paintings: (H) $3,850

JACQUET, Gustave Jean
French 1846-1909
paintings: (L) $1,870; (H) $30,800
drawings: (L) $275; (H) $4,400

JACQUET, Henry Leon
French b. 1856
drawings: (L) $137; (H) $1,925

JACQUET, Maurice
French b. 1877
paintings: (H) $1,540

JACQUETTE, Yvonne
American b. 1934
paintings: (L) $1,980; (H) $10,450
drawings: (L) $275; (H) $4,400

JACQUIN, F.
French 19th cent.
paintings: (H) $990

JACQUIN, Victorine
ac. 19th cent.
drawings: (H) $5,280

JACQUOT Y GARCIA
paintings: (H) $1,980

JADIN, Louis Godefroy
French 1805-1882
paintings: (H) $68,200

JAEGER
sculpture: (H) $1,100

JAEGER
German b. 1880
sculpture: (H) $825

JAEGER, Gotthilf
German b. 1871
sculpture: (H) $2,200

JAENISCH, Hans
contemporary
paintings: (L) $198; (H) $16,500

JAENSON, Charles
sculpture: (H) $2,420

JAGET, Paul Leon
French 19th cent.
paintings: (H) $715

JAGGER, Charles Sargeant
British 1855-1934
sculpture: (H) $6,600

JAHN, Adolf
German
sculpture: (L) $990; (H) $3,520

JAHN, Louis
German 1839-1911
paintings: (L) $770; (H) $1,210

JAKI, Bunsai
paintings: (H) $1,760

JAKOBS, Paul Emil
German 1802-1866
paintings: (H) $88,000

JAKOBSEN, Katherine
American b. 1952
paintings: (H) $6,600

JAMAR, Armand
paintings: (H) $660

JAMBOR, Louis
Hungarian/American 1884-1955
paintings: (L) $450; (H) $27,500

JAMES, A.
paintings: (H) $1,540

JAMES, Alice Archer Sewall
American 1870-1955
paintings: (L) $220; (H) $935

JAMES, David
English ac. 1881-1898
paintings: (L) $1,550; (H) $9,350

JAMES, Durno
English 1752-1795
paintings: (H) $2,200

JAMES, Frank
paintings: (H) $7,700

JAMES, Frederick
American 1845-1907
paintings: (H) $5,775
drawings: (H) $1,430

JAMES, H.
paintings: (H) $900

JAMES, John Seymore
paintings: (H) $1,540

JAMES, John Wells
American b. 1873
paintings: (L) $220; (H) $770

JAMES, Lydia P.
American
drawings: (H) $1,100

JAMES, Roy Walter
American b. 1897
paintings: (L) $357; (H) $2,750

JAMES, Will
American 1892-1942
drawings: (L) $175; (H) $1,540

JAMES, William
American b. 1882
paintings: (L) $24,200; (H) $110,000

JAMES, William
English ac. 1761-1771
paintings: (L) $25,000; (H) $110,000

JAMESON, Middleton
British d. 1919
paintings: (H) $19,800

JAMESON, T.S.
English 19th cent.
paintings: (H) $1,045

JAMIESON, Alexander
Scottish 1873-1937
paintings: (L) $1,100; (H) $1,210

JAMIESON, Mitchell
American b. 1915
paintings: (L) $110; (H) $1,045

JAMISON, Philip
American b. 1925
drawings: (L) $440; (H) $3,575

JAN, Elvire
Belgian b. 1904
paintings: (L) $302; (H) $1,870

JANAK, Frantisek
contemporary
sculpture: (H) $2,420

JANCE, Paul Claude
French b. 1840
paintings: (L) $577; (H) $9,000

JANCK, Angelo
German 1868-1956
paintings: (L) $825; (H) $6,050

JANCO, Marcel
Israeli b. 1895
paintings: (L) $2,090; (H) $39,600
drawings: (L) $1,200; (H) $1,980

JANECEK, Ota
Czeckoslovakian b. 1919
paintings: (H) $660

JANECKI-TEYRAL, Hazel
American b. 1918
paintings: (H) $935

JANENSCH, Gerhard Adolf
sculpture: (L) $770; (H) $935

JANESCH, Albert
Austrian b. 1889
paintings: (L) $880; (H) $5,280

JANIN, Charles
French 20th cent.
paintings: (L) $1,100; (H) $1,760

JANIN, Jean
French 1898-1970
paintings: (H) $880

JANK, Angelo
paintings: (H) $2,750

JANKOWSKI, Cheslas Bois De
Polish c. 1879
paintings: (H) $13,200

JANKOWSKI, F. Wilhelm
Austrian 19th cent.
paintings: (H) $2,200

JANNECK, Franz Christoph
Austrian 1703-1761
paintings: (L) $1,430; (H) $77,000

JANNSON, Alfred
Swedish/American 1863-1931
paintings: (L) $1,650; (H) $2,750

JANOUSEK, Frantisek
paintings: (L) $2,530; (H) $3,300

JANSE, Felix
French 19th/20th cent.
paintings: (H) $22,000

JANSEM, Jean
Armenian/French b. 1920
paintings: (L) $605; (H) $82,500
drawings: (L) $990; (H) $2,640

JANSEN, A.
paintings: (H) $770

JANSEN, Alfred J.
Belgian ca. 1910
paintings: (L) $550; (H) $1,500

JANSEN, Charles
Dutch 19th cent.
paintings: (H) $11,000

JANSEN, Jean
paintings: (H) $660

JANSEN, Joseph
German 1829-1905
paintings: (L) $1,210; (H) $11,000

JANSEN, Willem George Frederick
Dutch 1871-1949
paintings: (L) $33; (H) $2,200

JANSSEN, Gerhard
German b. 1863
paintings: (H) $1,100

JANSSENS, Cornelis
Dutch 1593-1664
paintings: (H) $12,100

JANSSENS, Hieronymous
1624-1693
paintings: (L) $15,400; (H) $28,600

JANSSENS, Jozef Marie Louis
Belgian 1854-1930
paintings: (H) $1,980

JANSSENS, Victor
German 1807-1845
paintings: (L) $4,400; (H) $4,840

JANSSENS VAN CEULEN, Cornelis
Dutch 1593-1664
paintings: (L) $13,200; (H) $41,800

JANSSENS VAN NUYSSEN,
Abraham
paintings: (H) $12,100

JANSSON, Alfred
Swedish/American 1863-1931
paintings: (L) $22; (H) $4,675

JANTZEN, Hans Henrik
Danish 1857-1897
paintings: (H) $1,320

JAPY, Louis Aime
French 1840-1916
paintings: (L) $990; (H) $8,800

JAQUEMIN
paintings: (H) $1,320

JAQUES, Francis Lee
American b. 1887
paintings: (L) $1,210; (H) $5,500

JARDIN, Du
paintings: (L) $176; (H) $880

JARDINE, William
drawings: (L) $1,760; (H) $5,225

JARDINES, Jose Maria
Spanish b. 1862
paintings: (L) $220; (H) $12,100

JARGETH
French 20th cent.
paintings: (H) $660

JAROCKI, Wladyslaw
Polish b. 1879
paintings: (L) $1,485; (H) $1,540

JARVIS, George
British 19th/20th cent.
paintings: (H) $3,025

JARVIS, John
American contemporary
drawings: (H) $3,000

JARVIS, John Wesley
American 1780-1839/40
paintings: (L) $528; (H) $71,500
drawings: (L) $528; (H) $880

JARVIS, W. Frederick
American 20th cent.
paintings: (L) $275; (H) $880

JASHIGGAK(?), V.
paintings: (H) $715

JASZAY, Jozsef
Hungarian 19th cent.
paintings: (L) $1,430; (H) $1,485

JAUDON, Valerie
American b. 1945
paintings: (L) $1,650; (H) $41,800
drawings: (H) $2,420

JAULMES, G.L.
paintings: (H) $770

Florida Auction

Headlines each season announce record-breaking prices for paintings sold in New York, but there are many other auctions held each year throughout the country. They range from informal country-style auctions to fine art auctions with elaborate catalogs. Some are estate auctions with mixed offerings.

In the winter of 1990, the Arthur James Gallery in Delray Beach, Florida, was consigned an estate. When the ads promoting the sale ran in *The Maine Antique Digest* and *The Newtown Bee*, the auction house received numerous inquiries regarding an oil by Jean Jansem (b. 1920). Jansem is a French painter of Armenian origin who studied in France at the École des Arts Decoratifs and first made a living by executing humorous drawings and movie posters. During the 1950s and 1960s, his work consisted primarily of realistic depictions of the poor and unfortunate. The painting of street urchins is representational of his *oeuvre*. Jansem has exhibited internationally and has received numerous awards for his work. (Jean Jansem, *Street Urchins*, oil on canvas, 45 ⅝ x 32 in., Arthur James, February 22, 1990, $55,000)

JAULMES, Gustave
contemporary
paintings: (H) $1,100

JAVIER, Maximino
Mexican contemporary
drawings: (L) $198; (H) $2,200

JAWLENSKY, Alexej von
German 1864-1941
paintings: (L) $20,900; (H) $748,000
drawings: (L) $3,575; (H) $52,250

JAWLENSKY, Andreas
paintings: (H) $1,980

JEAN, Edmund Francois Aman
French 1860-1935/1936
paintings: (H) $1,650

JEAN, Eugene
Haitian b. 1950
paintings: (H) $1,650

JEAN, Herve
Haitian 20th cent.
paintings: (H) $660

JEAN, J.
French 19th cent.
paintings: (H) $990

JEAN, Joseph Baptiste
20th cent.
paintings: (H) $715

JEAN, Marcel
drawings: (L) $358; (H) $2,420

JEANMOUGIN, Alfred Pierre Joseph
French 19th cent.
paintings: (H) $6,600

JEANNIN, Georges
French 1841-1925
paintings: (L) $2,200; (H) $3,850
drawings: (H) $352

JEANNIOT, Pierre Georges
French 1848-1934
paintings: (L) $1,870; (H) $8,800

JEANRON
French b. 19th cent.
paintings: (H) $770

JEAURAT DE BERTRY, Nicholas
Henry
French 1728-1796
paintings: (H) $2,640

JEBLUM, F.B.
American School 19th cent.
paintings: (H) $1,650

JEDIEY, Raoul Lamour
sculpture: (H) $1,100

JEFFERY, Dick
20th cent.
paintings: (H) $1,980

JELINEK, Rudolph
Austrian 19th/20th cent.
paintings: (L) $275; (H) $3,300

JELINEK, Vladimir
contemporary
sculpture: (H) $660

JELLINCK
paintings: (H) $1,650

JENKENS, Wilfred
paintings: (H) $1,210

JENKINS
American 19th cent.
paintings: (H) $935

JENKINS, F. Lynn
1870-1929
sculpture: (H) $1,045

JENKINS, George Henry
English 19th cent.
paintings: (L) $495; (H) $880
drawings: (H) $330

JENKINS, Paul
American b. 1923
paintings: (L) $1,400; (H) $55,000
drawings: (L) $440; (H) $9,350

JENKINS, Winfred
paintings: (L) $330; (H) $715

JENNEWEIN, Carl Paul
American 1890-1978
sculpture: (L) $11,000; (H) $11,000

JENNEY, Neil
American b. 1945
paintings: (L) $18,700; (H) $308,000
sculpture: (H) $4,180

JENNINGS, Jonathan
19th cent.
drawings: (H) $14,300

JENNINGS-BROWN, H.W.
British 19th cent.
paintings: (H) $22,000

JENNY, Heinrich
paintings: (H) $1,100

JENNYS, William
American ac. 1795-1810
paintings: (L) $990; (H) $12,100

JENS, Heinrich Engelbert Reynt
Dutch 1817-1878
paintings: (H) $1,800

JENSEM, Jean
contemporary
drawings: (H) $1,430

JENSEN, Alfred
American 1903-1981
paintings: (L) $2,750; (H) $77,000

JENSEN, Axel P.
Danish 1885-1972
paintings: (H) $880

JENSEN, Bill
American b. 1945
paintings: (L) $2,640; (H) $38,500
drawings: (H) $3,520

JENSEN, C. Hornung
Danish 20th cent.
paintings: (L) $220; (H) $8,250

JENSEN, Carl Milton
Danish b. 1855
paintings: (H) $1,320

JENSEN, George
American b. 1878
paintings: (L) $88; (H) $1,210

JENSEN, Holger W.
American b. Denmark 1880
paintings: (L) $187; (H) $1,870
drawings: (H) $308

JENSEN, Johan Laurentz
Danish 1800-1856
paintings: (L) $6,600; (H) $121,000
drawings: (H) $22,000

JENSEN, Laurits
Danish b. 1859
sculpture: (H) $7,150

JENSEN, Robert
American b. 1922
drawings: (H) $660

JENSON, R.
English late 19th/early 20th cent
paintings: (L) $385; (H) $660

JERDENS AND BETTRIDGE
American
paintings: (H) $715

JERICHAU, Holger Hvitfeldt
Danish 1861-1900
paintings: (L) $1,320; (H) $3,575

JERNBERG, Olaf August Andreas
Swedish b. 1855
paintings: (L) $990; (H) $2,860

JEROME
American
paintings: (H) $1,100

JEROME, Elizabeth Gilbert
American 1824-1910
paintings: (H) $1,210

JERRLICZ, G.
paintings: (H) $1,650

JERVAS, Charles
Irish c. 1675-1739
paintings: (L) $2,750; (H) $8,250

JERVIS, Margie and Susie
KRASNICAN
contemporary
sculpture: (H) $2,860

JESPERSEN, V.
paintings: (H) $770

JESS
American b. 1923
drawings: (H) $28,600

JETTEL, Eugene
Austrian 1845-1901
paintings: (L) $2,640; (H) $20,900

JEULLIN, A.
French/American 19th cent.
paintings: (H) $1,925

JEWELL, Elizabeth G.
American 1874-1956
paintings: (L) $110; (H) $880

JEWELL, Ruth
American 20th cent.
paintings: (H) $1,650

JEWETT, Maude Sherwood
American 1873-1953
sculpture: (L) $522; (H) $8,250

JEWETT, William Smith
American 1812-1873
paintings: (H) $44,000

JEX, Garnet W.
American b. 1895
paintings: (L) $385; (H) $1,210

JICARD, F.
sculpture: (H) $2,750

JIMENEZ, J.
paintings: (H) $4,620

JIMENEZ Y ARANDA, Jose
Spanish 1832-1903
paintings: (L) $9,900; (H) $99,000
drawings: (H) $29,700

JIMENEZ Y ARANDA, Luis
Spanish b. 1845
paintings: (L) $137; (H) $41,800
drawings: (H) $935

JIMENEZ Y MARTIN, Juan
Spanish b. 1858
paintings: (L) $10,450; (H) $44,000

JIMINEZ Y FERNANDEZ, Federico
paintings: (H) $990

JOACHEMS, Pieter Frans
Dutch b. 1929
paintings: (H) $1,210

JOANNAN
paintings: (H) $3,300

JOANOVITCH, Paul
Austrian b. 1859
paintings: (H) $41,800

JOBBE-DUVAL, Felix Armand Marie
French
paintings: (H) $7,150

JOCELYN, Nathaniel
American 1796-1881
paintings: (L) $247; (H) $3,850

JOCHEMSZ, P.F.
paintings: (L) $220; (H) $715

JOCHMUS, Harry
German 1855-1915
paintings: (L) $7,150; (H) $24,200

JODE, Hans de
paintings: (H) $3,850

JOFANO, E.
Italian? 19th cent.
drawings: (H) $2,420

JOHANN, Hermann
German 1821-1884
paintings: (H) $990

JOHANSEN, Anders D.
Danish/American 20th cent.
paintings: (H) $798
drawings: (H) $110

JOHANSEN, Jean MacLane
American 1878-1964
paintings: (H) $26,400

JOHANSEN, John C.
American 1876- c. 1969
paintings: (L) $110; (H) $1,100

JOHANSSON, Karl A.
Swedish b. 1863
paintings: (H) $880

JOHFRA
Dutch 1919-1963
paintings: (H) $825

JOHN, Augustus
British 1878-1961
paintings: (H) $4,950
drawings: (L) $275; (H) $4,180

JOHNS, Clarence M.
American 1843-1925
paintings: (L) $137; (H) $880

JOHNS, Jasper
American b. 1930
paintings: (L) $192,500; (H) $17,050,000
drawings: (L) $13,200; (H) $3,630,000
sculpture: (H) $385,000

JOHNSON
paintings: (H) $2,090

JOHNSON, A. Hale
American School 20th cent.
paintings: (H) $825
sculpture: (L) $1,320; (H) $1,320

JOHNSON, Avery
American b. 1906
drawings: (L) $330; (H) $1,980

JOHNSON, Ben
contemporary
paintings: (H) $880
drawings: (L) $660; (H) $660

JOHNSON, C.E.
paintings: (H) $715

JOHNSON, Charles Howard
American
drawings: (H) $770

JOHNSON, Clarence R.
American 1894-1981
paintings: (L) $13,200; (H) $121,000

JOHNSON, David
American 1827-1908
paintings: (L) $330; (H) $187,000
drawings: (L) $1,870; (H) $6,050

JOHNSON, Eastman
American 1824-1906
paintings: (L) $660; (H) $46,750
drawings: (L) $110; (H) $8,250

JOHNSON, Edward Killingworth
English 1825-1896
drawings: (L) $2,200; (H) $17,600

JOHNSON, Eldred Clark
American b. 1926
paintings: (L) $1,045; (H) $2,090

JOHNSON, Frank Tenney
American 1874-1939
paintings: (L) $825; (H) $71,500
drawings: (L) $313; (H) $3,300

JOHNSON, Frost
paintings: (H) $4,950

JOHNSON, Guy
American b. 1927
paintings: (L) $99; (H) $1,650

JOHNSON, J.
19th cent.
paintings: (H) $1,650

JOHNSON, J. William
American 19th/20th cent.
paintings: (H) $5,500

JOHNSON, J.W.A.
American late 19th/early 20th cent
paintings: (H) $990

JOHNSON, Jonathan Eastman
American 1824-1906
paintings: (L) $2,200; (H) $33,000
drawings: (H) $2,200

JOHNSON, Joshua
American c. 1769-1824
paintings: (L) $9,900; (H) $660,000

JOHNSON, Lester
contemporary
paintings: (L) $935; (H) $30,800
drawings: (L) $176; (H) $8,250

JOHNSON, Marshall
American 1846/50-1915/21
paintings: (L) $110; (H) $9,900
drawings: (H) $1,320

JOHNSON, Robert
American 1885-1933
paintings: (H) $4,180

JOHNSON, Robert
Australian 19th/20th cent.
paintings: (H) $4,950

JOHNSON, Sidney Yates
British 19th/20th cent.
paintings: (L) $412; (H) $770

JOHNSON, Theodore
drawings: (H) $1,100

JOHNSON, Wesley
drawings: (L) $2,475; (H) $5,500

JOHNSON, William H.
American 1901-1970
drawings: (H) $15,400

JOHNSTEDT, P.L.
American 20th cent.
paintings: (H) $1,045

JOHNSTON, C.W.
American first quarter 20th cent.
paintings: (H) $935

JOHNSTON, Frank Hans
Canadian 1888-1949
paintings: (H) $825

JOHNSTON, John
American 1753-1818
paintings: (H) $34,100

JOHNSTON, John Humphreys
American 1857-1941
paintings: (L) $1,870; (H) $2,420

JOHNSTON, John R.
American b. 1820's, ac. to 1872
paintings: (L) $990; (H) $1,320

JOHNSTON, L.
American 19th cent.
paintings: (H) $88,000

JOHNSTON, Reuben Le Grande
American 1850-1918
paintings: (L) $412; (H) $3,190
drawings: (L) $247; (H) $880

JOHNSTON, Robert E.
Canadian/American 1885-1933
paintings: (L) $715; (H) $7,150

JOHNSTON, T.
English 19th cent.
paintings: (L) $1,760; (H) $1,980

JOHNSTON, Thomas M.
19th/20th cent.
paintings: (H) $825

JOHNSTON, W.R.
paintings: (H) $1,980

JOHNSTONE, George Whitton
English 1849-1901
paintings: (H) $660

JOHNSTONE, Henry J.
British 19th cent.
drawings: (L) $4,125; (H) $6,050

JOHNSTONE, Henry James
British 1835-1907
paintings: (H) $19,800

Black Artist

Most of the works of William Johnson (1901-1970) are found in the Smithsonian and rarely are offered at auction. No auction records were available when James Bakker of Cambridge, Massachusetts, estimated a Johnson watercolor of a pushcart at $300-$500. When the dust had settled, *Pushcart* had sold to a Washington, D.C., collection for $15,400.

William Johnson was born to an impoverished family in 1901 in Florence, South Carolina. As a young boy he loved to draw, and at age seventeen he moved to New York City, where he worked for three years until he had saved enough money to attend the five-year course at the National Academy of Design. After graduation he received a private scholarship and traveled abroad to study. While in Paris he studied under Chaim Soutine, a European Expressionist. At an artists' colony at Cagnes-sur-Mer he met his future wife, Holcha Krake, a Danish designer, weaver, and ceramicist. They married in 1930 and returned to Denmark.

The Johnsons traveled extensively in Europe and Africa. During this period his works did not sell well in the United States but were well received in Scandinavia. In 1938 the Johnsons settled in New York. Johnson painted murals for the WPA and began to concentrate on religious subjects. During World War II he depicted Negro soldiers in action. In 1942 Holcha died, and after 1944 Johnson was too ill to paint. Following an extended illness he died in 1970. (William Johnson, *Pushcart*, watercolor on paper, 11 ¼ x 13 ¾ in., Bakker, June 7, 1989, $15,400)

JOINER, Harvey
American 1852-1932
paintings: (L) $440; (H) $2,750

JOINVILLE, E.
French 19th cent.
paintings: (H) $715

JOIRE, Jean
sculpture: (H) $990

JOLI, Antonio
Venetian 1700?-1777
paintings: (L) $17,600; (H) $176,000

JOLLIVET, Pierre Jules
French 1794-1871
paintings: (H) $11,000

JONAS, Louis Paul
American
sculpture: (H) $1,760

JONAS, Lucien Hector
French b. 1880
paintings: (H) $8,800
drawings: (L) $192; (H) $550

JONCIERES, Leonce J. V.
French b. 1871
paintings: (H) $2,200

JONES, Adolph Robert
Belgian 1806-1874
paintings: (H) $2,200
drawings: (H) $45

JONES, Allen
British b. 1937
paintings: (L) $275; (H) $22,000
sculpture: (L) $4,950; (H) $28,600

JONES, C.S.
drawings: (H) $1,650

JONES, Charles
British 1836-1892
paintings: (L) $1,100; (H) $5,000

JONES, Daniel Adolphe Robert
Belgian 1806-1874
paintings: (H) $5,225

JONES, Deborah
paintings: (L) $550; (H) $880

JONES, F. Eastman
paintings: (H) $880
drawings: (H) $99

JONES, Francis Coates
American 1857-1932
paintings: (L) $3,850; (H) $47,300
drawings: (H) $325

JONES, Grace Church
American 20th cent.
paintings: (L) $110; (H) $660

JONES, H.B.
paintings: (H) $1,210

JONES, H.F.
British 19th cent.
paintings: (L) $550; (H) $15,400

JONES, Herbert H.
British 19th/20th cent.
paintings: (H) $1,760
drawings: (H) $330

JONES, Hugh Bolton
American 1848-1927
paintings: (L) $440; (H) $30,800
drawings: (L) $154; (H) $3,025

JONES, J.
English 18th/19th cent.
drawings: (H) $1,210

JONES, Jessie
American 1865-1944
paintings: (L) $55; (H) $935
drawings: (H) $137

JONES, Joe
American 1909-1963
paintings: (L) $495; (H) $14,300

JONES, Mary Bacon
American 1868-1924
paintings: (H) $1,870

JONES, Maud Raphael
British ac. 1889-1907
paintings: (H) $4,950

JONES, Ott
American
sculpture: (H) $800

JONES, Paul
British 19th cent.
paintings: (L) $2,090; (H) $4,125

JONES, Richard
British 1767-1840
paintings: (L) $33,000; (H) $52,800

JONES, Robert Edmond
American b. 1887
drawings: (L) $330; (H) $2,420

JONES, Samuel John Egbert
English ac. 1820-1845
paintings: (L) $2,200; (H) $23,100

JONES, T.R.
19th cent.
paintings: (H) $770

JONES, William
paintings: (L) $8,250; (H) $8,800

JONG, Jacobus Sterre de
Dutch 1866-1920
paintings: (H) $1,210
drawings: (L) $770; (H) $3,300

JONG, Jan de
paintings: (H) $770

JONGERE, Marius de
Dutch b. 1912
paintings: (L) $440; (H) $2,250

JONGH, Ludolph de
1616-1679
paintings: (L) $1,870; (H) $6,600

JONGH, Oene Romkes de
Dutch 1812-1896
paintings: (L) $1,045; (H) $6,050

JONGHE, Gustave Leonhard de
Belgian 1828/29-1893
paintings: (L) $12,100; (H) $63,250

JONGKIND, Johan Barthold
Dutch 1819-1891
paintings: (L) $7,700; (H) $165,000
drawings: (L) $900; (H) $33,000

JONNEVOLD, Carl Henrik
American 1856-1930?
paintings: (L) $193; (H) $2,750

JONNIAUX, Alfred
Belgian/American b. 1882
paintings: (L) $137; (H) $18,700

JONSON, Raymond
American b. 1891
paintings: (L) $1,650; (H) $70,400

JOORS, Eugene
Belgian 1850-1910
paintings: (L) $3,300; (H) $8,800

JOORS, J.E.
paintings: (H) $660

JOORS, Van
19th cent.
paintings: (H) $16,500

JOOSTENS, Paul
Belgian 1889-1960
sculpture: (H) $6,380

JORDAENS, Hans, III Le Long
Jordaens
Flemish c. 1595-1643/44
paintings: (L) $2,970; (H) $13,200

JORDAENS, Jacob
Flemish 1593-1678
paintings: (H) $17,600

JORDAENS, Jacob, and studio
Flemish 1593-1678
paintings: (L) $44,000; (H) $55,000

JORDAN, Adolphe
paintings: (H) $3,300

JORDAN, Carl
paintings: (H) $990

JORDAN, R.
European 19th cent.
paintings: (H) $935

JORDAN, Samuel
American 1803/4-after 1831
paintings: (H) $2,640

JOREL, A.
sculpture: (H) $660

JORGENSEN, Christian
Norwegian/American 1860-1935
paintings: (L) $100; (H) $4,400
drawings: (L) $66; (H) $4,675

JORGENSEN, Willer
Danish 19th/20th cent.
paintings: (H) $660

JORGENSON, Nels Jorgenson
19th/20th cent.
paintings: (L) $1,650; (H) $1,980

JORISSEN, W.
Dutch 19th cent.
paintings: (L) $1,045; (H) $3,300

JORON, Maurice Paul
paintings: (H) $1,045

JOS, Julien
19th cent.
paintings: (L) $2,200; (H) $2,750

JOSEPH, George Frances
English 1764-1846
paintings: (H) $1,320

JOSEPH, Jaques Francois, called
SWEBACH-DESFONTAINES
paintings: (H) $8,800

JOSEPH, Josef
sculpture: (H) $1,870

JOSEPH, Julian
American 20th cent.
paintings: (L) $303; (H) $3,300
drawings: (L) $220; (H) $330

JOSEPH, Ronald
American 20th cent.
paintings: (H) $990

JOSEPH-VALCIN, Pierre
Haitian b. 1938
paintings: (H) $660

JOSI, Charles
British 19th cent.
paintings: (H) $24,200

JOSSELIN DE JONG, Pieter de
Dutch 1861-1906
paintings: (H) $1,760

JOST, Joseph
Austrian b. 1888
paintings: (H) $1,980

JOST, Joseph
German b. 1875
paintings: (H) $1,210

JOUBERT, J.B.
drawings: (H) $4,400

JOUBERT, Leon
French 19th cent.
paintings: (L) $412; (H) $3,300

JOUETT, Matthew Harris
American 1787/88-1827
paintings: (L) $5,500; (H) $9,900

JOUKOVSKY, Stanislav Joulianovich
paintings: (H) $3,080

JOULLIN, Amadee
American 1862-1917
paintings: (L) $577; (H) $4,400
drawings: (H) $1,210

JOURDAIN, Roger
Canadian b. 1914
paintings: (H) $2,420

JOURDAIN, Roger Joseph
French 1845-1918
paintings: (H) $13,200

JOURDAN, Adolphe
French 1825-1889
paintings: (L) $2,970; (H) $19,800

JOURDAN, Felix
paintings: (H) $1,540

JOURDEUIL, Louis Adrien
Russian/French 1849-1907
paintings: (H) $3,300

JOURGUENEFF, P.
sculpture: (H) $770

JOUVE, Paul
French 1880-1973
paintings: (L) $990; (H) $8,800
drawings: (L) $1,540; (H) $24,200
sculpture: (L) $880; (H) $9,460

JOUVENET, Jean Baptiste
paintings: (H) $1,650

JOUVRAY, Madeleine
sculpture: (H) $1,320

JOY, George William
British 1844-1925
paintings: (H) $7,975

JOY, Robert
American b. 1901
paintings: (H) $935

JOY, Thomas Musgrove
British 1812-1866
paintings: (L) $18,700; (H) $19,800

JOY, William and John
paintings: (H) $2,200

JOYCE, Marshall W.
American 20th cent.
paintings: (H) $700
drawings: (H) $275

JOYNER, Jacob
American 19th/20th cent.
sculpture: (H) $1,650

JOZAN, Jeanne
French 1868-1946
sculpture: (H) $13,750

JOZON, J.
French 19th cent.
sculpture: (H) $907

JPOLD, A.
Dutch late 19th cent.
paintings: (H) $1,430

JUAN Y AGRASOT, Joaquim
Spanish 19th/20th cent.
paintings: (H) $2,200

JUAREZ, Jose
paintings: (H) $16,500

JUAREZ, Nicholas Rodriguez
Mexican
paintings: (H) $24,200

JUAREZ, Roberto
American b. 1952?
paintings: (L) $3,850; (H) $7,975

JUDD, Donald
American b. 1928
drawings: (L) $2,090; (H) $13,200
sculpture: (L) $1,320; (H) $286,000

JUDSON, Alice
American d. 1948
paintings: (L) $220; (H) $2,750
drawings: (H) $55

JUDSON, William Lees
Anglo/American 1842-1928
paintings: (L) $495; (H) $3,850
drawings: (L) $302; (H) $825

JUERGENS, Alfred
American 1866-1934
paintings: (L) $55; (H) $990

JUETTE, G.
paintings: (H) $1,980

JUGLAR, Victor Henri
French b. 1826
paintings: (L) $770; (H) $1,650

JUKE
paintings: (H) $880

JULIANA Y ALBERT, Jose
Spanish 19th cent.
paintings: (H) $11,000
drawings: (H) $1,100

JULIEN, Joseph
Belgian 19th cent.
paintings: (H) $6,820

JULIENNE, Eugene
French c. 1800-1874
drawings: (H) $11,000

JUNG, Charles Jacob
American
paintings: (H) $3,850

JUNG, George
Austrian ac. 1930-1940
paintings: (H) $4,125

JUNGBLUT, Johann
German 1860-1912
paintings: (L) $1,430; (H) $4,400

JUNGHEIM, C.
German 19th cent.
paintings: (H) $990

JUNGHEIM, Jules
paintings: (H) $3,300

JUNGMAN, A.
paintings: (H) $825

JUNGMANN, Nico W.
Dutch 1872-1935
drawings: (H) $1,980

JUNGNICKEL, Ludwig Heinrich
drawings: (H) $935

JUNGWIRTH, Joseph
Austrian 20th cent.
drawings: (L) $660; (H) $1,900

JUNIOR, Emil Kosa
American 1903-1968
drawings: (H) $3,575

JUNYER, Joan
paintings: (H) $880

JUPP, G.H.
Continental 19th/20th cent.
paintings: (H) $4,675

JUPPEL, A.
Continental 19th/20th cent.
drawings: (H) $660

JURGENSEN, Louis Otto
French 19th cent.
paintings: (H) $715

JURUTKA, Josef
paintings: (H) $3,080

JUSTE, Estelle
French 20th cent.
paintings: (H) $1,925

JUSTIN, Auguste Francois
French b. 1847
paintings: (H) $2,310

JUTSUM, H.
English 1816-1869
paintings: (L) $330; (H) $1,320
drawings: (L) $907; (H) $1,650

JUTZ, Carl
German 1838-1916
paintings: (L) $15,950; (H) $27,500

KABAKOV, Ilya
Russian b. 1933
paintings: (H) $154,000

KABOTIE, Fred, NAKAYOMA, Day
After Day
American Indian b. 1900
paintings: (H) $990

KACERE, John
American b. 1920
paintings: (L) $5,280; (H) $33,000

KACZ, Komiomi
Hungarian b. 1880
paintings: (H) $770

KADAR, Bela
Hungarian 1877-1955
paintings: (H) $1,980
drawings: (L) $11; (H) $26,400

KADISHMAN, Menashe
Israeli b. 1932
paintings: (L) $715; (H) $22,000

KADLACSIK, Laszlo
Hungarian 1925-1989
paintings: (H) $12,100

KAELIN, Charles Salis
American 1858-1929
paintings: (L) $385; (H) $13,200
drawings: (L) $110; (H) $5,775

KAEMMERER, Frederik Hendrik
Dutch 1839-1902
paintings: (L) $1,870; (H) $1,320,000
drawings: (H) $1,650

KAERCHER, Amalie
American 19th cent.
paintings: (L) $2,310; (H) $66,000

KAESBACH, Rudolf
German b. 1873
sculpture: (L) $605; (H) $770

KAESEN, H.R.
Continental 19th cent.
paintings: (H) $5,500

KAGAN, Rod
sculpture: (H) $2,750

KAGANOVE, J.
Continental 20th cent.
paintings: (H) $715

KAGY, Wilhelm
Swedish 1889-1960
paintings: (H) $2,530

KAHAEB, M.
Russian 19th/20th cent.
sculpture: (H) $1,045

KAHL, Karl Soukowsky
Russian 1873-1935
paintings: (H) $1,210

KAHLER, Carl
Austrian/American b. 1855
paintings: (L) $715; (H) $17,600
drawings: (H) $165

KAHLO, Frida
Mexican 1907-1954
paintings: (L) $46,200; (H) $1,430,000
drawings: (L) $17,600; (H) $110,000

KAHN, Gary
contemporary
sculpture: (H) $1,980

KAHN, Susan B.
American 20th cent.
paintings: (H) $990

KAHN, Wolf
German/American b. 1927
paintings: (L) $2,420; (H) $18,700
drawings: (L) $825; (H) $2,310

KAIER, G. Prince
paintings: (H) $1,100

KAISER, Richard
German 1868-1941
paintings: (H) $1,760

KAISH, Louise
sculpture: (H) $1,375

KALBACH, F.
German 19th cent.
paintings: (H) $770

Cult Figure

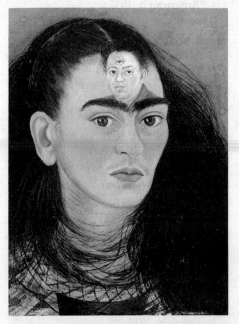

Frida Kahlo (1907-1954) has recently become a cult figure for many art lovers and feminists. Pop star Madonna, who is one of many collectors of Kahlo's paintings, has purchased the rights to the artist's life story. At the time of her death in 1954, Frida Kahlo was best known as the third and fourth wife of Mexican artist Diego Rivera. Born in a Mexico City suburb, she endured a bout of polio as a child. When she was in her teens, she was crippled in a streetcar accident, and the spinal injuries she suffered caused her to live with pain for the rest of her life. Frida met Diego Rivera when she was attending the National Preparatory School. They married in 1929, divorced in 1939, and remarried a year later.

Frida Kahlo's paintings were embraced by the Surrealists, but her style was her own–intimate and autobiographical, intense outpourings of personal pain and grief. Many of her self-portraits feature a little round window above her eyebrows filled with the subject of her thoughts. In 1948, Frida promised to paint a self-portrait for her American friend, Florence Arquin. Florence saw the original sketch in Mexico, but when she unwrapped the finished painting in Chicago, she saw that it had evolved very differently. Rather than her usual crown of braids, Frida's hair was stringy and wrapped around her throat, tears were in her eyes, and Diego was painted on her forehead. The painting *Diego y Yo* reflected Kahlo's anguish over another of Diego's escapades, this time with a Mexican movie star.

In 1978 the first of many biographies of Frida was published; 1983 saw an exhibition of Kahlo's work in New York, a documentary circulating in art film houses, and a biography featured in a cover article in *Art in America*. In 1984, Frida was added to the elite list of Mexican artists, including Rivera, Siqueiros, Orozco, Velasco, and Dr. Alt, whose works are considered a national patrimony; Mexican law forbids the export of works by these artists. Paintings by Kahlo that were already legally out of the country immediately appreciated in value. In 1990 the Metropolitan Museum of Art mounted a special exhibition of Mexican paintings and works by both Diego Rivera and Frida Kahlo were included. *Diego y Yo*, the catalog cover lot for Sotheby's May 1990 sale, set an auction record for the artist (and for any Latin American painting) when it sold for $1.43 million. (Frida Kahlo, *Diego y Yo*, oil on masonite, 11 5/8 x 8 13/16 in., Sotheby, May 2, 1990, $1,430,000)

KALCE, Alfredo
Mexican 20th cent.
paintings: (H) $1,650

KALCKREUTH, Patrick von
German 19th/20th cent.
paintings: (L) $990; (H) $1,100

KALF, Willem
Dutch 1619/22-1693
paintings: (H) $31,900

KALINA, Richard
paintings: (H) $660

KALISH, Max
Polish/American 1891-1945
sculpture: (L) $165; (H) $11,000

KALISKI, Henri
American ac. 1892-1893
paintings: (L) $715; (H) $3,300

KALLER, W.J.
American b. 1871
paintings: (H) $660

KALLMORGAN, Friedrich
German 1856-1924
paintings: (L) $1,320; (H) $2,970

KALLOS, Paul
American contemporary
paintings: (H) $18,700

KALLSTENIUS, Gottfried
Swedish 1861-1943
paintings: (H) $31,900

KALRAET, Abraham van
Dutch 1642/43-1721/22
paintings: (H) $36,300

KALTENMOSER, Karl
paintings: (H) $11,000

KALTENMOSER, Kaspar
German 1806-1867
paintings: (H) $9,350

KAMINSKY, Edward
American 20th cent.
paintings: (L) $440; (H) $990

KAMP, Louise M.
American 1867-1959
paintings: (H) $1,320

KANDINSKY, Wassily
Russian 1866-1944
paintings: (L) $38,500; (H) $20,900,000
drawings: (L) $1,760; (H) $715,000

KANE, Bob
American b. 1937
paintings: (L) $1,650; (H) $13,200
drawings: (H) $412

KANE, John
American 1860-1934
paintings: (L) $3,850; (H) $9,350

KANE, Paul
Canadian 1810-1871
paintings: (H) $275,000

KANEKO, Jun
contemporary
sculpture: (H) $990

KANIN, Michael
American 20th cent.
sculpture: (H) $3,080

KANNEMANS, Christian Cornelis
Dutch 1812-1884
paintings: (H) $2,500

KANTOR, Tadeusz
Polish b. 1915
paintings: (H) $1,210
drawings: (H) $715

KAPLAN, Joseph
American 1900-1982
paintings: (H) $2,000

KAPOOR, Amish
English b. India 1954
sculpture: (L) $18,700; (H) $41,250

KAPP, Gary
b. 1942
paintings: (L) $55; (H) $5,000

KAPPES, Alfred
American 1850-1894
paintings: (H) $1,100

KARAZIAN, Eduard
Russian b. 1939
paintings: (L) $1,980; (H) $4,400

KARBERG, L.
paintings: (H) $1,100

KARDEGG, L.
paintings: (H) $770

KARFIOL, Bernard
Hungarian/American 1866/86-1955
paintings: (L) $82; (H) $1,760

KARL, K.
English late 19th cent.
paintings: (H) $715

KARLOVSZKY, Bertalan
Hungarian 1858-1939
paintings: (L) $198; (H) $1,540

KARLSEN, Gardner
American 20th cent.
paintings: (H) $880

KAROLY, A. and SZANTOS, L.
drawings: (L) $88; (H) $660

KARPATHY, Jeno
Hungarian 1871-1950
paintings: (H) $2,860

KARRAS, Spiros John
American 1897-1941
paintings: (H) $1,760

KARSSEN, A.N.M.
Continental 20th cent.
paintings: (H) $1,650

KARSSEN, Anton
Dutch 20th cent.
paintings: (L) $1,210; (H) $1,540

KARTOCHVILL, Stephen
American b. 1876
paintings: (H) $2,200

KASPARIDES, Edouard
German 1858-1926
paintings: (H) $5,280

KASSACK, Lajos
drawings: (L) $2,090; (H) $2,860

KASUVIKOLZ, N.
German 20th cent.
paintings: (H) $935

KATE, Herman ten
Dutch 1822-1890
paintings: (H) $7,150

KATWIJK, Arthur Fuedel
European 19th cent.
drawings: (H) $880

KATZ, Alex
American b. 1927
paintings: (L) $1,650; (H) $121,000
drawings: (L) $358; (H) $14,300
sculpture: (H) $15,400

KATZ, William P.
sculpture: (H) $2,200

KATZEN, Lila
contemporary
sculpture: (H) $4,950

KAU, Georg
German b. 1870
paintings: (H) $660

KAUB-CASALONGA, Alice
French b. 1875
paintings: (H) $7,700

KAUBA, Carl
Austrian 1865-1922
sculpture: (L) $330; (H) $60,500

KAUFFER, Edward McKnight
American 1890-1954
drawings: (H) $1,045

KAUFFMAN, Angelica
Swiss 1740-1807
paintings: (L) $3,190; (H) $23,100

KAUFFMAN, Craig
contemporary
sculpture: (H) $9,900

KAUFFMAN, Max
German 19th cent.
paintings: (L) $660; (H) $715

KAUFFMANN, Hermann
German 1808-1889
paintings: (H) $7,150
drawings: (H) $1,045

KAUFFMANN, Hermann
German b. 1873
paintings: (H) $1,540

KAUFFMANN, Hugo
German 1844-1915
paintings: (L) $7,700; (H) $60,500

KAUFMAN, John Francois
Swiss/American b. 1870
paintings: (L) $522; (H) $990

KAUFMANN, Adolf
Austrian 1848-1916
paintings: (L) $550; (H) $5,225

KAUFMANN, Ferdinand
German/American 1864-after 1934
paintings: (L) $935; (H) $12,100

KAUFMANN, Isidor
Austrian 1853-1921
paintings: (L) $5,500; (H) $66,000

KAUFMANN, Karl
Austrian b. 1843
paintings: (L) $302; (H) $9,900

KAULA, Lee Lufkin
American 1865-1957
paintings: (L) $121; (H) $32,000
drawings: (H) $247

KAULA, William Jurian
American 1871-1953
paintings: (L) $248; (H) $52,800
drawings: (L) $225; (H) $3,190

KAULBACH, Anton
German 20th cent.
paintings: (L) $770; (H) $2,750

KAULBACH, Franz August von
paintings: (H) $2,090

KAULBACH, Friedrich August von
German 1850-1920
paintings: (L) $275; (H) $13,200

KAULBACH, Hermann
German 1846-1909
paintings: (L) $13,200; (H) $28,600

KAULBACH, Wilhelm von
paintings: (H) $6,050

KAUTZKY, Ted
American d. 1953
paintings: (L) $935; (H) $1,980
drawings: (H) $615

KAVANAGH, J.M.
paintings: (H) $1,900

KAVANAGH, Joseph M.
paintings: (H) $1,320

KAVANDOWSKI, Edmund D.
paintings: (H) $1,430

KAVEL, Martin
paintings: (L) $4,400; (H) $6,600

KAY, T.S.
Continental 19th century
paintings: (H) $4,400

KAYE, Otis
American 1885-1974
paintings: (L) $9,900; (H) $45,100

KAYN, Hilde
paintings: (H) $852

KEAHBONE, George Campbell, Asaute
American Indian b. 1916
paintings: (H) $770

KEARNEY, John
paintings: (H) $165
sculpture: (L) $198; (H) $715

KEARNS, Jerry
American b. 1943
paintings: (H) $17,600

KECK, Charles
American 1875-1951
sculpture: (L) $880; (H) $3,575

KECK, H.
German ac. 1900-1922
sculpture: (L) $440; (H) $770

KEECH, A.E.
paintings: (H) $1,210

KEEGAN, Marie
American b. 1941
paintings: (H) $2,750

KEELE (?), A.
American
paintings: (H) $1,100

KEELHOFF, Frans
Belgian 1820-1893
paintings: (L) $660; (H) $2,530

KEELING, Michael
British d. 1820
paintings: (H) $1,430

KEENAN, Ann Eckert
American 1904-1982
paintings: (H) $990

KEESEY, G.W.
American 19th cent.
paintings: (H) $1,760

KEFFER, Frances
American 1881-1954
paintings: (L) $550; (H) $715
drawings: (L) $82; (H) $82

KEIL, Bernhardt, called Monsu
Bernardo
Danish 1624-1687
paintings: (L) $5,225; (H) $22,000

KEIL, E.
French 20th cent.
paintings: (H) $660

KEIL, G.
American 19th cent.
paintings: (H) $825

KEINANEN, Sigfrid August
Finnish 1841-1914
paintings: (H) $1,430

KEIRINCX, Alexander
Flemish 1600-1652
paintings: (L) $44,000; (H) $60,500

KEISERMAN, Franz
Swiss 1765-1833
drawings: (H) $13,200

KEISTER, Roy
American b. 1886
paintings: (L) $550; (H) $1,430

KEISTER, Steve
American b. 1886
sculpture: (L) $220; (H) $7,308

KEITH, Dora Wheeler
American 1857-1940
paintings: (H) $935

KEITH, W. Castle
American 19th/20th cent.
paintings: (L) $935; (H) $2,200
drawings: (H) $715

KEITH, William
American 1839-1911
paintings: (L) $132; (H) $27,500
drawings: (H) $1,100

KELDERMAN, Jan
Dutch 1741-1820
paintings: (L) $330; (H) $1,320

KELETY, Alexander
Hungarian ac. 1918-1940
sculpture: (L) $825; (H) $37,400

KELLER, Adolphe
paintings: (H) $13,200

KELLER, Albert von
Swiss 1844-1920
paintings: (L) $770; (H) $2,475

KELLER, Arthur Ignatius
American 1866/67-1924
paintings: (H) $1,045
drawings: (L) $192; (H) $1,980

KELLER, Clyde Leon
American 1872-1941
paintings: (L) $137; (H) $880

KELLER, Edgar Martin
American 1868-1932
paintings: (H) $5,225

KELLER, F.
paintings: (L) $412; (H) $770

KELLER, F.
Carribean School late 19th cent.
paintings: (H) $1,320

KELLER, Ferdinand
German 1842-1922
paintings: (L) $7,150; (H) $22,000

KELLER, Henry G.
American 1870-1949
paintings: (L) $66; (H) $935
drawings: (L) $33; (H) $605

KELLER, J.
American c. 1886
paintings: (H) $687

KELLER, R.
Dutch 20th cent.
drawings: (H) $1,045

KELLER-KUHNE, Josef Waldemar
paintings: (H) $1,870

KELLER-REUTLINGEN, Paul Wilhelm
German 1854-1920
paintings: (L) $3,300; (H) $3,575

KELLEY, Ramon
American b. 1939
drawings: (L) $632; (H) $4,500

KELLOGG, Alfred G.
American d. 1935
paintings: (H) $825

KELLOGG, Harry J.
paintings: (L) $1,540; (H) $1,760

KELLY, Ellsworth
American b. 1923
paintings: (L) $110,000; (H) $715,000
drawings: (L) $6,050; (H) $35,750
sculpture: (L) $5,775; (H) $677,500

KELLY, Felix
British b. 1916
paintings: (H) $1,210

KELLY, James Edward
American 1855-1933
sculpture: (L) $121; (H) $3,575

KELLY, Leon
Franco/American b. 1901
paintings: (L) $110; (H) $2,750
drawings: (L) $165; (H) $1,760
sculpture: (H) $4,400

KELLY, Louise
American 20th cent.
paintings: (H) $1,760

KELLY, Sir Gerald
English 1879-1972
paintings: (L) $6,050; (H) $30,800

KELLY, Walt
American 1913-1973
paintings: (H) $1,540
drawings: (L) $275; (H) $4,950

KELMAN, Benjamin
American b. 1887
paintings: (L) $440; (H) $1,100

KELPE, Paul
American 1902-1985
paintings: (H) $38,500
drawings: (L) $9,350; (H) $14,300

KELS, Franz
German 1828-1893
paintings: (H) $41,250

KELSEY, C.
American ac. c. 1850
paintings: (L) $2,200; (H) $5,250

KEMBLE, Edward Windsor
American 1861-1933
drawings: (L) $165; (H) $4,620

KEMBLE, Kenneth
Argentinian b. 1912
paintings: (H) $5,500

KEMENY, Zoltan
contemporary
sculpture: (H) $1,760

KEMEYS, Edward
American 1843-1907
sculpture: (L) $550; (H) $14,300

KEMM, Robert
English ac. 1874-91
paintings: (L) $1,540; (H) $6,050

KEMMER, Hans
German c. 1495-after 1554
paintings: (H) $242,000

KEMP, Gerald van der
drawings: (H) $1,100

KEMP, Oliver
American 1887-1934
paintings: (L) $440; (H) $7,150

KEMPENEER, Pieter de, called Pedro
Campana
1503-1580
drawings: (H) $7,150

KEMPENER, Pieter de
paintings: (H) $990

KEMPER, Henry E.
American 19th cent.
paintings: (H) $880

KEMPSON, Julia Beers, nee Hart
American 1835-1913
paintings: (L) $110; (H) $1,650

KENARD, C.
British 19th cent.
paintings: (H) $1,430

KENDALL, Marie Boening
American 1885-1953
paintings: (L) $110; (H) $935

KENDALL, Sergeant
American 1869-1938
paintings: (L) $220; (H) $46,750
drawings: (L) $412; (H) $7,425

KENDRICK, Albert H.
British 19th cent.
paintings: (H) $2,750

KENDRICK, Mel
American b. 1949
drawings: (H) $17,600
sculpture: (L) $8,800; (H) $23,100

KENDRICK, Sydney P.
British 1874-1955
paintings: (H) $770

KENNEDY, Cecil
British b. 1905
paintings: (H) $3,520

KENNEDY, Charles Napier
English 1852-1898
paintings: (H) $1,980

KENNEDY, David
American 1816-1898
drawings: (L) $9,900; (H) $12,540

KENNEDY, H. Arthur
British 19th cent.
paintings: (H) $10,450

KENNEDY, M.W.
paintings: (H) $825

KENNEDY, S.J.
American b. 1877
paintings: (L) $275; (H) $880

KENNEDY, William
1818-1870
paintings: (L) $550; (H) $19,800

KENNEY, John T.
English 20th cent.
paintings: (H) $2,090

KENNINGTON, C.G.
British 19th cent.
paintings: (H) $1,210

KENNINGTON, Thomas Benjamin
British 1856-1916
paintings: (L) $14,300; (H) $28,600

KENSETT, John Frederick
American 1816/18-1872
paintings: (L) $2,420; (H) $616,000
drawings: (L) $1,100; (H) $5,775

KENT, Rockwell
American 1882-1971
paintings: (L) $495; (H) $64,900
drawings: (L) $88; (H) $7,150
sculpture: (L) $2,200; (H) $3,300

KENT, William
contemporary
sculpture: (H) $770

KENYON, Henry R.
American d. 1926
paintings: (L) $302; (H) $1,430

KEPES, Gyorgy
American b. Hungary 1906
paintings: (L) $264; (H) $3,080

KERCHER, Bob
American
paintings: (H) $1,000

KERCHER, Robert
American
drawings: (H) $1,400

KERCKHOVE, Auguste van den
Belgian 1825-1895
paintings: (H) $6,050

KERCKHOVEN, Jacob van de
Flemish 1667-1724
paintings: (H) $17,600

KERFOOT, Margaret
American b. 1901
drawings: (L) $385; (H) $797

KERKHAM, Earl
American c. 1890-1965
paintings: (H) $2,420
drawings: (L) $33; (H) $1,980

KERLING, Anna E.
Dutch b. 1862
paintings: (H) $5,500

KERN, Hermann
Hungarian 1839-1912
paintings: (L) $770; (H) $15,400

KERNAN, Joseph F.
American 1878-1958
paintings: (L) $400; (H) $6,200
drawings: (H) $330

KEROVINC, Constantin
American
drawings: (H) $990

KERR, Charles Henry Malcolm,
the elder
British 1858-1907
paintings: (H) $1,870

KERRN, Hansine Sophie Joachimine
Danish 1826-1860
paintings: (L) $6,600; (H) $8,800

KERSEBOOM, Friedrich
1632-1690
paintings: (H) $2,860

KESSEL, Hieronymus
1578-1636
paintings: (H) $3,850

KESSEL, Jan van
paintings: (H) $14,850

KESSEL, Jan van
Flemish 1626-1679
paintings: (L) $11,000; (H) $66,000

KESSEL, Jan van
Flemish
paintings: (H) $52,800

KESSEL, Peter van
d. 1668
paintings: (H) $22,000

KESSLER, August
paintings: (L) $990; (H) $17,600

KESSLER, Carl
German 19th/20th cent.
drawings: (H) $660

KETT, Emile
American c. 1838-1880
paintings: (H) $1,100

KETTEMANN, Erwin
German b. 1897
paintings: (H) $1,045

KETTLE, Tilly
English 1735-1786
paintings: (L) $440; (H) $37,400

KEULEYAN-LAFON, Jean
French b. 1886
paintings: (H) $1,210

KEVER, Jacob Simon Hendrik
Dutch 1854-1922
paintings: (L) $275; (H) $17,600
drawings: (L) $330; (H) $3,850

KEY, Adriaen Thomasz.
c. 1544-after 1589
paintings: (H) $18,700

KEY, John Ross
American 1832-1920
paintings: (L) $1,760; (H) $31,900
drawings: (H) $440

KEY, Mabel
American 1874-1926
drawings: (H) $6,325

KEY, William
Flemish 1515/20-1568
paintings: (L) $6,600; (H) $44,000

KEYES, Bernard M.
American 1898-1973
paintings: (L) $88; (H) $2,640

KEYSER, Ephraim
sculpture: (H) $880

KEYSER, Ernest Wise
American 1875-1951
sculpture: (L) $660; (H) $825

KEYSIL, William H.
American 19th cent.
paintings: (H) $907

KHMELUK, Vassyl
Russian b. 1903
paintings: (L) $247; (H) $660

KHNOPFF, Fernand
Belgian 1858-1912
paintings: (H) $132,000

KHODOROVICH, F.
sculpture: (H) $1,760

KHRUTSKY, Ivan
19th cent.
paintings: (H) $44,000

KIAERSKOU, Frederick
Danish 1805-1891
paintings: (H) $8,500

KIBALL, Alonzo Myron
American 1874-1923
paintings: (H) $660

KIECHLE, Edgar O.
American 20th cent.
paintings: (H) $770

KIEDERICH, Paul Joseph
German 1809-1850
paintings: (H) $6,600

KIEFER, Anselm
German b. 1945
paintings: (L) $16,500; (H) $418,000
drawings: (L) $77,000; (H) $165,000

KIENHOLZ, Edward
American b. 1927
paintings: (H) $1,980
drawings: (L) $2,200; (H) $176,000
sculpture: (H) $13,200

KIESEL, Conrad
German 1846-1921
paintings: (L) $2,420; (H) $60,500
drawings: (H) $550

KIESLING, Ferdinand
1810-1882
paintings: (H) $1,100

KIHN, William Langdon
American 1898-1957
paintings: (H) $4,700
drawings: (H) $3,850

KIKOINE, Michel
French 1892-1968
paintings: (L) $1,650; (H) $31,900

KILBOURNE, Samuel A.
American 1836-1881
paintings: (L) $660; (H) $2,310

KILBURNE, George Goodwin
British 1839-1924
paintings: (L) $1,870; (H) $12,100
drawings: (L) $220; (H) $7,150

KILGORE, Charles P.
American 20th cent.
paintings: (L) $247; (H) $2,090

KILLGORE, Charles
American 20th cent.
paintings: (H) $1,540

KILLINGBECK, Benjamin
British ac. 1769-1789
paintings: (L) $3,025; (H) $8,800

KILPATRICK, Aaron Edward
American 1872-1953
paintings: (L) $413; (H) $5,500

KILPIN, Zegh Mulhall
drawings: (H) $935

KILVERT, Benjamin Sayre Cory
American 1881-1946
drawings: (H) $1,430

KIMBALL, Charles Frederick
American 1835/36-1907
paintings: (L) $110; (H) $4,400

KIMBEL, Richard M.
American 1865-1942
paintings: (L) $385; (H) $3,080

KIMBLE, Colby
American
paintings: (H) $1,320

KIMBOCK, R.
paintings: (H) $3,850

KIMMEL, T.
20th cent.
paintings: (H) $1,430

KINDLER, Alice L. Riddle
American b. 1892
paintings: (H) $880

KING, Albert F.
American 1854-1945
paintings: (L) $220; (H) $9,350

KING, C.V,
American 20th cent.
paintings: (H) $935

KING, Charles Bird
American 1785-1862
paintings: (L) $1,100; (H) $385,000

KING, F.W.
American 19th cent.
paintings: (H) $1,430

KING, Frank
paintings: (H) $990

KING, G.
American 19th cent.
paintings: (H) $1,100

KING, George W.
American 1836-1922
paintings: (L) $280; (H) $3,300

KING, Gordon
British 20th cent.
paintings: (H) $1,045

KING, H.C.
British 19th cent.
paintings: (L) $110; (H) $715

KING, Haynes
British 1831-1904
paintings: (L) $660; (H) $3,850

KING, J.W.
American 19th cent.
paintings: (L) $176; (H) $10,450

KING, James
American 19th cent.
paintings: (H) $2,090

KING, James S.
American 1852-1925
paintings: (L) $330; (H) $2,310

KING, John Crookshanks
American 1806-1882
sculpture: (L) $2,970; (H) $9,900

KING, Joseph Wallace, called Vinciata
American b. 1912
paintings: (H) $1,320

KING, L. Adam
paintings: (H) $1,100

KING, Mary Elizabeth
paintings: (L) $220; (H) $770

KING, Paul
American 1867-1947
paintings: (L) $303; (H) $13,200

KING, Tony
American b. 1944
paintings: (L) $2,310; (H) $2,530

KING, William
American b. 1925
sculpture: (L) $165; (H) $6,600

KING, William Charles Holland
early 20th cent.
sculpture: (H) $2,200

KING, William Joseph
English b. 1857
paintings: (H) $1,210

KINGHAN, Charles
American b. 1895
paintings: (H) $700

KINGMAN, Dong
American b. 1911
paintings: (H) $495
drawings: (L) $137; (H) $26,400

KINGMAN, Eduardo
Ecuadorean b. 1913
paintings: (L) $550; (H) $7,700
drawings: (L) $110; (H) $1,760

KINGSLEY, Elbridge
American 1841-1918
paintings: (L) $110; (H) $770

KINGSMAN, Doug
American b. 1911
drawings: (H) $715

KINGZECA (?), A.
paintings: (H) $3,300

KINKADE, Thomas
American b. 1947
paintings: (L) $3,900; (H) $4,730

KINLOCH, E.L.
paintings: (L) $880; (H) $880

KINNAIRD, Frederick Gerald
British 19th cent.
paintings: (H) $2,640

KINNAIRD, Henry J.
British ac. 1880-c. 1920
paintings: (L) $770; (H) $3,960
drawings: (L) $825; (H) $4,950

KINNAIRD, Wiggs
English exhib. 1894-1911
paintings: (H) $550
drawings: (L) $880; (H) $990

KINSBURGER, Sylvain
French b. 1855
sculpture: (L) $192; (H) $1,870

KINSELLA, James
American 1857-1923
drawings: (H) $770

KINSEY, Alberta
American 1875-1955
paintings: (L) $137; (H) $5,170

KINSON
paintings: (H) $1,210

KINSON, Francis Joseph
Flemish 1771-1839
paintings: (H) $1,650

KINTZ, W.C.
19th/20th cent.
paintings: (H) $900

KINZEL, Josef
Austrian 1852-1925
paintings: (L) $1,100; (H) $11,000

KIOERBOE, Carl Fredrik
Swedish 1799-1876
paintings: (L) $1,210; (H) $1,870

KIPNESS, Robert
American b. 1931
paintings: (L) $825; (H) $3,080

KIRBERG, Otto Karl
German 1850-1926
paintings: (H) $18,700

KIRCHHOFF, Peter
sculpture: (H) $660

KIRCHNER, Ernst Ludwig
German 1880-1938
paintings: (L) $50,600; (H) $1,650,000
drawings: (L) $1,100; (H) $77,000
sculpture: (H) $825

KIRCHNER, Otto
German b. 1887
paintings: (L) $495; (H) $2,200

KIRCHNER, Raphael
Austrian 1876-1917
paintings: (H) $14,300

KIRILI, Alain
contemporary
paintings: (H) $5,720
sculpture: (H) $7,150

KIRIN, G. Vogt
20th cent.
paintings: (H) $1,100

KIRK, Marie Louise
drawings: (L) $358; (H) $660

KIRK, Thomas
English d. 1797
paintings: (L) $550; (H) $715

KIRKBY, Thomas
English ac. 1796-1847
paintings: (L) $1,760; (H) $3,300

KIRKEBY, Per
Danish b. 1938
paintings: (L) $18,700; (H) $39,600

KIRKPATRICK
English 19th cent.
paintings: (H) $3,850

KIRKPATRICK, Ethel
British 20th cent.
paintings: (H) $1,100

KIRKPATRICK, Frank LeBrun
American 1853-1917
paintings: (L) $467; (H) $17,602

KIRKPATRICK, William A.B.
American b. 1880
paintings: (L) $150; (H) $3,520

KIRMSE, Marguerite
Anglo/American 1885-1954
paintings: (H) $467
drawings: (L) $522; (H) $770
sculpture: (H) $132

KIRSCH, Johanna
paintings: (H) $825

KISCHKA, Isis
French 1908-1974
paintings: (L) $132; (H) $1,210

KISELEWSKI, Joseph
American 1901-1988
sculpture: (L) $330; (H) $48,400

KISH, Maurice
Russian/American b. 1898
paintings: (H) $880

KISLING, Moise
Polish/French 1891-1953
paintings: (L) $3,575; (H) $396,000

KISS, Rudolph
American 1898-1953
paintings: (L) $605; (H) $2,200

KISSACK, R.A.
American
paintings: (H) $4,400

KISSEL, Eleanora
American 1891-1966
paintings: (H) $1,100

KITA, Renzo
Japanese 19th/20th cent.
paintings: (H) $1,100

KITAJ, R.B.
American b. 1933
paintings: (L) $99,000; (H) $385,000

KITCHELL, Hudson M.
American 1862-1944
paintings: (L) $165; (H) $2,750

KITCHEN, Robert
drawings: (H) $825

KITCHEN, Tella
paintings: (L) $770; (H) $4,700

KITCHIN, Benjamin Spurgeon
American b. 1892
paintings: (H) $990
drawings: (H) $990

KITSON, Henry Hudson
American 1863-1947
sculpture: (L) $1,540; (H) $9,900

KITSON, Theo Alice Ruggles
American 1876-1932
sculpture: (H) $4,070

KITTELL, Nicholas Biddle
1822-1894
paintings: (L) $220; (H) $880

KITTY, N.
American 20th cent
paintings: (H) $770

KJAKOBSEN
contemporary
paintings: (H) $1,800

KLAER, T. van
German 19th/20th cent.
paintings: (H) $935

KLAPPER, Siegfried
paintings: (H) $2,420

KLAUS, Joseph
Belgian 19th cent.
paintings: (H) $8,800

KLEBE, Gene
American b. 1907
drawings: (L) $412; (H) $1,265
sculpture: (H) $165

KLECZYNSKI, Bodhan von
Polish d. 1850
paintings: (L) $8,800; (H) $18,700

KLECZYNSKI, Bohdan von
Polish 1851-1916
paintings: (L) $2,420; (H) $8,800

KLEE, Paul
Swiss 1879-1940
paintings: (L) $110,000; (H) $1,017,500
drawings: (L) $990; (H) $1,320,000

KLEEHAAS, Theodor
German b. 1854
paintings: (L) $3,080; (H) $38,500

KLEEMAN, Ron
American b. 1937
paintings: (L) $880; (H) $22,000

KLEIBER, Hans
paintings: (H) $192
drawings: (H) $660

KLEIN, Franz
Belgian 20th cent.
paintings: (H) $7,150

KLEIN, Phillip
drawings: (H) $2,640

KLEIN, Wilhelm
German 1821-1897
paintings: (H) $2,200

KLEIN, Yves
French 1928-1962
paintings: (L) $23,100; (H) $61,600

KLEINBARD, Alexa
contemporary
paintings: (L) $220; (H) $770

KLEINE, David
paintings: (H) $11,000

KLEINERT, Joseph Edgar
paintings: (H) $3,520

KLEINHOLZ, Frank
American b. 1901
paintings: (L) $302; (H) $935

KLEINMANN, Fryc
Polish
drawings: (H) $880

KLEINMEYER, B.
paintings: (H) $1,430

KLEINSCHMIDT, Paul
German b. 1883
paintings: (H) $19,800
drawings: (L) $550; (H) $2,420

KLEITSCH, Joseph
Hungarian/American 1885-1931
paintings: (L) $605; (H) $75,900

KLEMKE, Hans
paintings: (H) $880

KLEMM, E.
Austrian ac. 1850
paintings: (L) $1,210; (H) $1,980

KLENGEL, Johann Christian
drawings: (H) $1,650

KLEVER, Julius Sergius von
Russian 1850-1924
paintings: (L) $825; (H) $22,000

KLEY, George
German 20th cent.
paintings: (H) $990

KLEY, Heinrich
German 1863-1945
paintings: (L) $572; (H) $1,760
drawings: (L) $220; (H) $220

KLEY, Henri
German b. 1908
paintings: (L) $880; (H) $880

KLEY, Henry or Henri
French 20th cent.
paintings: (L) $330; (H) $715

KLEYN, Lodewyk Johannes
Dutch 1817-1897
paintings: (L) $880; (H) $25,300

KLIMT, Gustav
Austrian 1862-1918
paintings: (H) $3,850,000
drawings: (L) $1,045; (H) $41,800

KLINE, Franz
American 1910-1962
paintings: (L) $5,500; (H) $2,860,000
drawings: (L) $880; (H) $154,000

KLINE, William Fair
American 1870-1931
paintings: (H) $990

KLINGER, Max
German 1857-1920
drawings: (H) $1,540
sculpture: (H) $9,350

KLINGSBOG, M.
paintings: (H) $715

KLINGSBOGL, Rudolf
Austrian b. 1881
paintings: (H) $1,100

KLINKENBERG, Johannes Christiaan Karel
Dutch 1852-1924
paintings: (L) $825; (H) $3,300
drawings: (L) $1,540; (H) $11,000

KLINKENBURG
paintings: (H) $3,300

KLINKER
German 20th cent.
paintings: (H) $770

KLINKER, Orpha
American 1891-1964
paintings: (L) $330; (H) $770

KLITGAARD, Georgina
American b. 1893
paintings: (H) $880
drawings: (H) $66

KLIUN, Ivan
Russian 1873-1943
drawings: (H) $25,300

KLODNICKI, Taddeus
Polish/American 1904-1982
drawings: (H) $660

KLOMBECK, Johann Bernard
Dutch 1815-1893
paintings: (L) $15,400; (H) $35,200

KLOMBEECK, Johann Bernard and Eugene **VERBOECKHOVEN**
Belgian 19th cent.
paintings: (H) $105,600

KLOSSOWSKI, Erich
German 1875-1949
drawings: (H) $935

KLOVSTAD, Eric
Continental 19th/20th cent.
paintings: (H) $770

KLUGE, Constantine
Russian b. 1912, French
paintings: (L) $374; (H) $7,700

KLUM, I.H.E.
paintings: (H) $660

KLUMPKE, Anna Elisabeth
American 1856-1942
paintings: (L) $4,400; (H) $4,400

KLUMPP, Gustav
American 1902-1980
paintings: (L) $2,420; (H) $4,675

KLUTH, R.
paintings: (H) $715

KLUYVER, Pieter Lodewijk Francisco
Dutch 1816-1900
paintings: (H) $2,860

KNAPP, Charles W.
American 1822-1900
paintings: (L) $550; (H) $26,400

KNAPP, George Kasson
American 1833-1910
paintings: (H) $2,500

KNAPP, Johann
Austrian 1778-1833
paintings: (H) $3,850

KNAPP, N.A.
paintings: (H) $880

KNATHS, Karl
American 1891-1971
paintings: (L) $209; (H) $13,200
drawings: (L) $88; (H) $990

KNAUS, F.
German 19th cent.
paintings: (H) $1,100

KNAUS, Ludwig
German 1829-1910
paintings: (L) $6,050; (H) $99,000
drawings: (H) $550

KNAVER, Robert W.
American 20th cent.
drawings: (H) $770

KNEBEL, Franz, the younger
Swiss 1809-1877
paintings: (H) $4,950

KNEE, Gina
American b. 1898
drawings: (H) $3,300

KNEIP, Grebbard
paintings: (H) $1,980

KNELL, J.H.
English ac. 1833-1834
paintings: (H) $880

KNELL, William Adolphus
English c. 1805-1875
paintings: (L) $5,500; (H) $9,900

KNELL, William Calcott
English ac. 1848-1871
paintings: (L) $990; (H) $4,950
drawings: (H) $990

KNELLER, Sir Godfrey
German/English 1646-1723
paintings: (L) $880; (H) $20,900

KNIBBERGEN, Catharina van
Dutch 17th cent.
paintings: (H) $2,090

KNIGHT, A. Roland
British 19th cent.
paintings: (L) $5,500; (H) $7,700

KNIGHT, Aston
paintings: (H) $880

KNIGHT, Charles P.
paintings: (H) $1,045

KNIGHT, Charles R.
American 1874-1953
paintings: (L) $825; (H) $3,850

KNIGHT, Dame Laura
English 1877-1970
drawings: (L) $3,000; (H) $9,900

KNIGHT, Daniel Ridgway
American 1839-1924
paintings: (L) $2,750; (H) $71,500
drawings: (L) $990; (H) $3,850

KNIGHT, F.
English 19th cent.
paintings: (L) $715; (H) $935

KNIGHT, J.A.
British 19th cent.
paintings: (H) $880

KNIGHT, Louis Aston
American 1873-1948
paintings: (L) $110; (H) $30,800

KNIGHT, William Henry
British 1823-1863
paintings: (L) $1,870; (H) $13,200

KNIJFF, Wouter
Dutch c. 1607-c. 1693
paintings: (L) $11,000; (H) $23,100

KNIKKER, Aris
Dutch 19th cent.
paintings: (H) $1,210

KNIKKER, Jan Simon
Dutch b. 1911
paintings: (L) $715; (H) $1,100

KNIP, August
paintings: (H) $1,430

KNIP, William Alexander
Dutch 1883-1967
paintings: (L) $412; (H) $1,100

KNOCHL, Hans
German b. 1850
paintings: (H) $3,960

KNOEBEL, Imi
contemporary
paintings: (H) $8,250
drawings: (H) $3,850

KNOLL, Leon
American 1884-1975
paintings: (H) $1,320

KNOLLE, Helene Friedriks
ac. 20th cent.
drawings: (H) $770

KNOOP, August
German b. 1856
paintings: (L) $275; (H) $1,540

KNOPF, H.
paintings: (H) $1,375

KNOPF, Hermann
Austrian b. 1870
paintings: (L) $880; (H) $1,760

KNORR, Charles Emile
French b. 1890
paintings: (L) $1,650; (H) $1,650

KNOWLAND, Tom
20th cent.
sculpture: (H) $935

KNOWLES, C.B.
British 19th cent.
paintings: (H) $4,675

KNOWLES, Davidson
British 19th cent.
paintings: (H) $1,100

KNOWLES, Elizabeth A.
Canadian 1866-1928
paintings: (H) $660

KNOWLES, F. McGillvray
American 1860-1932
paintings: (H) $1,650
drawings: (H) $500

KNOWLES, Fred J.
paintings: (H) $1,650

KNOWLES, George Sheridan
English 1863-1931
paintings: (L) $935; (H) $16,500

KNOWLTON, Helen Mary
American 1832-1913/18
paintings: (H) $660
drawings: (H) $154

KNOWLTON, Win
American b. 1953
sculpture: (H) $22,000

KNOX, James
American b. 1866
paintings: (L) $110; (H) $4,400

KNOX, Susan Ricker
American 1875-1959
paintings: (L) $137; (H) $5,390
drawings: (L) $22; (H) $660

KNOX, W.
paintings: (H) $2,750

KNOX, Wilfred
American 1886-1966
paintings: (H) $2,750

KNUPFER, Benes
Czechoslovakian 1848-1910
paintings: (L) $176; (H) $10,450

KNYFF, Alfred de
Belgian 1819-1885
paintings: (H) $3,850

KNYFF, Wouter
Dutch c. 1607-c. 1693
paintings: (L) $5,775; (H) $11,000

KOBELL, Jan, III
Dutch 1800-1838
paintings: (L) $935; (H) $1,650

KOBELL, Wilhelm von
German 1766-1855
drawings: (H) $5,280

KOCH, A.
paintings: (H) $1,100

KOCH, Georg
German b. 1878
paintings: (L) $2,420; (H) $7,150

KOCH, H.
German 19th cent.
paintings: (H) $1,430

KOCH, John
American 1909/10-1978
paintings: (L) $462; (H) $363,000
drawings: (L) $220; (H) $6,380
sculpture: (L) $660; (H) $2,090

KOCH, Ludwig
Austrian 1866-1934
paintings: (H) $15,400

KOCH, Martin
20th cent.
paintings: (L) $1,045; (H) $1,100

KOCH, Peter
paintings: (H) $1,210

KOCH, Walter
German 1875-1915
paintings: (H) $1,760

KOCHANOWSKI, Roman
Polish 1856-1945
paintings: (H) $1,320

KOCHEISHVILI, Boris
Russian b. 1940
paintings: (H) $6,050
drawings: (L) $1,100; (H) $1,210

KOCHER, Fritz
German/American 1904-1973
paintings: (L) $165; (H) $1,100

KOECK, *P***
paintings: (H) $1,430

KOEHLER, Henry
American b. 1927
paintings: (H) $19,800

KOEHLER, Paul R.
American 1875-1909
drawings: (L) $330; (H) $1,760

KOEHLER, Robert
American 1850-1917
paintings: (H) $11,000

KOEKKEK, Frederick
Dutch 19th cent.
paintings: (H) $770

KOEKKOEK, Barend Cornelis
Dutch 1803-1862
paintings: (L) $880; (H) $165,000

KOEKKOEK, Hendrik Barend
Dutch 1849-1909
paintings: (L) $1,100; (H) $7,700

KOEKKOEK, Hendrik Pieter
Dutch 1843-1890
paintings: (L) $4,400; (H) $16,500

KOEKKOEK, Hermanus
paintings: (L) $3,520; (H) $15,400

KOEKKOEK, Hermanus, Sr.
Dutch 1815-1882
paintings: (L) $770; (H) $52,250

KOEKKOEK, Hermanus, called Jan
van COUVER Jr.
Dutch 1836-1909
paintings: (L) $99; (H) $5,500
drawings: (L) $121; (H) $660

KOEKKOEK, Hermanus Willem
Dutch 1867-1929
paintings: (H) $3,300

KOEKKOEK, Jan Hermanus
paintings: (H) $126,500

KOEKKOEK, Johannes Hermanus
Dutch 1778-1851
paintings: (L) $7,700; (H) $10,450

KOEKKOEK, Johannes Hermanus
Barend
Dutch 1840-1912
paintings: (L) $2,860; (H) $41,800

KOEKKOEK, Marinus Adrianus
Dutch 1807-1870
paintings: (L) $4,950; (H) $19,800

KOEKKOEK, Marinus Adrianus, II
Dutch 1873-1944
paintings: (H) $2,640

KOEKKOEK, Willem
Dutch 1839-1895
paintings: (L) $2,310; (H) $110,000

KOEKOER, John
paintings: (H) $825

KOELPIN, William J.
paintings: (H) $935

KOEMPOECZI, O.
Polish 20th cent.
paintings: (H) $3,300

KOENIGER, Walter
American b. 1881
paintings: (L) $500; (H) $17,600

KOENINCK, David de
paintings: (H) $19,800

KOERNER, Ernst Karl Eugen
German 1846-1927
paintings: (H) $10,450

KOERNER, Henry
drawings: (L) $2,310; (H) $3,300

KOERNER, Henry
Austrian/American b. 1915
drawings: (L) $55; (H) $3,300

KOERNER, William Henry Dethlef
German/American 1878-1938
paintings: (L) $462; (H) $27,000
drawings: (L) $1,100; (H) $2,475

KOESSLER, W.
German 19th/20th cent.
paintings: (L) $440; (H) $825

KOESTER, Alexander Max
German 1864-1932
paintings: (L) $2,750; (H) $264,000
drawings: (H) $286

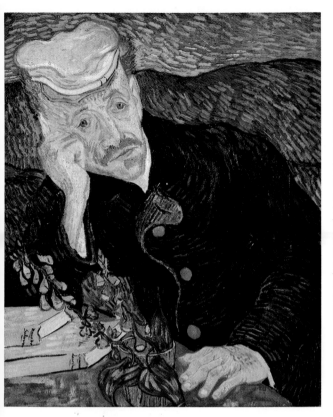

Post-Impressionist Vincent van Gogh's (1853-1890) *Portrait Du Dr. Gachet* had an impeccable provenance and had been widely exhibited, most recently at the Metropolitan Museum of Art in 1987. The oil (26 x 22½ in.) was painted in 1890, shortly before van Gogh's death. Consigned from the estate of Siegfried Kramarsky, it sold to a Japanese industrialist for $82.5 million, a record price for any work of art.
(Christie's, May 15, 1990)

Pierre Auguste Renoir's *Au Moulin de la Galette* is one of two versions of the same scene. The other, slightly larger oil hangs in the Musée d'Orsay in Paris. Consigned from the John Whitney Collection, the painting sold for $78.1 million to the same Japanese industrialist who had bought van Gogh's *Portrait Du Dr. Gachet* the previous day at Christie's.
(Sotheby's, May 17, 1990)

Joaquin Sorolla y Bastida was a prolific artist and painted a wide variety of subjects—genre, portraits, and landscapes. He lived in Valencia, Spain, and during the summers painted beach scenes. *Niños en la Playa* (28⅜ x 37⅜ in.), executed in 1904, set an auction record for the artist when it fetched $2.42 million. (Sotheby's, May 23, 1990)

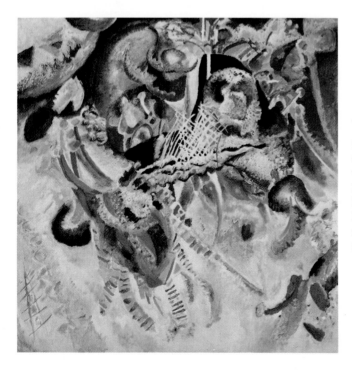

Wassily Kandinsky's oil *Fugue* (51 x 51 in.) was painted in 1914, a transitional painting as his works became more abstract. Deaccessioned by the Guggenheim Museum, the catalog cover lot sold for $20.9 million, a record for the artist.
(Sotheby's, May 17, 1990)

Jacopo da Carucci, called Pontormo, was a 15th-century Italian Mannerist painter. His *Portrait of Duke Cosimo I de' Medici* (36¼ x 28⅝ in.) is an oil on panel transferred to canvas in an early 17th-century Bolognese frame. With an extensive provenance and many citations in art publications, it has been widely exhibited. The painting was consigned from the collection of Chauncey D. Stillman and sold to the Getty Museum for $35.2 million. (Christie's, May 31, 1989)

Edouard Manet's Impressionist painting *La Rue Mosnier Aux Drapeaux* (25¾ x 31¾ in.) was the highlight of the sale of works of art from the Paul Mellon Collection. The painting, which was signed and dated 1878, was featured on the catalog cover. The oil, which Mellon had bought in 1958 for $316,400, sold to the Getty Museum for $26.4 million, a record for the artist. (Christie's, November 14, 1989)

Seductive adolescent girls are a favorite theme of Balthus. *La Toilette*, painted in 1957, depicts one of his favorite models, his nineteen-year-old niece, Frederique Tison. *La Toilette* (64 x 51¼ in.), the catalog cover lot for Sotheby's fall 1989 contemporary paintings sale, was deaccessioned by the Billy Wilder Collection; the sale set a record for the artist when the painting sold for $2.09 million. (Christie's, November 13, 1989)

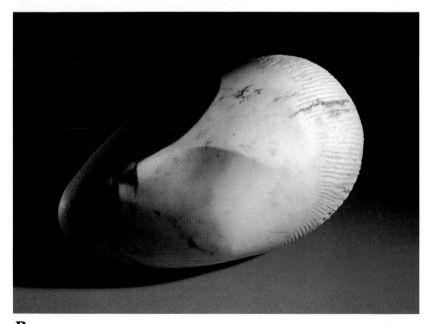

Brancusi received some formal academic training both in Budapest and Paris, but was mainly self-taught. Rejecting the tenets of both the Impressionists and the Cubists, he developed his own style, eliminating superfluous detail until his sculptures were reduced to a primordial form. *La Muse Endormie III* (7¼ x 11⅜ in.), executed in 1917, is a classic example of his work. Sold at Christie's in the fall of 1989, this unique marble, one of a series of three, fetched $8.25 million. (Christie's, November 14, 1989)

Marc Chagall's *Anniversaire* (31⅞ x 39½ in.), deaccessioned by the Guggenheim Museum, was executed in 1923. It is a replica of an earlier 1915 version which is in the collection of the Museum of Modern Art, New York. Purchased directly from the artist in 1926 by Solomon Guggenheim, it sold for $14.85 million, a record for the artist. (Sotheby's, May 17, 1990)

Thomas Eakins (1844-1916) was an American Realist painter and well-known teacher at the Pennsylvania Academy of Fine Arts. *John Biglin in a Single Scull,* executed in 1873, was one of a series of paintings of men sculling. The watercolor (16⅞ x 24 in.) had been missing for over 100 years. Featured on the catalog cover, the watercolor sold for $3.52 million to an American private collector. (Christie's, May 23, 1990)

Paul Gauguin painted *Mata Mua, In Olden Times* in 1892 during his first trip to Tahiti. An excellent example of his mature style, the oil set an auction record for the artist when it sold for $24.2 million. Only five years earlier, the same painting had fetched $3.8 million. The painting is in the Thyssen-Bornemisza Collection in Lugano, Switzerland.
(Sotheby's, May 9, 1989)

Claude Monet's *Le Parlement, Coucher de Soleil* (32¼ x 36½ in.) was one of his Thames series, which included a view of the Houses of Parliament as seen from across the river. The oil, from the Hal Wallis Collection, had been on loan to the Los Angeles Museum of Art from 1987 to 1989. The painting sold for $14.3 million, a record for a Monet painting.
(Christie's, May 10, 1989)

Au Lapin Agile (39 x 39½ in.) was painted by Pablo Picasso in 1904, just after he had moved to Paris. Consigned from the Payson Collection, the oil sold for $40.7 million to Walter Annenberg, and will eventually be part of the permanent collection at the Metropolitan Museum of Art. (Sotheby's, November 15, 1989)

Garçon à la Veste Bleue (36¼ x 24 in.) was painted by Amedeo Modigliani in 1918. Widely exhibited, the oil, one of a series of works deaccessioned by the Guggenheim Museum, sold for $11.55 million. (Sotheby's, May 17, 1990)

Abstract Expressionist Willem de Kooning's *Interchange* (79 x 69 in.) was painted in 1955, one of a series of paintings which redirected de Kooning's art. Featured on the catalog cover, the painting from the Edgar J. Kauffmann estate sold for $20.68 million, a record for the artist. (Sotheby's, November 8, 1989)

Jenny Holzer (b. 1950) is a Conceptualist artist whose works have been internationally recognized and who has won many awards. *Selections from the Survival Series*, executed in 1983 in an edition of five, is an electronic LED sign with red diodes (6½ x 121½ x 4 in.). The sign sold for $82,500, a record for the artist. (Christie's, May 8, 1990)

KOETS, Roelof, the elder
Dutch 1592/93-1655
paintings: (L) $33,000; (H) $99,000

KOFFA
paintings: (H) $1,100

KOGAN, Moissej
Russian 1879-1930
sculpture: (H) $3,575

KOGAN, Nina
drawings: (H) $16,500

KOGL, Benedict
German 1892-1969
paintings: (L) $1,650; (H) $3,850

KOHL, Clemens
1754-1807
drawings: (H) $1,650

KOHLBECK, John
Continental 19th cent.
paintings: (H) $1,210

KOHLEN, Carl
German 19th cent.
paintings: (H) $3,575

KOHLER, Gustav
German b. 1859
paintings: (L) $1,760; (H) $5,500

KOHLHOFER, Christof
contemporary
paintings: (H) $1,650

KOHLMEYER, Ida
American b. 1912
paintings: (L) $275; (H) $9,350
drawings: (H) $132

KOHRL, Ludwig
German b. 1858
paintings: (L) $247; (H) $1,760

KOKKEN, Henri
Belgian b. 1860
paintings: (H) $7,425

KOKO-MIKOLETZKY, F.
Austrian 19th/20th cent.
paintings: (L) $55; (H) $3,410

KOKOSCHKA, Oskar
Austrian 1886-1980
paintings: (L) $99,000; (H) $2,970,000
drawings: (L) $1,320; (H) $41,800

KOLAR, Jiri
Czechoslovakian b. 1919
drawings: (L) $715; (H) $4,950
sculpture: (L) $1,980; (H) $2,750

KOLBE, Georg
German 1877-1947
drawings: (L) $1,870; (H) $2,200
sculpture: (L) $2,200; (H) $26,400

KOLESNIKOFF, Sergei
Russian b. 1889
paintings: (L) $2,750; (H) $3,520

KOLIG, Anton
drawings: (H) $825

KOLITZ, Louis
German 1845-1914
paintings: (L) $880; (H) $5,280

KOLLER, Wilhelm, Guillaume
Austrian 1829-1884
paintings: (H) $1,870
drawings: (H) $1,870

KOLLNER, Augustus
American b. 1813
drawings: (L) $242; (H) $3,850

KOLLWITZ, Kathe
German 1867-1945
paintings: (H) $632
drawings: (L) $6,600; (H) $15,400
sculpture: (L) $13,000; (H) $37,400

KOLN, J.
Austrian 19th/20th cent.
paintings: (H) $8,800

KOLOKOLCHIK
Russian 20th cent.
paintings: (H) $1,100

KOLOSHVARY
paintings: (H) $2,200

KOMAR and MELAMID
contemporary
drawings: (H) $48,400

KOMAROMI-KACZ, Endre
Hungarian b. 1880
paintings: (H) $2,200

KONARSKI, Josef
Polish 19th cent.
paintings: (L) $242; (H) $1,540

KONDOS, Gregory
American b. 1923
paintings: (H) $6,050

KONEK, Ida
Austrian b. 1856
paintings: (H) $715

KONI, Nicolaus
Hungarian/American b. 1911
sculpture: (L) $440; (H) $3,960

KONIG, Johann
German
paintings: (H) $3,080

KONINCK, Andries de
Dutch ac. c. 1660
paintings: (L) $3,850; (H) $187,000

KONINCK, David de
Flemish c. 1636-1699
paintings: (H) $13,200

KONINCK, Philips
Dutch 1619-1688
drawings: (H) $28,600

KONING, Elisabeth Joanna
Dutch 1816-1888
paintings: (H) $4,400

KONING, Johannes
Dutch 19th cent.
paintings: (H) $935

KONINGH, Leendert de
Dutch 1777-1849
drawings: (L) $1,760; (H) $6,050

KONINGH, Leendert de
Dutch 1810-1887
paintings: (H) $880

KONO, Micao
Japanese contemporary
paintings: (L) $6,600; (H) $27,500

KONRAD, Adolf
American
paintings: (H) $935

KONTCHALOVSKY, Piotr
Russian b. 1876
paintings: (L) $825; (H) $2,200

KONTI, Isidore
Austrian/American 1862-1938
sculpture: (L) $605; (H) $6,050

KOOKEN, Olive
sculpture: (L) $99; (H) $1,210

KOOL, Willem Gillesz
Dutch c. 1608-1666
paintings: (L) $16,500; (H) $33,000

KOONS, Jeff
American b. 1955
sculpture: (H) $27,500

KOOPMAN, Augustus
American 1869-1914
paintings: (L) $220; (H) $1,540

KOPEL, G.F.
paintings: (H) $825

KOPF, Maxim
paintings: (L) $440; (H) $880

KOPMAN, Benjamin D.
Russian/American 1887-1965
paintings: (L) $66; (H) $5,280
drawings: (L) $55; (H) $220

KOPNER, P.
paintings: (H) $715

KOPP, J.
sculpture: (H) $660

KOPPAY, Joszi Arpad
Hungarian b. 1859
paintings: (H) $5,500
drawings: (H) $1,100

KOPPENOL, Cornelis
Dutch 1865-1946
paintings: (L) $385; (H) $6,500

KOPYSTIANSKY, Igor
Russian b. 1954
paintings: (L) $10,450; (H) $33,000
sculpture: (H) $11,000

KORBEL, J.P.M.
sculpture: (H) $1,100

KORBEL, Mario J.
b. Czechoslavakia 1882-1954
sculpture: (L) $330; (H) $9,900

KORIN, J.L.
European 19th cent.
paintings: (H) $880

KORNBECK, Hermann Julius
paintings: (H) $2,200

KOROVINE, Constantin Alexeievitch
Russian 1861-1939
paintings: (L) $1,100; (H) $26,400
drawings: (L) $275; (H) $275

KORSCHANN, Charles
Czechoslovakian b. 1872
sculpture: (L) $330; (H) $3,575

KORTE, H.G. de
Continental 19th/20th cent.
paintings: (H) $4,400

KOSA, E.
paintings: (H) $1,595

KOSA, Emil, Sr.
American 1876-1955
paintings: (L) $550; (H) $1,100

KOSA, Emil Jean, Jr.
American 1903-1968
paintings: (L) $1,650; (H) $12,100
drawings: (L) $440; (H) $2,475

KOSCIANSKI, Leonard
American 20th cent.
sculpture: (H) $990

KOSINSKY, Anna M.
American b.c. 1890-1961
paintings: (H) $16,500

KOSLER, Franz Xavier
Austrian b. 1864
paintings: (L) $1,760; (H) $18,700

KOSSAK, Jerzy
Polish 1890-1963
paintings: (L) $110; (H) $3,080

KOSSAK, Wojciech
Polish 1857-1942
paintings: (L) $1,320; (H) $5,500

KOSSOWSKI, Henryk, the younger
Polish 19th/20th cent.
sculpture: (L) $467; (H) $1,100

KOSSUTH, Egon Josef
German b. 1874
paintings: (H) $1,760

KOST, Frederick W.
American 1865-1923
paintings: (L) $220; (H) $1,540

KOST, Julius
German 1807-1888
paintings: (H) $2,860

KOSTA, Alex
contemporary
sculpture: (H) $4,125

KOSTABI, Mark
American b. 1960
paintings: (L) $4,400; (H) $12,100
drawings: (L) $220; (H) $1,100

KOSTER, Everhardus
Dutch 1817-1892
paintings: (L) $1,485; (H) $2,200

KOSTER, Paul
German b. 1855
paintings: (H) $3,300

KOSTRZEWSKI, F.
paintings: (H) $1,100

KOSUTH, Joseph
Hungarian/American b. 1945
drawings: (L) $2,860; (H) $49,500
sculpture: (H) $82,500

KOTAZOVOUCY
paintings: (H) $715

KOTCH, George J.
American
drawings: (H) $1,210

KOTSCHENREITER, Georg H.
paintings: (H) $2,640

KOTSCHENREITER, Hugo
German 1854-1908
paintings: (L) $3,080; (H) $7,150

KOTTLER, Howard
American b. 1930
sculpture: (H) $4,400

KOULICHE, M.
French 20th cent.
paintings: (L) $825; (H) $990

KOUNELLIS, Jannis
Greek/Italian b. 1936
paintings: (L) $14,300; (H) $148,500

KOUSNETSOFF, Constantine
Russian 19th cent.
paintings: (H) $1,870

KOUTROULIS, Aris
contemporary
paintings: (H) $1,320

KOVNER, Saul
American 1904-1982
paintings: (L) $1,650; (H) $4,950

KOWAK, Franz
paintings: (H) $825

KOWALCZEWSKI, Karl
German b. 1876
sculpture: (L) $220; (H) $3,025

KOWALCZEWSKI, P.
sculpture: (L) $308; (H) $770

KOWALSKI, Ivan Ivanovitch
Russian early 20th cent.
drawings: (L) $247; (H) $1,100

KOWALSKI, Leopold Franz
French b. 1856
paintings: (L) $77,000; (H) $132,000

KOWALSKI-WIERUSZ, Alfred von
Polish 1849-1915
paintings: (L) $4,400; (H) $33,000

KOWASKI, D.
European 19th cent.
paintings: (H) $2,750

KOWLASKI
Polish/American 20th cent.
paintings: (L) $715; (H) $715

KOZAKIEWICZ, Anton
paintings: (H) $5,500

KOZLOFF, Alexander I.
American 20th cent.
paintings: (H) $1,540

KOZLOFF, Joyce
American
paintings: (H) $1,650

KOZLOW, Richard
paintings: (L) $220; (H) $1,045

KOZMON, George
American b. 1960
drawings: (H) $715

KRABANSKY, Gustave
French ac. 1876-1897
sculpture: (H) $10,450

KRABBE, Hendrik Maarten
paintings: (L) $1,430; (H) $3,300

KRACK, L.
early 20th cent.
sculpture: (H) $660

KRAEMER, Peter
German b. 1857
paintings: (L) $6,600; (H) $7,150
drawings: (L) $1,320; (H) $11,000

KRAFFT, Carl R.
American 1884-1930
paintings: (L) $121; (H) $6,490

KRAFT, M.
paintings: (H) $742

KRAMER, Jack
American 1923-1983
paintings: (L) $99; (H) $1,760

KRAMER, James
American b. 1927
drawings: (H) $715

KRAMER, R.
paintings: (H) $660

KRANTZ, F.
French 19th cent.
paintings: (L) $1,210; (H) $1,760

KRANTZ, Robert B.
American 20th cent.
sculpture: (L) $660; (H) $880

KRASNER, Lee
American b. 1912
paintings: (L) $6,050; (H) $165,000
drawings: (L) $16,500; (H) $25,300

KRATKE, Charles Louis
French 1848-1921
paintings: (L) $1,430; (H) $4,950

KRATKY, A***
Continental School 19th/20th cent.
paintings: (H) $3,300

KRATKY, S.
European 19th/20th cent.
paintings: (H) $1,045

KRAULBACH, Friedrich August von
paintings: (H) $1,540

KRAUS, August
German b. 1868
paintings: (L) $1,870; (H) $3,300

KRAUS, Friederich
German 1826-1894
paintings: (H) $1,320

KRAUS, Georg Melchior
German 1737-1806
paintings: (H) $8,250

KRAUS, Jan
Polish b. 1760
paintings: (H) $4,125

KRAUSE, F.
19th cent.
paintings: (L) $330; (H) $1,650

KRAUSE, J.
paintings: (H) $1,210

KRAUSE, L.
paintings: (L) $550; (H) $770

KRAUSE, Laverne
American b. 1924
paintings: (H) $825

KRAUSE, Lina
German b. 1857
paintings: (L) $1,650; (H) $10,450

KRAUSE, S.
German 19th cent.
paintings: (L) $1,045; (H) $1,320

KRAUSKOPF, Bruno
German 1892-1962
paintings: (L) $550; (H) $5,500
drawings: (L) $220; (H) $1,870

KRAUSS, Robert Frank
paintings: (H) $1,540

KRAUSZ, Wilhelm Victor
Hungarian b. 1878
paintings: (L) $550; (H) $660

KRAUTIK, All.
Continental 19th cent.
paintings: (H) $2,200

KRAWIEC, Harriet
American 1894-1968
paintings: (L) $198; (H) $660
drawings: (L) $110; (H) $137

KRAY, Wilhelm
German 1828-1889
paintings: (L) $8,800; (H) $12,100

KREBS, Friederich
American d. 1815
drawings: (L) $5,775; (H) $17,600

KREHBIEL, Albert Henry
American 1875-1945
paintings: (L) $1,100; (H) $2,200

KREMEGNE, Pinchus
Russian b. 1890
paintings: (L) $550; (H) $10,450

KREMER, Pierre
Belgian 1801-1888
paintings: (H) $990

KRENGER, Tardos
paintings: (H) $1,430

KRENN, Edmund
Austrian 1846-1902
paintings: (H) $11,000

KRENTZIN, Earl
20th cent.
sculpture: (L) $247; (H) $770

KRENZEN, Earl
20th cent.
sculpture: (H) $770

KRESS, Frederick B.
American 1888-1970
paintings: (H) $935

KRESTIN, Lazar
paintings: (H) $5,225

KRETSCHMAR, Howard Sigesmund
American 1845-1933
sculpture: (L) $242; (H) $715

KRETZINGER, Clara
b. 1883
paintings: (H) $2,530

KRETZINGER, Clara Josephine
American b. 1883
paintings: (L) $880; (H) $7,975

KREUTZER
Canadian 19th/20th cent.
paintings: (H) $990

KREUTZER, B.
German 19th cent.
paintings: (L) $1,210; (H) $2,200

KREYDER, Alexis Joseph
French 1839-1912
paintings: (L) $6,600; (H) $16,500

KREYSSIG, Hugo
German 19th/20th cent.
paintings: (L) $66; (H) $880

KRICHELDORF, Carl
German b. 1863
paintings: (L) $55; (H) $5,500

KRICHELDORF, Hermann Gottlieb
German b. 1863
paintings: (H) $2,310

KRICKE, Norbert
German b. 1922
sculpture: (H) $38,500

KRIEGHOFF, Cornelius
Canadian 1815-1872
paintings: (L) $880; (H) $214,500
drawings: (L) $2,520; (H) $12,100

KRIEHUBER, Josef
German 1800-1876
paintings: (L) $176; (H) $2,200
drawings: (L) $2,640; (H) $2,860

KRIER
paintings: (H) $935

KRIER, E.
contemporary
paintings: (H) $1,760

KRIMMEL, John Lewis
American 1787-1821
drawings: (H) $8,800

KRIPPENDORF, William H.
German American b. 1910
paintings: (L) $110; (H) $880

KRISCHKE, Franz
Austrian 19th/20th cent.
paintings: (L) $715; (H) $1,650

KROHG, Per
paintings: (H) $935

KROHN, C.
Norwegian 19th cent.
paintings: (L) $770; (H) $2,200

KROLL, Abraham Leon
American 1884-1974
paintings: (L) $1,100; (H) $93,500
drawings: (L) $165; (H) $2,750

KRON, Paul
French 1869-1936
paintings: (L) $1,210; (H) $1,430

KRONBERG, Louis
American 1872-1965
paintings: (L) $110; (H) $25,300
drawings: (L) $38; (H) $3,575

KRONBERGER, Carl
Austrian 1841-1921
paintings: (L) $2,640; (H) $17,600

KROUTHEN, P.
early 20th cent.
paintings: (H) $2,860

KROYER, Peder Severin
Danish 1851-1909
paintings: (H) $374,000

KRUGER, Barbara
American b. 1945
drawings: (L) $17,600; (H) $49,500

KRUGER, Eugen
German 1832-1876
paintings: (H) $3,300

KRUGER, Franz
German 1797-1857
paintings: (H) $3,300

KRUGER, Richard
American b. 1880
paintings: (L) $193; (H) $1,100
drawings: (H) $220

KRUGNIAK
Continental 19th/20th cent.
paintings: (H) $770

KRUIP, Joop, II
Dutch 20th cent.
paintings: (H) $770

KRUMBACH, V.
American 19th/20th cent.
paintings: (H) $1,320

KRUPP, F.
paintings: (H) $1,320

KRUSE, Alexander Z.
American b. 1890
paintings: (H) $825
drawings: (H) $440

KRUSE, Bruno Freidrich Emile
German b. 1855
sculpture: (H) $3,575

KRUSEMAN, F.V.
paintings: (H) $7,700

KRUSEMAN, Frederik Marianus
Dutch 1816/17-1860/82
paintings: (L) $2,750; (H) $177,100

KRUSEMAN, Jan Theodor
Dutch 1835-1895
paintings: (H) $2,640

KRUSEMAN VAN ELTEN, Hendrik
Dirk
Dutch/American 1829-1904
paintings: (L) $165; (H) $12,100
drawings: (H) $528

KRUSHENICK, Nicholas
American b. 1929
paintings: (L) $198; (H) $13,200
drawings: (H) $605

KRUSZCINSKI, J.
late 19th cent.
drawings: (H) $2,750

KRUYS, Cornelis
Dutch d. 1660?
paintings: (H) $18,700

KUAPIL
paintings: (H) $3,575

KUBA, Ludvik
Czechoslovakian 1863-1956
paintings: (H) $7,425

KUBIN, Alfred
Austrian 1877-1959
drawings: (H) $5,775

KUCHLER, Rudolf
sculpture: (L) $264; (H) $770

KUEHL, Gottherd
paintings: (H) $1,100

KUEHN, Gary
contemporary
drawings: (L) $385; (H) $880

KUEHNE, Max
American 1880-1968
paintings: (L) $138; (H) $33,000
drawings: (H) $1,210

KUEN, Hendrik
drawings: (H) $660

KUGHLER, Francis Vandeveer
American b. 1901
paintings: (L) $440; (H) $825

KUHLMANN, Edward
American 1882-1973
paintings: (L) $110; (H) $990

KUHLMANN-REHER, E.
German 20th cent.
paintings: (H) $1,320

KUHN, Max
paintings: (H) $715

KUHN, Walt
American 1877/80-1949
paintings: (L) $660; (H) $192,500
drawings: (L) $27; (H) $15,400

KUHNE, Friedrich
German 1806-1834
paintings: (H) $770

KUHNE, Prof. A.
Austrian 1845-1895
sculpture: (H) $990

KUHNEN, Pieter Lodewyk
Belgian 1812-1877
paintings: (H) $1,100

KUHNERT, Wilhelm
German 1865-1926
paintings: (L) $220; (H) $28,600

KUIPERS, C.
Dutch 18th cent.
paintings: (H) $5,775

KUITCA, Guillermo
Argentinian b. 1961
paintings: (L) $5,500; (H) $14,300

KULICKE, Robert
American
paintings: (L) $682; (H) $682
drawings: (H) $770

KULIK, Karl
Austrian 1654-1713
paintings: (H) $37,400

KULMBACH, Hans Suess von, called
Hans von Kulmbach
German c. 1480-1522
drawings: (H) $82,500

KUMMER, Julius Hermann
German b. 1817
paintings: (L) $770; (H) $880

KUNADISKO, T.
drawings: (H) $660

KUNC, Milan
contemporary
paintings: (L) $4,400; (H) $8,250

KUNIYOSHI, Yasuo
American 1893-1953
paintings: (L) $12,100; (H) $616,000
drawings: (L) $165; (H) $57,200

KUNST, Pieter Cornelisz.
Dutch b. 1490
drawings: (L) $3,850; (H) $4,400

KUNSTLER, Mort
American b. 1931
paintings: (L) $1,870; (H) $2,090
drawings: (H) $770

KUNTZ, Carl
German 1770-1830
paintings: (H) $12,320

KUNTZ, Roger
American 20th cent.
paintings: (H) $4,400

KUNZ, Ludwig Adam
Austrian 1857-1929
paintings: (L) $935; (H) $8,250

KUPETSKY, Jan
1666-1740
paintings: (H) $1,100

KUPETZKI, Johann
German 1667-1740
paintings: (H) $1,100

KUPKA, Franz
Czechoslovakian 1871-1957
paintings: (H) $57,750
drawings: (L) $2,200; (H) $6,600

KURELEK, William
Canadian
drawings: (L) $5,500; (H) $13,200

KURELLA, Ludwik von
Polish 1834-1902
paintings: (L) $495; (H) $990

KURILOFF, Edna
Russian/American 1889-1979
paintings: (L) $110; (H) $3,080

KURLAND, Bruce
paintings: (L) $1,760; (H) $1,760

KURRINGER, G.A.
paintings: (H) $880

KURZ, L.
paintings: (H) $797

KURZBAUER, Eduard
German 1810-1879
paintings: (H) $1,100

KUSCHE, Carlton Julius
American 1873-1943
paintings: (L) $11; (H) $770

KUSHNER, Robert
American b. 1949
paintings: (L) $3,300; (H) $11,000
drawings: (L) $4,950; (H) $15,400
sculpture: (H) $1,430

KUSS, Ferdinand
Austrian 1800-1886
paintings: (H) $19,800

KUWASSEG, Charles Euphrasie
French 1833/38-1904
paintings: (L) $990; (H) $17,600

KUYCK, Frans Pieter van
Belgian 1852-1915
paintings: (L) $880; (H) $19,800

KUYCK, Jean Louis van
Belgian 1821-1871
paintings: (H) $3,190

KUYL, Gysbrecht van der
Dutch d. 1673
paintings: (H) $115,500

KUYPERS, Cornelis
Dutch b. 1864
paintings: (H) $1,210

KUYPERS, Dirk
Dutch 1733-1796
drawings: (H) $2,640

KVAPIL, Charles
Belgian 1884-1958
paintings: (L) $330; (H) $10,450

KWAFSEY
paintings: (H) $1,100

KYHN, Peter Wilhelm Karl
Danish 1819-1903
paintings: (L) $412; (H) $2,310

KYOKO
drawings: (H) $770

KYSER, H.L.
American 19th cent.
paintings: (L) $522; (H) $1,155

L'AIN, Girod de
contemporary
paintings: (L) $77; (H) $2,200

L'AINE, Louis Gabriel Moreau
paintings: (H) $9,350

L'AUBARDERE, Louis Paul de
paintings: (H) $1,550

L'AUBINIERE
paintings: (H) $660

L'ENGLE, William
American 1884-1957
paintings: (L) $330; (H) $1,210
drawings: (L) $50; (H) $880

L'HERMITE, Leon Augustin
French 1844-1925
paintings: (H) $6,050
drawings: (L) $440; (H) $26,400

L'HIVET, A.
French 19th cent.
paintings: (H) $2,310

L'HOSPITAL, J.F. de
French 18th/19th cent.
paintings: (H) $2,200

LA CAVE, Peter
English 18th/19th cent.
drawings: (H) $880

LA CHANCE, George
paintings: (H) $1,760

LA CORTE, Gabriel de
Spanish 1648-1694
paintings: (H) $132,000

LA COUR, Janus A.B.
Danish 1837-1909
paintings: (H) $2,750

LA CROIX
French 19th/20th cent.
paintings: (H) $1,100

LA CRUZ, Juan Pantoja de, studio of
paintings: (H) $7,150

LA FAGE, Raymond de
French c. 1650/56-1684
drawings: (L) $440; (H) $3,080

LA FARGE, John
American 1835-1910
paintings: (H) $110,000
drawings: (L) $770; (H) $93,500

LA FARGE, John and George Loring
BROWN
American
drawings: (H) $3,300

LA FONTAINE, Thomas Sherwood
English b. 1915
paintings: (L) $1,430; (H) $35,750

LA FOSSE, Charles de
French 1636-1716
paintings: (H) $13,750

LA FRESNAYE, Roger de
French 1885-1925
drawings: (L) $550; (H) $49,500

LA FUENTE, Manuel de
sculpture: (L) $7,150; (H) $20,900

LA GATTA, John
Italian/American 1894-1974
drawings: (L) $66; (H) $3,850

LA HAYE, *M*** de
paintings: (H) $3,850

LA HAYE, Reinier de
Dutch c. 1640-c.1684/95
paintings: (L) $8,250; (H) $35,200

LA HYRE, Laurent de
French 1606-1656
paintings: (H) $29,700
drawings: (H) $7,975

LA LYRE, Adolphe
French b. 1850
paintings: (L) $143; (H) $1,980

LA MARCHE, Nathalie de
drawings: (H) $4,620

LA MARE, Paul
paintings: (H) $1,980

LA MARIEE
French late 19th/20th cent.
sculpture: (H) $2,475

LA NOUE, Terence
contemporary
paintings: (H) $6,050
drawings: (H) $165

LA PIRA
Italian 19th/20th cent.
paintings: (H) $385
drawings: (H) $2,530

LA PORTE
sculpture: (H) $770

LA RICHE
sculpture: (H) $2,200

LA RUE, Louis Felix de
French 1720/31-1765
drawings: (L) $275; (H) $1,540

LA SERNA, Ismael Gonzalez de
Spanish 1900-1968
paintings: (L) $385; (H) $23,100
drawings: (L) $1,045; (H) $12,100

LA THANGUE, Henry Herbert
British 1859-1929
paintings: (L) $52,800; (H) $220,000

LA TORRE, Martin Nester de
Spanish 1888-1938
paintings: (H) $20,900

LA TOUCHE, Gaston de
French 1854-1913
paintings: (H) $660

LA VALLEY, Jonas Joseph
American 1858-1930
paintings: (L) $400; (H) $3,080
drawings: (H) $137

LA VERGNE, Adolphe Jean
French 19th cent.
sculpture: (H) $1,540

LA VILLEON, Emmanuel de
French 1858-1944
paintings: (L) $3,300; (H) $22,000

LAAN, Adolf van der
drawings: (L) $440; (H) $1,650

LAAN, Jan Zeeuw van der
Dutch 1832-1892
paintings: (H) $1,980

LAAR, Jan Hendrik van de
Dutch 1807-1874
paintings: (H) $4,950

LABASQUE, Henri
drawings: (H) $2,420

LABATUT, Jules Jacques
sculpture: (L) $825; (H) $3,025

LABAUDT, Lucien Adolph
American 1880-1943
paintings: (L) $357; (H) $1,210

LABBE, Emile Charles
before 1820-1885
drawings: (H) $1,650

LABINO, Dominick
American b. 1910
sculpture: (L) $1,045; (H) $13,200

LABISSE, Felix
paintings: (H) $4,400

LABOR, Charles
French 1813-1900
paintings: (H) $15,400

LABOUREUR, Jean Emile
French 1877-1943
paintings: (H) $19,800

LABROUCHE, Pierre
French 19th/20th cent.
paintings: (H) $1,265

LABRUZZI, Pietro
Italian 1739-1805
paintings: (L) $660; (H) $39,600

LACASSE, Joseph
1894-1975
paintings: (L) $715; (H) $1,210

LACAULT, Aquiles Leon
French b. 1866
paintings: (H) $1,870

LACAZE, Germaine
paintings: (H) $3,000

LACEY, Charles J. de
British 19th cent.
paintings: (H) $3,410

LACH, Andreas
Austrian 1817-1882
paintings: (L) $1,980; (H) $6,050

LACHAISE, Eugene A.
American 1857-1925
paintings: (H) $11,000

LACHAISE, Gaston
French 1882-1935
drawings: (L) $550; (H) $8,250
sculpture: (L) $2,750; (H) $165,000

LACHANCE, Georges
American b. 1880
paintings: (H) $3,080

LACHENWITZ, F. Sigmund
paintings: (H) $2,750

LACHMAN, Harry
American 1886-1974
paintings: (L) $605; (H) $7,700

LACHTROPIUS, Nicolas
Dutch ac. 1656-1700
paintings: (H) $56,000

LACOMBE
paintings: (H) $1,100

Inspiration

Gaston Lachaise (1882-1935) was born in Paris, the son of a decorator and cabinetmaker. He began to study sculpture at the age of thirteen, and at sixteen was admitted to the Academie Beaux-Arts. In 1902, while walking in the school gardens, he saw and fell instantly in love with a married woman from Boston, ten years his senior. His beloved, Isabel Nagle, returned home to her husband and child. Lachaise apprenticed himself to the workshop of René Lalique, saved his earnings, and in 1906 emigrated to America. He settled in Boston and worked for Henry Kitson, a sculptor of commemorative monuments. When Kitson moved to New York, Lachaise followed, but soon went to work in the studio of Art Deco sculptor Henry Manship. In 1917 Isabel divorced her husband, and she and Lachaise were married.

Isabel was the inspiration and model for much of Lachaise's work. He sculpted highly sensual, monumental women with bulbous breasts and slim legs. By 1927 his style had formed and he worked on variations on his heroic female nude. Lachaise was a meticulous craftsman and worked directly in stone. When he used bronze, his most successful medium, he polished it to an unnatural brightness. During his lifetime he was considered a preeminent sculptor. In 1935 a large exhibition of his work was held at the Museum of Modern Art in New York. Lachaise died later that same year of leukemia. (Gaston Lachaise, *Walking Woman*, polished bronze, 19 in. high, Doyle, October 5, 1988, $71,500)

LACOMBE, Georges
French 1868-1916
paintings: (L) $16,500; (H) $143,000

LACOMBLE, Adolphe
paintings: (H) $1,320

LACOMTE
sculpture: (H) $2,200

LACOUR, Janus Andreas Bartholin
Danish 1837-1909
paintings: (H) $11,000

LACRETELLE, Jean Edouard
French 1817-1900
paintings: (H) $13,200

LACROIX, Anton
French 1848-1896
paintings: (H) $3,300

LACROIX, Charles F. de,
called LACROIX de Marseille or DELACROIX
French d. 1782
paintings: (L) $935; (H) $192,500

LACROIX, Gaspard Jean
French 1810-1878
paintings: (H) $1,430

LACROIX, P.
paintings: (H) $825

LACROIX, Paul
American ac. 1858-1869
paintings: (L) $2,420; (H) $6,600

LACY, Charles John de
English ac. 1885-1918
paintings: (H) $2,750

LADBROOKE, H.
English 19th cent.
paintings: (H) $2,200

LADBROOKE, John Berney
English 1803-1879
paintings: (L) $660; (H) $1,925

LADBROOKE, Robert
British 1770-1842
paintings: (L) $2,420; (H) $12,100

LADD, Anna Coleman
American 1878-1939
sculpture: (L) $330; (H) $26,400

LADD, Laura D. Stroud
American 1863-1943
paintings: (L) $302; (H) $2,310

LADD, Lawrence T., The Utica Master
American ac. 1870-1892
drawings: (L) $3,300; (H) $38,500

LADDEY, Ernst
German 19th cent.
paintings: (H) $880

LADELL, Edward
British 1821-1886
paintings: (L) $1,650; (H) $35,200

LAECK, Reinier van der
paintings: (H) $8,800

LAER, Alexander T. van
American 1857-1920
paintings: (L) $550; (H) $2,600
drawings: (L) $110; (H) $750

LAESSIG, Robert
American b. 1920
paintings: (L) $550; (H) $715
drawings: (L) $110; (H) $715

LAESSLE, Albert
American 1877-1945
sculpture: (L) $330; (H) $770

LAEVERENZ, Gustav
German 1851-1909
paintings: (H) $8,250

LAEZZA, Giovanni
Italian d. 1905
paintings: (H) $1,155

LAEZZA, Giuseppe
Italian d. 1905
paintings: (L) $2,200; (H) $6,050

LAFITTE, Louis
French 1770-1828
drawings: (L) $132; (H) $3,080

LAFON, Francois
French ac. 1875-1890
paintings: (L) $935; (H) $1,980
drawings: (H) $660

LAFON, Marie Meloe, called Madam
MARSAUD
paintings: (H) $1,320

LAFONTAINE, Pierre Josephe
paintings: (H) $1,320

LAGAR, Celso
Spanish 1891-1966
paintings: (L) $660; (H) $825
drawings: (H) $990

LAGARDE, Pierre
French 1853-1910
paintings: (H) $1,925

LAGERCRANTZ, Ava Hedvig
Gustafva
Swedish b. 1862
paintings: (H) $1,100

LAGIER, Em.
paintings: (H) $660

LAGLENNE, Jean Francis
French b. 1899
drawings: (H) $715

LAGNDT, H.
paintings: (H) $3,300

LAGNEAU
drawings: (L) $209; (H) $6,600

LAGNEAU, Nicolas, LANNEAU
French 16th/17th cent.
drawings: (H) $30,800

LAGOOR, Johannes
ac. 1645-1659
paintings: (H) $14,300

LAGRANGE, Jacques
French b. 1917
paintings: (L) $77; (H) $770

LAGRENEE, Louis Jean Francois
French 1725-1805
paintings: (L) $6,600; (H) $88,000

LAGYE, Victor
Belgian 1829-1896
paintings: (L) $3,300; (H) $7,150

LAHNER, Emile
American 20th cent.
paintings: (L) $275; (H) $770
drawings: (L) $413; (H) $523

LAI-SUNG
Chinese 19th cent.
paintings: (H) $31,900

LAIDMAN, G.
paintings: (H) $880

LAIR, Franz Xavier
French 1812-1875
paintings: (H) $2,310

LAIRESSE, Gerard de
Flemish 1641-1711
paintings: (H) $60,500

LAISSEMENT, Henri Adolphe
French c. 1854-1921
paintings: (L) $13,200; (H) $13,200

LAJOIE, M.
Continental School 19th cent.
paintings: (H) $990

LAJOS, Gyenes
Hungarian 19th/20th cent.
paintings: (H) $990

LAJOUE, Jacques de
French 1687-1761
paintings: (L) $20,900; (H) $44,000

LAKEMAN, Nathaniel
American
paintings: (H) $10,450

LAKHOVSKY, Arnold
Russian b. 1885
paintings: (L) $908; (H) $1,870

LALANNE, Claude
b. Paris contemporary
sculpture: (L) $1,650; (H) $49,500

LALANNE, Francois Xavier
French b. 1924
sculpture: (L) $13,200; (H) $45,100

LALAUZE, Alphonse
French d. 1872
paintings: (H) $1,100

LALIQUE, Rene
French 1860-1945
drawings: (L) $2,860; (H) $3,080
sculpture: (H) $148,500

LALLEMAND, Georges
French c. 1575-c. 1635
drawings: (H) $3,300

LALLEMAND, Jean Baptiste
French c. 1710-c. 1803/1805
paintings: (H) $2,420
drawings: (L) $209; (H) $8,800

LALOUE, Eugene Galien
paintings: (H) $7,150

LAM, Wifredo
Cuban 1902-1982
paintings: (L) $4,675; (H) $605,000
drawings: (L) $990; (H) $121,000
sculpture: (L) $1,100; (H) $19,800

LAMARRE
French late 19th cent.
sculpture: (H) $82,500

LAMASURE, Edwin, Jr.
American b. 1866
drawings: (L) $44; (H) $660

LAMB, F. Mortimer
American 1861-1936
paintings: (L) $220; (H) $7,000
drawings: (L) $110; (H) $2,900

LAMB, G.
paintings: (H) $1,650

LAMBDIN, George Cochran
American 1830-1896
paintings: (L) $495; (H) $22,000
drawings: (L) $121; (H) $220

LAMBDIN, James Reid
American 1807-1889
paintings: (L) $880; (H) $1,155

LAMBEAUX, Joseph Maria Thomas, Jef
Belgian 1852-1908
sculpture: (L) $275; (H) $5,225

LAMBERT, B.
19th cent.
paintings: (L) $110; (H) $715

LAMBERT, Camille Nicolas
Belgian b. 1876
paintings: (L) $1,210; (H) $13,750

LAMBERT, Clement
English 1855-1925
paintings: (L) $275; (H) $1,320

LAMBERT, George
French 20th cent.
paintings: (H) $1,045

LAMBERT, Georges
French b. 1919
paintings: (L) $1,650; (H) $2,200

LAMBERT, Jack
American b. 1892
paintings: (H) $248
sculpture: (L) $330; (H) $1,210

LAMBERT, Jacques Henri Jean
French b. 1877
paintings: (H) $880

LAMBERT, Louis Eugene
French 1825-1900
paintings: (L) $330; (H) $5,500

LAMBERT, Theodore R.
American 1905-1960
paintings: (L) $1,210; (H) $8,525

LAMBERT-RUCKI, Jean
French 1888-1967
paintings: (L) $660; (H) $12,100
sculpture: (L) $5,500; (H) $33,000

LAMBERTI
Italian 19th cent.
drawings: (H) $4,620

LAMBIN, James Reid
paintings: (H) $1,870

LAMBINET, Emile Charles
French 1815-1877
paintings: (L) $1,155; (H) $6,600

LAMBINI, Alberto
paintings: (H) $1,540

LAMBORN
paintings: (H) $1,200

LAMBRECHT, Pat
American
drawings: (H) $750

LAMBRECHTS, Jan Baptist
Flemish 1680-after 1731
paintings: (L) $1,320; (H) $5,775

LAMBRICHS, Edmond Alphonse
Charles
Belgian 1830-1887
paintings: (L) $1,760; (H) $2,750

LAMDON, James Northcote
American
paintings: (H) $660

LAMEN, Christoffel Jacobsz van der
Flemish 1606/15-1651
paintings: (L) $2,090; (H) $28,600

LAMEN, Jacob van der
paintings: (H) $4,400

LAMI, Eugene Louis
French 1800-1890
paintings: (L) $275; (H) $9,900
drawings: (L) $1,100; (H) $1,980

LAMI, Stanislas
French 1858-1944
sculpture: (H) $3,025

LAMME, Arie Johannes
Dutch 1812-1900
paintings: (H) $5,500

LAMOND, W.B.
paintings: (H) $2,420

LAMOTTE, Bernard
French b. 1903
paintings: (L) $220; (H) $22,000
drawings: (L) $121; (H) $715

LAMOURDEIEU, Raoul
French b. 1877
sculpture: (L) $715; (H) $1,210

LAMPE, L.
Belgian 19th cent.
paintings: (H) $1,650

LAMPI, Giovanni Battista
paintings: (L) $4,950; (H) $11,550

LAMPI, Giovanni Battista
Italian 1755-1842
paintings: (H) $42,900

LAMPI, Giovanni Battista
Italian 1807-1857
paintings: (H) $8,250

LAMPI, Johan Baptist, the younger
Italian/Austrian 1775-1837
paintings: (H) $7,700

LAMPI, Johann B. Raph Ritter V.
German 19th cent.
paintings: (H) $2,200

LAMPLOUGH, Augustus Osborne
English 1877-1930
drawings: (L) $412; (H) $3,520

LAMPMAN, Sidney
paintings: (H) $990

LAMQUA
c. 1850
paintings: (H) $18,700

LAMY, Pierre Desire Eugene Franc
French 1855-1919
paintings: (L) $660; (H) $8,800

LANAZIN
Continental School 19th cent.
paintings: (H) $44,000

LANCARET, N.
sculpture: (H) $3,850

LANCE, George
English 1802-1864
paintings: (L) $1,200; (H) $5,500

LANCE, Orville
paintings: (H) $2,090

LANCERAY, Eugene Alexandrovitch
Russian 1848-1886
sculpture: (L) $440; (H) $16,500

LANCEROTTO, Egisto
Italian 1848-1916
paintings: (L) $4,400; (H) $22,000

LANCKEN, Frank von de
1872-1950
paintings: (L) $467; (H) $715

LANCKOD, L.
German 19th cent.
paintings: (H) $770

LANCKOW, L.
German 19th cent.
paintings: (L) $1,100; (H) $2,860

LANCON, Auguste Andre
French 1836-1887
paintings: (H) $2,420

LANCON, Edouard Michel
French b. 1854
paintings: (H) $7,150

LANCRET, Nicolas
French 1690-1743
paintings: (L) $22,000; (H) $187,000
drawings: (L) $9,350; (H) $93,500

LANDAU, Zygmunt
Polish 1898-1962
paintings: (L) $495; (H) $6,050

LANDELLE, Charles Zacherie
French 1812-1908
paintings: (L) $1,375; (H) $27,500

LANDFIELD, Ronnie
American b. 1947
paintings: (L) $1,045; (H) $1,430

LANDI, Gaspare
paintings: (H) $5,225

LANDI, Ricardo Verdugo
Italian 19th/20th cent.
paintings: (L) $7,425; (H) $8,800

LANDIS, H.W.
American 19th/20th cent.
paintings: (H) $1,430

LANDIS, John
American c. 1830
drawings: (H) $6,050

LANDOWSKI, Paul Maximilien
French 1875-1961
sculpture: (L) $770; (H) $4,950

LANDSEER, Charles
British 1802-1873
paintings: (H) $6,600

LANDSEER, E.
paintings: (H) $1,870

LANDSEER, Sir Edwin Henry
English 1802-1873
paintings: (L) $1,870; (H) $577,500
drawings: (H) $1,925

LANDSMAN, Stanley
American 1930-1984
paintings: (H) $1,870

LANDTSHEER, Jan Baptist
Belgian 1797-1845
paintings: (H) $1,925

LANDUYT, S.J. van
Belgian 19th/20th cent.
paintings: (H) $7,150

LANE, Fitz Hugh
American 1804-1865
paintings: (L) $33,000; (H) $825,000

LANE, Harry
American b. 1891
paintings: (L) $250; (H) $2,420

LANE, Katherine Ward, WEEM
American
sculpture: (H) $2,860

LANE, Leonard
Canadian 20th cent.
paintings: (H) $1,650

LANE, Lois
contemporary
paintings: (H) $4,675
drawings: (H) $770

LANE, Martella Cone
American 1875-1962
paintings: (L) $110; (H) $660

LANFAIR, Harold Edward
American b. 1898
drawings: (L) $220; (H) $935

LANFANT DE METZ, Francois Louis
French 1814-1892
paintings: (L) $880; (H) $11,000

LANFRANCO, Giovanni
Italian 1582-1647
drawings: (L) $2,200; (H) $5,500

LANG, A.
drawings: (H) $825

LANG, A.
German 19th cent.
paintings: (H) $990

LANG, A. and A. STEINHARDT
drawings: (H) $880

LANG, Albert
German b. 1847
paintings: (L) $990; (H) $1,320
drawings: (H) $605

LANG, G.C.
19th cent.
paintings: (H) $825

LANG, John F.
paintings: (L) $1,100; (H) $1,210

LANG, Louis
German/American 1814/24-1893
paintings: (L) $1,045; (H) $4,125

LANGASKINS, Maurice
Belgian b. 1884
paintings: (H) $4,675

LANGDALE, Marmaduke A.
British d. 1905
paintings: (H) $1,650

LANGE, Julius
paintings: (H) $3,520

LANGENBACH, Clara Emma
American b. 1871
paintings: (H) $1,540

LANGENDIJK, Dirk
Dutch 1748-1805
drawings: (L) $1,650; (H) $14,300

LANGEVELD, Frans
Dutch 1877-1939
paintings: (L) $495; (H) $2,200

LANGEVIN, C.
Canadian 20th cent.
paintings: (L) $495; (H) $825

LANGL, Josef
Austrian 1843-1920
paintings: (L) $24,200; (H) $27,500

LANGLAIS, Bernard
American 1921-1977
sculpture: (H) $18,700

LANGLEY, C.D.
British 19th cent.
paintings: (H) $7,150

LANGLEY, Edith May
American 19th/20th cent.
paintings: (H) $2,750

LANGLEY, Edward
British ac. 1904-1908
paintings: (L) $165; (H) $660

LANGLEY, W.
paintings: (L) $715; (H) $3,080

LANGLEY, Walter
English 1852-1922
paintings: (H) $660

LANGLEY, William
British 19th cent.
paintings: (L) $99; (H) $2,200

LANGLOIS, C.
British 19th cent.
paintings: (L) $1,430; (H) $8,250

LANGLOIS, J.
paintings: (H) $1,045

LANGLOIS, Jerome Martin
French 1779-1838
paintings: (L) $7,700; (H) $440,000

LANGLOIS, Mark W.
British 19th cent.
paintings: (L) $302; (H) $2,420

LANGOIS, Paul
paintings: (H) $2,420

LANGRAND, E *
French 19th cent.
paintings: (H) $7,425

LANGUE, L. de
19th cent.
paintings: (H) $2,200

LANGWORTHY, W.H.
paintings: (L) $165; (H) $850

LANMAN, Charles
American 1819-1895
paintings: (L) $275; (H) $1,540
drawings: (H) $110

LANNUDIUN, S.
paintings: (H) $1,210

LANOUX, B.
French 19th cent.
paintings: (L) $1,320; (H) $3,080

LANPANEAU, Sidney
paintings: (H) $1,045

LANSIL, Walter Franklin
American 1846-1925
paintings: (L) $165; (H) $4,675
drawings: (H) $300

LANSKOY, Andre
Russian/French 1902-1976
paintings: (L) $1,320; (H) $126,500
drawings: (L) $143; (H) $11,000

LANSON, F.
sculpture: (H) $1,320

LANSOT, Aimable Desire
French/American 1799-1851
paintings: (H) $2,200

LANTZ, Walter
drawings: (L) $135; (H) $935

LANYON, Ellen
paintings: (L) $33; (H) $660

LANZA
paintings: (H) $660

LANZANI, P.
Italian
paintings: (L) $550; (H) $880

LAOUST, Andre Louis Adolphe
French b. 1843
sculpture: (H) $4,400

LAPICQUE, Charles
French b. 1898
paintings: (L) $605; (H) $26,000

LAPIERRE, Louis Emile
French 1817-1886
paintings: (H) $2,860

LAPINI, C.
Italian b. 1848
sculpture: (L) $1,045; (H) $10,450

LAPINI, Cesare
Italian b. 1848
sculpture: (H) $14,300

LAPINI, Fratelli
sculpture: (H) $1,430

LAPINI, Gall
Italian 19th cent.
sculpture: (L) $2,420; (H) $3,190

LAPINI, T.
sculpture: (H) $1,485

LAPIRA
Italian 19th cent.
drawings: (L) $220; (H) $6,050

LAPIS, Gaetano
Italian 1706-1758
paintings: (L) $3,850; (H) $7,150

LAPITO, Louis Auguste
French 1803-1874
paintings: (H) $20,350

LAPLANCHE
sculpture: (H) $660

LAPORTE, Emile
French 1858-1907
sculpture: (L) $247; (H) $3,300

LAPORTE, George Henry
German/English 1799-1873
paintings: (L) $3,300; (H) $9,350

LAPORTE-BLAIRSY, Leo
sculpture: (H) $3,300

LAPOSTOLET, Charles
French 1824-1890
paintings: (L) $5,500; (H) $17,600

LAPU, Manuel
paintings: (H) $2,200

LARA, Ernest
English b. 1870
paintings: (H) $715

LARA, George
paintings: (H) $6,050

LARA, Georgina
British 19th cent.
paintings: (L) $1,650; (H) $8,250

LARA, J.G. de
Spanish 19th/20th cent.
paintings: (H) $1,100

LARA, William
British 19th cent.
paintings: (H) $1,760

LARCHE, Francois Raoul
French 1860-1912
sculpture: (L) $495; (H) $55,000

LARCOMBE, Ethel
drawings: (H) $3,300

LARD, Francois Maurice
French 1864-1908
paintings: (H) $13,200

LARENNE, Roger
American 20th cent.
paintings: (H) $715

LARGILLIERE, Nicolas de
French 1656-1746
paintings: (L) $16,500; (H) $74,250

LARIONOV, Mikhail
Russian/French 1881-1964
paintings: (L) $16,500; (H) $121,000
drawings: (L) $275; (H) $30,800

LARIVE-GODEFROY, Pierre Louis de
Swiss 1735-1817
paintings: (H) $12,100

LARMON, Kevin
contemporary
paintings: (H) $4,400

LARMOUR, William
American 1870-1943
drawings: (H) $935

LARONZE, Jean
paintings: (H) $4,400

LAROQUE, R.
French 19th cent.
paintings: (H) $1,100

LARRANGA, Enrique de
paintings: (H) $7,150

LARRAZ, Julio
Cuban/American b. 1944
paintings: (L) $4,400; (H) $46,200
drawings: (L) $132; (H) $4,675

LARREGIEU, Fulbert Pierre
sculpture: (H) $660

LARROFF, G.
sculpture: (H) $3,630

LARRUE
paintings: (H) $880

LARRUE, Guillaume
French b. 1851
paintings: (L) $935; (H) $7,150

LARSEN, Adolf Alfred
Danish 1856-1942
paintings: (L) $1,650; (H) $16,500

LARSEN, Knud
Danish 1865-1922
paintings: (L) $1,265; (H) $19,800

LARSEN, W.
paintings: (L) $1,430; (H) $2,310

LARSON, Cecil
Swedish/American b. 1908
paintings: (L) $660; (H) $1,650

LARSON, Edward
American contemporary
sculpture: (H) $825

LARSON, Jean Fred
American
paintings: (H) $1,100

LARSON, Marthe
American
sculpture: (H) $3,300

LARSON, Nils
paintings: (H) $4,400

LARSSON, Carl
Swedish 1853-1919
drawings: (L) $8,250; (H) $330,000

LASABTIER
paintings: (H) $1,650

LASALLE, L. (?)
paintings: (H) $825

LASAR, Charles A.
French 19th/20th cent.
paintings: (H) $880

LASCANO, Juan
Argentinian b. 1947
paintings: (L) $10,450; (H) $25,300

LASCARI, Salvatore
Italian/American 1884-1967
paintings: (L) $137; (H) $825
drawings: (H) $11

LASCAUX, Elie
paintings: (L) $577; (H) $2,860

LASCH, Carl Johann
German 1822-1888
paintings: (H) $715

LASCHI, G.
sculpture: (H) $1,210

LASELLAZ, Gustave Francois
French 19th cent.
paintings: (H) $15,400

LASH, Lee
American 1864-1935
paintings: (L) $5,225; (H) $66,000

LASKE, Oskar
Austrian 1874-1911
drawings: (L) $522; (H) $825

LASKER, Jonathan
American b. 1948
paintings: (L) $1,760; (H) $16,500

LASKY, Bessie Mona
American 1890-1972
paintings: (L) $550; (H) $1,210

LASSALLE, Camille Leopold
Cabaillot Dit
paintings: (H) $3,300

LASSAW, Ibram
American b. 1913
sculpture: (L) $880; (H) $23,100

LASSEN, Hans August
German b. 1857
paintings: (L) $660; (H) $4,290

LASSER, Hans
paintings: (H) $4,400

LASSONDE, Omer Thomas
American 1903-1980
paintings: (L) $412; (H) $907

LASTMAN, Pieter
Dutch 1583-1633
paintings: (L) $4,950; (H) $57,750

LASZLO, Aldor
paintings: (H) $990

LASZLO DE LOMBOS, Philip
Alexius de
Hungarian/English 1869-1937
paintings: (L) $220; (H) $12,100

LATHROP, Francis
American 1849-1909
paintings: (L) $825; (H) $1,760

LATHROP, Ida Pulis
American 1859-1937
paintings: (L) $165; (H) $1,100

LATHROP, William Langson
American 1859-1938
paintings: (L) $1,045; (H) $18,700
drawings: (L) $275; (H) $742

LATIMER, Lorenzo Palmer
American 1857-1941
paintings: (L) $330; (H) $1,100
drawings: (L) $88; (H) $1,320

LATOIX, Gaspard
American ac. 1890-1910
paintings: (L) $2,800; (H) $9,900
drawings: (H) $990

LATOIX, Paul
American
paintings: (H) $3,850

LATORTUE, Ph.
paintings: (H) $1,980

LATOUCHE, Gaston de
French 1854-1913
paintings: (L) $385; (H) $82,500
drawings: (L) $1,760; (H) $7,700

LATOUCHE, L.
French 19th cent.
paintings: (H) $880

LATOUR, Maurice Quentin de
French 1704-1788
drawings: (H) $79,750

LATTARD, Phillip
American 19th/20th cent.
paintings: (H) $12,100

LAU, Rex
contemporary
paintings: (H) $2,750

LAUBADERE, Louis Paul de
French 19th cent.
paintings: (H) $990

LAUDER, Charles James
English d. 1920
paintings: (L) $2,750; (H) $6,600
drawings: (L) $2,750; (H) $3,080

LAUDY, Jean
Belgian 20th cent.
paintings: (H) $8,800

LAUFMAN, Sidney
American b. 1891
paintings: (L) $66; (H)$2,420
drawings: (H) $82

LAUGE, Achille
French 1861-1944
paintings: (L) $1,650; (H) $17,600

LAUGEE, Desire Francois
French 1823-1896
paintings: (L) $3,740; (H) $8,800

LAUGEE, Georges
French b. 1853
paintings: (L) $1,540; (H) $8,250

LAUGHLIN
paintings: (H) $1,540

LAULIE, Joseph
French b. 1928
paintings: (H) $1,320

LAUNAY, Fernand de
French 19th cent.
paintings: (H) $13,200

LAUNAY, M. de
French 19th cent.
paintings: (H) $7,150

LAUPHEIMER, Anton
paintings: (H) $13,200

LAUR, Josef
paintings: (H) $12,100

LAUR, Yvonne Marie, called Yo
French b. 1879
paintings: (L) $4,180; (H) $16,500

LAURANT, Robert
American 1890-1970
drawings: (H) $935

LAURE, Jean Francois Hyacinthe Jules
French 1806-1861
paintings: (H) $4,950

LAUREL
sculpture: (H) $1,100

LAUREN, J.
paintings: (H) $660

LAURENCE, Sydney
American 1860/65-1940
paintings: (L) $660; (H) $187,000
drawings: (L) $220; (H) $6,050

LAURENCIN, Marie
French 1883-1956
paintings: (L) $13,200; (H) $1,430,000
drawings: (L) $605; (H) $1,100,000

LAURENS, Henri
French 1885-1954
drawings: (L) $2,090; (H) $40,700
sculpture: (L) $30,800; (H) $687,500

LAURENS, Jean Paul
French 1838-1921
paintings: (L) $3,850; (H) $5,225
drawings: (H) $275

LAURENS, Jules Joseph Augustin
French 1825-1901
paintings: (H) $16,500
drawings: (H) $440

LAURENS, Paul Albert
French 1870-1934
paintings: (H) $3,850

LAURENSON, Edward Louis
British b. 1868
paintings: (L) $302; (H) $850
drawings: (L) $300; (H) $425

Parisian Artist

Marie Laurencin (1883-1956) was a versatile artist. She is well known for her oil and watercolor portraits of women and young girls. Additionally, she was a designer, etcher, lithographer, and poet. Born in Paris, she attended evening classes at the School of Art in Sevres but was primarily self-taught. She frequented the Bateau-Lavoir, a group of artists' studios in Montmartre. Between 1907 and 1912 she lived with Guillaume Apollinaire, the poet who championed the first Cubists. His friends were the avant-garde– Picasso, Braque, Matisse, Gris, and Gertrude Stein.

Laurencin later married the German painter Otto van Waetjen and lived in Spain. After World War II they divorced and she returned to France. She illustrated more than thirty books, including Lewis Carroll's *Alice in Wonderland*, and designed costumes and sets for the Ballet Russe and Comedie Francaise. She was also a portraitist for Parisian female society. Laurencin's delicate, idyllic pictures of graceful young girls in pastel shades have a universal appeal, and her works have found great favor with the Japanese. The highlight of Grogan's February 1990 sale was Marie Laurencin's watercolor of two young girls. (Marie Laurencin, *Two Young Girls in a Forest*, watercolor over pencil on paper, 14⅞ x 11 in., Grogan, February 27, 1990, $79,750)

LAURENT, Ernest
French 1859-1929
paintings: (L) $5,500; (H) $17,600

LAURENT, Eugene
French 1832-1898
sculpture: (L) $770; (H) $1,540

LAURENT, Felix
French 1821-1908
paintings: (H) $19,800

LAURENT, G.H.
sculpture: (L) $990; (H) $1,320

LAURENT, Georges
sculpture: (H) $3,300

LAURENT, J.B.J.
French School 18th cent.
paintings: (H) $3,575

LAURENT, Jean
French b. 1906
paintings: (L) $1,100; (H) $4,125

LAURENT, Peterson
American
paintings: (H) $715

LAURENT, Robert
American 1890-1970
sculpture: (L) $440; (H) $11,000

LAURENT, V.
French School 19th cent.
paintings: (H) $880

LAURENTI, Cesare
Italian 1854-1936
paintings: (H) $25,300

LAURENTY, L.
French 19th cent.
paintings: (H) $1,100

LAURENTY, Remacle Joseph
drawings: (H) $2,310

LAURENTZ
Continental 19th cent.
paintings: (H) $2,090

LAURET, F.
paintings: (H) $2,200

LAURITZ, Jack
American 20th cent.
paintings: (L) $303; (H) $715

LAURITZ, Paul
Norwegian/American 1889-1975
paintings: (L) $550; (H) $14,300
drawings: (L) $220; (H) $715

LAURON, Albert Frederic
French b. 1841
paintings: (H) $4,400

LAUS, Marie Yvonne
French b. 1879
paintings: (H) $4,400

LAUTER, Henri
sculpture: (H) $990

LAUTERS, G.
European 19th cent.
paintings: (H) $1,320

LAUTERS, G. and F. van SEVERDONCK
paintings: (H) $1,320

LAUTH, Charles Frederic
French 1865-1922
paintings: (H) $2,475

LAUTIER, Henri
French 20th cent.
sculpture: (H) $715

LAUVERNAY-PETITJEAN, Jeanne
French b. 1875
paintings: (L) $825; (H) $2,420

LAUX, August
American 1847/53-1921
paintings: (L) $660; (H) $11,000

LAUZERO, Albert
French b. 1909
paintings: (H) $1,100

LAVALLE, John
American b. 1896
paintings: (L) $467; (H) $3,520
drawings: (L) $66; (H) $495

LAVALLEN, Julio
Argentinian b. 1957
paintings: (L) $3,300; (H) $3,850
drawings: (H) $1,925

LAVATELLI, Carla
contemporary
sculpture: (H) $2,750

LAVERENT, C.
French 19th cent.
paintings: (H) $990

LAVERGNE, Adolphe
French 19th cent.
sculpture: (L) $550; (H) $660

LAVERY, Sir John
Irish 1856-1941
paintings: (L) $10,725; (H) $286,000

LAVIEILLE, Eugene Antoine Samuel
French 1820-1889
paintings: (H) $2,860

LAVIEILLE, Marie Adrien
paintings: (H) $3,520

LAVILLE, Joy
English b. 1923
paintings: (L) $7,150; (H) $11,000
drawings: (L) $2,750; (H) $4,400

LAVOIS, E.
paintings: (H) $825

LAVOLPE, Alessandro
Italian 1820-1887
paintings: (L) $1,705; (H) $1,705

LAVOLPE, Nicola
paintings: (H) $2,640

LAVREINCE, Nicolas
1737-1807
paintings: (H) $39,600

LAVROFF, Georges
Russian/French b. 1895
sculpture: (L) $4,950; (H) $12,100

LAVRUT, Louise
French b. 1874
paintings: (H) $2,310

LAWLESS, Carl
American 1894-1964
paintings: (L) $715; (H) $2,860

LAWLOR, George Warren
American b. 1878
paintings: (L) $770; (H) $935

LAWMAN, Jasper Holman
American 1825-1906
paintings: (L) $770; (H) $52,800

LAWRENCE, Charles B.
American
paintings: (H) $1,980

LAWRENCE, Edna
American b. 1898
paintings: (L) $192; (H) $1,210
drawings: (L) $83; (H) $385

LAWRENCE, Jacob
American b. 1917
paintings: (L) $5,500; (H) $44,000
drawings: (L) $7,700; (H) $44,000

LAWRENCE, Sir Thomas
English 1769-1830
paintings: (L) $1,760; (H) $110,000
drawings: (H) $176

LAWRENCE, Sir Thomas, and studio
1768-1830
paintings: (H) $82,500

LAWRENCE, Sydney
American 1865-1940
paintings: (H) $8,000
drawings: (L) $550; (H) $2,200

LAWRENCE, William Goadby
paintings: (H) $9,350

LAWRENCE, William Hurd
American 1866-1938
paintings: (L) $440; (H) $1,980

LAWRIE, Alexander
American 1828-1917
paintings: (L) $935; (H) $8,800

LAWS, Arthur J.
American 1894-1960
paintings: (L) $82; (H) $1,430

LAWSHE, Hank
American b. 1835
paintings: (H) $1,000
drawings: (H) $700

LAWSON, Alexander
British 19th/20th cent.
paintings: (H) $715

LAWSON, David
paintings: (H) $1,045

LAWSON, E.I.
paintings: (H) $1,100

LAWSON, Ernest
American 1873-1939
paintings: (L) $605; (H) $528,000

LAWSON, Francis Wilfried
English 1842-1935
paintings: (H) $660

LAWSON, George Anderson
English ac. 1832-1904
sculpture: (H) $2,475

LAWSON, Joseph
American
paintings: (H) $1,045

LAY, Oliver Ingraham
American
paintings: (L) $660; (H) $4,950

LAZANO, Lee
contemporary
drawings: (L) $385; (H) $880

LAZAREV, V.
paintings: (H) $880

LAZARUS, Jacob Hart
American 1822-1891
paintings: (H) $1,540

LAZERGE, Jean Raymond Hippolyte
French 1817-1887
paintings: (L) $1,430; (H) $4,950

LAZERGES, Jean Baptiste Paul
French 1845-1902
paintings: (L) $660; (H) $8,800

LAZZARINI, Gregorio
paintings: (L) $6,600; (H) $7,150

LAZZELL, Blanche
American 1878-1956
paintings: (L) $715; (H) $26,400
drawings: (L) $495; (H) $4,950

LE BARBIER, Jean Jacques,
the younger
  French 1738-1826
  paintings: (H) $28,600
  drawings: (L) $2,200; (H) $5,225

LE BEY, Barbara
  b. 1939
  paintings: (H) $5,775

LE BIHAN, Alexandre
  French b. 1839
  paintings: (L) $2,200; (H) $12,650

LE BIHAN, Peter
  French 19th cent.
  paintings: (H) $19,800

LE BLANT, Julien
  French b. 1851
  drawings: (H) $1,950

LE BOEUFF, Pierre
  French 19th cent.
  paintings: (H) $1,320
  drawings: (H) $440

LE BROCQUY, Louis
  British b. 1916
  paintings: (L) $660; (H) $16,500

LE BRUN
  French? 19th cent.
  paintings: (H) $2,530

LE BRUN, Frederico, Rico
  Italian/American 1900-1964
  drawings: (L) $176; (H) $5,225

LE BRUN, Virginia
  paintings: (H) $2,090

LE CLERC, Sebastien Jacques, called
LECLERC des Gobelins
  French 1734-1785
  paintings: (L) $4,125; (H) $4,400

LE CLERCQ
  Flemish School d. 1826
  sculpture: (H) $1,045

LE COMPTE, Victor
  French 1856-1920
  paintings: (H) $2,090

LE CORBUSIER, Charles Edouard
JEANNERET
  Swiss/French 1887-1965
  paintings: (L) $34,100; (H) $148,500
  drawings: (L) $1,870; (H) $44,000

LE DUC, Victor Viollet
  French 1848-1901
  paintings: (L) $1,200; (H) $6,000

LE FAGUAYS, Pierre
  French b. 1892
  sculpture: (L) $550; (H) $22,000

LE FAUVRE
  French 19th/20th cent.
  sculpture: (H) $770

LE GUAY, Etienne Charles
  drawings: (H) $1,650

LE JEUNE, Eugene Joseph
  French 1818-1897
  paintings: (H) $2,200

LE JEUNE, Henry
  British 1819-1904
  paintings: (H) $9,900

LE JUENE, M.
  paintings: (H) $770

LE MASSON, Paul
  French 1898-1980
  paintings: (L) $1,100; (H) $3,300

LE MOAL, Jean
  French b. 1909
  paintings: (H) $5,775

LE MOINE, Elisabeth
  French 18th cent.
  paintings: (L) $9,900; (H) $14,300

LE MOPE
  paintings: (H) $1,320

LE PARC, Julio
  Argentinian b. 1928
  paintings: (H) $2,750
  drawings: (L) $143; (H) $165

LE PHO
  Vietnamese/French b. 1907
  paintings: (L) $110; (H) $5,500

LE PRINCE, Jean Baptiste
  French 1734-1781
  paintings: (H) $9,625

LE QUEU, Jean Jacques
  French 1757-c. 1825
  drawings: (H) $30,800

LE SIDANER, Henri
  French 1862-1939
  paintings: (L) $3,300; (H) $495,000

LE SUEUR, Eustache
French 1617-1655
paintings: (H) $154,000
drawings: (H) $49,500

LE VA, Barry
American b. 1941
drawings: (L) $550; (H) $17,600

LE VILAIN, Ernest Auguste
French d. 1916
paintings: (H) $880

LEACH, Ethel Pennewill Brown
American 1878-1960
paintings: (H) $2,090

LEADER, Benjamin Williams
English 1831-1923
paintings: (L) $660; (H) $52,800

LEADER, Charles
British 19th/20th cent.
paintings: (L) $412; (H) $1,210

LEAKE, Gerald
American 1885-1975
paintings: (L) $450; (H) $1,540

LEAL, Juan de Valdes
paintings: (H) $19,800

LEAR, Alexander Theobald van
American 1857-1920
paintings: (H) $3,300

LEAR, Edward
English 1812-1888
drawings: (L) $495; (H) $66,000

LEAVER, Charles
British 19th cent.
paintings: (H) $880

LEAVER, Noel H.
English 1889-1951
drawings: (L) $385; (H) $1,980

LEAVERS, Lucy A.
British ac. 1887-1898
paintings: (H) $13,200

LEAVITT, Edward Chalmers
American 1842-1904
paintings: (L) $165; (H) $8,250

LEAVITT, John F.
American 1905-1974
drawings: (L) $400; (H) $1,540

LEBARBIER, Jean Jacques Francois, the elder
French 1738-1826
paintings: (H) $31,900

LEBAS, H.
paintings: (H) $1,320

LEBAS, Jacques Philippe
1707-1783
drawings: (L) $2,475; (H) $2,750

LEBAS, Leonie
paintings: (H) $1,320

LEBASQUE, Henri
French 1865-1937
paintings: (L) $5,500; (H) $907,500
drawings: (L) $605; (H) $27,500

LEBASQUE, Marthe
French 19th/20th cent.
paintings: (L) $3,300; (H) $4,400

LEBDUSKA, Lawrence
American b. 1894
paintings: (L) $605; (H) $2,200

LEBDUSKA, Lawrence H.
American b. 1894
paintings: (L) $220; (H) $2,750

LEBEDEV, Vladimir
Russian 1891-1967
paintings: (L) $275; (H) $1,210
drawings: (L) $935; (H) $4,400

LEBEY, Barbara
American b. 1939
paintings: (L) $1,430; (H) $1,430

LEBLANC, Alexandre
French 1793-1866
paintings: (H) $2,750

LEBOT, V.
20th cent.
paintings: (L) $605; (H) $825

LEBOURG, Albert
French 1849-1928
paintings: (L) $880; (H) $82,500
drawings: (L) $990; (H) $1,650

LEBRET, Frans
Dutch 1820-1909
paintings: (L) $1,760; (H) $6,050

LEBRET, Paul
French b. 1875; ac. 1901-1907
drawings: (H) $1,900

LEBRUN, Christopher
British contemporary
paintings: (L) $20,900; (H) $33,000

LEBRUN, Eric
French 20th cent.
paintings: (H) $2,750

LEBRUN, Louis
Belgian 1844-1900
paintings: (L) $1,210; (H) $2,310

LEBRUN, Marcel
early 20th cent.
paintings: (H) $24,200

LEBRUN, Rico
Italian/American 1900-1964
drawings: (H) $2,600

LECAMUS, Jules Alexandre Duval
French 1814-1878
paintings: (H) $9,350

LECHESNE, Auguste
sculpture: (H) $3,080

LECLAIRE, Victor
French 1830-1885
paintings: (L) $13,200; (H) $33,000

LECLEAR, Thomas
American 1818-1882
paintings: (L) $209; (H) $2,090

LECLERCQ, A.
paintings: (H) $770

LECOCQ, Adrien
French 1832-1887
paintings: (H) $2,200

LECOINDRE, Eugene
French 19th cent.
paintings: (H) $13,200

LECOMTE, Hippolyte
French 1781-1857
paintings: (L) $1,760; (H) $7,700

LECOMTE, Paul Emile
French b. 1877
paintings: (L) $319; (H) $11,000
drawings: (L) $700; (H) $950

LECOMTE, Valentine
paintings: (H) $1,650

LECOMTE-VERNET, Charles Emile
Hippolyte
French 1821-1900
paintings: (L) $33,000; (H) $57,750

LECOQUE, Al
Czech/American 1891-1981
paintings: (L) $330; (H) $6,050

LECOUNT, J.
sculpture: (H) $1,100

LECOURNEY, Nicholas
French ac. 1880-1900
sculpture: (H) $1,210

LECOURTIER, Prosper
French 1855-1924
sculpture: (L) $495; (H) $2,860

LEDELI, Moritz
Czechoslovakian 1856-c. 1920
drawings: (H) $1,320

LEDESMA, Gabriel Fernandez
paintings: (H) $33,000

LEDOUX, Charles Alexandre Picart
French 1881-1959
drawings: (H) $770

LEDOUX, Jean Philiberte
drawings: (H) $7,150

LEDRU, Auguste
sculpture: (H) $3,850

LEDUC, Arthur
sculpture: (H) $4,180

LEDUC, P.
French 19th/20th cent.
paintings: (H) $7,150

LEDUC, Paul
Belgian 1876-1943
paintings: (L) $4,400; (H) $5,610

LEE, A.
English 19th cent.
paintings: (L) $330; (H) $715

LEE, Arthur
Norwegian/American 1881-1961
sculpture: (H) $18,700

LEE, Bertha Stringer
American 1873-1934/37
paintings: (L) $220; (H) $4,125

LEE, Chee Chin S. Cheung
Chinese/American b. 1896
paintings: (L) $110; (H) $660
drawings: (H) $1,210

LEE, Colin
contemporary
paintings: (H) $1,650

LEE, Doris
American b. 1905
paintings: (L) $880; (H) $33,000
drawings: (L) $412; (H) $1,980

LEE, Frederick Richard
British 1798-1879
paintings: (L) $358; (H) $8,250

LEE, H.
paintings: (H) $1,650

LEE, Laura
American b. 1867
paintings: (H) $1,870

LEE, Leslie
American b. 1871
paintings: (L) $2,090; (H) $2,750

LEE, Robert E.
American b. 1899
paintings: (H) $6,600

LEE, Walt
American 20th cent.
paintings: (L) $275; (H) $1,100

LEE, William
paintings: (H) $9,350

LEE-HANKEY, William
British 1869-1952
paintings: (H) $20,900

LEE-SMITH, Hughie
American 20th cent.
paintings: (L) $495; (H) $990

LEECH, John
English 1817-1864
paintings: (L) $1,100; (H) $3,300
drawings: (L) $165; (H) $825

LEEKE, Ferdinand
German b. 1859
paintings: (H) $1,650

LEEMANS, Antonius
Dutch 1631-1673
paintings: (L) $8,800; (H) $46,200

LEEMANS, Johannes
Dutch c. 1633-before 1689
paintings: (H) $33,000

LEEMPOELS, Jef
Belgian 1867-1935
paintings: (L) $13,750; (H) $38,500

LEEMPUTTEN, Cornelis van and Jan
David COL
Belgian late 19th/early 20th cent
paintings: (H) $4,125

LEEMPUTTEN, Cornelis van, and Lion
SCHULMAN
Belgian/Dutch 19th cent.
paintings: (H) $2,200

LEEMPUTTEN, Cornelius van
Belgian 1841-1902
paintings: (L) $935; (H) $7,700

LEEMPUTTEN, Cornelius van and
Alexis de LEEUW
Belgian 19th cent.
paintings: (H) $4,400

LEEMPUTTEN, Frans van
Belgian 1850-1914
paintings: (L) $853; (H) $4,950

LEEMPUTTEN, J.L. van
Belgian 1850-1914
paintings: (L) $468; (H) $2,200

LEEMPUTTEN, J.L. van
Belgian 19th cent.
drawings: (L) $495; (H) $4,400

LEEMPUTTEN, Jef Louis van
Belgian 1865-1948
paintings: (L) $880; (H) $1,430

LEEOVEN, A.E. de
Dutch 19th cent.
paintings: (H) $770

LEETEG, Edgar
American 20th cent.
paintings: (H) $3,300

LEEUW, A. de
British 19th cent.
paintings: (H) $2,200

LEEUW, Alexis de
Belgian ac. 1864
paintings: (L) $935; (H) $4,950

LEEUW, Alexis de and Cornelius van
LEEMPUTTEN
Belgian 19th cent.
paintings: (H) $13,200

LEFARGE, Mabel
drawings: (H) $660

LEFEBVRE, A.
Continental 19th cent.
paintings: (H) $3,410

LEFEBVRE, Augustin Francois
French 19th cent.
paintings: (H) $3,575

LEFEBVRE, Hippolyte
b. 1863
sculpture: (H) $6,050

LEFEBVRE, Jules Joseph
French 1834/36-1912
paintings: (L) $3,520; (H) $35,200

LEFEUVRE, Jean
French b. 1882
paintings: (L) $10,450; (H) $13,200

ALBERT-LEFEUVRE, Louis Etienne Marie
French ac. 1875-1905
sculpture: (L) $412; (H) $990

LEFEVRE, Marie
French 19th cent.
paintings: (L) $880; (H) $3,300

LEFEVRE, Marie
French 20th cent.
paintings: (H) $1,760

LEFEVRE, Robert
French 1755-1830
paintings: (L) $1,650; (H) $33,000
drawings: (H) $1,430

LEFEVRE, Robert Jacques Francois Faust
French 1755-1830
drawings: (H) $6,875

LEFLER, Franz
Czechoslovakian 1831-1898
paintings: (L) $3,575; (H) $16,500

LEFLER, Heinrich
Austrian 1863-1919
drawings: (H) $1,980

LEFORT, Jean Louis
French b. 1875
paintings: (L) $440; (H) $19,800

LEFORTIER, Henri Jean
paintings: (H) $1,760

LEFTROOK, Terry
contemporary
drawings: (H) $715

LEFTWICH, George R.
British ac. 1875-1880
paintings: (H) $27,500

LEGANGER, N.J.
paintings: (H) $880

LEGANGER, Nicolay Tysland
American 1832-1894
paintings: (L) $248; (H) $3,025

LEGAT, Leon
French b. 1829
paintings: (L) $7,700; (H) $20,900

LEGEAY, Jean Laurent
drawings: (H) $6,600

LEGENDRE, Eugene
Belgian 19th cent.
paintings: (L) $276; (H) $715

LEGER, Fernand
French 1881-1955
paintings: (L) $60,500; (H) $8,525,000
drawings: (L) $1,430; (H) $550,000
sculpture: (L) $935; (H) $220,000

LEGER, H.
paintings: (H) $1,100

LEGER, L.
paintings: (H) $880

LEGERE, Jon S.
American 20th cent.
paintings: (H) $1,100

LEGGETT, Alexander
English 19th cent.
paintings: (L) $660; (H) $770

LEGOUT-GERARD, Fernand Marie Eugene
French 1856-1924
paintings: (L) $4,125; (H) $15,400
drawings: (L) $660; (H) $2,860

LEGRAIN, Pierre
American
drawings: (L) $440; (H) $12,100

LEGRAND, Alexandre
paintings: (H) $1,100

LEGRAND, E**
French 19th/20th cent.
paintings: (H) $2,530

LEGRAND, Jenny
French ac. 1801-1831
paintings: (H) $39,600

LEGRAND, Louis
French 1863-1951
paintings: (L) $1,650; (H) $16,500
drawings: (H) $3,190

LEGRAND, Mercedes
French 20th cent.
paintings: (H) $1,925

LEGRAND, Paul
French 19th/20th cent.
paintings: (H) $1,100

LEGRAND, Rene
French b. 1923
paintings: (L) $880; (H) $6,050

LEGROS, Alphonse
paintings: (H) $9,350
drawings: (L) $660; (H) $5,280

LEGUAY, Charles Etienne
French 1762-1846
drawings: (L) $3,575; (H) $7,700

LEGUEULT, Raymond
French 1891-1971
drawings: (H) $4,675

LEGUILLEMIN, E.
sculpture: (H) $1,375

LEHMANN, Henri
drawings: (L) $495; (H) $715

LEHMANN, Wilhelm
German 1819-1905
paintings: (H) $1,100

LEHMBRUCK, Wilhelm
German 1881-1919
sculpture: (L) $4,950; (H) $143,000

LEHR, Adam
American 1853-1910?
paintings: (L) $99; (H) $2,860

LEIBL, Wilhelm Maria Hubertus
German 1844-1900
paintings: (H) $198,000
drawings: (H) $17,600

LEICKERT, Charles
Belgian 1816/18-1907
paintings: (L) $1,760; (H) $42,500

LEIENDECKER, Jon
paintings: (H) $700

LEIGH, William Robinson
American 1866-1955
paintings: (L) $660; (H) $187,000
drawings: (L) $1,430; (H) $5,500

LEIGHTON, Edmund Blair
British 1853-1922
paintings: (H) $6,600

LEIGHTON, Kathryn W.
American 1876-1952
paintings: (L) $660; (H) $10,450

LEIGHTON, Lord Frederick
British 1830-1896
paintings: (L) $4,400; (H) $165,000
drawings: (L) $440; (H) $4,950
sculpture: (L) $11,000; (H) $46,750

LEIGHTON, Scott
American 1849-1898
paintings: (L) $330; (H) $6,050
drawings: (L) $70; (H) $110

LEIGHTON-JONES, Barry
English 20th cent.
paintings: (L) $880; (H) $1,540

LEIJBICKEN (?)
paintings: (H) $825

LEISEK, Georg
sculpture: (H) $3,025

LEISSER, Martin B.
American 1846-1940
paintings: (L) $55; (H) $1,760
drawings: (L) $275; (H) $330

LEISSNER, Ed
paintings: (H) $935

LEISTEN, Jacobus
German 1844-1918
paintings: (H) $3,080

LEITCH, Richard P.
American 19th cent.
paintings: (H) $1,980

LEITCH, William Leighton
Scottish 1804-1883
drawings: (L) $82; (H) $660

LEITH-ROSS, Harry
American b. 1886
paintings: (L) $275; (H) $9,900
drawings: (L) $302; (H) $2,750

LEITZ, Robert
American
drawings: (H) $800

LEJEUNE, A.A.
18th cent.
drawings: (H) $7,700

LEJEUNE, Adolphe Frederic
French ac. 1879-1912
paintings: (H) $3,410

LEJEUNE, Eugene
French 1818-1897
paintings: (H) $2,090

LEJEUNE, H.
British 1820-1906
paintings: (H) $3,960

LEJEUNE, Henri Pierre
paintings: (L) $1,100; (H) $13,200

LEJEUNE, Louis
French 19th cent.
paintings: (H) $1,650

LELAND, Henry
American
paintings: (H) $935

LELAND, Joel
American 19th cent.
paintings: (H) $1,980

LELEU, Alexandre Felix
French b. 1871
paintings: (H) $3,850

LELEUX, Armand Hubert Simon
paintings: (H) $4,400

LELIE, Adriaen de
paintings: (H) $5,500

LELIENBERGH, Cornelis
paintings: (H) $10,450

LELIOR, Leon
paintings: (H) $1,320

LELOIR, Alexandre Louis
French 1843-1884
paintings: (L) $990; (H) $19,800
drawings: (L) $1,650; (H) $5,720

LELOIR, Jean Baptiste Auguste
French 1809-1892
paintings: (H) $66,000

LELOIR, Maurice
French 1853-1940
paintings: (L) $770; (H) $6,380
drawings: (L) $770; (H) $2,750

LELONG
French 19th cent.
drawings: (H) $2,860

LELONG, P.
French 20th cent.
paintings: (H) $880

LELONG, Rene
French 19th cent.
paintings: (L) $9,900; (H) $34,100

LELY, Sir Peter
British 1618-1680
paintings: (L) $1,210; (H) $17,600

LELY, Sir Peter, studio of
paintings: (L) $2,750; (H) $11,000

LEMAIRE, J.
French 19th cent.
paintings: (H) $660

LEMAIRE, Jean
paintings: (H) $4,400

LEMAIRE, Louis Marie
French 1824-1910
paintings: (H) $12,100

LEMAIRE, Madeleine
French 1845-1928
paintings: (L) $4,675; (H) $28,600
drawings: (L) $440; (H) $4,180

LEMAIRE, Marie Therese
paintings: (H) $6,050

LEMAIRE, R.
Continental 19th/20th cent.
drawings: (H) $2,750

LEMAITRE, Aline M.
French
sculpture: (H) $770

LEMAITRE, H.E.
Continental School 19th cent.
paintings: (H) $6,050

LEMAN, Jacques Edmond
French 1829-1889
paintings: (H) $2,640

LEMASSON, Paul
contemporary
paintings: (H) $935

LEMBECK, Jack
American b. 1942
paintings: (L) $5,500; (H) $15,400

LEMBERT, P.
Continental 19th/20th cent.
paintings: (H) $3,520

LEMEUNIER, Alfred Leon
drawings: (H) $770

LEMEUNIER, Basile
French b. 1852
paintings: (H) $10,450

LEMIEUX, Jean Paul
Canadian b. 1904
paintings: (L) $29,700; (H) $121,000

LEMIRE, F.
sculpture: (H) $880

LEMLY, Bessie Carrie
American b. 1871
drawings: (H) $2,750

LEMMEN, Georges
Belgian 1865-1916
paintings: (L) $20,900; (H) $121,000

LEMMENS, E.
French 19th cent.
paintings: (H) $1,100

LEMMENS, Theophile Victor Emile
French 1821-1867
paintings: (L) $990; (H) $2,310

LEMMERS, Georges Ferdinand
Belgian 1871-1944
paintings: (L) $418; (H) $1,650

LEMMI, Angelo
paintings: (H) $1,430

LEMMI, L**
Italian 19th cent.
paintings: (H) $1,650

LEMOINE, Jacques Antoine Marie
drawings: (H) $3,850

LEMOINE, Marie Victoire
French 1753/54-1820
paintings: (H) $18,700

LEMON, David
American 20th cent.
sculpture: (H) $1,870

LEMOS, Pedro Joseph
American 1882-1954
paintings: (H) $990
drawings: (H) $99

LEMOYNE, Francois
paintings: (H) $1,430

LEMOYNE, Jean Baptiste
sculpture: (H) $3,300

LEMPICKA, L.
Continental 19th cent.
paintings: (H) $3,025

LEMPICKA, Tamara de
Polish 1898-1980
paintings: (L) $2,860; (H) $1,320,000
drawings: (L) $880; (H) $33,000

LENAIL, Marie Joseph Ernest
paintings: (H) $3,850

LENBACH, Franz Seraph von
German 1836-1904
paintings: (L) $3,300; (H) $11,000

LENCK, Walter
sculpture: (H) $880

LENDT, Adrian van
Dutch 1901-1984
paintings: (H) $715

LENFESTEY, Giffard Hocart
British 1872-1943
drawings: (H) $880

LENGO Y MARTINEZ, Horacio
Spanish 1840-1890
paintings: (L) $3,080; (H) $8,800

LENKEY, J.
French 19th cent.
paintings: (H) $2,750

LENN, Judith
paintings: (H) $17,600

LENNON, John
British 1940-1980
paintings: (H) $5,500
drawings: (L) $825; (H) $4,950

LENNON, John and Yoko ONO
20th cent.
drawings: (L) $2,200; (H) $8,800

LENNON, Robert
American 19th cent.
paintings: (H) $852

LENOCK
sculpture: (H) $715

LENOIR, Charles Amable
French b. 1861
paintings: (L) $7,700; (H) $88,000

LENOIR, Marcel
paintings: (H) $4,950

LENOIR, Paul Marie
French 1843-1881
paintings: (H) $154,000

LENOIR, Pierre
sculpture: (L) $440; (H) $15,400

LENOIR, Simon Bernard
1729-1791
drawings: (H) $2,090

LENORDEZ, Pierre
French 19th cent.
sculpture: (L) $1,870; (H) $1,980

LENORDEZ, Pierre and V. BOYER
French 19th cent.
sculpture: (H) $6,050

LENS, Bernhard, the younger
English 1682-1740
paintings: (H) $17,600

LENZ, Alfred David
sculpture: (H) $1,760

LENZ, Maximilien
Austrian 1860-1948
drawings: (H) $880

LENZ, Norbert
American b. 1900
paintings: (H) $1,760

LEOCAT
drawings: (H) $990

LEON
Continental 19th cent.
paintings: (H) $1,430

LEON, Noe
Colombian b. 1907
paintings: (H) $7,700

LEON Y ESCOSURA, Ignacio de
Spanish 1834-1901
paintings: (L) $2,200; (H) $34,100

LEONARD, Agathon
French b. 1841
sculpture: (L) $176; (H) $17,600

LEONARD, George Henry
b. 1869
paintings: (H) $880

LEONARD, J.B.
sculpture: (H) $1,430

LEONARD, John Henry
paintings: (H) $3,520
drawings: (H) $440

LEONARD, Michael
paintings: (H) $660

LEONARDI, A.
Italian 19th cent.
paintings: (H) $1,320

LEONE, Colle
Italian 19th cent.
paintings: (H) $3,300

LEONE, John
American contemporary
paintings: (L) $2,310; (H) $7,040

LEONHARDT, Adolf
paintings: (H) $770

LEONI, Ottavio
drawings: (H) $2,420

LEONI, Ottavio Maria
Italian 1587-1630
drawings: (H) $39,600

LEPAGE, Celine
French
sculpture: (H) $17,600

LEPAGE, J.
French 19th cent.
paintings: (H) $2,750

LEPAGE-MARTIN, Louis
French b. 1850
paintings: (L) $605; (H) $935

LEPEINTRE, Charles
French 1735-1803
paintings: (L) $2,250; (H) $3,080

LEPICIE, Nicolas Bernard
French 1735-1784
paintings: (L) $7,150; (H) $16,500
drawings: (H) $9,625

LEPINAY, Paul Charles Emmanuel
Gallard
paintings: (L) $1,540; (H) $6,600

LEPINE
paintings: (H) $5,750

LEPINE, Stanislas
French 1835-1892
paintings: (L) $495; (H) $77,000
drawings: (H) $330

LEPOILTEVIN, Eugene Modeste
Edmond
French 1806-1870
paintings: (L) $138; (H) $1,100

LEPOITTEVIN, Louis
French 1847-1909
paintings: (L) $1,430; (H) $2,860

LEPRIN, Marcel
French 1891-1933
paintings: (L) $1,540; (H) $12,100

LEPRINCE, Auguste Xavier
French 1799-1826
paintings: (L) $990; (H) $10,450
drawings: (H) $825

LEPRINCE, Jean Baptiste
French 1734-1781
paintings: (L) $660; (H) $26,400
drawings: (L) $550; (H) $1,320

LEPSIUS, Reinhold
paintings: (H) $2,420

LEQUESNE, Eugene L.
French 1815-1887
sculpture: (H) $3,850

LEQUESUE, Eugene Louis
French 1815-1887
paintings: (H) $1,650
drawings: (H) $1,210

LERAUX, G.
French 19th cent.
paintings: (H) $1,100

LERAY, Prudent Louis
French 1820-1879
paintings: (L) $1,980; (H) $4,400

LERCHE, Hans Stotenberg
German late 19th cent.
sculpture: (H) $1,430

LERCHE, Vincent Stoltenberg
Norwegian 1837-1892
paintings: (H) $2,750

LERIUS, Joseph Henri Francois van
Belgian 1823-1876
paintings: (L) $2,750; (H) $16,500

LERMONT, E.
Continental School 19th cent.
paintings: (H) $1,540

LERMONTE, P.
Continental 19th cent.
paintings: (H) $4,950

LERNER, Leslie
American b. 1849
paintings: (H) $1,760

LEROLLE, Henry
French 1848-1929
paintings: (L) $1,100; (H) $3,300

LEROUX, Etienne
French 19th cent.
paintings: (H) $1,210

LEROUX, G.
paintings: (H) $550
sculpture: (H) $2,970

LEROUX, Gaston
French b. 1854
sculpture: (L) $550; (H) $11,000

LEROUX, Jules Marie Auguste
French b. 1871
paintings: (H) $8,250

LEROUX, Louis Hector
French 1829-1900
paintings: (L) $1,100; (H) $8,800

LEROY, Jules
French 1833-1865
paintings: (L) $3,300; (H) $22,000

LEROY, Paul Alexandre Alfred
French b. 1860
paintings: (L) $71,500; (H) $115,500

LEROY, S.
Continental 19th cent.
paintings: (H) $1,430

LERSY, Roger
French b. 1920
paintings: (L) $77; (H) $1,100

LESIEUR, Pierre
paintings: (L) $3,000; (H) $7,975

LESIO, A. de
drawings: (H) $660

LESLIE, Alfred
American b. 1927
paintings: (L) $1,650; (H) $49,500
drawings: (L) $3,025; (H) $8,250

LESLIE, Charles
British b. 1841
paintings: (L) $302; (H) $1,045

LESLIE, Charles Robert
English 1794-1859
paintings: (L) $110; (H) $11,000

LESLIE, George Dunlop
British 1835-1921
paintings: (L) $1,650; (H) $3,300

LESNE, Camille
paintings: (H) $4,180

LESOURD-BEAUREGARD, Ange
Louis Guillaume
French b. 1800
paintings: (H) $24,200

LESREL, Adolphe Alexandre
French 1839-1921
paintings: (L) $1,000; (H) $38,500

LESSER-URY
German 1861-1931
paintings: (L) $5,390; (H) $110,000
drawings: (L) $4,950; (H) $126,500

LESSI, Giovanni
Italian 1852-1922
drawings: (H) $825

LESSING, Carl Friedrich
German 1808-1880
paintings: (H) $17,600
drawings: (H) $6,750

LESSORE, Jules
French/British 1849-1892
drawings: (L) $247; (H) $1,870

LESTER, Ruth Wilson
American 20th cent.
paintings: (H) $1,320

LESTRADE, Jack
American contemporary
drawings: (H) $2,600

LESUR, Henri Victor
French b. 1863
paintings: (L) $2,860; (H) $20,900

LETHBRIDGE, Rodney
American b. 1891
paintings: (H) $880

LETHIERE, Guillaume
French 1760-1832
drawings: (L) $275; (H) $9,350

LETILLOIN
paintings: (H) $1,320

LETO, Antonio, called Leto de Capri
paintings: (H) $8,250

LETOUR, Julian
French 19th cent.
drawings: (L) $660; (H) $770

LETSCH, Louis
German b. 1856
paintings: (L) $990; (H) $1,045

LEU, August
paintings: (H) $3,300

LEU, August Wilhelm
German 1819-1897
paintings: (L) $4,125; (H) $9,075

LEU, Oscar
German 1864-1942
paintings: (L) $660; (H) $2,090

LEUDIK(?), F.
paintings: (H) $1,650

LEUSSESE, Andre Paul
French 19th/20th cent.
paintings: (H) $2,750

LEUTZE, Emanuel
American 1816-1868
paintings: (L) $1,430; (H) $15,400

LEUTZE, Emmanuel Gottlieb and
Henry Kirk BROWN
American
drawings: (H) $1,430

LEUUS, Jesus
Mexican 20th cent.
paintings: (L) $88; (H) $7,150

LEUX, Albert
Flemish early 20th cent.
paintings: (H) $1,430

LEVASSEUR, Henri Louis
French b. 1853
sculpture: (L) $550; (H) $8,800

LEVASSUR, A.
sculpture: (L) $1,100; (H) $5,500

LEVE, Frederic Louis
French b. 1877
paintings: (H) $13,200

LEVEE, John
contemporary
paintings: (L) $198; (H) $1,650
drawings: (L) $55; (H) $275

LEVENS, Hy
American 20th cent.
sculpture: (H) $3,300

LEVEQUE, Gabriel
Haitian b. 1923
paintings: (L) $143; (H) $715

LEVER, Richard Hayley
American 1876-1958
paintings: (L) $220; (H) $30,800
drawings: (L) $55; (H) $4,400

LEVERRIER, Max
French early 20th cent.
sculpture: (L) $3,080; (H) $6,600

LEVERS
paintings: (H) $660

LEVI, Carlo
paintings: (H) $4,620

LEVI, Julian E.
American 1900-after 1940
drawings: (H) $1,760

LEVIER, Charles
American (?) b. 1920
paintings: (L) $66; (H) $5,500
drawings: (L) $82; (H) $385

LEVIEUX, Reynier
paintings: (H) $7,700

LEVIGNE, Theodore
French 19th cent.
paintings: (L) $220; (H) $660

LEVIKOVA, Bela
Russian b. 1939
paintings: (H) $14,300

LEVIN, Robert
contemporary
sculpture: (L) $242; (H) $3,080

LEVIN, W.E.
paintings: (H) $770

LEVINE, David
paintings: (H) $880
drawings: (L) $462; (H) $1,760

LEVINE, David
American
paintings: (H) $4,620
drawings: (L) $605; (H) $4,620

LEVINE, Jack
American b. 1915
paintings: (L) $5,500; (H) $93,500
drawings: (L) $55; (H) $7,700

LEVINE, Les
contemporary
sculpture: (H) $3,300

LEVINE, Marilyn
Canadian b. 1935
sculpture: (L) $1,210; (H) $8,800

LEVINE, Sherrie
American b. 1947
paintings: (L) $7,700; (H) $14,300
drawings: (H) $7,700
sculpture: (H) $52,250

LEVINSON, Mon
contemporary
sculpture: (H) $660

LEVIS, Maurice
French 1860-after 1927
paintings: (L) $2,200; (H) $10,450

LEVITAN, Isaac Ilyitch
Lithuanian 1860-1900
drawings: (H) $1,320

LEVOLGER, A.J.P.
Dutch 1853-1952
paintings: (H) $6,325

LEVRAC-TOURNIERES, Robert
French 1667/68-1752
paintings: (L) $1,980; (H) $11,000

LEVY, Alexander O.
American 1881-1947
paintings: (L) $110; (H) $20,900

Art Students League

The post-Civil War prosperity of the 1870s fostered an artistic awakening in many parts of the United States. The center of this activity was New York, the home of the National Academy of Design, the major art institution in the country. Yet the National Academy was very conservative, and many young artists returning from abroad felt the need for a society or group that would support their radical ideas.

In 1875 the Art Students League was formed, and the League became the first independent art school in the country, founded on the premise that there would be no membership requirements and that study would be open to any candidate who had the ability to pay. The League offered a broad range of artistic study, favoring no particular school or specific approach to painting. In 1892 the League moved to West 57th Street, where it remains today. The school has been very influential, with a long and impressive roster of teachers that included William Merritt Chase, Robert Henri, John Sloan, Max Weber, Stuart Davis, Hans Hofmann, and Alexander Calder.

Richard Hayley Lever (1876-1958) was a teacher at the Art Students League from 1919 until 1931. Born in Australia, he studied in London and Cornwall, England. His paintings of the English coastline were done in a modified Impressionist manner and were well received. In 1911 he moved to New York City and became an American citizen. He later opened a summer studio in Gloucester, Massachusetts. During his years in New York he painted scenes of Manhattan, but he is best known for his colorful harbor scenes. (Richard Hayley Lever, *Downtown New York*, oil on board, 7 x 9 in., Young, June 2, 1990, $3,025)

LEVY, Alph
sculpture: (H) $1,210

LEVY, Charles Octave
late 19th cent.
sculpture: (L) $990; (H) $2,475

LEVY, Diane
American b. 1948
paintings: (H) $1,210

LEVY, G.
European 19th cent.
sculpture: (H) $935

LEVY, Henri Leopold
French 1840-1904
paintings: (H) $3,850
drawings: (H) $385

LEVY, Henry L.
American b. 1868
paintings: (L) $110; (H) $770

LEVY, Herbert
American
paintings: (H) $1,320

LEVY, J.
European 19th cent.
paintings: (H) $2,750

LEVY, J.
French 19th cent.
paintings: (H) $715

LEVY, Jule Benoit
paintings: (H) $2,750

LEVY, Margaret Wasserman
American b. 1899
sculpture: (H) $5,610

LEVY, Micael
sculpture: (H) $770

LEVY, Nat
American 1896-1984
drawings: (L) $220; (H) $2,475

LEVY-DHURMER, Lucien
French 1865-1953
paintings: (H)$264,000
drawings: (L) $1,100; (H) $33,000

LEWAN, Dennis
American b. 1943
paintings: (L) $715; (H) $825

LEWANDOWSKI, Edmund D.
American b. 1914
paintings: (H) $4,675

LEWIN, James
paintings: (H) $1,045

LEWIS, Charles James
British 1830-1892
paintings: (L) $770; (H) $1,980

LEWIS, Edmund Darch
American 1835-1910
paintings: (L) $198; (H) $20,900
drawings: (L) $110; (H) $7,425

LEWIS, Emerson
American b. 1892
paintings: (L) $467; (H) $2,090

LEWIS, Frederick Christian
English 1779-1856
drawings: (H) $3,080

LEWIS, Geoffrey
American 20th cent.
paintings: (L) $550; (H) $770

LEWIS, Harry Emerson
American b. 1892
paintings: (L) $138; (H) $1,650
drawings: (L) $385; (H) $660

LEWIS, Henry
English/German 1819-1904
paintings: (L) $495; (H) $6,050

LEWIS, Jeanette Maxfield
American 1894-1982
paintings: (H) $1,540

LEWIS, John
American b. 1942
sculpture: (L) $1,100; (H) $2,420

LEWIS, John Frederick
English 1805-1876
paintings: (L) $440; (H) $1,100,000
drawings: (H) $14,300

LEWIS, Martin
American 1881/83-1962
drawings: (L) $2,310; (H) $7,150

LEWIS, Percy Wyndham
British 1884-1957
drawings: (H) $8,250

LEWIS, Ruth
paintings: (H) $660

LEWIS, Thomas
American
paintings: (L) $198; (H) $1,430

LEWIS, Thomas E.
American 1909-1979
drawings: (H) $1,650

LEWISOHN, Raphael
German 1863-1923
paintings: (L) $412; (H) $3,300

LEWITT, Sol
American b. 1928
drawings: (L) $1,650; (H) $88,000
sculpture: (L) $4,950; (H) $165,000

LEWSEY, Tom
British 20th cent.
paintings: (H) $990

LEWY, James
American 19th/20th cent.
paintings: (H) $825

LEYENDECKER, Frank Xavier
American 1877/78-1924
paintings: (L) $1,925; (H) $4,125
drawings: (L) $825; (H) $7,975

LEYENDECKER, Joseph Christian
American 1874-1951
paintings: (L) $650; (H) $37,400
drawings: (L) $440; (H) $1,760

LEYENDECKER, Mathias
German 1822-1871
paintings: (H) $1,045

LEYENDECKER, Paul
French b. 1842
paintings: (L) $825; (H) $6,600

LEYS, Baron Hendrik
Belgian 1815-1869
paintings: (L) $5,500; (H) $15,400

LEYS, Henri Jan Augustyn
Belgium 1815-1869
paintings: (L) $412; (H) $9,350

LEYSTER, Judith
Dutch c. 1600-1660
paintings: (L) $143,000; (H) $528,000

LHERMITTE, Leon Augustin
French 1844-1925
paintings: (L) $3,850; (H) $363,000
drawings: (L) $1,650; (H) $68,200

LHOEST, E.
paintings: (H) $3,300

LHOTE, Andre
French 1885-1962
paintings: (L) $3,300; (H) $165,000
drawings: (L) $1,430; (H) $19,800

LI KUCHAN
Chinese 1898-1983
drawings: (H) $1,760

LIADINSKY
American 20th cent.
paintings: (H) $990

LIANCE(?), J.
sculpture: (H) $6,600

LIATAUD, Georges
Haitian b. 1899
sculpture: (H) $2,200

LIAUSU, Camille
French b. 1894
paintings: (L) $880; (H) $4,400

LIBBEY, Walter
American
paintings: (H) $5,500

LIBBY
American School 19th cent.
paintings: (H) $825

LIBENSKY, Stanislav and Jaroslava
BRYCHTOVA
Czechoslovakian b. 1921
sculpture: (H) $1,045

LIBERI, Marco
1640-1725
paintings: (H) $2,750

LIBERI, Pietro
Italian 1614-1687
paintings: (L) $7,700; (H) $33,000

LIBERICH, Nicolai Ivanovich
Russian 1828-1883
sculpture: (H) $3,300

LIBERIKH, Lapil
sculpture: (H) $880

LIBERMAN, Alexander
Russian/American b. 1912
paintings: (L) $4,620; (H) $9,350
drawings: (H) $1,210
sculpture: (H) $4,675

LIBERMANN, Max
German 1847-1935
drawings: (H) $880

Minimalism

Sol Lewitt, Carl Andre, Tony Smith, and Donald Judd are the leading exponents of Minimalism, a style of painting and sculpture in which only the most elemental geometric forms are used. The movement gained force in the late 1950s and early 1960s as a reaction to Abstract Expressionism and a desire to seek simplicity during a turbulent decade that saw the struggles of the Civil Rights movement and the Vietnam War. Minimalists sought to reduce their work to its essential elements, defining the artist's role as an originator and designer. The movement was aided by the rise in basic design courses in art schools in which pure geometric forms were studied both for their own sake and for their application to industrial design. In many cases, a Minimalist work is actually executed by a skilled craftsman after the artist's design.

Sol Lewitt (b. 1928) was born in Hartford, Connecticut, and was graduated from Syracuse University. He held his first one-man show in 1965, where he exhibited his earliest three-dimensional grids–one of the first Minimalist art shows. By 1969 he had abandoned architectural wood and painted aluminum constructions in favor of two-dimensional "wall drawings" executed in pencil directly on the gallery walls. The drawings, mathematical in concept but delicate and beautiful, were frequently destroyed after they had been exhibited.

At Christie's in 1987, the Gilman Paper Company sold its collection of Minimalist art, the first major sale of Minimalist art at auction. Lot #48, a black graphite drawing consisting of 10,000 lines drawn on the back wall of Christie's, was purchased for $26,400. The drawing, almost too faint to be seen, was sold with a certificate of authenticity from the artists and with exact instructions for its re-creation. A footnote in the catalog stated: "Studio assistants are available to re-create this work, all expenses to be borne by the buyer." When *B 2,5,8*, a sculpture by Lewitt executed in 1967, was auctioned at Christie's, it realized a record price. (Sol Lewitt, *B 2,5,8*, baked enamel on steel and plastic strips, 81 x 81 x 299 in., Christie's, May 8, 1990, $165,000)

LIBERT, George Emil
Danish 1820-1908
paintings: (L) $770; (H) $1,980

LICHTENBERG, Manes
American b. 1920
paintings: (H) $1,100

LICHTENHELD, Wilhelm
German 1817-1891
paintings: (L) $1,100; (H) $4,400

LICHTENSTEIN, Roy
American b. 1923
paintings: (L) $4,400; (H) $6,050,000
drawings: (L) $4,950; (H) $242,000
sculpture: (L) $990; (H) $1,100,000

LIDDERDALE, Charles Sillem
English 1831-1895
paintings: (L) $1,100; (H) $8,800

LIDOV, Arthur
American 1917-?
paintings: (H) $935

LIE, A.J.
paintings: (H) $1,100

LIE, Jonas
American 1880-1940
paintings: (L) $44; (H) $37,400
drawings: (H) $400

LIE, Robert
American/Norwegian 1899-1980
paintings: (L) $66; (H) $1,100

LIEBENWEIN, Maximilien
Austrian 1869-1926
drawings: (H) $2,420

LIEBER, Tom
American b. 1949
paintings: (L) $4,400; (H) $6,050

LIEBERICH, Nicolai
Russian 1828-1893
sculpture: (L) $1,760; (H) $1,870

LIEBERMANN, Ferdinand
sculpture: (L) $550; (H) $3,850

LIEBERMANN, Max
German 1847-1935
paintings: (L) $11,000; (H) $88,000
drawings: (L) $275; (H) $44,000

LIEBMANN
sculpture: (H) $660

LIEBSCHER, Karl
Polish 1851-1906
paintings: (H) $880

LIECK, Joseph
German b. 1849
paintings: (H) $1,320

LIECKERT, C.H.J.
paintings: (H) $687

LIENARD, Emile Desire
paintings: (H) $4,400

LIENDER, Paulus van
1731-1797
drawings: (H) $1,650

LIER, J. van
Belgian 20th cent.
paintings: (H) $1,540

LIES, Jozef Hendrik Hubert
paintings: (L) $2,860; (H) $4,950

LIESEGANG, Helmut
German b. 1858
paintings: (H) $2,200

LIESGANG, Helmuth
paintings: (H) $3,520

LIESTE, Cornelis
paintings: (H) $3,410

LIEVENS, Jan
Dutch 1607-1672/74
paintings: (L) $28,600; (H) $319,000
drawings: (H) $57,750

LIEVERICH, Nicolai Ivanovitch
sculpture: (H) $2,970

LIEVIN, Jacques
French b. 1850
paintings: (L) $1,650; (H) $6,600
drawings: (L) $2,475; (H) $7,700

LIEVIN, Jules
French 20th cent.
drawings: (H) $4,675

LIGER, F.
French 19th/20th cent.
paintings: (L) $3,300; (H) $5,500

LIGHT, Leonard Robert
American 19th/20th cent.
drawings: (H) $715

LIGKELIJN, E.
paintings: (H) $1,430

LIGNIER, J.
French 19th/20th cent.
drawings: (L) $770; (H) $1,210

LIGNON, Bernard
French b. 1928
paintings: (H) $1,100

LIGORIO, Pirro
Italian c. 1500-1583
drawings: (L) $495; (H) $15,400

LIGOZZI, Jacopo
Italian c. 1547-1627
paintings: (L) $22,000; (H) $396,000

LILIEVRE, E.
French
sculpture: (H) $4,400

LILIO, Andrea
Italian 1555-1610
drawings: (H) $2,640

LILJEFORS, Bruno
Swedish 1860-1939
paintings: (L) $2,860; (H) $82,500

LILJESTROM, Gustave
American b. 1882
paintings: (L) $495; (H) $2,090

LILLO, L. de
European 20th cent.
paintings: (H) $1,045

LIMBURG, Michiel D. van
paintings: (H) $1,430

LIMOUSE, Roger
American b. 1894
paintings: (L) $1,760; (H) $31,900

LIMOUSIN
sculpture: (H) $1,210

LINARD, Jacques
French c. 1600-1645
paintings: (H) $61,600

LINCK, Louis
American 20th cent.
sculpture: (H) $825

LINCOLN, Ephraim Frank
American 19th/20th cent.
paintings: (L) $550; (H) $1,500

LINDBERG, Arthur Harold
American
drawings: (L) $1,650; (H) $1,650

LINDBERG, Harald
Swedish 1901-1976
paintings: (H) $2,475

LINDE, Ossip L.
American 1871-1940
paintings: (L) $660; (H) $4,950
drawings: (H) $110

LINDEN, Carl
American 1869-1942
paintings: (L) $1,320; (H) $2,090

LINDENLAU, Rob
paintings: (H) $1,540

LINDENMUTH, Arlington N.
American b. 1867
paintings: (H) $880

LINDENMUTH, Tod
American 1885-1976
paintings: (L) $121; (H) $2,640

LINDENSCHMIT, Wilhelm van
German 1829-1895
paintings: (H) $1,540

LINDENSCHMIT, Wilhelm von
German b. 1857
paintings: (H) $1,430

LINDER, Harry
American 1886-1931
drawings: (L) $303; (H) $880

LINDER, Henry
American 1854-1910
paintings: (H) $1,200
sculpture: (L) $770; (H) $1,320

LINDER, J.
German 19th/20th cent.
paintings: (H) $2,420

LINDER, Lambert
paintings: (H) $6,050

LINDER, Philippe Jacques
French 19th cent.
paintings: (H) $2,750

LINDERUM, Richard
German b. 1851
paintings: (L) $2,200; (H) $5,500

LINDHOLM, Berndt
Finnish 1841-1914
paintings: (H) $9,350

LINDIN, Carl Olaf Eric
Swedish/American 1869-1942
paintings: (H) $3,300

LINDNER, Ernest
paintings: (H) $3,300

LINDNER, J.
paintings: (H) $935

LINDNER, Julius
paintings: (H) $4,400

LINDNER, Richard
German/American 1901-1978
paintings: (L) $66,000; (H) $418,000
drawings: (L) $450; (H) $71,500

LINDNEUX, Robert Ottokar
American 1871-1970
paintings: (L) $935; (H) $1,045

LINDO, P.
British 1821-1892
paintings: (H) $3,080

LINDSAY, Frank
English 19th cent.
paintings: (H) $1,100

LINDSAY, Thomas C.
American 1845-1907
paintings: (L) $220; (H) $1,870

LINDSELL, Violet
British 19th cent.
drawings: (H) $935

LINDSFORS
paintings: (H) $2,860

LINDSTROM, Bengt
Swedish b. 1925
paintings: (H) $4,125

LINFORD, Charles
American 1846-1897
paintings: (L) $413; (H) $2,200

LINGELBACH, Johannes
Dutch c. 1622-1674
paintings: (L) $17,050; (H) $55,000
drawings: (H) $1,980

LINGEN, A.V.
Dutch 19th/20th cent.
paintings: (H) $825

LINGKE, Albert Muller
German b. 1844
paintings: (H) $4,950

LINK, B. Lillian
American b. 1880
sculpture: (H) $715

LINNELL, J.
paintings: (H) $1,980

LINNELL, James Thomas
English 1826-1905
paintings: (L) $418; (H) $2,500

LINNELL, John, Sr.
English 1792-1882
paintings: (L) $1,265; (H) $44,000

LINNIG, Egidius
Flemish 1821-1860
paintings: (H) $6,050

LINNIG, Willem, Sr.
Belgian 1819-1885
paintings: (H) $2,750

LINNIG, Willem, Jr.
Belgian 1842/7/9-1890
paintings: (H) $2,090

LINS, Adolf
German 1856-1927
paintings: (L) $3,850; (H) $6,600

LINSEY, Martin
American 20th cent.
drawings: (L) $44; (H) $880

LINSON, Corwin Knapp
American b. 1864
paintings: (L) $66; (H) $42,900

LINT, Hendrik Frans van, called Studio
Flemish 1684-1763
paintings: (L) $36,300; (H) $165,000

LINT, Pieter van
Flemish 1609-1690
paintings: (L) $8,250; (H) $33,000

LINTON, Henry S.
English 19th/20th cent.
paintings: (H) $825

LINTON, William
British 1791-1876
paintings: (H) $17,600

LINTON, William Evans
English b. 1878
drawings: (H) $660

LINTOTT, Edward Barnard
American 1875-1951
paintings: (L) $220; (H) $4,400
drawings: (L) $88; (H) $1,320

LINTZ, Frederick
Belgian b. 1824
paintings: (H) $990

LION, Alois
paintings: (H) $770

LION, Flora
British 19th/20th cent.
paintings: (H) $825

LIONE, Andrea de
Italian 1595-1675
paintings: (H) $99,000

LIP
sculpture: (H) $7,700

LIPCHITZ, Jacques
French 1891-1973
drawings: (L) $825; (H) $17,600
sculpture: (L) $1,045; (H) $1,540,000

LIPCHYTZ, L.
sculpture: (H) $880

LIPINSKI, Hypolit
Czechoslovakian 1846-1884
paintings: (H) $3,520

LIPOFSKY, Marvin
American b. 1938
sculpture: (L) $2,310; (H) $18,700

LIPPERT, Leon
American d. 1950
paintings: (L) $154; (H) $4,950

LIPPI, Lorenzo
Italian 1606-1665
paintings: (H) $16,500

LIPPINCOTT, William Henry
American 1849-1920
paintings: (L) $330; (H) $18,700

LIPPMANN, Alphonse
French 19th cent.
sculpture: (H) $990

LIPSCHITZ, Jacques
drawings: (H) $3,300

LIPSKI, Donald
American b. 1947
sculpture: (L) $2,475; (H) $4,125

LIPSZYC, Samuel
sculpture: (H) $5,500

LIPTON, Seymour
American b. 1903
sculpture: (L) $1,100; (H) $24,200

LIRA, Benjamin
paintings: (H) $3,300

LISIO, Arnaldo de
Italian b. 1869
paintings: (H) $2,200

LISMER, Arthur
Canadian 1885-1911
paintings: (L) $4,070; (H) $30,800

LISSE, Dirck van der
Dutch d. 1669
paintings: (H) $6,050

LISSER, Onrico
Continental 19th cent.
paintings: (H) $8,800

LISSITSKY, El
Russian 1890-1941
drawings: (L) $57,750; (H) $605,000

LISTERE, A. de
French 18th cent.
paintings: (H) $2,420

LITHGOW, David Cummingham
English b. 1868
paintings: (L) $138; (H) $11,000

LITSCHAUR, Karl Joseph
paintings: (H) $5,500

LITTLE, J. Wetley
English 19th/20th cent.
drawings: (H) $880

LITTLE, John Geoffrey
paintings: (H) $4,125

LITTLE, John Wesley
American 1867-1923
drawings: (L) $55; (H) $742

LITTLE, Nat
American b. 1893
paintings: (H) $1,650

LITTLE, Philip
American 1857-1942
paintings: (L) $187; (H) $13,200
drawings: (L) $55; (H) $935

Cubist Sculptor

Jacques Lipchitz (1891-1973) was born in Lithuania, but after graduating from high school he went to Paris to study at the École des Beaux-Arts and the Academie Julian. By 1911 he had established his own studio in Montparnasse. In 1913 he met Picasso, and by 1914 his work began to show a Cubist influence. Lipchitz became particularly close friends with Juan Gris as well as with Amedeo Modigliani and Henri Matisse. By 1916 he was producing a wide variety of Cubist works in stone, bronze, and wood construction. During the 1920s he executed some of his most monumental Cubist works, such as the eleven-foot-high *Joie de Vivre* now at the Whitney Museum of American Art.

In the 1930s Lipchitz's work became more expressive; he turned away from specifically Cubist ideals, although he continued to use many of the Cubist forms. His themes during this period were variations of the Greek legend of Prometheus and the eagle. In 1940, when the Germans invaded France, Lipchitz left Paris, arriving in the United States in 1941. During the 1960s and 1970s he received commissions for many monumental sculptures, but he also continued to cast smaller maquettes. After 1941, Lipchitz's bronzes were cast by means of the lost-wax process. Concerned about recasts and fakes he impressed his finger into the wax next to his signature and edition number; his fingerprint on his bronzes showed he had authorized the casting.

Lipchitz received numerous awards and had one-man exhibitions in major museums throughout the United States and Europe. In 1989 the St. Louis court ordered the Mansion House Center Collection of Contemporary Sculpture to be sold at auction. Selkirk Galleries conducted the sale, and Lipchitz's *Reclining Figure with Guitar, circa 1923*, sold for $120,000. (Jacques Lipchitz, *Reclining Figure with Guitar*, bronze, 47 x 89 x 5 in., Selkirk, May 22, 1989, $120,000)

LITTLEFIELD, William H.
American 1902-1969
paintings: (L) $55; (H) $2,090
drawings: (L) $27; (H) $275

LITTLETON, Harvey K.
American b. 1922
sculpture: (L) $2,750; (H) $7,920

LITZINGER, Dorothea M.
American 1889-1925
paintings: (L) $412; (H) $7,150
drawings: (H) $440

LIVEMONT, Privat
Belgian 1861-1936
drawings: (L) $1,320; (H) $2,750

LIVENS, H.
English 19th cent.
paintings: (H) $797

LIVENS, Henry
19th cent.
paintings: (H) $990

LIVENS, Horace Mann
British b. 1862
paintings: (H) $715

LIVERATI, Carlo Ernesto
Italian 1805-1844
paintings: (H) $1,320

LIVINGSTON, N.C.
Scottish 19th cent.
paintings: (H) $825

LIZ, Domingo
Dominican b. 1931
paintings: (L) $3,300; (H) $5,500

LIZCANO Y ESTEBAN, Angel
Spanish b. 1846
paintings: (L) $165; (H) $2,640

LIZEN, M.
Belgian 19th cent.
paintings: (H) $1,650

LJUBA
paintings: (L) $7,150; (H) $10,450

LLEWELIN, Henry
drawings: (H) $770

LLONA, Ramiro
Peruvian b. 1947
paintings: (H) $4,950

LLOYD, C.
paintings: (H) $1,265

LLOYD, Edward
British ac. 1866
paintings: (H) $3,850

LLOYD, M.
paintings: (H) $1,210

LLOYD, Stanley
British 19th/20th cent.
paintings: (L) $990; (H) $1,210

LLOYD, Stuart
English 20th cent.
paintings: (L) $550; (H) $7,150
drawings: (L) $253; (H) $2,090

LLOYD, Thomas Ivester
British 19th cent.
paintings: (L) $880; (H) $10,450
drawings: (H) $1,320

LLOYD, Thomas James
English 1849-1910
drawings: (L) $357; (H) $2,860

LLOYD, W. Stuart
English ac. 1875-1929
drawings: (L) $220; (H) $1,320

LLULL, Jose Pinelo
Spanish 1861-1922
paintings: (H) $990

LLYOD, C.
Anglo/American School 19th cent.
paintings: (H) $935

LO GRIPPO
paintings: (H) $825

LOBER, Georg John
American
sculpture: (H) $880

LOBRICHON, Timoleon Marie
French 1831-1914
paintings: (L) $1,430; (H) $41,800

LOCATELLI, Andrea
Italian 1693-1741
paintings: (L) $9,075; (H) $88,000

LOCKE, Harry
British 20th cent.
paintings: (H) $660

LOCKER, John
British ac. 1802
paintings: (H) $5,610

LOCKET, D.H.
drawings: (H) $935

LOCKHART, William Ewart
British 1846-1900
paintings: (L) $330; (H) $825

LOCKHEAD, John
British b. 1866
paintings: (H) $3,080

LOCKHORST, Johan Nicolaus
paintings: (H) $825

LOCKMAN, Dewitt McClellan
American 1870-1957
paintings: (L) $468; (H) $4,950

LOCKWOOD, Ward
paintings: (H) $880

LODENKAMP
paintings: (H) $4,400

LODER, C.L.
paintings: (H) $990

LODER, James
British 1784-1860
paintings: (L) $1,650; (H) $8,800

LODER, James, of Bath
English 19th cent.
paintings: (L) $5,280; (H) $14,300

LODGE, George Edward
English 1860-1954
drawings: (H) $3,300

LODI, Gaetano
Italian 19th cent.
paintings: (L) $302; (H) $880

LODONE, Eusebio
Italian 19th cent.
paintings: (H) $3,630

LOEB, Dorothy
American b. 1887
paintings: (L) $3,850; (H) $4,125

LOEB, Louis
American 1866-1909
paintings: (L) $192; (H) $13,200

LOEDING, Harmen
Dutch 1637-1673
paintings: (L) $33,000; (H) $154,000

LOEFFLER, A**
American 19th/20th cent.
paintings: (H) $880

LOEMANS, Alexander F.
American
paintings: (L) $660; (H) $6,050

LOEWY, Raymond
French d. 1986
paintings: (H) $770

LOFEULARD, Alexandre
paintings: (H) $660

LOFFLER, Auguste
German 1822-1866
drawings: (L) $352; (H) $660

LOFFLER, Berthold
drawings: (H) $2,860

LOGAN, Maurice
American 1886-1977
paintings: (L) $550; (H) $2,090
drawings: (L) $495; (H) $1,210

LOGAN, Robert Fulton
Canadian b. 1899
paintings: (H) $5,500

LOGAN, Robert Henry
American 1874-1942
paintings: (L) $330; (H) $2,420

LOGSDAIL, William
English 1859-1944
paintings: (H) $5,280

LOGUE, John James
American
paintings: (H) $4,620

LOHR, August
German 19th cent.
paintings: (L) $3,850; (H) $49,500
drawings: (L) $220; (H) $8,800

LOHR, Hugo
German 19th cent.
paintings: (L) $935; (H) $1,430

LOHR, Otto
drawings: (L) $550; (H) $715

LOIR, Luigi
French 1845-1916
paintings: (L) $3,300; (H) $55,000
drawings: (L) $2,750; (H) $26,400

LOIR, Nicolas Pierre
1624-1679
paintings: (H) $17,600

LOISEAU, Gustave
French 1865-1935
paintings: (L) $8,800; (H) $308,000

LOJACONO, Francesco
Italian 1841-1915
paintings: (H) $2,640

LOKHARST, D.P. van
paintings: (H) $1,980

LOLLI, Giacomo
Italian b. 1857
paintings: (H) $770

LOMAX, John Arthur
British 1857-1923
paintings: (L) $2,200; (H) $3,520
drawings: (H) $165

LOMBARD, Henri Edward
sculpture: (H) $1,650

LOMBARD SCHOOL, CIRCA 1500
drawings: (H) $8,800

LOMBARDI, Giovanni Battista
Italian 1823-1880
sculpture: (L) $2,860; (H) $24,200

LOMBARDI, Giovanni Domenico,
called Omino
1682-1752
paintings: (H) $18,700

LOMBEAUX, Jules
Belgian 1858-1890
paintings: (H) $3,300

LOMI, Aurelio
Italian 1556-1622
paintings: (H) $28,600
drawings: (H) $605

LOMMEN, Wilhelm
German 1838-1895
paintings: (H) $7,700

LONCERRA, V.
paintings: (H) $3,300

LONE WOLF, Hart Merriam
SCHULTZ
American 1882-1970
paintings: (L) $880; (H) $7,700

LONEY, William G.
paintings: (H) $2,420

LONG, Christopher
contemporary
paintings: (H) $18,700

LONG, Edwin
English 1829-1891
paintings: (L) $330; (H) $5,225

LONG, Richard
American b. 1945
drawings: (L) $8,250; (H) $9,020
sculpture: (L) $46,750; (H) $209,000

LONG, Stanley M.
American 1892-1972
paintings: (L) $110; (H) $303
drawings: (L) $77; (H) $770

LONGENECKER, Paul
American 20th cent.
paintings: (L) $220; (H) $660

LONGFELLOW, Ernest Wadsworth
American 1845-1921
paintings: (L) $400; (H) $1,045

LONGFELLOW, Mary K.
American 1852-1945
drawings: (L) $110; (H) $1,045

LONGHI, Alessandro
Italian 1733-1813
paintings: (H) $5,775

LONGHI, Barbara
Italian 1552-1638
paintings: (H) $9,350

LONGHI, Luca
paintings: (H) $1,320

LONGMAID, William
English ac. 1886-1909
paintings: (H) $3,300

LONGMAN, Evelyn Beatrice
American b. 1874
sculpture: (H) $19,800

LONGO, Robert
American b. 1923
paintings: (H) $154,000
drawings: (L) $2,640; (H) $44,000
sculpture: (L) $4,950; (H) $41,250

LONGOBARDI, Nino
drawings: (H) $3,300

LONGOBARDI, Nino
contemporary
drawings: (L) $1,320; (H) $2,640

LONGONI, Emilio
Italian 1859-1933
paintings: (L) $935; (H) $935

LONGPRE, M. de
French 19th/20th cent.
drawings: (L) $220; (H) $1,430

LONGSTAFFE, E.
English
paintings: (H) $907

LONGSTAFFE, Edgar
British 1849-1912
paintings: (H) $1,100

LONGSTAFFE, Edward
paintings: (H) $1,045

LONSDALE, James
English 1777-1839
paintings: (H) $1,540

LONZA, Antonio
Italian b. 1846
paintings: (H) $2,310

LOO, Carle van
French 1705-1765
paintings: (L) $2,200; (H) $46,200
drawings: (L) $4,180; (H) $11,000

LOO, Cesare van
paintings: (H) $8,800

LOO, Jacob van
paintings: (H) $5,500

LOO, Jean Baptiste van
French 1684-1745
paintings: (L) $7,150; (H) $30,800
drawings: (H) $1,210

LOO, Louis Michel van
Flemish/French 1707-1771
paintings: (L) $3,300; (H) $231,000
drawings: (H) $715

LOO, Pieter van
drawings: (L) $495; (H) $13,200

LOOMIS, Albert B.
19th cent.
paintings: (H) $1,045

LOOMIS, Andrew
American b. 1892
paintings: (L) $250; (H) $3,025

LOOMIS, Charles Russell
American d. 1883
paintings: (L) $325; (H) $1,210
drawings: (L) $110; (H) $550

LOOMIS, Chester
American 1852-1924
paintings: (L) $550; (H) $770
drawings: (L) $385; (H) $385

LOOMIS, Osbert
paintings: (H) $825

LOON, J*** van
paintings: (H) $13,200

LOOP, Henry Augustus
American 1831-1895
paintings: (L) $1,540; (H) $1,980

LOORS
paintings: (H) $1,210

LOOS, A.
paintings: (H) $1,210

LOOS, John
19th/20th cent.
paintings: (H) $9,900

LOOS, John
Belgian 19th cent.
paintings: (H) $1,430

LOOSCHEN, Hans
paintings: (H) $1,760

LOOSE, Basile de
Dutch 1809-1885
paintings: (L) $4,125; (H) $8,800

LOPER, Edward
American 20th cent.
paintings: (H) $1,870

LOPEZ, Andreas
paintings: (H) $2,200

LOPEZ, Carlos
American b. 1935
paintings: (H) $1,540
drawings: (L) $14; (H) $55

LOPEZ, Gasparo, called Gasparo dei Fiori
Italian 1650-1732
paintings: (L) $22,000; (H) $22,000

LOPEZ, M.
Spanish 19th cent.
paintings: (H) $660

LOPEZ, R. Munoz
paintings: (H) $825

LOPEZ DE ALAYA, Manuel
Spanish 19th cent.
paintings: (H) $71,500

LOPEZ Y PORTANA, Vincente
Spanish 1772-1850
paintings: (L) $4,400; (H) $22,000

LORCK, Carl Julius
Norwegian 1829-1882
paintings: (L) $4,675; (H) $7,700

LORD, Andrew
contemporary
sculpture: (H) $9,350

LORENTZEN, Christian August
1749-1828
paintings: (H) $4,400

LORENZ, A.
paintings: (H) $1,320

LORENZ, Richard
German/American 1858-1915
paintings: (L) $495; (H) $8,800

LORENZINI, Gianantonio, called Fra
Antonio
1665-1740
drawings: (H) $4,125

LORENZL
sculpture: (L) $550; (H) $5,500

LORENZL, K.
ac. 1910-1930
sculpture: (H) $660

LORI, Guglielmo Amedeo
paintings: (H) $880

LORIA, Vincenzo
Italian b. 1850
paintings: (H) $523
drawings: (L) $110; (H) $1,870

LORIAN, Dolia
contemporary
paintings: (L) $770; (H) $2,970

LORING, Francis William
American 1838-1905
paintings: (H) $880

LORING, W.H.
American 19th cent.
paintings: (H) $660

LORING, William Cushing
American b. 1879
paintings: (H) $770

LORJOU, Bernard
French b. 1908
paintings: (L) $495; (H) $46,200
drawings: (L) $1,100; (H) $1,430

LORMIER, Edouard
French 1847-1919
sculpture: (H) $1,870

LORMIER, J***
sculpture: (H) $2,200

LORRAIN, Claude, Claude GELLEE,
called LE LORRAIN
French 1600-1682
paintings: (L) $1,870; (H) $550,000
drawings: (L) $4,400; (H) $374,000

LORRAINE, Claude
paintings: (H) $1,870

LORRIT
sculpture: (H) $8,800

LOS, H. de
paintings: (H) $2,090

LOS, Waldemar
Polish 1849-1888
paintings: (L) $1,320; (H) $9,350

LOSIK, Thomas
Polish 1849-1896
paintings: (H) $1,760

LOSSOW, Heinrich
German 1843-1897
paintings: (L) $550; (H) $2,090

LOSTUTTER, Robert
American
drawings: (L) $495; (H) $1,210

LOTH, Johann Carl
1625-1676
paintings: (H) $4,400

LOTH, Johann Karl
German 1632-1698
paintings: (L) $440; (H) $20,900
drawings: (L) $1,650; (H) $1,650

LOTHAR
sculpture: (H) $907

LOTTI, A.
drawings: (H) $1,320

LOTTO, Lorenzo
Italian 1480-1556
paintings: (L) $110,000; (H) $154,000

LOTZ, Matilda B.
American 1858-1923
paintings: (L) $2,090; (H) $9,900

LOUAU, Jacques
French 19th/20th cent.
paintings: (H) $3,300

LOUBON, Emile Charles Joseph
French 1809-1863
paintings: (H) $3,850

LOUBOT
paintings: (H) $715

LOUCHET, Charles
sculpture: (H) $2,970

LOUDERBACK, Walt
American 1887-1941
paintings: (L) $50; (H) $3,850
drawings: (H) $220

LOUDON, Terence
British ac. 1921-1940
paintings: (H) $825

LOUGHEED, Robert Elmer
American b. 1910
paintings: (L) $990; (H) $9,350

LOUIS, John P.
paintings: (H) $660

LOUIS, Morris
American 1912-1962
paintings: (L) $55,000; (H) $1,045,000
drawings: (H) $4,400

LOUNSBERY, Richard M.
American
sculpture: (H) $1,045

LOUSTAUNAU, Louis Auguste
Georges
French 1846-1898
paintings: (L) $2,310; (H) $4,400

LOUTHERBOURG, Philippe
Jacques de
French/English 1740-1812
paintings: (L) $825; (H) $121,000
drawings: (H) $1,980

LOUVAN, N. and P. ATETE
paintings: (H) $8,250

LOUVRIER, Maurice
contemporary
paintings: (H) $3,080

LOUYOT, Edmond
German 1861-ca. 1909
paintings: (L) $660; (H) $1,210

LOUYOT, Edmond
German 19th cent.
paintings: (L) $1,760; (H) $4,400

LOVATTI, Matteo
Italian b. 1861
paintings: (H) $4,840

LOVATTI?
paintings: (H) $6,600

LOVEJOY, Rupert Scott
American 1885-1975
paintings: (L) $1,100; (H) $2,585

LOVELL, Katherine A.
American 1877?-1955?
paintings: (L) $198; (H) $3,850

LOVELL, Tom
American b. 1909
paintings: (L) $385; (H) $22,000
drawings: (L) $440; (H) $7,700

LOVELY, Candace Whittemore
paintings: (H) $1,100

LOVEN, Frank W.
American 1869-1941
paintings: (L) $220; (H) $5,720

LOVER, S.
paintings: (H) $1,650

LOVER, Samuel
Irish 1797-1868
paintings: (H) $1,320

LOVERIDGE, Clinton
American 1824-1902
paintings: (L) $495; (H) $18,700
drawings: (H) $550

LOVET-LORSKI, Boris
Lithuanian/American 1894-1973
drawings: (H) $688
sculpture: (L) $1,650; (H) $60,500

LOVEWELL, Rominer
American 1853-1932
drawings: (H) $700

LOVICK, Annie Pescud
paintings: (H) $990

LOVING, James
American b. 1826
paintings: (H) $1,100

LOVMAND, Christine
Danish 1803-1872
paintings: (L) $9,900; (H) $29,700

LOVOTELLI, F.
Italian early 20th cent.
sculpture: (H) $770

LOVYOX, E.
paintings: (H) $1,430

LOW, Bertha Leo
American b. 1848
paintings: (H) $660

LOW, Fritzi, designed by
paintings: (H) $8,800

LOW, Mary Fairchild
American 1858-1946
paintings: (L) $165; (H) $2,750

LOW, Will Hicok
American 1853-1932
paintings: (L) $1,054; (H) $45,100
drawings: (L) $385; (H) $440

LOWCOCK, Charles Frederick
paintings: (L) $1,650; (H) $1,870

LOWCOCK, Charles Frederick
British ac. 1878-1922
paintings: (H) $2,475

LOWE, J.
American
paintings: (H) $935

LOWELL, M.H.
paintings: (H) $1,650

LOWELL, Milton H.
American 1848-1927
paintings: (L) $165; (H) $1,760

LOWELL, Orson Byron
American 1871-1956
drawings: (L) $55; (H) $2,090

LOWENICH
sculpture: (H) $1,540

LOWENTHAL, E.
paintings: (H) $2,200

LOWERY, Ronald W.
American
sculpture: (H) $700

LOWRY, Laurence Stephen
English 1887-1976
paintings: (H) $1,100
drawings: (L) $358; (H) $1,210

LOYALFIELD
paintings: (H) $1,210

LOYALFIELD, E.
American
paintings: (H) $935

LOYSEAU, A.
sculpture: (H) $4,620

LOZA, Luis Lopez
paintings: (L) $2,200; (H) $2,200

LOZANO, Manuel Rodriguez
Latin American
paintings: (H) $4,400

LOZANO, Margarita
b. France 1936
paintings: (H) $7,150

LOZOWICK, Louis
American 1892-1973
paintings: (L) $2,860; (H) $203,500
drawings: (L) $1,100; (H) $12,100

LUBBERS, Holger
Danish 1855-1928
paintings: (H) $8,800

LUBEN, Alolf
German 1837-1905
paintings: (H) $8,250

LUBIENIECKI, Christoffel
Polish 1660-1728
paintings: (H) $14,300

LUBIENIECKI, Christoph
paintings: (H) $2,640

LUBIN, Arieh
paintings: (H) $1,500

LUBUIS, Jean
French 19th cent.
paintings: (H) $8,250

LUCA, F. de
sculpture: (L) $330; (H) $2,530

LUCAS, Albert D.
paintings: (L) $715; (H) $770

LUCAS, Albert Durer
paintings: (L) $330; (H) $935

LUCAS, Albert Pike
American 1862-1945
paintings: (L) $440; (H) $2,420

LUCAS, G.A.
paintings: (L) $220; (H) $770

LUCAS, H.F. Lucas
English 1908-1943
paintings: (L) $1,320; (H) $1,650

LUCAS, Hippolyte
French 1854-1925
paintings: (L) $2,090; (H) $8,250

LUCAS, John Seymour
British 1849-1923
paintings: (L) $523; (H) $8,250
drawings: (H) $192

LUCAS, John Templeton
English 1836-1880
paintings: (L) $385; (H) $2,750

LUCAS, Wilhelm
contemporary
paintings: (H) $2,200

LUCAS Y PADILLA, Eugenio
Spanish 1824-1870
paintings: (L) $13,200; (H) $63,250

LUCAS Y VILLAAMIL, Eugenio
Spanish 1858-1918
paintings: (L) $9,900; (H) $17,600

LUCAS-LUCAS, Henry Frederick
British d. 1943
paintings: (L) $990; (H) $7,700

LUCAS-ROBIQUET, Marie Aimee
French b. 1864
paintings: (L) $4,675; (H) $44,000

LUCCHESI, Bruno
Italian/American b. 1926
sculpture: (L) $275; (H) $8,250

LUCCHESI, Giorgio
Italian 1855-1941
paintings: (L) $4,180; (H) $6,600

LUCCIONI, Luigi
American b. 1900
paintings: (H) $7,150

LUCE, Maximilien
French 1858-1941
paintings: (L) $2,200; (H) $550,000
drawings: (L) $55; (H) $13,200

LUCE, Molly
American 1896-1986
paintings: (L) $440; (H) $11,000

LUCEBERT, Jean
Dutch b. 1924
paintings: (L) $1,540; (H) $17,600
drawings: (H) $7,700

LUCENA, E.
paintings: (H) $715

LUCERO, Michael
American b. 1953
sculpture: (L) $2,640; (H) $20,900

LUCHINI, M.
Italian 19th cent.
paintings: (H) $4,070

LUCIEN-GILBERT, Darpy
French b. 1875
paintings: (H) $770

LUCIONI, Luigi
Italian/American 1900-1988?
paintings: (L) $522; (H) $77,000

LUCKENBACH, Reuben
American
paintings: (L) $4,400; (H) $4,400

LUCKER, William, Sr.
British c. 1820-1892
paintings: (H) $3,575

LUCO, A. Se
Italian
sculpture: (L) $2,200; (H) $2,475

LUCO, F.S. de
sculpture: (H) $6,050

LUCY, Charles
British 1814-1873
paintings: (H) $4,950

LUDLOW, Gabriel R.
American 1800-1838
drawings: (H) $24,200

LUDOVICI, Albert
British 19th cent.
paintings: (H) $2,420

LUDOVICI, Albert, Jr.
English 1852-1932
paintings: (H) $7,150

LUDOVICI, Julius
American b. Germany 1837-1906
paintings: (L) $1,760; (H) $2,750

LUDUENA, Jorge
paintings: (H) $2,640

LUDWIG, Helen
American 20th cent.
paintings: (H) $742

LUDWIG, Karl
paintings: (H) $3,300

LUERZER, F. von
Dutch 19th cent.
paintings: (L) $302; (H) $880

LUFBERY
sculpture: (H) $4,400

LUGERTH, Ferdinand
Austrian 1885-1915
sculpture: (L) $330; (H) $1,650

LUIGI, Ludovico de
Italian b. 1933
paintings: (H) $1,045
sculpture: (H) $2,200

LUIGINI, Ferdinand Jean
French 1870-1943
paintings: (L) $330; (H) $1,100

LUINI, Aurelio
drawings: (H) $1,100

LUINI, Bernardino
Italian 1480/85-1532
paintings: (L) $44,000; (H) $60,500

LUISE, Enrico de
paintings: (H) $935

LUKENS, Winfield S.
American 20th cent.
paintings: (H) $907

LUKER, William
British 19th cent.
paintings: (H) $880

LUKER, William, Sr.
English ac. 1852-1889
paintings: (L) $385; (H) $16,500

LUKS, Benjamin
drawings: (H) $880

LUKS, George
American 1867-1933
paintings: (L) $880; (H) $660,000
drawings: (L) $77; (H) $24,200

LUM, Bertha Boynton
American 1879-1954
paintings: (H) $3,025
drawings: (L) $550; (H) $880

LUMINAIS, Evariste Vital
French 1822-1896
paintings: (H) $660

LUMIS, Harriet Randall
American 1870-1953
paintings: (L) $220; (H) $16,500
drawings: (L) $2,420; (H) $14,300

LUMLEY, Augustus Savile
British ac. 1856-1880
paintings: (H) $1,760

LUNA, Mariano
Italian 19th cent.
drawings: (H) $4,400

LUND, Carl Ove Julian
Danish 1857-1936
paintings: (L) $154; (H) $8,250

LUND, T.
American
paintings: (H) $2,310

LUNDBERG, August F.
American 1878-1928
paintings: (L) $165; (H) $3,575

LUNDE, Emily
b. 1914
paintings: (L) $125; (H) $1,300

LUNDEAN, Louis
paintings: (H) $1,760

LUNDEBERG, Helen
American b. 1908
paintings: (L) $1,540; (H) $6,050

LUNDMARK, Leon
American b. 1875
paintings: (L) $88; (H) $1,100

LUNGLOIS, G.
English
paintings: (H) $852

LUNGLOIS, M.V.
paintings: (H) $1,100

LUNGREN, Fernand
American 1859-1932
paintings: (L) $1,100; (H) $6,050
drawings: (H) $1,760

LUNGT
sculpture: (H) $990

LUNTZ, Adolf
German 1875-1924
paintings: (H) $880

LUNY, Thomas
English 1759-1837
paintings: (L) $1,320; (H) $29,700

LUPERTZ, Markus
German b. 1941
paintings: (L) $16,500; (H) $44,000

LUPIN, C.
European 19th cent.
paintings: (H) $1,870

LUPPENS, H.
sculpture: (H) $715

LUQUES, F. A., and Harry RUSS
French 19th cent.
paintings: (H) $2,970

LURCAT, Jean
French 1892-1966
paintings: (L) $467; (H) $15,400
drawings: (L) $413; (H) $3,575

LUTEURGERT
paintings: (H) $1,100

LUTI, Benedetto
Italian 1666-1724
paintings: (L) $1,870; (H) $88,000
drawings: (L) $8,250; (H) $25,300

LUTTER, R.
sculpture: (H) $1,045

LUTTICHUYS, Simon
Dutch 1610-1662
paintings: (L) $5,500; (H) $35,200

LUTYENS, Charles Augustus Henry
British 19th cent.
paintings: (H) $7,150
sculpture: (H) $2,200

LUTZ, Dan
American 1906-1978
paintings: (L) $110; (H) $1,430
drawings: (H) $523

LUTZ, J.
paintings: (H) $715

LUYCKX, Christiaan
Flemish 1623-1653
paintings: (H) $28,600

LUYKEN, Jan
Dutch 1649-1712
drawings: (H) $660

LUZZI, Cleto
paintings: (H) $2,750
drawings: (H) $825

LYDIS, Mariette
Austrian 20th cent.
paintings: (L) $660; (H) $770
drawings: (H) $715

LYFORD, Philip
American 1887-1950
paintings: (L) $412; (H) $4,180
drawings: (H) $125

LYLE, Byron
British 19th cent.
paintings: (H) $5,500

LYMAN, Harry
paintings: (L) $1,760; (H) $2,640

LYMAN, Joseph
American 1843-1913
paintings: (L) $330; (H) $2,090

LYNCH, Albert
Peruvian b. 1851, ac. Paris 1930
paintings: (L) $715; (H) $28,600
drawings: (L) $357; (H) $605

LYND
English 20th cent.
paintings: (H) $1,815

LYNDE, R.
paintings: (H) $2,750

LYNDE, Raymonde
English 19th/20th cent.
paintings: (H) $3,300

LYNE, Michael
English b. 1912
paintings: (L) $1,100; (H) $15,400
drawings: (L) $660; (H) $4,400
sculpture: (L) $440; (H) $605

LYNER, T.R.
Continental 19th cent.
paintings: (H) $2,090

LYNGBYE, Lauritz B.
Danish 1805-1869
drawings: (H) $2,420

LYNN, John
English ac. 1826-1838
paintings: (H) $15,400

LYON, Corneille de
Flemish 16th cent.
paintings: (H) $46,750

LYON, Henry
paintings: (H) $2,750

LYON, Richard
American 20th cent.
paintings: (H) $907

LYPCHYTZ, Samuel
sculpture: (H) $2,970

MAAS, Dirk
Dutch 1659-1717
paintings: (L) $4,125; (H) $44,000
drawings: (H) $1,210

MAAS, Ray
American 20th cent.
paintings: (H) $687

MAASDIJK, Alexander Henri
Robert van
Dutch 1856-1931
paintings: (L) $825; (H) $1,650

MAASS, David
American 20th cent.
paintings: (L) $3,960; (H) $6,380

MABE, Manabu
Brazilian b. 1924 in Japan
paintings: (L) $3,300; (H) $18,700

MABERRY, Philip
American b. 1951
sculpture: (H) $1,100

MAC KAY, Edwin Murray
American
paintings: (H) $1,650

MACARRON, R.
Spanish 20th cent.
paintings: (L) $330; (H) $715

MACARTHUR, Blanche
paintings: (H) $2,200

MACARTNEY, Jack
American 1893-1976
paintings: (H) $715

MACARTY, Jessie
American 19th/20th cent.
paintings: (L) $440; (H) $660

MACAULIFFE, James J.
American 1848-1921
paintings: (L) $2,420; (H) $2,860

MACBETH, Robert Walker
English 1848-1910
paintings: (H) $6,050

MACBEY, James
drawings: (L) $308; (H) $880

MACCALLUM, Andrew
British 1821-1902
paintings: (H) $8,250

MACCAMERON, Robert Lee
American 1866-1912
paintings: (H) $715

MACCARI, Cesare
Italian 1840-1919
drawings: (H) $3,080

MACCARTAN, Edward
American 1878-1947
sculpture: (L) $660; (H) $14,300

MACCARTHY, Frank
American b. 1924
paintings: (H) $20,900

MACCARTHY, Paul
American 20th cent.
paintings: (H) $660

MACCHIATI, Serafino
Italian 1861-1916
drawings: (H) $880

MACCILVARY, Norwood Hodge
American 1874-1949
paintings: (H) $2,805

MACCIO, Romulo
Argentinian b. 1931
paintings: (L) $1,320; (H) $26,400
drawings: (H) $440

MACCOGM
sculpture: (H) $1,100

MACCONNEL, Kim
American b. 1946
paintings: (L) $5,500; (H) $14,300
drawings: (L) $1,980; (H) $4,125

MACDONALD, Chris
contemporary
drawings: (H) $137
sculpture: (H) $9,900

MACDONALD, Grant
Canadian b. 1909
paintings: (L) $5,000; (H) $11,000

MACDONALD, James Edward Hervey
Canadian 1873-1932
paintings: (L) $19,800; (H) $220,000

MACDONALD, Manly Edward
paintings: (L) $2,860; (H) $6,050

MACDONALD, W. Alister
British exhib. 1935-36
drawings: (L) $137; (H) $770

MACDONALD-WRIGHT, Stanton
American 1890-1973/74
paintings: (L) $2,200; (H) $484,000
drawings: (L) $192; (H) $6,600

MACE, Flora
contemporary
sculpture: (L) $770; (H) $1,210

MACENTYRE, Eduardo
Argentinian b. 1929
paintings: (L) $192; (H) $5,500

MACEWEN, Walter
American 1860-1943
paintings: (L) $770; (H) $15,400
drawings: (H) $275

MACFEE, S.
American
paintings: (H) $1,210

MACGEORGE, William Stewart
English 1861-1931
paintings: (L) $880; (H) $42,900
drawings: (H) $880

MACGILVARY, Norwood Hodge
American 1874-1950
paintings: (L) $247; (H) $3,300

MACGOUN, Hannah Claire Preston
British 19th cent.
paintings: (L) $220; (H) $1,650

MACGREGOR, Jessie
American 19th/20th cent.
paintings: (L) $330; (H) $4,400

MACGREGOR, Robert
Scottish 1848-1922
paintings: (H) $1,650

MACGREGOR, William York
Scottish 1855-1923
paintings: (H) $1,320

MACHARD, Jules Louis
paintings: (H) $4,950

MACHAULT, Pierre
sculpture: (L) $550; (H) $660

MACHEN, William H.
American 1832-1911
paintings: (L) $148; (H) $1,760

MACHETANZ, Fred
American b. 1908
paintings: (L) $3,300; (H) $17,600

MACIAS, Jose
Mexican 19th/20th cent.
paintings: (H) $825

MACINTOSH, David
American 20th cent.
paintings: (L) $165; (H) $880

MACINTOSH, Marian T.
American 1871-1936
paintings: (L) $660; (H) $2,530

MACK, Heinz
contemporary
sculpture: (H) $3,300

MACK, Leal
paintings: (H) $1,320

MACKAY, Edwin Murray
American 1869-1926
paintings: (L) $352; (H) $7,150

MACKAY, William Andrew
American
paintings: (H) $1,760

MACKAY, William Darling
British 1844-1924
paintings: (L) $825; (H) $2,200

MACKE, Auguste
drawings: (H) $3,300

MACKELLAR, Duncan
British 1849-1908
paintings: (L) $550; (H) $825

MACKENDRICK, Lillian
American b. 1906
paintings: (L) $385; (H) $1,870

MACKENZIE, Alexander
British b. 1848
paintings: (H) $770

MACKENZIE, Frank J.
English/American 1865/67-1939
paintings: (L) $523; (H) $935

MACKENZIE, Frederick
Scottish c. 1787-1854
drawings: (H) $2,750

MACKENZIE, Kenneth
Scottish 19th cent.
paintings: (H) $3,080

MACKLOT, Camill
20th cent.
paintings: (L) $825; (H) $1,320

MACKNIGHT, Dodge
American 1860-1950
drawings: (L) $522; (H) $9,350

MACKY, Eric Spencer
American 1880-1958
paintings: (L) $1,870; (H) $3,025
drawings: (H) $385

MACLELLAN, Charles A.
Canadian b. 1885
paintings: (L) $165; (H) $1,600

MACLEOD, Alexander
American b. 1888
paintings: (H) $825

MACLEOD, William
American 19th cent.
paintings: (H) $770

MACLEOD, William Douglas
American 1811-1892
paintings: (H) $990

MACLEOD, Yan
American 20th cent.
sculpture: (H) $4,125

MACLET, Elisee
French 1881-1962
paintings: (L) $660; (H) $37,400
drawings: (L) $440; (H) $4,950

MACLISE, Daniel
Irish 1806/11-1870
paintings: (L) $1,650; (H) $5,500

MACMONNIES, Frederick William
American 1863-1937
sculpture: (L) $770; (H) $104,500

MACMONNIES, Mary Fairchild
American 1859-1946
paintings: (H) $4,400

MACNEE, Sir Daniel
Scottish 1806-1882
paintings: (H) $1,100

MACNEIL, Ambrose
Scottish b. 1852
paintings: (L) $330; (H) $852

MACNEIL, Carol Brooks
American 1871-1944
sculpture: (L) $385; (H) $3,080

MACNEIL, Hermon Atkins
American 1866-1947
sculpture: (L) $1,430; (H) $25,300

MACOMBER, Mary L.
American 1861-1916
paintings: (L) $550; (H) $13,200

MACONIAZ, G.
Continental 20th cent.
paintings: (H) $990

MACRAE, Elmer Livingston
American 1875-1953
paintings: (L) $550; (H) $46,200
drawings: (L) $100; (H) $770

MACRAE, Emma Fordyce
American 1887-1974
paintings: (L) $1,760; (H) $8,800

MACRINO D'ALBA
Italian d. 1528
paintings: (H) $253,000

MACRUM, George
American 19th/20th cent.
paintings: (H) $6,600

MACWHIRTER, John
English 1839-1911
paintings: (L) $700; (H) $4,400
drawings: (H) $1,650

MACY, W. Ferdinand
American 19th cent.
paintings: (L) $660; (H) $1,100

MACY, Wendell
American 1845-1913
paintings: (L) $77; (H) $6,050

MACY, Wendell Ferdinand
American 1852-1902
paintings: (L) $385; (H) $2,420
drawings: (H) $385

MACY, William Starbuck
American 1853-1916
paintings: (L) $1,210; (H) $4,180

MADARASZ, Gyula von
Austrian b. 1858
paintings: (H) $12,100

MADDEN, Jan
American 20th cent.
paintings: (H) $1,980

MADDERSTEEG, Michiel
Dutch c. 1659-1709
paintings: (H) $28,600

MADELAIN, Gustave
French 1867-1944
paintings: (L) $2,200; (H) $24,200

MADELINE, Paul
French 1863-1920
paintings: (L) $4,620; (H) $6,325

MADERLINCK, L.
Continental 19th cent.
paintings: (H) $1,430

MADIOL, Adrien Jean
Dutch 1845-1892
paintings: (H) $660

MADIONO, Luis
Spanish 19th cent.
paintings: (H) $935

MADLENER, A. Joseph
German b. 1881
paintings: (L) $2,200; (H) $2,475

MADONINI, Giovanni
Italian b. 1915
paintings: (H) $935

MADOU, Jean Baptiste
Belgian 1796-1877
paintings: (L) $660; (H) $35,200
drawings: (H) $4,620

MADRASSI, Luca
Italian 19th/20th cent.
sculpture: (L) $687; (H) $4,125

MADRAZO, A.
Italian 19th cent.
paintings: (L) $412; (H) $660

MADRAZO Y GARRETA,
Raimundo de
Spanish 1841-1920
paintings: (L) $4,675; (H) $154,000

MADRAZO Y GARRETA, Ricardo de
Spanish 1852-1917
paintings: (H) $17,600

MADSON, Charles
American 20th cent.
drawings: (L) $825; (H) $880

MAECKER, Franz Wilhelm
German 1855-1913
paintings: (L) $60; (H) $1,320

MAELLA, Mariano Salvador de
Spanish 1739-1819
paintings: (H) $45,100

MAENTEL, Dr. Jacob
American 1763-1863
drawings: (L) $880; (H) $143,000

MAES, Eugene Remy
Belgian 1849-1912
paintings: (L) $990; (H) $20,900

MAES, Eugene Remy and Jan David
COLE
Belgian 19th/20th cent.
paintings: (H) $13,200

MAES, H.
British 19th cent.
paintings: (L) $880; (H) $1,045

MAES, Hendrik
Dutch 1793-1873
paintings: (L) $1,100; (H) $6,600

MAES, Nicolaes
Dutch 1632/34-1693
paintings: (L) $2,200; (H) $165,000

MAESTOSI, F.
Italian 19th cent.
paintings: (L) $1,100; (H) $7,500

MAFFEI, Francesco
Italian c. 1600/20-1660
paintings: (L) $1,210; (H) $5,500

MAFFEI, Guido von
paintings: (H) $3,850

MAGAFAN, Ethel
American b. 1916
paintings: (L) $176; (H) $1,320

MAGANZA, Alessandro
drawings: (H) $3,300

MAGAUD, Dominique Antoine Jean
Baptiste
French 1817-1899
paintings: (H) $12,100

MAGDANZ, Andrew
contemporary
sculpture: (L) $220; (H) $880

MAGEE, James C.
American 1846-1924
paintings: (L) $660; (H) $1,870

MAGERER, H.
Dutch 19th/20th cent.
paintings: (H) $770

MAGGI, Cesare
paintings: (H) $8,250

MAGGIOLO(?), Jarrier
drawings: (L) $330; (H) $715

MAGGIOTTO, Domenico
Italian 1713-1794
paintings: (L) $13,750; (H) $16,500

MAGGS, John Charles
English 1819-1895/96
paintings: (L) $1,430; (H) $14,300

MAGIE, Gertrude
American b. 1862
paintings: (H) $1,980

MAGINI, Carlo
Italian 1720-1806
paintings: (H) $85,250

MAGNASCO, Alessandro, Il
Lissandrino
Italian 1667-1749
paintings: (L) $2,750; (H) $88,000

MAGNE, Desire Alfred
French 1855-1936
paintings: (L) $467; (H) $4,950

MAGNENAT, Paul
French 1905-1970
paintings: (H) $743

MAGNI, Giuseppe
Italian b. 1869
paintings: (L) $1,760; (H) $71,500

MAGNUS, Camille
French 19th cent.
paintings: (L) $275; (H) $16,500

MAGRATH, Georges Achille de
French 19th cent.
drawings: (H) $2,530

MAGRATH, William
Irish 1838-1918
paintings: (H) $440
drawings: (H) $3,850

MAGRITTE, Rene
Belgian 1898-1967
paintings: (L) $1,870; (H) $1,650,000
drawings: (L) $440; (H) $352,000
sculpture: (L) $60,500; (H) $176,000

MAGUIRE, Jeanne
American 20th cent.
paintings: (H) $2,750

MAHAFFEY, Noel
American b. 1944
paintings: (L) $4,675; (H) $22,000

MAHER, Kate Heath
American 1860-1946
paintings: (H) $990

MAHER, Philip B.
drawings: (H) $990

MAHERBEST, William
American 20th cent.
paintings: (H) $1,320

MAHLKNECHT, Edmund
Austrian 1820-1903
paintings: (L) $550; (H) $9,075

MAHU, Cornelis
paintings: (L) $5,500; (H) $17,600

MAHUDEZ, Jeanne Louise Jacontot
French b. 1876
paintings: (L) $3,850; (H) $5,500

MAIDMENT, Henry
English 19th/20th cent.
paintings: (L) $990; (H) $1,045

MAIER, Claus
German School 19th/20th cent.
paintings: (H) $880

MAIER, Emil
paintings: (H) $1,650

MAIGE, Etienne Henri du
sculpture: (H) $660

MAIGNAN, Albert Pierre Rene
French 1845-1908
paintings: (L) $3,080; (H) $4,675

MAIGNON, A.
paintings: (H) $2,750

MAIL(?), A.
British 19th cent.
paintings: (H) $1,705

MAILE, George
drawings: (H) $770

MAILLARD, Claude
French 19th cent.
paintings: (L) $19,800; (H) $19,800

MAILLARD, Emile
French b. 1846; ac. 1884-1893
paintings: (H) $935

MAILLAUD, Fernand
French 1862-1948
paintings: (L) $880; (H) $14,300

MAILLET, Auguste, called Rigon
French d. 1844
paintings: (H) $1,760

MAILLOL, Aristide
French 1861-1944
drawings: (L) $633; (H) $17,600
sculpture: (L) $7,150; (H) $1,100,000

MAINARDI, Sebastiano
Italian c. 1460-1513
paintings: (H) $19,800

MAINELLA, Raffaele
Italian b. 1858
paintings: (L) $935; (H) $990
drawings: (L) $49; (H) $1,650

MAINERI, Gian Francesco de
Italian c. 1489-1504/05
paintings: (H) $154,000

MAIRE, E.
paintings: (H) $660

MAIROVICH, Zvi
1911-1974
paintings: (L) $440; (H) $1,540

MAISON, Mary Edith
American 1886-1954
paintings: (L) $330; (H) $1,650

MAIYE, M. Simon
sculpture: (H) $1,430

MAJEWSKI, F.
Russian late 19th/early 20th cent
paintings: (H) $3,740

MAJO, Paolo de
paintings: (H) $2,200

MAJOR, B.
19th/20th cent.
paintings: (L) $55; (H) $770

MAJOR, Ernest L.
American 1864-1950
paintings: (L) $330; (H) $8,250
drawings: (H) $165

MAJORE, Frank
American b. 1948
drawings: (H) $4,180

MAJORELLE, Jacques
French 19th/20th cent.
drawings: (H) $825

MAJORS, Robert J.
American b. 1913
drawings: (L) $302; (H) $715

MAKART, Hans
Austrian 1840-1884/85
paintings: (L) $4,400; (H) $23,100

MAKK, Americo
paintings: (H) $990

MAKOVSKAIA, A.E.
Russian b. 1837
paintings: (H) $2,200

MAKOVSKY, Alexander
Russian b. 1869
paintings: (H) $12,100

MAKOVSKY, Vladimir
Russian 1846-1920
paintings: (L) $990; (H) $13,200

MAKOWSKI, Alexander W.
Russian 19th cent.
paintings: (H) $660

MAKOWSKY, Constantin Jegorovich
Russian 1839-1915
paintings: (L) $1,870; (H) $18,700

MALAMPRE, Leo
British 19th cent.
paintings: (H) $6,600

MALANGA, Andy WARHOL and
Gerard
contemporary
drawings: (L) $17,600; (H) $18,700

MALATESTA, Narciso
Italian b. 1835
paintings: (L) $1,760; (H) $4,125

MALBET, Aurelie Leontine
French ac. 1868-1906
paintings: (H) $7,150

MALBRANCHE, Louis Claude
French 1790-1838
paintings: (L) $302; (H) $1,540

MALCOLM, Lloyd R.
drawings: (L) $550; (H) $750

MALDARELLI, Federico
Italian 1826-1893
paintings: (L) $440; (H) $8,800

MALDENER, Josef
German b. 1881
paintings: (H) $1,430

MALECZEVSKI, Jacek
paintings: (H) $4,950

MALEMPRE, Leo
English ac. 1887-1901
paintings: (L) $1,980; (H) $9,350

MALENFANT, J.F.
paintings: (H) $6,050

MALER, Hans
paintings: (H) $13,200

MALESPINA, Louis Ferdinand
paintings: (H) $2,860
drawings: (H) $825

MALET, Albert
French b. 1902
paintings: (L) $2,090; (H) $4,400

MALEVICH, Kasimir
Russian 1878-1935
drawings: (L) $880; (H) $19,800

MALFATTI, Andrea
Italian late 19th/early 20th cent
sculpture: (H) $6,600

MALFRAY, Charles Alexandre
French 1887-1940
sculpture: (L) $1,980; (H) $4,400

MALFROY, Charles
paintings: (H) $3,080

MALFROY, Henry
French b. 1895
paintings: (L) $935; (H) $4,400

MALHAUPT, Frederick J.
American 1871-1938
paintings: (L) $1,760; (H) $5,500

MALHERBE, William
French 19th/20th cent.
paintings: (L) $550; (H) $5,775

MALI, Christian Friedrich
German 1832-1906
paintings: (L) $28,600; (H) $46,750

MALIAVINE, Philippe
Russian 1869-1940
paintings: (H) $13,200
drawings: (L) $110; (H) $220

MALICOAT, Philip Cecil
American b. 1908
paintings: (H) $2,200

MALINCONICO, Niccolo
paintings: (H) $1,650

MALISSARD, Georges
French b. 1877
sculpture: (H) $3,850

MALLET, Jean Baptiste
French 1759-1835
drawings: (L) $10,450; (H) $39,600

MALLINDER, A.
English 19th cent.
paintings: (H) $880

MALLO, Maruja
Argentinian b. 1908
paintings: (L) $8,800; (H) $11,000

MALLOEB (?), C.
paintings: (H) $660

MALLORY, Ronald
paintings: (H) $1,320
sculpture: (L) $110; (H) $440

MALMSTROM, August
Swedish 1829-1901
paintings: (H) $99,000

MALNOVITZER, Zvi
paintings: (L) $7,150; (H) $14,300

MALO, Vincent
paintings: (H) $4,400

MALONEY, Dave
American
paintings: (H) $1,150

MALONEY, Louise B.
19th/20th cent.
paintings: (L) $55; (H) $1,100

MALTINO, F.
paintings: (H) $660

MALVANI, E.
sculpture: (H) $3,520

MALY, August Chevalier von
Austrian b. 1835
paintings: (H) $7,700

MAMANI, C.
Italian 19th cent.
sculpture: (H) $1,430

MAMANI, O.
sculpture: (H) $660

MANAGO, Vincent
paintings: (H) $1,100

MANARESI, Ugo
Italian 1851-1917
paintings: (H) $2,200

MANCCINI, A.
paintings: (H) $825

MANCHON, Raphael
paintings: (H) $1,210

MANCIN, Francesco
Italian 1830-1905
paintings: (H) $19,800

MANCINELLI, Giuseppe
Italian 1813-1875
paintings: (L) $6,500; (H) $13,200

MANCINI
Italian 19th cent.
drawings: (H) $3,080

MANCINI, Antonio
Italian 1852-1930
paintings: (L) $880; (H) $18,700

MANCINI, Emilio
sculpture: (H) $825

MANCINI, Francesco Longo
Italian 20th cent.
paintings: (L) $330; (H) $660

MANCINI, Francesco Paolo
Italian b. 1900
paintings: (H) $1,430

MANCLAIR, A.
British 19th cent.
paintings: (H) $990

MANDEL, John
contemporary
drawings: (H) $1,210

MANDER, William Henry
British ac. 1880-1922
paintings: (L) $275; (H) $3,575

MANDERLOS, V.M.
paintings: (H) $715

MANE-KATZ
French/Israeli 1894-1962
paintings: (L) $990; (H) $77,000
drawings: (L) $275; (H) $15,400
sculpture: (L) $330; (H) $8,800

MANES, Pablo Curatella
Latin American
sculpture: (H) $6,600

MANESSIER, Alfred
French b. 1941
paintings: (L) $17,600; (H) $68,200

MANET, Edouard
French 1832-1883
paintings: (L) $24,200; (H) $26,400,000
drawings: (H) $1,980

MANETTI, Mauro
European 20th cent.
sculpture: (H) $1,210

MANETTI, Rutilio di Lorenzo
Italian 1571-1639
paintings: (H) $22,000

MANGILLI, Ada
Italian b. 1863
paintings: (H) $40,700

MANGLARD, Adrien
French 1695-1760
paintings: (H) $11,000

MANGOLD, Robert
American b. 1937
paintings: (L) $2,750; (H) $88,000
drawings: (L) $2,640; (H) $176,000

MANGOLD, Sylvia
American b. 1938
paintings: (L) $1,870; (H) $3,850
drawings: (H) $1,760

MANGRAVITE, Peppino
Italian/American b. 1896
paintings: (L) $22; (H) $825

MANGUIN, Henri
French 1874-1943/49
paintings: (L) $14,300; (H) $77,000
drawings: (L) $440; (H) $14,300

MANHU
contemporary
paintings: (L) $825; (H) $880

MANIATTY, Stephen G.
American b. 1910
paintings: (L) $330; (H) $1,650

MANIGAULT, Edward Middleton
American 1887-1922
paintings: (L) $1,320; (H) $16,500
drawings: (L) $357; (H) $440

MANIQUE, R.
sculpture: (H) $660

MANLEY, Thomas R.
American 1853-1938
paintings: (L) $660; (H) $1,650

MANLIN, R.
French 19th/20th cent.
paintings: (H) $2,750

MANN, David
American b. 1948
paintings: (L) $440; (H) $14,850

MANN, Edith
American
paintings: (H) $2,420

MANN, Joshua Hargrave Sams
British 19th cent.
paintings: (H) $1,760
drawings: (H) $110

MANN, Parker
American 1852-1918
paintings: (L) $467; (H) $1,595
drawings: (H) $110

MANNERS, William
English ac. 1885-1910
paintings: (H) $880

MANNHEIM, Jean
German/American c. 1861/63-1945
paintings: (L) $495; (H) $33,000

MANNING, W.W.
American
paintings: (H) $2,640

MANNINGS, Sir Alfred
British 1878-1959
paintings: (L) $24,200; (H) $110,000

MANQUIN, Henri
French 1874-1949
drawings: (H) $2,750

MANSCH, Ignaz
sculpture: (H) $3,575

MANSELL, G. V.
paintings: (H) $4,180

MANSFELD, Josef
Austrian 1819-1894
paintings: (H) $3,300

MANSFELD, Moriz
Austrian ac. 1850-1900
paintings: (H) $687

MANSFIELD, Heinrich August
Austrian 1816-1901
paintings: (H) $8,250

MANSHIP, Paul Howard
American 1885-1966
sculpture: (L) $660; (H) $363,000

MANSOUROFF, Pavel
drawings: (H) $2,200

MANTECERDE
sculpture: (H) $990

MANTEGAZZA, Giacomo
Italian 1853-1920
paintings: (L) $3,575; (H) $9,350

MANTELET, Albert Goguet
French b. 1858
paintings: (H) $1,540

MANTELET-MARTEL, Andre
French b. 1876
paintings: (H) $7,425

MANTON, W.
British 19th cent.
paintings: (H) $715

MANUEL, Victor
Cuban 1867-1969
paintings: (L) $770; (H) $10,450

MANZANA-PISSARRO, Georges
French 1871-1961
paintings: (L) $5,060; (H) $7,150

MANZI, Jean
American 19th/20th cent.
paintings: (L) $605; (H) $1,320

MANZONI, Piero
Italian 1933-1963
paintings: (L) $2,860; (H) $220,000

MANZU, Giacomo
Italian b. 1908
sculpture: (L) $15,400; (H) $220,000

MANZUOLI, Egisto
Italian 19th cent.
paintings: (L) $495; (H) $1,210

MANZUOLI, Tommaso d'Antonio, called Maso da San Friano
Italian 1536-1571
drawings: (L) $3,850; (H) $16,500

MANZUR, David
Columbian b. 1929
paintings: (L) $1,980; (H) $4,400
drawings: (L) $1,760; (H) $15,400

MARA, Antonio, called LO SCARPETTA
Italian d.c. 1750
paintings: (H) $77,000

MARAGALL, Julio
sculpture: (L) $2,860; (H) $8,800

MARAIS, Adolph Charles
French b. 1856
paintings: (L) $660; (H) $2,750

MARAIS-MILTON, Victor
French b. 1872
paintings: (L) $3,850; (H) $9,900

MARANTONIO
paintings: (L) $110; (H) $990

MARASCO, Antonio
contemporary
paintings: (L) $7,425; (H) $15,400

MARATTA, Carlo
Italian 1625-1713
drawings: (L) $770; (H) $18,700

MARC, Franz
German 1880-1916
paintings: (L) $82,500; (H) $1,595,000
drawings: (L) $16,500; (H) $66,000

MARC, Wilhelm
German 1839-1907
paintings: (H) $6,050

MARCA-RELLI, Conrad
American b. 1913
paintings: (L) $15,400; (H) $88,000
drawings: (L) $385; (H) $46,750

MARCEL, Lawrence
American contemporary
sculpture: (H) $1,925

MARCEL, Normand S.
paintings: (H) $8,250

MARCEL-BERONNEAU, Pierre Amedee
French 1869-1937
paintings: (H) $9,350

MARCEL-CLEMENT, Amedee Julien
French b. 1873
paintings: (H) $9,075

MARCELLO, D.
European 20th cent.
paintings: (H) $1,540

MARCH, Reginald
American 1889-1954
drawings: (H) $2,860

MARCH Y MARCO, Vicente
Spanish 1859-1914
paintings: (L) $15,400; (H) $49,500

MARCHAND, Andre
French b. 1907
paintings: (L) $440; (H) $10,450
drawings: (H) $308

MARCHAND, Charles
German b. 1843
paintings: (L) $660; (H) $2,750

MARCHAND, E.
sculpture: (L) $1,540; (H) $2,420

MARCHAND, Jean
paintings: (H) $770

MARCHAND, Jean Baptiste
sculpture: (H) $660

MARCHAND, Jean Hippolyte
French 1883-1940
paintings: (H) $6,050

MARCHAND, John Norval
American 1875-1921
paintings: (H) $1,760
drawings: (L) $357; (H) $1,100

MARCHAND, Phillipe
French 20th cent.
paintings: (L) $440; (H) $4,400

MARCHAND(?)
sculpture: (H) $1,650

MARCHANT, Edward Dalton
American 1806-1887
paintings: (L) $550; (H) $9,900

MARCHE, Ernest Gaston
French 1864-1932
paintings: (L) $880; (H) $1,760

MARCHESE, Savario
Italian 19th cent.
paintings: (H) $1,045

MARCHESI, Giuseppe, called Il
Sansone
Italian 1699-1771
paintings: (L) $8,800; (H) $35,200
drawings: (H) $1,760

MARCHETTI, Ludovico
Italian 1853-1909
paintings: (L) $1,980; (H) $110,000
drawings: (H) $7,150

MARCHETTI, Marco, called Marco da
FAENZA
Italian d. 1588
drawings: (H) $9,900

MARCHI, Vincenzo
Italian 1818-1894
paintings: (L) $6,600; (H) $9,350
drawings: (H) $2,090

MARCHIS, Alessio de
drawings: (H) $2,200

MARCIUS-SIMONS, Pinky
American 1867-1909
paintings: (H) $8,250

MARCKE, Emile van
Belgian 1797-1839
paintings: (L) $330; (H) $1,650

MARCKE, Jean van
paintings: (L) $3,300; (H) $3,520

MARCKE DE LUMMEN, Emile van
French 1827-1890
paintings: (L) $715; (H) $13,200
drawings: (H) $660

MARCKS, Alexander
German 1864-1909
paintings: (H) $1,210

MARCKS, Gerhard
German b. 1889
drawings: (L) $28; (H) $308
sculpture: (L) $3,300; (H) $49,500

MARCOLA, Marco
c. 1740-1793
drawings: (H) $880

MARCON, Charles
drawings: (L) $10,000; (H) $11,000

MARCOUSSIS, Louis
French 1883-1941
paintings: (L) $33,000; (H) $99,000
drawings: (H) $2,750

MARCUSE, Rudolf
German b. 1878
sculpture: (L) $1,210; (H) $1,650

MARDEN, Brice
American b. 1938
paintings: (L) $110,000; (H) $1,100,000
drawings: (L) $3,500; (H) $220,000

MAREC, Victor
French 1862-1920
paintings: (H) $660

MARECHALLE, Elisa
French 19th cent.
paintings: (H) $9,350

MARENHART, T.
Dutch 19th cent.
paintings: (H) $990

MARESCA, M.
Italian
paintings: (L) $214; (H) $660

MAREVNA, Maria VOROBIEFF
Russian b. 1892
paintings: (L) $1,760; (H) $6,600

MARFFY, Odon Edmond
Hungarian 1878-1959
paintings: (H) $4,675

MARGAT, Andre
French b. 1903
drawings: (L) $1,320; (H) $3,300

MARGESON, Gilbert Tucker
American ac. 1873
paintings: (L) $110; (H) $1,485
drawings: (H) $350

MARGETSON, William Henry
British 1861-1940
paintings: (H) $4,125

MARGETTA, Mary
English d. 1886
drawings: (L) $1,540; (H) $6,050

MARGO, Boris
American
drawings: (L) $880; (H) $3,520

MARGOULIES, Berta
American b. 1907
sculpture: (L) $660; (H) $1,100

MARGRY, Antoine
paintings: (H) $9,350

MARGULIES, Joseph
American b. Austria 1896
paintings: (L) $375; (H) $3,300
drawings: (L) $77; (H) $3,080

MARIA, Francesco de
Italian 1845-1908
drawings: (L) $715; (H) $2,200

MARIANI, Carlo Maria
Italian contemporary
paintings: (H) $14,300
drawings: (L) $4,950; (H) $12,100

MARIANI, Pompeo
Italian 1857-1927
drawings: (H) $12,100

MARIE, Desire Pierre Louis
sculpture: (L) $550; (H) $1,760

MARIE, Jacques
French 19th/20th cent.
paintings: (H) $3,575

**MARIE LOUISE ALEXANDRINE
CAROLINE, COUNTESS OF
FLANDER,** nee Princesse de
Hohenzollern
German 1845-1905
paintings: (H) $660

MARIESCHI, Jacopo
Italian 1711-1791
paintings: (H) $88,000

MARIESCHI, Michele
Italian 1696-1743
paintings: (L) $30,800; (H) $220,000

MARIJNISSEN, Adrianus
Dutch b. 1899
paintings: (L) $330; (H) $1,430

MARILHAT, Prosper Georges Antoine
French 1811-1847
paintings: (L) $1,100; (H) $6,050
drawings: (H) $352

MARIMER, Alex
paintings: (H) $990

MARIN, John
American 1870-1953
paintings: (L) $440; (H) $40,700
drawings: (L) $550; (H) $165,000

MARIN, Joseph Charles
French 1759-1834
drawings: (H) $19,800
sculpture: (L) $41,800; (H) $68,750

MARIN, Tanger
paintings: (H) $880

MARINELLI, Vincenzo
Italian 1820-1892
paintings: (H) $4,180

MARINI, Leonardo
Italian c. 1730-1797
drawings: (L) $1,430; (H) $16,500

MARINI, Marino
Italian 1901-1980
paintings: (L) $3,520; (H) $308,000
drawings: (L) $990; (H) $57,200
sculpture: (L) $7,500; (H) $2,200,000

MARINKO
paintings: (H) $880

MARINKO, George
American 1908-1989
paintings: (L) $330; (H) $1,760
drawings: (L) $880; (H) $2,310

MARINO
paintings: (L) $77; (H) $357
sculpture: (H) $2,475

MARINUS, Ferdinand Joseph Bernard
Belgian 1808-1890
paintings: (L) $3,300; (H) $4,400

MARIO, A.
American 19th cent.
paintings: (L) $385; (H) $1,320

MARIO, Alessandro E.
Italian 19th cent.
paintings: (L) $800; (H) $1,210

MARIOLO, R.
Italian 19th cent.
paintings: (H) $935

MARIOTON
sculpture: (L) $440; (H) $1,210

MARIOTON, C.
French 1844-1919
sculpture: (H) $715

MARIOTON, Eugene
French b. 1854
sculpture: (L) $357; (H) $3,850

MARIOTON, Jean Alfred
French 1864-1903
paintings: (L) $13,200; (H) $14,300

MARIS, J.
paintings: (H) $2,860

MARIS, Jacob
Dutch 1837-1899
paintings: (L) $330; (H) $88,000

MARIS, Simon
Dutch 1873-1935
paintings: (L) $660; (H) $3,575

MARIS, Willem
Dutch 1844-1910
paintings: (L) $495; (H) $15,400
drawings: (L) $660; (H) $1,320

MARISOL, Marisol ESCOBAR
French/American b. 1930
drawings: (L) $1,210; (H) $4,180
sculpture: (L) $6,050; (H) $26,400

MARK, Brenda
Scottish 19th/20th cent.
paintings: (H) $2,200

MARK, D.
European 20th cent.
paintings: (H) $770

MARKART, Hans
1840-1883
paintings: (H) $2,420

MARKE, Louis
paintings: (H) $1,320

MARKEWITSCH, Arthur, or
MARKOWICZ
Polish 1872-1934
paintings: (L) $1,100; (H) $11,000

MARKHAM, Charles C.
American 1837-1907
paintings: (L) $8,250; (H) $9,900

MARKHAM, George
American
paintings: (H) $990

MARKHARM, Kyra
American 1891-1967
paintings: (L) $275; (H) $2,310
drawings: (H) $110

MARKO, Andreas
Austrian 1824-1895
paintings: (L) $4,400; (H) $8,360

MARKO, Carl
Austrian 19th cent.
paintings: (H) $1,210

MARKO, J.
paintings: (H) $990

MARKO, Karl
Hungarian 1822-1891
paintings: (L) $3,575; (H) $15,400

MARKOFF, Alexei
Russian 1802-1878
paintings: (H) $990

MARKOS, Lajos
American b. 1917
paintings: (L) $4,290; (H) $15,000

MARKS, George Washington
American d. 1879
paintings: (H) $3,575

MARKS, Graham
contemporary
sculpture: (L) $3,300; (H) $4,180

MARKS, Henry Stacy
English 1829-1898
paintings: (L) $2,475; (H) $9,350

MARLATT, H. Irving
American d. 1929
paintings: (L) $275; (H) $1,760
drawings: (L) $90; (H) $330

MARLE, Felix del
paintings: (H) $462
drawings: (H) $2,500

MARLOW, William
English 1740-1813
paintings: (H) $1,320
drawings: (H) $3,960

MARNE, Silas
19th cent.
paintings: (H) $1,320

MARNY, Paul
French 1829-1914
drawings: (L) $357; (H) $1,210

MAROHN, Ferdinand
German 1839-1859
paintings: (H) $1,100
drawings: (H) $935

MARONIEZ, G.
paintings: (H) $1,700

MARONIEZ, Georges Philibert Charles
French b. 1865
paintings: (L) $1,100; (H) $3,850

MARONTONIA(?)
Italian 19th cent.
paintings: (H) $1,980

MARPLE, William L.
American 1827-1910
paintings: (L) $303; (H) $2,200

MARQUESTE, Laurent Honore
sculpture: (L) $1,980; (H) $1,980

MARQUET
sculpture: (H) $1,430

MARQUET, Albert
French 1875-1947
paintings: (L) $16,500; (H) $506,000
drawings: (L) $275; (H) $22,000

MARQUET, Rene Paul
sculpture: (L) $880; (H) $2,530

MARQUIS, Richard
contemporary
sculpture: (H) $1,760

MARR, Carl
American 1858-1936
paintings: (L) $700; (H) $3,960

MARR, Joseph Heinrich Ludwig
German 1807-1871
paintings: (H) $3,575

MARRANI, A.
Italian School 20th cent.
drawings: (H) $660

MARREL, Jacob
Dutch 1614-1681
paintings: (H) $198,000

MARS, Peter Joseph Lawrence
paintings: (H) $1,320

MARSANS, Luis
paintings: (H) $16,500

MARSCHALL, Nicola
American 1829-1917
paintings: (L) $522; (H) $1,320

MARSDEN
paintings: (L) $825; (H) $1,540

MARSDEN, David
American 19th/20th cent.
paintings: (H) $825

MARSDEN, Theodore
paintings: (H) $11,550

MARSEUS VAN SCHRIECK, Otto, or
MARCELLIUS VAN SCHRIECK called
Snuffalaer
Dutch 1619-1678
paintings: (L) $38,500; (H) $104,500

MARSH, Fred Dana
American 1872-1961
paintings: (H) $2,200

MARSH, Reginald
American 1898-1954
paintings: (L) $990; (H) $363,000
drawings: (L) $193; (H) $46,200

MARSH, W., Jr.
American
drawings: (L) $99; (H) $935

MARSH, W.S.
American 20th cent.
paintings: (L) $88; (H) $770

City Life

Reginald Marsh (1898-1954) was born in Paris of American parents. The family returned to the United States when Marsh was two, and he grew up in New Jersey. Both his mother and father were painters, and Marsh began to draw while still a child. At Yale University he was a cartoonist for the *Yale Record* and served as its art editor in 1920. After graduation he became a staff artist for *Vanity Fair* and the New York *Daily News*, before traveling to Europe to study in 1924. Returning to New York in 1926, he studied at the Arts Students League under John Sloan, George Luks, Kenneth Hayes Miller, and Boardman Robinson, all of whom greatly influenced his work.

Marsh painted murals for the Post Office Building in Washington, D.C., and for the New York City Customs House; however, most of his *oeuvre* consisted of paintings, etchings, and lithographs depicting the energy and spirit of New York City life. He was influenced by the nineteenth-century drawings of Honore Daumier, and his study of the Old Masters is evidenced in his vigorous Baroque style and powerful draftsmanship. His favorite subjects were burlesque houses, shopgirls, the bums of the Bowery, Coney Island, subways, and everyday street activities. His choice of subjects grew out of the Social Realist school of the twentieth century following the tradition of Hogarth and Daumier. Line and design were more important than color to Marsh, and many of his works were lithographs or Chinese ink drawings. In the 1930s, he began to work with egg tempera, a medium that was quick-drying and translucent. When *Gayety Burlesk* was consigned by an estate to Barridoff Galleries in Portland, Maine, it was in need of a cleaning. Restoration is an art, and most buyers would have their own expert clean a piece. Sold in its "found" condition, the painting realized $231,000. Reports after the sale were that the painting cleaned beautifully. (Reginald Marsh, *Gayety Burlesk,* tempera on panel, 24 x 30 in., Barridoff, August 1, 1990, $231,000)

MARSHALL, Ben
  English 1767-1835
  paintings: (L) $7,700; (H) $220,000

MARSHALL, Charles
  British 1806-1890
  paintings: (L) $605; (H) $2,200

MARSHALL, Clark S.
  American 19th/20th cent.
  paintings: (L) $121; (H) $880

MARSHALL, Frank Warren
  American 1866-1930
  paintings: (L) $165; (H) $742
  drawings: (H) $83

MARSHALL, Herbert M.
  English 1841-1913
  paintings: (L) $2,090; (H) $9,680
  drawings: (H) $1,210

MARSHALL, John Miller
  British ac. 1881-1927
  paintings: (H) $770

MARSHALL, L.J.
American 20th cent.
paintings: (H) $1,430

MARSHALL, Lambert
British 1809-1870
paintings: (L) $13,200; (H) $16,500

MARSHALL, Mary E.
American 19th/20th cent.
paintings: (H) $800

MARSHALL, R.
British? 19th/20th cent.
paintings: (L) $192; (H) $770

MARSHALL, Roberto Angelo
Kittermaster
British 1849-1902
drawings: (L) $990; (H) $1,980

MARSHALL, Thomas Falcon
British 1818-1878
paintings: (H) $6,600

MARSHALL, Thomas William
American 1850-1874
paintings: (L) $522; (H) $4,675

MARTEL, Jan and Joel
French 1896-1966
sculpture: (L) $302; (H) $4,620

MARTEL, Paul Jean
American/Belgian 1879-1942
paintings: (H) $715

MARTELLI
paintings: (H) $1,760

MARTELLY, John de
paintings: (H) $1,760

MARTENS, Ernest Edouard
French b. 1865
paintings: (L) $2,750; (H) $18,700

MARTENS, Henry
British ac. 1828-1854
paintings: (H) $4,675

MARTENS, Willem Johannes
Dutch 1838-1895
paintings: (H) $7,700
drawings: (H) $468

MARTENS, Willy
Dutch 1856-1927
paintings: (H) $1,760

MARTIAL, A.
sculpture: (H) $3,850

MARTIAL, Armand
French early 20th cent.
sculpture: (H) $2,420

MARTIN, Agnes
Canadian/American b. 1912
paintings: (L) $12,100; (H) $385,000
drawings: (L) $2,750; (H) $44,000
sculpture: (H) $16,500

MARTIN, C.J.
paintings: (H) $12,100

MARTIN, Charles Badger
sculpture: (H) $990

MARTIN, David
British 1736/37-1798
paintings: (L) $1,870; (H) $49,500

MARTIN, E.
Spanish 19th cent.
paintings: (H) $2,860

MARTIN, Emma
American ac. 1850
drawings: (L) $1,980; (H) $3,410

MARTIN, Fletcher
American 1904-1979
paintings: (L) $633; (H) $60,500
drawings: (L) $770; (H) $3,850

MARTIN, Franc A.
paintings: (H) $4,620

MARTIN, Fritz
German 1859-1889
paintings: (L) $2,200; (H) $3,850

MARTIN, H.
paintings: (L) $198; (H) $660

MARTIN, Henri Jean Guillaume
French 1860-1943
paintings: (L) $1,430; (H) $632,500

MARTIN, Homer Dodge
American 1836-1897
paintings: (L) $550; (H) $33,000
drawings: (L) $247; (H) $1,650

MARTIN, J.
drawings: (H) $1,100

MARTIN, J. Edward B.
American 20th cent.
paintings: (L) $1,650; (H) $3,300

MARTIN, J.R.
19th cent.
paintings: (H) $45,100

MARTIN, Jean Baptiste, called Martin
des Batailles
French 1659-1735
paintings: (H) $2,750

MARTIN, K.
20th cent.
paintings: (H) $660

MARTIN, Knox
Colombian/American b. 1923
paintings: (L) $605; (H) $1,870
drawings: (L) $440; (H) $462

MARTIN, Scott
paintings: (H) $2,970

MARTIN, Sylvester
English ac. 1870-1899
paintings: (L) $2,420; (H) $11,000

MARTIN, Thomas Mower
Canadian 1838-1934
paintings: (L) $330; (H) $1,210
drawings: (L) $110; (H) $440

MARTIN, William Alison
British 19th cent.
paintings: (L) $770; (H) $1,100

MARTIN-DELESTRE, Adolphe
Alexandre
French 1823-1858
paintings: (L) $3,025; (H) $26,400

MARTIN-FERRIERES, Jac
French b. 1893
paintings: (L) $1,650; (H) $33,000

MARTIN-GAUTHERAU, Andre
French 19th/20th cent.
paintings: (H) $8,800

MARTIN-KAVEL, Francois
French 19th/20th cent.
paintings: (L) $550; (H) $7,700

MARTINDALE, G. Thomas
British 19th cent.
paintings: (L) $5,500; (H) $7,700

MARTINDALE, Percy H.
British b. 1869
paintings: (H) $2,640

MARTINELLI, Giovanni
Italian c. 1610-1659
paintings: (L) $2,860; (H) $170,500

MARTINETTI, Angelo
Italian 19th cent.
paintings: (L) $5,500; (H) $6,600

MARTINETTI, M. and G. FORTINATI
drawings: (H) $660

MARTINETTI, Maria
Italian b. 1864
paintings: (H) $19,800
drawings: (L) $1,760; (H) $3,300

MARTINEZ, Alfredo Ramos
Mexican 1872-1946
paintings: (L) $1,650; (H) $46,200
drawings: (L) $1,430; (H) $5,500

MARTINEZ, F.F.
Continental School 19th/20th cent.
paintings: (H) $1,320

MARTINEZ, F.E.
paintings: (H) $1,650

MARTINEZ, F.E.
Spanish 19th cent.
drawings: (H) $1,320

MARTINEZ, J.
European 19th cent.
paintings: (H) $1,540

MARTINEZ, John Paul
Spanish 20th cent.
paintings: (L) $550; (H) $2,860

MARTINEZ, Jose Ignacio Pinazo
Spanish b. 1879
paintings: (H) $7,700

MARTINEZ, Julian
American 1897-1943
drawings: (L) $825; (H) $1,870

MARTINEZ, Pedro-Luis
paintings: (H) $4,675

MARTINEZ, Raymundo
Mexican b. 1945
paintings: (H) $5,500

MARTINEZ, Ricardo
Mexican b. 1918
paintings: (L) $3,300; (H) $35,200
drawings: (H) $6,050

MARTINEZ, Richard, Opa Mu Nu
American Indian b. 1904
paintings: (L) $302; (H) $715

MARTINEZ, Xavier
Mexican/American 1869-1943
paintings: (L) $1,320; (H) $7,700
drawings: (L) $248; (H) $3,850

MARTINEZ CUBELLS, Salvador
Spanish 1845-1914
paintings: (H) $44,000

MARTINI, Alberto
Italian 1876-1954
paintings: (L) $2,200; (H) $4,950

MARTINI, Arturo
contemporary
sculpture: (L) $2,860; (H) $6,050

MARTINI, Gaetano de
paintings: (H) $7,700

MARTINI, Joseph de
American b. 1896
paintings: (L) $77; (H) $1,210

MARTINO, A.P.
paintings: (L) $1,980; (H) $4,675

MARTINO, Antonio Pietro
American b. 1902
paintings: (L) $330; (H) $6,160

MARTINO, D.
Italian contemporary
sculpture: (L) $220; (H) $3,190

MARTINO, Giovanni
American b. 1908
paintings: (L) $187; (H) $4,950

MARTINS, Maria
sculpture: (H) $11,550

MARTINUS
sculpture: (L) $4,400; (H) $4,950

MARTINUS, Elsa
American 20th cent.
sculpture: (L) $4,125; (H) $6,050

MARTIUS, Karl Friedrich Philipp von
drawings: (H) $11,550

MARTSZEN, Jan, the younger
d. after 1647
paintings: (H) $9,350

MARTY, Andre Edouard
drawings: (H) $660

MARUCCI, Lucio
drawings: (H) $2,200

MARUSSIG, Anton
Austrian 1868-1925
paintings: (H) $1,100

MARWEDE, Richard L.
paintings: (H) $880

MARX, Alphonse
paintings: (H) $9,900

MARX, Claude
English 19th cent.
paintings: (H) $660

MARX, Maurice Roger
sculpture: (L) $1,925; (H) $2,750

MARX, Sam
drawings: (H) $715

MARYAN, Maryan Pinchas
BURNSTEIN
American b. 1927
paintings: (L) $4,950; (H) $8,800
drawings: (L) $1,100; (H) $10,450

MARZANO, Pasquale Ruggiero Di San
Italian 1851-1916
paintings: (L) $715; (H) $880

MARZELLE, Jean
paintings: (H) $1,760

MARZI, Ergio
Italian 19th cent.
paintings: (H) $2,200

MARZOLO, Leo Aurelio
b. 1887
paintings: (L) $357; (H) $990

MAS Y FONDEVILA, Arcadio
Spanish b. 1850
paintings: (H) $1,100

MAS Y FONDEVILLA, Arturo
Spanish b. 1850
paintings: (H) $9,350

MASCART, Gustave
French 19th cent.
paintings: (L) $1,760; (H) $8,800

MASCHERINI, Marcello
Italian b. 1906
sculpture: (L) $1,100; (H) $6,050

MASEREEL, Frans
Belgian 1889-1971
drawings: (H) $900

MASIC, Nicholas
Yugoslavian 1852-1902
paintings: (H) $5,225

MASIP, Vincent Juan, called
Juan de Juanes
Spanish before 1523-1579
paintings: (H) $8,800

MASON, Alice Trumbull
American 1904-1971
paintings: (H) $22,000

MASON, Finch
British 1850-1915
drawings: (L) $192; (H) $1,100

MASON, Frank
American b. 1921
paintings: (H) $1,650

MASON, Frank Henry
English 1876-1965
drawings: (L) $1,100; (H) $7,700

MASON, John
contemporary
sculpture: (L) $3,300; (H) $5,500

MASON, Maud M.
American 1867-1956
paintings: (L) $605; (H) $3,025

MASON, Roy M.
American
paintings: (L) $330; (H) $2,090
drawings: (H) $330

MASON, Sanford
American 1798-1862
paintings: (H) $1,400

MASON, W.
drawings: (H) $1,265

MASON, William Sanford
American 1824-1864
paintings: (L) $1,430; (H) $4,400

MASON, Wisanford
late 19th cent.
paintings: (H) $880

MASONI, G.B.
19th cent.
sculpture: (H) $1,430

MASQUERIER, John James
British 1778-1855
paintings: (L) $1,100; (H) $2,200
drawings: (H) $2,090

MASRIERA, Francisco
paintings: (H) $2,200

MASRIERA, Frederico
paintings: (H) $6,380

MASSANI, Pompeo
Italian 1850-1920
paintings: (L) $468; (H) $13,200

MASSARI, Lucio
Italian 1569-1633
paintings: (H) $8,250
drawings: (H) $6,050

MASSE, Jules
French 1825-1899
paintings: (H) $1,760

MASSEAU, Pierre-Felix
sculpture: (L) $1,980; (H) $6,600

MASSELINK, Eugene
20th cent.
drawings: (L) $330; (H) $1,100

MASSON, Andre
French b. 1896
paintings: (L) $5,775; (H) $605,000
drawings: (L) $1,650; (H) $121,000
sculpture: (H) $14,300

MASSON, Clovis Edmond
French 1838-1913
sculpture: (L) $462; (H) $2,090

MASSON, Henri
Canadian b. 1907
paintings: (L) $3,575; (H) $5,500

MASSON, Jules Edmond
French b. 1871
sculpture: (L) $330; (H) $4,125

MASSON, Marcel
paintings: (H) $7,700

MASSONI, Egisto
Italian 19th cent.
paintings: (L) $990; (H) $1,650

MASSOULE, Andre Paul Arthur
French late 19th cent.
sculpture: (L) $1,650; (H) $3,740

MASSYS, Jan
Flemish d. 1592
paintings: (H) $9,900

MASTENBROEK, Johann Hendrik van
Dutch 1875-1945
paintings: (L) $880; (H) $17,600
drawings: (L) $1,320; (H) $2,640

MASTER A.C.
Italian 18th cent.
paintings: (H) $880

MASTER B.B.
first half 17th cent.
paintings: (L) $18,700; (H) $82,500

MASTER OF 1416
paintings: (H) $99,000

MASTER OF 1518
paintings: (H) $35,200

MASTER OF FRANKFORT
ac. 1493-1520
paintings: (H) $46,750

MASTER OF LANGEZENN, 15TH CENTURY
paintings: (H) $22,000

MASTER OF MARRADI
paintings: (H) $12,100

MASTER OF SANTA VERDIANA
paintings: (H) $66,000

MASTER OF SIGNA
paintings: (H) $16,500

MASTER OF THE BAMBINO VISPO
Italian 15th cent.
paintings: (H) $66,000

MASTER OF THE BERLIN ROUNDELS OF 1515
drawings: (H) $31,900

MASTER OF THE COBURG ROUNDELS
ac. c. 1475-1500
drawings: (H) $30,800

MASTER OF THE EGMONT ALBUMS
drawings: (H) $3,410

MASTER OF THE FEMALE HALF-LENGTHS, 16TH CENTURY
Dutch
paintings: (L) $8,800; (H) $55,000

MASTER OF THE GENRE FIGURES, CIRCA 1600
sculpture: (H) $66,000

MASTER OF THE GHISLIERI APSE
16th cent.
drawings: (H) $23,100

MASTER OF THE GREENVILLE TONDO, CIRCA 1500
paintings: (H) $71,500

MASTER OF THE HEILIGEN SIPPE
paintings: (H) $66,000

MASTER OF THE HOLDEN TONDO
paintings: (H) $6,050

MASTER OF THE JOHNSON NATIVITY
15th cent.
paintings: (H) $52,250

MASTER OF THE JOHNSON TABERNACLE
early 15th cent.
paintings: (H) $20,900

MASTER OF THE JUDGEMENT OF SOLOMON, 17TH CENTURY
paintings: (H) $38,500

MASTER OF THE KING SOLOMON TRIPTYCH
paintings: (H) $110,000

MASTER OF THE LEONARDESQUE FEMALE PORTRAITS
first half 16th cent.
paintings: (H) $385,000

MASTER OF THE MAGDALEN,
workshop of
paintings: (H) $82,500

MASTER OF THE MAGDALEN LEGEND
paintings: (L) $39,600; (H) $220,000

MASTER OF THE MAINZ MADONNA
paintings: (H) $11,000

MASTER OF THE MILLER TONDO
ac. late 15th cent.
paintings: (H) $275,000

MASTER OF THE NAUMBERG MADONNA, LATE 15TH CENTURY
paintings: (L) $25,300; (H) $55,000

MASTER OF THE PANZANO TRIPTYCH
paintings: (H) $176,000

MASTER OF THE PARROT, 16TH CENTURY
Flemish
paintings: (L) $12,100; (H) $16,500

MASTER OF THE RICHARDSON TABERNACLE
paintings: (H) $17,600

MASUCCI, Agostino
paintings: (H) $3,850

MASUREL, J. Eugel
Dutch 1826-1915
paintings: (H) $1,100

MASUROUSKY, Gregory
contemporary
drawings: (H) $825

MASWEINS, Joseph
Belgian 1828-1880
paintings: (L) $220; (H) $1,650

MATA, Emelio Garcia
French 1910-1985
paintings: (L) $550; (H) $825

MATANIA, E.
paintings: (H) $1,100

MATANIA, Fortunino
Italian b. 1881
drawings: (L) $250; (H) $1,100

MATARE, Ewald
German 1887-1965
sculpture: (L) $5,280; (H) $8,250

MATHER, John
Australian 1843-1916
drawings: (H) $935

MATHESON-DAEL, Louise
Belgian 1871-1945
paintings: (H) $1,650

MATHEWS, Alfred E.
American
paintings: (H) $1,045

MATHEWS, Arthur
American 1860-1945
paintings: (L) $16,500; (H) $110,000
drawings: (H) $17,600

MATHEWS, John Chester
English ac. 1884-1900
paintings: (H) $5,225

MATHEWS, Joseph
American 1863-1893
paintings: (H) $1,650

MATHEWS, Lucia Kleinhans
American 1870-1955
paintings: (H) $7,150

MATHEWS, Michael
British 20th cent.
paintings: (L) $1,760; (H) $1,870

MATHEWSON, F.W.
drawings: (H) $660

MATHEWSON, Frank Convers
American 1862-1941
paintings: (L) $165; (H) $3,300
drawings: (L) $165; (H) $900

MATHIESEN, Pat
sculpture: (L) $412; (H) $2,420

MATHIEU, Gabriel
paintings: (H) $1,155

MATHIEU, Georges
French b. 1921
paintings: (L) $770; (H) $132,000
drawings: (L) $2,475; (H) $11,000

MATHIEU, Paul
Belgian 1872-1932
paintings: (H) $14,300
drawings: (H) $88

MATHY, Andre
paintings: (H) $3,300

MATILLA, Segundo
Spanish 19th cent.
paintings: (H) $5,500

MATISSE, Camille
French 19th/20th cent.
paintings: (H) $880

MATISSE, Henri
French 1869-1954
paintings: (L) $71,500; (H) $12,375,000
drawings: (L) $6,050; (H) $1,650,000
sculpture: (L) $7,150; (H) $4,180,000

MATTA
Chilean b. 1911
paintings: (L) $33,000; (H) $264,000
drawings: (L) $3,850; (H) $8,800

MATTA, Roberto Echaurren
Chilean b. 1911
paintings: (L) $4,950; (H) $1,155,000
drawings: (L) $495; (H) $187,000

MATTEIS, Paolo de
Italian 1662-1728
paintings: (L) $5,500; (H) $35,200
drawings: (H) $2,860

MATTELE, G.
Belgian 19th cent.
paintings: (H) $5,500

MATTENHEIMER, Theodor
German 1787-1850
paintings: (H) $18,700

MATTER, Herbert
drawings: (H) $6,050

MATTESON, Tomkins Harrison
American 1813-1884
paintings: (H) $23,100

MATTHEWS, Michael
English b. 1933
paintings: (L) $137; (H) $3,520

MATTHEWS, William F.
American b. 1878
paintings: (L) $330; (H) $5,830

MATTHIASDOTTIR, Louisa
Icelandic b. 1917?
drawings: (H) $990

MATTHIEU, Cornelis
paintings: (H) $7,700

MATTIOLI, Armeno
Italian b. 1920
paintings: (L) $357; (H) $770

MATTO
sculpture: (H) $2,200

MATTSCHASS, Eric
paintings: (H) $2,530

MATTSON, Henry E.
American 1887-1971
paintings: (L) $302; (H) $935

MATULKA, Jan
Czechoslovakian/American 1890-1972
paintings: (L) $1,650; (H) $46,750
drawings: (L) $440; (H) $3,520

MATZINGER, Philip F.
American 1860-1942
paintings: (H) $880

MAUBACH, *****
sculpture: (H) $880

MAUBERT, James
paintings: (H) $2,860

MAUFRA, Maxime
French 1861/62-1918
paintings: (L) $4,400; (H) $82,500
drawings: (L) $715; (H) $2,750

MAUREL, Louis
French 19th cent.
paintings: (H) $990

MAURER, Alfred Henry
American 1868-1932
paintings: (L) $1,100; (H) $154,000
drawings: (L) $462; (H) $19,800

MAURER, Louis
German/American 1832-1932
paintings: (L) $3,520; (H) $99,000
drawings: (L) $253; (H) $2,310

MAURETE, P.
paintings: (H) $715

MAURICE, P.
paintings: (H) $880

MAURICE-MARTIN
French 1894-1978
paintings: (L) $880; (H) $1,870

MAURY, Francois
French 1861-1933
paintings: (L) $935; (H) $2,200

MAURY, Georges Sauveur
French b. 1872
paintings: (H) $6,050

MAUVE, Anton
Dutch 1838-1888
paintings: (L) $110; (H) $16,500
drawings: (L) $165; (H) $7,040

MAUZEY, Merritt
American
paintings: (H) $2,860

MAWLEY, George
British 1838-1873
paintings: (H) $1,045
drawings: (H) $55

MAX, Gabriel Cornelius von
Czechoslovakian 1840-1915
paintings: (L) $880; (H) $3,850

MAX, Peter
German/American b. 1937
paintings: (L) $4,180; (H) $4,400
drawings: (L) $88; (H) $220

MAXENCE, Edgard
French 1871-1954
paintings: (L) $5,775; (H) $16,500
drawings: (L) $3,080; (H) $7,150

MAXFIELD, J. Emery
American
paintings: (H) $2,200

MAXFIELD, James
American b. 1848
paintings: (L) $660; (H) $7,150

MAXWEYL
paintings: (H) $1,540

MAYBECK, Bernard
American 1862-1957
paintings: (H) $12,100
sculpture: (L) $2,750; (H) $3,850

MAYBURGER, Josef
Austrian 1813-1908
paintings: (H) $4,400

MAYDELL, Baron Ernst von
German b. 1888
drawings: (L) $110; (H) $660

**MAYER, Constance, M. F. Constance
La Martiniere**
French 1775-1821
paintings: (H) $132,000
drawings: (H) $2,640

MAYER, Constant
French/American 1829/32-1911
paintings: (L) $3,300; (H) $23,100

MAYER, F.V.F.W.
paintings: (H) $880

MAYER, Frank B.
American 1827-1899
paintings: (L) $1,760; (H) $12,100

MAYER, Nicolas
French early 20th cent.
sculpture: (L) $825; (H) $1,320

MAYER, Peter Bela
American b. 1888
paintings: (L) $412; (H) $6,600

MAYER, William C.
American 20th cent.
paintings: (H) $7,700

MAYET, Leon
French b. 1858
paintings: (L) $1,650; (H) $2,750

MAYHEW, Nell Brooker
American 1876-1940
paintings: (L) $412; (H) $990
drawings: (H) $55

MAYHEW, Thomas
American 19th cent.
paintings: (H) $700

MAYNARD, George Willoughby
American 1843-1923
paintings: (L) $165; (H) $4,180
drawings: (L) $1,100; (H) $1,650

MAYNARD, Richard Field
American b. 1875
paintings: (H) $880
drawings: (L) $250; (H) $1,430

MAYR, Heinrich von
German 1806-1871
paintings: (H) $7,150

MAYR, Peter
1758-1836
paintings: (H) $770

MAYR, V.
Continental 19th/20th cent.
paintings: (H) $1,300

MAYR-GRAETZ, Karl
German 1843-1912
paintings: (H) $770

MAYRHOFER, Johann Nepomuk
Austrian 1764-1832
paintings: (L) $5,500; (H) $39,600

MAYS, Paul Kirtland
American 1887-1961
paintings: (L) $880; (H) $1,870

MAZANOVICH, Lawrence
American b. 1872
paintings: (H) $10,450

MAZE, Paul
French b. 1928
paintings: (L) $2,200; (H) $13,200
drawings: (L) $605; (H) $3,300

MAZEROLLE, Alexis Joseph
French 1826-1889
paintings: (L) $2,970; (H) $4,400

MAZINI, Angelo
Italian 19th cent.
drawings: (L) $83; (H) $1,000

MAZOT, Angeline
French 19th cent.
drawings: (H) $10,450

MAZOTTI, R.
paintings: (H) $2,200

MAZURA
sculpture: (H) $770

MAZZALINI, Giuseppe
Italian 19th cent.
paintings: (H) $2,530

MAZZANOVICH, Lawrence
American b. 1872
paintings: (L) $1,320; (H) $11,000

MAZZANTI, Lodovico
Italian c. 1679-1775
paintings: (L) $4,950; (H) $7,150

MAZZELLA, J.
French 19th cent.
paintings: (H) $2,970

MAZZETTI, P.
Italian 19th/20th cent.
paintings: (H) $660

MAZZOLA, Filippo, called Filippo
dell Erbette
Italian 1460-1505
paintings: (H) $44,000

MAZZOLINI, Giuseppe
Italian 1806-1876
paintings: (L) $495; (H) $14,300

MAZZOLINI, Joseph
Italian 19th cent.
paintings: (H) $7,700

MAZZOLINO, Guiseppe
Italian 1748-1838
paintings: (H) $3,080

MAZZONI, Sebastiano
Italian 1611-1678
paintings: (H) $33,000

MAZZONOVICH, Lawrence
American b. 1872
paintings: (H) $9,625

MAZZOTTA, Federico
Italian 19th cent.
paintings: (L) $6,050; (H) $6,600

MAZZUCHELLI, Pier Francesco, called
IL MORAZZONE
drawings: (H) $1,540

MCAFEE, Ila
American b. 1900
paintings: (L) $330; (H) $660

MCALPINE
British 19th cent.
paintings: (H) $3,575

MCAULIFFE, James J.
American 1848-1921
paintings: (L) $715; (H) $37,400

MCAVOY(?), W.
paintings: (H) $660

MCBEY, James
British 1883-1959
paintings: (H) $852
drawings: (L) $385; (H) $1,375

MCCABE, A.
paintings: (H) $3,850

MCCARTAN, Edward
American 1879-1947
sculpture: (L) $1,210; (H) $44,000

MCCARTER, Henry
American 1866-1942
paintings: (L) $2,200; (H) $8,250
drawings: (L) $44; (H) $1,540

MCCARTHY, Frank C.
American b. 1924
paintings: (L) $6,600; (H) $55,000
drawings: (H) $4,400

MCCARTHY, Helen Kiner
American 1884-1927
paintings: (L) $352; (H) $990

MCCARTHY, Jack
American contemporary
sculpture: (H) $825

MCCARTHY, Justin
American 1891-1977
drawings: (L) $550; (H) $2,310

MCCAW, Dan
American b. 1942
paintings: (L) $2,900; (H) $4,500

MCCAY, Winsor
American 1871-1934
paintings: (H) $2,640
drawings: (L) $715; (H) $3,960

MCCLARD, Michael
contemporary
paintings: (H) $660

MCCLEOD, John
British b. 1872
paintings: (L) $3,850; (H) $7,700

MCCLINTOCK, Lucy
American
paintings: (H) $2,420

MCCLOSKEY, James
American contemporary
paintings: (L) $935; (H) $2,035

MCCLOSKEY, William J.
American 1859-1941
paintings: (L) $1,320; (H) $231,000

MCCLOSKY, A. Binford
paintings: (H) $5,500

MCCLOUD
American 20th cent.
paintings: (H) $1,045

MCCLYMONT, John
American 1858-1934
paintings: (H) $770

MCCOLLUM, Allan
contemporary
sculpture: (H) $8,580

MCCOMAS, Francis John
American 1874-1938
paintings: (H) $3,300
drawings: (L) $605; (H) $16,500

MCCONKEY, Murray M.
American contemporary
sculpture: (H) $2,970

MCCONKEY, William
ac. c. 1850
paintings: (H) $4,675

MCCONNELL, Emlen
American 1872-1947
paintings: (L) $40; (H) $75
drawings: (H) $1,400

MCCONNELL, George
American 1852-1929
paintings: (L) $55; (H) $2,200
drawings: (H) $66

MCCORD, George Herbert
American 1848-1909
paintings: (L) $66; (H) $5,500
drawings: (L) $275; (H) $550

MCCORMICK, Arthur David
British 1860-1943
paintings: (L) $1,045; (H) $4,950
drawings: (H) $660

MCCORMICK, Howard
American 1875-1943
paintings: (L) $220; (H) $2,200

MCCORMICK, M. Evelyn
American 20th cent.
paintings: (L) $220; (H) $770

MCCOY, Wilton
American ac. 1930s
paintings: (L) $522; (H) $660

MCCRACKEN, John
American b. 1934
paintings: (L) $880; (H) $4,620
sculpture: (H) $18,700

MCCRADY, John
American 1911-1968
paintings: (H) $3,300

MCCREA, Samuel Harkness
American b. 1867
paintings: (L) $220; (H) $770

MCCULLOCH, Horatio
British 1805-1867
paintings: (L) $99; (H) $6,050

MCCULVIN
paintings: (H) $715

MCDERMITT, William
American b. 1884
paintings: (H) $880
drawings: (L) $468; (H) $550

MCDERMOTT AND MCGOUGH
contemporary
paintings: (L) $8,800; (H) $17,600

MCDERMOTT and MCGOUGH
Americans b. 1950's
paintings: (L) $5,280; (H) $24,200

MCDONALD, Mason
American
paintings: (L) $357; (H) $2,090

MCDOWELL, Edward
American 19th cent.
paintings: (H) $1,760

MCDUFF, Frederick H.
American b. 1931
paintings: (L) $3,300; (H) $7,975

MCEHANEY, Laurence
19th cent.
paintings: (H) $770

MCENTEE, Jervis
American 1828-1891
paintings: (L) $935; (H) $35,200
drawings: (L) $27; (H) $1,760

MCENTEE, William H.
American 1857-1919
paintings: (L) $385; (H) $1,210

MCEVOY, Ambrose
British 1878-1927
drawings: (H) $1,980

MCEWAN, Thomas, "Tom"
British 1846-1914
paintings: (L) $605; (H) $3,520

MCEWAN, William
American ac. 1859-1869
paintings: (L) $550; (H) $3,300

MCEWEN, Walter
American 1860-1943
paintings: (L) $770; (H) $3,630
drawings: (H) $275

MCFEE, Henry Lee
American 1886-1953
paintings: (L) $1,430; (H) $22,000

MCGAUGHY, Clay
drawings: (H) $880

MCGEEHAN, Jessie M.
British ac. 1892-1913
paintings: (H) $12,650

MCGHIE, John
Scottish 1867-1941
paintings: (L) $357; (H) $5,500

MCGILL, Eloise Polk
American 20th cent.
paintings: (L) $330; (H) $770

MCGINNIS, Robert
American contemporary
paintings: (H) $9,000

MCGLYNN, Thomas A.
American 1878-1966
paintings: (L) $1,980; (H) $13,200

MCGRATH, Clarence
American b. 1938
paintings: (H) $5,225

MCGRAW, R. Brownell
drawings: (H) $825

MCGREGOR, Robert
British 1848-1922
paintings: (L) $3,080; (H) $5,500

MCGREGOR, Sarah
British 19th/20th cent.
paintings: (H) $770

MCGREGOR, William
British 20th cent.
paintings: (H) $1,320

MCGREW, Ralph Brownell
American b. 1916
paintings: (H) $6,050

MCHEE, Robert Russell
paintings: (H) $660

MCHURON, Gregory I.
American
paintings: (H) $2,700

MCILHENNY, Charles Morgan
American 1858-1908
paintings: (L) $352; (H) $1,430

MCINNES, Alex
paintings: (L) $275; (H) $935

MCINNES, Robert
British 1801-1886
paintings: (H) $3,850

MCINTOSH, Amanda
American 1865-1941
paintings: (H) $1,210

MCINTOSH, Pleasant Ray
American b. 1897
paintings: (L) $935; (H) $6,050
drawings: (H) $495

MCINTYRE, J.H.
British ac. 1896-1904
paintings: (H) $2,200

MCINTYRE, Peter
New Zealand b. 1910
drawings: (H) $715

MCINTYRE, Robert
American
paintings: (H) $1,210

MCKAIN, Bruce
American b. 1900
paintings: (H) $1,350

MCKAY, Edwin Murray
American 1869-1926
paintings: (L) $412; (H) $825

MCKAY, Winsor
drawings: (L) $4,675; (H) $5,225

MCKECHNIE, Alexander Bulfour
Scottish 1860-1930
drawings: (H) $660

MCKEE, V.
sculpture: (L) $660; (H) $935

MCKENNA, Stephen
contemporary
paintings: (L) $990; (H) $1,540

MCKENZIE, Robert Tait
Canadian/American 1867-1938
sculpture: (L) $330; (H) $24,200

MCKERN, Hugh F.
20th cent.
paintings: (H) $770

MCKERSON, V.D.
19th cent.
drawings: (H) $1,100

MCKEY, Edward M.
American
paintings: (H) $2,200

MCKILLOP, William
American early 20th cent.
paintings: (L) $1,320; (H) $1,980

MCKINSLEY, Grace
paintings: (H) $825

MCKITTRICK, William
paintings: (H) $660

MCKNIGHT, Dodge
American 1860-1950
drawings: (L) $1,870; (H) $2,090

MCKNIGHT, Thomas
American
paintings: (H) $6,380

MCLACHLAN, J.
British 19th cent.
paintings: (H) $2,500

MCLANE, Murtle Jean
American early 20th cent.
paintings: (H) $19,800

MCLAUCHLIN, Tom
contemporary
sculpture: (L) $1,100; (H) $1,540

MCLAUGHLIN, John
American b. 1898
paintings: (L) $6,050; (H) $60,500

MCLAUGHLIN, Mary Louise
American 1847-1939
drawings: (L) $220; (H) $1,017

MCLEAN, Bruce
contemporary
paintings: (L) $3,300; (H) $7,480

MCLEAN, Howard
American
paintings: (H) $880

MCLEAN, J.D.
paintings: (H) $715

MCLEAN, Richard
American b. 1934
paintings: (L) $26,400; (H) $38,500

MCLEARY, Bonnie
American
sculpture: (H) $7,150

MCLELLAN, Ralph
American
paintings: (H) $12,100

MCLEOD, John
paintings: (H) $2,200

MCLOUGHLIN, Gregory
American 20th cent.
paintings: (L) $55; (H) $1,540

MCMAHN, William F.
paintings: (H) $2,310

MCMANUS, George
American 1884-1954
paintings: (H) $209
drawings: (L) $165; (H) $770

MCMANUS, James Goodwin
American 1882-1958
paintings: (L) $110; (H) $1,870

MCMEE, J.W.
American 19th cent.
paintings: (H) $11,000

MCMULLIN, Jeanette W.
American 19th/20th cent.
paintings: (H) $2,970
drawings: (H) $660

MCNAHA, Eugene
sculpture: (H) $4,675

MCNAUGHTON, Robert
c. 1830
paintings: (H) $13,750

MCNEIL, George
American b. 1908
paintings: (L) $1,045; (H) $15,400

MCNEILLEDGE, Capt. Alexander
Canadian 1781-1874
drawings: (H) $6,600

MCNICOLL, Helen Galloway
paintings: (H) $7,150

MCNULTY, William Charles
American b. 1889
drawings: (L) $462; (H) $935

MCPHERSON, John
drawings: (H) $1,100

MCRAE, Elmer Livingston
American
drawings: (H) $990

MCRICKARD, James P.
American b. 1872
paintings: (H) $2,640

MEACCI, Ricciardo
Italian b. 1856
drawings: (L) $495; (H) $900

MEADE
sculpture: (H) $825

MEADE-KING, E.
British 20th cent.
drawings: (H) $1,320

MEADOR, Joshua
American b. 1911
paintings: (L) $192; (H) $825

MEADOWS, Arthur Joseph
English 1843-1907
paintings: (L) $715; (H) $24,200

MEADOWS, Gordon Arthur
British b. 1868
paintings: (H) $660

MEADOWS, James
English 1798-1864
paintings: (L) $1,320; (H) $7,150

MEADOWS, James Edwin
British 1828-1888
paintings: (L) $660; (H) $7,700
drawings: (H) $495

MEADOWS, W.
British ac. 1830-1832
paintings: (H) $1,870

MEADOWS, William
British 19th/20th cent.
paintings: (L) $440; (H) $5,500

MEADOWS, William G.
British ac. 1874
paintings: (L) $550; (H) $4,400

MEADOWS, William J.
English 19th cent.
paintings: (H) $6,600

MEAKIN, Louis Henry
American 1850/53-1917
paintings: (L) $330; (H) $9,900

MEANEIMI, A.
paintings: (H) $3,080

MEARS, George
British ac. 1870-1896
paintings: (L) $2,200; (H) $3,300

MEARS, Henrietta Dunn
American b. 1877
paintings: (L) $165; (H) $1,045

MEDARD, Jules Ferdinand
French 19th cent.
paintings: (H) $6,875

MEDCALF, William
American 20th cent.
paintings: (L) $990; (H) $2,200

MEDINA, A.
European 19th/20th cent.
drawings: (H) $1,980

MEDINA-CAMPENY, Xavier
contemporary
sculpture: (H) $17,600

MEECH(?), J.J.
English 19th cent.
drawings: (H) $935

MEEGEREN, Hans van
paintings: (H) $880

MEEKER, Edwin James
American 1853-1936
drawings: (L) $33; (H) $3,520

MEEKER, Joseph Rusling
American 1827-1889
paintings: (L) $220; (H) $38,500

MEEKS, Eugene
American b. 1843
paintings: (L) $350; (H) $4,400

MEER, Barend van der
Dutch 1659-1690/1702
paintings: (L) $11,000; (H) $68,500

MEER, Jan Van Der, the elder
Dutch 1628-1691
paintings: (H) $11,000

MEER, M. van der
drawings: (H) $907

MEERTS, Frans
Belgian 1836-1896
paintings: (L) $523; (H) $16,500

MEESER, Lillian B.
American 1864-1942
paintings: (L) $1,760; (H) $2,200
drawings: (H) $110

MEGARGEE, Lon
American 1883-1960
paintings: (L) $880; (H) $2,090

MEGE, Lydia Marie
French 19th cent.
drawings: (H) $1,320

MEGGENDORFER, Lothar
drawings: (H) $2,200

MEHEUT, Mathurain
sculpture: (H) $2,420

MEHNER, Walter
paintings: (H) $715

MEHNI, W. Roessler
paintings: (H) $660

MEHUS, Livio
Flemish 1630-1691
paintings: (L) $13,200; (H) $19,800

MEI, Paulo
Italian 19th cent.
paintings: (L) $468; (H) $6,875

MEIER, E.
sculpture: (H) $1,430

MEIERRHANS, Joseph
Swiss/American b. 1890
paintings: (H) $1,155

MEIERSDORF, Leo
American contemporary
paintings: (L) $825; (H) $880
drawings: (H) $275

MEIFREN Y ROIG, Eliseo
paintings: (H) $18,700

MEIGS, Walter
American b. 1918
paintings: (L) $247; (H) $742

MEILSNER, Ernst
paintings: (H) $18,700

MEINDL, Albert
Austrian 1891-1967
paintings: (L) $247; (H) $1,320

MEIRA, Monica
Colombian b. 1949
paintings: (H) $2,750

MEISSEL, Ernst
German 1838-1895
paintings: (H) $12,100

MEISSNER, Adolf Ernst
German 1837-1902
paintings: (L) $1,100; (H) $26,400

MEISSNER, Leo
American
paintings: (H) $990
drawings: (H) $330

Bayou Artist

Joseph Rusling Meeker (1827-1889) is best known for his paintings of the Louisiana bayous. Born in Newark, New Jersey, he studied at the National Academy of Design under Asher B. Durand, a leader of the Hudson River School of landscape painting, and Charles Loring Elliott, a prominent portrait painter. Meeker painted for several years in Buffalo, New York, and then worked in Louisville, Kentucky, from 1852 to 1859. He was living and painting in St. Louis when the Civil War broke out in 1861. Meeker entered the U.S. Navy and became a paymaster on a gunboat that traveled the Mississippi River.

On board he made many sketches of the Mississippi River and the Louisiana bayous and swamplands. At the end of the war he returned to St. Louis and used his sketches to paint numerous bayou and swamp landscapes. In their attention to detail and realistic depiction of nature, these paintings showed the strong influence of the Hudson River School.

Meeker made numerous trips back to Louisiana to study the unusual light and stillness of the swamps; his post-1870 paintings of the bayous show a concern with light and tonality and contain many Luminist elements. Meeker also traveled north around the Ohio River and the Great Lakes and painted many portraits of Indian chiefs. In his hometown of St. Louis, he was a leading figure in the art community and an active member of several art organizations. (Joseph Rusling Meeker, *West Bayou Plaquemines*, oil on canvas, 13 ¾ x 21 ½ in., Neal, October 7, 1989, $14,850)

MEISSONIER, Jean Charles
French 1848-1917
paintings: (L) $330; (H) $55,000
drawings: (H) $2,090
sculpture: (H) $4,675

MEISSONIER, Jean Louis Ernest
French 1815-1891
paintings: (L) $3,300; (H) $148,500
drawings: (H) $1,320
sculpture: (L) $4,950; (H) $11,000

MEISTER, Ernst
paintings: (H) $715

MEIXMORON DE DOMBASLE,
Charles de
French 1839-1912
paintings: (H) $3,850

MEIXNER, Ludwig
Bavarian 1828-1855
paintings: (L) $770; (H) $1,870

MEKELIN
paintings: (H) $4,400

MELBYE, Anton
paintings: (H) $3,300

MELBYE, Fritz Sigfried Georg
paintings: (H) $1,760

MELCARTH, Edward
American
paintings: (L) $220; (H) $1,100
drawings: (H) $330

MELCHER, George Henry
American 1881-1975
paintings: (H) $3,850

MELCHER, William
paintings: (H) $1,760

MELCHERS, Julius Gari
American 1860-1932
paintings: (L) $4,730; (H) $79,750
drawings: (L) $495; (H) $3,850

MELCHOIR, Wilhelm
German 1817-1860
paintings: (H) $3,575

MELCRATH
sculpture: (H) $1,100

MELDOLLA, Andrea, called Il
SCHIAVONE
ac. 1527-1563
paintings: (H) $18,700

MELE, Guiseppe
Italian 19th cent.
paintings: (H) $1,760

MELEZET, **** Du
ac. mid-17th cent.
paintings: (H) $550,000

MELINQUE, Etienne Marin
sculpture: (H) $935

MELLON, Eleanor M.
American 1894-1979
sculpture: (L) $330; (H) $2,860

MELLOR, William
British 1851-1931
paintings: (L) $110; (H) $3,960

MELLOR-GILL, Margaret Webster
American b. 1901
paintings: (L) $412; (H) $715

MELOHS, Charles
American 20th cent.
paintings: (L) $200; (H) $1,100

MELROSE, Andrew W.
American 1836-1901
paintings: (L) $330; (H) $28,600
drawings: (L) $495; (H) $880

MELTSNER, Paul R.
American b. 1905
paintings: (L) $495; (H) $4,400

MELTZER, Anna Elkan
American 1896-1974
paintings: (L) $1,320; (H) $3,575

MELTZER, Arthur
American b. 1893
paintings: (L) $440; (H) $8,800

MELVILLE, Alex
paintings: (L) $7,700; (H) $8,800

MELVILLE, Harden Sidney
British ac. 1837-1881
paintings: (L) $165; (H) $660
drawings: (H) $495

MELVILLE, R.
English 19th cent.
paintings: (H) $1,100

MELVIN, Terry
American
drawings: (L) $1,100; (H) $1,550

MELZI, Francesco
Italian c. 1491/93-c. 1568/70
paintings: (H) $38,500

MEMBLING, Jacob
Austrian 1855-1928
paintings: (H) $1,980

MENAGEOT, Francois Guillaume
French 1744-1816
paintings: (L) $6,600; (H) $28,600

MENARD, Ch.
paintings: (H) $1,430

MENARD, Marie Auguste Emile Rene
French 1862-1930
paintings: (L) $1,210; (H) $13,200

MENASCO, Milton
American
paintings: (L) $275; (H) $1,200

MENASSE, L.
French 18th/19th cent.
paintings: (L) $2,310; (H) $2,530

MENCIA, A.G.
Italian 19th cent.
paintings: (H) $2,750

MENCONI, D.
Italian/American 19th cent.
sculpture: (H) $3,850

MENDENHALL, Emma
American 20th cent.
drawings: (L) $192; (H) $770

MENDENHALL, Jack
American b. 1937
paintings: (H) $10,450

MENDENHALL, John
contemporary
paintings: (H) $17,600

MENDEZ, M.G.
paintings: (H) $990

MENDIETA, Ana
Cuban 1948-1985
sculpture: (H) $5,500

MENDJISKY, Serge
French b. 1929
paintings: (L) $605; (H) $6,160

MENDOZA, Carlos
sculpture: (H) $2,310

MENE, Pierre Jules
French 1810-1879
sculpture: (L) $143; (H) $17,600

MENEGAZZI, Carlo
Italian 19th cent.
drawings: (L) $605; (H) $1,045

MENEGHELLI, Enrico
Italian 19th cent.
paintings: (H) $1,210

MENGALLI, F.
Italian 19th cent.
paintings: (H) $990

MENGER, Edward
American b. c. 1832
paintings: (L) $110; (H) $1,650

MENGIN, Paul Eugene
sculpture: (H) $9,350

MENGS, Anton Raphael
German 1728-1779
paintings: (L) $2,200; (H) $104,500

MENGUY, Frederic
French b. 1927
paintings: (H) $3,300

MENKES, Sigmund
Polish/American b. 1896
paintings: (L) $209; (H) $9,350
drawings: (H) $1,320

MENNEVILLE
sculpture: (H) $880

MENNIE, Florence
American 20th cent.
paintings: (L) $275; (H) $660

MENNOR, A.
paintings: (H) $825

MENOCAL, Richard de
paintings: (L) $247; (H) $770
drawings: (H) $110

MENOTTI, P.
Italian 19th cent.
paintings: (H) $2,400

MENPES, Mortimer
British 1860-1938
paintings: (H) $3,850
drawings: (H) $143

MENTA, Edouard
French b. 1858
drawings: (H) $5,225

MENTOR, Huebner
20th cent.
paintings: (H) $1,430

MENTOR, Will
American b. 1958
paintings: (L) $6,600; (H) $12,100

MENZEL, Adolf von
German 1815-1905
drawings: (L) $1,100; (H) $60,500

MENZIES, William A.
British ac. 1886-1902
paintings: (L) $4,125; (H) $7,700

MENZINGER (?)
paintings: (H) $880

MENZLER-PEYTON, Bertha
American 1871-1950
paintings: (L) $2,860; (H) $6,050

MEOLA, Elizabeth Zullo
drawings: (L) $1,320; (H) $2,200

MERCIE, Marius Jean Antonin
French 1845-1916
sculpture: (L) $1,320; (H) $39,600

MERCIER, E.
French 19th cent.
paintings: (H) $1,980

MERCIER, Philippe
French 1689/91-1760
paintings: (H) $16,500

MERCKAERT, Jules
Belgian 1872-1924
paintings: (H) $3,575

MEREKAERTZ, Tul
Belgian 19th/20th cent.
paintings: (H) $3,025

MERET, Emile Louis
French 19th/20th cent.
paintings: (H) $1,320

MERFELD, Gerald
paintings: (L) $412; (H) $800

MERIDA, Carlos
Guatemalan 1891-1984
paintings: (L) $1,980; (H) $82,500
drawings: (L) $852; (H) $38,500

MERIDITH, Isaac
American 1878-1954
paintings: (H) $1,650

MERIE, D.
French 19th cent.
sculpture: (H) $2,750

MERIMEE, Prosper
drawings: (H) $1,980

MERK, Eduard
Bavarian 1816-1888
paintings: (L) $825; (H) $1,650

MERKE, Otto
American 19th cent.
paintings: (H) $990

MERLE, Georges
French 19th cent.
paintings: (L) $2,640; (H) $5,500

MERLE, Hugues
French 1823-1881
paintings: (L) $1,155; (H) $27,500
drawings: (H) $2,750

MERLIN, Daniel
French 1861-1933
paintings: (H) $7,750

MERLOT, Emile Justin
French 1839-1900
paintings: (H) $1,320

MERLROSE, Andrew W.
American 1836-1901
paintings: (H) $15,400

MERON, C.
paintings: (L) $605; (H) $880

MERRIAM, James Arthur
American 1880-1951
paintings: (L) $138; (H) $1,045

MERRIHAM(?), Joseph
paintings: (H) $1,980

MERRILL, Frank Thayer
American b. 1848
drawings: (L) $44; (H) $935

MERRILL, Robert S.
American 1842-1924
paintings: (L) $11; (H) $880
drawings: (L) $5; (H) $165

MERRITT, Anna Lea
American b. England 1844, d. 1930
paintings: (L) $550; (H) $1,320

MERRITT, Henry Samuel
British ac. 1908-1948
paintings: (L) $330; (H) $660

MERSFELDER, Jules
American 1865-1937
paintings: (L) $275; (H) $1,870
drawings: (H) $330

MERSON, Luc Olivier
French 1846-1920
paintings: (H) $12,100
drawings: (H) $605

MERTENS, S.
Flemish 18th cent.
paintings: (H) $6,600

MERTER, Albert
American 1871-1950
paintings: (H) $880

MERTRAND
paintings: (H) $1,430

MERWART, Paul
Polish 1855-1902
paintings: (H) $2,750

MERWIN, Antoinette deForest
American b. 1861
paintings: (H) $1,210

MERZ, Mario
Italian b. 1925
paintings: (H) $88,000

MESDACH, Salomon
paintings: (H) $1,320

MESDAG, Hendrik Willem
Dutch 1831-1915
paintings: (L) $660; (H) $17,600
drawings: (L) $605; (H) $6,050

MESGRIGNY, Claude Francois
Auguste de
French 1836-1884
paintings: (L) $5,775; (H) $7,150

MESLE, Joseph Paul
French 1855-1929
paintings: (L) $1,100; (H) $3,630

MESMER, G.
Swiss 19th cent.
paintings: (L) $990; (H) $1,760

MESPLES, Paul Eugene
French b. 1849
paintings: (L) $660; (H) $7,150
drawings: (H) $440

MESSEL, Oliver
British 20th cent.
drawings: (H) $770

MESSIER, Gregory F.
American 20th cent.
paintings: (L) $330; (H) $1,650
drawings: (L) $330; (H) $1,100

MESSINA, Francesco
Italian b. 1900
sculpture: (H) $4,950

METCALF, Conger
American b. 1914
paintings: (L) $495; (H) $715
drawings: (L) $110; (H) $1,540

METCALF, W.J.
British 19th cent.
paintings: (H) $8,800

METCALF, Willard Leroy
American 1858-1925
paintings: (L) $413; (H) $638,000
drawings: (L) $550; (H) $3,850

METEYARD, Thomas Buford
American 1865-1928
paintings: (H) $1,000

METHFESSEL, Adolf
paintings: (H) $4,950

METSU, Gabriel
Dutch 1629-1667
paintings: (H) $16,500

METTLING, Louis
French 1847-1904
paintings: (L) $3,740; (H) $6,050

METZINGER, Jean
French 1883-1956
paintings: (L) $3,850; (H) $632,500
drawings: (L) $2,090; (H) $18,700

METZLER, Karl Ernest
American b. 1909
paintings: (H) $880

METZMACHER, Emile Pierre
French 19th cent.
paintings: (L) $22,000; (H) $28,600

MEUCCI, Michelangelo
Italian 19th cent.
paintings: (L) $248; (H) $4,400

MEULEN, Adam Frans van der
Belgian 1632-1690
drawings: (L) $2,640; (H) $5,500

MEULENER, Pieter
Dutch 1602-1654
paintings: (H) $3,850

MEUNIER, Constantin Emile
Belgian 1831-1905
paintings: (H) $440
sculpture: (L) $110; (H) $13,200

MEUNIER, Georgette
Belgian 1859-1951
paintings: (H) $770

MEURER, Charles A.
American 1865-1955
paintings: (L) $209; (H) $18,700

MEVIUS, Herman
paintings: (H) $2,750

MEYER, Alvin
American
sculpture: (H) $1,650

MEYER, Claus
paintings: (H) $2,420

MEYER, Emile
French 19th cent.
paintings: (L) $6,600; (H) $20,900
drawings: (H) $165

MEYER, Ernest
Danish 1797-1861
paintings: (H) $1,375

MEYER, Ernest Frederick
American 1863-1961
paintings: (L) $165; (H) $1,375

MEYER, Felicia, Mrs. Reginald Marsh
American b. 1913
paintings: (L) $110; (H) $660

MEYER, Georges
French 19th cent.
paintings: (L) $330; (H) $1,980

MEYER, Hendrick de, the elder
Dutch c. 1600-before 1690
paintings: (L) $6,600; (H) $8,250

MEYER, Hendrik, the younger
paintings: (L) $15,400; (H) $16,500

MEYER, Herbert
American 1882-1960
paintings: (L) $302; (H) $2,750
drawings: (H) $715

MEYER, J.
American late 19th cent.
drawings: (H) $1,210

MEYER, Louis
Dutch 1809-1866
paintings: (L) $1,650; (H) $9,900

MEYER, Louise
German 1789-1861
paintings: (H) $28,600

MEYER, Maurice de
French b. 1911
paintings: (H) $770

MEYER DE HAAN, Jacob
paintings: (H) $3,300

MEYER VON BREMEN, Johann Georg
German 1813-1886
paintings: (L) $3,300; (H) $77,000
drawings: (H) $302

MEYER-KASSEL, Hans
paintings: (H) $660

MEYER-PYRITZ, Martin A.R.
German b. 1870
sculpture: (H) $880

MEYERHEIM, Frederick Edouard
German 1808-1879
paintings: (H) $3,850

MEYERHEIM, Hermann
German 19th cent.
paintings: (L) $4,675; (H) $16,500

MEYERHEIM, Paul
paintings: (L) $880; (H) $2,200

MEYERHEIM, Wilhelm Alexander
German 1814/15-1882
paintings: (L) $7,700; (H) $12,100

MEYERINGH, Albert
Dutch 1645-1714
paintings: (H) $17,600

MEYEROWITZ, William
Russian/American b.c. 1898, d. 1981
paintings: (L) $550; (H) $4,950

MEYERS, Frank Harmon
American 1899-1956
paintings: (L) $660; (H) $6,600

MEYERS, Harry
American 20th cent.
paintings: (L) $198; (H) $770

MEYERS, Jerome
American 1876-1940
drawings: (L) $440; (H) $935

MEYERSAHM, Exene Reed
American 20th cent.
paintings: (H) $2,200

MEYNER, Walter
American b. 1867
paintings: (H) $715

MEZA, Guillermo
Mexican b. 1917
paintings: (H) $3,300
drawings: (L) $1,210; (H) $5,500

MEZZERA, Rosa
Italian 1791-1826
paintings: (H) $14,300

MIARTANI, P.
British 19th cent.
paintings: (H) $2,750

MICAS, Jeanne Sarah Nathalie
French 19th cent.
paintings: (H) $3,080

MICH, Jean
sculpture: (H) $1,430

MICHAEL, H.
paintings: (H) $990

MICHAEL, Jo.
Dutch ? 17th cent.
paintings: (H) $5,500

MICHAEL, Max
German 1823-1891
paintings: (H) $1,650

MICHAEL, Schmitt
German ac. 1870-1890
paintings: (H) $1,760

MICHAELIS, Arthur
German b. 1864
paintings: (H) $1,045

MICHAELIS, Gerard Jan
drawings: (H) $2,420

MICHAL, W.
paintings: (L) $77; (H) $990

MICHALOWSKI, H.
19th cent.
paintings: (L) $275; (H) $2,090

MICHAU, Theobald
Flemish 1676-1765
paintings: (L) $2,860; (H) $26,400
drawings: (H) $10,450

MICHAUD, A.
French 19th/20th cent.
paintings: (L) $880; (H) $1,650

MICHAUD, Leonie
French 1873-1915
paintings: (H) $7,700

MICHAUX
French 19th/20th cent.
paintings: (H) $1,210

MICHAUX, Henri
Belgian b. 1899
paintings: (H) $110
drawings: (L) $4,620; (H) $8,250

MICHEEL, William
American d. 1986
paintings: (L) $99; (H) $880

MICHEL, C.
Belgian 1874-1940
drawings: (H) $2,420

MICHEL, Emile
French 1818-1909
paintings: (H) $1,100

MICHEL, Georges
French 1763-1843
paintings: (L) $220; (H) $33,000
drawings: (L) $55; (H) $2,640

MICHEL, Gustave Frederic
French 1851-1924
sculpture: (H) $2,640

MICHEL, Robert
paintings: (L) $7,700; (H) $10,450
drawings: (H) $165

MICHEL, Sally, AVERY
American 20th cent.
paintings: (L) $495; (H) $1,430

MICHELE
paintings: (H) $1,100

MICHELENA, Arturo
Venezuelan 1863-1898
paintings: (H) $4,400

MICHELET, G.
19th/20th cent.
drawings: (L) $1,320; (H) $1,650

MICHETTI, Francesco Paolo
Italian 1851/52-1929
paintings: (L) $14,300; (H) $24,200
drawings: (H) $1,540

MICHETTI, Othello
American 20th cent.
drawings: (L) $176; (H) $1,430

MICHIELI, Andrea, called Vicentino
1539?-1614
drawings: (L) $8,250; (H) $13,200

MICHIELI, G.
Italian 19th cent.
sculpture: (H) $715

MICKMANN
sculpture: (H) $1,045

MICLETZKY, F. Koko
paintings: (H) $660

MIDDENDORF, Helmut
German b. 1953
paintings: (L) $12,100; (H) $22,000
drawings: (L) $88; (H) $7,150

MIDDLETON, H.
paintings: (H) $715

MIDDLETON, J.
paintings: (L) $440; (H) $1,760

MIDDLETON, John
paintings: (H) $770

MIDDLETON, Stanley Grant
American b. 1852
paintings: (L) $192; (H) $8,800

MIDDLETON, Statler
paintings: (H) $660

MIDWOOD, William Henry
British 19th cent.
paintings: (L) $1,320; (H) $5,500

MIEDUCH, Dan
American b. 1947
paintings: (L) $5,170; (H) $8,000

MIEIRIS, Frans van, the elder
Dutch 1635-1681
paintings: (H) $726,000

MIEL, Jan
Flemish 1599-1663
paintings: (L) $2,200; (H) $36,300

MIELICH, Leopold Alphons
Austrian 1863-1929
paintings: (L) $440; (H) $5,500
drawings: (H) $440

MIELZINER, Jo
drawings: (H) $770

MIEREVELT, Michiel Jansz van
Dutch 1567-1641
paintings: (L) $3,300; (H) $15,400

MIERIS
19th cent.
paintings: (H) $935

MIERIS, Frans van, the elder
Dutch 1635-1681
paintings: (L) $660; (H) $407,000

MIERIS, Frans van, the younger
Dutch 1689-1763
paintings: (H) $19,800

MIERIS, Willem van
Dutch 1662-1747
paintings: (L) $2,200; (H) $82,500
drawings: (H) $7,150

MIFFLIN, Lloyd
American 1846-1921
paintings: (L) $550; (H) $2,970

MIGHELS
American 19th cent.
paintings: (H) $935

MIGLIARO, Vincenzo
Italian 1858-1938
paintings: (L) $165; (H) $63,250

MIGNARD, Pierre
French 1612-1695
paintings: (L) $1,045; (H) $77,000

MIGNON, Abraham
German 1640-1679
paintings: (L) $11,770; (H) $451,000

MIGNON, Leon
Belgian 1847-1898
sculpture: (L) $440; (H) $3,575

MIGNON, Lucien
paintings: (L) $1,320; (H) $1,650

MIGNOT, Louis Remy
American 1831-1870
paintings: (L) $385; (H) $82,500

MIJARES, Jose
Cuban b. 1921
paintings: (L) $1,760; (H) $2,200

MIKLOS, Gustave
French 1888-1967
sculpture: (L) $550; (H) $38,500

MIKULSKI, J.
paintings: (H) $990

MILANI, Aureliano
paintings: (H) $5,500

MILANO, Tabacchi
19th cent.
sculpture: (H) $1,870

MILARSKY, A.
American 20th cent.
paintings: (H) $825

MILBOURNE, Henri
French 1781-1826
paintings: (H) $1,045

MILDER, Jay
American b. 1934
paintings: (L) $22; (H) $7,150

MILES, J., of Northleach
English 19th cent.
paintings: (L) $5,775; (H) $9,900

MILES, John C.
American 1831/32-1911
paintings: (L) $75; (H) $825

MILES, Thomas Rose
English ac. 1869-1906
paintings: (L) $440; (H) $3,080

MILES, W**
British ac. 1841-1848
paintings: (H) $2,310

MILESI, Alessandro
Italian 1856-1945
paintings: (L) $3,300; (H) $8,800

MILEY, R.A.
British 19th cent.
paintings: (H) $4,125

MILIONE, A.
paintings: (H) $1,760

MILLAIS, John Guille
British 1865-1909
paintings: (H) $3,025

MILLAIS, Raoul
English 19th cent.
paintings: (L) $2,750; (H) $9,900

MILLAIS, Sir John Everett
English 1829-1896
paintings: (L) $880; (H) $407,000
drawings: (L) $1,650; (H) $2,750

MILLAR, Addison Thomas
American 1860-1913
paintings: (L) $220; (H) $33,000
drawings: (L) $165; (H) $990

MILLAR, H.B.
English 19th/20th cent.
paintings: (H) $1,430

MILLAR, J.H.C.
French 19th cent.
paintings: (L) $330; (H) $1,100

MILLARD, Frederick
British b. 1857
paintings: (H) $1,430

MILLARES, Manolo
Spanish 1926-1972
paintings: (L) $6,050; (H) $12,650
drawings: (L) $22,000; (H) $104,500

MILLE, Jan Baptiste
paintings: (H) $9,350

MILLER, Alfred Jacob
American 1810-1874
paintings: (L) $660; (H) $137,500
drawings: (L) $385; (H) $45,100

MILLER, Anton
Austrian 1853-1897
paintings: (H) $1,045

MILLER, Barse
American 1904-1973
paintings: (L) $2,475; (H) $3,300
drawings: (L) $660; (H) $1,320

MILLER, C.W.
American
paintings: (H) $3,000

MILLER, Carol
sculpture: (L) $2,420; (H) $8,250

MILLER, Charles Henry
American 1842-1922
paintings: (L) $375; (H) $9,350
drawings: (H) $88

MILLER, Charles K.
British 19th cent.
paintings: (L) $550; (H) $1,100

MILLER, Charles W.
American
paintings: (H) $4,100

MILLER, Evylena Nunn
American 1888-1966
paintings: (L) $110; (H) $4,950

MILLER, F.
American 19th/20th cent.
paintings: (H) $1,650

MILLER, F.H.
American 19th cent.
paintings: (H) $1,100

MILLER, Ferdinand von, II
American b. 1842
sculpture: (H) $4,400

MILLER, Francis
American 1885-1930
paintings: (L) $1,650; (H) $8,250

MILLER, Harriette G.
American 20th cent.
paintings: (H) $4,400

MILLER, Henry
American 20th cent.
drawings: (L) $88; (H) $7,700

MILLER, J.A.
paintings: (H) $825

MILLER, James Robertson
English ac. 1880-1912
paintings: (H) $275
drawings: (L) $60; (H) $1,430

MILLER, John
paintings: (H) $1,430

MILLER, Joseph
German 19th cent.
paintings: (H) $8,525

MILLER, Kate Reno
1874-1929
paintings: (H) $1,650

MILLER, Kenneth Hayes
American 1876-1952
paintings: (L) $935; (H) $7,700

MILLER, Melvin
American b. 1937
paintings: (H) $880

MILLER, Mildred Bunting
American 1892-1964?
paintings: (H) $1,000

MILLER, P.D.
American (?) 19th cent.
paintings: (H) $1,210

MILLER, Ralph Davison
American 1858-1945
paintings: (L) $165; (H) $2,200
drawings: (H) $302

MILLER, Richard
American 1875-1943
paintings: (L) $660; (H) $638,000

MILLER, W.E.
paintings: (H) $7,425

MILLER, William R.
American 1850-1923
paintings: (H) $2,750
drawings: (H) $330

MILLER, William Rickarby
English/American 1818-1893
paintings: (L) $550; (H) $38,500
drawings: (L) $358; (H) $2,530

MILLES, Carl
Swedish 1875-1955
sculpture: (L) $1,320; (H) $165,000

MILLESON, Royal Hill
American b. 1849
paintings: (L) $176; (H) $1,980
drawings: (H) $330

MILLET, Aime
sculpture: (H) $1,210

MILLET, Auguste, called Rigon
Continental 19th/20th cent.
paintings: (H) $2,640

MILLET, Clarence
American 1897-1959
paintings: (L) $247; (H) $6,600

MILLET, Francis Davis
American 1846-1912
paintings: (L) $2,860; (H) $5,250
drawings: (L) $880; (H) $1,100

American Impressionism

Impressionism, the most widely recognized of all art styles, originated in France in the 1870s. The Impressionists rejected artificially contrived subject matter and attempted to catch the natural "fleeting moment." They painted in a succession of discontinuous strokes of color, replacing the traditional technique of firm outlines and smooth surfaces. Pure colors were laid directly on the canvas, and at a distance the prismatic colors fused on the retina to give the illusion of flickering light and a vibrating atmosphere.

Athough the Impressionists announced no formal movement or doctrine, Claude Monet (1840-1926) was their acknowledged leader. The term "Impressionism" was coined by a Paris critic when he saw Monet's *Impression: Sunrise, Le Havre* at the group's first exhibition in Paris in 1874.

Impressionism was first introduced into the United States by American artists who had traveled and studied abroad. Some American artists, such as Richard Miller (1875-1943), became expatriates, staying in France to study and paint. Miller was from St. Louis, and after studying in his hometown he entered the Academie Julian in Paris in 1898. Several years later he took up residence in Giverny near the home of Monet. Each summer he taught classes for the students of Mary Wheeler's Providence, Rhode Island, school.

Miller almost invariably painted women, most often in luxurious settings. His paintings were very decorative, with strong patterns of color and light. Miller returned to the United States in 1916, during World War I, and eventually settled in Provincetown, Massachusetts. (Richard Miller, *Dancer Resting*, oil on board, 30 x 32 in., Hindman, May 13, 1990, $66,000)

MILLET, Francois
French 1851-1917
drawings: (H) $2,200

MILLET, Jean Francois
French 1814-1875
paintings: (L) $57,750; (H) $1,078,000
drawings: (L) $990; (H) $825,000

MILLEY, H.R.
paintings: (H) $1,210

MILLIER, Arthur Henry Thomas
American 1893-1975
drawings: (L) $302; (H) $880

MILLIERE, Maurice
French b. 1871
paintings: (L) $2,750; (H) $12,100

MILLIKEN, Robert W.
British 19th/20th cent.
drawings: (L) $220; (H) $3,025

MILLIOT, F.
sculpture: (H) $770

MILLITT
paintings: (H) $880

MILLNER, Karl
German 1825-1894
paintings: (L) $3,410; (H) $12,100

MILLS, I.
paintings: (H) $1,100

MILLSPAUGH, J.H.
paintings: (L) $715; (H) $1,760

MILNE, David Brown
paintings: (H) $33,000
drawings: (H) $9,350

MILNE, John MacLaughlan
contemporary
paintings: (H) $1,100

MILONE, A.
paintings: (L) $825; (H) $3,300

MILONE, Antonio
Italian 19th cent.
paintings: (H) $715

MILONE, G.
paintings: (L) $330; (H) $2,420

MILOTA, E.
Italian 19th cent.
paintings: (H) $1,870

MILOTA, F.
paintings: (H) $2,970

MILTON, John
British ac. 1767-1774
paintings: (H) $104,500

MILTON, Sydney H.
paintings: (H) $770

MILTON, Victor Marais
French b. 1872
paintings: (H) $4,400

MIMNAUGH, Terry
American
paintings: (H) $5,000
drawings: (H) $2,100

MINAUX, Andre
contemporary
paintings: (H) $2,090

MINAUX, Armand
French b. 1923
paintings: (H) $990

MINCHELL, Peter
American 1889-after 1972
drawings: (L) $550; (H) $660

MINE, Caspar
paintings: (H) $825

MINEL, Antonia
drawings: (H) $990

MINER, H.J.
paintings: (H) $715

MINET, Louis Emile
French c. 1850-c. 1920
paintings: (H) $14,300

MING, Y
contemporary
paintings: (H) $880

MINGERS, C.
paintings: (H) $5,060

MINGUZZI, Luciano
Italian b. 1911
sculpture: (L) $14,300; (H) $41,800

MINIER, Suzanne
French b. 1884
paintings: (H) $5,500

MINIFIE, C.
American 19th cent.
paintings: (H) $935

MINKOWSKI, Maurice
Polish 19th/20th cent.
paintings: (L) $3,300; (H) $7,700

MINNE, George
Belgian 1866-1941
sculpture: (H) $33,000

MINOR, Anne Rogers
American b. 1864
paintings: (L) $330; (H) $975

MINOR, Ferdinand
paintings: (H) $1,650

MINOR, Robert Crannell
American 1840-1904
paintings: (L) $176; (H) $6,600

MINOZZI, Flaminio
drawings: (H) $660

MINTCHINE, Abraham
Russian 1898-1931
paintings: (H) $1,650

MINTCHINE, Andre
Russian 20th cent.
paintings: (H) $715

MINUJIN, Marta
Argentinian b. 1943
sculpture: (L) $7,700; (H) $8,800

MINUMBOC, Rodolfo
Venezuelan b. 1933
sculpture: (L) $6,600; (H) $6,600

MIOLA, Camillo
Italian b. 1840
paintings: (H) $3,300

MIRA, Alfred S.
American 20th cent.
paintings: (L) $2,200; (H) $17,600

MIRABEL, Vicente, Chiu Tah
American Indian 1918-1946
paintings: (H) $2,090

MIRALLES, Francisco
Spanish b.c. 1850
paintings: (L) $715; (H) $242,000

MIRALLES, Jose Darmanin
Spanish fl. 1850-1900
drawings: (H) $3,300

MIRALLES Y GALUP, Francisco
Spanish 1848-1901
paintings: (H) $88,000

MIRALLES-DARMANIN, Jose
Spanish 19th cent.
paintings: (H) $2,090

MIRAM STOCKMAN, F.
early 20th cent.
sculpture: (H) $1,650

MIRAMONT, Hortense de
drawings: (H) $3,960

MIRANDA Y RENDON, Manuel
paintings: (H) $880

MIRIZON, Armaiud
paintings: (H) $660

MIRKO, Mirko BASALDELLA
contemporary
paintings: (L) $1,045; (H) $1,100
drawings: (L) $660; (H) $715
sculpture: (L) $825; (H) $1,980

MIRO, Joan
Spanish 1893-1983
paintings: (L) $1,540; (H) $9,350,000
drawings: (L) $1,430; (H) $2,695,000
sculpture: (L) $46,750; (H) $374,000

MIROU, Anton
Flemish 1586-1661
paintings: (H) $10,450

MIRRI, Sabina
contemporary
drawings: (H) $1,320

MIRSKY, Samuel
American
paintings: (L) $880; (H) $1,320

MIRVAL, C.
sculpture: (H) $15,400

MISCEVIC, Bogden
paintings: (H) $2,200

MITAI, Amohamen
American 20th cent.
paintings: (H) $1,650

MITCHELL, Alfred R.
American 1888-1972
paintings: (L) $303; (H) $16,500

Surrealist Painter

Surrealism first emerged in Paris in the early 1920s as a literary movement devoted to exploring the unconscious. Its leading figure was the poet Andre Breton. Surrealism was conceived as a revolutionary mode of thought and action, a way of life rather than a set of stylistic attitudes. The Surrealists borrowed heavily from the theories of Sigmund Freud; by liberating thought from the constraints of logic, they hoped to reveal a different super-reality, to give expression to the poetry of the subconscious.

As an art movement, the Surrealists first exhibited as a group in 1926. Like their literary counterparts, they tried to give free rein to the subconscious as a source of creativity and to liberate pictorial ideas from their traditional associations. The art of Surrealism took two directions. The first, associated with Pierre Roy, Salvador Dali, Yves Tinguely, and Rene Magritte, presents in meticulous detail recognizable scenes and objects that are taken out of natural context. Ordinary objects are juxtaposed in an atmosphere of fantasy. The second direction, called Organic Surrealism, is exemplified by the works of Joan Miro, Andre Masson, and later Matta. This group followed the dictates of thought without control of the mind. The results are generally close to abstraction. The work of Jackson Pollock and Arshile Gorky, pioneers of Abstract Expressionism and action painting, is rooted in the spontaneous irrational works of the Organic Surrealists.

Joan Miro (1893-1983) was a Spanish painter, graphic artist, ceramist, and scenic designer. The son of a goldsmith, he entered the Gali Art Academy in Barcelona in 1912. His early paintings were influenced by Fauvism and Cubism. In 1919 he traveled to Paris and visited his boyhood friend, Pablo Picasso. Miro spent the summers in Spain and winters in Paris.

Miro was exceptionally productive. In 1924 he met Andre Breton and joined his gatherings; in 1926 he exhibited in the first showing of Surrealist art; in 1929 he created his first collages composed of paper and objects; in 1930 he learned lithography; in 1932 he designed the sets and costumes for the Ballets Russes.

Miro worked constantly and explored different materials. He painted on sandpaper, copper, masonite, and burlap. In 1944, in collaboration with the Spanish ceramist Llorens Artigas, Miro produced his first ceramics. In the 1950s he created large murals at Harvard University in Cambridge, Massachusetts, and for the UNESCO building in Paris. In the 1960s he created large scale paintings. When he was in his eighties, he began to explore stained-glass designs. *Personnages Et Oiseaux Devant Le Soleil* was painted in 1939, one of a series of nine small paintings on burlap. (Joan Miro, *Personnages Et Oiseau Devant Le Soleil*, oil on burlap laid down on panel, 7 3/8 x 10 7/8 in., Sotheby's, May 16, 1990, $660,000)

MITCHELL, Ernest G.
British 20th cent.
paintings: (H) $715

MITCHELL, George Bertrand
American 1872-1966
paintings: (L) $110; (H) $5,225
drawings: (L) $330; (H) $1,045

MITCHELL, Glen
American 1894-1972
paintings: (L) $2,420; (H) $3,300
drawings: (L) $330; (H) $3,300

MITCHELL, James A.
American 20th cent.
paintings: (L) $220; (H) $1,155
drawings: (L) $82; (H) $495

MITCHELL, Joan
American b. 1926
paintings: (L) $4,180; (H) $506,000
drawings: (L) $8,800; (H) $20,900

MITCHELL, John Campbell
Scottish 1862-1922
paintings: (H) $4,180

MITCHELL, Neil Reed
American 1860-1934
drawings: (L) $165; (H) $1,210

MITCHELL, Thomas
American 1875-1940
paintings: (H) $1,760

MITCHELL (?)
American 20th cent.
paintings: (H) $770

MITELLI, Agostino
drawings: (H) $880

MITFORD, Robert
English 1781-1870
paintings: (L) $385; (H) $22,000
drawings: (H) $1,100

MIYASAKI, George
paintings: (H) $3,025

MIZEN, Frederick
American 1888-1964
paintings: (L) $495; (H) $3,200

MIZUNO, S.
Sino/Cont. School 19th cent.
paintings: (H) $7,150

MOBIUS, Karl
sculpture: (L) $825; (H) $1,980

MOCK, George A.
American 1886-1958
paintings: (L) $742; (H) $825

MODERSOHN, Otto
German 1865-1943
paintings: (L) $1,650; (H) $13,200

MODET, P.
sculpture: (H) $770

MODIGLIANI, Amedeo
Italian 1884-1920
paintings: (L) $385,000; (H) $11,550,000
drawings: (L) $2,200; (H) $357,500
sculpture: (L) $46,200; (H) $66,000

MODIGLIANI, Corinna
Italian 19th/20th cent.
paintings: (L) $132; (H) $2,420

MODRA, Theodore B.
American 1873-1930
drawings: (H) $2,750

MOELLER, Louis Charles
American 1855-1930
paintings: (L) $248; (H) $38,500

MOER, Jean Baptiste van
Belgian 1819-1884
paintings: (L) $1,430; (H) $1,980

MOERENHOUT, Joseph Jodocus
1801-1875
paintings: (H) $2,860

MOERMAN, E.
Belgian late 20th cent.
paintings: (L) $137; (H) $1,210

MOESELAGEN, Johannes
paintings: (H) $14,300

MOEST, Josef
sculpture: (H) $990

MOFFAT, Curtis
paintings: (H) $2,750

MOFFAT, Curtis
American 1887-1949
paintings: (H) $1,100

MOFFETT, Ross E.
American 1888-1971
paintings: (L) $247; (H) $1,870
drawings: (H) $330

MOGFORD, John
English 1821-1885
paintings: (L) $137; (H) $9,900
drawings: (H) $825

MOHALY, Yolanda
b. Hungary 1909-1978
paintings: (H) $3,410

MOHLER, Gustave Jean Louis
French b. 1836
sculpture: (H) $1,650

MOHLTE, John Alfred
Swedish/American 1865-1952
paintings: (L) $468; (H) $1,100

MOHOLY-NAGY, Laszlo
Hungarian 1895-1946
paintings: (L) $23,100; (H) $77,000
drawings: (L) $3,850; (H) $60,500
sculpture: (L) $24,200; (H) $33,000

MOHR, Karl
paintings: (L) $660; (H) $880

MOHRMANN, Henry
American 19th/20th cent.
paintings: (H) $8,250

MOHRMANN, J.H.
Danish 19th/20th cent.
paintings: (H) $7,150

MOHRMANN, John Henry
American 1857-1916
paintings: (L) $880; (H) $5,500

MOIGNIEZ, Jules
French 1835-1894
sculpture: (L) $247; (H) $11,000

MOINE, Charles le
French b. 1839
sculpture: (H) $880

MOISE
paintings: (H) $1,320

MOJIA, M. Tobon
paintings: (L) $770; (H) $1,320

MOLA, Pier Francesco
Italian 1612-1666
paintings: (L) $20,900; (H) $26,400
drawings: (L) $1,540; (H) $7,150

MOLARSKY, Abram
American b. 1883
paintings: (L) $330; (H) $935
drawings: (H) $2,090

MOLARSKY, Maurice
Russian/American 1885-1950
paintings: (L) $1,320; (H) $4,400
drawings: (L) $22; (H) $121

MOLAS, N. de
drawings: (H) $660

MOLDOBAN, Sacha
American 20th cent.
paintings: (L) $935; (H) $1,320

MOLE, John Henry
English 1814-1886
paintings: (L) $1,870; (H) $3,575
drawings: (L) $440; (H) $440

MOLENAER, Claes
Dutch before 1630-1676
paintings: (L) $1,045; (H) $57,750

MOLENAER, Jan Miense
Dutch c. 1610-1668
paintings: (L) $935; (H) $49,500

MOLES, E.
Continental 19th cent.
paintings: (H) $4,400

MOLET, Salvador
Spanish 1773-1836
paintings: (H) $99,000

MOLIJN, Pieter
1595-1661
paintings: (H) $7,700

MOLIN, Oreste da
Italian 1856-1921
paintings: (L) $2,750; (H) $3,960

MOLINA CAMPOS, Florencio
Argentinian 1891-1959
drawings: (H) $9,350

MOLINARI, Antonio
Italian d. 1642
paintings: (L) $33,000; (H) $37,400

MOLINARY, Andres
American 1847-1915
paintings: (L) $605; (H) $1,870

MOLINE, A. de
French ac. 1873
paintings: (L) $6,600; (H) $31,900

MOLINS, Ch.
Continental
sculpture: (H) $7,700

MOLINS, H.
sculpture: (L) $688; (H) $4,950

MOLKENBOER, Antoine
American
paintings: (H) $660

MOLL, Carl
Austrian 1861-1945
paintings: (L) $5,500; (H) $7,150

MOLL, Evert
Dutch 1878-1955
paintings: (L) $800; (H) $12,100

MOLLER, Carl
Danish 1845-1920
paintings: (L) $715; (H) $880

MOLLER, F.
German 19th cent.
paintings: (H) $1,760

MOLLER, Olaf
American b. 1903
paintings: (H) $660

MOLLET, Ernest
French 1831-1902
paintings: (H) $2,475

MOLLICA, Achille
Italian 19th cent.
paintings: (L) $1,980; (H) $16,500

MOLLICA, Emanuele
Italian 19th cent.
drawings: (H) $1,760

MOLLICK, A.
Continental 19th/20th cent.
paintings: (H) $3,850

MOLLINGS, P.A.
American
paintings: (H) $3,850

MOLLY
sculpture: (H) $1,540

MOLNARI, R.
paintings: (H) $852

MOLS, Adrienne
Belgian 19th/20th cent.
paintings: (H) $1,760

MOLS, Florent
paintings: (H) $5,500

MOLS, Robert Charles Gustave
Belgian 1848-1903
paintings: (L) $2,860; (H) $3,850

MOLSTED, Christian Ferdinand
Andreas
Danish 1862-1930
paintings: (H) $14,850

MOLT, Philippe le
French b. 1895
paintings: (H) $2,090

MOLYN, Pieter de, the elder
Dutch 1595-1661
paintings: (L) $1,650; (H) $28,600

MOLYNEUX, Edward
English 19th/20th cent.
paintings: (L) $1,100; (H) $1,980

MOMADAY, Al, War Lance
American Indian b. 1913
paintings: (L) $247; (H) $1,320

MOMBUR, Jean
sculpture: (H) $2,860

MOMI, De
paintings: (H) $660

MOMPER, Jocduas de, II
Flemish 1564-1635
paintings: (L) $55,000; (H) $77,000

MOMPER, Joos de, the younger
Flemish 1564-1635
paintings: (L) $16,500; (H) $176,000

MOMPER, Philips de, I
Flemish 1608?-1634
paintings: (H) $26,400

MOMPO, Manolo
drawings: (H) $1,100

MONACO, S.
sculpture: (L) $2,750; (H) $3,575

MONALDI, Paolo
Italian ac. c. 1760
paintings: (L) $2,200; (H) $28,600

MONAMY, Peter
English 1670/89-1749
paintings: (L) $990; (H) $6,600

MONANTE
sculpture: (H) $770

MONARD, Louis de
French b. 1873
sculpture: (L) $2,200; (H) $3,520

MONCHABLON, Jean Ferdinand,
called Jan
French 1855-1904
paintings: (L) $1,320; (H) $35,200

MONCOURT, Albert de
French b. 1858
paintings: (H) $825

MONDO, Domenico
drawings: (H) $880

MONDRIAN, Piet
Dutch 1872-1944
paintings: (L) $14,300; (H) $9,625,000
drawings: (L) $12,100; (H) $220,000

MONEDERO, Manuel
Spanish b. 1925
paintings: (H) $1,540

MONET, Claude
French 1840-1926
paintings: (L) $22,000; (H) $14,300,000
drawings: (L) $33,000; (H) $330,000

MONFALLET, Adolphe Francois
French 1816-1900
paintings: (L) $825; (H) $36,300

MONFREID, Georges Daniel de
French 1856-1929/30
paintings: (H) $9,900

MONGE, Luis
Ecuadorean b. 1920
paintings: (H) $18,700

MONGIN, Antoine Pierre
French 1761-1827
drawings: (H) $12,100

MONGINOT, C.
paintings: (L) $935; (H) $1,430

MONGINOT, Charles
French 1825-1900
paintings: (L) $2,200; (H) $63,250

MONI, Louis de
1698-1771
paintings: (L) $11,000; (H) $12,100

MONI, de
paintings: (H) $2,420

MONIEN, Julius
paintings: (H) $2,420

MONJO, Enrique
Spanish 20th cent.
drawings: (H) $22
sculpture: (L) $528; (H) $1,100

MONKS, John Austin Sands
American 1850-1917
paintings: (L) $385; (H) $1,870
drawings: (L) $247; (H) $715

MONLEY, T.R.
American 19th/20th cent.
paintings: (L) $1,100; (H) $1,320

MONNERET, Jean
drawings: (H) $2,200

MONNET-LAVERPILIERE, Estelle
French 19th cent.
paintings: (H) $660

MONNICKENDAM, J.
Dutch 19th cent.
paintings: (H) $990

MONNIER, Henri
French 1805-1877
drawings: (L) $121; (H) $1,500

MONNOT, Maurice Louis
French b. 1869
paintings: (H) $1,320

MONNOYER, Jean Baptiste
French 1636-1699
paintings: (L) $33,000; (H) $154,000

MONOGRAMMIST A.S.
German ac. 1530
drawings: (H) $48,400

MONOGRAMMIST GVD
Flemish c. 1700
paintings: (H) $3,575

MONREAL, Andres
paintings: (L) $2,200; (II) $4,400

MONSTED, Peder Mork
Danish 1859-1941
paintings: (L) $1,430; (H) $154,000

MONTAGNA, Bartolommeo
Italian c. 1450-1523
paintings: (H) $20,900

MONTAGNY, L.
paintings: (H) $990

MONTAGUE, Alfred
British ac. 1832-1883
paintings: (L) $412; (H) $5,500

de Stijl

Piet Mondrian (1872-1944) was one of the most influential artists of the twentieth century. Born in Holland, he earned two teaching degrees before entering Amsterdam Academy of Fine Arts in 1892 to study art. Naturalistic brown tones characterized his early landscapes. In 1908 he met the Dutch painter Johannes Toorop, and under his influence experimented with the Neo-Impressionist style. But Mondrian's first substantial contact with contemporary European artists came in 1910 when he visited Paris. His series, "Trees," documents his progression from Naturalism to Symbolism, Impressionism, Post-Impressionist, Fauvism, Expressionism, and finally Abstraction.

Mondrian spent the World War I years in Holland, studying abstraction and developing theories about horizontal-vertical axes while completely rejecting the curved line. In 1917, with artist Theo van Doesburg, he founded the periodical *de Stijl*, whose contributors were mainly Dutch artists and architects who used the straight line, the right angle and primary colors to underscore their principle of total abstraction. Mondrian wrote many theoretical articles promoting rigorously geometrical abstract painting.

In 1919 he returned to Paris and continued his explorations into horizontal-vertical theses. Mondrian believed in simplifying color and using the primary hues in addition to black and white; he painted in red, blue, and yellow relieved by black and white and shades of gray.

In 1924, as a reaction to Theo van Doesburg's use of the diagonal in his paintings, Mondrian began a series of sixteen paintings which emphasized diamond shapes. In 1925 he resigned from *de Stijl* and that same year the Bauhaus published his book *The New Form*. During the 1920s and 1930s Mondrian continued his exploration of compositions composed of vertical-horizontal linear patterns.

In 1938, anticipating the outbreak of war, Mondrian left Paris for London, and two years later he moved to New York. His New York years were productive. Mondrian finished many of the paintings he had started in Paris and worked on numerous abstract paintings of the city. Through the teachings of the Bauhaus in Germany and its offshoots in the United States, Mondrian's theories spread throughout the world. His influence is felt in today's architecture, art, fashion, commercial design, and advertising. The diamond shape has become synonymous with Mondrian and endures as one of the classic images of modern art. Only sixteen works were executed in this format; *Tableau Losangique II (Diamond Shaped Painting II)*, painted in 1925, was the catalog cover lot for Christie's May 1990 sale of Impressionist and Modern paintings. One of only three paintings from the series still in private hands, it realized $8,800,000. (Piet Mondrian, *Tableau Losangique II*, oil on canvas, 42⁷⁄₈ x 45¼ in., Christie's, May 15, 1990, $8,800,000)

MONTALLIER, Pierre
paintings: (H) $8,800

MONTANE, Roger
French b. 1916
paintings: (L) $385; (H) $1,760

MONTANER, Miguel
paintings: (L) $660; (H) $1,320

MONTAQUE, Clifford
English
paintings: (H) $1,320

MONTASSIER, Henri
French b. 1880
paintings: (H) $17,600

MONTCHABLON, Alphonse
French 1835-1907
paintings: (H) $880

MONTELATICI, Francesco, called
Cecco Bravo
Italian c. 1600-1661
paintings: (L) $33,000; (H) $35,200

MONTELATICI, Giovanni
Italian 19th cent.
sculpture: (H) $46,200

MONTEMEZZANO, Francesco
Italian c. 1540-after 1602
paintings: (H) $6,050

MONTEMEZZO, Antonio
German 1841-1898
paintings: (L) $6,050; (H) $11,000

MONTENBROOK, D.H.K.
drawings: (H) $770

MONTENEGRO, Jose
Spanish 19th/20th cent.
paintings: (L) $550; (H) $2,750

MONTENEGRO, Julio
Ecuadorean 1867-1932
paintings: (H) $1,100

MONTENEGRO, Roberto
Mexican b. 1885
paintings: (L) $1,980; (H) $22,000
drawings: (H) $1,100

MONTERO, Paulina
Spanish 19th/20th cent.
paintings: (H) $880

MONTERO Y CALVO, Arturo
paintings: (H) $1,870

MONTES DE OCA, Rafael
drawings: (H) $38,500

MONTESI, Carlo
Italian 20th cent.
paintings: (H) $660

MONTESIRO, A.
French contemporary
paintings: (H) $660

MONTEZIN, Pierre Eugene
French 1874-1946
paintings: (L) $3,300; (H) $99,000
drawings: (L) $4,950; (H) $20,900

MONTFALLET, Adolphe
French 1816-1900
paintings: (H) $1,760

MONTFORT, Antoine Alphonse
French 1802-1884
paintings: (H) $8,800
drawings: (H) $302

MONTGOMERY, Alfred
American 1857-1922
paintings: (L) $715; (H) $6,050

MONTGOMERY, S.N.
American late 19th cent.
paintings: (H) $825

MONTI, Francesco, called Brescianino
des Battaglie
Italian 1646-1712
paintings: (H) $3,300

MONTI, Francesco, called IL
BOLOGNESE
Italian 1685-1768
paintings: (L) $880; (H) $9,900

MONTI, Francesco and Nunzio
FERRAJOLI, called Il Bolognese
paintings: (H) $8,800

MONTI, John
contemporary
sculpture: (H) $1,980

MONTI, R.
paintings: (H) $715

MONTI, Rafaello
Italian 1818-1881
sculpture: (H) $41,800

MONTICELLI, Adolphe
French 1824-1886
paintings: (L) $935; (H) $74,250

MONTICELLI, Giuseppe
Italian 1841-1879
paintings: (H) $19,800

MONTILLO, E.
paintings: (H) $990

MONTINI, Giovanni
drawings: (H) $2,750

MONTOVA, J.
American 20th cent.
paintings: (H) $715

MONTOYA, Gustavo
Mexican b. 1905
paintings: (L) $1,650; (H) $7,150

MONTPEZAT, Henri D'Ainecy,
Comte de
French 1817-1859
paintings: (L) $2,090; (H) $18,700

MONTULLO
Continental 19th cent.
paintings: (L) $660; (H) $2,200

MONTZAIGNE, E.T.
drawings: (H) $935

MONVOISIN, Raymond Auguste
Quinsac
French 1794-1870
paintings: (H) $55,000

MONYO
sculpture: (L) $425; (H) $1,980

MONZINUT, Charles
French 20th cent.
paintings: (H) $7,920

MOON, Jeremy
contemporary
paintings: (H) $880

MOON, Carl
American 1879-1948
paintings: (L) $2,475; (H) $2,750
drawings: (H) $303

MOON, Samuel
1805-1860
paintings: (H) $4,950

MOONELIS, Judy
American b. 1953
sculpture: (H) $2,090

MOOR, Karel de
1656-1738
paintings: (H) $6,600

MOORE, Albert Joseph
British 1841-1893
paintings: (L) $5,500; (H) $715,000
drawings: (H) $22,000

MOORE, Augustus
American
paintings: (H) $750

MOORE, Benson Bond
American b. 1882
paintings: (L) $165; (H) $1,540
drawings: (L) $286; (H) $330

MOORE, Brett F.
American 20th cent.
paintings: (H) $4,125

MOORE, Bryan Holt
contemporary
sculpture: (H) $880

MOORE, Claude T. Stanfield
British 1853-1901
paintings: (L) $2,090; (H) $27,500

MOORE, David A.
American
drawings: (H) $990

MOORE, Ellen Marie
paintings: (H) $770

MOORE, Frank Montague
American 1877-1967
paintings: (L) $385; (H) $9,350

MOORE, Gertrude
American
paintings: (H) $1,650

MOORE, Guernsey
American 20th cent.
drawings: (L) $1,155; (H) $2,750

MOORE, Harry Humphrey
American 1844-1926
paintings: (H) $12,100
drawings: (H) $330

MOORE, Henry
English 1898-1986
paintings: (L) $1,320; (H) $1,320
drawings: (L) $4,400; (H) $165,000
sculpture: (L) $3,850; (H) $4,070,000

MOORE, Henry Wadsworth
American b. 1879
drawings: (H) $825

MOORE, James
paintings: (L) $1,430; (H) $4,950

MOORE, John
paintings: (H) $4,400

MOORE, John
contemporary
paintings: (H) $1,210
drawings: (H) $825

MOORE, Nelson Augustus
American 1824-1902
paintings: (L) $192; (H) $11,000

MOORE, Robert
British 20th cent.
paintings: (H) $1,100

MOORE, W.J.
American 19th cent.
paintings: (H) $1,100

MOORE, Will D.
British 20th cent.
paintings: (H) $800

MOORE, William
paintings: (H) $715

MOORE (?), I.
American
drawings: (H) $660

MOORE-PARK, Carton
American b. 1877
paintings: (L) $1,100; (H) $2,860

MOOTZKA, Waldo
American Indian 1903-1940
drawings: (L) $330; (H) $1,320

MOOY, Cornelis Pietersz.
Dutch d. 1693
paintings: (H) $24,200

MORA, Francis Luis
Uruguayan/American 1874-1940
paintings: (L) $82; (H) $30,800
drawings: (L) $11; (H) $5,500

MORA, Joseph Jacinto
American b. 1876
paintings: (H) $1,430

MORAGAS Y TORRES, Tomas
Spanish 1837-1906
drawings: (H) $8,800

MORAHAN, Eugene
American b. 1869
sculpture: (H) $1,925

MORALES, Armando
Nicaraguan/American b. 1927
paintings: (L) $467; (H) $66,000
drawings: (L) $1,980; (H) $27,500

MORALES, Dario
Columbian b. 1944
paintings: (L) $55,000; (H) $82,500
drawings: (L) $3,080; (H) $33,000
sculpture: (L) $5,500; (H) $38,500

MORALES, Luis de
paintings: (H) $15,400

MORALES, Rodolfo
Mexican b. 1925
paintings: (L) $2,200; (H) $33,000

MORALES, Ruiz
Spanish 20th cent.
paintings: (H) $990
drawings: (L) $220; (H) $418

MORALT, Willy
German 1884-1947
paintings: (H) $10,450

MORAN, Edward
American 1819-1878
paintings: (H) $31,900

MORAN, Edward
American 1829-1901
paintings: (L) $385; (H) $72,600
drawings: (L) $165; (H) $1,320

MORAN, Edward Percy
American 1862-1935
paintings: (L) $440; (H) $4,950
drawings: (L) $352; (H) $528

MORAN, H. Marcus
American
paintings: (H) $5,500

MORAN, John Leon
American 1864-1941
paintings: (L) $275; (H) $5,775
drawings: (L) $715; (H) $2,200

MORAN, Paul Nimmo
American 1864-1907
paintings: (H) $880

MORAN, Peter
American 1841-1914
paintings: (L) $110; (H) $13,200
drawings: (L) $154; (H) $4,180

MORAN, Thomas
American 1837-1926
paintings: (L) $3,575; (H) $374,000
drawings: (L) $605; (H) $38,500

MORAN, Thomas Sidney
American 19th/20th cent.
paintings: (H) $880
drawings: (H) $165

MORAN, Victor
American 19th cent.
paintings: (L) $193; (H) $990

MORANDI, Giorgio
Italian 1890-1964
paintings: (L) $72,600; (H) $1,485,000
drawings: (L) $3,850; (H) $18,700

MORANTE, J.P.
paintings: (H) $3,300

MORAS, Walter
German ac. 1876-1910
paintings: (L) $550; (H) $3,520

MORAT
paintings: (H) $990

MORATTI, P.
drawings: (H) $660

MORBIDO, Cesare
Italian 19th cent.
paintings: (H) $770

MORCAU, I***
paintings: (H) $3,575

MORCHAIN, Paul Bernard
French b. 1876
paintings: (H) $5,775

MORCILLO RAYA, Gabriel
Spanish b. 1888
paintings: (L) $11,000; (H) $39,600

MORDT, Gustave Adolph
Norwegian 1826-1856
paintings: (H) $5,500

MORDVINOFF
French 20th cent.
paintings: (H) $990

MORE, Jacob
drawings: (L) $1,760; (H) $1,980

MOREA
French
sculpture: (H) $3,520

MOREAU, Adrien
French 1843-1906
paintings: (L) $2,090; (H) $126,500
drawings: (H) $550

MOREAU, Auguste
French ac. 1860-1910
sculpture: (L) $99; (H) $4,840

MOREAU, Charles
French b. 1830
paintings: (H) $4,400

MOREAU, Chocarne
French 19th cent.
paintings: (L) $2,475; (H) $9,350

MOREAU, Gustave
French 1826-1898
paintings: (L) $726,000; (H) $2,750,000

MOREAU, Henri
paintings: (H) $660

MOREAU, Hippolyte Francois
French 1832-1917
paintings: (L) $1,210; (H) $1,980
sculpture: (L) $165; (H) $8,800

MOREAU, J.L.
19th cent.
paintings: (H) $770

MOREAU, Jean Michel, called
MOREAU Le Jeune
French 1741-1814
drawings: (H) $7,150

MOREAU, Louis Gabriel, called
Moreau L'Aine
French 1740-1806
paintings: (H) $4,180
drawings: (L) $1,100; (H) $46,200

MOREAU, Mathurin
French 1822-1912
sculpture: (L) $247; (H) $15,950

MOREAU, Paul Charles Chocarne
French 1855-1931
paintings: (L) $605; (H) $5,775

MOREAU-VAUTHIER, Paul
French b. 1871
sculpture: (L) $605; (H) $4,125

MOREELSE, Paulus
Dutch 1571-1638
paintings: (L) $13,200; (H) $49,500

MOREHOUSE, M.B.
paintings: (H) $715

MOREJAU?, E.
Italian 19th cent.
paintings: (H) $1,045

MOREL, Izak Vaerzon
Dutch 1803-1876
paintings: (H) $8,525

MOREL, J.E.
paintings: (H) $1,980

MOREL, Jan Baptiste
Flemish 1662-1732
paintings: (L) $8,800; (H) $9,900

MOREL, Jan Evert
Dutch 1777-1808
paintings: (H) $3,740

MOREL, Jan Evert, II
Dutch 1835-1905
paintings: (L) $880; (H) $4,950

MOREL, Jan Evert and Franz van
SEVERDONCK, II
Dutch 19th cent.
paintings: (H) $3,850

MOREL, Vaarzon
Dutch b. 1868
paintings: (H) $1,045

MORELLE, J.P.
paintings: (H) $1,210

MORELLI
sculpture: (H) $3,300

MORELLI, Domenico
Italian 1826-1901
paintings: (L) $880; (H) $5,500
sculpture: (H) $440

MORELLI, Eugene and Joan
ZYGMUNT
American
sculpture: (H) $2,200

MORELLI, F.
Italian 19th cent.
paintings: (L) $1,045; (H) $1,485

MORELLI, J. H.
paintings: (H) $935

MORENO, L. Marin
French 19th cent.
paintings: (L) $1,650; (H) $1,925

MORET, Henry
French 1856-1913
paintings: (L) $11,000; (H) $165,000

MORETTI, Alberto
paintings: (H) $3,300

MORETTI, G.
Italian early 20th cent.
sculpture: (H) $1,540

MORETTI, R.
Italian 19th cent.
drawings: (L) $385; (H) $1,100

MORGAN, Annie Laurie
American
paintings: (H) $1,760

MORGAN, Charles
paintings: (L) $220; (H) $1,870

MORGAN, Frederick
English c. 1856-1927
paintings: (L) $825; (H) $55,000

MORGAN, Ike
American b. 1958
drawings: (H) $880

MORGAN, John
British 1823-1886
paintings: (L) $3,300; (H) $24,200

MORGAN, Mary De Neale
American 1868-1948
paintings: (L) $413; (H) $9,350
drawings: (L) $220; (H) $3,300

MORGAN, Robert F.
American
paintings: (L) $1,000; (H) $1,600

MORGAN, Sister Gertrude
drawings: (L) $495; (H) $770

MORGAN, Theodore J.
American 1872-1947
paintings: (L) $1,045; (H) $1,265

MORGAN, William Penn
American 1826-1900
paintings: (L) $1,320; (H) $4,000
drawings: (H) $550

MORGANTI, Pompeo da Fano
Italian 1510-1569
drawings: (H) $7,700

MORGANTIN, L.
paintings: (H) $825

MORGENSTEIN, Carl
paintings: (H) $935

MORGENSTERN, Christian
German 1805-1867
paintings: (L) $385; (H) $1,980

MORGENSTERN, Friedrich Ernst
English 1853-1919
paintings: (H) $2,860

MORGENSTJERNE-MUNTHE,
Gerhard Arij Ludvig
Dutch b. 1875
paintings: (L) $440; (H) $990

MORGHEN, Antonio
Italian 1788-1853
paintings: (H) $8,800

MORGHEN, L.
Italian School 19th cent.
paintings: (H) $935

MORHAM, John Henry
paintings: (H) $715

MORIANY
paintings: (H) $1,540

MORICE
French
sculpture: (H) $770

MORICE, *****
sculpture: (H) $28,600

MORIER, David
paintings: (H) $15,400

MORIGGI, Artur
early 20th cent.
sculpture: (H) $4,950

MORIN, Adolphe
French b. 1841
paintings: (L) $660; (H) $2,860

MORIN, L.
paintings: (H) $5,500

MORIN, Louis
French b. 1855
paintings: (H) $110
drawings: (H) $935

MORIS, J.
paintings: (H) $1,875

MORIS, Marie Louis
French b. 1818
sculpture: (L) $1,540; (H) $6,600

MORISOT, Berthe
French 1841-1895
paintings: (L) $85,250; (H) $1,045,000
drawings: (L) $3,025; (H) $440,000

MORISOT, Henriette
French 19th cent.
paintings: (H) $935

MORISSET, Francois Henri
French b. 1870
paintings: (L) $2,860; (H) $2,860

MORISSET, Henri E.
paintings: (H) $8,800

MORIZOT, H.
paintings: (H) $880

MORLAND, George
British 1782-1854
drawings: (L) $385; (H) $2,420

MORLAND, George
English
paintings: (L) $495; (H) $18,700
drawings: (H) $330

MORLAND, George
English 1763-1804
paintings: (L) $1,430; (H) $22,000

MORLEY, Malcolm
American b. 1931
paintings: (L) $522; (H) $506,000
drawings: (L) $3,375; (H) $57,750

MORLEY, T.W.
English 1859-1925
drawings: (L) $137; (H) $770

MORLON, Pierre Alexandre
French b. 1878
sculpture: (H) $1,430

MORMIL, Andre
Haitian contemporary
paintings: (H) $990

MORMILE, Gaetano
Italian 1839-1890
paintings: (H) $4,180
drawings: (H) $2,860

MORMILE, George
Italian 1839-1890
paintings: (L) $550; (H) $3,410

MORO, Battista Angolo del
Italian 1514-1575
drawings: (L) $5,500; (H) $8,250

MOROAN
sculpture: (H) $990

MORON, Edward
American 1829-1901
paintings: (H) $5,500

MORONI, J.
Continental 18th cent.
paintings: (H) $1,320

MORREL, Owen
contemporary
drawings: (L) $825; (H) $935

MORRELL
American
paintings: (H) $825

MORRELL, Wayne
American b. 1923
paintings: (L) $110; (H) $1,700

MORREN, George
Belgian 1868-1941
paintings: (H) $15,950

MORRICE, James Wilson
Canadian 1865-1924
paintings: (L) $18,700; (H) $220,000

MORRIS, A.E.
English 20th cent.
paintings: (L) $110; (H) $1,870

MORRIS, Carl
American b. 1911
paintings: (L) $330; (H) $825

MORRIS, Charles
British 19th cent.
paintings: (H) $1,100

MORRIS, George Ford
American 1873-1960
paintings: (L) $198; (H) $2,090

MORRIS, George Lovett Kingsland
American 1905/06-1975
paintings: (L) $88; (H) $39,600
drawings: (L) $330; (H) $9,900

MORRIS, J.
English 19th cent.
paintings: (H) $1,980

MORRIS, James W.
English 19th cent.
paintings: (H) $6,050

MORRIS, John Floyd
paintings: (H) $8,800
drawings: (L) $132; (H) $1,430

MORRIS, Kyle
American 1918-1979
paintings: (L) $800; (H) $7,425

MORRIS, Philip Richard
English 1836/38-1902
paintings: (L) $330; (H) $12,100

MORRIS, Robert
American b. 1931
drawings: (L) $495; (H) $19,800
sculpture: (L) $165; (H) $63,250

MORRIS, William
contemporary
sculpture: (H) $2,200

MORRIS, William
English 1834-1896
paintings: (H) $4,950
drawings: (L) $2,200; (H) $27,500

MORRIS, William H.
paintings: (H) $3,300

MORRIS, William W.
paintings: (H) $1,650

MORRISH, Sydney S.
paintings: (H) $3,300

MORRISON, K.M.
British 20th cent.
paintings: (H) $770

MORRISON, Van
Continental School 19th/20th cent.
paintings: (H) $2,640

MORRISON, Zaidee Lincoln
American b. 1872
paintings: (H) $1,210

MORSDEN, Michael
paintings: (H) $5,775

MORSE, E.E.
American 19th cent.
paintings: (H) $1,210

MORSE, George R.
19th cent.
paintings: (H) $1,045

MORSE, Henry Dutton
American 1826-1888
paintings: (L) $302; (H) $6,325

MORSE, Jonathan Bradley
American 1834-1898
paintings: (L) $165; (H) $935

MORSE, Mary Minns
American b. 1859
drawings: (H) $660

MORSE, N.E.
American 19th cent.
paintings: (H) $1,430

MORSE, Ruth Eleanor
American b. 1887
paintings: (L) $110; (H) $715

MORSE, Samuel Finley Breese
American 1791-1872
paintings: (L) $1,155; (H) $57,200
drawings: (H) $330

MORSE, Vernon Jay
American 1898-1964
paintings: (L) $1,045; (H) $3,025

MORTEL, Jan
Dutch c. 1650-1719
paintings: (H) $22,000

MORTELMANS, Frans
Belgian 1865-1936
paintings: (L) $2,750; (H) $30,800

MORTIMER, John
paintings: (H) $12,100

MORTIMER, John Hamilton
English 1740/41-1779
drawings: (L) $715; (H) $4,400

MORTIMORE, Mary
British 19th cent.
paintings: (H) $3,300

MORTON, Christina
American 19th/20th cent.
paintings: (L) $220; (H) $770

MORTON, John Ludlow
American 1792-1871
paintings: (L) $8,800; (H) $13,200

MORTON, Thomas Corsan
British 19th cent.
paintings: (H) $880

MORTON, William
American 20th cent.
paintings: (L) $880; (H) $1,760

MORVILLER, Joseph
American ac. 1855-1870
paintings: (L) $440; (H) $8,800

MORZENTI
drawings: (L) $187; (H) $880

MOSER, Frank H.
American 1886-1964
paintings: (L) $110; (H) $2,200
drawings: (L) $220; (H) $220

MOSER, Kolo
Austrian 1868-1918
drawings: (H) $1,210

MOSERT, Zoe
American 20th cent.
paintings: (L) $660; (H) $990

MOSES, Anna Mary Robertson
("Grandma")
American 1860-1961
paintings: (L) $1,980; (H) $82,500

MOSES, Bernard
1860-1870
paintings: (H) $825

MOSES, Ed
American b. 1926
paintings: (L) $8,800; (H) $27,500
drawings: (L) $880; (H) $3,300

MOSES, Forrest K.
American 1893-1974
paintings: (L) $440; (H) $2,090

MOSES, Thomas G.
English/American 1856-1934
paintings: (L) $55; (H) $1,760
drawings: (L) $33; (H) $550

MOSES, Walter Farrington
American b. 1874
paintings: (L) $275; (H) $1,430

MOSKOWITZ
German 19th cent.
paintings: (H) $1,430

MOSKOWITZ, Robert
American b. 1935
paintings: (L) $3,960; (H) $286,000
drawings: (H) $2,970

MOSLER, Gustave Henry
1875-1906
paintings: (L) $247; (H) $1,210

MOSLER, Henry
American 1841-1920
paintings: (L) $1,100; (H) $22,000

MOSMAN, Gul.
paintings: (H) $1,900

MOSS, Charles E.
Canadian/American 1860-1901
paintings: (L) $605; (H) $41,250

MOSS, Kevin
contemporary
paintings: (L) $4,400; (H) $11,550

MOSS, Tom
American b. 1935
sculpture: (L) $1,540; (H) $5,200

MOSSA, Gustave Adolphe
French 1883-1971
drawings: (H) $715

MOSSLAR, L.
paintings: (H) $1,650

MOTE, George William
English 1832?-1909
paintings: (L) $550; (H) $6,600

MOTHERWELL, Robert
American b. 1915
paintings: (L) $4,500; (H) $1,100,000
drawings: (L) $1,980; (H) $121,000

MOTLEY, D.
English late 19th cent.
paintings: (H) $1,870

MOTLEY, Robert
American 20th cent.
paintings: (H) $1,045

MOTT-SMITH, May
American 1879-1952
paintings: (H) $660

MOTTA, Raffaellino, called Raffaellino
da Reggio
Italian c. 1550-1578
drawings: (L) $33,000; (H) $63,250

MOTTET, Jeanie Gallup
American 1864-1934
paintings: (H) $1,320

MOTTET, Yvonne
French 1906-1968
paintings: (H) $770

MOTTEZ, Victor
French 1809-1897
paintings: (H) $11,000

MOTTO
sculpture: (H) $1,320

MOTZ, Peter
paintings: (L) $495; (H) $660

MOUCHERON, Frederic de
Dutch 1633-1686
paintings: (L) $2,000; (H) $4,950

MOUCHERON, Isaac de
Dutch 1667-1744
paintings: (H) $24,200
drawings: (L) $4,400; (H) $20,900

MOUCHOT, Louis Claude
French 1830-1891
paintings: (L) $3,190; (H) $9,350

MOUCK, A.
Dutch 19th/20th cent.
paintings: (H) $2,530

MOUETTE, J.B.
sculpture: (H) $2,475

MOULINET, Antoine Edouard Joseph
French 1833-1891
paintings: (H) $6,050

MOULINS
sculpture: (H) $1,925

MOULTON, F.
American School 19th cent.
paintings: (H) $660

MOUNT, Shepard Alonzo
American 1804-1868
paintings: (L) $1,320; (H) $4,950

MOUNT, William Sidney
American 1807-1868
paintings: (L) $11,000; (H) $286,000
drawings: (L) $220; (H) $8,250

MOURIN, E.
drawings: (H) $770

MOUROT, A.
French 19th/20th cent.
paintings: (H) $1,100

MOUS, Morris
Austrian
sculpture: (H) $715

MOUSSET, Pierre
French d. 1894
paintings: (H) $3,025

MOWBRAY, Henry Siddons
English b. Egypt 1858, d. 1928
paintings: (L) $1,650; (H) $77,000

MOWER, Martin
American b. 1870
paintings: (H) $3,575

MOYA Y CALVO, Victor
paintings: (H) $880

MOYAERT, Claes
paintings: (H) $2,420

MOYAERT, Nicolas
Dutch 1592/1593-1655
paintings: (H) $35,200

MOYERS, William
American b. 1916
sculpture: (H) $2,750

MOYLAN, Lloyd
American b. 1893
paintings: (L) $880; (H) $2,475

MOZIN, C.
paintings: (H) $990

MOZIN, Leon
sculpture: (H) $1,540

MOZZIOLI, G.
Italian 19th cent.
paintings: (H) $20,900

MUCHA, Alphonse
Czechoslovakian 1860-1939
paintings: (L) $5,225; (H) $115,500
drawings: (L) $302; (H) $45,100

MUCKE, Prof. Carl Emil
German 1847-1923
paintings: (L) $2,750; (H) $4,400

MUCKLEY, William Jabez
British 1837-1905
paintings: (H) $2,750
drawings: (L) $2,860; (H) $4,950

MUELLER, Alexander
American
paintings: (H) $8,250

MUELLER, H.
German 20th cent.
sculpture: (H) $2,640

MUELLER, Louis F.
paintings: (H) $1,760

MUELLER, Ned
American
drawings: (H) $900

MUELLER, Otto
German 1874-1930
paintings: (L) $242,000; (H) $308,000
drawings: (L) $7,150; (H) $93,500

MUELLER, Rudolph
American 20th cent.
paintings: (L) $330; (H) $770

MUELLER, Stephen
contemporary
paintings: (L) $605; (H) $5,500

MUELLER-WACHSMUTH
paintings: (H) $880

MUENIER, Jules Alexis
French 1863-1934/1942
paintings: (L) $1,100; (H) $7,700
drawings: (H) $66

MUHL, Roger
French b. 1929
paintings: (L) $137; (H) $7,150

MUHLENFELD, Otto
American 1871-1907
paintings: (L) $1,400; (H) $4,400

MUHLIG, Bernhard
German 1829-1910
paintings: (L) $1,650; (H) $6,050

MUHLIG, Hugo
German 1854-1929
paintings: (H) $880

MUHLIG, Meno
German 1823-1873
paintings: (H) $3,960

MUHRMAN, Henry
American
drawings: (H) $1,760

MUIR, J.N.
American contemporary
sculpture: (H) $25,000

MUIRHEAD, John
English 1863-1927
paintings: (L) $137; (H) $770
drawings: (L) $192; (H) $330

MULENFELD, Otto
American 1871-1907
paintings: (H) $7,150

MULER, Eugene
Continental 19th/20th cent.
paintings: (H) $6,380

MULERTT, Carel Eugene
American b. 1869
paintings: (L) $770; (H) $2,250

MULHAUPT, Frederick John
American 1871-1938
paintings: (L) $357; (H) $26,400

MULHOLLAND, Sydney A.
British 19th cent.
paintings: (H) $7,700
drawings: (L) $138; (H) $715

MULIER, Pieter, called Il Cavaliere
Tempesta
Dutch c. 1637-1701
paintings: (H) $27,500

MULIER, Pieter, the elder
Dutch 1615-1670
paintings: (H) $16,500

MULIERE, Claude
French 20th cent.
paintings: (H) $1,650

MULL, Evert
Dutch 19th/20th cent.
paintings: (H) $660

MULLER
sculpture: (L) $220; (H) $1,650

MULLER, A.
Austrian 19th/20th cent.
paintings: (H) $935

MULLER, Alfredo
Italian 1869-1940
paintings: (H) $3,300

MULLER, Anton
paintings: (L) $49; (H) $1,540

MULLER, Arnold
drawings: (H) $935

MULLER, August
German 1836-1885
paintings: (L) $495; (H) $5,775

MULLER, C***
German 19th/20th cent.
paintings: (H) $1,100

MULLER, C.
paintings: (L) $440; (H) $2,750

MULLER, C.
German 19th cent.
paintings: (H) $3,300

MULLER, Camille
French 1861-1880
paintings: (H) $1,540

MULLER, Carl Friedrich Moritz
German 1807-1865
paintings: (L) $1,375; (H) $10,450

MULLER, Charles
French 1815-1892
paintings: (H) $6,050

MULLER, Charles Arthur
sculpture: (H) $990

MULLER, Charles Louis Lucien
French 1815-1892
paintings: (L) $1,320; (H) $14,300
drawings: (H) $165

MULLER, E.
paintings: (H) $1,210

MULLER, Emma von
German b. 1859
paintings: (H) $8,250

MULLER, Ernst
German 1823-1875
paintings: (H) $2,090

MULLER, Franz
paintings: (H) $8,800

MULLER, Fritz
Austrian b. 1901
paintings: (H) $797

MULLER, Fritz
German b. 1879
paintings: (L) $330; (H) $1,045

MULLER, Fritz
German b. 1913
paintings: (L) $330; (H) $1,210

MULLER, Gerard
Dutch 1861-1923
paintings: (H) $5,500

MULLER, Hans
German b. 1873
sculpture: (L) $209; (H) $1,925

MULLER, Heinz
German b. 1872
sculpture: (L) $660; (H) $715

MULLER, Jan
American 1922-1958
paintings: (H) $19,800
drawings: (L) $935; (H) $6,500

MULLER, K.
sculpture: (H) $770

MULLER, K.
probably American 19th cent.
paintings: (H) $1,500

MULLER, Karl
German 19th/20th cent.
paintings: (H) $880

MULLER, Leopold Karl
Austrian 1834-1892
paintings: (L) $10,450; (H) $60,500

MULLER, M.
German 19th cent.
paintings: (H) $1,650

MULLER, Maria
German 19th cent.(?)
paintings: (H) $2,310

MULLER, Moritz
German 1841-1899
paintings: (L) $1,100; (H) $8,800

MULLER, Moritz, Jr.
German 19th/20th cent.
paintings: (H) $880

MULLER, Moritz Karl Friedrich, called
FEUERMULLER
German 1807-1865
paintings: (H) $28,600

MULLER, Morten
Norwegian 1828-1911
paintings: (L) $357; (H) $9,350

MULLER, Paul Lother
German b. 1869
paintings: (H) $825

MULLER, Peter Paul
paintings: (H) $1,650

MULLER, R.
paintings: (H) $247
drawings: (H) $1,100

MULLER, Richard
Austrian 1874-1930
paintings: (H) $660

MULLER, Rudolph Gustav
German 1858-1888
paintings: (H) $5,225

MULLER, Victor
German 1829-1871
paintings: (H) $7,150

MULLER, William James
British 1812-1845
paintings: (L) $1,540; (H) $14,300

MULLER, Yves Edgard
French b. 1876
paintings: (H) $1,045

MULLER-GRANTZOW, Ad.
German 19th/20th cent.
paintings: (H) $2,750

MULLER-LINGKE, Albert
German b. 1844
paintings: (L) $2,750; (H) $3,850

MULLER-SCHEESSEL, Ernst
German b. 1863
paintings: (H) $2,750

MULLER-URY, Adolf Felix
American b.1862
paintings: (L) $220; (H) $3,410

MULLEY, Oskar
paintings: (L) $4,290; (H) $11,000

MULLHOLAND, S.J.
paintings: (H) $660

MULLICAN, Matt
American b. 1951
paintings: (L) $23,100; (H) $33,000
drawings: (L) $2,640; (H) $30,250

MULLIN, Willard
American
paintings: (H) $880

MULMAUPT, Frederick J.
b. 1871
paintings: (H) $1,045

MULREADY, William
Irish 1786-1863
paintings: (H) $1,980
drawings: (H) $660

MULVAD, Emma
Danish b. 1838
paintings: (H) $2,750

MULVANEY, John
American 1844-1904/06
paintings: (H) $1,045
drawings: (H) $2,420

MUNAKATA, Shiko
Japanese 1903-1975
drawings: (H) $57,750

MUNARI, Cristoforo
Italian 1648-1730
paintings: (L) $22,000; (H) $231,000

MUNCH, Edvard
Norwegian 1863-1944
paintings: (L) $704,000; (H) $3,300,000
drawings: (L) $6,600; (H) $30,800

MUNCHHAUSEN, A. von
German 19th/20th cent.
drawings: (L) $33; (H) $2,310

MUNDELL, J.G.
English 1818-1875
paintings: (H) $1,320

MUNDHENK, August
American 1848-1922
drawings: (H) $660

MUNEL
paintings: (H) $3,190

MUNGER, Gilbert Davis
American 1836/37-1903
paintings: (L) $770; (H) $9,350

MUNIER, Emile
French 1810-1885
paintings: (L) $660; (H) $93,500

MUNK, Loren
contemporary
sculpture: (H) $2,750

MUNKACSY, Michel van Lieb, called
Mihaly
Hungarian 1844-1900
paintings: (L) $1,100; (H) $96,250
drawings: (H) $1,000

MUNKINS, Cornelius
paintings: (H) $1,430

MUNNINGER, Ludwig
European 19th cent.
paintings: (H) $1,760

MUNNINGER, Ludwig
German 20th cent.
paintings: (H) $2,200

MUNNINGS, Sir Alfred J.
English 1878-1959
paintings: (L) $6,050; (H) $1,210,000
drawings: (L) $2,420; (H) $66,000

MUNOZ, Domingo
Spanish 1850-1912
paintings: (H) $990

MUNOZ, M.
Spanish 19th cent.
paintings: (H) $1,650
drawings: (H) $2,420

MUNOZ, Oscar
Colombian b. 1951
drawings: (L) $2,310; (H) $3,300

MUNOZ VERA, Guillermo
Chilean b. 1949
paintings: (H) $13,200

MUNOZ Y CUESTRA, Domingo
Spanish 1850-1912
paintings: (L) $3,300; (H) $22,000

MUNOZ Y LUCENA, Tomas
Spanish 1860-1942
paintings: (H) $11,000

MUNOZ-VERA, Guillermo
Chilean b. 1949
paintings: (L) $9,900; (H) $9,900
drawings: (H) $2,750

MUNRO, Janet
American b. 1949
paintings: (L) $110; (H) $4,675

MUNROE, Albert F.
American 19th/20th cent.
paintings: (L) $1,210; (H) $2,640

MUNSCH, Josef
Austrian 1832-1896
paintings: (H) $2,090

MUNSON, G.
paintings: (H) $660

MUNSTER, Franz Muller
paintings: (H) $3,520

MUNTER, David Heinrich
German 1816-1879
paintings: (L) $357; (H) $935

MUNTER, Gabriele
German 1877-1962
paintings: (L) $11,000; (H) $77,000
drawings: (H) $34,100

MUNTHE, Gerhard Morgen Sterne
Norwegian 1849-1929
paintings: (L) $605; (H) $660

MUNTHE, Ludwig
Norwegian 1841-1896
paintings: (L) $880; (H) $13,200

MUNZINGER
sculpture: (H) $687

MURA, E. Andre
paintings: (L) $1,210; (H) $1,430

MURA, Francesco de
Italian 1696-1782
paintings: (L) $3,960; (H) $66,000

MURATON, Euphemie
French b. 1840
paintings: (L) $2,640; (H) $3,080

MURATON, Frederick Alphonse
paintings: (H) $3,080

MURATON, Louis
French 19th/20th cent.
paintings: (H) $2,860

MURATTA, Kishio
Japanese 20th cent.
paintings: (H) $1,540

MURCH, Walter
American 1907-1967
paintings: (L) $275; (H) $52,800
drawings: (L) $880; (H) $8,250

MURDOCH, M. Burn
English 19th cent.
paintings: (H) $2,420

MURILLO, Bartolome Esteban
Spanish 1618-1682
paintings: (H) $308,000

MURINGER, Ludwig
paintings: (H) $660

MURPHY, Catherine
American b. 1941
paintings: (L) $17,600; (H) $27,500

MURPHY, Hermann Dudley
American 1867-1945
paintings: (L) $770; (H) $18,000
drawings: (L) $1,540; (H) $1,650

MURPHY, John Francis
American 1853-1921
paintings: (L) $385; (H) $16,500
drawings: (L) $55; (H) $4,950

MURPHY, Terry J.
sculpture: (L) $1,100; (H) $5,500

MURRAY, Eben H.
British ac. 1880-1886
paintings: (H) $8,800

MURRAY, Elizabeth
American b. 1940
paintings: (L) $3,080; (H) $16,500
drawings: (L) $99; (H) $24,750

MURRAY, Elizabeth Heaphy
English 1815-1882
paintings: (H) $2,850
drawings: (L) $247; (H) $302

MURRAY, F. Richardson
American 20th cent.
drawings: (L) $3,850; (H) $6,270

MURRAY, H.
English ac. 1850-1860
drawings: (L) $2,475; (H) $5,280

MURRAY, Jim
contemporary
drawings: (H) $1,100

MURRAY, John
American b. 1931
drawings: (L) $4,400; (H) $5,500

MURRAY, Sir David
British 1849-1933
paintings: (L) $1,100; (H) $7,700

MURRAY, William
American
drawings: (H) $10,450

MUSCHAMP, F. Sydney
English ac. 1870-1903, d. 1929
paintings: (L) $440; (H) $33,000
drawings: (H) $275

MUSGRAVE, Sylvester
American 19th cent.
paintings: (H) $1,300

MUSIC, Antonio
Italian 1909-1952
paintings: (H) $209,000
drawings: (L) $9,900; (H) $28,600

MUSIC, Zoran Antonio
Italian 1909-1952
paintings: (L) $9,900; (H) $60,000
drawings: (L) $1,000; (H) $17,600

MUSIN, Auguste Henri
Belgian 1852-1920
paintings: (L) $3,850; (H) $6,600

MUSIN, Francois Etienne
Belgian 1820-1888
paintings: (L) $11,000; (H) $29,700

MUSINGER
sculpture: (H) $2,420

MUSLVER, Gustav Henry
paintings: (H) $4,950

MUSS-ARNOLT, Gustav
American 1858-1927
paintings: (L) $3,520; (H) $7,700

MUSSCHER, Michiel van
Dutch 1645-1705
paintings: (H) $2,750
drawings: (H) $1,540

MUSSELMAN, Darwin B.
American b. 1916
paintings: (H) $1,210

MUTH, A.
American
paintings: (H) $1,320

MUTINELLI, Carlo Alberto
paintings: (H) $2,530

MUTTONI, Pietro de, called Pietro
della vecchia
1605-1678
paintings: (L) $3,300; (H) $27,500

MUYDEN, Evert Louis van
drawings: (H) $2,860

MY, Hieronymus van der
paintings: (H) $2,000

MYERS, Bob
American 20th cent.
paintings: (H) $3,300

MYERS, Ethel H. Klink
American 1881-1960
drawings: (H) $990

MYERS, Frank Harmon
American 1899-1956
paintings: (L) $165; (H) $3,850
drawings: (L) $138; (H) $468

MYERS, Harry
American 20th cent.
paintings: (H) $1,210

MYERS, Jerome
American 1867-1940/41
paintings: (L) $1,320; (H) $22,000
drawings: (L) $192; (H) $6,600

MYERS, Joel Philip
American b. 1934
sculpture: (L) $275; (H) $8,800

MYERS, Paul
paintings: (H) $1,650

MYERS, R.A.
American 20th cent.
paintings: (H) $2,200

MYGATT, Robertson K.
American d. 1919
paintings: (L) $38; (H) $1,100

MYLES, J.
ac. early 19th cent.
paintings: (H) $6,050

MYN, Herman van der
Dutch 1684-1741
paintings: (H) $33,000

MYRBACH-RHEINFELD, Baron
Felicien de
Austrian b. 1853
drawings: (L) $440; (H) $3,080

MYRBACH-RHEINFELD, Felician
Baron de
Austrian b. 1853
drawings: (H) $1,650

MYTENS, Daniel, studio of
paintings: (H) $7,150

MYTENS, Daniel, studio of
c. 1590-c. 1648
paintings: (H) $12,100

MYTENS, Martin
drawings: (L) $66; (H) $4,400

NAAGER, Franz
paintings: (H) $880

NABERT, Wilhelm Julius August
German 1830-1904
paintings: (H) $4,500

NADELMAN, Elie
American 1885-1946
drawings: (L) $1,650; (H) $6,050
sculpture: (L) $2,310; (H) $2,860,000

NAEGELE, Charles Frederick
American 1857-1944
paintings: (L) $150; (H) $1,980

NAGANO, Shozo
Japanese/American contemporary
paintings: (L) $2,200; (H) $2,640

NAGARE, Masayuki
contemporary
sculpture: (L) $2,860; (H) $6,050

NAGEL, Peter
German b. 1941
drawings: (L) $440; (H) $660

NAGLE, Ron
American b. 1939
sculpture: (L) $1,540; (H) $5,500

NAGLER, Edith Kroger
American 1890-1975?
paintings: (L) $467; (H) $1,650
drawings: (L) $25; (H) $137

NAGUCHI
American 20th cent.
sculpture: (H) $1,100

NAGY, Vilmos
Hungarian b. 1874
paintings: (H) $1,760

NAHA, Raymond
American b. 1933
paintings: (L) $220; (H) $715
drawings: (H) $412

NAHL, Charles Christian
American 1818-1878
paintings: (L) $5,500; (H) $42,900

NAHL, Hugo Wilhelm Arthur
American 1833-1889
paintings: (H) $3,300

NAHL, Perham Wilhelm
American b. 1869
paintings: (H) $15,400

NAILOR, Gerald, Toh YAH
American 1917-1952
paintings: (H) $1,980

NAISH, John George
British 1824-1905
paintings: (H) $88,000

NAIVEU, Matthys
Dutch 1647-1721
paintings: (L) $23,100; (H) $33,000

NAIWINCX, Herman
Dutch c. 1624-after 1654
drawings: (H) $13,200

NAKAGAWA, Hachiro
Japanese 1877-1922
paintings: (H) $3,500

NAKAGAWA, Naoto
Japanese 20th cent.
paintings: (H) $2,200

NAKANO, Emiko
drawings: (H) $1,870

NAKIAN, Reuben
American b. 1897
drawings: (L) $605; (H) $2,420
sculpture: (L) $1,760; (H) $14,300

NAKKEN, Willem Karel
Dutch 1835-1926
paintings: (L) $2,310; (H) $13,200
drawings: (H) $1,430

NALDINI, Giovanni Battista
1537-1591
drawings: (H) $12,100

NAMCHEONG
c. 1820
paintings: (H) $6,600

NAMMIN, R.
sculpture: (H) $2,200

NANKIVEL, Frank
American 1876-1950
paintings: (H) $3,300

NANKIVELL, Frank Arthur
American 1869-1959
paintings: (L) $330; (H) $1,980

NANKIVELL, John Frederick
American 1876-1950
paintings: (L) $110; (H) $3,575

NANNINI
sculpture: (H) $1,100

NANNINI, Raphael
Italian
sculpture: (H) $12,100

NANNYA, Jaap
Dutch 20th cent.
paintings: (H) $1,320

NANSEN, Eigil
drawings: (H) $660

NANTEUIL, Celestin Francois LeBoeuf
French 1813-1873
drawings: (L) $330; (H) $880

NAOUMOVA, Larissa
Russian b. 1945
paintings: (L) $4,950; (H) $16,500

NAPOLETANO, Filippo
paintings: (L) $7,700; (H) $14,300

NARDI, E.
Italian 19th cent.
drawings: (H) $7,700

NARDI, Enrico
drawings: (H) $2,200

NARDO, Francesco
drawings: (L) $935; (H) $1,100

NARIMANBEKOV, Togrul
Russian b. 1930
paintings: (L) $6,600; (H) $14,300

NARJOT, Ernest Etienne de
Francheville
American
paintings: (H) $1,760

NARVAEZ, Francisco
Venezuelan b. 1905/08
sculpture: (H) $26,400

NASAGI, J.
Continental 19th/20th cent.
drawings: (H) $1,100

NASH, E.R.
American 20th cent.
paintings: (L) $303; (H) $715

NASH, Frederick
British 1782-1856
drawings: (H) $3,520

NASH, John Northcote
British 1893-1977
drawings: (L) $715; (H) $770

NASH, Joseph
English 1808-1878
drawings: (L) $715; (H) $4,675

NASH, M. Hall
paintings: (H) $660

NASH, Manley Kerchaval
American
paintings: (H) $2,640

NASH, Paul
English 1889-1946
drawings: (L) $770; (H) $990

NASH, Willard
American 1898-1943
paintings: (L) $30,250; (H) $33,000

NASI, G.
Italian 19th cent.
paintings: (H) $1,430
drawings: (H) $935

NASINI, Giuseppe Nicola
1657-1736
drawings: (H) $1,100

NASMYTH, A.
paintings: (H) $1,320

NASMYTH, Charlotte
English b. 1804; ac. 1840-1862
paintings: (H) $2,200

NASMYTH, Patrick
British 1787-1831
paintings: (L) $1,100; (H) $3,850

NASON, Gertrude
American 1890-1968
paintings: (L) $220; (H) $14,850

NASON, Pieter
Dutch c. 1612-1688/90
paintings: (L) $5,500; (H) $16,500

NAST, Thomas
American 1840-1902
paintings: (H) $770
drawings: (L) $440; (H) $20,900

NATIORE, Charles
drawings: (H) $1,500

NATKIN, Robert
American b. 1930
paintings: (L) $308; (H) $29,700
drawings: (L) $121; (H) $4,400

NATOIRE, Charles Joseph
French 1700-1777
drawings: (L) $15,400; (H) $37,400

NATTIER, Jean Marc
French 1685-1766
paintings: (L) $3,740; (H) $148,500

NATTIER, Jean Marc, studio of
French 18th cent.
paintings: (L) $5,225; (H) $44,000

NATTONIER, C.
French 19th/20th cent.
paintings: (H) $1,320

NATWICK, Grim
drawings: (H) $1,210

NAUER, Albert
German b. 1873
paintings: (H) $2,475

NAUEZ, Joseph Francois
Belgian 1787-1869
paintings: (H) $1,650

NAUMAN, Bruce
American b. 1941
paintings: (L) $148,500; (H) $407,000
drawings: (L) $2,200; (H) $198,000
sculpture: (L) $13,200; (H) $429,000

NAUMANN, Carl Georg
German 1827-1902
paintings: (H) $6,325

NAUMANN, Johann
paintings: (H) $1,650

NAUMER, Helmuth
American b. 1907
drawings: (L) $302; (H) $1,430

NAVARRA, Pietro
Italian ac. 17th/18th cent.
paintings: (H) $24,200

NAVARRO, Gilberto Acedes
sculpture: (H) $3,080

NAVARRO, Jose
paintings: (L) $176; (H) $5,500

NAVARRO Y LLORENS, Jose
Spanish 1867-1923
paintings: (L) $4,400; (H) $8,030

NAVEZ, Francois Joseph
Belgian 1767-1869
paintings: (H) $11,000

NAVLET
sculpture: (H) $2,090

NAVLET, Joseph
drawings: (H) $3,850

NAVLET, Joseph
French 1821-1889
paintings: (H) $7,150

NAVONE, Edoardo
Italian 19th cent.
paintings: (H) $6,600
drawings: (H) $1,870

NAY, Ernst Wilhelm
German 1902-1968
paintings: (H) $12,100

NAYSMITH
English 18th/19th cent.
paintings: (H) $2,475

NAZZARI, Bartolomeo
1699-1758
drawings: (H) $1,100

NEAGLE, John
American 1796-1865
paintings: (L) $660; (H) $3,300

NEALE, Edward
paintings: (H) $2,860

NEALE, George Hall
English 1863-1940
paintings: (H) $6,270

NEALE, Maud Hall
paintings: (L) $770; (H) $2,860

NEANDROSS, Sigurd
American 1871-1958
sculpture: (H) $1,430

NEBBIA, Cesare
Italian c. 1536-1614
drawings: (L) $154; (H) $4,400

NEBEKER, Bill
b. 1942
sculpture: (H) $5,280

NEBEL, Otto
drawings: (L) $2,420; (H) $3,850

NEBOT, Balthasar
British 18th cent.
paintings: (L) $11,550; (H) $25,300

NECK, Jan van
Dutch 1635-1714
paintings: (L) $2,750; (H) $4,950

NEEBE, Louis Alexander
American b. 1873
paintings: (L) $220; (H) $1,430

NEEBE, Minnie Harms
American 1873-1946
paintings: (L) $660; (H) $1,430

NEEDHAM, D.
American (?) 19th/20th cent.
paintings: (H) $1,760

NEEDLOCK
paintings: (H) $1,980

NEEFFS, Pieter, the elder
Flemish 1578-1656/1661
paintings: (L) $30,800; (H) $66,000

NEEFFS, Pieter, the younger
Flemish b. 1620/d. after 1675
paintings: (L) $1,980; (H) $26,400

NEER, Aert van der
Dutch 17th cent.
paintings: (L) $14,300; (H) $34,100

NEER, Eglon Hendrik van der
paintings: (H) $8,800

NEERGARD, Hermania Sigvardine
Danish 1799-1874
paintings: (L) $7,700; (H) $68,750

NEFFLEN, Paul
paintings: (L) $660; (H) $1,760

NEGELY, G.
Hungarian early 20th cent.
paintings: (H) $715

NEGRE
Italian 19th cent.
sculpture: (H) $4,290

NEGRET, Edgar
Columbian b. 1920
sculpture: (L) $3,520; (H) $19,800

NEGRETTI, Angelo
Italian b. 1881
sculpture: (H) $880

NEGRETTI, Jacopo, called PALMA IL GIOVANE
drawings: (L) $660; (H) $935

NEGRI, Mario
contemporary
sculpture: (L) $660; (H) $35,750

NEGULESCO, Jean
Hungarian 19th/20th cent.
paintings: (H) $825

NEIER, Jacob
b. 1859
paintings: (H) $1,320

NEILL, Francis Isabel
American b. 1871
paintings: (L) $632; (H) $770

NEILSON, Raymond Perry Rodgers
American 1881-1964
paintings: (L) $770; (H) $14,850

NEIMAN, A.
American 20th cent.
paintings: (H) $825

NEIMAN, Leroy
American b. 1925
paintings: (L) $1,650; (H) $7,150
drawings: (L) $650; (H) $1,760

NEIZVESTNY, Ernst
Russian b. 1926
drawings: (L) $2,750; (H) $3,080
sculpture: (H) $12,650

NEL-DUMOUCHEL, Jules
French 19th cent.
paintings: (L) $990; (H) $14,850

NELL, Antonia
American 20th cent.
paintings: (H) $715

NELLIUS, Martinus
Dutch ac. 1670; d. 1706
paintings: (L) $10,450; (H) $12,100

NELSON, A.
sculpture: (H) $2,420

NELSON, Alphonse Henri
French b. 1854
sculpture: (H) $715

NELSON, Anna E.
American 19th/20th cent.
paintings: (H) $660

NELSON, C.
British 19th cent.
paintings: (H) $5,500

NELSON, Ernest Bruce
American 1888-1952
paintings: (L) $2,750; (H) $13,200

NELSON, Ernest O.
American 19th cent.
paintings: (H) $4,675

NELSON, George Laurence
American 1887-1978
paintings: (L) $55; (H) $3,960
drawings: (L) $39; (H) $1,100

NELSON, Joan
American b. 1958
paintings: (L) $7,700; (H) $19,800
drawings: (L) $3,850; (H) $14,300

NELSON, O.
paintings: (H) $3,300

NELSON, Roger Laux
contemporary
paintings: (H) $6,050

NELZER, A.
English 19th cent.
paintings: (H) $1,320

NEME, Clarel
Uruguayan b. 1926
paintings: (L) $4,950; (H) $8,250

NEMETH, Lajos
Hungarian b. 1861
paintings: (H) $770

NEMETHY, Albert
American 19th/20th cent.
paintings: (L) $880; (H) $3,190

NEMETHY, George
American 20th cent.
paintings: (L) $275; (H) $2,090

NEMETHY, Georgina
American 20th cent.
paintings: (L) $357; (H) $880

NEOGRADY, Laszlo
Hungarian 1861-1942
paintings: (L) $220; (H) $3,300

NEOGRADY, Laszlo
paintings: (L) $550; (H) $880

NEOGRADY, Laszlo
Hungarian b. 1900
paintings: (L) $220; (H) $6,050
drawings: (H) $715

NEPOTE, Alexander
American b. 1913
drawings: (L) $605; (H) $1,540

NER DI BICCI
Italian 1419-1491
paintings: (H) $121,000

NERENZ, Wilhelm
German 1804-1871
paintings: (H) $6,050

NERI
French 19th cent.
sculpture: (H) $660

NERI, F.
drawings: (H) $1,650

NERI, Manuel
American 20th cent.
paintings: (H) $1,100
drawings: (L) $1,430; (H) $3,025

NERLY, Frederick, Jr.
Italian 1824-1919
paintings: (H) $1,210

NERLY, Friedrich
paintings: (H) $1,980

NERLY, Friedrich
Italian/Austrian 1807-1878
paintings: (H) $18,700

NERONI, Bartolommeo, Il Riccio
Italian c. 1500-1571/73
paintings: (L) $3,850; (H) $13,200

NESBITT, John
Scottish 1831-1904
paintings: (H) $715

NESBITT, Lowell
American b. 1933
paintings: (L) $44; (H) $7,700
drawings: (L) $247; (H) $2,420

NESSI, Marie Lucie
French b. 1910
paintings: (L) $220; (H) $2,640

NESTEROV, Mikhail Vasilievich
Russian 1862-1942
paintings: (H) $19,800

NESTEROVA, Natalia
Russian b. 1944
paintings: (L) $4,400; (H) $13,200

NETER, Laurentius de
German b. c. 1600
paintings: (H) $6,600

NETO, Manuel Chong
paintings: (H) $6,600

NETSCHER, Caspar
Dutch 1639-1684
paintings: (L) $8,250; (H) $46,750

NETSCHER, Constantin
Dutch 1668-1723
paintings: (L) $2,530; (H) $26,400

NETTLESHIP, John Trivett
British 1841-1902
paintings: (H) $4,675

NETTLETON, Walter
American 1861-1936
paintings: (L) $440; (H) $3,025

NEU, Walther
paintings: (H) $852

NEUBERT, Ludwig
German 1846-1892
paintings: (H) $2,860

NEUCKENS, P.J.
Belgian 19th cent.
paintings: (H) $3,300

NEUENDAM, V.
Scandinavian 19th/20th cent.
paintings: (H) $5,500

NEUFELD, Woldemar
Russian/American b. 1909
paintings: (H) $1,870
drawings: (H) $220

NEUHAUS, Fritz
German b. 1852
paintings: (H) $1,100

NEUHAUS, Karl Eugen
American 1879-1963
paintings: (L) $660; (H) $3,025
drawings: (H) $550

NEUHUYS, Albert
Dutch 1844-1914
paintings: (L) $990; (H) $4,620
drawings: (L) $440; (H) $1,540

NEUHUYS, Joseph Hendrikus
paintings: (H) $3,080

NEUMANN, A.
paintings: (H) $770

NEUMANN, Alexander
paintings: (H) $1,980

NEUMANN, Arnold
German 1836-1920
paintings: (H) $1,650

NEUMANN, B.
American 20th cent.
paintings: (H) $660

NEUMANN, Carl
Danish 1833-1891
paintings: (H) $1,045

NEUMANN, Johan Jens
Danish 1860-1940
paintings: (H) $3,500

NEUMANN, Robert von
American 1888-1976
paintings: (L) $302; (H) $2,200

NEUMANS, H., Jr.
Dutch 19th cent.
paintings: (H) $1,870

NEUQUELMAN, Lucien
French b. 1909
paintings: (L) $3,250; (H) $11,000

NEUSER, Louis A. William
German/American ac. 1856-1902
paintings: (L) $165; (H) $660

NEUSTATTER, Ludwig
German 1829-1899
paintings: (H) $6,500

NEUVILLE, Alphonse Marie de
French 1835-1885
paintings: (L) $500; (H) $13,200
drawings: (L) $275; (H) $1,430

**NEUVILLE, Alphonse Marie de and
Edouard DETAILLE**
French 19th cent.
paintings: (H) $7,150

NEUVILLE, Bernard
French 19th/20th cent.
paintings: (H) $660

NEVELSON, Louise
Russian/American 1900-1988
drawings: (L) $468; (H) $9,900
sculpture: (L) $2,860; (H) $253,000

NEVIL, E.
Continental 19th cent.
drawings: (H) $880

NEVILL, Eunice M.
English 19th/20th cent.
drawings: (H) $1,100

NEWALL, Ray
American 20th cent.
paintings: (H) $935

NEWCOMBE, Warren A.
American b. 1894
paintings: (L) $880; (H) $880

NEWCOME
English 19th cent.
drawings: (H) $1,100

NEWELL, George Glen
American
paintings: (H) $2,750

NEWELL, George Glenn
American 1870-1947
paintings: (L) $55; (H) $2,200

NEWELL, Hugh
American 1830-1915
paintings: (L) $165; (H) $26,400
drawings: (L) $200; (H) $3,520

NEWELL, Peter S. H.
American 1862-1924
drawings: (L) $88; (H) $1,650

NEWHALL, Harriot B.
American b. 1874
paintings: (L) $467; (H) $1,430

NEWMAN, Allen George
sculpture: (H) $6,600

NEWMAN, Barnett
American 1905-1970
paintings: (L) $165,000; (H) $1,650,000
drawings: (H) $28,600

NEWMAN, Benjamin T.
American 1859-1940
paintings: (L) $99; (H) $3,850
drawings: (H) $220

NEWMAN, Donald
contemporary
drawings: (L) $418; (H) $3,080

NEWMAN, Elias
American b. 1903
paintings: (L) $66; (H)$1,650
drawings: (H) $55

NEWMAN, George
paintings: (H) $1,150

NEWMAN, Henry Roderick
American c. 1833-1918
drawings: (L) $2,860; (H) $71,500

NEWMAN, Howard
American 20th cent.
sculpture: (L) $550; (H) $9,350

NEWMAN, Robert Loftin
American 1827-1912
paintings: (L) $2,640; (H) $7,975
drawings: (H) $302

NEWMAN, Solon
American
drawings: (H) $6,600

NEWMARK, M.
sculpture: (H) $715

NEWQUIST, Marc
sculpture: (H) $1,760

NEWSWANGER, Kiehl
Primitive School 20th cent.
paintings: (H) $1,100

NEWTON, Gilbert Stuart
b. Canada, d. Eng. c. 1794-1835
paintings: (L) $600; (H) $1,980

NEWTON, Herbert H.
British b. 1881
paintings: (H) $770

NEWTON, Richard, Jr.
paintings: (L) $385; (H) $9,900

NEWTON, Richard, Jr.
American 20th cent.
paintings: (H) $990

NEWTON, William G.
American 19th cent.
drawings: (H) $770

NEWVILLE
paintings: (H) $825

NEYLAND, Harry A.
American 1877-1958
paintings: (H) $3,575

NEYLAND, Harry A.
American b. 1877
paintings: (L) $330; (H) $3,520

NEYMARK, Gustave Mardoche
French b. 1850
paintings: (L) $880; (H) $3,850

NEYN, Pieter de
Dutch 1597-1639
paintings: (L) $8,800; (H) $66,000

NEYTS, Aegidius
Flemish 1623-1687
drawings: (H) $12,100

NEYTS, Gillis
Flemish 1623-1687
paintings: (H) $12,100
drawings: (H) $4,950

NFAAM, Rita Letendre
paintings: (H) $3,300

NIBBRIG, Ferdinand Hart
Dutch 1866-1915
paintings: (H) $2,420

NIBBS, Richard Henry
British 1816-1893
paintings: (L) $1,045; (H) $11,500

NIBLETT, Gary
American b. 1943
paintings: (L) $2,640; (H) $7,500
drawings: (L) $660; (H) $1,430

NICE, Don
American b. 1923
paintings: (L) $242; (H) $8,800
drawings: (L) $825; (H) $6,050

NICHOL, Andrew
drawings: (H) $1,650

NICHOL, G.A.
American 19th cent.
paintings: (H) $700

NICHOLAS
English 19th cent.
paintings: (H) $935

NICHOLAS, Hobart
American 1869-1962
paintings: (H) $1,540

NICHOLL, Andrew
Irish 1804-1886
drawings: (H) $880

NICHOLL, Charles Wynn
Irish 1831-1903
paintings: (H) $3,500

NICHOLL, T.J.
American 19th cent.
paintings: (H) $770

NICHOLLS, Bertram
British b. 1883
paintings: (H) $3,410

NICHOLLS, Burr H.
American 1848-1915
paintings: (L) $375; (H) $17,600

NICHOLLS, George F.
British 1885-1937
drawings: (L) $770; (H) $1,430

NICHOLLS, Rhoda Holmes
Anglo/American 1854-1930
paintings: (L) $440; (H) $715
drawings: (L) $209; (H) $2,750

NICHOLS, Abel
American 19th cent.
paintings: (H) $1,100

NICHOLS, Alfred
British 19th cent.
paintings: (H) $1,650

NICHOLS, Carroll Leja
American b. 1882
paintings: (L) $275; (H) $1,540

NICHOLS, Dale
American b. 1904
paintings: (L) $330; (H) $24,200
drawings: (H) $2,200

NICHOLS, Henry Hobart
American 1869-1962
paintings: (L) $1,045; (H) $14,300
drawings: (L) $425; (H) $440

NICHOLS, Hubley
American 19th cent.
paintings: (H) $2,310

NICHOLS, William
American b. 1942
paintings: (H) $22,000

NICHOLSON, Ben
British 1894-1982
paintings: (L) $23,100; (H) $451,000
drawings: (L) $6,600; (H) $93,500

NICHOLSON, Captain John
American 1832-1915
drawings: (H) $16,500

NICHOLSON, Edward H.
American 1901-1966
paintings: (L) $440; (H) $2,200
drawings: (L) $137; (H) $770

NICHOLSON, George W.
American 1832-1912
paintings: (L) $192; (H) $8,250
drawings: (L) $358; (H) $1,100

NICHOLSON, Lillie May
American 1884-1964
paintings: (L) $220; (H) $1,980

NICKELE, Isaac van
paintings: (H) $11,000

NICODEMO, August
Italian 18th cent.
paintings: (H) $1,210

NICOL, Erskine
British 1825-1904
paintings: (L) $143; (H) $24,200

NICOL, H.
paintings: (H) $660

NICOLAS, Joep
Dutch b. 1898
paintings: (H) $9,350

NICOLAS, L.
paintings: (H) $1,400

NICOLE, Gabriel
paintings: (H) $4,675

NICOLET, Gabriel Emile Edouard
French 1856-1921
paintings: (H) $17,600
drawings: (H) $330

NICOLI, Charles
sculpture: (H) $2,970

NICOLIE, J.C.
paintings: (H) $1,650

NICOLIE, Josephus Christianus
paintings: (H) $3,850

NICOLIE, Paul Emile
Belgian 1828-1894
paintings: (H) $2,420

NICOLL, James Craig
American 1846-1918
paintings: (L) $165; (H) $3,850
drawings: (H) $715

NICOLLE, Victor Jean
French 1754-1826
drawings: (L) $385; (H) $3,850

NICOLS, Audley Dean
American 20th cent.
paintings: (H) $1,210

NICOT, Louis Henri
sculpture: (H) $2,090

NICZKY, Eduard
German 1850-1919
paintings: (L) $550; (H) $8,800

NIEDECKEN, George Mann
drawings: (L) $275; (H) $16,500

NIEDECKEN, George Mann and office
of Frank Lloyd WRIGHT
drawings: (L) $990; (H) $1,980

NIEDMANN, Erich
paintings: (H) $660

NIELSEN, Amaldus Clarin
Norwegian b. 1838
paintings: (H) $18,700

NIELSEN, Carl
Norwegian 1848-1908
paintings: (H) $1,650

NIELSEN, Kay
b. Denmark 1886-1957
drawings: (L) $715; (H) $19,800

NIELSON, Peter
American 20th cent.
paintings: (L) $357; (H) $15,400

NIEMAN, Leroy
American 20th cent.
drawings: (H) $770

NIEMANN, Edmund E.
American b. 1909
paintings: (H) $990

NIEMANN, Edmund John
British 1813-1876
paintings: (L) $176; (H) $16,500
drawings: (H) $110

NIEMANN, Edward H.
British 19th cent.
paintings: (H) $4,125

NIEMANN, J.
paintings: (H) $880

NIEMEYER, John Henry
American 1839-1932
paintings: (L) $1,870; (H) $14,300
drawings: (H) $200

NIEMIRSKI, N.
Polish 20th cent.
paintings: (H) $1,320

NIEPOLD, Frank
American b. 1890
paintings: (L) $825; (H) $1,430

NIERMAN, Leonardo
Mexican b. 1932
paintings: (L) $132; (H) $2,860

NIETO, Anselmo Miguel
paintings: (H) $770

NIETO, Rodolfo
Mexican b. 1936-1988
paintings: (L) $990; (H) $14,300
drawings: (L) $4,950; (H) $6,600

NIEULANDT, Willem van
paintings: (H) $4,400
drawings: (H) $2,200

NIEULANDT, Willem van, II
paintings: (H) $28,600

NIGG, Joseph
Austrian 1782-1863
paintings: (L) $3,740; (H) $44,000

NIGHTENGALE, Basil
British 1864-1940
drawings: (H) $5,280

NIGHTINGALE, Robert
British 1815-1895
paintings: (H) $4,180

NIJLAND, Gesina Christina
Dutch b. 1937
paintings: (H) $660

NIKICH, Anatol
Russian b. 1918
paintings: (L) $1,320; (H) $1,430

NIKUTOWSKI, Arthur
German 1830-1888
paintings: (H) $1,760

NILES, D.E.
American 19th cent.
paintings: (H) $990

NILES, George E.
American 1837-1898
paintings: (L) $220; (H) $1,100

NILSON, Johann Jacob
drawings: (H) $3,300

NILSSON, Gladys
contemporary
drawings: (L) $660; (H) $1,980

NILSSUN, R.E.
Scandinavian 20th cent.
paintings: (H) $800

NINO, Carmelo
Venezuelan b. 1951
paintings: (L) $3,850; (H) $6,600

NINVILLE, F. de
French (?) 19th cent.
paintings: (H) $990

NINVILLE, J. de
paintings: (H) $770

NISBET, Noel Laura
British 1887-1956
paintings: (H) $1,320

NISBET, Pollok Sinclair
British 1848-1922
paintings: (H) $1,870
drawings: (L) $715; (H) $2,750

NISBET, Robert Buchanan
Scottish b. 1857
paintings: (L) $1,100; (H) $2,200
drawings: (H) $935

NISBET, Robert H.
American 1879-1961
paintings: (L) $88; (H) $22,000
drawings: (L) $110; (H) $880

NISINI, G.
sculpture: (H) $1,100

NISSL, Rudolf
Austrian 1870-1955
paintings: (L) $1,650; (H) $4,950

NITTIS, Giuseppe de
Italian 1846-1884
paintings: (L) $3,025; (H) $440,000
drawings: (H) $4,400

NIXON, W.R.
British 19th cent.
paintings: (H) $1,200

NIXON, Warren
American 1793-1872
drawings: (H) $6,270

NOAILLES, Marie Laure de
drawings: (H) $2,420

NOBLE, John
American 1874-1935
paintings: (L) $300; (H) $1,320

NOBLE, John Sargeant
English 1848-1896
paintings: (L) $7,700; (H) $24,200

NOBLE, Matthew
English 19th cent.
sculpture: (H) $1,100

NOBLE, Robert
British ac. 1821-1860
paintings: (H) $3,850

NOBLE, Thomas S.
American 1835-1907
paintings: (H) $3,575

NOBLE, W.R.
English School 19th cent.
paintings: (H) $2,310

NOBLE, Will P.
American 19th cent.
paintings: (H) $660

NOCCHI, Bernardino
Italian 1741-1812
drawings: (L) $462; (H) $1,430

NOCK, F.
American 19th/20th cent.
sculpture: (H) $2,750

NODRICK, J.
American
paintings: (H) $1,100

NOE, Luis Felipe
Argentinian b. 1933
paintings: (L) $12,100; (H) $17,600

NOEL
contemporary
paintings: (H) $1,760

NOEL, A.J.
French or English 19th cent.
paintings: (H) $1,980

NOEL, Alexandre Jean
French 1752-1834
drawings: (L) $2,750; (H) $5,225

NOEL, Georges
French b. 1924
drawings: (L) $385; (H) $1,430

NOEL, J. (Jules Achille?)
French 1815-1881
paintings: (H) $770

NOEL, John Bates
English 19th cent.
paintings: (H) $743

NOEL, Jules Achille
French 1813/15-1881
paintings: (L) $330; (H) $24,200

NOELSMITH, Thomas
British 19th cent.
drawings: (L) $467; (H) $1,320

NOERR, Julius
German 1827-1897
paintings: (L) $4,400; (H) $7,150

NOGTOGAAL, J.F.
paintings: (H) $660

NOGUCHI, Isamu
American 1904-1988
sculpture: (L) $7,975; (H) $632,500

NOHEIMER, Mathias
American 20th cent.
paintings: (L) $3,080; (H) $3,080

NOLAN, Sidney
Australian b. 1917
paintings: (L) $3,300; (H) $6,050

NOLAND, Kenneth
American b. 1924
paintings: (L) $1,320; (H) $2,035,000
drawings: (L) $2,200; (H) $20,900

NOLDE, Emil
German 1867-1956
paintings: (L) $396,000; (H) $935,000
drawings: (L) $412; (H) $170,500

NOLF, John T.
1871-1954
paintings: (L) $484; (H) $687

NOLLE, Lambert
French 19th cent.
paintings: (H) $3,575

NOLPE, Pieter
Dutch 1613/14-1652/53
paintings: (H) $27,500

NOLTEN, M.
German 19th cent.
paintings: (H) $7,700

NONI, Luigi
Italian 19th cent.
paintings: (H) $2,310

NONNENBRUCH, Max
German 1857-1922
paintings: (L) $10,175; (H) $14,300

NONNOTTE, Donat
Italian 1708-1785
paintings: (L) $2,200; (H) $27,500

NONO, Luici
Italian
paintings: (H) $825

NOOMS, Reinier, called ZEEMAN
c. 1623-before 1667
paintings: (H) $13,200

NOORDT, Joannes van
Dutch 1620-1676
paintings: (H) $16,500

NOORT, Adam van
paintings: (L) $11,000; (H) $13,200

NOORT, Adrianus Cornelis van
Dutch b. 1914
paintings: (L) $825; (H) $4,950
drawings: (H) $330

NOORT, Jan van
paintings: (L) $990; (H) $990

NORBERT, Fridrich
paintings: (H) $1,430

NORDALM, Federico
Nicaraguan b. 1949
paintings: (L) $1,650; (H) $17,600

NORDELL, Carl J.
Danish/American b. 1885
paintings: (L) $302; (H) $4,125

NORDENBERG, Bengt
Swedish 1822-1902
paintings: (L) $17,600; (H) $39,600

NORDENBERG, Hendrik
paintings: (H) $9,350

NORDFELDT, Bror Julius Olsson
Swedish/American 1878-1955
paintings: (L) $715; (H) $33,000
drawings: (L) $82; (H) $3,740

NORDGREN, Anna
paintings: (H) $1,760

NORDGREN, Axel
Swedish 1828-1888
paintings: (L) $357; (H) $2,860

NORDHAUSEN, August Henry
American b. 1901
paintings: (L) $1,540; (H) $2,860
drawings: (H) $66

NORDIN, Alice Maria
sculpture: (H) $2,750

NORDSTROM, Carl
American 1876-1934
paintings: (L) $330; (H) $2,420
drawings: (L) $137; (H) $495

NORILY, Peter
English 19th/20th cent.
paintings: (H) $935

NORLING, Barry
sculpture: (H) $9,900

NORMANN, Adelsteen, or
NORMAND
Norwegian 1848-1918
paintings: (L) $990; (H) $19,250

NORMIL, Andre
Haitian 20th cent.
paintings: (L) $1,320; (H) $1,320

NORRETRANDERS, Johannes Carl
Ferdinand
  Danish b. 1871
  paintings: (H) $9,350
NORRIS, C.D.
  paintings: (H) $4,950
NORRIS, Walter S.
  American
  paintings: (H) $1,320
NORRMAN, Herman
  paintings: (H) $1,650
NORTH, Noah
  American 1809-1880
  paintings: (H) $39,600
NORTHCOTE, James
  paintings: (L) $660; (H) $14,300
NORTHCOTE, James
  American 1822-1904
  paintings: (L) $495; (H) $1,100
NORTHCOTE, James
  English 1746-1831
  paintings: (H) $1,650
  drawings: (H) $6,600
NORTHCOTE, Joseph
  American
  paintings: (H) $2,090
NORTHEN, Adolf
  German 1828-1876
  paintings: (H) $4,675
NORTON, Benjamin Cam
  British 1835-1900
  paintings: (L) $2,750; (H) $4,950
NORTON, Elizabeth
  American b. 1887
  sculpture: (H) $2,970
NORTON, Louis Dyle
  American b. 1867
  paintings: (L) $605; (H) $715
  drawings: (H) $77
NORTON, R.
  German late 19th cent.
  paintings: (H) $1,320
NORTON, William Edward
  American 1843-1916
  paintings: (L) $121; (H) $7,150
  drawings: (L) $550; (H) $3,025

NORWAG, J.
  German 19th cent.
  paintings: (H) $1,155
NOSSAL, J.
  Dutch 19th/20th cent.
  paintings: (H) $1,320
NOTER, David Emil Joseph de
  Belgian 1825-1880/1900
  paintings: (L) $7,150; (H) $15,400
NOTER, David Emil Joseph de and
Jules Adolphe GOUPIL
  Belgian
  paintings: (H) $27,500
NOTER, David Emile Joseph de
  French 1825-1887
  paintings: (L) $3,960; (H) $18,700
NOTER, David de
  Belgian 1825-1912
  paintings: (H) $8,800
NOTER, Louis de
  Flemish 19th cent.
  paintings: (H) $1,320
NOTERMAN, Emmanuel
  Flemish 1808-1863
  paintings: (L) $605; (H) $7,700
NOTERMAN, Zacharias
  Belgian 1820-1890
  paintings: (L) $990; (H) $8,525
NOTT, Raymond
  American 1888-1948
  paintings: (H) $247
  drawings: (L) $192; (H) $1,760
NOURSE, Elizabeth
  American 1859-1938
  paintings: (L) $22,000; (H) $82,500
  drawings: (L) $550; (H) $44,000
NOUY, Jean du
  sculpture: (L) $990; (H) $1,925
NOVAK, Ernst
  paintings: (H) $770
NOVATI, Marco
  paintings: (H) $3,575
NOVELLI, E.
  paintings: (H) $715
NOVELLI, Gastone
  paintings: (H) $7,150

Cincinnati Artist

Elizabeth Nourse (1859-1938) was born in Cincinnati, Ohio, a twin and one of ten children. Her early training was at the Cincinnati School of Design, and she earned her living by painting murals, illustrating magazine articles, and executing pen and ink sketches of private homes. At the age of twenty-eight she sailed to Paris with her older sister Louise, where she studied with Boulanger and Lefebvre at the Academie Julian. They advised her to study and work independently so her fresh creative style would not be lost. She studied with Carolus Duran and Jean Jacques Henner and was soon able to support herself through her painting.

Nourse was known for her strong draftsmanship and masterful handling of light. She worked in oil, watercolor, and pastels; although she painted landscapes, her favorite subjects were peasant women and children. In 1895 she became the first American woman to be accepted as an *associee* in the prestigious Société National des Beaux-Arts. In 1910 the French government bought her painting *Les Volets Clos (The Closed Shutters)* for its permanent collection of contemporary art at the Musée du Luxembourg. She achieved international recognition and exhibited regularly in Europe and the United States. When she died in 1938, the paintings in her studio were given to the Cincinnati Museum of Art. In 1983 the Smithsonian Institution and the Cincinnati Art Museum mounted a retrospective of her work. Prices for her drawings and paintings rose sharply after the show. (Elizabeth Nourse, *Le Baiser*, pastel and charcoal on paper laid down on board, 13 x 14 in., Doyle, December 7, 1989, $28,600)

NOVELLI, Pietro Antonio
  drawings: (L) $330; (H) $4,400

NOVELLI, Pietro Antonio, III
  1729-1804
  paintings: (L) $3,300; (H) $14,300
  drawings: (H) $1,980

NOVELLI, Rudolfo
  American b. 1879
  paintings: (H) $1,320

NOVILLE, Fr.
  paintings: (H) $2,640

NOVO, Stefano
  Italian b. 1862
  paintings: (L) $248; (H) $52,250

NOVOA, Gustavo
  paintings: (H) $825

NOVOTNY, Elmer L.
  American b. 1909
  paintings: (L) $220; (H) $9,900

NOVROS, David
  American b. 1941
  paintings: (L) $2,200; (H) $25,300

NOVY, Vilibald
  Czechoslovakian late 19th cent.
  paintings: (L) $880; (H) $1,375

NOWAK, Ernst
  paintings: (H) $4,125

NOWAK, Franz
paintings: (H) $770

NOWAK, Franz
Austrian 19th/20th cent.
paintings: (L) $770; (H) $1,100

NOWAK, Wilhelm
German 19th cent.
paintings: (H) $770

NOWELL, Arthur Trevithan
British 1862-1940
paintings: (H) $5,000

NOYER, Philippe
French b. 1917
paintings: (L) $440; (H) $8,250
drawings: (L) $605; (H) $4,125

NOYES, George Loftus
Canadian/American 1864-1951/54
paintings: (L) $220; (H) $25,000
drawings: (L) $55; (H) $3,080

NOYES, George Lufton
American
paintings: (H) $2,750

NUDERSCHER, Frank B.
American 1880-1959
paintings: (L) $247; (H) $8,800
drawings: (L) $187; (H) $550

NUMAN, Hermanus
drawings: (H) $3,300

NUNAMAKER, Kenneth
American 1890-1957
paintings: (L) $17,600; (H) $38,500

NUNCQUES, William Degouve de
Belgian 1867-1935
paintings: (H) $17,600

NUNEZ, Armando Garcia
paintings: (H) $8,800
drawings: (H) $2,860

NUNEZ DEL PRADO, Marina
Bolivian b. 1912
sculpture: (L) $935; (H) $3,300

NUNNS, J.W.
paintings: (H) $770

NUNZIO
contemporary
sculpture: (H) $3,850

NUTT, Jim
American b. 1938
paintings: (L) $6,600; (H) $38,500
drawings: (L) $1,980; (H) $2,475

NUVOLONE, Carlo Francesco
Italian 1608-1661/65
paintings: (L) $12,100; (H) $27,500
drawings: (H) $2,200

NUVOLONE, Giuseppe, called Panfilo
Italian 1619-1703
paintings: (H) $4,950

NUZZI, Mario, called Mario dei Fiori
Italian c. 1603-1673
paintings: (H) $17,600

NYE, Edgar
American 1879-1943
paintings: (L) $110; (H) $3,960
drawings: (L) $82; (H) $357

NYGREN, John
American b. 1940
sculpture: (L) $308; (H) $1,980

NYHOLM, Arvid Frederick
American 1866-1927
paintings: (L) $110; (H) $16,500
drawings: (H) $55

NYL-FROSCH, Marie
paintings: (H) $2,200

NYMEGEN, Dionys van
paintings: (H) $11,000

NYROP, Borge
Danish 1881-1948
paintings: (L) $193; (H) $1,100

NYS, Carl
Belgian b. 1858
paintings: (L) $880; (H) $4,950

O'BOURKE, Terina
American 20th cent.
paintings: (H) $750

O'BRIEN, Smith
American 1868–1952
paintings: (H) $660

O'CONNOR, A.
paintings: (H) $1,650

O'BOURKE, Terina
American 20th cent.
paintings: (H) $750

O'BRIEN, Smith
American 1868-1952
paintings: (H) $660

O'CONNOR, A.
paintings: (H) $1,650

O'CONNOR, James Arthur
Irish 1792-1841
paintings: (L) $550; (H) $22,000

O'CONNOR, John
paintings: (H) $1,540

O'CONNOR, Patrick
Irish 20th cent.
paintings: (H) $660

O'CONOR, Roderick
Irish 1860-1940
paintings: (L) $3,575; (H) $90,750

O'DONNELL, Hugh
English b. 1950
paintings: (L) $5,170; (H) $14,300
drawings: (L) $3,080; (H) $5,500

O'GORMAN, Juan
Mexican 1905-1982
paintings: (L) $7,150; (H) $550,000
drawings: (L) $990; (H) $24,200

O'HIGGINS, Pablo
Mexican b. 1904
paintings: (L) $1,320; (H) $12,100

O'KEEFFE, Georgia
American 1887-1986
paintings: (L) $126,500; (H) $1,800,000
drawings: (L) $33,000; (H) $605,000

O'KELLEY, Mattie Lou
American b. 1908
paintings: (L) $200; (H) $20,900
drawings: (H) $6,050

O'KELLY, Aloysius
Irish/American b. 1850/53
paintings: (L) $770; (H) $9,900
drawings: (H) $1,760

O'MALLEY, Joseph M.
American b. 1903
drawings: (H) $1,100

O'NEIL, George
paintings: (H) $660

O'NEIL, Henry Nelson
British 1817-1880
paintings: (L) $44,000; (H) $55,000

O'NEIL, Rooney
contemporary
paintings: (H) $2,200

O'NEILL, Daniel
Irish 20th cent.
paintings: (H) $11,000

O'NEILL, George Bernard
British 1828-1917
paintings: (L) $3,300; (H) $16,500

O'NEILL, Rose
American 1875-1944
paintings: (L) $523; (H) $1,650
drawings: (L) $302; (H) $6,600

O'SHEA, John
American 1876-1956
paintings: (H) $1,210

O'SHEE, G.P.
drawings: (H) $1,650

O'SICKEY, Joseph B.
American 20th cent.
paintings: (L) $440; (H) $990

O'SULLIVAN, Sean
drawings: (H) $1,210

O'TOOLE, Cathal
American b. 1903
paintings: (L) $275; (H) $2,310

OAKES, Ann T.
ac. 1852-1854
paintings: (H) $880

OAKES, John Wright
British 1820-1887
paintings: (L) $825; (H) $1,320

OAKES, Wilbur L.
American 1876-1934
paintings: (L) $220; (H) $2,970
drawings: (H) $242

OAKLEY, Octavius
English 1800-1867
drawings: (L) $990; (H) $1,155

OAKLEY, Thornton
American 1881-1953
paintings: (H) $9,900
drawings: (L) $38; (H) $550

OAKLEY, Violet
American 1874-1960/61
paintings: (H) $1,870
drawings: (L) $165; (H) $1,100

OBERHAUSER, Emanuel
Austrian 19th cent.
paintings: (L) $8,250; (H) $18,700

OBERMAN, Antonis
Dutch 1781-1845
paintings: (L) $6,875; (H) $8,800

OBERMULLER, F.
Austrian 19th cent.
paintings: (L) $1,760; (H) $4,125

OBERSTEINER, Ludwig
Austrian b. 1857
paintings: (L) $880; (H) $4,950

OBERTEUFFER, George
American 1878-1940
paintings: (L) $1,650; (H) $24,200

OBERTEUFFER, Henriette Amiard
American
paintings: (H) $660

OBIN, Philome
Haitian b. 1892
paintings: (L) $2,750; (H) $46,200

OBIN, Seneque
Haitian 1893-1977
paintings: (L) $1,980; (H) $9,900

OBIOLS, G.
sculpture: (L) $660; (H) $1,760

OBIT, L.
Bohemian 19th cent.
paintings: (L) $302; (H) $770

OBOLENSKY, Conservator Ivan
sculpture: (H) $4,400

OBREGON, Alejandro
Spanish/Colombian b. 1920
paintings: (L) $2,750; (H) $60,500
drawings: (H) $3,850
sculpture: (H) $16,500

OCHOA Y MADRAZO, Raphael de
Spanish b. 1858
paintings: (H) $6,325

OCHTERVELT, Jacob
Dutch 1635-1708/10
paintings: (L) $8,250; (H) $93,500

OCHTMAN, Dorothy
American 1892-1971
paintings: (L) $110; (H) $1,100

OCHTMAN, Leonard
Dutch/American 1854-1934
paintings: (L) $605; (H) $23,100
drawings: (H) $110

OCHTMAN, Mina Fonda
American 1862-1924
paintings: (L) $825; (H) $4,125
drawings: (H) $220

ODAZZI, Giovanni
Italian 1663-1731
paintings: (H) $6,600

ODDIE, Walter M.
American 1808-1865
paintings: (L) $1,650; (H) $3,850

ODER, A.
Russian 19th cent.
sculpture: (H) $880

ODIERNA, Guido
b. 1913
paintings: (L) $55; (H) $715

ODIN, Blanche
French b. 1865
drawings: (H) $660

ODIO, Saturnino Portuondo, Pucho
American b. 1928
sculpture: (L) $220; (H) $1,100

OEDER, Georg
German 1846-1931
paintings: (L) $3,300; (H) $3,520

OEHME, Ernst Erwin
German 1831-1907
paintings: (H) $3,575

OEHMICHEN, Hugo
Dutch 1843-1933
paintings: (H) $1,320

OEHRING, Hedwig
German b. 1855
paintings: (H) $1,210

OELSHIG, Augusta
American 20th cent.
paintings: (L) $220; (H) $1,100

OENICKE, Clara Wilhelmine
paintings: (H) $4,400

OERDER, Frans
Dutch 1866-1944
paintings: (H) $1,650

OERTEL, Johannes Simon
American 1823-1909
paintings: (L) $3,080; (H) $30,800

OERTEL, Wilhelm
German b. 1870
paintings: (L) $825; (H) $2,090

OESER, Friedrich Adam
German 1717-1799
drawings: (H) $2,420

OETS, Pieter
1721-1790
paintings: (L) $1,210; (H) $3,850

OFFER, F. Rawlings
British 19th cent.
paintings: (H) $1,045

OFFERMANN, Fried
sculpture: (H) $1,540

OFFERMANSS, Tony Lodewyk
George
Dutch 1854-1911
paintings: (L) $1,980; (H) $2,090

OFNER, Josef
American b. 1868
sculpture: (H) $11,550

OGDEN, Frederick D.
American 19th/20th cent.
paintings: (L) $200; (H) $660

OGDEN, Henry A.
American 1856-1936
drawings: (L) $220; (H) $3,080

OGE, Pierre
sculpture: (L) $1,870; (H) $2,200

OGIER, M.L.
French b. 1912
paintings: (L) $1,320; (H) $1,430

OGILVIE, Clinton
American 1838-1900
paintings: (L) $104; (H) $15,400
drawings: (H) $275

OGILVIE, John Clinton
British 19th cent.
paintings: (L) $1,650; (H) $6,600

OGUISS, Takanori
Japanese b. 1901
paintings: (L) $52,800; (H) $572,000

OHLSEN, Th.
paintings: (H) $660

OHTAKE, Tomie
Japanese/Brazilian b. 1913
paintings: (L) $3,850; (H) $7,700

OIESTAD, Steven
American
drawings: (H) $1,300

OJEDA, Gustavo
paintings: (H) $4,400

OKADA, Kenzo
Japanese/American b. 1902
paintings: (L) $16,500; (H) $66,000
drawings: (L) $4,400; (H) $28,600

OKADA, Koen
Japanese b. 1919
paintings: (H) $1,870

OKAMURA, Arthur
paintings: (L) $300; (H) $700

OKIMOTO
contemporary
paintings: (H) $2,420

OKULICK, John
contemporary
drawings: (L) $605; (H) $880

OLBRICH, W.
American late 19th cent.
paintings: (L) $220; (H) $825

OLDENBURG, Claes
Swedish/American b. 1929
paintings: (L) $24,750; (H) $34,100
drawings: (L) $3,025; (H) $88,000
sculpture: (L) $8,250; (H) $495,000

OLDFIELD, Fred
paintings: (H) $2,475

OLDFIELD, Otis
American 1890-1969
paintings: (L) $660; (H) $27,500

OLDS, Gary
American
sculpture: (H) $1,700

Pop Art

Pop Art was the name bestowed by English critic Lawrence Alloway on a movement that flourished from the late 1950s to the early 1970s, chiefly in Britain and the United States. Pop Art emphasized the anonymous, mechanized mass-produced objects and popular images of a consumer society promoted in advertisements, billboards, comic books, and packaging, as well as images from television and movies. Pop artists worked in a variety of media–painting, sculpture, collage, and photography.

Based in part on a rejection of Abstract Expressionism, it was immediately accepted by a public that was able to recognize its subject matter–comic-strip panels, press photos, coke bottles, flags, brand-name packages. The subject matter itself sprang from the paintings of Jasper Johns and Robert Rauschenberg, but pop artists substituted commercial art techniques and materials for conventional brushes and paint. Roy Lichtenstein, Andy Warhol, Tom Wesselmann, James Rosenquist, and Claes Oldenburg are the bright lights of Pop Art.

Claes Oldenburg (b. 1929) was the son of a Swedish diplomat and spent much of his childhood shuttling between Sweden and the United States. He graduated from Yale University in 1950 and then enrolled at the Art Institute of Chicago while working part-time as a newspaper reporter and illustrator. By 1960 he had met New York artists Robert Whitman, Jim Dine, Red Grooms, and Allan Kaprow, who were beginning to question the established boundaries between art and life. They initiated a new form of participatory art called "happenings" and "environments." The costumes and props Oldenburg created for the happenings formed the basis for many of his later sculptures.

In 1961, on the Lower East Side of New York, he opened "The Store," where he sold painted plaster replicas of food and other domestic objects, thus becoming one of the initiators of Pop Art. In 1962 he exhibited his first soft sculptures of hard objects. Created on a gigantic scale of sewn canvas stuffed with foam rubber and painted with Liquitex, his soft sculptures of typewriters, bathtubs, hamburgers, and ice cream cones were important sculptural innovations. In 1965 Oldenburg began a series of drawings of proposed monuments such as a colossal peeled banana for Times Square and a gigantic ironing board for New York's Lower Eastside. In the 1970s he created monumental sculptures for popular sites such as the GSA building in Chicago and Yale University.

At Christie's, in November 1989, Oldenburg's giant sculpture of a typewriter eraser, cast in 1977 and one of an edition of eighteen, sold for $253,000. (Claes Oldenburg, *Typewriter Eraser*, aluminum, pigment in concrete and steel, 32 x 35 x 23 in., Christie's, November 7, 1989, $253,000)

OLINSKY, Ivan G.
Russian/American 1878-1962
paintings: (L) $300; (H) $6,600
drawings: (H) $275

OLINSKY, Tosca
Italian/American b. 1909
paintings: (L) $138; (H) $1,980

OLIS, Jan
paintings: (H) $5,225

OLITSKI, Jules
American b. 1922
paintings: (L) $1,650; (H) $352,000
drawings: (L) $660; (H) $8,800

OLIVA, F.
paintings: (H) $2,500

OLIVA, F.
Spanish 19th cent.
paintings: (H) $1,100

OLIVA, F.
Spanish School
paintings: (H) $825

OLIVA Y RODRIGO, Eugenio
paintings: (H) $1,760

OLIVE, Jacinto
Spanish 1896-1967
paintings: (H) $7,700

OLIVEIRA, Nathan
American b. 1928
paintings: (L) $3,300; (H) $28,600
drawings: (L) $880; (H) $19,800
sculpture: (H) $1,320

OLIVER, Charles
American ac. c. 1842-1850
sculpture: (H) $33,000

OLIVER, Emma
paintings: (H) $825

OLIVER, Frederick W.
American b. 1876
paintings: (L) $220; (H) $1,760

OLIVER, J.
British 19th cent.
paintings: (H) $1,900

OLIVER, Thomas Clarkson
American 1827-1893
paintings: (L) $330; (H) $11,000
drawings: (H) $550

OLIVER, William
paintings: (L) $935; (H) $1,760

OLIVER, William
British 1805-1853
paintings: (L) $2,860; (H) $8,520

OLIVER, William
British 1881-1897
paintings: (H) $880

OLIVER, William
English ac. 1867-1882
paintings: (H) $1,320

OLIVETTI, Luigi
Italian 19th/20th cent.
drawings: (L) $247; (H) $2,475

OLIVIER, J.
French School 20th cent.
paintings: (H) $1,980

OLIVIER-MERSON, Luc
French 1846-1920
paintings: (H) $4,400

OLIVIERA, Nathan
contemporary
paintings: (H) $1,760

OLIVIERI, Pietro Paulo
Italian 1551-1599
sculpture: (H) $49,500

OLLER, Francisco
Puerto Rican 1833-1917
paintings: (L) $23,100; (H) $132,000

OLLIVARY, Annette
French 20th cent.
paintings: (L) $770; (H) $1,760

OLLIVIER, Michel Barthelemy
paintings: (H) $8,250

OLSEN, Chr Benjamin
Danish 1818-1878
paintings: (L) $935; (H) $1,870

OLSEN, Christian Benjamin
Danish 1873-1935
paintings: (H) $5,775

OLSEN, Einar
paintings: (H) $1,100

OLSEN, George Wallace
American 1876-1938
paintings: (L) $1,870; (H) $4,125

OLSON, Joseph Olaf
American 1894-1979
paintings: (L) $357; (H) $5,500
drawings: (L) $132; (H) $1,045

OLSON, Thomas
American
drawings: (H) $2,200

OMERTH
sculpture: (L) $385; (H) $825

OMERTH, Georges
French ac. 1895-1925
sculpture: (L) $1,760; (H) $17,600

OMGLEY, W.
British 19th cent.
paintings: (H) $715

OMMEGANCK, Balthasar Paul
Flemish 1755-1826
paintings: (L) $550; (H) $5,500

ONDERDONCK, Robert Jenkins
American 1853-1917
paintings: (L) $2,420; (H) $2,750

ONDERDONK, Julian
American 1882-1922
paintings: (L) $495; (H) $23,100

ONEILL, Rooney
contemporary
paintings: (H) $1,100

ONGLEY, W.
American 19th/20th cent.
paintings: (H) $880

ONGLY, W.
paintings: (L) $357; (H) $660

ONKEN, Karl
German 1846-1912
paintings: (H) $1,100

ONO, Yoko
Japanese/American b. 1933
drawings: (H) $4,400
sculpture: (H) $6,600

ONO, Yoko and KYOKO
drawings: (H) $2,750

ONOFRI, Crescenzio
drawings: (H) $770

ONSAGER, Soren
Norwegian 19th/20th cent.
paintings: (H) $5,225

ONSLOW-FORD, Gordon
paintings: (L) $1,045; (H) $6,600

ONTHANK, Nahum Ball
American 1823-1888
paintings: (L) $825; (H) $2,420

OOLEN, Adriaen van
Dutch d. 1694
paintings: (H) $9,900

OOST, Jacob van, the elder
Belgian 1601-1671
paintings: (L) $5,500; (H) $18,700

OOSTEN, Izaak van
Flemish 1613-1661
paintings: (L) $17,600; (H) $31,900

OPDENHOFF, George Willem
Dutch 1807-1873
paintings: (L) $2,500; (H) $3,740

OPERTI, Albert J.
Italian 1852-1927
paintings: (L) $247; (H) $660

OPHEY, Walter
German 1882-1930
paintings: (H) $4,675

OPIE, John
English 1761-1807
paintings: (L) $825; (H) $8,350

OPIE, Julian
American b. 1936
sculpture: (L) $8,800; (H) $11,550

OPPENHEIM
paintings: (H) $1,100

OPPENHEIM, Dennis
American b. 1938
paintings: (H) $3,300
drawings: (L) $825; (H) $7,700
sculpture: (L) $3,300; (H) $6,600

OPPENHEIM, Edmund
paintings: (L) $275; (H) $2,750

OPPENHEIM, Moritz Daniel
German 1800-1882
paintings: (L) $8,250; (H) $132,000

OPPENHEIMER, Josef
German b. 1876
drawings: (H) $825

OPPENORDT, Gilles Marie
drawings: (H) $2,750

OPSTAL, Gaspard Jacob van and
Others, the younger
17th cent.
paintings: (H) $48,400

ORANGE, Maurice Henri
French 1868-1916
paintings: (L) $1,320; (H) $3,025
drawings: (L) $880; (H) $1,650

ORCHARDSON, William Quiller
Scottish b. 1835
paintings: (H) $5,225

ORD, Joseph Bayas
American 1805-1865
paintings: (H) $13,750

ORDONEZ, Sylvia
Mexican b. 1956
paintings: (L) $1,100; (H) $3,575

ORDONO DE ROSALES, Emmanuele
sculpture: (L) $990; (H) $2,310

ORDWAY, Alfred
American 1819-1897
paintings: (L) $275; (H) $1,210

ORELLI, M. Sykes
paintings: (H) $1,210

ORETTI, A.P.
paintings: (H) $3,300

ORFEI, Orfeo
Italian 19th cent.
paintings: (H) $3,300

ORLANDI, Stefano
paintings: (H) $13,200

ORLEANS, Princess Marie Christine d'
sculpture: (H) $880

ORLEY, Barent van
Flemish 1490/95-1541/42
paintings: (L) $77,000; (H) $77,000

ORLIK, Emil
German 1870-1932
paintings: (L) $495; (H) $5,775

ORLOFF, Chana
Russian/French 1888-1968
sculpture: (L) $1,430; (H) $55,000

ORLOFF, J.
Russian 18th cent.
paintings: (L) $495; (H) $935

ORLOFF, Nicolas Wassilietch
Russian b. 1863
paintings: (H) $880

ORLOV, Igor
Russian b. 1935
paintings: (H) $1,100

ORMISTON, MacGregor
1899-1956
paintings: (L) $605; (H) $950
drawings: (H) $385

ORMSBY, Victor
British 19th cent.
paintings: (H) $15,400

OROPALLO, Deborah
paintings: (H) $3,850

OROZCO, Jose Clemente
Mexican 1883-1949
paintings: (L) $1,980; (H) $93,500
drawings: (L) $605; (H) $26,400

OROZCO ROMERO, Carlos
Mexican 1898-1984
paintings: (L) $6,600; (H) $13,200
drawings: (H) $6,050

ORPEN, Sir William Newenham
Montague
Irish 1878-1931
paintings: (L) $12,100; (H) $104,500

ORR, C.S.
American 19th cent.
paintings: (H) $220
drawings: (H) $1,100

ORR, Elliot
American b. 1904
paintings: (L) $300; (H) $700
drawings: (L) $200; (H) $200

ORR, Eric
contemporary
paintings: (H) $7,150

ORR, George P.
American 20th cent.
paintings: (H) $935

ORRENTE, Pedro
paintings: (H) $4,950

ORROCK, James
paintings: (H) $880

ORROCK, James
British 1829-1913
drawings: (H) $1,045

ORSELLI, A.
drawings: (H) $2,200

ORSELLI, Arturo
Italian 19th cent.
paintings: (H) $11,000
drawings: (L) $2,090; (H) $4,950

ORTADE
German 18th cent.
paintings: (H) $935

ORTIZ, Emilio
paintings: (L) $1,650; (H) $11,000

ORTKENS, Aert, or Pseudo Ortkens
Flemish ac. early 16th cent.
drawings: (H) $38,500

ORTLIEB, Friedrich
German 1839-1909
paintings: (L) $3,960; (H) $15,400

ORTMAN, George
sculpture: (H) $1,540

ORTMAN, George
contemporary
paintings: (H) $1,320

ORZE, Joseph
American
sculpture: (H) $1,980

OS, Georgius Jacobus Johannes van
Dutch 1782-1861
paintings: (H) $27,500
drawings: (H) $8,800

OS, Jan van
Dutch 1744-1808
paintings: (L) $605; (H) $126,500

OS, Marie Maguerite van
drawings: (H) $1,100

OS, Pieter Frederick van
Dutch 1808-1860
paintings: (H) $2,200

OS, Pieter Gerardus van
Dutch 1776-1839
paintings: (H) $6,600
drawings: (H) $1,540

OS-DELHEZ, Henri van
Dutch 1880-1976
paintings: (L) $1,430; (H) $1,540

OSBERT, Alphonse
French 1857-1939
paintings: (H) $4,950

OSBORNE, Elizabeth
contemporary
drawings: (H) $4,400

OSBORNE, William
paintings: (H) $1,980

OSEN, Erwin
drawings: (H) $8,800

OSGOOD, Edward E.
American 1849-1928
paintings: (H) $1,430

OSGOOD, N.
American
paintings: (H) $9,350

OSGOOD, Ruth
American d. 1977
paintings: (H) $1,650

OSGOOD, Samuel T.
American 19th cent.
paintings: (H) $1,320

OSHIVER, Harry James
American b. 1888
paintings: (L) $198; (H) $715

OSINAGHI, J.
Continental 19th cent.
paintings: (H) $1,045

OSKERCK, Robert Ward von
American b. 1855
paintings: (H) $4,125

OSNAGHI, J.
c. 1900
paintings: (H) $3,575

OSORIO, Alfonso
drawings: (H) $1,650

OSSLUND, Helmer Jonas H.
paintings: (H) $3,850

OSSORIO, Alfonso
American b. 1916
paintings: (H) $26,400
drawings: (L) $330; (H) $1,320
sculpture: (H) $6,050

OSSWALD, Eugene
German b. 1879
paintings: (H) $935

OSTADE, Adriaen van
Dutch 1610-1685
paintings: (L) $358; (H) $110,000

OSTADE, Isaac van and Cornelis
ĐUSART
17th cent.
drawings: (H) $4,180

OSTADE, Izaack van
Dutch 1621-1649
paintings: (L) $49,500; (H) $60,500
drawings: (H) $4,400

OSTERLIND, Allan
Swedish 1855-1938
paintings: (H) $3,080

OSTERLIND, Anders
French 1887-1960
paintings: (L) $660; (H) $2,200

OSTERMAN, Karl Emil
Swedish b. 1870
paintings: (H) $1,980

OSTERSETZER, Carl
German 1865-1914
paintings: (L) $500; (H) $5,500

OSTHAUS, Edmund H.
German/American 1858-1928
paintings: (L) $302; (H) $39,600
drawings: (L) $385; (H) $17,600

OSTMAN, Charles
American ac. 1902-1909
paintings: (H) $687

OSTMAN, Lempe
paintings: (L) $385; (H) $3,080

OSTRICAIA
sculpture: (H) $1,540

OSTROWSKY, Sam
American b. 1885
paintings: (L) $55; (H) $880

OSWALD, C.J.
English 19th cent.
paintings: (H) $825

OSWALD, C.W.
paintings: (L) $192; (H) $715

OSWALDO, Carlos
paintings: (H) $1,650

OTIS, Bass
American 1784-1861
paintings: (L) $522; (H) $9,075

OTIS, George Demont
American 1877/79-1962
paintings: (L) $1,540; (H) $30,250
drawings: (L) $550; (H) $4,125

OTIS, Samuel D.
American 1889-1961
drawings: (H) $1,000

OTT, Jerry
American b. 1947
paintings: (L) $1,100; (H) $7,975

OTTE, William Louis
American 1871-1957
paintings: (L) $138; (H) $1,045
drawings: (H) $660

OTTENFELD, Rudolf Otto von
German 1856-1913
paintings: (H) $11,000

OTTER, Thomas P.
American d. 1870
paintings: (L) $275; (H) $1,100

OTTERNESS, Tom
American b. 1952
sculpture: (H) $1,870

OTTERSON, Joel
American b. 1959
sculpture: (H) $14,300

OTTESEN, Otto Didrik
Danish 1816-1892
paintings: (L) $2,200; (H) $68,500

OTTINGER, George
American
paintings: (H) $1,100

OTTINGER, Ken
American b. 1945
sculpture: (L) $2,475; (H) $3,850

OTTMAN, Henri
paintings: (H) $2,860

OTTO, Carl
German 1830-1902
paintings: (H) $1,540

OUBORG, Piet
paintings: (H) $1,430

OUDENDORP, Wilhelmus Cornelius
Chimaer van
Belgian 1822-1873
paintings: (H) $2,750

OUDERAA, Pierre Jan van der
paintings: (H) $3,520

OUDINOT, Achille Francois
French 1820-1891
paintings: (L) $275; (H) $8,800

OUDOT, Roland
French b. 1897
paintings: (L) $302; (H) $9,900

OUDRY, Jacques Charles
French 1720-1778
paintings: (L) $29,700; (H) $55,000

OUDRY, Jean Baptiste
French 1686-1755
paintings: (L) $5,500; (H) $110,000
drawings: (L) $1,870; (H) $46,200

OUREN, Karl
American b. 1882
paintings: (L) $935; (H) $3,575

OURSLER, C. Leslie
American contemporary
paintings: (H) $850

OUTCAULT, R.F.
drawings: (L) $440; (H) $15,400

OUTIN, Pierre
French 1840-1899
paintings: (H) $5,500

OUVRIE, Pierre Justin
French 1806-1879
paintings: (H) $7,425

OVCHINNIKOV, Nikolai
Russian b. 1958
paintings: (L) $8,250; (H) $48,400

OVED, Moshe
1885-1958
sculpture: (H) $5,500

OVENS, Jurgen
Dutch 1623-1678
paintings: (L) $18,700; (H) $66,000

OVERFIELD, Richard
contemporary
drawings: (H) $880

OVERSCHEE, Pieter van
paintings: (H) $4,950

OVIEDO, Ramon
Dominican b. 1927
paintings: (L) $6,050; (H) $13,200
drawings: (H) $5,225

OWEN, Bill
American b. 1942
paintings: (H) $8,250

OWEN, Joel
Scottish (?) 19th/20th cent.
paintings: (H) $770

OWEN, Robert Emmett
American 1878-1957
paintings: (L) $165; (H) $13,200
drawings: (L) $100; (H) $275

OWEN, Samuel
drawings: (H) $990

OWEN, V.H.
American 20th cent.
paintings: (H) $1,870

OWEN, William
British 1769-1825
paintings: (L) $990; (H) $5,500

OWLES, Alfred
Anglo/American b. 1895/98
drawings: (L) $165; (H) $880

OZENFANT, Amedee
French 1886-1966
paintings: (L) $5,500; (H) $220,000
drawings: (H) $39,600

OZIER, Kenneth
American
paintings: (H) $2,640

PAALEN, Wolfgang
Mexican 1905/07-1959
paintings: (H) $52,250
drawings: (H) $7,700

PABST, Charles H.
American
paintings: (H) $6,875

PACH, Walter
American 1883-1958
paintings: (L) $550; (H) $990

PACHECO, Maria Luisa
Bolivian b. 1919
paintings: (L) $1,540; (H) $3,850
drawings: (H) $1,650

PACHECO ALTAMIRANO, Arturo
paintings: (H) $6,065

PACHER, Ferdinand
German 1852-1911
paintings: (L) $4,180; (H) $19,450

PACIA, G.
British 19th cent.
paintings: (H) $1,650

PACINO DE BONAGUIDA
Italian 14th cent.
paintings: (H) $33,000

PACIONI, Celestino
Italian/American b. 1888
paintings: (H) $4,620

PACKER, Frederick Little
American 1886-1956
paintings: (H) $2,200

PACZKA, Ferencz
Hungarian 1856-1925
paintings: (H) $1,650

PADDOCK, Ethel Louise
American b. 1887
drawings: (L) $165; (H) $935

PADDOCK, Willard
American 20th cent.
sculpture: (H) $715

PADUA
paintings: (H) $3,520

PAEZ, Jose de
Mexican 18th cent.
paintings: (L) $770; (H) $33,000

PAFSET, B.
French 19th/20th cent.
paintings: (L) $9,350; (H) $9,900

PAGANI, Gregorio
Italian 1558-1605
paintings: (H) $3,850

PAGANI, Paolo
paintings: (L) $1,320; (H) $1,980

PAGE, Bernard
English 19th/20th cent.
paintings: (H) $687

PAGE, Charles Jewett
American 19th/20th cent.
paintings: (H) $3,630
drawings: (H) $110

PAGE, Edward A.
1850-1928
paintings: (L) $440; (H) $2,400
drawings: (H) $220

PAGE, Henri Maurice
English ac. 1879-1890
paintings: (L) $1,320; (H) $1,430

PAGE, J.R.
American
paintings: (L) $3,410; (H) $4,180

PAGE, Josephine A.
American 20th cent.
paintings: (H) $935

PAGE, Marie Danforth
American 1869-1940
paintings: (L) $1,320; (H) $1,650
drawings: (H) $88

PAGE, Raymond
paintings: (H) $1,155

PAGE, Walter Gilman
American 1862-1934
paintings: (L) $302; (H) $13,200

PAGE, William
American 1811-1885
paintings: (L) $6,325; (H) $77,000

PAGEDAIEFF, Georges de
drawings: (L) $176; (H) $880

PAGELS, Herman Joachim
German b. 1876
sculpture: (H) $1,980

PAGES, Irene
French 20th cent.
paintings: (L) $110; (H) $1,210

PAGES, Jules
American 1867-1946
paintings: (L) $55; (H) $12,100

PAGES, Jules Francois
American 1833-1910
paintings: (H) $11,000

PAGGI, Giovanni Battista
paintings: (L) $1,650; (H) $5,500

PAGLIACCI, Aldo
Italian b. 1913
paintings: (L) $55; (H) $1,650

PAGON, Katherine Dunn
American b. 1892
paintings: (L) $77; (H) $660

PAICE, George
British 1854-1925
paintings: (L) $330; (H) $2,750

PAIK, Nam June
Korean/American b. 1932
sculpture: (L) $66,000; (H) $110,000

PAIL, Edouard
French b. 1851
paintings: (L) $2,420; (H) $20,900

PAILES, Isaac
French b. 1895
paintings: (L) $440; (H) $2,750

PAILLARD, Victor
French 19th cent.
sculpture: (H) $22,000

PAILLER, Henri
French 20th cent.
paintings: (L) $1,210; (H) $5,060

PAILLET, Charles
French b. 1871
sculpture: (L) $165; (H) $6,875

PAILLOU, Peter
drawings: (H) $990

PAINE, C.B.
American 19th cent.
paintings: (H) $770

PAINE, Dorothy P.
American 19th/20th cent.
drawings: (H) $1,100

PAJETTA, Pietro
paintings: (L) $1,430; (H) $1,650

PALACI, Fran
contemporary
paintings: (L) $880; (H) $1,045

PALACIOS, Alirio
Venezuelan b. 1944
paintings: (H) $12,100
drawings: (L) $6,050; (H) $16,500

PALADINO, Mimmo
Italian b. 1948
paintings: (L) $1,540; (H) $247,500
drawings: (L) $935; (H) $41,800
sculpture: (L) $29,700; (H) $44,000

PALAEZ, Amelia
paintings: (H) $9,350

PALAMEDES, Anthonie
Dutch 1601-1673
paintings: (L) $3,300; (H) $33,000

PALAMEDESZ, Palamedes, I
Dutch 1607-1638
paintings: (H) $25,300

PALAO Y ORTUBIA, L.
Spanish 19th cent.
paintings: (H) $12,100

PALAZZOLO, Carl
paintings: (H) $1,100

PALENCIA, Benjamin
Spanish b. 1902
paintings: (H) $1,320

PALERMO, Blinky, Peter
HEISTERKAMP
German? 1943-1977
paintings: (H) $42,900
drawings: (H) $38,500

PALIN, William Mainwaring
British 1862-1947
paintings: (L) $110; (H) $4,950

PALING, Johannes Jacobus
paintings: (H) $3,025

PALIZZI, Filippo
Italian 1818-1899
paintings: (L) $1,430; (H) $28,600

PALIZZI, Giuseppe
Italian 1810/13-1887/89
paintings: (H) $4,675

PALKO, Franz Xavier Karl
Austrian 1724-1767
paintings: (L) $220; (H) $24,200

PALLA, F.
Italian 19th cent.
sculpture: (H) $2,420

PALLARES, Allustante
Spanish
paintings: (H) $1,980

PALLARES Y ALLUSTANTE, Joaquin
Spanish 19th cent.
paintings: (L) $2,310; (H) $5,500

PALLENBURG, Joseph Franz
sculpture: (H) $935

PALLIERE, Armand Julien
paintings: (H) $7,700

PALLISER, Robert
American 19th/20th cent.
paintings: (H) $1,100

PALM, Anna
Norwegian 1854-1924
drawings: (L) $1,760; (H) $3,410

PALMA, Jacopo, Il Vecchio follower of
paintings: (H) $4,950

PALMA, Jacopo, called Il Giovane
Italian 1544-1628
paintings: (L) $4,400; (H) $16,500
drawings: (L) $2,860; (H) $20,900

PALMAROLI Y GONZALEZ, Vicente
Spanish 1834-1896
paintings: (L) $15,400; (H) $36,300

PALMER, Adelaide
American 1851-1928
paintings: (L) $330; (H) $2,420

PALMER, Cecil
paintings: (H) $880

PALMER, E.W.
American 19th cent.
sculpture: (H) $880

PALMER, Erastus Dow
American
sculpture: (L) $3,300; (H) $4,950

PALMER, Fanny Frances
American 1812-1876
paintings: (H) $715
drawings: (H) $440

PALMER, G.G.
paintings: (H) $2,200

PALMER, Harry Sutton
English 1854-1933
paintings: (H) $462
drawings: (L) $33; (H) $990

PALMER, J.
drawings: (H) $2,090

PALMER, James Lynwood
British 1865-1941
paintings: (L) $3,080; (H) $22,000

PALMER, Leigh
paintings: (L) $330; (H) $880

PALMER, Lynwood and Claude
PRESCOTT
paintings: (H) $1,320

PALMER, Pauline
American 1865-1938
paintings: (L) $247; (H) $45,100
drawings: (H) $165

PALMER, Samuel
British 1805-1881
drawings: (L) $23,100; (H) $187,000

PALMER, Walter Launt
American 1854-1932
paintings: (L) $2,200; (H) $143,000
drawings: (L) $1,430; (H) $13,200

PALMER, William
American
paintings: (H) $6,600

PALMER, William C.
American b. 1906
paintings: (L) $88; (H) $1,210

PALMERO
paintings: (H) $1,100

PALMESHOFER, Ant.
paintings: (L) $770; (H) $880

PALMEZZANO, Marco
Italian 1458/63-1539
paintings: (H) $29,700

PALMIER, R.
sculpture: (H) $715

PALMIERI, Pietro Giacomo
drawings: (L) $1,210; (H) $1,980

PALMORE, Tom
paintings: (L) $220; (H) $770

PALTRONIERI, Pietro
Italian 1673-1741
drawings: (H) $104,500

PALUMBO, Alphonse
American b. 1890
paintings: (L) $660; (H) $5,500

PALUMBO, L.
European 19th/20th cent.
paintings: (H) $1,320

PALUSKY, Robert
contemporary
sculpture: (H) $825

PANCOAST, Morris Hall
American b. 1877
paintings: (L) $385; (H) $6,050

PANCORBO, Alberto
Colombian b. 1956
paintings: (L) $11,000; (H) $13,200

PANDIANI, Antonio
Italian ac. late 19th cent.
sculpture: (L) $1,650; (H) $2,200

PANESCH, Hermine
Austrian 19th/20th cent.
paintings: (H) $1,430

PANFILI, Pio
drawings: (H) $1,650

PANINI
Continental School 18th cent.
drawings: (H) $880

PANK, Arthur A.
paintings: (H) $1,100

PANNETT, R.
drawings: (H) $4,950

PANNINI, Giovanni Paolo
Italian 1691/92-1765
paintings: (L) $9,900; (H) $275,000
drawings: (H) $5,170

PANNINI, Giovanni Paolo, and studio
Italian 18th cent.
paintings: (H) $44,000

PANORIOS, K.
Greek 19th/20th cent.
paintings: (H) $3,520

PANSING, Fred
American ac. c. 1818
paintings: (L) $1,045; (H) $44,000

PANTON, Alexander
British
paintings: (H) $1,045

PANZA, Giovanni
Italian 19th cent.
paintings: (H) $2,750

PANZANO MASTER
paintings: (H) $44,000

PAOLETTI, Antonio Ermolao
Italian 1834-1912
paintings: (L) $880; (H) $18,700

PAOLINI, Giulio
Italian b. 1940
sculpture: (H) $35,750

PAOLINI, Pietro
Italian 1603/05-1681/82
paintings: (L) $8,250; (H) $46,200

PAOLO DA VISSO
Italian ac. 1437-1481
paintings: (H) $46,200

PAOLOZZI, Eduardo
British b. 1924
sculpture: (L) $770; (H) $44,000

PAPA, R.
sculpture: (H) $825

PAPALOGER, L.
paintings: (H) $1,320

PAPALUCA, L.
paintings: (L) $770; (H) $1,650
drawings: (H) $2,750

PAPALUCA, L.
Italian 1842-1912
paintings: (L) $220; (H) $990
drawings: (L) $250; (H) $950

PAPART, Max
French b. 1911
paintings: (L) $935; (H) $4,675

PAPE, Abraham de
Dutch 1620-1666
paintings: (H) $41,800

PAPE, C.
French 19th/20th cent.
paintings: (H) $935

PAPE, Eric
American 1870-1938
paintings: (L) $275; (H) $12,100
drawings: (L) $302; (H) $5,500

PAPE, Frank C.
drawings: (H) $1,650

PAPE, Friedrich Edouard
German 1817-1905
paintings: (H) $6,600

PAPELEN, Victor de
French 1810-1881
paintings: (H) $4,950

PAPPAS, John
sculpture: (L) $192; (H) $880

PAPPERITZ, Fritz Georg
paintings: (H) $3,520

PARADES, Vicenta de
Spanish 19th cent.
paintings: (H) $4,400

PARADISE, Phil
American b. 1905
paintings: (H) $1,100
drawings: (L) $990; (H) $1,430

PARAPARNT, Th.
paintings: (H) $990

PAREDES, Vicenta de
Spanish 19th cent.
paintings: (L) $1,650; (H) $16,500
drawings: (L) $385; (H) $1,000

PARENT, Leon
French b. 1869
paintings: (H) $1,485

PARENTINO, Bernardino, called
Bernardin Parecan
Italian 1437-1531
paintings: (H) $8,800
drawings: (L) $3,575; (H) $74,800

PARIS, Alfred Jean Marie
French 1846-1908
drawings: (H) $4,620

PARIS, Camille Adrien
French 1834-1901
paintings: (H) $33,000

PARIS, George de
French 1829-1911
drawings: (H) $2,750

PARIS, Harold Persico
American b. 1925
drawings: (L) $990; (H) $1,320

PARIS, Pierre Adrien
1745-1819
drawings: (H) $700

PARIS, Rene
French b. 1881
sculpture: (L) $2,310; (H) $6,600

PARIS, Roland
German b. 1894
sculpture: (L) $825; (H) $3,575

PARIS, Walter
American 1842-1906
drawings: (L) $165; (H) $8,800

PARIZEAU, Philippe Louis
French 1740-1801
drawings: (L) $4,950; (H) $4,950

PARK, David
American 1911-1960
paintings: (L) $13,200; (H) $110,000
drawings: (L) $1,760; (H) $9,350

PARK, John Anthony
British 1888-1962
paintings: (L) $275; (H) $1,100

PARK, Patric
Scottish 1811-1855
sculpture: (H) $3,080

PARK, Richard Henry
American b. 1932
sculpture: (L) $880; (H) $13,200

PARK, Roswell
American 1807-1869
drawings: (H) $19,800

PARK, Stuart
British 1862-1933
paintings: (L) $400; (H) $1,430

PARKER, Bill
American b. 1922
paintings: (H) $3,300

PARKER, C.R.
paintings: (H) $2,200

PARKER, Cora
American
paintings: (H) $770

PARKER, George Waller
American 1888-1957
paintings: (L) $247; (H) $660

PARKER, H.E.
British 19th cent.
paintings: (H) $935

PARKER, Henry H.
English 1858-1930
paintings: (L) $330; (H) $8,525
drawings: (H) $88

PARKER, Henry Perlee
British 1785-1873
paintings: (H) $22,000

PARKER, John Adams
American 1829-c. 1905
paintings: (L) $1,320; (H) $2,750

PARKER, Lawton S.
American 1868-1954
paintings: (L) $413; (H) $198,000
drawings: (L) $220; (H) $1,430

PARKER, Ray
American b. 1922
paintings: (L) $198; (H) $6,600

PARKER, W.
British 19th cent.
paintings: (H) $990

PARKHURST
19th cent.
paintings: (H) $770

PARKHURST, Charles S.
American ac. 1880-1890
paintings: (H) $1,320

PARKHURST, Clifford Eugene
American
drawings: (H) $825

PARKHURST, Daniel
American b. 19th cent.
paintings: (H) $1,980

PARKHURST, E.W.
American 19th cent.
paintings: (H) $880

PARKHURST, Thomas
American 1853-1923
paintings: (H) $1,320

PARKS, Bob
sculpture: (L) $715; (H) $1,100

PARKS, Joel
American 19th cent.
paintings: (L) $9,900; (H) $14,300

PARKS, Madeleine
American
sculpture: (H) $2,860

PARKS (?), Ross
paintings: (H) $880

PARMANTIO, O.
sculpture: (H) $990

PARMENTER, Ramon
sculpture: (L) $4,290; (H) $4,290

PARMIGIANO, IL, Girolano Francesco
Maria MAZZOLA
Italian 1503-1540
paintings: (L) $3,300; (H) $286,000

PAROLARI, G.
drawings: (H) $2,090

PARRA, Carmen
Mexican b. 1944
paintings: (H) $15,400

PARRA, Gines
Spanish 1895-1960
paintings: (L) $880; (H) $880

PARRA, Jose Felipe
Spanish 19th cent.
paintings: (H) $4,400

PARRASIO, Micheli
Italian 1516-1578
paintings: (L) $2,860; (H) $3,300

PARRISH, David
American b. 1939
paintings: (H) $14,300

PARRISH, Maxfield
American 1870-1966
paintings: (L) $2,090; (H) $220,000
drawings: (L) $825; (H) $4,950

PARRISH, Stephen
American 1846-1938
paintings: (L) $825; (H) $5,500

PARROCEL, Charles
French 1688-1752
paintings: (H) $9,900
drawings: (L) $2,200; (H) $15,400

PARROCEL, Joseph
paintings: (H) $11,000

PARROCEL, Pierre
drawings: (H) $880

PARROCELL, Joseph
paintings: (H) $3,300

PARROT, Philippe
French 1831-1894
paintings: (H) $110,000

PARROT-LECOMTE, Philippe
French 19th cent.
paintings: (H) $1,870

PARROTT, William Samuel
American 1844-1915
paintings: (L) $605; (H) $4,675
drawings: (H) $357

PARRSINI, Guisi
paintings: (H) $1,540

PARSHALL, De Witt
American 1864-1956
paintings: (L) $330; (H) $1,650
drawings: (L) $247; (H) $770

PARSHALL, Douglas
American b. 1899
paintings: (L) $467; (H) $4,125
drawings: (L) $220; (H) $495

PARSONS, Alfred William
English 1847-1920
paintings: (H) $4,070
drawings: (L) $137; (H) $2,420

PARSONS, Arthur Wilde
British 1854-1931
drawings: (L) $550; (H) $1,760

PARSONS, Beatrice
English 1870-1955
drawings: (L) $418; (H) $3,740

PARSONS, Betty B.
American 20th cent.
paintings: (H) $1,045
drawings: (H) $165
sculpture: (L) $275; (H) $2,200

PARSONS, Edith Baretto Stevens
American 1878-1956
sculpture: (L) $220; (H) $33,000

PARSONS, Francis
British d. 1804
paintings: (H) $770

PARSONS, J.W.
American
paintings: (H) $990

PARSONS, John F.
British ac. 1880's
drawings: (H) $6,600

PARSONS, Marion
American 1880-1953
paintings: (L) $990; (H) $3,025

PARSONS, Orrin Sheldon
American 1866/68-1943
paintings: (L) $165; (H) $30,250

PARTINGTON, Richard Langtry
American 1868-1929
paintings: (L) $385; (H) $3,575
drawings: (L) $83; (H) $3,960

PARTON, Arthur
American 1842-1914
paintings: (L) $247; (H) $8,800

PARTON, Ernest
American 1845-1933
paintings: (L) $248; (H) $6,050
drawings: (H) $88

PARTON, Henry W.
American
paintings: (L) $605; (H) $935

PARTON, J.
paintings: (L) $770; (H) $1,045

PARTON, Professor B.
British 19th/20th cent.
paintings: (H) $2,750

PARTRIDGE, H.T.
English 19th cent.
paintings: (H) $797

PARTRIDGE, Joseph
American 1792-1833
drawings: (H) $6,600

PARTRIDGE, William H.
American b. 1858
paintings: (L) $33; (H) $1,155

PARTRIDGE, William Ordway
American 1861-1930
sculpture: (L) $550; (H) $3,520

PARYS, A.
French 19th cent.
drawings: (H) $7,150

PASCAL
sculpture: (H) $1,650

PASCAL, P.
French b. 1896
drawings: (H) $825

PASCAL, Paul
French
drawings: (H) $2,145

PASCAL, Paul
French 1832-1903
paintings: (H) $605
drawings: (L) $192; (H) $1,760

PASCAL, Paul
French b. 1867
paintings: (H) $715
drawings: (L) $440; (H) $1,760

PASCAL, Paul B.
drawings: (L) $715; (H) $825

PASCALIS, Louise
French 1893-1934
paintings: (H) $1,100

PASCHKE, Ed
American b. 1939
paintings: (L) $9,900; (H) $34,100

PASCIN, Jules
French/American 1885-1930
paintings: (L) $27,500; (H) $451,000
drawings: (L) $110; (H) $137,500

PASCOE, William
British 19th cent.
paintings: (L) $715; (H) $990

PASCUTTI, Antonio
Austrian 19th cent.
paintings: (L) $1,500; (H) $2,090

PASENE, L.
sculpture: (H) $6,875

PASINELLI, Lorenzo
paintings: (H) $1,100

PASINI, A.
paintings: (H) $660

PASINI, A.
European 20th cent.
paintings: (H) $1,100

PASINI, Alberto
Italian 1826-1899
paintings: (L) $3,300; (H) $198,000
drawings: (L) $880; (H) $3,300

PASKELL, William Frederick
American 1866-1951
paintings: (L) $83; (H) $1,320
drawings: (L) $49; (H) $900

PASMORE, F.G.
British 19th cent.
paintings: (L) $990; (H) $2,200

PASMORE, J.F.
paintings: (H) $990

PASS(?), C.
paintings: (H) $825

PASSANI, R.
sculpture: (H) $4,125

PASSARELLI, Carlo
paintings: (H) $1,100

PASSAROTTI, Bartolomeo
Italian 1529-1592
paintings: (H) $396,000
drawings: (L) $5,500; (H) $13,200

PASSAROTTI, Tiburzio
c. 1555-1612
drawings: (H) $29,700

PASSAVANT, Lucile
French b. 1910
sculpture: (H) $3,520

PASSERI, Giuseppe
Italian 1654-1714
drawings: (L) $1,650; (H) $9,350

PASSET, Gerard
French b. 1936
paintings: (L) $1,540; (H) $2,530

PASSEY, Charles H.
British 19th cent.
paintings: (L) $412; (H) $2,310

PASSINI, Ludwig
Austrian 1832-1903
drawings: (L) $2,200; (H) $20,900

PASTEGA, Luigi
Italian 1858-1927
paintings: (L) $4,675; (H) $7,700

PASTINA, Giuseppe
Italian b. 1863
paintings: (H) $2,475

PASTOUR, Louis
French b. 1876
paintings: (H) $825

PATA, Cherubin
French 19th cent.
paintings: (H) $8,800

PATCH, Thomas
English 1720-1782
paintings: (H) $49,500

PATEL, Antoine Pierre, II
French 1648-1707
paintings: (H) $24,200
drawings: (L) $2,750; (H) $8,800

PATEL, Pierre, the elder
paintings: (H) $4,950

PATELLIERE, Amedee de la
paintings: (H) $8,800

PATER, Jean Baptiste
French 1695-1736
paintings: (L) $28,600; (H) $143,000
drawings: (L) $4,400; (H) $16,500

PATERSON, George M.
English b. 1873
paintings: (H) $990

PATERSON, Mary Viola
American 1899-1982
paintings: (H) $2,530

PATERSSEN, Benjamin
drawings: (L) $880; (H) $1,100

PATI, Gasto
drawings: (H) $4,180

PATIGIAN, Haig
American
sculpture: (H) $9,350

PATIN, Ray
paintings: (H) $3,190
drawings: (H) $3,190

PATINIR, Joachim, workshop of
Flemish 15th/16th cent.
paintings: (H) $99,000

PATKIN, Itzar
Israli/American b. 1965
paintings: (H) $24,200

PATON, Frank
English 1856-1909
paintings: (H) $1,980
drawings: (L) $440; (H) $13,200

PATON, Hubert
American
drawings: (H) $880

PATON, Sir Joseph Noel
British 1821-1901
paintings: (L) $2,750; (H) $4,400

PATRICK, James McIntosh
British b. 1907
paintings: (H) $2,860
drawings: (H) $1,320

PATROFF, Alexandre Andre
paintings: (H) $1,870

PATROIS, Isidore
French 1815-1884
paintings: (H) $4,675

PATROT, Ferdinand
French
sculpture: (H) $1,210

PATTEIN, Cesar
b. Norway ac. 1882-1914 Paris
paintings: (L) $3,850; (H) $16,500

PATTEN, George
British 1801-1865
paintings: (H) $8,800

PATTERSON, Charles Robert
American 1875/78-1958
paintings: (L) $550; (H) $8,250
drawings: (L) $264; (H) $440

PATTERSON, Howard Ashman
American b. 1891
paintings: (L) $1,760; (H) $2,420

PATTERSON, Margaret Jordan
American 1868/69-1950
paintings: (L) $275; (H) $3,025
drawings: (L) $110; (H) $1,540

PATTERSON, Russell
American 1896-1977
paintings: (H) $4,400
drawings: (H) $600

PATTI, Tom
American b. 1946
sculpture: (L) $8,250; (H) $14,300

PATTISON, Abbott
American b. 1916
sculpture: (L) $66; (H) $5,390

PATTISON, Robert J.
American 1838-1903
paintings: (H) $3,300

PATTON, C.E.
paintings: (H) $875

PATTON, Katherine
American
paintings: (H) $880

PATTY, William Arthur
American 1889-1961
paintings: (L) $176; (H) $1,320

PAUL, *J***
18th/19th cent.
paintings: (H) $2,750

PAUL, John
British 19th cent.
paintings: (L) $2,310; (H) $15,400

PAUL, Sir John Dean
English 1755-1852
paintings: (L) $2,420; (H) $18,700

PAULEMILE-PISSARRO
French 1884-1972
paintings: (L) $550; (H) $7,700
drawings: (L) $550; (H) $5,775

PAULI, George Wilhelm
Swedish b. 1855
paintings: (H) $2,200

PAULI, Richard
1855-1892
paintings: (L) $605; (H) $770

PAULIN, Paul
sculpture: (L) $2,200; (H) $3,300

PAULMAN, Joseph
paintings: (H) $1,650

PAULSEN, N. Chr.
Danish 19th cent.
paintings: (H) $2,750

PAULUS, Francis Petrus
American 1862-1933
paintings: (L) $275; (H) $1,210

PAULY, Erik Bogdanffy
Hungarian b. 1869
paintings: (H) $825

PAUSINGER, Clemens von
German 1855-1936
drawings: (L) $1,980; (H) $2,420

PAUSINGER, Franz von
German 1839-1915
paintings: (H) $4,400
drawings: (H) $440

PAUSINGER, Helena Paula von
paintings: (H) $770

PAUTROT, Ferdinand
French 19th cent.
sculpture: (L) $247; (H) $4,950

PAUWELS, H.J.
Belgian 20th cent.
paintings: (H) $935

PAVESI, Pietro
Italian 19th cent.
drawings: (L) $990; (H) $3,575

PAVIL, Elie Anatole
French 1873-1948
paintings: (L) $302; (H) $2,310

PAVLIK, Michael
contemporary
sculpture: (H) $3,080

PAVY, Eugene
French 19th cent.
paintings: (L) $770; (H) $19,800

PAVY, P.
paintings: (H) $1,870

PAVY, Philippe
French 19th cent.
paintings: (L) $2,200; (H) $25,300

PAWLIKOWSKI, Andre
Polish/American b. 1940
paintings: (L) $550; (H) $825

PAXSON, Edgar Samuel
American 1852-1919
paintings: (L) $605; (H) $50,600
drawings: (L) $303; (H) $19,800

PAXSON, Ethel
American 1885-1982
paintings: (L) $110; (H) $2,860
drawings: (L) $55; (H) $247

PAXTON, Elizabeth V.O.
American 1877-1971
paintings: (L) $138; (H) $8,250

PAXTON, William McGregor
American 1869-1941
paintings: (L) $110; (H) $154,000
drawings: (L) $165; (H) $38,500

PAYER, H.
sculpture: (H) $770

PAYNE, Charlie Johnson, called
Snaffles
British 1884-1967
drawings: (H) $27,500

PAYNE, David
British 19th cent.
paintings: (L) $1,980; (H) $4,125

PAYNE, Edgar Alwin
American 1882-1947
paintings: (L) $550; (H) $49,500
drawings: (L) $66; (H) $3,300

Boston School

The years 1910-1930 were the heyday of the Boston School. Led by Edmund Tarbell, an important American Impressionist, artists of the Boston School painted idealized portraits, utilizing Impressionist color, fine draftsmanship, and compositions inspired by the Old Masters. During the same period in New York, members of movements such as the Ashcan School were painting contemporary urban life, depicting tenements and the poor with a vigorous realism. The Boston School ignored the social and economic changes occurring in the world. They studied the effects of light in the open air and in darkened interiors; their interior scenes featured predictable props—antique furniture, copies of Old Master pictures, flower arrangements, and most important, oriental jars, urns, and folding screens.

William McGregor Paxton (1869-1941), a native Bostonian, joined the staff of the Boston Museum School in 1906. He had studied with Gerome at the École des Beaux-Arts and the Academie Julian in Paris, and later under Joseph DeCamp in Boston. Paxton had adopted many of the techniques of the 17th-century Dutch painter Vermeer and was a fine draftsman and painter. By 1906 he was already known for his portraits of fashionable young women. *The One in Yellow* is a typical Boston School portrait; the sitter is stylish and has an aura of intelligence and accomplishment–an idealized embodiment of grace and refinement. (William Paxton, *The One in Yellow*, oil on academy board, 18 x 15 in., Barridoff, August 9, 1989, $104,500)

PAYNE, George S.
American
drawings: (H) $660

PAYNE, Ken
American
sculpture: (H) $1,500

PAYTON, Joseph
British ac. 1861-1870
paintings: (L) $770; (H) $1,100

PAYTON, Waller Hugh
English 1828-1895
paintings: (H) $2,640

PAYZANT, Charles
American 1898-1980
drawings: (L) $495; (H) $2,200

PAYZANT, Claude Louis
American 20th cent.
paintings: (L) $110; (H) $770

PEABODY, Ruth Eaton
American 1898-1967
paintings: (L) $275; (H) $4,675

PEALE, Anna Claypoole
American 1791-1878
paintings: (H) $8,250

PEALE, Charles Willson
American 1741-1827
paintings: (L) $3,740; (H) $451,000

PEALE, Harriet Cany
American 1800-1869
paintings: (H) $660

PEALE, J.
American 19th cent.
paintings: (H) $8,800

PEALE, James
paintings: (H) $660

PEALE, James
American 1749-1831
paintings: (L) $55,000; (H) $181,500
drawings: (H) $2,750

PEALE, Margaretta Angelica
American 1795-1882
paintings: (L) $5,225; (H) $12,100

PEALE, Mary Jane
American 1826-1902
paintings: (L) $2,750; (H) $12,100

PEALE, R.
paintings: (L) $935; (H) $935

PEALE, Raphaelle
American 1774-1825
paintings: (H) $495,000

PEALE, Rembrandt
American 1778-1860
paintings: (L) $2,200; (H) $4,070,000
drawings: (H) $24,200

PEALE, Sarah Miriam
American 1800-1885
paintings: (L) $2,860; (H) $42,900
drawings: (H) $138

PEALE, Titian Ramsey
American 1800-1885
paintings: (H) $2,475
drawings: (L) $33,000; (H) $35,000

PEALE(?), M.J.
paintings: (H) $660

PEAN, Louis Rene
French b. 1875
paintings: (H) $4,675

PEAN, Rene
French 20th cent.
paintings: (L) $2,310; (H) $2,310

PEARCE, Charles Sprague
American 1851-1914
paintings: (L) $192; (H) $57,750

PEARCE, Edgar Lewis
American b. 1885
paintings: (L) $550; (H) $1,100
drawings: (L) $77; (H) $88

PEARCE, L.J.
American contemporary
paintings: (L) $2,200; (H) $2,250

PEARCE, William Houghton Sprague
American 19th/20th cent.
paintings: (L) $132; (H) $1,650

PEARL, Moses P.
American 20th cent.
paintings: (H) $1,650
drawings: (H) $742

PEARLMUTTER, Stella
contemporary
paintings: (L) $550; (H) $687

PEARLSTEIN, Philip
American b. 1924
paintings: (L) $6,050; (H) $57,750
drawings: (L) $660; (H) $19,800

PEARSON, Marguerite Stuber
American 1898-1978
paintings: (L) $110; (H) $28,600
drawings: (L) $55; (H) $330

PEARSON, Mary Martha
English 1799-1871
paintings: (H) $935

PEARSON, Robert
American 19th cent.
paintings: (H) $1,650

PEARSON, William
American 19th cent.
paintings: (H) $715

PEBBLES, Frank M.
American 1839-1928
paintings: (L) $302; (H) $1,650

PECHAUBES, Eugene
French 1890-1967
paintings: (L) $330; (H) $18,700
drawings: (L) $33; (H) $330

PECHE, Dale
American
paintings: (L) $605; (H) $1,210

Detective Work

Charles Willson Peale (1741-1827) was a painter, patriot, museum founder, inventor, naturalist, and father of a distinguished family of artists. As a young boy in Maryland, Peale was apprenticed as a saddlemaker. He began to paint when he was in his twenties and traveled to London to study under Benjamin West. Peale fought in the Continental Army during the Revolutionary War and became a good friend of George Washington, who sat for his friend seven times. Peale painted more than sixty portraits of the President. In 1782, Peale opened America's first art gallery in Philadelphia and displayed his paintings of the leading personalities of the time. Peale fathered seventeen children by three wives; the children of his first wife were named after artists–Rembrandt, Titian, and Raphaelle Peale, also well-known artists.

In 1985 Cape Cod auctioneer Robert Eldred went through the papers of a Massachusetts estate and found mention of a portrait of David Rittenhouse by Charles Willson Peale. After exhaustive research, Eldred unearthed the portrait in a Philadelphia bank vault. David Rittenhouse was a statesman and a patriot and the first director of the United States mint. He was also a skilled clock maker, builder of scientific instruments, and respected scientist. The telescope in the portrait signifies his prominence as an astronomer. Estimated at $200,000-$300,000, the portrait sold to a Michigan collector for $451,000. (Charles Willson Peale, *David Rittenhouse*, oil on canvas, 50 x 40 in., Eldred, March 28, 1986, $451,000)

PECHEUR, Emile
French 19th cent.
paintings: (H) $15,400

PECHSTEIN, Max
German 1881-1955
paintings: (L) $33,000; (H) $440,000
drawings: (L) $165; (H) $57,750

PECK, Charles
American 1827-1900
paintings: (L) $192; (H) $918

PECK, Edith Hogen
American b. 1884
paintings: (H) $1,870

PECK, Fay
paintings: (L) $110; (H) $1,100

PECK, K.
sculpture: (H) $742

PECK, Orrin M.
American 1860-1921
paintings: (L) $165; (H) $2,750

PECK, Sheldon
American 1797-1868
paintings: (L) $7,975; (H) $79,750

PECKHAM, Robert
American 1785-1877
paintings: (L) $1,210; (H) $55,000

PECORARO, Gle.
sculpture: (H) $935

PECRUS, Camille
French 1826-1907
paintings: (H) $935

PECRUS, Charles
French 1826-1907
paintings: (L) $1,400; (H) $2,640

PECZELY, Antal
Hungarian b. 1891
paintings: (L) $192; (H) $715

PEDDER, J.
paintings: (H) $990

PEDERSEN, Finn
contemporary
paintings: (L) $990; (H) $6,380

PEDERSEN, Hugo Vilfred
Danish b. 1870
paintings: (H) $3,575

PEDERSEN, Viggo Christien Frederik Wilhelm
Danish 1854-1926
paintings: (H) $5,500

PEDERSEN-MOLS, Niels
Danish b. 1859
paintings: (H) $17,600

PEDONE, Bartolomeo
Italian 1665-1732
paintings: (H) $16,500

PEDRINI, Domenico
1728-1800
drawings: (H) $1,760

PEDULLI, Federigo
Italian b. 1860
drawings: (L) $850; (H) $1,210

PEEL
paintings: (H) $4,400

PEEL, James
English 1811-1906
paintings: (L) $935; (H) $3,850

PEEL, Paul
Canadian 1861-1892
paintings: (L) $19,250; (H) $121,000

PEELE, John Thomas
Anglo/American 1822-1897
paintings: (L) $440; (H) $16,500

PEETERS, Bonaventura
Flemish 1614-1652
paintings: (L) $1,980; (H) $19,800

PEETERS, Jacob
Flemish ac. 1675-1721
paintings: (H) $17,600

PEETERS, Jan
Flemish
paintings: (H) $14,300

PEIFFER, A.
sculpture: (H) $2,640

PEIFFER, August Joseph
French 1832-1879/1886
sculpture: (L) $440; (H) $2,475

PEIRCE, H. Winthrop
American 1850-1935/36
paintings: (L) $357; (H) $3,080
drawings: (L) $165; (H) $1,540

PEIRCE, Waldo
American 1884-1970
paintings: (L) $302; (H) $8,800
drawings: (L) $468; (H) $3,300

PEISER, Mark
American b. 1938
sculpture: (L) $5,500; (H) $15,400

PEISLEY, John Wilfred
paintings: (L) $770; (H) $880

PEIXOTTO, Ernest Clifford
American 1869-1940
paintings: (L) $247; (H) $3,300

PEIXOTTO, George
American 1869-1937
paintings: (L) $330; (H) $1,430

PELAEZ, Amelia
Cuban 1897-1968
paintings: (L) $9,900; (H) $22,000
drawings: (L) $1,100; (H) $15,400

PELAGI, Pelagio
drawings: (H) $1,320

PELHAM, J.
paintings: (H) $2,860

PELHAM, Thomas Kent
British 19th cent.
paintings: (L) $450; (H) $6,820

PELLAN, Alfred
Canadian b. 1906
paintings: (L) $25,300; (H) $59,400

PELLEGRIN, Honore
French 1800-1870
paintings: (L) $4,400; (H) $10,000
drawings: (L) $4,400; (H) $8,800

PELLEGRINI, Giovanni Antonio
Italian 1675-1741
paintings: (L) $5,500; (H) $66,000
drawings: (H) $3,300

PELLEGRINI, Ricardo
paintings: (H) $2,200

PELLEGRINI, Vincenzo
Italian 1575-1612
paintings: (H) $13,750

PELLEW, John
American 20th cent.
paintings: (L) $209; (H) $935

PELLICCIA, Fernando
Italian
sculpture: (H) $1,650

PELLIGRINI, Giovanni Antonio
Italian 1675-1741
paintings: (H) $198,000

PELOUSE, Leon Germain
French 1838-1891
paintings: (L) $385; (H) $12,100

PELS, Albert
American b. 1910
paintings: (L) $88; (H) $3,410

PELTON, Agnes
German/American 1881-1961
paintings: (L) $33; (H) $27,500
drawings: (L) $286; (H) $4,400

PELUSO, Francesco
Italian b. 1863
paintings: (L) $467; (H) $7,700

PEN, Rudolph
paintings: (H) $935

PENA, Angel
Venezuelan b. 1949
paintings: (L) $3,520; (H) $15,400

PENA, Jose Encarnacion, Soqween
American Indian b. 1902
paintings: (H) $192
drawings: (L) $275; (H) $715

PENA, Tonita, Quah Ah
San Ildefonso 1895-1949
paintings: (L) $357; (H) $2,420

PENALBA, Alicia
Argentinian b. 1918
sculpture: (L) $2,200; (H) $15,400

PENCK, A.R.
German b. 1939
paintings: (L) $7,700; (H) $242,000
drawings: (L) $3,300; (H) $38,500

PENDARIES, Jules Jean L.
sculpture: (H) $3,300

PENDERSEN, Robert Holm
American
paintings: (H) $990

PENDL, Erwin
drawings: (H) $1,430

PENDLETON, William Larned Marcy
American b. 1865
paintings: (H) $5,225

PENFIELD, Anna
paintings: (L) $770; (H) $12,100

PENFIELD, Edward
American 1866-1925
drawings: (L) $825; (H) $3,575

PENLEY, Aaron Edwin
English 1807-1870
drawings: (L) $357; (H) $5,280

PENN, Stanley
Scottish late 19th cent.
paintings: (L) $522; (H) $1,760

PENNACHINI, Domenico
paintings: (H) $2,750

PENNE, Charles Olivier de
French 1831-1897
paintings: (L) $550; (H) $66,000
drawings: (L) $247; (H) $1,210

PENNELL, Eugene Harry
British ac. 1885-1897
paintings: (H) $1,870

PENNELL, Joseph
American 1860-1926
drawings: (L) $132; (H) $14,300

PENNEY, Edwin
drawings: (H) $4,950

PENNEY, Frederick D.
American b. 1900
paintings: (L) $468; (H) $1,540
drawings: (L) $137; (H) $1,100

PENNIMAN, John Ritto
American 1782-1841
paintings: (H) $27,500

PENNINGTON, Harper
American 1854-1920
paintings: (H) $7,150
drawings: (H) $550

PENNOYER, Albert Sheldon
American 1888-1957
paintings: (L) $550; (H) $2,200
drawings: (L) $220; (H) $880

PENNY, Edward
English 1714-1791
paintings: (H) $44,000

PENNY, James
American
paintings: (H) $3,300

PENNY, William Daniel
British 1834-1924
paintings: (H) $2,700

PENOT
sculpture: (H) $770

PENOT, Albert Joseph
French ac. 1910
paintings: (L) $605; (H) $3,850
drawings: (H) $550

PENOT, Jean Valette-Falgores
French 1710-1777
paintings: (H) $88,000

PENTELEI-MOLNAR, Janos
Hungarian 1878-1924
paintings: (L) $143; (H) $1,980

PEPER, In. A.
paintings: (H) $1,100

PEPLOC, Fitzgerald
sculpture: (H) $990

PEPLOE, Samuel John
Scottish 1871-1935
paintings: (H) $46,750

PEPPER, Beverly
American b. 1924
sculpture: (L) $121; (H) $35,200

PEPPER, Charles Hovey
American 1864-1950
paintings: (L) $660; (H) $1,760
drawings: (L) $165; (H) $660

PEPPER, Meta
paintings: (H) $880

PEPPERCORN, Arthur Douglas
British 1847-1926
paintings: (H) $2,090

PERAIRE, Paul Emmanuel
French 1829-1893
paintings: (L) $14,300; (H) $20,900

PERALTA, Franco
drawings: (H) $770

PERALTA DEL CAMPO, Francisco
Spanish 1837-1897
paintings: (L) $8,250; (H) $29,700

PERBANDT, Carl von
American 1832-1911
paintings: (L) $715; (H) $5,225

PERBOYRE, Paul Emile Leon
French 1826-1907
paintings: (L) $1,210; (H) $10,450

PERCEVAL, Don
American 1908-1979
drawings: (H) $6,050

PERCHAUBES, Eugene
French 1890-1967
paintings: (H) $2,750

PERCIVICI-PALLAVICINI, Baron
sculpture: (H) $9,350

PERCY, Sidney Richard
English 1821-1886
paintings: (L) $1,430; (H) $52,800

PERDRIAT, Helene Marie Marguerite
French b. 1894
paintings: (H) $1,430

PEREDA, Raimondo
sculpture: (H) $4,675

PEREIRA, Irene Rice
American 1907-1971
paintings: (L) $440; (H) $10,450
drawings: (L) $55; (H) $1,430
sculpture: (H) $4,125

PERELLI, Achille
Italian/American 1822-1891
paintings: (L) $2,200; (H) $2,750
drawings: (L) $308; (H) $1,320

PERELMAGNE, Vladimir
sculpture: (L) $522; (H) $924

PERETTI, Achille
1847-1923
paintings: (H) $2,200

PEREZ
Spanish 19th/20th cent.
paintings: (H) $2,750

PEREZ, Alonso
Spanish 1858-1914
paintings: (L) $1,100; (H) $46,750
drawings: (H) $2,145

PEREZ, Bartolome
Spanish 1634-1693
paintings: (H) $17,600

PEREZ, C.A.
paintings: (H) $1,430

PEREZ, Cayetano
paintings: (H) $825

PERICONI, Domingo F.
American
paintings: (L) $660; (H) $2,090

PERIGAL, Arthur
paintings: (H) $3,300

PERIGAL, Arthur, Jr.
British 1816-1884
paintings: (L) $1,650; (H) $3,025

PERIGNON, Alexis Joseph
French 1806-1882
paintings: (H) $15,400

PERILLI, Achille
Italian b. 1927
drawings: (H) $1,485

PERILLO, Gregory
American b. 1929
paintings: (L) $440; (H) $2,420
sculpture: (H) $1,540

PERIN, E.**
late 19th cent.
sculpture: (H) $2,200

PERINI, G.
paintings: (H) $2,530

PERKINS, A.
American 19th cent.
paintings: (H) $660

PERKINS, C.R. 'Pa'
American b. 1906
paintings: (H) $1,320

PERKINS, Granville
American 1830-1895
paintings: (L) $55; (H) $14,300
drawings: (L) $154; (H) $3,850

PERKINS, Harley
American b. 1883
paintings: (L) $110; (H) $660
drawings: (L) $495; (H) $550

PERKINS, M.S.
American 19th/20th cent.
paintings: (H) $963

PERKINS, Parker S.
American b. 1862
paintings: (L) $220; (H) $1,400
drawings: (H) $440

PERKINS, Ruth Hunter 'Ma'
American b. 1911
paintings: (L) $935; (H) $3,960

PERL, Karl
Austrian b. 1876
sculpture: (L) $1,320; (H) $1,925

PERLA, L.
paintings: (H) $907

PERLBERG, Friedrich
German 1848-1921
drawings: (L) $880; (H) $4,400

PERLIN, Bernard
American b. 1918
paintings: (L) $880; (H) $11,000
drawings: (H) $385

PERLMAN, Joel
American b. 1943
sculpture: (L) $935; (H) $5,280

PERMEKE, Constant
Belgian 1886-1952
drawings: (H) $2,530

PERNET, Jean Henri Alexandre
French b. c. 1763
drawings: (L) $2,310; (H) $7,150

PERNOT, Henri
sculpture: (L) $770; (H) $1,430

PERRACHON, Andre
French 1827-1909
paintings: (L) $3,080; (H) $4,125

PERRAUD, Jean Joseph
sculpture: (H) $1,870

PERRAULT, Henry
French 1867-1932
paintings: (H) $11,000

PERRAULT, Leon Jean Basile
French 1832-1908
paintings: (L) $600; (H) $55,000
drawings: (H) $990

PERRAULT, Marie
American b. 1874
drawings: (H) $1,210

PERRET, Aime
French 1847-1927
paintings: (L) $522; (H) $15,400

PERRET, Paul C.
sculpture: (H) $4,950

PERRETT, S.
British 19th cent.
paintings: (H) $2,640

PERREY, Julien Auguste
paintings: (H) $1,650

PERRIE, Bertha Eversfield
America 1868-1921
paintings: (L) $1,045; (H) $2,800
drawings: (L) $66; (H) $357

PERRIN, A.F.
paintings: (H) $1,650

PERRIN, Henri
paintings: (H) $2,420

PERRIN, Victor Emile Cesar
paintings: (H) $1,430

PERRINE, Van Dearing
American 1868-1955
paintings: (L) $1,100; (H) $2,200

PERRON, Charles Clement Francis
French 1893-1958
paintings: (L) $2,100; (H) $6,250

PERRONEAU, Jean Baptiste
French 1715-1783
paintings: (L) $2,420; (H) $6,600

PERROT, F.J. Beth
b. 1807
sculpture: (H) $687

PERROTON, Philippe
French b. 1925
paintings: (H) $1,045

PERRUGIA, Plessner
sculpture: (H) $770

PERRY, Clara Fairfield
American d. 1941
paintings: (H) $825

PERRY, Clara Greenleaf
American 1871-1960
paintings: (L) $66; (H) $1,320
drawings: (H) $357
sculpture: (H) $715

PERRY, Enoch Wood, Jr.
American 1831-1915
paintings: (L) $220; (H) $30,800

PERRY, J.
drawings: (H) $1,210

PERRY, Lilla Cabot
American 1848-1933
paintings: (L) $440; (H) $33,000
drawings: (H) $9,900

PERRY, Lisa
sculpture: (H) $2,200

PERRY, Roland Hinton
American 1870-1941
paintings: (L) $22; (H) $8,250

PERRY, W.
English 19th cent.
paintings: (L) $908; (H) $935

PERSAN, Raffy le
paintings: (L) $209; (H) $1,430

PERSOGLIA, Franz Von
Austrian b. 1852
paintings: (L) $2,750; (H) $4,950

PERTAK, Diana Lily
drawings: (H) $715

PERTGEN, Karl Maria
German b. 1881
paintings: (H) $88,000

PERUGINI, Charles Edward
English, b. Naples 1839-c. 1918
paintings: (H) $22,000

PERUZZI, Baldassare
Italian 1481-1536
drawings: (L) $17,600; (H) $66,000

PERZL, L.
German or Austrian 19th cent.
paintings: (H) $1,320

PESAGE, A.
French 19th cent.
paintings: (H) $990

PESENTI, Domenico
Italian 1843-1918
paintings: (H) $2,860

PESKE, Geza
Austrian 1859-1934
paintings: (L) $2,750; (H) $3,300

PESKE, Jean
paintings: (H) $2,420

PESNE, Antoine
French 1683-1757
paintings: (L) $495; (H) $33,000

PETER, Emanuel
19th cent.
paintings: (H) $1,320
drawings: (H) $1,760

PETER, V.
sculpture: (H) $2,750

PETERDI, Gabor
Hungarian/American b. 1915
paintings: (L) $495; (H) $1,540

PETERICH, Paul
sculpture: (H) $6,600

PETERS, Anna
German 1843-1926
paintings: (L) $2,750; (H) $18,700

PETERS, Carl William
American 1897-1988
paintings: (L) $385; (H) $4,950

PETERS, Charles Rollo
American 1862-1928
paintings: (L) $495; (H) $17,600

PETERS, Constance
American 1878-1935
paintings: (H) $1,430

PETERS, Pearl L.
American ac. 1870-1890
paintings: (H) $660

PETERS, Pietronella
Dutch 1848-1924
paintings: (H) $14,300

PETERS, Rev. Matthew William
Irish 1741/42-1814
paintings: (H) $26,400

PETERS, Udo
contemporary
paintings: (H) $2,970

PETERSEN, Edvard Frederik
Danish 1841-1911
paintings: (H) $13,200

PETERSEN, Hans von Ritter
German 1850-1914
paintings: (L) $1,980; (H) $2,200

PETERSEN, Johann Erik Christian
Danish/American 1839-1874
paintings: (L) $2,750; (H) $8,800
drawings: (H) $1,100

PETERSEN, Martin
American b. 1870
paintings: (H) $2,475

PETERSEN, Roland
contemporary
paintings: (H) $1,045

PETERSEN-FLENSBURG, H.
German 1861-1908
paintings: (H) $770

PETERSON, H.
German 19th cent.
paintings: (H) $7,700

PETERSON, Jane
American 1876-1965/68
paintings: (L) $247; (H) $126,500
drawings: (L) $115; (H) $17,600

PETERSON, Margaret, Mrs. O'Hagen
American b. 1902
paintings: (L) $1,980; (H) $3,410

PETERSON, Martin
Danish/American b. 1870
paintings: (H) $5,280

PETERSON, Roland
paintings: (H) $825

PETHER, Abraham
English 1756-1812
paintings: (L) $1,650; (H) $2,860

PETHER, Henry
English ac. 1828-1865
paintings: (L) $9,900; (H) $11,000

PETHER, Sebastian
English 1790-1844
paintings: (H) $3,300

PETIL, C.
drawings: (H) $2,090

PETILLION, Jules
French 1845-1899
paintings: (H) $1,980

PETIT, B.
drawings: (H) $1,320

PETIT, Charles
French ac. 1884-1896
paintings: (L) $3,190; (H) $4,950

PETIT, Corneille
Belgian 19th cent.
paintings: (L) $1,980; (H) $5,500

PETIT, Eugene
French 1839-1886
paintings: (L) $660; (H) $8,250

PETIT DE VILLENEUVE, Claude
French 1760-1824
drawings: (H) $2,420

PETIT-GERARD, Pierre
French b. 1852
paintings: (L) $1,540; (H) $8,800

PETITJEAN, Edmond Marie
French 1844-1925
paintings: (L) $1,430; (H) $16,500

PETITJEAN, Hippolyte
French 1854-1929
paintings: (L) $605; (H) $143,000
drawings: (L) $660; (H) $24,200

PETO, John Frederick
American 1854-1907
paintings: (L) $4,840; (H) $418,000

PETO, John Frederick and H.H. STACY
American
paintings: (H) $9,900

PETRASSI, L.
paintings: (H) $660

PETRAZZI, Astolfo
drawings: (H) $1,650

PETREE, Will H.
paintings: (H) $1,075

PETRELLI, A.
20th cent.
sculpture: (H) $9,900

PETRI, P.
paintings: (L) $132; (H) $1,100

PETRIER
sculpture: (L) $2,860; (H) $4,620

PETRILLI, A.
sculpture: (H) $1,045

PETRILLI, Professor A.
sculpture: (L) $3,630; (H) $7,150

PETRINI, A**
Italian 19th cent.
paintings: (L) $935; (H) $1,210

PETRINIS
paintings: (H) $1,430

PETRO
Hungarian b. 1918
paintings: (H) $687

PETROCELLI, Arturo
Italian b. 1856
paintings: (L) $220; (H) $3,575

PETROSIAN, Rafael
sculpture: (H) $1,100

PETROV, Arkadi
Russian b. 1940
paintings: (H) $7,700

PETRUK, Yuri
Russian b. 1950
paintings: (H) $2,200

PETRUOLO, Salvatore
Italian 1857-1946
paintings: (L) $825; (H) $6,050

PETRY, Victor
American b. 1903
paintings: (L) $220; (H) $1,870

PETTENKOFEN, August Xavier
Carl von
Austrian 1822-1889
paintings: (H) $4,500

PETTER, Franz Xaver
Austrian 1791-1866
paintings: (L) $28,600; (H) $48,400

PETTIBONE, Richard
contemporary
paintings: (H) $3,520

PETTITT, Charles
English 1831-1885
paintings: (L) $137; (H) $11,000
drawings: (L) $165; (H) $440

PETTITT, Joseph Paul
English 1812-1882
paintings: (L) $1,210; (H) $3,300

PETTORUTI, Emilio
Argentinian 1892-1971
paintings: (L) $3,300; (H) $242,000
drawings: (L) $3,575; (H) $115,500

PETTY, George
American
drawings: (H) $2,420

PETTY, Mary
1898-1976
drawings: (H) $1,100

PETUA, Leon Jean
French 1846-1921
paintings: (H) $24,200

PEVSNER, Antoine
French 1884-1962
sculpture: (L) $77,000; (H) $82,500

PEXIOTTO, Ernest Clifford
American
paintings: (H) $880

PEXIOTTO, George
paintings: (H) $880

PEYNOT, E.
sculpture: (H) $2,970

PEYNOT, Emile Edmond
French 1850-1932
sculpture: (L) $1,760; (H) $4,620

PEYRAUD, Frank C.
American 1858-1928
paintings: (L) $330; (H) $4,400

PEYRE
sculpture: (H) $1,760

PEYRE, Raphael Charles
French b. 1872
paintings: (H) $4,400
sculpture: (L) $1,430; (H) $8,250

PEYROL-BONHEUR, Juliette
French 1830-1891
paintings: (H) $2,860

PEYTON, Bertha Menzler
American 1871-1950
paintings: (L) $2,310; (H) $3,300

PEZANT, Aymar
French 1846-after 1914
paintings: (H) $880

PEZZO, Lucio del
contemporary
paintings: (H) $82
sculpture: (L) $770; (H) $7,700

PFAFF, Judy
American b. 1946
sculpture: (L) $30,250; (H) $49,500

PFAHL, Charles
American b. 1946
paintings: (H) $4,125

PFALHER, Georg Karl
paintings: (L) $2,090; (H) $2,090

PFEIFFER, Fritz
American 1889-1960
paintings: (H) $3,630
drawings: (H) $742

PFEIFFER, Heinrich H., Harry R.
American 1874-1960
paintings: (L) $50; (H) $2,090

PFEIFFER, Wilhelm
German 1822-1891
paintings: (L) $3,850; (H) $4,620

PFLUG, Johanes Baptiste
German 1785-1866
paintings: (H) $143,000

PFREDA, R.
Swiss 1840-1915
sculpture: (H) $2,090

PFULLER, Minna
German 1824-1907
paintings: (L) $2,420; (H) $4,950

PHABOUS, A.
European 19th cent.
paintings: (H) $715

PHELAN, Charles T.
American b. 1840
paintings: (L) $352; (H) $675

PHELAN, Ellen
contemporary
paintings: (H) $6,600
drawings: (H) $2,640

PHELAN, Harold Leo
American b. 1881
paintings: (L) $495; (H) $660

PHELPS, Edith Catlin
American 1875/79-1961
paintings: (L) $138; (H) $5,500

PHELPS, William Preston
American 1848-1923
paintings: (L) $440; (H) $2,860

PHILIBERT, Georges and Charles
MARONIEZ
French
paintings: (H) $1,000

PHILIPP, Robert
American 1895-1981
paintings: (L) $50; (H) $20,900
drawings: (L) $99; (H) $3,300

PHILIPPAR-QUINET, Jeanne Charlotte
French late 19th cent.
paintings: (H) $14,300

PHILIPPE, A.R.
sculpture: (H) $1,430

PHILIPPE, Paul
French ac. 1900-1930
sculpture: (L) $1,430; (H) $20,900

PHILIPPE, Paul
Polish ac. 1900-1930
sculpture: (L) $1,210; (H) $5,775

PHILIPPEAU, Karel Frans
Dutch 1825-1897
paintings: (L) $3,300; (H) $7,150

PHILIPPOTEAUX, Henri Felix
Emmanuel
French 1815-1884
paintings: (H) $14,300

PHILIPS, Charles
paintings: (H) $1,540

PHILIPS, James March
drawings: (H) $935

PHILLIP, John
English 1817-1867
paintings: (L) $935; (H) $4,950

PHILLIPP, Werner
American 1897-1982
paintings: (L) $275; (H) $715
drawings: (H) $880

Specialties

Collecting has become highly specialized. Specialty sales include everything an aficionado interested in a sport or subject would want. At golf auctions the most collectible items are clubs, books, balls, and, within the last two years, artwork. The first golf auction was held in 1980 in Scotland by Sotheby's.

There are also specialty museums of every kind. In Far Hills, New Jersey, the United States Golf Association has a museum and library, both open to the public. The museum, which has been in existence since 1938, is located on sixty-two acres of grounds in a large Georgian colonial house. Exhibits include clubs and balls that trace the history of the game, as well as a collection of paintings of golfers and golf scenes, portraits of some of the game's memorable figures, and sculpture. There is even a Rembrandt etching depicting the game of kolven, a precursor of golf. (James March Philips, *Pebble Beach,* watercolor, 14½ x 21½ in., Oliver, June 21, 1988, $935)

PHILLIPPE, P. (Paul?)
French 19th cent.
paintings: (H) $770

PHILLIPS, Ammi
American 1788-1865
paintings: (L) $2,750; (H) $181,500

PHILLIPS, Bert Greer
American 1868-1956
paintings: (L) $1,980; (H) $41,250

PHILLIPS, Charles
paintings: (L) $3,300; (H) $8,250

PHILLIPS, Dorothy Sklar
American 20th cent.
drawings: (H) $825

PHILLIPS, Gordon
American b. 1927
paintings: (L) $440; (H) $6,050
sculpture: (L) $495; (H) $2,860

PHILLIPS, Henry Wyndham
British 1820-1868
paintings: (H) $3,575

PHILLIPS, James
American
paintings: (L) $770; (H) $1,100

PHILLIPS, James March
American b. 1913
drawings: (L) $77; (H) $1,045

PHILLIPS, John Campbell
American 1873-1949
paintings: (L) $220; (H) $3,300

PHILLIPS, Marjorie
American 1894-1985
paintings: (L) $154; (H) $2,420

PHILLIPS, Peter
contemporary
paintings: (H) $220
drawings: (H) $1,045

PHILLIPS, Prof. H.
paintings: (H) $1,320

PHILLIPS, S. George
American 20th cent.
paintings: (L) $385; (H) $9,350

PHILLIPS, Walter J.
Canadian 1884-1963
drawings: (H) $990

PHILPOT, Glyn
English 1884-1937
drawings: (H) $1,760

PHIPPEN, George
American 1916-1966
paintings: (L) $3,000; (H) $9,900
drawings: (L) $1,075; (H) $3,960

PHIPPS
British 19th cent.
paintings: (H) $2,310

PHISTER, Jean Jacques
paintings: (L) $330; (H) $660

PHLIPPEAU, Karel Frans
Dutch 1825-1897
paintings: (H) $4,400

PIANG, J.F.
French 19th/20th cent.
paintings: (H) $1,980

PIATEK, Frank
paintings: (H) $990

PIATTOLI, Giuseppe
1785-1807
drawings: (H) $770

PIAZZETTA, Giovanni Battista
Italian 1862-1754
paintings: (H) $605,000
drawings: (L) $17,050; (H) $50,600

PIAZZONI, Gottardo
American 1872-1945
paintings: (L) $468; (H) $3,850

PICABIA, Francis
French 1878-1953
paintings: (L) $4,400; (H) $528,000
drawings: (L) $275; (H) $495,000

PICABIA, Marie
American
drawings: (H) $660

PICARD, Georges
French b. 1857
drawings: (H) $3,520

PICART, Bernard
drawings: (H) $1,320

PICART, O.
European 20th cent.
paintings: (H) $2,310

PICART LE DOUX, Charles
French 1881-1959
paintings: (L) $440; (H) $1,100

PICASSO, Pablo
b. Spain 1881, d. France 1973
paintings: (L) $1,650; (H) $47,850,000
drawings: (L) $550; (H) $15,400,000
sculpture: (L) $770; (H) $2,750,000

PICAULT, Edouard
French late 19th cent.
sculpture: (L) $528; (H) $3,080

PICAULT, Emile Louis
French ac. 1863-1909
sculpture: (L) $99; (H) $12,100

PICCINELLI, Andrea, called Andrea
del Brescianino
Italian b. c. 1485
paintings: (H) $9,350

PICCINI, Gaetano
ac. 1724-1744
drawings: (H) $825

PICCIOLE, J.
sculpture: (H) $660

PICCIRILLI, Attilio
American 1866-1945
sculpture: (L) $2,200; (H) $13,200

PICENSTEIN (?), H.E.
sculpture: (H) $1,100

PICHE, Henri le
French 19th cent.
paintings: (H) $1,650

PICHETTE, James
paintings: (H) $9,350

PICHLER, Adolf
Hungarian 1835-1905
paintings: (H) $8,250

PICHLER, Rudolf
German b. 1863
paintings: (H) $935

PICHOT, Emile Jules
drawings: (L) $550; (H) $880

PICHOT, Emile Jules
French 19th/20th cent.
paintings: (L) $462; (H) $4,180
drawings: (L) $550; (H) $880

PICHOT, Marie Louise
French b. 1885
paintings: (H) $4,840

PICHOT, Ramon
Spanish 1872-1925
paintings: (L) $247; (H) $6,380

PICILLO, Joseph
contemporary
drawings: (L) $330; (H) $825

PICINICH, C.E.
American
paintings: (H) $935

PICIZYNSKI, E.
20th cent.
paintings: (H) $1,045

PICKENHAGEN
paintings: (L) $935; (H) $990

PICKERSGILL, Richard
paintings: (H) $1,650

PICKETT, Joseph
American 1848-1918
paintings: (L) $2,200; (H) $23,100

PICKHARDT, Carl E., Jr.
American
drawings: (H) $880

PICKNELL, George W.
American 1864-1943
paintings: (L) $385; (H) $1,650

PICKNELL, William Lamb
American 1854-1897
paintings: (L) $5,500; (H) $49,500
drawings: (H) $220

PICKTHORN, A. Nadine
American
drawings: (H) $1,500

PICOLO Y LOPEZ, Manuel
Spanish 1850-1892
paintings: (L) $2,750; (H) $5,225

PICOT, Francois Edouard
French 1786-1868
paintings: (H) $154,000

PICOU, Henri Pierre
French 1824-1895
paintings: (L) $495; (H) $8,250

PIE, Will
paintings: (H) $935

PIEL, Paul
sculpture: (H) $1,760

PIELER, Franz Xavier
Austrian 1879-1952
paintings: (L) $900; (H) $20,900

PIENE, Otto
German/American b. 1928
paintings: (L) $5,280; (H) $11,000
sculpture: (H) $935

PIENEMAN, Nikolaas
paintings: (H) $4,950

PIERCE, Charles Franklin
American 1844-1920
paintings: (L) $55; (H) $1,650
drawings: (L) $66; (H) $632

PIERCE, J.W.
paintings: (H) $2,750

PIERCE, Joseph W.
American 19th cent.
paintings: (H) $1,650

PIERCE, Lucy Valentine
American 1887-1947
paintings: (L) $468; (H) $935

PIERCE, M.W.
American School 19th cent.
drawings: (H) $990

PIERCE, R.E.
American
paintings: (H) $1,000

PIERCE, Waldo
American 1884-1970
paintings: (H) $2,420

PIERON, Henri
paintings: (L) $2,200; (H) $2,640

PIERRE, Jean Baptiste Marie
French 1713-1789
drawings: (L) $11,000; (H) $14,850

PIERRET
paintings: (H) $880

PIERRUGUES, J.
French 20th cent.
paintings: (L) $44; (H) $880

PIERSON, G.
American 19th cent.
paintings: (H) $8,800

PIETA, A.
paintings: (H) $880

PIETA, A.
Italian 19th cent.
paintings: (H) $770

PIETERS, Evert
Dutch 1856-1932
paintings: (L) $550; (H) $46,200

PIETERSZ, Bertus
American 1869-1938
paintings: (L) $110; (H) $990

PIETRI, Pietro dei
drawings: (H) $5,500

PIETRO, Cartaino Di Scarrino
American
sculpture: (L) $195; (H) $2,860

PIETRO DA CORTONA, Pietro
BERRETTINI
Italian 1596-1669
drawings: (L) $1,430; (H) $9,350

PIETRONI, Antonio
Italian 20th cent.
paintings: (L) $302; (H) $1,760

PIETTE, Ludovic
French 1826-1877
paintings: (H) $27,500

PIEXOTTO, Ernest Clifford
American 1869-1940
paintings: (L) $357; (H) $1,430

PIFFARD, Harold Hume
British ac. 1895-1899
paintings: (L) $412; (H) $33,000

PIGALLE
sculpture: (H) $990

PIGALLE
French
sculpture: (L) $715; (H) $2,310

PIGALLE, Jean Baptiste
French 1714-1785
sculpture: (H) $33,000

PIGAULT, Marie Celestine
French 1811-1859
paintings: (H) $2,530

PIGMA, A.
Italian 19th cent.
paintings: (H) $8,250

PIGNA, A.
Italian 19th cent.
paintings: (L) $7,150; (H) $8,250

PIGNON, Edouard
French b. 1905
paintings: (L) $1,760; (H) $30,800
drawings: (H) $7,150

PIGNONE, Simone
Italian 1614-1698
paintings: (L) $2,475; (H) $13,200

PIGOTT, Walter H.
English c. 1810-1901
drawings: (L) $440; (H) $1,320

PIJNACKER, Adam
Dutch 1622-1673
paintings: (H) $264,000

PIKE, Sidney
English ac. 1885-1901
paintings: (L) $275; (H) $660

PIKE, William Henry
British 1846-1908
paintings: (H) $880

PIKELNY, Robert
Polish b. 1904
paintings: (L) $495; (H) $1,870

PILCH, Adahbert
paintings: (L) $990; (H) $1,430

PILET, Leon
French 1839-1916
sculpture: (L) $264; (H) $1,100

PILLEMENT, Jean
French 1728-1808
paintings: (L) $3,300; (H) $33,000
drawings: (L) $1,100; (H) $18,700

PILNY, Otto
Swiss b. 1866
paintings: (L) $3,850; (H) $26,400

PILOT, Robert
American
paintings: (L) $2,750; (H) $2,750

PILOT, Robert Wakeham
Canadian 1898-1967/68
paintings: (L) $13,200; (H) $44,000

PILOTY, Carl Theodor von
German 1826-1886
paintings: (H) $33,000
drawings: (H) $660

PILS, Isidore Alexandre Augustin
French 1813-1875
paintings: (L) $6,600; (H) $18,700
drawings: (L) $275; (H) $27,500

PILTZ, Otto
German 1846-1910
paintings: (L) $13,750; (H) $46,200

PIMENTEL, Rodrigo Ramirez
paintings: (L) $4,620; (H) $13,200

PINA, Alfredo
sculpture: (L) $1,320; (H) $1,540

PINAL, Ferdinand
French b. 1881
paintings: (H) $3,520

PINAZO, Jose
paintings: (H) $1,980

PINCHART, Emile Auguste
French 1842-after 1930
paintings: (L) $3,410; (H) $11,000

PINCHON, Joseph Porphyre
French b. 1871
paintings: (H) $11,550

PINCHON, Robert
French 1886-1943
paintings: (L) $2,475; (H) $44,000

PINDELL, Howardina
American 20th cent.
drawings: (H) $1,045

PINE, Geri
American b. 1914
paintings: (H) $935

PINE, R.E.
paintings: (H) $825

PINE, Theodore E.
American 1828-1905
paintings: (L) $1,210; (H) $4,675

PINEDA, Jose
Spanish 19th cent.
drawings: (H) $1,000

PINEDO, Emile
French 19th cent.
sculpture: (L) $825; (H) $1,925

PINEL, Gustave Nicolas
French 1842-1896
paintings: (H) $11,000

PINEL DE GRANDCHAMP
French
drawings: (H) $880

PINELLO, Jose
drawings: (H) $4,950

PINETTI, Mario
French 20th cent.
paintings: (H) $715

PINGET, Henri Auguste
French 19th cent.
paintings: (H) $6,050

PINGGERA, Heinz
Italian 19th/20th cent.
paintings: (L) $935; (H) $2,475

PINGRET, Edouard
French 1788-1875
paintings: (H) $3,520

PINKERTON, Henrietta J.
Canadian 1852-1939
paintings: (H) $770

PINKHAM, D.W.
American contemporary
paintings: (H) $4,500

PINO, Marco
paintings: (H) $4,400

PINTO, Alberto
paintings: (H) $1,980

PINTO, Biagio
American b. 1911
paintings: (L) $522; (H) $2,200
drawings: (H) $1,100

PINTO, Jody
contemporary
drawings: (H) $1,210

PINTO, Lorraine
American
sculpture: (H) $660

PINTO, Salvatore
American 20th cent.
paintings: (L) $467; (H) $1,430

PIOLA, Domenico
drawings: (L) $1,650; (H) $1,650

PIOLA, Margherita
Spanish 19th cent.
paintings: (H) $700

PIOLA, Paolo Girolamo
paintings: (H) $8,250

PIOT, Adolphe
French 1850-1910
paintings: (L) $220; (H) $46,200

PIOT, Antoine
French 1869-1934
paintings: (H) $1,100

PIOTROWSKI, Antoni
Polish 1853-1924
paintings: (L) $3,575; (H) $6,325

PIOTROWSKI, Maksymiljan Antoni
Polish 1813-1875
paintings: (H) $8,525

PIPER, John
English b. 1903
paintings: (H) $5,500
drawings: (L) $1,100; (H) $15,400

PIPO, Manolo Ruiz
paintings: (L) $770; (H) $1,650

PIPPI, Giulio, called Giulio ROMANO
Italian c. 1499-1546
drawings: (L) $4,950; (H) $10,450

PIPPIN, Horace
American 1888-1947
paintings: (L) $9,350; (H) $385,000

PIQUEMAL, Francois Alphonse
sculpture: (H) $770

PIQUET, P.
French 19th cent.
paintings: (H) $1,705

PIRA, Gioacchino la
Italian 19th cent.
drawings: (H) $825

PIRA, La
Italian 19th cent.
drawings: (L) $1,320; (H) $1,760

PIRANDELLO, Fausto
paintings: (H) $9,350
drawings: (H) $14,300

PIRANESI, Giovanni Battista
Italian 1720-1778
drawings: (H) $10,450

PISIS, Filippo de
Italian 1896-1956
paintings: (L) $3,850; (H) $41,800

PISSARRO, Camille
French 1830-1903
paintings: (L) $77,000; (H) $3,190,000
drawings: (L) $440; (H) $484,000

PISSARRO, Claude
paintings: (L) $6,600; (H) $9,900

PISSARRO, H. Claude
French 20th cent.
paintings: (L) $4,950; (H) $22,000
drawings: (H) $2,090

PISSARRO, Lucien
French 1863-1944
paintings: (L) $2,310; (H) $55,000

PISSARRO, Ludovic Rodo
drawings: (H) $770

PISSARRO, Manzana
paintings: (H) $9,900

PISSARRO, P.
paintings: (H) $880

PISTOLETTO, Michelangelo
Italian b. 1933
paintings: (L) $14,300; (H) $35,750

PISTOR, Giovanti
paintings: (H) $6,875

PITALL, Rhoda Hahma
American
drawings: (H) $715

PITARD, Ferdinand
paintings: (H) $12,100

PITCHARD, W. Thompson
paintings: (H) $1,100

PITERS, Evert
Dutch b. 1856
paintings: (H) $3,080

PITT, William
English ac. 1849-1890
paintings: (L) $110; (H) $2,860

PITTARD, L.
American 19th cent.
paintings: (L) $1,100; (H) $1,760

PITTINGALI, W.E.
British
paintings: (L) $990; (H) $990

PITTMAN, Hobson
American 1898/1900-1972
paintings: (L) $495; (H) $4,950
drawings: (L) $99; (H) $1,210

PITTONI, Giovanni Battista
Italian 1687-1767
paintings: (L) $11,000; (H) $45,100

PITTS, Richard
paintings: (H) $770

PITZ, Henry Clarence
American 1895-1976
drawings: (L) $143; (H) $770

PITZNER, Max Joseph
paintings: (H) $6,050

PITZNER, S.
paintings: (H) $1,100

PIVOT, Louis
paintings: (H) $1,650

PIZZONI, Isa
sculpture: (H) $4,950

PIZZUTI, Michele
Italian b. 1882
drawings: (H) $1,430

PLA Y RUBIO, Alberto
Spanish b. 1867
paintings: (L) $11,000; (H) $12,100

PLACE, Vera Clark
American b. 1890
paintings: (H) $3,300

PLAGENS, Peter
contemporary
paintings: (H) $880

PLANAS, Juan Batlle
paintings: (H) $4,400

PLANQUETTE, Felix
French b. 1873
paintings: (L) $385; (H) $1,760

PLANSON, Andre
French b. 1898
paintings: (L) $1,400; (H) $2,860

PLAS, Lourentius
Dutch 1828-1888
paintings: (L) $605; (H) $1,870

PLAS, Pieter van
paintings: (H) $8,800

PLASCHKE
paintings: (H) $3,190

PLASSAN, Antoine Emile
French 1817-1903
paintings: (L) $935; (H) $8,250

PLATHNER, Hermann
German 1831-1902
paintings: (L) $2,860; (H) $9,350

PLATT, Alethea Hill
paintings: (H) $1,540

PLATT, Charles Adams
American 1861-1933
paintings: (L) $352; (H) $6,600
drawings: (H) $715

PLATT, George W.
American 1839-1899
paintings: (L) $467; (H) $715

PLATT, Martha A.
American 19th/20th cent.
paintings: (L) $660; (H) $880

PLATZER, Johann Georg
Austrian 1704-1761
paintings: (L) $44,000; (H) $253,000

PLAY, L.
European 19th cent.
paintings: (H) $825

PLAZA, N.
sculpture: (H) $2,475

PLAZZOTTA, Enzo
Italian ac. 1948
sculpture: (L) $1,100; (H) $6,820

PLE, Henri
French 1853-1922
sculpture: (L) $3,575; (H) $13,200

PLECHION, De
sculpture: (H) $4,180

PLEDGE, C. Terry
drawings: (H) $770

PLEISSNER, Ogden Minton
American 1905-1983
paintings: (L) $1,650; (H) $52,250
drawings: (L) $1,650; (H) $49,500

PLEPP, Hans Jacob
Swiss 1560-1595
drawings: (H) $7,150

PLESNER, R.
French 20th cent.
paintings: (L) $715; (H) $1,705

PLEUER, Hermann
German 1863-1911
paintings: (H) $24,200

PLEYSIER, Ary
Dutch 1809-1879
paintings: (L) $440; (H) $715

PLIMPTON, William E.
American
paintings: (H) $1,045

PLOLL, Victor
paintings: (H) $880

PLOQUIN, Gaston
paintings: (L) $3,300; (H) $5,000

PLUMLEY, P.
British 19th cent.
paintings: (H) $1,430

PLUMMER, Elmer Ginzel
American 1910-1987
drawings: (H) $880

PLUMMER, William H.
American ac. 1872-1876
paintings: (L) $44; (H) $9,350
drawings: (L) $44; (H) $165

PLUMOT, Andre
Belgian 1829-1906
paintings: (H) $1,980

PLUNKETT, Walter
drawings: (L) $3,250; (H) $9,900

PO, Giacomo del
Italian 1652-1726
paintings: (L) $1,650; (H) $154,000

PO, Teresa del
drawings: (H) $14,300

POBOGENSKY, Wjatscheslaw
Russian b. 1943
paintings: (H) $1,980

POCCETTI, Bernardino
Italian 1548-1612
drawings: (L) $605; (H) $880

POCOCK, Nicholas
English 1740-1821
paintings: (L) $5,775; (H) $6,600
drawings: (L) $187; (H) $3,080

PODCHERNIKOFF, Alexis
American b. 1912
paintings: (H) $5,280

PODCHERNIKOFF, Alexis M.
Russian/American 1886-1931
paintings: (L) $165; (H) $6,600

PODOLAK
American 19th/20th cent.
sculpture: (H) $1,430

PODRYSKI, Misha
American 20th cent.
paintings: (H) $3,850

POEL, A.D.
Dutch 17th cent.
paintings: (H) $3,080

POEL, Adriaen Lievensz van der
Dutch 1626-1685
paintings: (H) $1,870

POEL, Egbert van der
Dutch 1621-1664
paintings: (L) $1,320; (H) $3,300

POEL, Egbert van der and Adriaen van
OSTADE
paintings: (H) $35,200

POELENBURGH, Cornelis van
Dutch 1586-1667
paintings: (L) $5,775; (H) $176,000

POERSON, Charles
French 1653-1725
paintings: (H) $28,600

POERTZEL, Professor Otto
German b. 1876
sculpture: (L) $715; (H) $22,000

POGEDAIEFF, Georges de
drawings: (H) $1,100

POGGENBEEK, Geo
drawings: (H) $1,100

POHL
sculpture: (H) $3,300

POHLE, Hermann
German 1831-1901
paintings: (H) $660

POHLE, Leon
German 1841-1908
paintings: (H) $2,750

POINCY, Paul
American 1833-1909
paintings: (L) $825; (H) $1,320

POINGDESTRE, Charles H.
paintings: (H) $5,500

POINT, Armand
French 1860/61-1932
paintings: (H) $6,600
drawings: (H) $1,650

POIRIER, Anne and Patrick
contemporary
sculpture: (H) $9,900

POISSON, Louverature
Haitian b. 1914
paintings: (L) $248; (H) $13,200

POITEVIN, Auguste Flavien
French 19th cent.
paintings: (H) $15,400

POIX, Hugh de
paintings: (H) $1,430

POKITONOV, Ivan
Russian 1851-c. 1924
paintings: (L) $2,310; (H) $6,820

POL, Christian van
Dutch 1752-1813
paintings: (L) $2,750; (H) $187,000

POL, Louis
paintings: (H) $770

POL, Louis van der
paintings: (L) $110; (H) $1,760

POL, Louis van der
Dutch 1886-1956
paintings: (L) $412; (H) $2,310

POL, Louis van der
Dutch 1896-1982
paintings: (L) $77; (H) $2,090

POLAR, J.
drawings: (H) $770

POLASEK, Albin
Czechoslovakian b. 1897
sculpture: (L) $440; (H) $4,125

POLBRIG, H.
paintings: (L) $660; (H) $660

POLELONEMA, Otis
American Indian b. 1902
paintings: (H) $1,100

POLENBURGH, Cornelius van
Dutch 1586-1667
paintings: (H) $1,650

POLENOV, Vassily Dimitrievitch
Russian 1844-1927
paintings: (H) $9,350

POLEO, Hector
Venezuelan b. 1918
paintings: (L) $11,000; (H) $110,000
drawings: (H) $110
sculpture: (H) $8,800

POLESELLO, Rogelio
Argentinian b. 1939
paintings: (L) $330; (H) $5,500
drawings: (H) $880
sculpture: (H) $330

POLGARY, Geza
Hungarian b. 1862
paintings: (L) $220; (H) $2,860

POLIAKOFF, Serge
French 1900-1969
paintings: (L) $660; (H) $70,400
drawings: (H) $15,400

POLIDORI, C.
Continental 19th cent.
paintings: (H) $3,960

POLIDORI, C.
Italian 19th/20th cent.
drawings: (H) $660

POLIDORI, Gian Carlo
drawings: (H) $2,640

POLK, Charles Peale
American 1767-1822
paintings: (L) $9,350; (H) $110,000

POLK, Leonard
sculpture: (H) $1,100

POLKE, Sigmar
German b. 1941
paintings: (L) $15,400; (H) $286,000
drawings: (L) $13,200; (H) $253,000

POLL, Herbert van der
paintings: (H) $1,210

POLLAK, August
Austrian b. 1838
paintings: (H) $6,050

POLLAK, Sigismund
Austrian 19th cent.
paintings: (H) $7,700

POLLAND, Don
sculpture: (L) $143; (H) $1,100

POLLARD, James
English 1797-1859/67
paintings: (L) $2,860; (H) $26,400

POLLENTINE, Alfred
English ac. 1861-1880
paintings: (L) $275; (H) $9,350

POLLET, Jean
paintings: (H) $1,320

POLLET, Joseph
American 1897-1979
paintings: (H) $880

POLLINGER, Felix
German 1817-1877
paintings: (H) $715

POLLINI, Cesare
drawings: (H) $1,430

POLLOCK, Charles
American b. 1902
paintings: (H) $990

POLLOCK, Jackson
American 1912-1956
paintings: (L) $22,000; (H) $11,550,000
drawings: (L) $5,775; (H) $1,155,000

POLLOG, Robert Karl
German b. 1882
paintings: (H) $1,980

POLOS, Theodore
paintings: (H) $2,750

POLOSKY, Vladimir
paintings: (H) $1,980

POMERENKE, Heinrich
Continental 19th cent.
paintings: (H) $2,640

POMEROY, Frederick William
sculpture: (H) $935

POMMERANZ, M.
paintings: (H) $880

POMODORO, Arnaldo
Italian b. 1926
sculpture: (L) $770; (H) $66,000

POMODORO, Gio
Italian b. 1930
sculpture: (L) $1,760; (H) $10,780

POMPON, Francois
French 1855-1933
sculpture: (L) $1,980; (H) $8,250

PONCE, Antonio
Spanish 17th cent.
paintings: (H) $77,000

PONCE DE LEON, Fidelio
Latin American
paintings: (L) $1,320; (H) $14,850
drawings: (L) $82; (H) $4,180

PONCHIN, Antoine
French b. 1872
paintings: (H) $2,750

POND, Clayton
paintings: (L) $605; (H) $1,100

POND, Dana
American 1880-1962
paintings: (L) $88; (H) $4,070

PONDEL, Friedrich
German b. 1830
paintings: (L) $330; (H) $1,650

PONSARD, Paul
French 1882-1915
sculpture: (L) $1,650; (H) $2,420

PONSEN, Tunis
American 1891-1968
paintings: (L) $247; (H) $3,080
drawings: (L) $110; (H) $220

PONSON, Aime Etienne
French 1850-1924
paintings: (H) $1,760

PONSONELLI, Giacomo Antonio
Italian 1654-1735
drawings: (H) $3,850

PONTE, ***
paintings: (H) $880

PONTHIER, E.
European 20th cent.
paintings: (H) $715

PONTINI, Fritz
paintings: (H) $2,420

PONTORMO, Jacopo da CARUCCI
Italian 1494-1557
paintings: (L) $385,000; (H) $35,200,000

POOL, Paul Falconer
paintings: (H) $2,200

POOLE, A.E.
American
paintings: (H) $2,310

POOLE, Abram
American 1883-1961
paintings: (L) $4,620; (H) $4,785

POOLE, Eugene Alonzo
American 1841-1912
paintings: (L) $357; (H) $990

POOLE, Frederick Victor
American d. 1936
drawings: (L) $77; (H) $1,210

POOLE, Horatio Nelson
American 1884-1949
paintings: (H) $2,750

POOLE, James
British 1804-1886
paintings: (L) $578; (H) $1,100

POOLE, Paul Falconer
British 1807-1879
paintings: (L) $825; (H) $3,025

POOLE, Richard
paintings: (H) $825

POONS, Larry
American b. 1937
paintings: (L) $2,475; (H) $176,000
drawings: (L) $715; (H) $1,100

POOR, Henry Varnum
American 1888-1970
paintings: (L) $390; (H) $4,675
drawings: (H) $990

POORE, Henry Rankin
American 1859-1940
paintings: (L) $385; (H) $7,150
sculpture: (H) $4,400

POORTER, Willem de
Dutch 1608-1648
paintings: (L) $3,850; (H) $52,250

POOSCH, Max von
Austrian b. 1872
paintings: (H) $1,540

POOTEN, Jan de
paintings: (H) $12,100

POOTER, J. de
paintings: (H) $7,700

POPE, Alexander
American 1849-1924
paintings: (L) $770; (H) $19,800
drawings: (L) $110; (H) $660
sculpture: (L) $165; (H) $5,280

POPE, Gustav
British ac. 1852-1895
paintings: (H) $9,900

POPE, H.A.
American
paintings: (H) $1,210

POPE, J**
British 19th cent.
paintings: (H) $660

POPE, Thomas Benjamin
American d. 1891
paintings: (H) $770

POPELIN, Gustave Leon Antoine
Marie
French b. 1859
paintings: (H) $9,900

POPLASKI, A.
paintings: (H) $2,200

POPOVA, Liubov
Russian 1889-1924 or 1929
paintings: (H) $1,760,000
drawings: (L) $3,300; (H) $29,700

POPPE, Fedor
German b. 1850
paintings: (L) $220; (H) $2,860

POPPEL, Rudolph
paintings: (H) $2,750

POPPERITZ, Gustave
paintings: (II) $8,800

PORAY, Stanislaus P.
American 1888-1948
paintings: (L) $110; (H) $2,475

PORBANT, C.V.
paintings: (H) $990

PORCEL, Saturnino
Bolivian c. 1820-1892
paintings: (H) $3,300

PORCELLI, L.
sculpture: (H) $1,100

PORCELLIS, Jan
Dutch c. 1584-1632
paintings: (H) $13,200

PORCELLIS, Julius
Dutch c. 1609-1645
paintings: (H) $16,500

PORCHERON, Lucien Emile
French 1876-1957
paintings: (H) $22,000

PORGE, Gergely
Hungarian 1852-1912
paintings: (H) $935

PORPORA, Paolo
Italian 1617-1673
paintings: (H) $55,000

PORTA, Baccio della, called Fra
Bartolommeo, studio of
paintings: (H) $8,250

PORTA, Guglielmo della
sculpture: (H) $1,320

PORTER, Benjamin Curtis
American 1845-1908
paintings: (L) $220; (H) $1,210
drawings: (H) $55

PORTER, C.E.
paintings: (L) $1,870; (H) $9,500

PORTER, Charles Eaton
American 1850-1923
paintings: (L) $220; (H) $15,100

PORTER, Charles Ethan
American 1847-1923
paintings: (L) $550; (H) $4,750

PORTER, Fairfield
American 1907-1975
paintings: (L) $4,180; (H) $280,500
drawings: (L) $495; (H) $4,400

PORTER, John J.
American 19th cent.
paintings: (H) $7,150
drawings: (H) $3,850

PORTER, Katherine
American b. 1941
paintings: (L) $1,650; (H) $33,000
drawings: (L) $825; (H) $3,850

PORTER, M.F.
English 20th cent.
paintings: (H) $880

PORTER, R.T.
English 19th cent.
paintings: (H) $2,420

PORTER, Rufus
American 1792-1884
drawings: (L) $2,530; (H) $7,700

PORTER, Tom
American b. 1948
paintings: (L) $220; (H) $1,100

PORTER, Vivian Forsythe
1888-1982
paintings: (L) $110; (H) $990

PORTICELLI
Italian 19th cent.
paintings: (H) $715

PORTIELJE, Edward Antoon
Belgian 1861-1949
paintings: (L) $3,080; (H) $10,450
drawings: (L) $715; (H) $2,200

PORTIELJE, Gerard
Belgian 1856-1929
paintings: (L) $4,400; (H) $18,700

PORTIELJE, Jan Frederik Pieter
Belgian 1829-1895
paintings: (L) $1,210; (H) $19,800

PORTINARI, Candido
Brazilian 1903-1962
paintings: (L) $15,950; (H) $275,000
drawings: (L) $1,430; (H) $6,050

PORTMAN, Christian
Dutch 1799-1867
paintings: (H) $1,100

PORTOCARRERO, Rene
Cuban b. 1912
paintings: (L) $1,980; (H) $30,800
drawings: (L) $1,100; (H) $17,600

PORTOCARRERO, Wifredo
drawings: (H) $2,200

PORTSMOUTH, Percy
sculpture: (H) $7,150

PORTZLINE, Francis
American 1800-1847
drawings: (H) $8,800

POSEN, Leonid V.
Russian b. 1849
sculpture: (H) $4,400

POSEN, Steven
American b. 1939
paintings: (L) $3,850; (H) $41,250

POSEN, Tunis
American 20th cent.
paintings: (H) $770

POSILLIPO, Napolida
drawings: (H) $1,375

POSNER, A.
British 19th cent.
paintings: (H) $825

POSSART, Felix
German 1837-1928
paintings: (H) $1,760

POSSIN, Rudolf
German b. 1861
paintings: (H) $1,400

POSSNER, Hugo
paintings: (H) $2,420

POST, Eduard C.
German 1827-1882
paintings: (L) $5,500; (H) $6,600

POST, Frans Jansz
Dutch 1612-1680
paintings: (L) $440,000; (H) $962,500

POST, George Booth
American b. 1906
drawings: (L) $440; (H) $1,100

POST, William Merritt
American 1856-1935
paintings: (L) $110; (H) $4,400
drawings: (L) $275; (H) $2,200

POSTIGLIONE, L.
Italian 19th cent.
paintings: (H) $825

POSTIGLIONE, Luca
Italian 1876-1936
paintings: (L) $330; (H) $1,760

POSTIGLIONE, Salvatore
Italian 1861-1906
paintings: (L) $1,760; (H) $22,000

POT, Hendrick Gerritsz.
Dutch c. 1585-1657
paintings: (L) $4,400; (H) $24,200

POTERLET, Pierre Saint Ange
French 1804-1881
paintings: (H) $1,100

POTHAST, Bernard
Dutch 1882-1966
paintings: (L) $495; (H) $27,500

POTIER
18th cent.
drawings: (L) $660; (H) $1,540

POTT, Laslett John
British 1837-1898
paintings: (H) $60,500

POTTER, Beatrix
English 1866-1943
drawings: (L) $7,700; (H) $12,650

POTTER, Louis
American 1873-1912
sculpture: (L) $1,320; (H) $27,500

POTTER, Mary Kynaston
sculpture: (H) $9,900

POTTER, Paulus
Dutch 1625-1654
paintings: (H) $36,300

POTTER, William J.
American 1883-1964
paintings: (L) $264; (H) $1,320

POTTHAST, Edward Henry
American 1857-1927
paintings: (L) $605; (H) $253,000
drawings: (L) $330; (H) $22,000

POUGHEON, Eugene Robert
French b. 1886
drawings: (H) $6,600

POUGHEON, Robert Eugene
contemporary
drawings: (H) $3,300

POUGNY, Jean
French 1894-1956
paintings: (L) $935; (H) $1,650
drawings: (L) $5,775; (H) $5,775

POULAIN, Michel Marie
French b. 1906
paintings: (H) $990

POURBUS, Frans, the younger
Flemish 1569/70-1622
paintings: (L) $3,300; (H) $11,000

POURBUSI, Frans
paintings: (H) $9,350

POUSETTE-DART, Richard
American b. 1916
paintings: (L) $7,150; (H) $99,000
drawings: (L) $82; (H) $27,500

POUSIN, H.
French 19th cent.
paintings: (H) $990

POUSSIN, Charles Pierre
French d. 1905
paintings: (H) $3,025

POUSSIN, Nicholas
French 1594-1665
drawings: (H) $90,750

POUYLSON, J.
19th cent.
paintings: (H) $2,750

POVEDA, Carlos
Costa Rican b. 1940
drawings: (L) $3,300; (H) $5,225

POVEDA Y JUAN, Vicente
Spanish ? b. 1857; ac. 1895
paintings: (L) $17,600; (H) $28,600

POWELL, Ace
American 1912-1978
paintings: (L) $1,000; (H) $5,500
sculpture: (L) $1,000; (H) $1,600

POWELL, Arthur
American 1864-1956
paintings: (L) $385; (H) $1,540

POWELL, Arthur James Emery
American 1864-1956
paintings: (L) $550; (H) $7,975

POWELL, Charles Martin
British d. 1824
paintings: (H) $13,200

POWELL, Lucien Whiting
American 1846-1930
paintings: (L) $220; (H) $5,500
drawings: (L) $165; (H) $1,210

POWELL, William E.
British ac. 1900-1950
drawings: (L) $385; (H) $2,200

POWER, Thomas
American 20th cent.
paintings: (H) $1,980

POWERS, Amanda
American c. 1835
paintings: (L) $22,000; (H) $66,000

POWERS, Asahel L.
American b. 1813
paintings: (H) $19,800

POWERS, Hiram
American 1805-1873
sculpture: (L) $3,025; (H) $57,200

POWERS, Marilyn
1925-1976
paintings: (H) $1,300

POWERS, Marion
American ac. early 20th cent.
paintings: (L) $110; (H) $3,300
drawings: (L) $150; (H) $275

POWIS, Paul
19th/20th cent.
paintings: (L) $1,210; (H) $1,320

POYNTER, Sir Edward John, or
Sir Edward James
French/English 1836-1919
paintings: (L) $4,950; (H) $46,750
drawings: (L) $385; (H) $990

POZZI, Francesco
Italian 1779-1844
sculpture: (H) $88,000

POZZO, Pietro Antonio(?)
drawings: (H) $1,320

POZZO, Stefano
1707-1768
drawings: (H) $880

PRAAG, Alexander Salomon van
Dutch 1812-1865
paintings: (H) $13,200

PRADEL
Continental School 19th cent.
paintings: (H) $1,045

PRADES, Alfred F. de
British ac. 1844-1883
paintings: (L) $2,530; (H) $49,500
drawings: (H) $550

PRADIER, Jean Jacques
French 1792-1852
sculpture: (L) $440; (H) $11,000

PRADIER, P.
French 19th cent.
sculpture: (L) $2,200; (H) $2,530

PRADILLA Y ORTIZ, Francisco
Spanish 1848-1921
paintings: (L) $7,700; (H) $15,400
drawings: (L) $5,225; (H) $12,100

PRADO, Marina Nunez del
sculpture: (L) $2,750; (H) $4,180

PRAHAR, Renee
sculpture: (L) $550; (H) $2,860

PRAMPOLINI, Enrico
Italian 1894-1956
paintings: (L) $110,000; (H) $220,000
drawings: (H) $5,500

PRASSINOS, Mario
paintings: (L) $6,600; (H) $7,700

PRATCHENKO, Paul
American 20th cent.
paintings: (H) $1,540
drawings: (L) $275; (H) $412

PRATELLA, Antonio
paintings: (L) $275; (H) $1,320

PRATELLA, Attilio
Italian 1856-1949
paintings: (L) $770; (H) $38,500
drawings: (L) $1,800; (H) $4,620

PRATELLA, Fausto
Italian 1888-1964
paintings: (H) $1,980

PRATERE, Edmond Joseph de
Belgian 1826-1888
paintings: (H) $12,100

PRATT, Bela Lyon
American 1867-1917
sculpture: (L) $3,575; (H) $5,225

PRATT, Emmett A.
20th cent.
paintings: (H) $880

PRATT, Henry C.
American 19th cent.
paintings: (H) $1,100

PRATT, Hilton
paintings: (H) $5,280

PRATT, Jonathon
English 19th cent.
paintings: (H) $1,430

PRATT, Samuel Baldwin
American b. 1903
paintings: (L) $275; (H) $660

PRATT, William
English b. 1855
paintings: (H) $1,100

PRATZ, Ramon
Hungarian 20th cent.
paintings: (L) $1,210; (H) $1,210

PRAX, Valentine
French b. 1899
paintings: (L) $3,300; (H) $7,150
drawings: (H) $1,650

PRECHT, A.
paintings: (H) $935

PREGUIRE, F.
sculpture: (H) $2,750

PREHN, A.
European 19th/20th cent.
paintings: (H) $880

PREHN, A.
German 19th cent.
paintings: (H) $990

PREISLER, Johann Daniel
drawings: (H) $880

PREISS, Ferdinand, Fritz
German 1882-1943
sculpture: (L) $385; (H) $34,100

PREISTLY, E.
paintings: (H) $825

PRELL, Hermann
German 1854-1922
paintings: (H) $15,400

PRELL, Walter
French b. 1857
paintings: (H) $5,500

PRELLWITZ, Henry
American b. 1865
paintings: (H) $880

PREM, Heimrad
contemporary
paintings: (H) $6,050

PRENDERGAST, Charles
American 1868-1948
paintings: (H) $52,800
drawings: (H) $4,950
sculpture: (L) $550; (H) $4,400

PRENDERGAST, J.
Continental School
drawings: (H) $9,900

PRENDERGAST, Maurice
American 1859-1924
paintings: (L) $39,600; (H) $1,815,000
drawings: (L) $577; (H) $1,870,000

PRENT, Johan
Dutch 19th/20th cent.
paintings: (H) $935

PRENTICE, Levi Wells
American 1851-1935
paintings: (L) $132; (H) $50,600

PRENTISS, Thomas
American b. 1920
paintings: (H) $990
drawings: (H) $99

PRENTZEL, Hans
German School b. 1880
paintings: (H) $2,860

PRESCOTT, C.B.
American late 19th/20th cent.
paintings: (H) $1,430

PRESSMANE, Joseph
paintings: (H) $7,150

PRESTON, Alice Bolam
American 1889-1958
drawings: (H) $825

PRESTON, Edward
English 19th cent.
drawings: (H) $700

PRESTON, May Wilson
American 1873-1949
paintings: (L) $220; (H) $8,800
drawings: (L) $110; (H) $1,100

PRESTON, W.
British 19th cent.
paintings: (H) $2,250

PRESTOPINO, Gregorio
American b. 1907
paintings: (L) $1,650; (H) $13,200
drawings: (L) $770; (H) $880

PRETI, Mattia, called Il Cavaliere
Calabrese
Italian 1613-1699
paintings: (L) $46,750; (H) $1,155,000
drawings: (L) $715; (H) $2,420

PRETTI, Mattia, studio of
paintings: (H) $2,420

PRETTO, Rogelio
paintings: (H) $3,300

PREUSSEL, C.C.
American
paintings: (H) $990

PREUSSER, Robert Ormerod
American b. 1919
paintings: (L) $330; (H) $7,700

PREUX, Henri
French 19th cent.
drawings: (H) $660

PREVAL, Christiane de
French b. 1876
paintings: (H) $1,000

PREVERT, Jacques
French 1900-1977
drawings: (H) $1,100

PREVET, A. Collas
sculpture: (H) $1,320

PREVIATI, Gaetano
Italian 1852-1920
paintings: (L) $935; (H) $4,400

PREVOST
French 19th cent.
paintings: (H) $1,540

PREVOST, Nicholas
19th cent.
paintings: (H) $2,200

PREVOT-VALERI, Andre
French b. 1890
paintings: (H) $1,430

PREVOT-VALERI, Auguste
paintings: (H) $4,400

PREYER, Emilie
German 1849-1930
paintings: (L) $13,200; (H) $57,200

PREYER, Johann Wilhelm
German 1803-1889
paintings: (L) $13,200; (H) $110,000

PREZZI, Wilma
American 20th cent.
paintings: (H) $2,860

PRICE, Alan
American 20th cent.
paintings: (L) $193; (H) $4,675

PRICE, Clayton Sumner
American 1874-1950
paintings: (H) $1,100

PRICE, Kenneth
American b. 1935
drawings: (H) $1,760
sculpture: (L) $3,300; (H) $52,250

PRICE, Mary Elizabeth
American 1875-1960
paintings: (H) $550
drawings: (H) $770

PRICE, Norman Mills
American 1877-1951
paintings: (L) $770; (H) $1,485
drawings: (L) $121; (H) $1,600

PRICE, Robert
contemporary
sculpture: (H) $1,100

PRICE, William Henry
American 1864-1940
paintings: (H) $1,540

PRICE, William Lake
English 1810-1891
drawings: (H) $1,320

PRIDA, Fernando Ramos
paintings: (H) $2,750

PRIEBE, Karl
American 1914-1976
paintings: (L) $82; (H) $825
drawings: (L) $27; (H) $605

PRIECHENFRIED, Alois
Polish 1867-1953
paintings: (L) $550; (H) $6,325

PRIER-BARDIN, F. Leon
French 19th cent.
paintings: (H) $935

PRIESTLEY, E.
English 19th cent.
paintings: (L) $770; (H) $1,320

PRIESTLEY, Edward
English 19th cent.
paintings: (H) $825

PRIETO, Anthony
sculpture: (H) $3,575

PRIETO, Manuel Jimenez
Spanish 19th cent.
paintings: (H) $2,860

PRIEUR, Barthelemy
French d. 1611
sculpture: (H) $110,000

PRIKING, Frantz
German b. 1927
paintings: (L) $412; (H) $63,800

PRIMATICCIO, Francesco, called
Bologna
Italian 1504-1570
drawings: (H) $27,500

PRINCETEAU, Rene
French 1844-1914
paintings: (H) $33,000

PRINDLE
American 20th cent.
paintings: (H) $1,650

PRINET, Rene Francois Xavier
French 1861-1946
paintings: (L) $467; (H) $46,200

PRINGLE, J.
American 19th cent.
paintings: (L) $275; (H) $2,310

PRINGLE, Joseph Fulton
British/American 19th cent.
paintings: (L) $4,950; (H) $7,150

PRINGLE, William J.
British ac. 1834-1858
paintings: (H) $3,300

PRINS, Benjamin
paintings: (H) $2,090

PRINS, Pierre Ernest
French 1838-1913
paintings: (H) $17,600
drawings: (L) $275; (H) $1,540

PRINSEP, Valentine Cameron
English 1836-1904
paintings: (L) $1,100; (H) $41,800

PRINZ, A.E.
American 19th cent.
paintings: (H) $1,760

PRIOR, M. Elizabeth
American 20th cent.
paintings: (H) $700

PRIOR, Scott
20th cent.
paintings: (H) $1,100

PRIOR, William Matthew
American 1806-1873
paintings: (L) $550; (H) $53,900

PRIOR-HAMBLEN SCHOOL
paintings: (H) $36,300

PRIOTTI, Gloria
Latin American
sculpture: (H) $1,870

PRIOU, Louis
French b. 1845
paintings: (L) $4,400; (H) $7,700
drawings: (H) $220

PRITCHARD, Edward F.D.
British 1809-1905
paintings: (L) $357; (H) $3,740
drawings: (H) $467

PRITCHARD, F.
paintings: (H) $990

PRITCHARD, George Thompson
American 1878-1962
paintings: (L) $330; (H) $4,400
drawings: (H) $358

PRITCHARD, J. Ambrose
American 1858-1905
paintings: (L) $440; (H) $935
drawings: (L) $77; (H) $495

PRITCHETT, Edward
British ac. 1828-1864
paintings: (L) $660; (H) $18,700

PRITCHETT, S.
paintings: (H) $5,280

PRIVAT, Auguste Gilbert, called
Gilbert
French b. 1892
sculpture: (L) $385; (H) $5,500

PRIVAT-LIVEMONT
drawings: (H) $4,400

PROBST, Carl
Austrian 1854-1924
paintings: (L) $1,100; (H) $19,800

PROBST, Thorwald A.
American 1886-1948?
paintings: (L) $825; (H) $4,125

PROCACCINI, Andrea
drawings: (H) $1,980

PROCACCINI, Camillo
Italian 1546/51-1629
paintings: (L) $8,800; (H) $68,750
drawings: (L) $880; (H) $3,850

PROCACCINI, Carlantonio
Italian 1571-1630
paintings: (H) $19,800

PROCACCINI, Ercole
1596-1676
drawings: (H) $4,675

PROCACCINI, Giulio Cesare
Italian 1570-1625
paintings: (H) $18,700
drawings: (H) $8,250

PROCHAZKA, Josef
Hungarian b. 1909
paintings: (H) $770

PROCHAZKA, Karl
drawings: (H) $7,150

PROCHOROFF, Alexander
Vassilievitch
Russian b. 1848
paintings: (L) $1,760; (H) $3,520

PROCTOR, Alexander Phimister
American 1862-1950
drawings: (L) $138; (H) $770
sculpture: (L) $1,430; (H) $38,500

PROCTOR, Burt
American 1901-1980
paintings: (L) $1,980; (H) $12,000

PROFESSOR FIASCHI
sculpture: (H) $2,640

PROLSS, Friedrich Anton Otto
German b. 1855
paintings: (L) $6,380; (H) $33,000

PRON, Louis Hector
French 1817-1902
paintings: (H) $29,700

PRONK, Cornelis
Dutch 1691-1759
paintings: (H) $41,800

PROOGRUFF(?), A.
paintings: (H) $797

PROOM, A.
American 20th cent.
paintings: (H) $3,025

PROPER, Ida Sedgwick
American 1873-1957
paintings: (L) $1,430; (H) $31,900

PROSDOCINI, Alberto
Italian b. 1852
drawings: (L) $110; (H) $1,870

PROST, M.
sculpture: (H) $1,210

PROST, Maurice
French 1894-?
sculpture: (H) $880

PROTAIS, Paul Alexandre
French 1826-1890
paintings: (L) $495; (H) $3,300

PROTTI, Alfredo
Italian 1882-1949
paintings: (H) $715

PROUT, Margaret Fisher
English 1875-1963
paintings: (H) $825

PROUT, Samuel
English 1783-1852
paintings: (H) $935
drawings: (L) $121; (H) $17,600

PROUVE, Victor Emile
French 1858-1943
drawings: (H) $16,500

PROVIS, Alfred
British 19th cent.
paintings: (L) $1,430; (H) $2,420

PROVOST, Jan, II
Flemish 1462/65-1529
paintings: (H) $418,000

PROVOST, Jan, studio of
paintings: (H) $220,000

PRUCHA, Gustav
Austrian b. 1875
paintings: (L) $525; (H) $4,675

PRUD'HON, Pierre Paul
French 1758-1823
paintings: (L) $1,980; (H) $38,500
drawings: (L) $3,080; (H) $15,400

PRUEY, F.W.
paintings: (H) $1,760

PRUNA, Pedro
Spanish b. 1904
paintings: (L) $4,400; (H) $8,800

PRUNIER, Pierre
French
paintings: (H) $7,150

PRUSHECK, Harvey Gregory
American
paintings: (H) $2,640

PRY, Lamont "Old Ironsides"
American 1921-1987
paintings: (H) $2,420

PRYDE, James
Scottish 1866-1941
paintings: (L) $22,000; (H) $46,750

PRYOR, William Matthew
American 1806-1873
paintings: (H) $1,430

**PSEUDO PIER FRANCESCO
FIORENTINO**
Italian ac. 1470-1500
paintings: (H) $49,500

**PSEUDO PIER FRANCESCO
FIORENTINO,** studio of
paintings: (H) $18,700

PUECH, D.
sculpture: (L) $1,210; (H) $3,740

PUECH, Denys Pierre
French 1854-1942
sculpture: (L) $1,650; (H) $7,975

PUESTRE, Si
sculpture: (H) $715

PUGET, Pierre
French 1620-1694
paintings: (H) $36,300

PUGI
Italian
sculpture: (L) $352; (H) $1,430

PUGI, F.
sculpture: (L) $412; (H) $1,100

PUGIN, Augustus
French 1769-1832
drawings: (L) $990; (H) $2,090

PUHLMANN, Alexis
German ac. 1930's
paintings: (H) $1,100

PUIG-RODA, G.
Italian 19th/20th cent.
drawings: (H) $7,700

PUIGAUDEAU, Ferdinand du, or
Fernand du
French 1864/66-1930
paintings: (L) $23,100; (H) $77,000

PUIGI-RODA, G.
Spanish early 20th cent.
drawings: (H) $935

PUJOL DE GUASTAVINO, Clement
French 19th cent.
paintings: (L) $4,400; (H) $30,800

PULIGO, Domenico
Italian 1492-1527
paintings: (H) $110,000

PULINCKX, Louis
Belgian b. 1843
paintings: (H) $7,150

PULLER, John Anthony
British 19th cent.
paintings: (L) $1,320; (H) $3,300

PULZONE, Scipione, Il Gaetano
Italian c. 1550-1598
paintings: (H) $286,000

PUMMIL, Robert
American b. 1936
paintings: (L) $3,575; (H) $9,900

PUMMILL, Robert
American contemporary
paintings: (H) $6,500

PUPINI, Biagio, called Dalle Lame
Italian ac. 1511-1575
drawings: (L) $5,500; (H) $6,050

PURDY, Albert J.
American 1835-1909
paintings: (L) $165; (H) $6,380
drawings: (H) $495

PURGAU, Franz Michael
Siegmund von, the elder
1677/78-1754
paintings: (H) $10,450

PURY, Edmond Jean de
Swiss 1845-1911
paintings: (L) $3,300; (H) $4,950

PURYEAR, Martin
American contemporary
sculpture: (H) $44,000

PUSHMAN, Hovsep
American 1877-1966
paintings: (L) $825; (H) $28,600
drawings: (H) $220

PUTEANI, Friedrich von
German 1849-1917
paintings: (H) $3,850

PUTHUFF, Hanson Duvall
American 1875-1972
paintings: (L) $605; (H) $17,600
drawings: (H) $2,200

PUTNAM, Arthur
American 1873-1930
sculpture: (L) $880; (H) $4,400

PUTNAM, Brenda
sculpture: (H) $1,100

PUTTER, Pieter de
Dutch c. 1600-1659
paintings: (H) $2,860

PUTTNER, Josef Carl Berthold
Austrian 1821-1881
paintings: (L) $1,045; (H) $3,300

PUTZ, Leo
German 1869-1940
paintings: (H) $25,300

PUTZHOFEN-HAMBUCHE, Paul
German 19th/20th cent.
paintings: (H) $770

PUVIS DE CHAVANNES, Pierre
French 1824-1898
paintings: (H) $6,050
drawings: (L) $209; (H) $8,250

PUY, Jean
French b. 1876
paintings: (L) $3,080; (H) $22,000
drawings: (H) $2,860

PUYET, Jose
Spanish b. 1922
paintings: (H) $1,100

PUYL, Gerard van der
paintings: (H) $5,775

PUYL, Louis Francois Gerard van der
Dutch 1750-1824
paintings: (L) $1,870; (H) $5,775

PUYROCHE-WAGNER, Elise
German 1828-1895
paintings: (L) $2,090; (H) $9,900

PUYT, A.
French
sculpture: (L) $220; (H) $660

PYE, Williams
British 19th cent.
paintings: (H) $1,100

PYLABE, V.
French 19th cent.
paintings: (H) $990

PYLE, Howard
American 1853-1911
paintings: (L) $1,760; (H) $18,150
drawings: (L) $1,045; (H) $13,200

PYNACKER, Adam
Dutch 1622-1673
paintings: (L) $13,200; (H) $297,000

PYNAS, Jan
Dutch 1583/84-1631
paintings: (H) $880

PYNE, James Baker
British 1800-1870
paintings: (L) $110; (H) $8,250
drawings: (L) $412; (H) $2,640

QJAR DYNASTY
Persian late 18th cent.
paintings: (H) $16,500

QUA, Sun
c. 1860-1870
paintings: (L) $8,000; (H) $20,000
drawings: (H) $3,190

QUADAL, Martin Ferdinand
paintings: (L) $1,210; (H) $2,750

QUAEDVLIEG, Carel Max Gerlach
Anton
Dutch 1823-1874
paintings: (L) $1,650; (H) $12,100

QUAGLIO, Franz
German 1844-1920
paintings: (L) $1,760; (H) $1,980

QUAH-AHE TONITA
American 1895-1941
drawings: (H) $2,530

QUARENGHI, Giacomo
Italian 1744-1817
drawings: (L) $1,540; (H) $8,800

QUARTARARO, Riccardo
paintings: (H) $33,000

QUARTLEY, Arthur
American 1839-1886
paintings: (L) $440; (H) $9,680
drawings: (L) $330; (H) $385

QUAY, John
paintings: (H) $2,860

QUAYTMAN, Harvey
American b. 1937
paintings: (L) $3,520; (H) $3,520

QUELLINUS, Artus, the elder
Flemish c.1609-1668
sculpture: (H) $308,000

QUELLINUS, Erasmus, II
Flemish 1607-1678
paintings: (L) $12,100; (H) $46,750

QUENCE, Raymond
paintings: (H) $770

QUENTEL, Holt
contemporary
paintings: (H) $16,500

QUERENA, Luigi
Italian 1860-1890
paintings: (H) $3,520

QUERFURT, August
German 1696-1761
paintings: (L) $14,300; (H) $19,800

QUESNEL, E.
sculpture: (H) $660

QUESTA, Francesco della
Italian 1652-1723
paintings: (H) $39,600

QUIDOR, John
American 1801-1881
paintings: (L) $220; (H) $6,600

QUIGG, J.
American 19th cent.
paintings: (H) $5,280

QUIGLEY
paintings: (H) $1,540

QUIGNON, Fernand Just
French b. 1854
paintings: (H) $8,800

QUILLARD, Pierre Antoine
paintings: (L) $3,850; (H) $11,000

QUIMBEY, Fred G.
American 1863-1923
paintings: (H) $4,950

QUINCY, Edmund
American b. 1903
paintings: (L) $220; (H) $7,150

QUINN, Edmond T.
sculpture: (H) $1,650

QUINN, Noel
American 20th cent.
drawings: (H) $825

QUINN, Wayne
paintings: (H) $5,500

QUINONES, Lee
contemporary
paintings: (H) $3,025

QUINQUELA MARTIN, Benito
Argentinian 1890-1977
paintings: (L) $3,190; (H) $19,800

QUINSA, Giovanni
17th cent.
paintings: (L) $35,200; (H) $68,200

QUINSAC, Paul Francois
French b. 1858
paintings: (L) $2,860; (H) $39,600

QUINTANA, Ben, Ha A TEE
American Indian 1923-1944
paintings: (H) $825

QUINTERO, Daniel
Spanish contemporary
paintings: (L) $1,540; (H) $3,850

QUINTIN, H.J.
British 19th cent.
paintings: (H) $9,900

QUINTON, H**
British 19th cent.
paintings: (H) $4,675

QUINTON, J.
English 19th cent.
paintings: (L) $2,750; (H) $2,860

QUINTON, James
British 19th cent.
paintings: (L) $1,210; (H) $2,860

QUIROS, Bernaldo de
paintings: (L) $4,400; (H) $9,900

QUIRT, Walter
American 1902-1968
paintings: (L) $462; (H) $2,750

QUITTON, Edward
Belgian b. 1842
paintings: (L) $1,600; (H) $3,520

QUIVIERES, P. Marcotte de
French 19th cent.
paintings: (H) $1,980

QUIZET, Alphonse Leon
French 1885-1955
paintings: (L) $330; (H) $17,600

RAAPHORST, Cornelis
Dutch 1875-1974
paintings: (L) $3,520; (H) $4,950

RABES, Max Friedrich
German b. 1868
paintings: (H) $5,225

RABIN, Michael
sculpture: (H) $1,100

RACH, L.
paintings: (H) $1,210

RACHMIEL, A.
French 19th/20th cent.
paintings: (H) $1,210

RACKHAM, Arthur
English 1867-1939
drawings: (L) $1,320; (H) $45,100

RACOFF, Rotislaw
paintings: (L) $247; (H) $3,300

RADCLIFFE, Paul
paintings: (H) $1,980

RADEMAKER, Abraham
Dutch 1675-1735
drawings: (L) $605; (H) $7,150

RADICE, Casimiro
Italian 1834-1908
paintings: (H) $33,000

RAEBURN, Sir Henry
Scottish 1756-1823
paintings: (L) $385; (H) $110,000

RAEYMECKERS, Jules
Belgian 1833-1904
paintings: (H) $9,350

RAFFAEL, Joseph
American b. 1933
paintings: (L) $1,210; (H) $52,250
drawings: (L) $2,420; (H) $3,850

RAFFAELLI, Jean Francois
French 1850-1924
paintings: (L) $3,850; (H) $57,750
drawings: (L) $990; (H) $4,620

RAFFALT, Ignaz
Austrian 1800-1857
paintings: (L) $5,500; (H) $5,775

RAFFALT, Johann Gualbert
paintings: (H) $3,300

RAFFET, Denis Auguste Marie
French 1804-1860
paintings: (L) $302; (H) $8,800
drawings: (L) $550; (H) $1,540

RAGAN, Leslie
American b. 1897
drawings: (H) $2,200

RAGGI
drawings: (H) $1,155

RAGGI, E.
Italian 19th cent.
drawings: (L) $825; (H) $1,650

RAGGIO, Giuseppe
Italian 1823-1916
paintings: (L) $880; (H) $5,500

RAGIONE, Raffaele
Italian 1851-1925
paintings: (H) $6,050

RAGOT, Jules Felix
French ac. 1867-1882
paintings: (L) $715; (H) $2,750

RAHL, Carl
Austrian 1812-1865
paintings: (H) $1,760

RAI, A.E.
German 19th cent.
paintings: (H) $990

RAIANO, G.
Italian 19th/20th cent.
sculpture: (H) $1,320

RAIBOLINI, Francesco di Marco or
di Giacomo, called Il Francia
Italian 1450-1517
paintings: (H) $407,000

RAIGUE, G. de la
paintings: (H) $3,080

RAIMONDI, Roberto
Italian b. 1877
paintings: (H) $1,870

RAIN, Charles
American contemporary
paintings: (L) $66; (H) $2,860

RAINER, Arnulf
German b. 1929
paintings: (L) $2,750; (H) $3,960

RAIPON
sculpture: (H) $1,100

RAJNERE, Gabrielle
paintings: (H) $880

RAKEMANN, Carl
American 1878-1965
paintings: (H) $1,100

RAKOFF, A.
paintings: (H) $1,045

RALEIGH, Charles Sidney
American 1831-1925
paintings: (L) $3,500; (H) $14,300

RALEIGH, Henry Patrick
American 1880-1945
drawings: (L) $198; (H) $750

RALLI, Theodore Jacques
Greek 1852-1909
paintings: (L) $2,530; (H) $44,000

RAMBERG, Arthur George
Austrian 1819-1875
paintings: (H) $8,800

RAMBERT, Rene
French 20th cent.
paintings: (L) $1,045; (H) $2,200

RAMEL, Pierre
French b. 1927
paintings: (H) $1,870

RAMIREZ, Saturnino
Colombian b. 1946
paintings: (L) $2,640; (H) $2,970

RAMM, John Henry
American 1879-1948
paintings: (L) $66; (H) $1,045

RAMOS
sculpture: (H) $3,300

RAMOS, Carlos Jose
paintings: (H) $1,210

RAMOS, Domingo
Cuban b. 1894
paintings: (L) $2,750; (H) $15,400

RAMOS, Lita
contemporary
paintings: (H) $1,045

RAMOS, Mel
American b. 1935
paintings: (L) $6,600; (H) $187,000
drawings: (L) $1,320; (H) $44,000

RAMOS, Patricio
Mexican 19th cent.
paintings: (H) $22,000

RAMOS, Tod
British 20th cent.
paintings: (H) $11,000

RAMPAZO, Luciano
French b. 1936
paintings: (L) $495; (H) $2,200

RAMSAY, Allan
English 1713-1784
paintings: (L) $1,650; (H) $17,600

RAMSAY, Allan, studio of
paintings: (H) $40,700

RAMSAY, Martha D.
American 19th/20th cent.
drawings: (H) $1,540

RAMSAY, Milne
American 1847-1915
paintings: (L) $550; (H) $16,500
drawings: (H) $990

RAMSDELL, Fred Winthrop
American 1865-1915
paintings: (L) $880; (H) $1,540

RAMSDELL, M. Louise, Lee
American 1883-1970
paintings: (L) $55; (H) $1,430
drawings: (H) $110

RAMSEY, Charles Frederick
American
paintings: (H) $6,050

RAMSEY, William
English 19th cent.
drawings: (H) $880

RAMSOM, Fletcher
American
paintings: (H) $3,000

RAN, Emil
German b. 1858
paintings: (H) $1,430

RANC, Jean
French 1674-1735
paintings: (H) $40,700

RANCOULET
sculpture: (H) $2,200

RANCOULET, Ernest
French 19th cent.
sculpture: (L) $1,540; (H) $5,500

RAND, Ellen G. Emmet,
Mrs. William B.
American 1876-1941
paintings: (L) $165; (H) $1,760

RAND, Henry Asbury
American b. 1886
paintings: (H) $1,320

RANDALL, Sarah
American 19th cent.
paintings: (H) $1,870

RANDALL, Wallace
American 20th cent.
paintings: (L) $250; (H) $2,600

RANDANINI, Carlo
Italian ac. 1881, d. 1884
paintings: (H) $3,080

RANDLE, Frederic
American 19th cent.
paintings: (H) $700

RANDOLPH, John
British 19th/20th cent.
paintings: (H) $3,300

RANDOLPH, Lee Fritz
American 1880-1956
paintings: (L) $935; (H) $935

RANE, Bill
American 20th cent.
paintings: (H) $935

RANFT, Richard
Swiss 1862-1931
paintings: (L) $1,045; (H) $28,600

RANFTL, Johann Matthias
Austrian 1805-1854
paintings: (H) $1,210

RANGEL, Mario
Mexican b. 1938
drawings: (H) $2,200

RANGER, Henry Ward
American 1858-1916
paintings: (L) $605; (H) $9,075
drawings: (L) $138; (H) $2,310

RANKEN, William Bruce Ellis
English 1881-1941
paintings: (H) $2,200

RANNEY, William Tylee
American 1813-1857
paintings: (L) $8,800; (H) $104,500
drawings: (H) $8,800

RANSOM, Fletcher C.
American 19th cent.
paintings: (L) $7,150; (H) $16,500

RANSON, Paul
French 1864-1909
paintings: (L) $30,800; (H) $374,000

RANSWYK, J.
Dutch 19th/20th cent.
paintings: (H) $880

RANZONI, Hans, the elder
Austrian b. 1868
paintings: (L) $660; (H) $1,980

RAOULT, Th.
paintings: (L) $1,210; (H) $3,960

RAOUX, Jean
French 1677-1734
paintings: (L) $6,875; (H) $20,900

RAPHAEL, Raffaello SANZIO
Italian 1483-1520
drawings: (H) $605,000

RAPHAEL, Joseph
American 1869/72-1950
paintings: (L) $110; (H) $14,300
drawings: (L) $770; (H) $1,540

RAPHAEL, L.
sculpture: (H) $1,210

RAPHAEL, W.
American 19th cent.
paintings: (H) $770

RAPP, J.H.T.
American 19th/20th cent.
paintings: (H) $4,400

RAPPINI, Vittorio
drawings: (H) $4,400

RASCH, Gustav
American 1836-1906
paintings: (L) $357; (H) $1,760

RASCH, H.
Dutch 19th cent.
paintings: (H) $2,200

RASCH, Heinrich
German 1840-1913
paintings: (L) $605; (H) $3,300

RASCHEN, Henry
American 1856/57-1937/38
paintings: (L) $715; (H) $19,800
drawings: (H) $1,700

RASINELLI, Roberto
Italian 19th cent.
paintings: (H) $2,750

RASKIN, Joseph
American 1897-1981
paintings: (L) $1,320; (H) $6,050

RASMUSSEN, Georg Anton
Swedish, d. Germ. 1842-1914
paintings: (L) $2,500; (H) $8,250

RASMUSSEN, John
American 1828-1895
paintings: (H) $52,250

RASMUSSEN, Otto
German b. 1845
sculpture: (L) $330; (H) $660

RATEAU, Armand Albert
French 20th cent.
sculpture: (H) $66,000

RATHBONE, Harold S.
British 1850-1920
paintings: (H) $935

RATHBONE, John
English 1750-1807
paintings: (L) $605; (H) $1,980

RATTI, Eduard
German b. 1816
paintings: (H) $3,300

RATTNER, Abraham
American 1895-1978
paintings: (L) $330; (H) $12,100
drawings: (L) $440; (H) $1,100

RAU, Emil
German b. 1858
paintings: (L) $2,200; (H) $14,300

RAU, N.
paintings: (H) $715

RAUCH, Johann
Austrian 19th cent.
paintings: (H) $1,980

RAUCHINGER, Heinrich
Polish 1859-1942
paintings: (L) $550; (H) $1,430

RAUDNITZ, Albert
German 1814-1899
paintings: (L) $4,400; (H) $20,900

RAUFER, Aloys
German 1794-1856
paintings: (H) $3,190

RAUGHT, John Willard
American 1857-1931
paintings: (L) $110; (H) $715

RAULAND, Orland
American
paintings: (H) $4,180

RAUPP, Karl
German 1837-1918
paintings: (L) $3,850; (H) $24,200

RAUSCHENBERG, Robert
American b. 1925
paintings: (L) $5,500; (H) $6,325,000
drawings: (L) $4,400; (H) $330,000
sculpture: (L) $9,900; (H) $3,740,000

RAUSTEYN, Hubert van
Dutch 1640-1691
paintings: (H) $1,540

RAUX, Louis Marchand des
French 20th cent.
paintings: (L) $77; (H) $1,045

RAV, F.
German 19th cent.
paintings: (H) $1,045

RAVANNE, Leon Gustave
paintings: (H) $2,640

RAVEN, Samuel
British 1775-1847
paintings: (L) $1,320; (H) $3,025

RAVENSTEYN, *H***
paintings: (H) $2,200

RAVENZWAAY, Adriana van
Dutch 1816-1872
paintings: (H) $27,500

RAVESTEYN, Dirck de Quade van
Dutch c.1565/1570-d. after 1619
paintings: (H) $176,000

RAVESTEYN, Jan Antoinisz. van
Dutch c. 1570-1657
paintings: (L) $3,850; (H) $15,400

RAVESTEYN, Jan van
Dutch
paintings: (H) $5,500

RAVLIN, Grace
American b. 1885
paintings: (L) $715; (H) $1,760

RAWBON, J.L.
American School 19th cent.
paintings: (H) $1,265

RAWSON, A.L.
American 1829-1902
paintings: (H) $3,300

RAWSON, Carl W.
American b. 1884
paintings: (L) $137; (H) $1,045

RAY, Man
American 1890-1976
paintings: (L) $1,100; (H) $148,500
drawings: (L) $1,870; (H) $31,900
sculpture: (L) $1,980; (H) $26,400

RAY, Ruth
American d. 1977
paintings: (L) $412; (H) $1,870

RAYASSE, Martial
French contemporary
paintings: (H) $20,900

RAYMOND, H.
American 19th cent.
paintings: (H) $1,300
drawings: (H) $220

RAYMONDS, E.
European 20th cent.
paintings: (H) $1,045

RAYNER, Louise J.
English 1829-1924
drawings: (L) $1,540; (H) $3,740

RAYNER, Margaret
English 19th/20th cent.
drawings: (L) $220; (H) $660

RAYO, Omar
South American 20th cent.
paintings: (L) $1,320; (H) $8,800

REA, Louis Edward
American 1868-1927
paintings: (L) $1,320; (H) $1,650

REACH, C.T.
paintings: (H) $660

READ, Elmer Joseph
American b. 1862
drawings: (L) $165; (H) $660

READ, Thomas
British 19th cent.
paintings: (H) $4,400

READ, Thomas Buchanan
American 1822-1872
paintings: (L) $220; (H) $3,520

READEN, Eric
paintings: (H) $715

REALFONSO, Tommaso, called
Masillo
Italian 18th cent.
paintings: (H) $23,100

REAM, Carducius Plantagenet
American 1837-1917
paintings: (L) $825; (H) $11,550

REAM, Morston C.
American 1840-1898
paintings: (L) $3,300; (H) $10,450

REASER, Robert Alden
paintings: (L) $577; (H) $935

REASER, Wilbur Aaron
American 1860-1942
paintings: (L) $1,650; (H) $1,870

REASONER, Gladys Thayer
American b. 1886
drawings: (L) $165; (H) $660

REBAY, Hilla
American 1890-1967
paintings: (L) $2,200; (H) $14,300
drawings: (L) $495; (H) $3,575

REBELL, Joseph
Austrian 1787-1828
paintings: (H) $33,000

REBELO, Domingo
paintings: (H) $2,750

REBEYROLLE, Paul
French b. 1926
paintings: (H) $14,300

RECCO, Giuseppe
Italian 1634-1695
paintings: (L) $16,500; (H) $17,600

RECIPON, Georges
French b. 1860
sculpture: (L) $935; (H) $2,200

RECKHARD, Gardner Arnold
American 1858-1908
paintings: (L) $165; (H) $3,575

RECKNAGEL, Theodore
German 19th cent.
paintings: (H) $660

REDDIE, Mac Ivor
American 20th cent.
paintings: (L) $900; (H) $1,100
drawings: (H) $1,200

REDEIN, Alexander
American
paintings: (L) $99; (H) $770

REDELIUS, F.H.
American 20th cent.
paintings: (L) $165; (H) $1,650

REDER, Bernard
Rumanian/American 1897-1963
sculpture: (L) $605; (H) $5,500

Artist and Actor

Granville Redmond (1871-1935) is recognized as one of the most important California Impressionists. Stricken with scarlet fever at age three, he suffered a permanent loss of hearing and speech. His family migrated to California shortly after his illness and enrolled him at the California School for the Deaf at Berkeley. An art instructor recognized and encouraged his artistic ability and taught him pantomine. After graduation, he entered the San Francisco School of Design and then continued his studies in Paris at the Academie Julian.

Redmond returned to California in 1898, married, and settled in Los Angeles. There he painted with other leading landscape painters and, in the era of silent films, became a part-time actor. Redmond developed a friendship with Charlie Chaplin and helped him perfect his pantomime techniques. Chaplin gave him a studio on his lot and bought many of Redmond's paintings.

Redmond's best-known movie role was the sculptor in Chaplin's *City Lights*; as a painter he is best known for his landscapes of poppies and lupines. Although his paintings have been collected privately for some time, it wasn't until 1987 that his work sold at auction for more than $10,000. In 1990, *Rolling Fields of Poppies and Lupine* set a record at $132,000. (Granville Redmond, *Rolling Fields of Poppies and Lupine*, oil on canvas, 26 x 43 in., Butterfield's, June 12, 1990, $132,000)

REDFIELD, Edward W.
American 1869-1965
paintings: (L) $495; (H) $137,500
drawings: (H) $550

REDGRAVE, Richard
English 1804-1888
paintings: (L) $3,960; (H) $4,950

REDIG, Laurent Herman
Dutch 1822-1861
paintings: (L) $990; (H) $1,760

REDIN, Paul
American 20th cent.
paintings: (H) $8,250

REDMILE, Anthony
sculpture: (H) $1,650

REDMOND, Granville
American 1871-1935
paintings: (L) $248; (H) $132,000

REDMORE, Henry
English 1820-1887
paintings: (L) $2,200; (H) $6,875

REDON, Odilon
French 1840-1916
paintings: (L) $49,500; (H) $1,650,000
drawings: (L) $3,300; (H) $2,310,000

REDOUTE, Pierre Joseph
French 1759-1840
paintings: (L) $6,050; (H) $28,600
drawings: (L) $26,400; (H) $27,500

REDPATH, Anne
Scottish 1895-1965
paintings: (H) $1,650

REDWOOD, Allen Carter
American 1844-1922
paintings: (H) $7,150
drawings: (L) $385; (H) $4,950

REECE, Maynard
American contemporary
paintings: (L) $522; (H) $4,675

REED
American 20th cent.
paintings: (H) $1,100

REED, E., "Popeye" Reed
20th cent.
sculpture: (H) $4,400

REED, Joseph Charles
English 1822-1877
drawings: (H) $990

REED, Marjorie
American b. 1915
paintings: (L) $165; (H) $2,200

REED, Paul
contemporary
paintings: (L) $33; (H) $1,760

REED, Scott
American 20th cent.
paintings: (H) $1,100

REED, Thomas Buchanan
American 1822-1872
paintings: (L) $132; (H) $5,500

REED, W.T.
paintings: (H) $1,650

REEDY, Leonard Howard
American 1899-1956
paintings: (L) $522; (H) $2,475
drawings: (L) $275; (H) $1,595

REEKERS, Hendrik
Dutch 1815-1854
paintings: (H) $15,400

REESBROECK, Jacob van
paintings: (H) $2,200

REESE, William
American
paintings: (H) $1,000

REEVS, George M.
American
drawings: (H) $715

REFREGIER, Anton
American b. 1905
paintings: (L) $110; (H) $770

REGAGNON, Albert
paintings: (H) $2,640

REGGIANINI, Vittorio
Italian b. 1858
paintings: (L) $1,210; (H) $93,500

REGGIO, Raffaellino Motta da
drawings: (H) $4,620

REGINATO, Peter
contemporary
sculpture: (H) $6,600

REGNAULT, Henri Alexandre Georges
French 1843-1871
paintings: (H) $2,310
drawings: (L) $715; (H) $2,420

REGNAULT, Jean Baptiste
French 1754-1829
paintings: (L) $3,575; (H) $825,000
drawings: (L) $605; (H) $1,650

REGNIER
sculpture: (H) $1,100

REGNIER, Nicolas, called Nicola
RENIERI
Flemish 1590-1667
paintings: (L) $14,300; (H) $104,500

REHDER, J.
paintings: (H) $2,090

REHDER, Julius Christian
German/American b. 1861
paintings: (L) $137; (H) $3,575
drawings: (L) $55; (H) $110

REHN, Frank Knox Morton
American 1848-1914
paintings: (L) $165; (H) $7,425
drawings: (L) $247; (H) $1,760

REICH, Albert
German b. 1881
paintings: (H) $2,200

Botanticals

Pierre-Joseph Redouté (1759-1840) is one of the world's most famous botanical artists, known for the beauty of his paintings as well as for their scientific accuracy. Born in Belgium, the son of a minor painter, he studied the works of the Dutch and Flemish masters and then moved to Paris at the age of twenty-four. There he became acquainted with a botanist named L'Heritier, who trained the young man as a botanical artist and took him to London to learn the techniques of stipple engraving. Upon his return, he became Master of Drawing to Queen Marie-Antoinette.

After the French Revolution, Redouté was named official painter for the Empress Josephine. Josephine loved horticulture and botany and all plants and flowers, particularly exotic ones. She lavished large sums on her gardens.

For his empress, Redouté created *Les Liliacées*, a printed book that illustrated the lilies, irises, amaryllis, tulips, and other flowers of the imperial gardens; Redouté painted four hundred and eighty-six watercolors on vellum for the colorplates. Using his own refinement of stipple engraving, he printed two hundred copies of the sixteen-volume work. The watercolors, accompanied by a unique copy of the printed text on vellum, became the property of the Empress Josephine. Upon her death the volumes passed to her son, Prince Eugène.

Over the years, nineteen of the watercolors were lost. In 1935, at the sale of Prince Eugène's library, the remaining four hundred and sixty-seven watercolors were acquired by a New York dealer. In 1985 the complete set was offered at auction at Sotheby's. According to the terms of the sale, the entire four hundred and sixty-seven lots (estimated at $5-$7 million) were to be offered as a single lot. If they failed to reach the reserve, each lot would be offered separately in the course of the day. Forty-five bidding numbers were assigned, but at 10:15 A.M., a dealer from Pennsylvania, who had organized a syndicate just to purchase *Les Liliacées*, bid $5 million plus a ten percent buyer's premium ($5,500,000). After the sale, the works were distributed to members of his syndicate. Since 1985 individual pieces from that sale have come up at auction. The more lavish the flower, the higher the price. (Pierre-Joseph Redouté, *Ixia Miniata, Ixia Minium,* pencil and watercolor on vellum, 18½ x 13⅜ in., Christie's, February 23, 1989, $28,600)

REICHARDT, Ferdinand
American 1819-1895
paintings: (L) $3,850; (H) $17,050

REICHEL
drawings: (H) $770

REICHER, C. Franz
paintings: (H) $2,090

REICHERT, Carl
Austrian 1836-1918
paintings: (L) $715; (H) $10,450

REICHMAN, Josephine
American b. 1864
paintings: (H) $1,650

REICHMANN, Franz
Austrian b. 1868
drawings: (H) $1,760

REID, Flora M.
British ac. 1879-1929
paintings: (L) $4,400; (H) $41,800

REID, George Ogilvy
British 1851-1928
paintings: (L) $440; (H) $2,200

REID, John, Jr.
drawings: (H) $825

REID, John Robertson
British 1851-1926
paintings: (L) $1,100; (H) $15,400
drawings: (H) $770

REID, Patty
American
drawings: (L) $700; (H) $1,100

REID, Robert
American b. 1924
paintings: (L) $715; (H) $198,000

REID, Robert
American 1862-1929
paintings: (L) $1,100; (H) $341,000
drawings: (L) $220; (H) $4,125

REID, Robert Payton
British b. 1859
paintings: (L) $110; (H) $2,200

REID, Samuel
British 1854-1919
paintings: (L) $1,100; (H) $4,400

REID, Stephen
British b. 1873
paintings: (L) $1,650; (H) $2,475

REIDER, H.
sculpture: (H) $825

REIDER, Marcel
French b. 1852
paintings: (H) $2,530

REIFFEL, Charles
American 1862-1942
paintings: (L) $467; (H) $30,800

REILLE, Karl, Baron
paintings: (H) $6,380

REILLY, Frank Joseph
American 1906-1967
paintings: (L) $330; (H) $1,650

REIN, Johan Eimerich
Norwegian 1827-1900
paintings: (H) $2,420

REIN, Surica Singer
American 20th cent.
paintings: (H) $990

REINAGLE, George Phillip
British 1802-1835
paintings: (H) $1,100

REINAGLE, Philipp
paintings: (H) $3,850

REINAGLE, Richard Ramsay
British 1775-1862
paintings: (H) $6,600

REINAGLE, W.
drawings: (H) $797

REINBERG, Conrad
German 19th cent.
paintings: (L) $2,530; (H) $2,640

REINDEL, William George
American 1871-1948
paintings: (L) $88; (H) $935

REINE, Minnie B.
paintings: (H) $990

REINER, Wenzel Lorenz
1689-1743
drawings: (H) $3,300

REINERT, A.
paintings: (H) $1,650

REINHARDT, Ad
American 1913-1967
paintings: (L) $34,100; (H) $2,530,000
drawings: (H) $24,200

REINHARDT, Louis
German d. 1870
paintings: (H) $2,090

REINHARDT, Ludwig
German d. 1870
paintings: (L) $550; (H) $4,950

REINHARDT, Siegfried
German/American b. 1925
paintings: (L) $88; (H)$5,225
drawings: (H) $77

REINHARDT, Wilhelm
German 1815-1881
paintings: (L) $1,100; (H) $1,760

REINHART, Benjamin Franklin
American 1829-1885
paintings: (L) $1,650; (H) $4,675

REINHART, Charles Stanley
American 1844-1896
drawings: (L) $330; (H) $1,045

REINHART, Johann Christian
1761-1847
drawings: (H) $935

REINHOLD, Franz
Austrian 1816-1893
paintings: (L) $743; (H) $4,950

REINHOLD, Friedrich, the younger
Austrian 1814-1881
paintings: (H) $5,225

REINHOLD, Theobald, Baron
von OER
German 1807-1885
paintings: (H) $17,600

REINIGER, Otto
German 1863-1909
paintings: (H) $1,045

REINPRECHT, J.K.
Dutch School 19th cent.
paintings: (H) $1,760

REINPRECHT, Josef
late 19th/early 20th cent
paintings: (H) $687

REISMAN, Philip
American b. 1904
paintings: (L) $193; (H) $4,950
drawings: (L) $82; (H) $99

REISS, Lionel S.
American
paintings: (H) $1,980
drawings: (L) $440; (H) $880

REISS, Winold
German/American 1886-1953
drawings: (L) $82; (H) $5,775

REISZ, Frank
American 20th cent.
paintings: (L) $385; (H) $880

REISZ, Herman
Austrian b. 1865
paintings: (H) $3,300

REITER, Johan Baptist
American 1813-1890
paintings: (H) $13,750

REITZEL, Marques E.
American b. 1896
paintings: (H) $1,430

REKOWSKY, F.
Continental 19th/20th cent.
paintings: (H) $880

RELINGER, Joseph
American 19th cent.
paintings: (L) $4,180; (H) $7,700

RELLI, Conrad Marca
contemporary
drawings: (H) $935

REMBRANDT, Rembrandt Harmensz
van RIJN
Dutch 1606-1669
drawings: (L) $79,200; (H) $957,000

REMENICK, Seymour
American b. 1923
paintings: (L) $55; (H) $660
drawings: (H) $55

REMICK, Harry E.
American 1846-1877
drawings: (L) $165; (H) $4,400

REMINGTON, Deborah
American b. 1930/35
paintings: (L) $825; (H) $4,400

REMINGTON, Frederic Sackrider
American 1861-1909
paintings: (L) $3,960; (H) $4,730,000
drawings: (L) $1,100; (H) $170,500
sculpture: (L) $550; (H) $4,400,000

REMISOFF, Nicolai
Russian/American b. 1887
paintings: (L) $385; (H) $1,320
drawings: (L) $220; (H) $1,540

REMSEN, Ira, Rem
American 1876-1928
paintings: (H) $44,000

REMY, A.D.
Italian 19th cent.
paintings: (H) $1,650

REN, Chuck
American contemporary
paintings: (L) $5,500; (H) $40,700

RENARD, Charles
French 19th cent.
paintings: (H) $1,430

RENARD, Emile
paintings: (H) $880

RENARD, Emile
French 1850-1930
paintings: (H) $1,980

RENARD, Fernand
French? contemporary
paintings: (L) $550; (H) $1,320

RENARD, Jean Augustine
French 1744-1807
drawings: (H) $4,620

RENARD, Marcel
sculpture: (L) $880; (H) $1,540

RENARD, Paul
French 1871-1920
paintings: (H) $880
drawings: (L) $3,025; (H) $4,675

RENAUDIN, Alfred
French b. 1866
paintings: (L) $1,100; (H) $18,700

RENAUDOT, Paul
French 1871-1920
paintings: (H) $935

RENAULT, Charles Edmond
paintings: (H) $2,750

RENAULT, Gaston
French 19th cent.
paintings: (H) $3,520

RENAULT, Luigi P.
Italian ac. 1850-1880
paintings: (H) $2,310

RENCOULET
sculpture: (H) $660

RENDA, G.
Italian
sculpture: (H) $1,045

RENDEUSE, Renier, called Renier
Panhay De Rendeuse
1684-1754
drawings: (H) $1,700

RENDINA, Mario
American School 20th cent.
paintings: (H) $990

RENDON, Manuel
Ecuadorean b. 1894
paintings: (L) $715; (H) $2,750

RENE, Jean Jacques
French 20th cent.
paintings: (L) $715; (H) $1,980

RENEE, E.
French 19th cent.
paintings: (H) $3,300

RENESON, Chet
drawings: (L) $990; (H) $1,430

RENFROW, Greg
contemporary
paintings: (L) $440; (H) $1,100

RENHOF
French School mid-19th cent.
paintings: (H) $1,045

RENI, Guido
Italian 1575-1642
paintings: (H) $88,000
drawings: (L) $1,540; (H) $44,000

RENI, Guido, studio of
paintings: (H) $1,760

RENIER, Joseph Emile
American 1887-1966
sculpture: (H) $3,575

RENNER, O.
drawings: (L) $550; (H) $715

En Grisaille

Frederic Sackrider Remington (1861-1909) was an illustrator, painter, and sculptor of the American West. He was born in upstate New York and attended Yale but dropped out of school after his sophomore year when his father died. In 1880 he traveled throughout the West, prospecting, cowpunching, and sketching. By 1886 prints of his illustrations from *Collier's, Scribner's,* and *Harper's Weekly* had made his name a household word. In 1885 Remington was invited to exhibit at the National Academy of Art, a great honor for an illustrator. He began working as a sculptor the same year and soon became one of the most popular and prolific sculptors of the American West. He created twenty pieces of sculpture, among them some of his most valuable works. By 1905 Remington was painting almost exclusively for exhibition and began to incorporate some of the techniques of American Impressionism in his work. In 1909, at age 48, he died suddenly of complications from an appendicitis attack.

En grisaille is French for "shades of gray" and is used to describe paintings executed in black and white and shades of gray. During the last quarter of the nineteenth century many illustrators painted *en grisaille* because it reproduced best in photographs. Paintings were photographed and used as illustrations for news articles or books. (Frederic Sackrider Remington, *Mounted Lawman Shooting a Falling Outlaw,* oil on canvas, 34 x 22 in., Du Mouchelle, November 17, 1989, $165,000)

RENO, Jim
American
sculpture: (H) $13,000

RENOIR, Pierre Auguste
French 1841-1919
paintings: (L) $12,100; (H) $78,100,000
drawings: (L) $2,200; (H) $2,860,000
sculpture: (L) $5,225; (H) $242,000

RENOIR, Pierre Auguste and MOREL, Louis
sculpture: (H) $14,850

RENOIR, Pierre Auguste and Richard GUINO
sculpture: (L) $5,500; (H) $198,000

RENOUARD, George
American b. 1885
paintings: (L) $110; (H) $1,210

RENOUF, Edda
Mexican/American b. 1943
paintings: (H) $1,650
drawings: (L) $550; (H) $3,300

RENOUF, Emile
French 1845-1894
paintings: (L) $19,800; (H) $137,500

RENOUX, Charles Caius
French 1795-1846
paintings: (H) $7,700

RENOUX, Jules Ernest
French 1863-1932
paintings: (L) $935; (H) $6,050

RENSHAW, A.
paintings: (H) $1,540

RENSHAW, J.
paintings: (H) $715
drawings: (H) $44

RENTZ
European 20th cent.
paintings: (H) $1,100

RENYA, Antonio
paintings: (H) $7,480

REPIN, Ilya Efimovich
Russian 1844-1930
paintings: (L) $3,080; (H) $1,100,000

REPP, O.
Continental 19th cent.
paintings: (H) $935

RESCH, W.S.
sculpture: (H) $1,650

RESCHI, Pandolfo
Polish 1634 or 1643-1699
paintings: (L) $14,850; (H) $25,300

RESEDER, F.M.T.
American 19th cent.
paintings: (H) $1,980

RESIKA, Paul
American 20th cent.
paintings: (L) $715; (H) $1,430
drawings: (L) $550; (H) $770

RESNICK, Milton
American b. 1917
paintings: (L) $1,430; (H) $132,000

RESTORI, M.M.
paintings: (H) $8,250

RESTOUT, Jean
paintings: (L) $9,900; (H) $77,000

RESTOUT, Jean, the younger
French 1692-1768
paintings: (L) $3,850; (H) $9,900

RETH, Alfred
French 1884-1966
paintings: (L) $4,620; (H) $11,000
drawings: (H) $4,400

RETH, Caspar von
German 1858-1913
paintings: (H) $16,500

RETHEL, Alfred
German 1816-1859
paintings: (H) $22,000

RETTEGI, Steven
American 20th cent.
paintings: (H) $1,100

RETTIG, Heinrich
paintings: (H) $1,100

RETTIG, John
American 1860-1932
paintings: (L) $110; (H) $2,090
drawings: (L) $44; (H) $302

RETTIG, Martin
American 20th cent.
paintings: (L) $220; (H) $700

RETZ, Eudes Alfred Francois de
French b. 1857
paintings: (H) $2,420

REULANDT, Le Grand de
American
paintings: (H) $26,400

REUSENBERG, ***
paintings: (H) $660

REUSSWIG, William
American b. 1902
paintings: (H) $1,760

REUTERDAHL, Henry
American 1871-1925
drawings: (L) $247; (H) $1,430

REVEL, Gabriel
1642-1712
paintings: (H) $4,620

REVERON, Armando
Venezuelan 1889/90-1954
paintings: (L) $22,000; (H) $308,000
drawings: (H) $26,400

REVILLE, H. Whittaker
British ac. 1881-1903
paintings: (H) $7,975

REVOIL, Pierre
paintings: (H) $1,100

REVOL, Guy
French b. 1912
sculpture: (H) $1,045

REYES, Jesus
Mexican 20th cent.
paintings: (H) $660
drawings: (H) $66

REYES, Juan Cruz
sculpture: (H) $1,100

REYHER, Max
American 1862-1945
paintings: (H) $5,500

REYMANN, J.
paintings: (H) $1,650

REYMOND, Carlos
paintings: (H) $2,420

REYNA, Antonio
Spanish 19th/20th cent.
paintings: (L) $1,320; (H) $48,400
drawings: (L) $550; (H) $1,870

REYNARD, Flora C.
drawings: (H) $715

REYNARD, Grant
American 1887-1967
drawings: (L) $55; (H) $700

REYNAUD, Francois
French 1825-1909
paintings: (L) $440; (H) $1,100

REYNAUD, Marius
paintings: (H) $1,320

REYNOLD, A.
paintings: (H) $1,045

REYNOLDS, Alan
drawings: (H) $1,760

REYNOLDS, Frederick Thomas
American b. 1882
paintings: (L) $1,870; (H) $3,300

REYNOLDS, James E.
American b. 1926
paintings: (L) $1,760; (H) $35,000
drawings: (H) $55

REYNOLDS, Sir Joshua
English 1723-1792
paintings: (L) $1,100; (H) $363,000
drawings: (H) $303

REYNOLDS, W.J.
paintings: (H) $660

REYNOLDS, W.S.
paintings: (H) $1,760

REYNOLDS, W.S.
American 19th/20th cent.
paintings: (L) $4,400; (H) $17,600

REYNOLDS, Wellington Jarard
American b. 1866
paintings: (L) $77; (H) $1,100

REYNOT
sculpture: (H) $7,700

REYNTJENS, Henrich Engelbert
Dutch 1817-1859
paintings: (L) $550; (H) $3,850

REZIA, Felice A.
French 19th/20th cent.
paintings: (L) $825; (H) $1,210

REZIA, V.
19th/20th cent.
paintings: (H) $1,430

REZNIKOFF, Misha
American b. 1935
paintings: (H) $825
drawings: (L) $22; (H) $495

RHEAD, Louis
American 1857-1926
paintings: (H) $750
drawings: (H) $495

RHIJN, Abraham van
Dutch School 19th cent.
paintings: (H) $1,650

RHODES, Joseph
British 1782-1854
paintings: (H) $1,650

RHOMBERG, Hanno
German 1820-1869
paintings: (L) $770; (H) $11,000

RHYS, Oliver
British ac. 1876-1893
paintings: (L) $2,750; (H) $12,100

RIANCHO Y MORA, Augustin
paintings: (H) $5,280

RIBA, Paul
American b. 1912
paintings: (L) $1,210; (H) $3,300
drawings: (L) $55; (H) $1,650

RIBA-ROVIRA, Francois
paintings: (H) $4,950

RIBAK, Louis
American 1902/03-1980
paintings: (L) $528; (H) $2,420
drawings: (H) $121

RIBAK, Tzvi
Russian/Israeli b. 1910
paintings: (L) $3,300; (H) $13,200

RIBCOWSKY, Dey de
American 1880-1936
paintings: (L) $330; (H) $4,950

RIBERA, Jusepe de, called
L'Espagnolet
Spanish 1588-1656
paintings: (L) $8,250; (H) $350,000

RIBERA, Jusepe de, studio of
paintings: (L) $1,650; (H) $99,000

RIBERA, Pierre
French 1867-1932
paintings: (L) $5,500; (H) $121,000

RIBLOWSKY, D.
Polish/Russian 19th/20th cent.
paintings: (H) $1,540

RIBOT, Germain Theodore
French d. 1893
paintings: (L) $22,000; (H) $121,000

RIBOT, Theodule Augustin
French 1823-1891
paintings: (L) $770; (H) $90,200
drawings: (H) $1,100

RICARDI, G.
paintings: (H) $990

RICARDI, G.
Italian 19th cent.
paintings: (H) $1,430

RICARDI, G.
Italian 20th cent.
paintings: (H) $825

RICCHI, Pietro, Il Lucchese
1605-1675
paintings: (H) $2,200

RICCI, Alfredo
Italian 1864-1889
paintings: (H) $1,100

RICCI, Arturo
Italian b. 1854
paintings: (L) $880; (H) $27,500
drawings: (H) $1,650

RICCI, Dante
Italian 20th cent.
paintings: (L) $275; (H) $880
drawings: (L) $248; (H) $880

RICCI, E.
paintings: (H) $880

RICCI, Giovanni, called Gianpietrino
Italian ac. c. 1520-1540
paintings: (H) $49,500

RICCI, Guido
paintings: (H) $660

RICCI, M.
paintings: (H) $1,925

RICCI, Marco
Italian 1676-1729
drawings: (L) $4,400; (H) $26,400

RICCI, Michele
Italian 19th cent.
paintings: (H) $1,100

RICCI, Pio
Italian d. 1919
paintings: (L) $1,870; (H) $12,650
drawings: (H) $522

RICCI, Sebastiano
Italian 1659-1734
paintings: (L) $9,900; (H) $209,000

RICCIARDI
paintings: (H) $990

RICCIARDI, Cesare A.
American b. 1892
paintings: (L) $77; (H) $880
drawings: (H) $165

RICCIARDI, Oscar
Italian 1864-1935
paintings: (L) $110; (H) $4,675

RICCIARELLI, Daniele, called Daniele
da VOLTERRA
Italian 1509-1566
drawings: (H) $24,200

RICCO, A.
paintings: (H) $660

RICCU, J.
American
paintings: (H) $880

RICE, Henry Webster
American 1853-1933
drawings: (L) $55; (H) $825

RICE, Marion
American 20th cent.
paintings: (L) $60; (H) $1,045

RICH, John Hubbard
American 1876-1955?
paintings: (L) $88; (H) $3,300
drawings: (L) $275; (H) $1,650

RICHARD
paintings: (H) $137
sculpture: (L) $1,100; (H) $1,210

RICHARD, Durando T.
French/Argentinian 20th cent.
paintings: (H) $825

RICHARD, E.
German ac. 1720-1735
paintings: (L) $935; (H) $990

RICHARD, J.
American early 20th cent.
paintings: (H) $660

RICHARD, Jean Claude, ABBE DE
SAINT-NON
1727-1791
drawings: (H) $2,200

RICHARD, R.P.
English 19th cent.
paintings: (H) $660

RICHARD, Rene
Canadian 1895-1982
paintings: (L) $770; (H) $1,100

RICHARD-PUTZ, Michel
French b. 1868
paintings: (H) $17,600

RICHARDS, Addison T.
American 1820-1900
paintings: (H) $2,310

RICHARDS, Anne Marie
American 1870-1952
drawings: (H) $1,265

RICHARDS, C.
British 19th cent.
paintings: (H) $660

RICHARDS, Ella E.
American 20th cent.
paintings: (L) $220; (H) $1,980

RICHARDS, Frederick De Berg
American 1864-1921
paintings: (H) $3,080

RICHARDS, Frederick De Bourg
American 1822-1903
paintings: (L) $220; (H) $23,100
drawings: (L) $175; (H) $700

RICHARDS, Gustave
Continental 19th cent.
paintings: (L) $1,980; (H) $1,980

RICHARDS, J.
paintings: (H) $660

RICHARDS, John Inigo
English 1720-1810
paintings: (H) $110,000

RICHARDS, Lucy Currier
American
sculpture: (H) $1,870

RICHARDS, Thomas Addison
Anglo/American 1820-1900
paintings: (L) $550; (H) $4,950

RICHARDS, W.
English 19th cent.
paintings: (L) $193; (H) $2,420

RICHARDS, William Trost
American 1833-1905
paintings: (L) $137; (H) $275,000
drawings: (L) $55; (H) $41,800

RICHARDS, Wit.
paintings: (H) $660

RICHARDSON
American 19th cent.
paintings: (H) $660

RICHARDSON, C.
British 1853-1932
drawings: (H) $660

RICHARDSON, Francis Henry
American 1859-1934
paintings: (L) $357; (H) $935
drawings: (L) $83; (H) $550

RICHARDSON, G.M.
American 19th/20th cent.
paintings: (H) $797

RICHARDSON, G.S.
American 19th cent.
paintings: (H) $1,045

RICHARDSON, Jonathan
paintings: (H) $2,860

RICHARDSON, Louis H.
American 1853-1923
paintings: (L) $138; (H) $4,180

RICHARDSON, Mary Curtis
American 1848-1931
paintings: (L) $660; (H) $8,800
drawings: (L) $55; (H) $825

RICHARDSON, Paul
British b. 1943
paintings: (L) $412; (H) $825

RICHARDSON, Sam
American 20th cent.
paintings: (H) $1,100

RICHARDSON, T.M.
English 19th cent.
paintings: (H) $825

RICHARDSON, Theodore J.
American 1855-1914
drawings: (L) $192; (H) $1,540

RICHARDSON, Thomas Miles, Jr.
English 1813-1890
drawings: (L) $302; (H) $9,350

RICHARDSON, Volney Allan
American b. 1880
paintings: (L) $550; (H) $2,640

RICHARDSON, W.
European 19th cent.
paintings: (H) $1,320

RICHARDSON, William
American
drawings: (H) $3,575

RICHARDSON, William
British ac. 1842-1877
drawings: (H) $4,620

RICHARDT, Ferdinand
American 1819-1895
paintings: (L) $8,250; (H) $11,000
drawings: (H) $880

RICHE, Adele
French 1791-1878
paintings: (H) $12,100
drawings: (L) $440; (H) $1,430

RICHE, Louis
French b. 1887
sculpture: (L) $165; (H) $3,300

RICHEBE, Horace
French 1871-1937
paintings: (H) $715

RICHENBERG, Robert
contemporary
paintings: (H) $715

RICHENBURG, Robert B.
b. 1917
paintings: (L) $715; (H) $4,400
drawings: (H) $165

RICHER, B.
French 1849-1933
sculpture: (H) $850

RICHER, S.
paintings: (H) $990

RICHERT, Charles Henry
American b. 1880
paintings: (L) $82; (H) $1,210
drawings: (L) $92; (H) $468

RICHET, Jean
French b. 1929
paintings: (H) $1,045

RICHET, Leon
French 1847-1907
paintings: (L) $935; (H) $16,500

RICHEZ, Jean
French b. 1929
paintings: (L) $550; (H) $990

RICHIER, Germaine
French 1904-1959
sculpture: (L) $13,200; (H) $550,000

RICHIR, Herman Jean Joseph
Belgian b. 1866
paintings: (L) $1,870; (H) $12,100

RICHMOND, Agnes M.
American c. 1870-1964
paintings: (L) $800; (H) $14,300

RICHMOND, Leonard
British d. 1965
paintings: (L) $220; (H) $825
drawings: (L) $220; (H) $935

RICHTER, A.
German late 19th cent.
paintings: (H) $715

RICHTER, Edouard Frederic Wilhelm
French 1844-1913
paintings: (L) $4,950; (H) $33,000

RICHTER, Gerhard
American b. 1928
paintings: (L) $11,000; (H) $616,000
drawings: (L) $2,640; (H) $7,150

RICHTER, Guido Paul
German 1859-1941
paintings: (H) $121,000

RICHTER, Gustav
paintings: (H) $880

RICHTER, Gustav Karl
German 1823-1884
paintings: (H) $33,000

RICHTER, H. Davis
paintings: (L) $1,760; (H) $2,090

RICHTER, Henry
American 1870-1960
paintings: (L) $302; (H) $880
drawings: (L) $116; (H) $412

RICHTER, Herbert Davis
English 1874-1955
paintings: (H) $1,045

RICHTER, Johann
Swedish 1665/85-1745
paintings: (H) $429,000

RICHTER, Klaus
German b. 1887
paintings: (H) $1,100

RICHTER, Leopoldo
paintings: (H) $4,400
drawings: (H) $2,200

RICHTER, Luisa
paintings: (H) $1,980
drawings: (H) $880

RICHTER, Thomas E.
American
paintings: (H) $1,045

RICHTER-REICH, F.M.
paintings: (H) $2,420

RICKETSON, Walton
American b. 1839
sculpture: (H) $797

RICKEY, George
American b. 1907
sculpture: (L) $880; (H) $74,250

RICKMAN, Phillip
British b. 1891
drawings: (H) $1,980

RICKS, Don
American 20th cent.
paintings: (H) $770

RICKS, Douglas
American contemporary
paintings: (L) $4,200; (H) $6,500

RICKS, J.
British 19th/20th cent.
paintings: (H) $3,575

RICO Y CEJUDO, Jose
Spanish b. 1864
paintings: (H) $6,600

RICO Y ORTEGA, Martin
Spanish 1833-1908
paintings: (L) $220; (H) $165,000
drawings: (L) $990; (H) $15,400

RICOEUR, Nicolas
paintings: (H) $12,100

RICOIS, Frances Edme
French 1795-1881
paintings: (H) $3,190

RICQUIER, Louis
Belgian 1792-1884
paintings: (H) $7,975

RIDDEL, James
British 1858-1928
paintings: (H) $1,100

RIDDICK, Ron
American contemporary
paintings: (H) $4,000

RIDEOUT, Phillip H.
English 19th/20th cent.
paintings: (L) $468; (H) $7,150

RIDER, A.J.
paintings: (H) $4,400

RIDER, Arthur Grover
American 1886-1975
paintings: (L) $825; (H) $18,700
drawings: (L) $522; (H) $660

RIDER, Henry Orne, also RYDER
American b. 1860
paintings: (L) $50; (H) $1,100

RIDINGER, Johann Elias
German 1698-1767
drawings: (L) $2,090; (H) $8,800

RIDINGER, Martin Elias
drawings: (H) $715

RIDOLFI, Claudio
drawings: (H) $880

RIEBIR, Herman
paintings: (H) $1,210

RIECK, Ernst
German 19th cent.
paintings: (L) $1,320; (H) $2,750

RIECKE, George
American 1848-1924
paintings: (L) $330; (H) $3,190

RIECKE, Johann Georg Lodewyck
Dutch 1817-1898
paintings: (L) $330; (H) $2,860

RIED, Robert
American 1862-1929
paintings: (H) $4,400

RIEDER, D.
Continental 19th/20th cent.
sculpture: (H) $715

RIEDER, Marcel
French b. 1852
paintings: (H) $6,600

RIEDMAYER, Francesco Marie
late 18th cent.
paintings: (H) $3,300

RIEGEN, Nicholas
Dutch 1827-1889
paintings: (L) $880; (H) $2,475

RIEGER, Albert
Austrian b. 1834
paintings: (L) $1,600; (H) $15,400
drawings: (H) $137

RIELLE, Rainer Zstvanffy Gabinelle
drawings: (H) $1,045

RIEMERSCHMID, Rudolf
German b. 1873
paintings: (H) $8,800

RIESENBERG, Sidney H.
American b. 1885
paintings: (L) $248; (H) $2,475

RIESENER, Henri Francois
French 1767-1828
paintings: (H) $5,500

RIESTER, Garey
contemporary
paintings: (L) $412; (H) $880

RIESTRA, Adolfo
Mexican b. 1944
sculpture: (H) $3,575

RIETSCHEL, Ernest Friedrich August
German
sculpture: (L) $6,050; (H) $18,700

RIETSCHOOF, Jan Claes
Dutch 1652-1719
paintings: (L) $9,350; (H) $22,000

RIETVELD, Antonie
paintings: (L) $6,050; (H) $17,600

RIFKA, Judy
American b. 1945
paintings: (L) $1,540; (H) $6,820

RIGAUD, F.
French early 20th cent.
sculpture: (H) $4,950

RIGAUD, Gaspard
1661-1705
paintings: (H) $7,150

RIGAUD, Hyacinthe
French 1659-1743
paintings: (H) $110,000

RIGAUD, Jean
French b. 1912
paintings: (L) $660; (H) $2,090

RIGAUD, John Francis
English 1742-1810
paintings: (H) $34,100

RIGAUD, Pierre Gaston
French b. 1874
paintings: (L) $440; (H) $1,980

RIGBY
drawings: (H) $1,100

RIGGS, Robert
American 1896-1970
paintings: (L) $1,320; (H) $24,200
drawings: (H) $550

RIGHETTI, F.
Roman
sculpture: (H) $7,425

RIGNANO, Vittorio
Italian 1860-1916
paintings: (L) $742; (H) $2,860

RIGOLOT, Albert Gabriel
French 1862-1932
paintings: (L) $990; (H) $39,600

RIGOT, Georges
sculpture: (H) $3,850

RIGOTARD, Alexandre
French 19th cent.
paintings: (H) $880

RIGUIL
sculpture: (H) $1,210

RIJ-ROUSSEAU, Jeanne
French 1870-1956
drawings: (H) $1,320

RIJKELIJKHIJSEN, Hermanus Jan
Herndrick
Dutch 1813-1883
paintings: (L) $220; (H) $2,750

RIJSWIJCK, Jan van
Dutch 20th cent.
paintings: (L) $264; (H) $1,980

RIJSWIJK, Johanna van
Dutch School 1893-1956
paintings: (H) $1,045

RIKELME, Claudio
paintings: (L) $4,620; (H) $9,350

RIKET, Leon
European 19th cent.
paintings: (H) $2,530

RIKNER, H.
Continental 19th cent.
drawings: (H) $715

RILEY, Bridget
British b. 1931
paintings: (L) $26,400; (H) $93,500
drawings: (L) $1,980; (H) $5,720

RILEY, John
paintings: (L) $1,320; (H) $3,575

RILEY, Kenneth
American b. 1919
paintings: (L) $700; (H) $29,700

RILLA, Boemm
paintings: (H) $1,320

RIMBERT, Arthur
paintings: (H) $1,045

RIMBERT, Rene
French 20th cent.
paintings: (H) $7,700

RIMMER
paintings: (H) $660

RIMMER, William
American 1816-1879
sculpture: (H) $29,700

RIMSA, Juan
Lithuanian b. 1903
paintings: (H) $3,300

RINALDI, Claudio
Italian 19th/20th cent.
paintings: (L) $660; (H) $2,750

RINALDI, F.
Italian 19th cent.
paintings: (H) $2,200

RINALDI, Felice
Italian 18th cent.
paintings: (H) $14,300

RINCON, Agapito
drawings: (H) $3,080

RINEHARDT, Siegfried
American 1925-1984
paintings: (H) $1,650

RINEHART, William Henry
American 1825-1874
paintings: (L) $2,090; (H) $57,200

RING, Ole
paintings: (L) $1,210; (H) $1,980

RING, Pieter de
Dutch 1615-1660
paintings: (L) $49,500; (H) $264,000

RING, Sorenson
sculpture: (H) $2,035

RINOVIANA
paintings: (H) $825

RIO Y CEJUDO
paintings: (H) $880

RIOLO, T.
Italian 19th cent.
drawings: (H) $1,320

RION, Hanna
American 1875-1924
paintings: (H) $715

RIOPELLE, Jean Paul
Canadian b. 1922/23
paintings: (L) $4,400; (H) $1,540,000
drawings: (L) $6,250; (H) $30,800
sculpture: (H) $5,500

RIOS, A.
Spanish 20th cent.
paintings: (H) $715

RIOZELLA, I. Geo.
paintings: (H) $1,430

RIP, Willem Cornelis
Dutch 1856-1922
paintings: (L) $2,750; (H) $4,400
drawings: (L) $495; (H) $1,650

RIPAMONTE, R.R.
sculpture: (H) $1,650

RIPARI, Virgilio
Italian 1843/46-1902
paintings: (L) $88; (H) $2,200

RIPATRANSONE, Padre Francesco
Maria da
drawings: (H) $4,620

RIPLEY, Aiden Lassell
American 1896-1969
paintings: (L) $275; (H) $58,300
drawings: (L) $77; (H) $18,150

RIPPS, Rodney
American 20th cent.
paintings: (H) $2,200
sculpture: (H) $5,500

RISCHELL, Claude
American 20th cent.
paintings: (H) $907

RISHER, Anna Priscilla
American 1875-1946
paintings: (H) $1,210

RISING
paintings: (H) $825

RISSE, James
drawings: (H) $770

RISSE, Roland
German b. 1835
paintings: (H) $3,300

RITCHIE, Duncan S.
English 19th cent.
paintings: (H) $2,530

RITCHIE, John
paintings: (H) $9,350

RITCHIE, John
British ac. 1858-1875
paintings: (L) $2,750; (H) $4,070

RITMAN, Louis
American 1889-1963
paintings: (L) $715; (H) $451,000

RITSCHEL, William P.
German/American 1864-1949
paintings: (L) $550; (H) $66,000
drawings: (L) $242; (H) $6,050

RITSCHL, Otto
contemporary
paintings: (L) $2,310; (H) $3,500

RITT, Augustin
drawings: (H) $1,320

RITTENBERG, Henry R.
Russian/American 1879-1969
paintings: (L) $110; (H) $5,225

RITTER, Caspar
German 1861-1923
paintings: (L) $1,650; (H) $3,300

RITTER, Ernest W.
American
paintings: (H) $1,430

RITTER, Laslo
paintings: (H) $1,210

RITTER, Paul
German/American 1829-1907
paintings: (L) $467; (H) $3,850

RITTER, Paul
German/American 1859-1888
paintings: (H) $990

RITTER, Richard
contemporary
sculpture: (H) $2,860

RITTWEGER, J.G.
German 19th cent.
paintings: (H) $4,950

RITZ, Rafael
Swiss 1829-1894
paintings: (H) $30,800

RIVA
drawings: (H) $935

RIVA, Giussepe
Italian 19th cent.
drawings: (H) $1,210

RIVAS
drawings: (H) $825

RIVAS, Antonio
Italian 19th cent.
paintings: (L) $2,640; (H) $5,225

RIVAS, Antonio
Italian 19th/20th cent.
paintings: (L) $1,200; (H) $6,050

RIVAS, E.M.
drawings: (H) $687

RIVAS, J.M.
Spanish 19th/20th cent.
paintings: (H) $1,430

RIVERA, Carlos
Mexican 19th cent.
paintings: (H) $23,100

RIVERA, Diego
Mexican 1886-1957
paintings: (L) $9,900; (H) $605,000
drawings: (L) $275; (H) $77,000

RIVERA, Jose de
American b. 1904
sculpture: (L) $8,800; (H) $28,600

RIVERA, Manuel
b. Spain 1927
sculpture: (L) $1,650; (H) $14,300

RIVEROS, Jorge
paintings: (H) $4,400

RIVERS, Denton
English (?) 19th cent.
paintings: (H) $660

RIVERS, G.D.
British 19th cent.
paintings: (H) $660

RIVERS, Larry
American b. 1923
paintings: (L) $3,520; (H) $467,500
drawings: (L) $1,100; (H) $88,000
sculpture: (L) $11,000; (H) $27,500

RIVERS, Larry, collaboration with
Kenneth Koch
paintings: (H) $35,750

RIVERS, Leopold
British 1850/52-1905
paintings: (L) $600; (H) $825

RIVES, Anthony
English 19th cent.
paintings: (H) $1,760

RIVES, Frances E.
American 1890-1968
paintings: (H) $4,675

RIVIERE, Briton
British 1840-1920
paintings: (L) $1,650; (H) $7,150

RIVIERE, Henry Parsons
English 1811-1888
paintings: (L) $44; (H) $7,425

RIVIERE, J.L.
paintings: (H) $880

RIVIERE, Maurice Guiraud
French b. 1881
sculpture: (L) $660; (H) $17,600

RIVIERE, Theodore
French 1857-1912
sculpture: (L) $2,420; (H) $7,150

RIVOIRE, Francois
French 1842-1919
drawings: (L) $3,080; (H) $19,800

RIVOIRE, Raymond Leon
French b. 1884
sculpture: (L) $4,400; (H) $4,950

RIX, Julian Walbridge
American 1850-1903
paintings: (L) $412; (H) $10,450
drawings: (L) $467; (H) $1,980

RIZOS, Jacques
Greek 19th cent.
paintings: (H) $7,150

RIZZO, E.
Italian 19th/20th cent.
paintings: (H) $1,650

RIZZONI, Alexandre
Russian 1836-1902
paintings: (H) $4,400

ROBADI, V.
paintings: (H) $797

ROBB, Elizabeth B.
American 20th cent.
paintings: (L) $110; (H) $5,225

ROBB, J.E.
American 19th/20th cent.
paintings: (H) $14,300

ROBB, Samuel
American 1851-1928
sculpture: (L) $19,800; (H) $74,250

ROBBE, H.
paintings: (H) $880

ROBBE, Henri
Belgian 1807-1899
paintings: (L) $24,750; (H) $55,000

ROBBE, Louis Marie Dominique
Romaine
Belgian 1806-1887
paintings: (L) $990; (H) $16,500

ROBBINS, Bruce
American b. 1948
paintings: (L) $154; (H) $18,700
drawings: (H) $3,300

ROBBINS, Ellen
American 1828-1905
paintings: (L) $330; (H) $440
drawings: (L) $55; (H) $4,125

ROBBINS, Horace Wolcott, Jr.
American 1842-1904
paintings: (L) $12,100; (H) $26,400
drawings: (H) $1,650

ROBBINS, Nrice
sculpture: (H) $660

ROBERT, Anton
paintings: (H) $1,210

ROBERT, Hubert
French 1733-1808
paintings: (L) $11,000; (H) $484,000
drawings: (L) $495; (H) $28,600

ROBERT, Hubert, and studio
French 18th cent.
paintings: (H) $26,400

ROBERT, J.
French 19th cent.
paintings: (L) $247; (H) $742

ROBERT, Leopold Louis
Swiss/French 1794-1835
paintings: (H) $3,080
drawings: (H) $1,320

ROBERT, Louis Valentine Elias
sculpture: (H) $2,200

ROBERT-FLEURY, Joseph Nicolas
drawings: (L) $330; (H) $1,045

ROBERT-FLEURY, Tony
French 1837-1912
paintings: (H) $16,500

ROBERTI, Albert Pierre
Belgian 1811-1864
drawings: (H) $770

ROBERTO, Luigi
Italian 19th cent.
drawings: (L) $440; (H) $990

ROBERTS, Bruce Elliott
American 20th cent.
paintings: (L) $1,320; (H) $1,650

ROBERTS, Clifford
paintings: (H) $825

ROBERTS, David
British 1796-1864
paintings: (L) $605; (H) $41,800
drawings: (L) $303; (H) $2,420

ROBERTS, Edwin Thomas
English 1840-1917
paintings: (L) $2,200; (H) $26,400

ROBERTS, Elizabeth Wentworth
American 1871-1927
paintings: (L) $1,320; (H) $17,600
drawings: (L) $660; (H) $880

ROBERTS, Ellen J.
American 19th/20th cent.
paintings: (L) $330; (H) $1,100

ROBERTS, Fulton
paintings: (H) $935

ROBERTS, Goodridge
American 1904-1974
paintings: (H) $14,300

ROBERTS, Harold Greble
American 19th/20th cent.
paintings: (L) $605; (H) $770

ROBERTS, I.
19th cent.
paintings: (H) $1,760

ROBERTS, James
British ac. 1858-1876
paintings: (H) $18,700

ROBERTS, Joseph L.
American ac. 1850-1870
paintings: (H) $3,300

ROBERTS, Lewis
Continental 20th cent.
paintings: (H) $2,750

ROBERTS, Priscilla
American b. 1918
paintings: (L) $550; (H) $880

ROBERTS, S.
paintings: (H) $660

ROBERTS, Thomas, the elder
Irish c. 1749-1778
paintings: (H) $253,000

ROBERTS, William Goodridge
paintings: (L) $5,500; (H) $37,400

ROBERTSON, Charles
English 1844-1891
drawings: (H) $7,700

ROBERTSON, Struan
British 20th cent.
paintings: (L) $1,050; (H) $2,145

ROBICHON, Jules Paul Victor
French 19th cent.
paintings: (H) $1,100

ROBIE, Jean Baptiste
Belgian 1821-1910
paintings: (L) $1,320; (H) $27,500

ROBILLARD, Marcel
French 19th cent.
paintings: (H) $2,420

ROBIN, Jean Baptiste Claude
French 1734-1818
paintings: (H) $115,500

ROBINET, P.
French 1814-1878
sculpture: (H) $11,000

ROBINS, Thomas Sewell
English 1814-1880
paintings: (H) $990
drawings: (L) $605; (H) $4,400

ROBINSON
19th/20th cent.
paintings: (L) $413; (H) $1,100

ROBINSON, Albert Henry
paintings: (H) $11,000

ROBINSON, Alexander Charles
American b. 1867
paintings: (L) $192; (H) $3,025
drawings: (L) $220; (H) $770

ROBINSON, Boardman
American 1876-1952
paintings: (L) $192; (H) $1,100
drawings: (L) $137; (H) $250

ROBINSON, Charles Dorman
American 1847-1933
paintings: (L) $110; (H) $13,200
drawings: (L) $275; (H) $468

ROBINSON, Denton Moore
American 20th cent.
paintings: (H) $880

ROBINSON, Florence Vincent
American 1874-1937
paintings: (L) $110; (H) $2,200
drawings: (L) $275; (H) $1,210

ROBINSON, G.
British 19th ccent.
paintings: (H) $3,750

ROBINSON, Gladys Lloyd
American 20th cent.
paintings: (L) $55; (H) $715

ROBINSON, H.
American 19th/20th cent.
paintings: (H) $770

ROBINSON, Hal
American 1875-1933
paintings: (L) $275; (H) $4,400

ROBINSON, J.
paintings: (L) $770; (H) $825

ROBINSON, James
American b. 1944
paintings: (L) $2,310; (H) $2,750

ROBINSON, Jim
American
paintings: (H) $4,000

ROBINSON, John
English 20th cent.
sculpture: (H) $4,840

ROBINSON, Matthias
British ac. 1856-1884
paintings: (H) $2,750

ROBINSON, T.
paintings: (L) $715; (H) $907

ROBINSON, Theodore
American 1852-1896
paintings: (L) $4,400; (H) $522,500
drawings: (L) $11,000; (H) $104,500

ROBINSON, Thomas
American 1835-1888
paintings: (L) $220; (H) $990
drawings: (H) $1,265

ROBINSON, William S.
American 1861-1945
paintings: (L) $352; (H) $14,300
drawings: (H) $770

ROBINSON, William T.
American b. 1852
paintings: (L) $165; (H) $3,300

ROBUS, Hugo
American 1885-1964
paintings: (L) $3,080; (H) $18,700
drawings: (L) $2,090; (H) $3,300

ROBUSTI, Domenico, called
TINTORETTO
paintings: (H) $2,860

ROCA, Manuel de la
Spanish b. 1846
paintings: (H) $1,980

ROCCA, Giovanni della
19th cent.
paintings: (L) $1,320; (H) $3,080

ROCCA, J. Della
Italian 19th cent.
paintings: (H) $2,200

PARMIGIANINO, Michele ROCCA or
Micheleda PARMA the younger
Italian 1670/75-1751
paintings: (L) $11,000; (H) $15,400

ROCCHI, A.
Italian 19th cent.
paintings: (H) $1,100

ROCHE, Charles Ferdinand de la
French 19th cent.
paintings: (H) $1,210

ROCHE, P.
sculpture: (H) $825

ROCHEGROSSE, Georges Antoine
French 1859-1938
paintings: (L) $3,850; (H) $14,300

ROCHET, Louis
sculpture: (H) $2,860

ROCHUSSEN, Charles
Dutch 1824-1894
drawings: (L) $110; (H) $1,980

ROCKBURNE, Dorothea
Canadian ac. 1970-1974
paintings: (H) $46,200
drawings: (L) $2,200; (H) $24,200

ROCKENSCHAUB, Gerwald
Austrian b. 1952
paintings: (L) $1,650; (H) $3,300

ROCKHAND
paintings: (H) $880

ROCKMORE, Noel
American b. 1928
paintings: (L) $275; (H) $2,310
drawings: (L) $33; (H) $1,980

ROCKWELL, August
American 1822-1882
paintings: (H) $1,540

ROCKWELL, Augustus
American ac. 1855-after 1860
paintings: (H) $1,210

ROCKWELL, Cleveland
American 1837-1907
paintings: (L) $880; (H) $52,250
drawings: (L) $303; (H) $3,025

ROCKWELL, Norman
American 1894-1978
paintings: (L) $2,420; (H) $264,000
drawings: (L) $1,870; (H) $46,200

ROCKWELL, Peter Barstow
American b. 1936
sculpture: (L) $220; (H) $715

ROCKWELL, Robert Henry
American
sculpture: (L) $1,045; (H) $1,650

ROCQUEPLAN, Camille
paintings: (H) $2,200

RODCHENKO, Alexandre
Russian 1891-1956
drawings: (H) $22,000

RODDE, Michel
French b. 1913
paintings: (H) $4,400

RODE, Edmund A.
European School 19th/20th cent.
paintings: (H) $2,310

RODE, Gotfred
Danish 1862-1937
paintings: (H) $671

RODER, E.A.C.
Belgian? 19th/20th cent.
paintings: (L) $523; (H) $3,190

RODIN, Auguste
French 1840-1917
drawings: (L) $577; (H) $104,500
sculpture: (L) $1,980; (H) $4,290,000

RODO, Ludovic, Ludovic Rodolphe
PISSARRO
French 1878-1952
drawings: (H) $825

RODO BOULANGER, Graciela
Bolivian b. 1935
paintings: (L) $11,000; (H) $14,300

RODOCONACHI, Paul
paintings: (H) $880

RODON, Francisco
Puerto Rican b. 1934
paintings: (L) $49,500; (H) $104,500

RODRIGUE, George
Cajun/American 20th cent.
paintings: (L) $330; (H) $1,650

RODRIGUEZ, A.
Spanish 19th/20th cent.
paintings: (H) $880

RODRIGUEZ, Alirio
Venezuelan b. 1934
paintings: (H) $1,650
drawings: (H) $2,750

RODRIGUEZ, Mariano
Cuban b. 1912
paintings: (H) $15,400
drawings: (H) $9,900

RODRIGUEZ, Miguel
Spanish 19th cent.
paintings: (H) $3,575

RODRIGUEZ DE GUZMAN, Manuel
Spanish 1818-1867
paintings: (L) $5,500; (H) $19,800

RODRIGUEZ LOZANO, Manuel
Mexican 1896-1971
paintings: (L) $16,500; (H) $19,800

RODRIGUEZ SAINT CLEMENT, F.
paintings: (H) $2,200

RODRIGUEZ SAN CLEMENT,
Francisco
Spanish 1861-1956
paintings: (L) $12,100; (H) $16,500

RODRIGUEZ-ETCHART, Severo
Argentinian b. 1864
paintings: (H) $2,750

RODRIQUEZ, Manuel
drawings: (H) $2,860

RODRIQUEZ, Mariano
paintings: (H) $3,300

RODSINI, G.
sculpture: (H) $2,750

ROE, C.G.
paintings: (H) $1,210

ROE, Clarence
English ac. 1870; d. 1909
paintings: (L) $275; (H) $1,210

ROE, Colin Graeme
British ac. 1858-1913
paintings: (L) $1,320; (H) $7,150

ROE, Frederick Rushing, Fred
British 1864-1947
paintings: (L) $143; (H) $1,430

ROE, Walter Herbert
British ac. 1882-1893
paintings: (H) $3,630

ROEHN, Adolphe Eugene Gabriel
French 1780-1867
paintings: (H) $4,400

ROEHN, Jean Alphonse
French 1799-1864
paintings: (H) $7,150

ROEHNER, William
Austrian 19th cent.
paintings: (H) $1,705

ROELOFS, Willem, the elder
Dutch 1822-1897
paintings: (L) $440; (H) $33,000
drawings: (L) $220; (H) $9,075

ROELOFS, Willem Elisa, the younger
Dutch b. 1897
paintings: (H) $1,650

ROEPEL, Coenraet
Dutch 1678-1748
paintings: (L) $60,500; (H) $88,000

ROERICH, Nikolai K.
Russian 1874-1947
drawings: (H) $1,870

ROESEN, Severin
German/American d. 1871
paintings: (L) $1,980; (H) $115,500

ROESLER, August Wilhelm
Austrian b. 1837
paintings: (H) $9,900

ROESLER FRANZ, Ettore
Italian 1845-1907
drawings: (L) $385; (H) $13,200

ROESSLER, George
German 1861-1925
paintings: (L) $880; (H) $990

ROESSLER, W.
paintings: (H) $880

ROESSLER, Walter
Russian 19th/20th cent.
paintings: (L) $165; (H) $1,320

ROESTRATEN, Pieter Gerritsz van
Dutch 1630-1700
paintings: (L) $7,150; (H) $55,000

ROFFIAEN, Jean Francois Xavier
Belgian 1820-1898
paintings: (L) $220; (H) $4,180

ROGER
American early 19th cent.
drawings: (H) $1,045

ROGER, Suzanne
paintings: (H) $3,740

ROGERS, D.
American 19th cent.
paintings: (H) $3,575

ROGERS, Franklin Whiting
American b. 1854
paintings: (L) $198; (H) $1,320

ROGERS, Gretchen W.
American b. 1881
drawings: (L) $440; (H) $4,400

ROGERS, John
American 1829-1904
sculpture: (L) $137; (H) $2,200

ROGERS, John
American b. 1881
sculpture: (H) $2,750

ROGERS, Nathaniel
American 1788-1844
drawings: (H) $935

ROGERS, P.
paintings: (H) $1,320

ROGERS, Phillip Hutchins
British 1789-1853
paintings: (H) $3,300

ROGERS, Randolph
American 1825-1892
sculpture: (L) $825; (H) $16,500

ROGERS, T.
American 20th cent.
paintings: (H) $2,200

ROGERS, W.
British
paintings: (H) $1,540

ROGERS, William
English 19th cent.
paintings: (H) $3,190

ROGERS (?), Steve
paintings: (H) $1,210

ROGGE, Wilhelm
paintings: (H) $3,080

ROGHMAN, Roeland
paintings: (H) $11,550

ROGISONZKY, Joseph
Austrian b. 1821
paintings: (H) $1,100

ROHDE, H.
paintings: (H) $990

ROHL, Peter Karl
drawings: (H) $3,520

ROHL-SMITH, Carl Wilhelm Daniel
Danish 1848-1900
sculpture: (H) $770

ROHLFS, Christian
German 1849-1938
paintings: (H) $71,500
drawings: (L) $20,900; (H) $26,400

ROHNER, George
paintings: (H) $5,280

ROHR, Fred
paintings: (H) $3,850

ROHRBECK, E.
paintings: (L) $660; (H) $1,155

ROHRBECK, Franz
paintings: (L) $330; (H) $7,700

ROI, Charles Pears
paintings: (H) $2,640

ROIG, Jose
Spanish 19th/20th cent.
paintings: (L) $1,650; (H) $2,090

ROINA
paintings: (H) $880

ROJAS, Elmar
Guatemalan b. 1938
paintings: (L) $825; (H) $19,800

ROJO, Vincente
paintings: (L) $1,320; (H) $2,860

ROLAND
sculpture: (H) $3,575

ROLAND
French late 19th/20th cent.
sculpture: (H) $1,980

ROLAND, Edward
American b. 1911
sculpture: (H) $825

ROLAND, G.
paintings: (H) $1,540

ROLAND, R.
paintings: (H) $770

ROLAND, W.
paintings: (H) $660

ROLANDI, H.
Italian 19th cent.
paintings: (H) $1,980

ROLARD, Francois Laurent
French 1842-1912
sculpture: (L) $1,100; (H) $2,200

ROLDAN, Enrique
Spanish 19th/20th cent.
paintings: (L) $1,540; (H) $2,750

ROLDAN, Modesto
Spanish b. 1926
paintings: (H) $2,475

ROLFE, Alexander F.
paintings: (H) $30,800

ROLFE, Henry Leonidas
British ac. 1847-1881
paintings: (L) $6,325; (H) $9,900

ROLFE, Henry Leonidas and Joseph
Denovan Adam
English 19th cent.
paintings: (H) $16,500

ROLLAND, H.
paintings: (H) $2,090

ROLLE, August H.O.
American 1875-1941
paintings: (L) $1,210; (H) $4,510
drawings: (H) $825

ROLLE, Marie
sculpture: (H) $825

ROLLINS, J.
paintings: (H) $7,150

ROLLINS, Tim and K.O.S.
contemporary
paintings: (H) $6,600
sculpture: (H) $132

ROLLINS, Warren Eliphalet
American 1861-1962
paintings: (L) $275; (H) $27,500

ROLSHOVEN, Julius
American 1858-1930
paintings: (L) $192; (H) $16,500
drawings: (L) $660; (H) $1,650

ROMA, J. Ferranti
Italian 20th cent.
paintings: (H) $1,650

ROMAGNONI, Bepi
Italian 1930-1964
paintings: (H) $1,650

ROMAIN, Filippo
paintings: (H) $4,400

ROMANACH, Leopoldo
Cuban/American 1862-1951
paintings: (L) $1,650; (H) $4,400

ROMANELLI
sculpture: (H) $4,125

ROMANELLI, Giovanni Francesco
Italian 1610-1662
paintings: (L) $7,700; (H) $165,000

ROMANELLI, Pasquale
sculpture: (L) $605; (H) $3,300

ROMANELLI, Raffaello
Italian 1856-1928
sculpture: (L) $3,300; (H) $6,600

ROMANELLI, T.
sculpture: (H) $1,320

ROMANI, Juana
Italian 1869-1924
paintings: (L) $1,430; (H) $2,420

ROMANI, Mario
Italian 19th/20th cent.
paintings: (H) $3,850

ROMANI, R.
paintings: (H) $880

ROMANNE, Valentine
French 19th cent.
paintings: (L) $1,320; (H) $2,200

ROMANO, Il, Giulio Pippi, follower of
drawings: (H) $1,540

ROMANO, Pietro Paulo, called
GALEOTTI
d. 1584
sculpture: (H) $209,000

ROMANOWSKY, Dimitri
paintings: (L) $1,430; (H) $2,475

ROMBOUTS, Salomon
Dutch ac. c. 1652; d. c. 1702
paintings: (L) $4,675; (H) $38,500

ROMBOUTS, Theodor
Flemish 1597-1637
paintings: (H) $99,000

ROMEK, Arpad
Hungarian b. 1883
paintings: (L) $550; (H) $935

ROMER, I.
paintings: (H) $880

ROMER, Paul
paintings: (H) $715

ROMES, A.
Italian 19th cent.
paintings: (L) $770; (H) $1,100

ROMIROS, P.
paintings: (L) $770; (H) $935

ROMITI, Gino
Italian 1881-1967
paintings: (L) $247; (H) $1,155

ROMITI, Sergio
contemporary
paintings: (L) $220; (H) $1,760

ROMNEY, George
English 1734-1802
paintings: (L) $1,375; (H) $660,000
drawings: (L) $1,430; (H) $1,650

ROMULO, Teodulo
Mexican b. 1943
paintings: (L) $3,300; (H) $8,800
drawings: (H) $110

RONAI, Jozsef Rippl
paintings: (H) $3,080

RONALD, William
American b. 1926
paintings: (L) $880; (H) $990

RONAY, Camille
paintings: (H) $770

RONAY, J.L.
paintings: (H) $1,100

RONDEL
19th cent.
paintings: (H) $660

RONDEL, Alfred WAUD and Frederic
American 19th cent.
paintings: (H) $3,575

RONDEL, Frederick
American 1826-1892
paintings: (L) $715; (H) $22,000

RONDEL, Henri
French 1857-1919
paintings: (L) $1,650; (H) $5,500

RONEY, Harold Arthur
paintings: (L) $550; (H) $880

RONMY, Guillaume Frederic
French 1786-1854
paintings: (H) $7,700

RONNEBECK, Arnold
American 1885-1947
sculpture: (H) $3,520

RONNER, Alice
Belgian b. 1857
paintings: (H) $2,200

RONNER-KNIP, Henriette
Dutch 1821-1909
paintings: (L) $660; (H) $22,000

RONNOW, Cai
drawings: (L) $990; (H) $1,540

RONSON, Richard H.
English 19th cent.
paintings: (H) $2,300

RONTINI, Ferrucio
Italian 1893-1964
paintings: (L) $165; (H) $1,980

ROODENBURG, Hendrikus Elias
Dutch 1895-1983
paintings: (H) $2,200

ROOK, Edward F.
1870-1960
paintings: (H) $1,540

ROOKE, Henri
French 19th cent.
paintings: (H) $1,100

ROOS
paintings: (H) $2,200

ROOS, Eva
English b. 1872
paintings: (H) $66,000

ROOS, J.
paintings: (H) $2,090

ROOS, Johann Heinrich
German 1631-1685
paintings: (L) $1,650; (H) $16,500
drawings: (H) $220

ROOS, Joseph
1726-1805
paintings: (H) $9,900

ROOS, P.
19th cent.
paintings: (H) $1,430

ROOS, Peter
American b. 1850
paintings: (L) $110; (H) $2,860
drawings: (H) $990

ROOS, Philipp Peter, called Rosa da Tivoli
German 1657-1706
paintings: (L) $2,640; (H) $38,500

ROOSDORP, Frederik
Dutch 1839-1865
paintings: (L) $935; (H) $1,650

ROOSENBOOM, Albert
Belgian 1845-1875
paintings: (L) $1,430; (H) $12,100

ROOSENBOOM, Margarete
Dutch 1843-1896
paintings: (H) $23,100

ROOSENBOOM, Nicolas Jan
Dutch 1805-1880
paintings: (L) $2,640; (H) $4,675

ROOSKENS, Anton
Dutch 1906-1976
paintings: (H) $22,000
drawings: (H) $3,740

ROOY, Johannes Embrosius Wetering de
Dutch b. 1877
paintings: (H) $1,430

ROPER, Richard
English 18th century
paintings: (H) $20,900

ROPES, Joseph
American 1812-1885
paintings: (H) $2,090

ROPS, Felicien Joseph Victor
Belgian 1833-1898
paintings: (H) $2,750

ROSA, Francesco de, called Pacecco de ROSA
Italian c. 1600-1654
paintings: (H) $60,500

ROSA, Louis
paintings: (L) $495; (H) $1,320

ROSA, Salvator
Italian 1615-1673
paintings: (L) $4,400; (H) $93,500
drawings: (L) $8,250; (H) $23,100

ROSA DA TIVOLI, Philip Peter ROOS
German 1657-1706
paintings: (L) $6,050; (H) $13,750

ROSAI, Ottone
Italian 1895-1957
paintings: (L) $880; (H) $5,775
drawings: (H) $1,760

ROSAIRE, Arthur Dominique
Canadian 1879-1922
paintings: (H) $1,485

ROSAM, Walter Alfred
German 1883-1916
paintings: (H) $17,600

ROSANCE
ac. c. 1860
paintings: (H) $1,760

ROSANJIN, Kitaoji
Japanese 1883-1959
drawings: (H) $88,000

ROSATI, Giulio
Italian 1858-1917
paintings: (L) $6,050; (H) $29,700
drawings: (L) $2,310; (H) $16,500

ROSATI, James
American b. 1912
drawings: (H) $1,045
sculpture: (H) $6,050

ROSE, A. C. de
American
paintings: (H) $770

ROSE, Adam
American 19th cent.
sculpture: (H) $2,200

ROSE, Adama
contemporary
sculpture: (H) $990

ROSE, Guy
American 1867-1925
paintings: (L) $2,475; (H) $126,500

ROSE, Herman
American b. 1909
paintings: (L) $495; (H) $4,950

ROSE, Iver
American 1899-1972
paintings: (L) $110; (H) $2,310
drawings: (H) $880

ROSE, Julius
German 1828-1911
paintings: (L) $605; (H) $8,800

ROSE, Samuel
American b. 1941
paintings: (L) $1,210; (H) $2,970

ROSE, Walter
German 20th cent.
paintings: (L) $990; (H) $1,045

ROSE(?), A.
British 19th cent.
paintings: (H) $1,980

ROSELAND, Harry
American 1868-1950
paintings: (L) $412; (H) $66,000
drawings: (H) $385

ROSELL
paintings: (H) $1,650

ROSELL, A.
paintings: (H) $1,430

ROSELL, Alexander
paintings: (H) $1,210

ROSSELLI, Cosimo Di Lorenzo
Italian 1439-1507
paintings: (H) $52,800

ROSELLI, F.
drawings: (H) $770

ROSELLI, Pietro
drawings: (H) $715

ROSEN, A.
paintings: (H) $3,740

ROSEN, Charles
American 1878-1950
paintings: (L) $880; (H) $35,200

ROSEN, J.H.
European 19th cent.
paintings: (H) $1,265

ROSEN, Jan
Polish 1854-1936
paintings: (H) $7,810

ROSEN, Jane
drawings: (H) $800

ROSEN, K.
Dutch 20th cent.
paintings: (H) $3,850

ROSENBAUM, Richard
American 19th cent.
drawings: (H) $660

ROSENBERG, Alan
paintings: (H) $825

ROSENBERG, Charles G.
American ac. 1857-1866
paintings: (H) $660

ROSENBERG, Henry M.
Canadian 1858-1947
paintings: (H) $660

ROSENBERG, James N.
American b. 1874
paintings: (H) $1,100
drawings: (H) $440

ROSENBERG, O. von
American early 20th cent.
paintings: (H) $742

ROSENBERG, Samuel
paintings: (H) $770

ROSENFELD, Eugen
paintings: (H) $2,640

ROSENKRANZ, Clarence C.
paintings: (L) $110; (H) $1,320

ROSENMEYER, Bernard Jacob
b. 1870
paintings: (H) $660

ROSENQUIST, James
American b. 1933
paintings: (L) $4,400; (H) $2,090,000
drawings: (L) $3,300; (H) $88,000
sculpture: (L) $6,050; (H) $12,100

ROSENSTAND, Wilhelm J.
Danish 1838-1915
paintings: (L) $8,690; (H) $9,350

ROSENSTOCK, Isidore
French b. 1880
drawings: (L) $605; (H) $1,650

ROSENTHAL, Albert
American 1863-1939
paintings: (L) $220; (H) $1,760

ROSENTHAL, Bernard
drawings: (H) $55
sculpture: (H) $900

ROSENTHAL, Doris
American 1895-1971
paintings: (L) $110; (H) $742
drawings: (L) $44; (H) $132

ROSENTHAL, E.
paintings: (H) $715

ROSENTHAL, Lillian
American 20th cent.
paintings: (L) $93; (H) $908

ROSENTHAL, Toby Edward
American 1848-1917
paintings: (H) $6,050

ROSENTHAL, Tony
American b. 1914
sculpture: (L) $825; (H) $3,300

ROSIER, Amedee
French b. 1831
paintings: (L) $550; (H) $1,320

ROSIERSE, Johannes
Dutch 1818-1901
paintings: (L) $1,320; (H) $3,410

ROSLIN, Alexandre
Swedish 1718-1793
paintings: (L) $3,300; (H) $37,400

ROSPINI, L.
Italian 19th cent.
paintings: (H) $742

ROSS, Alvin
American b. 1920
paintings: (L) $385; (H) $1,430
drawings: (H) $352

ROSS, Barbara Ellis
paintings: (H) $1,100

ROSS, C. Chandler
American d. 1952
paintings: (H) $2,200

ROSS, Chandler R.
American
paintings: (H) $2,310

ROSS, Harry Leith
American 1886-1973
paintings: (L) $440; (H) $2,090

ROSS, Leith
paintings: (H) $4,400

ROSS, R.P.
British 19th cent.
paintings: (H) $1,430

ROSS, T.
paintings: (L) $55; (H) $6,600

ROSS, Thomas
American 1829-1896
paintings: (H) $19,800

ROSSE, F.
sculpture: (L) $528; (H) $880

ROSSE, Franz
sculpture: (H) $3,575

ROSSEAU, Percival Leonard
American 1859/69-1937
paintings: (L) $385; (H) $44,000

ROSSEELS, Jacob Cornelis
Belgian 1828-1912
paintings: (H) $3,300

ROSSELLI, Bernardo
paintings: (H) $8,800

ROSSELLI, Cosimo
Italian 1439-1507
paintings: (H) $44,000

ROSSERT, Paul
French 1851-1918
paintings: (H) $7,150

ROSSERT, Paul
French 19th cent.
paintings: (H) $19,800

ROSSET, Joseph, called Du Pont
sculpture: (H) $7,700

ROSSETTI, Antonio
Italian b. 1819
paintings: (H) $1,320
sculpture: (H) $3,630

ROSSETTI, Dante Gabriel
English 1828-1882
drawings: (L) $19,800; (H) $165,000

ROSSETTO
Italian 19th cent.
sculpture: (H) $13,200

ROSSI, A.M.
British 19th cent.
paintings: (H) $770

ROSSI, Alberto
Italian 1858-1936
paintings: (H) $4,675

ROSSI, Alexander M.
English ac. 1870-1903
paintings: (L) $8,800; (H) $25,300
drawings: (H) $6,600

ROSSI, Antonio
paintings: (H) $880

ROSSI, C. de
Italian 19th cent.
paintings: (H) $12,100

ROSSI, Egisto
Italian 1856-1916
sculpture: (H) $8,800

ROSSI, Francesco del, called Il Salviati
Italian 1510-1563
drawings: (H) $38,500

ROSSI, G. de
paintings: (L) $357; (H) $7,150

ROSSI, Joseph
paintings: (H) $770

ROSSI, L.
Italian 19th cent.
paintings: (H) $6,050

ROSSI, Lucius
French 1846-1913
paintings: (L) $1,100; (H) $35,750
drawings: (H) $4,180

ROSSI, Luigi
Swiss 1853-1923
paintings: (L) $9,900; (H) $60,500

ROSSITER, Charles
British b. 1827
paintings: (L) $2,200; (H) $17,600

ROSSITER, Thomas Pritchard
American 1818-1871
paintings: (L) $1,210; (H) $9,350

ROSSITER, Thomas Pritchard and
William Henry SNYDER
American 19th cent.
paintings: (H) $2,310

ROSSLER, Rudolf
Austrian b. 1864
paintings: (L) $7,150; (H) $7,975

ROSSO, *N**
paintings: (H) $3,575

ROSSO, Medardo
Italian 1858-1928
sculpture: (L) $137,500; (H) $242,000

ROSSUM DU CHATTEL, Fredericus
Jacobus van
Dutch 1856-1917
drawings: (H) $1,980

ROSTEL, Aga
German 19th cent.
paintings: (H) $1,210

ROSZAK, Theodore
contemporary
drawings: (L) $1,430; (H) $2,200

ROTARI, Pietro Antonio
Italian 1707-1762
paintings: (L) $1,100; (H) $77,000

ROTELLA, Mimmo
drawings: (L) $1,100; (H) $5,225

ROTENBERG, Harold
American b. 1905
paintings: (L) $357; (H) $880

ROTERS, Carl
paintings: (L) $495; (H) $2,200

ROTH, Ernest David
American 1879-1964
paintings: (L) $302; (H) $1,210
drawings: (H) $330

ROTH, Frederick George Richard
American 1872-1944
sculpture: (L) $715; (H) $11,000

ROTH, G.
sculpture: (H) $1,430

ROTH, Mark
contemporary
paintings: (H) $2,200

ROTH, N.
drawings: (H) $715

ROTH, Peter
Dutch 20th cent.
paintings: (H) $660

ROTH, Phillip
German 1841-1921
paintings: (L) $192; (H) $3,575

ROTHAUG, Alexander
Austrian b. 1870
paintings: (L) $22,000; (H) $39,600

ROTHAUG, Leopold
Austrian 1868-1959
paintings: (H) $660
drawings: (H) $1,045

ROTHBORT, Laurence
American 20th cent.
paintings: (H) $1,100

ROTHBORT, Samuel
American 1882-1971
paintings: (L) $550; (H) $8,250
drawings: (H) $165

ROTHENBERG, Susan
American b. 1945
paintings: (L) $31,900; (H) $550,000
drawings: (L) $25,300; (H) $38,500

ROTHENSTEIN, William
British 1872-1945
paintings: (H) $66,000

ROTHERMEL, Peter Frederick
American 1817-1895
paintings: (L) $350; (H) $3,850

ROTHKO, Mark
Russian/American 1903-1970
paintings: (L) $5,170; (H) $3,630,000
drawings: (L) $1,320; (H) $176,000

ROTIER, Peter
American b. 1888
paintings: (L) $66; (H) $1,320

ROTIG, Georges Frederic
French 1873-1961
paintings: (L) $1,430; (H) $5,775

ROTINI, Giulio, called Guilio da
VICCHIO
Italian b. 1925
paintings: (H) $770

ROTTENHAMMER, Hans
German
paintings: (H) $19,800

ROTTENHAMMER, Johann
German 1564-1625
drawings: (H) $104,500

ROTTERDAM, Paul
contemporary
paintings: (H) $7,700

Color Field Painting

Color Field painting is the term used to describe abstract paintings that lack a single central image and focus on large expanses of unmodulated color. A movement of the late 1940s and early 1950s, its leading exponents were Barnett Newmann and Mark Rothko.

Mark Rothko (1903-1970) was born in Russia, but when he was ten years old his family resettled in Portland, Oregon. He attended Yale University, then moved to New York, where he studied briefly with Max Weber at the Art Students League. In the 1930s he painted urban scenes, but his work gradually evolved toward a Surrealist style. After meeting Robert Motherwell and Barnett Newman in 1948, he experimented with Expressionism but soon turned to large fields of color, painting both dense and luminous fields. By the late 1950s he was world-famous for his Color Field paintings. In 1961 the Museum of Modern Art in New York City held a retrospective of his work. During the 1960s he painted large wall paintings and murals; in 1969 he completed murals for a nondenominational chapel in Houston, Texas, which he considered his masterpiece. (Mark Rothko, *Brown, Black & Blue*, oil on canvas, 69½ x 60 in., Christie's, May 7, 1990, $3,080,000)

ROTTMAN, Mozart
Hungarian b. 1874
paintings: (L) $3,300; (H) $11,000

ROTTONARA, Franz Angelo
Austrian b. 1848
drawings: (H) $1,100

ROUART, Henri Stanislas
French 1833-1912
paintings: (H) $4,950

ROUAS, Ferdinand
Spanish 1843-1897
paintings: (H) $1,045

ROUAULT, Georges
French 1871-1958
paintings: (L) $19,800; (H) $1,210,000
drawings: (L) $4,400; (H) $220,000

ROUAULT, Georges Dominique
French b. 1904
paintings: (L) $880; (H) $2,200
drawings: (L) $165; (H) $467

ROUBAUD, Franz
Russian 1856-1928
paintings: (L) $1,870; (H) $15,400

ROUBAUD, G.
contemporary
paintings: (H) $2,200

ROUBEA
paintings: (H) $1,980

ROUBY, Alfred
French b. 1849
paintings: (L) $3,575; (H) $5,500

ROUERE, Pietro Lonte de la
Italian 19th/20th cent.
paintings: (H) $6,325

ROUGELET, Benoit
sculpture: (H) $2,750

ROUGGO
paintings: (H) $1,870

ROULAND, Orlando
American 1871-1945
paintings: (L) $550; (H) $7,260

ROULIN, Louis Francois Marie
drawings: (H) $1,540

ROUMEGOUS, Auguste Francois
French 19th cent.
paintings: (L) $1,980; (H) $2,200

ROUSE, A.F.
British 19th cent.
paintings: (H) $1,320

ROUSE, Robert William Arthur
English 19th/20th cent.
paintings: (L) $44; (H) $935
drawings: (H) $44

ROUSSE, Charles
American 19th/20th cent.
drawings: (H) $660

ROUSSEAU
sculpture: (L) $357; (H) $1,980

ROUSSEAU, Alain
French contemporary
paintings: (H) $1,760

ROUSSEAU, Charles
paintings: (L) $3,850; (H) $4,400

ROUSSEAU, Ed.
French 19th cent.
paintings: (H) $5,225

ROUSSEAU, Etienne Pierre Theodore
French 1812-1867
paintings: (L) $7,975; (H) $418,000
drawings: (L) $1,650; (H) $8,800

ROUSSEAU, Helen
American b. 1898
paintings: (L) $1,650; (H) $3,300

ROUSSEAU, Henri, Le Douanier
French 1844-1910
paintings: (H) $66,000

ROUSSEAU, Henri Emilien
French 1875-1933
paintings: (L) $1,980; (H) $22,000
drawings: (H) $1,540

ROUSSEAU, Jean
French b. 1813
sculpture: (H) $1,595

ROUSSEAU, M***
French 19th/20th cent.
paintings: (H) $3,750

ROUSSEAU, Marguerite
Belgian 1888-1948
paintings: (L) $1,650; (H) $9,350
sculpture: (L) $5,500; (H) $8,250

ROUSSEAU, Percival
American 1859/69-1937
paintings: (L) $9,350; (H) $22,000
drawings: (H) $770

ROUSSEAU, Philippe
French 1816-1887
paintings: (L) $4,400; (H) $8,800

ROUSSEAU, Theodore
French 1812-1867
paintings: (L) $3,300; (H) $26,400
drawings: (L) $770; (H) $3,740

ROUSSEAU (?), T.
paintings: (H) $5,225

ROUSSEL, H.A.
paintings: (H) $770

ROUSSEL, Ker Xavier
French 1867-1944
drawings: (L) $550; (H) $28,600

ROUSSEL, Leon
sculpture: (H) $2,420

ROUSSEL, Paul
sculpture: (H) $2,475

ROUSSEL, Pierre
French b. 1927
paintings: (L) $495; (H) $10,725
drawings: (H) $3,300

ROUSSEL-MASURE
contemporary
paintings: (H) $3,520

ROUVIERE, Daniel
paintings: (L) $22; (H) $1,210

ROUWETTE, Paul
paintings: (H) $1,760

ROUX, Antoine
French 1765-1835
drawings: (H) $3,080

ROUX, Antoine
French 1799-1872
drawings: (H) $900

ROUX, Anton
French 19th cent.
drawings: (H) $11,000

ROUX, Constant Ambroise
sculpture: (H) $935

ROUX, F.
18th cent.
paintings: (H) $7,700

ROUX, Frederick
paintings: (H) $3,740
drawings: (H) $6,600

ROUX, Guillermo
Argentinian b. 1929
drawings: (H) $2,750

ROUX, Joseph Ange Antoine
French 1765-1835
drawings: (L) $5,500; (H) $8,250

ROUX, Louis
French 1817-1903
paintings: (H) $16,000
drawings: (L) $6,000; (H) $6,875

ROUZEE, M.
French 19th cent.
paintings: (H) $1,100

ROVERE, Giovanni Battista Della
Italian 1561-c. 1628
drawings: (H) $1,320

ROVERE, Giovanni Mauro Della
Italian c. 1575-1640
drawings: (L) $990; (H) $3,300

ROVIER, E.
paintings: (H) $660

ROWAN, Marian Ellis
Australian 1848-1922
drawings: (H) $1,210

ROWBOTHAM, Charles
English ac. 1877-1913
drawings: (L) $250; (H) $880

ROWE, L.K.
paintings: (H) $4,950

ROWE, Rd.
English 3rd quarter 18th cent.
drawings: (H) $990

ROWE, Sydney Grant
British 1861-1928
drawings: (L) $550; (H) $990

ROWELL, John Thomas
Australian b. 1894
paintings: (H) $1,100

ROWELL, William
Australian 1898-1946
paintings: (H) $990

ROWLAND, William
paintings: (H) $798

ROWLANDSON, George Derville
British b. 1861
paintings: (L) $2,750; (H) $6,050

ROWLANDSON, Thomas
English 1756-1827
drawings: (L) $154; (H) $16,500

ROWORTH, Ivania
paintings: (H) $1,210

ROWSE, Samuel W.
American
drawings: (H) $660

ROY, J.
Continental School
drawings: (H) $1,870

ROY, Marius
French b. 1833
paintings: (L) $1,210; (H) $1,760

ROY, Norman
American 20th cent.
paintings: (L) $33; (H) $660

ROY, Pierre
French 1880-1950
paintings: (L) $44,000; (H) $143,000
drawings: (L) $4,180; (H) $6,050

ROYAL, Alexander
paintings: (H) $660

ROYBET, Ferdinand
French 1840-1920
paintings: (L) $825; (H) $8,800
drawings: (H) $220

ROYER, Henri
drawings: (L) $110; (H) $1,210

ROYER, Lionel Noel
French 1852-1926
paintings: (L) $440; (H) $6,600

ROYLE, Herbert
English ac. 1929
paintings: (L) $413; (H) $9,680

ROYLE, Stanley
paintings: (H) $2,200

ROYTINA, Alfred
paintings: (H) $2,200

ROZEN, J.
American 20th cent.
paintings: (H) $660

ROZET, Fanny
sculpture: (L) $1,430; (H) $1,760

ROZIER, Dominique
paintings: (H) $715

ROZIER, Jules
French 1821-1882
paintings: (L) $660; (H) $1,320

ROZYNSKI, Kurt von
German b. 1864
paintings: (L) $495; (H) $1,210

ROZZI, Jim
paintings: (H) $990

RUBEN, Franz Leo
Austrian/Czech 1842-1920
paintings: (L) $8,800; (H) $25,300
drawings: (H) $1,980

RUBENS, Jos.
late 18th - 19th cent.
paintings: (H) $1,540

RUBENS, Sir Peter Paul
Flemish 1577-1640
paintings: (L) $462,000; (H) $528,000
drawings: (H) $41,250

RUBENS, Sir Peter Paul, studio of
1577-1640
paintings: (H) $24,200

RUBENSEN, G.
European 19th cent.
paintings: (H) $3,000

RUBERSTEIN, Barnet
drawings: (H) $2,090

RUBIN
Israeli 20th cent.
paintings: (H) $1,017

RUBIN, Reuven
Israeli 1893-1974
paintings: (L) $7,700; (H) $49,500
drawings: (L) $1,100; (H) $6,600

RUBIO, Antonio Perez
paintings: (H) $3,300

RUBIO, Luigi
Italian d. 1882
paintings: (H) $3,300

RUCKER, Robert
American 20th cent.
paintings: (L) $715; (H) $1,540
drawings: (H) $412

RUCKREIM, Ulrich
contemporary
sculpture: (H) $19,800

RUDD, N.
American 19th cent.
paintings: (H) $2,750

RUDDER, Isidore de
Belgian b. 1855
sculpture: (H) $2,310

RUDE, Francois
French 1784-1855
sculpture: (L) $660; (H) $26,400

RUDE, Olaf
paintings: (H) $6,600

RUDE, Sophie, born Fremiet
French 1797-1867
paintings: (L) $2,090; (H) $137,500

RUDISUHLI, Hermann
Swiss 1864-1945
paintings: (H) $3,080

RUDNIK, D.
paintings: (H) $1,320

RUDOLPH, Harold
American 1850-1884
paintings: (L) $495; (H) $4,400

RUE, De La
French contemporary
paintings: (H) $825

RUELAS, Julio
Mexican 1870-1907
paintings: (H) $57,750

RUELLAN, Andree
American b. 1905
paintings: (H) $3,520
drawings: (L) $66; (H) $110

RUEPING, K.
American
drawings: (H) $1,430

RUETER, Georg
Dutch b. 1875
paintings: (H) $1,210

RUFF
sculpture: (L) $330; (H) $1,100

RUFFIER
paintings: (H) $1,100

RUFFIER, Noel
French late 19th cent.
sculpture: (H) $880

RUGENDAS, Georg Philipp
German 1666-1742
paintings: (H) $2,200

RUGENDAS, Johann Moritz
German 1802-1858
paintings: (L) $5,500; (H) $88,000
drawings: (L) $8,800; (H) $15,400

RUGER, H. Otto
German 19th cent.
paintings: (H) $2,000

RUGGIERI, or RUGGIERO
paintings: (L) $825; (H) $935

RUGMAN, J.L.L.
paintings: (H) $1,430

RUIPEREZ, Luis
Spanish 1832-1867
paintings: (H) $1,540

RUIS, Johanes Porticus
16th cent.
paintings: (H) $3,080

RUISDAEL, Jacob Salomonsz van
Dutch 1630-1681
paintings: (L) $16,500; (H) $440,000

RUISDAEL, Salomon van
Dutch c. 1600-1670
paintings: (L) $22,000; (H) $907,500

RUMMELHOFF, John
American b. 1942
paintings: (L) $825; (H) $2,420

RUMPLER, Franz
Austrian 1848-1922
paintings: (L) $3,300; (H) $8,800

RUMSEY, Charles Cary
American
sculpture: (H) $5,280

RUNGE, John
American
drawings: (H) $1,320

RUNGIUS, Carl
American 1869-1959
paintings: (L) $605; (H) $63,250
sculpture: (H) $60,500

RUNKEL, A.
paintings: (H) $4,620

RUNKEL, August
German ac. 1785-1825
paintings: (H) $5,500

RUNZE, Wilhelm
German b. 1887
paintings: (H) $2,640

RUOKOKOSKI, Jali
Scandinavian 1886-1936
paintings: (H) $770

RUOPPOLO, Giovanni Battista
Italian 1629-1693
paintings: (L) $22,000; (H) $297,000

RUPPERT, Otto von
German b. 1841
paintings: (L) $330; (H) $3,850

RUPPRECHT, Tini
German b. 1868
drawings: (H) $990

RUPRECHT, H.
European 20th cent.
paintings: (L) $55; (H) $1,100

RURIER, E.
paintings: (H) $3,575

RUSCH, B.W.
Continental 19th cent.
drawings: (H) $3,575

RUSCHA, Ed
American b. 1937
paintings: (L) $7,700; (H) $297,000
drawings: (L) $2,750; (H) $82,500

RUSH, Olive
paintings: (H) $1,430

RUSH, William
American 1756-1833
sculpture: (H) $23,100

RUSHOUT, Lady Anne
English 1768?-1849
drawings: (L) $88; (H) $770

RUSINOL, Santiago
Spanish 1861-1931
paintings: (L) $63,250; (H) $352,000

RUSS, C.B.
American ac. 1880-1920
paintings: (L) $330; (H) $770
drawings: (L) $110; (H) $248

RUSS, Harry
American 19th/20th cent.
paintings: (H) $5,500

RUSS, Robert
Austrian 1847-1922
paintings: (H) $68,750

RUSSELL, A.C.
American
paintings: (H) $880

RUSSELL, Bella
American
paintings: (H) $2,750

RUSSELL, Benjamin
American 1804-1885
drawings: (L) $990; (H) $4,500

RUSSELL, Charles Marion
American 1864-1926
paintings: (L) $11,000; (H) $1,100,000
drawings: (L) $770; (H) $209,000
sculpture: (L) $303; (H) $39,600

RUSSELL, E.W.
American 20th cent.
sculpture: (H) $1,430

RUSSELL, Edward John
Canadian/American 1832-1906
paintings: (L) $110; (H) $3,190
drawings: (H) $990

RUSSELL, Edward N.
American 1852-1927
paintings: (H) $770

RUSSELL, George William
Irish 1867-1935
paintings: (L) $605; (H) $3,025

RUSSELL, Gyrth
Canadian b. 1892
paintings: (L) $330; (H) $715

RUSSELL, J.
paintings: (H) $1,430

RUSSELL, J.A.
British 19th cent.
paintings: (H) $1,045

RUSSELL, J.B.
English 19th/20th cent.
paintings: (H) $990

RUSSELL, John
paintings: (L) $220; (H) $2,750
drawings: (L) $2,530; (H) $4,950

RUSSELL, John
English 1745-1806
paintings: (L) $880; (H) $7,150
drawings: (L) $2,090; (H) $10,450

RUSSELL, John
British 19th cent.
paintings: (H) $17,600

RUSSELL, John
English 19th cent.
paintings: (H) $3,300

RUSSELL, Laura
American 20th cent.
sculpture: (H) $2,475

RUSSELL, Morgan
American 1886-1953
paintings: (L) $660; (H) $176,000
drawings: (L) $49; (H) $5,500

RUSSELL, Walter
paintings: (H) $770

RUSSIN
paintings: (L) $55; (H) $715

RUSSMAN, Felix
American 1888-1962
paintings: (H) $1,100

RUSSO, B.
drawings: (H) $2,640

RUSSO, Germano
French b. 1928
paintings: (H) $770

RUSSO, Mario
Italian b. 1925
paintings: (L) $55; (H) $1,100

RUSSOLO, Luigi
Italian 1885-1947
paintings: (H) $462,000

RUST
paintings: (H) $1,870

RUST, Johan Adolph
Dutch 1828-1915
paintings: (L) $990; (H) $16,500

RUTHERFORD, A.
paintings: (H) $3,960

RUTHVEN, Jerry
American
paintings: (L) $4,000; (H) $7,500

RUTTEN, Jan
Dutch 1809-1884
paintings: (H) $11,000

RUTTEN, V***
Dutch ac. 1869
drawings: (H) $1,760

RUTTER, Frank
English 19th/20th cent.
paintings: (H) $660

RUTTER, W.B.
American 19th cent.
paintings: (H) $770

RUYS, William
paintings: (H) $770

RUYSCH, Rachel
Dutch 1664-1750
paintings: (L) $33,000; (H) $165,000

RUYTEN, Jan Michiel
Belgian 1813-1881
paintings: (L) $550; (H) $9,900

RUYTEN, Jean
paintings: (H) $8,800

RUYTENBACH, *E***
2nd half 17th cent.
paintings: (H) $11,000

RUYTIN, Alfred
Belgian b. 1871
paintings: (L) $3,520; (H) $9,075

RY, Peter Danckerts de
paintings: (H) $2,200

RYAN, Anne
American 1889-1954
paintings: (L) $2,750; (H) $4,125
drawings: (H) $357

RYAN, Patrick
Continental 19th/20th cent.
paintings: (H) $5,280

RYAN, Tom
American b. 1922
paintings: (H) $5,500
drawings: (H) $5,500

RYBACK, Issachar
Russian b. 1897
paintings: (L) $825; (H) $9,900
drawings: (L) $2,530; (H) $9,900

RYCKAERT, David, the younger
paintings: (L) $5,500; (H) $7,150

RYCKAERT, Marten
Flemish 1587/91-1631/38
paintings: (L) $3,575; (H) $35,200

RYDER, Albert Pinkham
American 1847-1917
paintings: (H) $1,540

RYDER, Chauncey Foster
American 1868-1949
paintings: (L) $330; (H) $31,900
drawings: (L) $125; (H) $6,875

RYDER, J.S.
paintings: (H) $660

RYDER, J.S.
American 19th cent.
paintings: (L) $165; (H) $2,750

RYDER, Jack van
American 1898-1968
paintings: (L) $165; (H) $1,045

RYDER, Platt Powell
American 1821-1896
paintings: (L) $120; (H) $1,760
drawings: (H) $2,530

RYER, L.
paintings: (H) $2,200

RYERSON, Margery
American b. 1886
paintings: (H) $7,150

RYLAND, Henry
English 1856/59-1924
drawings: (H) $2,750

RYLAND, Robert Knight
American 1873-1951
paintings: (L) $192; (H) $3,080

RYMAN, Robert
American b. 1930
paintings: (L) $33,000; (H) $2,310,000
drawings: (L) $27,500; (H) $82,500

RYSBRACK, John Michael
1693-1770
drawings: (H) $1,300

RYSSELBERGHE, Theo van
Belgian 1862-1926
paintings: (L) $6,600; (H) $770,000
drawings: (L) $605; (H) $38,500

SAAR, Alison
American 20th cent.
drawings: (H) $1,210

SAAR, Betye
American b. 1926
drawings: (L) $330; (H) $1,100

SAARI, Peter
American b. 1951
paintings: (L) $3,025; (H) $11,550

SABATINI, I.
Continental 19th/20th cent.
paintings: (H) $4,620

SABATINI, I.
Italian 19th cent.
paintings: (H) $39,600

SABATINO, J.
American 20th cent.
paintings: (H) $715

SABBAGH, George Hanna
Egyptian/French 1887-1951
paintings: (H) $1,430

SABBATINI, Andrea, called Sabbatini
da SALERNO
Italian c. 1487-1530
paintings: (H) $52,250

SABBATINI, Lorenzo
c. 1530-1576
drawings: (H) $4,400

SABELA, H.J.
American 19th/20th cent.
paintings: (H) $1,000

SABLET, Jacques
Swiss 1720-1798
paintings: (H) $22,000

SABOURAUD, Emile
French b. 1900
paintings: (L) $302; (H) $1,980

SACCAGI, Cesare
Italian 1868-1934
paintings: (H) $13,200

SACCARDI, A.
Italian 20th cent.
sculpture: (H) $5,720

SACCARO, John
American 1913-1981
paintings: (H) $4,675
drawings: (L) $1,045; (H) $7,700

SACCHI, Andrea
Italian 1599-1661
drawings: (H) $880

SACCO, Luca
American 1858-1912
paintings: (L) $990; (H) $2,750

SACKLARIAN, Stephen
Bulgarian/American b. 1899
paintings: (L) $13,200; (H) $52,800
drawings: (H) $8,250

SACKS, Joseph
American b. 1887
paintings: (L) $302; (H) $2,640

SACKS, Walter T.
American b. 1895
paintings: (L) $605; (H) $715
drawings: (H) $220

SADEE, Philippe Lodowyck Jacob
Frederik
Dutch 1837-1904
paintings: (L) $16,500; (H) $26,400
drawings: (H) $7,700

SADLER, Walter Dendy
English 1854-1923
paintings: (L) $1,320; (H) $33,000

SADLER, William
British 1782-1839
paintings: (H) $2,750

SADONA, Matteo
American 1881-1964
drawings: (H) $1,100

SAEDELEER, Valerius de
Belgian 1867-1941
paintings: (H) $3,740

SAETTI, Bruno
drawings: (H) $5,500

SAFFORD, Charles
paintings: (H) $880

SAFFORD, Fannie
paintings: (H) $770

SAFTLEVEN, Cornelis
Dutch 1607-1681
drawings: (L) $3,575; (H) $7,150

SAFTLEVEN, Herman
Dutch
drawings: (H) $39,600

SAFTLEVEN, Herman
Dutch 1609-1685
paintings: (L) $15,400; (H) $121,000
drawings: (L) $7,700; (H) $20,900

SAGE, Kay
American 1848-1963
paintings: (L) $3,300; (H) $12,100
drawings: (H) $1,760

SAGRESTANI, Giovanni Camillo
Italian 1660-1731
paintings: (L) $1,760; (H) $4,400

SAIN, Edouard Alexandre
French 1830-1910
paintings: (L) $660; (H) $23,100

SAIN, Paul Jean Marie
French 1853-1908
paintings: (L) $880; (H) $3,960

SAINSBURY, Grace E.
English ac. 1889-1904
drawings: (H) $1,870

SAINT A. MOIR
sculpture: (H) $1,100

SAINT ANDRE, Simon Renard de
French 1614-1677
paintings: (L) $55,000; (H) $187,000

SAINT AUBIN, Augustin de
paintings: (H) $880

SAINT AUBIN, Gabriel de
French 1724-1780
drawings: (L) $198; (H) $25,300

SAINT BRICE, Robert
Haitian 1893-1973
paintings: (H) $880

SAINT EVRE, Gillot
French 1791-1858
paintings: (H) $1,100
drawings: (H) $660

SAINT GAUDENS, Augustus
American 1848-1907
sculpture: (L) $165; (H) $242,000

SAINT JOHN, Susan Hely
paintings: (H) $1,980

SAINT LERCHE, Hans
sculpture: (H) $1,100

SAINT MARCEAUX, Charles Rene de
sculpture: (L) $2,640; (H) $2,860

SAINT MEMIN, Charles Balthazar
Julien
French/American 1770-1852
drawings: (H) $6,600

SAINT PHALLE, Niki de
French b. 1930
drawings: (L) $13,200; (H) $15,400
sculpture: (L) $2,200; (H) $110,000

SAINT PHALLE, Niki de and Jean
TINGUELY
contemporary
sculpture: (L) $3,850; (H) $33,000

SAINT PIERRE DE MONTZAIGLE,
Edgard de
French b. 1867
drawings: (H) $8,800

SAINTIN, Jules Emile
American 1829-1894
paintings: (H) $4,950
drawings: (L) $660; (H) $3,080

SAINTPIERRE, Gaston Casimir
French 1833-1916
paintings: (H) $4,950

SAITER, Johann Gottfried
1717-1800
drawings: (H) $880

SAITO, Kikuo
paintings: (L) $440; (H) $1,760

SAKAI, Kazuya
Argentinian b. 1927/31
paintings: (L) $440; (H) $3,300

SAKS, Joseph
American 1887-1974
paintings: (H) $1,320

SALA, Paolo
Italian 1859-1924
paintings: (L) $4,125; (H) $7,700
drawings: (H) $99

SALA, Ventura Alvarez
Spanish b. 1871
paintings: (H) $6,600

SALA Y FRANCES, Emilio
Spanish 1850-1910
paintings: (L) $2,310; (H) $33,000

SALABET, Jean
French 20th cent.
paintings: (L) $165; (H) $4,400

SALADINI, A.
paintings: (L) $418; (H) $660

SALANSON, Eugenie Marie
French ac. 1864-1892
paintings: (L) $1,045; (H) $20,900

SALANSON, G.
paintings: (H) $3,850

SALAS, M.
drawings: (H) $880

SALAS, Tito
South American b. 1887
paintings: (H) $3,300

SALASKI, Michael
American contemporary
sculpture: (L) $132; (H) $990

SALAZAR, Carlos
Colombian b. 1956
paintings: (L) $4,400; (H) $4,675

SALAZAR, Ignacio
Mexican b. 1947
paintings: (H) $5,500

SALAZAR Y MENDOZA, Jose
Francisco Xavier de
Mexican d. 1802
paintings: (H) $68,200

SALDANA, Mateo
paintings: (H) $2,860

SALEH, Raden
Dutch 1816-1880
paintings: (H) $1,100

SALEMME, Attilio
American 1911-1955
paintings: (L) $3,300; (H) $6,050
drawings: (L) $1,100; (H) $3,575

SALENTIN, Hubert
German 1822-1910
paintings: (L) $6,050; (H) $33,000

SALESION, L.
Italian ac. 1890-1925
sculpture: (H) $770

SALICETI, Jeanne
French 1873-1950
paintings: (H) $660

SALIGO, Charles Louis
paintings: (H) $3,850

SALIMBENI, Lorenzo
Italian c. 1374-c. 1416
paintings: (H) $9,350

SALINAS
paintings: (H) $990

SALINAS, Pablo
Spanish 1871-1946
paintings: (L) $1,540; (H) $44,000

SALINAS, Porfirio
American 1910-1972
paintings: (L) $467; (H) $7,700

SALINAS Y TERUEL, Augustin
Spanish b. 1862
paintings: (L) $2,475; (H) $3,520

SALING, Paul E.
American 1876-1936
paintings: (L) $330; (H) $1,320

SALISBURY, Alta West
American 1879-1933
paintings: (L) $132; (H) $1,430

SALISBURY, Frank O.
English b. 1874
paintings: (L) $248; (H) $2,310

SALLA, Salvatore
American
paintings: (H) $770

SALLAI
Continental 19th cent.
paintings: (H) $2,200

SALLE, David
American b. 1952
paintings: (L) $14,300; (H) $550,000
drawings: (L) $880; (H) $28,600

SALMON, John Cuthbert
British 1844-1917
paintings: (H) $1,210
drawings: (L) $330; (H) $990

SALMON, R.
American School 19th cent.
drawings: (H) $1,760

SALMON, Robert
Anglo/American 1775-c. 1842/44
paintings: (L) $31,900; (H) $126,500

SALMSON, Hugo Frederik
Swedish 1844-1894
paintings: (L) $4,400; (H) $17,600

SALMSON, Jean Jules
French 1823-1902
sculpture: (L) $413; (H) $3,300

SALOME, Wolfgang Gilarz
German b. 1954
paintings: (L) $3,300; (H) $24,750

SALOME
German 20th cent.
paintings: (L) $3,300; (H) $24,750

SALOMON, Gabriel
drawings: (H) $2,200

SALSA, Philip van
drawings: (H) $1,100

SALT, J.
paintings: (H) $1,210

SALT, James
British 19th cent.
paintings: (L) $467; (H) $3,575

SALT, John
American b. 1937
paintings: (H) $46,750

SALTINI, Pietro
Italian 1839-1908
paintings: (H) $16,500

SALTOFT, Edvard Anders
Danish b. 1883
drawings: (H) $1,320

SALV
paintings: (H) $60,500

SALVAT, Francois
French b. 1892
paintings: (L) $302; (H) $770

SALVI, Ensel
paintings: (L) $495; (H) $990

SALVI, Giovanni Battista, called Il
Sassoferrato
Italian 1609-1685
paintings: (L) $5,500; (H) $37,400

SALVIN, M.A. de
Italian 19th cent.
paintings: (L) $880; (H) $3,300

SALVO
paintings: (L) $3,575; (H) $4,620

SAM, Joe
American 20th cent.
drawings: (H) $1,760

SAMACCHINI, Orazio
Italian 1532-1577
drawings: (L) $11,000; (H) $17,600

SAMANIEGO Y JARAMILLO,
Manuel
Ecuadorean b. c. 1767-1824
paintings: (H) $23,100

SAMARAS, Lucas
Greek/American b. 1936
paintings: (L) $462; (H) $5,500
drawings: (L) $1,540; (H) $23,100
sculpture: (L) $3,080; (H) $132,000

SAMBROOK, Russell
American 20th cent.
paintings: (H) $715

SAMMACCHINI, Orazio
drawings: (H) $3,410

SAMMANN, Detlef
American 1857-1938
paintings: (L) $880; (H) $5,500

SAMMONS, Carl
American 1853-1917
paintings: (L) $1,320; (H) $1,320

SAMMONS, Carl
American 1886-1968
paintings: (L) $275; (H) $4,400
drawings: (L) $440; (H) $990

SAMPLE, Paul Starrett
American 1896-1974
paintings: (L) $400; (H) $19,800
drawings: (L) $440; (H) $3,300

SAMPSON, H.
American 19th cent.
paintings: (H) $742

SAMSON, Jeanne
French 19th cent.
paintings: (L) $1,980; (H) $6,050

SAMSTAG, Gordon
American b. 1906
paintings: (L) $275; (H) $1,320

SAN MARTIN, C.
Continental 19th cent.
paintings: (H) $1,540

SANBORN
paintings: (H) $3,300

SANBORN, Percy
American 1849-1929
paintings: (L) $660; (H) $9,900

SANCHES, Harriet de
American
paintings: (L) $1,540; (H) $2,860

SANCHES, Manuel
paintings: (H) $4,180

SANCHEZ, Adolfo
contemporary
paintings: (H) $1,760

SANCHEZ, Edgar
Venezuelan b. 1940
paintings: (L) $5,500; (H) $7,700

SANCHEZ, Emilio
Cuban b. 1921
paintings: (L) $5,500; (H) $9,350
drawings: (L) $770; (H) $2,200

SANCHEZ, Enrique
paintings: (L) $4,400; (H) $8,800

SANCHEZ, Mario
paintings: (H) $770

SANCHEZ, Tomas
Cuban b. 1948
paintings: (L) $7,150; (H) $12,100

SANCHEZ PESCADO, F.
Spanish 19th cent.
drawings: (H) $880

SANCHEZ-PERRIER, Emilio
Spanish 1855-1907
paintings: (L) $2,750; (H) $35,200

SANCTIS, Guglielmo de
paintings: (H) $660

SAND, Maximilen E.
American 19th cent.
drawings: (H) $935

SANDBACK, Fred
American b. 1943
sculpture: (L) $6,875; (H) $38,500

SANDBY, Paul
English 1725-1809
drawings: (L) $660; (H) $4,400

SANDER, Ludwig
American 1906-1975
paintings: (L) $990; (H) $5,280

SANDER, Sherry
American b. 1941
sculpture: (L) $1,500; (H) $6,100

SANDER, Tom
American
paintings: (L) $1,500; (H) $3,100
drawings: (H) $1,600
sculpture: (H) $800

SANDERS
paintings: (H) $330
drawings: (H) $2,090

SANDERS, Hercules
Dutch 1606-1663
paintings: (H) $2,750

SANDERS, Phillip
British 20th cent.
paintings: (H) $770

SANDERS, Robert
paintings: (L) $440; (H) $660

SANDERS, Walter G.
British fl. 1884-1901
paintings: (H) $3,025

SANDERSON-WELLS, J.S.
paintings: (L) $5,500; (H) $5,500

SANDFORD, Edward Field
American
sculpture: (H) $3,850

SANDORFI, Istvan
contemporary
paintings: (H) $16,500

SANDORHAZL, W.B.
American 19th cent.
paintings: (H) $1,870

SANDOZ, E.M.
sculpture: (L) $770; (H) $1,540

SANDOZ, Edouard Marcel
Swiss 1881-1971
sculpture: (L) $330; (H) $5,500

SANDRUCCI, G.
Italian 19th/20th cent.
paintings: (H) $3,575

SANDRUCCI, Giovanni
Italian 19th cent.
paintings: (L) $1,650; (H) $15,400

SANDS, Harry H.
paintings: (H) $880

SANDYS, Anthony Frederick
Augustus
British 1829-1904
drawings: (H) $4,400

SANDZEN, Sven Birger
American 1871-1954
paintings: (L) $220; (H) $6,600

SANESI, Niccolo
Italian 1818-1889
paintings: (H) $2,200

SANFORD, E.
American 19th cent.
paintings: (H) $715

SANFORD, Marion
American
sculpture: (H) $4,620

SANFORD, W.G.
American 20th cent.
paintings: (H) $1,980

SANFORD, Walter
American b. 1915
paintings: (L) $412; (H) $660
drawings: (L) $154; (H) $385

SANGUINO
sculpture: (L) $1,210; (H) $2,750

SANI, Alessandro
Italian 19th cent.
paintings: (L) $247; (H) $8,800

SANI, David
Italian 19th cent.
paintings: (L) $605; (H) $6,050

SANIN, Fanny
Colombian b. 1938
paintings: (H) $16,500

SANO DI PIETRO
Italian 1406-1481
paintings: (L) $27,500; (H) $77,000

SANOJA, Miguel
sculpture: (H) $3,520

SANT, James
English 1820-1916
paintings: (L) $880; (H) $33,000

SANT, de
paintings: (H) $2,200

SANTA CROCE, Francesco di Simone da
Italian c. 1443-1508
paintings: (H) $38,500

SANTACROCE, Girolamo da
Italian ac. 1503-d. 1556
paintings: (H) $17,600

SANTAFEDE, Francesco
Italian b. c. 1519
paintings: (H) $16,500

SANTERRE, Jean Baptiste
French 1651/58-1771
paintings: (L) $18,700; (H) $30,800

SANTHO, Maria
Hungarian b. 1898
paintings: (H) $935

SANTI
sculpture: (H) $935

SANTINI, Giuseppe
ac. 1663
drawings: (L) $660; (H) $880

SANTOMASSO, Giuseppe
Italian b. 1907
drawings: (H) $16,500

SANTORO, Rubens
Italian 1843/59-1942
paintings: (L) $2,750; (H) $35,200
drawings: (H) $1,430

SANTOS, S.L. Gonzales
Spanish 19th/20th cent.
paintings: (H) $2,420

SANTRY, Daniel
American 1867-1951
paintings: (L) $385; (H) $1,320

SANTVOORT, Dirk
Dutch 1610-1680
paintings: (H) $20,900

SANZEL, F.
Continental 19th cent.
sculpture: (H) $1,045

SANZEL, Felix
French 1829-1883
sculpture: (H) $990

SAPONARI, G.
Italian 19th/20th cent.
paintings: (H) $1,650

SARASSIN, Jean Philippe
late 17th cent.
paintings: (H) $1,650

SARDE
sculpture: (H) $1,100

SARDI, Istvan
1846-1901
paintings: (L) $1,155; (H) $1,155

SARDI, Richard C.
late 19th/early 20th cent
paintings: (H) $660

SARET, Alan
American b. 1944
drawings: (L) $1,100; (H) $3,300
sculpture: (H) $14,300

SARG, Tony
drawings: (H) $6,050

SARGEANT, Geneve Rixford
American 1868-1957
paintings: (L) $275; (H) $1,540
drawings: (L) $330; (H) $405

SARGENT, Carroll, Jr.
American 1877-1956
paintings: (H) $3,025

SARGENT, G. Henry
American
paintings: (H) $2,200

SARGENT, John S.
drawings: (H) $880

SARGENT, John Singer
American 1856-1925
paintings: (L) $2,750; (H) $1,485,000
drawings: (L) $1,320; (H) $203,500
sculpture: (L) $4,675; (H) $6,050

SARGENT, Louis Augustus
British b. 1881
paintings: (L) $137; (H) $715

SARGENT, Margarett W.
American b. 1892
paintings: (H) $715

SARGENT, Paul Turner
American b. 1880
paintings: (L) $715; (H) $1,045

SARGENT, Richard
1911-1978
drawings: (L) $110; (H) $7,000

SARGENT, Walter
American 1868-1927
paintings: (L) $220; (H) $10,340

SARISAWA
paintings: (H) $2,640

SARKISIAN, Paul
American b. 1928
paintings: (H) $19,800
drawings: (H) $2,740

SARKISIAN, Sarkis
American 1909-1977
paintings: (L) $220; (H) $1,540
drawings: (L) $77; (H) $880

SARLE, Sister Cora Helena
American 1867-1956
paintings: (H) $1,540

SARNOFF, Arthur
American b. 1912
paintings: (L) $137; (H) $1,705
drawings: (H) $852

SARSONY, Robert
American b. 1938
paintings: (H) $2,860

SARTAIN, Emily
American d. 1927
paintings: (H) $2,200

SARTAIN, William
American 1843-1924
paintings: (L) $418; (H) $3,300

SARTORELLI, Francesco
Italian 1856-1939
paintings: (H) $7,700

SARTORIO, Giulio Aristide
Italian 1860-1932
paintings: (L) $3,520; (H) $9,350
drawings: (L) $11; (H) $2,200

SARTORIUS, Francis
English 1734-1804
paintings: (L) $4,510; (H) $46,200

SARTORIUS, John Francis
English c. 1775-1831
paintings: (H) $13,200

SARTORIUS, John Nost
English 1759-1828
paintings: (L) $1,210; (H) $93,500

SARTORIUS, Virginie de
Belgian b. 1828
paintings: (L) $11,000; (H) $24,200

SASSONE, Marco
Italian/American b. 1942
paintings: (H) $12,100

SASSONS, Amory C.
sculpture: (H) $4,840

SATCHELL, Theodore
British 1854-1919
paintings: (H) $1,540

SATLOFT, Edward A.
Danish 20th cent.
drawings: (H) $3,300

SATO, Key
Japanese b. 1906
paintings: (H) $5,775

SATRIANO, Conda De
paintings: (H) $12,100

SATTERLEE, Walter
American 1844-1908
paintings: (L) $300; (H) $2,035
drawings: (L) $82; (H) $220

SATTLER, Hubert
Austrian 1817-1904
paintings: (H) $1,100

SAUBERT, Tom
American
drawings: (H) $1,050

SAUER, Walter
Belgian 1889-1972
drawings: (L) $3,850; (H) $10,450

SAUERFELT, Leonard
paintings: (H) $990

SAUFELT, Leonard
French 19th cent.
paintings: (H) $3,575

SAUL, Peter
American b. 1934
paintings: (H) $24,200
drawings: (L) $1,100; (H) $12,100

SAULACROY, F.
paintings: (H) $1,210

SAULNER, F.
sculpture: (H) $715

SAUNDERS, Ella G.
American 19th cent.
paintings: (H) $4,950

SAUNDERS, Norman
paintings: (L) $1,100; (H) $1,800

SAUNDERS, Theodore
French 19th cent.
paintings: (L) $935; (H) $1,870

SAUNIER, Noel
French 1847-1890
paintings: (L) $7,700; (H) $29,700

SAURA, Antonio
Spanish b. 1930
paintings: (L) $29,700; (H) $96,250
drawings: (L) $17,600; (H) $19,800

SAURA, Fra Domingo Texdury
paintings: (H) $2,420

SAURET, M.
paintings: (H) $715

SAURFELT, Leonard
French 19th cent.
paintings: (L) $165; (H) $7,150

SAURFIN
paintings: (H) $1,100

SAUSSURE, Theodore de
Swiss 1824-1903
paintings: (L) $660; (H) $1,320

SAUSSY, Hattie
American
paintings: (H) $2,970

SAUVAGE, Arsene Symphorien
paintings: (H) $1,650

SAUVAGE, Philip
French
paintings: (H) $2,420

SAUVAGE, Piat Joseph
Flemish 1744-1818
paintings: (L) $3,300; (H) $12,100

SAUVAGE, Piet
French 19th cent.
paintings: (H) $1,320

SAUVAGE, Pieter Joseph
Flemish 1744-1818
paintings: (H) $3,300

SAUZAY, Adrien Jacques
French 1841-1928
paintings: (H) $6,600

SAVAGE, Edward
American 19th cent.
paintings: (H) $963

SAVAGE, R.A.
American 19th cent.
paintings: (H) $18,700

SAVELLO, Leon
Italian 19th cent.
paintings: (H) $4,400

SAVERY, Jacob
Dutch c. 1565-1603
drawings: (H) $24,200

SAVERY, Roelandt
Flemish 1576-1639
paintings: (H) $49,500

SAVERYS, Albert
paintings: (H) $2,860

SAVILE
drawings: (H) $660

SAVILLA, L. Aguila
paintings: (H) $1,650

SAVIN, Maurice
French 1894-1973
paintings: (L) $3,960; (H) $25,300

SAVINE, Leopold Pierre
paintings: (H) $1,650

SAVINI, A**
Italian 19th cent.
paintings: (H) $990

SAVINI, Alfonso
Italian 1836-1908
paintings: (H) $6,050

SAVINIO, Alberto
drawings: (H) $7,700

SAVITSKY, Jack
American b. 1910
paintings: (L) $225; (H) $3,960

SAVOURG, R.
paintings: (H) $715

SAVRASOV, Aleksei Kondratievitch
Russian 1830-1897
paintings: (H) $880

SAVRY, Hendrick
Dutch 1823-1907
paintings: (L) $935; (H) $3,520

SAWYER, Helen
American b. 1900
paintings: (L) $44; (H) $1,210
drawings: (H) $385

SAWYER, Warren F.
20th cent.
paintings: (L) $770; (H) $3,410
drawings: (H) $3,520

SAWYER, Wells M.
American 1863-c. 1960
paintings: (L) $247; (H) $1,925

SAWYIER, Paul
American 1865-1917
drawings: (L) $5,500; (H) $23,100

SAXILD, Carl R.
American 20th cent.
paintings: (L) $468; (H) $3,300

SAXON, Lulu King
American 1855-1927
paintings: (H) $2,750

SAY, Frederick Richard
paintings: (H) $1,650

SAYRE, Fred Grayson
American 1879-1938/39
paintings: (L) $1,430; (H) $11,000
drawings: (L) $99; (H) $440

SCACCIATTI, Andrea
paintings: (H) $6,050

SCAEFER, Henry Thomas
British ac. 1873-1915
paintings: (H) $7,150

SCAFFAI, Luigi
Italian b. 1837
paintings: (L) $990; (H) $19,800

SCAGLIONE, Carlos
paintings: (H) $2,860

SCALBERT, J.
paintings: (H) $775
drawings: (H) $550

SCALBERT, Jules
French b. 1851, ac. 1876-1891
paintings: (L) $7,700; (H) $9,900
drawings: (H) $2,200

SCALINI, F.
Italian 19th/20th cent.
paintings: (H) $7,425

SCAMPERLE, Livio
paintings: (L) $3,300; (H) $3,520

SCANGA, Italo
American b. 1932
drawings: (L) $1,100; (H) $1,760
sculpture: (L) $2,090; (H) $17,600

SCARLETT, Rolph
American 1889-1984
paintings: (L) $2,750; (H) $22,000
drawings: (L) $715; (H) $6,600

SCARPITTA, G. Salvatore Cartland
sculpture: (H) $880

SCARSELLINO, Ippolito
paintings: (H) $770

SCARVELLI
Italian 19th/20th cent.
drawings: (L) $110; (H) $935

SCATTOLA, F.
paintings: (H) $2,200

SCATTOLA, Ferruccio
Italian 1873-1950
paintings: (H) $715

SCETTOLIN (?), Viti
Italian 20th cent.
paintings: (L) $412; (H) $660

SCEVOLA, Lucien Guirard de
French 1871-1950
paintings: (H) $2,750

SCHAAN, Paul
French 19th-20th cent.
paintings: (L) $1,650; (H) $3,520

SCHABE, Emile
German b. 1856
paintings: (H) $907

SCHABELITZ, Rudolph F.
American 1884-1959
paintings: (L) $770; (H) $2,750

SCHACHINGER, Gabriel
German 1850-1912
paintings: (H) $6,050

SCHACHTEL, H.
paintings: (H) $1,430

SCHAD-ROSSA, Paul
German 1862-1916
paintings: (H) $1,210

SCHAEFELS, Henri Francois, or
Hendrik Frans
Belgian 1827-1904
paintings: (L) $2,310; (H) $5,500

SCHAEFELS, Lucas
Belgian 1824-1885
paintings: (L) $1,650; (H) $33,000

SCHAEFER, D.
sculpture: (H) $2,200

SCHAEFFER, August
Austrian 1833-1916
paintings: (H) $41,250

SCHAEFFER, H.
French b. 1926
paintings: (H) $770

SCHAEFFER, Heinrich
German 19th cent.
paintings: (H) $2,200

SCHAEFFER, Henri
French 1900-1975
paintings: (H) $6,050

SCHAEFFER, Henri
French b. 1924
paintings: (L) $2,860; (H) $2,860

SCHAEFFER, John Simon
American
paintings: (H) $1,980

SCHAEFFER, Mead
American 1898-1980
paintings: (L) $77; (H) $6,600
drawings: (H) $440

SCHAEP, Henri Adolphe
Dutch 1826-1870
paintings: (H) $2,420

SCHAETTE, C.
paintings: (H) $1,320

SCHAFER, Dirch
Dutch 1864-1941
paintings: (H) $1,870

SCHAFER, Frederick
German/American 1839-1927
paintings: (L) $220; (H) $8,800

SCHAFER, Heinrich
German b. 1815
paintings: (H) $990
drawings: (L) $220; (H) $1,210

SCHAFER, Henry
British/French 19th cent.
paintings: (L) $495; (H) $3,080
drawings: (L) $154; (H) $1,540

SCHAFER, Henry Thomas
English b. 1854
paintings: (L) $1,320; (H) $8,250
drawings: (L) $660; (H) $2,420

SCHAFER, Hermann
German b. 1880
paintings: (L) $770; (H) $1,650
drawings: (L) $330; (H) $385

SCHAFFER, Adalbert
paintings: (H) $6,600

SCHAFFER, Don
drawings: (H) $2,200

SCHAFFER, H.
Belgian 20th cent.
paintings: (H) $1,045

SCHAGEN, Gerbrand Frederick van
Dutch 1880-1968
paintings: (L) $1,155; (H) $1,210

SCHAGGI, R.
sculpture: (H) $990

SCHALCKEN, Godfried
Dutch 1643-1706
paintings: (L) $3,300; (H) $16,500

SCHALDACH, William J.
American b. 1896
paintings: (H) $1,100
drawings: (L) $192; (H) $1,430

SCHALL, F.
paintings: (H) $2,420

SCHALL, Jean Frederic
French 1752-1825
paintings: (L) $6,600; (H) $148,500

SCHAMBERG, Morton Livingston
American 1881-1918
paintings: (L) $4,125; (H) $308,000
drawings: (L) $110; (H) $23,100

Precisionism

Precisionism, an indigenous movement in American art, originated in 1915 and flourished through the 1920s. Precisionists emphasized draftsmanship and geometry in their compositions. Their subject matter was urban and industrial, devoid of any human element. Precisionism was not a formal movement, but its leaders, Charles Demuth, Georgia O'Keeffe, and Charles Sheeler, often exhibited together.

The works of Morton Livingston Schamberg (1881-1918) foreshadowed the beginning of the Precisionist movement. Born in Philadelphia, he studied architecture at the University of Pennsylvania. After graduation he attended the Pennsylvania Academy of the Fine Arts, where he studied with William Merritt Chase. Charles Sheeler was another student at the Academy, and the two became close friends and shared a studio. Schamberg's arbitrarily colored landscapes appeared in the historic 1913 New York Armory Show, which introduced modern art to the United States.

Schamberg and Sheeler made numerous trips abroad and were influenced by Cezanne, Matisse, and the Cubist movement. In New York, at the salon of Walter H. Annenberg, the two met French Dada artists Marcel Duchamp, Man Ray, and Francis Picabia. By 1912 Schamberg was painting partially abstract pictures while supporting himself as a photographer. In 1914 he began to paint machines, and his training in architecture and his experience in photography led to paintings with mechanical lines and carefully arranged flat shapes. He painted numerous pastels and sketches and some oils. Not all of his works are signed. In 1918, when mail began to pile up outside his door, a neighbor called his good friend Charles Sheeler, who discovered that Schamberg had died, a victim of the flu epidemic.

In 1986 two oils by Schamberg were consigned to Weschler's Galleries in Washington, D.C. The two paintings had once been owned by John Quinn, a legendary collector of modern art and organizer of the 1913 Armory Show. Fresh to the market, and the first time works by Schamberg had been offered at auction, the pair sold for $127,600. (Morton Livingston Schamberg, *Victory* and *Houses*, oils on panel, 14 x 10 in., Weschler, March 7, 1986, $127,600)

SCHAMPHELLEER, Edmond de
Belgian 1824-1899
paintings: (H) $2,090

SCHAMS, Franz
Austrian 1823-1883
paintings: (H) $715

SCHANKER, Louis
American b. 1903
paintings: (L) $825; (H) $13,200
drawings: (L) $440; (H) $1,980

SCHAPHERDERS, Jaak
Dutch 19th/20th cent.
paintings: (H) $935

SCHARF, Kenny
American b. 1958
paintings: (L) $5,720; (H) $93,500
drawings: (L) $990; (H) $3,850
sculpture: (L) $1,100; (H) $14,300

SCHARF, Viktor
Austrian b. 1872
paintings: (H) $12,100

SCHARL, Joseph
German 1896-1954
paintings: (L) $10,450; (H) $20,900
drawings: (L) $198; (H) $1,320

SCHATTENSTEIN, Nicol
American 1877-1954
paintings: (L) $302; (H) $11,550

SCHATZ, Manfred
German 20th cent.
paintings: (H) $2,200

SCHATZ, Professor Boris
sculpture: (L) $715; (H) $935

SCHAUTA(?), F.
paintings: (H) $2,200

SCHDOL, Max
Austrian 1834-1921
paintings: (H) $1,650

SCHEBEK, Ferdinand
Austrian 1875-1949
paintings: (H) $1,100

SCHEDELBAUER, Eduard
Austrian 19th/20th cent.
paintings: (H) $660

SCHEERES, Hendricus Johannes
Dutch 1829-1864
paintings: (L) $660; (H) $1,650

SCHEFFER, Ary
Dutch/French 1795-1858
paintings: (L) $550; (H) $26,400

SCHEFFLER, Rudolf
American b. Germany 1884
paintings: (H) $31,900
drawings: (L) $1,320; (H) $1,430

SCHEGGI, A.
Italian 19th cent.
sculpture: (H) $825

SCHEIBER, Hugo
Hungarian 1873-1950
paintings: (L) $3,300; (H) $8,800
drawings: (L) $275; (H) $5,280

SCHEIBL, Hubert
contemporary
paintings: (H) $1,320

SCHEIDEL, Franz Anton von
Austrian 1731-1801
drawings: (L) $770; (H) $3,300

SCHELFHAUT, A.
paintings: (H) $825

SCHELFHOUT, Andreas
Dutch 1787-1870
paintings: (L) $6,600; (H) $25,300

SCHELL, Frank H.
American 1830/34-1909
drawings: (L) $770; (H) $2,860

SCHELL, Frank H. and Thomas
HOGAN
American
drawings: (L) $550; (H) $1,650

SCHELLBACH, Karl Hermann
German 1850-1921
paintings: (H) $990

SCHELLEIN, A.
Austrian 19th cent.
paintings: (H) $1,980

SCHELLINK, Hendrik
Dutch 1795-1848
paintings: (H) $4,950

SCHELOUMOFF, A.
Continental 19th cent.
paintings: (H) $935

SCHELOUMOFF, A. and A. SCHEM
paintings: (H) $2,200

SCHEMPP, Theodore
paintings: (H) $1,760

SCHENAU, Johann Eleazar
German 1737-1806
drawings: (L) $385; (H) $880

SCHENAU, Johann Eleazar Zeizig
sculpture: (H) $935

SCHENCK, August Friedrich Albrecht
Danish 1828-1901
paintings: (L) $1,100; (H) $4,840

SCHENCK, Penelope Josephine
American b. 1883
drawings: (H) $1,430

SCHENCKS, J.
paintings: (H) $880

SCHENDEL, Petrus van
Belgian 1806-1870
paintings: (L) $275; (H) $77,000

SCHENFELDER
paintings: (H) $1,100

SCHEPERS, Maria
paintings: (H) $33,000

SCHERAN, P.
paintings: (H) $1,210

SCHERMAN, Tony
paintings: (H) $3,500

SCHERMER, Cornelis Albertus
Johannes
drawings: (H) $4,180

SCHERRER, Jean Jacques
French 19th cent.
paintings: (H) $3,300

SCHERREWITZ, Johan
Dutch 1868-1951
paintings: (L) $302; (H) $24,200

SCHETLEY, J.S.
paintings: (H) $2,420

SCHEUERER, Julius
German 1859-1913
paintings: (L) $550; (H) $5,500

SCHEUERER, Otto
German 1862-1934
paintings: (L) $1,760; (H) $4,180

SCHEUERLE, Joseph
American 19th/20th cent.
drawings: (L) $825; (H) $825

SCHEUREN, Caspar Johann Nepomuk
German 1810-1887
paintings: (L) $935; (H) $8,250

SCHEURER, Julius
German 1859-1913
paintings: (L) $2,475; (H) $8,800

SCHEURER, Julius
German d. 1819
paintings: (L) $2,750; (H) $6,325

SCHEURSTEEN, Thomas
American 19th cent.
paintings: (H) $1,045

SCHEVILL, W.V.
American b. 1864
paintings: (H) $1,485

SCHIAVI, G. and G. ROSSI
drawings: (H) $660

SCHIAVONE, Andrea, called Meldolla
Italian 1522-1563
paintings: (L) $7,975; (H) $55,000

SCHIAVONI, N.
paintings: (H) $2,310

SCHIEDGES, P.P.
Dutch 19th cent.
paintings: (H) $1,320

SCHIEDGES, Peter Paulus
Dutch 1812-1876
paintings: (H) $990

SCHIELE, Egon
German 1890-1918
paintings: (L) $38,500; (H) $5,940,000
drawings: (L) $9,900; (H) $880,000

SCHIERL, Josef
German ac. c. 1835
paintings: (H) $3,300

SCHIFANO, Mario
Italian contemporary
paintings: (L) $8,250; (H) $13,200

SCHIFFER, Anton
paintings: (H) $8,250

SCHIFFNER, Barbara
English 20th cent.
paintings: (H) $935

SCHILDER, Andrei Nicolajevitch
Russian b. 1861
paintings: (H) $6,050

SCHILDT, Gary
American
paintings: (L) $600; (H) $750
sculpture: (H) $700

SCHILKING, Heinrich
German 1815-1895
paintings: (H) $7,975

SCHILL, Adrien
Dutch 1849-1902
paintings: (H) $825

SCHILL, Emil
Swiss b. 1870
paintings: (H) $6,600
drawings: (H) $412

SCHILLE, Alice
American d. 1955
drawings: (L) $55; (H) $6,050

SCHILLINGER, J.
drawings: (H) $1,540

SCHILSKY, Eric
sculpture: (H) $660

SCHIMMEL, Wilhelm
American b. 1817
sculpture: (H) $2,750

SCHIMMELFENNIG, Oswalt
sculpture: (H) $1,870

SCHINDLER, Emil Jacob
Austrian 1842-1892
paintings: (L) $3,850; (H) $28,600
drawings: (H) $4,400

SCHINDLER, Jakob Emil
Austrian 1842-1892
paintings: (H) $29,700

SCHINDLER, Thomas
German b. 1959
paintings: (L) $2,750; (H) $6,600

SCHIODTE, Harald Valdemar
Immanuel
Danish 1852-1924
paintings: (H) $7,700

SCHIOTTZ-JENSEN, Niels Frederik
Danish b. 1855
paintings: (L) $4,400; (H) $10,450

SCHIPPERS, Joseph
Belgian 1868-1950
paintings: (L) $990; (H) $4,400

SCHIPPERUS, Pieter Adrianus
Dutch 1840-1929
paintings: (H) $2,200

SCHIRMER, Johann Wilhelm
German 1807-1863
paintings: (L) $9,900; (H) $18,700
drawings: (H) $2,420

SCHIRREN, Ferdinand
Belgian 1872
drawings: (H) $1,100

SCHIVERT, Victor
Rumanian b. 1863
paintings: (L) $220; (H) $3,575

SCHJELDERUP, Leis
Norwegian 19th/20th cent.
paintings: (H) $12,650

SCHLEICH, Eduard
paintings: (H) $2,640

SCHLEICH, Eduard, Jr.
German 19th cent.
paintings: (L) $880; (H) $7,150

SCHLEICH, Robert
German 1845-1934
paintings: (L) $3,850; (H) $16,500

SCHLEICHER, Carl
Austrian ac. 1859-1871
paintings: (L) $660; (H) $1,650

SCHLEIER, T.M.
American 19th cent.
paintings: (H) $935

SCHLEMMER, Oskar
German 1888-1943
sculpture: (H) $46,200

SCHLESINGER, Carl
Swiss 1825-1893
paintings: (L) $3,575; (H) $8,250

SCHLESINGER, Felix
German 1833-1910
paintings: (L) $4,840; (H) $38,500

SCHLESINGER, Henri Guillaume
French 1814-1893
paintings: (L) $2,510; (H) $12,100
drawings: (H) $1,650

SCHLESINGER, Johann
German 1768-1848
paintings: (L) $3,025; (H) $4,400

SCHLESINGER, Karl
Swiss 1825/26-1893
paintings: (H) $1,760

SCHLESINGER, Mark
contemporary
paintings: (L) $2,750; (H) $2,860
drawings: (H) $880

SCHLETTER
paintings: (H) $990

SCHLICHTING, Waldemar
German 20th cent.
paintings: (H) $880

SCHLICHTING, Walter
American 20th cent.
paintings: (H) $770

SCHLICK, Benjamin
French ac. 19th/20th cent.
drawings: (L) $4,675; (H) $11,550

SCHLIMARSKI, Heinrich Hans
Austrian
paintings: (H) $1,485

SCHLISINGER, C.
German 19th cent.
paintings: (H) $1,540

SCHLITT, Heinrich
German b. 1849
paintings: (L) $275; (H) $9,350

SCHLITTGEN, Hermann
contemporary
paintings: (H) $2,640

SCHLOESSER, Carl Bernhard
German 1832-after 1914
paintings: (H) $11,000

SCHMALIX, Hubert
contemporary
paintings: (H) $4,620

SCHMALNT
paintings: (H) $880

SCHMALZ, Herbert Gustave
British 1865-1935
paintings: (H) $14,300

SCHMALZIGAUG, Friedrich
Ferdinand
German 1847-1902
paintings: (H) $9,350

SCHMAUSS, Peter
American 1868-1938
paintings: (H) $935

SCHMID, Davi Alois
Swiss 1791-1861
drawings: (H) $4,400

SCHMID, Richard
American b. 1934
paintings: (L) $550; (H) $8,800

SCHMIDT, Adolf
German b. 1804
paintings: (H) $8,250

SCHMIDT, Albert H.
American 1885-1957
paintings: (L) $1,320; (H) $8,250

SCHMIDT, Alfred
German b. 1867
paintings: (H) $1,760

SCHMIDT, Bruno
paintings: (H) $770

SCHMIDT, Carl
American 1885-1969
paintings: (L) $495; (H) $3,575

SCHMIDT, Carl
American b. 1855
paintings: (L) $385; (H) $880
drawings: (H) $330

SCHMIDT, Eduard
German 1806-1862
paintings: (H) $7,150

SCHMIDT, Eric von
paintings: (L) $412; (H) $1,650

SCHMIDT, Franz
German 19th/20th cent.
drawings: (L) $550; (H) $1,100

SCHMIDT, Frederic Albert
French 1846-1916
paintings: (H) $1,650

SCHMIDT, H.
paintings: (H) $1,650

SCHMIDT, Hans
American
paintings: (H) $880

SCHMIDT, Harold von
American 1893-1982
paintings: (L) $350; (H) $33,000
drawings: (L) $800; (H) $2,200

SCHMIDT, Jay
American 20th cent.
paintings: (H) $1,540

SCHMIDT, Johann Georg, called
Wienerschmidt
Austrian 1694-1765
paintings: (H) $6,600

SCHMIDT, Julius
American b. 1923
sculpture: (H) $660

SCHMIDT, Karl
American 1890-1962
paintings: (L) $330; (H) $5,500
drawings: (L) $770; (H) $2,200

SCHMIDT, Kaspar
paintings: (H) $1,210

SCHMIDT, Katherine
American b. 1898
paintings: (L) $440; (H) $4,950

SCHMIDT, Martin Johann, Kremser-
Schmidt
Austrian 1718-1801
drawings: (H) $5,280

SCHMIDT, Oscar
German 19th cent.
paintings: (H) $3,300

SCHMIDT, Rudolf
Austrian b. 1873
drawings: (H) $1,760

SCHMIDT, W.
Dutch 19th cent.
paintings: (H) $3,575

SCHMIDT-CASSEL
sculpture: (H) $1,045

SCHMIDT-FELLING
c. 1895-1930
sculpture: (L) $143; (H) $1,980

SCHMIDT-ROTTLUFF, Karl
German 1884-1976
paintings: (L) $115,500; (H) $396,000
drawings: (L) $6,050; (H) $60,500

SCHMIED, Francois Louis
drawings: (H) $2,860

SCHMITS
paintings: (H) $880

SCHMITT, *D***
paintings: (H) $4,950

SCHMITT, Carl
American b. 1889
paintings: (H) $715

SCHMITT, Georg Philipp
German 1808-1873
paintings: (H) $1,210

SCHMITT, Nathaniel
German 1847-1918
paintings: (L) $2,420; (H) $5,225

SCHMITT, Paul Leon Felix
French 1856-1902
paintings: (H) $2,750

SCHMITZ, Georg
German b. 1851
paintings: (H) $3,575

SCHMITZ, Jean Paul
German 19th cent.
paintings: (H) $1,320

SCHMUTZER, Jakob Mathias, the
younger
Austrian 1733-1811
drawings: (L) $220; (H) $6,050

SCHMUTZLER, Leopold
German 1864-1941
paintings: (L) $1,100; (H) $22,000

SCHNABEL, Julian
American b. 1951
paintings: (L) $4,400; (H) $242,000
drawings: (L) $2,750; (H) $33,000
sculpture: (H) $165,000

SCHNAKENBERG, Henry Ernest
American 1892-1970
paintings: (L) $110; (H) $4,125
drawings: (L) $33; (H) $550

SCHNAUER, R.
sculpture: (H) $935

SCHNEE, Hermann
paintings: (H) $6,875

SCHNEIDAU, Christian von
American 1893-1976
paintings: (L) $275; (H) $4,125

SCHNEIDER
German 19th cent.
paintings: (H) $1,650

SCHNEIDER, B.
Continental 19th cent.
paintings: (H) $880

SCHNEIDER, F.
paintings: (H) $990

SCHNEIDER, F.
American ac. early 20th cent.
paintings: (L) $700; (H) $1,265

SCHNEIDER, F.
German late 19th cent.
paintings: (H) $660

SCHNEIDER, G.
Belgian 19th cent.
paintings: (H) $660

SCHNEIDER, G.
European 19th cent.
paintings: (H) $660

SCHNEIDER, George
American contemporary
paintings: (L) $1,870; (H) $19,800

SCHNEIDER, Gerard
French 1896-1948
paintings: (L) $8,250; (H) $28,600

SCHNEIDER, Hermann
German 1847-1918
paintings: (H) $3,300

SCHNEIDER, Jose
Spanish/American 1848-1893
paintings: (H) $3,300

SCHNEIDER, Otto Henry
American 1865-1950
paintings: (H) $22,000

SCHNEIDER, William G.
American 1863-1912.
paintings: (H) $1,182

SCHNEIDR, J.
paintings: (H) $880

SCHNETZ, Jean Victor
drawings: (H) $2,420

SCHNIDT, Nicolaus
sculpture: (H) $3,575

SCHNITZLER, Fritz
paintings: (H) $7,700

SCHOBER, Peter Jakob
German b. 1897
paintings: (H) $4,400

SCHODL, Max
Austrian 1834-1921
paintings: (L) $880; (H) $3,300

SCHOENFELD, Flora
American 1873-1960
paintings: (L) $770; (H) $1,870

SCHOENHAUER (?), T.E.
American 20th cent.
paintings: (H) $1,870

SCHOENN, Alois
Austrian 1826-1897
paintings: (H) $1,650

SCHOETER, M.
paintings: (H) $1,925

SCHOFIELD, John William
English 19th/20th cent.
paintings: (L) $522; (H) $715

SCHOFIELD, Kershaw
British 19th/20th cent.
paintings: (L) $990; (H) $4,950

SCHOFIELD, Walter Elmer
American 1867-1944
paintings: (L) $1,100; (H) $55,000

SCHOLDER, Fritz
American b. 1937
paintings: (L) $1,100; (H) $34,100
drawings: (H) $110

SCHOLTEN, Hendrik Jacobs
Dutch 1824-1907
paintings: (H) $1,430

SCHOLZ, Max
German b. 1855
paintings: (L) $2,750; (H) $9,350

SCHOMMER, Francois
French 1850-1935
paintings: (H) $1,210

SCHONBAUER, Henry
American b. 1895
sculpture: (H) $1,980

SCHONBRUNNER, Ignaz
paintings: (H) $1,430

SCHONIAN, Alfred
German b. 1856
paintings: (L) $1,100; (H) $3,520

SCHONLEBER, Gustav
German 1851-1917
paintings: (L) $1,650; (H) $7,150
drawings: (H) $3,520

SCHONTON
European 19th cent.
paintings: (H) $1,017

SCHONVERK
sculpture: (H) $2,475

SCHONZEIT, Ben
American b. 1942
paintings: (L) $2,750; (H) $11,000
drawings: (L) $523; (H) $770

SCHOONLINGEN, J.H.
Dutch 20th cent.
paintings: (H) $990

SCHOONOVER, Frank E.
American 1877-1972
paintings: (L) $715; (H) $28,600

SCHOOTEN, Floris van
Dutch c. 1590-1655
paintings: (L) $33,000; (H) $66,000

SCHOPIN, Frederic Henri
French 1804-1880
paintings: (L) $605; (H) $126,500

SCHOR, Ilya
American 20th cent.
paintings: (L) $1,980; (H) $4,400

SCHORDER, Paul
Continental 19th cent.
paintings: (H) $2,860

SCHORK, Hans
Austrian early 20th cent.
sculpture: (H) $2,420

SCHOTEL, Anthonie Pieter
Dutch 1890-1958
paintings: (L) $330; (H) $3,850

SCHOTEL, E.C.
Dutch 20th cent.
paintings: (H) $1,045

SCHOTEL, Jan Christianus
Dutch 1787-1838
paintings: (L) $2,200; (H) $3,575

SCHOTEL, Petrus Jan
Dutch 1808-1865
paintings: (H) $6,050

SCHOTT, Walter
sculpture: (L) $467; (H) $1,210

SCHOUMAN, Aert
Dutch 1710-1792
paintings: (H) $77,000
drawings: (L) $660; (H) $11,000

SCHOUMANN, Martinus
Dutch 1770-1848
paintings: (H) $11,000

SCHOUT, A.
Belgian 19th cent.
paintings: (H) $900

SCHOUTEN, Henri
Belgian 1864-1927
paintings: (L) $550; (H) $5,500

SCHOUTEN, Henry
Dutch 1791-1835
paintings: (H) $1,870

SCHOYERER, Josef
German 1844-1923
paintings: (L) $1,100; (H) $2,860

SCHRADER, Julius Friedrich Anton
German 1815-1900
paintings: (L) $4,950; (H) $46,750

SCHRADER, R.
paintings: (H) $4,620

SCHRADER, Theodore
Continental 19th cent.
paintings: (H) $7,700

SCHRAEGLE, Gustave
German
paintings: (H) $880

SCHRAG, Karl
American b. 1912
paintings: (H) $4,125
drawings: (L) $88; (H) $1,980

SCHRAM, Alois Hans
Austrian 1864-1919
paintings: (L) $1,100; (H) $4,950

SCHRANZ, Anton
German 1769-1839
paintings: (H) $8,800

SCHRECKENGOST, Viktor
American b. 1906
drawings: (L) $88; (H) $1,375

SCHREIBER, Charles Baptiste
French d. 1903
paintings: (L) $1,100; (H) $8,800

SCHREIBER, George
American 20th cent.
paintings: (L) $1,650; (H) $6,600
drawings: (L) $550; (H) $2,200

SCHREIBER, Georges
Belgian/American 1904-1977
drawings: (H) $2,860

SCHREIBER, Hugo
drawings: (L) $770; (H) $825

SCHREIGER, L.
paintings: (H) $880

SCHREPLER, L.
paintings: (H) $660

SCHREUDER, F.J.
Dutch 19th/20th cent.
paintings: (H) $715

SCHREYER, A. de
paintings: (H) $9,000

SCHREYER, Adolf
German 1828-1899
paintings: (L) $1,320; (H) $148,500

SCHREYER, C.W.
German 19th cent.
paintings: (L) $192; (H) $935

SCHREYVOGEL, Charles
American 1861-1912
paintings: (L) $352; (H) $198,000
drawings: (L) $13,200; (H) $17,600
sculpture: (H) $19,800

SCHRIMPF, Georg
German 1889-1938
paintings: (H) $52,800

SCHRODER, Albert Friedrich
German b. 1854
paintings: (L) $825; (H) $9,900

SCHRODER, Povl
Danish 1894-1957
paintings: (H) $770

SCHRODER-SONNENSTERN,
Friedrich
German b. 1892
drawings: (H) $9,350

SCHROEDER, H.
American 19th/20th cent.
paintings: (H) $687

SCHROEDER, Heinrich Johan
German 1866-1935
paintings: (H) $715

SCHROETER, Mathias
German 19th/20th cent.
paintings: (L) $935; (H) $935

SCHROETER, Paul K.
German b. 1866
paintings: (H) $1,100

SCHROFF, Alfred H.
American b. 1863
paintings: (L) $110; (H) $880
drawings: (H) $150

SCHROFFER, A. von
paintings: (H) $1,320

SCHROTER, G.
paintings: (L) $330; (H) $715

SCHROTH, L.D.
American 20th cent.
paintings: (H) $1,430

SCHROTTER, Alfred von
Austrian 1856-1935
paintings: (H) $1,100

SCHRUTEK (?), Franz von
paintings: (H) $715

SCHRYVER, Louis Marie de
French 1862-1942
paintings: (L) $4,400; (H) $209,000

SCHUBACK, Emil Gottlieb
German 1820-1902
paintings: (L) $8,250; (H) $10,450

SCHUBERT, V.
German 19th cent.
paintings: (H) $660

SCHUCK, A.
Austrian 20th cent.
paintings: (H) $5,500

SCHUERER, Julius
German 1859-1913
paintings: (H) $12,100

SCHUERER, S.
German/Austrian 19th cent.
paintings: (H) $1,650

SCHUESSLE, Christian
American 19th cent.
drawings: (H) $770

SCHUFFENECKER, Claude Emile
French 1851-1934
paintings: (L) $17,600; (H) $132,000
drawings: (L) $302; (H) $13,200

SCHULDT, Fritiof Johannes
Swedish 1891-1978
paintings: (H) $1,210

SCHULE, Hillard
American
paintings: (H) $660

SCHULLER, Joseph Charles Paul
French ac. 1880-1910
paintings: (H) $7,700

SCHULMAN, David
Dutch 1881-1966
paintings: (H) $1,540

SCHULMAN, Lion
Dutch 1851-1942
paintings: (H) $1,320

SCHULTE, Antoinette
American 1897-1981
paintings: (H) $825

SCHULTZ, Charles
American
paintings: (H) $880

SCHULTZ, George F.
American b. 1869
paintings: (L) $66; (H) $2,750
drawings: (L) $154; (H) $1,925

SCHULTZBERG, Anshelm Leonard
Swedish 1862-1945
paintings: (L) $1,320; (H) $16,500

SCHULTZE, Bernard
German b. 1915
drawings: (L) $8,250; (H) $15,400
sculpture: (L) $2,200; (H) $6,820

SCHULTZE, Carl
paintings: (H) $4,400

SCHULTZE, Jean
paintings: (H) $990

SCHULTZE, Louis
American late 19th cent.
paintings: (L) $121; (H) $660

SCHULTZE, Robert
German b. 1828
paintings: (L) $577; (H) $6,600

SCHULZ, Adolph Robert
American 1869-1963
paintings: (L) $770; (H) $2,750

SCHULZ, Adrien
paintings: (L) $100; (H) $1,870

SCHULZ, Charles
American b. 1922
paintings: (H) $165
drawings: (L) $247; (H) $1,045

SCHULZ-STRADTMANN, Otto
American 20th cent.
paintings: (H) $825

SCHUMACHER, Charles J.
American 19th cent.
paintings: (H) $1,210

SCHUMACHER, Emil
German b. 1912
paintings: (H) $1,210

SCHUMAKER, Philip
American 20th cent.
paintings: (H) $3,300

SCHUPPLER, H.
sculpture: (H) $1,210

SCHURR, Claude
paintings: (H) $990

SCHUSTER, Donna
American 1883-1953
paintings: (L) $660; (H) $8,800
drawings: (L) $412; (H) $2,200

SCHUSTER, Josef
Austrian 1812-1890
paintings: (L) $1,760; (H) $27,500

SCHUSTER, Karl Maria
Austrian 1871-1953
paintings: (L) $8,800; (H) $60,500

SCHUT, Cornelis
Flemish 1597-1655
paintings: (L) $4,180; (H) $35,200
drawings: (H) $770

SCHUTZ, Christian Georg
German 1718-1791
paintings: (L) $2,475; (H) $18,700

SCHUTZ, E.
German early 20th cent.
drawings: (H) $880

SCHUTZ, Edward
paintings: (H) $4,620

SCHUTZ, Erich
drawings: (H) $1,430

SCHUTZ, Johannes F.
paintings: (H) $2,530

SCHUTZ, Willem Joannes
Dutch 1854-1933
paintings: (H) $1,045

SCHUTZE, August
German 1805-1847
paintings: (H) $11,000

SCHUTZE, Wilhelm
paintings: (L) $550; (H) $8,250

SCHUTZENBERGER, Paul Rene
French 1860-1916
paintings: (H) $5,500

SCHUYFF, Peter
Dutch b. 1958
paintings: (L) $2,750; (H) $33,000
drawings: (H) $1,760

SCHUYLER, Remington
American 1884/87-1955
paintings: (L) $1,870; (H) $2,475

SCHUZ, Friedrick
German
paintings: (H) $6,775

SCHUZ, Theodor
German 1830-1900
paintings: (H) $10,120

SCHWABAUER, Lyle
American
sculpture: (H) $850

SCHWABEDA, Johann Michael
German 1734-1794
paintings: (H) $10,725

SCHWACHA, George
American b. 1908
paintings: (L) $880; (H) $1,045

SCHWANFELDER, Charles Henry
English 1774-1837
paintings: (L) $7,150; (H) $14,300

SCHWANKOVSKY, Frederick John
American 1885-1974
paintings: (L) $330; (H) $715

SCHWAR, Wilhelm
German b. 1860
paintings: (L) $1,430; (H) $2,500

SCHWARTZ, Albert Gustav
German b. 1833
paintings: (L) $5,500; (H) $6,875

SCHWARTZ, Andrew T.
American 1867-1942
paintings: (L) $154; (H) $22,000

SCHWARTZ, Daniel
paintings: (L) $55; (H) $1,045

SCHWARTZ, Davis Francis
American 1879-1969
paintings: (L) $358; (H) $3,300
drawings: (L) $165; (H) $660

SCHWARTZ, William S.
Russian/American b. 1896, d. 1977?
paintings: (L) $99; (H) $8,250
drawings: (L) $495; (H) $2,310

SCHWARTZE, Theresa
Dutch 1851-1918
paintings: (L) $385; (H) $4,125

SCHWARZ, A.
German 19th cent.
paintings: (H) $1,430

SCHWARZSCHILD, Alfred
German b. 1874
paintings: (H) $3,850

SCHWEBLER, William
American 20th cent.
paintings: (L) $66; (H) $770
drawings: (L) $66; (II) $330

SCHWEICKHARDT, Hendrick Willem
German 1746-1797
paintings: (H) $66,000

SCHWEINITZ, Graf
German b. 1910
paintings: (H) $660

SCHWEIRING
American 20th cent.
paintings: (H) $1,870

SCHWEIZER, J. Otto
b. 1863
sculpture: (H) $660

SCHWEMMINGER, Josef
paintings: (H) $1,100

SCHWENINGER, Carl, Jr.
Austrian 1854-1903
paintings: (L) $5,720; (H) $11,000

SCHWENINGER, Carl
Austrian 19th cent.
paintings: (H) $26,400

SCHWENINGER, Carl
Austrian 1818-1887
paintings: (L) $8,250; (H) $30,250

SCHWENINGER, Rosa
Austrian b. 1849
paintings: (H) $17,600

SCHWIERING, O. Conrad
paintings: (L) $275; (H) $2,090

SCHWIND, Edouard
French 19th cent.
paintings: (H) $2,750

SCHWITTERS, Kurt
German 1887-1948
paintings: (L) $1,210; (H) $115,500
drawings: (L) $5,500; (H) $148,500

SCIALOJA, Toti
Italian b. 1914
paintings: (L) $330; (H) $4,180
drawings: (H) $55

SCIORTINO, A.
sculpture: (H) $3,300

SCIVER, Pearl Aiman van
b. 1896
paintings: (L) $220; (H) $800

SCKELL, Ludwig
German 1833-1912
paintings: (H) $12,100

SCNACKENBERG, Henry Ernest
American 1892-1970
paintings: (H) $2,640

SCOGNAMIGLIO
Italian 18th/19th cent.
paintings: (H) $2,310

SCOGNAMIGLIO, Giovanni
paintings: (H) $4,620

SCOPPA, Giuseppe
Italian 19th cent.
drawings: (L) $4,125; (H) $7,150

SCOPPETTA, Pietro
Italian 1863-1920
paintings: (L) $3,080; (H) $6,600

SCOREL, Jan van
Flemish 1495-1562
paintings: (L) $12,100; (H) $38,500

SCOTT, Alexander
British 19th/20th cent.
paintings: (H) $1,100

SCOTT, Campbell
British 19th/20th cent.
paintings: (L) $330; (H) $3,080

SCOTT, Edith
19th/20th cent.
paintings: (H) $900

SCOTT, Edwin
19th/20th cent.
paintings: (L) $440; (H) $1,210

SCOTT, Frank Edwin
American 1862-1929
paintings: (L) $303; (H) $3,850
drawings: (H) $99

SCOTT, Georges
French b. 1873
paintings: (H) $3,740

SCOTT, Henry Edward
American b. 1900
paintings: (L) $7,975; (H) $8,250

SCOTT, Henry Louis
French 1846-1884
paintings: (H) $17,600

SCOTT, J.W.A.
paintings: (H) $2,420

SCOTT, James Powell
American b. 1909
paintings: (H) $880

SCOTT, John
American
paintings: (H) $3,520

SCOTT, John
American b. 1907
paintings: (L) $523; (H) $4,510

SCOTT, John
British 1802-1885
paintings: (H) $12,100

SCOTT, John White Allen
American 1815-1907
paintings: (L) $330; (H) $12,100

SCOTT, Julian
American 1846-1901
paintings: (L) $3,300; (H) $7,150
drawings: (L) $550; (H) $1,650

SCOTT, Louise
American 20th cent.
paintings: (H) $1,320

SCOTT, Nellie E. Burrell
American 1856-1913
paintings: (H) $715

SCOTT, Peter
paintings: (L) $385; (H) $660

SCOTT, Peter
English 20th cent.
paintings: (L) $3,300; (H) $3,740

SCOTT, R. Bagge
English 19th cent.
paintings: (H) $880

SCOTT, Samuel
English 1703-1772
paintings: (H) $26,400

SCOTT, T.J.
British 19th cent.
paintings: (H) $880

SCOTT, Thomas Jefferson
paintings: (H) $7,700

SCOTT, Tom
English 1859-1927
drawings: (H) $770

SCOTT, W.J.
English 19th cent.
paintings: (H) $825

SCOTT, William
paintings: (L) $770; (H) $18,150

SCOTT, William Bell
Scottish 1811-1890
paintings: (L) $22,000; (H) $44,000
drawings: (H) $3,850

SCOUTEN
Belgian 19th cent.
paintings: (H) $880

SCREY, Anterio
paintings: (H) $1,045

SCRIVER, Bob
American b. 1914
sculpture: (L) $1,100; (H) $4,800

SCRIVER, Robert
American b. 1917
sculpture: (H) $3,575

SCUDDER, Janet
American 1875-1940
paintings: (H) $715
sculpture: (L) $5,500; (H) $66,000

SCULLY, Sean
Irish b. 1945
paintings: (L) $3,850; (H) $341,000
drawings: (L) $4,400; (H) $28,600

SCULLY, Sean and Catherine LEE
contemporary
drawings: (H) $880

SCUTARY
drawings: (H) $990

SCUTENAIRE, Jean
drawings: (H) $2,200

SCWEININGER, Carl
German or Austrian 19th cent.
paintings: (H) $4,675

SEABROOKE, Elliot
British 1886-1950
paintings: (H) $1,100

SEAFORTH, Charles Henry
paintings: (H) $4,400

SEAGER, ***
American 19th cent.
drawings: (H) $6,600

SEAGER, Edward
American 1809-1886
drawings: (L) $11; (H) $1,100

SEAGO, Edward
British 1910-1974
paintings: (L) $770; (H) $46,200
drawings: (L) $440; (H) $6,050

SEALY, Alfred
English 19th/20th cent.
paintings: (H) $715

SEALY, Allen Culpepper
British 19th/20th cent.
paintings: (L) $2,400; (H) $9,900

SEARLE, Helen
American 19th cent.
paintings: (H) $7,425

SEARLE, Ronald
English b. 1920
drawings: (L) $110; (H) $660

SEARS, Benjamin W.
American 1846-1905
paintings: (L) $165; (H) $1,650

SEARS, Cynthia L.
American c. 1830
drawings: (H) $33,000

SEARS, Francis
British 1873-1933
paintings: (L) $2,090; (H) $4,675

SEARS, Sarah Choate
American 1858-1935
drawings: (H) $1,650

SEARS, Taber
American 1870-1950
paintings: (L) $935; (H) $990
drawings: (L) $385; (H) $2,200

SEAVEY, George W.
American 1841-1916
paintings: (L) $467; (H) $1,430

SEAVEY, L.B.
American
paintings: (H) $1,100

SEAWELL, Harry Washington
American ac. 1906-1933
paintings: (H) $715

SEBEN, Henri van
Belgian 1825-1913
paintings: (L) $1,045; (H) $3,740
drawings: (H) $1,100

SEBES, Pieter Willem
Dutch 1830-1906
paintings: (L) $1,650; (H) $8,800

SEBIRE, Gaston
French b. c. 1920/25
paintings: (L) $220; (H) $6,600

SEBOTH, Josef
Austrian 1814-1883
paintings: (H) $34,100

SEBREE, Charles
American
paintings: (H) $1,320

SEBRIGHT, George
paintings: (H) $7,150

SECOLA, A.
Italian 19th/20th cent.
paintings: (L) $1,320; (H) $6,050

SEDGLEY, Peter
contemporary
paintings: (L) $770; (H) $2,750
drawings: (H) $110

SEDGWICK, G.V.
19th cent.
paintings: (H) $3,850

SEDLACEK, Stephan
Czechoslovakian 19th cent.
paintings: (L) $605; (H) $7,700

SEDLICKY, J.
paintings: (H) $1,210

SEECK, Otto
paintings: (H) $880

SEEGER, Hermann
German b. 1857
paintings: (H) $29,700

SEEL, Adolf
German 1829-1907
paintings: (L) $2,750; (H) $46,200

SEERY, John
American b. 1914
paintings: (L) $1,980; (H) $2,860

SEEVAGEN, Lucien
French 1887-1959
paintings: (L) $440; (H) $7,425

SEGAL, Arthur
Rumanian 1875-1944
paintings: (H) $12,100

SEGAL, G.
European 20th cent.
paintings: (H) $1,650

SEGAL, George
American b. 1924
drawings: (L) $880; (H) $44,000
sculpture: (L) $2,200; (H) $528,000

SEGALL, Lasar
Brazilian 1890-1957
drawings: (L) $2,860; (H) $22,550

SEGANTINI, Giovanni
Italian 1858-1899
paintings: (H) $39,600

SEGAR, Sir William
English ac. 1858, d. 1633
paintings: (H) $38,500

SEGIN
paintings: (H) $16,500

SEGOVIA, Andres
Spanish b. 1929
paintings: (L) $308; (H) $2,420

SEGUI, Antonio
Argentinian b. 1934
paintings: (L) $220; (H) $15,400
drawings: (L) $143; (H) $19,800

SEGUIN, Armand, or Fortune Armand
French 1869-1903
paintings: (H) $143,000

SEGUIN, Jocelyne
French 20th cent.
paintings: (L) $154; (H) $660

SEGUIN, Oliver
Mexican 20th cent.
sculpture: (H) $1,320

SEHRING, Adolf
Russian b. 1930
paintings: (L) $8,800; (H) $9,900

SEIDEL, Gustav
German 1819-1901
paintings: (H) $5,500

SEIDENECK, George Joseph
American 1885-1972
paintings: (H) $770

SEIFERT, Alfred
Czechoslovakian 1850-1901
paintings: (L) $770; (H) $18,700

SEIFERT, Paul
American 1840-1921
drawings: (H) $25,300

SEIFERT, Victor Heinrich
German b. 1870
sculpture: (L) $385; (H) $1,650

SEIGLER, Charles
American
drawings: (H) $1,045

SEIGNAC, Guillaume
French ac. c. 1903
paintings: (L) $935; (H) $99,000

SEIGNAC, Paul
French 1826-1904
paintings: (L) $1,430; (H) $20,900

SEIGNEURGENS, Ernest Louis
Augustin
French d. 1904
paintings: (H) $1,210

SEIGNOL
French 20th cent.
paintings: (H) $880

SEILER, Carl Wilhelm
German 1846-1921
paintings: (L) $2,200; (H) $5,500

SEITER, Daniel
Italian 1649-1705
paintings: (H) $8,800

SEITZ, Alexander Maximilian
German 1811-1888
paintings: (H) $5,500

SEITZ, Anton
German 1829-1900
paintings: (L) $9,900; (H) $13,200

SEITZ, Johann Georg
German 1810-1870
paintings: (L) $4,400; (H) $11,000

SEKINE, Yoshio
contemporary
paintings: (H) $2,420

SEKOTO, G.
Japanese 20th cent.
paintings: (H) $1,100

SEKOTO, Gerard
paintings: (H) $990

SELBY, Prideaux John
English 1788-1867
drawings: (L) $770; (H) $57,750

SELDEN, Henry Bill
American 1886-1934
paintings: (L) $1,045; (H) $1,870

SELDON, Richard
American 20th cent.
paintings: (H) $1,210

SELDRON, Alisabeth
Dutch/Flemish 18th/19th cent.
paintings: (H) $5,225

SELFE, Madeline
paintings: (L) $605; (H) $880

SELFRIDGE, Reynolds L.
19th/20th cent.
paintings: (H) $660

SELIGER, Charles
contemporary
paintings: (L) $330; (H) $3,520

SELIGMANN, Kurt
Swiss 1900-1962
paintings: (L) $8,250; (H) $20,900
drawings: (L) $2,310; (H) $3,575

SELINGER, Emily
American b. 1854
paintings: (L) $400; (H) $1,650
drawings: (L) $77; (H) $88

SELINGER, Jean Paul
American 1850-1909
paintings: (L) $220; (H) $990

SELL, Christian
German 1831-1883
paintings: (L) $605; (H) $4,400

SELLAER, Vincent, or Zeelare
Flemish b. c. 1539
paintings: (L) $7,700; (H) $29,700

SELLSTEDT, Lars Gustav
American 1819-1911
paintings: (H) $660

SELOUS, Henry Courtney
British 1811-1890
paintings: (L) $248; (H) $23,100

SELTZER, Olaf Carl
American 1877-1957
paintings: (L) $2,475; (H) $88,000
drawings: (L) $1,430; (H) $27,500

SELTZER, W. Steve
American
paintings: (L) $2,900; (H) $3,100

SELTZER, William S.
American
drawings: (H) $4,400

SELUCA, A.
sculpture: (H) $2,310

SELYHR, Conrad
Scandinavian 19th/20th cent.
paintings: (H) $775

SELZER, Frank
American 19th/20th cent.
paintings: (L) $302; (H) $1,155

SEMENOWSKY, Eisman
French 19th cent.
paintings: (L) $660; (H) $24,200

SEMINO, Andrea
paintings: (H) $825

SEMINO, Ottavio
paintings: (L) $3,850; (H) $5,280

SEMON, John
American d. 1917
paintings: (L) $104; (H) $1,210
drawings: (L) $93; (H) $413

SEN, Sarbani
paintings: (H) $3,850

SENAPE, Antonio
drawings: (H) $770

SENART, R.
paintings: (H) $935

SENAT, Prosper L.
American 1852-1925
paintings: (L) $200; (H) $7,150
drawings: (L) $132; (H) $1,430

SENDAK, Maurice
American b. 1928
drawings: (L) $77; (H) $8,800

SENDALL, J.
English 19th cent.
paintings: (H) $2,200

SENET, Rafael
Spanish b. 1856
paintings: (L) $12,100; (H) $17,600
drawings: (L) $110; (H) $1,980

SENEZCOURT, Charlotte de
French 19th cent.
paintings: (H) $3,500

SENEZCOURT, Jules de
French 1818-1866
paintings: (H) $6,600

SENNHAUSER, John
American
drawings: (H) $660

SENNO, Pietro
Italian 1831-1904
paintings: (L) $220; (H) $1,980

SENQUIST, Raphael
American
paintings: (H) $700

SENSEMAN, Raphael
American 1870-1965
paintings: (L) $154; (H) $770
drawings: (L) $88; (H) $110

SENTENIS, Renee
contemporary
sculpture: (H) $4,950

SEPESHKY, Zoltan L.
Hungarian/American b. 1898
paintings: (L) $220; (H) $9,350
drawings: (L) $27; (H) $2,530

SEQUIERA, Julio
paintings: (H) $1,210

SEQUIN-BERTAULT, Paul
contemporary
paintings: (H) $3,520

SERBIE, Gaston
paintings: (H) $2,090

SEREBRIAKOFF, Alexandre
Russian 20th cent.
drawings: (L) $5,500; (H) $18,700

SERENA, Luigi
Italian 1855-1911
paintings: (H) $6,380

SERENI, G.
drawings: (H) $1,980

SERGEANT, Edgar
American
paintings: (L) $385; (H) $1,100

SERGEIEV, F.
Russian 19th cent.
paintings: (H) $2,200

SERGENT, Lucien Pierre
French 1849-1904
paintings: (L) $880; (H) $8,800

SERGONE
paintings: (H) $1,018

SERIN, Hermann
Flemish 1678-1765
paintings: (L) $1,100; (H) $2,420

SERNESI, Raffaello
Italian 1838-1866
paintings: (H) $19,800

SERPAN, Jaroslav
contemporary
paintings: (H) $3,520

SERRA, Richard
American b. 1939
paintings: (L) $22,000; (H) $121,000
drawings: (L) $8,250; (H) $66,000
sculpture: (H) $49,500

SERRA Y AUQUE, Enrique
Spanish 1859-1918
paintings: (L) $1,760; (H) $20,900

SERRANO, Manuel Gonzalez
paintings: (L) $2,750; (H) $9,350

SERRAO, Luella M. Varney
sculpture: (H) $1,100

SERRAS, John Thomas
British 1759-1825
paintings: (H) $5,500

SERRES, Antony
French 1828-1898
paintings: (L) $825; (H) $1,320

SERRES, D***
British 18th cent.
paintings: (H) $1,430

SERRES, Dominic
English 1722-1793
paintings: (H) $38,500
drawings: (H) $1,210

SERRET, Alan
contemporary
drawings: (H) $1,210

SERRI, Alfredo
Italian 1897-1972
paintings: (L) $385; (H) $1,980

SERRURE, Auguste
Flemish 1825-1903
paintings: (L) $13,200; (H) $16,500

SERUSIER, Louis Paul Henri
French 1863-1927
drawings: (L) $4,675; (H) $5,280

SERUSIER, Paul
French 1863-1927
paintings: (L) $9,350; (H) $440,000
drawings: (L) $770; (H) $1,650

SERVEAU, Clement
French 1886-1972
paintings: (L) $55; (H) $6,600

SERVERINI, Gino
paintings: (H) $19,800

SESSIA, B.C.
paintings: (H) $4,400

SESSIONS, James Milton
American 1882-1962
drawings: (L) $187; (H) $4,675

SETHER, Gulbrand
American 20th cent.
paintings: (L) $88; (H) $6,600
drawings: (L) $38; (H) $962

SETTANNI, Luigi
Italian/American 1908-1984
paintings: (L) $330; (H) $7,920

SETTLE, William Frederick
English 1821-1897
drawings: (H) $1,045

SEULBO, F.
paintings: (H) $1,210

SEURAT, Georges
French 1859-1891
paintings: (H) $132,000
drawings: (L) $16,500; (H) $407,000

SEVERDONCK, A. van
paintings: (H) $1,210

SEVERDONCK, Franz van
Belgian 1809-1889
paintings: (L) $605; (H) $6,600

SEVERDONCK, Joseph van
Belgian 1819-1905
paintings: (L) $1,650; (H) $2,750

SEVERINI, Gino
Italian 1883-1966
paintings: (L) $37,400; (H) $3,630,000
drawings: (L) $2,310; (H) $550,000
sculpture: (H) $24,200

SEVERINO DA CINGOLI, Messer
Ulisse
Italian 16th cent.
drawings: (L) $2,310; (H) $25,300

SEVERO DA RAVENA, workshop of
Italian 15th/16th cent.
sculpture: (L) $16,500; (H) $44,000

SEWELL, Amanda Brewster
paintings: (H) $2,200

SEWELL, Amos
American 1901-1983
paintings: (L) $1,045; (H) $1,100
drawings: (L) $850; (H) $990

SEWELL, Robert van Vorst
American 1860-1924
paintings: (L) $660; (H) $4,840

SEXTIE, William A.
paintings: (H) $2,200

SEXTON, Frederick Lester
American b. 1889
paintings: (L) $440; (H) $3,575
drawings: (H) $550

SEYBOLD, Louis
American 19th/20th cent.
paintings: (L) $770; (H) $770

SEYDEL, Edouard Gustav
paintings: (H) $2,420

SEYFERT
paintings: (H) $1,430

SEYFFERT, Leopold Gould
American 1887-1956
paintings: (H) $1,210
drawings: (H) $165

SEYLER, Julius
German 1873-1958
paintings: (L) $4,125; (H) $7,700
drawings: (L) $880; (H) $1,870

SEYMOUR, George L.
English 19th cent.
paintings: (L) $880; (H) $2,640
drawings: (H) $358

SEYMOUR, James
English 1702-1752
paintings: (L) $18,700; (H) $71,500

SEYMOUR, Robert
Irish 1819-1883
paintings: (H) $3,300

SEYMOUR, Tom
British 19th cent.
paintings: (L) $412; (H) $1,100

SEYPPEL, Carl Maria
German 1847-1913
paintings: (H) $11,550

SEYSSAUD, Rene
French 1867-1952
paintings: (L) $1,540; (H) $20,900

SEYSSES, Auguste
sculpture: (H) $1,265

SHABANAUD
contemporary
sculpture: (H) $1,210

SHADDIX, Bill
American b. 1931
paintings: (H) $660

SHAFER, L.E. "Gus"
sculpture: (H) $715

SHAFER, S.P.
American School 19th cent.
paintings: (L) $440; (H) $1,320

SHAFFER, Mary
American b. 1947
sculpture: (L) $3,960; (H) $5,500

SHAHN, Ben
American 1898-1969
paintings: (L) $8,250; (H) $121,000
drawings: (L) $385; (H) $57,750

SHALDERS, G. and G. COLE
paintings: (H) $935

SHALDERS, George
English 1826-1873
paintings: (L) $2,640; (H) $4,950

SHALOM OF SAFED, Shalom
Moskovitz
b. 1892
paintings: (L) $2,200; (H) $3,300
drawings: (L) $1,100; (H) $2,475

SHAMBERK, Vladimer
Russian 19th cent.
paintings: (H) $2,310

SHANNON, Charles Haslewood
English 1863-1937
paintings: (H) $4,950
drawings: (H) $990

SHANNON, Sir James Jebusa
British 1862-1923
paintings: (L) $3,850; (H) $687,500

SHANNONHOUSE, Sandra
contemporary
sculpture: (H) $660

SHANOSKI, Michael P.
drawings: (H) $990

SHAPIRO, Joel
American b. 1941
paintings: (H) $7,700
drawings: (L) $3,850; (H) $88,000
sculpture: (L) $8,800; (H) $242,000

SHAPLAND, John
British 1901-1929
paintings: (H) $2,200

SHAPLEIGH, Frank Henry
American 1842-1906
paintings: (L) $385; (H) $15,400
drawings: (L) $275; (H) $2,310

SHAPLEY, Miss A. Foster
paintings: (H) $1,045

SHARMAN, John
American 20th cent.
paintings: (L) $990; (H) $2,860

SHARON, L.
late 20th cent.
paintings: (H) $2,640

SHARP, David
paintings: (H) $1,045

SHARP, John
American 20th cent.
paintings: (H) $715

SHARP, Joseph Henry
American 1859-1953
paintings: (L) $150; (H) $77,000
drawings: (L) $165; (H) $1,650

SHARP, Louis Hovey
American 1875-1946
paintings: (L) $110; (H) $1,650

SHARP, M.R.
American/Canadian 19th/20th cent.
paintings: (H) $1,045

SHARP, William Alexander
American 1864-1944
drawings: (L) $247; (H) $2,475

SHARPLES, James
American
drawings: (H) $22,000

SHATTENSTEIN, Nikol
American
paintings: (H) $880

SHATTUCK, Aaron Draper
American 1832-1928
paintings: (L) $385; (H) $10,450
drawings: (L) $330; (H) $2,860

SHATTUCK, E.J.
American 19th cent.
drawings: (H) $6,600

SHAVER, L.P.
American 19th cent.
paintings: (L) $143; (H) $1,650

SHAW
paintings: (L) $33; (H) $935

SHAW, Alan Winter
American b. 1894
paintings: (L) $38; (H) $825
drawings: (H) $825

SHAW, Annie Cornelia
American 1852-1887
paintings: (H) $825

SHAW, Charles Green
American 1892-1974
paintings: (L) $143; (H) $24,200

SHAW, John Byam Liston, or
Byan John
British 1872-1919
paintings: (L) $1,650; (H) $104,500

SHAW, Joshua
American 1776-1860
drawings: (H) $660

SHAW, Katherine H.
paintings: (H) $770

SHAW, Sydney Dale
American 1879-1946
paintings: (L) $77; (H) $1,540
drawings: (H) $1,100

SHAW, William
British d. 1773
paintings: (L) $5,775; (H) $68,750

SHAYER, Charles Waller
British ac. 1860-1880
paintings: (L) $1,760; (H) $14,300

SHAYER, Henry Thring and Charles
Waller SHAYER
British 19th/20th cent.
paintings: (L) $2,750; (H) $18,700

SHAYER, William
paintings: (H) $715

SHAYER, William J., Sr.
English 1788-1879
paintings: (L) $825; (H) $42,900

SHAYER, William J.
English 19th cent.
paintings: (L) $302; (H) $29,700

SHAYER, William Joseph, Jr.
English 1811-1892
paintings: (L) $3,300; (H) $19,800

SHEAN, Charles M.
American
drawings: (H) $880

SHEARBON, Andrew
British 19th cent.
paintings: (L) $2,200; (H) $3,850

SHEARER, Christopher H.
American 1840-1926
paintings: (L) $330; (H) $5,170
drawings: (H) $250

SHEE, Sir Martin Archer
Irish 1769-1850
paintings: (L) $2,750; (H) $22,000

SHEELER, Charles
American 1883-1965
paintings: (L) $15,400; (H) $242,000
drawings: (L) $22,000; (H) $55,000

SHEERBOOM, A.
paintings: (H) $1,980

SHEETS, Frank M.
American 19th cent.
paintings: (H) $3,850

SHEETS, Millard
American 1907-1989
paintings: (L) $6,050; (H) $35,750
drawings: (L) $302; (H) $27,500

SHEETS, Nan
American 1889-1976
paintings: (L) $110; (H) $2,640

SHEFFER, Glen C.
American 1881-1948
paintings: (L) $121; (H) $2,750

SHEFFIELD, I.
paintings: (H) $2,090

SHEFFIELD, Isaac
American 1798-1845
paintings: (L) $2,090; (H) $41,250

SHEILS, William
British 1785-1857
paintings: (H) $6,600

SHEIRE, Mary
Continental School 19th cent.
paintings: (H) $1,045

SHELBY
20th cent.
drawings: (H) $880

SHELDON, Joshua
American ac. mid-19th cent.
paintings: (H) $990

SHELLEY, Samuel
English c. 1750-1808
drawings: (L) $247; (H) $660

SHELTON, Peter
American Indian
paintings: (L) $385; (H) $687

SHELTON, William H.
American 1840-1932
paintings: (L) $165; (H) $660
drawings: (L) $330; (H) $770

SHEPARD, Ernest H.
English 1879-1976
drawings: (L) $3,575; (H) $24,200

SHEPHARD, Warren J.
American 1859-1937
paintings: (L) $660; (H) $3,300

SHEPHERD, David
paintings: (H) $8,800

SHEPHERD, George Sydney
British d. 1858
drawings: (L) $660; (H) $13,750

SHEPHERD, J. Clinton
American b. 1888
paintings: (L) $110; (H) $2,475

SHEPHERD, S.
English 19th cent.
drawings: (H) $1,045

SHEPPARD, Joseph Sherly
American b. 1930
paintings: (L) $137; (H) $2,200

SHEPPARD, Warren
American 1858-1937
paintings: (L) $495; (H) $19,250
drawings: (L) $110; (H) $2,200

SHEPPARD, William Ludwell
American 1833-1912
drawings: (L) $495; (H) $5,280

SHERBELL, Rhoda
drawings: (H) $77
sculpture: (L) $220; (H)$12,100

SHERIDAN, Claire
sculpture: (H) $1,650

SHERIRN, D.
paintings: (H) $770

SHERLINGH, A.
British 19th cent.
paintings: (H) $990

SHERMAN, Cindy
American contemporary
drawings: (L) $6,600; (H) $19,800

SHERMAN, G.
American 20th cent.
paintings: (L) $242; (H) $4,675

SHERMAN, John W.
American ac. 1930's
paintings: (H) $825

SHERRIN, Daniel
British ac. 1895-1915
paintings: (L) $110; (H) $2,750
drawings: (L) $220; (H) $880

SHERRIN, John
English 1819-1896
drawings: (H) $1,045

SHERWOOD, Rosina Emmet
American b. 1854
drawings: (L) $220; (H) $3,300

SHERWOOD, Vladimir Osipovich
Russian 1832-1897
paintings: (H) $6,600

SHERWOOD, William Anderson
American 1875-1951
paintings: (L) $66; (H) $2,860

SHICKLER, Aaron
drawings: (H) $660

English Illustrator

Interest in collecting drawings and watercolors produced for book illustrations has surged in the last few years. Once favored only by book collectors for their literary associations, these illustrations have become a separate field of collecting. Often larger than their published size, they are appealing for their visual impact and artistic merit as well as for the memories they evoke.

The value of a book illustration is determined by the artist's reputation and the demand for his work. The well-known English artists who worked primarily as illustrators for children's books include Kate Greenaway, Kay Nielsen, Arthur Rackham, and Ernest H. Shepard.

Ernest H. Shepard (1879-1976) was born in England, the son of an architect and the grandson of a well-known watercolorist. He first exhibited at the Royal Academy when he was only twenty-one. In 1907 he started drawing for *Punch* magazine and came into prominence in 1924, when he began to work with A. A. Milne, creating the drawings for his first book, *When We Were Very Young*. In 1926 he illustrated Milne's first volume of *Winnie the Pooh*. In the 1930s he worked on *The Wind in the Willows* and other books for Kenneth Grahame.

Shepard, using pen and ink as well as watercolor and gouache, illustrated more than thirty books. The original drawings for *Winnie the Pooh* are highly collectible; if both Christopher Robin and Pooh appear, the price rises. (Ernest H. Shepard, *Christopher Robin Gives Extract of Malt All Around*, watercolor, 5 ½ x 7¹³/₁₆ in., Sloan, March 31, 1989, $24,200)

SHIELDS, Alan
American b. 1944
paintings: (L) $1,540; (H) $3,300
drawings: (L) $308; (H) $660
sculpture: (H) $4,400

SHIELDS, Frederick James
British 1833-1911
paintings: (H) $38,500

SHIELDS, So.
American 19th cent.
paintings: (H) $2,200

SHIELDS, Thomas W.
American 1849/50-1920
paintings: (L) $990; (H) $2,750

SHIKLER, Aaron
American b. 1922
paintings: (L) $715; (H) $9,350
drawings: (L) $2,420; (H) $3,520

SHIKO, Munakata
Japanese 1903-1975
drawings: (H) $14,300

SHILLING, Alexander
American
paintings: (H) $770

SHILLING, Arthur
Canadian
paintings: (H) $12,100

SHIMIDZU, H.
paintings: (H) $715

SHIMIDZU, H.
Japanese 19th/20th cent.
paintings: (H) $1,980

SHINN, Everett
American 1876-1953
paintings: (L) $1,980; (H) $52,800
drawings: (L) $99; (H) $308,000

SHIPLEY
English 19th/20th cent.
paintings: (H) $2,970

SHIRE, Peter
sculpture: (H) $1,760

SHIRK, Jeanette Campbell
American b. 1898
paintings: (H) $880

SHIRLAW, Walter
Scots/American 1838-1909
paintings: (L) $440; (H) $10,450
drawings: (L) $50; (H) $880

SHKURKIN, Vladimir
American b. 1900
paintings: (H) $935

SHLEPPY, Rose Blanton
American 20th cent.
paintings: (H) $1,760

SHOEMAKER, Vaughn
American b. 1902
drawings: (L) $110; (H) $660

SHOKHIN, M.
Russian late 19th cent.
sculpture: (H) $6,600

SHOKLER, Harry
American b. 1895
paintings: (H) $2,090
drawings: (H) $220

SHONBORN, John Lewis
English 19th cent.
paintings: (H) $770

SHOPE, Irvin Shorty
American
paintings: (H) $2,200

SHORE, Henrietta
American 1880-1963
paintings: (H) $1,430

SHORES, J.W.
English 19th cent.
paintings: (H) $660

SHORT, Frederick Golden
English ac. 1882-1908
paintings: (L) $165; (H) $2,310

SHORT, Sir Frank
English 1857-1945
paintings: (H) $990

SHOTWELL, Helen Harvey
American b. 1908
paintings: (L) $100; (H) $770

SHOUP, Charles
American 20th cent.
paintings: (L) $3,850; (H) $6,050
drawings: (H) $495

SHOVE, John J.
American
drawings: (H) $2,750

SHOWELL, Ken
contemporary
paintings: (L) $330; (H) $825

SHRADER, Roscoe
American 1879-1960
paintings: (H) $1,430

SHRADY, Henry Merwin
American 1871-1922
sculpture: (L) $550; (H) $30,800

SHROEDER
American 19th cent.
paintings: (H) $880

SHROETER, Mathias
German 19th/20th cent.
paintings: (H) $1,045

SHUHO, Ikegami
Japanese 1874-1944
drawings: (H) $22,000

SHULGOLD, William Robert
American 20th cent.
paintings: (L) $495; (H) $2,915

SHULTZ, James Willard, Lone Wolf
paintings: (H) $1,980

SHULZ, Ada M.
American 20th cent.
paintings: (H) $9,075

SHULZ, Adolph Robert
American 1870-1928
paintings: (L) $137; (H) $2,420

SHUMWAY, H.I.
American 20th cent.
paintings: (H) $1,760

SHURTLEFF, Roswell Morse
American 1838-1915
paintings: (L) $522; (H) $2,640
drawings: (H) $440

SHUTE, Mrs. R.W.
American 19th cent.
drawings: (H) $41,800

SHUTE, R.W. and S.A.
American 19th cent.
drawings: (L) $11,550; (H) $28,600

SHUTTLEWORTH, Claire
American
paintings: (H) $2,200

SIBERDT, Eugene
Belgian 1851-1931
paintings: (H) $1,210

SIBERECHTS, Jan
Flemish 1627-c. 1703
paintings: (L) $19,800; (H) $110,000

SIBEUD
French early 20th cent.
sculpture: (H) $2,860

SICARD, Francois Leon
French 1862-1934
sculpture: (L) $522; (H) $880

SICERI, Eugene
drawings: (H) $1,430

SICHEL, Harold M.
American b. 1881
paintings: (L) $176; (H) $4,125

SICHEL, Nathaniel
German 1843-1907
paintings: (L) $385; (H) $9,350
drawings: (H) $220

SICILIA, Jose Maria
Spanish b. 1954
paintings: (L) $15,400; (H) $71,500

SICKERT, Walter Richard
English 1860-1942
paintings: (L) $3,300; (H) $34,100
drawings: (L) $385; (H) $1,760

SIDLEY, Samuel
English 1829-1896
paintings: (H) $660

SIDNEY, Herbert
paintings: (H) $1,650

SIEBERT, Edward S.
American 1856-1944
paintings: (L) $72; (H) $19,800

SIEFERT, August Friedrich
German 1820-1883
paintings: (H) $1,430

SIEFFERT, Paul
French b. 1874
paintings: (L) $1,540; (H) $3,080

SIEGEL, Alan
contemporary
sculpture: (H) $3,080

SIEGEN, A. von
German 19th cent.
paintings: (H) $1,760

SIEGERT, August
German 1786-1869
paintings: (L) $3,025; (H) $4,950

SIEGERT, August Friedrich
German 1820-1883
paintings: (L) $1,320; (H) $1,650

SIEGFRIED, Edwin C.
American 1889-1955
drawings: (L) $413; (H) $1,870

SIEGRIEST, Louis B.
American b. 1899
paintings: (L) $935; (H) $4,400
drawings: (H) $193

SIEMER, Christian
American 1874-1940
paintings: (L) $2,090; (H) $10,450

SIEMIRADZKI, Hendryk
Russian 1843-1902
paintings: (H) $8,250

SIEVERS, Gregory
American
paintings: (H) $900

SIGLER, Hollis
contemporary
paintings: (H) $7,700

SIGMUND, Benjamin D.
English ac. 1879-1904
drawings: (H) $3,080

SIGNAC, Paul
French 1863-1935
paintings: (L) $24,200; (H) $2,750,000
drawings: (L) $1,210; (H) $52,800

SIGNORELLI, Luca
Italian 1441-1523
drawings: (H) $66,000

SIGNORELLI, Luca, and studio
Italian 1441/1445-1523
paintings: (H) $93,500

SIGNORET, Charles Louis Eugene
French 1867-1932
paintings: (L) $660; (H) $17,600

SIGNORI, Sergio
sculpture: (H) $2,600

SIGNORINI, Giovanni
Italian c. 1808-c. 1858
paintings: (L) $1,760; (H) $7,150

SIGNORINI, Giuseppe
Italian 1857-1932
paintings: (L) $5,500; (H) $11,000
drawings: (L) $330; (H) $6,325

SIGNORINI, Telemaco
Italian 1835-1901
paintings: (L) $12,100; (H) $60,500

SIGNORINI, Telemaco and Gugliemo
STELLA
Italian 19th/20th cent.
paintings: (H) $18,700

SIGRISTE, Guido
Swiss 1864-1915
paintings: (L) $2,860; (H) $6,600

SIJAN, Marc
American contemporary
sculpture: (H) $2,420

SIKIERS, A. von
Continental 19th cent.
paintings: (H) $990

SILBERT, Max
French b. 1871
paintings: (L) $1,320; (H) $24,200

SILISEO, F.
paintings: (H) $3,080

SILLEN, Herman Gustav
Swedish 1857-1908
paintings: (H) $17,600

SILLETT, James
English 1764-1840
paintings: (H) $12,100

SILLS, Thomas
paintings: (H) $2,475

SILVA, Benjamin
paintings: (L) $715; (H) $5,500

SILVA, Francis Augustus
American 1835-1886
paintings: (L) $3,960; (H) $60,500
drawings: (L) $2,750; (H) $77,000

SILVA, Jose da
paintings: (H) $2,200

SILVA, William Posey
American 1859-1948
paintings: (L) $247; (H) $6,050

SILVERMAN, Burton
American b. 1928
drawings: (L) $132; (H) $660

SILVERMAN, Martin
American
sculpture: (L) $1,100; (H) $6,600

SILVERT, Max
French b. 1871
paintings: (H) $2,200

SILVESTRE, Israel
drawings: (H) $770

SILVESTRE, Israel, the younger
1621-1691
paintings: (H) $8,800
drawings: (H) $2,860

SILVESTRE, Louis de
paintings: (H) $27,500

SILVESTRE, Paul
French b. 1884
sculpture: (L) $2,200; (H) $4,400

SIMARD, L.C.
French 20th cent.
sculpture: (H) $2,640

SIMAU, Hermann
Continental School 19th cent.
paintings: (H) $4,950

SIMBARI, Nicola
Italian b. 1927
paintings: (L) $110; (H) $19,800
drawings: (L) $440; (H) $4,950

SIME, Sidney Herbert
English 1867-1944
drawings: (L) $1,100; (H) $3,520

SIMEON-CHARBONNIEZ
paintings: (H) $880

SIMKIN, Richard
Scottish 1840-1926
drawings: (L) $770; (H) $1,430

SIMKHOVITCH, Simka
American b. Russia 1893
paintings: (L) $715; (H) $3,960
drawings: (H) $412

SIMM, Franz Xaver
Austrian 1853-1918
paintings: (L) $4,950; (H) $9,900

SIMMONDS, Charles
American b. 1945
sculpture: (H) $11,000

SIMMONS, Edward Emerson
American 1852-1931
paintings: (L) $220; (H) $66,000
drawings: (L) $110; (H) $7,150

SIMMONS, Franklin
American 1893-1913
paintings: (H) $330
sculpture: (L) $1,320; (H) $4,400

SIMON, Herman
American b. 1846
paintings: (L) $165; (H) $825

SIMON, Hermann Gustav
American 19th cent.
paintings: (H) $3,300

SIMON, J.
French 19th/20th cent.
paintings: (H) $660

SIMON, L.
paintings: (H) $880

SIMON, Lucien
French 1861-1945
paintings: (L) $110; (H) $11,000

SIMON, Mollie
paintings: (L) $715; (H) $715

SIMON, Sidney
American b. 1917
paintings: (H) $1,210

SIMON, Tavik Franktisek
Czechoslovakian b. 1877
paintings: (H) $2,750

SIMONAU, Gustave Adolphe
Belgian 1810-1870
drawings: (L) $440; (H) $1,100

SIMONDS, Charles
American b. 1945
sculpture: (H) $22,000

SIMONE, A. de
Italian late 19th cent.
paintings: (H) $9,900

SIMONE, E.
French 19th cent.
sculpture: (H) $1,980

SIMONE, Francesco de
Italian 19th cent.
paintings: (H) $935

SIMONE, Tomaso de
Italian ac. 1852-1857
paintings: (L) $8,250; (H) $18,700
drawings: (L) $467; (H) $2,090

SIMONELLI, Giuseppe
1649-1710
paintings: (H) $990

SIMONET, Augustin
French 19th cent.
paintings: (H) $5,500

SIMONET-CASTRO, Bernardo
20th cent.
paintings: (L) $605; (H) $2,640

SIMONETTI, Amedeo Momo
Italian 1874-1922
drawings: (L) $577; (H) $4,400

SIMONETTI, Attilio
Italian 1843-1925
paintings: (L) $1,320; (H) $6,600
drawings: (L) $275; (H) $2,750

SIMONETTI, C.A.
Italian 19th cent.
paintings: (H) $4,675

SIMONETTI, C.G.
Italian 19th cent.
drawings: (H) $770

SIMONETTI, Ettore
Italian 19th cent.
paintings: (L) $880; (H) $33,000
drawings: (L) $1,650; (H) $26,400

SIMONETTI, L.
drawings: (H) $4,180

SIMONETTI, R.
Italian 19th/20th cent.
paintings: (H) $1,980

SIMONI, Alfredo de
Italian 19th cent.
paintings: (L) $4,180; (H) $6,050

SIMONI, Gustavo
Italian b. 1846
paintings: (L) $1,100; (H) $16,500
drawings: (L) $715; (H) $17,600

SIMONI, Scipione
Italian 19th/20th cent.
paintings: (L) $165; (H) $1,980
drawings: (H) $1,210

SIMONIDY, Michel
Romanian 1870-1933
paintings: (L) $495; (H) $1,760

SIMONINI, Francesco
Italian 1686-1753
paintings: (L) $2,750; (H) $49,500
drawings: (L) $1,100; (H) $4,400

SIMONNER, L.
paintings: (H) $1,320

SIMONS, Bernard
sculpture: (H) $1,760

SIMONS, Frans
Belgian 1855-1916
paintings: (H) $11,550

SIMONS, Michiel
Dutch d. 1673
paintings: (L) $6,500; (H) $63,250

SIMONS, Paul Henri
paintings: (H) $1,320

SIMONS, Pinky Marcius
American
paintings: (H) $2,200

SIMONSEN, Niels
Danish 1807-1885
paintings: (L) $12,100; (H) $28,600

SIMONSEN, Simon Ludvig Ditlev
Danish 1841-1928
paintings: (H) $6,600

SIMONSEN, Soren
Danish 1843-1900
paintings: (H) $1,650

SIMONSON, David
German 1831-1896
paintings: (H) $11,000

SIMONSON, J.T.
American 19th/20th cent.
paintings: (H) $770

SIMPLOT, Alexander
American 1837-1914
drawings: (L) $165; (H) $770

SIMPSON, Alexander Brantingham
British exhib. 1904-1931
paintings: (L) $330; (H) $2,310

SIMPSON, Charles Walter
English 1885-1971
paintings: (L) $1,705; (H) $13,200
drawings: (H) $7,700

SIMPSON, Frank H.
paintings: (H) $715

SIMPSON, Harry
American 20th cent.
paintings: (H) $1,100

SIMPSON, Henry
English 1853-1921
paintings: (H) $1,100
drawings: (L) $275; (H) $302

SIMPSON, John
paintings: (H) $3,300

SIMPSON, Manville Stewart
paintings: (H) $935

SIMPSON, Maxwell Stuart
American b. 1896
paintings: (L) $176; (H) $1,210

SIMS, Charles
British 1873-1928
paintings: (L) $1,045; (H) $4,180

SIMS, J.W.
British 19th cent.
paintings: (H) $3,300

SIMSON, J.A.
18th cent.
drawings: (H) $20,900

SINCLAIR, G.
paintings: (H) $1,980

SINCLAIR, G.
British 19th cent.
paintings: (H) $825

SINCLAIR, Gerrit
American 1890-1955
paintings: (L) $300; (H) $825

SINCLAIR, John
English ac. 1872-1890
paintings: (H) $16,500

SINCLAIR, M.
British 19th cent.
paintings: (L) $1,540; (H) $5,280

SINCLAIR, Olga
paintings: (H) $6,600

SINDING, Otto Ludwig
paintings: (H) $1,650

SINDING, Stephen
sculpture: (L) $1,980; (H) $3,575

SINGER, Burr
American b. 1912
paintings: (L) $467; (H) $8,250

SINGER, Clyde
American b. 1908
paintings: (L) $82; (H) $9,900
drawings: (L) $110; (H) $1,760

SINGER, William Henry, Jr.
American 1868-1943
paintings: (L) $880; (H) $6,050
drawings: (H) $2,970

SINGIER, Gustave
French 1909-1984
paintings: (L) $7,700; (H) $23,100
drawings: (L) $2,420; (H) $2,860

SINGLETON, Henry
English 1766-1839
paintings: (H) $3,300

SINIBALDI, Jean Paul
French 1857-1909
paintings: (L) $3,520; (H) $20,900

SINIBALDI, Nino
European 19th/20th cent.
paintings: (H) $1,100

SINIBALDI, T.
paintings: (H) $1,320

SINTENIS, Renee
German 1888-1965
sculpture: (L) $770; (H) $9,075

SIQUEIROS, David Alfaro
Mexican 1896/98-1974
paintings: (L) $1,980; (H) $363,000
drawings: (L) $715; (H) $4,950

SIQUEIROS, Jose Alfaro
paintings: (L) $15,400; (H) $25,300

SIRANI, Giovanni Andrea
paintings: (L) $3,300; (H) $16,500

SIRONI, Mario
Italian 1885-1961
paintings: (L) $3,080; (H) $20,900
drawings: (L) $2,090; (H) $330,000

SISLEY, Alfred
French 1839-1899
paintings: (L) $121,000; (H) $3,630,000
drawings: (L) $5,280; (H) $192,500

SISQUELLA, Alfredo
paintings: (H) $1,100

SISS, W.
paintings: (H) $1,210

SISSON, Frederick Rhodes
American 1893-1962
paintings: (L) $990; (H) $1,320

SISSON, Laurence P.
American b. 1928
paintings: (L) $1,650; (H) $4,675
drawings: (L) $330; (H) $1,760

SISTERE, A** de
French 19th cent.
paintings: (H) $1,210

SITNIKOV, Alexander
Russian b. 1945
paintings: (H) $44,000

SITZMAN, Edward R.
American b. 1874
paintings: (L) $220; (H) $275
drawings: (L) $38; (H) $935

SJAMAAR, Pieter Geerard
Dutch 1819-1876
paintings: (H) $1,430

SJOSTRAND, Carl Johan
Swedish 19th cent.
paintings: (H) $7,150

SKALA, H.
Czechoslovakian 19th/20th cent.
paintings: (H) $715

SKARBINA, Franz
German 1849-1910
drawings: (L) $385; (H) $770

SKEAPING, John Rattenbury
British 1901-1980
paintings: (L) $1,870; (H) $1,980
drawings: (L) $770; (H) $4,180
sculpture: (H) $1,870

SKELTON, Red
American b. 1916
paintings: (L) $500; (H) $1,760

SKEMP, Robert Oliver
American 1907-1979
paintings: (L) $495; (H) $1,870

SKILLING, William
British/American 20th cent.
paintings: (L) $154; (H) $9,900

SKINNER, Thomas C.
American 1888-1955
paintings: (H) $1,045

SKIPWORTH, Frank Markham
British 1854-1929
paintings: (H) $88,000

SKOU, Sigurd
Norwegian/American 1878-1929
paintings: (L) $242; (H) $7,150
drawings: (L) $110; (H) $330

SKRAMSTAD, Ludvig
Norwegian 1855-1912
paintings: (H) $3,520

SKRETA, Karel
drawings: (H) $3,850

SKUTEZKY, Dominic
Hungarian 1850-1921
paintings: (L) $1,980; (H) $16,500

SKYNNER, Thomas
American 19th cent.
paintings: (H) $107,250
drawings: (H) $1,100

SLADE, Caleb Arnold
American 1882-1961
paintings: (L) $165; (H) $2,090
drawings: (H) $578

SLATER, John Falconar
British 1857-1937
paintings: (L) $275; (H) $3,300

SLAVIN, Arne
paintings: (H) $1,210

SLEETER
paintings: (H) $880

SLEPYSHEV, Anatoli
Russian b. 1932
paintings: (L) $6,600; (H) $44,000

SLEVOGT, Max
German 1868-1932
drawings: (L) $330; (H) $1,980

SLOAN, John
American 1871-1951
paintings: (L) $385; (H) $209,000
drawings: (L) $550; (H) $7,700

SLOAN, Junius R.
American 1827-1900
paintings: (L) $440; (H) $2,475
drawings: (L) $83; (H) $990

SLOAN, Marianna
American 1875-1954
paintings: (H) $825
drawings: (H) $66

SLOANE, Eric
American 1905/10-1985
paintings: (L) $770; (H) $15,400
drawings: (L) $357; (H) $550

SLOANE, George
American 19th/20th cent.
paintings: (L) $2,200; (H) $5,500
drawings: (H) $110

SLOANE, Marian Parkhurst
American d. 1955
paintings: (L) $165; (H) $2,310

SLOCOMBE, Frederick Albert
English 1847-1920
paintings: (H) $12,100

SLONE, Sandi
contemporary
paintings: (L) $825; (H) $2,090

SLOUN, Frank van
American 1879-1938
paintings: (L) $330; (H) $11,000
drawings: (L) $193; (H) $1,870

SLOWSKY, T.
paintings: (L) $495; (H) $880

SLUCA(?), A.
sculpture: (H) $19,251

SLUIS, Jacobus van der
Dutch 1660-1732
paintings: (H) $12,100

SLUSSER, Jean Paul
American
paintings: (L) $220; (H) $2,860

SLUYS, Theo van
Belgian 1849-1931
paintings: (L) $550; (H) $3,850

SLUYTERS, Jan
paintings: (H) $1,100

SMALL, Arthur
American 20th cent.
paintings: (H) $1,100
drawings: (H) $132

SMALL, Florence Veric Hardy
paintings: (H) $2,420

SMALL, H.
paintings: (H) $2,200

SMALL, William
paintings: (H) $660

SMARKUSZ, Vincent T.
American 1919-1974
paintings: (L) $165; (H) $880

SMART, J.
Scottish 19th cent.
paintings: (H) $715

SMART, John
British 1838-1899
paintings: (H) $1,650
drawings: (H) $550

SMEDLEY, William Thomas
American 1858-1920
paintings: (L) $4,400; (H) $15,950
drawings: (L) $110; (H) $2,420

SMEERS, Frans
Belgian b. 1873
paintings: (H) $2,420

SMET, F.
Belgian 19th cent.
paintings: (H) $3,520

SMET, Gustave de
paintings: (H) $9,350

SMET, Leon de
Belgian b. 1881
paintings: (H) $8,800

SMETS, A.
Continental 19th cent.
paintings: (L) $1,870; (H) $5,500

SMETS, Louis
Dutch 19th cent.
paintings: (L) $3,850; (H) $7,500

SMIBERT, John
American 1688-1751
paintings: (H) $28,600

SMIBERT, Nathaniel
American 1734-1756
paintings: (H) $8,525

SMILLIE, George Henry
American 1840-1921
paintings: (L) $440; (H) $9,900
drawings: (L) $165; (H) $2,640

SMILLIE, James David
American 1833-1909
paintings: (L) $357; (H) $20,900
drawings: (L) $300; (H) $990

SMIRNOV, Nikolai
Russian b. 1938
paintings: (L) $14,300; (H) $38,500

SMISSEN, Leon van der
contemporary
paintings: (H) $715

SMIT, Jan Borritsz.
Dutch ac. 1721-1768
paintings: (H) $49,500

SMITH, A.M.
American School 20th cent.
paintings: (H) $770

SMITH, Albert Delmont
American 1886-1962
paintings: (H) $880

SMITH, Alfred
American 1863-1955
paintings: (H) $15,950

SMITH, Allen
American 1810-1890
paintings: (H) $715

SMITH, Anita Miller
American b. 1893
paintings: (L) $990; (H) $1,045

SMITH, Archibald Cary
American 1837-1911
paintings: (L) $3,300; (H) $15,400

SMITH, Augustus Morton Hely
British 1862-1930's
drawings: (H) $900

SMITH, C.R.
British 19th cent.
paintings: (H) $3,025

SMITH, Carlton Alfred
British 1853-1946
paintings: (L) $3,300; (H) $5,500
drawings: (L) $2,860; (H) $9,350

SMITH, Cedric
contemporary
paintings: (H) $2,090

SMITH, Charles
paintings: (H) $1,320

SMITH, Charles L.A.
American 1871-1937
paintings: (L) $770; (H) $1,760
drawings: (L) $413; (H) $880

SMITH, Charles Lorraine
English 1751-1835
paintings: (H) $1,650

SMITH, Clarendon
English 19th cent.
paintings: (H) $1,210

SMITH, Dan W.
paintings: (H) $6,050
drawings: (L) $275; (H) $900

SMITH, David
American 1906-1965
paintings: (L) $4,400; (H) $17,600
drawings: (L) $3,850; (H) $18,700
sculpture: (L) $4,400; (H) $1,320,000

SMITH, DeCost
American 1864-1939
paintings: (H) $14,300
drawings: (H) $880

SMITH, Denzil
British 20th cent.
paintings: (L) $990; (H) $1,870

SMITH, E. Gregory
American 1881-1963
paintings: (H) $2,585

SMITH, Elmer Boyd
American 1860-1943
paintings: (L) $247; (H) $20,900
drawings: (H) $660

SMITH, Ernest Browning
American 1866-1951
paintings: (L) $303; (H) $6,600

SMITH, F. Rollin
European 19th cent.
paintings: (L) $935; (H) $3,300

SMITH, F.E.D.
American ac. c. 1875
paintings: (H) $79,750

SMITH, Francis
English 1881-1961
paintings: (H) $2,750

SMITH, Francis Hopkinson
American 1838-1915
drawings: (L) $248; (H) $46,200

SMITH, Frank Hill
American 1841-1901
paintings: (L) $330; (H) $880

SMITH, Frank Vining
American 1879-1967
paintings: (L) $137; (H) $6,600
drawings: (H) $125

SMITH, Frederick Carl
American 1868-1955
paintings: (L) $192; (H) $2,750
drawings: (L) $385; (H) $770

SMITH, Frederick W.
American b. 1885
paintings: (H) $1,430

SMITH, G. Binney
American 20th cent.
paintings: (L) $165; (H) $660

SMITH, G.F.
paintings: (H) $660

SMITH, Gean
American 1851-1928
paintings: (L) $165; (H) $4,290

SMITH, George
British
paintings: (H) $1,100

SMITH, George
British 1829-1901
paintings: (H) $3,300

SMITH, George, of Chichester
English 1714-1776
paintings: (L) $935; (H) $9,900

SMITH, George Melville
paintings: (L) $1,045; (H) $1,870

SMITH, Graham
British d. 1951
drawings: (L) $385; (H) $2,585

SMITH, H.
American b. 1885
paintings: (H) $1,100

SMITH, H.
English 19th cent.
paintings: (L) $440; (H) $1,100

SMITH, Harry Knox
American 1879-1934
paintings: (H) $165
drawings: (L) $165; (H) $1,430

SMITH, Hassel
American b. 1915
paintings: (L) $3,850; (H) $12,100
drawings: (H) $1,210

SMITH, Hely Augustus Morton
English 1862-1941
paintings: (L) $220; (H) $715
drawings: (L) $220; (H) $770

SMITH, Henry Pember
American 1854-1907
paintings: (L) $550; (H) $9,625
drawings: (L) $110; (H) $2,860

SMITH, Hobbe
Dutch 1862-1942
paintings: (L) $770; (H) $880
drawings: (H) $55

SMITH, Howard Everett
American 1885-1970
paintings: (L) $220; (H) $8,250
drawings: (H) $137

SMITH, Hughie Lee
paintings: (L) $220; (H) $1,210

SMITH, J. Christopher
American 1891-1943
paintings: (H) $3,025

SMITH, J. Henry
American 19th cent.
paintings: (H) $715

SMITH, J. Stewart
Scottish 19th cent.
paintings: (H) $880

SMITH, J. Wells
English ac. 1870-1875
paintings: (H) $990

SMITH, J.B.
paintings: (L) $880; (H) $2,200

SMITH, J.R.
paintings: (H) $1,760

SMITH, Jack
paintings: (H) $1,045

SMITH, Jack Wilkinson
American 1873-1949
paintings: (L) $935; (H) $49,500

SMITH, James B.
American early 19th cent.
paintings: (H) $6,325

SMITH, James Burrell
English 1822-1897
paintings: (L) $1,540; (H) $1,980
drawings: (H) $1,540

SMITH, Jessie Willcox
American 1863-1935
paintings: (L) $2,420; (H) $27,500
drawings: (L) $1,210; (H) $22,000

SMITH, Joelle
American
drawings: (H) $1,200

SMITH, John Brandon
British 1848-1884
paintings: (L) $2,090; (H) $14,300

SMITH, John Rubens
American 1775-1849
paintings: (H) $2,750

SMITH, John Warwick
British 1749-1831
drawings: (H) $9,900

SMITH, Joseph Lindon
American 1863-1950
paintings: (L) $330; (H) $3,575
drawings: (L) $550; (H) $5,775

SMITH, Joseph Marshall, Jr.
American 1854-1923
drawings: (L) $1,100; (H) $5,500

SMITH, Juanita
American
paintings: (H) $1,760

SMITH, Lawrence Beall
American
paintings: (L) $550; (H) $3,850

SMITH, Leon Polk
American b. 1906
paintings: (L) $13,200; (H) $44,000
drawings: (H) $1,540

SMITH, Letta Crapo
American 1862-1921
drawings: (H) $16,500

SMITH, Lowell Ellsworth
American b. 1924
drawings: (L) $55; (H) $3,410

SMITH, M.T.
American 19th/20th cent.
paintings: (H) $1,540

SMITH, Marshall, Jr.
paintings: (H) $3,300

SMITH, Martin
contemporary
sculpture: (H) $770

SMITH, Mary
American 1842-1878
paintings: (L) $192; (H) $8,250

SMITH, Miriam Tindall
American 20th cent.
paintings: (L) $495; (H) $3,960

SMITH, Mortimer L.
American
paintings: (H) $14,300

SMITH, Myrtle Holm
American b. 1875
paintings: (L) $357; (H) $935

SMITH, Patti
American contemporary
drawings: (L) $770; (H) $880

SMITH, Reginald
English c. 1855/70-c. 1925
paintings: (H) $770

SMITH, Richard
sculpture: (H) $2,200

SMITH, Richard
contemporary
drawings: (L) $550; (H) $770
sculpture: (H) $2,200

SMITH, Rosamond Lombard
American 20th cent.
paintings: (L) $13,200; (H) $28,600

SMITH, Royal Brewster
American 1801-1849
paintings: (L) $6,600; (H) $41,800

SMITH, Rufus Way
American late 19th cent.
paintings: (H) $852

Woman Illustrator

Jessie Willcox Smith (1863-1935) became a kindergarten teacher when she was seventeen. Almost by chance a young cousin taught her to draw, and she soon left teaching to enter the Pennsylvania Academy of the Fine Arts. In 1888 Smith left the Academy to become a full-time artist.

This was the Golden Age of Illustration (1880-1914). The advent of the half-tone and color processes had spurred a phenomenal growth in the printing industry and increased the demand for illustrators. Smith's first regular paycheck came from *The Ladies' Home Journal* for which she drew advertising illustrations. She specialized in portraying mothers, babies, and young children; there was an unspoken rule in the nineteenth century that women should not draw men!

In 1904, Howard Pyle, a famous illustrator, began teaching classes at Drexel Institute in Philadelphia. Jessie was one of his first students; two other students, Violet Oakley and Elizabeth Shippen Green, became her close friends. After leaving the Institute the three shared a studio and soon became widely recognized illustrators. In 1917 Smith began the first of her nearly two hundred covers for *Good Housekeeping* magazine. Her book illustrations included *Heidi*, *Little Women*, and *A Child's Garden of Verses*. In the spring of 1989, Freeman/Fine Arts in Philadelphia sold an illustration from George MacDonald's *At the Back of the North Wind* for $10,100. (Jessie Willcox Smith, *Are You Ill, Dear North Wind?* watercolor and gouache on board, sight size 23 x 18 in., Freeman/Fine Arts, June 16, 1989, $10,100)

SMITH, Russell
  Scottish/American 1812-1896
  paintings: (L) $55; (H) $8,800
  drawings: (L) $88; (H) $138

SMITH, Sarah K.
  American 20th cent.
  drawings: (H) $660

SMITH, Stephen Catterson, the elder
  British 1806-1872
  paintings: (L) $715; (H) $27,500

SMITH, T. Henry
  American 19th cent.
  paintings: (H) $660

SMITH, T.A.
  American 19th cent.
  paintings: (H) $770

SMITH, T.L.
  American
  paintings: (H) $2,420

SMITH, Thomas Henry
  American 19th cent.
  paintings: (H) $1,375

SMITH, Thomas Lochlan
  American 1835-1884
  paintings: (L) $2,530; (H) $3,080

SMITH, Tony
American b. 1912
paintings: (L) $7,700; (H) $16,500
sculpture: (L) $2,310; (H) $165,000

SMITH, Vernon B.
American b. 1894
paintings: (L) $55; (H) $2,200
drawings: (L) $61; (H) $825
sculpture: (H) $715

SMITH, William Collingwood
British 1815-1887
paintings: (H) $660
drawings: (L) $385; (H) $1,210

SMITH, William Harding
English 1848-1922
paintings: (L) $1,045; (H) $3,850

SMITH, William Thompson Russell
American 1812-1896
paintings: (L) $3,850; (H) $10,450

SMITH, Xanthus R.
American 1838/39-1929
paintings: (L) $110; (H) $26,400
drawings: (L) $99; (H) $5,500

SMITH, de Cost
American 1864-1939
paintings: (L) $3,080; (H) $7,975

SMITHE, William, of Chichester
1707-1764
paintings: (H) $5,500

SMITHSON, Robert
American 1938-1972/73
drawings: (L) $1,100; (H) $25,300
sculpture: (H) $165,000

SMITS, Jakob
Belgian 1856-1928
paintings: (H) $2,750

SMITS, Jan Geerard
Dutch 1823-1910
paintings: (L) $935; (H) $1,210

SMOLIN, Nat
American
sculpture: (H) $3,080

SMOOTHY, Derrich
paintings: (H) $1,760

SMYTH, Eugene Leslie
American 1857-1932
paintings: (L) $250; (H) $1,320

SMYTH, H.
British 19th cent.
paintings: (L) $154; (H) $2,200

SMYTH, Ned
sculpture: (H) $4,180

SMYTHE, Edward Robert
English 1810-1899
paintings: (L) $605; (H) $6,600

SMYTHE, Eugene Leslie
American 1857-1932
paintings: (L) $165; (H) $715

SMYTHE, F.
American 19th cent.
paintings: (H) $880

SMYTHE, L.
British 19th cent.
paintings: (H) $825

SMYTHE, Minnie
English d. 1955
drawings: (H) $26,400

SMYTHE, Thomas
English 1825-1906/07
paintings: (L) $770; (H) $14,300

SNAYERS, Pieter
Flemish 1592-1667
paintings: (L) $2,200; (H) $55,000

SNELL, G.
Continental 19th cent.
paintings: (H) $880

SNELL, Henry Bayley
American 1858-1943
paintings: (L) $715; (H) $6,600
drawings: (L) $150; (H) $412

SNELLING, Lilian
drawings: (H) $825

SNELSON, Kenneth
American b. 1927
drawings: (H) $275
sculpture: (L) $2,860; (H) $46,200

SNIDER, Dan L.
American
sculpture: (H) $700

SNIJERS, Peeter
Flemish 1681-1752
paintings: (H) $52,250

SNOECK, Jacques
Dutch 1881-1921
paintings: (L) $605; (H) $1,980

SNOWDEN, Mary
contemporary
drawings: (H) $880

SNOWDON, Margaret Kemplay
English ac. 1918-1938
paintings: (H) $1,650

SNYDER, A.
American 20th cent.
paintings: (L) $253; (H) $2,640

SNYDER, Joan
American b. 1940
paintings: (L) $3,850; (H) $24,200
drawings: (H) $20,900

SNYDER, Peter Etril
paintings: (H) $2,420

SNYDER, W. Mek
Danish 19th cent.
paintings: (H) $1,650

SNYDER, William
American 20th cent.
paintings: (H) $1,540

SNYDER, William H.
American 1829-1910
paintings: (L) $165; (H) $2,310

SNYDERS, Frans
Flemish 1579-1657
paintings: (L) $33,000; (H) $77,000

SNYERS, Pieter
Flemish 1681-1752
paintings: (L) $4,950; (H) $132,000

SOARES, Antonio
paintings: (H) $6,600

SOARES, Pablo
paintings: (H) $3,300

SOBEL, Ida
20th cent.
paintings: (H) $715

SOCCORRDA, Andrea
Spanish 19th cent.
paintings: (H) $935

SOCHOR, Richard
Continental 19th cent.
drawings: (L) $825; (H) $1,430

SODAR, Andre
Belgian 1829-1903
paintings: (H) $1,430

SODERSTON, Herman
Swedish/American 1862-1926
paintings: (L) $825; (H) $1,210

SOELLNER, Oscar Daniel
American b. 1890
paintings: (L) $11; (H) $1,210

SOENS, Jan
Dutch 1547/48-1611/14
paintings: (H) $60,500

SOEST, Gerard
English 1600-1681
paintings: (H) $4,400

SOETE
French 19th cent.
paintings: (L) $6,600; (H) $7,700

SOEVOLA, Guirdarne de
paintings: (H) $880

SOFFICI, Ardengo
Italian 1879-1964
paintings: (H) $10,175

SOHIER, Alice Ruggles
American b. 1880
paintings: (L) $7,700; (H) $9,900

SOKOFF, Alexander Petrovitch
paintings: (H) $3,520

SOKOLOFF, Anatolio
Russian 1891-1971
paintings: (H) $1,650

SOLANA, Jose Gutierrez
Spanish 1885-1945
paintings: (H) $101,750

SOLAR, Xul
b. Argentina 1887-1963
paintings: (H) $9,350
drawings: (L) $22,000; (H) $24,200

SOLBRIG, E. or H.(?)
19th cent.
paintings: (H) $2,420

SOLDE, Alexandre
French 1822-1893
drawings: (H) $1,650

SOLDENHOFF, Alexander B.
paintings: (H) $2,200

SOLDI, Andrea
Italian c. 1703-after 1771
paintings: (H) $49,500

SOLDNER, Paul
American b. 1921
sculpture: (L) $1,650; (H) $1,980

SOLDWEDEL, Frederic
American b. 1886
drawings: (L) $55; (H) $1,100

SOLER, F.
paintings: (H) $1,540

SOLER, Rogobento
paintings: (H) $3,300

SOLER Y LLOPIS, Eduardo
Spanish 1829-1928
paintings: (H) $3,300

SOLIMENA, Francesco
Italian 1657-1747
paintings: (L) $22,000; (H) $44,000
drawings: (H) $935

SOLIMENA, Francesco, studio of
paintings: (H) $3,080

SOLIN, Suzanne Daynes Grassot
French b. 1884
paintings: (H) $14,300

SOLLET(?)
sculpture: (H) $11,000

SOLMAN, Joseph
Russian/American b. 1909
paintings: (L) $495; (H) $4,400
drawings: (L) $187; (H) $2,310

SOLOMON, Abraham
English 1823/24-1862
paintings: (L) $1,540; (H) $19,800

SOLOMON, Frederick
German/American 1899-1980
paintings: (L) $247; (H) $770

SOLOMON, Harry
American b. 1873
drawings: (H) $1,100

SOLOMON, Simeon
British 1840-1905
paintings: (L) $5,500; (H) $15,400
drawings: (L) $3,575; (H) $16,500

SOLOMON, Solomon Joseph
British 1860-1927
paintings: (L) $9,900; (H) $52,250

SOLOMON, Syd
American b. 1917
paintings: (H) $880

SOLOWEY, Ben
Polish/American 1900/01-1978
paintings: (L) $165; (H) $3,300
drawings: (H) $522

SOMAINI, Francesco
contemporary
sculpture: (L) $467; (H) $2,475

SOMELLI, Guido
Italian b. 1881
paintings: (H) $2,750

SOMER
20th cent.
paintings: (H) $770

SOMER, Hendrick van
Dutch 1615-c. 1684/85
paintings: (H) $71,500

SOMER, Paul van
paintings: (H) $23,100

SOMERS, F.
paintings: (H) $880

SOMERS, G.
paintings: (H) $1,540

SOMERS, Otto
German/American 19th cent.
paintings: (H) $715

SOMERSCALES, Thomas
English 1842-1927
paintings: (H) $7,150

SOMERSET, Richard Gay
paintings: (H) $2,640

SOMES, C.
paintings: (H) $660

SOMME, Theophile Francois
French b. 1871
sculpture: (L) $742; (H) $2,640

SOMMER, Carl August
American 1839-1921
paintings: (H) $3,300

SOMMER, Jorg
paintings: (H) $715

SOMMER, Otto, or SOMMERS
American ac. 1860-1870s
paintings: (L) $358; (H) $39,600

SOMMER, R.
German 19th cent.
paintings: (H) $2,310

SOMMER, William
American 1867-1949
paintings: (L) $137; (H) $6,600
drawings: (L) $77; (H) $1,760

SOMMERSCALES, Thomas
paintings: (H) $2,200

SOMNIAVILLA, A.
paintings: (H) $880

SOMOGYI, D.
paintings: (H) $1,650

SON, Joris van, or Georg van
Flemish 1623-1667
paintings: (L) $22,000; (H) $242,000

SONDERBORG, Kurt
Danish b. 1923
paintings: (H) $20,900

SONDERLAND, Fritz
German 1836-1896
paintings: (L) $4,950; (H) $12,100

SONDERMANN, Hermann
German 1832-1901
paintings: (L) $5,720; (H) $14,300

SONJE, Jan Gabrielsz
Dutch 1625-1707
paintings: (H) $9,900

SONNENSTERN, Friedrich Schroder
drawings: (L) $1,100; (H) $6,050

SONNER, J***
paintings: (H) $935

SONNIER, Keith
American b. 1941
drawings: (H) $6,050
sculpture: (L) $19,800; (H) $41,250

SONNTAG, W.H.
paintings: (H) $880

SONNTAG, William Louis
American
paintings: (L) $4,400; (H) $55,000
drawings: (H) $2,860

SONNTAG, William Louis, Jr.
American b. 1870
paintings: (L) $1,045; (H) $1,155
drawings: (L) $990; (H) $13,200

SONNTAG, William Louis, Sr.
American 1822-1900
paintings: (L) $1,045; (H) $37,400
drawings: (L) $1,320; (H) $1,760

SONNTAG, William Louis and Arthur Fitzwilliam TAIT
American
paintings: (H) $13,200

SONREL, Elisabeth
French b. 1874
paintings: (H) $2,200

SONREL, Elsa
French
paintings: (H) $2,035

SOONIUS, Louis
Dutch 20th cent.
paintings: (H) $880

SOPER, Thomas James
British ac. 1836-1890
paintings: (H) $935

SORBI, Rafaello
Italian 1844-1931
paintings: (H) $28,600

SORBINI, A.
Italian 19th cent.
paintings: (H) $16,500

SORENSEN, Carl Frederick
Danish 1818-1879
paintings: (L) $3,850; (H) $4,675

SORENSEN, Carl Sofus Wilhelm
American b. 1864
sculpture: (H) $770

SORENSEN, Karin
Danish 19th cent.
paintings: (L) $3,300; (H) $3,575

SORGH, Hendrick Maartensz Rokes
Dutch c. 1611-1670
paintings: (H) $6,050

SORIANO, Juan
Mexican b. 1919/20
paintings: (L) $1,430; (H) $35,200
drawings: (L) $660; (H) $4,675

SORINE, Saveli
drawings: (H) $880

SORMAN, Steven
contemporary
paintings: (L) $550; (H) $880

SORMITT, Carl
American
paintings: (H) $4,400

SOROKOPOODOFF, Goryushkin
Russian 19th/20th cent.
paintings: (H) $2,475

SOROLA, Diaz
paintings: (H) $1,320

SOROLLA Y BASTIDA, Joaquin
Spanish 1863-1923
paintings: (L) $5,775; (H) $2,420,000
drawings: (H) $2,420

SORTA, Salvador
contemporary
sculpture: (H) $1,210

SOSPATAK, Laszlo Potaky von
Continental 1857-1912
paintings: (H) $1,320

SOSSON, L.
sculpture: (L) $880; (H) $1,045

SOTHERLAND
paintings: (H) $935

SOTO, Jesus Raphael
Venezuelan b. 1923
paintings: (L) $1,540; (H) $9,350
drawings: (L) $15,400; (H) $28,600
sculpture: (L) $660; (H) $71,500

SOTOMAYOR Y ZARAGOZA,
Fernando Alvarez de
Spanish b. 1875
paintings: (H) $143,000

SOTTER, George William
American 1879-1953
paintings: (L) $5,400; (H) $29,500

SOTTOCORNOLA, Giovanni
Italian 1855-1917
paintings: (L) $7,700; (H) $35,200

SOUDEIKINE, Sergei
Russian/American 1883/86-1946
paintings: (L) $110; (H) $935
drawings: (L) $165; (H) $1,500

SOULACROIX, Charles, or Joseph
Frederic Charles or Frederigo
French 1825-1877
paintings: (L) $3,300; (H) $110,000
drawings: (H) $110

SOULACRUY, E.
paintings: (H) $825

SOULAGES, Pierre
French b. 1919
paintings: (L) $20,900; (H) $242,000
drawings: (H) $47,300

SOULE, Carleton M.
American b. 1911
paintings: (L) $220; (H) $660

SOULE, Charles
American
paintings: (H) $825

SOULEN, Henry
paintings: (H) $880

SOULEN, Henry James
American 1888-1965
paintings: (L) $440; (H) $8,250

SOULES, Eugene Edouard
drawings: (H) $2,860

SOUTER, George
paintings: (H) $770

SOUTHER, J.K.
American b. 1869
paintings: (H) $935

SOUTHERN, J.M.
American 19th cent.
paintings: (L) $770; (H) $1,155

SOUTHILL, F.
paintings: (H) $1,210

SOUTINE, Chaim
Russian 1894-1943
paintings: (L) $52,800; (H) $880,000

SOUVERBIE, Jean
French b. 1891
paintings: (L) $5,500; (H) $6,600
drawings: (H) $137

SOUZA-PINTO, Jose Julio de
Portuguese 1855-1939
paintings: (L) $24,750; (H) $46,750

SOYER, Isaac
Russian/American b. 1907
paintings: (L) $220; (H) $26,400
drawings: (H) $412

SOYER, Moses
Russian/American 1899-1974
paintings: (L) $440; (H) $19,800
drawings: (L) $22; (H) $1,320

SOYER, Paul Constant
French 1823-1903
paintings: (L) $770; (H) $11,000

SOYER, Raphael
American 1899-1987
paintings: (L) $1,100; (H) $93,500
drawings: (L) $165; (H) $16,500

SOYVER, J.D.
paintings: (H) $770

SPADA, Lionello
Italian 1576-1622
paintings: (H) $66,000

SPAENDONCK, Cornelis van
French 1756-1840
paintings: (L) $28,600; (H) $115,500

SPAENDONCK, Gerard de, or
Gerardus van S.
French 1746-1822
paintings: (L) $9,900; (H) $797,500

SPAKENBURG
German 19th cent.
paintings: (L) $605; (H) $715

SPALATIN, Marko
American b. 1945
paintings: (H) $990

SPALDING, C.B.
British ac. 1832-1875
paintings: (H) $7,150

SPALDING, Charles B.
paintings: (H) $1,100

SPAMAAR, Pieter Gerardus
paintings: (H) $2,640

SPAMPINATO, Clem
American b. 1912
sculpture: (L) $385; (H) $8,250

SPANG, Frederick
American 1831-1909
paintings: (H) $1,650

SPANG, Michael Henry
sculpture: (H) $3,300

SPANGENBERG, Ferdinand T.
American ac. 1859-1866
paintings: (H) $4,950
drawings: (H) $302

SPANGENBERG, George
American 20th cent.
paintings: (H) $880

SPANGENBERG, Gustav Adolf
German 1828-1891
paintings: (H) $3,300

SPANISH FORGER
late 19th cent.
paintings: (H) $3,850

SPANZOTTI, Giovanni Martino,
studio of
Italian before 1456-1526/28
paintings: (H) $8,250

SPARE, Austin Osman
British 1888-1956
drawings: (L) $220; (H) $660

SPARKS, Arthur Watson
American 1870-1919
paintings: (L) $2,310; (H) $3,300

SPARKS, Will
American 1862-1937
paintings: (L) $825; (H) $3,850

SPAT, Gabriel
American 1890-1967
paintings: (L) $165; (H) $12,100
drawings: (L) $121; (H) $385

SPAULDING, Henry Plympton
American b. 1868
paintings: (L) $522; (H) $660
drawings: (L) $110; (H) $495

SPAZZAPAN, Luigi
paintings: (H) $2,420

SPEAR, Arthur P.
American 1879-1959
paintings: (L) $2,200; (H) $7,425
drawings: (L) $220; (H) $770

SPEAR, Ruskin
English b. 1911
paintings: (H) $6,600

SPEAR, Thomas Truman
American 1803-1882
paintings: (H) $990

SPEED, Ulyssess Grant
American b. 1930
sculpture: (L) $2,090; (H) $9,000

SPEER
American
paintings: (H) $660

SPEICHER, Eugene
American 1883-1962
paintings: (L) $165; (H) $15,400
drawings: (L) $110; (H) $770

SPELMAN, John A.
American 1880-1941
paintings: (L) $154; (H) $1,100

SPENCE, B.E.
sculpture: (H) $3,080

SPENCE, Ernest
British ac. 1884-1894
paintings: (H) $3,300

SPENCE, R.
English 19th cent.
paintings: (H) $880

SPENCE, Thomas Ralph
British b. 1855
paintings: (L) $660; (H) $10,450

SPENCELAYH, Charles
English 1865-1958
paintings: (L) $2,310; (H) $7,700

SPENCER, Asa
Anglo/American c. 1805-1847
paintings: (L) $121; (H) $1,155

SPENCER, C.W.
English 19th cent.
paintings: (H) $2,750

SPENCER, Frederick R.
American 1806-1875
paintings: (L) $1,210; (H) $12,100

SPENCER, Howard Bonnell
American early 20th cent.
paintings: (L) $440; (H) $990

SPENCER, J. Clinton
paintings: (H) $1,210

SPENCER, J.C.
American 19th/20th cent.
paintings: (L) $302; (H) $2,310
drawings: (H) $275

SPENCER, John C.
American late 19th/early 20th cent
paintings: (L) $193; (H) $2,090

SPENCER, Lilly Martin
American 1822-1902
paintings: (L) $330; (H) $12,100
drawings: (L) $55; (H) $9,350

SPENCER, Niles
American 1893-1952
paintings: (L) $550; (H) $47,300
drawings: (H) $3,520

SPENCER, R.B.
British ac. 1805-1870
paintings: (L) $3,025; (H) $44,000
drawings: (H) $77

SPENCER, Robert
American 1879-1931
paintings: (L) $1,430; (H) $99,000

SPENCER, Stanley
drawings: (H) $1,900

SPENCER, Thomas
British c. 1700-1767
paintings: (H) $14,300

SPENCER, W. Clyde
paintings: (H) $1,100

SPENCER, W.B.
American
paintings: (H) $6,160

SPENCER-STANHOPE, John Roddam
British 1829-1908
paintings: (H) $121,000

SPENLOVE, Frank Spenlove
paintings: (L) $440; (H) $990

SPERL, Johann
German 1840-1914
paintings: (L) $34,100; (H) $52,800

SPERLICH, Sophie
German 19th cent.
paintings: (H) $2,530

SPERLING, Heinrich
German 1844-1924
paintings: (L) $2,750; (H) $13,200

SPICER-SIMSON, Theodore
American 1871-1959
sculpture: (H) $1,650

SPICUZZA, Francesco J.
Italian/American 1883-1962
paintings: (L) $11; (H) $3,000
drawings: (L) $44; (H) $1,980

SPIECHER, Eugene
American
paintings: (H) $1,980

SPIEGAL, A.
American 20th cent.
paintings: (H) $825

SPIELTER, Carl Johann
German 1851-1922
paintings: (H) $5,500

SPIERS, Harry
English/American 1869-after 1934
drawings: (L) $88; (H) $1,045

SPILIMBERGO, Lino Eneas
paintings: (H) $3,080

SPILSBURY, Edgar Ashe
paintings: (H) $3,300

SPINELLI, Giovanni Battista
ac. c. 1630-1647
drawings: (H) $2,970

SPINELLI, Luca, called Spinello
ARETINO
c. 1350-1410
paintings: (H) $104,500

SPINETTI, Mario
Italian 19th/20th cent.
paintings: (H) $2,420
drawings: (L) $880; (H) $4,400

SPINKS, Thomas
British ac. 1872-1907
paintings: (L) $900; (H) $2,640

SPIRIDON, Ignace
Italian ac. 1889-1900
paintings: (L) $7,700; (H) $17,600

SPIRO, G.
European 19th cent.
paintings: (H) $1,210

SPIRO, Georges
French b. 1909
paintings: (L) $1,210; (H) $3,850

SPISANO, Vincenzo, Il Spisanelli
paintings: (H) $3,300

SPITZER, Walter
Polish b. 1927
paintings: (L) $825; (H) $8,800

SPITZLER, Carl
German 20th cent.
paintings: (H) $660

SPITZWEG, Carl
German 1808-1885
paintings: (H) $55,000
drawings: (H) $1,650

SPODE, John
English 19th cent.
paintings: (H) $4,950

SPODE, Samuel
paintings: (L) $1,320; (H) $8,800

SPOEL, Jacob
paintings: (L) $1,320; (H) $2,420

SPOERRI, Daniel
contemporary
sculpture: (H) $1,650

SPOHLER, J.F.
paintings: (H) $1,540

SPOHLER, Jan Jacob, or Jean Jacques
Dutch 1811-1879
paintings: (L) $660; (H) $49,500

SPOHLER, Jan Jacob Coenraad
Dutch 1837-1923
paintings: (L) $3,300; (H) $7,150

SPOHLER, Johannes Franciscus
Dutch 1853-1894
paintings: (L) $2,420; (H) $10,450

SPOHN, Clay
contemporary
paintings: (L) $132; (H) $2,310

SPOLVERINI, Ilario, called Il Mercanti
Italian 1657-1734
paintings: (H) $44,000

SPOONER, C.H.
American 19th cent.
paintings: (H) $2,860

SPORER, Fidelis Joseph, of Constance
sculpture: (H) $6,600

SPRAGUE, Howard F.
American 1871-1899
paintings: (L) $3,300; (H) $9,900

SPRAGUE, Huldah M.
American
drawings: (H) $770

SPRENG, Anton
paintings: (L) $660; (H) $1,100

SPRINCHORN, Carl
American 1887-1971
paintings: (L) $165; (H) $4,950
drawings: (L) $110; (H) $990

SPRING, Alfons
German 1843-1908
paintings: (L) $4,750; (H) $19,800

SPRINGER, C.
paintings: (H) $770

SPRINGER, Charles Henry
American 1857-1920
paintings: (L) $605; (H) $715

SPRINGER, Cornelis
Dutch 1817-1891
paintings: (L) $4,400; (H) $82,250
drawings: (L) $495; (H) $880

SPRUCE, Everett Franklin
American b. 1907
paintings: (L) $2,310; (H) $6,600

SPRY, William
drawings: (H) $1,760

SPUEHLER, Ernst A.
American 1900-1973
paintings: (H) $660

SPULAK, A.
paintings: (H) $4,400

SQUIER, Donald Gordon
American 1895-1987
paintings: (L) $55; (H) $2,640
drawings: (L) $66; (H) $165

SQUIRES, C. Clyde
American 1883-1970
paintings: (H) $1,210

STAATEN, Louis van
Dutch 19th/20th cent.
paintings: (L) $660; (H) $660
drawings: (L) $303; (H) $880

STABILE, Judy
American 20th cent.
drawings: (L) $660; (H) $990

STACEY, Anna Lee
American 1871-1943
paintings: (L) $440; (H) $6,050

STACEY, John F.
American b. 1859
paintings: (H) $9,900

STACHOUWER, Willem Tjarda van
Starkenborgh
Dutch 1823-1885
paintings: (H) $1,320

STACK, Josef Magnus
Swedish 1812-1868
paintings: (H) $1,320

STACKHOUSE, Robert
drawings: (H) $2,250

STACKHOUSE, Robert
contemporary
drawings: (L) $3,850; (H) $6,600

STACQUET, Henry
drawings: (H) $990

STADEMANN, Adolf
German 1824-1895
paintings: (L) $3,520; (H) $18,150

STAEL, Nicolas de
French 1914-1955
paintings: (L) $38,500; (H) $1,320,000
drawings: (L) $5,500; (H) $20,900

STAFANORI, Attillio
paintings: (H) $1,210

STAFFANONI, Luigi
French 1905-1984
paintings: (L) $990; (H) $2,090

STAFFELORM, Prof. Reich
European 19th cent.
paintings: (H) $880

STAGLIANO, Arturo
Italian 1870-1936
paintings: (L) $825; (H) $6,600

STAGURA, Albert
German 1866-1947
paintings: (H) $660

STAHL, Benjamin A.
American 1910-1987
paintings: (L) $300; (H) $5,940
drawings: (H) $605

STAHL, Marie Louise
American 20th cent.
paintings: (H) $900

STAHLEY, J.
paintings: (H) $770

STAHLY, Francois
sculpture: (H) $990

STAHR, Paul
American b. 1883
paintings: (H) $850

STAINFORTH, Martin
Australian 20th cent.
paintings: (H) $1,650

STALBEMT, Adriaen van
Flemish 1580-1662
paintings: (L) $12,100; (H) $16,500

STALSER, Hans
paintings: (H) $715

STAMMEL, Eberhard
German 1832/33-1906
paintings: (L) $550; (H) $4,675

STAMOS, Theodoros
American b. 1922
paintings: (L) $1,100; (H) $192,500
drawings: (L) $1,210; (H) $17,600

STAMPER, James William
British b. 1873
paintings: (H) $1,320

STANARD, Lilian
drawings: (H) $1,100

STANCZAK, Julian
American b. 1928
paintings: (L) $1,210; (H) $2,750

STANDING, William
American
paintings: (L) $2,000; (H) $7,000
drawings: (H) $900

STANDISH, Frank B.
American 1860-1944
paintings: (H) $2,090

STANFIELD, George Clarkson
English 1828-1878
paintings: (L) $1,540; (H) $4,675

STANFIELD, William Clarkson
English 1793-1867
paintings: (L) $467; (H) $7,700
drawings: (L) $110; (H) $187

STANGER, Alois
German 1836-1870
paintings: (H) $1,100

STANIER, Henry
British 19th cent.
drawings: (L) $220; (H) $3,520

STANIFORD, Lydia S.
American c. 1830
drawings: (H) $11,550

STANIFORD, W.M.
paintings: (H) $770

STANILAND, Charles Joseph
English 1838-1916
paintings: (H) $2,750

STANISLAW, Ejsmond
Polish 19th/20th cent.
drawings: (H) $5,500

STANKIEWICZ, Richard
American b. 1922
sculpture: (L) $4,675; (H) $18,700

STANLEY, Bob
contemporary
paintings: (H) $880

STANLEY, John Mix
American 1814-1872
paintings: (L) $6,050; (H) $46,750

STANNARD, Cecil
paintings: (H) $660

STANNARD, Emily
1875-1907
paintings: (H) $1,045

STANNARD, Henry
British 1844-1920
drawings: (L) $605; (H) $935

STANNARD, Henry Sylvester
English 1870-1951
drawings: (L) $660; (H) $14,300

STANNARD, John
paintings: (H) $770

STANNARD, Lilian
British b. 1884
drawings: (L) $825; (H) $2,640

STANNARD, Theresa Sylvester
drawings: (L) $1,870; (H) $1,870

STANNUS, Anthony Carey
English 19th/20th cent.
drawings: (L) $110; (H) $2,420

STANTON, Gideon
American b. 1855
paintings: (L) $176; (H) $990

STANTON, John A.
American 1857-1929
paintings: (L) $275; (H) $1,650

STANWOOD, Franklin
American 1856-1888
paintings: (L) $605; (H) $5,940

STANZIONE, Massimo, called
Cavaliere Massimo
Italian 1585-1656
paintings: (L) $55,000; (H) $242,000

STAPLES, John
English mid-19th cent.
paintings: (H) $1,045

STAPLES, Sir Robert Ponsonby
British 1853-1943
paintings: (H) $23,100
drawings: (H) $275

STAPPERS, Julien
Belgian 19th cent.
paintings: (L) $2,750; (H) $4,400

STAPRANS, Raimonds
American b. 1926
paintings: (L) $468; (H) $1,760

STAR, Kevin Red
American Indian (Crow) b. 1943
drawings: (H) $825

STARACE, Girolamo
paintings: (H) $5,500

STARK, Arthur James
English 1831-1902
paintings: (L) $1,540; (H) $4,125

STARK, Bruce
drawings: (H) $2,420

STARK, Jack Gage
American 1882-1950
paintings: (L) $358; (H) $1,430

STARK, James
British 1794-1859
paintings: (L) $4,675; (H) $7,425

STARK, Otto
American 1859-1926
paintings: (H) $17,600
drawings: (L) $385; (H) $880

STARK, Robert
paintings: (H) $1,100

STARKENBORGH, Jacobus Nicolaus,
Baron Tjarda van
Dutch/American 1822-1895
paintings: (H) $1,760

STARKEY, George
paintings: (H) $1,320

STARKWEATHER, William Edward
Bloomfield
American 1879-1969
paintings: (L) $55; (H) $4,950

STARKWEATHER, William H.B.
American
paintings: (H) $1,540

STARN TWINS
American b. 1961
drawings: (L) $4,400; (H) $55,000

STASCHUS, Daniel
paintings: (H) $770

STASIAK, Ludwik
Polish 1858-1924
paintings: (H) $2,860

STAUDER, Jacob Carl
1694-1756
paintings: (H) $3,300

STAUDER, Karl
paintings: (H) $3,300

STAUNTON, Phineas, Jr.
American 1817-1867
paintings: (H) $1,100

STAVE, George
contemporary
paintings: (H) $825

STAVEART
Dutch School
paintings: (H) $2,310

STAVROWSKY, Oleg
American b. 1927
paintings: (L) $770; (H) $15,400

STAYNES, Percy Angelo
British 1875-1953
drawings: (H) $1,100

STEAD, Frederick
British b. 1863
paintings: (H) $12,100

STEADMAN, J.T.
British 1887-1891
paintings: (H) $990

STEARNS, Junius Brutus
American 1810-1885
paintings: (L) $2,200; (H) $66,000

STEBBINS, Roland Stewart
American 1883-1974
paintings: (L) $605; (H) $1,210

STECK, G.
paintings: (H) $660

STEEGMAN, Philip
Italian b. 1926
paintings: (H) $1,155

STEELE, Edwin
British 19th cent.
paintings: (L) $143; (H) $2,200

STEELE, Gourlay
drawings: (H) $8,250

STEELE, J.
American 19th cent.
paintings: (H) $715

STEELE, Marian Williams
American b. 1916
paintings: (L) $385; (H) $880

STEELE, Theodore Clement
American 1847-1926
paintings: (L) $2,200; (H) $18,700

STEELE, Thomas Sedgwick
American 1845-1903
paintings: (L) $330; (H) $4,730

STEELE, William
American 1888-1965
paintings: (H) $3,300

STEELE, Zulma
American 1881-1979
paintings: (L) $110; (H) $495
drawings: (L) $302; (H) $880

STEELINK, Willem
Dutch 1826-1913
paintings: (L) $220; (H) $825
drawings: (L) $467; (H) $1,320

STEELINK, Willem, Jr.
Dutch 1856-1928
paintings: (H) $990
drawings: (L) $467; (H) $550

STEELL, Gourlay
Scottish 1819-1894
paintings: (L) $6,600; (H) $33,000

STEELL, John
English 1804-1891
sculpture: (H) $1,100

STEEN, Jan
Dutch
paintings: (L) $18,700; (H) $330,000

STEEN, Jan Havicksz
Dutch 1626-1679
paintings: (L) $4,950; (H) $2,970,000

STEENS, D****
paintings: (H) $4,400

STEENSEL, Jan van
Belgian 19th cent.
paintings: (H) $1,100

STEENWIJCK, Hendrik van, the younger
b. Antwerp 1580 d. London 1649
paintings: (L) $22,000; (H) $52,800

STEENWYCK, Harmen van
Dutch 1612-after 1656
paintings: (H) $17,600

STEEPLE, John
English exhib. 1846-1852, d. 1887
drawings: (H) $1,100

STEER, Philip Wilson
English 1860-1942
paintings: (L) $4,290; (H) $84,700
drawings: (L) $88; (H) $660

STEER, R.C.
paintings: (H) $962

STEFAN, Ross
American b. 1934
paintings: (L) $1,210; (H) $9,900

STEFANELL, L.
paintings: (H) $1,760

STEFANELLI, Romano
paintings: (H) $1,540

STEFFAN, F.
paintings: (H) $715

STEFFAN, Johann Gottfried
Swiss 1815-1905
paintings: (H) $15,400

STEFFANI, Luigi
Italian 1827-1898
paintings: (L) $192; (H) $880

STEICHEN, Edward J.
American 1879-1973
paintings: (L) $10,450; (H) $33,000
drawings: (L) $275; (H) $6,325

STEIDMANN, Eugene M.
American early 20th cent.
paintings: (L) $550; (H) $1,375

STEIG, William
American
sculpture: (H) $1,540

STEIN, Georges
French 20th cent.
paintings: (L) $7,700; (H) $26,400
drawings: (L) $990; (H) $9,900

STEINBACH, Haim
Israeli/American b. 1944
sculpture: (L) $28,600; (H) $29,700

STEINBERG, Saul
Rumanian/American b. 1914
paintings: (L) $13,200; (H) $31,900
drawings: (L) $33; (H) $110,000
sculpture: (L) $26,400; (H) $44,800

STEINBERGER
sculpture: (H) $2,860

STEINBRUCK, Eduard
paintings: (H) $9,900

STEINER, Agnes
German 1845-1925
paintings: (H) $1,210

STEINER, Clement Leopold
sculpture: (H) $3,080

STEINER, Michael
American b. 1945
paintings: (L) $550; (H) $770
sculpture: (L) $2,200; (H) $17,600

STEINER, William
20th cent.
paintings: (H) $1,430

STEINHARDT, Jakob
Israeli b. 1887
paintings: (H) $880
drawings: (L) $495; (H) $1,760

STEINHAUSER, Carl Johann
German 1813-1879
sculpture: (H) $22,000

STEINLEN, Theophile Alexandre
Swiss/French 1859-1923
paintings: (L) $3,080; (H) $16,500
drawings: (L) $165; (H) $7,150
sculpture: (H) $660

STEINMETZ-NORIS, Fritz
German 1860-after 1937
paintings: (H) $8,250

STEIR, Pat
American b. 1938
paintings: (L) $11,000; (H) $33,000
drawings: (H) $2,750

STELLA
sculpture: (H) $1,320

STELLA, Etienne Alexandre
French 19th cent.
sculpture: (H) $2,750

STELLA, Frank
American b. 1936
paintings: (L) $16,500; (H) $5,060,000
drawings: (L) $7,150; (H) $440,000
sculpture: (L) $9,900; (H) $660,000

STELLA, Guglielmo
Italian 1828-1888
paintings: (H) $4,400

STELLA, Jacques
French 1596-1657
drawings: (L) $2,200; (H) $17,600

STELLA, Joseph
American, b. Italy 1880-1946
paintings: (L) $1,100; (H) $2,200,000
drawings: (L) $132; (H) $24,200

STELZNER, Heinrich
German 1833-1910
paintings: (H) $7,425

STEMERER, von der
sculpture: (H) $935

STENBERRY, Algot
American b. 1902
paintings: (H) $2,090

STENNETT, Ralph
drawings: (H) $770

STEPHAN, A.
Dutch late 19th/20th cent.
paintings: (L) $1,100; (H) $1,925

STEPHAN, Gary
American b. 1942
paintings: (L) $1,100; (H) $13,200
drawings: (L) $990; (H) $1,430
sculpture: (L) $3,150; (H) $7,425

STEPHANOFF, Francis Philip
British 1790-1860
paintings: (H) $4,950

STEPHENS, Alice Barber
American 1858-1932
paintings: (L) $1,375; (H) $2,200
drawings: (H) $3,850

STEPHENSON, Benjamin Turner
American 1886-1973
paintings: (L) $825; (H) $1,650

STEPHENSON, J.G.
paintings: (H) $825

STEPPE, Romain
Belgian 1859-1927
paintings: (L) $660; (H) $2,200

STERCHI, Edna
American 19th/20th cent.
paintings: (L) $330; (H) $825

STERCHINE, Stephanie von
German b. 1858
paintings: (H) $935

STERLING, J.O.
American 20th cent.
paintings: (H) $770

STERLING, Lindsey Morris
American 1876-1931
sculpture: (L) $1,100; (H) $6,050

STERMERER, von der
sculpture: (H) $935

STERN, Bernard
British
paintings: (L) $14,300; (H) $26,400

STERN, Ignaz, called Stella
German 1680-1748
paintings: (H) $44,000

STERN, Max
German 1872-1943
paintings: (L) $3,190; (H) $16,500
drawings: (H) $88

STERNBERG, Harry
American b. 1904
paintings: (H) $38,500

STERNE, Hedda
Rumanian/American b. 1916
paintings: (L) $110; (H) $800

STERNE, Maurice
American 1877-1957
paintings: (L) $550; (H) $13,200
drawings: (L) $33; (H) $1,870

STERNER, Albert E.
American 1863-1946
paintings: (L) $350; (H) $4,290
drawings: (L) $27; (H) $990

STERNER, Harold
American
paintings: (H) $1,210
drawings: (L) $110; (H) $990

STERNER, William
paintings: (L) $165; (H) $770

STERRETT, Cliff
American contemporary
paintings: (H) $550
drawings: (L) $330; (H) $660

STETINA, Bruce S. von
American contemporary
paintings: (H) $3,025

STETSON, Charles Walter
American 1858-1911
paintings: (L) $192; (H) $6,050
drawings: (L) $357; (H) $550

STETTHEIMER, Florine
American 1871-1948
paintings: (H) $60,500

STEUER, Bernard Adrian
sculpture: (H) $3,520

STEUMPFIG, Walter
American 1914-1970
paintings: (H) $2,420

STEVENS, A.
paintings: (L) $935; (H) $1,320

STEVENS, A.
French 19th/20th cent.
paintings: (H) $4,675

STEVENS, Agapit
Belgian 19th cent.
paintings: (L) $1,650; (H) $2,750

STEVENS, Aime
Belgian b. 1879
paintings: (H) $41,250

STEVENS, Alfred
sculpture: (H) $2,475

STEVENS, Alfred
Belgian 1823-1906
paintings: (L) $330; (H) $462,000
drawings: (L) $220; (H) $3,850

STEVENS, Edward Dalton
American 1878-1939
paintings: (H) $990

STEVENS, Gustav Max
Belgian b. 1871
paintings: (H) $1,650
drawings: (H) $440

STEVENS, John Calvin
American b. 1855
paintings: (L) $935; (H) $1,210

STEVENS, L.S.
American mid-19th cent.
paintings: (H) $908

STEVENS, Lawrence Tenney
American
sculpture: (L) $825; (H) $1,100

STEVENS, M***
British School 19th/20th cent.
paintings: (H) $2,200

STEVENS, Pieter
Flemish 1567-1624
drawings: (H) $35,200

STEVENS, Thomas Pope
Irish d. 1771
paintings: (H) $15,950

STEVENS, W.L.
paintings: (H) $1,210

STEVENS, Will Henry
American b. 1881
paintings: (L) $1,540; (H) $3,850

STEVENS, William Lester
American 1888-1969
paintings: (L) $82; (H) $12,100
drawings: (L) $83; (H) $1,870
sculpture: (H) $880

STEVENSON, Alfred
American 19th cent.
paintings: (L) $700; (H) $880

STEVENSON, William Henry
American
drawings: (L) $880; (H) $1,540

STEVER, Jorge
drawings: (H) $770

STEWARD, Olive
American 19th cent.
paintings: (H) $660

STEWARD, S.W.
paintings: (H) $2,970

STEWARD, Seth W.
American 19th/20th cent.
paintings: (L) $825; (H) $2,970

STEWART, A.M.
English 19th cent.
paintings: (H) $660

STEWART, Allan
British 1865-1951
paintings: (H) $4,950

STEWART, B.P.
paintings: (L) $770; (H) $1,650

STEWART, Charles Edward
English ac. 1890-c. 1930
paintings: (H) $2,750

STEWART, E.
British 19th cent.
paintings: (H) $3,000

STEWART, Frank Algernon
American 1877-1945
drawings: (L) $2,640; (H) $17,600

STEWART, J. Malcolm
British 1829-1916
paintings: (H) $1,760

STEWART, Julius L.
American 1855-1919
paintings: (L) $1,980; (H) $38,500

STEWART, Lizbeth
contemporary
sculpture: (H) $3,740

STEWART, Robert W.
paintings: (H) $5,000

STEWART, Ron
American
drawings: (H) $850

STEYNOVITZ, Zamy
paintings: (H) $2,750

STICK, Frank
American 1884-1966
paintings: (L) $1,320; (H) $3,300

STICKROTH, Harry I.
American d. 1922
paintings: (H) $770

STICKS, C.B.
paintings: (H) $2,420

STICKS, G.B.
British 19th cent.
paintings: (H) $1,045

STICKS, George Blackie
British 1843-1938
paintings: (H) $880

STIEGELMEYER, Norman
contemporary
paintings: (H) $880

STIEPEVICH, Vincent G.
Russian ac. 1890
paintings: (L) $1,650; (H) $19,800
drawings: (H) $650

STIFTER, Moritz
Austrian 1857-1905
paintings: (L) $2,750; (H) $19,800

STIHA, Vladhan
American 20th cent.
paintings: (L) $550; (H) $1,870

STILKE, Hermann Anton
German 1803-1860
paintings: (H) $22,000

STILL, Clyfford
American b. 1904
paintings: (L) $4,400; (H) $1,100,000

STILLMAN-MYERS, Joyce
contemporary
paintings: (H) $4,180

STILLWELL, B.W.
American 19th cent.
paintings: (L) $605; (H) $1,500

STILSON (?), A.T.
American 20th cent.
paintings: (H) $1,320

STIMSON, John Ward
American 1850-1930
paintings: (H) $935
drawings: (L) $88; (H) $550

STINSKI, Gerald
American b. 1929
paintings: (L) $2,200; (H) $4,125

STITES, Caribel
American 19th/20th cent.
paintings: (H) $1,540

STITES, John Randolph
American b. 1836
paintings: (L) $660; (H) $880

STITT, Herbert D.
b. 1880
paintings: (H) $880

STOBART, John
paintings: (H) $8,800

STOBBE, Marie
American b. 1915
paintings: (L) $1,650; (H) $2,530
drawings: (H) $385

STOBIE, Charles Stewart
American 1845-1931
paintings: (L) $220; (H) $7,150

STOBWASSER, Gustav
German 19th cent.
paintings: (H) $3,850

STOCK, Ernest
American 20th cent.
paintings: (H) $1,925

STOCK, H.J.
paintings: (H) $2,750

STOCK, Henry John
British 1853-1931
paintings: (H) $715

STOCK, Ignatius van der
Dutch 17th cent.
paintings: (H) $15,400

STOCK, Joseph Whiting
American 1815-1855
paintings: (L) $1,595; (H) $85,250

STOCKLIN, Christian
Swiss 1741-1795
paintings: (H) $12,650

STOCKS, Arthur
paintings: (H) $3,850

STODDARD, Alice Kent
American 1885/93-1976
paintings: (L) $192; (H) $24,200
drawings: (L) $55; (H) $110

STODDARD, Frederick Lincoln
American 1861-1940
paintings: (H) $935
drawings: (H) $110

STOFFE, Jan Jacobsz van der
Dutch 1611-1682
paintings: (L) $4,400; (H) $6,600

STOFFE, Jan van der
paintings: (L) $3,300; (H) $6,600

STOHR, Julia W. Collins
American b. 1866
paintings: (H) $715
drawings: (H) $154

STOILOFF, Constantin
Russian 1850-1924
paintings: (L) $1,760; (H) $12,650

STOILOFF, Constantin and H.
BAUMGARTNER
Bulgarian 19th cent.
paintings: (H) $7,700

STOITZNER, Carl Sigfried
Austrian 1866-1943
paintings: (L) $880; (H) $1,650

STOITZNER, Constantin
Austrian 1863-1934
paintings: (L) $400; (H) $1,650

STOITZNER, Josef
Austrian b. 1884
paintings: (L) $2,310; (H) $7,700

STOJANOFF, C.
Russian 19th cent.
paintings: (H) $1,870

STOJANOW, C.
paintings: (H) $1,210

STOJNOV (?), Joseph
paintings: (H) $18,700

STOK, Jacobus van der
paintings: (H) $2,090

STOKES, Adrian
British 1854-1935
paintings: (H) $15,400

STOKES, Frank Wilbert
American 1854-1927
paintings: (L) $385; (H) $990

STOKES, George Vernon
drawings: (L) $550; (H) $1,980

STOKES, Marianne Preindlsberger
British 1855-1927
paintings: (H) $77,000

STOLK, Alida Elizabeth van
Dutch 1830-1884
paintings: (H) $3,575

STOLL, Leopold van
Dutch ac. 1828-1874
paintings: (H) $9,900

STOLL, Rolf
German/American b. 1892
paintings: (L) $2,090; (H) $2,530
drawings: (H) $55

STOLTENBERG, Hans John
American 1880-1963
paintings: (L) $55; (H) $1,210

STOLZENBERG, A.F.
paintings: (H) $935

STOMER, Mathaus
Flemish
paintings: (L) $5,500; (H) $16,500

STOMER, Mathaus, the elder
Flemish 1598/1600-after 1650
paintings: (H) $132,000

STOMME, Jan Jansz de
Dutch ac. 1643-1657
paintings: (H) $1,430

BOELEMA DE STOMME, Maerten, or
BOELSEMA DE STOMME
Dutch ac. 1642-1664
paintings: (H) $71,500

STONE, A.
paintings: (L) $770; (H) $825

STONE, A.
Continental 19th cent.
paintings: (H) $1,650

STONE, A.
English 19th cent.
paintings: (H) $2,420

STONE, Don
American b. 1929
paintings: (H) $275
drawings: (L) $165; (H) $1,100

STONE, Gilbert
1940-1984
paintings: (H) $800

STONE, H.
English 19th cent.
paintings: (L) $2,200; (H) $2,750

STONE, Marcus
English 1840-1921
paintings: (L) $440; (H) $99,000

STONE, Robert
British 19th cent.
paintings: (L) $990; (H) $17,600

STONE, Rudolf
paintings: (H) $9,350

STONE, Sarah
British 18th cent.
drawings: (H) $5,500

STONE, Seymour Millais
American b. 1877
paintings: (H) $1,045

STONE, Sylvia
American 20th cent.
paintings: (H) $660
drawings: (H) $11

STONE, W.
English 19th cent.
paintings: (H) $1,155

STONE, William R.
English 19th cent.
paintings: (H) $6,380

STONEY, Eleanor E.
American 19th cent.
paintings: (H) $742

STOOP, Dirk
Dutch 1610/18-1681/86
paintings: (H) $11,000

STOOPENDAAL, Mosse
Swedish 1901-1948
paintings: (H) $14,300

STOOPS, Herbert Morton
American 1888-1948
paintings: (L) $880; (H) $2,000
drawings: (H) $1,595

STORCK, Abraham
Dutch c. 1635-c. 1710
paintings: (L) $3,000; (H) $101,750

STORCK, Jacobus
Dutch ac. 1610-1686
paintings: (H) $7,700

STORER, Charles
American 1817-1907
paintings: (L) $357; (H) $3,025
drawings: (H) $192

STOREY, George Adolphus
English 1834-1919
paintings: (L) $935; (H) $38,500

STORIE, Jose
Belgian b. 1899
paintings: (H) $11,000

STORK, J.
Dutch 20th cent.
paintings: (H) $1,320

STORK, Lisl
American b. 1888
paintings: (H) $880

STORM, H.J.
Continental 20th cent.
paintings: (H) $880

STORM, Mark
American b. 1911
paintings: (H) $8,000

STORRS, Francis H.
19th/20th cent.
paintings: (L) $275; (H) $1,500

STORRS, John Henry Bradley
American 1885-1956
sculpture: (L) $36,300; (H) $126,500

STORY, George Henry
American 1835-1923
paintings: (L) $385; (H) $12,650

STORY, Julian Russel
American 1850-1919
paintings: (H) $2,200

STORY, Waldo Thomas
English 1855-1915
sculpture: (H) $12,100

STOTHARD, Thomas
British 1755-1834
paintings: (L) $2,090; (H) $2,970

STOTT, Edward
drawings: (H) $715

STOTT, W.R.S.
American
paintings: (H) $8,250

STOTZ, C.
sculpture: (H) $660

STOUT, Frank
paintings: (L) $11; (H) $825

STOUT, I. Mc.
sculpture: (H) $660

STOUT, Ida McClelland
American d. 1827
sculpture: (L) $660; (H) $825

STOUT, Myron
American b. 1908
paintings: (H) $52,800
drawings: (L) $8,800; (H) $44,000

STOVEHOUSE, Brian
drawings: (H) $715

STOVER, A.
American 19th cent.
paintings: (H) $935

STOVER, Allen James
American b. 1887
paintings: (H) $770

STOWARD, F.
American 19th cent.
paintings: (H) $1,430

STOWARD, F.
British 19th cent.
paintings: (H) $2,420

STRAAT, Jan van der, IL
STRADANUS, circle of
drawings: (H) $1,045

STRACHAN, Claude
English b. 1865, ac. 1885-1929
drawings: (L) $2,750; (H) $6,600

STRADNER, Lukas
drawings: (H) $1,320

STRADONE, Giovanni
paintings: (H) $990

STRAET, Jan van der, called Stradanus
Flemish 1523-1605
drawings: (L) $11,000; (H) $47,300

STRAETEN, Georges van der
Belgian b. 1856
sculpture: (L) $137; (H) $4,400

STRAFER, A.
sculpture: (H) $1,210

STRAIN, John Paul
American b. 1955
drawings: (L) $2,700; (H) $6,000

STRANG, Ray
American 1893-1954/57
paintings: (L) $82; (H) $4,400

STRANG, William
Scottish 1859-1921
paintings: (H) $2,750

STRANOVER, Tobias
Czechoslovakian 1684-1724
paintings: (L) $4,400; (H) $44,000

STRAOUTEN, B.V.
Belgian 19th cent.
paintings: (H) $4,125

STRASSER, Arthur
sculpture: (H) $3,300

STRASSER, Matthaus
German d. 1659
drawings: (H) $6,050

STRATER, Henry
American b. 1896
paintings: (L) $825; (H) $3,300

STRATHMANN, Carl
German 1866-1939
paintings: (H) $8,250
drawings: (H) $3,850

STRATTON, Alfred A.
Canadian b. 19th cent.
paintings: (H) $1,650

STRATZER
sculpture: (H) $4,125

STRAUS, M.
Continental 19th cent.
paintings: (H) $6,820

STRAUS, Meyer
American 1831-1905
paintings: (L) $248; (H) $15,400
drawings: (L) $220; (H) $605

STRAUSS, Andre
contemporary
paintings: (H) $770

STRAUSS, L. von
Austrian (?) b. 1929
paintings: (L) $550; (H) $660

STRAUSS, Malcolm Mitteldorfer
paintings: (H) $3,850

STRAUSS, Raphael
American ac. 1859-1897
paintings: (H) $3,575

STRAVROWSKY, Oleg
American
paintings: (H) $9,000

STRAWBRIDGE, Anne West
American 1883-1944
paintings: (H) $9,900

STRAYER, Paul
American b. 1885
paintings: (L) $55; (H) $1,705

STREATOR, Harold A.
American 1861-1926
paintings: (L) $440; (H) $1,540

STREECK, Hendrik van, or STREEK
Dutch 1659-1719
paintings: (L) $1,650; (H) $60,500

STREEFKERK, Carl August
Dutch b. 1894
paintings: (H) $687

STREET, Frank
American 1893-1944
paintings: (L) $77; (H) $3,200

STREET, Robert
American 1796-1865, ac. 1840
paintings: (L) $468; (H) $16,500

STREET, Rubens C.
American b. 1826
paintings: (H) $5,225

STREETER, J. van der
Dutch 19th cent.
sculpture: (H) $1,650

STREIT, Robert
Austrian b. 1883
paintings: (H) $6,380

STRETTON, Philip Eustace
British ac. 1884-1915
paintings: (L) $1,100; (H) $4,950

STREVENS, Frederick
English b. 1902
paintings: (H) $1,320

STRICKLAND, George
drawings: (L) $797; (H) $797

STRICKLAND, Juliana Sabina
British 19th cent.
drawings: (L) $440; (H) $1,210

STRICKLAND, William
drawings: (L) $412; (H) $2,530

STRIGELLY, E.
Continental 19th cent.
paintings: (H) $1,100

STRIJ, Jacob van
Netherlandish 1756-1815
paintings: (H) $880

STRINGER, Francis
British active 1760-1772
paintings: (L) $15,400; (H) $19,800

STRISIK, Paul
American b. 1918
paintings: (L) $110; (H) $1,540
drawings: (H) $1,210

STROBEL, Christian
Austrian 1855-1899
paintings: (H) $1,017

STROEBEL, Johann Anthonie Balthasar
Dutch 1821-1905
paintings: (L) $605; (H) $3,300

STROHLING, Peter Eduard
Russian 1768-1826
paintings: (H) $14,300

STROITZNER, Joseph
Austrian 1884-1951
paintings: (H) $1,320

STROJOINOW
paintings: (H) $1,760

STRONG, Elizabeth
American 1855-1941
paintings: (L) $192; (H) $8,250

STRONG, Joseph D., Jr.
American 1852-1899
paintings: (L) $523; (H) $4,675

STROOBANT, Francois
Belgian 1819-1916
paintings: (H) $3,000

STROUD, Ida Wells
American b. 1869
drawings: (L) $70; (H) $990

STROZZI, Bernardo
Italian 1581-1644
paintings: (H) $88,000

STRUCK, Herman G.
American 1887-1954
paintings: (L) $1,100; (H) $3,575

STRUTHERS
paintings: (H) $935

STRUTT, Jacob George
British 1790-1864
paintings: (L) $1,760; (H) $2,750

STRUTT, William
British 1825-1915
paintings: (L) $5,500; (H) $8,800

STRUTZEL, Leopold Otto
German 1855-1930
paintings: (L) $1,100; (H) $14,850

STRUYS, Alexandre
paintings: (H) $1,430

STRY, Abraham van
Dutch 18th/19th cent.
paintings: (H) $1,100

STRY, Jacob van
Dutch 1756-1815
paintings: (L) $6,600; (H) $27,500

STRYDONCK, Guillaume van
Belgian 1861-1937
paintings: (H) $24,200

STRYMANS, Adolphe Joseph
Belgian School b. 1866
sculpture: (H) $5,060

STUART, Charles
British ac. 1880-1904
paintings: (L) $308; (H) $5,500

STUART, Charles Alexander
American 1831-1898
paintings: (H) $2,860

STUART, Gilbert
American 1755-1828
paintings: (L) $1,155; (H) $990,000

STUART, J.R.
paintings: (H) $1,700

STUART, James Everett
American 1852-1941
paintings: (L) $138; (H) $6,050
drawings: (H) $220

STUART, Jane
American 1816-1888
paintings: (L) $1,760; (H) $12,100

STUART, John, 3rd Earl of Bute
British 1713-1792
paintings: (H) $4,950

STUART, R. Easton
British 19th/20th cent.
paintings: (L) $275; (H) $8,800

STUART, R. James
American 20th cent.
paintings: (H) $825

STUART, R.T.
American 19th cent.
paintings: (L) $275; (H) $687

STUART, William
British 19th cent.
paintings: (H) $15,400

STUBBS, George
British 1724-1806
paintings: (L) $176,000; (H) $2,420,000

STUBBS, Ralph
British 19th cent.
paintings: (H) $1,100

STUBBS, W.
American 19th cent.
paintings: (H) $2,200

STUBBS, William Pierce
American 1842-1909
paintings: (L) $990; (H) $11,000

STUBER, Dedrick B.
American 1878-1954
paintings: (L) $770; (H) $4,400

STUCK, Carl
German 19/20th cent.
paintings: (H) $1,210

STUCK, Franz von
German 1863-1928
paintings: (L) $24,200; (H) $27,500
drawings: (L) $1,100; (H) $3,300
sculpture: (L) $1,870; (H) $8,800

STUECREA, Karl W.
drawings: (H) $660

STUEMPFIG, Walter
American 1914-1970
paintings: (L) $220; (H) $18,700

STUHLMULLER, Karl
French 1858-1930
paintings: (L) $8,800; (H) $13,750

STULL, Henry
American 1851-1913
paintings: (L) $1,430; (H) $20,900

STURGESS, John
British ac. 1875-1884
paintings: (L) $2,860; (H) $15,400
drawings: (L) $990; (H) $2,200

STURGESS, Reginald Ward
Australian 1890-1932
drawings: (H) $1,210

STURGIS, Katherine
American
paintings: (H) $825

STURSA, Jan
sculpture: (H) $2,200

STURTEVANT, Elaine F.
American b. 1926
paintings: (L) $55; (H) $8,250

STURTEVANT, Helena
American 1872-1946
paintings: (L) $121; (H) $27,500
drawings: (L) $110; (H) $275

STURTEVANT, J.B.
American
paintings: (H) $1,540

STUUBBE, W.R.
paintings: (H) $12,650

STUVEN, Ernst
German 1657/60-1712
paintings: (H) $93,500

STYKA, Adam
French 1890-1959
paintings: (L) $2,750; (H) $11,000

STYKA, Tade
French b. 1889
paintings: (L) $352; (H) $2,200

SUAREZ, Libredo
Spanish 19th cent.
paintings: (H) $825

SUBIT, Aline
American 1819-1896
drawings: (H) $1,650

SUCH, B.J.
American
paintings: (H) $1,650

SUCH, William Thomas
British 1820-1893
paintings: (H) $1,980

SUCHY, Adalbert
drawings: (H) $770

SUCUI, Edmond
paintings: (H) $990

SUDKOVSKY, Rufin
paintings: (H) $2,420

SUDRE, Raymond
sculpture: (H) $4,180

SUERMANN, Edna
drawings: (L) $468; (H) $5,225

SUETIN, Nikolai
drawings: (H) $4,675

SUGAI, Kumi
Japanese b. 1919
paintings: (L) $16,500; (H) $132,000
drawings: (L) $3,300; (H) $9,020

SUGARMAN, George
contemporary
drawings: (H) $1,100

SUHRLANDT, Carl
German 1828-1919
paintings: (H) $27,500

SUISSE, Gaston
paintings: (H) $770

SULLIVAN, Blanche
American 19th/20th cent.
paintings: (H) $1,430

SULLIVAN, Louis Henry
American 1865-1924
drawings: (L) $6,600; (H) $8,250

SULLIVAN, William Holmes
British d. 1908
paintings: (H) $18,700

SULLIVANT, Thomas S.
American b. 1854-after 1926
drawings: (L) $700; (H) $935

SULLY, Alfred
American 19th cent.
drawings: (H) $2,200

SULLY, Thomas
American 1783-1872
paintings: (L) $743; (H) $143,000
drawings: (L) $715; (H) $11,000

SULLY, Thomas, Jr.
American 1811-1847
paintings: (L) $412; (H) $3,850

SULTAN, Altoon
contemporary
paintings: (H) $3,300

SULTAN, Donald
American b. 1951
paintings: (L) $16,500; (H) $440,000
drawings: (L) $3,300; (H) $115,000
sculpture: (H) $2,640

SULYON-PAPP, J.
American(?) 20th cent.
paintings: (H) $935

SUMMA, Emily B.
American b. 1875
paintings: (L) $247; (H) $1,760

SUMMERS, Alick D.
British 1864-1938
paintings: (L) $1,430; (H) $1,870

SUMMERS, Ivan
American d. 1964
paintings: (L) $330; (H) $1,045

SUMMERS, Robert
American b. 1940
paintings: (L) $4,510; (H) $17,600
sculpture: (L) $825; (H) $10,500

SUMMERS(?), A.
English 20th cent.
paintings: (H) $825

SUN KE GANG
Chinese b. 1923
drawings: (H) $770

SUNDBLOM, Haddon Hubbard
American 20th cent.
paintings: (L) $660; (H) $10,725

SUNG, Lai
Chinese 19th cent.
paintings: (H) $8,525

SUNQUA
mid-19th cent.
drawings: (H) $2,200

SUNTER
paintings: (H) $1,045

SUNYER, Joaquin S.Y. Myro
Spanish 1875-1956
drawings: (L) $3,300; (H) $14,300

SUREDA, Andre
French 1872-1930
drawings: (H) $825

SURENDORF, Charles Frederick
American 1906-1979
paintings: (L) $468; (H) $1,100
drawings: (L) $220; (H) $550

SURLS, James
American b. 1943
sculpture: (L) $16,500; (H) $19,800

SURTEES, John
British b. 1817
paintings: (H) $2,500

SURVAGE, Leopold
French 1879-1968
paintings: (L) $467; (H) $71,500
drawings: (L) $220; (H) $17,600

SUSENIER, Abraham
Dutch 1620-after 1668
paintings: (L) $37,400; (H) $81,400

SUSS, Johann
Austrian b. 1857
paintings: (L) $220; (H) $1,980

SUSTERMANS, Justus
Flemish 1597-1681
paintings: (L) $19,800; (H) $28,600

SUTER, Jakob
drawings: (H) $3,850

SUTHERLAND, Graham
English b. 1903
paintings: (H) $55,000

SUTHERLAND, J.N.
paintings: (H) $1,650

SUTIL, Francisca
Chilean b. 1952
drawings: (H) $3,850

SUTTER, Walter Samuel
American b. 1888
paintings: (L) $165; (H) $1,430

SUTTON, Harry, Jr.
American 1897-1984
paintings: (L) $22; (H) $687
drawings: (L) $165; (H) $6,600

SUTTON, J.
paintings: (H) $4,950

SUTZ, Robert
paintings: (L) $4,950; (H) $7,700

SUYDAM, James Augustus
American 1819-1865
paintings: (L) $6,050; (H) $88,000

SUYKER, Reyer Claesz.
c. 1590-c. 1653/5
paintings: (H) $8,800

SUZOR-COTE, Marc Aurele de Foy
sculpture: (H) $7,150

SUZUKI, James Hiroshi
Japanese b. 1933
paintings: (H) $5,720

SVARTEK, Aranca
paintings: (H) $4,620

SVENDSEN, Svend
Norwegian/American 1864-1915
paintings: (L) $33; (H) $3,080
drawings: (L) $110; (H) $357

SVERTSCHKOFF, Nicolas
Gregorovitch
Russian 1817-1898
paintings: (L) $2,420; (H) $2,860

SWAGERS, Frans
Dutch 1756-1836
paintings: (H) $5,500

SWAIM, Robert
American
paintings: (L) $110; (H) $700

SWAINE, Francis
British 1740-1782
paintings: (L) $4,500; (H) $10,450

SWAN, Cuthbert Edmund
Irish 1870/73-1931
paintings: (H) $4,400

SWAN, Emma Levina
American 1853-1927
paintings: (L) $770; (H) $1,100

SWAN, John Macallan
British 1847-1910
paintings: (H) $11,000

SWAN, Robert John
British b. 1888
paintings: (H) $990

SWANEVELT, Herman van
Dutch 1600-1665
paintings: (L) $1,540; (H) $2,640

SWANSON, Frank
American contemporary
sculpture: (H) $1,155

SWANSON, Mark
American contemporary
paintings: (L) $3,300; (H) $4,500

SWANSON, Ray
American b. 1937
paintings: (L) $7,000; (H) $20,000

SWANWICK, Harold
paintings: (H) $990

SWART VAN GRONINGEN, Jan
Dutch 1520-1558
drawings: (L) $660; (H) $14,300

SWEAT, Jonathan
drawings: (H) $4,125

SWEBACH, Bernard Edouard
French 1800-1870
paintings: (L) $3,000; (H) $14,300
drawings: (H) $770

SWEBACH-DESFONTAINES, Jacques
Francois
drawings: (H) $4,950

SWEERTS, Michael
Dutch 1624-1664
paintings: (H) $88,000

SWEISZEWSKI, Alexander
paintings: (H) $1,760

SWERINGEN, Ron van
American b. 1936
paintings: (L) $88; (H) $1,760

SWETT, William Otis, Jr.
American 1859-1938
paintings: (L) $165; (H) $4,730

SWIFT, Clement
American 1846-1918
paintings: (L) $330; (H) $4,400

SWINNERTON, James G.
American 1875-1974
paintings: (L) $330; (H) $11,000
drawings: (H) $220

SWINTON, Marion
American
paintings: (L) $61; (H) $1,045

SWOPE, H. Vance
American b. 1879
paintings: (L) $990; (H) $2,530

SWORD, James Brade
American 1839-1915
paintings: (L) $330; (H) $10,175
drawings: (L) $77; (H) $935

SWORTSCHKOFF, Wladimir
paintings: (H) $1,100

SYBORCK, R.
paintings: (H) $1,980

SYER, John
English 1815-1885
paintings: (L) $550; (H) $4,675
drawings: (H) $150

SYKES, Charles
English 1875-1950
sculpture: (L) $1,650; (H) $4,950

SYKORA, G.
paintings: (H) $3,300

SYLVAIN
Haitian 20th cent.
paintings: (H) $1,430

SYLVESTER, Frederick Oakes
American 1869-1915
paintings: (L) $330; (H) $9,350
drawings: (H) $495

SYLVESTRE, Joseph Noel
French 1847-1926
paintings: (L) $1,430; (H) $2,090

SYMES, John
American d. 1888
paintings: (H) $1,650

SYMONS, George Gardner
American 1863-1930
paintings: (L) $330; (H) $52,250
drawings: (L) $330; (H) $1,045

SYMONSZ, Jan, Pynas
paintings: (H) $2,530

SYNAVE, Tancrede
French b. 1880
paintings: (L) $715; (H) $31,900

SYNDER, W.P.
American
drawings: (H) $1,100

SYP, A. van der
paintings: (L) $385; (H) $660

SYTHOFF, G.
Dutch 19th cent.
paintings: (L) $1,650; (H) $3,300

SZABO, L.
Hungarian 20th cent.
paintings: (H) $660

SZAION, J.
sculpture: (H) $2,475

SZALAI, B.
Hungarian 19th cent.
paintings: (H) $693

SZANTHO, Maria
Hungarian b. 1898
paintings: (L) $220; (H) $3,850

SZCZEBLEWSKI, V.
French/Polish 19th cent.
sculpture: (L) $412; (H) $1,540

SZETO, Keung
paintings: (H) $660

SZEWCZENKO, Konstanty
Czechoslovakian b. 1909
paintings: (L) $440; (H) $935

SZIKELY, P.
paintings: (H) $715

SZOLBO, F.
paintings: (H) $1,100

SZTROYNOY, *Jos***
paintings: (H) $9,900

SZUKALSKI, Stanislaus
American
sculpture: (H) $3,300

SZYK, Arthur
Polish/American 1894-1951
drawings: (L) $220; (H) $2,860

SZYKIER, Fiekierz
Polish 19th cent.
paintings: (L) $4,950; (H) $7,150

SZYMANOWSKA, Lozyriska
paintings: (H) $1,100

SZYSZLO, Fernando de
Peruvian b. 1925
paintings: (L) $1,760; (H) $24,200
drawings: (L) $1,210; (H) $8,800

TAAFFE, Philip
American contemporary
paintings: (L) $3,520; (H) $49,500
drawings: (H) $6,600

TAANMAN, Jacob
Dutch 1836-1923
paintings: (H) $1,265

TABAR, Francois Germain Leopold
French 1818-1869
paintings: (H) $1,540

TABER, Isaac Walton
American 1830-1916
paintings: (H) $1,760
drawings: (L) $66; (H) $3,300

TABRIZI, S.
paintings: (H) $1,540

TACCA, Pietro, workshop of
first third of 17th cent.
sculpture: (H) $88,000

TACK, Augustus Vincent
American 1870-1949
paintings: (L) $330; (H) $220,000

TADDEO DI BARTOLO
Italian c. 1363-1422
paintings: (H) $126,500

TADOLINI, Giulio
Italian 1849-1918
sculpture: (L) $14,300; (H) $26,400

TAES
paintings: (H) $1,050

TAEUBER-ARP, Sophie
Swiss 1889-1943
paintings: (H) $30,800
drawings: (L) $7,150; (H) $19,800

TAFURI, Clemente
Italian 1903-1971
paintings: (H) $5,775

TAGGART, George Henry
American b. 1865
paintings: (L) $357; (H) $990

TAGGART, Lucy M.
American b. 19th cent.
paintings: (H) $1,430

TAGGIONI, Ch.
sculpture: (H) $1,650

TAHOMA, Quincy
American 1921-1956
paintings: (L) $715; (H) $1,100

TAIT, A.F.
paintings: (H) $2,200

TAIT, Agnes
American b. 1897
paintings: (H) $880
drawings: (H) $302

TAIT, Arthur Fitzwilliam
American 1819-1905
paintings: (L) $660; (H) $418,000
drawings: (L) $990; (H) $1,870

TAIT, John Robinson
American 1834-1909
paintings: (H) $935

TAITE, A.S.
American
paintings: (H) $41,800

TAKESHIRO, Kanokogi
Japanese 1874-1941
drawings: (H) $12,100

TAKIS, Nicholas
American 1903-1965
paintings: (L) $330; (H) $440
sculpture: (H) $2,750

TAKIS, Vassilakis
sculpture: (H) $7,920

TAL-COAT, Pierre
French b. 1905
paintings: (H) $8,250

TALAS
Austrian
sculpture: (H) $1,100

TALBOT, Grace Helen
American
sculpture: (H) $3,520

TALBOT, Henry S.
American 19th cent.
paintings: (H) $1,430

TALBOT, Jesse
American 1806-1879
paintings: (L) $220; (H) $6,600

TALBOT, Thomas
paintings: (H) $770

TALBOT, Tom
American contemporary
paintings: (H) $2,400

TALCOTT, Sarah Whiting
paintings: (L) $275; (H) $1,540

TALENGHI, Enrico
Italian b. 1848
drawings: (H) $2,200

TALLANT, Richard H.
American 1853-1934
paintings: (L) $1,430; (H) $1,760

TALLONE, Guido
paintings: (L) $1,100; (H) $1,210

TALMAGE, Algernon
English 1871-1939
paintings: (L) $715; (H) $16,500

TAM, Reuben
American b. 1916
paintings: (L) $660; (H) $2,090

TAMARIZ, Eduardo
Mexican contemporary
paintings: (L) $935; (H) $1,540

TAMAYO, Rufino
Mexican b. 1899
paintings: (L) $3,575; (H) $770,000
drawings: (L) $357; (H) $77,000

TAMBURINI, A.
20th cent.
paintings: (L) $55; (H) $770

TAMBURINI, Arnaldo
Italian b. 1843
paintings: (L) $357; (H) $5,500
drawings: (L) $605; (H) $660

TAMLIN, John
British 19th cent.
paintings: (H) $1,320

TAMM, Frans Werner von
German 1658-1724
paintings: (H) $29,700

TANAKA
paintings: (H) $1,320

TANAKA, Akira
Japanese b. 1918
paintings: (L) $3,575; (H) $6,325

TANAKA, Yasushi
Japanese 20th cent.
paintings: (H) $3,575

TANCREDI, Raffaello
paintings: (H) $2,310

TANGUY, Yves
French/American 1900-1955
paintings: (L) $143,000; (H) $506,000
drawings: (L) $1,155; (H) $209,000

TANHOLM, William
British or Amer. 19th cent.
paintings: (H) $2,000

TANKA, N.W.
American
paintings: (H) $715

TANNER, Henry Ossawa
American 1859-1937
paintings: (L) $2,475; (H) $27,500
drawings: (H) $1,980

TANNER, O.
paintings: (L) $550; (H) $1,650

TANNERT, Volker
contemporary
drawings: (H) $3,300

TANNING, Dorothea
American b. 1912
paintings: (L) $22,000; (H) $33,000

TANOUX, Adrien Henri
French 1865-1923
paintings: (L) $1,430; (H) $7,700

TANZELLA, B.
paintings: (H) $1,650

TANZI, Leon Louis Antoine
French 1846-1913
paintings: (H) $4,730

TAPIES, Antoni
Spanish b. 1923
paintings: (L) $46,200; (H) $165,000
drawings: (L) $3,740; (H) $176,000
sculpture: (H) $46,200

TAPIRO Y BARO, Jose
Spanish 1830-1913
drawings: (L) $2,200; (H) $9,350

TAPPAN, Roger
American 19th/20th cent.
drawings: (H) $4,950

TAPPERT, Georg
German 1880-1957
paintings: (L) $110,000; (H) $638,000

TARAVAL, Guillaume Thomas
Raphael
French 1701-1750
paintings: (H) $38,500

TARAVAL, Hugues
French 1728/29-1785
paintings: (H) $7,700
drawings: (H) $2,420

TARBELL, Edmund Charles
American 1862-1938
paintings: (L) $1,540; (H) $412,500
drawings: (L) $400; (H) $4,620

TARENGHI, Enrico
Italian b. 1848
paintings: (L) $1,650; (H) $3,300
drawings: (L) $1,045; (H) $4,180

TARENNE, Roger
paintings: (L) $357; (H) $715

TARENTE, G.
sculpture: (H) $880

TARNOWSKI, Michael de
sculpture: (H) $825

TASHA, Carl
American 20th cent.
sculpture: (H) $660

TASKER, William
English 1808-1852
paintings: (H) $33,000

TASLEY, Matthew
drawings: (H) $1,100

TASSAERT, Octave
French 1800-1874
paintings: (L) $605; (H) $2,310
drawings: (H) $990

TATE, A.F.
paintings: (H) $3,575

TATE, Gayle B.
American b. 1944
paintings: (L) $1,760; (H) $3,740

TAUBERT, Bertoldo
French b. 1915
paintings: (H) $770

TAUBES, Frederick
American 1900-1981
paintings: (L) $50; (H) $3,740
drawings: (L) $220; (H) $495

TAUBMAN, Frank Mowbray
English b. 1868
paintings: (H) $1,155
sculpture: (H) $14,850

TAUNAY, Nicolas Antoine
French 1755-1830
paintings: (L) $6,600; (H) $74,800

TAUPENOT, Mademoiselle
French 19th/20th cent.
paintings: (H) $3,300

TAVELLA, Carlo Antonio, called Il
Solfarola
Italian 1668-1738
paintings: (L) $10,450; (H) $19,800

TAVERNIER, Jules
French/American 1844-1889/99
paintings: (L) $1,210; (H) $66,000

TAVERNIER, Paul
French b. 1852
paintings: (L) $990; (H) $22,000

TAYLER, Albert Chevallier
British 1862-1925
paintings: (L) $330; (H) $22,000

TAYLER, D.
paintings: (H) $2,090

TAYLER, Minna
paintings: (H) $4,400

TAYLOR
paintings: (L) $660; (H) $715

TAYLOR, C.
English 19th cent.
paintings: (H) $1,045

TAYLOR, C.B.
American early 20th cent.
paintings: (H) $2,750

TAYLOR, Charles, Jr.
British 19th cent.
drawings: (L) $550; (H) $1,430

TAYLOR, D.
paintings: (L) $577; (H) $1,155

TAYLOR, Edward R.
British 1838-1911
paintings: (H) $8,800

TAYLOR, Francis
paintings: (H) $990

TAYLOR, Frank Walter
American b. 1874
paintings: (L) $220; (H) $880

TAYLOR, G.J.
American
paintings: (H) $1,430

TAYLOR, Gage
contemporary
paintings: (H) $770

TAYLOR, J.
paintings: (H) $770

TAYLOR, J.
British 19th cent.
paintings: (H) $4,125
drawings: (H) $3,575

TAYLOR, James
American 20th cent.
paintings: (H) $1,540

TAYLOR, James E.
drawings: (H) $1,760

TAYLOR, John, of Bath
1735-1806
paintings: (H) $5,500

TAYLOR, John D.
English 19th cent.
paintings: (H) $770

TAYLOR, Leonard Campbell
British 1874-1969
paintings: (H) $16,200

TAYLOR, Marie
American b. 1904
sculpture: (H) $2,200

TAYLOR, Ralph
American b. 1896
paintings: (L) $880; (H) $11,000

TAYLOR, Rolla S.
American b. 1874
paintings: (L) $440; (H) $1,155

TAYLOR, William Francis
paintings: (H) $715

TCHELITCHEW, Pavel
Russian/American 1898-1957
paintings: (L) $770; (H) $19,800
drawings: (L) $440; (H) $34,100

TCHERIKOVA, Ludmilla
contemporary
drawings: (H) $1,100

TEAGUE, Donald
American b. 1897
paintings: (H) $7,150
drawings: (L) $88; (H) $27,500

TEAL, Raymond
American 20th cent.
drawings: (H) $825

TEBARIN, A.
paintings: (H) $1,430

TECHOUYERES, C.
sculpture: (H) $5,500

TEED, Douglas Arthur
American 1864-1929
paintings: (L) $440; (H) $3,300

TEEL, Lewis Woods
American b. 1883
paintings: (L) $242; (H) $935

TEERLINK, Abraham
Dutch 1776-1857
paintings: (H) $5,500

TEESDALE, K.
English 19th cent.
paintings: (H) $715

TEGNER, Rudolf Christopher Puggard
Danish b. 1873
sculpture: (H) $9,350

TEIGEN, Peter
American 20th cent.
drawings: (H) $1,650

TELARICK, A.
paintings: (H) $660

TELES, Jose Jeronimo, Jr.
paintings: (H) $13,750

TELLANDER, Frederic A.
American b. 1878
paintings: (L) $825; (H) $935

TELSER, A.
Continental 19th/20th cent.
paintings: (H) $1,430

TELSIC, A.
Scandinavian 19th/20th cent.
paintings: (H) $2,200

TELTSCHER, Joseph Eduard
1807-1837
paintings: (H) $2,420

TELVATICO, Lino
paintings: (H) $1,650

TEMI
paintings: (H) $1,100

TEMMINCK, H.C.
Dutch 1813-1886
paintings: (H) $1,650

TEMMINCK, Leonard
Dutch 1753-1813
paintings: (H) $1,100

TEMPEST, Cyril
British 19th/20th cent.
paintings: (L) $990; (H) $1,540

TEMPESTA, Antonio
Italian 1555-1630
drawings: (L) $385; (H) $2,640

TEMPLE, Hans
Austrian 1857-1931
paintings: (L) $3,850; (H) $6,600

TEMPLE, Ruth Anderson
1884-1939
paintings: (L) $357; (H) $6,000

TEN HOVEN, Hendrik
Dutch 19th/20th cent.
paintings: (L) $192; (H) $2,750

TEN KATE, Hendrik Gerrit
Dutch 1803-1856
drawings: (L) $385; (H) $990

TEN KATE, Herman
Dutch 1822-1891
paintings: (L) $357; (H) $17,600
drawings: (H) $2,750

TEN KATE, Johan Marie Henri
Dutch 1831-1910
paintings: (L) $3,000; (H) $38,500
drawings: (L) $770; (H) $3,500

TENCY, Jean Baptiste
paintings: (H) $9,350

TENGGREN, Gustaf
Swedish/American 1896-1970
drawings: (L) $275; (H) $4,950

TENIERS, David, the younger
Flemish 1610-1690
paintings: (L) $5,225; (H) $572,000

TENIERS, David, the younger after
Domenico Feti
Flemish 1610-1690
paintings: (H) $55,000

TENNANT, John T.
British 1796-1872
paintings: (H) $7,150

TENOT, Charles
French 19th cent.
paintings: (H) $3,850

TENRE, Charles Henry
French 1864-1926
paintings: (L) $1,100; (H) $9,460
drawings: (H) $1,045

TEPPER, Saul
American 1899-1987
paintings: (L) $660; (H) $5,170

TER BORCH, Gerard
Dutch 1617-1681
paintings: (L) $13,200; (H) $478,500

TER BORCH, Gerard, studio of
paintings: (H) $7,150

TER MEULEN, Frans Pieter
Dutch 1843-1927
paintings: (L) $825; (H) $4,840

TERAOKA, Masami
contemporary
drawings: (L) $2,750; (H) $4,125

TERECHKOVITCH, Konstantin,
Kostia
Russian/French b. 1902
paintings: (L) $4,125; (H) $79,200
drawings: (L) $2,420; (H) $8,250

TERESCZUK, Peter
European 19th/20th cent.
sculpture: (L) $137; (H) $2,860

TERESZCZUK, F.
Austrian 19th/20th cent.
sculpture: (H) $2,530

TERKLIKOWSKI, Vladimir de
Polish 1873-1951
paintings: (H) $1,375

TERMAHLEN, Karl E.
American b. 1863
paintings: (L) $22; (H) $660

TERNEU, Alb.
paintings: (H) $825

TERPNING, Howard
American b. 1927
paintings: (L) $12,500; (H) $138,600

TERRELL, Allen Townsend
American
paintings: (H) $1,100

TERUZ, Orlando
paintings: (H) $26,400

TESAR, Joseph
American 19th/20th cent.
paintings: (H) $660

TESCHENDORFF, Emil
German 1833-1894
paintings: (H) $6,600

TESSARI, Vittorio
Italian b. 1860
paintings: (L) $143; (H) $660
drawings: (L) $192; (H) $495

TESSIER, Louis Adolphe
French 19th cent.
paintings: (H) $6,600

TESSON, Louis
French b. 19th cent.
paintings: (H) $4,950
drawings: (H) $352

TESTA, Pietro
Italian 1611-1650
drawings: (L) $5,500; (H) $29,700

TESTI, L.
Italian 19th cent.
paintings: (H) $1,760

TESTU, Paul
French 19th/20th cent.
paintings: (L) $467; (H) $4,180

TETAR VAN ELVEN
Dutch 19th/20th cent.
paintings: (H) $1,650

TETAR VAN ELVEN, Jan Baptiste
Dutch 1805-1879
paintings: (H) $1,430

TETAR VAN ELVEN, Pierre
Dutch 1831-1908
paintings: (L) $3,575; (H) $49,500

TEUBER, Hermann
paintings: (H) $2,640

TEWI, Thea
American 20th cent.
sculpture: (H) $1,210

TEYRAL, Hazel Janecki
American b. 1918
paintings: (L) $165; (H) $715

THALINGER, E. Oscar
American b. 1885
paintings: (L) $55; (H) $1,100

THARRATS
Spanish 20th cent.
paintings: (H) $1,100

THAULOW, Frits
Norwegian 1847-1906
paintings: (L) $15,400; (H) $126,500
drawings: (H) $3,150

THAXTER, Edward R.
American 1857-1881
sculpture: (L) $4,400; (H) $4,400

THAYER, Abbott Handerson
American 1849-1921
paintings: (L) $605; (H) $39,600
drawings: (L) $2,200; (H) $3,575

THAYER, Albert R.
American 19th/20th cent.
paintings: (L) $715; (H) $1,210

THAYER, Karen
American
paintings: (L) $1,700; (H) $2,100

BEARDSLEY LIMNER, Sarah Perkins
American late 18th cent.
drawings: (H) $5,775

THEBAULT, ***
Austrian (?) 19th cent.
paintings: (H) $2,530

THEER, Robert
1808-1863
paintings: (H) $2,420

THEK, Paul
contemporary
sculpture: (L) $440; (H) $8,800

THEMMEN, C.
German 19th cent.
paintings: (L) $1,750; (H) $3,000

THEMMEN, Charles
American 19th cent.
paintings: (L) $550; (H) $1,650

THENARD
French late 19th cent.
sculpture: (H) $660

THEOBALD, Samuel, Jr.
American b. 1872
paintings: (L) $350; (H) $1,320

THEODOR
German 19th cent.
paintings: (H) $3,960

THERKILDSEN, Michael
Danish 1850-1925
paintings: (H) $6,600

THERRIEN, Robert
contemporary
paintings: (L) $7,700; (H) $30,800

THEUS, Jeremiah
American c. 1716-1774
paintings: (L) $17,600; (H) $24,200

THEVENER, Louis
Belgian 1874-1930
paintings: (H) $990

THIBAULT, Jean Thomas
French 1757-1826
drawings: (H) $3,520

THIBON, Jean Maurice
French 19th cent.
paintings: (L) $275; (H) $2,750

THIEBAUD, Wayne
American b. 1920
paintings: (L) $17,600; (H) $605,000
drawings: (L) $2,420; (H) $143,000

THIEBAULT, Henri Leon
French b. 1855
paintings: (H) $5,500

THIEBLIN, Reine Josephine
French 19th cent.
paintings: (L) $3,575; (H) $7,700

THIECK, Arthur
paintings: (H) $990

THIELEMANN, A.
Continental 19th cent.
paintings: (H) $1,760

THIELEN, Jan Philips van
Flemish 1618-1667
paintings: (H) $110,000

THIEME, Anthony
Dutch/American 1888-1954
paintings: (L) $192; (H) $36,300
drawings: (L) $412; (H) $2,475

THIEME, Carl
German 1816-1884
paintings: (H) $1,320

THIER, Barend Hendrik
paintings: (H) $880

THIERRENS, Jacques Favre de
contemporary
paintings: (H) $2,200

THIERRIAT, Augustin Alexandre
French 1789-1870
drawings: (H) $1,760

THIESE, A.
American School 19th cent.
paintings: (L) $750; (H) $3,000

THIEVAERT, Daniel Jansz
Dutch c. 1613-1658
paintings: (H) $110,000

THIL, Jeanne
French b. 1887
paintings: (H) $1,320

THILLMANY
sculpture: (H) $1,980

THIREL, V.
German 19th cent.
paintings: (H) $1,100

THIRION, Charles Victor
French 1833-1878
paintings: (L) $5,500; (H) $19,800

THIRONET, Mathieu
paintings: (H) $4,400

THIVIER, Simeon Eugene
ac. 2nd half 19th cent.
sculpture: (H) $660

THOM, James Crawford
American 1838/42-1898
paintings: (L) $357; (H) $3,520
drawings: (L) $275; (H) $2,420

THOMA, Hans
German 1839-1924
paintings: (L) $1,320; (H) $19,800
drawings: (H) $2,200

THOMA, Josef
Austrian 1828-1899
paintings: (L) $1,210; (H) $4,675

THOMA, Josef
Austrian b. 1800
paintings: (H) $1,760

THOMA-HOFELE, Karl
paintings: (H) $8,800

THOMAS, Bernard P.
paintings: (L) $99; (H) $825

THOMAS, Charles
American 19th cent.
paintings: (H) $935

THOMAS, G.
English 19th cent.
paintings: (H) $1,265

THOMAS, Grosvenor
British 1856-1923
paintings: (H) $660

THOMAS, Lloyd H.
paintings: (H) $2,090

THOMAS, M.
European 20th cent.
paintings: (H) $990

THOMAS, P***
sculpture: (H) $1,650

THOMAS, P.
British 19th cent.
paintings: (H) $880

THOMAS, Pat, Lucille
American 1918-1985
paintings: (L) $550; (H) $715

THOMAS, Paul Kirk Middlebrook
American b. 1875
paintings: (H) $413
sculpture: (H) $1,320

THOMAS, Stephen Seymour
American 1868-1956
paintings: (L) $165; (H) $11,000
drawings: (L) $55; (H) $935

THOMASON, John
American 1893-1944
paintings: (H) $1,540

THOMASSE, Adolphe
French 1850-1930
paintings: (H) $1,980

THOMASSIN, Desire
German 1858-1933
paintings: (L) $660; (H) $7,700

THOMON, Thomas de
drawings: (H) $1,870

THOMPKINS, Frank Hector
American 1847-1922
paintings: (H) $2,530

THOMPSON, Albert
American b. 1853
paintings: (L) $176; (H) $2,200

THOMPSON, Alfred
paintings: (H) $3,850

THOMPSON, Alfred Wordsworth
American 1840-1896
paintings: (L) $275; (H) $44,000

THOMPSON, Arthur
American 19th cent.
paintings: (H) $3,960

THOMPSON, Bob
American 1937-1966
paintings: (L) $3,520; (H) $17,600

THOMPSON, C.A.
American 19th cent.
paintings: (L) $2,200; (H) $3,850

THOMPSON, C.L.
American 19th cent.
paintings: (H) $660

THOMPSON, Cephas Giovanni
American 1809-1888
paintings: (L) $165; (H) $4,950

THOMPSON, Frederick Louis
American b. 1868
paintings: (L) $192; (H) $5,000

THOMPSON, George Albert
American 1868-1938
paintings: (L) $150; (H) $5,225

THOMPSON, Guy H.
American 19th/20th cent.
paintings: (L) $55; (H) $880

THOMPSON, Harry
British d. 1901
paintings: (H) $2,200

THOMPSON, Harry Ives
American 1840-1906
paintings: (H) $1,375

THOMPSON, Henry
paintings: (H) $14,300

THOMPSON, J. Leslie
Continental 19th/20th cent.
paintings: (H) $2,200

THOMPSON, J.C.
American
paintings: (H) $1,320

THOMPSON, Jacob
paintings: (H) $1,100

THOMPSON, Jerome
American 1814-1886
paintings: (L) $248; (H) $22,000

THOMPSON, John Murray
paintings: (H) $1,320

THOMPSON, John S.
British 19th/20th cent.
paintings: (H) $880

THOMPSON, Leslie Prince
American 1880-1963
paintings: (L) $467; (H) $26,400

THOMPSON, Terry
drawings: (H) $2,090

THOMPSON, Y.
paintings: (H) $770

THOMSEN, August Karl Vilhelm
Danish 1813-1886
paintings: (H) $3,410

THOMSON, Carl Christian Frederik
Jakob
Danish 1847-1912
paintings: (L) $2,970; (H) $15,400

THOMSON, George
paintings: (H) $2,750

THOMSON, Henry Grinnell
American 1850-1939
paintings: (L) $715; (H) $27,500

THOMSON, Hugh
British 1860-1920
drawings: (L) $330; (H) $1,650

THOMSON, John Murray
British 19th/20th cent.
paintings: (H) $6,600

THOMSON, Tom
Canadian 1877-1917
paintings: (L) $3,740; (H) $176,000

THOMSON, W. Taylor
drawings: (H) $770

THONY, Eduard
American
drawings: (L) $605; (H) $1,430

THORBURN, Archibald
Scottish 1860-1935
paintings: (H) $385
drawings: (L) $660; (H) $47,300

THOREN, Karl Kasimir Otto von
Austrian 1828-1889
paintings: (L) $550; (H) $4,400

THORENFELD, Anton Erik Christian
Danish 1839-1907
paintings: (H) $17,600

THORNAM, Emmy Marie Caroline
Danish 1852-1935
paintings: (H) $1,300

THORNE, Alfred
paintings: (H) $770

THORNE, Diana
American b. 1895
paintings: (L) $165; (H) $1,430

THORNE, Joan
contemporary
paintings: (L) $880; (H) $4,125

THORNELEY, J.
British 19th cent.
paintings: (H) $1,000

THORNELY, Charles
paintings: (L) $2,200; (H) $3,300

THORNLEY, G.W.
paintings: (H) $1,100

THORNLEY, J.W.
British 19th cent.
paintings: (H) $5,225

THORNLEY, L.
German b. 1800
paintings: (H) $880

THORNLEY, William
British 19th/20th cent.
paintings: (L) $1,210; (H) $4,125

THORNLEY, William
French b. 1857
paintings: (H) $1,210

THORNTON, R.
English 20th cent.
drawings: (H) $715

THORS, James
English 19th cent.
paintings: (H) $1,100

THORS, Joseph
English exhib. 1883-1898
paintings: (L) $495; (H) $9,350

THORTON, Thomas H.
Continental 19th/20th cent.
paintings: (H) $825

THORVALD, H.
Norwegian 19th cent.
paintings: (H) $1,320

THORVALDSEN, Bertel
Danish 1768-1844
drawings: (H) $9,350
sculpture: (L) $14,300; (H) $275,000

THRASH, Dox
American 1892-1965
paintings: (L) $77; (H) $385
drawings: (L) $77; (H) $742

THRASHER, Leslie
American 1889-1936
paintings: (L) $302; (H) $3,600

THROOP, Frances Hunt
American 19th cent.
paintings: (L) $440; (H) $660

THULDEN, Theodor van
Dutch 1606-1669
paintings: (H) $49,500

THULSTRUP, Thure de
American 1848-1930
paintings: (L) $550; (H) $1,540
drawings: (L) $220; (H) $1,980

THURBER, James
American 1894-1961
drawings: (L) $1,320; (H) $3,300

THYLSTRUP, Georg
sculpture: (H) $3,520

THYS, Pieter
paintings: (H) $16,500

THYSEN, C.J.
Dutch b. 1867
paintings: (L) $1,320; (H) $1,980

TIARINI, Alessandro
Italian 1577-1668
drawings: (H) $55,000

TICE, M.E.
American School 19th cent.
paintings: (H) $660

TICHY, Dalibor
contemporary
sculpture: (H) $1,100

TIDDLE, Walter
American 1883-1966
paintings: (L) $440; (H) $1,650

TIDEMAND, Adolf
Norwegian 1814-1876
paintings: (H) $121,000

TIDEY, Henry F.
drawings: (L) $176; (H) $3,630

TIEDEMAN, Theodor
paintings: (H) $2,200

TIELE, Hans
Austrian b. 1850
paintings: (H) $660

TIELEMANS, Lodewyk
Belgian 1826-1856
paintings: (H) $3,575

TIELENS, Alexandre
Belgian 1868-1959
paintings: (L) $1,210; (H) $3,850

TIEPOLO, Giovanni Battista
Italian 1696-1770
paintings: (H) $82,500
drawings: (L) $2,475; (H) $126,500

TIEPOLO, Giovanni Domenico
Italian 1727-1804
drawings: (L) $2,200; (H) $159,500

TIEPOLO, Lorenzo
drawings: (H) $6,050

TIFFANY, Louis Comfort
American 1848-1933
paintings: (L) $1,100; (H) $15,400
drawings: (L) $550; (H) $4,675

TIGER, Jerome Richard
American 1941-1967
paintings: (H) $1,760

TILBORCH, Gillis van, the younger
Flemish c.1625-c.1678
paintings: (L) $5,500; (H) $110,000

TILCHE, H.O.
19th cent.
drawings: (H) $990

TILGNER, A.
paintings: (H) $1,980

TILGNER, E.
paintings: (H) $1,100

TILGNER, F.
paintings: (L) $385; (H) $1,100

TILGNER, Victor Oskar
sculpture: (H) $1,320

TILL, Leopold
Austrian 1830-1893
paintings: (H) $7,150

TILLEMANS, P.J.
Flemish 17th century
paintings: (H) $1,980

TILMANS, Simon Peter
paintings: (H) $2,750

TILTON, J. Rollin
American 1828-1888
paintings: (H) $3,300
drawings: (H) $137

TILYARD, Philip
American 1785-1830
paintings: (H) $24,200

TIMLIN, W.B.
American
paintings: (H) $880

TIMMERMANS, Louis
French 1846-1910
paintings: (L) $1,430; (H) $1,980
drawings: (L) $302; (H) $825

TIMMONS, Edward J. Finley
American b. 1882
paintings: (L) $132; (H) $880

TIMOCK, George
contemporary
sculpture: (H) $1,100

TINDELL, Benjamin
English ac. 1846-1889
paintings: (L) $2,000; (H) $3,960

TINELLI, Tiberio
paintings: (H) $1,100

TING, Nam
Chinese mid 19th cent.
paintings: (H) $1,000

TING, Walasse
contemporary
paintings: (L) $605; (H) $10,120

TINGKUN, Xu
19th cent.
drawings: (H) $6,875

TINGUELY, Jean
Swiss b. 1925
drawings: (L) $1,320; (H) $4,180
sculpture: (L) $5,500; (H) $198,000

TINTORETTO, Jacopo ROBUSTI
Italian 1518/19-1594
paintings: (L) $44,000; (H) $99,000
drawings: (H) $25,300

TINTORETTO, Domenico Robusti
Italian 1560-1635
paintings: (L) $2,860; (H) $35,200
drawings: (H) $11,000

TIRATELLI, Arturo
paintings: (H) $660

TIRATELLI, Aurelio
Italian 1842-1900
paintings: (L) $6,600; (H) $29,700
drawings: (H) $8,800

TIRATELLI, Cesare
Italian b. 1864
paintings: (H) $26,400

TIRINNANZI, Nino
contemporary
paintings: (L) $550; (H) $1,100

TIRONI, Francesco
Italian 18th/19th cent.
paintings: (L) $27,500; (H) $60,500

TIRRELL, George A.
American 19th/20th cent.
paintings: (L) $247; (H) $2,200

TISCHBEIN, Johann Heinrich,
the elder
German 1722-1789
paintings: (H) $7,975

TISIO, Benvenuto, called Il Garofalo
Italian 1481-1559
paintings: (L) $15,400; (H) $126,500

TISSOT, James Jacques Joseph
French 1836-1902
paintings: (L) $4,950; (H) $1,375,000
drawings: (L) $5,775; (H) $1,100,000

TITCOMB, Mary Bradish
American 1856-1927
paintings: (L) $7,700; (H) $33,000
drawings: (L) $550; (H) $1,870

TITCOMB, William H.
American 1824-1888
paintings: (L) $2,310; (H) $2,310

TITI, Tiberio
Italian 1573-1627
paintings: (H) $18,700

TITIAN, Tiziano Vecellio
Italian c. 1488-1576
paintings: (H) $2,640,000

TITIAN, studio of
Italian 16th cent.
paintings: (L) $9,350; (H) $44,000

TITIAN, workshop of
paintings: (H) $7,700

TITLE, Christian
American 20th cent.
paintings: (L) $3,080; (H) $3,300

TITO, Santi di
Italian 1536-1603
paintings: (L) $45,100; (H) $187,000

TITO, Santi di, studio of
paintings: (H) $15,400

TITTLE, Walter
American 1880/83-1960
paintings: (L) $165; (H) $2,200
drawings: (L) $121; (H) $385

TITUS, Enoch A.
American
drawings: (H) $2,640

TITZE, A.
sculpture: (L) $165; (H) $1,100

TIVOLI, Rosa da
paintings: (H) $3,520

TIZARD, K.
French
sculpture: (H) $770

TNLAY
paintings: (H) $660

TOBAR, Alonso Miguel de
1678-1758
paintings: (H) $3,850

TOBEY, Mark
American 1890-1976
paintings: (L) $770; (H) $68,750
drawings: (L) $440; (H) $55,000

TOBIASSE, Theo
Israeli/French b. 1927
paintings: (L) $2,090; (H) $41,800
drawings: (L) $632; (H) $13,200

TOBIN, R.
paintings: (H) $880

TOBUENA, Romeo V.
Mexican 20th cent.
paintings: (H) $770

TOCQUE, Louis
French 1696-1772
paintings: (L) $20,900; (H) $44,000

TODD, G.
drawings: (H) $1,320

TODD, Henry George
British 1847-1898
paintings: (L) $660; (H) $8,800

TODHUNTER, Francis
American 1884-1963
paintings: (L) $550; (H) $4,400
drawings: (L) $467; (H) $1,540

TODT, Max
paintings: (L) $1,100; (H) $5,280

TOECHE, Carl Johann Friedrich
German 1814-1890
paintings: (H) $2,420

TOEPP, Wayne
paintings: (H) $880

TOEPUT, Lodewijk, Il Pozzoserrato
drawings: (L) $935; (H) $2,970

TOESCHI, G.
Continental 19th/20th cent.
paintings: (H) $3,300

TOESCHI, G.
Italian 19th cent.
paintings: (H) $7,700

TOFANELLI, Agostino
drawings: (H) $1,650

National Museum of Women in the Arts

The National Museum of Women in the Arts was founded in Washington, D.C., in 1981 and now occupies a site in a restored Masonic temple two blocks east of the White House. The nucleus of the collection is the five hundred paintings by women artists donated by Wallace and Wilhelmina Holiday. The museum houses the single most important collection of art by women in the world; its library has information on more than twelve thousand women artists of all periods and countries. The museum also mounts exhibitions of contemporary women artists. Its opening exhibition in 1987 was "American Women Artists, 1830-1930" and featured more than seventy-five artists, many of whom had been honored in their day but since forgotten. The exhibitions have spurred renewed interest in their works.

Mary Bradish Titcomb (1858-1927) was among the women artists featured in the opening exhibition. Born in New Hampshire, she taught drawing in the Brockton, Massachusetts, public schools. At forty, she entered the School of the Museum of Fine Arts, Boston, and studied under Edmund Tarbell and Frank W. Benson. She also traveled to France, Spain, Italy, and England and studied under Jules Joseph Lefebvre in Paris in the early 1890s. When she returned to Boston, she rented a studio adjoining Tarbell's. In the summers she traveled and painted landscapes; during the winter she painted interior scenes in her studio. The highlight of her career occurred when President Woodrow Wilson purchased her portrait of *Geraldine J* in 1915. (Many years later actress Jane Russell identified Geraldine J. as her mother.) During her lifetime Titcomb exhibited widely and received many awards. (Mary Bradish Titcomb, *Landscape with Figures, Fort Park (?) Gloucester,* oil on canvas, 22 x 27 in., Moran, June 12, 1990, $30,250)

TOFANELLI, Stefano
drawings: (H) $1,210

TOFANO, Eduardo
Italian 1838-1920
drawings: (L) $495; (H) $770

TOFSOERT, P.J.
18th cent.
paintings: (H) $1,210

TOHER, Thomas M.
paintings: (H) $1,650

TOJETTI, Domenico
Italian/American ac. 1871-1892
paintings: (L) $770; (H) $16,500

TOJETTI, Eduardo
Italian/American 1852-1930
paintings: (L) $99; (H) $2,200

TOJETTI, Virgilio
Italian/American 1849-1901
paintings: (L) $660; (H) $14,300

TOL, Dominicus van
Dutch c. 1635-1676
paintings: (L) $1,430; (H) $17,600

TOLEDO, Francisco
Mexican b. 1940
paintings: (L) $6,050; (H) $308,000
drawings: (L) $440; (H) $57,750

TOLEGIAN, Manuel J.
paintings: (H) $4,125

TOLENTINO, Nikolo
paintings: (H) $1,320

TOLGYESSY, Artur
Hungarian 1823-1920
paintings: (H) $1,650

TOLLEY, Edward
British ac. 1848-1867
paintings: (L) $3,190; (H) $11,000

TOLLIVER, Mose
American c. 1919
paintings: (H) $2,640

TOLMAN, Ruel Pardee
American b. 1878
paintings: (L) $44; (H) $1,430

TOLMAN, Stacy
American 1860-1935
paintings: (L) $275; (H) $770
drawings: (L) $39; (H) $935

TOLSON, Edgar
American 1904-1984/86
sculpture: (L) $1,980; (H) $10,450

TOM, Jan Bedys
Dutch 1813-1894
drawings: (H) $825

TOM OF FINLAND
drawings: (L) $2,200; (H) $4,400

TOMA, Giovacchino
Italian 1836/38-1891
paintings: (H) $30,800

TOMAN, Leigh S.
American 19th/20th cent.
paintings: (H) $3,850

TOMANEK, Joseph
American b. Czechoslovakia 1889
paintings: (L) $247; (H) $1,650

TOMANEK, Joseph
French 1824-1898
paintings: (L) $242; (H) $962

TOMASO, Rico
American 1898-1985
paintings: (L) $220; (H) $3,000

TOMBA, Casimiro
Italian 1857-1929
drawings: (L) $2,200; (H) $2,860

TOMBROS, Michael
sculpture: (H) $1,100

TOMINETTI, A.
paintings: (H) $1,045

TOMINZ, Alfredo
Italian 1854-1936
paintings: (L) $7,150; (H) $8,800

TOMIOKA, Saichiko
Japanese 20th cent.
paintings: (H) $1,100

TOMLIN, Bradley Walker
American 1899-1953
paintings: (L) $3,300; (H) $572,000
drawings: (L) $132; (H) $825

TOMLINSON, Lorena
American first quarter 19th cent.
drawings: (H) $6,600

TOMLINSON, R.
paintings: (H) $3,080

TOMMACK, Jacob
  paintings: (H) $1,430

TOMMASI, Ludovico
  Italian 1866-1941
  paintings: (H) $2,200

TOMMASI, Publio de
  Italian b. 1849
  drawings: (L) $110; (H) $3,300

TOMMASO
  late 15th cent.
  paintings: (H) $7,700

TOMPKINS, Francis
  American
  paintings: (H) $1,540

TOMPKINS, Frank Hector
  American 1847-1922
  paintings: (L) $165; (H) $16,500
  drawings: (H) $990

TOMSON, Clifton
  English 1775-1835
  paintings: (L) $3,850; (H) $7,150

TONCHERY
  sculpture: (H) $1,045

TONGE, Louis Lammert Leire van der
  Dutch 1871-1937
  paintings: (L) $1,045; (H) $4,675
  drawings: (H) $770

TONGEREN, Herk van
  American b. 1943
  sculpture: (H) $1,430

TONGIANI, V.
  Continental/Amer. 19th/20th cent.
  paintings: (H) $2,200

TONK, Ernest
  American b. 1889
  paintings: (L) $2,750; (H) $4,290

TONSBERG, Gertrude Martin
  American 1902-1973
  paintings: (L) $121; (H) $3,575

TOOK, William
  drawings: (H) $1,870

TOOKER, George
  American b. 1920
  paintings: (L) $28,600; (H) $396,000
  drawings: (H) $20,900

TOORENVLIET, Jacob
  paintings: (L) $8,800; (H) $14,300

TOORNVLIET, Jacob
  Dutch 1635-1719
  paintings: (H) $44,000

TOOROP, Jan
  Dutch 1858-1928
  paintings: (H) $77,000
  drawings: (L) $715; (H) $12,100

TOPHAM, Frank William Warwick
  British 1838-1924
  paintings: (L) $2,530; (H) $19,800

TOPHAM, J.
  English 19th cent.
  paintings: (H) $935

TOPOR, Roland
  drawings: (H) $990

TOPPI, B.
  French School 20th cent.
  paintings: (H) $660

TOPPING, James
  American 1879-1949
  paintings: (L) $550; (H) $1,320
  drawings: (H) $165

TORAL, Tabo
  paintings: (H) $2,750

TORDI, Sinibaldo
  Italian 1876-1955
  paintings: (L) $1,650; (H) $11,000

TORELLI, Jafet
  sculpture: (H) $4,950

TOREY, T.
  paintings: (H) $1,100

TORGERSON, William
  American 19th cent.
  paintings: (H) $22,000

TORI, Giuseppe
  Italian 19th cent.
  paintings: (H) $1,100

TORINI, Pietro
  paintings: (H) $1,100

TORINO, Lombardi
  sculpture: (H) $1,430

TORLAKSON, James
  American b. 1951
  drawings: (L) $880; (H) $2,750

TORO, Atillio
  Italian b. 1892
  paintings: (L) $550; (H) $2,420

TORRALBA MASTER
paintings: (H) $26,400

TORREANO, John
American b. 1941
paintings: (L) $1,100; (H) $6,325
sculpture: (L) $2,200; (H) $6,600

TORRES, Antonio
Spanish 19th cent.
paintings: (L) $880; (H) $1,650

TORRES, Horacio
American 1924-1976
paintings: (L) $13,200; (H) $60,500

TORRES-GARCIA, Joaquin
Uruguayan 1874-1949
paintings: (L) $4,620; (H) $550,000
drawings: (L) $6,600; (H) $22,000

TORREY, Charles
American 1859-1921
paintings: (L) $715; (H) $5,500

TORREY, Elliot
American 1867-1949
paintings: (L) $192; (H) $3,025
drawings: (H) $800

TORREY, Marjorie
American 20th cent.
drawings: (L) $418; (H) $715

TORRICINI, A.
sculpture: (H) $880

TORRIGLIA, Giovanni Battista
Italian 1858-1937
paintings: (L) $7,150; (H) $25,300

TORRINI, E.
Italian 19th cent.
paintings: (L) $1,430; (H) $2,970
drawings: (L) $413; (H) $990

TORRINI, Girolamo
sculpture: (H) $9,350

TORRINI, Pietro
Italian b. 1852
paintings: (H) $12,100
drawings: (H) $495

TORSLEFF, August
Danish 1884-1968
paintings: (H) $4,950

TORTELLI, Giuseppe
drawings: (H) $715

TOSCANI, Giovanni di Francesco
Italian 1370-1430
paintings: (H) $77,000

TOSI, Professor G.
Italian
sculpture: (H) $660

TOSINI, Michele, called Michele di
RIDOLFO
Italian 1503-1577
paintings: (L) $6,930; (H) $16,500

TOSSEY, Verne
American
paintings: (H) $1,250

TOTSUGEN, Tanaka
Japanese 1760-1823
drawings: (H) $7,700

TOUCHE, Gaston de la
French 1854-1913
paintings: (L) $1,100; (H) $1,210

TOUCHEMOLIN
paintings: (H) $1,045

TOUDOUZE, Edouard
French 1848-1907
paintings: (L) $3,300; (H) $24,200
drawings: (H) $3,850

TOULMOUCHE, Auguste
French 1829-1890
paintings: (L) $11,000; (H) $41,800

TOULOUSE-LAUTREC, Henri de
French 1864-1901
paintings: (L) $132,000; (H) $12,980,000
drawings: (L) $1,485; (H) $3,080,000
sculpture: (H) $6,875

TOURGUENEFF, Pierre Nicolas
Russian late 19th/early 20th cent
sculpture: (L) $357; (H) $6,050

TOURNACHON, Gaspard Felix, called
Nadar
drawings: (H) $5,500

TOURNAY, H.
Swiss b. 1890
paintings: (H) $660

TOURNES, Etienne
French 1857-1931
paintings: (H) $1,540

TOURNIER, Nicolas
French 1590-1657
paintings: (L) $33,000; (H) $39,600

TOURNOVA, Natasha
Russian b. 1957
paintings: (H) $2,860

TOURS, Georges Moreau de
French 1848-1901
paintings: (H) $2,970

TOUSER, Henry E.
English 19th cent.
paintings: (H) $770

TOUSSAINT, Fernand
Belgian 1873-1955
paintings: (L) $3,740; (H) $16,500

TOUSSAINT, H.
French 19th cent.
drawings: (H) $660

TOUSSAINT, L.
paintings: (H) $1,045

TOUSSAINT, Louis
German b. 1826
paintings: (H) $990

TOUSSAINT, Pierre, le Chevalier
French b. 1825
paintings: (H) $6,325

TOUSSAINT, Pierre Joseph
paintings: (L) $4,400; (H) $7,700

TOUTENEL, Lodewuk Jan Petrus
Belgian 1819-1883
paintings: (H) $3,300

TOVAR, Ivan
Czechoslovakian 20th cent.
paintings: (L) $825; (H) $9,350

TOVAR Y TOVAR, Martin
Venezuelan 1827-1902
paintings: (L) $5,500; (H) $16,500

TOWNE, Charles
British 1763-1840
paintings: (L) $2,970; (H) $74,250

TOWNE, Charles
English 1781-1854
paintings: (H) $11,000

TOWNSEND, Diane
contemporary
drawings: (H) $5,500

TOWNSEND, Lee
American 1895-1965
paintings: (L) $176; (H) $880
drawings: (H) $605

TOWNSLEY, Channel Pickering
American 1867-1921
paintings: (L) $248; (H) $2,090

TOZZI, Claudio
paintings: (H) $1,100

TOZZINI, P.
paintings: (H) $2,090

TRACY, John M.
American 1844-1893
paintings: (L) $660; (H) $27,500

TRACY, Michael
contemporary
sculpture: (L) $2,640; (H) $5,500

TRACY, R.
paintings: (H) $660

TRACY, Scogin
paintings: (H) $4,400

TRAFELI, M.
sculpture: (H) $1,430

TRAIES, William
English 1789-1872
paintings: (H) $2,200

TRAMKA
European 20th cent.
paintings: (H) $742

TRAQUAIR, Phoebe Anna
paintings: (H) $7,700

TRAULLWEILER
Continental 20th cent.
paintings: (H) $4,180

TRAUTMANN, Johann George
paintings: (H) $3,300

TRAUTTWEILLER
paintings: (L) $550; (H) $660

TRAVER, George A.
American b. 1864
paintings: (L) $330; (H) $2,200
drawings: (L) $231; (H) $495

TRAVER, Marion Gray
American 1892-after 1934
paintings: (L) $715; (H) $935

TRAVERSE, Pierre
French b. 1892
sculpture: (L) $1,430; (H) $4,400

TRAVIS, Paul B.
American b. 1891
paintings: (H) $55
drawings: (L) $27; (H) $825

TRAYER, Jean Baptiste Jules
French 1824-1908/09
paintings: (L) $7,700; (H) $11,000
drawings: (H) $825

TRAYLOR, Bill
American 1854-1947
drawings: (L) $7,700; (H) $17,600

TRAYNER, John C.
American 20th cent.
paintings: (H) $1,430

TREADWELL, Charles A.
1827-1890
paintings: (L) $330; (H) $880

TREBACZ, Maurycy
Polish b. 1861
paintings: (H) $770

TREBILCOCK, Paul
American 1902-1981
paintings: (L) $330; (H) $1,540

TREDUPP, C.
Dutch 19th/20th cent.
paintings: (L) $82; (H) $825

TREFETHEN, Jessie B.
American 20th cent.
paintings: (L) $330; (H) $770

TREFLETH, E.J.
American 19th cent.
paintings: (H) $990

TREGO, William T.
American 1859-1909
paintings: (H) $2,200

TREIMAN, Joyce
American 20th cent.
paintings: (H) $935
drawings: (H) $66
sculpture: (H) $1,870

TRENHOLM, William Carpenter
American 1856-1931
paintings: (L) $825; (H) $11,000

TRENTANOVE, Raimondo
Italian 1792-1832
sculpture: (L) $2,200; (H) $7,480

TRESZCZUK, P.
sculpture: (H) $2,090

TREUX, Van Day
Continental 20th cent.
drawings: (L) $660; (H) $1,430

TREVISANI, Francesco
Italian 1656-1746
paintings: (L) $8,800; (H) $28,600
drawings: (L) $880; (H) $1,430

TREVISANI, Francesco, studio of
Italian 1656-1746
paintings: (H) $2,750

TRIBOUT, G.
paintings: (L) $2,750; (H) $2,750

TRIEBEL, Carl
German 1823-1885
paintings: (L) $3,630; (H) $5,280

TRIMINH, Nquyen
American 20th cent.
paintings: (H) $880

TRINCOT, G.
paintings: (H) $990

TRINQUE, George
sculpture: (H) $4,675

TRIPET, Alfred
French ac. 1861-1882
paintings: (H) $16,500

TRIPPEL, Albert Ludwig
German 1813-1854
paintings: (H) $2,640

TRIRUM, Johannes Woutres van
Dutch b. 1924
paintings: (L) $330; (H) $825

TRISCOTT, Samuel Peter Rolt
American 1846-1925
drawings: (L) $220; (H) $1,430

TRISTAN, Luis
Spanish 1586?-1624
paintings: (H) $13,200

TRIVILINI, Armand
American 20th cent.
paintings: (H) $825

TROCCOLI, Giovanni Battista
American 1882-1940
paintings: (H) $1,210

TROEKES, Heinz
drawings: (H) $1,650

TROGER, F.
German 19th cent.
paintings: (H) $6,325

TROGER, Paul
1698-1762
paintings: (H) $9,900

TROMP, Jan Zoetelief
Dutch 1872-1947
paintings: (L) $2,090; (H) $52,250

TROMPIZ, Virgilio
Latin American
paintings: (L) $3,850; (H) $13,200

TROPP, P.
American
paintings: (H) $880

TROPPA, Girolamo
Italian c. 1636-after 1706
paintings: (H) $37,400

TROSSARELLI, Gaspare
paintings: (H) $900

TROTTER, Newbold Hough
American 1827-1898
paintings: (L) $44; (H) $6,600

TROUBETZKOY, Prince Pierre
Russian/American b. 1864
paintings: (H) $8,800

TROUBETZKOY, Prince Paul
Russian/American 1866-1933/38
paintings: (L) $198; (H) $2,090
sculpture: (L) $1,540; (H) $18,700

TROUILLEBERT, Paul Desire
French 1829-1900
paintings: (L) $3,300; (H) $29,700

TROUPEAU, Ferdinand
French ac. 1880-1890
paintings: (H) $990

TROUTOVSKY, Konstantin
Alexandrovitch
Russian 1826-1893
paintings: (H) $3,080

TROVA, Ernest
American b. 1927
paintings: (L) $1,980; (H) $22,000
drawings: (L) $550; (H) $1,320
sculpture: (L) $770; (H) $110,000

TROY, Jean Francois de
French 1697-1752
paintings: (L) $7,700; (H) $132,000
drawings: (H) $7,700

TROYA, Rafael
paintings: (H) $4,400

TROYE, Edward
American 1808-1874
paintings: (L) $6,050; (H) $33,000

TROYEN, Michael
French 1875-1915
paintings: (H) $3,080

TROYON, Constant
French 1810-1865
paintings: (L) $935; (H) $110,000
drawings: (L) $825; (H) $3,300

TRUBNER, W.
paintings: (H) $1,650

TRUCHET, Abel
French 1857-1918
paintings: (H) $3,250
drawings: (H) $990

TRUCHET, Antoine Gaspard
drawings: (H) $2,750

TRUDEAU, Garry
drawings: (L) $302; (H) $770

TRUE, David
American b. 1942
paintings: (L) $5,500; (H) $14,300
drawings: (L) $1,100; (H) $2,420

TRUE, Dorothy
American 20th cent.
paintings: (H) $825

TRUELSEN, H.
American
paintings: (H) $700

TRUESDELL, Gaylord Sangston
American 1850-1899
paintings: (L) $2,200; (H) $3,520

TRUFFAUT, Georges
French 1857-1882
paintings: (L) $660; (H) $660

TRUIJEN, Johannes Paulus Franciscus
Dutch b. 1928
paintings: (H) $880

TRUITT, Anne
contemporary
drawings: (L) $275; (H) $935

TRUJILLO, Guillermo
Panamanian b. 1927
paintings: (H) $1,760

TRUMBULL, Edward
American 20th cent.
paintings: (H) $825
drawings: (H) $1,320

TRUMBULL, John
American 1756-1843
paintings: (L) $2,640; (H) $286,000

TRUMP, Petronella
Dutch 19th/20th cent.
paintings: (H) $1,870

TRUPHEME, Auguste Joseph
French 1836-1898
paintings: (L) $22,000; (H) $26,400

TRYER, George E.
paintings: (H) $1,320

TRYON, Benjamin F.
American b. 1824
paintings: (H) $770

TRYON, Constant
paintings: (H) $2,475

TRYON, Dwight W.
American 1849-1925
paintings: (L) $935; (H) $71,500
drawings: (L) $660; (H) $7,150

TSCHACBASOV, Nahum
American b. 1899
paintings: (L) $275; (H) $1,210

TSCHAGGENY, Charles Philogene
Belgian 1815-1894
paintings: (L) $385; (H) $5,500

TSCHAGGENY, Edmond Jean Baptiste
Belgian 1818-1873
paintings: (L) $5,225; (H) $16,500

TSCHAPLOWITZ, E.
German 19th/20th cent.
paintings: (L) $192; (H) $770

TSCHELAN, Hans
Austrian 1873-1964
paintings: (H) $880

TSCHUDL, Rudolf
European 19th cent.
paintings: (H) $1,100

TSEREGOTY, N.G.
Russian 19th cent.
paintings: (H) $3,000

TSUCHIYA, Tilsa
drawings: (L) $1,100; (H) $4,180

TSUNENOBU, Kano
Japanese 1636-1713
drawings: (H) $825

TUCEK, Karl
b. 1889
paintings: (H) $715

TUCKER, Ada Eliza
English ac. 1879-1884
paintings: (L) $2,970; (H) $3,300

TUCKER, Allen
American 1866-1939
paintings: (L) $330; (H) $13,200
drawings: (L) $357; (H) $1,540

TUCKER, Arthur
British 1864-1929
drawings: (L) $935; (H) $1,650

TUCKER, John Wallace
English 18th/19th cent.
paintings: (H) $3,850

TUCKER, Mary B.
American
drawings: (H) $4,400

TUCKER, William
contemporary
drawings: (H) $2,860
sculpture: (H) $2,420

TUCKERMAN, Stephen Salisbury
American 1830-1904
paintings: (H) $1,000

TUDGAY, F.J.
British 19th cent.
paintings: (L) $8,800; (H) $9,350

TUDGAY, Frederick
British ac. 1850-1877
paintings: (H) $22,000

TUDGAY, J.
British mid-19th cent.
paintings: (H) $6,750

TUDOR, Robert M.
American 19th cent.
paintings: (H) $17,050

TUER, Herbert
paintings: (H) $2,420

TUERENHOUT, Jef van
drawings: (H) $4,400

TUFNELL, E.
American/British 20th cent.
drawings: (L) $440; (H) $1,045

TUKE, Henry Scott
English 1858-1929
paintings: (L) $2,860; (H) $66,000
drawings: (H) $715

TULLEN, R.
American late 19th/early 20th cent
paintings: (H) $1,430

TULLIDGE, J.
American 19th/20th cent.
paintings: (H) $715

TUNNARD, John C.
English 1900-1971
paintings: (L) $110; (H) $22,000

TUNNICLIFFE, Charles Frederick
American 1859/69-1937
drawings: (H) $2,420

TURCAN, Jean
French 1846-1895
sculpture: (H) $3,190

TURCATO, Giulio
Italian contemporary
paintings: (L) $935; (H) $5,000

TURCHI, Alessandro, called Orbetto
Italian 1578-1649
paintings: (L) $29,700; (H) $88,000

TURCK, Eliza
British 1832-1891
paintings: (H) $7,700

TURGOT, F.
French 19th cent.
paintings: (H) $2,750

TURNBULL, William
contemporary
paintings: (H) $1,100
sculpture: (H) $8,250

TURNER, A.D.
paintings: (H) $1,430

TURNER, Alan
contemporary
paintings: (H) $1,320

TURNER, Alfred M.
American 1851/52-1932
paintings: (L) $1,430; (H) $6,600
drawings: (L) $385; (H) $4,620

TURNER, Charles H.
American b. 1848
paintings: (L) $220; (H) $7,150
drawings: (L) $132; (H) $275

TURNER, Charles Yardley
American 1850-1919
paintings: (L) $220; (H) $9,350
drawings: (L) $247; (H) $3,190

TURNER, Daniel
English ac. 1782-1801
paintings: (L) $440; (H) $1,320

TURNER, E.
paintings: (H) $2,090

TURNER, Frances Lee
American b. 1875
paintings: (H) $990

TURNER, Francis Calcraft
English ac. 1782-1846
paintings: (L) $2,200; (H) $44,000

TURNER, Frank
English 19th cent.
paintings: (L) $522; (H) $1,100

TURNER, G.A.
British 19th cent.
paintings: (H) $1,320

TURNER, George
paintings: (H) $1,870

TURNER, George
British 1843-1910
paintings: (L) $1,430; (H) $3,520

TURNER, George
English 1873-1920
paintings: (L) $358; (H) $7,425

TURNER, George
English 19th cent.
paintings: (L) $770; (H) $2,750

TURNER, George A.
English ac. 1845
paintings: (H) $1,100

TURNER, Helen M.
American 1858-1958
paintings: (L) $2,640; (H) $5,500

TURNER, J.
paintings: (H) $2,860

TURNER, J.A.
British 19th cent.
paintings: (H) $1,320

TURNER, Joseph Mallord William
English 1775-1851
drawings: (L) $2,200; (H) $577,500

TURNER, Joseph Mallord William and
Thomas GIRTIN
drawings: (L) $1,760; (H) $4,400

TURNER, Michael
drawings: (H) $1,650

TURNER, Raymond
sculpture: (L) $1,100; (H) $1,870

TURNER, Robert
American b. 1913
sculpture: (L) $2,200; (H) $3,300

TURNER, Ross Sterling
American 1847-1915
paintings: (L) $1,925; (H) $2,090
drawings: (L) $275; (H) $1,485

TURNER, W.H.
paintings: (H) $2,420
drawings: (H) $605

TURNER, W.H.M.
paintings: (H) $6,600

TUTTLE, Macowin
American 1861-1935
paintings: (L) $66; (H) $660

TUTTLE, Richard
American 20th cent.
paintings: (L) $2,860; (H) $44,000
drawings: (L) $2,860; (H) $12,100
sculpture: (L) $4,400; (H) $5,500

TUTUNDJIAN, Leon
French 1906-1968
paintings: (H) $4,950

TWACHTMAN, John Henry
American 1853-1902
paintings: (L) $1,980; (H) $605,000
drawings: (L) $3,080; (H) $19,800

TWARDZIK, Henryk
b. 1900
paintings: (H) $850

TWEDDLE, John
contemporary
paintings: (H) $770

TWELVETREES, C.
American
drawings: (H) $935

TWINING, Yvonne
American b. 1907
paintings: (L) $2,310; (H) $9,350

TWITCHELL, Asa Weston
American 1820-1904
paintings: (L) $121; (H) $770

TWITTY, James
American contemporary
paintings: (H) $1,045

TWOMBLY, Cy
American b. 1929
paintings: (L) $8,800; (H) $5,500,000
drawings: (L) $3,300; (H) $561,000

TWORKOV, Jack
Polish/American b. 1900
paintings: (L) $2,200; (H) $63,250
drawings: (L) $770; (H) $13,200

TYLER, Bayard Henry
American 1855-1931
paintings: (L) $55; (H) $5,500

TYLER, George Washington
American 1803-1833
paintings: (H) $825

TYLER, James Gale
American 1855-1931
paintings: (L) $280; (H) $20,000
drawings: (L) $770; (H) $1,200

TYLER, Stella Elkins
sculpture: (H) $880

TYLER, William Richardson
American 1825-1896
paintings: (L) $900; (H) $6,875

TYNER, Wm. P.
drawings: (H) $880

TYPALDOS, Nicolaos Xydias
Continental 19th cent.
paintings: (H) $4,620

TYSON, Caroll Sargent, Jr.
American 1878-1956
paintings: (L) $220; (H) $5,280
drawings: (L) $990; (H) $2,860

TYTGAT, Edgard
Flemish 1879-1957
drawings: (H) $7,150

UBAGHS, Jean
Belgian b. 1852
paintings: (L) $1,650; (H) $4,400

UBEDA, Augustin
Spanish b. 1925
paintings: (L) $550; (H) $14,300

UBERT, L.
French 19th cent.
paintings: (H) $660

UBERTINI, Francesco, called Il
Bacchiacca
Italian 1494/95-1557
paintings: (H) $66,000

UDEN, Lucas van
Flemish 1595-1672/73
paintings: (L) $6,600; (H) $19,800

UDVARDY, Flora N.
Hungarian 20th cent.
paintings: (H) $770

UEMURA, Kimio
contemporary
sculpture: (H) $770

UFER, Walter
American 1876-1936
paintings: (L) $9,350; (H) $121,000
drawings: (H) $297

UHL, Louis
Austrian 1860-1909
paintings: (H) $11,550

UHLE, Bernard
American b. 1847
paintings: (L) $330; (H) $1,870

UHLMANN, Hans
sculpture: (L) $220; (H) $2,310

UHRIG, Albert E.
paintings: (H) $660

ULFT, Jacob van der
Dutch 1627-1689
paintings: (H) $50,600
drawings: (H) $36,300

ULLMAN, Th.
sculpture: (L) $605; (H) $2,970

ULLMANN, Julius
German 1861-1918
paintings: (H) $660

ULNITZ, E.C.
Danish 19th cent.
paintings: (H) $4,950

ULP, Clifford
American 1885-1957
paintings: (L) $385; (H) $825

ULRICH, J.
sculpture: (L) $1,100; (H) $2,860

ULYSSE-ROY, Jean
French 19th cent.
paintings: (H) $7,150

UNDE, Fritz von
paintings: (H) $1,045

UNDERHILL, Georgia E.
American 19th/20th cent.
paintings: (H) $1,320

UNDERHILL, T.
paintings: (H) $2,000

UNDERHILL, W.
paintings: (H) $1,760

UNDERWOOD, Clarence F.
American 1871-1929
paintings: (H) $495
drawings: (L) $143; (H) $660

UNDERWOOD, Leon
American
sculpture: (H) $770

UNGER, Hans
German 1872-1936
paintings: (H) $1,100

UNSWORTH, Edna Ganzhorn
American b. 1890
paintings: (H) $2,200

UNTERBERGER
Austrian 18th cent.
paintings: (H) $770

UNTERBERGER, Franz Richard
Belgian 1838-1902
paintings: (L) $2,200; (H) $63,250

URBAHN, O.
German 19th cent.
paintings: (H) $2,530

URBAN
paintings: (H) $1,320

URBAN, Humberto
Mexican b. 1936
paintings: (L) $3,300; (H) $3,575

UREN, John Clarkson
English 1885-1898
drawings: (L) $143; (H) $825

URIANO
sculpture: (L) $550; (H) $1,760

URIBE-HOLGUIN, Santiago
Colombian b. 1957
drawings: (H) $1,320

URLAUB, Georg Anton Abraham
German 1744-1788
paintings: (H) $23,100

URLAUB, Georg Johann Christian
German 1844-1914
paintings: (H) $5,500

URLAUB, R.
German 19th cent.
paintings: (H) $4,400

URUETA, Cordelia
Mexican b. 1908
paintings: (L) $1,320; (H) $28,600

URY, A. Muller
German 19th cent.
paintings: (H) $1,210

USALDE (?), E. Patello
19th/20th cent.
paintings: (H) $715

UTAMARO
Chinese School late 19th cent.
paintings: (H) $3,300

UTRECHT, Adriaen van
Flemish 1599-1652/53
paintings: (L) $28,600; (H) $47,300

UTRILLO, Maurice
French 1883-1955
paintings: (L) $11,550; (H) $990,000
drawings: (L) $1,210; (H) $181,500

UTTER, Andre
paintings: (L) $6,820; (H) $6,820

UTTER, Andre
contemporary
paintings: (L) $165; (H) $4,950

UYL, Jan Jansz den
Dutch 1595/96-1639/40
paintings: (H) $2,200,000

UYTEWAEL, Joachim
Dutch c. 1566-1638
paintings: (H) $22,000

UZELAI, Jose
paintings: (H) $1,760

VAARBERG, Johannes Christoffel
Dutch 1825-1871
paintings: (L) $1,210; (H) $1,430

VAART, W. van der
Dutch 19th/20th cent.
paintings: (H) $660

VACCARO, Andrea
Italian 1598(?)-1670
paintings: (H) $3,520

VACCARO, Mario D.J.
Italian 1869-1934
paintings: (L) $825; (H) $2,530

VACCARO, Nicola
Italian 1637-1717
paintings: (H) $20,900

VADDER, Lodewyk de
Flemish 1605-1655
paintings: (H) $24,200

VAERE, Jean Antoine de, John
Flemish 1754-1830
sculpture: (H) $60,500

VAFFLARD, Pierre Antoine Augustin
French 1777-1840
paintings: (H) $3,850

VAGO, Sandor
Hungarian/American b. 1887
paintings: (L) $385; (H) $1,320
drawings: (L) $33; (H) $220

VAIL, Eugene Laurent
American 1857-1934
paintings: (L) $440; (H) $10,450

VAILLANT, Louis David
American b. 1875
paintings: (H) $660

VAILLANT, Wallerant
Dutch 1623-1677
paintings: (H) $1,540
drawings: (H) $4,180

VAJDA, Zsigmond
Hungarian 1860-1931
paintings: (L) $1,980; (H) $2,860

VALADE, Gabrielle Marie Marguerite
French 19th cent.
paintings: (H) $12,100

VALADON, Suzanne
French 1865-1938
paintings: (L) $8,250; (H) $187,000
drawings: (L) $440; (H) $57,200

VALANTIN, Paul
French 19th cent.
paintings: (H) $11,000

VALAPERTA, F.
European 19th cent.
paintings: (H) $715

VALBUENA, Ricardo
Colombian b. 1960
drawings: (H) $13,200

VALCKENBORCH, Frederik van
drawings: (H) $5,225

VALCKENBORCH, Lucas van
Flemish c. 1530/35-1597
paintings: (H) $77,000

VALCKENBORCH, Lucas van,
studio of
paintings: (H) $13,200

VALCKERT, Werner van den
paintings: (H) $2,530

VALDES, G.
paintings: (H) $1,100

VALDES LEAL, called Juan de Nisa
Spanish 1622-1690
paintings: (L) $16,500; (H) $79,750

VALDRON, C.
American 19th cent.
paintings: (H) $825

VALE, R.
paintings: (H) $15,400

VALENCIA, Manuel
American 1856-1935/36
paintings: (L) $193; (H) $6,050
drawings: (H) $330

VALENKAMPH, Theodore Victor Carl
American 1868-1924
paintings: (L) $55; (H) $4,180

VALENSI, Henry
French 1883-1960
paintings: (H) $1,870

VALENSTEIN, Alice
paintings: (H) $660

VALENTE, Paolo
Italian 19th cent.
paintings: (L) $2,750; (H) $3,300

VALENTI, Paul
Italian (?)
paintings: (H) $1,430

VALENTIN
European 19th/20th cent.
paintings: (H) $825

VALENTINE, Jane H.
American 1866-1934
paintings: (L) $121; (H) $1,540

VALENTINI, Va
Italian 19th cent.
paintings: (H) $2,860

VALER, G.
sculpture: (H) $3,300

VALERI, Silvestro
Italian 1814-1902
drawings: (H) $1,320

VALERI-PREVOT, Andre
French b. 1890
paintings: (H) $880

VALERIO, James
contemporary
paintings: (H) $16,500

VALERIO, Pietro
19th/20th cent.
paintings: (L) $660; (H) $990

VALERIO, Theodore
French 1819-1879
drawings: (L) $110; (H) $1,100

VALERO, D.C.
Continental 19th cent.
paintings: (H) $1,760

VALERO, J. Pio
Spanish 1830-1911
paintings: (H) $4,400

Artist, Model, and Mother

French painter Suzanne Valadon (1865-1938) is sometimes better remembered for her scandalous life than for her art. As a young girl she worked as a circus acrobat but left the circus after she was injured in a fall and became an artist's model in Montmartre. Much esteemed for her beauty, she modeled for Renoir, Puvis de Chavannes, Degas, and Toulouse-Lautrec. At eighteen she bore an illegitimate child–the painter Maurice Utrillo.

After her son was born, she began to draw. She was largely self-taught, though Lautrec and Degas gave her encouragement, and Degas provided instruction in the techniques of engraving. Her favorite subjects were female nudes, with her charwoman or a servant girl serving as models. She exhibited in her twenties, and her works sold well. From 1894 to 1908 she lived a sedate, although unmarried, life with a rich banker and worked prolifically. During this period she taught her son Maurice how to paint.

In 1908 she fell in love with an artist friend of her son's, Andre Utter, who was twenty-one years her junior, and went to live with him.

In 1909 she gave up drawing and engraving and began to paint, mostly landscapes or still lifes. *Nature Morte Au Compotier* was painted in 1918 and is a good example of her still lifes. The painting, which was the catalog cover illustration for the sale, realized a record price for the artist, $187,000. (Suzanne Valadon, *Nature Morte Au Compotier*, oil on canvas, 24 x 19¾ in., Christie's, February 26, 1990, $187,000)

VALETTE, Rene
French 19th cent.
paintings: (H) $4,400
drawings: (H) $385

VALIN-ISZLAY (?), M.V.
paintings: (H) $825

VALKENBORCH, Martin van
1535-1612
drawings: (H) $20,350

VALKENBURG, Dirk
Dutch 1675-1727
paintings: (H) $11,000

VALKENBURG, Hendrik
Dutch 1826-1896
paintings: (L) $1,100; (H) $3,850

VALKERS, A.
paintings: (H) $880

VALLAYER-COSTER, Anne
French 1744-1818
paintings: (H) $341,000

VALLEE, Etienne Maxime
French ac. 1873-1881
paintings: (L) $880; (H) $880

VALLEE, Geex de la
paintings: (H) $6,050

VALLES, Lorenzo
Spanish 1830-1910
paintings: (L) $1,870; (H) $2,420
drawings: (H) $330

VALLET, Jean Emile Pierre
French d. 1889
paintings: (H) $3,300

VALLET-BISSON, Frederique
French b. 1865
paintings: (L) $3,850; (H) $7,150
drawings: (H) $16,500

VALLETT, Mars. **
sculpture: (H) $2,750

VALLIANCE, R.B.
paintings: (H) $1,045

VALLIEN, Bertil
contemporary
sculpture: (L) $605; (H) $1,650

VALLOIS, Paul Felix
French 19th cent.
paintings: (L) $385; (H) $2,640

VALLOTTON, Felix
Swiss 1865-1925
paintings: (L) $24,200; (H) $104,500
drawings: (H) $192

VALMIER, Georges
French 1885-1937
paintings: (L) $5,280; (H) $28,600
drawings: (L) $1,650; (H) $8,800

VALTAT, Louis
French 1869-1952
paintings: (L) $1,650; (H) $242,000
drawings: (L) $605; (H) $46,200

VALTON, Charles
French 1851-1918
sculpture: (L) $275; (H) $3,300

VALVERANE, L. Denis
French 19th/20th cent.
paintings: (H) $1,650

VALVERO
paintings: (H) $770

VAN CLEAVE, Joe
American 20th cent.
drawings: (H) $935

VAN DER HOT
paintings: (H) $880

VAN DOORN, J.
Dutch 19th/20th cent.
paintings: (H) $3,575

VAN DYCK, Sir Anthony, studio of
17th cent.
paintings: (L) $9,350; (H) $30,800

VAN ELK, Ger
German contemporary
sculpture: (H) $33,000

VAN GORDER, Luther Emerson
paintings: (H) $2,750

VAN GUNTEN, Roger
paintings: (H) $11,000

VAN HEYDEN
drawings: (H) $770

VAN HUYSAM
paintings: (H) $4,950

VAN LAER, A.T.
American b. 1857
paintings: (H) $1,850

VAN LOAN, Dorothy L.
American b. 1904
paintings: (L) $220; (H) $935

VAN RYDER, Jack
American 20th cent.
paintings: (H) $1,980

VAN SHELDON
paintings: (H) $2,200

VAN SLOUN, Frank
American 1878-1938
drawings: (H) $660

VAN SLUYS
Dutch 19th cent.
paintings: (H) $2,530

VAN?, H.
mid-19th cent.
paintings: (H) $2,200

VANAISE, Gustave
Belgian 1854-1902
paintings: (L) $1,045; (H) $9,900

VANARDEN, George
American 19th cent.
paintings: (H) $1,650

VANBRABANT, Victor
paintings: (H) $825
VANDEHOUSE
paintings: (H) $880
VANDENBERG, Willem
paintings: (H) $715
VANDENBERGE, Peter
American b. Holland 1935
sculpture: (L) $550; (H) $4,400
VANDERBANK, John
English c. 1694-1739
paintings: (L) $1,100; (H) $7,150
VANDERBERG (?), B.
paintings: (H) $2,420
VANDERHOOF, Charles A.
American d. 1918
drawings: (L) $55; (H) $1,100
VANDERPOEL, Louis
Dutch 1896-1987
paintings: (H) $715
VANDERVENNE, Fritz
German b. 1900
paintings: (H) $1,925
VANDEVERDOUCK, Francis
Dutch 19th cent.
paintings: (H) $4,125
VANDIEVORT, Louis
Belgian b. 1875
paintings: (H) $6,600
VANGORP, Henry Nicholas
French 1756-1819
drawings: (H) $5,500
VANLOO, Jean Baptiste, studio of
paintings: (H) $2,310
VANNI, Guido
paintings: (H) $2,200
VANNINI, Ottavio
Italian 1585-1643
paintings: (H) $55,000
VANNUTELLI, Scipione
Italian 1834-1894
paintings: (L) $1,100; (H) $2,530
VANTONGERLOO, Frans Joseph
Belgian 1882-1965
paintings: (H) $6,875

VARADY, Frederic
American b. 1908
drawings: (L) $770; (H) $1,400
VARDA, Jean
paintings: (H) $660
VARDUCCA, E.
paintings: (H) $715
VARELA, Abigail
Venezuelan b. 1948
sculpture: (L) $3,850; (H) $52,800
VARGA
sculpture: (H) $2,090
VARGA, Albert
drawings: (H) $1,870
VARGAS, Alberto
American 1926-1983
drawings: (L) $2,500; (H) $12,100
VARI, Sofia
contemporary
sculpture: (H) $8,800
VARIAN, George Edmund
American 1865-1923
paintings: (L) $357; (H) $660
drawings: (H) $900
VARLEY, Frederick Horsman
Canadian 1881-1969
paintings: (L) $96,800; (H) $363,000
drawings: (H) $900
VARLEY, John
English 1778-1842
drawings: (L) $110; (H) $2,200
VARNIER, Pierre
sculpture: (H) $1,925
VARO, Remedios
Mexican, b. Spain 1908-1963
paintings: (L) $13,200; (H) $825,000
drawings: (L) $4,400; (H) $71,500
VARRE, Albert
paintings: (H) $1,430
VARRIALE, W. Stella
American b. 1927
paintings: (L) $1,650; (H) $2,310
VASA, Velizar
Yugoslav/American b. 1933
sculpture: (L) $770; (H) $825

VASARELY, Victor
French b. 1908
paintings: (L) $2,640; (H) $88,000
drawings: (L) $2,530; (H) $13,200
sculpture: (L) $302; (H) $9,350

VASARI, Giorgio
Italian 1511-1574
paintings: (L) $22,000; (H) $137,500
drawings: (L) $16,500; (H) $143,000

VASARRI, Emilio
Italian ac. 1900-1904
paintings: (L) $1,540; (H) $41,800

VASEILEV, B.
Russian 20th cent.
paintings: (H) $660

VASILIEFF, Nicholas
Russian/American 1892-1970
paintings: (L) $660; (H) $3,080
drawings: (H) $66

VASQUEZ, Gregorio
paintings: (H) $4,950

VASQUEZ BRITO, Ramon
Venezuelan b. 1927
paintings: (L) $6,600; (H) $9,350

VASSELIN, Jean E.
French 19th cent.
paintings: (H) $770

VASSEUR, Charles le
French 19th cent.
paintings: (H) $935

VASSILIEFF, Marie
paintings: (H) $20,900

VASSOS, John
drawings: (L) $3,960; (H) $6,050

VASTAG, Gyorgy
Hungarian 1834-1922
paintings: (H) $10,450

VASTAGH, Geza
Hungarian 1866-1919
paintings: (L) $550; (H) $3,850

VAUDECHAMP, Jean Joseph
paintings: (H) $9,625

VAUGHAN, Keith
English b. 1912
paintings: (H) $770
drawings: (H) $2,970

VAUREAL, De
sculpture: (H) $29,700

VAUTHIER, Pierre Louis Leger
French 1845-1916
paintings: (L) $715; (H) $55,000

VAUTIER, Marc Louis Benjamin
Swiss 1829-1898
paintings: (H) $9,350

VAUX, Jules Ernest de
French b. 1837
paintings: (H) $3,025

VAVRA, Frank Joseph
American 1898-1967
paintings: (H) $660

VAYANA, Nunzio
American 1887-1960
paintings: (L) $192; (H) $1,210

VAYSON, Paul
French 1842-1911
paintings: (H) $3,300

VEA, Van
Continental 20th cent.
paintings: (H) $825

VECCHI, Francesco di Bernardo de,
called Francesco Rizzo, workshop of
ac. 1490-after 1548
paintings: (H) $3,850

VECOLI
sculpture: (H) $9,350

VEDDER, Elihu
American 1836-1923
paintings: (L) $77; (H) $55,000
drawings: (L) $220; (H) $24,200
sculpture: (L) $7,700; (H) $33,000

VEDDER, Elihu and Alfred PARSONS
American
drawings: (H) $6,050

VEDOVA, Emilio
contemporary
paintings: (H) $7,700

VEEGAN, Anna
Belgian 19th/20th cent.
paintings: (H) $3,520

VEEN, Otto van
Dutch 1558-1629
paintings: (L) $5,500; (H) $17,600

VEEN, Pieter van
Dutch/American b. 1875
paintings: (L) $715; (H) $1,430

VEENFLIET, Richard
American
drawings: (L) $247; (H) $715

VEERENDAEL, Nicolaes van
Flemish 1640-1691
paintings: (H) $165,000

VEGA, Jose de la
Spanish 19th cent.
paintings: (H) $1,980

VEGA, Manolo de la
Spanish 19th cent.
paintings: (L) $3,520; (H) $16,500

VEGA Y MUNOZ, Pedro
Spanish 19th cent.
paintings: (L) $1,320; (H) $4,950

VEGER
19th/20th cent.
paintings: (H) $770

VEGER, Hermanus Johannes
Dutch b. 1910
paintings: (L) $550; (H) $825

VEILLON, Auguste-Louis
Swiss 1834-1890
paintings: (H) $8,250

VEJARANO, Gustavo
Colombian b. 1952
paintings: (H) $1,650

VELA, Alberto R.
Mexican b. 1920
paintings: (L) $1,430; (H) $1,650

VELA, Vincenzo
Italian 1820-1891
sculpture: (L) $1,320; (H) $7,150

VELARDE, Pablita
American b. 1918
paintings: (L) $88; (H) $715

VELASCO, Jose Maria
Mexican 1840-1912
paintings: (L) $7,150; (H) $341,000
drawings: (L) $7,700; (H) $11,000

VELASQUEZ, Jose Antonio
Honduran b. 1906
paintings: (L) $1,210; (H) $46,200

VELASQUEZ, Juan Ramon
Puerto Rican b. 1950
drawings: (H) $660

VELDE, Adriaen van de
Dutch 1636-1672
paintings: (L) $4,400; (H) $34,100

VELDE, Bram van
Dutch 1895-after 1980
paintings: (H) $19,800

VELDE, Esaias van de
Dutch 1587-1630
paintings: (L) $12,100; (H) $181,500
drawings: (L) $1,870; (H) $15,400

VELDE, Geer van
Dutch b. 1898
paintings: (L) $3,300; (H) $28,600

VELDE, Hanny Vander
b. 1883
paintings: (L) $357; (H) $1,320

VELDE, Peter van de
paintings: (H) $3,575

VELDE, Willem van de, studio of
paintings: (H) $17,600

VELDE, Willem van de, studio of,
the younger
1633-1707
paintings: (H) $16,500

VELDE, Willem van de, the elder
Dutch 1611-1693
paintings: (H) $462,000
drawings: (L) $4,125; (H) $11,000

VELDE, Willem van de, the younger
Dutch 1633-1707
paintings: (L) $49,500; (H) $132,000
drawings: (L) $550; (H) $7,700

VELDEN, Petrus van der
drawings: (H) $1,430

VELDHUIJZEN, Johannes Hendrik
Dutch 1831-1910
paintings: (H) $4,400

VELLAERT, Dirk Jacobsz
Flemish 16th cent.
paintings: (H) $26,400

VELLOSO, Fernando Magalhaes
sculpture: (H) $2,750

VELTEN, Wilhelm
Russian 1847-1929
paintings: (L) $1,000; (H) $24,200

VELY, Anatole
French 1838-1882
paintings: (L) $715; (H) $3,300

VELZEN, Johannes Petrus van
Dutch 1816-1853
paintings: (H) $1,320

VENARD, Claude
French b. 1913
paintings: (L) $154; (H) $46,200
drawings: (H) $825

VENDERBANK, John
paintings: (H) $2,310

VENDITTI, Jerry
American b. 1942
paintings: (L) $2,500; (H) $13,200

VENET, Bernard and Mimmo
ROTELLA
contemporary
drawings: (H) $3,850

VENET, Gabriel
French b. 1884
paintings: (H) $880

VENETO, SCHOOL OF, CIRCA 1400
paintings: (H) $55,000

VENITIEN, Jean
contemporary
paintings: (H) $660

VENNE, Adolf van der
Austrian 1828-1911
paintings: (L) $1,430; (H) $4,400

VENNE, Adriaen van de
Dutch 1589-1662
paintings: (H) $9,900

VENNE, Fritz van der
German c. 1900
paintings: (L) $1,045; (H) $6,050

VENNEMAN, Charles
Flemish 1802-1875
paintings: (L) $2,090; (H) $7,975

VENNEMAN, Rosa
Belgian 19th cent.
paintings: (H) $9,350

VENNER, W.H.T.
paintings: (H) $1,210

VENTORE, Roberto
paintings: (H) $1,650

VENTURRI, Achille
Italian 1826-1897
paintings: (H) $5,775

VENUTI, Filippo
Italian 19th cent.
drawings: (H) $1,870

VER BECK, Frank
American 1858-1933
drawings: (H) $1,100

VERA Y CALVO, Juan Antonio
Spanish 19th cent.
paintings: (H) $1,320

VERAY, Joe
paintings: (L) $330; (H) $880

VERBEECK, Pieter Cornelisz.
paintings: (H) $990

VERBEEK, J.
paintings: (H) $660

VERBERGHEN, P.
Dutch early 20th cent.
paintings: (H) $660

VERBOECKHOVEN, Charles Louis
Belgian 1802-1889
paintings: (L) $8,800; (H) $12,100

VERBOECKHOVEN, Eugene Joseph
Belgian 1798/99-1881
paintings: (L) $1,540; (H) $38,500
drawings: (L) $275; (H) $770

VERBOECKHOVEN, Eugene Joseph
and Edouard de VIGNE
Belgian 19th cent.
paintings: (H) $11,000

VERBOECKHOVEN, Eugene Joseph
and Frans KEELHOFF
Belgian 18th/19th cent.
paintings: (H) $4,125

VERBOECKHOVEN, Eugene Joseph
and Nicolas Jan ROSENBOOM
Belgian 18th/19th cent.
paintings: (H) $33,000

VERBOOM, Adriaen
Dutch c. 1628-1670
paintings: (H) $4,400

VERBRUGGEN, Gaspar Pieter
paintings: (L) $6,600; (H) $12,100

VERBRUGGEN, Gaspar Pieter, the elder
Flemish 1635-1687
paintings: (L) $11,000; (H) $13,200

VERBRUGGEN, Gaspar Pieter, the younger
Flemish 1664-1730
paintings: (L) $9,350; (H) $71,500

VERBRUGGHE, Charles
paintings: (H) $1,650

VERBURGH, Dionijs
d. 1722
paintings: (H) $12,100

VERBURGH, Rutger
paintings: (H) $8,800

VERCKER, J.G.P.
paintings: (H) $3,300

VERDEVOYE, L.
Belgian 19th/20th cent.
paintings: (H) $3,080

VERDI, A.
paintings: (H) $1,045

VERDI, A.
Italian 19th cent.
paintings: (H) $4,125

VERDIER, Francois
French 1651-1730
drawings: (L) $220; (H) $990

VERDIER, Jules Victor
paintings: (H) $1,980

VERDILHAN, Louis Mathieu
contemporary
paintings: (H) $6,600

VERDURA, Fulco
Italian 20th cent.
drawings: (L) $1,430; (H) $1,760
sculpture: (H) $2,530

VERDUSSEN, Jan Peeter
Flemish c. 1700-1763
paintings: (H) $8,250

VERELST, Simon Pietersz.
Dutch 1644-1721
paintings: (L) $49,500; (H) $495,000

VERELST, William
ac. 1734-d. c. 1756
paintings: (L) $11,550; (H) $12,100

VERESMITH, Daniel Albert, or
WEHRSCHMIDT
American 1861-1932
paintings: (H) $1,430

VERESS, T. Zoltan
paintings: (H) $935

VERETSHCHAGIN, Piotr Petrovitch
Russian 1836-1886
paintings: (L) $6,600; (H) $7,700

VEREY, A.
French 19th cent.
paintings: (H) $1,500

VEREY, Johanna Louise Antoinette
Dutch 1886-1966
paintings: (H) $1,320

VERGER, Carlos
Spanish 1872-1929
paintings: (H) $715

VERHAECHT, Tobias
Flemish 1561-1631
paintings: (H) $38,500

VERHAERT, Dirck
Dutch 1631-1664
paintings: (L) $2,090; (H) $3,850

VERHAERT, Piet
Dutch 1852-1903
paintings: (H) $1,100

VERHAS, Frans
Belgian 1827-1897
paintings: (H) $19,800

VERHAS, Jan Francois
Belgian 1834-1896
paintings: (L) $385; (H) $24,200

VERHEIJEN, Jan Hendrik
Dutch 1778-1846
paintings: (H) $28,600

VERHEYDEN, Francois
Belgian 1806-1890(?)
paintings: (L) $990; (H) $2,750

VERHEYDEN, Isidore
Belgian 1846-1905
paintings: (L) $1,650; (H) $1,760

VERHOESEN, Albertus
Dutch 1806-1881
paintings: (L) $770; (H) $7,150

VERHOEVEN-BALL, Adrien Joseph
paintings: (L) $1,045; (H) $5,500

VERLAT, Charles Michel Maria
Belgian 1824-1890
paintings: (L) $1,100; (H) $6,050

VERLET, Charles Raoul
sculpture: (H) $1,980

VERLIN, Venceslao
paintings: (H) $2,200

VERLINDE, Pierre Antoine Augustin
paintings: (H) $3,300

VERLINGEN, A.
paintings: (H) $770

VERLOT, O.
French 19th/20th cent.
paintings: (L) $3,300; (H) $4,950

VERMEER, Jan van der MEER, the younger
Dutch 1656-1705
paintings: (H) $16,500

VERMEHREN, Johan Frederick Nicolai
Danish 1823-1910
paintings: (H) $15,400

VERMEHREN, Otto
German mid-19th cent.
paintings: (H) $1,200

VERMEHREN, Sophus
Danish b. 1866
paintings: (H) $3,410

VERMEULEN
paintings: (H) $715

VERMEULEN, Andreas Franciscus
Dutch 1821-1884
paintings: (L) $3,080; (H) $7,975

VERMEULEN, Andries
Dutch 1763-1814
paintings: (H) $19,800

VERMEULEN, Cornelis
Dutch 1732-1813
paintings: (H) $2,200

VERMORCKEN, Frederic Marie
b. 1860
paintings: (L) $770; (H) $990

VERNARD, Claude
French b. 1913
paintings: (L) $605; (H) $853

VERNE, La
sculpture: (H) $660

VERNEER, Abraham
Dutch School 19th cent.
paintings: (H) $2,200

VERNER, Elizabeth O'Neill
American b. 1883
drawings: (L) $2,090; (H) $4,840

VERNER, Frederick Arthur
Canadian 1836-1928
paintings: (L) $4,290; (H) $88,000
drawings: (L) $2,200; (H) $8,800

VERNET, Antoine Charles Horace, called Carle
French 1758-1836
drawings: (L) $2,420; (H) $8,800

VERNET, C.
French 19th cent.
paintings: (H) $5,500

VERNET, Claude Joseph
French 1714-1789
paintings: (L) $286; (H) $880,000
drawings: (H) $302

VERNET, Emile Jean Horace, called Horace
French 1789-1863
paintings: (L) $3,300; (H) $484,000
drawings: (H) $495
sculpture: (H) $1,705

VERNIER, Emile
Swiss 1829-1887
paintings: (L) $495; (H) $3,520

VERNIER, Fortune
paintings: (H) $825

VERNIER, L.
French 1829-1887
paintings: (H) $1,045

VERNIER, T.
paintings: (H) $880

VERNILE
Italian 19th cent.
paintings: (H) $4,400

VERNON
paintings: (H) $990

VERNON, Alexandre Rene
French 1826-1897
paintings: (L) $715; (H) $3,080

VERNON, Arthur Langley
British ac. 1871-1922
paintings: (L) $770; (H) $4,920

VERNON, Emile
British ac. 1904
paintings: (L) $6,600; (H) $68,750

VERNON, P.
paintings: (H) $825

VERNON, Paul
French 19th cent.
paintings: (H) $1,320

VERNON, W.
British 19th cent.
paintings: (H) $4,400

VERON, Jules
French 19th cent.
paintings: (L) $1,045; (H) $1,870

VERON, Theodore
French 19th cent.
paintings: (H) $1,320

VERON-FARE, Jules Henri
French 1839-1890
paintings: (L) $1,430; (H) $2,310

VERONESE, Bonifazio, studio of
drawings: (H) $880

VERONESE, Paolo, Paolo CALIARI,
called Paul
Italian 1528-1588
paintings: (H) $2,970,000
drawings: (H) $440,000

VERONESE, Paolo, studio of
drawings: (H) $770

VERPOEKEN, Hendrik
Dutch 1791-1869
paintings: (H) $7,700

VERREAUX, Louis Leon Nicholas
paintings: (H) $1,100

VERREYDT, Pierre
paintings: (H) $2,200

VERRIER, Max le
sculpture: (L) $44; (H) $3,300

VERRYK, T.
paintings: (H) $2,860

VERSCHAFFELT, Edward
Belgian b. 1874
paintings: (H) $11,000

VERSCHUIER, Lieve
Dutch 1630-1686
paintings: (H) $85,800

VERSCHURING, Hendrik
Dutch 1627-1690
paintings: (L) $6,050; (H) $33,000

VERSCHUUR
paintings: (H) $1,760

VERSCHUUR, Wouter
Dutch 1812-1874
paintings: (L) $6,600; (H) $88,000

VERSCHUUR, Wouter, Jr.
Dutch 1841-1936
paintings: (L) $880; (H) $1,430

VERSPRONCK, Johannes Cornelisz
Dutch 1575-1642/53
paintings: (L) $3,080; (H) $39,600

VERSTRAETE, Theodore and Cornelis
van LEEMPUTTEN
Belgian 1850-1907/1841-1902
paintings: (H) $2,860

VERSTRALEN, Antoni
Dutch c. 1594-1641
paintings: (H) $121,000

VERTANGEN, Daniel
Dutch c. 1598-before 1684
paintings: (L) $4,400; (H) $12,100

VERTES, Marcel
French 1895-1961
paintings: (L) $770; (H) $13,200
drawings: (L) $44; (H) $1,650
sculpture: (L) $550; (H) $715

VERTIN, Pieter Gerardus
Dutch 1819-1893
paintings: (L) $1,760; (H) $6,050

VERTUNNI, Achille
paintings: (H) $5,060

VERVEER, Salomon Leonardus
Dutch 1813-1876
paintings: (L) $1,870; (H) $9,900
drawings: (L) $440; (H) $550

VERVOORT, M.
Flemish 19th cent.
paintings: (H) $2,090

VERWEE, Charles Louis
paintings: (H) $3,300

VERWEE, Louis Pierre
Belgian 1807-1877
paintings: (H) $2,200

VERWEST, Jules
Belgian 1883-1957
paintings: (H) $3,850

VESIN, Jaroslav Fr. Julius
Bulgarian d. 1915
paintings: (L) $1,430; (H) $24,200

VESPIGNANI, Renzo
Italian b. 1924
paintings: (H) $3,080
drawings: (H) $1,045

VESSELY, Boris-Theo
French 19th/20th cent.
paintings: (H) $6,600

VESTER, Willem
Dutch 1824-1871
paintings: (L) $2,530; (H) $33,000

VESTIER, Antoine
French 1740-1824
paintings: (H) $1,320

VEYRASSAT, Jules Jacques
French 1828-1893
paintings: (L) $550; (H) $11,000

VEZIEN, Elie Jean
sculpture: (H) $770

VEZIN, Charles
American 1858-1942
paintings: (L) $467; (H) $4,840

VIANDEN, Heinrich
American 1814-1899
paintings: (H) $2,475

VIANELLO, Cesare
Italian 19th cent.
paintings: (L) $3,520; (H) $6,050

VIANI, Giovanni Maria
1636-1700
paintings: (H) $16,500

VIANI, Lorenzo
Italian 1882-1936
paintings: (L) $825; (H) $3,740

VIARD, Georges
French ac. 1831-1848
paintings: (H) $15,400

VIAVANT, George Louis
drawings: (L) $715; (H) $1,100

VIBERT, Alexandre
sculpture: (H) $3,410

VIBERT, Jean Georges
French 1840-1902
paintings: (L) $770; (H) $44,000
drawings: (L) $220; (H) $203,500

VICCARI, C.
sculpture: (L) $495; (H) $1,210

VICENTE, Esteban
Spanish/American b. 1904/06
paintings: (L) $880; (H) $8,800
drawings: (L) $522; (H) $5,500

VICENTINO, Andrea
paintings: (H) $5,500

VICHI, F.
Italian 19th cent.
sculpture: (L) $550; (H) $20,900

VICHI, J.
sculpture: (H) $1,100

VICKERS, A.H.
paintings: (L) $77; (H) $935

VICKERS, Alfred
British 1786-1868
paintings: (L) $1,100; (H) $2,310

VICKERS, Alfred H.
British 19th cent.
paintings: (L) $550; (H) $687

VICKERS, C.
English 19th cent.
paintings: (H) $1,045

VICKERS, Charles
American
paintings: (H) $1,210

VICKERS, Henry Harold
British 1851-1919
paintings: (L) $1,100; (H) $1,540

VICKERY, Charles
paintings: (L) $121; (H) $2,640

VICKERY, John
Australian early 20th cent.
paintings: (H) $1,485

VICKREY, Robert
American b. 1926
paintings: (L) $1,540; (H) $12,100
drawings: (L) $1,650; (H) $4,400

VICTOR
sculpture: (L) $330; (H) $2,750

VICTORS, Jacobus
Dutch 1640-1705
paintings: (L) $6,600; (H) $16,500

VICTORS, Jan
Dutch 1620-1676
paintings: (L) $8,800; (H) $63,250

VICTORYNS, Anthonie
paintings: (L) $2,970; (H) $6,050

VIDAL
American
sculpture: (H) $800

VIDAL, Louis, known as Navatel
sculpture: (L) $242; (H) $1,760

VIEGERS, B.
paintings: (L) $33; (H) $825

VIEHL, F.
sculpture: (H) $3,575

VIEIRA DA SILVA, Maria Elena
French b. 1908
paintings: (L) $44,000; (H) $286,000
drawings: (L) $8,250; (H) $99,000

VIEN, Joseph Marie
1716-1809
paintings: (H) $13,200

VIEN, Joseph Marie, the younger
French 1762-1848
paintings: (H) $9,900

VIENA, F.
late 19th cent.
paintings: (H) $2,420

VIERIN, Emmanuel
Belgian b. 1869
paintings: (L) $1,100; (H) $4,400

VIERKANT, Brigitte
paintings: (H) $4,950

VIGEE-LEBRUN, Marie Louise
Elisabeth
French 1755-1842
paintings: (L) $16,500; (H) $300,000
drawings: (L) $1,100; (H) $33,000

VIGIL, Romando, Tse-Ye-Mu
American b. 1902
paintings: (L) $330; (H) $1,540
drawings: (H) $192

VIGNALI, Jacopo
paintings: (L) $715; (H) $7,700

VIGNAUD
Continental 19th cent.
paintings: (H) $1,540

VIGNERON, Pierre Roch
French 1789-1872
paintings: (L) $12,100; (H) $23,100

VIGNET, Henri
paintings: (H) $3,850

VIGNEY, Sylvain
French 1902-1970
paintings: (H) $475
drawings: (H) $660

VIGNOLES, Andre
French 20th cent.
paintings: (L) $308; (H) $3,575

VIGNON, Claude
French 1593-1670
paintings: (H) $22,000
drawings: (H) $41,250

VIGNON, Victor
French 1847-1909
paintings: (L) $2,750; (H) $24,200

VIGNOUX, A.
paintings: (H) $1,870

VIGOR, Charles
British ac. 1882-1917
paintings: (H) $1,320

VILA Y PRADES, Julio
Spanish 1875-1930
paintings: (H) $5,500

VILAS, R.
paintings: (H) $715

VILATO, Javier
French b. 1921
paintings: (L) $55; (H) $4,400

VILLA, Emile
paintings: (H) $2,090

VILLA, Hernando Gonzallo
American 1881-1952
paintings: (L) $303; (H) $2,750
drawings: (L) $220; (H) $1,980

VILLA Y PRADES, Julio
Spanish 19th/20th cent.
paintings: (H) $4,950

VILLACRES, Cesar A.
Ecuadorean b. 1880
paintings: (L) $110; (H) $5,500

VILLALOBOS MASTER
paintings: (H) $2,860

VILLAMIL, P.
ac. 1838-1870
paintings: (H) $990

VILLAMIZAR, Eduardo Ramirez
sculpture: (H) $11,000

VILLANAIS, Emmanuel
sculpture: (L) $242; (H) $3,575

VILLANDS(?), P.
French 19th/20th cent.
paintings: (H) $1,980

VILLANUEVA, Juan P.
Continental School 19th cent.
paintings: (L) $770; (H) $1,210

VILLANUEVA, Leoncio
Peruvian b. 1936
paintings: (L) $8,800; (H) $12,100

VILLEGAS
Spanish 19th cent.
paintings: (H) $1,870

VILLEGAS BRIEVA, Manuel
Spanish School 19th cent.
paintings: (H) $3,300

VILLEGAS Y CORDERO, Jose
Spanish 1848-1922
paintings: (L) $16,500; (H) $770,000
drawings: (L) $4,400; (H) $14,300

VILLEGAS Y CORDERO, Ricardo
Spanish b. 1852
paintings: (L) $13,200; (H) $30,800

VILLERS, Auguste de
French 19th cent.
paintings: (L) $1,100; (H) $1,980

VILLETTE, Elodie
French b. 1848
paintings: (H) $1,540

VILLIERS, T.
paintings: (H) $1,650

VILLON, Eugene
French b. 1879
drawings: (H) $1,540

VILLON, Jacques
French 1875-1963
paintings: (L) $4,950; (H) $363,000
drawings: (L) $330; (H) $30,800
sculpture: (H) $8,800

VILLORESI, Franco
paintings: (L) $247; (H) $1,045

VINALL, Joseph Williams Topham
British b. 1873
paintings: (H) $880

VINCELET, Victor
French d. 1871
paintings: (H) $1,210

VINCENNES, Charles Baillou
paintings: (H) $3,300

VINCENT
English 19th cent.
paintings: (H) $1,650

VINCENT, Francois Andre
French 1746-1816
paintings: (H) $462,000

VINCENT, George
English 1796-1831
paintings: (L) $1,100; (H) $1,650

VINCENT, H.
paintings: (H) $1,320

VINCENT, Harry Aiken
American 1864-1931
paintings: (L) $220; (H) $12,100

VINCENZA
paintings: (H) $5,500

VINCENZI, A.
paintings: (H) $1,650

VINCI, Leonardo da
Italian 1452-1519
drawings: (H) $3,630,000

VINCK, Franz
Belgian 19th cent.
paintings: (H) $1,210

VINCKE
paintings: (H) $2,970

VINE, J.
paintings: (H) $2,750

VINE, J.
English 19th cent.
paintings: (H) $2,200

VINEA, Francesco
Italian 1845/46-1902/04
paintings: (L) $1,320; (H) $2,310
drawings: (H) $2,860

VINEA (?), F. de
paintings: (H) $715

VINIEGRA Y LASSO, Salvador
Spanish 1862-1915
paintings: (H) $4,400

VINO, G.
contemporary
sculpture: (L) $385; (H) $1,320

VINTER, John Alfred
paintings: (H) $2,420

VINTERFROY
paintings: (H) $1,100

VINTON, Frederick Porter
American 1846-1911
paintings: (L) $330; (H) $3,250

VIOLET, Laurent
French 20th cent.
paintings: (H) $1,320

VIOLLET-LE-DUC, Victor
French 1848-1901
paintings: (L) $3,025; (H) $3,850

VIOLTI, E.
sculpture: (H) $715

VIPAUR, J.
European 19th cent.
paintings: (L) $990; (H) $1,320

VIRANO, A.J.
Italian 19th cent.
paintings: (L) $770; (H) $2,310

VIRY, Paul
French 1861-1881
paintings: (L) $6,325; (H) $15,400

VISCONTI, A.
paintings: (H) $1,210

VISCONTI, Alphonse Adolfo Ferraguti
French 1850-1924
paintings: (H) $7,700

VISKI, Janos
Hungarian b. 1891
paintings: (L) $330; (H) $935

VISKOLATY, W.E.
French 19th cent.
paintings: (H) $660

VISO, Nicola
paintings: (L) $2,860; (H) $12,100

VISPRE, Francois Xavier
paintings: (H) $5,500

VISSER, Adrianus de
paintings: (H) $8,250

VITAL-CORNU, Charles
French c. 1851-1927
sculpture: (H) $9,350

VITALI, E.
Italian 19th cent.
drawings: (L) $104; (H) $1,540

VITOLLO, A.
paintings: (H) $1,100

VITRINGA, Wigerus
paintings: (H) $7,700

VITTORIO
Italian 19th cent.
drawings: (L) $209; (H) $770

VITTOZ
sculpture: (H) $3,300

VITY, Andre de
French 20th cent.
paintings: (H) $1,045

VITY, Antonio de
Italian b. 1901
paintings: (L) $440; (H) $1,540

VIVANCOY, G.
paintings: (H) $1,045

VIVANT-DENON, Baron Dominique
1747-1825
drawings: (L) $770; (H) $1,980

VIVAR, Juan Correa de
ac. 1561
paintings: (H) $9,900

VIVARINI, Antonio
Italian c. 1415-1476/84
paintings: (H) $143,000

VIVIAN, Calthea
American 1857-1943
paintings: (H) $1,045
drawings: (H) $412

VIVIAN, G.
paintings: (L) $357; (H) $1,760

VIVIAN, J.
British 19th cent.
paintings: (H) $1,650

VIVIAN, John
paintings: (H) $2,420

VIVIN, Louis
French 1861-1936
paintings: (L) $605; (H) $16,500

VIVO, Pio
paintings: (H) $2,420

VIVREL, Andre Leon
French 1896-1976
paintings: (L) $715; (H) $880

VIZERS, Frederick
paintings: (H) $1,870

VIZKELETI, W.E.
Hungarian 1819-1895
paintings: (L) $950; (H) $1,650

VIZZOTTO-ALBERTI, Giuseppe
Italian 1862-1931
drawings: (H) $2,200

VLAMINCK, Maurice de
French 1876-1958
paintings: (L) $16,500; (H) $7,150,000
drawings: (L) $330; (H) $99,000

VLIEGER, Simon de
Dutch b.c. 1600, buried 1653
paintings: (H) $770,000

VLIET, Don van
contemporary
paintings: (H) $1,760

VLIET, Hendrick van
Dutch 1611-1675
paintings: (L) $4,400; (H) $148,500

VLIET, K.V.
Dutch 19th cent.
paintings: (L) $3,575; (H) $4,400

VLIET, Willem van der
Dutch c. 1584-1642
paintings: (L) $13,200; (H) $18,700

VOEGELE, A.
German 19th cent.
paintings: (H) $1,210

VOELLE, F.
19th cent.
paintings: (H) $715

VOERMIBURGH, V.
sculpture: (H) $1,320

VOET, Ferdinand
paintings: (L) $2,860; (H) $4,400

VOGEL, Cornelis Jan de and Eugene
VERBOECKHOVEN
paintings: (H) $12,100

VOGEL, Cornelis Jan de and Joseph
van SEVERDONCK
19th/20th cent.
paintings: (H) $3,850

VOGEL, Cornelius Jan de
Dutch 1824-1879
paintings: (L) $1,045; (H) $1,815

VOGEL, Donald
paintings: (H) $5,225

VOGELAER, Karel van, Carlo Dei Fiori
or Distelboom
Dutch 1653-1695
paintings: (L) $35,200; (H) $66,000

VOGELSANG, Christian Rudolph
paintings: (H) $1,650

VOGLER, Fritz
French 19th cent.
paintings: (H) $1,870

VOGT, Fritz G.
American ac. 1890-1900
drawings: (L) $1,100; (H) $6,600

VOGT, Louis Charles
American b. 1864
paintings: (L) $220; (H) $2,420
drawings: (L) $247; (H) $4,950

VOILLE, Jean
French 1744-1796
paintings: (H) $28,600

VOILLEMOT, Andre Charles
French 1823-1893
paintings: (L) $1,320; (H) $4,620

VOILLEMOT, Charles
French 1833-1887
paintings: (H) $1,320

VOIRIN, Jules Antoine
French 1833-1898
paintings: (L) $715; (H) $6,050

VOIRIN, Leon Joseph
French 1833-1887
paintings: (L) $13,200; (H) $148,500

VOIRIOT, Guillaume
French 1713-1799
paintings: (H) $52,800

VOISARD-MARGERIE, Adrien
Gabriel
French 19th cent.
paintings: (H) $12,100

VOISIN, A.
sculpture: (H) $660

VOLA, Joseph
paintings: (H) $1,320

VOLAIRE, Pierre Jacques
French 1729-1802
drawings: (L) $247; (H) $2,090

VOLCK, Adalbert John
American 1828-1912
paintings: (L) $495; (H) $2,860

VOLCKER, Robert
German 1854-1924
paintings: (H) $1,320

VOLDINI, Enrico
Italian 19th cent.
paintings: (H) $715

VOLEKER, Rob
paintings: (H) $1,045

VOLINGER, Wm.
paintings: (H) $770

VOLK, Douglas
American 1856-1935
paintings: (L) $110; (H) $8,800
drawings: (H) $220

VOLK, Leonard Wells
American 1828-1895
sculpture: (L) $1,980; (H) $9,900

VOLK, Leonard Wells and Augustus
SAINT GAUDENS
American 1828-1895
sculpture: (L) $8,800; (H) $15,400

VOLKART, Max
paintings: (H) $935

VOLKERS, A**
Dutch 19th cent.
paintings: (H) $1,210

VOLKERS, Adrianus
Dutch b. 1904
paintings: (H) $6,050

VOLKERS, Emil
German 1831-1905
paintings: (L) $1,650; (H) $18,700

VOLKERT, Edward Charles
American 1871-1935
paintings: (L) $550; (H) $5,720
drawings: (H) $605

VOLKHART, Max
German 1848-1924/35
paintings: (L) $9,900; (H) $41,800

VOLKMAR, Charles
American 1841-1914
paintings: (L) $660; (H) $2,900

VOLKMER, Bernard
American 1865-1929
paintings: (H) $550
drawings: (L) $55; (H) $715

VOLKMER, Hans
German 19th/20th cent.
paintings: (H) $660

VOLKOV, Sergei
Russian b. 1956
paintings: (L) $8,250; (H) $13,200

VOLL, F. Usher de
American 1873-1941
paintings: (L) $165; (H) $2,090

VOLLERDT, Johann Christian
German 1708/09-1769
paintings: (L) $11,000; (H) $24,200

VOLLET, H.
French 19th cent.
paintings: (L) $1,100; (H) $1,870

VOLLET, Henry Emile
French 19th cent.
paintings: (H) $1,100

VOLLMAR, Ludwig
German 1842-1884
paintings: (L) $15,400; (H) $19,800

VOLLMARK, K.
paintings: (H) $660

VOLLMER, Grace Libby
American 1884-1977
paintings: (L) $523; (H) $1,100

VOLLMER, Ruth
sculpture: (H) $1,210

VOLLMERING, Joseph
American 1810-1887
paintings: (L) $418; (H) $9,350

VOLLON, A.
19th/20th cent.
paintings: (H) $770

VOLLON, Alexis
French b. 1865
paintings: (L) $440; (H) $27,500

VOLLON, Antoine
French 1833-1900
paintings: (L) $193; (H) $44,000
drawings: (H) $385

VOLLWEIDER, Johann Jacob
German 1834-1891
paintings: (L) $3,300; (H) $4,400

VOLPE, Vincenzo
Italian 1855-1929
paintings: (L) $770; (H) $10,450

VOLTI
paintings: (H) $55
sculpture: (L) $1,210; (H) $3,025

VOLTI, Antoniucci
sculpture: (H) $7,700

VOLTOLINA, Pierd
Italian 19th/20th cent.
drawings: (H) $3,850

VOLTZ, Friedrich Johann
German 1817-1886
paintings: (L) $3,850; (H) $37,400
drawings: (H) $1,210

VOLTZ, J.
paintings: (H) $1,100

VON GUNTEN, Roger
Swiss/American b. 1933
paintings: (L) $660; (H) $880

VON SCHMIDT, Harold
American 1893-1982
paintings: (L) $2,860; (H) $3,080
drawings: (L) $350; (H) $418

VONCK, Jan
paintings: (H) $3,300

VONGLRIE, La
sculpture: (H) $880

VONNOH, Bessie Potter
American 1872-1955
sculpture: (L) $550; (H) $143,000

VONNOH, Robert William
American 1858-1933
paintings: (L) $440; (H) $44,000

VOOGD, Hendrick
Dutch 1768-1839
paintings: (H) $33,000

VOORBAES, J.
Continental 19th cent.
paintings: (H) $2,200

VOORDECKER, Henri
Belgian 1766-1839
paintings: (H) $4,400

VOORHEES, Clark Greenwood
American 1871-1933
paintings: (L) $715; (H) $12,100

VOORT, Cornelis van de
Flemish c. 1576-1624
paintings: (H) $52,800

VOORT, V. ver
paintings: (H) $11,000

VOORTMAN, Clara
German 19th cent.
paintings: (H) $1,540

VOOS, Von
Dutch 19th cent.
paintings: (H) $715

VOROBIEFF, Marvena Rosanovitch
paintings: (H) $7,700

VOROS, Bela
Hungarian 20th cent.
sculpture: (H) $2,200

VOS, Cornelis de
Flemish 1585-1651
paintings: (L) $4,675; (H) $10,450

VOS, Hubert
Dutch/American 1855-1935
paintings: (L) $495; (H) $1,980
drawings: (H) $880

VOS, J.D.
Dutch 19th cent.
paintings: (H) $8,250

VOS, Martin de
Flemish 1531/32-1603
paintings: (L) $2,200; (H) $44,000
drawings: (L) $3,520; (H) $5,225

VOS, Paul de
paintings: (H) $6,600

VOS, Simon de
1603-1676
paintings: (H) $4,180

VOS, Vincent de
Belgian 1829-1875
paintings: (L) $220; (H) $3,520

VOSEHER, Leopold
Austrian 1830-1877
paintings: (H) $3,025

VOSS, Carl Leopold
German 1856-1921
paintings: (L) $3,750; (H) $8,250

VOSS, Franklin Brooke
American 1880-1953
paintings: (L) $1,870; (H) $12,100

VOUET, Simon
French 1590-1641/49
paintings: (L) $104,500; (H) $275,000

VOULKOS, Peter
American b. 1924
sculpture: (L) $1,650; (H) $55,000

VOYET, Jacques
French b. 1927
paintings: (L) $770; (H) $880

VRANCX, Sebastian
Flemish 1573/78-1647
paintings: (L) $1,100; (H) $187,000

VREEDENBURGH, Cornelius
Dutch 1880-1946
paintings: (L) $3,850; (H) $6,820

VREELAND, F. van
Dutch 19th/20th cent.
paintings: (L) $242; (H) $880
drawings: (L) $198; (H) $715

VREELAND, S. Van
Dutch 19th/20th cent.
paintings: (H) $770

VREESE, G. de
sculpture: (H) $1,430

VRIENDT, Juliaan de
paintings: (H) $1,870

VRIES, Abraham de
paintings: (H) $6,380

VRIES, Paul Vredemann de
Flemish c. 1567-after 1630
paintings: (H) $52,250

VRIES, Roelof van
Dutch c. 1631-after 1681
paintings: (L) $1,045; (H) $14,300

VRIES, Sjoerd de
Dutch 20th cent.
paintings: (L) $550; (H) $660

VRIES, Sophia de
Dutch b. 1915
paintings: (H) $880

VROLYK, Jan
Dutch 1845-1894
paintings: (H) $3,300

VROOM, Cornelis
paintings: (H) $2,200

VUCHT, Gerrit van
Dutch ac. 1658-1697
paintings: (H) $22,000

VUCHT, Jan van der
paintings: (H) $1,760

VUILLARD, Edouard
French 1868-1940
paintings: (L) $2,420; (H) $7,700,000
drawings: (L) $440; (H) $550,000

VUILLEFROY, Felix de
French b. 1841
paintings: (L) $880; (H) $1,760

VULLIAMY, Gerard
French b. 1909
paintings: (H) $1,210

VYLDER, C. de
Dutch 19th cent.
paintings: (H) $14,300

VYTLACIL, Vaclav
American b. 1892
paintings: (L) $165; (H) $4,675
drawings: (L) $660; (H) $2,475

WAAGEN
German ac. 1860's
paintings: (H) $6,600

Guru Sculptor

Peter Voulkos (b. 1924) is an important and influential contemporary American sculptor. Born in Bozeman, Montana, he attended Montana State College and the California College of Arts and Crafts in Oakland, where he received an M.F.A. degree. He rapidly gained an international reputation as an excellent ceramist, receiving the Rodin Museum Prize in sculpture at the First Paris Biennial and the Gold Medal at the International Ceramic Exhibition at Cannes, France, in 1955. In 1959 he taught at Black Mountain College, an important creative arts school in North Carolina, where he met Jasper Johns, Robert Rauschenberg, and Franz Kline.

Under the influence of these Abstract Expressionists, Voulkos began to experiment with the form and surface of clay as a means of expression in itself; he abandoned the concept of the pot as a vessel and molded his clay into monumental sculptures. In the 1960s, he began to cast large slabs of bronze to create his sculptures. His innovative works have influenced many other sculptors including Kenneth Price, John Mason, and Ron Nagle. Voulkos also has been instrumental in founding many ceramics and sculpture workshops. Until 1988 he taught at the University of California, Berkeley. In 1991 he was still actively working and exhibiting. (Peter Voulkos, *Bird Table*, bronze, 13 in. high, Butterfield, October 11, 1989, $11,000)

WAAGEN, Adalbert
  German 1833-1898
  paintings: (H) $14,850

WAAY, Nicolaes van der
  Dutch 1855-1936
  paintings: (L) $3,850; (H) $12,100

WACHSMUTH, Ferdinand
  French 1802-1869
  paintings: (H) $8,800

WACHSMUTH, Maximilian
  German 1859-1912
  paintings: (L) $3,960; (H) $5,500

WACHTEL, Elmer
American 1864-1929
paintings: (L) $325; (H) $27,500
drawings: (L) $990; (H) $3,850

WACHTEL, Marion Kavanaugh
American 1875-1954
paintings: (L) $2,090; (H) $8,250
drawings: (L) $1,100; (H) $66,000

WACHTEL, Wilhelm
Polish 1875-1942
paintings: (L) $1,650; (H) $3,300
drawings: (H) $1,430

WADSWORTH, Frank Russell
American 1874-1905
paintings: (L) $825; (H) $880

WADSWORTH, Wedworth
American 1846-1927
drawings: (L) $55; (H) $990

WAEL, Cornelis de
Flemish 1592-1667
drawings: (H) $1,320

WAELPUT, C.L.
American 19th cent.
paintings: (H) $8,250

WAGEMAEKERS, Victor
Flemish b. 1876
paintings: (H) $935

WAGEMANS, Maurice
paintings: (H) $4,400

WAGMANS, Pieter Johannes
Dutch 1879-1955
paintings: (H) $1,100

WAGNER
sculpture: (H) $1,045

WAGNER, Alexander von
Hungarian 1838-1919
paintings: (H) $35,200

WAGNER, Carl
paintings: (H) $7,700

WAGNER, Edmund
German 1830-1859
paintings: (H) $2,640

WAGNER, Ferdinand, Jr.
German 1847-1927
paintings: (L) $2,200; (H) $5,775

WAGNER, Ferdinand, Sr.
German 1819-1881
paintings: (L) $577; (H) $49,500

WAGNER, Fred
American 1864-1940
paintings: (L) $110; (H) $880
drawings: (L) $33; (H) $990

WAGNER, Fritz
German 1896-1939
paintings: (L) $440; (H) $4,180

WAGNER, Fritz
Swiss b. 1872
paintings: (L) $467; (H) $4,950

WAGNER, George
American 19th/20th cent.
sculpture: (H) $4,125

WAGNER, H.
Austrian late 19th/early 20th cent
paintings: (H) $715

WAGNER, Helene
German 19th cent.
paintings: (H) $3,300

WAGNER, J.
paintings: (H) $935

WAGNER, Jacob
American 1852-1898
paintings: (L) $1,210; (H) $8,800

WAGNER, Karl
German/Austrian 19th cent.
paintings: (L) $302; (H) $4,950

WAGNER, Paul
paintings: (H) $2,750

WAGNER, Paul Hermann
German b. 1852
paintings: (H) $8,250

WAGNER, Wilhelm George
Dutch b. 1814
paintings: (H) $1,980

WAGONER, Harry B.
American 1889-1950
paintings: (L) $495; (H) $825
drawings: (H) $110

WAGONER, Robert B.
American 20th cent.
paintings: (H) $1,320

WAGREZ, Jacques Clement
French 1846/50-1908
paintings: (H) $18,700

WAHLBERG, Alfred
Swedish 1834-1906
paintings: (L) $1,200; (H) $17,600

WAHLQVIST, Ehrnfried
Swedish 1815-1895
paintings: (H) $9,900

WAIN, Louis William
English 1860-1939
paintings: (H) $11,000
drawings: (H) $522

WAINEWRIGHT, Thomas Francis
French 19th cent.
paintings: (H) $4,400
drawings: (L) $275; (H) $2,475

WAINRIGHT, John
paintings: (H) $3,080

WAINWRIGHT, John
British ac. 1859-1869
paintings: (H) $1,650

WAINWRIGHT, William John
British 1855-1931
drawings: (H) $9,350

WAITE, E.
paintings: (H) $880

WAITT, Marion Martha Parkhurst
American b. 1875
paintings: (H) $770

WAKEFIELD, M.B.
American 20th cent.
paintings: (H) $825

WALBOURN, Ernest
British ac. 1895-1920
paintings: (L) $275; (H) $29,150

WALCH, Charles
French 1898-1948
paintings: (H) $3,850

WALCOTT, Harry Mills
American 1870-1944
paintings: (L) $1,980; (H) $159,500
drawings: (H) $24,200

WALCUTT, William
American 1819-1895
paintings: (L) $412; (H) $1,210

WALD, A.
German 19th cent.
paintings: (H) $687

WALD, Carol
paintings: (L) $19; (H) $770
drawings: (H) $33

WALDE, Alfons
Austrian b. 1891
paintings: (L) $880; (H) $41,250

WALDECK, Kunz Meyer
paintings: (H) $2,750

WALDEIM, Auguste
German 19th cent.
paintings: (H) $1,485

WALDEN, Lionel
American 1861-1933
paintings: (L) $418; (H) $2,200
drawings: (L) $220; (H) $275

WALDHAUSER, Anton
paintings: (H) $715

WALDMULLER, Ferdinand Georg
Austrian 1793-1865
paintings: (H) $198,000

WALDO, J. Frank
paintings: (L) $22; (H) $660
drawings: (L) $165; (H) $330

WALDO, Samuel Lovett
American 1783-1861
paintings: (L) $660; (H) $4,400

WALDO, Samuel Lovett and William
JEWETT
American 19th cent.
paintings: (L) $220; (H) $2,200

WALDORP, Antoine
Dutch 1803-1866
paintings: (H) $13,200

WALE, Samuel
paintings: (H) $20,350

WALES, Orlando G.
American 20th cent.
paintings: (L) $330; (H) $1,430

WALKER, Addison
American 20th cent.
paintings: (L) $220; (H) $1,650
drawings: (H) $522

WALKER, Arthur George
British 1861-1939
paintings: (H) $7,700

WALKER, Barvo
American 20th cent.
sculpture: (L) $990; (H) $4,125

WALKER, Charles Howard
American 1857-1936
drawings: (L) $55; (H) $2,640

WALKER, Charles J.
British ac. 1860-1870
paintings: (H) $1,760

WALKER, Dame Ethel
English 1861-1951
paintings: (H) $1,320

WALKER, Edna M.
drawings: (H) $770

WALKER, Frank H.
British ac. 1878-1893
drawings: (H) $1,540

WALKER, Frederick R.
American 20th cent.
paintings: (H) $1,980

WALKER, George
sculpture: (H) $4,125

WALKER, Henry Oliver
American 1843-1929
paintings: (L) $1,100; (H) $1,760
drawings: (H) $825

WALKER, Horatio
Canadian 1858-1938
paintings: (L) $825; (H) $14,300

WALKER, Inez (Nathaniel)
American 1911-after 1977
drawings: (L) $325; (H) $660

WALKER, J.F.
British 20th cent.
paintings: (H) $1,100

WALKER, James
American 1819-1889
paintings: (H) $33,000

WALKER, James Alexander
British 1831-1898
paintings: (L) $2,200; (H) $132,000

WALKER, John
British b. 1939
paintings: (L) $4,950; (H) $35,750
drawings: (L) $825; (H) $2,860

WALKER, John Eaton
British ac. 1855-1865
paintings: (L) $462; (H) $7,700

WALKER, John Hanson
paintings: (L) $242; (H) $2,860

WALKER, John Rawson
British 1796-1873
paintings: (H) $935

WALKER, Joseph Francis
British ac. 1857-1889
paintings: (H) $63,250

WALKER, M.J.
American 19th/20th cent.
paintings: (H) $1,650

WALKER, Martha
American
paintings: (H) $3,850

WALKER, Robert Hollands
British 19th/20th cent.
drawings: (L) $440; (H) $4,675

WALKER, S.S.
paintings: (H) $880

WALKER, Samuel Edmund
paintings: (H) $1,320

WALKER, T. Dart
American 1869-1914
drawings: (L) $1,540; (H) $1,760

WALKER, William Aiken
American c. 1838-1921
paintings: (L) $550; (H) $31,900
drawings: (L) $1,210; (H) $2,310

WALKLEY, David Birdsey
American 1849-1934
paintings: (L) $396; (H) $2,090

WALKOWITZ, Abraham
American 1880-1965
paintings: (L) $550; (H) $22,000
drawings: (L) $83; (H) $4,180

WALL, A.
paintings: (H) $1,650

WALL, A. Bryan
American 1872-1937
paintings: (L) $150; (H) $6,325

WALL, Alfred S.
American 1825-1896
paintings: (L) $275; (H) $1,320

WALL, Bruce
contemporary
sculpture: (H) $7,150

WALL, W.
paintings: (H) $1,210

WALL, W.
19th/20th cent.
paintings: (H) $715

WALL, W.C.
paintings: (H) $1,650

WALL, William Allen
American 1801-1885
paintings: (L) $660; (H) $2,200
drawings: (L) $220; (H) $2,700

WALL, William Archibald
British b. 1828
paintings: (H) $2,640

WALL, William Coventry
American 1810-1886
paintings: (H) $770

WALL, William Guy
American 1792-after 1864
paintings: (L) $3,300; (H) $15,400

WALLACE, David
American 20th cent.
drawings: (H) $880

WALLACE, James
British 1872-1911
paintings: (L) $132; (H) $1,045

WALLACE, Lillie T.
American early 20th cent.
paintings: (L) $77; (H) $1,100

WALLACE, Moira
American 1911-1979
paintings: (H) $880

WALLENDORF, Hans Diehl
German b. 1877
paintings: (H) $6,050

WALLER, Frank
American 1842-1923
paintings: (L) $247; (H) $3,300

WALLER, Mary Lemon
English d. 1931
paintings: (H) $770

WALLER, Samuel Edmund
British 1850-1903
paintings: (L) $2,200; (H) $27,500

WALLIN, Carl E.
paintings: (L) $412; (H) $3,300

WALLIS, Alfred
British 1855-1942
paintings: (H) $1,210

WALLIS, F.
paintings: (L) $55; (H) $715

WALLIS, T.W.
Irish 19th cent.
sculpture: (H) $1,540

WALRAVEN, Jan
Dutch 1827-after 1874
paintings: (L) $1,980; (H) $5,500

WALRAVENT, J.
paintings: (H) $2,860

WALROND, E.M.
American 20th cent.
paintings: (H) $715

WALSCAPELLE, Jacob van
Dutch 1644-1727
paintings: (H) $181,500

WALSH, A.A.
American 19th/20th cent.
paintings: (H) $935

WALT, Anna
drawings: (H) $3,300

WALTENSPERGER, Charles
American 1871-1931
paintings: (L) $55; (H) $2,420

WALTER, Adele
paintings: (H) $1,540

WALTER, Christian J.
American 1872-1938
paintings: (H) $3,520

WALTER, Emma
British 19th cent.
paintings: (L) $1,045; (H) $1,100

WALTER, Martha
American 1875-1976
paintings: (L) $990; (H) $44,000
drawings: (L) $220; (H) $1,320

WALTER, T.C.
English? 19th/20th cent.
paintings: (H) $715

WALTER, Valerie Harrisse
American
sculpture: (L) $3,850; (H) $7,700

WALTER, W.G.
Dutch 20th cent.
paintings: (H) $1,540

WALTERS, Carl
American
sculpture: (H) $5,500

WALTERS, Emile
American b. 1893
paintings: (L) $110; (H) $1,320

WALTERS, G.J.
drawings: (H) $825

WALTERS, George Stanfield
British 1838-1924
paintings: (L) $1,650; (H) $4,675
drawings: (L) $302; (H) $1,320

WALTERS, John
American late 18th cent.
drawings: (H) $1,430

WALTERS, Joseph
English 1783-1856
paintings: (H) $28,600

WALTERS, Samuel
British 1811-1882
paintings: (L) $700; (H) $79,750

WALTHER, Charles H.
American 1879-1937
paintings: (L) $192; (H) $4,400

WALTHER, Jakob
c. 1570-1604
drawings: (H) $7,700

WALTON, F.
English 19th cent.
paintings: (H) $4,675

WALTON, Frank
English 1840-1928
paintings: (L) $242; (H) $3,520

WALTON, Henry
American 1746-1813
paintings: (H) $96,250

WALTON, Henry
American 1804-1865
drawings: (H) $9,900

WALTON, John W.
paintings: (H) $880

WALTON, William
American 1843-1915
paintings: (H) $3,025
drawings: (L) $88; (H) $3,025

WAN, J.C.
American 20th cent.
paintings: (H) $715

WANDESFORDE, Juan B.
American 1817-1872
paintings: (L) $1,540; (H) $4,400

WANING-STEVELS, Marie van
Dutch b. 1874
paintings: (H) $1,320

WANKIE, Wladyslaw
Polish 1860-1925
paintings: (L) $308; (H) $4,400

WANLASS, Stanley
sculpture: (L) $7,700; (H) $18,700

WANTE, E.
sculpture: (L) $440; (H) $770

WARBURG, Stephanie
sculpture: (H) $1,430

WARD
English b. 1902
drawings: (H) $660

WARD, Charles C.
American b. 1900
paintings: (H) $1,870

WARD, Charles Caleb
American c. 1831-1896
paintings: (H) $30,800
drawings: (H) $1,320

WARD, Edgar Melville, Jr.
French/American b. 1887
paintings: (L) $137; (H) $770

WARD, Edmund F.
American b. 1892
paintings: (L) $550; (H) $5,225

WARD, Edward Matthew
English 1816-1879
paintings: (L) $715; (H) $33,000

WARD, Edward N.
American contemporary
paintings: (H) $1,800

WARD, Ellen
American 19th/20th cent.
paintings: (L) $248; (H) $660

WARD, J. Stephen
American b. 1876
paintings: (L) $385; (H) $660

WARD, James
paintings: (L) $3,520; (H) $71,500

WARD, James
British 1769-1859
paintings: (L) $1,980; (H) $297,000
drawings: (L) $110; (H) $440

WARD, John Quincy Adams
American 1830-1910
sculpture: (L) $385; (H) $30,800

WARD, M.T.
paintings: (H) $935

WARD, William, Jr.
American
paintings: (L) $148; (H) $1,210
drawings: (H) $440

WARD, William, Jr.
American 20th cent.
paintings: (L) $467; (H) $935

WARDLE, Arthur
English 1864-1949
paintings: (L) $2,750; (H) $46,750
drawings: (L) $187; (H) $5,500

WARDLEWORTH, J.L.
English 19th cent.
paintings: (L) $330; (H) $825
drawings: (H) $165

WARE, Thomas
American c. 1820
paintings: (H) $5,225

WARFF, Ann
contemporary
sculpture: (H) $5,280

WARHOL, Andy
American 1928/31-1987
paintings: (L) $1,430; (H) $4,070,000
drawings: (L) $99; (H) $93,500
sculpture: (L) $1,100; (H) $77,000

WARHOL, Andy and Gerard
MALANGA
contemporary
drawings: (L) $11,000; (II) $17,600

WARNEKE, Heinrich
sculpture: (H) $1,210

WARNER, Everett Longley
American 1877-1963
paintings: (L) $715; (H) $5,500
drawings: (L) $660; (H) $1,980

WARNER, Nell Walker
American 1891-1970
paintings: (L) $303; (H) $4,400
drawings: (L) $275; (H) $303

WARNER, Olin Levi
American
sculpture: (L) $770; (H) $880

WARREN, A. Coolidge
American 1819-1904
paintings: (H) $1,045

WARREN, Andrew W.
American d. 1873
paintings: (L) $825; (H) $1,210

WARREN, Edmund George
drawings: (L) $528; (H) $5,280

WARREN, Edward L.
American
drawings: (H) $770

WARREN, Henry
British 1794-1879
drawings: (H) $1,210

WARREN, Melvin C.
American b. 1920
paintings: (L) $17,600; (H) $45,100

WARREN, Russ
American 20th cent.
paintings: (L) $715; (H) $2,200

WARREN, W.
British 19th cent.
paintings: (H) $2,200

WARREN, William White
British c. 1832-1912
paintings: (H) $1,760

WARSHAW, Howard
American b. 1920
paintings: (L) $468; (H) $2,475

WARSHAWSKY, Abel George
American 1873-1959
paintings: (L) $220; (H) $26,400

WASHBURN, Mary May Nightingale
American 1861-1932
paintings: (H) $3,850

WASHINGTON, Elizabeth Fisher
American 20th cent.
paintings: (L) $522; (H) $1,430
drawings: (L) $66; (H) $990

WASHINGTON, Georges
French 1827-1910
paintings: (L) $1,210; (H) $30,800

WASLEY, Frank
English b. 1854, ac. 1880-1914
paintings: (H) $770

WASMULLER, J.H.
American 19th cent.
paintings: (H) $11,000

WASSENBERG, Matthieu
Belgian b. 1939
paintings: (H) $1,100

WASSERMAN-LEVY, Margaret
American b. 1899
sculpture: (H) $9,900

WASSNETZOFF, Apolinarji
Michailovitch
Russian 1858-1933
paintings: (H) $715

WASSON, George Savary
American 1855-1926
paintings: (H) $1,210

WATCHEL, Elmer
American 1864-1929
drawings: (H) $1,100

WATELET, Charles Joseph
Belgian 1867-1954
paintings: (L) $5,775; (H) $11,000

WATELET, Louis Etienne
French 1780-1866
paintings: (H) $4,290

WATELIN, Louis
French 1838-1905
paintings: (L) $1,210; (H) $3,520

WATERHOUSE, John William
British 1849-1917
paintings: (L) $8,250; (H) $8,800
drawings: (H) $38,500

WATERLOO, Anthonie
Dutch 1609/10-1690
paintings: (H) $1,331
drawings: (L) $2,200; (H) $11,000

WATERLOW, Sir Ernest Albert
English 1850-1919
paintings: (H) $2,310
drawings: (L) $110; (H) $825

WATERMAN, Marcus A.
American 1834-1914
paintings: (L) $220; (H) $1,980
drawings: (H) $110

WATERMAN, Marge
paintings: (H) $1,045

WATERS, George W.
American 1832-1912
paintings: (L) $193; (H) $1,980
drawings: (H) $462

WATERS, Susan C.
American 1823-1900
paintings: (L) $907; (H) $15,400

WATKINS, Franklin Chenault
American 1894-1972
paintings: (L) $1,210; (H) $9,900
drawings: (L) $55; (H) $330

WATMOUGH, G.
paintings: (H) $15,400

WATRIN, Etienne
sculpture: (H) $1,980

WATRIN, Fred
American 20th cent.
paintings: (H) $1,430

WATROUS, Harry Willson
American 1857-1940
paintings: (L) $330; (H) $27,500
drawings: (L) $357; (H) $1,320

WATSON, Adele
American 1873-1947
paintings: (H) $2,090

WATSON, Charles Augustus
American 1857-1923
paintings: (L) $203; (H) $1,100

WATSON, Charles Edward
English 19th/20th cent.
paintings: (L) $302; (H) $1,320

WATSON, George
British 1767-1837
paintings: (L) $2,420; (H) $2,750

WATSON, Hamilton
20th cent.
paintings: (L) $880; (H) $2,090

WATSON, Homer Ransford
Canadian 1855-1936
paintings: (L) $770; (H) $6,050

WATSON, J.
American 19th cent.
paintings: (H) $26,400

WATSON, Nan
American 19th/20th cent.
paintings: (L) $550; (H) $880

WATSON, P. Fletcher
British 1842-1907
drawings: (H) $990

WATSON, Richard
paintings: (H) $770

WATSON, Robert
British active 1877-1915
paintings: (L) $880; (H) $2,090

WATSON, Robert
English ac. 1845-1866
paintings: (L) $1,155; (H) $4,400

WATSON, Syd
paintings: (H) $1,925

WATSON, W.
paintings: (H) $3,575

WATSON, Walter J.
British b. 1879
paintings: (L) $550; (H) $2,475

WATSON, William
British 19th/20th cent.
paintings: (L) $2,640; (H) $7,150

WATSON, William, Jr.
British d. 1921
paintings: (L) $385; (H) $19,250
drawings: (H) $385

WATSON-GORDON, Sir John
English 1790-1864
paintings: (H) $17,600

WATT, Linnie
English 19th/20th cent.
paintings: (H) $9,350

WATTEAU, Antoine
French 1684-1721
drawings: (L) $55,000; (H) $852,500

WATTEAU, Louis Joseph, called
WATTEAU De Lille
French 1731-1798
paintings: (L) $16,500; (H) $71,500

WATTER, Joseph
German 1838-1913
paintings: (L) $4,125; (H) $5,500

WATTS, D.
American 20th cent.
paintings: (L) $198; (H) $715

WATTS, F.W.
paintings: (H) $5,500

WATTS, Frederick W.
English 1800-1862
paintings: (L) $1,650; (H) $57,200

WATTS, George Frederick
British 1817-1904
paintings: (L) $2,200; (H) $143,000
drawings: (H) $7,700

WATTS, Robert
contemporary
sculpture: (H) $880

WATTS, Sidney
English 19th/20th cent.
paintings: (H) $687

WATTS, William Clothier
American 1869-1961
drawings: (L) $550; (H) $1,980

WATZDORF, M.
German 19th cent.
paintings: (L) $990; (H) $4,400

WATZELHAN, Carl
German 1867-1942
paintings: (H) $6,820

WAUD, Alfred R.
American 1828-1891
drawings: (L) $770; (H) $6,050

WAUGH, Coulton
American 1896-1973
paintings: (L) $137; (H) $880
drawings: (L) $110; (H) $825

WAUGH, Frederick Judd
American 1861-1940
paintings: (L) $330; (H) $28,600
drawings: (L) $275; (H) $1,210

WAUGH, Ida
American d. 1919
paintings: (L) $495; (H) $3,690

WAUGH, Samuel Bell
American 1814-1884
paintings: (L) $264; (H) $3,520

WAUTERS, Camille
Belgian 1856-1919
paintings: (L) $7,150; (H) $11,000

WAY, Andrew John Henry
American 1826-1888
paintings: (L) $1,320; (H) $20,900

WAY, Charles Jones
English/Canadian 1834-1919
paintings: (L) $700; (H) $3,630
drawings: (H) $1,540

WAY, George Brevitt
American b. 1854
paintings: (L) $192; (H) $880

WAY, Tom Robert
drawings: (L) $660; (H) $1,650

WAYANKE, R.
German 19th cent.
paintings: (H) $1,980

WAYCOTT, Hedley
American 1865-1937
paintings: (L) $110; (H) $4,620

WAYNE, June Claire
American
paintings: (L) $715; (H) $770

WEATHERBEE, George Faulkner
American 1851-1920
paintings: (H) $4,950

WEATHERBY, Richard C.
British ac. 1919-1948
paintings: (L) $522; (H) $15,950

WEATHERHEAD, William Haris
British 19th cent.
paintings: (H) $3,500

WEAVER, Arthur
paintings: (H) $440
drawings: (L) $1,430; (H) $1,650

WEAVER, Jay
American 20th cent.
paintings: (L) $220; (H) $2,100

WEAVER, Thomas
English 1774-1844
paintings: (L) $357; (H) $20,900

WEBB, Byron
British ac. 1846-1866
paintings: (L) $1,980; (H) $3,080

WEBB, Charles Meer
British 1830-1895
paintings: (L) $2,475; (H) $7,260

WEBB, Edward Walter
British 1810-1851
paintings: (H) $3,300

WEBB, J.
English 20th cent.
paintings: (L) $550; (H) $1,045

WEBB, James
English 1825-1895
paintings: (L) $880; (H) $49,500
drawings: (L) $66; (H) $275

WEBB, W.
Canadian ac. 1869-1870
paintings: (L) $175; (H) $4,250

WEBB, W.G.
English 19th cent.
paintings: (L) $605; (H) $770

WEBB, William
British ac. 1819-1850
paintings: (H) $18,700

WEBB, William Edward
British c. 1862-1903
paintings: (L) $1,870; (H) $11,000

WEBBE, William J.
British ac. 1853-1878
paintings: (L) $935; (H) $2,970

WEBBER, Charles T.
American 1825-1911
paintings: (L) $302; (H) $13,200

WEBBER, Otis S.
paintings: (L) $2,200; (H) $2,420

WEBBER, W.
American
paintings: (L) $66; (H) $990

WEBBER, Wesley
American 1839/41-1914
paintings: (L) $165; (H) $4,950

WEBER, A.
French 19th/20th cent.
paintings: (H) $3,300

WEBER, Alfred
Swiss b. 1859
paintings: (L) $1,210; (H) $1,320

WEBER, Alfred Charles
French 1862-1922
paintings: (L) $770; (H) $3,080

WEBER, Anton
German 1833-1909
drawings: (H) $1,870

WEBER, C.
American 19th cent.
paintings: (H) $1,430

WEBER, Carl
American 1850-1921
paintings: (L) $412; (H) $4,620
drawings: (L) $110; (H) $2,145

WEBER, C. Phillip
American b. 1849
paintings: (L) $77; (H) $8,800
drawings: (H) $220

WEBER, Frederick T.
American 1883-1956
paintings: (L) $358; (H) $660
drawings: (L) $220; (H) $440

WEBER, Gottlieb Daniel Paul
German 1823-1916
paintings: (H) $38,500

WEBER, Heinrich
German 1843-1913
paintings: (H) $770

WEBER, Heinrich
Swiss b. 1892
paintings: (H) $4,125

WEBER, Heinz
paintings: (H) $1,650

WEBER, Henrich A.
Continental 19th cent.
paintings: (H) $1,430

WEBER, M.
German 19th cent.
paintings: (H) $11,000

WEBER, Marie, PHILIPS-WEBER
Dutch ac. 1873
paintings: (H) $1,210

WEBER, Max
American 1881-1961
paintings: (L) $2,860; (H) $38,500
drawings: (L) $605; (H) $52,800
sculpture: (L) $2,970; (H) $9,350

WEBER, Otis R.
American 19th cent.
paintings: (H) $1,320

WEBER, Otis S.
American
paintings: (L) $275; (H) $4,250
drawings: (L) $77; (H) $413

WEBER, Otto
German 1832-1888
paintings: (H) $880

WEBER, Paul
German/American 1823-1916
paintings: (L) $385; (H) $19,800
drawings: (L) $110; (H) $385

WEBER, R.
paintings: (H) $825

WEBER, Rudolf
Austrian b. 1872
paintings: (L) $176; (H) $3,080

WEBER, S.
American
paintings: (H) $1,100

WEBER, Theodore
French 1838-1907
paintings: (L) $1,320; (H) $22,000
drawings: (H) $275

WEBER, W.
British 19th cent.
paintings: (H) $1,980

WEBSTER, George
English ac. 1797-1832
paintings: (L) $1,650; (H) $4,950

WEBSTER, J.
paintings: (H) $660

WEBSTER, Thomas
British 1800-1886
paintings: (L) $1,045; (H) $4,950

WEEDEN, Eleanor Revere
American b. 1898
paintings: (H) $825

WEEKES, Henry, Jr.
British ac. 1849-1888
paintings: (L) $5,500; (H) $6,050

WEEKES, Herbert William
British ac. 1864-1904
paintings: (L) $7,150; (H) $11,000

WEEKES, William Henry
British ac. 1851-1884
paintings: (L) $1,210; (H) $2,750

WEEKS, Edwin Lord
American 1849-1903
paintings: (L) $440; (H) $242,000
drawings: (H) $467

WEEKS, James
American b. 1922
paintings: (H) $11,000
drawings: (H) $1,980

WEEKS, T.
paintings: (H) $1,650

WEELE, Herman Johannes van der
Dutch 1852-1930
paintings: (L) $550; (H) $3,025

WEENIX, Jan
Dutch 1640-1719
paintings: (L) $22,000; (H) $539,000

WEENIX, Jan Baptist
Dutch 1621-1663
paintings: (L) $20,900; (H) $41,800

WEERTS, Jean Joseph
French 1847-1927
paintings: (H) $5,500

WEGER, Marie
American b. 1882
paintings: (L) $467; (H) $3,520

WEGMAN, William
American b. 1943
paintings: (H) $82,500
drawings: (L) $1,100; (H) $4,180

WEGMAYR, Sebastian
Austrian 1776-1857
paintings: (H) $12,100

WEGUELIN, John Reinhard
British 1849-1927
paintings: (L) $5,500; (H) $26,400
drawings: (H) $330

WEHR, M.
paintings: (H) $935

WEICHBERGER, Eduard
German 1843-1913
paintings: (H) $6,600
drawings: (H) $1,045

WEIDELL
German ? 19th cent.
paintings: (L) $825; (H) $825

WEIDENBACH, Augustus
American ac. 1853-1869
drawings: (H) $5,775

WEIGALL, Arthur Howes
British ac. 1856-1892
paintings: (L) $990; (H) $8,800

WEIGAND, Gustave
German/American 1870-1957
paintings: (L) $55; (H) $3,960

WEIGELE, Henry
sculpture: (L) $1,925; (H) $13,200

WEIL, Harrison
drawings: (H) $2,640

WEIL, M.
paintings: (H) $990

WEILAND, Johannes
Dutch 1856-1909
paintings: (L) $4,675; (H) $5,500
drawings: (L) $170; (H) $660

WEILER, Milton
paintings: (H) $2,860
drawings: (L) $605; (H) $2,640

WEINBERG, Elbert
sculpture: (L) $660; (H) $3,025

WEINBERG, Steven
contemporary
sculpture: (H) $3,960

WEINBERGER
sculpture: (H) $1,100

WEINDORF, Arthur
American b. 1885
paintings: (H) $715

WEINER, A.
sculpture: (H) $770

WEINER, Egon
Austrian/American b. 1906
drawings: (H) $33
sculpture: (H) $715

WEINGAERTNER, Hans
American 1896-1970
drawings: (L) $880; (H) $2,200

WEINMAN, Adolph Alexander
German/American 1870-1952
sculpture: (L) $550; (H) $39,600

WEINRICH, Agnes
American 1873-1946
paintings: (L) $55; (H) $3,300
drawings: (L) $110; (H) $770

WEIR, John Ferguson
American 1841-1926
paintings: (L) $2,200; (H) $3,630

WEIR, Julian Alden
American 1852-1919
paintings: (L) $770; (H) $440,000
drawings: (L) $550; (H) $42,900

WEIR, Robert Walter
American 1803-1889
paintings: (H) $4,730
drawings: (L) $33; (H) $24,200

WEIR, Robert Walter, Jr.
American 1836-1905
paintings: (L) $3,960; (H) $88,000
drawings: (H) $1,100

WEIROTTER, Franz Edmond
German 1730-1771
drawings: (H) $1,045

WEIS, John Ellsworth
American b. 1892
paintings: (L) $1,045; (H) $2,750

WEISBUCH, Claude
French b. 1927
paintings: (L) $605; (H) $9,900

WEISE, Karl
German 19th cent.
paintings: (H) $1,100

WEISHAUPT, Victor
paintings: (H) $1,980

WEISMAN, W.H.
American 19th/20th cent.
paintings: (L) $99; (H) $1,100

WEISMANN, J.
paintings: (H) $660

WEISS, Emil Rudolf
German 1875-1942
paintings: (H) $3,080

WEISS, Georges, or Emile Georges,
called Geo WEISS
French b. 1861
paintings: (L) $3,300; (H) $22,000

WEISS, H.
paintings: (H) $770

WEISS, Johann Baptist
German 1812-1879
paintings: (H) $4,400

WEISS, Jose
British 1859-1929
paintings: (L) $660; (H) $11,000

WEISS, Samuel A.
American b. 1874
paintings: (H) $3,025

WEISSE, Rudolf
Swiss b. 1846
paintings: (H) $48,400

WEISSE, Rudolph
Austrian b. 1869
paintings: (L) $44,000; (H) $71,500

WEISSENBRUCH, Jan Hendrik
Dutch 1824-1903
paintings: (L) $1,320; (H) $28,600
drawings: (L) $770; (H) $1,210

WEISSMAN, W.H.
American 19th/20th cent.
paintings: (H) $880

WEISZ, Adolphe
French b. 1868; ac. 1875-1900
paintings: (L) $2,200; (H) $27,500
drawings: (H) $468

WELCH, Guy M.
American ac. 1870-1910
paintings: (L) $440; (H) $1,320

WELCH, Jack
American b. 1905
paintings: (H) $3,400
drawings: (H) $121

WELCH, Ludmilla Pilat
American 1867-1925
paintings: (L) $330; (H) $2,475

WELCH, Rosemary Sarah
British 20th cent.
paintings: (L) $110; (H) $660

WELCH, Thaddeus
American 1844-1919
paintings: (L) $220; (H) $7,700
drawings: (L) $165; (H) $715

WELDON, Charles Dater
American
paintings: (H) $55
drawings: (H) $935

WELDON, Felix Weihs de
American b. 1907
sculpture: (H) $23,100

WELL, John Sanderson
British ac. 1872-1943
drawings: (H) $3,300

WELLIVER, Neil
American b. 1929
paintings: (L) $2,750; (H) $38,500

WELLS, Benjamin
American 1856-1923
paintings: (H) $1,100

WELLS, Cady
drawings: (H) $2,420

WELLS, George
American 1842-1888
paintings: (H) $1,650

WELLS, John Sanderson
British ac. 1890-1940
paintings: (L) $660; (H) $24,200

WELLS, Lynton
American b. 1940
paintings: (L) $385; (H) $6,600
drawings: (H) $6,875

WELLS, Mark
drawings: (H) $770

WELLS, Newton Alonzo
American b. 1852
paintings: (H) $660

WELLS, Peter
paintings: (H) $1,100

WELLS, Timothy Waite
American 20th cent.
paintings: (L) $400; (H) $1,500

WELLS, William L.
American 20th cent.
paintings: (L) $412; (H) $1,320

WELONSKI, Pio
sculpture: (H) $1,760

WELSCH, F.C.
English 19th cent.
paintings: (H) $825

WELSH, H. Devitt
American d. 1942
paintings: (H) $3,300

WELTE, Gottlieb
German ca. 1745-ca. 1790
drawings: (H) $880

WENBAN, Sion Longley
American 1848-1897
paintings: (H) $825

WENDEL, Theodore
American 1857-1932
paintings: (L) $2,750; (H) $30,800
drawings: (L) $352; (H) $7,700

WENDEROTH, A.
paintings: (H) $3,520

WENDEROTH, August
German b. c. 1817
paintings: (H) $41,250

WENDLING, Gustav
German b. 1862
paintings: (L) $950; (H) $1,650

WENDT, Julia Bracken
American 1871-1942
sculpture: (H) $8,250

WENDT, William
American 1865-1946
paintings: (L) $550; (H) $70,400
drawings: (H) $3,850

WENFNER, Johann Conrad
German 1728-1806
drawings: (H) $1,650

WENGENROTH, Stow
American 1906-1978
drawings: (L) $385; (H) $1,600

WENGER, John
American b. Russia 1891
paintings: (H) $1,870
drawings: (L) $17; (H) $1,760

WENGLEIN, Joseph
German 1845-1919
paintings: (L) $2,640; (H) $46,750

WENKEBACH, L.W.R.
Continental 19th/20th cent.
paintings: (H) $1,650

WENRICH, John
American
drawings: (H) $1,540

WENS, H.L.
paintings: (H) $1,375

WENTORF, Carl Christian Ferdinand
Danish 1863-1914
paintings: (L) $6,050; (H) $6,600

WENTWORTH, D.F.
American 1850-1934
paintings: (L) $209; (H) $700
drawings: (L) $220; (H) $700

WENTZ, Henry Frederick
American 20th cent.
paintings: (H) $4,950

WENZEL, Au
Continental 19th cent.
paintings: (H) $715

WENZEL, Meredith
contemporary
sculpture: (H) $770

WENZELL, Albert Beck
American 1864-1917
paintings: (L) $165; (H) $1,980
drawings: (L) $220; (H) $9,900

WERENSKIOLD, Erik Theodor
Norwegian 1855-1938
paintings: (H) $15,400

WERETSHCHAGIN, Piotr Petrovitch
Russian 1836-1886
paintings: (H) $24,200

WERFF, Adriaen van der
Dutch 1659-1722
paintings: (H) $6,600
drawings: (H) $800

WERFF, Pieter van der
Dutch 1665-1722
paintings: (L) $3,520; (H) $93,500

WERGELAND, Oscar
Scandinavian 1844-1910
paintings: (H) $1,760

WERLEMANN, Carl
Belgian 19th cent.
paintings: (H) $1,045

WERNER, Alexander Friedrich, Fritz
German 1827-1908
paintings: (H) $13,200

WERNER, B.
Austro/Hungarian early 20th cent.
paintings: (H) $1,650

WERNER, Carl
German 1809-1894
drawings: (H) $22,000

WERNER, Conrad
German late 19th cent.
paintings: (H) $1,540

WERNER, Hermann
German 1816-1905
paintings: (L) $6,270; (H) $7,150

WERNTZ, Carl N.
American 1874-1944
paintings: (L) $165; (H) $9,900

WERTHEIMER, Gustav
Austrian 1847-1904
paintings: (H) $11,000

WESCOTT, Paul
American
paintings: (L) $495; (H) $2,420

WESLEY, John
American b. 1928
paintings: (L) $110; (H) $1,760

WESSEL, Herman H.
American 1878-1969
paintings: (L) $330; (H) $2,970
drawings: (H) $330

WESSELMANN, Tom
American b. 1931
paintings: (L) $3,080; (H) $528,000
drawings: (L) $1,320; (H) $462,000
sculpture: (L) $5,280; (H) $495,000

WESSELS, Glenn
American 20th cent.
drawings: (H) $2,200

WESSLEY, Anton
Austrian b. 1848
paintings: (H) $5,500

WESSON, Robert Shaw
American 1902-1967
paintings: (L) $83; (H) $1,045

WEST, Benjamin
American 1738-1820
paintings: (H) $24,200
drawings: (L) $825; (H) $12,650

WEST, Edgar E.
English ac. 1857-1889
drawings: (L) $935; (H) $1,045

WEST, Edith
British 19th/20th cent.
paintings: (H) $4,950

WEST, Francis
late 19th cent.
sculpture: (H) $1,100

WEST, Levon
American
drawings: (L) $825; (H) $2,090

WEST, Raphael Lamar
1769-1850
drawings: (L) $550; (H) $7,150

WEST, Walter J.
English 19th/20th cent.
paintings: (L) $425; (H) $2,090

WEST, William
British 1801-1861
paintings: (H) $3,300

WESTALL, J.
British 19th cent.
paintings: (H) $825

WESTALL, Richard
English 1765-1836
paintings: (H) $2,200

WESTCHILOFF, Constantin
Russian 1880-1945
paintings: (L) $104; (H) $3,025
drawings: (H) $2,090

WESTCOTT, Phillip
British 1815-1878
paintings: (H) $2,090

WESTERBEEK, Cornelis
Dutch 1844-1903
paintings: (L) $990; (H) $2,530

WESTERMANN, H.C.
American b. 1922
drawings: (L) $4,180; (H) $132,000
sculpture: (L) $1,760; (H) $110,000

WESTEROP, B.
British 19th/20th cent.
paintings: (H) $3,850

WESTFELD, Max
German b. 1882
paintings: (H) $1,210

WESTON, Harold
American 1894-1972
paintings: (L) $1,045; (H) $2,200
drawings: (L) $110; (H) $660

WESTON, James L.
American 19th/20th cent.
paintings: (H) $715

WESTON, M.
20th cent.
paintings: (H) $1,045

WESTWOOD, Susan
English b. 1942
paintings: (L) $275; (H) $935

WET, Gerrit de
Dutch
paintings: (H) $1,320

WET, Jacob Willemsz de
1610-1671
paintings: (L) $2,090; (H) $9,350

WET, Jacob de, the younger
paintings: (H) $770

WETHERBEE, George Faulkner
American 1851-1920
paintings: (L) $742; (H) $3,850

WETHERBY, Isaac Augustus
American 1819-1904
paintings: (H) $660

WETHERILL, Elisha Kent Kane
American 1874-1929
paintings: (L) $1,100; (H) $17,600

WETZEL, Richard
American contemporary
paintings: (H) $1,045

WEVER, August de
French b. 1836
sculpture: (L) $495; (H) $715

WEX, Willibald
paintings: (L) $1,760; (H) $3,520

WEYDEN, Harry van der
American/English 1868-after 1935
paintings: (L) $220; (H) $8,800
drawings: (H) $247

WEYER, Jacob Matthias
drawings: (H) $935

WEYL, Max
American 1837-1914
paintings: (L) $302; (H) $4,675
drawings: (L) $412; (H) $495

WEYMOUTH, Frolic
American 20th cent.
drawings: (H) $825

WHALE, John H.
paintings: (H) $3,300

WHANG, Jang Har
Korean 20th cent.
drawings: (L) $440; (H) $1,650

WHARTON-EDWARDS, George
American 1859-1950
paintings: (H) $880

WHEAT, John
American b. 1920
paintings: (H) $3,575

WHEAT, John Potter
paintings: (H) $825

WHEATLEY, Francis
English 1747-1801
paintings: (L) $935; (H) $66,000
drawings: (L) $264; (H) $302

WHEATLEY, G.H.
American 20th cent.
paintings: (L) $132; (H) $1,320

WHEATLEY, W.H.
paintings: (H) $715

WHEATLEY, Warik
American b. 1928
paintings: (H) $715

WHEATLY, Francis
drawings: (H) $4,675

WHEATON, Francis
American b. 1849
paintings: (L) $357; (H) $2,200
drawings: (L) $385; (H) $4,675

WHEELER
German 20th cent.
paintings: (H) $5,500

WHEELER, Alfred
British 1851-1932
paintings: (L) $1,650; (H) $17,600

WHEELER, C.L.
American
sculpture: (H) $6,000

WHEELER, C.V.
paintings: (L) $715; (H) $825

WHEELER, Clifton
American
paintings: (H) $2,090

WHEELER, Hughlette
sculpture: (L) $880; (H) $2,750

WHEELER, J.
British 19th cent.
paintings: (H) $3,575

WHEELER, J. Alfred
British 1852-1932
paintings: (H) $7,150

WHEELER, James, of Bath
British 1820-1885
paintings: (H) $9,075

WHEELER, James Thomas
British 1849-1888
paintings: (H) $2,420

WHEELER, John, Jr.
British 1875-1930
paintings: (L) $4,180; (H) $6,050

WHEELER, John Alfred
English 1821-1903
paintings: (L) $2,200; (H) $9,625

WHEELER, John Arnold
paintings: (L) $880; (H) $16,500

WHEELER, John Arnold, of Bath
English 1821-1877
paintings: (L) $880; (H) $24,750

WHEELER, L.F.
paintings: (H) $990

WHEELER, William Ruthven
American 1832-c. 1895
paintings: (L) $715; (H) $4,180
drawings: (H) $770

WHEELOCK, Lila Audubon
American 20th cent.
sculpture: (H) $1,760

WHEELOCK, Merrill Greene
1822-1866
drawings: (L) $1,072; (H) $1,870

WHEELOCK, Warren
American 1880-1960
paintings: (H) $880
sculpture: (L) $522; (H) $3,520

WHEELWRIGHT, Rowland
British 1870-1955
paintings: (L) $33,000; (H) $38,500

WHEELWRIGHT, W.H.
British ac. 1857-1897
paintings: (H) $22,000

WHEETE, Treva
American b. 1890
paintings: (H) $1,045

WHIPPLE, Charles Ayer
American 1859-1928
paintings: (L) $247; (H) $1,760

WHIPPLE, Seth Arca
American 1855-1901
paintings: (H) $4,400

WHISTLER, James Abbott McNeill
American 1834-1903
paintings: (L) $35,200; (H) $2,585,000
drawings: (L) $2,200; (H) $154,000

WHISTLER, Rex
English 1905-1944
paintings: (L) $1,760; (H) $1,760

WHITAKER, Frederic
American b. 1891
drawings: (L) $154; (H) $935

WHITAKER, George William
American 1841-1916
paintings: (L) $137; (H) $4,125

WHITAKER, William
American b. 1943
paintings: (L) $522; (H) $9,500
drawings: (H) $4,000

WHITCOMB, Jon
American b. 1906
drawings: (L) $66; (H) $1,300

WHITCOMBE, H.
British 19th cent.
paintings: (H) $3,300

WHITCOMBE, Thomas
English c. 1760-c. 1824
paintings: (L) $3,575; (H) $35,200

WHITE, Clarence Scott
American b. 1872
paintings: (L) $412; (H) $660
drawings: (L) $220; (H) $275

WHITE, Edith
American 1855-1946
paintings: (L) $495; (H) $5,225

WHITE, Edwin
American
paintings: (L) $715; (H) $2,200

WHITE, F.
paintings: (H) $880

WHITE, Fritz
American b. 1930
sculpture: (L) $5,000; (H) $7,150

WHITE, H.M.
sculpture: (L) $715; (H) $1,980

WHITE, Henry Cooke
American b. 1861
paintings: (L) $1,430; (H) $1,980

WHITE, Joseph
American 20th cent.
paintings: (L) $330; (H) $1,320

WHITE, Mary
drawings: (H) $6,600

WHITE, Nelson Cooke
American b. 1902
paintings: (L) $1,760; (H) $1,760

WHITE, Nelson H.
20th cent.
paintings: (H) $825

WHITE, Newton H.
American 19th cent.
paintings: (H) $1,210

WHITE, Orrin A.
American 1883-1969
paintings: (L) $440; (H) $5,775
drawings: (H) $1,045

WHITE, Phillip
paintings: (L) $44; (H) $660

WHITE, R.C.
paintings: (H) $880

WHITE, Robert (Winthrop)
sculpture: (L) $66; (H) $1,320

WHITE, T.
British 19th cent.
paintings: (H) $9,625

WHITE, Thomas Gilbert
American 1877-1939
paintings: (L) $2,200; (H) $5,500

WHITE(?), John
English 19th cent.
paintings: (H) $1,320

WHITEFIELD, Edwin
American 1816-1892
drawings: (L) $110; (H) $1,320

WHITEHEAD, Frederick William
Newton
English 1853-1938
paintings: (H) $4,400

WHITELEY, Brett
paintings: (H) $8,800
drawings: (H) $1,870

WHITHY, W.R.
paintings: (H) $1,760

WHITING, Henry H.
American 19th cent.
paintings: (H) $3,850

WHITING, Henry W.
paintings: (H) $1,980

WHITLEY, G.
paintings: (H) $1,320

WHITLEY, Thomas W.
American b. 1835
paintings: (L) $137; (H) $4,125

WHITMORE, Coby
1913-1988
paintings: (L) $1,000; (H) $7,975

WHITNEY, Albertus D.
American ac. c. 1839
paintings: (H) $4,125

WHITNEY, E.S.
American 19th cent.
paintings: (H) $660

WHITNEY, Gertrude Vanderbilt
American 1878-1942
sculpture: (L) $1,760; (H) $2,640

WHITNEY, Richard
American 20th cent.
paintings: (L) $110; (H) $990

WHITTAKER, George W.
American 1841-1916
paintings: (L) $357; (H) $770

WHITTAKER, James
English 1828-1876
paintings: (H) $5,280

WHITTAKER, John Barnard and
Edwin A. PETTIT
paintings: (H) $2,090

WHITTEKER, Lilian
American 20th cent.
paintings: (H) $4,400
drawings: (H) $275

WHITTEMORE, C. Helen Simpson
American 20th cent.
drawings: (H) $1,100

WHITTEMORE, William
paintings: (H) $770

WHITTEMORE, William John
American 1860-1955
paintings: (L) $550; (H) $6,050
drawings: (L) $660; (H) $3,630

WHITTLE, Thomas
English 19th cent.
paintings: (H) $3,300

WHITTLESEN, Thomas
English 19th cent.
paintings: (H) $1,430

WHITTLEY, T.
paintings: (H) $990

WHITTREDGE, Worthington
American 1820-1910
paintings: (L) $2,530; (H) $1,870,000

WHORF, John
American 1903-1959
paintings: (L) $462; (H) $23,100
drawings: (L) $357; (H) $33,000

WHYMPER, Josiah Wood
English 1813-1903
drawings: (H) $880

Watercolor Artist

John Whorf (1903-1959) used modified Impressionist techniques in his
watercolors. Born in Winthrop, Massachusetts, the son of a commercial artist
and graphic designer, he enrolled at age fourteen in the Boston Museum Fine
Arts School and studied under Philip James and Charles Hawthorne. At age
sixteen he studied briefly in Paris, where he began to favor watercolor as a
medium for his brightly colored sketches. In 1924 he had his first solo
exhibition in Boston. John Singer Sargent, an accomplished watercolor artist,
purchased one of his paintings and later gave Whorf informal instruction.

Whorf was a popular and prolific painter, exhibiting regularly for over thirty
years. In 1938 he was one of two contemporary Massachusetts painters
represented in the Museum of Modern Art's exhibition of American art in Paris.
Whorf is best known for his sporting scenes, city views, and landscapes. When
his painting of a ballerina was offered for sale in the summer of 1990, many
judged the subject matter atypical for this artist. In fact, he painted a series of
ballerinas, most of which are held in private collections. The painting received
much attention at the preview; the sale set a record for a John Whorf
watercolor. (John Whorf, *Waiting in the Wings*, watercolor and gouache on
paper, 27 ½ x 22½ in., Bourne, August 7, 1990, $33,000)

WHYTE, Duncan McGregor
British 20th cent.
paintings: (H) $3,960

WIBBY, W.E.
paintings: (H) $770

WICHERA, Raimund
Austrian 1862-1925
paintings: (L) $880; (H) $7,150

WICKENDEN, Robert J.
English b. 1861
paintings: (L) $357; (H) $875

WICKEY, Harry
sculpture: (H) $2,090

WICKMAN, Julia M.
American 1866-1952
paintings: (H) $660

WICKS, Heppie E.
American 19th/20th cent.
paintings: (L) $1,980; (H) $7,150

WIDDAS, Richard Dodd
British 1826-1885
paintings: (L) $2,090; (H) $34,100

WIDER, Wilhelm
German 1818-1884
paintings: (L) $8,525; (H) $16,500

WIDFORSS, Gunnar Mauritz
Swedish/American 1879-1934
drawings: (L) $715; (H) $16,500

WIDGERY, Frederick John
English 1861-1942
paintings: (L) $522; (H) $2,640
drawings: (L) $385; (H) $440

WIDGERY, William
1822-1893
paintings: (L) $550; (H) $2,200
drawings: (H) $220

WIDMANN AND WALSH
American
drawings: (H) $1,650

WIECK, Johann
German b. 1855
paintings: (H) $825

WIEDEMANN, Guillermo
contemporary
paintings: (H) $1,210
drawings: (H) $1,210

WIEDEN, W.
American
paintings: (H) $797

WIEGAND, Charmion von
American b. 1899/1900
paintings: (L) $3,080; (H) $17,600

WIEGAND, Gustave Adolph
German/American 1870-1957
paintings: (L) $154; (H) $6,050
drawings: (H) $990

WIEGANDT, Bernhard
German 1851-1918
drawings: (L) $13,200; (H) $17,600

WIEGHORST, Olaf
American 1899-1988
paintings: (L) $1,760; (H) $57,750
drawings: (L) $308; (H) $7,500

WIELAND, Hans Beat
Swiss 1867-1945
paintings: (II) $8,250

WIER, Julian Alden
American 1852-1919
paintings: (H) $4,950

WIERICX, Jan
Flemish c. 1549-after 1615
drawings: (H) $4,400

WIERINGA, Harmen Willems
paintings: (H) $18,700

WIERINGEN, Cornelis Claesz. van
Dutch c. 1580-1633
paintings: (H) $11,000
drawings: (H) $6,600

WIERIX, Johan
Dutch c. 1549-after 1615
drawings: (H) $10,450

WIERTZ, Antoine
paintings: (H) $715

WIERUSZ-KOWALSKI, Alfred von
Polish 1849-1915
paintings: (L) $9,350; (H) $41,250

WIESCHEBRINK, Franz
German 1818-1884
paintings: (L) $7,700; (H) $8,250

WIESENTHAL, Franz
Hungarian b. 1856
paintings: (L) $1,650; (H) $7,700

WIESNER, Hella
German ac. 1910
paintings: (H) $7,700

WIGGINS, Carleton, John Carleton
WIGGINS
American 1848-1932
paintings: (L) $412; (H) $12,100
drawings: (L) $385; (H) $4,400

WIGGINS, Guy Carleton
American 1883-1962
paintings: (L) $385; (H) $46,200
drawings: (H) $2,090

WIGGLESWORTH
sculpture: (H) $880

WIGHT, Frederick S.
American contemporary
paintings: (L) $1,100; (H) $7,700

WIGHT, Moses
American 1827-1895
paintings: (L) $2,200; (H) $13,200

WIJNGAERDT, Anthonie Jacobus van
Dutch 1808-1887
paintings: (H) $1,210

WIJSMULLER, Jan Hillebrand
Dutch 1855-1925
paintings: (L) $1,540; (H) $5,500

WIKSTROM, Bror Anders
Swedish c. 1840-1909
paintings: (L) $1,045; (H) $1,540

WILBUR, Isaac E.
American 19th cent.
paintings: (H) $1,650

WILBUR, Lawrence Nelson
American b. 1897
paintings: (L) $467; (H) $4,125

WILCKENS, August
paintings: (H) $935

WILCOX, Frank
American b. 1887
drawings: (L) $30; (H) $3,630

WILCOX, Leslie A.
paintings: (L) $2,970; (H) $8,525
drawings: (H) $77

WILCOX, Ray D.
American b. 1883
paintings: (L) $250; (H) $1,100

WILDA, Charles
Austrian 1854-1907
paintings: (H) $8,800

WILDA, Gottfried Heinrich
drawings: (H) $3,080

WILDE, C.
British 19th cent.
paintings: (H) $825

WILDE, Frans de
paintings: (H) $5,500

WILDE, John
American b. 1919
paintings: (L) $1,430; (H) $15,400

WILDENS, Jan
Flemish 1586-1653
paintings: (L) $4,950; (H) $24,200

WILDER, Andre
French 1871-1965
paintings: (H) $2,200

WILDER, Arthur B.
American b. 1857
paintings: (L) $275; (H) $1,320

WILDER, J.
American 19th/20th cent.
paintings: (H) $4,290

WILDER, Louise Hibbard
American b. 1898
sculpture: (H) $2,475

WILDHABER, Paul, Jr.
American 20th cent.
paintings: (L) $385; (H) $660
drawings: (L) $165; (H) $550

WILDING, R.T.
British 20th cent.
drawings: (H) $1,045

WILES, Irving Ramsay
American 1861-1948
paintings: (L) $220; (H) $77,000
drawings: (L) $302; (H) $46,750

WILES, Lemuel Maynard
American 1826-1905
paintings: (L) $797; (H) $14,300

WILEY, Catherine
American
paintings: (H) $7,480

WILEY, J.G.
American 20th cent.
paintings: (H) $660

WILEY, W.S.
paintings: (H) $2,860

WILEY, William T.
American b. 1937
paintings: (L) $7,150; (H) $35,200
drawings: (L) $1,210; (H) $6,600
sculpture: (H)$5,225

WILGUS, William John
American 1819-1853
paintings: (H) $143,000

WILHELMI, Heinrich
German 1816-1902
paintings: (L) $7,150; (H) $20,900

WILHEM, A. Wayne
American
paintings: (H) $1,540

WILKIE, D.
paintings: (H) $1,320
drawings: (H) $125

WILKIE, Robert D.
American 1828-1903
paintings: (L) $1,760; (H) $16,000
drawings: (H) $550

WILKINS, John G.
American 20th cent.
paintings: (L) $1,760; (H) $1,870

WILKINSON, E.
American
paintings: (H) $880

WILKINSON, Norman
British 19th/20th cent.
paintings: (H) $660
drawings: (L) $150; (H) $1,540

WILKS, Maurice C.
British ac. 1933-1940
paintings: (L) $825; (H) $1,540

WILL, August
American 1834-1910
drawings: (L) $137; (H) $1,320

WILL, Frank
French 1900-1951
paintings: (L) $660; (H) $1,100
drawings: (L) $275; (H) $2,750

WILLAERT, Ferdinand
Belgian 1861-1938
paintings: (L) $1,320; (H) $6,325

WILLAERTS, A.
Dutch 17th cent.
paintings: (H) $2,640

WILLAERTS, Isaac
Dutch c. 1620-1693
paintings: (H) $33,000

WILLARD, Archibald M.
American 1836/37-1918
paintings: (L) $330; (H) $5,280

WILLCOCK, George Barrell
British 1811-1852
paintings: (L) $330; (H) $1,760

WILLCOX, W.H.
American b. 1831
paintings: (L) $1,100; (H) $2,640

WILLE, August von
German 1829-1887
paintings: (H) $3,300

WILLE, Fritz von
German 1860-1961
paintings: (H) $825

WILLE, Johann Georg
1715-1808
drawings: (H) $6,270

WILLE, O.
paintings: (H) $935

WILLEMS, Florent
Belgian 1823-1905
paintings: (L) $3,850; (H) $4,950

WILLERBEETS
paintings: (H) $1,760

WILLERS, William
American contemporary
sculpture: (H) $825

WILLETT, J.
paintings: (H) $880

WILLEY, Philo Levy "Chief"
American c. 1887-1980
paintings: (L) $200; (H) $1,300

WILLGAN, H.
paintings: (H) $825

WILLHIS, Albert
19th cent.
paintings: (H) $935

WILLIAM, Edward Charles
British ac. 1839-1845
paintings: (H) $3,850

WILLIAM, Henry
English 19th cent.
drawings: (H) $1,320

WILLIAM, John Haynes
British 19th cent.
paintings: (H) $11,000

WILLIAMS, A.
American 19th cent.
paintings: (L) $3,300; (H) $4,950

WILLIAMS, Albert
French 19th/20th cent.
paintings: (H) $2,750

WILLIAMS, Alfred Walter
British 1824-1905
paintings: (L) $412; (H) $5,500

WILLIAMS, Charles H.
paintings: (H) $2,640

WILLIAMS David
American Indian b. 1933
paintings: (H) $880

WILLIAMS, Dwight
American 1856-1932
paintings: (H) $990
drawings: (H) $165

WILLIAMS, E.
paintings: (H) $990
sculpture: (H) $1,650

WILLIAMS, E.
British 1807-1881
paintings: (L) $302; (H) $5,280

WILLIAMS, E.D.
paintings: (H) $770

WILLIAMS, Edward
paintings: (H) $2,310

WILLIAMS, Edward
British 1782-1855
paintings: (L) $1,210; (H) $1,540

WILLIAMS, Edward Charles
English ac. 1839-1845
paintings: (L) $16; (H) $37,400

WILLIAMS, Edward Charles and
William SHAYER, Sr.
British 18th/19th cent.
paintings: (L) $9,350; (H) $19,800

WILLIAMS, Edward K.
American b. 1870
paintings: (H) $2,090

WILLIAMS, Emily
paintings: (H) $1,100

WILLIAMS, Ewart Lyle
20th cent.
paintings: (H) $900

WILLIAMS, F.
paintings: (H) $850

WILLIAMS, F.H.
British 19th cent.
paintings: (H) $1,100

WILLIAMS, Florence White
American d. 1953
paintings: (L) $110; (H) $4,150
drawings: (L) $27; (H) $357

WILLIAMS, Frederick
paintings: (H) $715

WILLIAMS, Frederick Ballard
American 1871-1956
paintings: (L) $220; (H) $4,000
drawings: (L) $605; (H) $770

WILLIAMS, Frederick Dickinson
American 1829-1915
paintings: (L) $110; (H) $1,980
drawings: (H) $715

WILLIAMS, George Alfred
American 1875-1932
paintings: (L) $550; (H) $1,430
drawings: (L) $632; (H) $1,100

WILLIAMS, George Augustus
British 1814-1901
paintings: (L) $1,650; (H) $4,950

WILLIAMS, George Augustus and
John Frederick HERRING Jr.
British
paintings: (H) $8,800

WILLIAMS, Graham
British 19th cent.
paintings: (L) $522; (H) $2,090

WILLIAMS, Henry
American 1787-1830
paintings: (L) $440; (H) $1,210

WILLIAMS, J.
British 19th cent.
paintings: (H) $1,100

WILLIAMS, J. Insco
paintings: (L) $6,050; (H) $7,700

WILLIAMS, J.L.
British 19th cent.
paintings: (H) $1,760

WILLIAMS, J.W.
American 19th cent.
paintings: (L) $4,400; (H) $8,525

WILLIAMS, James Francis
British 1785-1846
paintings: (L) $605; (H) $2,420

WILLIAMS, Mary Belle
American 1873-1943
paintings: (L) $138; (H) $3,025

WILLIAMS, Mary R.
American 1857-1907
paintings: (H) $2,090
drawings: (H) $330

WILLIAMS, Micah
American 1782/83-1837
paintings: (L) $2,090; (H) $19,800
drawings: (H) $1,760

WILLIAMS, Mildred Emerson
American b. 1892
paintings: (L) $110; (H) $1,760

WILLIAMS, P.
American 19th cent.
paintings: (H) $935

WILLIAMS, Paul A.
American b. 1934
paintings: (L) $550; (H) $7,150

WILLIAMS, Pauline Bliss
American b. 1888
paintings: (L) $138; (H) $2,420

WILLIAMS, Penry
English, d. Rome 1798-1885
paintings: (L) $715; (H) $4,400

WILLIAMS, Robert F.
American 20th cent.
paintings: (H) $935

WILLIAMS, Sheldon
paintings: (H) $3,850

WILLIAMS, T.
British 19th/20th cent.
paintings: (H) $7,700

WILLIAMS, Tennessee
paintings: (H) $3,850

WILLIAMS, Terrick
English 1860-1936
paintings: (L) $137; (H) $30,800
drawings: (H) $5,500

WILLIAMS, Virgil
American 1830-1886
paintings: (L) $770; (H) $16,500
drawings: (H) $1,650

WILLIAMS, W.
paintings: (L) $550; (H) $990

WILLIAMS, W.
English 19th cent.
paintings: (L) $165; (H) $1,980

WILLIAMS, Walter
paintings: (L) $880; (H) $2,860

WILLIAMS, Walter
English 1835-1906
paintings: (L) $110; (H) $8,800

WILLIAMS, Walter
English 19th cent.
paintings: (L) $495; (H) $2,860

WILLIAMS, Walter Heath
British 19th cent.
paintings: (L) $110; (H) $2,200

WILLIAMS, Wheeler
American 1897-1972
sculpture: (L) $770; (H) $14,300

WILLIAMS, William
ac. 1758-1797
paintings: (H) $8,800

WILLIAMSON, Al and Frank
FRAZETTA
American
drawings: (H) $1,980

WILLIAMSON, E.E.
American 19th cent.
paintings: (H) $715

WILLIAMSON, Frederick
paintings: (H) $1,595

WILLIAMSON, Harold
contemporary
paintings: (H) $4,675

WILLIAMSON, John
American
paintings: (H) $1,980

WILLIAMSON, John
American 1826-1885
paintings: (L) $825; (H) $7,700

WILLIAMSON, R.
English 19th/20th cent.
paintings: (H) $935

WILLIAMSON, William Henry
British 1820-1883
paintings: (L) $495; (H) $1,650

WILLIE, Pierre Alexander
paintings: (H) $37,400

WILLIE, Robt. D.
English School 19th cent.
paintings: (H) $1,760

WILLIGEN, Claes Jansz van der
c. 1630-1676
paintings: (L) $3,520; (H) $6,600

WILLIOT, J.
paintings: (H) $1,210

WILLIS, A.V.
paintings: (H) $3,300

WILLIS, Edmund Aylburton
American 1808-1899
paintings: (L) $577; (H) $3,300

WILLIS, Henry Brittan
English 1810-1884
paintings: (L) $2,420; (H) $27,500

WILLIS, John
English 19th cent.
paintings: (H) $1,540

WILLIS, Luster
American b. 1913
drawings: (L) $660; (H) $660

WILLIS, Richard
paintings: (H) $1,100

WILLIS, Thomas H.
American 1850-1912
paintings: (L) $330; (H) $4,950

WILLIS, Thornton
American b. 1936
paintings: (L) $2,750; (H) $4,400

WILLISON, George
British 1741-1797
paintings: (H) $20,900

WILLNIS, Albert
American School 19th/20th cent.
paintings: (H) $2,200

WILLOUGHBY, W.
British 19th cent.
paintings: (H) $715

WILLROIDER, Ludwig
German 1845-1910
paintings: (L) $2,530; (H) $4,500

WILLS (?), E.C.
paintings: (H) $935

WILLSON, Robert
contemporary
sculpture: (H) $3,300

WILMARTH, Christopher
American b. 1943
drawings: (L) $13,200; (H) $19,800
sculpture: (L) $1,540; (H) $99,000

WILMARTH, Lemuel Everett
American 1835-1918
paintings: (L) $1,760; (H) $11,000

WILSON, Alexander
British 1803-1846
paintings: (H) $1,210

WILSON, Benjamin
paintings: (H) $1,210

WILSON, Bryan
contemporary
paintings: (L) $275; (H) $3,300

WILSON, Caroline
American 1810-1890
sculpture: (H) $7,150

WILSON, Charles Edward
English ac. 1889, d.c. 1936
drawings: (L) $3,850; (H) $13,200

WILSON, Charles J.A.
Scottish/American 1880-1965
drawings: (L) $605; (H) $660

WILSON, D.
English 19th cent.
paintings: (H) $715

WILSON, David Forrester
British 1873-1950
paintings: (L) $4,750; (H) $110,000

WILSON, E.
paintings: (H) $990

WILSON, Frederick
American b. 1858
paintings: (L) $850; (H) $880

WILSON, G.
British 19th cent.
paintings: (H) $5,775

WILSON, G.B.
British 19th cent.
paintings: (H) $4,950

WILSON, George
English 19th cent.
paintings: (H) $880

WILSON, J.
paintings: (H) $825

WILSON, J.
American 19th cent.
paintings: (H) $1,540

WILSON, J.
British 19th cent.
paintings: (L) $2,200; (H) $3,850

WILSON, J.
English early 19th cent.
paintings: (H) $1,870

WILSON, J. Coggeshall
American 19th cent.
paintings: (H) $770

WILSON, J.J.
paintings: (H) $1,320

WILSON, J.T.
paintings: (H) $2,750

WILSON, James Perry
American 1889-1976
paintings: (L) $328; (H) $770

WILSON, Jane
American b. 1924
paintings: (L) $715; (H) $2,090

WILSON, Jock
British 19th/20th cent.
paintings: (L) $250; (H) $1,210

WILSON, John
paintings: (H) $1,540

WILSON, John
English School 19th cent.
paintings: (H) $660

WILSON, John, Jock
English 1774-1855
paintings: (H) $825

WILSON, John James
British 1818-1875
paintings: (L) $330; (H) $4,620

WILSON, Laurence W.
drawings: (H) $1,760

WILSON, Margaret E.
British b. 1890
paintings: (L) $302; (H) $1,540

WILSON, Mortimer
American b. 1906
paintings: (L) $3,200; (H) $5,200

WILSON, Raymond
American 1906-1972
drawings: (L) $880; (H) $1,210

WILSON, Richard
British 1714-1782
paintings: (L) $330; (H) $1,650
drawings: (H) $660

WILSON, Robert
American contemporary
drawings: (L) $1,045; (H) $26,400

WILSON, Sol
Polish/American 1894/96-1974
paintings: (L) $11; (H) $1,210
drawings: (L) $22; (H) $440

WILSON, Thomas Fairbairn
British ac. 1808-1846
paintings: (H) $8,800

WILSON, Thomas Harrington
paintings: (L) $1,100; (H) $1,540

WILSON, W.A.
American
paintings: (H) $770

WILTON, Olive M.
British 20th cent.
paintings: (H) $2,090

WIMAR, Charles
American 1828-1863
paintings: (L) $4,950; (H) $52,250

WIMBUSH, Henry B.
  paintings: (H) $3,080
  drawings: (H) $165

WIMMER, Rudolf
  paintings: (H) $660

WIMPERIS, Edmund Morison
  English 1835-1900
  drawings: (H) $880

WINANS, Walter
  English 1852-1920
  sculpture: (L) $4,400; (H) $17,600

WINCK, Christian
  German 1738-1797
  paintings: (L) $2,200; (H) $2,420

WIND, D.W.
  paintings: (H) $715

WINDMAIER, Anton
  German 1840-1896
  paintings: (H) $6,050

WINDT, Phillip Peter
  Dutch 1847-1921
  paintings: (H) $2,750

WINEGAR, Samuel P.
  American b. 1845
  paintings: (H) $1,430
  drawings: (L) $550; (H) $1,050

WINELAND, N.W.
  American
  drawings: (H) $1,600

WINENSKI, Bronsilav
  Polish 19th cent.
  paintings: (H) $1,100

WINES, James
  American b. 1932
  sculpture: (L) $495; (H) $15,400

WINFIELD, Rodney M.
  American b. 1925
  paintings: (L) $220; (H) $275
  sculpture: (L) $110; (H) $2,750

WINGATE, Sir James Lawton
  Scottish 1846-1924
  paintings: (L) $85; (H) $1,540

WINGERT, Edward Oswald
  American b. 1864
  paintings: (H) $1,540
  drawings: (H) $275

WINGFIELD, James Digman
  British d. 1872
  paintings: (L) $1,430; (H) $2,420

WINHART, A.
  German 20th cent.
  paintings: (H) $935

WINK, Johann Amandus
  German 1748-1817
  paintings: (H) $19,800

WINKLER
  sculpture: (H) $1,250

WINMAR, Charles
  American 1828-1862
  paintings: (H) $4,950

WINNER, William E.
  American c. 1815-1883
  paintings: (L) $715; (H) $19,800

WINSOR, Helen A.
  American 19th cent.
  paintings: (L) $352; (H) $990

WINSTANLEY, Henri
  English 19th cent.
  paintings: (H) $1,155

WINT, Peter de
  British 1784-1849
  drawings: (L) $468; (H) $4,400

WINTER, Alice Beach
  American 1877-1970
  paintings: (L) $165; (H) $1,650
  drawings: (L) $220; (H) $660

WINTER, Andrew
  American 1893-1958
  paintings: (L) $385; (H) $18,700

WINTER, Charles Allan
  American 1869-1942
  paintings: (L) $77; (H) $7,700
  drawings: (H) $1,320

WINTER, Ezra
  American 1886-1949
  paintings: (H) $1,100

WINTER, Fritz
  German 1905-1978
  paintings: (L) $330; (H) $17,600
  drawings: (H) $2,530

WINTER, George
  American 1810-1876
  paintings: (L) $220; (H) $5,500

WINTER, H. Edward
American b. 1908
paintings: (H) $825

WINTER, Robin
contemporary
drawings: (H) $880

WINTER, William Arthur
Canadian b. 1909
paintings: (H) $1,045

WINTER-SHAW, Arthur
British 1869-1948
paintings: (H) $4,125

WINTERHALTER, Franz Xaver
German 1806-1873
paintings: (L) $3,300; (H) $137,500

WINTERHALTER, Hermann
paintings: (H) $6,380

WINTERS, Robin
American b. 1950
paintings: (L) $3,850; (H) $4,950
drawings: (L) $3,080; (H) $3,850

WINTERS, Terry
American b. 1949
paintings: (H) $60,500
drawings: (L) $1,650; (H) $28,600

WINTHER, Frederik
Danish 1853-1916
paintings: (H) $1,045

WINTZ, R.
paintings: (H) $935

WIREMAN, Eugenie M.
19th/20th cent.
paintings: (L) $297; (H) $990

WIRSUM, Karl
American contemporary
paintings: (H) $4,950

WIRTH, Paul
ac. 1571-1578
paintings: (H) $7,700

WISBY, Jack
American 1870-1940
paintings: (L) $330; (H) $1,760

WISDOM, K.
paintings: (H) $935

WISEMAN, Robert P.
American b. 1891
paintings: (L) $165; (H) $1,430

WISSING, William
paintings: (L) $1,650; (H) $3,080

WISTEHUFF, Revere F.
1900-1971
paintings: (H) $3,000

WIT, Jakob de
Dutch 1695-1754
paintings: (L) $660; (H) $16,500
drawings: (L) $2,420; (H) $3,520

WITCOWSKY, Karl
American 1860-1910
paintings: (H) $4,125

WITHEMS, J.
Continental 19th/20th cent.
paintings: (H) $1,400

WITHEREINGTON, William Frederick
British 1785-1865
paintings: (L) $467; (H) $28,600

WITHERSTINE, Donald
American 1896-1961
paintings: (L) $1,100; (H) $1,320

WITHOOS, Alida
Dutch c. 1660-after 1715
paintings: (H) $1,320

WITHOOS, Franz
paintings: (H) $14,300

WITHOOS, Matthias
Dutch 1627-1703
paintings: (L) $3,300; (H) $15,400

WITHROW, Eva Almond
American 1858-1928
paintings: (L) $275; (H) $1,540

WITJENS, Willem
Dutch 1884-1962
paintings: (H) $990

WITKIN, Isaac
sculpture: (L) $440; (H) $3,520

WITKIN, Jerome
American 20th cent.
drawings: (H) $1,100

WITKOWSKI, Karl
American 1860-1910
paintings: (L) $1,650; (H) $14,300

WITMAN, C.F.
American 19th cent.
paintings: (H) $2,475

WITT, John Henry Harrison
American 1840-1901
paintings: (L) $302; (H) $17,600

WITTE, Emanuel de
Dutch 1617/18-1692
paintings: (H) $330,000

WITTE, O.
Dutch 19th/20th cent.
paintings: (H) $1,210

WITTE, Pieter de, called Pietro
CANDIDO
Flemish 1548-1628
paintings: (H) $15,400

WITTEL, Gaspar van, Il Vanvitelli
Dutch 1653-1736
paintings: (H)$242,000
drawings: (L) $2,420; (H) $37,400

WITTEMORE, William J.
American 1860-1955
drawings: (H) $6,600

WITTERWULGHE, J.
sculpture: (L) $418; (H) $1,650

WITTKAMP, Johann Bernhard
German 1820-1885
paintings: (L) $2,750; (H) $3,300

WITTMANN, Ernest
French b. 1846
paintings: (H) $3,190

WITTRUP, Jack
American 1913-1987
paintings: (L) $1,430; (H) $1,980

WITTRUP, John S.
b. 1872
paintings: (L) $154; (H) $660

WODNASKY, Wilhelm
paintings: (H) $1,100

WOELFE, Ingeborg
paintings: (H) $1,100

WOELFFER, Emerson
American 20th cent.
paintings: (L) $99; (H) $660
drawings: (L) $55; (H) $55
sculpture: (H) $121

WOELFLE, Arthur William
American 1873-1936
paintings: (L) $154; (H) $1,430

WOERFFEL, C.F.
Russian
sculpture: (L) $407; (H) $2,860

WOFFORD, Philip
contemporary
paintings: (H) $1,100
drawings: (L) $99; (H) $176

WOHL, Mildred
American 20th cent.
paintings: (L) $275; (H) $1,980

WOICESKE, Ronau William
American 1887-1953
paintings: (L) $192; (H) $825

WOJNAROWICZ, David
American b. 1954
paintings: (L) $2,200; (H) $3,300
sculpture: (L) $4,400; (H) $5,280

WOJNAROWICZ, David, and
Marion S.
American contemporary
paintings: (H) $3,300

WOJTKIEWICZ, W.
Polish 1879-1909
drawings: (H) $963

WOLBERS, Hermanus Gerhardus
Dutch 1856-1926
paintings: (H) $1,430
drawings: (H) $275

WOLCOTT, Harold
American 20th cent.
paintings: (L) $715; (H) $2,750

WOLCOTT, J.
British 19th cent.
paintings: (H) $1,045

WOLEVER, Adeleine
American b. 1886
paintings: (H) $990

WOLF, A.
Continental 19th cent.
paintings: (H) $2,640

WOLF, F.
paintings: (L) $550; (H) $1,980

WOLF, Franz Xaver
Austrian b. 1896
paintings: (L) $410; (H) $5,500

WOLF, Franz Xavier and Julius
WOLFLE
paintings: (H) $660

WOLF, George
paintings: (H) $715

WOLF, Hamilton Achille
paintings: (L) $880; (H) $1,045

WOLF, Jacques
French 19th/20th cent.
paintings: (H) $1,210

WOLF, Lone
paintings: (H) $1,540

WOLFE, Byron B.
American 1904-1973
drawings: (H) $660

WOLFE, Edith Grace
British 1888-1970
paintings: (H) $3,080

WOLFE, Edward
American 20th cent.
paintings: (H) $6,050

WOLFE, George
English 1834-1890
drawings: (L) $440; (H) $1,760

WOLFE, Gustave
paintings: (H) $742

WOLFE, James
American b. 1944
sculpture: (H) $1,100

WOLFE, Sarah Bender de
American 1885-1915
paintings: (H) $1,045

WOLFE, Thomas
paintings: (L) $247; (H) $935

WOLFENSBERGER, Johann Jakob
Swedish 1797-1850
drawings: (L) $247; (H) $3,300

WOLFERT, C.H.
paintings: (H) $935

WOLFERT, Ch.
paintings: (H) $1,540

WOLFF, Franz Alexander Freidrich
Wilhelm
sculpture: (H) $3,300

WOLFF, Gustave
German/American 1863-1935
paintings: (L) $357; (H) $2,090

WOLFFORT, Artus
paintings: (H) $71,500

WOLFLE, G.
paintings: (H) $1,210

WOLFLE, Inge
Austrian 19th/20th cent.
paintings: (L) $220; (H) $825

WOLFORT, Charles
paintings: (H) $770

WOLFROM, Friedrich Ernst
German b. 1857
paintings: (H) $825

WOLINS, Joseph
American b. 1915
paintings: (L) $66; (H) $1,430

WOLKIE, D.
English 19th cent.
paintings: (H) $1,650

WOLKOV, Andrian
paintings: (H) $880

WOLLASTON, John
English b. 1672
paintings: (H) $20,900

WOLLASTON, John
English d. 1770
paintings: (H) $1,045

WOLLEN, William Barns
British b. 1857
paintings: (L) $1,430; (H) $3,520

WOLLENTINE, Gunnar
European 20th cent.
paintings: (H) $1,045

WOLMARK, Alfred Aaron
British 1877-1961
paintings: (H) $2,640

WOLMUET, Paulus
ac. 1587
drawings: (H) $9,350

WOLRING, F.
German 19th/20th cent.
drawings: (H) $5,500

WOLRUNG, F.
drawings: (H) $3,850

WOLSFELD, Erich
Continental School 19th cent.
paintings: (H) $9,625

WOLSKI, J.
Polish 19th/20th cent.
paintings: (H) $3,630

WOLSKI, Stanislaw Politan
paintings: (H) $6,600

WOLSTENHOLME, Dean
English 18th/19th cent.
paintings: (L) $4,620; (H) $18,700

WOLSTENHOLME, Dean, Jr.
English 1798-1882
paintings: (L) $5,500; (H) $6,050

WOLSTENHOLME, Dean, Sr.
English 1757-1837
paintings: (L) $7,700; (H) $49,500

WOLTER, Hendrik Jan
Dutch 1873-1952
paintings: (H) $13,200

WOLTON, Alan
American contemporary
paintings: (H) $9,500

WON, Jack C.
American 20th cent.
paintings: (H) $1,760

WONDER, L.
paintings: (H) $1,650

WONNER, Paul
American b. 1924
paintings: (H) $30,800
drawings: (H) $3,850

WONTNER, William Clarke
British 19th/20th cent.
paintings: (L) $12,100; (H) $33,000

WOOD, Alexander M.
American 19th cent.
paintings: (L) $99; (H) $825

WOOD, Beatrice
American contemporary
sculpture: (L) $2,750; (H) $2,750

WOOD, Bertha R.
paintings: (H) $2,750

WOOD, Charles Haigh
British 1856-1927
paintings: (H) $26,400

WOOD, George Albert
American 1845-1910
paintings: (L) $110; (H) $660

WOOD, George B., Jr.
American 1832-1910
drawings: (L) $165; (H) $2,090

WOOD, Grant
American 1892-1942
paintings: (L) $1,760; (H) $77,000
drawings: (L) $715; (H) $148,500
sculpture: (L) $4,620; (H) $6,050

WOOD, Hunter
American b. 1908
paintings: (L) $357; (H) $2,970

WOOD, J.
American 19th cent.
paintings: (H) $688

WOOD, John
British 1801-1870
paintings: (H) $1,650

WOOD, Lewis John
British 1813-1901
paintings: (L) $1,210; (H) $3,025

WOOD, Ogden
American 1852-1912
paintings: (L) $880; (H) $1,925

WOOD, Robert
paintings: (L) $1,100; (H) $6,050

WOOD, Robert
American 1926-1979
paintings: (L) $605; (H) $13,200

WOOD, Robert
British 1807-1879
paintings: (H) $1,870

WOOD, Robert E.
American 1889-1979
paintings: (L) $880; (H) $8,800
drawings: (L) $495; (H) $1,210

WOOD, Robert W.
paintings: (H) $1,045

WOOD, Silas
American 19th cent.
paintings: (H) $14,850

WOOD, T.
paintings: (H) $770

WOOD, Thomas Waterman
American 1823-1903
paintings: (L) $770; (H) $65,000
drawings: (L) $8,250; (H) $93,500

WOOD, William R.C.
American 1875-1915
paintings: (L) $121; (H) $1,980

WOOD, Worden
American ac. 1912-1937
paintings: (L) $82; (H) $247
drawings: (L) $70; (H) $1,100

WOODALL, Francis
American 20th cent.
paintings: (H) $1,650

WOODBURY, Charles Herbert
American 1864-1940
paintings: (L) $220; (H) $82,500
drawings: (L) $110; (H) $1,540

WOODCOCK, Hartwell L.
American 1852-1929
drawings: (L) $55; (H) $1,600

WOODFORDE, Samuel
British 1763-1817
paintings: (H) $2,750

WOODHOUSE, Frederick
paintings: (H) $2,200

WOODHOUSE, William
British 1857-1935
paintings: (L) $825; (H) $34,100

WOODLEIGH, Alma
American ac. 1880-1890
paintings: (L) $220; (H) $2,090

WOODMAN, Betty
contemporary
sculpture: (L) $1,045; (H) $2,750

WOODMAN, F.
English (?) 19th/20th cent.
paintings: (H) $880

WOODMAN, Tim
contemporary
sculpture: (L) $1,540; (H) $1,870

WOODROW, Bill
British b. 1948
sculpture: (L) $13,200; (H) $33,000

WOODRUFF, Jonah
paintings: (H) $4,050

WOODS, Robert
paintings: (H) $6,325

WOODSIDE, John Archibald, Sr.
American 1781-1852
paintings: (L) $1,815; (H) $41,800

WOODVILLE, Richard Caton
American 1825-1856
paintings: (H) $440
drawings: (H) $990

WOODVILLE, Richard Caton
British 1856-1927
paintings: (H) $12,100
drawings: (L) $110; (H) $220

WOODWARD, E.
drawings: (L) $495; (H) $715

WOODWARD, Ellsworth
American 1861-1939
paintings: (L) $1,100; (H) $5,500
drawings: (L) $247; (H) $6,600

WOODWARD, Laura
paintings: (H) $1,870

WOODWARD, Laura
American 19th cent.
paintings: (L) $1,320; (H) $2,090
drawings: (L) $220; (H) $275

WOODWARD, Lee
paintings: (H) $2,750

WOODWARD, M.T.
American 20th cent.
paintings: (H) $660

WOODWARD, Mabel May
American 1877-1945
paintings: (L) $275; (H) $24,200
drawings: (L) $495; (H) $1,430

WOODWARD, Robert Strong
American b. 1885
paintings: (L) $660; (H) $3,025

WOODWARD, Stanley Wingate
American 1890-1970
paintings: (L) $220; (H) $2,475
drawings: (L) $44; (H) $330

WOODWARD, Thomas
British 1801-1852
paintings: (L) $6,600; (H) $8,250

WOODWARD, William
American 1859-1939
paintings: (L) $357; (H) $4,675
drawings: (L) $825; (H) $4,400

WOODWELL, Joseph R.
American 19th cent.
paintings: (H) $4,620

WOODWOARD, Ellsworth
drawings: (H) $3,300

WOOG, Raymond
French b. 1875
paintings: (L) $440; (H) $6,600

WOOL
paintings: (H) $1,870

WOOL, Christopher
American b. 1955
paintings: (H) $26,400

WOOLARD, William
British 19th cent.
paintings: (H) $1,100

WOOLF, Samuel Johnson
American 1880-1948
paintings: (L) $880; (H) $3,300

WOOLFORD, John Elliot
19th cent.
paintings: (H) $13,200

WOOLLETT, Henry Charles
British ac. 1851-1872
paintings: (L) $468; (H) $3,850

WOOLLETT, Hy
British 19th cent.
paintings: (H) $1,430

WOOLMAN, A.L.
paintings: (H) $770

WOOLMER, Alfred Joseph
English 1805-1892
paintings: (L) $462; (H) $5,500

WOOLRYCH, F. Humphry W.
American b. 1868
paintings: (L) $247; (H) $1,980
drawings: (L) $192; (H) $522

WOOLSEY, C.E.
paintings: (H) $1,100

WOOLSEY, Wood W.
American b. 1899
paintings: (L) $275; (H) $1,430

WOOSTER, A.C.
American 19th cent.
paintings: (H) $990

WOOSTER, Austin C.
American ac. 1910
paintings: (L) $990; (H) $25,300

WOOTTON, Frank
British b. 1914
paintings: (H) $2,530

WOOTTON, John
English c. 1686-1765
paintings: (L) $10,450; (H) $99,000

WOPFNER, Joseph
Austrian 1843-1927
paintings: (H) $23,100

WORES, Theodore
American 1859/60-1939
paintings: (L) $137; (H) $19,800
drawings: (L) $1,100; (H) $5,500

WORMS, Jules
French 1832-1924
paintings: (L) $880; (H) $41,800
drawings: (L) $880; (H) $3,850

WORRELL, Abraham Bruiningh van
Dutch/English b. 1787, ac. 1820-1849
paintings: (H) $715

WORSEY, Thomas
English 1829-1875
paintings: (H) $3,850

WORTHAM, L.
paintings: (H) $1,760

WOSTRY, Carlo
Italian 1865-1943
paintings: (H) $82,500

WOTRUBA, Fritz
German 1907-1975
paintings: (H) $715
sculpture: (L) $5,500; (H) $38,500

WOU, Claesz Claesz
Dutch c. 1592-1665
paintings: (H) $20,900

WOUTERMAERTENS, Edouard
Belgian 1819-1897
paintings: (H) $1,100

WOUTERS, Constant
Belgian 1826-1853
paintings: (H) $1,320

WOUTERS, Frans
Flemish 1612/14-1659/60
paintings: (L) $2,420; (H) $17,600

WOUTERSZ. VOSMAER, Jan
1584-1641
paintings: (H) $8,800

WOUWERMAN, Philips
paintings: (H) $1,540

WOUWERMAN, Pieter
Dutch 1623-1682
paintings: (L) $3,190; (H) $22,000

WOUWERMANS, Jan Pauwelsz.
Dutch 1629-1666
paintings: (L) $13,200; (H) $25,300

WOUWERMANS, Philips
Dutch 1619-1668
paintings: (L) $26,400; (H) $638,000

WRAY, Henry Russell
American
paintings: (L) $1,100; (H) $1,650

WREFORD, Denis
British b. 1910
drawings: (H) $1,320

WRIGHT, Charles Lennox
American b. 1876
paintings: (L) $110; (H) $1,980
drawings: (H) $220

WRIGHT, Cory B.
American 19th/20th cent.
paintings: (H) $1,320

WRIGHT, David
American contemporary
paintings: (L) $7,000; (H) $10,800

WRIGHT, Ethel
British ac. 1893-1898
paintings: (H) $11,000

WRIGHT, Frank Lloyd
American 1869-1959
drawings: (L) $1,430; (H) $176,000

WRIGHT, George
paintings: (L) $2,640; (H) $28,600

WRIGHT, George
American
paintings: (H) $4,950

WRIGHT, George
British 1860-1942
paintings: (L) $2,200; (H) $19,800

WRIGHT, George Hand
American 1872-1951
paintings: (L) $1,320; (H) $2,090
drawings: (L) $33; (H) $2,200

WRIGHT, Gilbert Scott
British 1880-1958
paintings: (L) $11,000; (H) $28,600

WRIGHT, James Couper
Scottish/American b. 1906
drawings: (L) $88; (H) $880

WRIGHT, James Henry
American 1813-1883
paintings: (L) $660; (H) $715

WRIGHT, John Lloyd and Alfonso
IANNELLI
drawings: (H) $935

WRIGHT, John Michael
paintings: (H) $6,600

WRIGHT, Joseph, of Derby
British 1734-1797
paintings: (L) $44,000; (H) $71,500

WRIGHT, Louise Wood
paintings: (H) $1,210

WRIGHT, P.J.
English 19th cent.
paintings: (H) $4,400

WRIGHT, Redmond Stephens
American b. 1903
paintings: (L) $412; (H) $660

WRIGHT, Richard, Wright of
Liverpool
English 1735-1774
paintings: (H) $49,500

WRIGHT, Richard Henry
English 1857-1930
drawings: (L) $330; (H) $1,100

WRIGHT, Robert W.
English 19th/20th cent.
paintings: (H) $1,210

WRIGHT, W. Spencer
American 19th/20th cent.
paintings: (H) $850

WSSEL, Manuel
Spanish 19th cent.
drawings: (H) $1,650

WTEWAEL, Joachim
Dutch 1566-1638
paintings: (H) $33,000

WU GUANZHONG
Chinese b. 1915
drawings: (H) $825

WU (CHANGSHUO)
paintings: (H) $1,210

WUERMER, Carl
American 1900-1983
paintings: (L) $2,750; (H) $17,600
drawings: (L) $220; (H) $2,200

WUERPEL, Edmund Henry
American 1866-1958
paintings: (L) $605; (H) $990

WUEST, A.
paintings: (H) $880

WUGER, Eduard
Austrian 19th cent.
paintings: (L) $3,300; (H) $6,325

WUILLERMET, Charles
Swedish 19th cent.
paintings: (H) $3,630

WUNDERLICH, Paul
German b. 1927
paintings: (L) $5,280; (H) $24,200
drawings: (L) $660; (H) $13,200
sculpture: (L) $990; (H) $2,200

WUNNENBERG, Carl
German 1850-1929
paintings: (L) $2,420; (H) $11,000

WUNSCH, Marie
paintings: (H) $8,800

WURSTER, William W.
drawings: (L) $1,650; (H) $1,650

WURTZ, Adam
American
drawings: (H) $4,400

WUSMULLER, J.H.
German 19th/20th cent.
paintings: (H) $660

WUST, Alexander
American 1837-1876
paintings: (L) $1,045; (H) $13,200
drawings: (H) $1,650

WUTTKE, Carl
German 1849-1927
paintings: (L) $2,970; (H) $11,000

WYANT, Alexander Helwig
American 1836-1892
paintings: (L) $110; (H) $55,000
drawings: (L) $1,980; (H) $6,600

WYATT, Greg
American contemporary
sculpture: (H) $2,640

WYATT, Kenneth
American 20th cent.
paintings: (L) $165; (H) $660

WYBRANT
drawings: (H) $990

WYCK, Jan
Dutch 1640-1700
paintings: (H) $22,000

WYCK, Thomas
Dutch 1616-1677
drawings: (H) $715

WYCKOFF, J.H.
American 19th cent.
paintings: (H) $1,100

WYDEVELD, Arnoud
American ac. 1855-1862
paintings: (L) $330; (H) $3,575

WYETH, Andrew
American b. 1917
paintings: (L) $22,000; (H) $385,000
drawings: (L) $330; (H) $319,000

WYETH, James
American b. 1946
paintings: (H) $52,250
drawings: (L) $4,950; (H) $23,100

WYETH, John Allan
American 20th cent.
paintings: (L) $220; (H) $1,320

WYETH, Newell Convers
American 1882-1945
paintings: (L) $1,100; (H) $77,000
drawings: (L) $880; (H) $8,800

WYETH, Paul
paintings: (H) $880

WYGAERD, A.W.
Dutch 19th cent.
paintings: (H) $1,650

WYGANT, Bob
American b. 1927
paintings: (L) $6,600; (H) $12,000

WYK, Henri van
Dutch b. 1833
paintings: (L) $220; (H) $4,180

WYLD, William
English 1806-1889
paintings: (L) $220; (H) $6,050
drawings: (L) $1,320; (H) $1,760

WYLE, Florence
American 18th/19th cent.
sculpture: (H) $2,200

WYLIE, Robert
American 1839-1877
paintings: (H) $1,100

WYLLIE, Charles William
English 1853-1923
paintings: (H) $19,800

WYLLIE, William Lionel
British 1851-1931
paintings: (L) $264; (H) $2,750

WYMAN, William
contemporary
sculpture: (H) $4,180

WYNANTS, Jan
Dutch c. 1630/35-1684
paintings: (L) $16,500; (H) $46,750

WYNANTS, Jan and Johannes
LINGELBACH
17th cent.
paintings: (H) $22,000

WYNFIELD, David Wilkie
British 1837-1887
paintings: (H) $3,300

WYNGAERDE, Anthonie J. van, Jr.
Dutch 1808-1887
paintings: (L) $385; (H) $12,650

WYNGAERDT, Petrus Theodorus van
Dutch 1816-1893
paintings: (H) $4,950

WYON, Allan G.
English 1882-?
sculpture: (H) $4,400

WYSMULLER, Jan Hillebrand
Dutch 1855-1925
paintings: (L) $440; (H) $1,980

WYWIORSKI, Michal Gorstkin
Polish 1861-1926
paintings: (L) $3,300; (H) $13,200

XAVERY, Jakob
Dutch 1736-1769
paintings: (H) $14,300
drawings: (H) $1,650

XCERON, Jean
Greek/American 1890-1967
paintings: (L) $715; (H) $15,400
drawings: (H) $495

XIMENES, Ettore
Italian 1855-1926
drawings: (H) $1,100

XOERON, John
American
drawings: (H) $3,850

XUL SOLAR, Alejandro
Argentinian b. 1887-1963
drawings: (L) $20,900; (H) $28,600

YANDELL, Enid
American 1870-1936
sculpture: (L) $660; (H) $11,000

YANKILEVSKY, Vladimir
Russian b. 1938
sculpture: (H) $19,800

YAO, C.J.
paintings: (H) $8,800

YARBER, Robert
American b. 1948
paintings: (L) $7,700; (H) $23,100
drawings: (L) $3,300; (H) $6,050

YARD, Sydney Janis
American 1855/57-1907/09
paintings: (L) $660; (H) $3,850
drawings: (L) $55; (H) $7,150

YARNOLD, B.
British 19th cent.
paintings: (H) $1,045

YARNOLD, George B.
British b. 1874-1876
paintings: (H) $1,430

YARNOLD, M.
English 19th cent.
paintings: (H) $2,200

YARROW, William H.K.
American 1891-1941
paintings: (L) $495; (H) $4,070
drawings: (H) $220

YATES, Cullen
American 1866-1945
paintings: (L) $247; (H) $18,700

YATES, Julian E.
American 1872-1953
paintings: (L) $1,870; (H) $2,200

YATES, Thomas
English d. 1796
paintings: (H) $49,500

YATES, William Henry
American 1848-1934
paintings: (L) $275; (H) $1,430

YATRIDES, Georges
French b. 1931
paintings: (H) $11,000

YAUSS, G.
Continental 19th/20th cent.
paintings: (H) $1,320

YDEMA, Egnatius
Dutch 1876-1937
paintings: (H) $1,100

YEAGER, Ira
American 20th cent.
paintings: (L) $413; (H) $1,650

YEAMES, William Frederick
English 1835-1918
paintings: (H) $2,310

YEATS, Jack Butler
Irish 1871-1957
paintings: (L) $15,400; (H) $26,400

YEEND-KING, Henry John
British 1855-1924
paintings: (L) $330; (H) $20,900
drawings: (L) $253; (H) $1,430

YEKTAI, Manucher
b. 1922
paintings: (H) $1,100

YELLAND, Raymond Dab
American 1848-1900
paintings: (L) $330; (H) $24,750

YENS, Karl
American 1868-1945
paintings: (L) $99; (H) $37,400
drawings: (L) $220; (H) $880

YEPES, Tomas
Spanish d. 1674
paintings: (L) $319,000; (H) $1,017,500

YEWELL, George Henry
American 1830-1923
paintings: (L) $275; (H) $14,300

YGLESIAS, Vincent Philip
Scottish 1845-1910
paintings: (L) $330; (H) $715

YO LAUR, Yvonne Marie
French b. 1879
paintings: (H) $5,500

YOAKUM, Joseph E.
American 1886-1973
paintings: (L) $880; (H) $3,960
drawings: (H) $880

YOHN, Frederick C.
American 1875-1933
paintings: (H) $3,600
drawings: (L) $192; (H) $440

YON, Edmond Charles Joseph
French 1836-1897
paintings: (H) $8,800

YORK, Jeremiah
American
paintings: (H) $3,300

YORKE, William Guy
British 1817-1882
paintings: (L) $2,420; (H) $25,300

YORKE, William Hoard
English ac. 1858-after 1913
paintings: (L) $1,870; (H) $33,000

YOSHIDA, Hiroshi
Japanese 1876-1950
drawings: (L) $154; (H) $2,090

YOUNG, Alexander
English ac. 1889-1893
paintings: (L) $660; (H) $880

YOUNG, Brinton S.
paintings: (H) $770

YOUNG, Charles Morris
American 1869-1964
paintings: (L) $413; (H) $9,350

Plein Air

Plein air (pronounced "plane air") is the French term for open air. Prior to 1841, when the collapsible metal tube was invented, all paintings, even landscape paintings, were done wholly in the studio. Once paints were packaged in portable metal tubes, artists could carry them anywhere. The mid-century artists of the Barbizon School were the first to work outdoors, but the artists most often associated with *plein-air* painting are the Impressionists who moved outdoors to study the effects of light and to catch the spontaneity of the "fleeting moment."

Karl Yens (1868-1945) was a painter, illustrator, etcher, and muralist. Born in Germany, he studied under Constant and Laurens in Paris. He emigrated to the United States in 1901. During his first decade in the U.S. he worked as a muralist in New York City and Washington, D.C.

In 1911 he settled in California and became a member of the South California School of Impressionists and co-founder of the Laguna Beach Art Museum. Yens was a well-known exponent of *plein-air* painting, and the museum has numerous photos of Yens in the open air with his easels and paints on his back. Yens received many awards during his lifetime, but when *Her Finishing Touches* came up for sale at Foster's Auction Gallery in August of 1981, very few people were familiar with his work and the painting sold for $24,200. Since that time works by California Impressionists have become a specialized field of collecting. In 1990, *Her Finishing Touches* was once again offered for sale, this time at Butterfield's in San Francisco. The price the second time around was $30,250, an average annual rate of appreciation of three percent. (Karl Yens, *Her Finishing Touches*, oil on canvas, 38 x 40 in., Butterfield, $30,250)

YOUNG, E. Brown
American 19th cent.
paintings: (H) $660

YOUNG, Florence Upson
American b. 1872
paintings: (L) $275; (H) $880
drawings: (H) $357

YOUNG, H.
American 19th/20th cent.
paintings: (H) $770

YOUNG, Harry
American 19th cent.
paintings: (H) $2,100

YOUNG, Harvey Otis
American 1840-1901
paintings: (L) $99; (H) $5,500
drawings: (L) $165; (H) $385

YOUNG, J.P.
Continental 19th cent.
paintings: (H) $3,300

YOUNG, James Harvey
American 1830-1918
paintings: (H) $2,640

YOUNG, Mahonri MacKintosh
American 1877-1957
paintings: (L) $352; (H) $440
drawings: (L) $66; (H) $1,650
sculpture: (L) $1,650; (H) $30,800

YOUNG, Peter
contemporary
paintings: (L) $715; (H) $3,850

YOUNG, William S.
American active 1850-1870
paintings: (L) $1,760; (H) $8,250

YOUNG-HUNTER, John
American 1874-1955
paintings: (H) $797

YOUNGERMAN, Jack
American b. 1926
paintings: (L) $2,310; (H) $11,000
drawings: (L) $220; (H) $660

YRISARRY, Mario
contemporary
paintings: (H) $660

YUAN, S.C.
American 20th cent.
paintings: (L) $3,850; (H) $7,700

YUANQI, Wang
Chinese 1642-1715
drawings: (H) $19,800

YVARAL, Jean Pierre
French b. 1934
paintings: (H) $660
sculpture: (L) $330; (H) $357

YVON, Adolphe
French 1817-1893
paintings: (H) $2,200

ZAAN, Jan van der
paintings: (H) $1,100

ZABALETA, Vladimir
Venezuelan b. 1944
paintings: (L) $9,350; (H) $14,300

ZABELITZKY, A.
German School 19th cent.
paintings: (H) $5,225

ZACH, Bruno, or ZACK
Austrian early 20th cent.
sculpture: (L) $220; (H) $20,350

ZACHARIE, Ernest Philippe
French 1849-1915
paintings: (H) $8,525

ZACK, Leon
paintings: (H) $18,700

ZADKINE, Ossip
Russian/French 1890-1967
drawings: (L) $660; (H) $22,000
sculpture: (L) $3,300; (H) $297,000

ZADORECHI, M.J.
paintings: (L) $605; (H) $880

ZADOROJNY, Vasiliy
Russian 20th cent.
paintings: (H) $1,650

ZAFEA
paintings: (H) $880

ZAHN, Albert
American c. 1930
sculpture: (H) $2,310

ZAIS, Giuseppe
Italian 1709-1784
paintings: (L) $4,180; (H) $46,750

ZAJAC, Jack
American b. 1929
sculpture: (L) $3,300; (H) $8,800

ZAK, Eugene
Polish 1884-1926
drawings: (H) $2,750

ZAKANITCH, Robert, or ZAKANYCH
American b. 1935
paintings: (L) $357; (H) $17,600

ZAKHAROV, Feodor
Russian/American 1882-1935
paintings: (L) $990; (H) $990

ZAKHAROV, Vadim
Russian b. 1959
paintings: (L) $20,900; (H) $28,600

ZALCE, Alfredo
Mexican b. 1908
paintings: (H) $110
drawings: (H) $1,100

ZAMACOIS Y ZABALA, Eduardo
Spanish 1842-1871
paintings: (L) $1,870; (H) $104,500
drawings: (H) $4,400

ZAMORA, Jesus Maria
Columbian 1875-1949
paintings: (H) $3,300

ZAMORA, Mario
American
sculpture: (L) $2,200; (H) $3,740

ZAMPIGHI, Eugenio
Italian 1859-1944
paintings: (L) $825; (H) $39,600
drawings: (L) $715; (H) $4,400

ZANAZIO, G.
Italian 19th/20th cent.
paintings: (H) $880

ZANCHI, Antonio
drawings: (H) $1,430

ZANDOMENEGHI, Federigo
Italian 1841-1917
paintings: (L) $209,000; (H) $462,000
drawings: (L) $1,650; (H) $165,000

ZANDT, Thomas Kirby van
American 1814-1886
paintings: (L) $418; (H) $935

ZANDT, William C. van
paintings: (H) $1,760

ZANETTI ZELLA, Vetorre
Italian 1864-1945
paintings: (H) $2,200
drawings: (L) $440; (H) $1,430

ZANFANI, Enrico
Italian 19th cent.
paintings: (H) $715

ZANG, John J.
American ac. 1883
paintings: (L) $5; (H) $3,300

ZANGUIDI, Jacopo, called Il Bertoja
drawings: (H) $27,500

ZANIERI, Arturo
b. 1870
paintings: (H) $1,540

ZANIN, Francesco
Italian 19th cent.
drawings: (L) $1,650; (H) $2,640

ZANNONI, Giuseppe
Italian 1849-1903
paintings: (L) $660; (H) $2,970

ZAO-WOU-KI
Chinese/French b. 1921
paintings: (L) $825; (H) $104,500
drawings: (L) $3,850; (H) $9,350

ZARDO, Alberto
paintings: (H) $880

ZARITZKY, Joseph
paintings: (H) $9,900

ZARRAGA, Angel
Mexican 1886-1946
paintings: (L) $19,800; (H) $88,000

ZATZKA, Hans
Austrian b. 1859
paintings: (L) $605; (H) $18,700
drawings: (H) $1,320

ZAVERST, Simon
paintings: (H) $1,760

ZAWISKI, Edouard
French 19th/20th cent.
paintings: (H) $1,650

ZEEBROECK, Van
Dutch d. 1844
paintings: (H) $2,200

ZEHME, Werner
German b. 1859
paintings: (H) $33,000

ZEIZIG, Johann Eleazer, called
Schenau
paintings: (H) $2,640

ZELDIS, Malcah
American b. 1931
paintings: (H) $2,750

ZELIKSON, Serge
sculpture: (H) $715

ZELLER, Pakos Palota
American
paintings: (H) $1,430

ZELLINSKY, C.L.
American 19th cent.
paintings: (L) $2,310; (H) $9,350

ZELLOS, Z.
drawings: (H) $1,320

ZELONI, R.
Italian
paintings: (H) $3,850

ZEMSKY, Jessica
American
drawings: (L) $1,600; (H) $2,700

ZENDEJAS, Miguel Jeronimo
paintings: (H) $1,100

ZENIL, Nahum B.
Mexican b. 1947
drawings: (H) $8,250

ZENISEK, Josef
Czechoslovakian b. 1855
paintings: (H) $2,200

ZENO, Jorge
b. Washington, D.C 1956
paintings: (L) $3,850; (H) $5,225

ZENSETSU
Japanese 1599-1680
drawings: (H) $77,000

ZERBE, Karl
German/American 1903-1972
paintings: (H) $825
drawings: (L) $165; (H) $1,540

ZERMATI, Jules
Italian 19th/20th cent.
paintings: (L) $990; (H) $1,760

ZEROLO, Martin
contemporary
paintings: (L) $330; (H) $770

ZETSCHE, Eduard
Austrian 1844-1927
paintings: (L) $770; (H) $1,650
drawings: (L) $1,100; (H) $1,870

ZETTERSTROM, Gunard
paintings: (H) $770

ZEUNER
Dutch 18th cent.
paintings: (H) $1,320

ZEUNER, I.
paintings: (H) $3,850

ZEVENBERGHEN, Georges
Antoine van
Belgian b. 1877
paintings: (L) $550; (H) $7,150

ZEWY, Karl
Austrian 1855-1929
paintings: (H) $4,400

ZHANG DAQIAN
Chinese 1899-1983
drawings: (L) $2,475; (H) $9,350

ZHANG YU
Chinese
drawings: (H) $1,760

ZIC, Z.
paintings: (L) $220; (H) $1,540

ZICHY, Mihaly von
Hungarian 1827-1960
drawings: (H) $1,760

ZICK, Januarius Johann Rasso
German 1730-1797
paintings: (L) $2,200; (H) $6,600

ZICKENDRAUGHT, Bernhard
German 1854-1937
paintings: (H) $660

ZIEGLER, Eustace Paul
American 1881-1969
paintings: (L) $605; (H) $41,250
drawings: (L) $110; (H) $3,300

ZIEGLER, Henry Bryan
English 1793-1874
paintings: (H) $1,210

ZIEGLER, Karl
paintings: (H) $2,640

ZIEGLER, Nellie Evelyn
American 20th cent.
paintings: (L) $1,540; (H) $4,675

ZIEM, Felix Francois Georges Philbert
French 1821-1911
paintings: (L) $825; (H) $60,500
drawings: (L) $440; (H) $1,760

ZIER, Francois Edouard
French 1856-1924
paintings: (L) $308; (H) $18,700

ZIER, Victor Casimir
Polish b. 1822
paintings: (L) $1,045; (H) $1,320

ZIG
drawings: (L) $3,850; (H) $4,620

ZIGLIARA, Eugene Louis Leopold
Tripard
French 1873-1918
paintings: (L) $1,650; (H) $1,760

ZILLA, Vettore Zanetti
Italian 1866-1945
paintings: (L) $522; (H) $1,320
drawings: (H) $825

ZILLE, Heinrich
German 1858/64-1929
drawings: (L) $275; (H) $1,760

ZILLER
Continental 19th/20th cent.
paintings: (H) $1,980

ZIMMER, Chris
paintings: (H) $1,025

ZIMMER, Wilhelm Carl August
German 1853-1937
paintings: (H) $33,000

ZIMMERMAN, Carl
American b. 1900
paintings: (L) $660; (H) $1,650
drawings: (H) $247

ZIMMERMAN, Frederick Almond
American 1886-1974
paintings: (L) $165; (H) $2,750

ZIMMERMAN, Karl
German 1796-1857
paintings: (H) $17,600

ZIMMERMAN, Richard August
German 1820-1875
paintings: (H) $2,420

ZIMMERMANN, Albert
paintings: (H) $3,740

ZIMMERMANN, E.
paintings: (H) $990

ZIMMERMANN, Jan Wendel
Gerstenhauer
Dutch 1816-1887
paintings: (H) $5,500

ZIMMERMANN, Reinhard Sebastian
German 1815-1893
paintings: (L) $660; (H) $35,200

ZINGG, Jules Emile
French 1882-1942
paintings: (H) $3,740

ZINGONI, Aurelio
paintings: (H) $3,850

ZINKEISEN, Doris Clare
English b. 1898
paintings: (L) $715; (H) $1,430
drawings: (H) $1,540

ZINNOGGER, Leopold
Austrian 1811-1872
paintings: (H) $8,800

ZINOVIEV, Andre
drawings: (H) $880

ZLATUSCHUKA, Josef
paintings: (H) $715

ZLOTNIKOV, Yuri
Russian b. 1930
drawings: (L) $1,100; (H) $2,090

ZMURKO, Franciszek
Polish 1859-1910
paintings: (H) $4,400

ZO, Henri
French 1873-1933
paintings: (L) $3,300; (H) $22,000

ZO, Jean Baptiste Achille
French 1826-1901
paintings: (H) $16,500

ZOARCH, William
American 1887-1966
drawings: (H) $900

ZOBEL, B.
British 18th/19th cent.
paintings: (H) $4,125

ZOCCHI, Guglielmo
Italian b. 1874
paintings: (L) $605; (H) $14,850

ZOCCHI, Silvio
paintings: (H) $3,080

ZOFF, Alfred
Austrian 1852-1927
paintings: (L) $1,760; (H) $3,300

ZOFFOLI, A.
Italian 19th cent.
paintings: (L) $358; (H) $17,600

ZOFFOLI, G.
late 18th cent.
sculpture: (H) $3,850

ZOFFOLI, Giacomo and Giovanni
last 3rd 18th cent.
sculpture: (H) $6,600

ZOGBAUM, Rufus Fairchild
American 1849-1925
paintings: (L) $605; (H) $1,210
drawings: (L) $715; (H) $2,420

ZOI, D.
sculpture: (L) $165; (H) $5,775

ZOIR, Emil
Swedish b. 1867
paintings: (H) $1,100

ZOLNAY, George Julian
Rumanian/American b. 1863
sculpture: (H) $770

ZONARO, Faust
Italian 1854-1929
paintings: (H) $1,650

ZOPPI, Antonio
Italian 1860-1926
paintings: (L) $418; (H) $6,600

ZORACH, Marguerite
American 1887-1968
paintings: (L) $2,200; (H) $28,600
drawings: (L) $2,200; (H) $8,800

ZORACH, Marguerite and William
American late 19th/20th cent.
paintings: (H) $38,500

ZORACH, William
Lithuanian/American 1887-1966
paintings: (L) $330; (H) $66,000
drawings: (L) $55; (H) $12,100
sculpture: (L) $1,100; (H) $55,000

ZORICAK, Yan
contemporary
sculpture: (H) $1,540

ZORKOCZY, Gyula
Hungarian 1873-1932
paintings: (H) $880

ZORN, Anders
Swedish 1860-1920
paintings: (L) $880; (H) $1,375,000
drawings: (L) $1,100; (H) $704,000

ZORNES, James Milford
American b. 1908
paintings: (H) $4,675
drawings: (L) $165; (H) $6,600

ZORTHIAN, Jirayr H.
American b. 1912
drawings: (H) $825

ZOX, Larry
American contemporary
paintings: (L) $165; (H) $3,300
drawings: (L) $110; (H) $330

ZTERMIDA (?), Juan de
paintings: (H) $880

ZUBER, Henri
French 1844-1909
paintings: (H) $14,300

ZUBER, Julius
paintings: (H) $2,750

ZUBER-BUHLER, Fritz
Swiss 1822-1896
paintings: (L) $715; (H) $55,000
drawings: (L) $990; (H) $1,650

ZUBIAURRE, Ramon de
Spanish b. 1882
paintings: (L) $3,300; (H) $14,300

ZUBIAURRE, Valentin de
Spanish 1879-1963
paintings: (L) $8,250; (H) $20,900

ZUBRARAN, Francisco de
Spanish 1598-1664
paintings: (H) $24,200

ZUCCARELLI, Francesco
Italian 1701/02-1788
paintings: (L) $5,500; (H) $26,400
drawings: (L) $2,860; (H) $63,250

ZUCCARO, Federico
Italian 1542/43-1609
drawings: (L) $7,975; (H) $2,530,000

ZUCCARO, Taddeo
Italian 1529-1566
drawings: (L) $4,950; (H) $137,500

ZUCCARO, Taddeo and Giovanni
ANTINORO
Italian 16th cent.
drawings: (H) $319,000

ZUCCHI, Antonio Pietro Francesco
Italian 1726-1795
drawings: (H) $3,080

ZUCKER, Joe
American b. 1941
paintings: (L) $1,540; (H) $17,600
drawings: (L) $467; (H) $1,980

ZUGEL, Heinrich Johann
German 1850-1941
paintings: (L) $33,000; (H) $143,000

ZUGNO, Francesco, II
Italian 1709-1787
paintings: (L) $2,860; (H) $70,400

ZUILL, Abbie Luella
American 1856-1921
paintings: (L) $325; (H) $1,600

ZUILL, Alice E.
American 19th cent.
paintings: (H) $1,980

ZULOAGA Y ZABALETA, Ignacio
Spanish 1870-1945
paintings: (L) $4,400; (H) $341,000
drawings: (L) $522; (H) $6,050

ZUNIGA, Francisco
Mexican b. 1913
paintings: (H) $2,420
drawings: (L) $1,210; (H) $22,000
sculpture: (L) $4,070; (H) $90,750

ZUPAN, Bruno
American 20th cent.
paintings: (H) $1,320

ZURBARAN, Francisco de
Spanish 1598-1664
paintings: (L) $57,750; (H) $286,000

ZUYDERHOUDT, C. van
paintings: (H) $4,400

ZUYDERLAND, Siet
paintings: (H) $770

ZUYLEN, Jan Hendricksz van
Dutch ac. 1644
paintings: (H) $22,000

ZWAAN, Cornelis Christian
Dutch/American 1882-1964
paintings: (L) $27; (H) $5,500

ZWACK, Michael
contemporary
drawings: (H) $2,200

ZWART, A.J.
Dutch 19th cent.
paintings: (H) $770

ZWART, Willemus H.P.J. de
Dutch 1862-1931
paintings: (H) $1,430

Appendix A: Museums

ALABAMA

Birmingham
Birmingham Museum of Art

Huntsville
Huntsville Museum of Art

Montgomery
Montgomery Museum of Fine Arts

Tuscaloosa
Warner Collection of Gulf States
Paper Corporation

ALASKA

Anchorage
Anchorage Museum of History and
Art

Juneau
Alaska State Museum

ARIZONA

Phoenix
Heard Art Museum
Phoenix Art Museum

Tempe
University Art Centers, Arizona State
University

Tucson
Tucson Museum of Art
University of Arizona Museum of Art

ARKANSAS

Little Rock
Arkansas Arts Center

CALIFORNIA

Berkeley
University Art Museum, University of
California, Berkeley

La Jolla
La Jolla Museum of Contemporary
Art

Los Angeles
Los Angeles County Museum of Art

Malibu
J. Paul Getty Museum

Pasadena
Norton Simon Museum of Art

Sacramento
Crocker Art Museum

San Diego
San Diego Museum of Art
Timken Art Gallery

San Francisco
M.H. de Young Memorial Museum
California Palace of the Legion of
Honor
San Francisco Museum of Modern Art

San Marino
Huntington Library, Art Collection
and Botanical Gardens

Santa Barbara
Santa Barbara Museum of Art

Stockton
The Haggin Museum

COLORADO

Colorado Springs
Colorado Springs Fine Art Center

Denver
Denver Art Museum
Museum of Western Art

CONNECTICUT

Bridgeport
Housatonic Museum of Art

Farmington
Hill-Stead Museum

Hartford
Wadsworth Atheneum

New Britain
New Britain Museum of American Art

New Haven
Yale University Art Gallery
Yale Center for British Art

New London
Lyman Allyn Museum

Ridgefield
Aldrich Museum of Contemporary
Art

Stamford
Whitney Museum of American Arts

795

Storrs
William Benton Museum of Art,
  University of Connecticut

DELAWARE

Wilmington
Delaware Art Museum

Winterthur
Winterthur Museum and Gardens

DISTRICT OF COLUMBIA

Washington
Corcoran Gallery of Art
Hirshhorn Museum and Sculpture
  Garden
National Museum of American Art
National Gallery of Art
National Portrait Gallery
The Phillips Collection

FLORIDA

Coral Gables
Lowe Art Museum, University of
  Miami
Metropolitan Museum and Art
  Centers

Fort Lauderdale
Museum of Art

Jacksonville
Cummer Gallery of Art

Miami Beach
Bass Museum of Art

Orlando
Orlando Museum of Art

St. Petersburg
Museum of Fine Arts

Sarasota
The John and Mable Ringling
  Museum of Art

West Palm Beach
Norton Gallery and School of Art

GEORGIA

Albany
Museum of Art

Athens
Georgia Museum of Art, University of
  Georgia

Atlanta
High Museum of Art

Savannah
Telfair Academy of Arts and Sciences,
  Inc.

HAWAII

Honolulu
Contemporary Museum
Honolulu Academy of Arts

IDAHO

Boise
Boise Gallery of Art

ILLINOIS

Champaign
Krannert Art Museum, University of
  Illinois

Chicago
Art Institute of Chicago
Museum of Contemporary Art
Terra Art Museum

INDIANA

Bloomington
Indiana University Art Museum

Evansville
Evansville Museum of Arts and
  Science

Indianapolis
Indianapolis Museum of Art

Notre Dame
Smite Museum of Art, University of
  Notre Dame

Terre Haute
Sheldon Swope Art Gallery

IOWA

Cedar Falls
Gallery of Art, University of Northern
  Iowa

Cedar Rapids
Cedar Rapids Museum of Art

Davenport
Davenport Museum of Art

Des Moines
Des Moines Art Center

Fort Dodge
Blanden Memorial Art Museum

Iowa City
University of Iowa Museum of Art

Mason City
Charles H. MacNider Museum

KANSAS

Lawrence
Spencer Museum of Art, University of
  Kansas

Wichita
Edwin A. Ulrich Museum of Art,
  Wichita State University
Wichita Art Museum

KENTUCKY

Lexington
University of Kentucky Art Museum

Louisville
J.B. Speed Art Museum

Owensboro
Owensboro Museum of Fine Art

LOUISIANA

Jennings
Zigler Museum

New Orleans
New Orleans Museum of Art

Shreveport
R.W. Norton Art Gallery

MAINE

Brunswick
Bowdoin College Museum of Art

Portland
Portland Museum of Art

Rockland
William A. Farnsworth Library and
  Art Museum

Waterville
Colby College Museum of Art

MARYLAND

Baltimore
Baltimore Museum of Art
Walters Art Gallery

MASSACHUSETTS

Andover
Addison Gallery of American Art

Boston
The Institute of Contemporary Art
Museum of Fine Arts
Isabella Stewart Gardener Museum

Brockton
Brockton Art Museum

Cambridge
Arthur M. Sackler Art Museum
Busch-Reisinger Museum
Fogg Art Museum

Framingham
Danforth Museum

Northhampton
Smith College Museum of Art

Salem
Peabody Museum of Salem

Springfield
Museum of Fine Arts

Waltham
Rose Art Museum, Brandeis
  University

Wellesley
Wellesley College Museum, Jewett
  Art Center

Williamstown
Sterling and Francine Clark Art
  Institute

Worcester
Worcester Art Museum

MICHIGAN

Ann Arbor
University of Michigan Museum of
  Art

Detroit
Detroit Institute of Arts

Flint
Flint Institute of Arts

Grand Rapids
Grand Rapids Art Museum

MINNESOTA

Duluth
Tweed Museum of Art, University of
  Minnesota

Minneapolis
Minneapolis Institute of Arts
University Gallery, University of
  Minnesota
Walker Art Center

St. Paul
Minnesota Museum of Art

MISSISSIPPI

Laurel
Lauren Rogers Museum of Art

MISSOURI

Kansas City
Nelson-Atkins Museum of Art

St. Louis
St. Louis Art Museum

MONTANA

Billings
Yellowstone Art Center

Great Falls
C.M. Russell Museum

NEBRASKA

Lincoln
Sheldon Memorial Art Gallery,
  University of Nebraska Art Gallery

Omaha
Joslyn Art Museum

NEVADA

Las Vegas
Las Vegas Art Museum

NEW HAMPSHIRE

Hanover
Hood Museum of Art, Dartmouth
  College

Manchester
Currier Gallery of Art

NEW JERSEY

Newark
Newark Museum

Princeton
The Art Museum, Princeton
  University

Trenton
New Jersey State Museum

NEW MEXICO

Albuquerque
Albuquerque Museum
Jonson Gallery, University of New
  Mexico

Santa Fe
Museum of Fine Arts, Museum of
  New Mexico

NEW YORK

Buffalo
Albright-Knox Art Gallery

Canajoharie
Canajoharie Library and Art Gallery

Corning
The Rockwell Museum

Elmira
Arnot Art Museum

Glens Falls
Hyde Collection

Huntington
Heckscher Museum

Ithaca
Herbert F. Johnson Museum of Art,
  Cornell University

New York City
The Bronx Museum of the Arts
Cooper-Hewitt Museum
The Frick Collection
Solomon R. Guggenheim Museum
Jewish Museum
Metropolitan Museum of Art
Museum of American Folk Art
Museum of Modern Art
New Museum of Contemporary Art
New York Historical Society
Whitney Museum of American Art
The Brooklyn Museum

Poughkeepsie
Vassar College Art Gallery

Rochester
Memorial Art Gallery of the
  University of Rochester

Syracuse
Everson Museum of Art of Syracuse
  and Onondaga County

Utica
Munson-Williams-Proctor Institute,
  Museum of Art

NORTH CAROLINA

Charlotte
Mint Museum of Art

Greensboro
Weatherspoon Art Gallery

Raleigh
North Carolina Museum of Art

OHIO

Akron
Akron Art Museum

Cincinnati
Cincinnati Art Museum
Taft Museum

Cleveland
Cleveland Center for Contemporary
  Art
Cleveland Museum of Art

Columbus
Columbus Museum of Art
Wexner Center for the Visual Arts,
  Ohio State University

Dayton
Dayton Art Institute

Oberlin
Allen Memorial Art Museum, Oberlin
  College

Oxford
Miami University Art Museum

Toledo
Toledo Museum of Art

OKLAHOMA

Norman
Museum of Art, University of
  Oklahoma

Oklahoma City
National Cowboy Hall of Fame and
  Western Heritage Center Oklahoma
  Museum of Art
Oklahoma City Art Museum

Tulsa
Philbrook Museum of Art
Thomas Gilcrease Institute of
  American History and Art

OREGON

Eugene
Museum of Art, University of Oregon

Portland
Portland Art Museum

PENNSYLVANIA

Bethlehem
Lehigh University Art Galleries

Chadds Ford
Brandywine River Museum

Philadelphia
Barnes Foundation
Institute of Contemporary Art,
  University of Pennsylvania
Pennsylvania Academy of the Fine
  Arts
Philadelphia Museum of Art

Pittsburgh
Museum of Art, Carnegie Institute

RHODE ISLAND

Providence
Museum of Art, Rhode Island School
  of Design

SOUTH CAROLINA

Greenville
Greenville County Museum of Art

Murrells Inlet
Brookgreen Gardens

SOUTH DAKOTA

Brookings
South Dakota Art Museum

TENNESSEE

Chattanooga
Hunter Museum of Art

Memphis
Memphis Brooks Museum of Art
Dixon Gallery and Gardens

Nashville
Tennessee Botanical Gardens and Fine
  Arts Center, Inc.
Carl Van Vechten Gallery of Fine Arts,
  Fisk University
Vanderbilt Art Gallery

TEXAS

Austin
Archer M. Huntington Art Gallery,
  University of Texas at Austin

Dallas
Dallas Museum of Art

El Paso
El Paso Museum of Art

Fort Worth
Amon Carter Museum
Kimbell Art Museum
Modern Art Museum of Fort Worth

Houston
Contemporary Art Museum
Museum of Fine Arts, Houston

UTAH

Provo
B.F. Larsen Gallery
Brigham Young University Art
  Museum

Salt Lake City
Utah Museum of Fine Arts, University
  of Utah

Springville
Springville Museum of Art

VERMONT

Bennington
Bennington Museum

Middlebury
Christian A. Johnson Gallery,
  Middlebury College

Shelburne
Shelburne Museum, Inc.

VIRGINIA

Charlottesville
University of Virginia Art Museum

Newport News
Mariners Museum

Norfolk
Chrysler Museum

Richmond
Virginia Museum of Fine Arts

Williamsburg
Abby Aldrich Rockefeller Folk Art
  Center

WASHINGTON

Pullman
Museum of Art, Washington State
  University

Seattle
Seattle Art Museum
Henry Art Gallery, University of
  Washington

Tacoma
Tacoma Art Museum

WEST VIRGINIA

Huntington
Huntington Museum of Art

WISCONSIN

Madison
Elvehjem Museum of Art, University
  of Wisconsin-Madison

Milwaukee
Milwaukee Art Museum

WYOMING

Cody
Buffalo Bill Historical Center, The
  Whitney Gallery of Western Art

Laramie
Art Museum, University of Wyoming

Rock Springs
Community Fine Arts Center

Appendix B: Publications* ──────────

AMERICAN ARTIST (M)
1515 Broadway
New York, NY 10036

**AMERICAN COLLECTORS
JOURNAL (T)**
P.O. Box 407
Kewanee, IL 61443

AMERICANA (M)
29 West 38th Street
New York, NY 10018

THE ANTIQUE GAZETTE (T)
6949 Charlotte Pike
Suite #106
Nashville, TN 37205

ANTIQUE MARKET REPORT (M)
650 Westdale Drive
Suite #100
Wichita, KS 67209

ANTIQUE MONTHLY (T)
2100 Powerburg
Atlanta, GA 30339

ANTIQUE PRESS (T)
12403 N. Florida Avenue
Tampa, FL 33612

THE ANTIQUE REVIEW
P. O. Box 538
Worthington, OH 43085

**THE ANTIQUE TRADER
WEEKLY (T)**
P.O. Box 1050
Dubuque, IA 52001

ANTIQUE WEEK (T)
27 N. Jefferson
P.O. Box 90
Knightstown, IN 46168

**ANTIQUES (THE
MAGAZINE ANTIQUES) (M)**
575 Broadway
New York, NY 10012

**ANTIQUES & COLLECTING
HOBBIES (M)**
1006 South Michigan Avenue
Chicago, IL 60605

**ANTIQUES AND THE ARTS
WEEKLY/THE NEWTOWN BEE (T)**
5 Church Hill Road
Newtown, CT 06470

ANTIQUES WEST (T)
3315 Sacramento Street
San Francisco, CA 94118

ART & ANTIQUES (M)
633 3rd Avenue
New York, NY 10017

ART & AUCTION (M)
250 West 57th Street, Room 215
New York, NY 10019

**THE ART/ANTIQUES
INVESTMENT REPORT (N)**
99 Wall Street
New York, NY 10005

ART IN AMERICA (M)
575 Broadway
New York, NY 10012

ARTFORUM
65 Bleeker Street
New York, NY 10012

ARTNEWS (N)
48 West 38th Street
New York, NY 10018

THE ARTNEWSLETTER (N)
48 West 38th Street
New York, NY 10018

ART TODAY (M)
650 Westdale
Wichita, KS 67209

ARTWEEK (T)
12 South First Street
Suite 520
San Jose, CA 95113

───────
*Key: (J) - Journal, (M) - Magazine, (N) - Newsletter, (T) - Tabloid.

ART/WORLD (T)
55 Wheatly Road
Glen Head, NY 11545

ANTIQUES & FINE ART (M)
255 North Market Street
San Jose, CA 95110

COLLECTOR (T)
P. O. Box 601
1800 West Q. Street
Pomona, CA 91768

THE COLLECTOR (T)
Box 158
105 South Buchanan
Heyworth, IL 61745

COLLECTORS JOURNAL (T)
421 First Avenue, Box 601
Vinton, IA 52349

**COLLECTOR'S NEWS &
THE ANTIQUE REPORTER (T)**
P.O. Box 156
506 Second Street
Grundy Center, IA 50638

THE CONNOISSEUR (M)
1790 Broadway
New York, NY 10019

**FINE ART AND AUCTION
REVIEW (T)**
1683 Chestnut Street
Vancouver, B.C. V6J 4M6
Canada

**JOEL SATER'S ANTIQUES AND
AUCTION NEWS (T)**
P.O. Box 500
Mount Joy, PA 17552

**KOVELS ON ANTIQUES AND
COLLECTIBLES (N)**
P.O. Box 22200
Beachwood, OH 44122

**LEONARD'S ANNUAL PRICE
INDEX OF ART AUCTIONS (J)**
30 Valentine Park
Newton, MA 02165

**MAINE ANTIQUE DIGEST
(M.A.D.) (T)**
P.O. Box 1429
911 Main Street
Waldoboro, ME 04572

MASS BAY ANTIQUES (T)
Box 929
Danvers, MA 01923

**MIDATLANTIC ANTIQUES
MAGAZINE (T)**
P.O. Box 908
Henderson, NC 27536

**NEW ENGLAND ANTIQUES
JOURNAL (T)**
4 Church Street
Ware, MA 01082

THE NEW YORK ALMANAC (T)
P.O. Box 335
Lawrence, NY 11559

**NEW YORK-PENNSYLVANIA
COLLECTOR (T)**
P. O. Box C
Fishers, NY 14453

**RENNINGER'S ANTIQUE
GUIDE (T)**
P.O. Box 495
Lafayette Hill, PA 19444

SOUTHWEST ART (M)
P. O. Box 460535
Houston, TX 77256

WEST ART (T)
P.O. Box 6868
Auburn, CA 95604

WEST COAST PEDDLER (T)
P.O. Box 5134
Whittier, CA 90607

Appendix C: Auction Houses

ALTERMANN & MORRIS
3461 West Alabama
Houston, Texas 77027
(713) 840-1922

F.O. BAILEY AUCTION GALLERY
141 Middle Street
Portland, Maine 04101
(207) 774-1479

JAMES R. BAKKER
370 Broadway
Cambridge, MA 02139
(617) 864-7067

BARRIDOFF GALLERIES
26 Free Street
Portland, Maine 04101
(207) 772-5011

FREDERICK A. BAUER
RFD 1, Box 460
New Sharon, Maine 04955
(207) 778-9682

FRANK H. BOOS GALLERY, INC.
420 Enterprise Court
Bloomfield Hills, Michigan 48013
(313) 332-1500

RICHARD A. BOURNE CO., INC.
Corporation Road
Hyannis, Massachusetts 02601
Mail: P.O. Box 141
Hyannis Port, Massachusetts 02647
(508) 775-0797

JEFFREY BURCHARD GALLERIES
2528 30th Avenue North
St. Petersburg, Florida 33713
(813) 823-4156

BUTTERFIELD & BUTTERFIELD
220 San Bruno Avenue
San Francisco, California 94103
(415) 861-7500

CAROPRESO GALLERY
136 High Street
Lee, Massachusetts 01238
(413) 243-3424

CHICAGO ART GALLERIES, INC.
5039 Oakton Street
Skokie, Illinois 60077
(708) 677-6080

CHRISTIE, MANSON & WOODS INTERNATIONAL, INC.
502 Park Avenue
New York, New York 10022
(212) 546-1000

CHRISTIE'S EAST
219 East 67th Street
New York, New York 10021
(212) 606-0400

CLEARING HOUSE AUCTION GALLERIES
207 Church Street
Wethersfield, Connecticut 06019
(203) 529-3344

BRUCE D. COLLINS FINE ART
RR1, Box 113
Denmark, Maine 04022
(207) 452-2197

DECARO AUCTION SALES
105 New Street
Seaford, Delaware 19973
(302) 629-4643

JIM DEPEW GALLERIES
1860 Piedmont Road, NE
Atlanta, Georgia 30324
(404) 874-2286

J.C. DEVINE, INC.
Auctioneers and Appraisers
P.O. Box 413, Savage Road
Milford, New Hampshire 03055
(603) 673-4967

DOUGLAS AUCTIONEERS
Route 5
South Deerfield, Massachusetts 01373
(413) 665-2877

WILLIAM DOYLE GALLERIES
175 East 87th Street
New York, New York 10128
(212) 427-2730

DU MOUCHELLE ART GALLERIES
409 E. Jefferson
Detroit, Michigan 48226
(313) 963-6255

DUNNING'S AUCTION SERVICE, INC.
P.O. Box 866
Elgin, IL 60121
(708) 741-3483

ROBERT C. ELDRED CO., INC.
Route 6A, Box 796
East Dennis, Massachusetts 02641
(508) 385-3116

FREEMAN/FINE ARTS COMPANY
1808-10 Chestnut Street
Philadelphia, Pennsylvania 19103
(215) 563-9275

FOSTER'S AUCTIONS
Route 1, P. O. Box 203
Newcastle, Maine 04553
(207) 563-8110

GARTH'S AUCTIONS, INC.
2690 Stratford Road
P.O. Box 369
Delaware, Ohio 43015
(614) 362-4771

MORTON M. GOLDBERG AUCTION GALLERIES, INC.
547 Baronne Street
New Orleans, Louisiana 70113
(504) 592-2300

GREAT GATSBYS
91 University Place
New York, NY 10003
1 (800) 342-1744

GROGAN & COMPANY
890 Commonwealth Avenue
Boston, Massachusetts 02215
(617) 566-4100

GUERNSEY'S
108-1/2 East 73rd Street
New York, New York 10021
(212) 794-2280

HABSBURG, FELDMAN
36 East 75th Street
New York, New York 10021
(212) 570-4040

HANZEL GALLERIES
1120 South Michigan Avenue
Chicago, Illinois 60605
(312) 922-6234

WILLIS HENRY AUCTIONS
22 Main Street
Marshfield, Massachusetts 02050
(617) 834-7774

LESLIE HINDMAN AUCTIONEERS
215 West Ohio Street
Chicago, Illinois 60610
(312) 670-0010

F.B. HUBLEY & CO., INC.
364 Broadway
Cambridge, Massachusetts 02139
(617) 876-2030

ILLUSTRATION HOUSE, INC.
96 Spring Street, 7th Floor
New York, New York 10012
(212) 966-9444

ARTHUR JAMES GALLERIES
615 East Atlantic Avenue
Delray Beach, Florida 33483
(407) 278-2373

JAMES D. JULIA
Box 830
Route 201
Fairfield, Maine 04937
(207) 453-7904

FRANK C. KAMINSKI COMPANY
193 Franklin Street
Stoneham, Massachusetts 02180
(617) 665-8380

LINCOLN GALLERIES
225 Scotland Road
Orange, New Jersey 07050
(201) 677-2000

LITCHFIELD AUCTION GALLERY
P. O. Box 1337
425 Phantom Road
Litchfield, Connecticut 06759
(203) 567-3126

LOUISIANA AUCTION EXCHANGE
2031 Government Street
Baton Rouge, Louisiana 70806
(504) 924-1803

LUBIN GALLERIES
30 West 26th Street
New York, New York 10010
(212) 924-3777

MAPES AUCTIONEERS AND APPRAISERS
1600 Vestal Parkway West
Vestal, New York 13850
(607) 754-9193

MATZ & PRIBELL GALLERY
366-1/2 Broadway
Cambridge, Massachusetts 02139
(617) 661-6200

PAUL MCINNIS
356 Exeter Road
Hampton Falls, New Hampshire
  03844
(603) 778-8989

DUANE MERRILL
32 Beacon Street
S. Burlington, Vermont 05401
(802) 878-2625

JOHN MORAN AUCTIONEERS
3202 East Foothill Boulevard
Pasadena, California 91107
(818) 793-1833

MYSTIC FINE ARTS
47 Holmes Street
Mystic, Connecticut 06355
(203) 572-8873

NADEAU'S AUCTION GALLERY
489 Old Hartford Road
Colchester, Connecticut 06415
(203) 246-2444

NEAL AUCTION COMPANY
4038 Magazine Street
New Orleans, Louisiana 70115
(504) 899-5329

NORTHEAST AUCTIONS
Ronald Bourgeault Auctioneer
694 Lafayette Road
Hampton, New Hampshire 03842
(603) 926-8222

OLIVER'S
P. O. Box 337
Kennebunk, Maine 04043
(207) 985-3600

PETTIGREW AUCTION COMPANY
405 South Nevada Avenue
Colorado Springs, Colorado 80903
(719) 633-7963

PHILLIPS SON & NEALE, INC.
406 East 79th Street
New York, New York 10021
(212) 570-4830

PIONEER AUCTION OF AMHERST
P. O. Box 593
Jct. Rt. 116 and 63
N. Amherst, Massachusetts 01059
(413) 253-9914

JOHN C. ROSSELLE CO.
182 Cherry Street
Middleborough, Massachusetts 02346
(508) 947-2122

SANDERS & MOCK ASSOCIATES
Box 37
Tamworth, New Hampshire 03886
(603) 323-8749

SELKIRK GALLERIES
4166 Olive Street
St. Louis, Missouri 63108
(314) 533-1700

ROBERT W. SKINNER, INC.
Route 117
Bolton, Massachusetts 01740
(617) 779-6241

C.G. SLOAN & COMPANY, INC.
4920 Wyaconda Road
North Bethesda, Maryland 20852
(301) 468-4911

SOTHEBY'S, INC.
1334 York Avenue
New York, New York 10021
(212) 606-7000

SOTHEBY'S ARCADE AUCTIONS
1334 York Avenue
New York, New York 10021
(212) 606-7516

SWANN GALLERIES
104 East 25th Street
New York, New York 10010
(212) 254-4710

TEPPER GALLERIES
221 West 17th Street
New York, New York 10011
(212) 677-5300

TEXAS ART GALLERY
1400 Main Street
Dallas, Texas 75202
(214) 747-8158

KENNETH W. VAN BLARCOM AUCTIONEERS
63 Eliot Street
South Natick, Massachusetts 01760
(508) 653-7017

WESCHLER'S
905 E St., N.W.
Washington, D.C. 20004
(202) 628-1281

RICHARD W. WITHINGTON, INC.
Auctioneer & Appraiser
R.R.2, Box 440
Hillsboro, New Hampshire 03244
(603) 464-3232

GUSTAVE WHITE AUCTIONEERS
38 Bellevue Avenue
Newport, Rhode Island 02840
(401) 849-3000

WINTER ASSOCIATES
Box 823
21 Cooke Street
Plainville, Connecticut 06062
(203) 793-0288

WOLF'S AUCTION GALLERY
1239 West 6th Street
Cleveland, Ohio 44113
(216) 575-9653

YOUNG FINE ARTS GALLERY, INC.
Post Office Box 313
North Berwick, Maine 03906
(207) 676-3104

Appendix D: Indexing Guidelines ————————

Guidelines for Listing Artists' Last Names

These fundamental rules are based on the *Anglo-American Cataloguing Rules* revised in 1979 and published by the American Library Association.*

Try to ascertain how the artist signed his name, or the most common listing of the name, before turning to the general rules.

Ex. The famous American cartoonist Al Capp is listed "CAPP, Al," and not by his given name, Alfred Gerald Caplin.

English — Names are listed under the prefix.
Ex. DECAMP, Joseph Rodefer

Dutch — The listing is under the part of the name that follows the prefix unless the prefix is "ver."
Ex. GOGH, Vincent van

French — Look under the prefix if it is an article (le, la les) or a contraction of an article and a preposition (du, des, de le, del).
Ex. LE SIDANER, Henri
If the article and preposition are separate words, look under the part of the name following the preposition.
Ex. LA PAGE, Raymond de

German — If the prefix is an article or a contraction of an article and a preposition, look under the prefix (Am, Aus'm, Vom, Zum, Zur). Otherwise, look under the name following the prefix.
Ex. SCHWIND, Moritz Ludwig von

Italian — Modern names are catalogued under the prefix.
Ex. DEL LUNGO, Isidoro
Medieval names are listed under the name that follows the prefix.
Ex. ROBBIA, Luca della

Spanish — If the prefix is an article only, look under the article.
Ex. LAS HERAS, Manual Antonio
Look for other Spanish names under the part following the prefix (de, del, de las).

Exceptions — There are exceptions to every rule. If you can't find a name where you think it should be, look under the variants.
Ex. MEYER VON BREMEN, George

———————
*Indexes of names in books published prior to 1979 may not confirm to these rules.

Appendix E: Classification Index ——————

For the purpose of this price guide it was necessary to divide all works of art into one of three categories—paintings, drawings, and sculpture. When defining categories, the media *and* the support were considered. Examples of the media by category are listed below.

PAINTINGS	DRAWINGS	SCULPTURE
acrylic on canvas	acrylic and charcoal on	anything 2 or 3
acrylic on paper	paper	dimensional
acrylic, oil, India ink	assemblage	anything listed as "cast
and graphite on canvas	bistre	from a model by"
aquatec	body color on vellum	bas relief
casein	brush and ink	bronze
en grisaille on board	casein on paper	construction
distemper	chalk	Cornell boxes
dry-brush	charcoal	Earthworks
enamel	collage	ivory relief
encaustic	colored graphite	lacquered wood
epoxy	conte crayon	marble
etched and painted	crayon	mosaic tile
fresco	drawing	plaster
gesso	gouache on canvas	polyester resin
gold ground, oil on	gouache on paper	steatite
panel	gouache on vellum	steel
leimfarbe	gouache on panel/artist	terracotta
mirrored glass	board/ canvas board	wood
monoprint	mixed media	
oil on canvas	mixed media on paper	
oil on board	oil and pencil	
oil on copper	oil stick on paper	
oil on masonite	oil crayon on paper	
oil on paper	pastel	
oil on panel	pen and ink	
oil on wood	photography collage	
oil on paper laid down	pochoir	
oil and sand	sanguine	
poly-vinyl emulsion	sepia ink	
poster acrylic	tissue collage on paper	
sand painting	wash	
tempera on paper	watercolor	
tempera on canvas	watercolor on canvas	
tempera on panel		
tempera on artistboard		
tempera on canvas		
board		
velum		
Verre eglomise		

Appendix F: List of Illustrations* ————————

————
*Italicized pages numbers refer to artwork in the color insert.

Permissions

The author would like to acknowledge the following for use of photographs (works are listed in the order in which they appear in the book):

Heliodore's Woodstar with a Pink Orchid, courtesy Richard A. Bourne Co.; *Still Life of White Roses,* courtesy Auction Index, Inc.; *A Roman Scribe Writing Dispatches,* copyright © 1990 by Sotheby's, Inc.; *The Shepherdess,* courtesy Robert W. Skinner, Inc.; *Spring Storm,* courtesy Wolf's Auction Galleries; *Ferry Boat Interior,* courtesy Nadeau's Auction Gallery; *Le Havre,* courtesy Butterfield & Butterfield; *Le Tampon Buvard,* courtesy Christie's New York; *White Mountain Landscape,* courtesy Sanders & Mock Associates; *The Pont Neuf, Wrapped, Project for Paris,* courtesy Christie's New York; *Home by the Lake,* copyright © 1989 by Sotheby's, Inc.; *Study for the Deluge,* courtesy Christie's New York; *The Deluge,* John H. and Ernestine A. Payne Fund, courtesy Museum of Fine Arts, Boston; *Ajax,* courtesy Christie's New York; *Osceola, War Chief of the Seminoles (1803-1838),* courtesy William Reese Co.; *An Allegory with a Male and Female Figure,* courtesy Christie's New York; *Cheetah,* copyright © 1990 by Sotheby's, Inc.; *New Year's Day in Smolenski,* courtesy Frank H. Boos Gallery; *March Snow,* courtesy Blackwood/March Auctioneers; *All About Eve,* courtesy William Doyle Galleries; *On the Beach,* courtesy Robert W. Skinner, Inc.; *View of Benjamin Reber Farm in Lower Heidelberg Township, Berks County, Pennsylvania,* copyright © 1988 by Sotheby's, Inc.; *Abstract,* courtesy Mystic Fine Arts; *Young Man in a Courtyard Reading a Book,* courtesy Gustave White Auctioneers; *Washday at Melrose,* courtesy Morton M. Goldberg Auction Galleries; *Street Urchins,* courtesy Arthur James Galleries; *Pushcarts,* courtesy James R. Bakker Galleries; *Diego y Yo,* copyright © 1990 by Sotheby's, Inc.; *Walking Woman,* courtesy William Doyle Galleries; *Two Young Girls in a Forest,* courtesy Grogan & Company; *Downtown New York,* courtesy Young Fine Arts Gallery; *B 2, 5, 8,* courtesy Christie's New York; *Reclining Figure with Guitar,* courtesy Selkirk Galleries; *Gayety Burlesk,* courtesy Barridoff Galleries; *West Bayou Plaquemines,* courtesy Neal Auction Company; *Dancer Resting,* courtesy Leslie Hindman Auctioneers; *Personnages Et Oiseau Devant Le Soleil,* copyright © 1990 by Sotheby's, Inc.; *Tableau Losangique II,* copyright © Estate of Piet Mondrian/VAGA, New York 1991, courtesy Christie's New York; *Le Baiser,* courtesy William Doyle Galleries; *Typewriter Eraser,* courtesy Christie's New York; *The One in Yellow,* courtesy Barridoff Galleries; *David Rittenhouse,* courtesy Robert C. Eldred Company; *Pebble Beach,* courtesy Morton M. Goldberg Auction Galleries; *Rolling Fields of Poppies and Lupine,* courtesy Butterfield & Butterfield; *Ixia Miniata, Ixia Minium,* courtesy Christie's New York; *Mounted Lawman Shooting a Falling Outlaw,* courtesy DuMouchelle Art Galleries; *Brown, Black & Blue,* courtesy Christie's New York; *Victory* and *Houses,* courtesy Weschler's; *Christopher Robin Gives Extract of Malt All Around,* courtesy C. G. Sloan & Company; *Are You Ill, Dear North Wind?,* courtesy Freeman/Fine Arts Company; *Landscape with Figures, Fort Park (?) Gloucester,* courtesy John Moran Auctioneers; *Nature Morte Au Compotier,* courtesy Christie's New York; *Bird Table,* courtesy Butterfield & Butterfield; *Waiting in the Wings,* courtesy Richard A. Bourne Co.; *Her Finishing Touches,* courtesy Foster's Auctions.

Color Insert

Christie's New York: *Portrait Du Dr. Gachet; Portrait of Duke Cosimo I de' Medici; La Rue Mosnier Aux Drapeaux; La Toilette; La Muse Endormie III; John Biglin in a Single Scull; Le Parlement, Coucher de Soleil; Selections from the Survival Series.*

Sotheby's, Inc.: *Au Moulin de la Galette* © 1990; *Niños en la Playa* © 1990; *Fugue* © 1990; *Anniversaire* © 1990; *Mata Mua, In Olden Times* © 1989; *Au Lapin Agile* © 1989; *Garçon à la Veste Bleue* © 1990; *Interchange* © 1989.